State of Louisiana

WADE O. MARTIN, JR.

I, THE UNDERSIGNED SECRETARY of STATE, OF THE STATE OF LOUISIANA, DO HEREBY CERTIFY THAT

the Text of the Louisiana Code of Civil Procedure as contained in West's Louisiana Statutes Annotated is a true and correct copy of the Louisiana Code of Civil Procedure enacted by Act No. 15 of 1960, the original of which is on file and a matter of record in this office.

Given under my signature, authenticated with the impress of my Seal of office, at the City of Baton Rouge, this 17th *day of* June *A.D. 19*60

Wade O. Martin Jr.
Secretary of State

WEST'S
LOUISIANA STATUTES
ANNOTATED

CODE OF CIVIL PROCEDURE

*Under Arrangement of the Official
Louisiana Code of Civil Procedure*

TEXT—COMMENTS—TABLES—INDEX

Edited by

HENRY G. McMAHON
Professor of Law, Louisiana State University
Coordinator and Reporter, Louisiana Code of Civil Procedure

LEON D. HUBERT, Jr.
Professor of Law, Tulane University of Louisiana
Reporter, Louisiana Code of Civil Procedure

LEON SARPY
Professor of Law, Loyola University of the South
Reporter, Louisiana Code of Civil Procedure

Volume 1

ST. PAUL, MINN.
WEST PUBLISHING CO.

DEDICATION

This volume containing the official text of the Louisiana Code of Civil Procedure is dedicated with reverence to the memory of

ROBERT WYNESS MILLAR

late professor of law, Northwestern University School of Law, whose research and writings have contributed so much to the civil procedure of Louisiana

— The Editors.

Copyright, 1960
by
WEST PUBLISHING CO.

1 LSA–C.C.P.

PREFACE

The Louisiana Code of Civil Procedure, adopted by Act 15 of 1960, effective January 1, 1961, is the culmination of twelve years' study and research by the Louisiana State Law Institute as authorized by Act 335 of 1948. The new Code consolidates the procedural rules applicable generally to civil actions and proceedings, modernizes the state's system of civil procedure and adapts it for efficient use under modern social and economic conditions.

Judges, lawyers, law teachers and law students will find this volume a convenient desk book and a practical reference work on Louisiana civil practice and procedure.

Edited by Henry G. McMahon, Leon D. Hubert, Jr., and Leon Sarpy, this volume presents the complete official Text of the Code of Civil Procedure, with the official Comments, a detailed Index to the Code, and Concordance Tables between the new Code and the former Code of Practice, the Louisiana Revised Statutes and the Revised Civil Code.

A special Table shows the effect of the implementation Acts of 1960 on designated sections and articles of the Revised Statutes and the Revised Civil Code. Thus, the practitioner, by reference to this Table, may evaluate the impact of the new Code of Civil Procedure on the procedural law formerly found in the Revised Statutes and the Revised Civil Code.

The Publisher is indebted to the Louisiana State Law Institute, to John H. Tucker, jr., President, and to the Officers and Members of the Institute, for permission to include in this edition of the Code the Report to the Legislature and the complementary materials appearing in the Projet of the Louisiana Code of Civil Procedure prepared and submitted to the Legislature by the Institute.

Special acknowledgment is made to the State Officials, to the members of the Legislature, to the members of the Bar and the Judiciary, and to the Law Teachers who have contributed, and continue to contribute, so much of their time, effort and practical experience to the work of law revision in Louisiana.

THE PUBLISHER

July, 1960

 **LOUISIANA STATE LAW INSTITUTE**
UNIVERSITY STATION
BATON ROUGE, LA.

1 July 1959

To the Honorables, the Governor, and the Members of the Legislature, of the State of Louisiana:

The Louisiana State Law Institute is pleased to report that it has completed the revision of the Code of Practice, as directed by Act No. 335 of 1948.

The Institute construed its legislative mandate to contemplate a revision of all of the general procedural law of the State relating to civil actions and proceedings.

The Civil Code has always contained much civil procedure regulating, at least in part, successions, tutorships, emancipations, interdictions, curatorships, divorces and separations from bed and board. Since 1870 our procedural law has been developed mostly by the adoption of special statutes which have not been incorporated in the Code of Practice.

Many important rules are to be found only in the jurisprudence, and they should be codified. Considerable probate procedure is based on custom and varies from parish to parish. Here legislative selection and unification are long overdue.

Under these circumstances, it was considered both practicable and desirable to bring together in one comprehensive code the rules relating to procedure in civil actions of all kinds, except those rules relating to highly specialized types of action created by statutes which they are designed to implement and beyond which they have no effect.

The Institute recommends that this new Code be entitled "The Louisiana Code of Civil Procedure," as an indication of its broadened and inclusive nature.

This new Code is still essentially the Louisiana practice and procedure known to the bench and bar, and the transition from practice under rules drawn from several sources to practice under the single source of the new Code should present no difficulty whatsoever.

In a comprehensive Code of this kind, wrought out of the legislative accumulation of nearly a century, with the gloss given by the jurisprudence of the Supreme Court, there were many instances where conflicts had to be resolved, errors corrected, and deficiencies supplied. The source notes and comments which accompany each article of the Code explain in detail the reasons underlying such action.

The projet of the new Code, prepared by the Institute, is transmitted herewith to the Secretary of State, and copies thereof delivered to him for official distribution.

The adoption of this Code will require the concurrent amendment or repeal of some provisions of the Civil Code and the Revised Statutes. Proposed legislation to accomplish these purposes has been prepared by the Institute and will be submitted at the proper time.

Article III, Section 16, of the Constitution of Louisiana, as amended in 1948, empowers the Legislature to adopt a code of this nature by means of a single statute which shall be deemed to embrace but one object, and the title of which need only to refer to the general purpose and scope of the statute. Under authority of Article III, Section 24, of the Constitution of the state, the Legislature is given authority to cause bills revising any code to be read and promulgated in such manner as the Legislature may prescribe.

Both of these matters concern legislative processes and are entirely within the discretion of the Legislature. For its consideration, the Law Institute has prepared and will submit a suggested bill for the adoption of the proposed Code, and a suggested concurrent resolution which may be of some assistance in establishing the legislative rules for reading and promulgating the bill to adopt the Louisiana Code of Civil Procedure.

It is also suggested that procedures be devised by the Legislature to obtain consideration and adoption of this Code and supplementary legislation as expeditiously as possible, in order to effect distribution thereof at the earliest possible date.

You are fully cognizant of the techniques of preparation used by the Institute. The criterion of decision by the Institute has always been the best interests of Louisiana. This <u>projet</u> of the Code of Civil Procedure was prepared in that tradition, and we hope that you will find that it merits your confidence.

Respectfully,

John H. Tucker, jr.
President

Monte M. Lemann
Vice-President

C. C. Bird, Jr.
Vice-President

LeDoux R. Provosty
Vice-President

Thomas W. Leigh
Vice-President

J. Denson Smith
Director

Paul M. Hebert
Secretary

Charles F. Fletchinger
Treasurer

TABLE OF CONTENTS

	Page
Preface	III
Letter of Transmittal	V
Report to Accompany the Project of the Proposed Louisiana Code of Civil Procedure	XI
Revision Organization	XIX
The Louisiana State Law Institute	XXI
Key to Authorities Cited Through Abbreviations in Source Notes and Comments	XXIII
Analysis	XXV
A Short History of Louisiana Civil Procedure by Henry G. McMahon	LXV

Book

I. Courts, Actions, and Parties ... 1
   Title
    I. Courts ... 1
    II. Actions ... 69
    III. Parties ... 99

II. Ordinary Proceedings ... 140
   Title
    I. Pleading ... 140
    II. Citation and Service of Process ... 205
    III. Production of Evidence ... 220
    IV. Pre-Trial Procedure ... 254
    V. Trial ... 255
    VI. Judgments ... 283

III. Proceedings in Appellate Courts ... 313
   Title
    I. Appellate Procedure ... 313
    II. Supervisory Procedure ... 340

IV. Execution of Judgments ... 341
   Title
    I. General Dispositions ... 341
    II. Money Judgments ... 346
    III. Judgments Other Than Money Judgments ... 371
    IV. Foreign Judgments ... 375

V. Summary and Executory Proceedings ... 377
   Title
    I. Summary Proceedings ... 378
    II. Executory Proceedings ... 384

TABLE OF CONTENTS

Book		Page
VI.	Probate Procedure	415
	Title	
	I. General Dispositions	415
	II. Acceptance of Successions Without Administration	443
	III. Administration of Successions	458
	IV. Ancillary Probate Procedure	533
	V. Small Successions	537
	VI. Partition of Successions	544
VII.	Special Proceedings	546
	Title	
	I. Provisional Remedies	546
	II. Real Actions	572
	III. Extraordinary Remedies	591
	IV. Annulment of Marriage, Separation from Bed and Board, and Divorce	605
	V. Judicial Emancipation	611
	VI. Tutorship	614
	VII. Administration of Minor's Property During Marriage of Parents	660
	VIII. Interdiction and Curatorship of Interdicts	662
	IX. Partition between Co-Owners	672
	X. Concursus Proceedings	687
	XI. Eviction of Tenants and Occupants	697
VIII.	Trial Courts of Limited Jurisdiction	702
	Title	
	I. General Dispositions	702
	II. Cases Involving One Hundred Dollars or Less	710
	III. Cases Involving More Than One Hundred Dollars	720
IX.	Miscellaneous Provisions and Definitions	722
	Title	
	I. Miscellaneous Provisions	722
	II. Definitions	744

Concordance Table

1. Replacement in the Code of Civil Procedure, the Civil Code, and in the Revised Statutes of Articles in the Code of Practice ____ 751
2. Replacement in the Code of Civil Procedure and in the Revised Statutes of the Civil Code Articles Repealed ____ 761
3. Replacement in the Code of Civil Procedure of Repealed Sections of the Revised Statutes ____ 765
4. Implementation Table ____ 769

Index to Code of Civil Procedure ____ 773

REPORT
TO ACCOMPANY THE PROJET OF THE PROPOSED LOUISIANA CODE OF CIVIL PROCEDURE

TO THE LEGISLATURE OF LOUISIANA:

The Louisiana State Law Institute has completed the revision of the Code of Practice and civil procedural statutes which it was directed to prepare by Act 335 of the Louisiana Legislature of 1948. This revision is contained in the *"Projet* of the Louisiana Code of Civil Procedure", which is submitted to the Legislature with a view to its adoption, in accordance with the provisions of Article III, Sections 16 and 24, of the Constitution of Louisiana.

The importance and the broad coverage of the proposed procedural code submitted for adoption calls for more information thereon and more detailed explanation thereof than is usually necessary for the consideration of bills presented for legislative adoption. The Legislature, therefore, is entitled to a report from the Law Institute explaining the organization set up to comply with this legislative mandate, the methods used in the revision process, and the policies followed by the Institute in its revision of the civil procedure of the state.

The reasons which prompted the Legislature to mandate the Law Institute to revise the civil procedure of Louisiana may be summarized as follows: (1) legislative revision of the rules on the subject was long overdue, since none had been attempted since the revision of the Code of Practice in 1870, which had been limited to the elimination of all references to the institution of slavery and the incorporation of special legislation on procedural matters adopted during the period 1825 to 1870; and (2) considerable bodies of procedural law were embodied in the Civil Code, in the mass of special statutes adopted since 1870, and in the jurisprudence of the courts, all of which required incorporation into the procedural code.

COVERAGE OF THE PROPOSED CODE

The scope of the proposed Code of Civil Procedure is very considerably broader than the coverage of its predecessors, the Codes of Practice of 1825 and 1870. The proposed new code includes all of the retained procedural rules of the Code of Practice of 1870, the numerous procedural rules formerly contained in the Civil Code, a considerable body of special legislation on the subject of civil procedure, the large number of procedural rules to be found heretofore only in the

PROJET—CODE OF CIVIL PROCEDURE

jurisprudence, and the smaller number of procedural rules which have been sanctioned heretofore only by custom and long-continued usage by the profession.

Some idea of the broadened coverage of the proposed new code, as compared with that of its predecessors, can be gleaned from a comparison of the articles in Book VI of the former with the corresponding segments of the preceding codification.

Such a comparison will also provide evidence of the improvement in the civil procedure of the state to be effected through the adoption of the proposed new code. Heretofore, the probate procedure of Louisiana was to be found in duplicate (but by no means identical) articles of the Code of Practice and of the Civil Code, in the mass of special legislation on the subject adopted since 1870, in hundreds of decisions of the Supreme Court of Louisiana since 1825, and in local customs and practices. To further compound these difficulties, the whole theory of succession procedure was changed through the adoption of the Inheritance Tax Acts, and there has been inadequate legislative implementation of social and economic progress of the state since 1870.

REVISION POLICIES

The cardinal policy of the Law Institute in its revision of the civil procedural code was expressed in its rule that there should be no change recommended in the procedural law for the mere sake of change. Numerous procedural devices and rules of other jurisdictions were studied and considered to determine their availability to the civil procedure of this state, and some of these have been incorporated in the proposed new code; but none has been borrowed without convincing proof of its greater utility and workability than its present Louisiana counterpart.

In the drafting of this proposed code, every care and precaution was taken to include therein only those procedural rules and concepts which were adapted to the implementation of the substantive law of Louisiana, and which would prove workable in actual use. Each of the reporters on this project had been engaged in the active practice of law for more than ten years, and possessed some knowledge of the operation of procedural rules in actual use. The organizational setup for this revision work was designed to insure the utility, workability, and practicability of every procedural concept and rule recommended for legislative adoption.

Of necessity, a number of changes in the present procedural law are recommended. These consist principally of the modification and modernization of the present rules rather than the adoption of new ones. Despite the excellent work done by our appellate courts during the past quarter-century in the discarding of hypertechnical jurisprudential rules, a large number of these remain in our procedural law. They are anachronistic relics of the era when a lawsuit was regarded merely as a duel between skilled protagonists. These unfortunate jurisprudential rules are recommended for legislative overruling.

Probably the three greatest, and certainly the most controversial, changes made in our procedural law during the past forty years resulted from the adoption of pretrial and discovery procedures, and of third party practice. All of these changes were effected by the Legislature on its own initiative in 1952 and 1954, respectively. In the few years which have passed since their adoption, the workability of all of these procedural devices has been demonstrated most convincingly, with the result that the original professional opposition to their adoption has now melted away. All three of these procedural devices are recommended for retention in the proposed new code. By comparison, the changes in the procedural law recommended by the Law Institute are relatively minor.

The benefits to be derived from having rules of procedure in the state courts which are identical with or similar to those used in the federal courts in Louisiana are obvious. The Law Institute, therefore, has adapted the rules proposed in this *projet* to the Federal Rules of Civil Procedure whenever it could do so without violating the settled and basic theory of the procedural concepts of Louisiana. The recommended synchronization of these dual systems of procedure will result in a highly desirable similarity, but not in complete identity.

The procedural philosophy of the proposed new code is reflected in a number of its articles. While differently phrased, all of these provisions are based on the simple premise that lawsuits should be decided on their merits, and should not turn on arbitrary or technical rules of procedure. Perhaps this procedural philosophy is summarized by Article 5051 of the proposed new code, recommended for adoption as a perpetual reminder to the courts:

> "The articles of this Code are to be construed liberally, and with due regard for the fact that rules of procedure implement the substantive law and are not an end in themselves."

THE WORK OF REVISION

Organization

In preparing for its task of revising the civil procedural law of the state, the Law Institute modeled its organization largely upon that which had been used so successfully in the Revised Statutes project.

PROJET—CODE OF CIVIL PROCEDURE

Three reporters were selected from the principal law faculties of Louisiana, and research assistants were provided to assist them. One of these reporters was charged with the task of coordinating all phases of the revision work, and given the responsibility for over-all coverage and correlation of materials in the various books, titles, chapters, and sections of the proposed codification. These reporters and their research assistants did the necessary spade work in research and in initial preparation of drafts of recommended articles for group consideration.

Two separate advisory groups were appointed to assist the reporters: the first, known as the Advisory Committee, was composed of representatives from the practicing lawyers, chosen on the dual bases of geographical representation and experience in litigation; and a second, known as the Liaison Committee of the Judiciary, was composed of representatives of all of the courts of Louisiana. When the extremely important task of revising the probate procedure of the state was reached, a third committee, known as the Probate Advisory Committee, was selected. This committee was composed of practicing lawyers who were regarded in the profession as specialists in the field of probate law and procedure.

The Legislature, of course, is familiar with the composition of the Council of the Law Institute, which made the final decisions as to the procedural rules to be recommended to the Legislature for adoption. Consisting of representatives of the Legislature, the courts, the practicing lawyers, and the law faculties, the Council provides an effective medium for the determination of professional opinion.

The selection of the format for publishing the *projet*, insuring the uniformity of citation of legal authorities, and the determination of editorial style were the responsibilities of the Institute's Committee on Semantics, Style, and Publications. A very comprehensive set of "Drafting Rules" was adopted by the committee, for the guidance of the editor appointed by the Council to do the necessary editorial work on the manuscript of the *projet* to carry into effect the rules and policies of the committee.

Plant

Through the courtesy of the West Publishing Company, triplicate plants of procedural materials to be considered were provided on manuscript cards containing the provisions of each article of the Code of Practice of 1870 and all amendments thereof, and the provisions of each section of Title 13 of the Revised Statutes and the source provisions and amendments thereof.

REPORT—LOUISIANA STATE LAW INSTITUTE

The initial task of the reporters was the preparation of an outline of the proposed new procedural code, with a breakdown thereof into books, titles, chapters, and sections. Supplementing this outline was a list allocating each article of the Code of Practice of 1870, each section of Title 13, and each article of the Civil Code and section of Title 9 of the Revised Statutes on procedural subjects, to the proper subdivision of the proposed new code. After consideration and approval of both by the Council, this outline was printed and distributed widely throughout the state to receive the suggestions and constructive criticism of the legal profession. The proposed outline was amended to incorporate a number of valuable suggestions for the improvement of our civil procedure received from these sources.

This outline of the proposed new code, and its accompanying list of procedural materials to be included therein, served two very useful purposes. Firstly, they provided a tentative blueprint and guide for the actual revision work. Secondly, they constituted an effective guaranty that all of the positive law of Louisiana on civil procedure would receive due consideration in the drafting of the proposed new code.

Consideration of Materials

The first drafts of segments of the proposed code were prepared by the reporters, after an extensive research of the law and jurisprudence applicable not only in Louisiana but on the Continent and in other American jurisdictions as well. These initial drafts of articles and comments were mimeographed and copies thereof distributed to the members of the advisory committees three to four weeks in advance of scheduled meetings, to afford committee members ample opportunity for the study thereof before consideration by the committees. Initially, these materials were presented to and considered by the committees separately, but later it was found that better results were obtained from joint meetings and consideration by the advisory groups. At these meetings, the reporters' materials were criticized, and constructive criticism offered, by the members of the advisory committees.

The tentative drafts of the materials were then restudied and redrafted by the reporters in the light of the committees' criticism and suggestions, and mimeographed copies of the redrafted material were then distributed to the members of the Council from three to four weeks in advance of the meeting at which they were scheduled for consideration. Council members were thus afforded ample opportunity to study the materials submitted prior to Council consideration.

During the period of more than eight years during which this revision work was in progress, the Council averaged one two-day meeting a month, the great bulk of the time of which was devoted to the consideration of the tentative drafts of segments of the new code. At these meetings, the material was presented in detail by the particular reporter who submitted it, and discussed at considerable length by members of the Council. Important and controversial subjects were debated extensively prior to reaching a decision thereon. In a few areas, where the subject matter was involved or extremely close decisions were required, the Council was assisted by the findings and recommendations of special committees of the Council membership appointed by the president of the Law Institute. In all instances where the Council was not completely satisfied with the proposed article or comment, the matter was recommitted to the particular reporter for further study and necessary redrafting. All decisions reached by the Council while the revision work was in progress were understood to be tentative only, and a number of these decisions were reconsidered later at the request of members or of the coordinator.

Publicizing of the Revision Work

Every effort has been made by the Law Institute to keep members of the legal profession in Louisiana fully advised of the procedural rules which were being recommended tentatively for legislative adoption, and of the reasons why they were being recommended. In the second and third years of this revision work, the president of the Law Institute and the three reporters conducted a series of short institutes in New Orleans, Shreveport, Baton Rouge, Alexandria, Monroe, Lafayette, and Lake Charles at which the work previously done, and the Law Institute's plans for the future, were reviewed in some detail. Valuable suggestions and constructive criticism were received at the time from those present at these well-attended meetings. At each of the annual meetings of the Law Institute, held jointly with the annual conventions of the Louisiana State Bar Association, a half-day program was conducted at which the reporters reviewed the work completed during the past year. At several of these meetings, alternative solutions of significant procedural problems were presented, debated by members of the audience, and advisory opinions secured through the polling of members of the profession in attendance.

Copies of all mimeographed material have been distributed to the large membership of the Law Institute, and to all others who requested copies thereof. Until the current fiscal year, when lack of funds prevented, all titles of the proposed code tentatively approved by the Council were printed in the various *Exposés des Motifs* published by the Institute. Copies of these printed pamphlets were likewise distributed to the large Institute membership, and to all others who requested copies. Additionally, several hundred copies of each were distributed to the members of the legal profession attending the annual conventions of the Louisiana State Bar Association.

REPORT—LOUISIANA STATE LAW INSTITUTE

THE RECOMMENDED CHANGE OF NAME OF THE CODE

The Law Institute recommends that the official title of the revision codification submitted herewith, on adoption, be "Louisiana Code of Civil Procedure". This decision to recommend a change in the name of the state's civil procedural code was made after careful consideration and deliberation, and is grounded on the following reasons: (1) the scope of the accompanying codification has been broadened very appreciably as compared with the coverage of its predecessors, the Codes of Practice of 1825 and 1870; (2) the narrow word "practice" would be neither an apt nor an accurate indication of the coverage of the codification submitted herewith, which includes numerous procedural rules embraced only within the broader term "civil procedure"; (3) the great majority of the jurisdictions, Anglo-American and civilian, which have adopted legislative codes of procedural rules in civil causes have adopted officially the title "Code of Civil Procedure", and even those American jurisdictions which have followed the federal example of adopting judicial rules on the subject have invariably designated these as "Rules of Civil Procedure"; and (4) confusion in comparisons of the procedural rules of the new code with those of its predecessors can be avoided through the adoption of a completely different title for the former.

EFFECTIVE DATE

The Law Institute proposes that the effective date of the Code be made not less than six months after the date of its adoption by the Legislature. This recommendation is made because (1) it will be necessary to officially print and distribute the Code after it has been adopted; and (2) it will permit members of the bench and bar to become thoroughly familiar with the provisions of the new Code prior to its effective date. Plans are under consideration by which the Law Institute, the law faculties of Louisiana State University, Loyola University, and Tulane University, and the state and local bar associations will hold institutes, seminars, and meetings for discussion, at which the new Code may be completely and thoroughly explained.

There is nothing difficult or complex about the proposed Code, for it is essentially made up from the prevailing rules and practices, scientifically classified and concisely and clearly stated.

CONTINUOUS REVISION

The bill prepared by the Law Institute for the adoption of the proposed Code of Civil Procedure provides for its continuous revision, through the same system used so successfully for the continuous revision of the Revised Statutes of 1950.

PROJET—CODE OF CIVIL PROCEDURE

Continuous code revision is based on the sensible proposition that once a code has been adopted, the law embodied therein should be kept up-to-date. If civil procedural statutes adopted subsequently by the Legislature are permitted to accumulate for an extended period of time without incorporating them in the code, they will become a mass of unorganized legislation, often in conflict and inconsistent with the original code provisions. In a short time, Louisiana would find itself in the same situation that it was prior to the adoption of the code.

The proposed code in one respect departs from the traditional arrangement of prior Louisiana codes: while all the articles within each unit of the proposed code are numbered consecutively, wide gaps in article numbers are left between all units of the proposed codification. Under this system of numbering the articles, continuous code revision is made possible.

Under the proposed continuous revision, at the end of each legislative session the Law Institute will incorporate in appropriate places in the new code the texts of all amendments thereof and all new legislation on the subject of civil procedure, and will delete the language of all articles which are repealed expressly or impliedly thereby. No substantive change in the law will be made, but the Law Institute will have authority to renumber articles, change the wording of headnotes, correct grammatical errors, and the like, to preserve the original pattern of the code and to insure uniformity of its provisions.

REVISION ORGANIZATION

1. LOUISIANA STATE LAW INSTITUTE MEMBERSHIP

2. COUNCIL OF THE LOUISIANA STATE LAW INSTITUTE

3. REPORTERS' ADVISORY COMMITTEE

   RICHARD A. ANDERSON
   JEROME A. BROUSSARD*
   ALVIN R. CHRISTOVICH
   SIDNEY M. COOK
   FRED G. HUDSON*
   VAL IRION
   ALVIN O. KING*

   SUMTER D. MARKS, JR.
   BEN R. MILLER
   LEON O'QUIN
   G. T. OWEN, JR.
   CHARLES J. RIVET
   NELSON S. WOODDY*
   M. TRUMAN WOODWARD, JR.

   SOLOMON S. GOLDMAN, *Chairman*

4. LIAISON COMMITTEE OF THE JUDICIARY

   JUDGE ROBERT S. ELLIS, JR.
   JUDGE EDWARD L. GLADNEY, JR.
   JUDGE RICHARD T. McBRIDE

   JUSTICE HAROLD A. MOISE*
   JUDGE ALBERT TATE, JR.
   JUDGE LOUIS H. YARRUT

   JUDGE JOHN T. HOOD, JR., *Chairman*

5. SPECIAL PROBATE ADVISORY COMMITTEE

   WOOD BROWN
   JOHN T. CHARBONNET
   RAYMOND GAUCHE
   EDWIN W. GOETZ, JR.
   LOUIS C. GUIDRY

   G. T. OWEN, JR.
   GEORGE M. SNELLINGS, JR.
   GROVE STAFFORD
   BASCOM D. TALLEY, JR.
   BENNETT J. VOORHIES

   VICTOR A. SACHSE, *Chairman*

6. COMMITTEE ON SEMANTICS, STYLE, AND PUBLICATIONS

   C. C. BIRD, JR.
   ALEX F. SMITH

   WALTER J. SUTHON
   LEDOUX R. PROVOSTY, *Chairman*

7. COORDINATOR

   HENRY G. McMAHON

---

* Deceased.

PROJET—CODE OF CIVIL PROCEDURE

8. **REPORTERS**

    LEON D. HUBERT, JR.
    Book II: Titles II, III, V, and VI
    Book III
    Book VI: Titles III (Chapters 4 and 5), and VI
    Book VII: Titles II, IX, and XI
    Book VIII

    (MRS. MAY B. HUBERT, *Research Assistant*)

    HENRY G. McMAHON
    Book I: Titles I (Chapters 1, and 3–7), II, and III
    Book II: Title I
    Book V
    Book VI: Titles I, II, III (Chapters 1–3), and V
    Book IX

    (MRS. MARTHA C. INNES, *Research Assistant*)

    LEON SARPY
    Book I: Title I (Chapter 2)
    Book II: Title IV
    Book IV
    Book VI: Titles III (Chapters 6–12), and IV
    Book VII: Titles I, III–VIII, and X

    (ADRIAN G. DUPLANTIER, *Research Assistant*)

9. **COORDINATOR OF RESEARCH**

    CARLOS E. LAZARUS

10. **EDITOR**

    MARY ELLEN CALDWELL

THE LOUISIANA STATE LAW INSTITUTE

The Louisiana State Law Institute was chartered, created, and organized as an official advisory law revision commission, and law reform agency of the State of Louisiana, by Act 166 of 1938.

The act which created it provides that the general purposes for which it was formed are "to promote and encourage the clarification and simplification of the law of Louisiana, and its better adaptation to present social needs; to secure the better administration of justice; to carry on scholarly legal research and scientific legal work."

Its officers are:

JOHN H. TUCKER, jr.	President
MONTE M. LEMANN	Vice-President
C. C. BIRD, JR.	Vice-President
LEDOUX R. PROVOSTY	Vice-President
THOS. W. LEIGH	Vice-President
J. DENSON SMITH	Director
CHARLES F. FLETCHINGER	Treasurer
PAUL M. HEBERT	Secretary
T. HALLER JACKSON, JR.	Asst. Secretary
MICHAEL J. MOLONY, JR.	Asst. Secretary

The members of its council (as of January 1, 1959) are:

CUTHBERT S. BALDWIN	Practicing attorney
D. ELMORE BECNEL	Chairman of Judiciary "A" Committee of the House of Representatives
DALE E. BENNETT	Member of faculty of L.S.U. Law School
RICHARD J. BERTRAND	Chairman of Judiciary "C" Committee of the House of Representatives
ROBERT E. BRUMBY	Practicing attorney
HARRIET S. DAGGETT	Emeritus member
JOSEPH DAINOW	Member of faculty of L.S.U. Law School
J. J. DAVIDSON, JR.	Practicing attorney
BEN C. DAWKINS	Emeritus member
C. H. DOWNS	Chairman of Judiciary "B" Committee of the Senate
CHARLES E. DUNBAR, JR.	Member of Council of American Law Institute
CLARENCE M. EAST, JR.	Member of faculty of Loyola University School of Law
RAY FORRESTER	Dean of Tulane University School of Law
J. CLEVELAND FRUGÉ	Judge, 13th Judicial District Court
HOWARD B. GIST	Practicing attorney
EDWARD L. GLADNEY, JR.	Judge, Court of Appeal
SOLOMON S. GOLDMAN	Practicing attorney
JACK P. F. GREMILLION	Attorney General
JOE B. HAMITER	Associate Justice, Supreme Court of Louisiana
MILTON M. HARRISON	Dean of L.S.U. Law School

THE LOUISIANA STATE LAW INSTITUTE

N. SMITH HOFFPAUIR	Judge, 15th Judicial District Court
LEON D. HUBERT, JR.	Member of faculty of Tulane University School of Law
WELLBORN JACK	Designated representative of the Chairman of Judiciary "B" Committee of the House of Representatives
JOHN J. McAULAY	Member of faculty of Loyola University School of Law
HARRY McCALL	President of Louisiana State Bar Association
HENRY G. McMAHON	Member of faculty of L.S.U. Law School
GEORGE T. MADISON	Practicing attorney
JOHN M. MADISON	Practicing attorney
SUMTER D. MARKS, JR.	Practicing attorney
WM. F. M. MEADORS	Practicing attorney
BEN R. MILLER	Member of House of Delegates of American Bar Association
RICHARD B. MONTGOMERY	Member of House of Delegates of American Bar Association
EUGENE A. NABORS	Member of faculty of Tulane University School of Law
LEONARD OPPENHEIM	Member of faculty of Tulane University School of Law
A. E. PAPALE	Dean of Loyola University School of Law
S. W. PLAUCHÉ, JR.	Practicing attorney
JOHN R. PLEASANT	Practicing attorney
CHARLES J. RIVET	Practicing attorney
VICTOR A. SACHSE	Practicing attorney
LEON SARPY	Member of faculty of Loyola University School of Law
ANDREW L. SEVIER	Chairman of Judiciary "A" Committee of the Senate
ALEX F. SMITH	Practicing attorney
FRANK J. STICH*	Judge, Civil District Court
OLIVER P. STOCKWELL	Practicing attorney
WALTER J. SUTHON, JR.	Practicing attorney
BASCOM D. TALLEY, JR.	Practicing attorney
PAUL C. TATE	Practicing attorney
B. B. TAYLOR	Emeritus member
THOMAS C. WICKER, JR.	Chairman, Junior Bar Section of Louisiana State Bar Association
M. TRUMAN WOODWARD, JR.	Practicing attorney
J. SKELLY WRIGHT	Judge, U. S. District Court

Representatives of Junior Bar Section at Council Meetings:
GEORGE B. HALL
GEORGE W. PUGH

Observers for Junior Bar Section at Council Meetings:
ROBERT L. KLEINPETER
J. WALTER WARD

* Deceased.

KEY TO AUTHORITIES CITED THROUGH ABBREVIATIONS

IN

SOURCE NOTES AND COMMENTS

OF THE

LOUISIANA CODE OF CIVIL PROCEDURE

(References to compilations of statutes include references
to the latest supplements thereto)

Admiralty Rule ——	Rule ——, Federal Admiralty Rules
Ala.Code	The Code of Alabama (1940)
Ann.Pract. (1950)	Burnand, Burnett-Hall & Watts, The Annual Practice (1950)
Arizona Rev.Stats.Anno.	Arizona Revised Statutes Annotated (1956)
Ark.Stats.	Arkansas Statutes (1947) Annotated
Calif.Code of Civil Proc.	West's Annotated Code of Civil Procedure of the State of California (1954)
C.C.	Louisiana Civil Code of 1870
Conn.Gen.Stats.	The General Statutes of Connecticut (Revision of 1958)
C.P.	Louisiana Code of Practice of 1870
Eng.Rules of Supreme Court	Rules of the Supreme Court of Judicature (England)
Fed.Rule ——	Rule ——, Federal Rules of Civil Procedure
Fed.Rules Serv.	Federal Rules Service
Florida Stats. Anno.	Florida Statutes Annotated (1943–1944)
Idaho Stats.	Idaho Laws Annotated (1943)
Ill.Civil Practice Act	Illinois Civil Practice Act Annotated (1933)
Ill.L.Rev.	Illinois Law Review (now Northwestern Law Review)
Ill.Anno.Stats.	Smith-Hurd, Illinois Annotated Statutes (permanent edition)
Indiana Stats.Anno.	Indiana Statutes Annotated (1953)
Ins.L.J.	Insurance Law Journal
La.Bar J.	Louisiana Bar Journal
La.L.Rev.	Louisiana Law Review
Loyola L.Rev.	Loyola Law Review
L.S.A.	Louisiana Statutes Annotated (1951–1955)
McMahon	McMahon, Louisiana Practice (1939)
McMahon (1956 Supp.)	Supplement (1956) to McMahon, Louisiana Practice (1939)
Minn.Stats.Anno.	Minnesota Statutes Annotated (1946)
Model Probate Code	Model Probate Code, reproduced in Simes, Problems in Probate Law (1946)
N.Dakota Rev.Code	North Dakota Revised Code of 1943

1 LSA–C.C.P.

PROJET—CODE OF CIVIL PROCEDURE

Nev.Rules of Civil Procedure	Nevada Rules of Civil Procedure (1953) in 1 Nevada Revised Statutes (1957)
N.Y.Civil Practice Act	New York Civil Practice Act
New Mexico Stats.Anno.	New Mexico Statutes (1953) Annotated
Ohio St.L.J.	Ohio State University Law Journal
Okla.Stats.Anno.	Oklahoma Statutes Annotated (permanent edition)
Op.Atty.Gen.	Opinions of the Attorney General of Louisiana
Restatement of Conflicts	Restatement of the Law of Conflict of Laws (1934)
Restatement of Conflicts, 2d	. . . Restatement of the Law Second. Conflict of Laws . . . (1956)
Restatement of Judgments	Restatement of the Law of Judgments (1942)
R.S.	Louisiana Revised Statutes of 1950
R.S. of 1870	Louisiana Revised Statutes of 1870
Rules of Civil District Court	Rules of the Civil District Court for the Parish of Orleans (1954)
S.C.Code	Code of Laws of South Carolina (1952) Annotated
Texas Rule ——	Rule ——, Texas Rules of Civil Procedure (1939), reproduced in Vernon's Annotated Texas Rules of Civil Procedure (Franki's edition, 1955)
Tul.L.Rev.	Tulane Law Review
U.L.A.	Uniform Laws Annotated (1957)
U. of Cin.L.Rev.	University of Cincinnati Law Review
U.S.C.	United States Code
Utah Code Anno.	Utah Code Annotated (1953)
Va.Code	Virginia Code (1950)
Vand.L.Rev.	Vanderbilt Law Review
Vernon's Anno.Civil Stats.	Vernon's Revised Civil Statutes of the State of Texas (1947–1956)
Wis.Stats.	Wisconsin Statutes (1957)

ANALYSIS

BOOK I—COURTS, ACTIONS, AND PARTIES
TITLE I—COURTS
CHAPTER 1. JURISDICTION

Art.
1. Jurisdiction defined.
2. Jurisdiction over subject matter.
3. Same; cannot be conferred by consent.
4. Same; determination when dependent on amount in dispute or value of right asserted.
5. Same; effect of reduction of claim.
6. Jurisdiction over the person.
7. Same; implied waiver of objections by general appearance.
8. Jurisdiction over property; in rem.
9. Same; quasi in rem; attachment.
10. Jurisdiction over status.

CHAPTER 2. VENUE

Section 1. General Dispositions

41. Definition.
42. General rules.
43. Exception to general rules.
44. Waiver of objections to venue.
45. Conflict between two or more articles in Chapter.

Section 2. Exceptions to General Rules

71. Action against individual who has changed domicile.
72. Certain actions involving property; effect of judgment.
73. Action against joint or solidary obligors.
74. Action on offense or quasi offense.
75. Action on judicial bond.
76. Action on insurance policy.
77. Action against person doing business in another parish.
78. Action against partners of existing partnership.
79. Action to dissolve partnership.
80. Action involving immovable property.
81. Action involving succession.
82. Action to partition community property.
83. Action to partition partnership property.

ANALYSIS

Section 3. Change of Venue

Art.
121. Action brought in improper venue; transfer.
122. Change of proper venue.

Chapter 3. Recusation of Judges

151. Grounds.
152. Recusation on court's own motion or by supreme court.
153. Judge may act until recused or motion for recusation filed.
154. Procedure for recusation.
155. Selection of judge to try motion to recuse; court having two or more judges.
156. Same; court having single judge.
157. Judge ad hoc appointed to try cause when judge recused; power of judge ad hoc.
158. Supreme court appointment of district judge to try cause when judge recused.
159. Recusation of supreme court justice.
160. Recusation of judge of court of appeal.
161. Recusation of judge ad hoc.

Chapter 4. Power and Authority

Section 1. General Dispositions

191. Inherent judicial power.
192. Authority of trial court to appoint experts.
193. Power to adopt local rules; publication.
194. Power of district court to act in chambers; signing orders and judgments.
195. Same; judicial proceedings.
196. Power of district court to act in vacation.

Section 2. Power To Punish For Contempt

221. Kinds of contempt.
222. Direct contempt.
223. Same; procedure for punishing.
224. Constructive contempt.
225. Same; procedure for punishing.
226. Same; imprisonment until performance
227. Punishment for contempt.

Chapter 5. Clerks

Section 1. General Dispositions

251. Custodian of court records; certified copies; records public.
252. Issuance of process.

ANALYSIS

Art.
253. Pleadings, documents, and exhibits to be filed with clerk.
254. Docket and minute books.
255. Deputy clerks and other employees.
256. Minute clerk.
257. Neglect, failure, or refusal of clerk, deputy, or other employee to perform duty subjects him to punishment for contempt.

Section 2. Clerks of District Courts

281. Certain articles not applicable to Civil District Court for the Parish of Orleans.
282. Acts which may be done by district court clerk.
283. Orders and judgments which may be signed by district court clerk.
284. Judicial powers of district court clerk.
285. Powers of district court clerk may be exercised whether judge absent from parish or not.
286. Powers of district court clerk which may not be exercised by deputy; powers of chief deputy clerk.
287. District court clerk ex officio notary.
288. Functions which district court clerk may exercise on holiday.

CHAPTER 6. SHERIFFS

321. Executive officer of district court; serves process, executes writs and mandates directed to him by courts.
322. Exercises civil functions only in own parish; exception.
323. Writs executed on holiday.
324. Returns on process served, and writs and judgments executed.
325. Right of entry for execution; may require assistance of others if resistance offered or threatened.
326. Protection and preservation of property seized.
327. Seizure of rents, fruits, and revenue of property under seizure.
328. Power of administration of property under seizure.
329. Disbursements for protection, preservation, and administration of seized property.
330. Collection of fines from, and imprisonment of, persons found guilty of contempt of court.
331. Deputy sheriffs and other employees.
332. Service or execution by constable or marshal.
333. Crier.
334. Neglect, failure, or refusal of sheriff, deputy sheriff, or employee to perform duty subjects him to punishment for contempt.

CHAPTER 7. OTHER OFFICERS OF THE COURT

371. Attorney.
372. Court reporter.

ANALYSIS

Art.
373. Expert appointed by court.
374. Legal representative.
375. Neglect, failure, or refusal of expert or legal representative to perform a legal duty when ordered to do so, subjects him to punishment for contempt of court.

TITLE II—ACTIONS

CHAPTER 1. GENERAL DISPOSITIONS

421. Civil action; commencement; amicable demand unnecessary.
422. Personal, real, mixed actions.
423. Implied right to enforce obligation; prematurity.
424. Cause of action as a defense.
425. Division of cause of action, effect.
426. Transmission of action and of right to enforce obligation.
427. Action against obligor's heirs or legatees.
428. No abatement on death of party.

CHAPTER 2. CUMULATION OF ACTIONS

461. Cumulation of actions defined.
462. Cumulation by single plaintiff against single defendant.
463. Cumulation, plural plaintiffs or defendants.
464. Improper cumulation, effect.
465. Separate trials of cumulated actions.

CHAPTER 3. LIS PENDENS

531. Suits pending in Louisiana court or courts.
532. Suits pending in Louisiana and federal or foreign court.

CHAPTER 4. ABANDONMENT OF ACTION

561. Abandonment in trial and appellate court.

CHAPTER 5. CLASS AND SECONDARY ACTIONS

Section 1. Class Actions

591. Prerequisites.
592. Representation.
593. Venue.
594. Dismissal or compromise.
595. Award of expenses of litigation; security for costs.
596. Petition in shareholder's secondary action.
597. Effect of judgment.

XXVIII

ANALYSIS

Section 2. Secondary Actions

Art.
611. Shareholder's secondary action when not impracticable to join all shareholders or members.

TITLE III—PARTIES

CHAPTER 1. JOINDER

641. Compulsory joinder; indispensable parties.
642. Same; necessary parties.
643. Same; necessary parties; joint and solidary obligees and obligors.
644. Same; joinder of indispensable or necessary party plaintiff who refuses to sue.
645. Same; pleading nonjoinder of indispensable or necessary party.
646. Same; amendment of petition to join indispensable or necessary party.
647. Permissive joinder governed by rules of cumulation of actions.

CHAPTER 2. PARTIES PLAINTIFF

681. Real and actual interest required.
682. Individuals having procedural capacity.
683. Unemancipated minor.
684. Mental incompetent; interdict.
685. Succession.
686. Marital community.
687. Person doing business under trade name.
688. Partnership.
689. Unincorporated association.
690. Domestic corporation or insurer.
691. Foreign corporation; foreign or alien insurance corporation.
692. Corporation or partnership in receivership or liquidation.
693. Insurer in receivership.
694. Agent.
695. Same; wife as agent of husband.
696. Pledgor and pledgee.
697. Subrogor and subrogee.
698. Assignor and assignee.
699. Trust estate.
700. Authority or qualification of plaintiff suing in representative capacity.

CHAPTER 3. PARTIES DEFENDANT

731. Individuals having procedural capacity.
732. Unemancipated minor.

ANALYSIS

Art.
733. Mental incompetent; interdict.
734. Succession.
735. Marital community.
736. Person doing business under trade name.
737. Partnership; partners.
738. Unincorporated association; members.
739. Corporation; insurance corporation.
740. Corporation or partnership in receivership or liquidation.
741. Insurer in receivership.
742. Trust estate.

CHAPTER 4. PARTIES TO INCIDENTAL DEMANDS

771. Rules applicable.

CHAPTER 5. SUBSTITUTION OF PARTIES

SECTION 1. IN TRIAL COURTS

801. Voluntary substitution for deceased party; legal successor.
802. Compulsory substitution for deceased party; summons.
803. Same; service or publication of summons.
804. Same; effect of failure of legal successor to appear.
805. Legal representative; successor.
806. Public officer.
807. Transfer of interest.

SECTION 2. IN APPELLATE COURTS

821. Rules of Chapter applicable to district courts; rules of other appellate courts applicable.

BOOK II—ORDINARY PROCEEDINGS

TITLE I—PLEADING

CHAPTER 1. GENERAL DISPOSITIONS

851. Three modes of procedure; Book II governs ordinary proceedings.
852. Pleadings allowed; replicatory pleadings prohibited.
853. Caption of pleadings; adoption by reference; exhibits.
854. Form of pleading.
855. Pleading special matters; capacity.
856. Same; fraud, mistake, or condition of the mind.
857. Same; suspensive conditions.

ANALYSIS

Art.
858. Same; official document or act.
859. Same; judgment or decision.
860. Same; time and place.
861. Same; special damage.
862. Relief granted under pleadings; sufficiency of prayer.
863. Signing of pleadings, effect.
864. Attorney subject to disciplinary action.
865. Construction of pleadings.

CHAPTER 2. PETITION

891. Form of petition.
892. Alternative causes of action.

CHAPTER 3. EXCEPTIONS

921. Exception defined.
922. Kinds of exceptions.
923. Functions of exceptions.
924. Form of exceptions.
925. Objections raised by declinatory exception; waiver.
926. Objections raised by dilatory exception; waiver.
927. Objections raised by peremptory exception.
928. Time of pleading exceptions.
929. Time of trial of exceptions.
930. Evidence on trial of declinatory and dilatory exceptions.
931. Evidence on trial of peremptory exception.
932. Effect of sustaining declinatory exception.
933. Effect of sustaining dilatory exception.
934. Effect of sustaining peremptory exception.

CHAPTER 4. WRITTEN MOTIONS

961. Written motion required; exception.
962. Form of written motion.
963. Ex parte and contradictory motions; rule to show cause.
964. Motion to strike.
965. Motion for judgment on pleadings.
966. Motion for summary judgment; procedure.
967. Same; affidavits.
968. Effect of judgment on pleadings and summary judgment.
969. Judgment on pleadings and summary judgment not permitted in certain cases.

CHAPTER 5. ANSWER

1001. Delay for answering.
1002. Answer filed prior to confirmation of default.
1003. Form of answer.

ANALYSIS

Art.
1004. Denials.
1005. Affirmative defenses.
1006. Alternative defenses.

CHAPTER 6. INCIDENTAL ACTIONS

Section 1. General Dispositions

1031. Incidental demands allowed.
1032. Form of petition.
1033. Delay for filing incidental demand.
1034. Exceptions and motions.
1035. Answer.
1036. Jurisdiction; mode of procedure.
1037. Action instituted separately.
1038. Separate trial; separate judgment.
1039. Effect of dismissal of principal action.
1040. Words "plaintiff" and "defendant" include plaintiff and defendant in an incidental action.

Section 2. Reconvention

1061. Actions pleaded in reconventional demand.
1062. Pleading compensation.
1063. Service of reconventional demand; citation unnecessary.
1064. Additional parties.
1065. Reconventional demand exceeding principal demand.
1066. Action matured or acquired after pleading.

Section 3. Intervention

1091. Third person may intervene.
1092. Third person asserting ownership of, or mortgage or privilege on, seized property.
1093. Service of petition; citation unnecessary.
1094. Intervener accepts proceedings.

Section 4. Demand Against Third Party

1111. Defendant may bring in third person.
1112. Defendant in reconvention may bring in third person.
1113. Effect of failure to bring in third party.
1114. Service of citation and pleadings.
1115. Defenses of original defendant available to third party defendant.
1116. Third party defendant may bring in third person.

ANALYSIS

Art.
- 858. Same; official document or act.
- 859. Same; judgment or decision.
- 860. Same; time and place.
- 861. Same; special damage.
- 862. Relief granted under pleadings; sufficiency of prayer.
- 863. Signing of pleadings, effect.
- 864. Attorney subject to disciplinary action.
- 865. Construction of pleadings.

CHAPTER 2. PETITION

- 891. Form of petition.
- 892. Alternative causes of action.

CHAPTER 3. EXCEPTIONS

- 921. Exception defined.
- 922. Kinds of exceptions.
- 923. Functions of exceptions.
- 924. Form of exceptions.
- 925. Objections raised by declinatory exception; waiver.
- 926. Objections raised by dilatory exception; waiver.
- 927. Objections raised by peremptory exception.
- 928. Time of pleading exceptions.
- 929. Time of trial of exceptions.
- 930. Evidence on trial of declinatory and dilatory exceptions.
- 931. Evidence on trial of peremptory exception.
- 932. Effect of sustaining declinatory exception.
- 933. Effect of sustaining dilatory exception.
- 934. Effect of sustaining peremptory exception.

CHAPTER 4. WRITTEN MOTIONS

- 961. Written motion required; exception.
- 962. Form of written motion.
- 963. Ex parte and contradictory motions; rule to show cause.
- 964. Motion to strike.
- 965. Motion for judgment on pleadings.
- 966. Motion for summary judgment; procedure.
- 967. Same; affidavits.
- 968. Effect of judgment on pleadings and summary judgment.
- 969. Judgment on pleadings and summary judgment not permitted in certain cases.

CHAPTER 5. ANSWER

- 1001. Delay for answering.
- 1002. Answer filed prior to confirmation of default.
- 1003. Form of answer.

ANALYSIS

Art.
1004. Denials.
1005. Affirmative defenses.
1006. Alternative defenses.

CHAPTER 6. INCIDENTAL ACTIONS

Section 1. General Dispositions

1031. Incidental demands allowed.
1032. Form of petition.
1033. Delay for filing incidental demand.
1034. Exceptions and motions.
1035. Answer.
1036. Jurisdiction; mode of procedure.
1037. Action instituted separately.
1038. Separate trial; separate judgment.
1039. Effect of dismissal of principal action.
1040. Words "plaintiff" and "defendant" include plaintiff and defendant in an incidental action.

Section 2. Reconvention

1061. Actions pleaded in reconventional demand.
1062. Pleading compensation.
1063. Service of reconventional demand; citation unnecessary.
1064. Additional parties.
1065. Reconventional demand exceeding principal demand.
1066. Action matured or acquired after pleading.

Section 3. Intervention

1091. Third person may intervene.
1092. Third person asserting ownership of, or mortgage or privilege on, seized property.
1093. Service of petition; citation unnecessary.
1094. Intervener accepts proceedings.

Section 4. Demand Against Third Party

1111. Defendant may bring in third person.
1112. Defendant in reconvention may bring in third person.
1113. Effect of failure to bring in third party.
1114. Service of citation and pleadings.
1115. Defenses of original defendant available to third party defendant.
1116. Third party defendant may bring in third person.

ANALYSIS

CHAPTER 7. AMENDED AND SUPPLEMENTAL PLEADINGS

Art.
1151. Amendment of petition and answer; answer to amended petition.
1152. Amendment of exceptions.
1153. Amendment relates back.
1154. Amendment to conform to evidence.
1155. Supplemental pleadings.
1156. Amended and supplemental pleadings in incidental action.

TITLE II—CITATION AND SERVICE OF PROCESS

CHAPTER 1. CITATION

1201. Citation; waiver.
1202. Form of citation.
1203. Citation to legal representative of multiple defendants.

CHAPTER 2. SERVICE ON PERSONS

1231. Types of service; time of making
1232. Personal service.
1233. Same; where made.
1234. Domiciliary service.
1235. Service on representative.

CHAPTER 3. SERVICE ON LEGAL AND QUASI LEGAL ENTITIES

1261. Domestic or foreign corporation.
1262. Same; secretary of state.
1263. Partnership.
1264. Unincorporated association.
1265. Political entity; public officer.

CHAPTER 4. PERSONS AUTHORIZED TO MAKE SERVICE

1291. Service by sheriff.
1292. Sheriff's return.
1293. Service by private person.

ANALYSIS

CHAPTER 5. SERVICE OF PLEADINGS

Art.
1311. Service of copy of exhibit to pleading unnecessary.
1312. Service of pleadings subsequent to petition; exceptions.
1313. Same; service by mail or delivery.
1314. Same; service by sheriff.

TITLE III—PRODUCTION OF EVIDENCE

CHAPTER 1. SUBPOENAS

1351. Issuance; form.
1352. Restrictions on subpoena.
1353. Prepayment of fees.
1354. Subpoena duces tecum.
1355. Service of subpoena.
1356. Subpoenas and subpoenas duces tecum for depositions.
1357. Failure to comply with subpoena.

CHAPTER 2. PROOF OF OFFICIAL RECORDS

1391. Judicial notice of laws.
1392. Proof of statutes.
1393. Proof of official records by official publication.
1394. Proof of official records by certified copy: Louisiana records.
1395. Same; out of state records.
1396. Proof of lack of record.
1397. Other proof.

CHAPTER 3. DEPOSITIONS AND DISCOVERY

Section 1. General Dispositions

1421. Stipulation regarding the taking of depositions.
1422. Place of taking deposition.
1423. Person before whom deposition taken.
1424. Objection to irregularities in notice; waiver.
1425. Objection as to disqualification of officer; waiver.
1426. Objections to competency of witnesses, relevancy of testimony, manner or form of taking deposition.
1427. Objections as to completion and return of deposition.
1428. Use of deposition.
1429. Objection to admissibility.
1430. Effect of taking or using deposition.
1431. Deposition taken outside Louisiana.

XXXIV

ANALYSIS

Art.
1432. Perpetuation of testimony; petition.
1433. Notice and service of petition for perpetuation of testimony.
1434. Order and examination for perpetuation of testimony.
1435. Use of deposition to perpetuate testimony.
1436. Deposition pending action; scope of examination and cross examination of deponent.
1437. Deposition after trial.

Section 2. Depositions Upon Oral Examination

1451. Notice of examination; time and place.
1452. Orders for the protection of parties and deponents.
1453. Record of examination; oath; objections.
1454. Motion to terminate or limit examination.
1455. Submission to witness; changes; signing.
1456. Certification and filing by officer; copies; notice of filing.
1457. Failure to attend or to serve subpoena; expenses.

Section 3. Depositions Upon Written Interrogatories

1471. Notice and service of interrogatories.
1472. Taking of testimony and preparation of record; notice of filing of deposition.
1473. Orders for the protection of parties and deponents.

Section 4. Other Discovery Devices

1491. Interrogatories to parties.
1492. Discovery and production of documents and things for inspection, copying, or photographing.
1493. Physical and mental examination of parties.
1494. Same; report of findings; delivery of copies to parties; waiver of privilege of party examined.
1495. Right of party examined to other medical reports.
1496. Admission of facts and of genuineness of documents.

Section 5. Refusal to Make Discovery

1511. Refusal of deponent to answer oral or written interrogatories; order compelling answer; costs of obtaining order.
1512. Contempt.
1513. Failure to comply with orders, penalty.
1514. Refusal to admit, expenses.
1515. Failure to attend or serve answers.

TITLE IV—PRE-TRIAL PROCEDURE

1551. Pre-trial conference; order.

ANALYSIS

TITLE V—TRIAL

CHAPTER 1. CONSOLIDATION OF CASES

Art.
1561. Consolidation for trial; joint trial of common issues.

CHAPTER 2. ASSIGNMENT OF CASES FOR TRIAL

1571. Assignment by court rule.
1572. Written request for notice of trial.

CHAPTER 3. CONTINUANCE

1601. Discretionary grounds.
1602. Peremptory grounds.
1603. Motion for continuance.
1604. Prevention of continuance by admission of adverse party.
1605. Trial of motion; order.

CHAPTER 4. TRIAL PROCEDURE

1631. Power of court over proceedings.
1632. Order of trial.
1633. Oath or affirmation of witnesses; refusal to testify.
1634. Cross examination of party or representative by adverse party.
1635. Exceptions unnecessary.
1636. Evidence held inadmissible; record or statement as to nature thereof.
1637. Completion of trial; pronouncement of judgment.

CHAPTER 5. DISMISSAL

1671. Voluntary dismissal.
1672. Involuntary dismissal.
1673. Effect of dismissal with or without prejudice.

CHAPTER 6. DEFAULT

1701. Judgment by default.
1702. Confirmation of default judgment.
1703. Scope of judgment.

ANALYSIS

CHAPTER 7. JURY TRIAL

SECTION 1. RIGHT TO TRIAL BY JURY

Art.
1731. Issues triable by jury.
1732. Demand for jury trial.
1733. Limitation upon jury trials.
1734. Specification of issues.
1735. Trial of less than all issues; stipulation.

SECTION 2. SELECTION OF JURY

1751. Qualification and exemptions of jurors.

SECTION 3. PROCEDURE FOR CALLING AND EXAMINING JURORS

1761. Procedure in general.
1762. Swearing of juror before examination.
1763. Examination of juror.
1764. Peremptory challenges.
1765. Challenges for cause.
1766. Time for peremptory challenge.
1767. Challenging or excusing jurors after acceptance.
1768. Swearing of jurors; selection of foreman.
1769. Alternate jurors.

SECTION 4. PROCEDURE IN JURY TRIALS

1791. Time for charging the jury; recordation of charge.
1792. Contents of charge to jury.
1793. Instruction to jury; objections.
1794. Taking evidence to jury room.
1795. Number required for verdict; stipulation.

SECTION 5. VERDICTS

1811. Special verdicts.
1812. General verdict accompanied by answer to interrogatories.
1813. Remittitur or additur as alternative to new trial; reformation of verdict.
1814. New trial on showing of misconduct by jury.

TITLE VI—JUDGMENTS

CHAPTER 1. GENERAL DISPOSITIONS

1841. Judgments, interlocutory and final.
1842. Definitive judgment.
1843. Judgment by default.
1844. Judgment of dismissal; effect.

ANALYSIS

CHAPTER 2. DECLARATORY JUDGMENTS

Art.
1871. Declaratory judgments; scope.
1872. Interested parties may obtain declaration of rights, status, or other legal relations.
1873. Construction of contract.
1874. Interested person may obtain declaration of rights; purpose.
1875. Powers enumerated not exclusive.
1876. Court may refuse declaratory judgment.
1877. Review of judgments and decrees.
1878. Supplemental relief.
1879. Trial and determination of issue of fact.
1880. Parties.
1881. Construction.
1882. Provisions independent and severable.
1883. Uniformity of interpretation.

CHAPTER 3. RENDITION

1911. Final judgments read and signed in open court.
1912. Final judgment read and signed in any parish in district.
1913. Notice of judgment.
1914. Interlocutory order or judgment when case under advisement; notice; delay for further action when notice required.
1915. Partial judgment.
1916. Jury cases; signature of judgment by the court.
1917. Written findings of fact and reasons for judgment.
1918. Form of final judgment.
1919. Judgment affecting immovable property; particular description.
1920. Costs; parties liable; procedure for taxing.
1921. Interest allowed by the judgment.

CHAPTER 4. MODIFICATION IN TRIAL COURT

SECTION 1. AMENDMENT

1951. Amendment of judgment.

SECTION 2. NEW TRIAL

1971. Granting of new trial.
1972. Peremptory grounds.
1973. Discretionary grounds.
1974. Delay for applying for new trial.
1975. Application for new trial; verifying affidavit.
1976. Service of notice.

ANALYSIS

Art.
1977. Assignment of new trial.
1978. Method of procedure.
1979. Summary decision on motion; maximum delays.

Section 3. Action of Nullity

2001. Grounds in general.
2002. Annulment for vices of form; time for action.
2003. Same; action lost through acquiescence.
2004. Annulment for vices of substance; peremption of action.
2005. Annulment of judgments; effect of appeal.
2006. Court where action brought.

CHAPTER 5. REVIVAL

2031. Revival of judgments.

BOOK III—PROCEEDINGS IN APPELLATE COURTS

TITLE I—APPELLATE PROCEDURE

CHAPTER 1. GENERAL DISPOSITIONS

2081. Applicability of Title.
2082. Definition of appeal.
2083. Judgments appealable.
2084. Legal representative may appeal.
2085. Limitations on appeals.
2086. Right of third person to appeal.
2087. Delay for taking devolutive appeal.
2088. Divesting of jurisdiction of trial court.
2089. Description required of immovable property affected by judgments or decrees.

CHAPTER 2. PROCEDURE FOR APPEALING

2121. Method of appealing.
2122. Appointment or removal of legal representative not suspended by appeal; effect of vacating appointment on appeal.
2123. Delay for taking suspensive appeal.
2124. Security to be furnished for an appeal.
2125. Return day.
2126. Payment of costs.
2127. Record on appeal; preparation; prepayment of fees.
2128. Same; determination of content.

ANALYSIS

Art.
2129. Assignment of errors unnecessary; exception.
2130. Record on appeal; statement of facts.
2131. Same; narrative of facts.
2132. Same; correction.
2133. Answer of appellee; when necessary.

CHAPTER 3. PROCEDURE IN APPELLATE COURT

2161. Dismissal for irregularities.
2162. Dismissal by consent of parties, or because of lack of jurisdiction or right to appeal, or abandonment; transfer.
2163. Peremptory exception filed in appellate court; remand if prescription pleaded.
2164. Scope of appeal and action to be taken; costs.
2165. Dismissal of appeal for want of prosecution.
2166. Rehearing.
2167. Finality of judgment.

TITLE II—SUPERVISORY PROCEDURE

2201. Supervisory writs.

BOOK IV—EXECUTION OF JUDGMENTS

TITLE I—GENERAL DISPOSITIONS

2251. Execution only in trial court; appellate court judgment.
2252. Delay before proceeding with execution.
2253. Writ from clerk to sheriff.
2254. Execution by sheriff; return.

TITLE II—MONEY JUDGMENTS

CHAPTER 1. WRIT OF FIERI FACIAS

2291. Money judgment; fieri facias.
2292. Privilege of creditor on seized property; successive seizures.
2293. Notice to judgment debtor.
2294. Time for seizure; return.
2295. Order of sale; sale in globo.
2296. Reduction of excessive seizure.
2297. Alias fieri facias.
2298. Injunction prohibiting sale.
2299. Order prohibiting payment of proceeds of sale.

ANALYSIS

CHAPTER 2. JUDICIAL SALE UNDER FIERI FACIAS

Art.
2331. Publication of notice of sale.
2332. Appraisal.
2333. Sale of perishable property.
2334. Reading of advertisement and certificates.
2335. Superior mortgage or privilege.
2336. Minimum price; second offering, if bid is less than two-thirds of appraised value.
2337. Price insufficient to discharge superior privileges; property not sold.
2338. Judgment creditor having superior privilege; price insufficient to satisfy inferior mortgage.
2339. Judgment debtor and creditor may bid.
2340. Payment of debt prior to adjudication.
2341. Sale when installment not due.
2342. Act of sale by sheriff.
2343. Sheriff's return after sale.

CHAPTER 3. THE ADJUDICATION AND ITS EFFECT

2371. Effect of adjudication.
2372. Sale subject to superior real charge or lease.
2373. Distribution of proceeds of sale.
2374. Property subject to superior mortgage; payment of price.
2375. Purchaser's liability; property subject to inferior mortgages.
2376. Release of inferior mortgages.
2377. Inferior mortgages; payment; reference to proceeds.
2378. Enforcement of mortgage or privilege superior to that of seizing creditor.
2379. Rights of buyer in case of eviction.
2380. Loss of recourse when purchaser fails to give judgment debtor timely notice.
2381. Action by seizing creditor who has been compelled to reimburse purchaser.

CHAPTER 4. GARNISHMENT UNDER A WRIT OF FIERI FACIAS

2411. Garnishee; effect of service.
2412. Method of service; delay for answering.
2413. Effect of garnishee's failure to answer.
2414. Notice of answer; traversing.

ANALYSIS

Art.
2415. Delivery of property or payment of indebtedness to sheriff.
2416. Venue of garnishment proceedings.
2417. Garnishment elsewhere than in parish of main action; procedure.

CHAPTER 5. EXAMINATION OF JUDGMENT DEBTOR

2451. Examination of judgment debtor; depositions.
2452. Court where motion filed and examination conducted.
2453. Motion; order; service.
2454. Oath; testimony not used in criminal proceedings.
2455. Costs.
2456. Contempt.

TITLE III—JUDGMENTS OTHER THAN MONEY JUDGMENTS

2501. Judgment ordering delivery of possession; writ of possession.
2502. Writ of distringas; contempt; damages.
2503. Distringas, execution and revocation.
2504. Specific performance; court directing performance by third party.

TITLE IV—FOREIGN JUDGMENTS

2541. Execution of foreign judgments.

BOOK V—SUMMARY AND EXECUTORY PROCEEDINGS

TITLE I—SUMMARY PROCEEDINGS

2591. Proceedings conducted with rapidity.
2592. Use of summary proceedings.
2593. Pleadings.
2594. Service of process.
2595. Trial; decision.
2596. Rules of ordinary proceedings applicable; exceptions.

TITLE II—EXECUTORY PROCEEDINGS

CHAPTER 1. GENERAL DISPOSITIONS

2631. Use of executory proceedings.
2632. Act importing a confession of judgment.

ANALYSIS

Art.
2633. Venue.
2634. Petition.
2635. Authentic evidence submitted with petition.
2636. Authentic evidence.
2637. Evidence which need not be authentic.
2638. Order for issuance of writ of seizure and sale.
2639. Demand for payment.
2640. Citation unnecessary; service of demand for payment.
2641. Service upon, and seizure and sale prosecuted against, attorney for unrepresented defendant.
2642. Assertion of defenses; appeal.
2643. Third person claiming mortgage or privilege on property seized.
2644. Conversion to ordinary proceeding.

CHAPTER 2. PROCEEDING AGAINST SURVIVING SPOUSE, SUCCESSION, OR HEIR

2671. Proceeding against surviving spouse in community.
2672. Proceeding against heirs or legatees.
2673. Proceeding against legal representative.
2674. Attorney appointed to represent unrepresented defendant.
2675. Case falling within application of two or more articles; plaintiff may bring proceeding under any applicable article.

CHAPTER 3. PROCEEDINGS WHEN PROPERTY IN POSSESSION OF THIRD PERSON

2701. Alienation of property to third person disregarded.
2702. Rights of third person who has acquired property and assumed indebtedness.
2703. Rights of third possessor.

CHAPTER 4. EXECUTION OF WRIT OF SEIZURE AND SALE

2721. Seizure of property; notice.
2722. Advertisement of sale.
2723. Appraisal of property, unless waived.
2724. Articles relating to sales under fieri facias applicable.

CHAPTER 5. INJUNCTION TO ARREST SEIZURE AND SALE

2751. Grounds for arresting seizure and sale.
2752. Injunction procedure.
2753. Security not required in certain cases.
2754. Security otherwise required.

ANALYSIS

CHAPTER 6. DEFICIENCY JUDGMENT

Art.
2771. When deficiency judgment obtainable.
2772. Procedure to obtain deficiency judgment.

CHAPTER 7. MAKING JUDGMENTS OF OTHER LOUISIANA COURTS EXECUTORY

2781. When judgments may be made executory by other courts.
2782. Procedure; execution of executory judgment.
2783. Injunction to arrest execution of judgment made executory.

BOOK VI—PROBATE PROCEDURE

TITLE I—GENERAL DISPOSITIONS

CHAPTER 1. JURISDICTION

2811. Court in which succession opened.
2812. Proceedings in different courts; stay; adoption of proceedings by court retaining jurisdiction.

CHAPTER 2. EVIDENCE OF JURISDICTION AND HEIRSHIP

2821. Evidence of jurisdiction, death, and relationship.
2822. Requirements of affidavit evidence.
2823. Additional evidence.
2824. No affidavit evidence of factual issues.
2825. Costs.
2826. Definition of certain terms used in Book VI.

CHAPTER 3. PROBATE AND REGISTRY OF TESTAMENTS

SECTION 1. PROCEDURE PRELIMINARY TO PROBATE

2851. Petition for probate.
2852. Documents submitted with petition for probate.
2853. Purported testament must be filed, though possessor doubts validity.

ANALYSIS

Art.
2854. Search for testament.
2855. Return to order to search for testament.
2856. Probate hearing; probate forthwith if witnesses present.
2857. Proponent must produce witnesses; subpoenas.

Section 2. Ex Parte Probate of Testaments

2881. Ex parte probate if no objection.
2882. Proceedings at probate hearing.
2883. Olographic testament.
2884. Nuncupative testament by private act.
2885. Mystic testament.
2886. Probate of nuncupative testament by private act or mystic testament, when witnesses dead or absent.
2887. Statutory testament.
2888. Foreign testament.
2889. Depositions of witnesses.
2890. Procès verbal of probate.
2891. Nuncupative testament by public act executed without probate.
2892. Use of probate testimony in subsequent action.
2893. Period within which will must be probated.

Section 3. Contradictory Probate of Testaments

2901. Contradictory trial required; time to file opposition.
2902. Opposition to petition for probate.
2903. Proponent bears burden of proof.

CHAPTER 4. ANNULMENT OF PROBATED TESTAMENTS

2931. Annulment of probated testament by direct action; defendants.
2932. Burden of proof in nullity action.
2933. Action to annul nuncupative testament by public act.

CHAPTER 5. PAYMENT OF STATE INHERITANCE TAXES

2951. No judgment of possession or delivery of legacy or inheritance until inheritance taxes paid or deposited.
2952. Descriptive list of property, if no inventory.
2953. Evidence as to taxes due, receipt of payment.
2954. Rule to determine inheritance taxes due.

CHAPTER 6. GENERAL RULES OF PROCEDURE

2971. Pleading and service of process.
2972. Oppositions.

ANALYSIS

Art.
2973. Responsive pleadings to opposition.
2974. Appeals.

TITLE II—ACCEPTANCE OF SUCCESSIONS WITHOUT ADMINISTRATION

CHAPTER 1. INTESTATE SUCCESSIONS

3001. Unconditional acceptance.
3002. Same; petition for possession.
3003. Same; evidence of allegations of petition for possession.
3004. Discretionary power to send heirs and surviving spouse into possession.
3005. Same; petition for possession; evidence.
3006. Same; when one of competent heirs cannot join in petition for possession.
3007. Creditor may demand security when heirs sent into possession.
3008. Administration in default of security.

CHAPTER 2. TESTATE SUCCESSIONS

3031. Sending legatees into possession without administration.
3032. Same; petition for possession; evidence.
3033. Same; compensation of executor.
3034. Creditor may demand security when legatees sent into possession; administration in default of security.
3035. Particular legatee may demand security for delivery of legacy; administration in default of security.

CHAPTER 3. JUDGMENTS OF POSSESSION

3061. Judgment rendered and signed immediately.
3062. Effect of judgment of possession.

TITLE III—ADMINISTRATION OF SUCCESSIONS

CHAPTER 1. QUALIFICATION OF SUCCESSION REPRESENTATIVES

Section 1. Executors

3081. Petition for confirmation.
3082. Order of confirmation; letters.
3083. Appointment of dative testamentary executor.

ANALYSIS

Section 2. Administrators

Art.
- 3091. Petition for notice of application for appointment.
- 3092. Form of petition for notice of application for appointment.
- 3093. Notice in compliance with petition.
- 3094. Order on application for appointment.
- 3095. Opposition to application for appointment.
- 3096. Appointment when no opposition; appointment after trial of opposition.
- 3097. Disqualifications.
- 3098. Priority of appointment.

Section 3. Provisional Administrators

- 3111. Appointment.
- 3112. Security; oath; tenure; rights and duties.
- 3113. Inventory taken when appointment made.

Section 4. Administrators of Vacant Successions

- 3121. Clerk of court as administrator of vacant successions, Orleans Parish excepted.
- 3122. Public administrator as administrator of vacant successions in Orleans Parish.

Section 5. Inventory of Succession Property

- 3131. Notary appointed for inventory in each parish.
- 3132. Public inventory.
- 3133. Procès verbal of inventory.
- 3134. Return of procès verbal of inventory.
- 3135. Procès verbal of inventory prima facie proof; traverse.
- 3136. Descriptive list of property in lieu of inventory.
- 3137. Descriptive list prima facie correct; amendment or traverse; reduction or increase of security.

Section 6. Security, Oath and Letters of Succession Representative

- 3151. Security of administrator.
- 3152. Security of provisional administrator.
- 3153. Security of testamentary executor.
- 3154. Forced heirs and surviving spouse in community may compel executor to furnish security.
- 3155. Creditor may compel executor to furnish security.
- 3156. Maximum security of executor.
- 3157. Special mortgage in lieu of bond.
- 3158. Oath of succession representative.
- 3159. Issuance of letters to succession representative.

ANALYSIS

CHAPTER 2. ATTORNEY FOR ABSENT HEIRS AND LEGATEES

Art.
3171. Appointment.
3172. Duties.
3173. Removal; appointment of successor.
3174. Compensation.

CHAPTER 3. REVOCATION OF APPOINTMENT, AND REMOVAL OF SUCCESSION REPRESENTATIVE

3181. Revocation of appointment or confirmation; extension of time to qualify.
3182. Removal.

CHAPTER 4. GENERAL FUNCTIONS, POWERS, AND DUTIES OF SUCCESSION REPRESENTATIVE

SECTION 1. GENERAL DISPOSITIONS

3191. General duties.
3192. Duties and powers of multiple representatives.
3193. Powers of surviving representatives.
3194. Contracts between succession representative and succession prohibited; penalties for failure to comply.
3195. Contracts between succession representative and succession; exceptions.
3196. Procedural rights of succession representative.
3197. Duty to close succession.
3198. Compromise and modification of obligations.

SECTION 2. COLLECTION OF SUCCESSION PROPERTY

3211. Duty to take possession; enforcement of claims and obligations.

SECTION 3. PRESERVATION AND MANAGEMENT OF SUCCESSION PROPERTY

3221. Preservation of succession property.
3222. Deposit of succession funds; unauthorized withdrawals prohibited; penalty.
3223. Investment of succession funds.
3224. Continuation of business.

ANALYSIS

Art.
- 3225. Continuation of business; interim order unappealable.
- 3226. Lease of succession property.
- 3227. Execution of contracts.
- 3228. Loans to succession representative for specific purposes; authority to mortgage and pledge succession property as security therefor.
- 3229. Notice by publication of application for court order; opposition.

CHAPTER 5. ENFORCEMENT OF CLAIMS AGAINST SUCCESSIONS

- 3241. Presenting claim against succession.
- 3242. Acknowledgment or rejection of claim by representative.
- 3243. Effect of acknowledgment of claim by representative.
- 3244. Effect of inclusion of claim in petition or in tableau of distribution.
- 3245. Submission of formal proof of claim to suspend prescription.
- 3246. Rejection of claim; prerequisite to judicial enforcement.
- 3247. Execution against succession property prohibited.
- 3248. Enforcement of conventional mortgage or pledge.
- 3249. Succession representative as party defendant.

CHAPTER 6. SALE OF SUCCESSION PROPERTY

SECTION 1. GENERAL DISPOSITIONS

- 3261. Purpose of sale.
- 3262. No priority as between movables and immovables.
- 3263. Terms of sale.
- 3264. Perishable property; crops.

SECTION 2. PUBLIC SALE

- 3271. Petition; order.
- 3272. Publication of notice of sale; place of sale.
- 3273. Minimum price; second offering.

SECTION 3. PRIVATE SALE

- 3281. Petition.
- 3282. Publication.
- 3283. Who may file opposition.
- 3284. Order; hearing.
- 3285. Bonds and stocks.

ANALYSIS

CHAPTER 7. PAYMENT OF DEBTS AND CHARGES OF SUCCESSIONS

Art.
3301. Payment of debts or charges; court order.
3302. Time for payment of debts; urgent debts.
3303. Petition for authority; tableau of distribution.
3304. Notice of filing of petition; publication.
3305. Petition for notice of filing of tableau of distribution.
3306. Notice of filing of tableau of distribution; effect of failure to serve.
3307. Homologation; payment.
3308. Appeal.

CHAPTER 8. INTERIM ALLOWANCE TO HEIRS AND LEGATEES

3321. Interim allowance for maintenance during administration.

CHAPTER 9. ACCOUNTING BY SUCCESSION REPRESENTATIVE

3331. Time for filing account.
3332. Final account.
3333. Contents of account.
3334. Failure to file account; penalty.
3335. Notice to heirs and residuary legatees.
3336. Opposition; homologation.
3337. Effect of homologation.
3338. Deceased or interdicted succession representative.

CHAPTER 10. COMPENSATION OF SUCCESSION REPRESENTATIVE

3351. Amount of compensation; when due.
3352. More than one succession representative.
3353. Legacy to executor.

CHAPTER 11. SENDING HEIRS AND LEGATEES INTO POSSESSION

Section 1. Intestate Succession

3361. After homologation of final tableau of distribution.
3362. Prior to homologation of final tableau of distribution.

ANALYSIS

Section 2. Testate Succession

Art.
3371. After homologation of final tableau of distribution.
3372. Prior to homologation of final tableau of distribution.

Section 3. Judgment of Possession

3381. Judgment of possession.

CHAPTER 12. DISCHARGE OF SUCCESSION REPRESENTATIVE

3391. Discharge of succession representative.
3392. Effect of judgment of discharge.
3393. Reopening of succession.
3394. Refusal or inability to accept funds; deposit in bank.
3395. Disposition of movables not accepted by heir.

TITLE IV—ANCILLARY PROBATE PROCEDURE

3401. Jurisdiction; procedure.
3402. Foreign representative; qualification.
3403. Capacity to sue.
3404. Priority in appointment.
3405. Testament probated outside Louisiana.

TITLE V—SMALL SUCCESSIONS

CHAPTER 1. GENERAL DISPOSITIONS

3421. Small succession defined.
3422. Court costs.

CHAPTER 2. WHEN JUDICIAL PROCEEDINGS UNNECESSARY

3431. Small successions; judicial opening unnecessary.
3432. Submission of affidavit to inheritance tax collector.
3433. Endorsement that no inheritance taxes due.
3434. Endorsed copy of affidavit authority for delivery of property.

CHAPTER 3. JUDICIAL PROCEEDINGS

3441. Acceptance without administration; procedure.
3442. Administration of successions; procedure.
3443. Sale of succession property; publication of notice of sale.

ANALYSIS

TITLE VI—PARTITION OF SUCCESSIONS

Art.
3461. Venue; procedure.
3462. Partition of succession property.

BOOK VII—SPECIAL PROCEEDINGS

TITLE I—PROVISIONAL REMEDIES

CHAPTER 1. ATTACHMENT AND SEQUESTRATION

Section 1. General Dispositions

3501. Petition; affidavit; security.
3502. Issuance of writ before petition filed.
3503. Garnishment under writs of attachment or of sequestration.
3504. Return of sheriff; inventory.
3505. Reduction of excessive seizure.
3506. Dissolution of writ; damages.
3507. Release of property by defendant; security.
3508. Amount of security for release of attached or sequestered property.
3509. Release of property by third person.
3510. Necessity for judgment and execution.
3511. Attachment and sequestration; privilege.
3512. Release of plaintiff's security.
3513. Sale of perishable property.
3514. Release not to affect right to damages.

Section 2. Attachment

3541. Grounds for attachment.
3542. Actions in which attachment can issue.
3543. Issuance of a writ of attachment before debt due.
3544. Plaintiff's security.
3545. Nonresident attachment; venue.

Section 3. Sequestration

3571. Grounds for sequestration.
3572. Sequestration before rent due.
3573. Sequestration by court on its own motion.
3574. Plaintiff's security.
3575. Lessor's privilege.
3576. Release of property under sequestration.

ANALYSIS

CHAPTER 2. INJUNCTION

Art.
3601. Injunction, grounds for issuance; preliminary injunction; temporary restraining order.
3602. Preliminary injunction; notice; hearing.
3603. Temporary restraining order; affidavit of irreparable injury.
3604. Form, contents, and duration of restraining order.
3605. Content and scope of injunction or restraining order.
3606. Temporary restraining order; hearing on preliminary injunction.
3607. Dissolution or modification of temporary restraining order or preliminary injunction.
3608. Damages for wrongful issuance of temporary restraining order or preliminary injunction.
3609. Proof at hearings; affidavits.
3610. Security for temporary restraining order or preliminary injunction.
3611. Penalty for disobedience; damages.
3612. Appeals.
3613. Jurisdiction not limited.

TITLE II—REAL ACTIONS

CHAPTER 1. ACTIONS TO DETERMINE OWNERSHIP OR POSSESSION

3651. Petitory action.
3652. Same; parties; venue.
3653. Same; proof of title.
3654. Proof of title in action for declaratory judgment, concursus, expropriation, or similar proceeding.
3655. Possessory action.
3656. Same; parties; venue.
3657. Same; cumulation with petitory action prohibited; conversion into or separate petitory action by defendant.
3658. Same; requisites.
3659. Same; disturbance in fact and in law defined.
3660. Same; possession.
3661. Same; title not at issue; limited admissibility of evidence of title.
3662. Same; relief which may be granted successful plaintiff in judgment; appeal.
3663. Sequestration; injunctive relief.
3664. Real rights under contracts to reduce minerals to possession.

ANALYSIS

CHAPTER 2. BOUNDARY ACTION

Art.
3691. Right to compel fixing of boundaries.
3692. Appointment of surveyor by court.
3693. Determination of boundary rights.

CHAPTER 3. HYPOTHECARY ACTION

Section 1. General Dispositions

3721. Methods of enforcing mortgage.
3722. Enforcement by ordinary proceeding.
3723. Enforcement by executory proceeding.

Section 2. Hypothecary Action Against Third Person

3741. Right of enforcement.
3742. Notice of seizure.
3743. Rights of third possessor.

CHAPTER 4. NOTICE OF PENDENCY OF ACTION

3751. Notice to be recorded to affect third persons.
3752. Requirements of notice; recordation.
3753. Cancellation of notice of pendency.

TITLE III—EXTRAORDINARY REMEDIES

CHAPTER 1. GENERAL DISPOSITIONS

3781. Petition; summary trial; issuance of writs.
3782. Return date.
3783. Answer.
3784. Hearing.
3785. Disobedience of writ or judgment; contempt.

CHAPTER 2. HABEAS CORPUS

3821. Definition.
3822. Venue.
3823. Persons authorized to make service; proof of service.
3824. Method of service.
3825. Answer; production of person in custody.
3826. Transfer of custody; answer.

ANALYSIS

Art.
3827. Inability to produce person in custody.
3828. Custody pendente lite.
3829. Notice of hearing.
3830. Judgment.
3831. Appeal not to suspend execution of judgment.

CHAPTER 3. MANDAMUS

3861. Definition.
3862. Cases in which mandamus issues.
3863. Person against whom writ directed.
3864. Mandamus against corporation or corporate officer.
3865. Alternative writ.
3866. Judgment.

CHAPTER 4. QUO WARRANTO

3901. Definition.
3902. Judgment.

TITLE IV—ANNULMENT OF MARRIAGE, SEPARATION FROM BED AND BOARD, AND DIVORCE

3941. Court where action brought; nullity of judgment of court of improper venue.
3942. Appeal from judgment granting or refusing annulment, separation, or divorce.
3943. Appeal from judgment awarding custody or alimony.
3944. Injunctive relief.
3945. Execution of alimony judgments in arrears.

TITLE V—JUDICIAL EMANCIPATION

3991. Petition; court where proceeding brought.
3992. Consent of parent or tutor.
3993. Hearing; judgment.
3994. Expenses of proceeding.

TITLE VI—TUTORSHIP

CHAPTER 1. COURT WHERE PROCEEDINGS ARE BROUGHT

4031. Minor domiciled in the state.
4032. Minor not domiciled in the state.

ANALYSIS

Art.
4033. Petitions filed in two or more courts; stay of proceedings in second and subsequent courts; adoption of proceedings by first court.
4034. Proceedings subsequent to appointment of tutor.

CHAPTER 2. APPOINTMENT OF PARTICULAR TUTORS

4061. Natural tutor; general obligations.
4062. Tutorship by will.
4063. Legal tutor.
4064. Dative tutor.
4065. Legal or dative tutor; petition for appointment; publication of notice.
4066. Opposition to application of legal or dative tutor.
4067. Appointment of legal or dative tutor.
4068. Appeal from judgment confirming, appointing, or removing tutor or undertutor; effect.
4069. Separate tutor of property.
4070. Provisional tutor.
4071. Security, oath, and tenure of provisional tutor.
4072. Inventory on appointment of provisional tutor.
4073. Functions, duties, and authority of provisional tutor.

CHAPTER 3. INVENTORY OF MINOR'S PROPERTY

4101. Inventory and appraisement.
4102. Procedure for inventory; procès verbal; return.

CHAPTER 4. SECURITY OF TUTOR

4131. Amount.
4132. Nature of security.
4133. Special mortgage instead of bond.
4134. Natural tutor; bond; recordation of certificate of inventory.
4135. Security instead of legal mortgage.
4136. Substitution of one kind of security for another.

CHAPTER 5. OATH AND LETTERS OF TUTORSHIP

4171. Oath.
4172. Issuance of letters.

ANALYSIS

CHAPTER 6. UNDERTUTOR

Art.
4201. Appointment; oath.
4202. General duties of undertutor.
4203. Compelling tutor to account.
4204. Security of tutor, undertutor's duty regarding sufficiency.
4205. Vacancy in tutorship, duty of undertutor.
4206. Termination of duties.

CHAPTER 7. DISQUALIFICATION, REVOCATION OF APPOINTMENT, RESIGNATION, AND REMOVAL

4231. Disqualification of tutor.
4232. Revocation of appointment; extension of time to qualify.
4233. Resignation of tutor.
4234. Removal of tutor.
4235. Authority and liability of tutor after resignation or removal.
4236. Undertutor, grounds for disqualification, revocation, or removal.
4237. Appointment of successor tutor or undertutor.
4238. Heirs of tutor; responsibility.

CHAPTER 8. GENERAL FUNCTIONS, POWERS, AND DUTIES OF TUTOR

4261. Care of person of minor; expenses.
4262. Administration of minor's property.
4263. Contracts between tutor and minor.
4264. Tutor's administration in his own name; procedural rights.
4265. Compromise and modification of obligations.
4266. Continuation of business.
4267. Loans to tutor for specific purposes; authority to mortgage and pledge minor's property.
4268. Lease of minor's property; mineral contracts.
4269. Investment and management of minor's property.
4270. Procedure for investing funds.
4271. Court approval of action affecting minor's interest.
4272. Court approval of payments to minor.
4273. Temporary absence; appointment of agent.
4274. Compensation of tutor.
4275. Donations to or by minor.

CHAPTER 9. SALE OF MINOR'S PROPERTY

Section 1. General Dispositions

4301. Purpose of sale.
4302. Terms of sale.

ANALYSIS

Art.
4303. Perishable property; crops.
4304. Additional bond prior to sale of immovables.

Section 2. Public Sale

4321. Petition; order.
4322. Publication; place of sale.
4323. Minimum price; subsequent offering.

Section 3. Private Sale

4341. Petition.
4342. Bonds and stocks.

Section 4. Adjudication To Parent

4361. Adjudication of minor's interest to parent co-owner.
4362. Recordation of judgment; mortgage in favor of minor.
4363. Security instead of mortgage.

CHAPTER 10. ACCOUNTING BY TUTOR

4391. Duty to account; annual accounts.
4392. Final account.
4393. Contents of account.
4394. Service of account.
4395. Opposition; homologation.
4396. Effect of homologation.
4397. Deceased or interdicted tutor.
4398. Cost of accounting.

CHAPTER 11. ANCILLARY TUTORSHIP PROCEDURE

4431. Foreign tutor; authority and powers.
4432. Possession or removal of property from state.
4433. Foreign tutor qualifying in Louisiana; authority.

CHAPTER 12. SMALL TUTORSHIPS

4461. Small tutorship defined.
4462. Inventory dispensed with.
4463. Dative tutor without bond.
4464. Court costs.

TITLE VII—ADMINISTRATION OF MINOR'S PROPERTY DURING MARRIAGE OF PARENTS

4501. Father as administrator of minor's property.
4502. Rights of mother when father is a mental incompetent or absentee.

ANALYSIS

TITLE VIII—INTERDICTION AND CURATORSHIP OF INTERDICTS

Art.
- 4541. Court in which interdiction proceedings brought.
- 4542. Proceedings subsequent to appointment of curator.
- 4543. Who may file petition.
- 4544. Service of process; appointment of attorney.
- 4545. Defendant confined outside Louisiana.
- 4546. Summary trial.
- 4547. Interrogation and examination of defendant.
- 4548. Effect of appeal.
- 4549. Appointment and qualification of provisional curator; functions, duties, authority.
- 4550. Appointment of curator.
- 4551. Costs.
- 4552. Recordation of notice of suit and of judgment.
- 4553. Undercurator.
- 4554. Tutorship rules applicable.
- 4555. Custody of interdict.
- 4556. Expenses for care of interdict and legal dependents.
- 4557. Termination of interdiction.

TITLE IX—PARTITION BETWEEN CO-OWNERS

CHAPTER 1. GENERAL DISPOSITIONS

- 4601. Methods of partition.
- 4602. Judicial partition.
- 4603. Same; procedure; venue.
- 4604. Inventory.
- 4605. Preference; appointment of notary; discretion of court.
- 4606. Partition in kind.
- 4607. Partition by licitation.
- 4608. Controversy before notary effecting partition.
- 4609. Homologation of partition.
- 4610. Opposition to homologation.
- 4611. Supplementary partition when rule to reject or opposition to homologation sustained.
- 4612. Finality of partition when rule to reject or opposition unfounded.
- 4613. Attorney's fee in uncontested proceedings.
- 4614. Purchase by co-owner of property or interest sold.

CHAPTER 2. PARTITION WHEN CO-OWNER AN ABSENTEE

- 4621. Partition by licitation.
- 4622. Petition.

ANALYSIS

Art.
4623. Order; service of citation; contradictory proceedings.
4624. Publication of notice.
4625. Trial; judgment ordering sale.
4626. Judgment ordering reimbursement or payment of amounts due co-owner out of proceeds of sale.
4627. Effect of judgment and sale.
4628. Deposit of absentee's share into registry of court.
4629. Articles applicable to partition by licitation.
4630. Partition in kind when defendant appears and prays therefor.

CHAPTER 3. PARTITION WHEN CO-OWNER A MINOR OR INTERDICT

4641. Sale of interest of minor or interdict to effect partition.
4642. Partition in kind, dispensing with drawing of lots when authorized by court.

TITLE X—CONCURSUS PROCEEDINGS

4651. Definition.
4652. Claimants who may be impleaded.
4653. Parish where proceeding brought.
4654. Petition.
4655. Service of process; delay for answer.
4656. Each defendant both plaintiff and defendant; no responsive pleadings to answer; no default required.
4657. Failure of defendant to answer timely.
4658. Deposit of money into registry of court.
4659. Costs.
4660. Injunctive relief.
4661. Applicability of articles to proceedings under certain special statutes.
4662. Rules of ordinary proceeding applicable.

TITLE XI—EVICTION OF TENANTS AND OCCUPANTS

CHAPTER 1. GENERAL DISPOSITIONS

4701. Termination of lease; notice to vacate.
4702. Notice to occupant other than tenant to vacate.
4703. Delivery or service when premises abandoned or closed, or whereabouts of tenant or occupant unknown.
4704. Definitions.
4705. Lessors' rights or real actions not affected.

ANALYSIS

CHAPTER 2. PROCEDURE

Art.
4731. Rule to show cause why possession should not be delivered.
4732. Trial of rule; judgment of eviction.
4733. Warrant for possession if judgment of eviction not complied with.
4734. Execution of warrant.
4735. Appeal; bond.

BOOK VIII—TRIAL COURTS OF LIMITED JURISDICTION

TITLE I—GENERAL DISPOSITIONS

4831. Applicability of Book VIII.
4832. Jurisdiction of city courts in municipalities of less than 10,000 population, and justice of the peace courts.
4833. Jurisdiction of city courts in municipalities of 10,000 to 20,000 population.
4834. Jurisdiction of city courts in municipalities of 20,000 or more population, New Orleans city courts excepted.
4835. Jurisdiction of New Orleans city courts.
4836. Limitations on jurisdiction.
4837. Limitations on power and authority.
4838. Power to punish for contempt.
4839. Venue.
4840. Jury trial prohibited.
4841. Illness or absence of justice of the peace, or judge of city court; New Orleans city courts excepted.
4842. Illness or absence of judge of New Orleans city court.
4843. Recusation; grounds.
4844. Recusation of justice of the peace or city court judge; trial of motion to recuse; exceptions.
4845. Trial of motion to recuse; judges of city courts having more than one judge; Second City Court of New Orleans.
4846. Power and authority of judge ad hoc.
4847. Rules of court.

TITLE II—CASES INVOLVING ONE HUNDRED DOLLARS OR LESS

CHAPTER 1. CITY COURTS

SECTION 1. CITY COURTS, NEW ORLEANS EXCEPTED

4891. Procedure.
4892. Pleadings.

ANALYSIS

Art.
- 4893. Record of case; subsequent entries.
- 4894. Citation.
- 4895. Delay for answering.
- 4896. Defendant's failure to answer or parties' failure to appear; effect; proof of open account; judgment.
- 4897. Form of judgment; new trial not permitted; execution of judgment.
- 4898. Notice of judgment.
- 4899. Appeal.
- 4900. Appeal bond.
- 4901. Record on appeal.

Section 2. New Orleans City Courts

- 4921. Procedure in cases involving less than twenty-five dollars.
- 4922. Procedure in cases involving twenty-five to one hundred dollars.

CHAPTER 2. JUSTICE OF THE PEACE COURTS

- 4941. Procedure.
- 4942. Appeal.

CHAPTER 3. DISTRICT COURTS WHERE JURISDICTION CONCURRENT WITH JUSTICE OF THE PEACE COURTS

- 4971. Procedure.
- 4972. Rendition of judgment; cases where judgment rendered by clerk; time for applying for new trial.

TITLE III—CASES INVOLVING MORE THAN ONE HUNDRED DOLLARS

- 5001. Procedure.
- 5002. Delays for answering; incorporation of exceptions in answer; prior default unnecessary; notice of judgment; new trial; appeals.

BOOK IX—MISCELLANEOUS PROVISIONS AND DEFINITIONS

TITLE I—MISCELLANEOUS PROVISIONS

CHAPTER 1. RULES OF CONSTRUCTION

- 5051. Liberal construction of articles.
- 5052. Unambiguous language not to be disregarded.

ANALYSIS

Art.
- 5053. Words and phrases.
- 5054. Clerical and typographical errors disregarded.
- 5055. Number; gender.
- 5056. Conjunctive, disjunctive, or both.
- 5057. Headings, source notes, cross references.
- 5058. References to code articles or statutory sections.
- 5059. Computation of time.

CHAPTER 2. ATTORNEY APPOINTED TO REPRESENT UNREPRESENTED DEFENDANTS

- 5091. Appointment; contradictory proceedings against attorney; improper designation immaterial.
- 5092. Qualifications; suggestions for appointment not permitted.
- 5093. Oath not required; waiver of citation and acceptance of service.
- 5094. Duties; notice to nonresident or absentee.
- 5095. Same; defense of action.
- 5096. Compensation.
- 5097. Attorney appointed to represent claimant in workmen's compensation case.
- 5098. Validity of proceeding not affected by failure of attorney to perform duties; punishment of attorney.

CHAPTER 3. BONDS IN JUDICIAL PROCEEDINGS

- 5121. Bond payable to clerk; person in interest may sue.
- 5122. Oath of surety and principal on bond.
- 5123. Testing sufficiency and validity of bond.
- 5124. Furnishing new or supplemental bond to correct defects of original.
- 5125. Insufficiency or invalidity of bond; effect on orders or judgments; appeal from order for supplemental bond.
- 5126. Insufficiency or invalidity of new or supplemental bond.
- 5127. Release bond.

CHAPTER 4. DISCUSSION

- 5151. Discussion defined.
- 5152. Surety's right to plead.
- 5153. Transferee in revocatory action; right to plead discussion.
- 5154. Third possessor's right to plead.
- 5155. Pleading discussion.
- 5156. Effect of discussion.

ANALYSIS

CHAPTER 5. WAIVER OF COSTS FOR INDIGENT PARTY

Art.
5181. Privilege of litigating without prior payment of costs.
5182. Restrictions on privilege.
5183. Affidavits of poverty; order.
5184. Traverse of affidavits of poverty.
5185. Rights of party permitted to litigate without payment of costs.
5186. Account and payment of costs.
5187. Compromise; dismissal of proceeding prior to judgment.
5188. Unsuccessful party condemned to pay costs.

TITLE II—DEFINITIONS

5251. Words and terms defined.

A Short History of Louisiana Civil Procedure

By

HENRY G. McMAHON

Professor of Law, Louisiana State University

Coordinator and Reporter, Louisiana Code of Civil Procedure

A Short History of
Louisiana Civil Procedure

By

HENRY G. McMAHON

Professor of Law, Louisiana State University

Coordinator and Reporter, Louisiana Code
of Civil Procedure

A SHORT HISTORY OF LOUISIANA CIVIL PROCEDURE*

By Henry G. McMahon,
Professor of Law, Louisiana State University
Coordinator and Reporter, Louisiana Code of Civil Procedure.

INTRODUCTION

For the past century and a half Louisiana has been a veritable laboratory of comparative law. Its juridical heritage from France and Spain, and its acquisition by the United States, precipitated an immediate struggle between the Romanistic and English systems of law. Louisiana's admission into the Union required adoption of the constitutional and public law of America. A flourishing trade and commercial intercourse with its sister states made the adoption of Anglo-American commercial law expedient. The failure of the Louisiana Legislature, in 1824, to adopt Edward Livingston's enlightened penal code resulted in a juridical vacuum which the Anglo-American common law of crimes and criminal procedure found relatively easy to fill. But in the extremely important area of private law the Romanistic system emerged triumphant: the civilian customs and institutions of the former colony were retained and perpetuated through the 1808 codification and the Louisiana Civil Code of 1825, the latter modeled upon the Code Napoléon. A lesser victory was scored by the Romanistic system in the field of civil procedure, where Livingston skilfully blended Continental procedural principles with judicial administrative provisions of Anglo-American origin.

Competition between these two great legal systems did not end, however, with this early demarcation of spheres of influence. The training of Louisiana lawyers in the national law schools of America, the ultimate loss by the Louisiana practitioner and judge of the ability to read French and Spanish, and the greater availability of American legal literature, all permitted the influence of Anglo-American law to erode the civil law and procedure of the state. These inroads of the English common law, however, were the result of interstitial seepage

---

* This paper constitutes the initial portion of the author's article, *The Louisiana Code of Civil Procedure*, 21 LOUISIANA LAW REVIEW 1 (1960), and is published here, without supporting documentation, with the permission and through the courtesy of the Louisiana Law Review.

between the provisions of the positive law of Louisiana, rather than an undermining of its foundations. In due time a reaction was to set in.

The great improvement in legal education in Louisiana, which commenced roughly thirty-five years ago, brought an almost immediate revival of interest in its civil law and procedure. The publication of law reviews by the three law schools of the state provided, for the first time, the scholarly research and doctrinal writings so necessary for the nourishment of any civilian system. A decade or so later, the Louisiana State Law Institute was established as the official research and law reform agency of the state, with generous support from public funds. The Institute, utilizing as it does the combined knowledge and energies of members of the legislature, the judiciary, the bar, and of the law faculties, has given a tremendous impetus to law reform and improvement in Louisiana. Its work in the drafting of the *projet* of the new procedural code was much more than a consolidation and editorial revision of the pre-existing rules of civil procedure. True, those principles, concepts, and devices which have proven effective and workable in actual practice are retained. But the improvements in procedure achieved under the Federal Rules of Civil Procedure, by the more recent procedural codes of the various American states, and by the more advanced codes of civil procedure of Continental countries were studied carefully, with the view of improving Louisiana's procedure through a borrowing of the more effective procedural principles and devices of other states and countries. More than any other American code, the Louisiana Code of Civil Procedure is a product of the comparative method.

Procedure is only the means of enforcing and implementing the substantive law. To perform its proper role, it must be correlated to the substantive law which it is designed to enforce. As the substantive law of Louisiana is partly of Romanistic and partly of English origin, it is not surprising to find that in the past its civil procedure has been a blend of Continental and Anglo-American procedures.

An appraisal of the procedural system which will be ushered in through the adoption of the Louisiana Code of Civil Procedure, and an evaluation of the contributions which are made thereto by both Continental and Anglo-American civil procedures, is one of the objects of the present article. Such an analysis, however, would be impossible without some mention of the various procedural systems in effect in Louisiana in the past.

PROCEDURAL SYSTEMS PRIOR TO 1825

Though France claimed the vast Louisiana territory as early as 1682, by virtue of the explorations of La Salle, no serious effort was made to colonize any part of the vast expanse until 1699, when d'Iberville set up the first settlement on the coast of the Gulf of Mexico. No civil government worthy of the name was established until 1712, when the colony was granted to Crozat. Under the latter's charter, it was provided that the Custom of Paris—that most interesting combination of Germanic custom and Roman law which had been codified in the sixteenth century—should be in effect throughout the territory. The expense of colonization proved too great a drain upon the resources of even the immensely wealthy Crozat, so that in 1717 he was compelled to surrender his charter. Thereupon, a grant of the colony was made to John Law's Company of the West, under a charter which confirmed the applicability of the Custom of Paris to the Louisiana territory. After the bankruptcy of the Company of the West in 1732, the French monarch was forced to take over the Louisiana territory as a crown colony; but until the Spanish took possession of Louisiana under the cession of 1762, the Custom of Paris continued to be the basic private law of the colony, modified slightly from time to time by royal ordinances.

The judicial system of Louisiana may be said to have been founded during the Crozat administration, with the establishment of the Superior Council as the first court of the territory. The procedure employed in civil cases in the Superior Council of the colony was based primarily upon the four titles of the Custom of Paris relating to real actions, actions generally, arrests and executions, and the seizure and sale of movables. Otherwise, the procedure applicable was that employed in cases before the Châtelet of Paris. From an examination of Pigeau's work on the subject, it appears that the procedure of the Châtelet was based largely upon the Ordonnance Civile of 1667, Louis XIV's famed procedural code, generally regarded as the foundation of the present French Code of Civil Procedure.

Few lawyers were to be found in the colony at this time, and little litigation occurred during this period of French dominion. This procedural system thus failed to make any lasting impression upon the small population, with the result that French civil procedure played a relatively minor initial role in shaping the adjective law of Louisiana.

Under the secret Treaty of Fontainebleau in 1762, France ceded the entire Louisiana territory to Spain. The latter's initial attempt, under the timid de Ulloa, to take possession of the colony three years later resulted in resistance from the French colonists, which permitted Louisiana to remain under the *de facto* control of the French commander until 1769. In that year, Don Alejandro O'Reilly took possession of the territory with a strong Spanish force, ruthlessly punished the leaders of the resistance, and firmly established Spanish rule over the colony. His first official acts were proclamations issued in the name of His Most Catholic Majesty, abolishing the colonial government, establishing the new Spanish Province of Louisiana, abrogating French law in the colony, and establishing a short code of laws for the people. This code was intended only for temporary use, and only until the colonists could become more familiar with the laws of Spain.

The judicial system created under O'Reilly's Proclamation consisted of regional trial courts throughout the territory under Alcaldes Ordinary, with an appeal in petty cases to the Cabildo, or municipal council of New Orleans, and in the more important cases to the Audiencia in Havana, with the Council of the Indies as the appellate court of last resort.

Annexed to the brief code embodied in O'Reilly's Proclamation was a set of "instructions as to the manner of instituting suits, civil and criminal, and of pronouncing judgments in general," compiled by two of the Spanish lawyers on O'Reilly's staff. The headnote thereon evidences the fact that both O'Reilly's "code" and the instructions annexed thereto were based upon the Recopilación de las Indias, the great digest of the laws and regulations enacted by Spain during the preceding centuries for the people of their colonial empire, and the Recopilación de Castilla. Both of these latter codes contained references to the monumental Código de las Siete Partidas and the Nueva Recopilación de las Leyes de España, as well as the earlier Spanish codifications, the Fuero Real, the Fuero Viejo de Castilla, and even to the ancient Forum Juzgo. From the numerous citations of these Spanish codes by the courts of Louisiana during the initial period of American dominion, it seems reasonable to conclude that the colonial lawyers were completely familiar therewith. The same evidence indicates that the works of Gregario López, of Hevia Bolaños, and of Febrero likewise were available, and were accepted as authoritative in procedural matters during the Spanish regime. Although Spain held the colony for little more than a third of a century, its procedural law played an extremely important role in shaping the subsequent civil procedure of Louisiana.

Under the secret treaty of San Ildefonso in 1800, Spain retroceded the Louisiana territory to France. The latter, however, made no effort to regain possession of the colony until late in 1803. Prior to taking possession, France sold the entire territory to the United States of America, which assumed control thereof on December 20, 1803.

As France exercised sovereignty over the colony in this period for less than a month, no effort was made to abrogate the Spanish laws then in force. The American government, after taking over the colony, moved slowly in effecting changes in the law of Louisiana. The former French colony was first divided. That portion north of the present northern boundary of the State of Louisiana was organized as the District, then the Territory, of Louisiana, and finally as the Territory of Missouri. The remainder of the former colony, comprising all of the present State of Louisiana except the West Florida Parishes, was organized as the Territory of Orleans. Three acts of the Congress of the United States affecting the latter territory were passed during the first two years after the Louisiana Purchase. The first left unchanged all of the laws then in force, simply vesting the administrative power in different officers. The second and third of these congressional acts reorganized the territorial government to conform to the American pattern, provided for the writ of habeas corpus and for trial by jury, but expressly declared that all laws in force in the territory should continue in effect until changed by subsequent legislation.

The Legislative Council of the Territory of Orleans, empowered by Congress to legislate for this new American possession, made more significant changes almost immediately. The Crimes Act of 1805 defined a large number of felonies and misdemeanors, repealed all prior criminal legislation, recognized the accused's right to a trial by jury, and provided that all of such trials should be conducted according to the common law of England. The most important of these early territorial statutes, subsequently known as the Practice Act of 1805, recognized the Superior Court of the Territory, previously established in New Orleans by the territorial governor, and provided a simple procedure for the trial of cases therein. A third act divided the territory into counties, created county and justice of the peace courts, and adopted a simplified version of the procedure embodied in the Practice Act of 1805 for the trial of cases in these courts.

The Practice Act of 1805 merits extended consideration here for at least two reasons. For one thing, it was the handiwork of the distinguished Edward Livingston, who, ruined financially by the defalcations of a subordinate while holding the office of Mayor of New York, emigrated to Louisiana to regain his fortune, subsequently became an enthusiastic convert to the civil law, and led the fight for codification in Louisiana. For another, important segments of the Louisiana Code of Practice of 1825 were taken bodily from the 1805 legislation.

The most radical changes made in the civil procedure of Louisiana by the Practice Act of 1805 were the establishment of the trial by jury, and the requirement that the testimony of all available witnesses be taken in open court, with depositions permitted only for witnesses who were ill, aged, or beyond the control of the court. Other provisions established a simplified form of pleading, created the provisional remedies of attachment and arrest, provided for the enforcement of judgments under the writs of fieri facias and distringas, and authorized the court to issue writs of quo warranto, procedendo, mandamus, and prohibition. The statute went into great detail in prescribing the form of citations, writs, and other mandates to be issued by the court. As Livingston was a staunch disciple of the great English reformer, Jeremy Bentham, the simplified procedure embodied in the Practice Act of 1805 reflected Bentham's influence.

Considerable difference of opinion exists today as to the sources of this legislation. Mr. Benjamin Wall Dart, the distinguished editor of the last edition of the Louisiana Code of Practice, and the son of Louisiana's leading legal historian, has voiced the opinion that the provisions of the Practice Act of 1805 "were in effect restatements of the Spanish procedure with additions made necessary by the new order resulting from France's transfer of Louisiana to the United States." On the other hand, America's most distinguished student of comparative civil procedure, the late Professor Robert Wyness Millar, of the Northwestern University School of Law, is of the opinion that the Practice Act of 1805 was primarily a refinement and simplification of contemporary American chancery practice, a view in which the present writer originally concurred. Further research by the writer over a period of years, however, has convinced him that there is considerably more validity in Mr. Dart's position than the writer had originally thought.

A determination of the primary sources of the Practice Act is made extremely difficult by the very fact which, paradoxically enough, appears to lend support to the views of both Mr. Dart and Professor Millar: the striking similarity between many aspects of Anglo-American chancery practice and Spanish procedure. This is not surprising, in view of the fact that the equity system of England initially was administered by the ecclesiastics, who applied the procedural principles of canonical procedure in developing chancery practice. Since the adjective law of Spain was also a legitimate descendant of Romano-canonical law, many similarities of the two procedural systems are to be expected.

The present writer has been unable to find any recorded expression of the views of Edward Livingston on the subject. Fairly convincing evidence is available, however, to indicate that the courts and legal profession of Louisiana regarded the Practice Act of 1805 as being based primarily upon Spanish procedure.

The last section of this 1805 statute authorized the Superior Court to issue writs of quo warranto, procedendo, mandamus, and prohibition. The first year after the admission of Louisiana to statehood, the newly created Supreme Court found it necessary to determine whether the common law rules relating to mandamus or the rules relating to its Spanish counterpart, incitativo, were applicable in Louisiana. In determining this issue the court observed:

SHORT HISTORY—HENRY G. McMAHON

> "The common law names in judicial proceedings have naturally been adopted in a practice which is carried on in the English language, but they ought to be considered rather as a translation of the names formerly used, than as emanations from the English jurisprudence; the words mandamus, procedendo, certiorari, prohibition, &c., sometimes employed in our practice, may be good equivalents for incitativo, evocación, inhibición, &c; but their adoption as words can, by no rule of law, or common sense, be considered as having introduced the English practice itself."

This was the language of a court composed, not exclusively of native Louisianians who might be expected to be unsympathetic to any attempt to supersede the Spanish procedural rules with which they were familiar, but of a court having a majority of its judges trained initially under the common law system.

A later case, although decided three years after the end of the period which we are now considering, in answering a somewhat similar question, confirmed the judicial view quoted above. In this later case, speaking through Justice Porter, the court said:

> "The repeal of laws is never presumed; and if the new and old laws can stand together, they should be so construed. It would be going far, to hold that the special enactment of a remedy which previously existed, should introduce the consequences that attended that remedy in another system of jurisprudence. In this respect there is a material difference between this case and that construction which should be given to our laws introducing jury trial, and the writ of habeas corpus; for they being unknown to our jurisprudence, the understanding of them was ex necessitate, to be sought somewhere else. The use of common law terms is easily accounted for, in the desire of the legislature to use those words which would convey in the most clear and concise manner, to persons acquainted with the English language alone, the remedies defined."

Louisiana was admitted as a member state of the North American union in 1812, under a constitution adopted earlier in that year. Neither this constitution nor the statutes implementing its provisions made any substantial changes in the procedural law of Louisiana, other than the creation of a system of courts based on the American pattern, and consisting of a supreme court, district courts, and justice of the peace courts. The Practice Act of 1805 remained in effect until its repeal when the Code of Practice went into effect in 1825.

The civil procedure of Louisiana at the end of this period, therefore, was based primarily upon the Spanish procedure in force during the period of Spanish dominion. Two significant changes had been made therein by the Practice Act: the adoption of the institution of jury trial; and the requirement that the testimony of all available witnesses be given in open court. The common law rules of evidence followed in the wake of the adoption of the jury trial almost as a necessary consequence. The requirement of *viva voce* testimony in open court resulted in the direct and cross-examination of witnesses as under the English practice. As a result of these changes, the trial of litigation in Louisiana, at least during this period, took on the complexion of the common law trial. But otherwise, except to the extent that it ran counter to the provisions of the Practice Act and other legislation, Spanish influence upon the civil procedure of the state during this period remained paramount.

THE CODE OF PRACTICE OF 1825

Pursuant to a legislative resolution of March 14, 1822, L. Moreau-Lislet, Edward Livingston, and Pierre Derbigny were appointed as a committee to revise and amend the so-called Civil Code of 1808, to prepare a commercial code, and to submit "a treatise on the rules of civil actions and a system of the practice to be observed before our courts." No more able a group of jurisconsults could have been selected for these tasks. Livingston, who had come to Louisiana in 1804, probably was the most distinguished American legal scholar of his day, entirely familiar not only with the common law, but with Roman, French, and Spanish law as well. Derbigny had been an outstanding practitioner before the Spanish courts of the colony, one of the first justices of the Supreme Court of Louisiana, and subsequently Secretary of State and Governor. Moreau-Lislet, a distinguished veteran of the colonial period, had previously served as Attorney General of the state, and with Henry Carleton, had prepared the first English translation of the Siete Partidas.

Early in 1823, the three redactors submitted to the Legislature the *projet* of the new procedural code, which was subsequently approved and went into effect in 1825. This Code of Practice, in form and arrangement, was typically civilian, consisting of 1155 articles numbered consecutively, and divided into titles, chapters, and sections. As Colonel Tucker, the distinguished President of the Louisiana State Law Institute, has pointed out, it was "the product of a mixture of French, Spanish, and Roman law elements, together with common law elements of English origin."

The draftsmen of this procedural code, in the comments in their *projet*, not only gave their reasons for the adoption of controversial principles and procedural devices, but listed the sources of the more important articles of the code. An examination of these source notes is extremely interesting. The direct Roman law influence was slight, only eight references having been made to the Digest and three to the Institutes, all in the title dealing with actions. Spanish procedural law, as might be expected, served as the basis of a number of extremely important segments of the new codification, with sixty-three references to the Spanish codes and procedure writers. There must be considered in this connection, however, the forty-five references to the Practice Act of 1805 (the majority of which in turn were bottomed upon Spanish procedure), and the sixty-nine references to Louisiana statutes (a number of which were predicated on general concepts of Spanish law). French procedural theory, which had played a rather negligible role in the preceding era, increased its influence upon the adoption of the Code of Practice. Thirty references in the redactors' source notes were to works of French commentators, with the more indirect influence reflected through the twenty-six references to the Civil Code of 1808, which was based largely upon the Code Napoléon.

The Spanish procedural law constituting direct sources of the procedural code was drawn principally from the Siete Partidas, and the procedural works of Febrero and Hevia Bolaños. The writings of Domat and Pothier constituted the direct borrowings from French pre-code procedural theory. Important segments of Louisiana's procedural law, such as succession and injunction procedure, reflected the indirect influence of French procedure.

One of the deficiencies of the redactors' source notes is that very few references to Anglo-American law are listed, although even a cursory examination of this code indicates quite clearly that the Anglo-American contribution, though lesser than the Romanistic one, was considerable. Some idea of the relative weight thereof can be gleaned from the brief analysis of Louisiana's first procedural code which follows.

Procedural concepts and devices which reflect the primary influence of Continental law include the code provisions relating to actions generally; real actions; jurisdiction (*ratione materiae et personae*); demands and incidental demands; cumulation of actions; consolidation of actions; pleading (including the exceptions); the provisional remedies of arrest, sequestration, provisional seizure, and injunction; interrogatories on facts and articles; *contestatio litis*; real tenders; judgments; nullity and rescission of judgments; ordinary, summary, and executory procedures; and succession procedure. The primary influence of Anglo-American law was reflected in the code provisions relating to judicial administration (composition of courts, functions of judicial officers, assignment and continuance of cases, et cetera); the provisional remedy of attachment; production of evidence; trial of cases (including trial by jury); new trial; execution of judgments (particularly the enforcement of money judgments); and the extraordinary remedies. Both systems of procedural law appear to have contributed to the code provisions relating to citation and service of process, depositions, appellate procedure, and proceedings before justice of the peace courts.

We have seen heretofore that, under the Practice Act of 1805, the institution of jury trial had been adopted, and that this led to the jurisprudential adoption of the common law rules of evidence. Under the Anglo-American system, the appellate court reviewed only questions of law and ordinarily would not reverse the jury verdict on factual issues. Under the Continental system, the appellate court reviewed both legal and factual issues, as presented by the record. A compromise had been effected for the Superior Court of the Territory of Orleans: the court reviewed issues of law on appeal, and if any appellate review of factual questions was desired, the case was completely retried by a new jury selected in the appellate court. Very shortly after Louisiana's admission to the Union, its Supreme Court held that, under the Constitution of 1812, no retrial of a factual issue could be had before a new jury. This was followed shortly by a decision holding that the appellate court could review the transcript of the evidence presented in the trial court, to determine the correctness of the jury's findings of fact. The principle of appellate review of the facts thus adopted was repeatedly affirmed by the court, and was confirmed in subsequent constitutions of the state, at first impliedly, and then expressly.

The effects of these decisions, which did not make themselves evident for some years, were to prove far-reaching. As the appellate courts were free to substitute their findings on factual issues of the trial jury's verdict, and not infrequently did so, jury trials in civil cases ultimately were had with relative infrequence. As a result, the technique of applying the common law rules of evidence completely changed in the vast majority of civil cases. Instead of being used to determine the *admissibility* of evidence sought to be presented to the lay jury, they were now used by the trial judge, skilled through experience in the marshaling and evaluation of testimony, to *weigh* evidence, usually admitted subject to the objections urged. In the area of the trial, Continental procedure had regained much of the ground previously lost to Anglo-American procedure, and had neutralized much of the latter's earlier victory.

The influence of Anglo-American procedure, however, continued to increase during this period, as a reading knowledge of Spanish and French grew rarer in the profession, and Anglo-American legal literature became increasingly available. Members of the Louisiana Bench and Bar began to turn to English and American precedents in the solution of procedural problems really calling for the application of the principles of Continental civil procedure. Not a great deal of damage was done thereby, but this interstitial seepage subsequently was to pave the way for an increased reception of Anglo-American procedural law.

THE CODE OF PRACTICE OF 1870

The purposes of the revision of Louisiana's two codes following the Civil War were the elimination of all references therein to the institution of slavery, and the incorporation therein of all related special procedural legislation adopted since 1825. The Code of Practice of 1870 went no further than this, and did little to change the civil procedure of Louisiana.

THE PERIOD 1870–1960

Important changes of procedure were brought about during the early years of this period. The former judicial view that common law terms in the procedural code and statutes were to be regarded merely as translations of the names of their Continental counterparts now yielded to an excessively generous appraisal of the common law contribution to the procedure of the state, and increased resort to the legal compendia then being published in America.

Somewhat later, the American code procedure movement, which was ushered in by New York's adoption of the David Dudley Field Code of Procedure in 1848, and which spread like wildfire throughout America during this period, had much to do in extending the influence of Anglo-American procedure over Louisiana practice. Paradoxically enough, the initial flow of influence was thus reversed, for it was the Louisiana Code of Practice of 1825 which provided the inspiration for the Field Code, and "from it very many of the best portions of the Field Code were adopted." During this period, the current reversed its direction.

The Field Code, figuratively speaking, was a protest against the complexities and technicalities of contemporary Anglo-American procedure. It unified common law procedure and chancery practice as far as was then practicable, and it sought to eliminate unnecessary technicalities and to simplify procedure. But it was a procedural system designed to implement Anglo-American law, and consequently was an Anglo-American code; and it, and its offspring in the various American states, had to be interpreted and applied largely by lawyers and judges whose mental processes were molded by the "inexorable

LOUISIANA CIVIL PROCEDURE

logic" of common law procedure, and who were still dominated by the procedural philosophy of the old system. Considering the background of these American procedure codes, cases interpreting their provisions should never have been accepted by the Louisiana courts in the solution of the procedural problems of Louisiana; but unfortunately they were.

The system of pleading developed by these American codes was intended to require brief, simple statements of the controlling facts on which each litigant's position was based. As ultimately developed by judicial interpretation, there evolved a system of pleading rules almost as technical as the common law rules which they displaced. No lessening of the importance of the role played by pleading in Anglo-American procedure resulted from the adoption of American code pleading. In the present writer's opinion, the Louisiana courts adopted the system of "fact pleading" of the American codes shortly after the turn of the present century, through acceptance of the judicial decisions of the various American states on the subject, and froze it into our system somewhat later through the adoption of the Pleading and Practice Act. The original simplicity of the system of pleading in the Louisiana Code of Practice gradually ossified into a harsher and more technical system, with penalties for a breach of what actually were rules of judicial etiquette ranging from time-consuming amendments of the pleadings to the more drastic dismissal of the suit. This system of pleading obtains today in Louisiana, although its rigors have been tempered appreciably in recent years through the commendably liberal attitude of the Louisiana courts, and the Louisiana Code of Civil Procedure has further liberalized the system by both authorizing and encouraging amendment at every stage of the proceeding.

At just about the same time that the rules of fact pleading were received in Louisiana, the common law rules of joinder of parties effected a partial entry into the jurisprudence of the state. The provisions of the Codes of Practice relating to cumulation of actions, taken directly from Spanish procedure, as the redactors' source notes indicate, contained no requirement of connexity with respect to subjective cumulation (*litisconsortium*). The early Louisiana jurisprudence had solved the problem through the jurisprudential adoption of the requirement of a common interest, or community of interest, between the plaintiffs joining, or the defendant joined, in the suit—substantially the same concept as the "community of jural interest" of the German Code of Civil Procedure. In 1909, objection was raised by the defendant in a case to the union of actions by a plurality of plaintiffs. The result reached by the court was completely sound, and thoroughly harmonious both with the earlier jurisprudence of the state and with generally accepted Continental principles of subjective cumulation. However, three gratuitous and erroneous observations were voiced in the opinion, to the effect that: (1) Spanish and French procedure had no rules which would afford any solution of the problem present; (2) the early Louisiana jurisprudential rules on the subject were derived from Anglo-American procedure; and (3) a resort should be made "to the books of the common law" for aid in the solution of related problems. Since the only non-Louisiana authorities cited in this opinion were equity precedents applying the negative test of multifariousness, derived from the same Romano-canonical principles which constitute the source of Continental rules of cumulation of actions, it seems clear that the court did not intend to invite a resort to the applicable common law rules, but rather to the pertinent rules of chancery practice. Subsequent cases, however, misconstrued the quoted language as vouching for the acceptability in Louisiana of the common law rules of joinder of parties, which were designed to implement the substantive rules of the common law joint, several, and joint and several, obligations—concepts completely alien to the civil law of Louisiana. Not too much damage was done through the application of these common law procedural rules in isolated cases. The alarming potential of these unfortunate decisions has now been removed through the Louisiana Code of Civil Procedure.

The adoption, since 1870, of a small number of procedural statutes has further increased the content of Anglo-American procedure in Louisiana practice. Limitations of space permit the writer to refer only to the most important of these legislative acts.

The code provisions relating to injunctions originally were taken indirectly from French procedure, through the medium of provisions of the so-called Civil Code of 1808. With the rapid social and economic development in Louisiana, this injunction procedure had proven inadequate, and even anachronistic. Considerable improvement in the injunction practice had been made in prior years in several American jurisdictions. The injunction practice in the federal courts particularly had been improved through the adoption of a statute drafted by an extremely able congressional committee after an extended study of the subject. In 1924, Louisiana adopted a statute regulating the issuance of interlocutory injunctions, which was taken almost verbatim from this federal statute. The adoption of this legislation, and the gradual reception of equity principles relating to the issuance of injunctions which occurred both before and after this enactment, have resulted in an injunction procedure virtually of Anglo-American origin.

LOUISIANA CIVIL PROCEDURE

THE LOUISIANA CODE OF CIVIL PROCEDURE

The new procedural code which has just been adopted, and which becomes effective on January 1, 1961, is the product of ten years of painstaking work by the Louisiana State Law Institute, the members of its council, the three reporters and their research assistants, and the members of the Institute's advisory and special committees. The Institute's organization for this project, and the manner in which this work was done, has been described in some detail in the Institute's Report to the Louisiana Legislature which submitted the completed *projet*, and need not be repeated here.

Structure and Organization

Except in the two respects mentioned later, the Louisiana Code of Civil Procedure follows the conventional pattern of structure and organization of codes of civilian jurisdictions. It is divided into 9 books, 36 titles, 117 chapters, and 1029 articles. It departs from this conventional pattern, however, in two respects—the numbering of the code articles, and the inclusion of the redactors' comments in the code itself.

In lieu of the consecutive numbering of code articles from the first to the last, the new code employs the split number system, with all articles in a particular chapter or section numbered consecutively, but with wide gaps between the number of the last article in a particular chapter or section and the number of the initial article in the next book, title, chapter, or section. This system was adopted to permit the continuous revision of the new code after adoption, by the inclusion in appropriate places thereof of special procedural statutes adopted by the legislature in the future.

The inclusion of the redactors' comments in the code itself is a departure from traditional civilian redaction techniques, and was adopted over the objections of a few of the old-school civilians in Louisiana. This system was first employed by the Louisiana State Law Institute, as an experiment, in the *projet* of the Louisiana Criminal Code of 1942. The official comments in the latter have proved so helpful to the courts and practicing lawyers of the state that there was a strong professional demand for the employment of this technique in the *projet* of the new procedural code. Judicial precedent plays a more important role in Louisiana than in any other civilian jurisdiction, and the consideration of the prior jurisprudence was deemed helpful in all cases. The citation of prior cases was absolutely necessary in those instances where the jurisprudential rule was being reversed legislatively.

SHORT HISTORY—HENRY G. McMAHON

Objectives

Through the redaction of the Louisiana Code of Civil Procedure, the Louisiana State Law Institute sought to accomplish the following objectives:

(1) The consolidation of all procedural rules relating generally to civil actions and proceedings. Prior to the adoption of the new code, these rules were to be found in the Code of Practice, a large number of special statutes adopted since 1870, a much larger number of judicial decisions, and in the Civil Code. The latter contained large segments of our adjective law, including the procedural rules relating to successions, tutorship, judicial emancipation, interdiction, curatorship, annulment of marriage, separation from bed and board, and divorce.

(2) The elimination of many unnecessarily technical rules and results which served more to defeat than to further the ends of justice. A few of these were to be found in the positive law, but many more lurked in the prior decisions of the courts.

(3) The revision and reformation of those procedural devices and concepts of some efficacy and workability, which could be improved either through simplification or expansion, so as to operate more efficiently under modern economic or social conditions.

(4) The borrowing of some of the newer and more effective procedural devices in Anglo-American and Continental procedure which could be assimilated by and integrated into our adjective law.

(5) The granting of more power, authority, and discretion to the trial judge. The shackling of the trial judge in the United States during the past century and a quarter was largely a result of the influence of Jacksonian democracy, which was distrustful of the judiciary and sought to control procedural decisions through the adoption of minute and rigid statutory rules. The Code of Practice, largely the handiwork of Edward Livingston, one of the leaders of this school of political thought, hamstrung the trial judge unnecessarily in many respects. Here, the new code has adopted the approach of the Federal Rules of Civil Procedure in granting necessary power, authority, and discretion to the trial judge.

(6) The statement of procedural rules in clear, simple English. The Code of Practice of 1825 was drafted in French, with the English version an imperfect translation. The revision of 1870 left the latter as the only official version, but did nothing to remove its many awkward and cumbersome phrases. The procedural statutes adopted since 1870, most of which were replete with hackneyed legal terms and expressions which obscured their meaning, had further aggravated this unfortunate situation.

LOUISIANA CIVIL PROCEDURE

Redaction Policies

For nearly a century and a half the civil procedure of Louisiana has been a blend, or synthesis, of Continental and Anglo-American civil procedures. One of the initial decisions of the Louisiana State Law Institute, when it commenced work on the new procedural codification, was that there would be no discarding of the basic Louisiana procedure to accept a new system based upon either the Federal Rules of Civil Procedure or the procedural code of another American state.

The pragmatic justification of comparative law is the opportunity afforded for the improvement and enrichment of one legal system through the intelligent borrowing of more effective concepts and principles from other systems. The comparative method was utilized throughout the redaction of the new code. The latter contains some procedural devices and concepts borrowed from the latest and most advanced Anglo-American "codification"—the Federal Rules of Civil Procedure. These, however, have largely been in replacement of Louisiana counterparts of Anglo-American origin. Less extensive borrowings have been made from modern Continental procedural systems, and these largely in replacement of Louisiana analogues of Continental origin. As each procedural device and concept was considered by the Law Institute, it was compared carefully with its Continental and Anglo-American counterparts. If any of the latter clearly proved more useful and more workable, it was borrowed and incorporated into the new code. In some instances where no actual borrowing resulted, the comparison indicated the desirability of a more precise or clearer statement of the Louisiana rule which was to be retained.

Throughout the work of the redaction of the new code the Louisiana State Law Institute followed one cardinal policy: there should be no change for the mere sake of change. No matter how appealingly novel or intriguing the suggestion, no matter what its theoretical appeal, no change was made except upon convincing evidence that it would prove more useful and workable than its Louisiana counterpart. The result is that no radical or revolutionary changes were made in the civil procedure of the state through the adoption of the new code.

Procedural Philosophy

Every codification reflects, in large measure, the legal philosophy of its redactors. The procedural philosophy of the Louisiana Code of Civil Procedure is essentially pragmatic. While recognizing the need for symmetry and the correlation of the articles of this code, in its redaction the Louisiana State Law Institute was more concerned with the utility and workability of the procedural rules embodied therein than with any "science of civil procedure". The Code of Practice of

1825 provided an excellent base for an effective administration of civil justice in Louisiana, but for roughly half of the one hundred and thirty-five years which have elapsed since its adoption, its spirit was overlooked by both the legislatures and the courts of the state. During this period, both of the latter were largely under the influence of the procedural philosophy of Anglo-American law, which then regarded a lawsuit as a duel between skilled protagonists. Both shook off this influence more than a quarter of a century ago, but many legislative and jurisprudential rules overturned by the new code reflected this misconception of the function of procedure. The new code embodies procedural rules designed to permit the trial of a case to serve as a search for the truth, and to have its decision based on the substantive law applicable, rather than upon technical rules of procedure.

The procedural philosophy of the Louisiana Code of Civil Procedure is summed up by the language of its Article 5051: "The articles of this Code are to be construed liberally, and with due regard for the fact that rules of procedure implement the substantive law and are not an end in themselves."

†

Louisiana
Code of Civil Procedure

Act 15 of 1960

Approved June 16, 1960

Effective January 1, 1961

An Act

To revise the Code of Practice of the State of Louisiana by adopting a system of laws consolidating the procedural rules applicable generally to civil actions and proceedings, to be known as the Louisiana Code of Civil Procedure; to provide for the continuous revision thereof; to repeal the Code of Practice of the State of Louisiana, and all other laws in conflict or inconsistent with the provisions of the code hereby adopted; to provide that the provisions of this act shall prevail over the conflicting provisions of any other act adopted at this legislative session; and to provide the effective date of this act.

BE IT ENACTED BY THE LEGISLATURE OF LOUISIANA:

SECTION 1. The Louisiana Code of Civil Procedure, as set forth hereinafter in this section, is hereby adopted and enacted into law:

BOOK I
COURTS, ACTIONS, AND PARTIES

TITLE I
COURTS

Chap.		Art.
1.	Jurisdiction	1
2.	Venue	41
	Sec.	
	1. General Dispositions	41
	2. Exceptions to General Rules	71
	3. Change of Venue	121
3.	Recusation of Judges	151
4.	Power and Authority	191
	Sec.	
	1. General Dispositions	191
	2. Power to Punish for Contempt	221
5.	Clerks	251
	Sec.	
	1. General Dispositions	251
	2. Clerks of District Courts	281
6.	Sheriffs	321
7.	Other Officers of the Court	371

INTRODUCTION

The concept of jurisdiction, under the Codes of Practice of 1825 and 1870, was subdivided into "jurisdiction ratione materiae" and "jurisdiction ratione personae". This classification was patterned upon the "compétence ratione materiae" and "compétence ratione personae" of French procedure. Comment, Jurisdiction Ratione Materiae et Personae in Louisiana, 12 La.L. Rev. 210 (1951). These twin concepts of Louisiana procedure correspond closely with the "jurisdiction over subject matter" and "venue" of Anglo-American law.

Prior to 1878, the problems solved by the Anglo-American concept of "jurisdiction over the person" were solved by Louisiana procedure, under a different approach, by an application of the code requirements of citation and service of process. *Cf.* Art. 206, Louisiana Codes of Practice of 1825 and 1870. The decision of the United States Supreme Court in Pennoyer v. Neff, 95 U.S. 714, 24 L.Ed. 565 (1878), not only engrafted the concept of "jurisdiction over the person" onto our procedural system, as requirements of due process of law and full faith and credit, but also introduced the by-products of this concept, the classification of "jurisdiction in personam", "jurisdiction in rem", and "jurisdiction quasi in rem". A modern Louisiana codification of procedural law would be unrealistic if it failed to give recognition to all of these important procedural concepts.

Recent decisions of the Louisiana courts have served to obscure to some extent the line of demarcation between the twin civilian concepts of jurisdiction ratione materiae and jurisdiction ratione personae. *Cf.* Bercegeay v. Techeland Oil Corporation, 209 La. 33, 24 So.2d 242 (1945), noted 7 La.L.Rev. 437 (1947). See also, Mitcham v. Mitcham, 186 La. 641, 173 So. 132 (1937); Johnston v. Burton, 202 La. 182, 11 So.2d 513 (1942); and Comment, Jurisdiction Ratione Materiae et Personae in Louisiana, 12 La. L.Rev. 210 (1951). Additional confusion might possibly result from the majority opinion in Tanner v. Beverly Country Club, 217 La. 1043, 47 So.2d 906 (1950), noted 25 Tul.L.Rev. 399 (1951), in which the civilian concept of jurisdiction ratione personae was treated as if identical with the Anglo-American "jurisdiction over the person".

For these reasons, this Code adopts the Anglo-American concepts of jurisdiction, jurisdiction over the subject matter, jurisdiction over the person, and venue. In view of the constitutional requirements of due process of law and full faith and credit, this represents little more than a realistic change of terminology.

CHAPTER 1. JURISDICTION

Art.
1. Jurisdiction defined.
2. Jurisdiction over subject matter.
3. Same; cannot be conferred by consent.
4. Same; determination when dependent on amount in dispute or value of right asserted.
5. Same; effect of reduction of claim.
6. Jurisdiction over the person.
7. Same; implied waiver of objections by general appearance.
8. Jurisdiction over property; in rem.
9. Same; quasi in rem; attachment.
10. Jurisdiction over status.

Art. 1. Jurisdiction defined

Jurisdiction is the legal power and authority of a court to hear and determine an action or proceeding involving the legal relations of the parties, and to grant the relief to which they are entitled.

Source: New; cf. C.P. Art. 76.

Comments

(a) See Introduction to this Title.

(b) In this article there is presented a definition of sufficient accuracy to include all elements of the term, and yet of sufficient breadth and flexibility to avoid undue restraint on the courts in their empirical development of the concept of jurisdiction, and its application to new remedies.

For the derivation of the word "jurisdiction" and a general definition thereof, see Wedding v. Meyler, 192 U.S. 573, 24 S.Ct. 122, 48 L.Ed. 570, 66 L.R.A. 833 (1904); Central R. Co. v. Jersey City, 209 U.S. 473, 28 S.Ct. 592, 52 L.Ed. 896 (1909); Nielson v. State of Oregon, 212 U.S. 315, 29 S.Ct. 383, 53 L.Ed. 528 (1910).

Aside from the indirect source provision of this article and Succession of Weigel, 17 La.Ann. 70 (1865), the Louisiana law afforded little help in providing an accurate definition of jurisdiction. See State ex rel. Phelps v. Judge, 45 La.Ann. 1250, 14 So. 310 (1893); Allen v. Shreveport Mut. Bldg. Ass'n, 183 La. 521, 164 So. 328 (1935); and 7 La.L.Rev. 437, 439, n. 9 (1947).

Some courts define jurisdiction merely in terms of judicial power. See Johnson v. McKinnon, 54 Fla. 221, 45 So. 23 (1907) and cases cited. One of the most complete definitions of the term is to be found in Black on Judgments (2d ed.) 322 (1902). But it is entirely too complex and lengthy to serve as the predicate of a code definition. The majority of cases define the term as "the power to hear and determine a cause" or "the authority to hear and determine a cause." See the cases cited in 23 Words & Phrases (Perm.ed.) 367 (1940). See, also, General Invest. Co. v. New York Cent. R. Co., 271 U.S. 228, 46 S.Ct. 497, 70 L.Ed. 920 (1926); State ex rel. Shoemaker v. Hall, 257 S.W. 1047 (Mo.1924); United Cemeteries Co. v. Strother, 119 S.W.2d 764 (Mo.1938); Clark v. Arizona Mut. Savings & Loan Ass'n, 217 F. 640 (D.C.Ariz.1914).

One element of the definition of this term not usually recognized expressly in the cases, but necessarily implied, is that it is the *legal* power and authority of a court. This means authority under the constitutions and laws of both the state and the United States. Withers v. Patterson, 27 Tex. 491, 86 Am.Dec. 643 (1864); In re Harkness' Estate, 83 Okla. 107, 204 P. 911 (1921). Another important limitation on the definition of the term is that the action or proceeding must involve the legal relations of the parties. Stumberg, Principles of Conflict of Laws (2d ed.) 59 (1951).

There is not included within this definition the power to enforce execution of the judgment rendered by the court, which is considered an integral part of the definition by some courts. See Worcester v. Georgia, 6 Pet. 515, 8 L.Ed. 483 (1832); In re Ferguson, 9 John. 239 (N.Y.1812); and Dickson Fruit Co. v. District Court of Sac County, 203 Iowa 1028, 213 N.W. 803 (1927). Aside from the fact that such a definition might cause difficulty with respect to the declaratory and other types of judgments which require no enforcement, there are many valid judgments which courts have jurisdiction to render, but which they may be powerless to enforce, *e. g.*, a judgment against a nonresident who owns no property in the state and who was served with process personally while transiently in the state. In this Code the power of a court to enforce its judgment is no element of jurisdiction except to the extent that such power is included within the phrase "legal power and authority."

(c) The articles of this Title differentiate sharply the concepts of jurisdiction and venue. Generally, jurisdiction denotes the power or authority of a court to adjudicate; while venue signifies the place where the action or proceeding is to be brought and tried. *Cf.* Paige v. Sinclair, 217 Mass. 482, 130 N.E. 177 (1921); Shaffer v. Bank, 201 N.C. 415, 160 S.E. 481 (1931); National Ass'n of Creditors v. Brown, 147 Wash. 1, 264 P. 1005 (1928). See, also, Jurisdiction or Venue?, 19 U. of Cin.L.Rev. 493 (1950); and 7 La.L.Rev. 437 (1947).

Notwithstanding the fact that prior Louisiana decisions have often obscured the line of demarcation between jurisdiction ratione materiae and jurisdiction ratione personae, every effort has been made in the articles in this Title to keep the line of demarcation between jurisdiction and venue as clear and as distinct as possible. There are, however, some instances where public policy requires the institution of certain actions or proceedings in certain parishes only, under penalty of the nullity of the judgments. These exceptional cases are enumerated in the second paragraph of Art. 44, *infra*.

Art. 2. Jurisdiction over subject matter

Jurisdiction over the subject matter is the legal power and authority of a court to hear and determine a particular class of actions or proceedings, based upon the object of the demand, the amount in dispute, or the value of the right asserted.

Source: New; cf. C.P. Arts. 87, 88, 91.

Comments

(a) See Introduction to this Title.

(b) Jurisdiction over the subject matter, as defined in this article, is the "jurisdiction ratione materiae" of Louisiana procedure prior to its confusion with "jurisdiction ratione personae" by recent cases. It appears to be the same as "competency of the court" of the Restatement of Judgments, § 7; and is the exact counterpart of the French concept of "compétence ratione materiae".

(c) This definition is based largely upon the following cases: Clark v. Arizona Mut. Savings & Loan Ass'n, 217 F. 640 (D.C. Ariz.1914); Woodward v. Ruel, 355 Ill. 163, 188 N.E. 911 (1934); State ex rel. Shoemaker v. Hall, 257 S.W. 1047 (Mo.1924); United Cemeteries Co. v. Strother, 119 S.W.2d 762 (Mo.1938); Londagin v. McDuff, 207 Okla. 594, 251 P.2d 496 (1952); Honea v. Graham, 66 S.W.2d 802 (Tex.Civ.App.1934); Rolando v. Third Dist. Court of Salt Lake County, 72 Utah 459, 271 P. 225 (1928).

(d) See, also, Comments under Arts. 3, 422, 925, *infra*.

Art. 3. Same; cannot be conferred by consent

The jurisdiction of a court over the subject matter of an action or proceeding cannot be conferred by consent of the parties. A judgment rendered by a court which has no jurisdiction over the subject matter of the action or proceeding is void.

Source: C.P. Art. 92.

Comments

(a) See Comments under Art. 2, *supra*.

(b) Even though a judgment may be null, there are circumstances which would preclude a court from declaring its nullity, and invalidating a judicial sale under execution. See Arts. 2002 and 2003, *infra*. This procedural bar is established for the protection of third persons.

(c) See, also, Comments under Art. 925, *infra*.

Art. 4. Same; determination when dependent on amount in dispute or value of right asserted

When the jurisdiction of a court over the subject matter of an action depends upon the amount in dispute, or value of the right asserted, it shall be determined by the amount demanded or value asserted in good faith by the plaintiff.

Except as otherwise provided by law, the amount in dispute consists of the principal sum, and the attorney's fees and penalties provided by agreement or by law, demanded by the plaintiff. Interest and court costs are not a part of the amount in dispute.

Source: C.P. Art. 91(1); cf. Comments following.

Comments

(a) It is settled that the attorney's fees and penalties granted by law or by convention ordinarily must be considered part of the amount in dispute for purposes of determining the jurisdiction of the court. Thompson v. Jones, 200 La. 437, 8 So.2d 286 (1942); Hammack v. Resolute Fire Ins. Co., 223 La. 655, 66 So. 2d 583 (1953); Foundation Finance Co. v. Robbins, 144 So. 293 (La.App.1932); Perrault v. Proffer, 33 So.2d 579 (La.App.1947); Guinn Motors v. Looney, 81 So.2d 112 (La.App.1955). The above article is declaratory of this jurisprudential rule.

(b) The exception in the above article is included to avoid any clash with conflicting provisions of the constitution. For instance, Const. Art. VII, § 51 excludes attorney's fees from the jurisdictional amount with respect to the authority granted to the legislature to confer jurisdiction upon certain classes of city courts. Similarly, Const. Art. VII, §§ 91 and 92, exclude penalties from the grant of jurisdiction to the city courts of New Orleans.

(c) This article applies not only to the principal demand, but to the incidental demands as well, except as otherwise provided by law. See Art. 1036, *infra*.

Art. 5. Same; effect of reduction of claim

When a plaintiff reduces his claim on a single cause of action to bring it within the jurisdiction of a court and judgment is rendered thereon, he remits the portion of his claim for which he did not pray for judgment, and is precluded thereafter from demanding it judicially.

Source: C.P. Art. 91(2).

Comment

This rule is based on the same principle of law as that which forbids the splitting of the cause of action. The rule governing the latter is set forth in Art. 425, *infra*.

Art. 6. Jurisdiction over the person

Jurisdiction over the person is the legal power and authority of a court to render a personal judgment against a party to an action or proceeding. This jurisdiction must be based upon:

(1) The service of process on the defendant, or on his agent for the service of process;

(2) The service of process on the attorney at law appointed by the court to defend an action or proceeding brought against an absent or incompetent defendant who is domiciled in this state; or

(3) The submission of the party to the exercise of jurisdiction over him personally by the court, or his express or implied waiver of objections thereto.

Source: New; cf. Comments following.

Comments

(a) The Anglo-American concept of jurisdiction over the person was brought into the procedural law of Louisiana as one of the requirements of due process of law by Pennoyer v. Neff, 95 U.S. 714, 24 L.Ed. 565 (1878). See Introduction to this Title.

The language of the above article, while couched in terms giving effect to the principles of procedural law peculiar to Louisiana, such as those providing for the appointment of an attorney to defend the suit when the defendant is absent or incompetent, are well within the permissible legal limits of due process of law. See Restatement of Conflict of Laws, § 42(1).

(b) For a definition of "agent for the service of process", see Art. 5251, *infra*. The words in that article, "designated . . . by law" refer to those statutes which provide that the doing of an act is deemed equivalent to the appointment of the secretary of state as the agent for the service of process in all actions brought against the person in connection with the doing of the act. See former R.S. 13:3471(5) (c), 13:3474, 13:3475, 13:3479–13:3482, and R.S. 22:1253.

(c) Art. 6(2) is declaratory of the prior law which recognized that valid service of process might be made on an attorney at law appointed by the court to defend the suit when the defendant is either an absentee or an incompetent. See Arts. 116, 294, 964, Code of Practice of 1870; Civil Code, Art. 56; former R.S. 13:3471(14). In personal actions, this substituted service is valid only as to Louisiana domiciliaries. Restatement of Conflict of Laws, § 42(1). See Art. 5091, *infra*.

(d) Art. 6(3) is declaratory of the former procedural law. See comments under Art. 7, *infra*.

(e) Since the objection to the court's lack of jurisdiction over the person of the defendant is waivable, this objection must be pleaded through the declinatory exception. Art. 925, *infra*.

(f) The service of process contemplated by this article includes either personal or domiciliary service on the defendant. See Arts. 1233 and 1234, *infra*.

(g) This article is broad enough to include the extension of the limits of jurisdiction over the person recently made by McGee v. International Life Ins. Co., 355 U.S. 220, 78 S.Ct. 199, 2 L. Ed.2d 223 (1957).

(h) See, also, Comments under Arts. 422, 925, *infra*.

Art. 7. **Same; implied waiver of objections by general appearance**

Except as otherwise provided in this article, a party makes a general appearance which subjects him to the jurisdiction of the court and impliedly waives all objections thereto when, either personally or through counsel, he seeks therein any relief other than:

(1) Entry or removal of the name of an attorney as counsel of record;

(2) Extension of time within which to plead;

(3) Security for costs;

(4) Dissolution of an attachment issued on the ground of the nonresidence of the defendant; or

(5) Dismissal of the action on the ground that the court has no jurisdiction over the defendant.

This article does not apply to an incompetent defendant who attempts to appear personally, or to an absent or incompetent defendant who appears through the attorney at law appointed by the court to represent him.

When a defendant files a declinatory exception which includes a prayer for the dismissal of the action on the ground that the court has no jurisdiction over him, the pleading of other objections therein, the filing of the dilatory exception therewith, or the filing of the peremptory exception or an answer therewith when required by law, does not constitute a general appearance.

Source: New.
Cross Reference: Art. 2002.

Comments

(a) See Comment (a) under Art. 8, *infra*.

(b) The above article to some extent is based upon similar but narrower provisions of N.Y. Civil Practice Act, Art. 26, §§ 236–240, and Wisconsin Stats., §§ 262.17 and 543.15.

While it effects some changes, most of the provisions of this article are declaratory of the Louisiana procedural law. Art. 7(1) probably changes the law, but no case in point was found. Art. 7(3) is declaratory of the rule of Collier v. Morgan's L. & T. R. Co., 41 La.Ann. 37, 5 So. 537 (1889). Art. 7(4) codifies the jurisprudential rule applied in Chapman v. Irwin, 157 La. 920, 103 So. 263 (1925) and cases cited therein. Art. 7(5) is declaratory of the prior law.

(c) Art. 7(2) changes the law. Heretofore, when a defendant moved for an extension of time to plead, this motion constituted a general appearance which subjected him to the jurisdiction of the court for all purposes. Modisette & Adams v. Lorenze, 163 La. 505, 112 So. 397 (1927); Stanley v. Jones, 197 La. 627, 2 So.2d 45 (1941). Under federal practice, when an enlargement of the time for answering is granted, the order automatically extends the time for filing a motion to dismiss. Fed.Rules 6(b) and 12(a). Hence, the motion does not constitute a general appearance. Orange Theatre Corp. v. Rayhertz Amusement Corp., 139 F.2d 871 (3 Cir.1944); Blanton v. Pacific Mutual Life Ins. Co., 4 F.R.D. 200 (D.C.N.Y.1944). The above article legislatively overrules the unduly technical and harsh Louisiana rule.

(d) See, also, Comments under Art. 6, *supra*, and Arts. 9, 1001, 1201, 1672, 3544, *infra*.

Art. 8. Jurisdiction over property; in rem

A court which is otherwise competent under the laws of this state has jurisdiction to enforce a right in, to, or against property having a situs in this state, claimed or owned by a nonresident not subject personally to the jurisdiction of the court.

Source: New.

Comments

(a) For the definition of "competent court", see Art. 5251, *infra*. This definition is declaratory of the former procedural law. See Art. 87, Code of Practice of 1870; Flowers v. Pugh, 51 So.2d 136 (La.App.1951); Comment, 14 Tul.L.Rev. 601, 603 (1940).

(b) The language of this article does not expressly include the case of an action in rem against property in this state owned by a Louisiana domiciliary, as such a case presents no jurisdictional problem. Not only would the court have jurisdiction over the property, but the defendant may be served with process personally, thus giving the court jurisdiction over him personally.

Service of process upon the owner of property situated in this state is not a requirement of due process of law in an action in rem under Pennoyer v. Neff, 95 U.S. 714, 24 L.Ed. 565 (1878), and its progeny.

(c) This article bases the court's jurisdiction in rem upon the legal situs of the property, and leaves the courts free to apply the rules with respect to situs to the particular cases.

No problem is presented with respect to immovable property, whether corporeal or incorporeal, when the immovable is actually situated in this state. See Restatement of Conflict of Laws, § 48. Except under the circumstances discussed in Comment (d), no problem is presented with respect to corporeal movables. Restatement of Conflict of Laws, § 49. Except under the circumstances discussed in Comments (d) and (e), no problem is presented with respect to an incorporeal movable. If not evidenced by a negotiable instrument or corporation stock certificate, the situs of the incorporeal movable is the state having jurisdiction over the debtor. See Restatement of Conflict of Laws, §§ 108, 51, Comment (b). Usually, the case would be one of a claimant seeking to subject a debt due his debtor to the payment of his claim, and if the debtor was not subject to the jurisdiction of the court, but his debtor was, the incorporeal movable would be attached, and the case would fall under Art. 9, *infra*. In the unusual case in which it was sought to enforce a right of ownership of the incorporeal movable, the situs of the latter would be the state having jurisdiction over the debtor.

(d) The Restatement of Conflict of Laws, § 50 covers an exceptional set of circumstances which requires explanation. A typical illustration of the factual situation covered by this section is the negotiable bill of lading on property being transported. Under this article, it is not necessary to spell out the rules governing such an exceptional case. Within the intendment of this article, except for the purposes of enforcing the costs of preservation or condemnation, the "property" would be the document evidencing the title, and not the corporeal movables. Unless this document were in the state, the property would have no situs in Louisiana affording a basis for the court's jurisdiction in rem.

(e) Two more sets of exceptional circumstances are governed by the rules of the Restatement of Conflict of Laws, §§ 52, 53. A typical illustration of the situation covered by Sec. 52 is the negotiable instrument; while an example of the situation governed by Sec. 53 is the corporation stock certificate. However, under the above article no problem is presented with respect to either. The property, with respect to the negotiable instrument, and with respect to the corporation stock certificate allowed by the law of the state of incorporation, would be the instrument itself; and if this would not be in Louisiana, the court would have no jurisdiction in rem.

For a definition of "property", see Art. 5251, *infra*.

(f) See, also, Comments under Art. 7, *supra*, and Arts. 9, 10, *infra*.

Art. 9. Same; quasi in rem; attachment

A court which is otherwise competent under the laws of this state has jurisdiction to render a money judgment against a nonresident not subject personally to the jurisdiction of the court only if the action is commenced by an attachment of his property in this state. Unless the nonresident subjects himself personally to the jurisdiction of the court, the judgment may be executed only against the property attached.

Source: New.

Comments

(a) See Comment (a) under Art. 8, *supra*.

(b) The rule expressed in this article is sanctioned by Pennoyer v. Neff, 95 U.S. 714, 24 L.Ed. 565 (1878), and the cases based thereon. See also, Restatement of Judgments, § 76.

(c) See Art. 7, *supra*, with reference to general appearances.

(d) See, also, Comments under Art. 8, *supra*, and Art. 422, *infra*.

Art. 10. Jurisdiction over status

A court which is otherwise competent under the laws of this state has jurisdiction of the following actions or proceedings only under the following conditions:

(1) An adoption proceeding if the person who has legal custody of the child is domiciled, or the child is lawfully, in this state, and the court has personal jurisdiction over the adoptive parent; or if the latter is domiciled in this state, and the court has personal jurisdiction over the legal custodian;

(2) An emancipation proceeding if the minor is domiciled in this state;

(3) An interdiction proceeding if the person sought to be interdicted is domiciled in this state, or is in this state and has property herein;

(4) A tutorship or curatorship proceeding if the minor, interdict, or absentee, as the case may be, is domiciled in this state or has property herein;

(5) A proceeding to obtain the legal custody of a minor if he is domiciled in, or is in, this state;

(6) An action to annul a marriage if one or both of the parties are domiciled in this state; and

(7) An action of divorce, or of separation from bed and board, if one or both of the spouses are domiciled in this state and, except as otherwise provided by law, the grounds therefor were committed or occurred in this state, or while the matrimonial domicile was in this state.

Source: New.

Comments

(a) See Comment (a) under Art. 8, *supra*.

(b) Art. 10(1) expresses substantially the rule of the proposed Restatement of Conflict of Laws 2d, § 142, but for the sake of greater clarity uses the language "the child is lawfully in the state" rather than the more nebulous language of the Restatement, "has personal jurisdiction over . . . the adopted child." This provision is supported partially and inferentially by R.S. 9:423, and even more strongly by Succession of Caldwell, 114 La. 195, 38 So. 140, 108 Am.St.Rep. 341 (1905). See also, State ex rel. Horner v. Karpe, 151 La. 583, 92 So. 124 (1922).

(c) Arts. 10(2) and 3991, *infra*, require that emancipation proceedings in this state be limited to Louisiana domiciliaries. The above article overrules Succession of Gaines, 42 La.Ann. 699, 7 So. 788 (1890) which at least inferred that a minor who resides but is not domiciled in this state may be emancipated here.

(d) In so far as Art. 10(3) recognizes the right to interdict a Louisiana domiciliary, it accords with Restatement of Conflict of

Laws, § 194. It changes the procedural law of the state with respect to the interdiction of a Louisiana domiciliary who is confined, or is being treated, in another state. Interdiction of Dumas, 33 La.Ann. 679 (1880), held that a Louisiana court could not legally interdict a Louisiana domiciliary living outside of the state because there was no way in which valid service of process might be made. This objection was removed by the 1948 amendment of Civil Code Art. 391; but despite this, it was held in Interdiction of Toca, 217 La. 465, 46 So.2d 737 (1950), that the courts of this state could not interdict a Louisiana domiciliary confined to a District of Columbia institution. This unfortunate decision may create a judicial vacuum which would make it impossible to ever interdict a Louisiana domiciliary in an institution in another state which limits incompetency proceedings to its own domiciliaries. This provision and Art. 4541, *infra*, overrules Interdiction of Dumas, *supra*; Interdiction of Lepine, 160 La. 953, 107 So. 708 (1926); and Interdiction of Toca, *supra*.

The rule of this article that a person who is in Louisiana and has property herein, though not domiciled here, may be interdicted by a Louisiana court is declaratory of the decision in Interdiction of Stith, 161 La. 490, 109 So. 41 (1926). Interdiction, in such a case, is a mere preliminary to the administration of the property by a curator; and since both the person of the defendant and his property are subject to the jurisdiction of the courts of this state, there can be no constitutional objection to such a proceeding, in so far as the judgment therein is applied or enforced only in Louisiana. Under these facts another state may not have to recognize this judgment, under either full faith and credit or comity. Restatement of Conflict of Laws, §§ 149, 151. Under certain variations of these facts, however, the Louisiana judgment would be entitled to full faith and credit. *Cf.* Restatement of Conflict of Laws, § 40 and Comment (f) thereof.

No provision is made in this article for the interdiction of a person who has property in Louisiana, but is neither domiciled nor present in this state. Jurisdiction could not be conferred constitutionally on the Louisiana courts under these circumstances. This presents no hiatus, however, since such a person is regarded as an absentee, and may be proceeded against as such. Hansell v. Hansell, 44 La.Ann. 548, 10 So. 941 (1892); and Adler v. Adler, 126 La. 472, 52 So. 668 (1910).

(e) The proceeding for the appointment of a curator for a war veteran under the Uniform Veterans' Guardianship Law, R.S. 29:351 through 29:379, is not an interdiction proceeding R.S. 29:358.

(f) Art. 10(4), in so far as it refers to jurisdiction over the tutorship proceeding, is in accord with the prior law. Civil

Code Art. 307; Art. 946 of the 1870 Code of Practice; Succession of Cass, 42 La.Ann. 381, 7 So. 617 (1890); Succession of Gaines, 42 La.Ann. 699, 7 So. 788 (1890). See Arts. 4031 and 4431, *infra*. In so far as this article refers to jurisdiction over the curatorship proceeding of an interdict, it also accords with former law. Civil Code Arts. 307, 405, 415; Arts. 962, 964, Code of Practice of 1870. *Cf*. Smith v. Burt, 46 F.2d 306 (D.C.La. 1930), and Art. 4541, *infra*.

The rules of this article as to both tutorship and curatorship proceedings for Louisiana domiciliaries accords with Restatement of Conflict of Laws, §§ 30, 32, 149, 151. With respect to a minor or interdict domiciled in another state, but who has property in Louisiana, the courts of other states would not have to recognize the Louisiana judgment, under either full faith and credit or comity. Restatement of Conflict of Laws, §§ 149, 151. But there can be no constitutional objection to the administration of the property in this state by a Louisiana court.

A tutor, curator, or guardian of a minor or mental incompetent appointed by a court of another state or foreign country need not qualify here to administer his ward's property in this state. Civil Code Art. 363; Interdiction of Parker, 39 La.Ann. 333, 1 So. 891 (1887). This rule has been retained. The foreign tutor, curator, or guardian may qualify in Louisiana, however, if he so desires. Arts. 4433 and 4554, *infra*.

(g) Arts. 10(5) and 3822, *infra*, are declaratory of the former law. Art. 792, Code of Practice of 1870; Person v. Person, 172 La. 740, 135 So. 225 (1931). *Cf*. In re Owen, 170 La. 255, 127 So. 619 (1930). They also accord with Restatement of Conflict of Laws, §§ 144–148.

(h) The rule of Art. 10(6), relating to jurisdiction to annul a marriage, accords with the rationale of Williams v. North Carolina, 317 U.S. 287, 63 S.Ct. 207, 87 L.Ed. 279, 143 A.L.R. 1273 (1942), noted 17 Tul.L.Rev. 500 (1943), and 5 La.L.Rev. 319 (1943); and Williams v. North Carolina, 325 U.S. 226, 65 S.Ct. 1092, 89 L.Ed. 1577, 157 A.L.R. 1366 (1945), noted 6 La.L.Rev. 290 (1945). It is slightly broader than the rule of the Restatement of Conflict of Laws, §§ 113, 115.

The policy considerations which have limited the jurisdiction of Louisiana courts with respect to divorces and separations from bed and board do not require similar limitation of the jurisdiction to annul marriages, hence the full potential jurisdiction allowed by the twin cases of Williams v. North Carolina, *supra*, is permitted.

(i) The rule of Art. 10(7), with respect to jurisdiction over actions for divorce and separation from bed and board is sanctioned

Tit. 1   VENUE

by, though considerably narrower than that permitted under the two cases of Williams v. North Carolina, *supra*. In a number of respects the rule of this Code provision is narrower, and in one respect broader, than Restatement of Conflict of Laws, § 113.

For years, Louisiana courts have generally limited their jurisdiction to grant a divorce or separation to causes of action which occurred in this state, or while the parties were domiciled in this state. Mathews v. Mathews, 157 La. 930, 103 So. 267 (1925); Evans v. Evans, 166 La. 145, 116 So. 831 (1928); Mann v. Mann, 170 La. 958, 129 So. 543 (1930); Peeples v. Land, 181 La. 925, 160 So. 631 (1935); Hockaday v. Hockaday, 183 La. 88, 161 So. 164 (1935). The Louisiana courts, however, have exercised jurisdiction to grant a divorce or separation from bed and board on grounds which occurred elsewhere, but while the parties were domiciled in Louisiana. D'Auvilliers v. De Livaudais, 32 La.Ann. 605 (1880); Stevens v. Allen, 139 La. 658, 71 So. 936 (1916). The rule of this code provision is declaratory of the rules of these cases.

The exceptions referred to in Art. 10(7) are those sanctioned by Civil Code Art. 142 and R.S. 9:301.

(j) See, also, Comments under Arts. 422, 3941, *infra*.

CHAPTER 2. VENUE

SECTION 1. GENERAL DISPOSITIONS

Art.
41. Definition.
42. General rules.
43. Exception to general rules.
44. Waiver of objections to venue.
45. Conflict between two or more articles in Chapter.

SECTION 2. EXCEPTIONS TO GENERAL RULES

71. Action against individual who has changed domicile.
72. Certain actions involving property; effect of judgment.
73. Action against joint or solidary obligors.
74. Action on offense or quasi offense.
75. Action on judicial bond.
76. Action on insurance policy.
77. Action against person doing business in another parish.
78. Action against partners of existing partnership.
79. Action to dissolve partnership.
80. Action involving immovable property.
81. Action involving succession.
82. Action to partition community property.
83. Action to partition partnership property.

SECTION 3. CHANGE OF VENUE

Art.
121. Action brought in improper venue; transfer.
122. Change of proper venue.

PRELIMINARY STATEMENT

In this Chapter are included the broad general rules of venue and the more important particular provisions. Provisions dealing with narrow or infrequent situations are retained in the Revised Statutes.

The Code of Practice of 1870 sets out the general rule as to venue in Art. 162, and some of the exceptions to the general rule are stated in Arts. 163 through 168. In addition, there are numerous provisions elsewhere in the 1870 Code, as well as in the Civil Code and the Revised Statutes. In the statute enacting this Code, specific provision has been made for the repeal or amendment of certain Civil Code articles and sections of the Revised Statutes relating to venue.

In Louisiana the parishes fixed for the venue of most actions are the defendant's domicile or place of business, the situs of property involved in the suit, or the place where the cause of action arose. The substance of these rules has been retained in this Code. However, one important change is a specific provision dealing with the waiver of an objection to the venue by failure to object timely. See Art. 44, *infra*. Another innovation, Art. 121, *infra*, gives the court authority to transfer a case brought in a court of improper venue rather than dismiss it.

This Chapter does not include articles fixing the venue for opening successions; for divorce, separation and annulment suits; for emancipation and tutorship; for interdiction; and for adoption. However, appropriate venue provisions for these and other proceedings are included elsewhere in this Code involving the particular subject matter.

SECTION 1. GENERAL DISPOSITIONS

Art. 41. Definition

Venue means the parish where an action or proceeding may properly be brought and tried under the rules regulating the subject.

Source: New.

Cross Reference: Art. 4839.

Comment

This article parallels the definition articles in Chapter 1, Jurisdiction.

Art. 42. General rules

The general rules of venue are that an action against:

(1) An individual who is domiciled in the state shall be brought in the parish of his domicile;

(2) A domestic corporation, or a domestic insurer, shall be brought in the parish where its registered office is located;

(3) A domestic partnership, or a domestic unincorporated association, shall be brought in the parish where its principal business establishment is located;

(4) A foreign corporation licensed to do business in this state shall be brought in the parish where its principal business establishment in the state is located, as designated in its application to do business in the state;

(5) A foreign corporation not licensed to do business in the state, or a nonresident who has not appointed an agent for the service of process in the manner provided by law, other than a foreign or alien insurer, shall be brought in a parish where the process may be, and subsequently is, served on the defendant;

(6) A nonresident, other than a foreign corporation or a foreign or alien insurer, who has appointed an agent for the service of process in the manner provided by law, shall be brought in the parish of the designated post office address of an agent for the service of process; and

(7) A foreign or alien insurer shall be brought in the parish of East Baton Rouge.

Source: C.P. Arts. 89, 162, 165(2), 165(5); former R.S. 13:3234, 13:3235, 13:3471(5) (d); R.S. 22:985; cf. Comments following.

Cross References: Arts. 43, 45, 73, 77, 2416, 2633, 4653, 4839.

Comments

(a) Heretofore, there has been no statute fixing the venue of a suit against a domestic corporation, but the general rule of domicile has been held applicable. Ramey v. Cudahy Packing Co., 200 So. 333 (La.App.1941). R.S. 12:37 provides that a corporation's registered office shall be considered its domicile.

(b) Likewise, prior to the adoption of this Code, there was no provision in Louisiana fixing the venue of suits against unincorporated associations. For similar provisions, see N.Y.Gen.Assn. Law, Art. 3, § 13 (McKinney's Consol. Laws of N. Y., Book 18–A); Code of Alabama (1940), Title 7, § 56; Vernon's Tex. Rules Civil Procedure, Vernon Anno.Civil Stats., Art. 1995(23); Conn.Gen. Stats., §§ 52–42, 52–43; Fed. Rule 17(b).

(c) Former R.S. 13:3234 and 13:3235, which fixed the venue in suits against foreign corporations, have been judicially recognized as irreconcilable. Abadie v. National Petroleum Corp., 150 La. 1076, 91 So. 516 (1922). The statute enacting this Code specifically repeals both of these sections.

The term "principal business establishment" is used in paragraph (4) because R.S. 12:202 requires a foreign corporation to designate in writing the place of its "principal business establishment."

(d) Heretofore, nonresident individuals could be sued where service could be made, whether or not they had appointed agents. The above article restricts the venue as to nonresident individuals who have appointed agents. Otherwise, there is no change as to nonresident individuals. Paragraph (6) does not apply to a nonresident for whom, by operation of law, the secretary of state is made the agent for service of process, for in such a case the nonresident has not "appointed" an agent. See Roper v. Brooks, 201 La. 135, 9 So.2d 485 (1942) to the effect that a nonresident sued in connection with a motor vehicle accident is subject to nonresident attachment, even though by statute service may be made on the secretary of state. For the venue of a suit in which the jurisdiction is based upon a nonresident attachment, see Art. 3545, *infra*.

(e) Paragraphs (6) and (7) effect no change in the rules found in the Insurance Code relating to insurers.

(f) Paragraph (5) retains the 1954 amendment to former R.S. 13:3471(5)(d), which recognizes the state jurisdiction announced in International Shoe Co. v. State of Washington, 326 U.S. 310, 66 S.Ct. 154, 90 L.Ed. 95 (1945).

(g) The term "individual" is used in paragraph (1) instead of "person" for the reason that the definition of person in Art. 5251, *infra*, also includes unincorporated associations, partnerships, and domestic or foreign corporations.

(h) Under Art. 165(5) of the 1870 Code, nonresident individuals may be sued where service may be made, whether or not they have appointed agents. Paragraph (5) of the above article limits and restricts the venue for nonresident individuals who have appointed agents.

(i) Art. 165(2) of the 1870 Code provides that where a partnership has more than one place of business, suit must be brought in the parish where the obligation is entered into. That part has been omitted here, and the situation is covered by Art. 77, *infra*. Otherwise, there is no change with respect to partnerships. Suits against partners are governed by Art. 78, *infra*.

(j) Heretofore, there has been no established procedure for registration of appointments of agents for service of process by a nonresident individual, partnership, or association. Former R.S. 13:3471(19) permits but does not require the depositing of such an appointment with the sheriff. Thus, despite the fact that such an appointment protects a nonresident from nonresident attachment, and will under the above article limit the venue as to such nonresident, there is no certain method by which a local creditor can determine whether an agent has been appointed, who he is, or what his address is. Therefore, in order to effectuate the purposes of this Code, there has been submitted proposed legislation, revised R.S. 13:3485, which provides a procedure for registration with the secretary of state of appointments of agents for service of process by all nonresidents, and providing further that unless the nonresident registers the appointment, he cannot take advantage of it. *Cf.* a similar provision relating to foreign corporations at R.S. 12:202(A)(2).

(k) See, also, Comments under Art. 593, *infra*.

Art. 43. Exceptions to general rules

The general rules of venue provided in Article 42 are subject to the exceptions provided in Articles 71 through 83 and otherwise provided by law.

Source: New.

Cross References: Art. 4830.

Art. 44. Waiver of objections to venue

An objection to the venue may not be waived prior to the institution of the action.

The venue provided in Articles 2006, 2811, 2812, 3941, 3991, 4031, and 4541 may not be waived.

Except as otherwise provided in this article or by other law, any objection to the venue, including one based on any article in this Chapter, is waived by the failure of the defendant to plead the declinatory exception timely as provided in Article 928.

Source: C.P. Art. 162; cf. Comments following.

Cross References: Arts. 1631, 4839.

Comments

(a) The first paragraph clarifies Art. 162, Code of Practice of 1870, which provides that a defendant "shall not be permitted to elect any other domicile or residence for the purpose of being sued." See Jex v. Keary, 18 La.Ann. 81 (1866).

(b) The general rule under the 1870 Code seems to be that venue is waivable, either by an appearance without objection to the venue, or by default. But the question is not free from doubt. In a recent court of appeal decision, it was held that the right to be sued at one's domicile is jurisdictional and can be urged even after default, and by the court on its own motion. Automobile Insurance Co. of Hartford, Conn. v. Thornton, 56 So.2d 308 (La.App. 1951). Under the above article an objection to the venue is waivable, except in the special types of cases covered in the second paragraph.

(c) The article referred to in the last sentence of the above article sets forth the time within which an objection to the venue must be filed.

(d) See, also, Comments under Art. 1, *supra*, and Art. 75, *infra*.

Art. 45. Conflict between two or more articles in Chapter

The following rules determine the proper venue in cases where two or more articles in this Chapter may conflict:

(1) Article 78, 79, 80, 81, 82, or 83 governs the venue exclusively, if this article conflicts with any of Articles 42 and 71 through 77;

(2) If there is a conflict between two or more Articles 78 through 83, the plaintiff may bring the action in any venue provided by any applicable article; and

(3) If Article 78, 79, 80, 81, 82, or 83 is not applicable, and there is a conflict between two or more of Articles 42 and 71 through 77, the plaintiff may bring the action in any venue provided by any applicable article.

Source: New.

Cross Reference: Art. 4839.

Comments

This article covers the situation where more than one article is applicable to a particular case. In Williams' Heirs v. Zengel, 117 La. 599, 42 So. 153 (1906), the court held that a suit within the terms of two of the former mandatory provisions could have been brought in the venue provided in either.

See, also, Comments under Art. 81, *infra*.

SECTION 2. EXCEPTIONS TO GENERAL RULES

Art. 71. Action against individual who has changed domicile

An action against an individual who has changed his domicile from one parish to another may be brought in either parish for a period of one year from the date of the change, unless he has filed a declaration of intention to change his domicile, in the manner provided by law.

Source: C.P. Arts. 167, 168.

Cross References: Arts. 43, 45, 4839.

Comments

(a) This article makes no change in the law. Art. 42 of the Civil Code sets forth the method of making the declaration concerning a change of domicile.

(b) Art. 38 of the Civil Code defines domicile and provides that either of two places where one resides alternately may be considered his domicile, in the absence of a declaration. Art. 166, Code of Practice of 1870, covers the same situation. Since the problem is really one of fixing domicile, a substantive question, it has been retained in the Civil Code, and no counterpart to Art. 166 of the 1870 Code of Practice is included herein.

Art. 72. Certain actions involving property; effect of judgment

An action in which a sequestration is sought, or an action to enforce a mortgage or privilege by an ordinary proceeding, may be brought in the parish where the property, or any portion thereof, is situated.

The court may render a personal judgment against the defendant if prayed for, unless he objects to the venue of the personal action by the timely filing of the declinatory exception, as provided in Article 928. If this exception is maintained, the judgment shall be effective only against the property.

Source: C.P. Arts. 163, 165(8).

Cross References: Arts. 43, 45, 80, 4839.

Comments

(a) The first paragraph of this article is almost completely new. It applies to all property, movable and immovable, and covers the same situations included in Arts. 163 and 165(8) of the 1870 Code.

(b) The second paragraph is intended to remedy situations presented in Franck v. Turner, 164 La. 532, 114 So. 148 (1927), and Robin v. J. Thomas Driscoll, Inc., 197 So. 307 (La.App.1940). In these cases the court held that if a suit is brought in a parish where the defendant owns property and the property is sequestered or provisionally seized, the judgment can be operative only to the amount of the property involved, even though the defendant allows a default judgment to be entered against him. This article sets forth the general rule that a valid default judgment may be rendered by a court of improper venue in the actions specified herein. Under this article, however, if the defendant makes an appearance and fails to urge the limitation, judgment for the full amount of the claim may be rendered.

(c) The venue of executory proceedings is governed by Art. 2633, *infra*.

(d) Because of the lack of jurisdiction under Pennoyer v. Neff, 95 U.S. 714, 24 L.Ed. 565 (1877), no Louisiana court could render a personal judgment against a nonresident who is not served personally, even though he does not object to the venue. The last paragraph of this article is not intended to affect nonresidents who are not before the court.

(e) Art. 126, Code of Practice of 1870, provides that whenever a conflict of privileges arises between different creditors, all claims shall be transferred to the court which first seized the property, which court shall rank the privileges. This provision is unnecessary and has not been included in this Code. In the case of Bank of West Feliciana v. Clark, 127 La. 909, 54 So. 145 (1911), the court indicated that Art. 126 has never been applied.

Art. 73. Action against joint or solidary obligors

An action against joint or solidary obligors may be brought in any parish of proper venue, under Article 42, as to any obligor who is made a defendant.

If the action against this defendant is compromised prior to judgment, or dismissed after a trial on the merits, the venue shall remain proper as to the other defendants, unless the joinder was made for the sole purpose of establishing venue as to the other defendants.

Source: C.P. Art. 165(6).

Cross References: Arts. 43, 45, 4839.

Comments

(a) Under this article, the rule that a suit on a solidary obligation can be maintained at the domicile of any of the obligors only if the resident obligor is made a defendant, remains in effect. See Hillebrandt v. Home Indemnity Co., 177 La. 349, 148 So. 254 (1933); Pittman Bros. Constr. Co. v. American Indem. Co., 194 La. 437, 193 So. 699 (1940).

(b) In several cases the question has been presented as to what effect the dismissal of the suit against the resident defendant has on the suit against the nonresident solidary obligor, and the courts have held consistently that under such circumstances the suit against the nonresident must be dismissed for want of jurisdiction. In DeBouchel v. Koss Const. Co., 180 La. 615, 157 So. 270 (1934), the suit against the resident was dismissed on an exception of prescription; in Tate v. Dupuis, 195 So. 810 (La.App.1940), the suit against the resident was dismissed on an exception of no cause of action; in State v. Younger, 206 La. 1037, 20 So.2d 305 (1944), the suit against the resident defendants was compromised and therefore dismissed; in Reich v. Reich, 23 So.2d 566 (La. App.1945), the suit against the resident was dismissed on exceptions of no right or cause of action; and in Gordon v. Bates-Crumley Chevrolet Co., 182 La. 795, 162 So. 624 (1935), a damage suit was dismissed as to the resident defendant after trial on the merits on the ground that he was not guilty of negligence. In all of the above cases the suit against the nonresident defendant was subsequently dismissed on exceptions to the jurisdiction, on the theory that there were no joint or solidary obligors. The second paragraph of the above article overturns the principle of the cited cases in so far as compromise or dismissal after trial is concerned.

Art. 74. Action on offense or quasi offense

An action for the recovery of damages for an offense or quasi offense may be brought in the parish where the wrongful conduct occurred, or in the parish where the damages were sustained.

Source: C.P. Art. 165(9).

Cross References: Arts. 43, 45, 4839.

Comments

Several changes are made by this article. The source article applied to acts of commission of individuals, partnerships, and corporations, but to acts of omissions of corporations only. See Police Jury v. Texas & P. R. Co., 122 La. 388, 47 So. 692 (1908); Tripani v. Meraux, 184 La. 66, 153 So. 453 (1936). The "wrongful conduct" of the above article applies to acts of both omission and commission, and applies equally to all defendants.

The source article was interpreted as applying to actions for damages ex contractu as well as those ex delicto. City of Lafayette v. Wells, Fargo & Co., 129 La. 323, 56 So. 257 (1911); O'Brien v. Delta Air Corporation, 188 La. 911, 178 So. 489 (1938); T. A. Dubell v. Union Central Life Ins. Co., 211 La. 167, 29 So.2d 709 (1947). As this rule was considered very difficult to apply, the above article limits its application to damages resulting from offenses and quasi offenses.

Art. 75. Action on judicial bond

An action against the principal or surety, or both, on a bond filed in a judicial proceeding may be brought in the court where the bond was filed.

Source: C.C. Art. 3042; former R.S. 13:3238.

Cross References: Arts. 43, 45, 4839.

Comments

(a) This article broadens the Louisiana law so as to make it applicable to all bonds filed in judicial proceedings. Arts. 3042 and 3064 of the Civil Code, when read together, apparently apply only in cases where bonds are required to be furnished. The above article applies to all bonds in connection with judicial proceedings, including those furnished voluntarily, such as release bonds.

(b) Former R.S. 13:3238 provides that the principal and surety on a bond furnished by a seizing creditor when a third party claims ownership of the seized property may be sued thereon in the parish where the process was executed. This situation is covered by the above article, and the statute enacting this Code repeals former R.S. 13:3238.

(c) Art. 165(7) of the 1870 Code of Practice provides that suits to enforce the collection of bonds of state officers may be brought in the parish in which the officers exercise their duties, no matter where the sureties reside. A surety on a bond is liable in solido with the principal thereon, and under the terms of Art. 165(6), Code of Practice of 1870, may be sued in any parish in which the principal may be sued. See Rosenberg v. Derbes, 161 La. 1070, 109 So. 841 (1926). Suits against the surety sounding in damages ex contractu may be brought under the above article, whereas suits ex delicto may be brought pursuant to Art. 74, *supra*.

Art. 76. Action on insurance policy

An action on a life insurance policy may be brought in the parish where the deceased died, the parish where he was domiciled, or the parish where any beneficiary is domiciled.

An action on a health and accident insurance policy may be brought in the parish where the insured is domiciled, or in the parish where the accident or illness occurred.

An action on any other type of insurance policy may be brought in the parish where the loss occurred or the insured is domiciled.

Source: C.P. Art. 165(10).

Cross References: Arts. 43, 45, 4839.

Tit. 1   VENUE   Art. 78

Comments

(a) Except for minor changes in terminology to conform to the terms used in the Insurance Code, the above article does not change the law, except in one immaterial respect.

(b) This article also applies to policies issued by a fraternal benefit society.

(c) For the definition of "insurance policy", see Art. 5251, *infra*.

Art. 77. Action against person doing business in another parish

An action against a person having a business office or establishment in a parish other than that where he may be sued under Article 42, on a matter over which this office or establishment had supervision, may be brought in the parish where this office or establishment is located.

Source: Former R.S. 13:3236.

Cross References: Arts. 43, 45, 4839.

Comments

(a) This article is broader than the source article, which is restricted to persons engaged in "commercial business."

(b) This article applies to all "persons" which, by definition, includes corporations and partnerships, resident and nonresident.

(c) See, also, Comments under Art. 42, *supra*.

Art. 78. Action against partners of existing partnership

Except as provided in Article 79, an action against a partner of an existing partnership on an obligation of the latter, or on an obligation growing out of the partnership, shall be brought in any parish of proper venue as to the partnership.

Source: C.P. Art. 165(2).

Cross References: Arts. 43, 45, 4839.

Comments

(a) This article makes no change in the law. Art. 165(2), Code of Practice of 1870, has been interpreted as requiring a suit against partners during the existence of the partnership to be brought in a parish in which the partnership is susceptible to suit. Hayes Machinery Co. v. Eastham, 147 La. 347, 84 So. 898 (1920); Rheuark v. Terminal Mud & Chem. Co., 213 La. 732, 35 So.2d 592 (1948). See also, Wolf v. N. O. Tailor-Made Pants Co., 52 La.Ann. 1357, 27 So. 893 (1900).

(b) Under the above article, the partner may object to his being sued at his domicile.

(c) This provision does not absolutely limit the venue to the parish of the partnership's place of business, however, because in many instances the partnership may be sued elsewhere, *e. g.*, as a solidary obligor, or as a defendant in a tort action.

(d) With regard to incidental demands, Art. 165(4) of the 1870 Code of Practice designates the venue for matters of warranty; Art. 392 for interventions; and Art. 397 for third oppositions. Because the articles of this Code which define incidental demands require that they be filed in the court where the main demand is pending, no provisions for venue of incidental demands are included in this Chapter.

(e) See, also, Comments under Art. 42, *supra*.

Art. 79. Action to dissolve partnership

An action for the dissolution of a partnership shall be brought in the parish where it has or had its principal business establishment.

Source: C.P. Art. 165(2).

Cross References: Arts. 43, 45, 78, 4839.

Art. 80. Action involving immovable property

The following actions shall be brought in the parish where the immovable property is situated:

(1) An action to assert an interest in immovable property, or a right in, to, or against immovable property, except as otherwise provided in Articles 72 and 2633; and

(2) An action to partition immovable property, except as otherwise provided in Articles 81, 82, and 83.

If the immovable property, consisting of one or more tracts, is situated in more than one parish, the action may be brought in any of these parishes.

Source: C.P. Arts. 165(1), 165(8); C.C. Arts. 840, 1290, 1291.

Cross References: Arts. 43, 45, 3652, 3656, 4603.

Comments

(a) The last paragraph of this article changes the law by broadening the rule of Art. 1291 of the Civil Code, so as to permit one court to adjudicate all issues, even though separate tracts situated in different parishes are involved.

(b) The exceptions in Art. 80(1) refer to the articles providing the venue in proceedings to enforce a mortgage or privilege, in both ordinary and executory process.

(c) This article provides the venue in an action of boundary. See, also, Art. 840 of the Civil Code.

(d) The second paragraph of Art. 1290, and Art. 1291, of the Civil Code are superseded by this article.

(e) See, also, Comments under Arts. 81, 83, *infra*.

Art. 81. Action involving succession

When a succession has been opened judicially, until rendition of the judgment of possession, the following actions shall be brought in the court in which the succession proceeding is pending:

(1) A personal action by a creditor of the deceased; but an action brought against the deceased prior to his death may be prosecuted against his succession representative in the court in which it was brought;

(2) An action to partition the succession;

(3) An action to annul the testament of the deceased; and

(4) An action to assert a right to the succession of the deceased, either under his testament or by effect of law.

Source: C.P. Arts. 164, 1022; C.C. Arts. 1137, 1327.

Cross References: Arts. 43, 45, 80, 3461.

Comments

(a) This article includes the situations covered by Art. 164 of the 1870 Code of Practice relative to succession matters generally; Art. 1022 of the 1870 Code, and Arts. 1137 and 1327 of the Civil Code, regarding partition of succession property.

(b) Civil Code Art. 1113 sets out the venue in suits against vacant successions. Since such suits are included within the general terms of the above article, proposed legislation has been submitted recommending that Civil Code Art. 1113 be amended so as to delete the venue provision.

(c) Art. 1000, Civil Code, provides that the heir who "suffers judgment to be given against him" on a succession debt thereby accepts the succession. Such a suit is against the heir himself, does not involve the succession except incidentally, and should be brought at the domicile of the heir under Art. 42, *supra*, particularly since it is a personal judgment which is sought against the heir.

(d) This article covers only partitions "between coheirs", that is, those which take place as part of the succession proceeding.

Art. 81

Once the heirs become co-owners by virtue of a judgment of possession, Art. 80, *supra,* will apply to a partition suit between them. Freret v. Freret, 31 La.Ann. 506 (1879); Medicis v. Medicis, 155 La. 171, 99 So. 27 (1924).

(e) An action against a succession to partition property owned in indivision by the succession and another person is not governed by this article.

Art. 82. Action to partition community property

Except as otherwise provided in the second paragraph of this article, an action to partition community property shall be brought either as an incident of the action which would result in a dissolution of the community, or as a separate action in the parish where the judgment dissolving the community was rendered.

If the community owns immovable property, the action to partition the community property, movable and immovable, may be brought in the parish where any of the immovable property is situated.

Source: New.

Cross References: Arts. 45, 80.

Comments

(a) Until 1954, there was no rule of venue provided by positive law, and only one reported case, which gave no definite answers to the various problems presented. See Demourelle v. Allen, 218 La. 603, 50 So.2d 208 (1950). R.S. 13:4991, adopted as La.Act 448 of 1954, excluded the parish in which the court which rendered the judgment was situated as a possible venue, to accept alternative venues based primarily on the last matrimonial domicile. In Steere v. Marston, 228 La. 94, 81 So.2d 822 (1955), the court refused to apply the 1954 statute retroactively.

(b) This article changes the law, but is declaratory of what are generally accepted in the profession as the soundest solutions of the problems possible. R.S. 13:4991 is recommended for repeal.

Art. 83. Action to partition partnership property

Except as otherwise provided in the second paragraph of this article, an action to partition partnership property shall be brought either as an incident of the action to dissolve the partnership, or as a separate action in the court which·rendered the judgment dissolving the partnership.

If the partnership owns immovable property, the action to partition the partnership property, movable and immovable, may be brought in the parish where any of the immovable property is situated.

Source: New.

Cross References: Arts. 45, 80.

Comments

(a) Heretofore, no specific provision covered this situation. Although no case was found directly in point, it seems that under prior law this type of partition suit would have to be brought at the situs of the property, 1870 Code of Practice Art. 165(1), and Civil Code Art. 1291. The above article was included because it seemed advisable to make the court which handled the dissolution proceeding a court of proper venue for the partition.

(b) In cases where the partnership owns property in indivision with a person not a member of the partnership, actions to partition such property should be brought under the general partition article, Art. 80, *supra*.

SECTION 3. CHANGE OF VENUE

Art. 121. Action brought in improper venue; transfer

When an action is brought in a court of improper venue, the court may dismiss the action, or in the interest of justice transfer it to a court of proper venue.

Source: New.

Comments

(a) This represents an innovation in Louisiana procedure. Former R.S. 13:4441 contains a somewhat similar provision with respect to appeals taken to the wrong court. See, also, Rule 89, Texas Rules of Civil Procedure. The reason for the rule is, of course, to eliminate needless costs and delays.

(b) This article presupposes a timely objection to the venue; otherwise the defendant waives the improper venue.

(c) See Art. 421 *infra*, Comment (e), and Art. 932, *infra*, for a discussion of the effect of transfer on prescription.

(d) See, also, Comments under Arts. 464, 932, *infra*.

Art. 122. Change of proper venue

Any party by contradictory motion may obtain a change of venue upon proof that he cannot obtain a fair and impartial trial because of

Art. 122 COURTS Bk. 1

the undue influence of an adverse party, prejudice existing in the public mind, or some other sufficient cause. If the motion is granted, the action shall be transferred to a parish wherein no party is domiciled.

Source: Former R.S. 13:3271–13:3274.

Comments

(a) This article applies to a change of venue requested even after answer is filed. It is not related to the waiver of the exception to venue referred to in the preceding articles.

(b) One change effected by this article is the elimination of the requirement of former R.S. 13:3274 that the application be accompanied by an affidavit. Art. 863, *infra*, a general provision to the effect that a signature on a pleading amounts to a certificate as to the truth of the allegations contained therein and the good faith of the party filing the pleading, obviates the need for most of the special affidavit provisions.

(c) Another change is the elimination of the requirement that the action must be transferred to a parish in the same district or an adjoining district. Such a requirement is too restrictive and unnecessary, for it is unlikely that a judge will order a case transferred to a parish a great distance away from that in which it was originally brought.

CHAPTER 3. RECUSATION OF JUDGES

Art.
151. Grounds.
152. Recusation on court's own motion or by supreme court.
153. Judge may act until recused or motion for recusation filed.
154. Procedure for recusation.
155. Selection of judge to try motion to recuse; court having two or more judges.
156. Same; court having single judge.
157. Judge ad hoc appointed to try cause when judge recused; power of judge ad hoc.
158. Supreme court appointment of district judge to try cause when judge recused.
159. Recusation of supreme court justice.
160. Recusation of judge of court of appeal.
161. Recusation of judge ad hoc.

Art. 151. Grounds

A judge of any court, trial or appellate, may be recused when he:

(1) Is a material witness in the cause;

(2) Has been employed or consulted as an attorney in the cause, or has been associated with an attorney during the latter's employment in the cause;

(3) Has performed a judicial act in the cause in another court;

(4) Is the spouse of a party, or of an attorney employed in the cause; or is related to a party, or to the spouse of a party, within the fourth degree; or is related to an attorney employed in the cause, or to the spouse of the attorney, within the second degree; or

(5) Is interested in the cause.

In any cause in which the state, or a political subdivision thereof, or a religious body or corporation is interested, the fact that the judge is a citizen of the state or a resident of the political subdivision, or pays taxes thereto, or is a member of the religious body or corporation, is not a ground for recusation.

Source: C.P. Arts. 337, 881, 1072.

Cross Reference: Art. 4843.

Comment

The provisions of the source articles relating to the grounds for the recusation of a judge ad hoc and a justice of the peace are made applicable to each by Art. 161 and Art. 4845 *infra*, respectively.

See, also, Comments under Arts. 4845–4847, *infra*.

Art. 152. Recusation on court's own motion or by supreme court

A judge may recuse himself, whether a motion for his recusation has been filed by a party or not, in any cause in which a ground for recusation exists.

On the written application of a district judge, the supreme court may recuse him for any reason which it considers sufficient.

Source: C.P. Arts. 338(2), 881; *cf.* Comments following.

Comments

(a) No change in the law is effected by the first paragraph. The second paragraph makes a change by empowering the supreme court to recuse a district judge, on his written application, in any case where the supreme court considers that his application for recusation should be granted in the interests of justice or to avoid embarrassment, even though no ground for recusation otherwise exists.

(b) Nothing in this article prevents the transfer or re-allotment of cases in a court having two or more judges, in accordance with its rules.

Art. 153. Judge may act until recused or motion for recusation filed

Until a judge has recused himself, or a motion for his recusation has been filed, he has full power and authority to act in the cause.

Source: C.P. Art. 338(2).

Comment

This article effects no change in Louisiana procedure.

Art. 154. Procedure for recusation

A party desiring to recuse a judge of a district court shall file a written motion therefor assigning the ground for recusation. This motion shall be filed prior to trial or hearing unless the party discovers the facts constituting the ground for recusation thereafter, in which event it shall be filed immediately after these facts are discovered, but prior to judgment. If a valid ground for recusation is set forth in the motion, the judge shall either recuse himself, or refer the motion to another judge or a judge ad hoc, as provided in Articles 155 and 156, for a hearing.

Source: C.P. Art. 338(1).

Comment

This article effects no change in the law.

Art. 155. Selection of judge to try motion to recuse; court having two or more judges

In a district court having two or more judges, the judge who is sought to be recused shall have the motion to recuse referred to another judge of the court for trial, in accordance with the rules of the court.

Source: C.P. Art. 339.

Cross References: Arts. 154, 157.

Comment

This article is declaratory of the law enunciated by the source provision.

Art. 156. Same; court having single judge

The judge of a district court having a single judge shall appoint a district judge of an adjoining district to try the motion to recuse.

The order of court appointing the judge ad hoc shall be entered on its minutes, and a certified copy of the order shall be sent to the judge ad hoc.

Source: New; *cf.* C.P. Art. 340.

Cross References: Arts. 154, 157.

Comment

The indirect source provision of this article permitted the appointment of a judge of an adjoining district or of a lawyer to try the case. However, in view of the increase in the number of district judges in recent years, the above article permits only the judges of an adjoining district to try the motion to recuse.

Art. 157. Judge ad hoc appointed to try cause when judge recused; power of judge ad hoc

After a trial judge recuses himself he shall appoint a judge ad hoc to try the cause in the manner provided by Articles 155 and 156 for the appointment of a judge ad hoc to try the motion to recuse. When a trial judge is recused after a trial of the motion therefor, the judge ad hoc appointed to try the motion to recuse shall continue to act as judge ad hoc for the trial of the cause.

The judge ad hoc has the same power and authority to dispose of the cause as the recused judge has in cases in which no ground for recusation exists.

Source: C.P. Arts. 339, 340, 342.

Cross Reference: Art. 158.

Comment

This article makes no change in Louisiana procedure.

Art. 158. Supreme court appointment of district judge to try cause when judge recused

In a cause in which the district judge is recused, even when a judge ad hoc has been appointed for the trial of the cause under Article 157, a party may apply to the supreme court for the appointment of another district judge as judge ad hoc to try the cause. If the supreme court deems it in the interest of justice, such appointment shall be made.

Art. 158

The order of the supreme court appointing a judge ad hoc shall be entered on its minutes. The clerk of the supreme court shall forward two certified copies of the order, one to the judge ad hoc appointed and the other to the clerk of the district court where the cause is pending, for entry in its minutes.

Source: C.P. Art. 341.

Comment

This article makes no change in the law.

Art. 159. Recusation of supreme court justice

When a written motion is filed to recuse a justice of the supreme court, he may recuse himself or the motion shall be heard by the other justices of the court.

When a justice of the supreme court recuses himself, or is recused, the court may (1) have the cause argued before and disposed of by the other justices, or (2) appoint a judge of a district court or a court of appeal having the qualifications of a justice of the supreme court to act for the recused justice in the hearing and disposition of the cause.

Source: New; cf. C.P. Art. 881.

Comment

Former R.S. 13:101 provided that in any case when a justice of the supreme court may be recused, he shall select a judge of a court of appeal or a district court to sit in the trial of the case. This provision is superseded by the above article.

Art. 160. Recusation of judge of court of appeal

When a written motion is filed to recuse a judge of a court of appeal, he may recuse himself or the motion shall be heard by the other judges on the panel to which the cause is assigned, or by all judges of the court, except the judge sought to be recused, sitting en banc.

When a judge of a court of appeal recuses himself, or is recused, the court may (1) have the cause argued before and disposed of by the other judges of the panel to which it is assigned, or (2) appoint another of its judges, a judge of a district court or a lawyer having the qualifications of a judge of a court of appeal to act for the recused judge in the hearing and disposition of the cause.

Source: New; cf. Const. Art. VII, § 26; C.P. Art. 881.

Comment

This article makes only the changes necessary to implement the changes in the appellate court system recently effected by constitutional amendment.

Art. 161. Recusation of judge ad hoc

A judge ad hoc appointed to try a motion to recuse a judge, or appointed to try the cause, may be recused on the grounds and in the manner provided in this Chapter for the recusation of judges.

Source: New; cf. C.P. Arts. 337–342.

Comment

See Comment under Art. 151, *supra*.

CHAPTER 4. POWER AND AUTHORITY

SECTION 1. GENERAL DISPOSITIONS

Art.
191. Inherent judicial power.
192. Authority of trial court to appoint experts.
193. Power to adopt local rules; publication.
194. Power of district court to act in chambers; signing orders and judgments.
195. Same; judicial proceedings.
196. Power of district court to act in vacation.

SECTION 2. POWER TO PUNISH FOR CONTEMPT

221. Kinds of contempt.
222. Direct contempt.
223. Same; procedure for punishing.
224. Constructive contempt.
225. Same; procedure for punishing.
226. Same; imprisonment until performance.
227. Punishment for contempt.

SECTION 1. GENERAL DISPOSITIONS

Art. 191. Inherent judicial power

A court possesses inherently all of the power necessary for the exercise of its jurisdiction even though not granted expressly by law.

Source: C.P. Arts. 130, 877.

Comment

This article makes no change in the procedural law of Louisiana.

Art. 192. Authority of trial court to appoint experts

A trial court, on its own motion or on motion of a party, may appoint persons learned or skilled in a science, art, profession, or calling as experts to assist it in the adjudication of any case in which their special knowledge or skill may aid the court.

The reasonable fees and expenses of these experts shall be taxed as costs of court.

Source: New; *cf.* C.P. Arts. 441–443, 446, 462.

Comment

This article is a simplification and restatement of its indirect source provisions.

See, also, Comment under Art. 373, *infra*.

Art. 193. Power to adopt local rules; publication

A court may adopt rules for the conduct of judicial business before it, including those governing matters of practice and procedure which are not contrary to the rules provided by law. When a court has more than one judge, its rules shall be adopted or amended by a majority of the judges thereof, sitting en banc.

The rules may provide that the court may call a special session of court during vacation, and that any action, proceeding, or matter otherwise required by law to be tried or heard in open court during the regular session may be tried or heard during the special session.

The rules shall be entered on the minutes of the court. Rules adopted by an appellate court shall be published in the manner which the court considers most effective and practicable. Rules adopted by a district court shall be printed in pamphlet form, and a copy shall be furnished on request to any attorney licensed to practice law in this state.

Source: C.P. 145; R.S. 13:72, 13:73, 13:1147; *cf.* Const. Art. VII, §§ 18, 81.

Cross Reference: Art. 4847.

Comments

(a) No change in the law is made by the first and third paragraphs of this article.

(b) In view of the renovation and air-conditioning of many of the district court rooms throughout the state, and the considerable professional and popular demand for the continuation of court throughout some part of the summer, each district court is given the power to hold such special sessions during the summer, and to try such matters at this special session, as each district court may deem in the interests of justice.

(c) See, also, Comments under Arts. 196, 2121, *infra*.

Art. 194. Power of district court to act in chambers; signing orders and judgments

The following orders and judgments may be signed by the district judge in chambers:

(1) Order directing the taking of an inventory; judgment decreeing or homologating a partition, when unopposed; judgment probating a testament ex parte; order directing the execution of a testament; order confirming or appointing a legal representative, when unopposed; order appointing an undertutor or an undercurator; order appointing an attorney at law to represent an absent, incompetent, or unrepresented person, or an attorney for an absent heir; order authorizing the sale of property of an estate administered by a legal representative; order directing the publication of the notice of the filing of a tableau of distribution, or of an account, by a legal representative; judgment recognizing heirs or legatees and sending them into possession, when unopposed; all orders for the administration and settlement of a succession, or for the administration of an estate by a legal representative;

(2) Order to show cause; order directing the issuance and providing the security to be furnished by a party for the issuance of a writ of attachment or sequestration; order directing the release of property seized under a writ of attachment or sequestration and providing the security to be furnished therefor; order for the issuance of a temporary restraining order and providing the security therefor; order for the issuance of a writ, or alternative writ, of habeas corpus, mandamus, or quo warranto;

(3) Order for the seizure and sale of property in an executory proceeding;

(4) Order for the taking of testimony by deposition; for the production of documentary evidence; for the production of documents and things for inspection, copying, or photographing; for permission to enter land for the purpose of measuring, surveying, or photographing;

(5) Order or judgment deciding or otherwise disposing of an action, proceeding, or matter which may be tried or heard in chambers;

(6) Order or judgment which may be granted on ex parte motion or application, except an order of appeal on an oral motion and a judgment granting or confirming a default; and

(7) Any other order or judgment not specifically required by law to be signed in open court.

Source: New; *cf.* former R.S. 13:581, 13:3751, 13:3752, 13:3782, 13:3783; La. Act 77 of 1924; La. Act 15 of 1882; R.S. of 1870, §§ 1746, 1936.

Cross Reference: Art. 196.

Comments

(a) This article recognizes the authority of the district judge to sign in chambers any judgment or order which he is now so authorized to sign, but extends this power appreciably, as pointed out in Comments (b) and (c).

(b) The former law authorized the judge to confirm or appoint an executor, administrator, tutor, or curator in chambers. This article extends this power by authorizing his appointment, in chambers, of any legal representative. This term, as defined in Art. 5251, *infra*, includes an administrator, provisional administrator, administrator of a vacant succession, executor, dative testamentary executor, tutor, curator, receiver, liquidator, and trustee. This power, however, is limited to those instances where there is no opposition to the confirmation or appointment.

(c) This article further extends the authority of the judge to sign an order or judgment in chambers to all cases, except an order of appeal on oral motion, or a default judgment, which may be granted on ex parte motion or application.

(d) See, also, Comments under Arts. 1911, 2121, 3612, 3993, *infra*.

Art. 195. Same; judicial proceedings

The following judicial proceedings may be conducted by the district judge in chambers:

(1) Hearing on an application by a legal representative for authority, whether opposed or unopposed, and on a petition for emancipation;

(2) Homologation of a tableau of distribution, or of an account, filed by a legal representative, so far as unopposed;

(3) Trial of a rule to determine the nonexempt portion of wages, salaries, or commissions seized under garnishment and to direct the payment thereof periodically by the garnishee to the sheriff;

Tit. 1 POWER AND AUTHORITY Art. 196

(4) Examination of a judgment debtor; and

(5) Trial of or hearing on any other action, proceeding, or matter which the law expressly provides may be tried or heard in chambers.

Source: New; cf. former R.S. 13:581; La. Act 77 of 1924, La. Act 15 of 1882; R.S. of 1870, §§ 1746, 1936.

Cross Reference: Art. 196.

Comments

(a) Art. 195(1) and 195(2) broaden, to a considerable extent, the trial judge's power to act in chambers. Under the former law, he was empowered to act in chambers on applications by a tutor or curator for authority, and to homologate, so far as unopposed, tableaus of distribution or accounts filed by administrators, executors, tutors, and curators. Under this article the trial judge is empowered to act in chambers on applications for authority, or to homologate tableaus of distribution or accounts, filed by any legal representative, as defined in Art. 5251, *infra*.

(b) Art. 195(3) and 195(4) are in accord with the prior law. See former R.S. 13:3921–13:3927 and 13:4311–13:4315.

(c) See, also, Comments under Arts. 1911, 2595, 3381, 3612, 3993, 4271, *infra*.

Art. 196. Power of district court to act in vacation

The following judicial acts or proceedings may be performed or conducted by the district court during vacation:

(1) Signing of an order or judgment which, under Article 194, may be signed in chambers; and signing of any order or judgment in an action or proceeding which is tried in vacation;

(2) Trial of or hearing on an action, proceeding, or matter which, under Article 195, may be tried or heard in chambers;

(3) Trial of a rule for a preliminary injunction, or for the dissolution or modification of any injunctive order;

(4) Trial of a habeas corpus, mandamus, quo warranto, or partition proceeding;

(5) Trial of a motion for a change of venue;

(6) Trial of or hearing on any other action, proceeding, or matter which the law expressly provides may be tried or heard during vacation, or in which the parties thereto have consented to the trial or hearing thereof during vacation;

(7) Signing of an order of appeal requested by petition, providing the security therefor, and trying a rule to test the surety on an appeal bond; and

Art. 196

(8) Trial of or hearing on an action, proceeding, or matter in a special session which, under the rules of the court, may be tried or heard therein.

Source: Former R.S. 13:4070.

Comments

(a) There is no reason why a court should not be empowered to do or perform any judicial act during vacation which it is authorized to do or perform in chambers. Art. 196(1) and 196(2) grant this power and authority.

(b) Art. 196(6) applies to two different classes of cases. First, it applies to all actions, proceedings, or matters which may now be tried in vacation under special statutes. It also grants authority to try during vacation any action, proceeding, or matter when the parties consent to such trial.

(c) Art. 196(8) implements the provisions of the second paragraph of Art. 193, *supra*.

(d) See, also, Comments under Arts. 1911, 2121, 2595, 3606, 3612, 3993, 4271, 4603, *infra*.

SECTION 2. POWER TO PUNISH FOR CONTEMPT

Art. 221. Kinds of contempt

A contempt of court is any act or omission tending to obstruct or interfere with the orderly administration of justice, or to impair the dignity of the court or respect for its authority.

Contempts of court are of two kinds, direct and constructive.

Source: New; *cf.* Comment following.

Comment

This is the uniform classification of contempts of court in America, recognized and applied in State ex rel. DeBuys v. Judges of Civil District Court, 32 La.Ann. 1256 (1880); and Graham v. Jones, 200 La. 137, 7 So.2d 688 (1942). See 17 Tul.L.Rev. 655 (1943), and 38 Minn.Stats.Anno., § 588.01(1).

See, also, Comments under Art. 3611, *infra*.

Art. 222. Direct contempt

A direct contempt of court is one committed in the immediate view and presence of the court and of which it has personal knowledge, or a contumacious failure to comply with a subpoena or summons, proof of service of which appears of record.

Any of the following acts constitutes a direct contempt of court:

(1) Contumacious, insolent, or disorderly behavior toward the judge, or an attorney or other officer of the court, tending to interrupt or interfere with the business of the court, or to impair its dignity or respect for its authority;

(2) Breach of the peace, boisterous conduct, or violent disturbance tending to interrupt or interfere with the business of the court, or to impair its dignity or respect for its authority;

(3) Use of insulting, abusive, or discourteous language by an attorney or other person in open court, or in a pleading, brief, or other document filed with the court in irrelevant criticism of another attorney or of a judge or officer of the court;

(4) Violation of a rule of the court adopted to maintain order and decorum in the court room;

(5) Contumacious failure to comply with a subpoena, proof of service of which appears of record, or refusal to take the oath or affirmation as a witness, or refusal of a witness to answer a non-incriminating question when ordered to do so by the court; and

(6) Contumacious failure to attend court to serve as a juror after being accepted as such, or to attend court as a member of a jury venire, when proof of service of the summons appears of record.

Source: New; *cf.* Rules of the Supreme Court of Louisiana, Rule X, § 4; 38 Minn.Stats.Anno., § 588.01(1), (2); 29 McKinney's Consol.Laws of N.Y. Anno., Art. 19, § 753.

Cross Reference: Art. 4838.

Comments

(a) While this article is patterned to some extent upon the Minnesota law, which is the most complete statute found, it has been broadened appreciably so as to include all applicable and useful provisions of the other indirect sources, and to cover the case discussed in Comment (b).

(b) Under the Minnesota and other statutes on the subject, the definition of direct contempt is not broad enough to cover the case of the contumacious refusal or failure of a witness or juror to attend court when subpoenaed or summoned. Yet the whole theory of the direct contempt is that the judge does not need the introduction of evidence to reach his finding, and certainly these cases fall within this theory. Actually, no proof is needed, as the return on the subpoena or summons is in the record, and there is no reason why these cases should not be considered direct contempts. When a witness refuses to be sworn, or to answer a question, all of this occurs in the immediate view and presence of the court. For this reason, the first paragraph of this article has been broadened to include them within the definition of direct contempt, and Art. 222(5) and 222(6) expressly make them a direct contempt.

(c) See, also, Comments under Arts. 224, 864, 3611, *infra*.

Art. 223. Same; procedure for punishing

A person who has committed a direct contempt of court may be found guilty and punished therefor by the court forthwith, without any trial other than affording him an opportunity to be heard orally by way of defense or mitigation. The court shall render an order reciting the facts constituting the contempt, adjudging the person guilty thereof, and specifying the punishment imposed.

Source: New; *cf.* 38 Minn.Stats.Anno., § 588.03.

Comment

This article goes beyond its indirect source provision in affording the person charged with contempt an opportunity to make an oral statement by way of defense or mitigation. This accords with customary judicial practices in Louisiana.

See, also, Comments under Arts. 224, 864, 3611, *infra*.

Art. 224. Constructive contempt

A constructive contempt of court is any contempt other than a direct one.

Any of the following acts constitutes a constructive contempt of court:

(1) Wilful neglect or violation of duty by a clerk, sheriff, or other person elected, appointed, or employed to assist the court in the administration of justice;

(2) Wilful disobedience of any lawful judgment, order, mandate, writ, or process of the court;

(3) Removal or attempted removal of any person or property in the custody of an officer acting under authority of a judgment, order, mandate, writ, or process of the court;

(4) Deceit or abuse of the process or procedure of the court by a party to an action or proceeding, or by his attorney;

(5) Unlawful detention of a witness, party, or his attorney, while going to, remaining at, or returning from the court where the action or proceeding is to be tried;

(6) Improper conversation by a juror or venireman with a party to an action which is being, or may be, tried by a jury of which the juror is a member, or of which the venireman may be a member, or with any person relative to the merits of such an action; or receipt by a juror or venireman of a communication from any person with reference to such an action, without making an immediate disclosure to the court of the substance thereof;

(7) Assuming to act as a juror, or as an attorney or other officer of the court, without lawful authority;

(8) Comment by a newspaper or other medium for the dissemination of news upon a case or proceeding, then pending and undecided, which constitutes a clear, present, and imminent danger of obstructing or interfering with the orderly administration of justice, by either influencing the court to reach a particular decision, or embarrassing it in the discharge of its judicial duties;

(9) Wilful disobedience by an inferior court, judge, or other officer thereof, of the lawful judgment, order, mandate, writ, or process of an appellate court, rendered in connection with an appeal from a judgment or order of the inferior court, or in connection with a review of such judgment or order under a supervisory writ issued by the appellate court; and

(10) Any other act or omission punishable by law as a contempt of court, or intended to obstruct or interfere with the orderly administration of justice, or to impair the dignity of the court or respect for its authority, and which is not a direct contempt.

Source: New; *cf.* 38 Minn.Stats.Anno., § 588.01(3); 29 McKinney's Consol. Laws of N.Y., Art. 19, § 753.

Comments

(a) See Comment (b) under Art. 222, *supra*.

(b) Art. 224(8) is declaratory of the rule of Graham v. Jones, 200 La. 195, 7 So.2d 695 (1942), and is within the constitutional limitations imposed by Bridges v. State of California, 314 U.S. 252, 62 S.Ct. 190, 86 L.Ed. 193 (1941).

(c) Art. 224(10) is an omnibus provision which includes: (1) all acts or omissions punishable as a contempt of court under special statutes, and which are not direct contempts; and (2) all other intentional acts or omissions which fall within the definition of contempt of court, and which are not direct contempts.

(d) See, also, Comments under Arts. 864, 3611, *infra*.

Art. 225. Same; procedure for punishing

Except as otherwise provided by law, a person charged with committing a constructive contempt of court may be found guilty thereof and punished therefor only after the trial by the judge of a rule against him to show cause why he should not be adjudged guilty of contempt, and punished accordingly. The rule to show cause may issue on the court's own motion, or on motion of a party to the action or proceeding, and shall state the facts alleged to constitute the contempt. A certified copy of the motion, and of the rule to show cause, shall be served upon the person charged with contempt in the same manner as a subpoena, at least forty-eight hours before the time assigned for the trial of the rule.

If the person charged with contempt is found guilty, the court shall render an order reciting the facts constituting the contempt, adjudging the person charged with contempt guilty thereof, and specifying the punishment imposed.

Source: New; cf. C.P. Art. 132; 38 Minn.Stats.Anno., § 588.04.

Comments

(a) The procedure in this article employs a rule to show cause, which may issue on the court's own motion or on the motion of a party, and the motion for the rule to show cause sets forth the facts alleged to constitute the constructive contempt. Further, the person charged with committing the constructive contempt is allowed at least forty-eight hours to prepare his defense.

(b) The language "Except as otherwise provided by law" is necessary to avoid any conflict with the provisions of R.S. 23:848, covering charges of contempt for violating an injunctive order issued in a labor relations case, and providing a completely different procedure, including the right to trial by jury, and the right to recuse the trial judge in certain instances, where a person is charged with an "indirect contempt" which is undefined but means the "constructive contempt" of this article.

The provisions of this article contemplate a trial by the judge alone, and negative any right to a trial by jury.

(c) See, also, Comments under Arts. 257, 3611, *infra*.

Art. 226. Same; imprisonment until performance

When a contempt of court consists of the omission to perform an act which is yet in the power of the person charged with contempt to perform, he may be imprisoned until he performs it, and in such a case this shall be specified in the court's order.

Source: New; cf. 38 Minn.Stats.Anno., § 588.12.

Comment

This article is necessary in rare cases of civil contempt, so as to permit the court to enforce its order or judgment. It accords with the 1870 Code of Practice Art. 937, but overrules legislatively Haffner v. Judge of First Judicial District, 50 La.Ann. 552, 23 So. 478 (1898).

See, also, Comments under Art. 3611, *infra.*

Art. 227. Punishment for contempt

A person may not be adjudged guilty of a contempt of court except for misconduct defined as such, or made punishable as such, expressly by law.

The punishment which a court may impose upon a person adjudged guilty of contempt of court is provided in R.S. 13:4611.

Source: New.

Comment

This article implements the provisions of Const. Art. XIX, § 17, providing that, "The power of the courts to punish for contempt shall be limited by law." This article limits such power to two classes of cases, both of which must be provided expressly by law: (1) misconduct defined as such by a code or statutory provision; and (2) misconduct which a code or statutory section provides is punishable as a contempt. The numerous statutes of Louisiana fall into both categories.

See, also, Comments under Arts. 1357, 3611, *infra.*

CHAPTER 5. CLERKS

SECTION 1. GENERAL DISPOSITIONS

Art.
251. Custodian of court records; certified copies; records public.
252. Issuance of process.
253. Pleadings, documents, and exhibits to be filed with clerk.
254. Docket and minute books.
255. Deputy clerks and other employees.
256. Minute clerk.
257. Neglect, failure, or refusal of clerk, deputy, or other employee to perform duty subjects him to punishment for contempt.

SECTION 2. CLERKS OF DISTRICT COURTS

281. Certain articles not applicable to Civil District Court for the Parish of Orleans.

Art.
282. Acts which may be done by district court clerk.
283. Orders and judgments which may be signed by district court clerk.
284. Judicial powers of district court clerk.
285. Powers of district court clerk may be exercised whether judge absent from parish or not.
286. Powers of district court clerk which may not be exercised by deputy; powers of chief deputy clerk.
287. District court clerk ex officio notary.
288. Functions which district court clerk may exercise on holiday.

SECTION 1. GENERAL DISPOSITIONS

Art. 251. Custodian of court records; certified copies; records public

The clerk of a court is the legal custodian of all of its records, and is responsible for their safekeeping and preservation. He may issue a copy of any of these records, certified by him under the seal of the court to be a correct copy of the original. Except as otherwise provided by law, he shall permit any person to examine, copy, photograph, or make a memorandum of any of these records at any time during which the clerk's office is required by law to be open.

Source: New; *cf.* C.P. Arts. 775–779.

Comments

(a) The first and third sentences of this article restate the basic principles of the indirect source provisions, and make no change in the law. The second sentence states expressly the recognized power of the clerk to issue certified copies of the records of the court. The third sentence, based to some extent on the provisions of Art. 778, Code of Practice of 1870, has been expanded to accord with the principles of the Public Records Act, R.S. 44:1–44:7, 44:31–44:38.

(b) The exception at the beginning of the third sentence avoids conflict with statutes requiring certain records to be kept confidential, particularly those relating to juveniles. See, for instance, R.S. 9:427.

(c) For the requirements of proof in a Louisiana court of a record of another Louisiana court, see Art. 1394, *infra*.

Art. 252. Issuance of process

The clerk of a court shall issue all citations, writs, mandates, summons, subpoenas, and other process of the court in the name of the

State of Louisiana. He shall indicate thereon the court from which they issue, sign them in his official capacity, and affix the seal of the court thereto. If service by the sheriff is required, the clerk shall deliver or mail them to the sheriff who is to make the service.

Source: C.P. Art. 774.

Comments

(a) This article effects no change in the law.

(b) The second sentence indicates the requirements common to all process to be issued. Additional requirements are to be found in the various articles regulating the citation, the different writs, the subpoena, and other forms of process.

(c) See, also, Comments under Art. 1202, *infra*.

Art. 253. Pleadings, documents, and exhibits to be filed with clerk

All pleadings or documents to be filed in an action or proceeding instituted or pending in a court, and all exhibits introduced in evidence, shall be delivered to the clerk of the court for such purpose. The clerk shall endorse thereon the fact and date of filing, and shall retain possession thereof for inclusion in the record, or in the files of his office, as required by law.

Source: New.

Comments

(a) While it has no counterpart in the 1870 Code of Practice, this article is declaratory of recognized practices and customs throughout the state today.

(b) There is no conflict between this and Art. 256, *infra*. When the minute clerk of a trial court receives exhibits introduced in evidence, and notes thereon the fact that they are filed, he acts for the clerk, and discharges the duty imposed on the latter by this article.

(c) In some instances, during a trial or hearing, counsel offers an original document in evidence, and with leave of court introduces and files in evidence a photostatic or other copy thereof. In such cases, the clerk receives the copy introduced, and notes thereon the fact that it has been filed. The original document offered, but not introduced and filed, is no part of the records of the court.

(d) See, also, Comments under Art. 1354, *infra*.

Art. 254. Docket and minute books

In addition to other record books required by law, each court shall keep docket and minute books.

The clerk of the court shall enter in the docket book the number and title of each action or proceeding filed in the court, the date of filing of the petition, exceptions, answers, and other pleadings, and the court costs paid by and the names of counsel of record for each of the parties.

All orders and judgments rendered, all motions made, all proceedings conducted, and all judicial acts of the court during each day it is in session shall be entered in the minute book.

Source: C.P. Arts. 544, 775-777.

Cross Reference: Art. 256.

Comment

This article merely increases the number of required entries in the docket and minute books, but is declaratory of established customs and practices throughout the state.

Art. 255. Deputy clerks and other employees

Except as otherwise provided by law, a deputy clerk of a court possesses all of the powers and authority granted by law to the clerk, and may perform any of the duties and exercise any of the functions of the clerk.

Deputy clerks and other employees of a clerk of court are subject to his direction and supervision, and shall perform the duties assigned to them by law, the court, and the clerk.

The clerk of a court is responsible for the performance or nonperformance of their official duties by his deputies and other employees.

Source: New; cf. R.S. 13:910.

Comments

(a) This article makes no change in the law.

(b) Since the appointment and tenure of deputy clerks, including minute clerks, of the Civil District Court for the Parish of Orleans and the other district courts of the state are governed by different statutes, these subjects are not covered by this Code.

(c) The limitations upon the power and authority of deputy clerks of district courts outside of New Orleans are set forth in Art. 286, *infra*.

(d) See, also, Comments under Art. 286, *infra*.

Art. 256. Minute clerk

The minute clerk of a court shall keep the minutes of the court daily when in session and transcribe them into the minute book, as required by Article 254; shall file all pleadings and documents tendered for filing in open court; and shall perform such other duties as are assigned to him by law, the court, and the clerk with the approval of the court.

The minute clerk of a trial court shall administer the oath to jurors and witnesses and shall file all exhibits offered in evidence, when directed to do so by the court. If there are two or more judges on a trial court, its rules may require a minute clerk for each division thereof.

When a court has no minute clerk, and there is no deputy clerk available for such duty, the clerk shall perform all of the duties of the minute clerk.

Source: New; cf. C.P. Art. 782; R.S. 13:1, 13:910.

Comments

(a) This article makes no change in the law, but prescribes those duties of a minute clerk which are common to the minute clerks of all courts.

(b) The minute clerks of the Civil District Court for the Parish of Orleans are required to perform a number of duties, under former R.S. 13:1, which are not generally required of the minute clerks of the other district courts of the state. There is no intention to have this article repeal or conflict with R.S. 13:1. The language of this article "and shall perform such other duties as are assigned to him by law" refers to this, and similar, statutory provisions.

(c) See, also, Comments under Art. 253, *supra*.

Art. 257. Neglect, failure, or refusal of clerk, deputy, or other employee to perform duty subjects him to punishment for contempt

The neglect, failure, or refusal of a clerk, deputy clerk, or other employee of a clerk of court to perform any ministerial duty subjects him to punishment for contempt of court.

Source: New; cf. C.P. Art. 780.

Comments

(a) This article broadens the provisions of its indirect source in two respects: (1) by providing for punishment for contempt of court for the neglect, failure, or refusal to perform any ministerial duty; and (2) by subjecting deputies and other employees of the clerk to punishment for contempt.

(b) The offenses covered by this article would constitute an indirect contempt of court under Art. 224(1), the punishment for which would be a fine of not more than $250, or imprisonment for not more than thirty days, or both. R.S. 13:4511(A) (4). The procedure for trying the offender for contempt is provided in Art. 225, *supra*.

(c) See, also, Comments under Art. 375, *infra*.

SECTION 2. CLERKS OF DISTRICT COURTS

Art. 281. Certain articles not applicable to Civil District Court for the Parish of Orleans

The provisions of Articles 282 through 286 do not apply to the clerk and the deputy clerks of the Civil District Court for the Parish of Orleans.

Source: R.S. 13:471.

Comment

This article makes no change in the law; but prevents the application of the articles referred to, to the clerks and deputy clerks of the Civil District Court for the Parish of Orleans.

See, also, Comments under Arts. 282, 283, 284, 285, 286, *infra*.

Art. 282. Acts which may be done by district court clerk

The clerk of a district court may:

(1) Grant an appeal and fix the return day thereof; fix the amount of the bond for an appeal, or for the issuance of a writ of attachment or of sequestration, or for the release of property seized under any writ, unless fixed by law; appoint an attorney at law to represent a nonresident, absent, incompetent, or unrepresented defendant; or dismiss without prejudice, on application of plaintiff, an action or proceeding in which no exception, answer, or intervention has been filed; and

(2) Probate a testament, when there is no opposition thereto; homologate an inventory; confirm or appoint a tutor, undertutor, undertutor ad hoc, curator, undercurator, undercurator ad hoc, administrator, executor, or dative testamentary executor, when there is no opposition thereto; appoint an attorney for absent heirs; and approve and accept the bond required of a legal representative for the faithful performance of his duties.

Source: Former R.S. 13:901–13:905.

Cross References: Arts. 281, 283, 285, 286.

Comments

(a) The provisions of this article do not apply to the Clerk of the Civil District Court for the Parish of Orleans. Art. 281, *supra*.

(b) This article and Art. 283, *infra*, confer on the clerk of a district court the power and authority to do certain acts, and render and sign certain orders and judgments, which normally are done by the judge himself. Most of these are of a ministerial nature, while the remainder, although involving the exercise of some discretion cannot be classified as strictly judicial. On the other hand, admittedly judicial powers are conferred on these clerks in Art. 284, *infra*. The great majority of these powers have been vested in district court clerks for years, and both the statutes heretofore adopted and the provisions of these articles appear to be clearly constitutional. See Const. Art. VII, §§ 37, 66.

(c) Not all of the provisions of the sources of this article are incorporated herein. There are included in this article all of the acts which the clerk of a district court had the power and authority to do, and in Art. 283, *infra*, the orders and judgments which the clerk of a district court was authorized to render and sign.

(d) None of the powers and authority of district court clerks has been curtailed or diminished in this and the succeeding two articles, except to the extent mentioned in the Comments under Art. 283, *infra*. In some instances, they have been broadened. This article increases the powers and authority of district court clerks in the following respects:

(1) Under the pertinent source provision, the clerk is authorized to appoint "advocates for absentees." This article broadens this power to enable him to "appoint an attorney at law to represent a nonresident, absent, incompetent, or unrepresented defendant";

(2) Under the pertinent source provision, the clerk is authorized to "take the necessary bond required of tutors, dative testamentary executors, administrators, curators of vacant successions, curators of interdicted persons, syndics of insolvent debtors, syndics of insolvent successions." This article shortens the language, but broadens the power to "approve and accept the bond required of a legal representative for the faithful performance of his duties."

(e) The obsolete provisions of the sources which have not been carried over into this and Art. 283 are enumerated in Comment (d) of Art. 283.

(f) See, also, Comments under Arts. 284, 3508, *infra*.

Art. 283. Orders and judgments which may be signed by district court clerk

The clerk of a district court may sign any of the following orders or judgments:

(1) An order or judgment effecting or evidencing the doing of any of the acts authorized in Article 282;

(2) An order for the issuance of executory process, of a writ of attachment or of sequestration, or of garnishment process under a writ of fieri facias, attachment, or of sequestration; the release under bond of property seized under a writ of attachment or of sequestration; or to permit the filing of an intervention;

(3) An order for the execution of a probated testament; the affixing of seals; the taking of an inventory; the public sale of succession property to pay debts, on the written application of the succession representative accompanied by a list of the debts of the succession; the advertisement of the filing of a tableau of distribution or of an account by a legal representative; or requiring a legal representative to file an account; or

(4) An order for the issuance of a rule against the inheritance tax collector to show cause why inheritance taxes should or should not be decreed due; or to permit a party to institute and prosecute, or to defend, a suit without the payment of costs, under the provisions of Articles 5181 through 5188.

When an order signed by the clerk requires the services of a notary, the clerk shall appoint the notary suggested by the party obtaining the order.

Source: Former R.S. 13:901–13:907.

Cross References: Arts. 281, 285, 286.

Comments

(a) The provisions of this article do not apply to the clerk of the Civil District Court for the Parish of Orleans. Art. 281, *supra*.

(b) See Comments (b), (c) and (d) under Art. 282, *supra*.

(c) This article increases the power of district court clerks in the following respects:

(1) One of the sources of this article authorized the clerk to "grant orders of garnishment under writs of fieri facias and attachment." Since garnishment may now issue also under the writ of sequestration, Art. 3503, *infra*, this article also empowers the clerk to grant orders of garnishment under sequestration;

(2) A source of this article empowered the clerk to "issue orders for the advertisement of the filing of accounts and tableaux of tu-

tors, of executors, of administrators, [of] curators of vacant successions, of curators of interdicted persons, of syndics of insolvent successions, and of syndics of insolvent debtors." This article broadens the power to order "the advertisement of the filing of a tableau of distribution or of an account by a legal representative"; and

(3) One of the source provisions of this article empowered the clerk to "order executors, tutors, administrators, curators and syndics to file accounts." This article broadens the power by authorizing the clerk to sign orders "requiring a legal representative to file an account."

(d) The following obsolete or unnecessary language of the source provisions was not retained:

(1) Writs of arrest, syndics of insolvent debtors or successions, and family meetings which are now obsolete;

(2) Under this Code provisional seizure is merged with sequestration, third oppositions are merged with interventions, and the third party demand has been substituted for the call in warranty. Therefore, references to these outmoded procedural devices are not necessary. However, see Comment (g), *infra*;

(3) One of the sources of this article provided that "in all cases of opposition filed in the clerk's office, he shall place the opposition on the docket of the court." This language is unnecessary, since the trial of oppositions is left to the local rules of the court or to the attorneys concerned; and

(4) One of the sources of this article empowered the clerk to "order executors, tutors, administrators, curators and syndics to file accounts." This language has been retained in broadened form. See Comment (c) (4), *supra*.

This article grants the clerk the power to require such an accounting, but does not impose a mandatory duty on him in connection therewith. Further, the time in which the legal representative must file his account is no longer determined by code provision, but is left to the discretion of the court. *Cf.* Arts. 3331 and 3332, *infra*. This article similarly leaves the time of filing the account to be determined by the clerk.

(e) Provision for the private sale of succession property was made some few years ago. Former R.S. 9:1451 *et seq.* These rules are retained in Arts. 3281 through 3285, *infra*. Authority for the private sale of succession property always involves a judicial determination of fair value, and may involve a contradictory proceeding. These are matters which are reserved to the judge exclusively. Hence, this article is restricted to "the public sale of succession property."

(f) With respect to the taking of testimony by deposition, the only orders which are now required are: (1) to permit taking of depositions before the action is filed; (2) permit the taking of depositions within fifteen days of the filing of the petition; (3) taking of depositions after trial; (4) to enlarge or shorten the time for taking depositions; (5) to call off, restrict, or limit the examination; (6) to compel the witness to answer; and (7) to punish a witness who refuses to be sworn, or refuses to answer when ordered by the court to do so. Arts. 1434, 1436, 1437, 1451, 1452, 1454 and 1511, *infra,* respectively. All of these are matters of such importance that they are reserved for determination by the judge exclusively. Hence this article and Art. 282, *supra,* contain no references to the taking of depositions.

(g) Although the third party demand has been substituted for the old call in warranty, Art. 282, *supra,* and this article do not empower the clerk to permit the filing of a third party demand. The latter may be filed without leave of court at any time up to and including the time the answer is filed; and thereafter only with leave of court. Art. 1033, *infra.* Hence no order is required for the filing of a third party demand, unless it is filed after the filing of an answer. In such a case, the judge exclusively exercises the judicial discretion to permit or not to permit its filing.

(h) Under a source provision of this article, the district court clerk is empowered to appoint curators of vacant successions. These functions are performed by the public administrator in Orleans Parish, and in all other parishes by the district court clerks, as administrators of vacant successions. Arts. 3121 and 3122, *infra.* Since such cases always involve the judicial determination of whether the succession actually is vacant, the appointment in such cases is left to the judge exclusively.

(i) The power of district court clerks to administer oaths is included in Art. 287, *infra.*

(j) See, also, Comments under Art. 282, *supra.*

Art. 284. Judicial powers of district court clerk

The clerk of a district court may render, confirm, and sign judgments by default or by confession in cases where the jurisdiction of the court is concurrent with that of justices of the peace, as provided in Article 4972.

Source: Const. Art. VII, § 37; former R.S. 13:3335.

Cross References: Arts. 281, 285, 286.

Comments

(a) The provisions of this article do not apply to the clerk of the Civil District Court for the Parish of Orleans. Art. 281, *supra.*

(b) See Comment (b) under Art. 282, *supra.*

(c) See Art. 4972, *infra.*

Art. 285. Powers of district court clerk may be exercised whether judge absent from parish or not

The powers and authority granted to the clerk of a district court under Articles 282 through 284 may be exercised by him whether the judge of the district court is absent from the parish or not.

Source: Former R.S. 13:908.

Cross Reference: Art. 281.

Comments

(a) The provisions of this article do not apply to the clerk of the the Civil District Court for the Parish of Orleans. Art. 281, *supra*.

(b) See Comment (b) under Art. 282, *supra*.

Art. 286. Powers of district court clerk which may not be exercised by deputy; powers of chief deputy clerk

No deputy clerk of a district court may exercise any of the judicial powers and authority granted to the clerk of a district court under Article 284. No deputy clerk of a district court, except the chief deputy clerk, may exercise any of the powers and authority granted to the clerk of the district court under Articles 282 and 283.

Whether the judge or the clerk, or both, are absent from the parish or not, the chief deputy clerk of a district court may exercise all of the powers and authority granted to the clerk of a district court under Articles 282 and 283.

Source: Former R.S. 13:909; R.S. 13:910.

Cross Reference: Art. 281.

Comments

(a) This article does not apply to the clerk and deputy clerks of the Civil District Court for the Parish of Orleans. Art. 281, *supra*.

(b) This article is authorized under Const. Art. VII, § 67.

The chief deputy and other deputy clerks of a district court possess the same powers as the district court clerk except: (1) the judicial powers conferred on the clerk under Const. Art. VII, § 37; and (2) those powers specifically withheld by law. Op.Atty.Gen. 195 (1942–1944).

(c) Former R.S. 13:910 conferred on the chief deputy clerk all of the powers of the district court clerk except the judicial power conferred under Const. Art. VII, § 37, and the power "to bond any conservatory writ." The Institute was of the opinion that the chief deputy should exercise all of the power of the district court clerk except the latter's judicial power.

Art. 286

Otherwise, this article makes no change in the law, except indirectly through the broadening of the power and authority of the district court clerk by Arts. 282 and 283, *supra*.

(d) See Art. 255, *supra*.

(e) See, also, Comments under Art. 255, *supra*.

Art. 287. District court clerk ex officio notary

The clerk of a district court is ex officio a notary; and, as such, may administer oaths and exercise all of the other functions, powers, and authority of a notary.

Source: New; *cf.* R.S. 13:751, former R.S. 13:902.

Comments

This article applies to all clerks of district courts, including the clerk of the Civil District Court for the Parish of Orleans.

See, also, Comments under Art. 283, *supra*.

Art. 288. Functions which district court clerk may exercise on holiday

The only functions which a clerk of a district court may exercise on a legal holiday are:

(1) The signing of an order for the issuance of a writ of attachment or of sequestration by a clerk of a district court other than the Civil District Court for the Parish of Orleans; and

(2) The issuance of a writ of attachment, sequestration, or injunction.

Source: C.P. Art. 207.

Comment

This article does not change the law, and applies to all clerks of district courts.

CHAPTER 6. SHERIFFS

Art.
321. Executive officer of district court; serves process, executes writs and mandates directed to him by courts.
322. Exercises civil functions only in own parish; exception.
323. Writs executed on holiday.
324. Returns on process served, and writs and judgments executed.
325. Right of entry for execution; may require assistance of others if resistance offered or threatened.

Art.
326. Protection and preservation of property seized.
327. Seizure of rents, fruits, and revenue of property under seizure.
328. Power of administration of property under seizure.
329. Disbursements for protection, preservation, and administration of seized property.
330. Collection of fines from, and imprisonment of, persons found guilty of contempt of court.
331. Deputy sheriffs and other employees.
332. Service or execution by constable or marshal.
333. Crier.
334. Neglect, failure, or refusal of sheriff, deputy sheriff, or employee to perform duty subjects him to punishment for contempt.

Art. 321. Executive officer of district court; serves process, executes writs and mandates directed to him by courts

The sheriff is the executive officer of the district court.

He shall serve citations, summons, subpoenas, notices, and other process, and shall execute writs, mandates, orders, and judgments directed to him by the district courts, the courts of appeal, and the supreme court.

Source: New; cf. C.P. Art. 760.

Comments

This article makes no change in the law.

See, also, Comments under Art. 3504, *infra*.

Art. 322. Exercises civil functions only in own parish; exception

Except as otherwise provided in Article 1291, the sheriff may exercise his civil functions only in the parish for which he was elected.

Source: C.P. Art. 761.

Comments

(a) Except as mentioned in Comment (c) below, this article makes no change in the law.

(b) Art. 1291, *infra*, provides that "Service shall be made by the sheriff of the parish where service is to be made or of the parish were the action is pending". This was the law under the Service of Process Act. See former R.S. 13:3471(12), 13:3471(13).

(c) Since writs of arrest have been abolished, there is no necessity to embody in this article this exception in its source provision.

Art. 323. Writs executed on holiday

The sheriff shall not execute any writ, mandate, order, or judgment of a court in a civil case on a legal holiday, except a writ of attachment, sequestration, or injunction.

Source: C.P. Arts. 207, 763.

Comments

(a) Art. 207 of the Code of Practice of 1870 authorized the issuance and execution of writs of attachment, sequestration, and injunction on a legal holiday. The above article makes no change of the law in this respect.

(b) Art. 1231, *infra*, expressly provides that service of process, whether personal or domiciliary, may be made at any time of day or night, including a legal holiday. This article was drafted so as to avoid a conflict therewith.

(c) Since the writ of arrest has been abolished, the references thereto in both of the source provisions have not been carried over into the above article.

(d) See, also, Comments under Art. 3504, *infra*.

Art. 324. Returns on process served, and writs and judgments executed

The sheriff shall make a return to the issuing court on citations, summons, subpoenas, notices, and other process, and on writs, mandates, orders, and judgments, showing the date on which and the manner in which they were served or executed.

Source: New.

Comments

This article makes no change in the law, and is intended as a substitute for numerous provisions in the 1870 Code of Practice, specifying minutely the details of the return with respect to the various writs. Because of the complexity of the subjects, separate provisions are set forth with respect to the service of citation, the execution of the writ of fieri facias, and by reference the writ of seizure and sale. See Arts. 1292, 2254, 2343, and 2724, *infra*.

See, also, Comments under Art. 2503, *infra*.

Art. 325. Right of entry for execution; may require assistance of others if resistance offered or threatened

In the execution of a writ, mandate, order, or judgment of a court, the sheriff may enter on the lands, and into the residence or other building, owned or occupied by the judgment debtor or defendant. If necessary to effect entry, he may break open any door or window. If resistance is offered or threatened, he may require the assistance of the police, of neighbors, and of persons present or passing by.

Source: C.P. Art. 762.

Comments

(a) This article makes no change in the law.

(b) The failure of an able-bodied inhabitant of the parish to comply with the sheriff's orders, when pressed into service as a member of the posse comitatus, is a misdemeanor. R.S. 33:1436.

Art. 326. Protection and preservation of property seized

The sheriff shall take actual possession of all movable property seized which is susceptible of actual possession and may remove it to a warehouse or other place of safekeeping.

He may take actual possession of all immovable property seized, unless it is under lease or occupied by an owner.

He shall safeguard, protect, and preserve all property seized of which he has taken or is required to take actual possession; and for such purposes may appoint a keeper of the property.

Source: New; cf. C.P. Arts. 657, 659, 660.

Comments

(a) This article makes a number of changes in the law, as noted in the comments below. Cf. former R.S. 13:3851–13:3861.

(b) For a definition of the word "property", see Art. 5251, infra.

(c) Unless incorporeal movables are in the form of evidences of debt, they are not susceptible of actual possession. The first sentence of this article makes recognition of this fact.

(d) The language of Art. 660, Code of Practice of 1870, prohibiting the sheriff from removing from lands and plantations "the implements of agriculture, [and] the cattle employed in cultivating them" is not carried over into this article. This prohibition is both too broad and too restrictive. It was probably adopted to implement the rule that immovables by destination cannot be seized separately from the land to which they are attached. Here, the prohibition is too broad, as it is only the implements and work stock placed on the land *by the owner of the land* which are immovables by destination. Art. 468, Civil Code; Fallin v. J. J. Stovall & Sons, 141 La. 220, 74 So. 911 (1917). Hence, this theory should not bar the sheriff's right to remove implements and work stock placed on a farm or plantation by a tenant, or lessee. Further, even if placed there by the owner of the land, if subject to a chattel mortgage, they are movables in so far as a proceeding to enforce the chattel mortgage is concerned; and here again theory should not bar the sheriff's right of removal.

If farm implements and work stock are movables, then there appears to be no sound reason for prohibiting the sheriff from removing them to a place of greater safety, if he or the seizing creditor thinks it advisable. If the farm implements and work stock are immovables by destination, this article has no application.

(e) The second paragraph of this article permits the sheriff to take actual possession of the immovables seized, but does not require him to. If he does not take actual possession, then he must comply with R.S. 13:3851 et seq.

The second paragraph further excludes authority for the sheriff to take actual possession of immovable property under lease, or which is occupied by an owner. As a practical matter, this makes no change in the present law and practices. *Cf.* Art. 657 of the 1870 Code; and Conte v. Handy, 34 La.Ann. 862 (1882).

(f) The last paragraph of this article imposes on the sheriff the duty of safeguarding, protecting, and preserving only: (1) the property which he is required to take possession of; and (2) the property which he is not required to, but has actually taken possession of. He should not be held accountable for any other property.

Art. 327. Seizure of rents, fruits, and revenue of property under seizure

The seizure of property by the sheriff effects the seizure of the fruits and issues which it produces while under seizure. The sheriff shall collect all rents and revenue produced by property under seizure.

Source: C.P. Art. 656.

Comment

In New Orleans Compress Co. v. Katz, 185 La. 723, 170 So. 244 (1936), it was held that the source provision was as applicable to a seizure in executory process as to a seizure under the writ of fieri facias. It is intended that this article should apply to all seizures, regardless of the particular writ under which they were made.

Art. 328. Power of administration of property under seizure

The sheriff has the power of administration of all property under seizure, regardless of the type of writ or mandate under authority of which the property was seized.

If immovable property is not occupied by an owner and is not under lease, the sheriff may lease it for a term not beyond the date of judicial sale. He cannot lease movable property under seizure unless authorized by the court with the consent of the parties.

The sheriff may, and if the necessary funds therefor are advanced or satisfactory security is furnished him by any interested person shall, continue the operation of any property under seizure, including a business, farm, or plantation. For such purposes, the sheriff may employ a manager and such other employees as he may consider necessary.

Source: New; *cf.* C.P. Arts. 657, 658, 662.

Comments

(a) This article makes three rather important changes in the procedural law. See Comments *infra*.

(b) Under the Code of Practice of 1870, the sheriff had the power of administration over immovable property seized only under a writ of fieri facias, sequestration, or seizure and sale. Learned v. Walton, 42 La.Ann. 455, 7 So. 723 (1890); American Nat. Bank v. Childs, 49 La.Ann. 1359, 22 So. 384 (1897). The sheriff had no power to administer property seized under a writ of attachment, American Nat. Bank v. Childs, *supra*; and apparently had no power of administration of property seized under any writ other than those named above. There is just as much need of the sheriff's power of administration when a farm or plantation with a growing crop is seized under a writ of attachment or distringas, as when it is seized under a writ of fieri facias, sequestration, or seizure and sale. This article extends the sheriff's power of administration to property seized under any writ.

(c) While the jurisprudence on the subject leaves much to be desired, it appears at least possible that under the 1870 Code the sheriff had the power of administration of movables, such as a herd of dairy cattle, seized under a writ of provisional seizure, in the enforcement of a predial lease. *Cf.* L. H. Hayward & Co. v. Jules Catering Co., 160 So. 821 (La.App.1935). This article expressly grants the sheriff a limited power of administration, within the provisions of this article, over all movables seized by the sheriff, even though the farm or plantation on which these movables were situated was only leased by the judgment debtor, and hence had not been seized.

(d) Art. 657 of the 1870 Code prohibited the sheriff from leasing immovables under seizure which were leased at the time of the seizure. The jurisprudence under this article prohibits the sheriff from leasing immovable property seized which is occupied by an owner. Conte v. Handy, 34 La.Ann. 862 (1882). This article makes no change of the law in these respects.

(e) Art. 662 of the Code of Practice of 1870 prohibited the sheriff from leasing the animals seized by him, without the authority of a court order and the consent of the parties. There is at least dictum to the effect that this prohibition extends to all movables seized. Jones v. Robeline Garage, 16 La.App. 601, 135 So. 120 (1931). This article extends the prohibition to all movables under seizure.

(f) Under the 1870 Code of Practice, it was clear that the sheriff might continue the cultivation, and harvest and sell a crop on a farm or plantation seized under a writ of fieri facias, sequestration, or seizure and sale. Lambeth v. Joffrion, 41 La.Ann. 749, 6 So. 558 (1889); Learned v. Walton, *supra;* and American Nat. Bank v. Childs, *supra.* Cf. State ex rel. Vial v. Judge, 36 La.Ann. 910 (1884). It was by no means clear, however, that the sheriff could continue the operation of a farm or plantation which was not, in the strictest sense, in cultivation, such as a dairy farm or beef cattle ranch. This article expressly grants such authority.

(g) The price which will be brought by the sale of a going commercial business will usually be considerably higher than the price realized from a sale of the merchandise, fixtures, and equipment of a business which ceased to operate when the seizure was made. Authorization for the continuance of such a business after seizure makes it possible to avoid this loss.

Under this article, if the judgment debtor is the owner of both a business and the premises in which it is conducted, and both are seized, the sheriff cannot continue the operation of this business in the premises without the consent of the debtor.

(h) See, also, Comments under Art. 3504, *infra.*

Art. 329. Disbursements for protection, preservation, and administration of seized property

The sheriff may make all necessary disbursements for the protection, preservation, and administration of property under seizure, which shall be taxed as costs of the seizure.

Source: New; *cf.* C.P. Art. 661.

Comment

This article makes no change in the law.

Art. 330. Collection of fines from, and imprisonment of, persons found guilty of contempt of court

The sheriff shall collect the fines which persons found guilty of contempt of court are sentenced to pay, and pay them over to the official entitled by law to receive them. He shall take into custody and imprison individuals found guilty of contempt of court and sentenced to imprisonment in the parish jail.

Source: New; cf. C.P. Arts. 768, 769.

Comments

(a) This article makes no change in the law. The use of the word "persons" in the first sentence of this article, and of the word "individuals" in the second sentence is advised. A corporation or partnership, which is a person within the intendment of the articles of this code (see Art. 5251, *infra*), could be sentenced to pay a fine for contempt of court, but could not be imprisoned. An individual, who is also within the definition of "person", could be fined or imprisoned.

(b) If the sheriff fails to pay over to the proper official the fines which he has collected, he may be adjudged in contempt of court. Art. 334, *infra*.

(c) The second sentence rounds out the duty of the sheriff with respect to effectuating the sentence of the court for contempt.

Art. 331. Deputy sheriffs and other employees

Except as otherwise provided by law, a deputy sheriff possesses all of the powers and authority granted by law to the sheriff, and may perform any of the duties and exercise any of the functions of the sheriff.

Deputy sheriffs and other employees of the sheriff are subject to his direction and supervision, and shall perform the duties assigned to them by law, and by the sheriff.

The sheriff is responsible for the performance or nonperformance of their official duties by his deputies and other employees.

Source: New; cf. C.P. Art. 771.

Comments

This article makes no change in the law.

See, also, Comments under Arts. 1291, 3823, *infra*.

Art. 332. Service or execution by constable or marshal

When authorized to do so by the sheriff, a constable of a justice of the peace court, or a constable or marshal of a city court, within the territorial jurisdiction of his court, may serve any process and execute any writ or mandate which the sheriff is authorized to serve or execute.

For such purpose, the constable or marshal possesses the powers and authority of the sheriff; a service or execution so made has the same effect as if made by the sheriff; and the latter is responsible for the performance or nonperformance of his duties by a constable or marshal in such cases.

Source: New; *cf.* C.P. Art. 765.

Comments

This article does not change the law. It merely restates the authority conferred in the source provision, and makes it clear that the services of the executive officer of a city court, whether he may be called a constable or a marshal, may be utilized under the authority conferred.

See R.S. 13:3484, relating to the constable and marshal.

See, also, Comments under Art. 1291, *infra*.

Art. 333. Crier

The crier of a court shall attend all sessions thereof; under the direction of the judge shall open and close court at each session, and maintain order and decorum in the court room; and shall perform such other duties as are assigned to him by law, the court, or the sheriff.

The crier of a trial court, when requested to do so, shall call all witnesses in the building whose testimony is desired by the court or by a party.

When a court has no crier, and there is no deputy sheriff available for such duty, the sheriff shall perform the duties of crier.

Source: New; *cf.* C.P. Arts. 758, 784; R.S. 13:74, 13:381.

Comment

This article makes no change in the law, but does set forth generally the duties of the crier, who is the counterpart of the bailiff in the courts of Anglo-American jurisdictions.

Art. 334. Neglect, failure, or refusal of sheriff, deputy sheriff, or employee to perform duty subjects him to punishment for contempt

The neglect, failure, or refusal of a sheriff, deputy sheriff, or other employee of a sheriff to perform any ministerial duty subjects him to punishment for contempt of court.

Source: New; *cf.* C.P. Arts. 766-769.

Comments

(a) One change made in the law by this article is the elimination of the penalty of twenty percent per annum on all funds collected by the sheriff, and withheld illegally or without reasonable excuse.

(b) The most effective remedy for the neglect, failure, or refusal of a sheriff, deputy, or other employee of a sheriff is punishment for contempt. The claimant would still have his remedy against the sheriff to recover the damages sustained thereby. This article extends punishment for contempt to the deputies and employees of the sheriff.

(c) The conditions under which a public official may now be removed from office are now prescribed by Const. Art. IX, § 6. In view of this, all statutory provisions conflicting therewith are unconstitutional. For this reason, the removal from office provisions of the indirect sources of this article have not been retained.

(d) See, also, Comments under Art. 330, *supra*, and Art. 375, *infra*.

CHAPTER 7. OTHER OFFICERS OF THE COURT

Art.
371. Attorney.
372. Court reporter.
373. Expert appointed by court.
374. Legal representative.
375. Neglect, failure, or refusal of expert or legal representative to perform a legal duty when ordered to do so, subjects him to punishment for contempt of court.

Art. 371. Attorney

An attorney at law is an officer of the court. He shall conduct himself at all times with decorum, and in a manner consistent with the dignity and authority of the court and the role which he himself should play in the administration of justice.

Art. 371

He shall treat the court, its officers, jurors, witnesses, opposing party, and opposing counsel with due respect; shall not interrupt opposing counsel, or otherwise interfere with or impede the orderly dispatch of judicial business by the court; shall not knowingly encourage or produce false evidence; and shall not knowingly make any misrepresentation, or otherwise impose upon or deceive the court.

For a violation of any of the provisions of this article, the attorney at law subjects himself to punishment for contempt of court, and such further disciplinary action as is otherwise provided by law.

Source: New; *cf.* C.P. Art. 486.

Cross Reference: Art. 1631.

Comments

This article is a restatement of the duty and obligation of an attorney at law to the court. For the disbarment and other discipline of members, and the Canons of Ethics of the Louisiana State Bar Association, see 21 L.S.A. 377 (1951).

See, also, Comments under Art. 375, *infra*.

Art. 372. Court reporter

The court reporter of a trial court, when directed by the court, shall report verbatim in shorthand by stenography or stenotype, or by voice recording or any other recognized manner when the equipment therefor has been approved by the court, the testimony of all witnesses, the other evidence introduced or offered, the objections thereto, and the rulings of the court thereon, on the trial of any appealable civil case or matter.

When the court so directs, or the fees therefor have been paid or secured, or when an appeal has been granted in cases in which a party has been permitted to litigate without the payment of costs, he shall transcribe verbatim in a manner approved by the supreme court, all of his notes taken at the trial, or such portion thereof as is designated. He shall file one copy of the transcript in the trial court; shall deliver a copy thereof to each of the parties who has paid therefor; and, when an appeal has been granted, he shall furnish to the clerk of the trial court the number of copies of the transcript required by law.

In any appealable civil case or matter in which he has not transcribed all of his notes taken at the trial, he shall preserve them for a period of one year after the judgment is signed.

He shall perform such other duties as are assigned to him by law or by the court.

Source: New; *cf.* R.S. 13:961(C), 13:962(E), 13:963(B), 13:964(D), 13:965(D), 13:967(B), 13:967(C), 13:968(D).

Comments

(a) This article is a composite of the salient features of all of its indirect source provisions.

(b) The provisions of this article recognize recent improvements in the verbatim reporting at the trial by specifically sanctioning the use of stenotype and, when the court has approved the equipment therefor, of authorizing the use of voice recording or any other recognized manner of reproducing the testimony verbatim.

(c) The manner of transcribing the shorthand notes is regulated by the rules of the various appellate courts. The requirements of the supreme court are broad enough to cover those of all other appellate courts. See Rules of the Supreme Court of Louisiana, Rule I, § 1 (1952).

Art. 373. Expert appointed by court

An expert appointed by a trial court to assist it in the adjudication of a case in which his special skill and knowledge may aid the court is an officer of the court from the time of his qualification until the rendition of final judgment in the case.

Source: New.

Comment

Authority to appoint experts, and to allow them reasonable compensation for their services, is expressly granted to the court by Art. 192, *supra*. This article implements the former by expressly recognizing these experts as officers of the court pro tempore, and impliedly subjecting them to the supervision and control of the court.

Art. 374. Legal representative

A legal representative appointed or confirmed by a court is an officer of this court from the time of his qualification for the office until his discharge.

Source: New.

Comments

(a) For a definition of "legal representative", see Art. 5251, *infra*.

(b) This article is declaratory of the settled jurisprudential rules, but its express recognition thereof serves as recognition of the fact that, in the performance of their official duties, legal representatives are under the supervision and control of the court.

Art. 375. **Neglect, failure, or refusal of expert or legal representative to perform a legal duty when ordered to do so, subjects him to punishment for contempt of court**

The neglect, failure, or refusal of an expert appointed by the court, or a legal representative appointed or confirmed by the court, to perform a legal duty when ordered to do so by the court, subjects him to punishment for contempt of the court.

Source: New.

Comments

See Arts. 257, 334, and 371, *supra*.

Experts appointed by the court, and legal representatives appointed or confirmed by the court, are on a somewhat different basis from permanent officers of the courts. For these reasons, punishment for contempt as to the expert and legal representative is allowed only for the failure to perform a legal duty, after being ordered to do so by the court.

TITLE II
ACTIONS

Chap.		Art.
1.	General Dispositions	421
2.	Cumulation of Actions	461
3.	Lis Pendens	531
4.	Abandonment of Action	561
5.	Class and Secondary Actions	591
	Sec.	
	1. Class Actions	591
	2. Secondary Actions	611

CHAPTER 1. GENERAL DISPOSITIONS

Art.
421. Civil action; commencement; amicable demand unnecessary.
422. Personal, real, mixed actions.
423. Implied right to enforce obligation; prematurity.
424. Cause of action as a defense.
425. Division of cause of action, effect.
426. Transmission of action and of right to enforce obligation.
427. Action against obligor's heirs or legatees.
428. No abatement on death of party.

Art. 421. Civil action; commencement; amicable demand unnecessary

A civil action is a demand for the enforcement of a legal right. It is commenced by the filing of a pleading presenting the demand to a court of competent jurisdiction. Amicable demand is not a condition precedent to a civil action, unless specifically required by law.

Source: C.P. Arts. 1, 147, 169, 170; R.S. 9:5801.

Comments

(a) The word "action" has a double meaning under the language of Art. 1 of the 1870 Code of Practice—meaning both the "instituted action" and the "right to institute the action." This double meaning has proved most unfortunate whenever the word "action" is employed in other code provisions or in statutes. See the dissenting opinion of Justice Blanchard in Chivers v. Roger, 50 La.Ann. 57, 23 So. 100 (1898). To avoid this difficulty, throughout this Code "action" has been given only the meaning ascribed to it in the definition of the above article—"instituted action." Whenever the "right to institute the action," is meant express language to this effect clearly indicating this meaning is employed. See Arts. 424, 427, 428, *infra*.

(b) The phrase "to a court of competent jurisdiction" retains the Louisiana rules concerning the interruption of prescription by the filing of suit. See Art. 5251, *infra*. The latter article tracks substantially the language of R.S. 9:5801 which has been interpreted to mean a court possessing both jurisdiction ratione materiae and jurisdiction ratione personae. Flowers v. Pugh, 51 So.2d 136 (La. App.1951). Cf. 14 Tul.L.Rev. 601 (1940).

(c) In view of the fact that under Louisiana law amicable demand is sometimes required as a condition precedent to suit, recognition of these exceptions was made in the third sentence of this article. Illustrations of the requirement of amicable demand are R.S. 23:1314, workmen's compensation suits, and R.S. 23:845, suits for injunctive relief in labor disputes.

(d) The dilatory exception of want of amicable demand, if sustained, has the effect of imposing the costs of suit on the plaintiff in those instances where no amicable demand has been made and the defendant is willing to comply with the plaintiff's demand. Babcock v. Shirley, 11 La. 73 (1837); Amory v. Black, 13 La. 264 (1839); Saillard v. Turner, 14 La. 259 (1840); Orleans Nav. Co. v. Municipality No. Two, 17 La. 269 (1841); Wood v. Hennen, 9 La. Ann. 264 (1854); and Flournoy v. Robinson-Slagle Lumber Co., 173 La. 989, 139 So. 321 (1932). This rule appears to have proven satisfactory and for this reason has been retained. See Arts. 926, 933, *infra*.

(e) While this article is based in part on the provisions of R.S. 9:5801, the statute contains additional language which is quite necessary. In order to effectuate the purposes of this Code, legislation has been recommended proposing that R.S. 9:5801 be amended and as amended it incorporates the rule of Art. 3518 of the Civil Code and the jurisprudence to the effect that even though the action is filed in an improper venue or in a court which has no jurisdiction, prescription is interrupted by the service of citation upon the defendant. Barrow v. Shields, 13 La.Ann. 57 (1858); Blume v. City of New Orleans, 104 La. 345, 29 So. 106 (1900); Board of Com'rs v. Toyo Kisen Kaisha, 163 La. 865, 113 So. 127 (1927); cf. Hotard v. Brodr Wilhelmsen Aktieselskabet, 23 F.2d 668 (5 Cir. 1928); Brandon v. Kansas City So. Ry., 7 F.Supp. 1008 (D.C.La. 1934); 14 Tul.L.Rev. 601 (1940); 13 Tul.L.Rev. 312 (1939).

(f) See, also, Comments under Art. 121, *supra*, and Art. 933, *infra*.

Tit. 2   GENERAL DISPOSITIONS   Art. 423

Art. 422. Personal, real, mixed actions

A personal action is one brought to enforce an obligation against the obligor, personally and independently of the property which he may own, claim, or possess.

A real action is one brought to enforce rights in, to, or upon immovable property.

A mixed action is one brought to enforce both rights in, to, or upon immovable property, and a related obligation against the owner, claimant, or possessor thereof.

Source: C.P. Arts. 3, 4, 7, 12, 26, 28, 41.

Comments

(a) The word "obligation" used throughout this Title means the legally enforceable "civil or perfect obligation", and not the partially enforceable "natural obligation" or the unenforceable "imperfect obligation." See Art. 1757 of the Civil Code.

(b) No definitions were included here of the action in personam, in rem, and quasi in rem—concepts which were brought into the procedure of Louisiana through the jurisdictional requirements of due process of law and full faith and credit under the federal constitution, as interpreted in Pennoyer v. Neff, 95 U.S. 714, 24 L.Ed. 565 (1879), and subsequent cases. See Arts. 2, 6, 9, and 10, *supra*.

Art. 423. Implied right to enforce obligation; prematurity

An obligation implies a right to enforce it which may or may not accrue immediately upon the creation of the obligation. When the obligation allows a term for its performance, the right to enforce it does not accrue until the term has elapsed. If the obligation depends upon a suspensive condition, the right to enforce it does not accrue until the occurrence or performance of the condition.

When an action is brought on an obligation before the right to enforce it has accrued, the action shall be dismissed as premature, but it may be brought again after this right has accrued.

Source: C.P. Arts. 14, 158.

Comments

(a) This article expresses the rules enunciated in the two source provisions and states more clearly the accrual of the right of action with respect to the obligation dependent upon a suspensive condition.

Illustrations of actions brought prematurely, because the obligations were based upon suspensive conditions which had not yet occurred or been performed, are afforded by H. B. Claflin Co. v. Feibleman, 44 La.Ann. 518, 10 So. 862 (1892); Sugar Field Oil Co. v. Carter, 207 La. 453, 21 So.2d 495 (1945); and Halbert v. Klauer Mfg. Co., 181 So. 75 (La.App.1938).

(b) In the case of prematurity because the term allowed for performance has not yet elapsed, the obligation comes into existence at the moment the contract is entered into, though it does not become exigible until the end of the term allowed for performance. For this reason it has been held that this type of prematurity must be raised through the exception of prematurity. Hart v. Springfield Fire & Marine Ins. Co., 136 La. 114, 66 So. 558 (1914); Williams v. Washington Nat. Ins. Co., 180 La. 423, 156 So. 453 (1934). Under this Code, this procedural objection may be raised only through the dilatory exception. See Arts. 926, 933, *infra*.

If the obligation is dependent upon the suspensive condition, the right to enforce it does not come into existence until the occurrence or the performance of the condition, which may never happen; therefore, under the 1870 Code this objection was raised through an exception of no cause of action. H. B. Claflin Co. v. Feibleman, *supra*; Halbert v. Klauer Mfg. Co., supra. Under this Code, this type of prematurity may be raised through the peremptory exception. See Arts. 927, 934, *infra*.

Art. 424. Cause of action as a defense

A person who has a right to enforce an obligation also has a right to use his cause of action as a defense. A prescribed obligation may be used as a defense if it is incidental to, or connected with, the obligation sought to be enforced by the plaintiff.

Source: C.P. Art. 20; *cf.* Comments following.

Comments

(a) Much of the language of the source provisions of this article is either archaic or somewhat confusing, and for these reasons has been changed in the above article. Thus, the word "exception" used in Art. 20 of the 1870 Code of Practice was not intended to be limited to the "procedural exceptions," but was intended rather to have its ancient and generic meaning of "defense." Also, the obligee never really has a "right yet more evident" to use his obligation as a defense. In fact, when the obligation interposed as a defense is prescribed, the fact that it may be interposed as a defense is not at all evident. But the obligee in such a case does have a "right" to use his cause of action as a defense, since he could not have successfully brought the action, if it had been prescribed. Further, the dual meaning of "action", as defined in Art. 1 of the 1870 Code of Practice, made it necessary in the subsequent articles of that Code to use the term "right of action" where "right to bring the action", rather than "instituted action", was intended. The result in the 1870 Code in several instances is a rather confusing jumble of the concepts of "right of action" and "cause of action". The above article eliminates this confusion.

(b) Art. 20 of the 1870 Code of Practice has long been recognized as the positive law basis in Louisiana for the Roman law maxim: *Quae temporalia sunt ad agendum perpetua sunt ad excipiendum* (Things which are temporary for the purposes of attack are permanent for the purposes of defense). Under this maxim, the courts have repeatedly held that a cause of action which would be prescribed if the obligee attempted to sue the obligor, can nevertheless be used as a defense to an action. Thompson v. Milburn, 1 Mart. (N.S.) 468 (La.1823); Davenport's Heirs v. Fortier, 3 Mart. (N.S.) 695 (La.1825); Bushnell v. Brown's Heirs, 4 Mart. (N.S.) 499 (La.1826); Nichols v. Hanse & Hepp, 2 La. 382 (1831); Delahoussaye v. Dumartrait, 16 La. 91 (1840); Lafiton v. Doiron, 12 La.Ann. 164 (1857); Riddle v. Kreinbiehl, 12 La.Ann. 297 (1857); Davis v. Millaudon, 14 La.Ann. 868 (1859); Lastrapes v. Rocquet, 23 La.Ann. 68 (1871); Succession of Harvey v. Harvey, 44 La.Ann. 80, 10 So. 410 (1891); Edwards v. Plaquemine Ice & Cold-Storage Co., 46 La.Ann. 360, 15 So. 61 (1894); Otis v. Texas Co., 153 La. 384, 96 So. 1 (1922); J. B. Beaird Co. v. Burris Bros., 216 La. 655, 44 So.2d 693 (1949); Dileo v. Dileo, 217 La. 103, 46 So.2d 53 (1950); Holcomb & Hoke Mfg. Co. v. Theodora, 1 La.App. 445 (1925); Crown Cork & Seal Co. v. Grapico Bottling Works, 1 La. App. 638 (1925); Colt Co. v. Seal, 4 La.App. 618 (1926); J. A. Fay & Egan Co. v. Lafayette Lumber Co., 9 La.App. 674, 119 So. 781 (1929).

In such cases, of course, there must be connexity—"a visceral connection"—between the obligation sued on by plaintiff and the prescribed obligation interposed as a defense. Girod v. His Creditors, 2 La.Ann. 546 (1847); Boeto v. Laine, 3 La.Ann. 141 (1848); Harris v. N. O. Opelousas & G. W. R.R. Co., 16 La.Ann. 140 (1861); Walker v. Villavaso, 18 La.Ann. 715 (1866); Chadwick v. Menard, 104 La. 38, 28 So. 933 (1900); Roper v. Monroe Grocer Co., 171 La. 181, 129 So. 811 (1930); Rapides Grocery Co. v. Clopton, 171 La. 632, 131 So. 734 (1930); Wolff v. Warden, 141 So. 821 (La.App. 1932); Foster Mfg. Co. v. Gerth, 144 So. 142 (La.App.1932). The second sentence of the above article enunciates this rule expressly.

Art. 425. Division of cause of action, effect

An obligee cannot divide an obligation due him for the purpose of bringing separate actions on different portions thereof. If he brings an action to enforce only a portion of the obligation, and does not

Art. 425 ACTIONS Bk. 1

amend his pleading to demand the enforcement of the full obligation, he shall lose his right to enforce the remaining portion.

Source: C.P. Arts. 91(2), 156; Art. 87(2), Quebec Code of Civil Procedure; cf. Comments following.

Comments

(a) No change in the procedural law of Louisiana is intended.

(b) The rationale on which the above article is based does not in any way exclude the enforcement of the different installments of a conjunctive obligation separately as they mature, if there is no acceleration clause in the agreement. Cf. Art. 2065 of the Civil Code and Brandagee v. Chamberlin, 2 Rob. 207 (La.1842); Kearney v. Fenerty, 185 La. 862, 171 So. 57 (1936). However, this article does preclude the division of any single installment for procedural purposes.

(c) The rule of Art. 87 of the Quebec Code of Civil Procedure is well established by the jurisprudence of Louisiana. See State ex. rel. Dobson v. Newman, 49 La.Ann. 52, 21 So. 189 (1897); Kearney v. Fenerty, 185 La. 862, 171 So. 57 (1936). Cf. Reynolds & Henry Const. Co. v. Mayor, etc., of Monroe, 47 La.Ann. 1289, 17 So. 802 (1895).

(d) See, also, Comments under Art. 5, *supra*.

Art. 426. Transmission of action and of right to enforce obligation

An action to enforce an obligation is the property of the obligee which on his death is transmitted with his estate to his heirs, universal legatees, or legatees under a universal title, except as otherwise provided by law. An action to enforce an obligation is transmitted to the obligee's legatee under a particular title only when it relates to the property disposed of under the particular title.

These rules apply also to a right to enforce an obligation, when no action thereon was commenced prior to the obligee's death.

Source: C.P. Arts. 22, 23, 24.

Comments

(a) The meaning of the terms "universal legatee," "legatee under a universal title," and "legatee under a particular title," used in the above article are set forth in Arts. 1606, 1612, and 1625 of the Civil Code.

(b) The last clause of the first sentence of this article, reading "except as otherwise provided by law," was inserted to except from the application thereof the "strictly personal obligation" of Civil Code Art. 1997, and other obligations which, under the provisions of positive law, only the original obligee might have the the right to enforce.

(c) The last paragraph of this article was included to retain the full meaning of the source provisions. The use of the language "right to enforce the obligation" indicates the obligee's right prior to the institution of an action thereon. *Cf.* Comment (a), Art. 424, *supra*.

(d) See, also, Comments under Art. 421, *supra*.

Art. 427. Action against obligor's heirs or legatees

An action to enforce an obligation, if the obligor is dead, may be brought against the heirs, universal legatees, or legatees under a universal title, who have accepted his succession, except as otherwise provided by law. The liability of these heirs and legatees is determined by the provisions of the Civil Code.

Source: C.P. Arts. 25, 27, 40.

Comments

(a) This article does not change the law.

(b) The language of Art. 25 of the 1870 Code of Practice expressly stating that the heirs or legatees are liable for the obligations of the decedent arising ex delicto or quasi ex delicto is included in the broad language of the above article. The necessity for originally incorporating such an express provision in the Code of Practice of 1825 appears in the explanation by the Livingston Committee in the Projet of the Code of Practice of 1825 at 2 Louisiana Legal Archives 6 (1937).

(c) The liability of heirs who have accepted the succession of their ancestor unconditionally is set forth in Art. 1013 of the Civil Code, and the proportion of liability of the individual heir is established by Art. 40 of the 1870 Code of Practice. The liability of the heirs who have accepted the succession under benefit of inventory is established by Civil Code Art. 1054.

Arts. 1611, 1614, and 1642 of the Civil Code provide the liability of the universal legatee, the legatee under a universal title, and the legatee under a particular title, respectively.

(d) The clause "except as otherwise provided by law" appearing at the end of the first sentence of this article, excepts the obligation personal as to both obligor and obligee, or personal as to the obligor, from the application of the rule of this article. *Cf.* Civil Code Art. 1997.

(e) This article does not deal with the subject of parties plaintiff or defendant, and for that reason no effort was made to reflect the right of the obligee to bring the action against the personal representative of the deceased, when the heirs or legatees have not accepted the succession, or when the latter is still under administration. See Art. 734, and Arts. 3196, 3246 and 3249, *infra*.

(f) See Art. 428, *infra*, and Comments thereunder.

Art. 428. No abatement on death of party

An action does not abate on the death of a party. The only exception to this rule is an action to enforce a right or obligation which is strictly personal.

Source: C.P. Art. 21; former R.S. 13:3349.

Comments

(a) Perhaps no single article of the 1870 Code of Practice has been so completely misinterpreted by the courts as Art. 21 of that Code.

The problems presented by the death of a party while the action is pending in the court were solved by Anglo-American common law through the application of its rules on abatement of actions, and survival of actions—rules which, while relatively easy to apply, produced results so harsh and unjust that they have now been abrogated, in whole or in part, by statute in every single Anglo-American jurisdiction. Roman law solved these problems more equitably through application of less technical procedural rules, which Spanish law retained. The more highly developed law of post-revolutionary France adopted Domat's theories, and solved these problems through the application of substantive rules implementing the doctrine of universal succession. The redactors of the twin Louisiana Codes of 1825 made every effort possible to prevent judicial acceptance by Louisiana of the harsh and technical common law rules of abatement and survival of actions. Yet, within the century, under the dominance of common law procedural philosophy, the Louisiana courts misinterpreted these code rules, and reached results diametrically opposite to those intended by the redactors. For a brief explanation of these points, see Comment, Abatement of Actions in Louisiana, 15 La.L.Rev. 722 (1955).

An amendment to Civil Code Art. 2315 and the adoption of the above article abrogate the harsh jurisprudential rules of Louisiana on the subject, and attain the original objectives of the Livingston committee which drafted the 1825 Codes.

(b) The rule of Art. 21 of the 1870 Code providing that actions do not abate after answer filed, had a rational basis, and served a useful purpose, in early Roman law, which regarded the joinder of issue as the line of demarcation between the proceedings before the praetor (*in jure*) and those conducted by the judex (*in ju-*

dicio). This rule was anachronistic and without a rational basis even in early Spanish procedure, where no such distinction was made. It was even more anachronistic and irrational in modern Louisiana procedure, and for these reasons this rule has been discarded. Now the line of demarcation is the institution of suit. *Cf.* Art. 421, *supra*. If the plaintiff has elected to enforce a right of action by instituting suit thereon, then his heirs, or his survivors under the amended Art. 2315 of the Civil Code, have the right to continue its prosecution, if the plaintiff dies.

(c) Art. 21 of the 1870 Code of Practice contained no express recognition of any exceptions to the rule that an action does not abate on the death of the party; while former R.S. 13:3349 expressly provided that there were no such exceptions. Both of these provisions were unfortunate, since, of necessity, there must be exceptions to this rule. Thus, if a citizen seeks to mandamus the registrar of voters to register him as an elector, or a wife sues her husband to obtain a divorce, both of these actions abate on the death of the plaintiff. They do so for the reason that the rights sought to be enforced judicially are strictly personal to the plaintiffs, and cannot be enforced by their heirs. For these reasons, this article provides that the "only exceptions to this rule are actions to enforce rights and obligations which are strictly personal." For the definition of strictly personal rights and obligations, see Art. 1997 of the Civil Code.

Actions to recover damages for wrongful death, characterized as "strictly personal" under the prior jurisprudence of Louisiana, are now heritable under the amendment of Art. 2315 of the Civil Code.

(d) The amendment of Art. 2315 of the Civil Code, proposed as companion legislation to this article, changes the substantive law of Louisiana in four respects:

(1) Under the former Art. 2315, the right to recover property damage caused by an offense or quasi offense is transmitted only to the survivors of the deceased designated by this article. Young v. McCullium, 74 So.2d 339 (La.App.1954); Covey v. Marquette Cas. Co., 84 So.2d 217 (La.App.1955); Guidry v. Crowther, 96 So. 2d 71 (La.App.1957). Under amended Art. 2315, the right to recover such property damages is inherited by the heirs of the deceased, or such heirs and the surviving spouse, if the damaged property was owned by the community.

(2) Under former Art. 2315, the highest class of survivors are the surviving spouse and minor children and a major child has no right of action if either exists. Under the amended Art. 2315, the highest class of survivors are the surviving spouse and children, major and minor.

(3) Under Chivers v. Roger, 50 La.Ann. 57, 23 So. 100 (1898) and its progeny, if the survivor designated by former Art. 2315

sued to recover damages for wrongful death, and died prior to rendition of judgment, the action abated. The amended Art. 2315 overrules legislatively this line of cases, and under it in such a case the right of action is transmitted to the survivor's heirs.

(4) Under Kerner v. Trans-Mississippi Terminal R. Co., 158 La. 853, 104 So. 740 (1925), if a right to recover damages for wrongful death accrued to the survivor named in the former Art. 2315, and this survivor died before instituting suit, the right of action died with him. Under the amended Art. 2315, this right is transmitted to the survivor's heirs "whether suit has been instituted thereon by the survivor or not."

(e) See, also, Comments under Art. 427, *supra*.

CHAPTER 2. CUMULATION OF ACTIONS

Art.
461. Cumulation of actions defined.
462. Cumulation by single plaintiff against single defendant.
463. Cumulation, plural plaintiffs or defendants.
464. Improper cumulation, effect.
465. Separate trials of cumulated actions.

PRELIMINARY STATEMENT

Cumulation of actions in the procedure of civilian jurisdictions is the counterpart of both joinder of actions and joinder of parties of Anglo-American procedure. The civilian visualizes suits by plural plaintiffs or against plural defendants as the cumulation in the same suit of a number of separate and distinct actions: in the case of plural plaintiffs, a union of the actions by each plaintiff against the defendant; and when plural defendants are sued in the same suit, a union of the separate actions by the plaintiff against each defendant. The early Louisiana cases recognized and applied this broad concept, but the failure of the two Codes of Practice to impose expressly the requirement of a community of interest in cases where there were plural parties on one side or the other ultimately led to the erroneous statements in Gill v. City of Lake Charles, 119 La. 17, 43 So. 897 (1907) that: (1) the code rules on cumulation of actions were not applicable; and (2) we must look for guidance on the subject "to the books of the common law". Actually, the result in the Gill case was entirely sound, as the court merely applied the test of community of interest of the earlier Louisiana cases, and considered no common law cases at all, but only equity precedents on the kindred subject of multifariousness. Later Louisiana decisions, however, misinterpreted the Gill case, and applied common law rules on the subject. The latter were based on concepts of joint, several, and joint and several obligations which are completely foreign to our substantive law. The result was that these later Louisiana cases adopted rules which are completely unworkable, and which in some instances lead us into vicious circles.

This Chapter restores the simple rules of cumulation, with specific rules covering all aspects of the subject.

For a detailed discussion of the subject, and the problems presented, see 19 La.L.Rev. 1 (1958).

Art. 461. Cumulation of actions defined

Cumulation of actions is the joinder of separate actions in the same judicial demand, whether by a single plaintiff against a single defendant, or by one or more plaintiffs against one or more defendants.

Source: C.P. Art. 148; Arts. 153, 156, Spanish Code of Civil Procedure; Arts. 153, 156, Cuban Code of Civil Procedure; *cf.* Comments following.

Comments

(a) Although Arts. 149, 151, and 152 of the Code of Practice of 1825 were phrased so narrowly that they appeared to contemplate only the cumulation of actions by a single plaintiff against a single defendant, Art. 148 of the 1825 Code did not limit the concept to this type of joinder. The early Louisiana cases treated cumulation as including the joinder of actions by a plurality of plaintiffs or against a plurality of defendants. Kennedy v. Oakey, 3 Rob. 404 (La.1843); Theurer v. Schmidt, 10 La.Ann. 293 (1855); Waldo & Hughes v. Angomar, 12 La.Ann. 74 (1857); Mavor v. Armant, 14 La.Ann. 181 (1859); Dyas & Co. v. Dinkgrave, 15 La.Ann. 502, 77 Am.Dec. 196 (1860).

(b) One of the reasons why the civilian rules of cumulation of actions have failed to operate as intended by the redactors of the Code of Practice of 1825 was the failure of Art. 148 of that Code to state expressly that cumulation embraced the union of actions by plural plaintiffs or against plural defendants. Hence, the resort to the common law rules of "joinder of parties" which, being based upon completely different concepts, have caused a good bit of confusion in the law. The definition of this article expressly states that it includes both types of cumulation.

Art. 462. Cumulation by single plaintiff against single defendant

A plaintiff may cumulate against the same defendant two or more actions even though based on different grounds, if:

(1) Each of the actions cumulated is within the jurisdiction of the court and is brought in the proper venue; and

Art. 462

(2) All of the actions cumulated are mutually consistent and employ the same form of procedure.

Except as otherwise provided in Article 3657, inconsistent or mutually exclusive actions may be cumulated in the same judicial demand if pleaded in the alternative.

Source: C.P. Arts. 149, 151; cf. Comments following and Arts. 153, 154, Spanish Code of Civil Procedure; Arts. 153, 154, Cuban Code of Civil Procedure; Arts. 87, 177(6), Quebec Code of Civil Procedure; § 260, German Code of Civil Procedure.

Comments

(a) Despite the prohibition in Arts. 149 and 151 of the 1870 Code of Practice against the joining of inconsistent or mutually exclusive demands in the same action, the jurisprudence of Louisiana has always permitted inconsistent demands to be joined in the same action, if they were pleaded in the alternative. Smith v. Donnelly, 27 La.Ann. 98 (1875); Haas v. McCain, 161 La. 114, 108 So. 305 (1926); Board of Com'rs of Orleans Levee Dist. v. Shushan, 197 La. 598, 2 So.2d 35 (1941); Templet v. Babbitt, 198 La. 810, 5 So.2d 13 (1941); Boxwell v. Department of Highways, 203 La. 760, 14 So.2d 627 (1943); Bullis v. Town of Jackson, 4 So.2d 550 (La.App.1941). See, also, Succession of Markham, 180 La. 211, 156 So. 225 (1934).

The prohibition against the cumulation of inconsistent or mutually exclusive actions in the same demand is one of the oldest civilian rules of cumulation. In so far as Louisiana procedure is concerned, the fountainhead of this rule is Las Siete Partidas, Partida 3.10.7. Spanish procedure permitted, however, the cumulation of contrary and inconsistent actions in the alternative, where the plaintiff was not required to make an election between the two. Millar, The Joinder of Actions in Continental Civil Procedure, 28 Ill.L.Rev. 177, 193 (1933). Similarly, as illustrated in the cases cited *supra*, Louisiana's procedural law has always permitted complete freedom of joinder of inconsistent and mutually exclusive actions in the same suit if they were pleaded in the alternative.

(b) Likewise the requirement that the court must be competent to adjudicate all of the actions cumulated in the same suit is universal in all of the civilian jurisdictions except France. It is specifically required by Art. 154 of the Codes of Civil Procedure of both Spain and Cuba, and by Sec. 260 of the Code of Civil Procedure of Germany. The most recent, and the great majority, of the Louisiana cases also apply this rule. Prevost v. Greig, 5 Mart. (N.S.) 87 (La.1826); Boulden v. Hughes, 8 Mart. (N.S.) 285 (La.1829); Merritt v. Hozey, 4 Rob. 319 (La.1843); United States v. Cochrane, 5 Rob. 120 (La.1843); Armitage v. Barrow & St. John, 10 La.Ann. 78 (1855); Bazoni v. Marcera, 18 La.Ann. 136 (1866); Broadwell v. Smith, 28 La.Ann. 172 (1876); Stevenson v. Weber, 29 La.Ann. 105

(1877); Favrot v. Parish of East Baton Rouge, 30 La.Ann. 606 (1878); Larrieux v. Crescent City L. S. L. & S. H. Co., 30 La.Ann. 609 (1878); Louisiana Western R. Co. v. Hopkins, 33 La.Ann. 806 (1881); Tague v. Royal Insurance Co., 38 La.Ann. 456 (1886); Marshall v. Holmes, 39 La.Ann. 313, 1 So. 610 (1887); State Nat. Bank v. Allen, 39 La.Ann. 806, 2 So. 600 (1887); Harrison v. Moss & Co., 41 La.Ann. 239, 6 So. 528 (1889); Fredericks v. Donaldson, 50 La.Ann. 471, 23 So. 446 (1898); Landry v. Caffery Cent. Sugar Refinery & R. Co., 104 La. 757, 29 So. 349 (1901); State ex rel. Sumner Building & Supply Co. v. Judges of Court of Appeals, 105 La. 333, 29 So. 892 (1901); Southern Timber & Land Co. v. Wartell, 109 La. 453, 33 So. 559 (1903); Sewerage & Water Board v. Thelen, 117 La. 923, 42 So. 426 (1906); Bloch & Levy v. Lambert, 130 La. 977, 58 So. 849 (1912); State ex rel. North v. Ermon, 133 La. 952, 63 So. 479 (1913); Alessi v. Town of Independence, 142 La. 338, 76 So. 792 (1917); Hotard v. Perilloux, 160 La. 752, 107 So. 515 (1926); Vogt v. Jannarelli, 195 La. 277, 196 So. 346 (1940); Seybold v. Fidelity & Deposit Co. of Maryland, 197 La. 287, 1 So.2d 522 (1941); State ex rel. Nunez v. Baynard, 203 La. 711, 14 So.2d 611 (1943); Sheffield v. Jefferson Parish Developers, 213 La. 799, 35 So.2d 737 (1948); State ex rel. Langlois v. Lancaster, 218 La. 1052, 51 So.2d 622 (1951); Parker v. T. Smith & Son, 222 La. 1061, 64 So. 2d 432 (1953); Taylor v. American Bank & Trust Co., 17 La.App. 458, 133 So. 402 (1931); Shreveport Laundries v. Red Iron Drilling Co., 192 So. 895 (La.App.1939); Lopez v. Bertel, 198 So. 185 (La. App.1940).

However, there are a substantial number of Louisiana cases applying the contrary rule, and providing that the jurisdictional amount of a suit in which several actions are cumulated in the same suit is the aggregate of the cumulated actions. Offut's Heirs v. Roberts, 12 Mart. (O.S.) 300 (La.1822); Heirs of Ballio v. Poisset, 8 Mart. (N.S.) 338 (La.1829); Rhodes v. Scholfield, 6 La.Ann. 251 (1851); Lartigue v. White, 25 La.Ann. 291 (1873); Bowman v. City of New Orleans, 27 La.Ann. 501 (1875); State ex rel. St. Cyr v. Jumel, 34 La.Ann. 201 (1882); Dalcour v. McCan, 37 La. Ann. 7 (1885); Armstrong v. Vicksburg, S. & P. R. Co., 46 La.Ann. 1448, 16 So. 468 (1894); Amato v. Ermann & Cohn, 47 La.Ann. 967, 17 So. 505 (1895); A. Lehman & Co. v. Coulon, 105 La. 431, 29 So. 879 (1901); La Groue v. City of New Orleans, 114 La. 253, 38 So. 160 (1905); Learned & Koontz v. Texas & P. R. Co., 128 La. 430, 54 So. 931 (1911); Sandlin v. Coyle, 143 La. 121, 78 So. 261, L.R.A. 1918D, 389 (1918); Meyer v. Blanchard, Gunby's Dec. 11 (La.App. 1885); Granier v. Bourgeois, 189 So. 474 (La.App.1939).

With reference to the requirement of the above article that each of the actions must be within the jurisdiction of the court and in the proper venue, see Chapters 1 and 2 of Book I, Title 1, which set forth the use of these terms in this Code.

Art. 462

(c) Art. 3657, *infra*, prohibits the alternative pleading of the petitory and possessory actions.

(d) See, also, Comments under Art. 463, *infra*.

Art. 463. Cumulation, plural plaintiffs or defendants

Two or more parties may be joined in the same suit, either as plaintiffs or as defendants, if:

(1) There is a community of interest between the parties joined;

(2) Each of the actions cumulated is within the jurisdiction of the court and is brought in the proper venue; and

(3) All of the actions cumulated are mutually consistent and employ the same form of procedure.

Except as otherwise provided in Article 3657, inconsistent or mutually exclusive actions may be cumulated in the same suit if pleaded in the alternative.

> **Source:** C.P. Art. 149; *cf.* Comments following, and Arts. 154, 156, Spanish Code of Civil Procedure; Arts. 154, 156, Cuban Code of Civil Procedure; Arts. 87, 177(6), Quebec Code of Civil Procedure; §§ 59, 260, German Code of Civil Procedure.
>
> **Cross Reference:** Art. 647.

Comments

(a) This article is similar to Art. 462, *supra*, relating to cumulation of actions against the same defendant. The requirements common to both types of cumulation are: (1) each of the actions cumulated must be within the jurisdiction of the court and brought in the proper venue; (2) all of the actions cumulated must be enforceable by the same *form* of procedure, *i. e.*, ordinary, executory, or summary procedure; and (3) all of the actions cumulated must be mutually consistent, although inconsistent or mutually exclusive actions may be cumulated if pleaded in the alternative. *Cf.* Comments (a), (b), and (c) under Art. 462, *supra*.

While a single plaintiff may cumulate in the same suit two or more actions against the same defendant having no connection with each other, and based on different causes of actions, of necessity, greater restriction on the privilege of cumulating actions must be imposed when the suit is brought by plural plaintiffs or against plural defendants. The test to be employed in the latter case is the traditional one of a "community of interest between the parties joined." For an explanation of this concept, see Comments (b), (c), and (d), hereof, *infra*.

(b) The test of proper joinder applied by the majority of the Louisiana cases is the "common interest" of the plaintiffs joined in bringing the actions, or of the defendants joined in defending the actions. Waldo & Hughes v. Angomar, 12 La.Ann. 74 (1857); New Orleans Ins. Ass'n v. Harper, 32 La.Ann. 1165 (1880); State v. State Tax Collector, 39 La.Ann. 530, 2 So. 59 (1887); Riggs v. Bell, 39 La.Ann. 1030, 3 So. 183 (1887); State v. Shakspeare, 43 La.Ann. 92, 8 So. 893 (1890); Neugass v. City of New Orleans, 43 La.Ann. 78, 9 So. 25 (1891); Gill v. City of Lake Charles, 119 La. 17, 43 So. 897 (1907); Davidson v. Fletcher, 126 La. 535, 52 So. 761 (1910); Davidson v. Frost-Johnson Lumber Co., 126 La. 542, 52 So. 759 (1910); Strong v. Robbins, 137 La. 680, 69 So. 93 (1915); Reardon v. Dickinson, 156 La. 556, 100 So. 715 (1924); Erskine Heirs v. Gardiner, 166 La. 1098, 118 So. 453 (1928); Castille v. Texas Co., 170 La. 887, 129 So. 518 (1930); Buras v. Machella, 172 La. 580, 134 So. 751 (1931); State v. Parish Democratic Executive Committee, 173 La. 844, 138 So. 857 (1931); State v. Grace, 191 La. 15, 184 So. 527 (1938); Seybold v. Fidelity & Deposit Co. of Maryland, 197 La. 287, 1 So.2d 522 (1941); Watson v. Bethany, 209 La. 989, 26 So.2d 12 (1946); Reynaud v. Champagne, 14 Orl.App. 179 (La.App. 1917); Morgan's La. & Tex. R. R. Co. v. Godchaux Sugars, Inc., 3 La.App. 236 (1925); Carona v. Cangemi, 13 La.App. 699, 129 So. 189 (1930); McCaskey Register Co. v. Barnes, 146 So. 714 (La.App. 1933); Succession of Coles v. Pontchartrain Apartment Hotel, 172 So. 28 (La.App.1937); Delesdernier Estate v. Zettwoch, 175 So. 137 (La.App.1937); Granier v. Bourgeois, 188 So. 423 (La.App. 1939); Pryor v. Pryor, 22 So.2d 831 (La.App.1945); Tucker v. Snyder, 30 So.2d 160 (La.App.1947).

A few of the Louisiana cases apply the test of "community of interest" in determining whether the cumulation of actions has been proper. Favrot v. Parish of East Baton Rouge, 30 La.Ann. 606 (1878); La. Western R. R. Co. v. Hopkins, 33 La.Ann. 806 (1881); State Nat. Bank v. Allen, 39 La.Ann. 806, 2 So. 600 (1887); McGee v. Collins, 156 La. 291, 100 So. 430 (1924). It is apparent, however, that "community of interest" and "common interest" refer to exactly the same concept, as a number of the Louisiana cases use both terms, and in a manner which indicates definitely that they are considered as synonymous. Briel v. Postal Telegraph Co., 112 La. 412, 36 So. 477 (1904); Smith v. Phillips, 171 La. 291, 131 So. 23 (1930); Lykes Bros Ripley S.S. Co. v. Wiegand Marionneaux L. Co., 185 La. 1085, 171 So. 453 (1936); Keel v. Rodessa Oil & Land Co., 189 La. 732, 180 So. 502 (1938); Board of Com'rs of Orleans Levee District v. Shushan, 197 La. 598, 2 So.2d 35 (1941). As used in this article, "community of interest" is considered as being synonymous with "common interest" and is used in exactly the same sense in which the latter term is used in Gill v. City of Lake Charles, *supra*.

(c) The term "community of interest" retains the same meaning assigned to it and to "common interest" in Gill v. City of Lake

Charles, 119 La. 17, 43 So. 879 (1907), and subsequent cases based thereon, namely, actions arising out of the same facts, or presenting the same factual and legal issues.

(d) See, also, Comments under Arts. 462, 591, *infra*.

Art. 464. Improper cumulation, effect

When the court lacks jurisdiction of, or when the venue is improper as to, one of the actions cumulated, that action shall be dismissed.

When the cumulation is improper for any other reason, the court may: (1) order separate trials of the actions; or (2) order the plaintiff to elect which actions he shall proceed with, and to amend his petition so as to delete therefrom all allegations relating to the action which he elects to discontinue. The penalty for noncompliance with an order to amend is a dismissal of plaintiff's suit.

Source: C.P. Art. 152; Fed. Rule 21; Ill.Civil Practice Act, § 44; *cf.* Art. 177(6), Quebec Code of Civil Procedure; Art. 103, Italian Code of Civil Procedure.

Cross Reference: Art. 647.

Comments

(a) The provisions of the first paragraph of the above article make no change in the procedural law of Louisiana. No cases were found directly in point, but the principles of law applicable appear to be settled beyond question. If an action is filed in a court of improper jurisdiction or venue, it seems clear that it would be dismissed upon exception. There is no reason to believe that a contrary result would follow if the action, instead of being filed singly, were cumulated with other actions.

If an action is filed in a court of improper jurisdiction or venue, the trial judge is empowered to transfer it to a proper Court under Arts. 121 and 932, *infra*. When a single action is filed in a court of improper jurisdiction or venue, the entire suit may be transferred to a proper court. But if the court has no jurisdiction over, or the venue is improper with respect to, only one of several actions cumulated, separation of this single action from the others, and its transfer to another court would present many difficulties. Therefore, no provision is made for such transfers with reference to actions improperly cumulated.

(b) Fed.Rule 21, Ill.Civil Practice Act, § 44, and Art. 103 of the Italian Code of Civil Procedure are the sources of the principal idea embodied in the second paragraph of this article: that if actions are improperly cumulated, the result should be either separate trials of the actions, or requiring plaintiff to elect as to which actions he would continue to prosecute, and *not* the dismissal of the suit.

Tit. 2   CUMULATION OF ACTIONS   Art. 464

(c) For years, in the procedure of both common law and civil law jurisdictions, a misjoinder of parties (or an improper cumulation of actions by or against plural parties) was regarded as presenting a problem of pleading. It is now recognized, in many jurisdictions of both systems, that this actually presents only a matter of inconvenience in the trial of actions improperly joined. Hence, in these jurisdictions, the problem of improper joinder is solved by severance—the separate trials of such actions. Fed.Rule 21; Ill.Civil Practice Act, § 44; Art. 103, Italian Code of Civil Procedure.

The penalty of forcing the plaintiff to elect has always been applied by the Louisiana courts with respect to the improper cumulation of actions by a single plaintiff against a single defendant. However, the penalty for the improper cumulation of actions by or against plural parties is not quite clear. Under traditional civilian judicial techniques, Art. 152 of the 1870 Code of Practice should have been applied to this type of improper cumulation, as well as to the other, and in at least two cases this was done. Briel v. Postal Telegraph Co., 112 La. 412, 36 So. 477 (1904); Davidson v. Fletcher, 126 La. 535, 52 So. 761 (1910). The majority of Louisiana cases, however, have imposed the penalty of dismissal of the suit for an improper cumulation of actions by or against plural parties. New Orleans Ins. Ass'n v. Harper, 32 La.Ann. 1165 (1880); Davidson v. Frost-Johnson Lumber Co., 126 La. 542, 52 So. 759 (1910); State v. Grace, 191 La. 15, 184 So. 527 (1938); Babineaux v. Miller, 5 La.App. 605 (1927); Delesdernier Estate v. Zettwoch, 175 So. 137 (La.App.1937); Copellar v. Britt, 188 So. 403 (La.App.1939); Pryor v. Pryor, 22 So.2d 831 (La.App.1945). *Cf.* McGee v. Collins, 156 La. 291, 100 So. 430 (1924).

In cases of improper cumulation for reasons other than those set forth in the first paragraph of the above article, the penalty therefor is not as drastic as the dismissal of the suit. In these instances the trial judge has discretion either to sever the actions for the purposes of trial, or to require plaintiff to elect as to which actions he would continue to prosecute, and which he would discontinue. Separate trials of the actions improperly cumulated is the usual solution of the problem, and requiring the plaintiff to elect would be ordered only in those unusual cases where separate trials of the actions is not feasible.

(d) The objection of improper cumulation, under this Code, is raised through the dilatory exception, Art. 926, *infra*, and hence must be raised thereunder prior to answer or judgment by default. Art. 928, *infra*. Hence, if this objection is not raised timely, it is considered waived, although the trial judge may order separate trials of the actions under Art. 465, *infra*.

Art. 465. Separate trials of cumulated actions

When the court is of the opinion that it would simplify the proceedings, would permit a more orderly disposition of the case, or would otherwise be in the interest of justice, at any time prior to trial, it may order a separate trial of cumulated actions, even if the cumulation is proper.

Source: Fed.Rules 21, 42(b); Art. 103, Italian Code of Civil Procedure; *cf.* Comments following.

Cross Reference: Art. 647.

Comments

(a) The right of the trial judge to grant a severance, or separate trials, of actions even though cumulated properly, when these actions cannot be tried conveniently together, or when one of the defendants will be prejudiced thereby, is well recognized in Louisiana. Probably due to the rarity of jury trials in civil cases, this right has been very seldom invoked and in three recent cases in which severance was demanded, the applicable rules were confused with those relating to cumulation. *Cf.* In re Cummings, 196 La. 493, 199 So. 402 (1940); Driefus v. Levy, 140 So. 259 (La.App.1932); Brewer v. Foshee, 178 So. 778 (La.App.1937).

(b) Severance, in all probability borrowed from common law procedure, has had an interesting history in Louisiana. Prior to the adoption of the Code of Practice of 1825, it was granted in Sere v. Armitage, 9 Mart. (O.S.) 394, 13 Am.Dec. 321 (La.1821); but after the adoption of that Code it was first held that severance would not be granted, as the Code made no provision therefor. Prall v. Peet's Curator, 3 La. 274 (1832). Subsequent decisions, however, expressly recognized the right of the trial judge to order separate trials within his discretion, even if the cumulation was proper, if the judge was of the opinion that the actions cumulated could not be tried conveniently together, or if a joint trial would prejudice the rights of one of the defendants. Arrowsmith v. Mayor, 17 La. 419 (1841); Borne v. Porter, 4 Rob. 57 (La.1843); Clement v. Wafer, 12 La.Ann. 599 (1857); Fonda v. Broom, 12 La.Ann. 768 (1857); Riggs v. Bell, 39 La.Ann. 1030, 3 So. 183 (1887); Williams v. Pullman Palace Car Co., 40 La.Ann. 417, 4 So. 85, 8 Am.St.Rep. 538 (1888); Cline v. Crescent City R. Co., 41 La.Ann. 1031, 6 So. 851 (1889). *Cf.* Holzab v. New Orleans & Carrollton R. Co., 38 La.Ann. 185 (1886); State v. St. Paul, 110 La. 722, 34 So. 750 (1903); Schwing v. Dunlap, 130 La. 498, 58 So. 162 (1912).

(c) The retention of the Louisiana rules of severance is necessary to permit the trial judge to take care of those situations when the actions cumulated, even though properly, cannot conveniently be tried together. The above article is also necessary to permit the orderly trial and disposition, through separate trials, of actions cumulated improperly, when the defendants do not object timely or properly to the improper joinder.

(d) See, also, Comments under Art. 464, *supra*.

CHAPTER 3. LIS PENDENS

Art.
531. Suits pending in Louisiana court or courts.
532. Suits pending in Louisiana and federal or foreign court.

Art. 531. Suits pending in Louisiana court or courts

When two or more suits are pending in a Louisiana court or courts on the same cause of action, between the same parties in the same capacities, and having the same object, the defendant may have all but the first suit dismissed by excepting thereto as provided in Article 925. When the defendant does not so except, the plaintiff may continue the prosecution of any of the suits, but the first final judgment rendered shall be conclusive of all.

Source: C.P. Arts. 94, 335(2).

Cross Reference: Art. 932.

Comments

(a) This article is declaratory of the rules of Arts. 94 and 335(2) of the 1870 Code of Practice, and of the jurisprudence interpreting them. State ex rel. Immanuel Presbyterian Church v. Riedy, 50 La.Ann. 258, 23 So. 327 (1898); Lorio v. Gladney, 147 La. 930, 86 So. 365 (1920); Liverpool & L. & G. Ins. Co. v. Aleman Planting & Mfg. Co., 166 La. 457, 117 So. 554 (1928); Treigle Sash Factory v. Saladino, 211 La. 945, 31 So.2d 172 (1947); Griffin v. Motor Transit Co., 133 So. 456 (La.App.1931). *Cf.* State v. City of Hammond, 184 La. 13, 165 So. 314 (1936); General Finance Co. of Louisiana v. Veith, 184 So. 364 (La.App.1938); State ex rel. Divens v. Johnson, 207 La. 23, 20 So.2d 412 (1944).

(b) The phrase "between the same parties in the same capacities" is a more accurate expression of the requirement of Civil Code Art. 2286 that the two demands be between the same parties in the same qualities. Even though Art. 94 of the 1870 Code of Practice does not employ this phrase, it is necessarily implied by reference to Art. 2286 of the Civil Code. *Cf.* Griffith's Estate v. Glaze's Heirs, 199 La. 800, 7 So.2d 62 (1942), and hence should be closely correlated.

(c) This article makes it clear that the strict rules of lis pendens apply only when the two suits are pending in Louisiana courts. This is well settled by the jurisprudence. See the cases cited under Comment (a) of Art. 532, *infra*.

(d) See, also, Comments under Art. 925, *infra*.

Art. 532. Suits pending in Louisiana and federal or foreign court

When a suit is brought in a Louisiana court while another is pending in a court of another state or of the United States on the same cause of action, between the same parties in the same capacities, and having the same object, on motion of the defendant or on its own motion, the court may stay all proceedings in the second suit until the first has been discontinued or final judgment has been rendered.

Source: New; *cf.* Comments following.

Comments

(a) The jurisprudence of Louisiana is well settled that the strict rules of lis pendens will not be applied unless the suits are pending in Louisiana courts, and that these rules do not apply when the first action is pending either in a federal court, or in a court of another state or a foreign country. Stone v. Vincent, 6 Mart. (N.S.) 517 (La.1828); Godfrey v. Hall, 4 La. 158 (1832); West v. McConnell, 5 La. 424 (1833); Hampton's Heirs v. Barrett, 9 La. 336 (1836); *Id.*, 12 La. 159 (1838); Peyroux v. Davis, 17 La. 479 (1841); Wright, Williams & Co. v. E. Hill & Co., 13 La.Ann. 233 (1858); State v. New Orleans & N. E. R. Co., 42 La.Ann. 11, 7 So. 84 (1890); Ferriday v. Middlesex Banking Co., 118 La. 770, 43 So. 403 (1907); Iatt Lumber Co. v. Faircloth, 132 La. 906, 61 So. 866 (1913); Lorio v. Gladney, 147 La. 930, 86 So. 365 (1920). See, also, Hope v. Madison, 191 La. 1075, 187 So. 28 (1939).

When the action is one in rem, however, through comity the Louisiana court will stay all proceedings in a second suit, so as to recognize, and avoid any interference with, the jurisdiction of a federal court in which the action was first brought. Ferriday v. Middlesex Banking Co., *supra*. It seems clear that the same rule would apply under similar circumstances if the action were one quasi in rem.

(b) This article changes the law in two respects: (1) it broadens the rule of Ferriday v. Middlesex Banking Co., *supra*, to extend it to actions in personam, as well as to actions in rem or quasi in rem; and (2) it grants the trial judge discretion to stay or not to stay the proceedings in the Louisiana case.

The object of this article is to curtail as far as practicable the practice of filing the same action in both a Louisiana court and a federal court, and prosecuting to final judgment the proceeding in which plaintiff feels he has the best chance of succeeding.

(c) This article applies only where the suit in the foreign jurisdiction or in the federal court is filed first. To extend the provisions of the article to cases where the Louisiana action has been filed first would require the Louisiana courts to abdicate their judicatory power.

(d) See, also, Comments under Art. 531, *supra,* and Art. 925, *infra.*

CHAPTER 4. ABANDONMENT OF ACTION

Art.
561. Abandonment in trial and appellate court.

Art. 561. Abandonment in trial and appellate court

An action is abandoned when the parties fail to take any steps in its prosecution or defense in the trial court for a period of five years. This provision shall be operative without formal order, but on ex parte motion of any party or other interested person, the trial court shall enter a formal order or dismissal as of the date of its abandonment.

An appeal is abandoned when the parties fail to take any step in its prosecution or disposition for a period of five years; and the appellate court shall dismiss the appeal summarily.

Source: C.C. Art. 3519.

Comments

(a) In Evans v. Hamner, 209 La. 442, 24 So.2d 814 (1946) and Sandfield Oil & Gas Co. v. Paul, 7 So.2d 725 (La.App.1942), Art. 3519(2) of the Civil Code was held to be self-operative, and no action need be taken by defendant to have the action dismissed upon its abandonment.

(b) Under the decision in Carmody v. Land, 207 La. 652, 21 So. 2d 764 (1945), it was held that Art. 3519(2) of the Civil Code is applicable only to principal demands, and does not apply to reconventional demands. The word "action" is used in this article instead of "demand" in order to make it applicable to the principal as well as to the incidental actions.

This article treats the action as abandoned only if five years has elapsed without any steps being taken by *any of the parties* in the prosecution *or defense* thereof. This change was made to provide for the case where the defendant has taken some step in the defense of the action, but subsequently moves to have the action declared abandoned because the plaintiff has failed to take any step in the prosecution thereof for five years.

(c) Prior to the decisions cited in Comment (a) hereof, two exceptions were recognized to the presumption of abandonment through the plaintiff's failure to prosecute his demand for a period of five years. The first of these recognized the plaintiff's right to resist the dismissal by proving that the failure to prosecute was caused by circumstances beyond his control. Burton v. Burbank, 138 La. 997, 71 So. 134 (1916); Bell v. Staring, 170 So. 502 (La. App.1936); Harrisonburg-Catahoula State Bank v. Myers, 185 So. 96 (La.App.1938), noted 13 Tul.L.Rev. 641 (1939); Metairie Bank in Liquidation v. Lecler, 1 So.2d 710 (La.App.1941). *Cf.* Sliman v. Araguel, 196 La. 859, 200 So. 280 (1941). The second was the rule that when the defendant takes any action in the case inconsistent with an intention to have the demand treated as abandoned, he waives his right to have the abandonment decreed. Geisenberger v. Cotton, 116 La. 651, 40 So. 929 (1906); Continental Supply Co. v. Fisher, 156 La. 101, 100 So. 64 (1924); King v. Illinois Cent. R. Co., 143 So. 95 (La.App.1932). For a time there was considerable doubt as to whether these cases had not been overruled sub silentio by Evans v. Hamner, *supra*, holding that the abandonment operates automatically when plaintiff fails to take any step in the prosecution of the case for a period of five years; although subsequently an intermediate appellate court continued to recognize the first exception. Zatarain v. Portera, 63 So.2d 477 (La.App.1953). Some time later, this doubt was dispelled by cases holding that, even though the code rule was self-operative and no further proceedings need be taken except to strike the case from the docket, this rule would not apply when the defendant had waived his right to treat the case as abandoned by taking any action inconsistent with such waiver. State v. United Dredging Co., 218 La. 744, 50 So.2d 826 (1951); Green v. Small, 227 La. 401, 79 So.2d 497 (1955); State ex rel. Shields v. Southport Petroleum Corporation of Del., 230 La. 199, 88 So.2d 25 (1956).

With respect to the exception to the rule of abandonment based on the defendant's waiver thereof, the point is moot under the above article, as the problem is solved by its broadened language "when *the parties* fail to take any steps in its prosecution *or defense*" for a period of five years. But the rationale of the three supreme court cases cited above necessarily reconciles the rule of Evans v. Hamner, *supra*, with earlier decisions recognizing that there should be no dismissal when the plaintiff's failure to prosecute was caused by circumstances beyond his control. See Note, 16 La.L.Rev. 199 (1955).

When the court dismisses a suit on the ex parte motion of defendant and plaintiff's failure to prosecute is due to circumstances beyond his control, plaintiff should rule defendant into court to show cause why the ex parte dismissal should not be vacated, alleging that plaintiff's failure to prosecute was due to circumstances beyond his control. A similar procedure should be followed in a case where the court inadvertently dismisses the suit without noticing that defendant has taken a step in the defense of the suit within the previous five years.

(d) In 1932, the supreme court expressly overruled its earlier decisions and held that Art. 3519(2) of the Civil Code had no application to cases pending on appeal. Veret v. Savoie, 174 La. 844, 141 So. 854 (1932); United Railway Men's Oil Assn. v. Dupuy, 175 La. 177, 143 So. 41 (1932). See, also, New Orleans Loan & Investment Co. v. Montagnet, 143 So. 721 (La.App.1932). Subsequently, the supreme court adopted its own rule on the subject, quite similar to the Code provision. Rule VIII, § 3, Revised Rules of Supreme Court of Louisiana (1951). See, also, McCaleb, The New Rules of the Supreme Court of Louisiana, 26 Tul.L.Rev. 491 (1952). In 1954, the legislature amended the Civil Code provision so as to make it apply to cases pending on appeal. The second paragraph of this article retains this change made by the legislature.

(e) In order to effectuate the purposes of the above article, proposed legislation was submitted recommending that Art. 3519 of the Civil Code be amended to provide that if the plaintiff, after having made his demand, abandons or discontinues it, the interruption shall be considered as having never happened.

(f) See, also, Comments under Art. 1672, *infra*.

CHAPTER 5. CLASS AND SECONDARY ACTIONS

SECTION 1. CLASS ACTIONS

Art.
591. Prerequisites.
592. Representation.
593. Venue.
594. Dismissal or compromise.
595. Award of expenses of litigation; security for costs.
596. Petition in shareholder's secondary action.
597. Effect of judgment.

SECTION 2. SECONDARY ACTIONS

611. Shareholder's secondary action when not impracticable to join all shareholders or members.

SECTION 1. CLASS ACTIONS

Art. 591. Prerequisites

A class action may be instituted when the persons constituting the class are so numerous as to make it impracticable for all of them to join or be joined as parties, and the character of the right sought to be enforced for or against the members of the class is:

(1) Common to all members of the class; or

Art. 591

(2) Secondary, in the sense that the owner of a primary right refuses to enforce it, and a member of the class thereby becomes entitled to enforce the right.

Source: New; *cf.* Fed. Rule 23(a) (1).

Comments

(a) The class action has been recognized and utilized in at least one Louisiana case. Executive Committee of French Opera Trades Ball v. Tarrant, 164 La. 83, 113 So. 774, 53 A.L.R. 1233 (1927). Further, the shareholder's secondary action has been repeatedly recognized in this state. See cases cited in Comments under Art. 596, *infra*. A few of these cases have been secondary class actions.

(b) This article is a modification of the indirect source provision to conform with Louisiana terminology. The word "joint" in Fed. Rule 23(a) (1) was eliminated since the phrase "common to all members of the class" includes the Louisiana joint right or obligation. The only similarity between the joint obligation of Anglo-American law and the joint obligation of Louisiana (the conjoint obligation of the civil law) is the name. See Preliminary Statement to Book I, Title III, Chapter 1, *infra*.

(c) Under federal practice Fed. Rule 23 covers three separate and distinct types of class actions: the true class action, the hybrid class action, and the spurious class action.

In the true class action, if the representation of the members of the class is adequate, the judgment concludes not only the representative parties, but all other members of the class who are not joined as parties. In strict theory the judgment in the hybrid class action concludes only the representative parties and persons who subsequently join in the action, but, as a practical matter, since there is a disposition of the property involved under the judgment, the latter may be prejudicial to those members of the class who do not join in the action. In the spurious class action, only the parties who actually join in the action are concluded by the judgment, and their rights would not be affected by their failure to join. "It is an invitation and not a command performance." 3 Moore's Federal Practice (2d ed.) 3443 (1948).

Both the hybrid and the spurious class actions are permissive joinder devices which are badly needed in federal practice where the jurisdiction of the court often depends upon diversity of citizenship. Joinder of all members of the class in the original complaint, or by intervention, would otherwise deprive a federal court of jurisdiction in all cases where a plaintiff and a defendant are citizens of the same state. But through the use of this permissive joinder device, the representative plaintiffs or defendants can be so selected as to afford the necessary diversity of citizenship; and once the court has acquired jurisdiction over the class action, it has ancillary jurisdiction to permit the subsequent joinder, or to adjudicate the rights of, all other members of the class. Hence, under its ancillary jurisdiction, the federal court may render judgment on the claims of those members of the class who subsequently join in the action.

There is no need for either the hybrid or the spurious class action in Louisiana, and therefore this Code provides for only the true class action.

(d) The liberality of cumulation of actions and of intervention accomplish the same purposes of the spurious class action directly and much more simply. *Cf.* Arts. 463, *supra*, and 1091, *infra*. For an illustration of the efficacy of our liberal rules of cumulation of actions, see Hernandez v. Ethyl Corp., 224 La. 470, 70 So.2d 92 (1954); and *Id.*, 83 So.2d 150 (La.App.1955).

(e) The primary need, in federal practice, of the hybrid class action is the creditors' bill for the appointment of a receiver. 3 Moore's Federal Practice (2d ed.) 3439 (1948). There is no corresponding need in Louisiana, since our receivership act expressly provides that a single creditor or shareholder may sue to provoke the appointment of a receiver. R.S. 12:752.

The second need therefor in federal practice is the equitable bill of peace with multiple parties, *i. e.*, where many persons are asserting claims to property held by a stakeholder. The concursus procedure of Louisiana is broad enough to provide the necessary remedy in such a case. See Arts. 4651 through 4662, *infra*.

Art. 592. Representation

One or more members of a class, who will fairly insure the adequate representation of all members, may sue or be sued in a class action on behalf of all members.

Source: New; *cf.* Fed. Rule 23(a) (1).

Comment

See Comment (a) under Art. 591, *supra*.

Art. 593. Venue

A secondary action of a shareholder or member to enforce a right of a corporation or unincorporated association shall be brought in the parish of proper venue as to the corporation or unincorporated association. All other class actions to enforce a right of all members of the class shall be brought in a parish of proper venue as to the defendant.

Art. 593.

A class action to enforce a right against all members of the class shall be brought in a parish of proper venue as to any member made a defendant.

"Proper venue" as used in this article means the venue provided in Article 42.

Source: New.

Cross Reference: Art. 611.

Comments

(a) Usually, in a secondary action of a shareholder or member much of the evidence presented consists of the books and other records of the corporation or unincorporated association. For this reason, this article requires such an action to be brought at the registered office of the corporation or the principal business establishment of the unincorporated association.

(b) Except for a larger number of defendants, an action brought to enforce an obligation against members of a class is similar to one brought to enforce an obligation against joint or solidary obligors, and under this article the plaintiff has the same option to sue in a parish of proper venue as to any member made a defendant.

Art. 594. Dismissal or compromise

A class action shall not be dismissed or compromised without the approval of the court. Notice of the proposed dismissal or compromise shall be given to all members of the class in such manner as the court directs.

Source: New; cf. Fed. Rule 23(c).

Cross Reference: Art. 611.

Comment

This article accords with the rule applicable to the true class action in Fed. Rule 23(c).

Art. 595. Award of expenses of litigation; security for costs

The court may allow the representative parties their reasonable expenses of litigation, including attorney's fees, when as a result of the class action a fund is made available, or a recovery or compromise is had which is beneficial, to the class.

The court, on contradictory motion at any stage of the proceeding in the trial court prior to judgment, may require the plaintiff in a class action to furnish security for the court costs which a defendant may be compelled to pay. This security for costs may be increased or

Tit. 2   CLASS AND SECONDARY ACTIONS   Art. 596

decreased by the court, on contradictory motion of any interested party, on a showing that the security furnished has become inadequate or excessive.

Source: New.

Cross Reference: Art. 611.

Comments

(a) It is intended, in the first paragraph, that the reasonable expenses of litigation allowed the successful representative parties is to be paid out of the fund or benefits made available by their efforts. If the action is a secondary shareholder's suit, these expenses are to be paid by the corporation which is to receive the fund or benefit. See Comment (b).

(b) The consistent policy of Louisiana heretofore has been to allow a successful litigant only his taxable costs, and not to award attorney's fees, unless provided by statute or convention. Under the general equity jurisprudence, reasonable expenses of litigation in a class action, including attorney's fees, may be allowed the successful litigant. See 3 Moore's Federal Practice (2d ed.) 3433, 3502 (1948) and cases cited. The above article retains the consistent Louisiana policy with respect to the class action.

(c) In some states, the security for costs which the plaintiffs in a class action may be required to furnish may include the attorney's fees which the defendants might be awarded, if successful. The result is that, at least in some instances, plaintiffs have been unable to continue the prosecution of a just claim, because they were unable to post the large bond required as security for costs. Since attorney's fees are not to be allowed the successful litigant, except as provided in the first paragraph of this article, the security for costs governed by the second paragraph of this article will include only the estimated taxable costs of the defendants.

Art. 596.   Petition in shareholder's secondary action

The petition in a class action brought by a shareholder or member of a corporation or unincorporated association because it refuses to enforce a right which it may enforce shall:

(1) Allege that the plaintiff was a shareholder or member at the time of the occurrence or transaction of which he complains, or that his share or membership thereafter devolved on him by operation of law;

(2) Allege with particularity the efforts of the plaintiff to secure from the managing directors, governors, or trustees and, if necessary, from the shareholders or members, the enforcement of the right; and

the reasons for his failure to secure such enforcement; or the reason for not making such an effort to secure enforcement of the right;

(3) Join as defendants the corporation or unincorporated association and the obligor against whom the obligation is sought to be enforced;

(4) Include a prayer for judgment in favor of the corporation or unincorporated association and against the obligor on the obligation sought to be enforced; and

(5) Be verified by the affidavit of the plaintiff or his counsel.

Source: New; *cf.* Fed. Rule 23(b).

Cross Reference: Art. 611.

Comments

(a) Louisiana recognizes the shareholder's secondary action to enforce a right which the corporation refuses to assert. Watkins v. North American Land & Timber Co., 107 La. 107, 31 So. 683 (1902). See, also, Dawkins v. Mitchell, 149 La. 1038, 90 So. 396 (1922); Viley v. Wall, 154 La. 221, 97 So. 409 (1923); *Id.*, 159 La. 627, 105 So. 794 (1925); Orlando v. Nix, 171 La. 176, 129 So. 810 (1930); and 20 Tul.L.Rev. 271 (1945). *Cf.* Marcuse v. Gullett Gin Mfg. Co., 52 La.Ann. 1383, 27 So. 846 (1900). No change in the procedural law is effected by this article.

(b) The rule stated in Art. 596(1) accords with Louisiana law. *Cf.* Von Schlemmer v. Keystone Life Ins. Co., 121 La. 987, 46 So. 991 (1908); Gordon v. Business Men's Racing Ass'n, 141 La. 819, 75 So. 735 (1917). See, also, Mullins v. De Soto Securities Co., 45 F.Supp. 871 (D.C.La.1942); and *Id.*, 3 F.R.D. 271 (D.C.La.1943).

(c) The rule set forth in Art. 596(3) is not embodied in its indirect source provision, but is declaratory of the general law on the subject. See 3 Moore's Federal Practice (2d ed.) 3436, 3437 (1948). Similarly, the rule of Art. 596(4) is not taken from the indirect source provision; but has been incorporated into the article to set forth more fully the general procedural law on the subject. In such an action, the plaintiff is not entitled to recover personally on the corporate right asserted, but only to obtain judgment in favor of the corporation on the obligation sought to be enforced.

(d) See, also, Comments under Art. 591, *supra*.

Art. 597. Effect of judgment

A definitive judgment on the merits rendered in a class action concludes all members of the class, whether joined in the action or not, if the members who were joined as parties fairly insured adequate representation of all members of the class.

Source: New.

Comments

(a) This article is merely declaratory of the settled law on the subject under federal practice. Supreme Tribe of Ben Hur v. Cauble, 255 U.S. 356, 41 S.Ct. 338, 65 L.Ed. 673 (1921), as modified by Hansberry v. Lee, 311 U.S. 32, 61 S.Ct. 115, 85 L.Ed. 22, 132 A.L.R. 741 (1940).

The United States Supreme Court Rules Advisory Committee did not recommend a rule covering the effect of the judgment rendered in the three types of class actions recognized by the federal rules as it felt that the subject was substantive, rather than procedural, law. 3 Moore's Federal Practice (2d ed.) 3456 (1948). Professor Moore has suggested a Subdivision (d), in the event that it might be deemed advisable to embody in Rule 23 the law on the effect of the judgment rendered in the various types of class actions. *Id.* at page 3472. This article accords with the suggested rule on the effect of judgment in a true class action.

(b) There was no need to include in this article any rule on the subject of the effect of judgment rendered in a shareholder's secondary action in which all of the shareholders are joined either as parties plaintiff or defendants. Since all are parties, all would be concluded by the judgment under the Louisiana rules of res judicata.

SECTION 2. SECONDARY ACTIONS

Art. 611. *Shareholder's secondary action when not impracticable to join all shareholders or members*

When it is not impracticable for all of the shareholders or members of a corporation or unincorporated association to join or to be joined as parties to a secondary action to enforce a right of the corporation or unincorporated association which it refuses to enforce, all of the shareholders or members who refuse or fail to join as plaintiffs in such an action shall be joined as defendants.

In all other respects, such an action is governed by the provisions of Articles 593 through 596.

Source: New.

Comments

(a) The action governed by this article is not a class action since it is practicable to join all members of the class in the action. It applies to a case where a corporation, with only a few shareholders, is controlled by the holders of a majority interest, who refuse to permit it to assert a corporate right. The only difference between such an action and the representative shareholder's secondary action is that in the latter the shareholders are so numerous as to make it impracticable to join all, hence representatives must be permitted to bring the action for the benefit of all.

(b) At least two cases in the federal courts have held that a shareholder's secondary action brought under Fed.Rule 23(b) is not subject to the requirements of Fed.Rule 23(a) as to the parties being so numerous as to make it impracticable to bring them all before the court, adequate representation, and so forth. Galdi v. Jones, 141 F.2d 984, 7 F.R.Serv. 23b.1, Case 3(2 Cir.1944); Topping v. Certain-teed Products Corp., 10 F.R.Serv. 23a.2, Case 2 (D.C.Ill.1947). Both have been criticized on the ground that the shareholder's secondary action under Fed.Rule 23(b) is a class action which must also meet the requirements of Rule 23(a). 3 Moore's Federal Practice (2d ed.) 3423, n. 2 (1948).

Conceding the validity of Professor Moore's criticism, it is not difficult to understand why a federal court would wish to apply the requirements of Fed.Rule 23(b) to a shareholder's secondary action where the shareholders were not so numerous as to make it impracticable to bring them all before the court. If all shareholders are joined, either as plaintiffs or defendants, then there is no need to resort to the fiction of the class action, as there is no problem of indispensable parties. This is the theory on which the above article is based.

TITLE III
PARTIES

Chap.		Art.
1.	Joinder	641
2.	Parties Plaintiff	681
3.	Parties Defendant	731
4.	Parties to Incidental Demands	771
5.	Substitution of Parties	801
	Sec.	
	1. In Trial Courts	801
	2. In Appellate Courts	821

CHAPTER 1. JOINDER

Art.
641. Compulsory joinder; indispensable parties.
642. Same; necessary parties.
643. Same; necessary parties; joint and solidary obligees and obligors.
644. Same; joinder of indispensable or necessary party plaintiff who refuses to sue.
645. Same; pleading nonjoinder of indispensable or necessary party.
646. Same; amendment of petition to join indispensable or necessary party.
647. Permissive joinder governed by rules of cumulation of actions.

PRELIMINARY STATEMENT

Under federal practice, and under modern American code procedure, parties are classified as: (1) formal; (2) proper; (3) necessary; and (4) indispensable. 3 Moore's Federal Practice (2d ed.) 2103 (1948); 2 Barron & Holtzoff, Federal Practice and Procedure 52 et seq. (1950); Clark on Code Pleading (2d ed.) 158 et seq. (1957). Formal parties are purely nominal, and are procedural vehicles who have no real interest in the controversy, such as the next friend who brings a suit to enforce a right of a minor, or a public official named as the obligee on a bond, who sues to enforce it for the benefit of persons in interest. Proper parties are those who must or may be joined in the action, whether such joinder is compulsory or permissive. Necessary parties are those whose interests in the subject matter of the action are separable, and whose absence would not prevent proper relief to the parties joined; but who should be joined, if feasible, to avoid a multiplicity of action and permit a complete adjudication of the controversy. Indispensable parties are those without whom the action cannot proceed.

Under Louisiana practice, the concept of formal parties has no usefulness, since either the actual parties in interest or their legal representatives must sue or be sued. The classification of proper parties serves a useful purpose in Anglo-American civil procedure in determining whether there has been a misjoinder of parties. It serves much the same purpose in Louisiana in determining whether there has been an improper cumulation of actions; but it is not so essential as to require express code recognition.

Every procedural system finds it necessary to have some counterpart to the concept of indispensable parties, without whose joinder the court cannot adjudicate; and to a lesser extent, to the concept of necessary parties, whose joinder is desirable, but not so indispensable as to prevent an adjudication of the action if they are not joined.

While not heretofore the subject of express recognition by the positive law of Louisiana, these two latter concepts have been recognized and utilized by the jurisprudence whenever necessary. Unfortunately, due to the failure to use precise terminology consistently and to recognize the differences between these two concepts, the jurisprudence is not as satisfactory as might be desired. Thus, in Ashbey v. Ashbey, 41 La.Ann. 138, 5 So. 546 (1889) and Succession of Todd, 165 La. 453, 115 So. 653 (1928), the court recognized and utilized the concept of indispensable parties, without labeling it as such. In both cases the suit was dismissed because all parties whose rights would be directly affected by any judgment which would be rendered were not before the court. Even though the defendant's exception of nonjoinder of parties defendant was not before the appellate court in either case, on its own motion in both the court noticed the defect and refused to adjudicate. At least three subsequent cases recognized and properly labeled the concept of indispensable parties. Horn v. Skelly Oil Co., 221 La. 626, 60 So.2d 65 (1952); State v. Ferris, 227 La. 13, 78 So.2d 493 (1955); Baton Rouge Production Credit Ass'n. v. Alford, 102 So.2d 866 (La.1958). On the other hand, the concept of necessary parties was expressly recognized and properly labeled in Reed v. Warren, 172 La. 1082, 136 So. 59 (1931) and its progeny.

The procedure for pleading the lack of indispensable parties or the nonjoinder of necessary parties has caused some confusion in the jurisprudence. Heretofore, only one exception, nonjoinder of parties, has been utilized for both purposes. The exception has long been recognized as a dilatory one which must be pleaded prior to answer or default, otherwise the objection sought to be raised thereby would be waived. This exception serves well to plead a nonjoinder of necessary parties, but was never designed to raise the issue of lack of indispensable parties. Since the latter defect may be noticed by either the trial or appellate court on its own motion, it can-

Tit. 3 JOINDER Art. 641

not be waived. Hence, it should be raised by a peremptory, and not a dilatory, exception. Utilizing the exception of nonjoinder of parties to raise the issue of lack of indispensable parties has worked confusion and presented difficulties. See De Hart v. Continental Land & Fur Co., 196 La. 701, 200 So. 9 (1941); and Ott v. Grace, 13 So.2d 138 (La.App.1943).

For a more detailed consideration and discussion of these matters, see McMahon, Joinder of Parties in Louisiana, 19 La.L.Rev. 1 (1958).

One great difference in the law of civilian and Anglo-American jurisdictions necessarily produced differences in results in the application of the rules relating to necessary and indispensable parties. The only similarity between the common law joint obligation and the joint obligation of Louisiana law is the name. Under Anglo-American law, the obligation in favor of joint obligees may be enforced only by the joint obligees collectively, hence all are indispensable parties to an action to enforce the obligation. The full obligation may be enforced against any joint obligor, hence the interests of these obligors is separable. But to avoid a multiplicity of actions, either against the other joint obligors, or by one against others to enforce contribution, it is highly desirable that all be joined as defendants in an action to enforce the obligation, if feasible. Hence, they are characterized as necessary parties. The joint obligation of Louisiana, the conjoint obligation of the civil law, is a divisible and not a collective obligation; each joint obligee may recover only his proportional part of the obligation; and each joint obligor is liable only for his proportional part of the obligation. Hence, while all joint obligees or obligors are proper parties to an action to enforce the obligation, heretofore they have been regarded as neither indispensable nor necessary parties, and have been permitted to sue or be sued singly. This leads to one further procedural difference between the joint and several obligation of the common law and the solidary obligation of the civil law. Under the common law, the creditor may elect to sue joint and several obligors either severally or jointly, but he may not sue some jointly and others severally. Under Louisiana law, the creditor may sue one or more, but need not sue all, of the solidary obligors. These differences in the two systems of law lead to important differences in the application of the rules of necessary and indispensable parties. The subject is discussed in 14 La.L.Rev. 828 (1954).

Art. 641. Compulsory joinder; indispensable parties

Indispensable parties to an action are those whose interests in the subject matter are so interrelated, and would be so directly affected by the judgment, that a complete and equitable adjudication of the controversy cannot be made unless they are joined in the action.

Art. 641

No adjudication of an action can be made unless all indispensable parties are joined therein.

Source: New.

Cross Reference: Art. 771.

Comments

(a) See Preliminary Statement to this Chapter.

(b) No attempt has as yet been made by any Louisiana case to define or delimit indispensable parties. This article accords with the leading case of Shields v. Barrow, 17 How. 130, 15 L.Ed. 158 (1854). The latter has been followed consistently by the United States Supreme Court: Barney v. Baltimore City, 6 Wall. 280, 18 L. Ed. 825 (1868); Waterman v. Canal-Louisiana Bank & Trust Co., 215 U.S. 33, 30 S.Ct. 10, 54 L.Ed. 80 (1909); Niles-Bement-Pond Co. v. Iron Moulders Union, 254 U.S. 77, 41 S.Ct. 39, 65 L.Ed. 145 (1920); and in the lower federal courts. See 3 Moore's Federal Practice (2d ed.) 2150 (1948); 2 Barron & Holtzoff, Federal Practice and Procedure 52 et seq. (1950).

(c) The second paragraph accords with the federal cases cited *supra* and with the jurisprudence of Louisiana. Ashbey v. Ashbey, 41 La.Ann. 138, 5 So. 546 (1899); Succession of Todd, 165 La. 453, 115 So. 653 (1928); and cases cited in McMahon (1956 Supp.) 73, n. 74.4.

(d) See, also, Comments under Art. 642, *infra*.

Art. 642. Same; necessary parties

Necessary parties to an action are those whose interests in the subject matter are separable and would not be directly affected by the judgment if they were not before the court, but whose joinder would be necessary for a complete adjudication of the controversy.

An adjudication of an action may be made even if all necessary parties are not joined therein, but when timely objection is made to the nonjoinder of a necessary party the court shall require his joinder if he is subject to its jurisdiction.

Source: New.

Cross Reference: Art. 771.

Comments

(a) See Preliminary Statement to this Chapter.

(b) The Louisiana cases thus far have not attempted to define and delimit necessary parties, but the first paragraph of this article accords with the authorities cited in Comment (b) of Art. 641, *supra*.

(c) The second paragraph of this article accords with the Louisiana jurisprudence. See Reed v. Warren, 172 La. 1082, 136 So. 59 (1931); Pierce v. Robertson, 190 La. 377, 182 So. 544 (1938); Neal v. Hall, 28 So.2d 131 (La.App.1946).

(d) See, also, Comments under Arts. 644, 697, 698, *infra*.

Art. 643. Same; necessary parties; joint and solidary obligees and obligors

All joint obligees are necessary parties to an action to enforce a joint right, and all joint obligors are necessary parties to an action to enforce a joint obligation.

One or more solidary obligees may sue to enforce a solidary right, and one or more solidary obligors may be sued to enforce a solidary obligation, without the necessity of joining all others in the action.

Source: New.

Cross Reference: Art. 771.

Comments

(a) A change in the procedural law is made by the first paragraph of this article with respect to joint obligees and joint obligors. The pertinent language is declaratory of what was once the law of this state. Formerly, all joint obligees had to join in an action to enforce a joint right, Alling v. Woodruff, 16 La.Ann. 6 (1861); and all joint obligors were required to be joined in an action to enforce a joint obligation. Civil Code Art. 2085. However, both aspects of the rule have been changed. Hincks v. Converse, 38 La.Ann. 873 (1886) overruled Alling v. Woodruff, *supra*; and held that, since a joint obligation in Louisiana was divisible and a joint obligee could recover only his virile share of the obligation, it was not necessary that all join in an action to enforce a joint right. La. Act 103, Ex.Sess. of 1870, § 2 adopted a rule diametrically opposite to that enunciated in Art. 2085 of the Civil Code, and repealed the latter by implication.

There is no theoretical base which requires the joinder of all joint obligees and joint obligors in Louisiana, as there is under Anglo-American law. Under the latter, the idea of collectivity requires the joinder. In Louisiana, the obligation is divisible and not collective. See Preliminary Statement to this Chapter.

There is, however, one very compelling practical reason supporting the rule of this article, and one which makes a strong appeal to any sound system of administering justice. The required joinder avoids a multiplicity of action; and in the case of the enforcement of the joint right, prevents the judicial harassment of the obligor. These are the bases on which the supreme court, in Reed v. Warren,

172 La. 1082, 136 So. 59 (1931) and its progeny, rested the jurisprudential rule that all beneficiaries suing to recover damages for the wrongful death of a relative were necessary parties plaintiff to an action to recover any of such damages. The change effected by the above article is not unduly technical or burdensome, since a necessary party who is not subject to the jurisdiction of the court need not be joined. Further, a defendant is not required to plead the nonjoinder of a necessary party unless he wishes to do so; and the court cannot notice the defect on its own motion.

(b) No change in the procedural law is made by the second paragraph of this article. All solidary obligees are not necessary parties to an action to enforce a solidary right, and all solidary obligors are not necessary parties to an action to enforce a solidary obligation. One or more may sue or be sued; and those not joined are not necessary parties. See Breedlove v. Nicolet, 7 Pet. 413, 8 L. Ed. 731 (1833).

Art. 644. Same; joinder of indispensable or necessary party plaintiff who refuses to sue

If an indispensable party, or a necessary party subject to the jurisdiction of the court, who should join as a plaintiff refuses or fails to do so, he may be joined as a defendant and required to assert his rights in the action or be precluded thereafter from asserting them.

Source: New; cf. Comments following.
Cross Reference: Art. 771.

Comments

(a) This article codifies the rule suggested in Reed v. Warren, 172 La. 1082, 136 So. 59 (1931).

(b) Since the action may proceed without a necessary party who is not subject to the jurisdiction of the court, and his joinder cannot be required, under Art. 642, *supra*, no problem is presented by the rare case where a nonresident who is a necessary party plaintiff refuses or fails to sue.

(c) The equally rare case where a nonresident who is an indispensable party plaintiff refuses or fails to sue presents much more of a problem. Some doubt exists as to whether such a nonresident may be joined as a defendant. The majority of the Council, however, was of the opinion that in such a case he may be joined, and served through an attorney at law appointed by the court to represent him. The basis of this opinion is that the incorporeal right which should be asserted in the action is a *res*; and since the alleged obligor is subject to the jurisdiction of the Louisiana court, the *res* has a situs in this state, and a Louisiana court would have jurisdiction to compel the nonresident to assert his right in the pending action. *Cf.* Herbert v. American Soc. of Composers, etc., 210 La. 240, 26 So.2d 732 (1946). A contrary view might make it impossible for the plaintiff in the pending suit to enforce his right anywhere.

(d) See, also, Comments under Art. 645, *infra*.

Art. 645. Same; pleading nonjoinder of indispensable or necessary party

The failure to join an indispensable party to an action may be pleaded in the peremptory exception, or may be noticed by the trial or appellate court on its own motion.

The failure to join a necessary party to an action may be pleaded only in the dilatory exception.

Source: New.

Cross Reference: Art. 771.

Comments

(a) Both paragraphs of this article accord with Louisiana jurisprudence. See the cases cited and discussed in the Preliminary Statement to this Chapter.

(b) The only change which this article makes with respect to indispensable parties is to provide workable procedure for raising the issue, and thus avoid procedural difficulties presented by the customary practice in the past of raising this issue through the dilatory exception of nonjoinder of parties. Since a lack of indispensable parties may be noticed by the court on its own motion, there can be no waiver of the objection by the defendant, and the issue should be raised through the peremptory exception.

(c) If either the peremptory or the dilatory exception is sustained because of the failure to join an indispensable or a necessary party plaintiff, the plaintiff may amend his petition and join him as a defendant, should he refuse to join as a plaintiff. See Art. 644, *supra*, and Comments thereunder.

Art. 646. Same; amendment of petition to join indispensable or necessary party

When the failure to join an indispensable party is pleaded successfully in or noticed by a trial court, the latter may permit amendment of the petition so as to make him a party, and may reopen the case if it has been submitted and further evidence is necessary. When such failure is pleaded successfully in or noticed by an appellate court, the latter may remand the case for such amendment and further evidence.

Art. 646.

When the failure to join a necessary party is pleaded successfully, the court shall permit an amendment of the petition to join him.

Source: New.

Cross Reference: Art. 771.

Comments

(a) See Preliminary Statement to this Chapter.

(b) Although Louisiana cases may be found where the courts dismissed the action because of a failure to join a necessary or indispensable party, whenever the right to amend has been requested of the courts, they have granted it to permit plaintiff to effect joinder. Even when the defect has been noticed by the appellate courts, they have remanded the cases to permit the necessary joinder. See cases cited in McMahon 415, n. 74.

(c) The right to reopen a submitted case to permit the reception of further evidence accords with the liberality of procedure applied in recent years. *Cf.* Succession of Robinson, 186 La. 389, 172 So. 429 (1937).

Art. 647. Permissive joinder governed by rules of cumulation of actions

The permissive joinder of two or more plaintiffs or defendants in the same suit is governed by the rules regulating the cumulation of actions provided in Articles 463 through 465.

Source: New.

Cross Reference: Art. 771.

Comment

Under the procedural theory of civilian jurisdictions the joinder of a plurality of plaintiffs or of defendants, or of both, in the same suit is regarded as the union of plural actions in the same suit, of separate actions by each plaintiff against each defendant. Hence, the subject is regulated by the rules relating to the cumulation of actions.

CHAPTER 2. PARTIES PLAINTIFF

Art.
681. Real and actual interest required.
682. Individuals having procedural capacity.
683. Unemancipated minor.
684. Mental incompetent; interdict.

Art.
685. Succession.
686. Marital community.
687. Person doing business under trade name.
688. Partnership.
689. Unincorporated association.
690. Domestic corporation or insurer.
691. Foreign corporation; foreign or alien insurance corporation.
692. Corporation or partnership in receivership or liquidation.
693. Insurer in receivership.
694. Agent.
695. Same; wife as agent of husband.
696. Pledgor and pledgee.
697. Subrogor and subrogee.
698. Assignor and assignee.
699. Trust estate.
700. Authority or qualification of plaintiff suing in representative capacity.

Art. 681. Real and actual interest required

Except as otherwise provided by law, an action can be brought only by a person having a real and actual interest which he asserts.

Source: C.P. Art. 15; *cf.* Fed. Rule 17(a).

Cross Reference: Art. 771.

Comments

(a) This article expresses only a general rule with respect to a litigant who seeks to enforce his own right, and clear exceptions thereto are afforded by all of the rules respecting a plaintiff who sues in a representative capacity. The exception in the first clause of this article avoids a conflict between it and Arts. 683, 684, 692 through 695, and 700, *infra*.

(b) This article also serves as the basis of the peremptory exception urging the objection that the plaintiff has no right of action. See the cases cited in McMahon 455–459 (1956 Supp. 75 76).

(c) See, also, Comments under Art. 698, *infra*.

Art. 682. Individuals having procedural capacity

A competent major and a competent emancipated minor have the procedural capacity to sue.

Source: C.P. Arts. 102, 110; C.C. Arts. 867, 370, 371, 382, 385.

Cross Reference: Art. 771.

Art. 682

Comments

(a) This article makes no change in the law.

(b) The terms "competent major" and "emancipated minor" include a married woman, now completely emancipated by R.S. 9:101–9:105. A married woman, however, enforces only her own right, *i. e.*, a right of her separate estate; and she may not sue to enforce a community right, unless authorized by her husband. *Cf.* Arts. 686 and 695, *infra*.

(c) An emancipated minor, regardless of the manner in which he is emancipated, has the procedural capacity to enforce his rights judicially. Beauchamp v. Whittington, 10 La.Ann. 646 (1855); Richardson v. Richardson, 38 La.Ann. 639 (1886).

Art. 375 of the Civil Code, providing that "the minor who is emancipated otherwise than by marriage, cannot appear in courts of justice without the assistance of a curator ad litem" was repealed impliedly by Art. 958 of the 1870 Code of Practice. Richardson v. Richardson, *supra*. *Cf.* Beauchamp v. Whittington, *supra*. Consequently, it is recommended that C.C. Art. 375 be repealed expressly.

(d) See, also, Comments under Art. 4394, *infra*.

Art. 683. Unemancipated minor

An unemancipated minor does not have the procedural capacity to sue.

Except as otherwise provided in Article 4431, the tutor appointed by a court of this state is the proper plaintiff to sue to enforce a right of an unemancipated minor, when (1) one or both of the parents are dead, (2) the parents are divorced or judicially separated, or (3) the minor is an illegitimate child.

The father, as administrator of the estate of his minor child, is the proper plaintiff to sue to enforce a right of an unemancipated minor who is the legitimate issue of living parents who are not divorced or judicially separated. The mother, as the administratrix of the estate of her minor child, is the proper plaintiff in such an action, when the father is a mental incompetent or an absentee.

Source: C.P. Arts. 108, 109; C.C. Arts. 157, 221, 246, 250.

Cross Reference: Art. 771.

Comments

(a) This article effects no change in the law.

(b) The exception at the beginning of the second paragraph avoids a conflict with the article which recognizes the right of a

Tit. 3 PARTIES PLAINTIFF Art. 684

tutor or guardian of a nonresident minor appointed by a court of another state to act in Louisiana without the necessity of appointment and qualification by a court of this state. See Art. 4431, *infra*. Under this article and Art. 4073, *infra*, a provisional tutor may sue to enforce a right of an unemancipated minor.

(c) See, also, Comments under Art. 681, *supra*, and Art. 684, *infra*.

Art. 684. Mental incompetent; interdict

A mental incompetent does not have the procedural capacity to sue.

Except as otherwise provided in Articles 4431, 4554, and 4557, the curator is the proper plaintiff to sue to enforce a right of an interdict.

Source: C.P. Arts. 108, 109; C.C. Art. 422.

Cross Reference: Art. 771.

Comments

(a) The above article does not change the law.

(b) The exception at the beginning of the second paragraph avoids a conflict with the articles recognizing: (1) the right of a guardian of a nonresident incompetent appointed by a court of another state to act in Louisiana without the necessity of appointment and qualification by a court of this state; and (2) the right of an interdict to sue to terminate the interdiction. See Arts. 4431 and 4554, *infra*.

A mental incompetent who is a minor is under the tutelage of his father, as administrator of the estate of the minor, or of a tutor, until he reaches the age of majority. There is neither a need nor a possibility of having him interdicted until he becomes a major. During his minority the proper plaintiff to sue to enforce his rights, and the proper defendant to be sued to enforce obligations against him, is his father, as administrator of the estate of the minor, or his tutor. Art. 389, Civil Code; Kerwin v. Hibernia Ins. Co., 35 La. Ann. 33 (1883). See Art. 683, *supra*, and Art. 733, *infra*.

(c) This article is declaratory of the prior procedural rules that a mental incompetent has no procedural capacity to sue; and the proper plaintiff to enforce the rights of a mental incompetent is the curator appointed after his interdiction.

Though a mental incompetent not interdicted has no procedural capacity to sue, if the defendant does not timely except thereto, the judgment rendered is not void, but only voidable. *Cf.* Vance v. Ellerbe, 150 La. 388, 90 So. 735 (1922) The defendant may protect himself in such a case by challenging the procedural capacity of the plaintiff through the timely filing of the dilatory exception. See Arts. 926 and 928, *infra*.

(d) See, also, Comments under Art. 681, *supra,* and Art. 733, *infra.*

Art. 685. Succession

Except as otherwise provided by law, the succession representative appointed by a court of this state is the proper plaintiff to sue to enforce a right of the deceased or of his succession, while the latter is under administration. The heirs or legatees of the deceased, whether present or represented in the state or not, need not be joined as parties, whether the action is personal, real, or mixed.

Source: New; cf. C.P. Art. 111; C.C. Arts. 1049, 1676.

Cross Reference: Art. 771.

Comments

(a) The exception in the first sentence of this article avoids a conflict with R.S. 13:3331, permitting the administrator or executor appointed or confirmed by a court of another state to sue in the courts of this state for damages for the wrongful death of the deceased, without qualifying as ancillary administrator or executor.

(b) This article is declaratory of the jurisprudence so far as it recognizes the right of an administrator alone to institute and prosecute a personal action. Fluker v. Kent, 27 La.Ann. 37 (1875); Labit v. Perry, 28 La.Ann. 591 (1876); Woodward v. Thomas, 38 La.Ann. 591 (1886); Gurley v. City of New Orleans, 124 La. 390, 50 So. 411 (1909). It is similarly declaratory of the jurisprudence to the extent that it recognizes the right of an executor alone to institute and prosecute a personal action. Hicky v. Sharp, 4 La. 335 (1832); Keane v. Goldsmith, Haber & Co., 14 La.Ann. 349 (1859); Eskridge v. Farrar, 30 La.Ann. 718 (1878); Smith v. Sinnott, 44 La.Ann. 51, 10 So. 413 (1892); Benton v. Benton, 106 La. 99, 30 So. 137 (1901).

Prior jurisprudential rules with respect to the right of an administrator alone to bring a real action to enforce a right of the succession were neither rational nor workable. There was authority for the proposition that when the succession owed debts, the administrator had procedural capacity to institute and prosecute a real action in behalf of the succession, without any necessity of joining the heirs. Woodward v. Thomas, *supra.* See also, Pauline v. Hubert, 14 La.Ann. 161 (1859); and Succession of Delaneuville v. Duhé, 114 La. 62, 38 So. 20 (1905). On the other hand, it had been held that where there was no proof that the succession owed debts, the administrator had no procedural capacity to bring a real action in behalf of the succession without joining the heirs. Ledoux v. Burton, 30 La.Ann. 576 (1878); Succession of Preston v. Brady,

125 La. 535, 51 So. 579 (1910); Griffith's Estate v. Glaze's Heirs, 199 La. 800, 7 So.2d 62 (1942). And, in at least one case, it was held that even when the succession owed debts, if it was solvent the administrator alone could not bring the real action. Bull v. Andrus, 137 La. 982, 68 So. 799 (1915).

The prior jurisprudence is in a similarly unsatisfactory state with respect to the right of an executor alone to institute and prosecute a real action. See Executors of Hart v. Boni, 6 La. 97 (1833); Smith v. Sinnot, *supra;* and Benton v. Benton, *supra.*

The lack of any rational basis for these different rules is demonstrated rather convincingly. Under Civil Code Art. 1049, the rules which govern the curator of a vacant succession apply equally to the administrator. Woodward v. Thomas, *supra.* Yet, the curator of a vacant succession was expressly empowered by positive law to bring a real action to enforce a right of the succession, whether it owed debts or not. Causey v. Opelousas-St. Landry Securities Co., 187 La. 659, 175 So. 448 (1937).

Both succession practice and succession theory have changed to a very considerable extent since the adoption of the 1825 Code of Practice and Civil Code. Prior to the advent of inheritance taxes, there was absolutely no necessity for the judicial opening of a succession which owed no debts, where all of the heirs were competent majors. Under the tax acts, however, any succession of any consequence must be opened judicially. When it is opened it invariably has debts—if nothing more, for the court costs and attorney's fees incurred in opening the succession. Years ago, the only reason for having an administrator appointed was to pay the debts of the deceased; hence the administrator represented the creditors rather than the heirs. Today there are many reasons for administering a succession, including tax avoidance or reduction. In this code the succession representative, regardless of his title, represents both creditors, and heirs or legatees; and he has been granted powers to act for the benefit of the heirs or legatees, primarily if not exclusively. See Arts. 3198, 3211, 3221, and 3223 through 3228, *infra.*

In the light of these developments the prior jurisprudential rules on the subject have become anachronistic. There is no reason today why a succession representative alone should not be able to enforce judicially all rights of the deceased, or of his succession, whether the action is personal, real or mixed. This article accomplishes this result, and the language employed is emphatic enough to indicate clearly the legislative intent to overrule all cases to the contrary.

(c) See, also, Comments under Arts. 734, 3196, 3246, *infra.*

Art. 686. Marital community

The husband is the proper plaintiff, during the existence of the marital community, to sue to enforce a right of the community.

Where doubt exists whether the right sought to be enforced belongs to the marital community or to the separate estate of the wife, the husband and wife may sue in the alternative to enforce the right.

Source: New; *cf.* C.C. Art. 2404.

Cross Reference: Art. 771.

Comments

(a) The first paragraph of this article is declaratory of the settled jurisprudence. See cases cited in McMahon 147–150 (1956 Supp. 30–33).

(b) No decided cases squarely support the rule of the second paragraph, although in principle it accords with the jurisprudential rules on alternative pleading. *Cf.* Wells v. Davidson, 149 So. 246 (La.App.1933); and see cases cited in McMahon 207–213 (1956 Supp. 40, 41).

One of the greatest reproaches to the administration of civil justice in Louisiana has been the manner in which our courts have permitted defendants to invoke substantive rules of community property to defeat the enforcement of the rights of husband and wife. The cases are collected and criticized in McMahon (1956 Supp.) 30, 31. It may be extremely difficult prior to suit to determine whether a particular right to be enforced belongs to the paraphernal estate of the wife or to the community estate. See State ex rel. Fields v. Rapides Parish School Board, 227 La. 290, 79 So.2d 312 (1955). Even when this matter can be determined prior to suit, the slightest inadvertence on the part of counsel for plaintiff in the submission of his proof may permit the defendant to defeat the action. See Howell v. Harris, 18 So.2d 668 (La. App.1944).

The substantive rules of community property are legal rules of accounting between the community and separate estates which usually are of no concern to the defendant. The only justification for procedural rules on the subject are: (1) a recognition of the husband as head and master of the community to prevent any unauthorized assertion by the wife of a community right; (2) protection of the rights of the forced heirs and creditors of the husband; and (3) protection of a defendant against double recovery. Time and time again the courts have permitted a defendant, completely protected against double recovery, to defeat a wife's suit when the evidence technically showed that the right sought to be enforced by the wife, with the husband's approval, was a community right; or when the evidence failed to rebut the presumption that it was a community right.

Tit. 3   PARTIES PLAINTIFF   Art. 688

The alternative pleading sanctioned by the second paragraph of this article affords an effective solution of the problems in this area.

(c) See, also, Comments under Art. 682, *supra*, and Art. 735, *infra*.

Art. 687. Person doing business under trade name

A person who does business under a trade name shall sue in his own name to enforce a right created by or arising out of the doing of such business.

Source: New; *cf.* Comment following.

Cross Reference: Art. 771.

Comment

This article is declaratory of the sounder jurisprudence. Wolfe v. Youbert, 45 La.Ann. 1100, 13 So. 806, 21 L.R.A. 772 (1893); In re Pelican Ins. Co. of New Orleans, 47 La.Ann. 935, 17 So. 427 (1895); Smith v. Williams, 152 La. 948, 94 So. 859 (1922); Tyler Co. v. Sutton, 51 So.2d 401 (La.App.1951); Palmer v. Presswood, 81 So.2d 116 (La.App.1955). But see Kent & Co. v. Mojonier, 36 La.Ann. 259 (1884); Rea v. Dow Motor Co., 36 So.2d 750 (La.App. 1948).

Art. 688. Partnership

A partnership has the procedural capacity to sue to enforce its rights in the partnership name, and appears through and is represented by an authorized partner.

Source: New.

Cross Reference: Art. 771.

Comments

(a) Under the civil law a partnership, regardless of the type thereof, is a legal entity, and may sue and be sued in the partnership name. Key v. Box, 14 La.Ann. 497 (1859); Wolf v. New Orleans Tailor-Made Pants Co., 52 La.Ann. 1357, 27 So. 893 (1900); Hayes Machinery Co. v. Eastham, 147 La. 347, 84 So. 898 (1920); American Photo Player Co. v. Simon, 151 La. 708, 92 So. 307 (1922); Snyder v. Davison, 172 La. 274, 134 So. 89 (1931); First Nat. Bank in Gibsland v. Knighton Bros., 16 La.App. 407, 134 So. 706 (1931). *Cf.* Empire Rice Mill Co. v. K. & E. Neumond, 199 F. 800 (D.C.La.1912).

(b) Under the prior cases, the partnership had to appear through and be represented by all of its partners, whose names and domiciles had to be listed in the petition. This article relaxes the rule, and permits a partnership to appear through and be represented by one or more of the partners. This change was made for two reasons: (1) the increased number of partnerships with numerous partners, which makes it difficult to secure the assent of all of the partners and to list their names and domiciles in the petition; and (2) the danger that the prior rule might subject partners in commendam to liability for all of the debts of the partnership.

(c) The partner or partners through whom the partnership appears, and who represent the partnership, must either have general authority under the articles of partnership or otherwise to cause the institution of the suit, or must be specially authorized to do so by the other partners.

Art. 689. Unincorporated association

An unincorporated association has the procedural capacity to sue to enforce its rights in its own name, and appears through and is represented by its president or other authorized officer.

Source: New; *cf.* Fed. Rule 17(b).

Cross Reference: Art. 771.

Comments

(a) This article changes the procedural law. Heretofore, an unincorporated association had no procedural capacity to enforce its rights judicially, since it was not a legal entity; and such a right had to be enforced by an action brought by all of the individual members of the association. Civil Code Art. 446; Soller v. Mouton, 3 La.Ann. 541 (1848); Workingmen's Accommodation Bank v. Converse, 29 La.Ann. 369 (1877); Anti-Vice Committee of Shreveport v. Simon, 151 La. 494, 91 So. 851 (1922); Klein v. Anderson, 4 Orl.App. 262 (1907). See also, Sheridan v. Thibodaux Benevolent Ass'n, 19 La.App. 762, 134 So. 360 (1931).

(b) Even though this article prevents the individual members of an unincorporated association from enforcing judicially a right of the association as long as it continues in existence, this effects no injury, since the association may sue in its own name.

(c) This article recognizes the authority of the president to authorize the institution and prosecution of a suit in the name of the association and to represent the association in all cases. It further permits similar action by any other officer of the association who is specially authorized to do so by the members.

Art. 690. Domestic corporation or insurer

Except as otherwise provided in Articles 692 and 693, a domestic corporation, and a domestic insurer, has the procedural capacity to sue to enforce its rights in the corporate name.

Source: C.P. Art. 112; C.C. Art. 432; R.S. 12:12(B) (3), 12:109, 12:210(A).

Cross Reference: Art. 771.

Comments

(a) This article makes no change in the procedural law.

(b) For the definition of "insurer", see Art. 5251, *infra*.

Art. 691. Foreign corporation; foreign or alien insurance corporation

Except as otherwise provided in Articles 692 and 693, a foreign corporation, and a foreign or alien insurance corporation, has the procedural capacity to sue to enforce its rights in the corporate name.

Source: C.P. Art. 112; C.C. Art. 432; R.S. 12:210(A).

Cross Reference: Art. 771.

Comments

(a) This article effects no change in the law.

(b) For a definition of "insurer", see Art. 5251, *infra*. Not all foreign or alien insurers are insurance corporations. For the rules as to the proper parties plaintiffs to enforce the rights of reciprocal insurers, and Lloyd's plan insurers, see R.S. 22:433, 22:492.

(c) A foreign corporation doing business in this state may not sue in a court of this state on an intrastate transaction until it is licensed to do business here, and has paid all taxes due the state. R.S. 12:211.

Art. 692. Corporation or partnership in receivership or liquidation

Except as otherwise provided by law, the receiver or liquidator appointed for a domestic or foreign corporation or partnership by a court of this state is the proper plaintiff to sue to enforce a right of the corporation or partnership, or of its receiver or liquidator. These rules apply whether, under the law of its domicile, the existence of the corporation or partnership continues or is terminated.

The receiver or liquidator may institute and prosecute any action without special authorization from the court which appointed him.

Source: New.

Cross References: Arts. 690, 691, 771.

Comments

(a) "Corporation" as used in this article does not include an insurance corporation. See Art. 693, *infra*.

(b) This article is largely declaratory of the Louisiana jurisprudence on the subjects of the receivership and liquidation of corporations, and the liquidation of partnerships. It makes a few changes therein, which are discussed in the following comments.

(c) Receiverships of corporations are generally classified as being of two types: equity and statutory. The first type derives its name from the fact that originally the receiver was appointed by the chancellor under his broad equity powers. It is the type used for the receivership of business corporations, where continued solvency is not a requisite to the continued corporate existence and there is no forfeiture of the corporate charter on the appointment of the receiver, no termination of the corporate existence, and the corporation retains legal title to all of its property during the receivership. The equity receiver merely acts as the agent or officer of the appointing court in the operation of the corporation. The equity receiver, who has no legal title to the corporate property, may sue to enforce a corporate right only if he is given general authority to sue either by statute or by an order of the appointing court, or is given special authorization to sue in the particular case by the appointing court.

The statutory receivership, as its name implies, is a creature of statute, and usually is employed for the liquidation of banks, insurance companies, and other corporations where corporate continuance requires solvency. Generally, under the various applicable statutes, the charters of these corporations are forfeited by the adjudication of insolvency, and legal title to all of their property is vested in the receivers or liquidators appointed by the courts. Since the statutory receiver or liquidator usually has legal title to all of the corporate property, in such cases he is the only person who can enforce judicially a right of the defunct corporation.

Whether the receiver or liquidator has procedural capacity to sue in a jurisdiction other than the one in which he was appointed usually turns on the type of receivership. The statutory receiver or liquidator who has legal title to the corporate property may sue in any other state without appointment or qualification by a court of the latter, in the absence of contrary statute. The equity receiver who has no legal title to the corporate property is merely the creature of the appointing court, whose authority need not be recognized beyond the territorial limits of the state in which he was appointed. Hence, his authority to sue in another state depends on whether the courts of the latter will recognize his authority through comity. The majority of American jurisdictions do not; and in these, the primary receiver must be appointed and qualified in ancillary proceedings brought in a court of the second state, before he may judicially enforce a corporate right therein. An increasing number in the minority of states, either through judicial comity or through statute requiring comity, recognize the authority of a receiver appointed by a court of another state, and permit him to sue without appointment and qualification in ancillary proceedings in the second state. For a complete discussion of these principles, see High on Receivers (4th ed.) 237 *et seq.* (1910); 8 Thompson on Corporations (3d ed.) 539 *et seq.* (1927); 16 Fletcher Cyclopedia Corporations (Perm. ed.) 322 *et seq.* (1942); and McMahon 158 *et seq.*

(d) Louisiana recognizes and applies the general principles discussed above. Michel v. Southern Insurance Co., 128 La. 562, 54 So. 1010, Ann.Cas.1912C, 810 (1911); Levy v. Union Indemnity Co., 146 So. 182 (La.App.1933). See also, Helme v. Littlejohn, 12 La.Ann. 298 (1857); Lichtenstein Bros. & Co. v. Gillett Bros., 37 La.Ann. 522 (1885); and Texas Mutual Insurance Co. v. Stutes, 77 So.2d 43 (La.App.1954). *Cf.* Owens v. Allied Underwriters, 207 La. 437, 21 So.2d 490 (1945); Mobley v. Hibernia Bank & Trust Co., 19 La.App. 414, 140 So. 251 (1932); and Tangipahoa Bank & Trust Co. v. Guwang, 15 So.2d 148, 616 (La.App.1943).

Louisiana follows the majority view that an equity receiver appointed by a court of another state is a mere creature of the appointing court, whose authority does not extend beyond the confines of the state in which he was appointed, and who must be appointed ancillary receiver by a Louisiana court before suing in the courts of this state. Mobley v. Hibernia Bank & Trust Co., *supra.* See also, Helme v. Littlejohn, *supra*; and Lichtenstein Bros. & Co. v. Gillett Bros., *supra*. This rule is not changed. Citizens of Louisiana having a claim against the corporation should not be forced to enforce their claims in the primary receivership in another state, when the corporation has assets here which could be distributed by an ancillary receiver in satisfaction of their claims.

For similar reasons, the above article changes the rule permitting a statutory receiver or liquidator appointed by a court of another state to sue in Louisiana without appointment and qualification by a Louisiana court. This article requires that the action be brought by the ancillary receiver or liquidator appointed by a Louisiana court.

(e) In so far as this article applies to partnerships, it accords with Helme v. Littlejohn, *supra;* and Lichtenstein Bros. & Co. v. Gillett Bros., *supra.*

No Louisiana statute authorizes a receiver or liquidator appointed by a court of this state to institute and prosecute such actions as he may deem necessary, with the result that such authority must be conferred either generally in the order appointing the receiver, or specially from time to time as the need for a suit by the receiver arises. These orders are perfunctory, invariably granted on request, and the necessity for obtaining them is a waste of the time of the appointing court.

The second paragraph of this article, which confers such authority on all receivers and liquidators, serves two purposes: (1) it saves the time of the appointing court; and (2) it provides legal justification for the rule that an equity receiver is the proper plaintiff to enforce a corporate right in all cases.

(f) The exception at the beginning of this article avoids a conflict with two important Louisiana statutes:

(1) The Business Corporation Act provides for the judicial liquidation of business corporations, either judicially or nonjudicially. R.S. 12:56, 12:57. The corporation is not dissolved until after the liquidation proceedings have been completed, and the proper certificate thereof is furnished the Secretary of State. R.S. 12:62. The statute expressly provides that, in the nonjudicial liquidation, a suit to enforce a corporate right is to be brought in the name of the corporation. R.S. 12:57(A) (1). It is silent with respect to the judicial liquidation; but the same rule should apply, both by analogy and from the fact that the corporation retains legal title to all of its property.

(2) Under the statutes governing the liquidation of state banks, it has been held that the bank's corporate existence is not terminated on the adjudication of insolvency, and that hence a suit to enforce a right of the bank may be brought either by the liquidators, or by the bank through the liquidators. Tangipahoa Bank & Trust Co. v. Guwang, 15 So.2d 148, 616 (La.App.1943). *Cf.* R.S. 6:383, 6:384, 6:397.

(g) See, also, Comments under Art. 681, *supra*, and Art. 740, *infra*.

Art. 693. Insurer in receivership

The receiver appointed by a court of this state for a domestic insurer is the proper plaintiff to sue to enforce a right of the domestic insurer, or of its receiver.

Except as otherwise provided by law, the ancillary receiver appointed by a court of this state for a foreign or alien insurer is the proper plaintiff to sue to enforce a right of the foreign or alien insurer, or of its domiciliary or ancillary receiver.

As used herein and in Article 741, "receiver" includes liquidator, rehabilitator, and conservator.

Source: R.S. 22:736, 22:757, 22:758.

Cross References: Arts. 690, 691, 771.

Comments

(a) For a definition of "insurer", see Art. 5251, *infra*.

(b) The exception in the second paragraph avoids a conflict with the Uniform Insurers Liquidation Law, R.S. 22:757 *et seq*. Under the latter, the Insurance Commissioner shall provoke the appointment of an ancillary receiver if (1) there are sufficient assets in the state to justify the appointment; and (2) ten or more resident creditors petition him to provoke such appointment. Unless an ancillary receiver is appointed, the domiciliary receiver may sue to recover the assets of the insurer in this state. R.S. 22:758 (B), (C).

(c) See, also, Comments under Art. 681, *supra*, and Art. 741, *infra*.

Art. 694. Agent

An agent has the procedural capacity to sue to enforce a right of his principal, when specially authorized to do so.

For all procedural purposes, the principal is considered the plaintiff in such an action. The defendant may assert any defense available against the principal, and may enforce his rights against the principal in a reconventional demand.

Source: New; *cf.* Comments following.

Cross Reference: Art. 771.

Comments

(a) This article makes no change in the law.

(b) Contrary to the rule obtaining at common law, in civilian jurisdictions the agent for a disclosed principal may sue to enforce the rights of the latter. Eggleston v. Colfax, 4 Mart. (N.S.) 481 (La.1826); Frazier v. Willcox, 4 Rob. 517 (La.1843); Frazier v. Dick, 5 Rob. 249 (La.1843); Ricard v. Harrison, 19 La.Ann. 181 (1867); Willard v. Lugenbuhl, 24 La.Ann. 18 (1872); Smith v. Atlas Cordage Co., 41 La.Ann. 1, 5 So. 413 (1888); Casanas v. Audubon Hotel Co., 124 La. 786, 50 So. 714 (1909); Reisz v. Kansas City Southern R. Co., 148 La. 929, 88 So. 120 (1921); Pearson v. Louisiana & Arkansas Ry. Co., 226 La. 834, 77 So.2d 411 (1954). To institute and prosecute the action to enforce the rights of his principal, however, the agent must be specially authorized to do so by the principal. Frazier v. Willcox, *supra*; Wallace, Lithgow & Co. v. Byrne, 17 La.Ann. 8 (1865); Casanas v. Audubon Hotel Co., *supra*. *Cf.* Art. 320 of the 1870 Code of Practice.

(c) The second paragraph sets forth rules which the courts would apply in subsequent cases if none were provided by positive law. *Cf.* Smith v. Atlas Cordage Co., 41 La.Ann. 1, 5 So. 413 (1888). A declaration thereof in this Code, however, serves very useful purposes. When the principal is an indispensable or necessary party plaintiff, this article makes it clear that he is considered as being joined in an action brought by his agent to enforce a right of the principal. The last sentence precludes any possibility of the principal sidestepping an anticipated defense or reconventional demand by having the suit filed by the agent.

(d) See, also, Comments under Art. 681, *supra*.

Art. 695. Same; wife as agent of husband

A wife, as the agent of her husband, may sue to enforce a right of his separate estate, or a right of the marital community, when specially authorized to do so by her husband.

Source: C.C. Art. 1787.

Cross Reference: Art. 771.

Comments

This article employs express language to accomplish what was sought to be accomplished in the source provision. The source of this article expressly authorizes the wife to act as the agent of her husband. It does not spell out the right of the wife to sue as agent to enforce a community right, and hence does not completely remove all doubt thereof. The earlier cases expressly recognized the right of the wife to act as agent of the community when specially authorized to do so by the husband. Succession of Brown, Mann. Unrep.Cas. 216 (La.1877–1880); Perfection Garment Co. v. Lanasa, 7 La.App. 31 (1931). Yet despite this, it had been held that the wife could not sue as agent to enforce a community right. Mitchell v. Dixie Ice Co., 157 La. 383, 102 So. 497 (1924). The point is considered in Oppenheim, The Significance of Recent Louisiana Legislation Concerning the Marital Community—Louisiana Acts 49 and 286 of 1944, 19 Tul.L.Rev. 200, 209 (1944); and McMahon 30, 31 (Supp. 1956). This article completely spells out the procedural capacity of the wife to sue as agent to enforce a community right, when authorized to do so by the husband.

See, also, Comments under Arts. 681, 682, *supra*.

Art. 696. Pledgor and pledgee

The pledgee of a real right, or of a negotiable instrument or other incorporeal right, is the proper plaintiff to sue to enforce the pledged right.

The pledgee may enforce the entire right judicially, unless it is an obligation of the pledgor, in which event it may be enforced only to the extent of the indebtedness secured by the pledge.

Source: New.

Cross Reference: Art. 771.

Comments

(a) The reference to the pledge of a real right gives procedural effect to R.S. 9:4301 *et seq.*, authorizing the pledge of rents, royalties, bonuses, and other payments under mineral leases and contracts.

If the pledgee fails or neglects to enforce the pledged right, the pledgor has a secondary right to enforce it. O'Kelley v. Ferguson, 49 La.Ann. 1230, 22 So. 783 (1897).

(b) The first clause of the second paragraph is declaratory of the positive law and jurisprudence on the subject. The pledgee, however, must pay or account to the pledgor for any amount recovered in excess of the indebtedness secured by the pledge. Civil Code Art. 3170; Mechanics' & Traders' Ins. Co. v. Lozano, 39 La. Ann. 321, 1 So. 608 (1887); Fidelity & Deposit Co. of Maryland v. Johnston, 117 La. 880, 42 So. 357 (1906); Freiler Mercantile Co. v. Chatney, 146 La. 188, 83 So. 436 (1919); Zibilich v. Rouseo, 157 La. 936, 103 So. 269 (1925).

(c) A common security arrangement is for the borrower to secure the loan by a mortgage on his property in an amount larger than the amount borrowed; and to pledge the mortgage note to the lender to secure the payment of the loan. On the maturity of the obligation, the pledgee may judicially enforce the mortgage, but only to the extent of the indebtedness secured by the pledge. Chaffe v. Whitfield, 40 La.Ann. 631, 4 So. 563 (1888); Crowley Bank & Trust Co. v. Hurd, 137 La. 787, 69 So. 175 (1915). See also, Canal Bank & Trust Co. v. Greco, 177 La. 507, 148 So. 693 (1933). The last clause of the second paragraph of this article is declaratory of the rule of these cases.

Art. 697. Subrogor and subrogee

An incorporeal right to which a person has been subrogated, either conventionally or by effect of law, shall be enforced judicially by:

(1) The subrogor and the subrogee, when the subrogation is partial; or

(2) The subrogee, when the entire right is subrogated.

Source: New.

Cross Reference: Art. 771.

Comments

(a) This article provides a workable rule to bring order out of the chaos of the Louisiana jurisprudence on the subject.

(b) The common law originally did not recognize subrogation. Consequently, a subrogated right could be enforced by the subrogee only in equity; and originally in an action at law the action had to be brought by the subrogor. Later, this strict rule was relaxed in cases of total subrogation, and the subrogee was permitted to bring the action in the name of the subrogor, but for the use and benefit of the subrogee. The adoption of code procedure in America, with its requirement that an action be brought by the actual party in interest, served to permit the subrogee to sue in his own name when the subrogation was total; but the prohibition against splitting the cause of action has prevented complete solutions of the various problems presented.

In Louisiana, under Art. 15 of the 1870 Code of Practice, which requires the action to be brought by the person having the real and actual interest, the subrogee should be the proper plaintiff in such cases, at least to the extent of his interest. This rule finds recognition in the jurisprudence. Reisz v. Kansas City Southern R. Co., 148 La. 929, 88 So. 120 (1921); London Guarantee & Acc. Ins. Co. v. Vicksburg, S. & P. R. Co., 153 La. 287, 95 So. 771 (1923). See also, Globe Indemnity Co. v. Toye Bros. Auto & Taxicab Co., 14 La.App. 142, 129 So. 234 (1930); Motors Ins. Co. v. Employers' Liability Assur. Corp., 52 So.2d 311 (La.App.1951).

On the other hand, the common law rule recognizing the subrogor as the proper plaintiff to bring the action in such cases has found a much more frequent recognition and application. Hanton v. New Orleans & C. R., Light & Power Co., 124 La. 562, 50 So. 544 (1909) and cases cited; and the Louisiana cases cited in Miller, Who Must Assert a Subrogation Claim? 312 Ins.L.J. 15, 20, n. 11 (1949).

The jurisprudence is further confused by recent holdings, rendering lip service to the requirement that the actual party in interest must sue, but holding that the subrogor must sue unless the defendant has consented to the subrogation. Dupuy v. Graeme Spring & Axle Service, 19 So.2d 657 (La.App.1944); Stein v. Williams Lumber Co., 36 So.2d 62 (La.App.1948); Marmol v. Wright, 62 So.2d 528 (La.App.1953); and Emmco Ins. Co. v. Erickson, 63 So.2d 747 (La.App.1953). These cases work a confusion of the rules of subrogation and assignment; cf. Taylor v. Fidelity & Casualty Ins. Co. of New York, 55 So.2d 307 (La.App.1951); Comment, 25 Tul.L.Rev. 358, 368 (1951); and their faulty reasoning has been convincingly exposed in Miller, op. cit. *supra* at 15, 16.

When the subrogation is partial, or when the entire right is subrogated to different subrogees, the common law rule requiring the subrogor to sue serves useful purposes in avoiding a multiplicity of actions and protecting an obligor from the harassment of multiple suits on the same controversy. But it does violence to the procedure of a jurisdiction which requires the actual party in interest to sue, and further makes it more difficult for the obligor to assert defenses against one or more subrogees which are not available against the subrogor.

Tit. 3   PARTIES PLAINTIFF   Art. 698

The soundest rules on the subject, and which have the added attraction of being harmonious with civilian procedural principles, are those recognized and applied in Reisz v. Kansas City Southern R. Co., *supra*. There, the court held that: (1) under Art. 15 of the 1870 Code the subrogees were the real parties in interest who should bring suit to assert their own interests; and (2) the subrogor alone could bring the action, individually to the extent of his retained interest, and as agent for all of the subrogees. These rules have all of the advantages of the common law rule and are subject to none of the objections thereto.

(c) A failure to comply with this article produces different results, depending on the circumstances. If there has been a total subrogation and the suit is brought in the name of the subrogor, the latter has no right of action, and the court cannot adjudicate in the absence of the indispensable party plaintiff—the subrogee. If there has been a partial subrogation, and the suit is brought only by the subrogor or the subrogee, there is a nonjoinder of a necessary party. See Art. 642, *supra*. If the defendant fails to object timely to the nonjoinder of a necessary party, in a case of partial subrogation, the objection is waived and the court may make an adjudication. But if, in such a case, the partial subrogation is proven, the plaintiff may recover only his interest in the partially subrogated claim.

(d) See, also, Comments under Art. 698, *infra*.

Art. 698.   Assignor and assignee

An incorporeal right which has been assigned, whether unconditionally or conditionally for purposes of collection or security, shall be enforced judicially by:

(1) The assignor and the assignee, when the assignment is partial; or

(2) The assignee, when the entire right is assigned.

Source: New.

Cross Reference: Art. 771.

Comments

(a) This article provides definite and workable rules on the subject which are consistent with the procedural theory of Louisiana, and which afford protection of the rights of all persons concerned.

(b) The development of procedural rules on the subject in Anglo-American law was impeded to a considerable extent by the original refusal, and subsequent reluctance, of the common law to recognize assignments. *Cf.* Comment (b) under Art. 697, *supra*. Its subsequent development in American code procedure has been impeded, as it has been complicated under all procedural systems, by the rule that the obligor is not compelled to recognize partial assignments, and cannot be subjected to the harassment of multiple suits on a single obligation.

Under Art. 15 of the 1870 Code requiring the person having the real and actual interest to bring the action, the assignee should be the proper plaintiff in all cases where there has been a total assignment. Some of the Louisiana cases have so held. Sedwell's Assignee v. Moore, 10 Mart. (O.S.) 117 (La.1821); Kilgour v. Ratcliff's Heirs, 2 Mart. (N.S.) 292 (La.1824); Smith v. Richland Compress & Warehouse Co., 153 La. 820, 96 So. 668 (1923). See Viguerie v. Hall, 107 La. 767, 31 So. 1019 (1902); and Orleans Discount Co. v. Cartwright, 10 La.App. 304, 121 So. 677 (1929).

Despite the original rejection of the common law rule that the assignor must bring the action in Sedwell's Assignee v. Moore, *supra*, a number of subsequent cases have held, where the assignment was total, that the assignor must bring the action for the use of the assignee. Dicks v. O'Connor, 5 Mart. (N.S.) 547 (La.1827); Towne v. Couch, 7 La.Ann. 93 (1852); Ruddock Cypress Co. v. Peyret, 111 La. 1019, 36 So. 105 (1904).

These conflicting rules subsequently were reconciled through the simple expedient of holding that in such cases either the assignee or the assignor may sue. Dugue v. Levy, 120 La. 369, 45 So. 280 (1907); Miller v. Bonner, 163 La. 332, 111 So. 776 (1926).

With respect to the partial assignment, the Louisiana cases originally applied principles of French and Spanish law, and reached substantially the same results as those reached in Anglo-American jurisdictions. Since an obligor is not compelled to recognize partial assignments, the assignee of only a portion of the obligation may not sue alone to enforce the interest assigned to him. King v. Havard, 5 Mart. (N.S.) 193 (La.1826); Russell v. Ferguson, 7 Mart. (N.S.) 519 (La.1829); Miller v. Brigot, 8 La. 533 (1835); Cantrelle v. Le Goaster, 3 Rob. 432 (La.1843); Le Blanc v. Parish of East Baton Rouge, 10 Rob. 25 (La.1845); Belden v. Butchers' Union Slaughter-House Co., 38 La.Ann. 391 (1886); Red River Valley Bank & Trust Co. v. Louisiana P. C. Co., 142 La. 838, 77 So. 763 (1918). See also, Interstate Trust & Banking Co. v. Young, 135 La. 465, 65 So. 611 (1914). *Cf.* Kelso v. Beaman, 6 La. 87 (1833).

Where the obligation has been partially assigned, it would appear that, under Art. 15 of the 1870 Code, the action to enforce the obligation should be brought by both the assignor and the assignee. This rule apparently was recognized in Smith v. Richland Compress & Warehouse Co., 153 La. 820, 96 So. 668 (1923); yet in Torian v. Weeks, 46 La.Ann. 1502, 16 So. 405 (1894), the assignor was permitted to sue to enforce his individual retained interest, and for the use of the assignees to whom portions of the debt had been assigned.

(c) The rules set forth in this article accord with the procedural theory of Louisiana, *cf.* Art. 681, *supra*; and afford adequate protection to the rights of all persons concerned. They are similar to the rules adopted on subrogated rights, and are based on the analogy offered by Reisz v. Kansas City Southern R. Co., 148 La. 929, 88 So. 120 (1921). See Comment (b) under Art. 697, *supra*.

The obligor is completely protected against the harassment of multiple suits on the same obligation, since all interested parties must join in the action.

(d) A failure to comply with this article produces different results, depending on the facts. If there has been an assignment of the entire right and the suit is brought in the name of the assignor, the latter has no right of action, and the court cannot adjudicate in the absence of the indispensable party plaintiff, the assignee. If there has been a partial assignment, and the suit is brought only by the assignor or the assignee, there is a nonjoinder of a necessary party. See Art. 642, *supra*. If the defendant fails to object timely to the nonjoinder of a necessary party, in a case of partial assignment, the objection is waived and the court may make an adjudication. The defendant has consented to the partial assignment. But if, in such a case, the partial assignment is proven, the plaintiff may recover only his interest in the partially assigned claim.

(e) On the subject of the conditional assignment for collection, see R.S. 9:3051. If the entire obligation is assigned conditionally for security, the assignee has the right to enforce the entire obligation judicially, but is required to either pay the excess of the amount collected over the secured indebtedness to the assignor, or to account to him for this excess. See 25 Tul.L.Rev. 358, 368 (1951).

Art. 699. Trust estate

Except as otherwise provided by law, the trustee of an express trust is the proper plaintiff to sue to enforce a right of the trust estate.

Source: New; *cf.* R.S. 9:1811, 9:1962(7) (9), 9:1001(2), 9:2000, 9:2093.

Cross Reference: Art. 771.

Comments

(a) No change. The Trust Estates Law does not expressly provide the rule of this article, but it is implicit in all of the indirect source provisions of this article.

(b) The exception at the commencement of this article was inserted to avoid conflict with the provisions of the Trust Estates Law giving the beneficiary and the settlor certain rights against

Art. 699

the trustee. See R.S. 9:2031, 9:2151, 9:2191–9:2194. It also preserves the beneficiary's secondary right to enforce a claim of the trust estate against a third person which the trustee has failed or refused to enforce. See R.S. 9:2031, and Restatement of Trusts, §§ 281(2), 282(3), 282(4) and 294.

Art. 700. Authority or qualification of plaintiff suing in representative capacity

When a plaintiff sues as an agent to enforce a right of his principal, or as a legal representative, his authority or qualification is presumed, unless challenged by the defendant by the timely filing of the dilatory exception. When so challenged, the plaintiff shall prove his authority or qualification on the trial of the exception.

Source: New; *cf.* Comments following.

Cross Reference: Art. 771.

Comments

(a) The first sentence of this article restates the settled rule in Louisiana. See Arts. 320 and 321 of the 1870 Code of Practice; Cartwright v. Puissigur, 125 La. 700, 51 So. 692 (1910). The second sentence is declaratory of the jurisprudential rule. See M. & F. Gayoso de Lemos v. Garcia, 1 Mart. (N.S.) 324, 330–331 (La. 1823); Guaranty Discount & Collection Co. v. McClure, 172 So. 564 (La.App.1937).

(b) For the definition of legal representative, see Art. 5251, *infra*.

(c) See, also, Comments under Art. 681, *supra*.

CHAPTER 3. PARTIES DEFENDANT

Art.
731. Individuals having procedural capacity.
732. Unemancipated minor.
733. Mental incompetent; interdict.
734. Succession.
735. Marital community.
736. Person doing business under trade name.
737. Partnership; partners.
738. Unincorporated association; members.
739. Corporation; insurance corporation.
740. Corporation or partnership in receivership or liquidation.
741. Insurer in receivership.
742. Trust estate.

Art. 731. Individuals having procedural capacity

A competent major and a competent emancipated minor have the procedural capacity to be sued.

Source: C.P. Art. 114; C.C. Arts. 367, 370, 371, 382, 385.

Cross Reference: Art. 771.

Comments

(a) This article makes no change in the procedural law.

(b) The terms "competent major" and "competent emancipated minor" include a married woman, now completely emancipated by R.S. 9:101–9:105. A married woman, however, can only be sued on an obligation of her separate estate, and may not be held on a community obligation unless she has assumed it. *Cf.* Art. 735, *infra*.

(c) An emancipated minor, regardless of the manner in which he is emancipated, has the procedural capacity to defend a suit against him and to stand in judgment therein. *Cf.* Beauchamp v. Whittington, 10 La.Ann. 646 (1855); and Richardson v. Richardson, 38 La.Ann. 639 (1886).

(d) See, also, Comments under Art. 4394, *infra*.

Art. 732. Unemancipated minor

An unemancipated minor has no procedural capacity to be sued.

Except as otherwise provided in Article 4431, the tutor appointed by a court of this state is the proper defendant in an action to enforce an obligation against an unemancipated minor, when (1) one or both of the parents are dead, (2) the parents are divorced or judicially separated, or (3) the minor is an illegitimate child. If such a minor has no tutor, the action may be brought against the minor, but the court shall appoint an attorney at law to represent him.

The father, as administrator of the estate of his minor child, is the proper defendant in an action to enforce an obligation against an unemancipated minor who is the legitimate issue of living parents who are not divorced or judicially separated. The mother, as the administratrix of the estate of her minor child, is the proper defendant in such an action, when the father is a mental incompetent or an absentee.

Source: C.P. Arts. 115, 964; C.C. Arts. 157, 221, 246, 250.

Cross References: Arts. 733, 771.

Art. 732

Comments

(a) No change is effected by this article.

(b) The exception at the beginning of the second paragraph avoids a conflict with the article recognizing the right of a tutor or guardian of a nonresident minor appointed by a court of another state to act in Louisiana without the necessity of appointment and qualification by a court of this state. See Art. 4431, *infra*. If process can be served upon the foreign tutor or guardian, the latter is a proper defendant.

(c) The term "tutor" includes a provisional tutor under Art. 4073, *infra*.

(d) See, also, Comments under Arts. 4264, 5091, *infra*.

Art. 733. Mental incompetent; interdict

A mental incompetent has no procedural capacity to be sued.

Except as otherwise provided in Articles 732, 4431, and 4554, the curator appointed by a court of this state is the proper defendant in an action to enforce an obligation against a mental incompetent or an interdict. If an incompetent has no curator, but is interdicted, or committed to or confined in a mental institution, the action shall be brought against him, but the court shall appoint an attorney at law to represent him.

Source: C.P. Arts. 115, 964.

Cross Reference: Art. 771.

Comments

The exception at the beginning of the second paragraph avoids a conflict with the article recognizing the right of a guardian of a nonresident mental incompetent appointed by a court of another state to act in Louisiana without the necessity of appointment and qualification by a court of this state. See Arts. 4431 and 4554, *infra*. Such a guardian is a proper defendant if process can be served on him. This exception also avoids a conflict, in the case of a mentally incompetent minor, with the preceding article.

See Comment (b) under Art. 684, *supra*.

See, also, Comments under Arts. 4264, 5091, *infra*.

Art. 734. Succession

The succession representative appointed by a court of this state is the proper defendant in an action to enforce an obligation of the deceased or of his succession, while the latter is under administration.

The heirs or legatees of the deceased, whether present or represented in the state or not, need not be joined as parties, whether the action is personal, real, or mixed.

Source: New.

Cross Reference: Art. 771.

Comments

Under the 1870 Code of Practice, the proper defendants in an action to enforce an obligation of the deceased depended largely upon whether the heirs were present or represented in the state, or were absent. Thus, under Art. 122, the curator of a vacant succession and the heirs present or represented had to be joined as defendants in both personal and real actions. Under Art. 123, the executor alone might be sued in a personal action, but the heirs present or represented had to be joined with him in a real action. A conflict existed on the question of whether the administrator alone might be sued in a real action. There was some authority for the proposition that in such a case the heirs present and represented had to be joined as parties defendant. Scott v. Key, 9 La.Ann. 519 (1942). Cf. Johnston v. Burton, 202 La. 152, 111 So.2d 519 (1942). Other cases held that the administrator alone might be sued in such a case. Pauline v. Hubert, 14 La.Ann. 161 (1859); Vicksburg, S. & P. Ry. Co. v. Tibbs, 112 La. 51, 36 So. 223 (1904); Veith v. Meyer, 166 La. 453, 117 So. 552 (1928).

Since the heirs or legatees have only a residual interest in the succession property, there is no justification for the complicated and unworkable rules of the 1870 Code of Practice and of prior jurisprudence. This article adopts a single, simple rule in all cases: the succession representative alone is the proper defendant. If the heirs or legatees wish to join in order to resist the plaintiff's demand individually, they may do so through intervention.

See Comments under Art. 685, *supra*.

See, also, Comments under Arts. 427, 428, *supra*, and Arts. 3196, 3246, *infra*.

Art. 735. Marital community

The husband is the proper defendant in an action to enforce an obligation against the marital community.

When doubt exists whether the obligation sought to be enforced is that of the marital community or of the separate estate of the wife, the husband and wife may be sued in the alternative.

Source: New; *cf.* C.C. Art. 2404; Comments following.

Cross Reference: Art. 771.

Art. 735   PARTIES

Comments

(a) The first paragraph of this article is declaratory of the jurisprudential rule. Knoblock & Rainold v. Posey, 126 La. 610, 52 So. 847 (1910); Reneau v. Brown, 9 La.App. 375, 158 So. 406 (1928); Fairbanks, Morse & Co. v. Bordelon, 198 So. 391 (La.App.1940); Breaux v. Decuir, 49 So.2d 495 (La.App.1950).

(b) The second paragraph is based on Wells v. Davidson, 149 So. 246 (La.App.1933). For the reason for its inclusion, see Comment (b) under Art. 686, *supra*.

(c) See, also, Comments under Art. 731, *supra*.

Art. 736.   Person doing business under trade name

A person who does business under a trade name is the proper defendant in an action to enforce an obligation created by or arising out of the doing of such business.

Source: New.

Cross Reference: Art. 771.

Comment

It has been held that a suit brought against the owner only in the trade name used was sufficient to justify rendition of judgment against the owner. Rea v. Dow Motor Co., 36 So.2d 750, 755–756 (La.App.1948). This results from an excessive liberality of pleading which disregards all of the basic principles of procedure, and will inevitably lead to difficulties. It is regarded as being completely unsound, since the business being done under a trade name is not a legal entity, and is without procedural capacity or status. This article legislatively overrules the Rea decision.

Art. 737.   Partnership; partners

A partnership has the procedural capacity to be sued in its partnership name.

The partners of an existing partnership may not be sued on a partnership obligation unless the partnership is joined as a defendant.

Source: New; *cf.* Comments following.

Cross Reference: Art. 771.

Comments

(a) This article makes no change in the procedural law.

(b) This article is declaratory of the rule established by the jurisprudence. Key v. Box, 14 La.Ann. 497 (1859); Hayes Machinery Co. v. Eastham, 147 La. 347, 84 So. 898 (1920); American Photo Player Co. v. Simon, 151 La. 708, 92 So. 307 (1922); Snyder v. Davison, 172 La. 274, 134 So. 89 (1931); Rheuark v. Terminal Mud & Chemical Co., 213 La. 732, 35 So.2d 592 (1948); Elfer v. Mintz, 7 So.2d 416 (La.App.1942); Moore v. Easom, 46 So.2d 162 (La.App.1950); Harrison v. Frye, 46 So.2d 382 (La.App.1950).

It is optional with the plaintiff as to whether the partners are to be joined as defendants with the partnership or not. First Nat. Bank in Gibsland v. Knighton, 16 La.App. 407, 134 So. 706 (1931).

Art. 738. Unincorporated association; members

An unincorporated association has the procedural capacity to be sued in its own name. The members of an unincorporated association may be sued jointly on an obligation of the association and the association may be joined as a defendant in such an action.

Source: New.

Cross Reference: Art. 771.

Comments

(a) This article changes the procedural law, but is merely the culmination of a definite trend in this direction under both the positive law and the jurisprudence.

(b) Originally, an unincorporated association had no status whatsoever as a legal entity, and hence could not be sued. Its obligation was enforced judicially only by an action brought against its members. Civil Code Art. 446. *Cf.* Hincks v. Converse, 37 La. Ann. 484 (1885). A statute, originally adopted in 1918, permitted an action to be brought against the association, with service to be made on an officer thereof. Former R.S. 13:3471. Recent cases have extended the statutory provisions by holding, at least insofar as labor unions are concerned, that an unincorporated association may be sued in its own name, and service may be made upon either an officer or a member. Godchaux Sugars v. Chaisson, 227 La. 146, 78 So.2d 673 (1955); Hanson v. International Union of Operating Eng., 79 So.2d 199 (La.App.1955). See also, Douglas Public Service v. Gaspard, 225 La. 972, 74 So.2d 182 (1954). This article is declaratory of these rules.

(c) Service on an unincorporated association may be made on a registered agent, or on any member. Art. 1264, *infra*.

(d) It has been held that the statute originally adopted in 1918 authorizes only an action seeking to enforce an obligation of the association. Doane v. General Longshore Workers, 61 So.2d 747 (La. App.1952). This article permits any action to be brought against the association itself.

Art. 738

(e) The last paragraph makes it clear that the plaintiff, at his option, may sue the members of the association on any obligation of the latter, and is intended to overrule the unfortunate contrary decision in Squaire v. Polk, 153 So. 504 (La.App.1934).

(f) See, also, Comments under Art. 1264, *infra.*

Art. 739. Corporation; insurance corporation

Except as otherwise provided in Articles 740 and 741, a domestic or foreign corporation, or a domestic, foreign, or alien insurance corporation, has the procedural capacity to be sued in its corporate name.

Source: C.P. Art. 119; C.C. Art. 432; R.S. 12:12(B) (3), 12:203(A).

Cross Reference: Art. 771.

Comments

(a) This article makes no change in the procedural law.

(b) Reciprocal insurers and Lloyd's plan insurers are included within the definition of "insurer" in R.S. 22:5, but are not corporations. Fraternal benefit societies are not included within the definition of "insurer" in R.S. 22:5. None of these are included within the scope of this article. Reciprocal insurers, Lloyd's plan insurers, and fraternal benefit societies are sued as provided in R.S. 22:433, 22:504, and 22:558, respectively.

Art. 740. Corporation or partnership in receivership or liquidation

Except as otherwise provided by law, the receiver or liquidator of a domestic or foreign corporation or partnership appointed by a court of this state is the proper defendant in an action to enforce an obligation of the corporation or partnership, or of its receiver or liquidator.

The receiver or liquidator may be sued without the necessity of obtaining permission therefor from the court which appointed him.

Source: New.

Cross References: Arts. 739, 771.

Comments

(a) "Corporation" as used in this article does not include an insurance corporation. See Art. 741, *infra.*

(b) See Comment (f) under Art. 692, *supra,* for the reasons for the exception in the first paragraph of this article.

(c) There is a conflict of opinion in America as to whether a receiver may be sued for a tort committed by the corporation prior to the appointment of a receiver. 16 Fletcher Cyclopedia Corporations (Perm. ed.) 430 *et seq.* (1942). Louisiana has not yet had occasion to decide the question. This article settles the matter by providing that the receiver may be sued in such a case.

(d) The receiver, rather than the corporation, has been recognized as the proper defendant in a case brought to recover damages for an offense or quasi offense committed during the operation of the corporation's property by a receiver. Anding v. Texas & P. Ry. Co., 158 La. 412, 104 So. 190 (1925); Harris v. Texas & P. Ry. Co., 2 La.App. 501 (1925); King v. Illinois Cent. R. Co., 15 La. App. 1, 131 So. 68 (1930). This article adopts this rule.

(e) The second paragraph of this article adopts the rule of 28 U.S.C. § 959, and legislatively overrules Godchaux v. Texas & P. Ry. Co., 151 La. 955, 92 So. 398 (1922); and Winn v. Veal-Winn Co.'s Receiver, 16 La.App. 323, 134 So. 264 (1931).

(f) The general rule recognized throughout America is that, though a receiver may be sued (usually with the permission of the appointing court), his possession and control of the corporate property cannot be interfered with either through mesne or final execution. The judgment against the receiver obtained in a plenary proceeding may be enforced only in the receivership proceeding in due course of administration. There is no intention to have these rules changed by this article. R.S. 13:4101, 13:4102 are statutory exceptions to these general rules.

Art. 741. Insurer in receivership

The receiver appointed by a court of this state for a domestic insurer is the proper defendant in an action to enforce an obligation of the insurer, or of its receiver.

Except as otherwise provided by law, the ancillary receiver appointed by a court of this state for a foreign or alien insurer is the proper defendant in an action to enforce an obligation of the insurer, or of its domiciliary or ancillary receiver.

Source: R.S. 22:736, 22:757, 22:758.

Cross References: Arts. 693, 730, 771.

Comments

(a) The above article effects no change in the procedural law.

(b) For the definition of "insurer", see Art. 5251, *infra*. "Receiver", as used herein, includes a liquidator, rehabilitator, and conservator. Art. 693, *supra*; R.S. 22:757(12).

(c) See Comment (b) under Art. 693, *supra*, for the reason for the exception made in the second paragraph.

(d) See, also, Comments under Art. 740, *supra*.

Art. 742. Trust estate

The trustee of an express trust is the proper defendant in an action to enforce an obligation against a trust estate.

Source: R.S. 9:1811, 9:1962(10), 9:2003, 9:2004.

Cross Reference: Art. 771.

Comments

(a) This article effects no change in the procedural law.

(b) The beneficiaries of the trust must be notified of the institution of the action within thirty days thereof, and more than thirty days prior to judgment, as provided in R.S. 9:2003(B) and 9:2004(C).

(c) Under the circumstances provided in R.S. 9:2003(C) and 9:2004(D), the trustee may also be held liable personally and individually.

CHAPTER 4. PARTIES TO INCIDENTAL DEMANDS

Art.
771. Rules applicable.

Art. 771. Rules applicable

Articles 641 through 742 and 801 through 821 are applicable to the parties to an incidental demand.

Source: New.

Comment

This article expressly makes the rules as to parties applicable to the parties to an incidental demand.

CHAPTER 5. SUBSTITUTION OF PARTIES

SECTION 1. IN TRIAL COURTS

Art.
801. Voluntary substitution for deceased party; legal successor.
802. Compulsory substitution for deceased party; summons.
803. Same; service or publication of summons.
804. Same; effect of failure of legal successor to appear.
805. Legal representative; successor.
806. Public officer.
807. Transfer of interest.

SECTION 2. IN APPELLATE COURTS

Art.
821. Rules of Chapter applicable to district courts; rules of other appellate courts applicable.

SECTION 1. IN TRIAL COURTS

Art. 801. Voluntary substitution for deceased party; legal successor

When a party dies during the pendency of an action which is not extinguished by his death, his legal successor may have himself substituted for the deceased party, on ex parte written motion supported by proof of his quality.

Legal successor, as used in Articles 801 through 804, means the succession representative of the deceased appointed by a court of this state, if the succession is under administration; and otherwise means the heirs or legatees of the deceased.

Source: New; *cf.* Rule XIV, § 1, Supreme Court of Louisiana; Fed. Rule 25(a) (1).

Cross References: Arts. 771, 805, 821.

Comment

These are the first rules governing the substitution of parties in the trial courts to apply uniformly throughout the state. Heretofore, the regulations on the subject were found only in the local rules of some district courts, which varied considerably.

Art. 802. Compulsory substitution for deceased party; summons

On ex parte written motion of any other party, supported by an affidavit of the truth of the facts alleged, the court may order the issuance of a summons to the legal successor to appear and substitute himself for the deceased party. This summons shall show the title and docket number of the action, and the name and address of the court where the action is pending.

Source: New; *cf.* Rule XIV, § 2, Supreme Court of Louisiana.

Cross References: Arts. 771, 801, 805, 821.

Art. 802

Comment

This article adopts the same approach as its indirect source, but is more specific as to the information to be furnished by the summons.

Art. 803. Same; service or publication of summons

When the name and address of the legal successor is known, and he is a resident of the state, he shall be summoned to appear and substitute himself for the deceased party within thirty days of the date the summons is served on him.

When the name and address of the legal successor is known, but he is a nonresident or absentee, he shall be summoned to appear and substitute himself for the deceased party within sixty days of the receipt of the summons through registered or certified mail.

If the name or address of the legal successor is unknown, the summons shall be by two publications not less than fifteen days apart in a newspaper published in the parish where the action is pending, which shall summon him to appear and substitute himself for the deceased party within sixty days of the first publication. The summons shall be addressed to the legal successor by name, if the latter is known; and otherwise shall be addressed to "The legal successor of ─────────────, deceased".

Source: New; *cf.* Rule XIV, §§ 2, 3, Supreme Court of Louisiana.

Cross References: Arts. 771, 801, 805, 821.

Comment

The delays in the indirect source were not consistent as between themselves, and not completely consistent with the delays provided in the appropriate rules of other appellate courts of the state. *Cf.* Rule VI, Court of Appeal for the Parish of Orleans; Rule 13, Court of Appeal for the Second Circuit.

Art. 804. Same; effect of failure of legal successor to appear

When the legal successor fails to appear and substitute himself for the deceased party within the delay allowed in the summons, on ex parte written motion of any other party, the court may:

(1) Dismiss the action as to the deceased party, with or without prejudice, if the deceased was a plaintiff; or

(2) Appoint an attorney at law to represent the legal successor of the deceased party, if the deceased was a defendant; and the action shall be proceeded with contradictorily against this attorney at law.

Source: New.

Cross References: Arts. 771, 801, 805, 821.

Comments

(a) The differences between the dismissal or hearing of an appeal, and the dismissal or proceeding to trial and judgment in the trial courts, made it impossible to follow the procedures prescribed in Rule XIV of the Supreme Court.

(b) Ordinarily, when a plaintiff dies pending trial, and his legal successor neglects to appear and substitute himself as a party, the case should be dismissed without prejudice. But there are circumstances which would make it inequitable to leave the defendant exposed to a second action in such a case. For this reason, the determination of whether the action should be dismissed with prejudice, or without prejudice, is left to the sound judicial discretion of the trial judge.

(c) Under this article, when a defendant dies pending trial, and his legal successor fails to appear and substitute himself, and his name and address are unknown to the plaintiff, an attorney is to be appointed to represent the legal successor, and the trial is to be had contradictorily against this attorney. Since the defendant was cited prior to his death, there can be no question as to the jurisdiction of the court to render judgment in such a case.

The judgment to be rendered in such a case would be against the succession of the deceased defendant, and not against his succession representative or heirs personally. This judgment could be enforced later in the succession proceeding, if one is opened; and otherwise against the heirs who accepted the succession of the deceased.

Art. 805. Legal representative; successor

Articles 801 through 804 apply to the substitution of a legal representative of any party other than a deceased person, and to the substitution of the successor of any legal representative appointed by a court of this state, except that the term "legal successor", as used therein, shall be considered as referring to such legal representative, or successor, as the case may be.

Source: New.

Cross References: Arts. 771, 821.

Comments

(a) This article makes the rules of the preceding articles in this Chapter applicable to cases where a curator is appointed for a mental incompetent, or a receiver or liquidator is appointed for a corporate party, pending trial.

(b) Ordinarily, the word "successor" in this article would mean a successor legal representative, but it is also intended to cover the case of the substitution of an individual party who attains majority, or is emancipated, or whose interdiction has been lifted, after institution of the action but prior to trial. In all these cases, the legal representative would be discharged, and the individual should be substituted as a party in the pending action.

(c) For the definition of "legal representative," see Art. 5251, *infra*.

Art. 806. Public officer

When an officer of the state, or of a municipality, parish, political subdivision, agency, or public corporation, who is a party dies, resigns, or otherwise ceases to hold office, his successor may be substituted therefor on ex parte written motion of the successor or any other party, supported by an affidavit of the truth of the facts alleged. A copy of the order substituting the successor shall be served on the adverse party by mail.

Source: New; *cf.* Fed. Rule 25(d).

Cross References: Arts. 771, 821.

Comment

The substitution of a state, parochial, or municipal officer in the courts of this state is a much more simple matter than the substitution of an officer of the United States in a federal court, and hence permits of a much simpler solution in this article than is possible in its indirect source.

Art. 807. Transfer of interest

When a party to an action transfers an interest in the subject matter thereof, the action shall be continued by or against such party, unless the court directs that the transferee be substituted for or joined with the transferor.

Source: New; *cf.* Fed. Rule 25(c).

Cross References: Arts. 771, 821.

Comments

(a) This article makes it possible for the trial court to order the substitution or joinder of the transferee, when a party has transferred an interest in the subject matter of the action after its institution, but prior to trial. At the same time, it insures the validity of the judgment for and against the original parties, if the transferee is not subject to the jurisdiction of the court, or if for any other reason the trial court feels it unnecessary or inadvisable to require the substitution or joinder.

(b) If the transfer was of the entire interest in the subject matter of the action, the transferee would be substituted. If it was only of a partial interest, the transferee would be joined. The substitution or joinder here is effected through amendment of the pleadings, and service of a copy thereof and the court order, on the transferee.

(c) This article is not intended to affect in any way the rules in the Civil Code on litigious rights.

SECTION 2. IN APPELLATE COURTS

Art. 821. Rules of Chapter applicable to district courts; rules of other appellate courts applicable

Articles 801 through 807 govern the substitution of parties in a case pending in a district court on appeal from a justice of the peace or city court.

The substitution of parties in an action pending in the supreme court or in a court of appeal is governed by the rules of the appellate court.

Source: New.

Cross Reference: Art. 771.

Comment

The second paragraph of this article makes it clear that the rules of the major appellate courts are not affected by the provisions of this chapter. See Rule XIV, Supreme Court of Louisiana; Rule VI, Court of Appeal for the Parish of Orleans; and Rule 13, Second Circuit Court of Appeals.

BOOK II.
ORDINARY PROCEEDINGS

TITLE I
PLEADING

Chap.		Art.
1.	General Dispositions	851
2.	Petition	891
3.	Exceptions	921
4.	Written Motions	961
5.	Answer	1001
6.	Incidental Actions	1031
	Sec.	
	1. General Dispositions	1031
	2. Reconvention	1061
	3. Intervention	1091
	4. Demand Against Third Party	1111
7.	Amended and Supplemental Pleadings	1151

INTRODUCTION

The articles in this Title retain the basic principles of the Louisiana law of pleading. In some instances, however, it was advisable to borrow from the Federal Rules of Civil Procedure some of the more effective procedural devices, such as the motion for summary judgment and the enumeration of affirmative defenses. The third party practice, which was also borrowed from the federal rules, had already been adopted by La.Act 433 of 1954, replacing the call in warranty. Third party practice is included in this Title.

While the articles in this Title have the effect of simplifying and liberalizing the procedural rules and increasing their effectiveness, there are really no radical changes embodied herein.

Three significant modifications, however, should be noted:

(1) Verification and certification of pleadings are no longer required as a general rule, the signature of the attorney implying the accuracy and truthfulness of the allegations as is the case under the federal rules.

(2) The number of formal exceptions has been reduced to three. The thirty-odd nominate exceptions recognized by the Louisiana procedural law, however, are not completely abolished, but are retained as specific objections which may be raised through the three exceptions, i. e., the declinatory exception, the dilatory exception, and the peremptory exception.

(3) The incidental demands have been reduced in number to three, through the broadening of reconvention to include compensation and the merger of intervention and third opposition.

CHAPTER 1. GENERAL DISPOSITIONS

Art.
851. Three modes of procedure; Book II governs ordinary proceedings.
852. Pleadings allowed; replicatory pleadings prohibited.
853. Caption of pleadings; adoption by reference; exhibits.
854. Form of pleading.
855. Pleading special matters; capacity.
856. Same; fraud, mistake, or condition of the mind.
857. Same; suspensive conditions.
858. Same; official document or act.
859. Same; judgment or decision.
860. Same; time and place.
861. Same; special damage.
862. Relief granted under pleadings; sufficiency of prayer.
863. Signing of pleadings, effect.
864. Attorney subject to disciplinary action.
865. Construction of pleadings.

Art. 851. Three modes of procedure; Book II governs ordinary proceedings

Three different modes of procedure are used in civil matters in the trial courts of this state: ordinary, summary, and executory.

The articles in this Book govern ordinary proceedings, which are to be used in the district courts in all cases, except as otherwise provided by law.

Summary and executory proceedings are regulated by the provisions of Book V.

Source: C.P. Arts. 98, 124.

Comments

(a) This Code retains the three modes of procedure recognized by the Codes of Practice of 1825 and 1870.

(b) The provisions of Book II relate only to ordinary proceedings in the trial courts of general jurisdiction. The simpler practice to be used in trial courts of limited jurisdiction, and in the district courts in cases where they have concurrent jurisdiction with justices of the peace, are included in Book VIII. Many of the articles of Book II, of course, are applicable to the latter two types of cases, and express provisions in Book VIII make such rules apply through appropriate cross references therein.

Probate procedure is regulated by the provisions of Book VI.

Art. 852. Pleadings allowed; replicatory pleadings prohibited

The pleadings allowed in civil actions, whether in a principal or incidental action, shall be in writing and shall consist of petitions, exceptions, written motions, and answers. No replicatory pleadings shall be used and all new matter alleged in exceptions, contradictory motions, and answers, whether in a principal or incidental action, shall be considered denied or avoided.

Source: New; *cf.* C.P. Arts. 170, 319, 327, 329, 365; Fed. Rules 7, 8(d).

Comments

(a) The provisions of this article are substantially similar to those of the Code of Practice of 1870. One difference between the two is reflected in the pleadings which a defendant in an incidental action must or may file. This Code provides that an answer must be filed, and that exceptions and written motions may be filed in incidental actions. *Cf.* Arts. 1034 and 1035, *infra*. Under the Code of Practice of 1870 there is no uniformity on the subject as to the various incidental demands. Thus the call in warranty and the intervention both require answers and permit exceptions. Arts. 381, 384, 393, Code of Practice of 1870. *Cf.* former R.S. 13:3601(7). Neither answer nor exceptions are permitted to the demand in compensation; and there is some doubt as to what responsive pleadings are permitted to the reconventional demand, though the probabilities are that answer and exceptions are not allowed. Pierce v. Millar, 3 Mart. (N.S.) 354 (La.1825); Suarez v. Duralde, 1 La. 260 (1830); Stone v. Carter, 5 La. 448 (1833); Bayly & Pond v. Stacey & Poland, 30 La.Ann. 1210 (1878); Loews v. Don George, 227 La. 127, 78 So.2d 534 (1955); Evans v. District Grand Lodge No. 21, G. U. O. O. F. 151 So. 664 (La.App.1933). But see contra: General Accident, Fire & Life Assur. Corp. v. Ross, 155 La. 545, 99 So. 443 (1924); Woodward-Wight & Co. v. Haas, 149 So. 161 (La. App.1933).

The requirement that all pleadings be in writing is expressed or implied by Arts. 159, 170, 319, 327, 333, and 365, Code of Practice of 1870. Abolition of replicatory pleadings, and denial of allega-

Tit. 1 GENERAL DISPOSITIONS Art. 853

tions in the answer by effect of law is provided by Art. 329 of the 1870 Code. *Cf.* Fed. Rule 8(d).

(b) In view of the provisions of this Title requiring answer and permitting motions and exceptions in all incidental actions, the system of pleadings proposed is quite similar to that recognized in the federal courts. The latter, however, still possesses at least the theoretical possibility of replicatory pleading, in those infrequent instances when the court exercises its power to order a reply to an answer or third party answer. See Fed. Rule 7(a).

(c) Though the federal rules do not treat written motions as pleadings in the technical sense of the word, they do provide that all of the rules respecting the form of pleadings shall apply to such motions. See Fed. Rule 7(b) (2). In Louisiana, the written motion traditionally has been considered a pleading. *Cf.* Art. 401, Code of Practice of 1870; former R.S. 13:3601(4). The provisions of this article retain the Louisiana viewpoint.

(d) The requirement as to written pleadings did not preclude oral pleadings in cases to be tried by justices of the peace (Art. 1073, Code of Practice of 1870), before city courts in certain cases (former R.S. 13:1878), and in district courts in cases in which they had concurrent jurisdiction with justices of the peace (former R.S. 13:3331). See Art. 851 and Comments following, *supra*. Under express provisions of Book VIII, oral pleadings are permitted in these cases.

(e) See, also, Comments under Arts. 921, 924, 930, 1034, 1035, 1111, 1156, 1312, 1701, 2973, *infra*.

Art. 853. Caption of pleadings; adoption by reference; exhibits

Every pleading shall contain a caption setting forth the name of the court, the title and number of the action, and a designation of the pleading. The title of the action shall state the name of the first party on each side with an appropriate indication of other parties.

A statement in a pleading may be adopted by reference in a different part of the same pleading or in another pleading in the same court. A copy of any written instrument which is an exhibit to a pleading is a part thereof for all purposes.

Source: C.P. Art. 172; Fed. Rule 10(a), (c).

Cross References: Arts. 891, 924, 962, 1003, 2972.

Comments

(a) Although heretofore there was no legal requirement for a caption, it had been customary to insert one in most pleadings. McMahon, 136, n. 2. If the petition had a caption, it might be considered as a part thereof in determining whether it complied with the requisites of law. Richardson v. Newman, 12 La.App. 646, 126 So. 575 (1930).

(b) This article differs from Fed. Rule 10(a) in that it does not require the names of all parties to be set out in the caption of the initial pleading.

(c) Adoption by reference has been employed in Louisiana for many years. McMahon 623, n. 42. Differently from the language of Rule 10(c) of the Federal Rules of Civil Procedure, adoption by reference is limited to statements made "in a different part of the same pleading or in another pleading *in the same court.*" The italicized words limit the pleadings referred to, to those of which the court can take judicial cognizance.

(d) Annexing a copy of a written instrument to a pleading, with the recital that it is made a part thereof for all purposes, has been a procedural device successfully employed in Louisiana for many years. Tremont Lumber Co. v. May, 143 La. 389, 78 So. 650 (1918). The last sentence of this article makes unnecessary any specific recital that the written instrument is made a part of the pleading.

Art. 854. Form of pleading

No technical forms of pleading are required.

All allegations of fact of the petition, exceptions, or answer shall be simple, concise, and direct, and shall be set forth in numbered paragraphs. As far as practicable, the contents of each paragraph shall be limited to a single set of circumstances.

Source: C.P. Arts. 160, 328, 329; former R.S. 13:3601; *cf.* Fed. Rules 8(e)(1), 10(b).

Cross References: Arts. 891, 924, 962, 1003, 2972.

Comments

(a) This article preserves the Louisiana system of pleading facts as being preferable to the notice pleading of the Federal Rules of Civil Procedure, or to any other modified system of notice pleading. *Cf.* Tucker, Proposal for Retention of the Louisiana System of Fact Pleading; Exposé des Motifs, 13 La.L.Rev. 395 (1953) and McMahon, The Case Against Fact Pleading in Louisiana, 13 La.L.Rev. 369 (1953).

Although it has always been necessary to state a cause of action and to allege the material facts constituting the cause of action, it is not necessary to allege evidence. Neither the Pleading and Practice Act of 1912 (La.Act 157 of 1912) nor State v. Hackley, Hume and Joyce, 124 La. 854, 50 So. 772 (1909), made or effected any change in these basic rules. Moreover, in the interest of upholding substantive rights instead of technicalities, amendment of a petition which fails to state a cause of action because of insufficient allegations is allowed. Douglas v. Haro, 214 La. 1099, 30 So.2d 774 (1949).

(b) Prior to the adoption of this Code, Louisiana adopted pretrial and deposition and discovery statutes, former R.S. 13:5151, and 13:3741–13:3794, respectively, and they have been incorporated in this Code at Arts. 1551, and 1421 through 1515. The rules of pleading contained in this Book provide also for a motion for summary judgment based upon similar procedure in the Federal Rules of Civil Procedure. With these provisions for simplifying the issues and for disclosing the facts, and the liberality of amendment provided by Art. 1154, *infra*, there is no reason why a plaintiff should not be required to state his cause of action when he comes into court, and a defendant to answer in like manner.

In Louisiana it is well settled that the pleadings are enlarged by evidence adduced without objection which is not pertinent to any of the issues raised by the pleadings, and hence would have been excluded if objected to timely. In fact, the end results of Art. 1154, *infra*, and the jurisprudential rules in Louisiana are substantially identical, except as respects deficiencies in the answer. The rule against replication in Louisiana has been interpreted as preventing discussion in the pleading state. Art. 1154, *infra*, however, should remove that possible source of difficulty. See Hope v. Madison, 191 La. 1075, 187 So. 28 (1939) and see the Comments under Art. 1154, *infra*.

(c) For obvious reasons, there is no necessity for articulate pleading in a short written motion. Hence, separate paragraphs are not required except in the case of lengthy written motions. See Art. 962, *infra*.

(d) See, also, Comments under Arts. 856, 860, 861, 892, 1004, 1154, *infra*.

Art. 855. Pleading special matters; capacity

It is not necessary to allege the capacity of a party to sue or be sued or the authority of a party to sue or be sued in a representative capacity or the legal existence of a legal entity or an organized association of persons made a party. Such procedural capacity shall be presumed, unless challenged by the dilatory exception.

Source: Fed. Rule 9(a).

Cross References: Arts. 891, 924, 962, 1003, 2972.

Comments

(a) The language of Fed. Rule 9 was changed only to the extent necessary to employ Louisiana terminology in Arts. 857 through 860, *infra*.

Art. 855 PLEADING Bk. 2

(b) Under Louisiana law, capacity is presumed, Broussard v. Rosenblum, 5 La.App. 245 (1926); and capacity of the plaintiff must be challenged through the dilatory exception to procedural capacity. Montfort v. Schmidt, 36 La.Ann. 750 (1884); Dickens v. Singer Sewing Machine Co., 19 La.App. 735, 140 So. 296 (1932); Guaranty Discount & Collection Co. v. McClure, 172 So. 564 (La. App.1937). See, also, Outdoor Electric Advertising, Inc. v. Saurage, 207 La. 344, 21 So.2d 375 (1945). This paragraph of the article, however, goes somewhat further than Art. 320, Code of Practice of 1870, in relieving the pleader from the necessity of averring allegations which show the authority of the party to sue in a representative capacity.

(c) See, also, Comments under Arts. 934, 1671, *infra*.

Art. 856. Same; fraud, mistake, or condition of the mind

In pleading fraud or mistake, the circumstances constituting fraud or mistake shall be alleged with particularity. Malice, intent, knowledge, and other condition of mind of a person may be alleged generally.

Source: Fed. Rule 9(b).

Cross References: Arts. 891, 924, 962, 1003, 2972.

Comments

Louisiana law is in accord with the rules set forth in this article. For the necessity of pleading with particularity the circumstances constituting fraud, see State v. Hackley, Hume & Joyce, 124 La. 854, 50 So. 772 (1909); Moss v. Drost, 130 La. 285, 57 So. 929 (1912); Losavio v. Losavio Realty Co., 212 La. 23, 31 So. 2d 412 (1947); Latham v. Latham, 216 La. 791, 44 So.2d 870 (1950); Brenard Mfg. Co. v. Gibbs, 9 La.App. 137, 119 So. 483 (1928); Masters v. Cleveland, 158 So. 382 (La.App.1935); Horney v. Scott, 171 So. 172 (La.App.1936); Williams v. Bush, 184 So. 583 (La.App.1938); Walker v. Fontenot, 22 So.2d 127 (La. App.1945). Likewise, mistake must be pleaded with particularity. See Sellwood v. Phillips, 185 La. 1045, 171 So. 440 (1936).

Even under a modified system of notice pleading, where factual particulars are required only in exceptional cases, a special rule must be adopted for these exceptional cases where the full circumstances are needed to afford adequate notice to the opposing litigant. That is why averments of the circumstances constituting fraud and mistake are required under Fed. Rule 9(b). Under the system of fact pleading retained in this Code, all material allegations of the cause of action or defense must be pleaded, Art. 854, *supra*, and Arts. 891, 1003 through 1005, *infra*. Hence, there was no actual need for the first sentence of this article, but it has been included to emphasize the necessity of pleading full particulars of the fraud or mistake averred.

Of necessity, malice, intent, knowledge, and other conditions of mind of a person cannot be particularized, and can only be raised through a general allegation thereof. This would appear to be sufficient under the Louisiana jurisprudence. *Cf.* Brian v. Harper, 144 La. 585, 80 So. 885 (1919); Little v. Campbell, 20 So.2d 627 (La.App.1945).

Art. 857. Same; suspensive conditions

In pleading the performance or occurrence of suspensive conditions, it is sufficient to allege generally that all such conditions have been performed or have occurred. A denial of performance or occurrence shall be alleged specifically and with particularity.

Source: Fed. Rule 9(c).

Cross References: Arts. 891, 924, 962, 1003, 2972.

Comments

The civilian term "suspensive condition" has been substituted for the words "condition precedent" of the source provision. For a definition of the suspensive condition, see Art. 2021 of the Civil Code.

See, also, Comments under Art. 855, *supra*.

Art. 858. Same; official document or act

In pleading an official document or official act, it is sufficient to allege that the document was issued or the act done in compliance with law.

Source: Fed. Rule 9(d).

Cross References: Arts. 891, 924, 962, 1003, 2972.

Comments to Articles 858 and 859

Although no cases were found expressly in point, the rules set forth in this article and Article 859 may represent a change in the law. The required pleading of all material allegations, however, imposes an almost impossible burden upon the pleader, and in the vast majority of these suits there seldom is any real issue with respect thereto. Permitting the pleader to allege these matters generally, and requiring the opposing litigant to allege the invalidity of the law, or the lack of jurisdiction, on specific grounds simplifies pleading to a considerable extent.

See, also, Comments under Art. 855, *supra*.

Art. 859. Same; judgment or decision

In pleading a judgment of a domestic or foreign court, or a decision of a judicial or quasi judicial tribunal, or of a board, commission, or officer, it is sufficient to allege the judgment or decision without setting forth matter showing jurisdiction to render it.

Source: Fed. Rule 9(e).

Cross References: Arts. 891, 924, 962, 1003, 2972.

Comments

See Comments under Art. 858, *supra*.
See, also, Comments under Art. 855.

Art. 860. Same; time and place

For the purpose of testing the sufficiency of a pleading, allegations of time and place are material and shall be considered as all other allegations of material matter.

Source: Fed. Rule 9(f).

Cross References: Arts. 891, 924, 962, 1003, 2972.

Comments to Articles 860 and 861

The rules of the sources of this article and Art. 861, *infra*, are essential to the system of pleading in federal practice. These rules are even more essential to the system of fact pleading in this Code. See Comments under Art. 934, *infra*.

Art. 861. Same; special damage

When items of special damage are claimed, they shall be specifically alleged.

Source: Fed. Rule 9(g).

Cross References: Arts. 891, 924, 962, 1003, 2972.

Comments

See Comments under Art. 860, *supra*.
See, also, Comments under Art. 855, *supra*.

Art. 862. Relief granted under pleadings; sufficiency of prayer

Except as provided in Article 1703, a final judgment shall grant the relief to which the party in whose favor it is rendered is entitled, even if the party has not demanded such relief in his pleadings and the latter contain no prayer for general and equitable relief.

Source: Fed. Rule 54(c); *cf.* Fed. Rules 8(e), 15(b).

Cross Reference: Art. 2972.

Comments

(a) This article eliminates the necessity for the prayer for general and equitable relief, as it automatically performs the function of such prayer. The exception to the rule established to protect a person against whom a default judgment is rendered accords with the strict requirement imposed upon a plaintiff who takes judgment by default against the defendant. *Cf.* Louisiana State Bank v. Senecal, 9 La. 225 (1836).

(b) Even more important, this article, together with Art. 1154, *infra*, suppresses the harsh and unduly technical "theory of the case" doctrine in Louisiana, under which the litigant must select a theory of his case or defense and adhere to it throughout the litigation and which has been severely criticized. See Hubert, The Theory of a Case in Louisiana, 24 Tul.L.Rev. 66 (1949). Rules 8(e), 15(b), and 54(c) of the Federal Rules of Civil Procedure, from which the above article is taken were likewise intended to abrogate the "theory of the case" doctrine in the federal courts. See Matarese v. Moore-McCormack Lines, 158 F.2d 631 (2 Cir. 1946); Nester v. Western Union Tel. Co., 25 F.Supp. 478 (D.C.Cal. 1938); Mitchell Novelty Co. v. United Manufacturing Co., 94 F. Supp. 612 (D.C.Ill.1950). See also Clark on Code Pleading (2d ed.) 234 (1947); Commentary, Pleading of "Theory" of Recovery, 3 Fed. Rules Serv. 667 (1940).

Art. 863. Signing of pleadings, effect

Every pleading of a party represented by an attorney shall be signed by at least one attorney of record in his individual name, whose address shall be stated. A party who is not represented by an attorney shall sign his pleading and state his address.

Pleadings need not be verified, or accompanied by affidavit or certificate, except as otherwise provided by law, but the signature of an attorney constitutes a certificate by him that he has read the pleading; that to the best of his knowledge, information, and belief there is good ground to support it; and that it is not interposed for delay.

Source: Fed. Rule 11.

Cross References: Arts. 864, 891, 892, 924, 962, 1003, 1006, 1603, 2972.

Art. 863

Comments

This article abolishes the necessity for verification and certification of pleadings required by former R.S. 13:3601(5) and 13:3601(6). It places the responsibility for truthful and accurate allegations upon the attorney. No verification and certification was required under the Codes of Practice of 1825 and 1870, except verification of the petition in conservatory writ and extraordinary writ cases.

See, also, Comments under Art. 122, *supra*, and Arts. 1975, 2411, *infra*.

Art. 864. Attorney subject to disciplinary action

An attorney may be subjected to appropriate disciplinary action for a wilful violation of any provision of Article 863, or for the insertion of scandalous or indecent matter in a pleading.

Source: Fed. Rule 11; *cf.* C.P. Arts. 172(5), 319.

Comments

(a) This article provides an effective sanction to observance of the ethical proprieties in the drafting of pleadings. See also Arts. 222 and 223, *supra*, providing that the court may punish an attorney for contempt for making false or fraudulent allegations in a pleading.

(b) The above article also follows the implied prohibition in Arts. 172(5) and 319, Code of Practice of 1870, against the petition or answer containing any insulting, impertinent, abusive, or defamatory expressions. However, it goes much further than the 1870 Code provisions in making any violation of the provisions of Art. 863, *supra*, punishable under the disciplinary powers of the court.

(c) See, also, Comments under Art. 892, *infra*.

Art. 865. Construction of pleadings

Every pleading shall be so construed as to do substantial justice.

Source: Fed. Rule 8(f).

Comments

(a) The source provision has served as a constant reminder to federal judges that pleading is not an end in itself but merely a means to an end, and the above article is included in this Code for the same purpose.

(b) The courts of this state have always professed never to favor technical objections and harsh rules of pleadings, and their decisions during the past quarter century have been in accord with their professed philosophy. For the more recent Louisiana cases reflecting a liberal trend, see West v. Ray, 210 La. 25, 26 So.2d 221 (1946); Seale v. Stephens, 210 La. 1068, 29 So.2d 65 (1946), noted 21 Tul.L.Rev. 703 (1947); Rials v. Davis, 212 La. 161, 31 So.2d 726 (1947); Althans v. Toye Bros. Yellow Cab Co., 191 So. 717 (La.App.1939), noted 14 Tul.L.Rev. 306 (1940); Davies v. Consolidated Underwriters, 14 So.2d 494 (La.App.1943).

CHAPTER 2. PETITION

Art.
891. Form of petition.
892. Alternative causes of action.

Art. 891. Form of petition

The petition shall comply with Articles 853, 854, and 863, and, whenever applicable, with Articles 855 through 861. It shall set forth the name, surname, and domicile of the parties; shall contain a short, clear, and concise statement of the object of the demand and of the material facts upon which the cause of action is based; and shall conclude with a prayer for judgment for the relief sought. Relief may be prayed for in the alternative.

Source: C.P. Arts. 171–173; former R.S. 13:3601; Fed. Rule 8(a).

Cross References: Arts. 926, 1032, 2634, 2703, 2782.

Comments

(a) This article retains the system of fact pleading in effect in Louisiana (see Comments under Art. 854, *supra*), modified through the adoption of a most liberal rule with respect to amendments. See Arts. 1151 and 1154, *infra*.

(b) This article accords with the 1870 Code provisions except that: (1) there will no longer be any requirement for a salutation or address to the court (*cf.* Arts. 171, 172(1), Code of Practice of 1870), although the name of the court will be set forth in the caption required by Art. 853, *supra*; (2) the prohibition against inserting insulting or impertinent expressions in the petition will now be set forth impliedly in Art. 964, *infra*, which states the function of the motion to strike, and is also covered obliquely in Art. 864, *supra*, under which the attorney may be subjected to disciplinary action for signing a pleading which contains scandalous or indecent matter; (3) the obsolete requirement of Art. 172(6), Code of Practice of 1870, that the petition end with the pleader's conclusions, has not been retained; and (4) no verification or certification of the petition, as is required by former R.S. 13:3601, will be necessary. See Comments under Art. 863, *supra*.

(c) See, also, Comments under Arts. 856, 860, 861, *supra*, and Arts. 892, 1154, 3821, *infra*.

Art. 892.   Alternative causes of action

Except as otherwise provided in Article 3657, a petition may set forth two or more causes of action in the alternative, even though the legal or factual bases thereof may be inconsistent or mutually exclusive. In such cases all allegations shall be made subject to the obligations set forth in Article 863.

Source: *Cf.* Fed. Rule 8(e) (2), and Comments following.

Comments

In view of the retention of the system of fact pleading under Arts. 854, 891, *supra*, and 1003 through 1005, *infra*, the rules set forth in this article are substantially identical with the Louisiana jurisprudential rules. Smith v. Donnelly, 27 La.Ann. 98 (1875); Haas v. McCain, 161 La. 114, 108 So. 305 (1926); Board of Com'rs of Orleans Levee Dist. v. Shushan, 197 La. 598, 2 So.2d 35 (1941); Boxwell v. Department of Highways, 203 La. 760, 14 So.2d 627 (1943); Bullis v. Town of Jackson, 4 So.2d 550 (La.App.1941). These cases consistently hold that the prohibition against the cumulation of inconsistent demands, Arts. 149, 152, Code of Practice of 1870, has no application to inconsistent demands pleaded in the alternative.

This article adopts the federal approach of not prohibiting the pleading of alternative causes of action based upon diametrically opposed factual bases, but rather of holding the attorney responsible for fraudulent or untruthful allegations. See Art. 864, *supra*. The pleading in the alternative of causes of action based upon conflicting factual allegations where the plaintiff has no knowledge of the actual facts was permitted in Succession of Markham, 180 La. 211, 156 So. 225 (1934).

Art. 3657, *infra*, prohibits the alternative pleading of the petitory and possessory actions.

CHAPTER 3. EXCEPTIONS

Art.
921. Exception defined.
922. Kinds of exceptions.
923. Functions of exceptions.
924. Form of exceptions.
925. Objections raised by declinatory exception; waiver.
926. Objections raised by dilatory exception; waiver.
927. Objections raised by peremptory exception.
928. Time of pleading exceptions.
929. Time of trial of exceptions.
930. Evidence on trial of declinatory and dilatory exceptions.
931. Evidence on trial of peremptory exception.
932. Effect of sustaining declinatory exception.
933. Effect of sustaining dilatory exception.
934. Effect of sustaining peremptory exception.

Art. 921. Exception defined

An exception is a means of defense, other than a denial or avoidance of the demand, used by the defendant, whether in the principal or an incidental action, to retard, dismiss, or defeat the demand brought against him.

Source: C.P. Art. 330.

Cross Reference: Art. 1111.

Comments

(a) The dual meaning, generic and specific, of the word "exception" in the source provision of the 1870 Code, and in the early Louisiana cases, has proved both confusing and unsatisfactory. For this reason, the definition in the above article was restricted to the specific meaning of the term, by the language "means of defense, other than a denial or avoidance of the demand."

(b) This definition has been rendered more concrete and precise by the enumerations of the objections to be raised through each of the three exceptions. See Arts. 925 through 927, *infra*.

(c) The definition above has been broadened over that contained in Art. 330, Code of Practice of 1870, so as to make it entirely clear that exceptions will be permitted in both the principal and incidental actions. See Comments under Art. 852, *supra*.

Art. 922. Kinds of exceptions

Three exceptions and no others shall be allowed: the declinatory exception, the dilatory exception, and the peremptory exception.

Source: New; *cf.* C.P. Arts. 331, 343.

Cross Reference: Art. 1111.

Comments

(a) This article, though different in theory from the system used heretofore, should not prove too different or difficult of application in practice.

(b) Two important changes in Louisiana procedural law are effected by the above article.

(1) The kinds and classes of the exceptions are abolished. At least one of these classes of exceptions—the exception peremptory as to form—is not and has never been employed in this state. This is due to the fact that, while the Livingston committee, appointed by the legislature in 1822 to prepare a "system of practice to be observed before the courts," adopted Pothier's classification of the exceptions, the jurisprudence recognized the exceptions employed under contemporary Spanish procedure, and there were no exceptions which could be included within the classification "exception peremptory as to form." See McMahon 452, n. 82. Further, the dichotomous terminology of "dilatory exception" and "dilatory exception, properly speaking" has caused considerable confusion and difficulty. See Chaffe v. Ludeling, 34 La.Ann. 962 (1882); State v. Younger, 206 La. 1037, 20 So.2d 305 (1944), noted 19 Tul.L.Rev. 460 (1945).

(2) The above article eliminates the numerous specific exceptions available in Louisiana's armory of defensive weapons. While the courts seldom regard the *label* of the exception as sacramental, the number of exceptions available and the fine line of demarcation between the functions of several make the system too cumbersome and too technical. The reduction of the exceptions to three, and the specific enumerations as to what procedural objections may be raised by each are intended to simplify the system. See Arts. 925 through 927, *infra*.

(c) See, also, Comments under Art. 923, *infra*.

Art. 923. Functions of exceptions

The function of the declinatory exception is to decline the jurisdiction of the court, while the dilatory exception merely retards the progress of the action, but neither exception tends to defeat the action. The function of the peremptory exception is to have the plaintiff's action declared legally nonexistent, or barred by effect of law, and hence this exception tends to dismiss or defeat the action.

Source: C.P. Arts. 332, 334, 343.

Cross Reference: Art. 1111.

Comments

(a) The three exceptions of this article serve the identical functions as the various declinatory, dilatory, and peremptory exceptions, respectively, served under the 1870 Code.

(b) Due allowance being made of the reduction of the exceptions to three under Art. 922, *supra*, this article is a simplified restatement of the three source articles in the 1870 Code of Practice.

Art. 924. Form of exceptions

All exceptions shall comply with Articles 853, 854, and 863, and, whenever applicable, with Articles 855 through 861. They shall set forth the name and surname of the exceptor, shall state with particularity the objections urged and the grounds thereof, and shall contain a prayer for the relief sought.

Source: New.

Cross References: Arts. 1034, 1111.

Comments

(a) Heretofore, the procedural law of Louisiana had no requisites of form for the exceptions, other than the requirement that they be pleaded specially. Phillips v. Preston, 5 How. 278, 12 L.Ed. 152 (1847). The form of the exception required by this article is very similar to the form customarily used. See the annotated forms contained in McMahon, Chapter 5.

(b) The most important change believed to have been made under the above article is the elimination of the "blanket" exception through the new requirement that the exception "state with particularity the objections urged and the grounds thereof." The adoption of such a requirement has been recommended for a number of years. McMahon, The Exception of No Cause of Action in Louisiana, 9 Tul.L.Rev. 17, 26, nn. 51, 52 (1934). A second difference is that the above article requires no verification or certification of the exception, as required by former R.S. 13:3601. These have been dispensed with under this Code. See Comments under Art. 852, *supra*.

(c) See, also, Comments under Art. 930, *infra*.

Art. 925. Objections raised by declinatory exception; waiver

The objections which may be raised through the declinatory exception include, but are not limited to, the following:

(1) Insufficiency of citation;

(2) Insufficiency of service of process;

(3) Pendency of another action between the same parties, in the same capacities, on the same cause of action, and having the same object;

(4) Improper venue;

(5) The court's lack of jurisdiction over the person of defendant; and

(6) The court's lack of jurisdiction over the subject matter of the action.

When two or more of these objections are pleaded in the declinatory exception, they need not be pleaded in the alternative or in any particular order.

When a defendant makes an appearance, all objections which may be raised through the declinatory exception, except the court's lack of jurisdiction over the subject matter of the action, are waived unless pleaded therein.

Source: New; *cf.* C.P. Arts. 92–94, 334–336.

Cross References: Arts. 1034, 1111.

Comments

(a) The enumeration of objections which may be raised through the declinatory exception includes all of the present declinatory exceptions. See McMahon 259 ff. This enumeration was made illustrative, rather than restrictive, so as to permit any other possible objection which presently might be urged through a declinatory exception to be raised through this exception.

(b) For an explanation of the function and scope of the objection of lis pendens, see Arts. 531 and 532, *supra*, and Comments thereunder.

(c) For the rules applicable to the court's jurisdiction over the subject matter and jurisdiction over the person, see Arts. 2, 3, and 6, *supra*.

(d) The second paragraph of this article constitutes a legislative overruling of the cases of State v. Younger, 206 La. 1037, 20 So.2d 305 (1944), noted 19 Tul.L.Rev. 460 (1945); George W. Garig Transfer v. Harris, 226 La. 117, 75 So.2d 28 (1954), noted 15 La. L.Rev. 849 (1955); and Mitchell v. Gulf Finance Corp., 226 La. 1008, 78 So.2d 3 (1955).

(e) See, also, Comments under Arts. 6, 921, 922, *supra*, and Art. 928, *infra*.

Art. 926. Objections raised by dilatory exception; waiver

The objections which may be raised through the dilatory exception include, but are not limited to, the following:

(1) Prematurity;

(2) Want of amicable demand;

(3) Unauthorized use of summary proceeding;

(4) Nonconformity of the petition with any of the requirements of Article 891;

(5) Vagueness or ambiguity of the petition;

(6) Lack of procedural capacity;

(7) Improper cumulation of actions, including improper joinder of parties;

(8) Nonjoinder of necessary party; and

(9) Discussion.

All objections which may be raised through the dilatory exception are waived unless pleaded therein.

Source: C.P. Arts. 332, 333; *cf.* Comments following.

Cross References: Arts. 1034, 1111.

Comments

(a) Except for item 4 above, which is restricted to the function of objecting to the failure of the petition to comply with any formal requirements, all of the objections enumerated in this article are considered dilatory exceptions under the 1870 Code and the Louisiana jurisprudence:

1. Prematurity: Arts. 158, 333, Code of Practice of 1870; Hart v. Springfield Fire & Marine Ins. Co., 136 La. 114, 66 So. 558 (1914); Williams v. Washington Nat. Ins. Co., 180 La. 423, 156 So. 453 (1934).

2. Want of amicable demand: Fox v. Bebee, 4 La. 104 (1832). *Cf.* Howard v. Owners S. B. Columbia, 1 La. 417 (1830); Phelps v. Coggeshall, 13 La.Ann. 440 (1858); Nelligan & Von Zinken v. Musbach, 20 La.Ann. 547 (1868); Porter v. Town of Ville Platte, 158 La. 342, 104 So. 67 (1925); Piazza v. Zimmerman, 49 So.2d 491 (La.App.1950).

3. Unauthorized use of summary proceeding: Butchert v. Ricker, 11 La.Ann. 489 (1856); Younger Bros. v. Spell, 194 La. 16, 193 So. 354 (1939); Alfonso v. Ruiz, 2 So.2d 480 (La.App.1941); Roper

v. Brooks, 9 So.2d 497 (La.App.1942); Cryer v. Cryer, 44 So.2d 517 (La.App.1950). See also, Dussin v. Delaroderie, 5 Rob. 202 (La.1843); LeBoeuf v. Merle, 1 La.Ann. 144 (1846); Conery v. Heno, 9 La.Ann. 587 (1854); Succession of Moore, 18 La.Ann. 512 (1866); Succession of Esteves, 182 La. 604, 162 So. 194 (1935); Bloomenstiel v. Tridico, 156 So. 793 (La.App.1934); Foret v. Stark, 16 So.2d 79 (La.App.1943).

5. Vagueness: Doullut v. McManus, 37 La.Ann. 800 (1885); Foster & Glassell Corp. v. Ackel, 166 So. 885 (La.App.1936).

There was a hiatus in the former law with respect to the vagueness or generality of the allegations of the answer, since the defendant was not permitted to amend his answer when plaintiff objected to the admission of evidence on the trial on the ground that no proper foundation therefor was laid in the answer; and this harsh result has been criticized vigorously. See McMahon, The Exception of No Cause of Action in Louisiana, 9 Tul.L.Rev. 17, 34–36 (1934).

The grounds of this criticism, however, are now removed through the provisions of Art. 1154, *infra*, under which the trial court is not only authorized, but is directed, to permit amendment of the answer in such cases. If plaintiff is surprised by the allegations of the amended answer, he may request a continuance to meet the new issues. Under this Code, the plaintiff's right to object to evidence when no foundation for its admission is provided in the answer, and the defendant's right to amend his answer so as to provide such foundation, constitutes an effective substitute for a plaintiff's motion for a bill of particulars.

6. Lack of procedural capacity: Arts. 320, 333, Code of Practice of 1870; Cartwright v. Puissigur, 125 La. 700, 51 So. 692 (1910); Central Surety & Ins. Corp. v. Canulette Shipbuilding Co., 195 So. 114 (La.App.1940); Wiseman v. Begnaud, 35 So.2d 836 (La.App. 1948).

7. Improper cumulation of actions: Cuny v. Brown, 12 Rob. 82 (La.1845); Mackoy v. J. B. Holton & Co., 8 La.Ann. 48 (1853); Gribble v. McKleroy & Bradford, 14 La.Ann. 793 (1859); Maisonneuve v. Dalferes, 133 La. 666, 63 So. 261 (1913). This subject has been complicated tremendously through the unfortunate borrowing of common law terminology and the creation of the so-called exception of misjoinder of parties. On this point, see McMahon 379–381, n. 71; and McMahon, Parties Litigant in Louisiana-III, 13 Tul.L.Rev. 385, 385–401 (1939). The objection to misjoinder of parties has been considered a dilatory exception. Kenney v. Dow, 10 Mart.(O.S.) 577, 13 Am.Dec. 342 (1822); Reardon v. Dickinson, 156 La. 556, 100 So. 715 (1924); Mitchell v. Holomon, 10 La. App. 219, 120 So. 672 (1929).

8. Nonjoinder of a necessary party: Although usually referred to as the exception of nonjoinder of proper parties, when used to

raise the objection that a necessary party has not been joined, this exception has always been classified as dilatory. Brown v. Robinson, 6 La.Ann. 423 (1851); Tanner v. King, 10 La.Ann. 485 (1855); Brewer v. Cook, 11 La.Ann. 637 (1856); Dyer and Stevenson v. Drew, 14 La.Ann. 657 (1859); Moore v. Gray, 22 La.Ann. 289 (1870).

See Arts. 641, 642, *supra*, and Comments thereunder. This objection should be distinguished from that of nonjoinder of an indispensable party. See Art. 641, *supra*, and Art. 927, *infra*.

9. Discussion: This exception has always been classified as a dilatory one. Art. 333, Codes of Practice of 1825 and 1870.

(b) See, also, Comments under Arts. 421, 464, 684, 921, 922, *supra*, and Arts. 1005, 2593, *infra*.

Art. 927.   Objections raised by peremptory exception

The objections which may be raised through the peremptory exception include, but are not limited to, the following:

(1) Prescription;

(2) Res judicata;

(3) Nonjoinder of an indispensable party;

(4) No cause of action; and

(5) No right of action, or no interest in the plaintiff to institute the suit.

The court cannot supply the objections of prescription and res judicata, which must be specially pleaded. The nonjoinder of an indispensable party, or the failure to disclose a cause of action or a right or interest in the plaintiff to institute the suit, may be noticed by either the trial or appellate court of its own motion.

Source: C.P. Arts. 343, 345; *cf.* Comments following.

Cross References: Arts. 1034, 1111.

Comments

(a) The peremptory exception of division, McCausland v. Lyons, 4 La.Ann. 273 (1874), Kilgore v. Tippit, 26 La.Ann. 624 (1874), has been converted into an affirmative defense in this Code. Its function is not to defeat the demand, but only to regulate the enforcement of the judgment; hence, in this Code the objection is raised through an affirmative defense, rather than through the peremptory exception. See Comments under Art. 1005, *infra*.

(b) Other than the change noted above with respect to division, and the consolidation of the several peremptory exceptions into a single one, no change has been made. The rules contained in the above article are supported, with respect to the various objections enumerated, by the following:

1. Prescription: Arts. 345, 346, 902, Code of Practice of 1870; Art. 3464, Civil Code; Dunbar v. Nichols, 10 Mart.(O.S.) 184 (1821); Ashbey v. Ashbey, 41 La.Ann. 102, 5 So. 539 (1889); Dunlap v. Berthelot, 122 La. 531, 47 So. 882 (1908).

2. Res judicata: Arts. 345, 346, Code of Practice of 1870; Williams v. Bethany, 1 La. 315 (1830); Zollicoffer v. Briggs, 3 Rob. 236 (La.1842); Carpenter v. Beatty, 12 Rob. 540 (1846); State v. Alexander, 106 La. 460, 31 So. 60 (1901); Lewis v. Lewis, 155 La. 231, 99 So. 202 (1924).

3. Nonjoinder of an indispensable party: Cucullu v. Walker, 16 La.Ann. 198 (1861); Ashbey v. Ashbey, 41 La.Ann. 138, 5 So. 546 (1889); Heirs of Burney v. Ludeling, 41 La.Ann. 627, 6 So. 248 (1889); Willis v. Wasey, 42 La.Ann. 876, 8 So. 591 (1890); Blum & Co. v. Wyly, 111 La. 1092, 36 So. 202 (1904); Succession of Todd, 165 La. 453, 115 So. 653 (1928); Commercial Nat. Bank in Shreveport v. Haas, 182 La. 502, 162 So. 57 (1935); Harvey v. Engler, 184 La. 858, 168 So. 81 (1936); Douglas v. Haro, 214 La. 1099, 39 So.2d 744 (1949); Jamison v. Superior Oil Co., 220 La. 923, 57 So.2d 896 (1952); Horn v. Skelly Oil Co., 221 La. 626, 60 So.2d 65 (1952); Kinchen v. Ligamari, 14 La.App. 497, 130 So. 228 (1930); Holicer Gas Co. v. Wilson, 39 So.2d 637 (La.App. 1949); Greer v. Sumney, 41 So.2d 526 (La.App.1949); Breazel v. Taylor, 46 So.2d 138 (La.App.1950); Chiasson v. Duplechain, 56 So.2d 615 (La.App.1952). The exceptions of nonjoinder of necessary parties (dilatory) and of indispensable parties (peremptory) have been confused in the opinions in DeHart v. Continental Land & Fur Co., 196 La. 701, 200 So. 9 (1940); and Ott v. Grace, 13 So. 2d 138 (La.App.1943). The above and the preceding articles serve to differentiate the functions of these two objections.

4. No cause of action: Arts. 345, 346, 902, Code of Practice of 1870; Fletcher v. Dunbar, 21 La.Ann. 150 (1869); Tarleton v. Kennedy, 21 La.Ann. 500 (1869); McCubbin v. Hastings, 27 La. Ann. 713 (1875); Weller v. VanHoven, 42 La.Ann. 600, 7 So. 702 (1890); Godwin v. Neustadt, 42 La.Ann. 735, 7 So. 744 (1890); Succession of Curtis, 156 La. 243, 100 So. 412 (1924). No cases were found which expressly held that the exception of no cause of action need not be pleaded; but it is obvious that if the petition does not state a cause of action, unless evidence is introduced without objection which would cure the defect, the court cannot render judgment for plaintiff. McMahon, Parties Litigant in Louisiana— III, 11 Tul.L.Rev. 527 (1937). Cf. Brown & Sons v. Saul, 4 Mart. (N.S.) 434, 16 Am.Dec. 175 (1826).

5. No right of action or no interest of plaintiff: Arts. 345, 346, 902, Code of Practice of 1870; Brown & Sons v. Saul, 4 Mart. (N.S.) 434, 16 Am.Dec. 175 (1826); Outdoor Electric Advertising,

Inc. v. Saurage, 207 La. 344, 21 So.2d 375 (1945); Termini v. McCormick, 208 La. 221, 23 So.2d 52 (1945); Ritsch Alluvial Land Co. v. Adema, 211 La. 675, 30 So.2d 753 (1947); Brooks v. Smith, 35 So.2d 613 (La.App.1948). See Comments under Art. 681, *infra*.

(c) Though cases can be found in which estoppel has been treated as an exception, Coco v. Nolin, 56 So.2d 204 (La.App.1951), in the vast majority of instances when the defendant has pleaded estoppel, it is set forth as an affirmative defense. Further, estoppel is as available to a plaintiff as it is to a defendant, and hence cannot be treated exclusively as an exception. For these reasons this objection is not included in the enumeration of the above article, but it is required that estoppel be pleaded by the plaintiff in the petition, and by the defendant as an affirmative defense. See Art. 1005, *infra*.

(d) See, also, Comments under Arts. 423, 921, 922, 926, *supra*, and Arts. 1064, 2163, *infra*.

Art. 928. Time of pleading exceptions

The declinatory exception and the dilatory exception shall be pleaded prior to answer or judgment by default. When both exceptions are pleaded, they shall be filed at the same time, and may be incorporated in the same pleading. When filed at the same time or in the same pleading, these exceptions need not be pleaded in the alternative or in a particular order.

The peremptory exception may be pleaded at any stage of the proceeding in the trial court prior to a submission of the case for a decision.

Source: C.P. Arts. 333, 346, 902.

Cross References: Arts. 44, 72, 1034, 1111.

Comments

(a) This article has adopted "prior to answer or judgment by default" as the deadline for filing the declinatory and dilatory exceptions, instead of "before issue joined" or "in limine litis". These latter concepts are anachronistic throwbacks to the early periods of Roman law, 15 La.L.Rev. 722, 723–724 (1955); and not only have no rational basis in modern procedure, but they have proven nebulous and unworkable.

Further, under Art. 902, Code of Practice of 1870, the appellate court in its discretion might consider a peremptory exception filed in the appellate court, but was under no compulsion to do so. Succession of Douglass, 225 La. 65, 72 So.2d 262 (1954), discussed in 15 La.L.Rev. 393, 394 (1955). There is no intention to change the rule of the *Douglass* case.

(b) This article changes the procedural law in one respect: it suppresses the rule of State v. Younger, 206 La. 1037, 20 So.2d 305 (1944), noted 19 Tul.L.Rev. 460 (1945), requiring pleading of the dilatory exception in the alternative when joined with the declinatory exception. This jurisprudential rule is unnecessarily technical, and is out of harmony with the procedural philosophy on which this Code is based. See, also, Comment (d) of Art. 925, *supra*.

(c) The second paragraph of this article is declaratory of the rule of Gayarre v. Millaudon, 23 La.Ann. 305 (1871), and by analogy, of the rule of O'Hara v. City of New Orleans, 30 La.Ann. 152 (1878). It qualifies the decision in Motors Ins. Corp. v. Employers' Liability Assur. Corp., 52 So.2d 311 (La.App.1951), which is believed to be too broad to prove workable.

(d) For the rule as to the filing of the peremptory exception for the first time in the appellate court, see Art. 2163, *infra*, and Comments thereunder.

(e) See, also, Comments under Art. 684, *supra*, and Arts. 1152, 1201, 2163, *infra*.

Art. 929. Time of trial of exceptions

The declinatory exception, the dilatory exception, and the peremptory exception when pleaded before answer, shall be tried and decided in advance of the trial of the case.

If the peremptory exception has been pleaded in the answer, or subsequently, but at or prior to the trial of the case, it shall be tried and disposed of on the trial. If the peremptory exception has been pleaded after the trial of the case, the court may rule thereon at any time unless the party against whom it has been pleaded desires and is entitled to introduce evidence thereon. In the latter event, the peremptory exception shall be tried specially.

Source: C.P. Arts. 346, 902; *cf.* Comments following.

Cross References: Arts. 1034, 1111.

Comments

(a) Under the jurisprudential rules, declinatory and dilatory exceptions ordinarily must be tried and decided preliminarily and prior to the trial of the case on its merits. Under exceptional and unusual cases, however, the trial judge might have no alternative but to refer a declinatory exception to the merits, and decide it after the trial of the case. *Cf.* Gordon v. Bates-Crumley Chevrolet Co., 182 La. 795, 162 So. 624 (1935).

(b) While the practice of referring peremptory exceptions to the merits has sometimes been criticized by the supreme court, Jennings v. Vickers, 31 La.Ann. 679 (1879), Farmer v. Hafley, 38 La. Ann. 232 (1886), Zerega v. Percival, 46 La.Ann. 590, 15 So. 476 (1894), later cases have recognized the discretion of the trial judge to refer the exception to the merits rather than attempt to dispose of it prior to the trial of the case. Saint v. Martel, 123 La. 815, 49 So. 582, 586 (1909). See, also, City of New Orleans v. Salmen Brick & Lumber Co., 135 La. 828, 66 So. 237 (1914). The rules enunciated in the above article with respect to the trial of the peremptory exception do not interfere in any way with the trial judge's discretion in such cases. They merely prevent the defendant's using dilatory tactics in filing the exception after answer, and then insisting upon the trial of the exception in an effort to delay the trial of the case on its merits.

Art. 930. Evidence on trial of declinatory and dilatory exceptions

On the trial of the declinatory exception, evidence may be introduced to support or controvert any of the objections pleaded, when the grounds thereof do not appear from the petition, the citation, or return thereon.

On the trial of the dilatory exception, evidence may be introduced to support or controvert any of the objections pleaded, when the grounds thereof do not appear from the petition.

Source: New; *cf.* Comments following.

Cross References: Arts. 1034, 1111.

Comments

The grounds of objections urged by the dilatory exceptions might appear from the face of the petition, while the grounds of objections pleaded in the declinatory exception might appear on the face of the petition, the citation, or the return thereon. In none of these circumstances would there be any necessity of introducing evidence either to support or to controvert any of the objections pleaded. Since under Art. 924, *supra*, the exceptions must "state with particularity the objections urged and the grounds thereof," adequate foundation for the introduction of evidence to support any of the objections is always provided by the exception. Similarly, since under Art. 852, *supra*, "[a]ll new matter alleged in exceptions . . . shall be considered denied or avoided," the plaintiff is always permitted to introduce evidence to controvert the objections pleaded in the exception.

See, also, Comments under Art. 931, *infra*.

Art. 931. Evidence on trial of peremptory exception

On the trial of the peremptory exception pleaded at or prior to the trial of the case, evidence may be introduced to support or controvert any of the objections pleaded, when the grounds thereof do not appear from the petition.

When the peremptory exception is pleaded in the trial court after the trial of the case, but prior to a submission for a decision, the plaintiff may introduce evidence in opposition thereto, but the defendant may introduce no evidence except to rebut that offered by plaintiff.

No evidence may be introduced at any time to support or controvert the objection that the petition fails to state a cause of action.

Source: C.P. Arts. 346, 902; cf. Comments following.

Cross References: Arts. 1034, 1111.

Comments

(a) See Comments under Art. 930, *supra*.

(b) Arts. 346 and 902 of the Code of Practice of 1870 preclude the exceptor's depriving the plaintiff of the opportunity of adducing evidence by pleading the exception after the trial of the case, or in the appellate court, and provide that in such cases the plaintiff is to be given an opportunity to produce his evidence, even though this may require a remand of the case from the appellate to the trial court. The rules set forth in the above article are based upon the rationale of these two 1870 Code provisions, but have been expanded to cover all phases of the problem.

(c) This article retains the rule that no evidence is to be admitted at any time to support or controvert the objection that the petition fails to state a cause of action.

(d) For the rule applicable when the peremptory exception is filed for the first time in the appellate court, see Art. 2163, *infra*.

Art. 932. Effect of sustaining declinatory exception

When the grounds of the objections pleaded in the declinatory exception may be removed by amendment of the petition or other action of plaintiff, the judgment sustaining the exception shall order the plaintiff to remove them within the delay allowed by the court.

If the grounds of the objection cannot be so removed, or if the plaintiff fails to comply with an order requiring such removal, the action shall be dismissed; except that if it has been brought in a court of improper jurisdiction or venue, the court may transfer the action to a proper court in the interest of justice.

Source: C.P. Art. 334; *cf.* Comments following.

Cross References: Arts. 1034, 1111, 1151.

Comments

(a) With the single exception noted in Comment (b) hereof, this article works no change in the procedural law of Louisiana, and is quite in accord with the liberality of amendment characterizing the most recent decisions of the Supreme Court of Louisiana. See, also, Art. 1152, *infra*.

(b) No dismissal of the action would necessarily result from a sustaining of the declinatory exception under this article if the objection were either to the venue or to the jurisdiction of the court, and if the interests of justice required its transfer to the proper court. It is contemplated that dismissal would result only in those cases where such a transfer would not be possible or would not be conducive to the administration of justice. Such a dismissal would not preclude the filing of an action in the proper court.

A transfer clause similar to that of the above article, but restricted to cases involving improper venue, is provided by Art. 121, *supra*.

(c) The machinery for effecting the transfer of the action under this article is provided in R.S. 13:3271 through 13:3274.

(d) See, also, Comments under Arts. 121, 464, *supra*.

Art. 933. Effect of sustaining dilatory exception

If the dilatory exception pleading want of amicable demand is sustained, the final judgment shall impose all court costs upon the plaintiff. If the dilatory exception pleading prematurity is sustained, the suit shall be dismissed.

When the grounds of the other objections pleaded in the dilatory exception may be removed by amendment of the petition or other action by plaintiff, the judgment sustaining the exception shall order plaintiff to remove them within the delay allowed by the court; and the suit shall be dismissed only for a noncompliance with this order.

Source: C.P. Arts. 158, 332; *cf.* Comments following.

Cross References: Arts. 1034, 1111, 1151.

Comments

(a) The rules announced by this article effect no change in the law since they are simply declaratory of the liberality of amendment characterizing the most recent decisions of the Supreme Court of Louisiana. See Comments under Art. 934, *supra*.

(b) Special provision was made for the effect of the sustaining of the dilatory exception pleading the objection of want of amicable demand, which can only be raised by a defendant willing to comply with the plaintiff's demand, and which relieves defendant from the payment of court costs. See cases cited under Comment (d) of Art. 421, *supra*.

(c) Under Art. 158, Code of Practice of 1870, the effect of sustaining the exception pleading the prematurity of the action is the dismissal of the action. This rule has been retained. Such dismissal, however, is without prejudice to the plaintiff's right to bring the action anew when matured.

(d) See, also, Comments under Art. 421, *supra*.

Art. 934. Effect of sustaining peremptory exception

When the grounds of the objection pleaded by the peremptory exception may be removed by amendment of the petition, the judgment sustaining the exception shall order such amendment within the delay allowed by the court. If the grounds of the objection cannot be so removed, or if plaintiff fails to comply with the order to amend, the action shall be dismissed.

Source: C.P. Art. 343; *cf.* Comments following.

Cross References: Arts. 1034, 1111, 1151.

Comments

Though it is contemplated that in most instances the maintaining of the peremptory exception will necessarily result in a judgment dismissing the action, this article authorizes the trial judge to permit amendment of the petition whenever possible and whenever dismissal of the suit would not be in the interests of justice. This rule is simply declaratory of the liberality of amendment characterizing the recent decisions of our appellate courts. See Reeves v. Globe Indemnity Co. of New York, 185 La. 42, 168 So. 488 (1936); Reagor v. First Nat. Life Ins. Co., 212 La. 789, 33 So. 2d 521 (1948); Douglas v. Haro, 214 La. 1099, 39 So.2d 744 (1949); Bailey v. Simon, 199 So. 185 (La.App.1940); Arceneaux v. Louisiana Highway Commission, 5 So.2d 20 (La.App.1941); Pancoast v. Cooperative Cab Co., 37 So.2d 452 (La.App.1948); Turner v. Maryland Casualty Co., 44 So.2d 374 (La.App.1950); Doyle v. Thompson, 50 So.2d 505 (La.App.1951).

See, also, Comments under Art. 933, *supra*.

CHAPTER 4. WRITTEN MOTIONS

Art.
961. Written motion required; exception.
962. Form of written motion.
963. Ex parte and contradictory motions; rule to show cause.
964. Motion to strike.
965. Motion for judgment on pleadings.
966. Motion for summary judgment; procedure.
967. Same; affidavits.
968. Effect of judgment on pleadings and summary judgment.
969. Judgment on pleadings and summary judgment not permitted in certain cases.

PRELIMINARY STATEMENT

Although motions are not considered to be pleadings under the Federal Rules of Civil Procedure, many of the pleading requirements have been made applicable to written motions. See Fed. Rule 7. In Louisiana, written motions have always been considered as pleadings under former R.S. 13:3601 and Art. 401, Code of Practice of 1870, and for this reason the rules applicable thereto are included in this Title.

While it was deemed necessary in the initial article to distinguish between oral and written motions, the articles of this Chapter otherwise apply only to written motions.

Art. 961. Written motion required; exception

An application to the court for an order, if not presented in some other pleading, shall be by motion which, unless made during trial or hearing or in open court, shall be in writing.

Source: Fed. Rule 7(b) (1); cf. Comments following.

Cross References: Arts. 1034, 1111.

Comments

(a) Fed. Rule 7(b) (1) provides: "An application to the court for an order shall be by motion which, unless made during a hearing or trial, shall be made in writing, shall state with particularity the grounds therefor, and shall set forth the relief or order sought. The requirement of writing is fulfilled if the motion is stated in a written notice of the hearing of the motion."

The requirement of the Federal Rules of Civil Procedure that motions be in writing unless made at a trial or hearing goes far beyond the Louisiana rule under which, unless the rules of the trial

Art. 961

court provide otherwise, there is no requirement that motions be in writing, only that they be entered on the minutes of the court. Anderson v. Thomas, 166 La. 512, 117 So. 573 (1928) and cases cited therein. The above article retains the Louisiana practice which permits oral motions when made during a trial or hearing or in open court.

(b) Although in one sense of the word a subpoena or a writ issued by the court is an "order," the word "order" as used in the above article is not intended to include subpoenas or writs.

(c) See, also, Comments under Arts. 1603, 1971, 1972, 1973, 1975, *infra*.

Art. 962. Form of written motion

A written motion shall comply with Articles 853 and 863, and shall state the grounds therefor, and the relief or order sought. It must also comply with Article 854 if the motion is lengthy, and whenever applicable, with Articles 855 through 861.

Source: Fed. Rules 7(b), 10.

Cross References: Arts. 1034, 1111.

Comments

(a) The formal requirements of the above article are in accord with the preferred practice in Louisiana. For the form of the motions and rules employed in many Louisiana jurisdictions, see McMahon, 531, 533.

(b) Pleading in separately numbered paragraphs is unnecessary in short written motions. It is extremely helpful in lengthy written motions. It is left to the discretion of the trial court to draw the line between "short" and "lengthy" written motions, and to determine specifically when separately numbered paragraphs are necessary.

(c) See, also, Comments under Art. 854, *supra*, and Art. 1975, *infra*.

Art. 963. Ex parte and contradictory motions; rule to show cause

If the order applied for by written motion is one to which mover is clearly entitled without supporting proof, the court may grant the order ex parte and without hearing the adverse party.

If the order applied for by written motion is one to which the mover is not clearly entitled, or which requires supporting proof, the motion shall be served on and tried contradictorily with the adverse party.

The rule to show cause is a contradictory motion.

Source: New; *cf.* Comments following.

Cross References: Arts. 1034, 1111.

Comments

(a) The "ex parte motion" of the first paragraph of this article is often referred to simply as a "motion". *Cf.* McMahon 524.

(b) Contradictory motions are of two types. Usually, they are in the form of a "rule to show cause", which is a hybrid pleading commencing with a written, ex parte motion by a party through counsel, suggesting the need or desirability of granting certain relief to mover, at the bottom of which is a blank order to be signed by the judge, requiring the adverse party to show cause at a designated time why mover should not be granted the suggested relief. This pleading is filed in court, presented to the judge in due course, and if the judge considers that the rule should be tried, he signs the order and fills in the appropriate blank to designate the time at which it should be tried. This combined motion and order is then served on the adverse party. See McMahon, Summary Procedure: A Comparative Study, 31 Tul.L.Rev. 573, 586, n. 50 (1957); and McMahon 525. *Cf.* former R.S. 13:3601(4).

Less frequently, the contradictory motion is in the form of that used in federal practice—a written motion filed in court suggesting the need or desirability of granting certain relief to mover, with a copy thereof served on the adverse party prior to a filing of the original in court. Subsequently, if the court considers that the motion should be heard, it assigns a time for the hearing, and has both parties notified thereof.

Under this article, either form of the contradictory motion may be used, at the option of the mover.

(c) See, also, Comments under Arts. 1312, 1975, 3505, *infra*.

Art. 964. Motion to strike

The court on motion of a party or on its own motion may at any time and after a hearing order stricken from any pleading any insufficient demand or defense or any redundant, immaterial, impertinent, or scandalous matter. The motion of a party shall be filed within ten days after service of the pleading upon mover, except that a defendant may move to strike any matter from the petition at any time within fifteen days of the service.

Source: Fed. Rule 12(f); *cf.* Comments following.

Cross References: Arts. 1034, 1111.

Comments

(a) The motion to strike from the pleadings formerly was recognized by the jurisprudence. Frank v. Magee, 49 La.Ann. 1250, 22 So. 739 (1897); Vicknair v. Terracina, 164 La. 117, 113 So. 787 (1927); In re Buller's Estates, 192 La. 644, 188 So. 728 (1939); Cox v. Cox, 193 La. 268, 190 So. 401 (1939). Later decisions of the supreme court, however, expressly repudiated the earlier position, and announced that the motion to strike had no place in the procedure of Louisiana. State ex rel. Sutton v. Caldwell, 195 La. 507, 197 So. 214 (1940); Perez v. Meraux, 195 La. 987, 197 So. 683 (1940); Stanley v. Jones, 197 La. 627, 2 So.2d 45 (1941); Central Sav. Bank & Trust Co. v. Oilfield Supply & S. Mat. Co., 202 La. 787, 12 So.2d 819 (1943); *Id.*, 12 So.2d 815 (La.App.1942); Atchley v. Horne, 13 So.2d 75 (La.App.1943); Davies v. Consolidated Underwriters, 14 So.2d 494 (La.App.1943). However, it was reinstated for the reason that there is no other procedural device, either in the 1870 Code of Practice or under the system proposed by this Code, which would effectively perform the functions of the motion to strike.

(b) Fed. Rule 12(f) provides that "Upon motion made by a party before responding to a pleading or, if no responsive pleading is permitted by these rules, upon motion made by a party within 20 days after the service of the pleading upon him or upon the court's own initiative at any time, the court may order stricken from any pleading any insufficient defense or any redundant, immaterial, impertinent, or scandalous matter." However, to prevent its use for dilatory tactics, fifteen days is provided in this article as a reasonable delay for filing a motion to strike matter from the petition and ten days is allowed for moving to strike matter from other pleadings. The motion to strike is made available to a defendant wishing to strike an insufficient demand from a petition, as well as to a plaintiff wishing to strike an insufficient defense from an answer.

Art. 965. Motion for judgment on pleadings

Any party may move for judgment on the pleadings after the answer is filed, or if an incidental demand has been instituted after the answer thereto has been filed, but within such time as not to delay the trial. For the purposes of this motion, all allegations of fact in mover's pleadings not denied by the adverse party or by effect of law, and all allegations of fact in the adverse party's pleadings shall be considered true.

Source: Former R.S. 13:3601(4); Fed. Rule 12(c).

Cross References: Arts. 1034, 1111, 1915.

Tit. 1 WRITTEN MOTIONS Art. 966

Comments

(a) This article follows Fed. Rule 12(c), and changes the rule of former R.S. 13:3601(4), so as to extend the motion for judgment on the pleadings to any party, and not restrict the availability of the device to the plaintiff. This extension increases its effectiveness and provides a needed procedural device for both plaintiff and defendant in incidental actions, where, under Art. 1035, *infra*, answers to incidental demands are required. This article further changes the rule of former R.S. 13:3601(4), which precludes the use of the motion for judgment on the pleadings in any case where there is a demand in warranty by defendant, or petition of intervention or third opposition, unless the state of the pleadings is such as to justify a judgment upon these demands. Since within the discretion of the trial judge, separate trials may be allowed, and separate judgments rendered, in incidental actions (Art. 1038, *infra*), there is no reason why the trial judge should not render judgment on the pleadings in either the principal demand or incidental demand, if he deems it in the interest of justice. Except for the changes indicated above, this article is a simplification of former R.S. 13:3601(4).

(b) Arts. 968 and 969, *infra*, provide additional rules for the motion for judgment on the pleadings.

Art. 966. Motion for summary judgment; procedure

The plaintiff or defendant in the principal or any incidental action, with or without supporting affidavits, may move for a summary judgment in his favor for all or part of the relief for which he has prayed. The plaintiff's motion may be made at any time after the answer has been filed. The defendant's motion may be made at any time.

The motion for summary judgment shall be served at least ten days before the time specified for the hearing. The adverse party may serve opposing affidavits prior to the day of the hearing. The judgment sought shall be rendered forthwith if the pleadings, depositions, and admissions on file, together with the affidavits, if any, show that there is no genuine issue as to material fact, and that mover is entitled to judgment as a matter of law.

Source: Fed. Rule 56(a)-(c).

Cross References: Arts. 1034, 1111, 1915.

Comments

(a) Under the 1870 Code of Practice there is no counterpart to the motion for summary judgment. Even though, in all probability, it will not be successfully utilized often, the availability of the device and its potential for expeditious disposition of frivolous, but well pleaded, demands and defenses should go very far in discouraging such demands and defenses.

(b) Though based upon Fed. Rule 56(a)–(c), the above article does not embody two changes in the federal rule made through the 1946 amendments thereof. Under this article the plaintiff in a principal or incidental action is not forced to wait twenty days after the commencement of the action, or until after a motion for summary judgment is served by the adverse party, before moving for summary judgment. Instead, the plaintiff is permitted to move for a summary judgment at any time after the answer is filed. Fed. Rule 56(c) was considered unnecessary in Louisiana. Such a provision is helpful in federal litigation, where otherwise all issues would have to go to the jury if there is an issue as to the amount of damages, with the consequent waste of the time of the court and attorneys. But in Louisiana, where civil jury trials are a rarity and the entire case usually is tried by the judge alone, no appreciable saving of time would be effected through such a provision.

(c) Arts. 967, 968, and 969, *infra*, provide additional rules for the motion for summary judgment.

Art. 967. Same; affidavits

Supporting and opposing affidavits shall be made on personal knowledge, shall set forth such facts as would be admissible in evidence, and shall show affirmatively that the affiant is competent to testify to the matters stated therein. Sworn or certified copies of all papers or parts thereof referred to in an affidavit shall be attached thereto or served therewith. The court may permit affidavits to be supplemented or opposed by depositions or by further affidavits.

If it appears from the affidavits of a party opposing the motion that for reasons stated he cannot present by affidavits facts essential to justify his opposition, the court may refuse the application for judgment or may order a continuance to permit affidavits to be obtained or depositions to be taken or discovery to be had or may make such other order as is just.

If it appears to the satisfaction of the court at any time that any of the affidavits presented pursuant to this article are presented in bad faith or solely for the purposes of delay, the court immediately shall order the party employing them to pay to the other party the amount of the reasonable expenses which the filing of the affidavits caused him to incur, including reasonable attorney's fees. Any offending party or attorney may be adjudged guilty of contempt.

Source: Fed. Rule 56(e)–(g).
Cross References: Arts. 1034, 1111.

Comments

(a) This article is substantially the same as Fed. Rule 56(e)–(g).

(b) See Comments under Arts. 966, *supra*, and 968 and 969, *infra*.

Art. 968. Effect of judgment on pleadings and summary judgment

Judgments on the pleadings, and summary judgments, are final judgments and shall be rendered and signed in the same manner and with the same effect as if a trial had been had upon evidence regularly adduced. If the judgment does not grant mover all of the relief prayed for, jurisdiction shall be retained in order to adjudicate on mover's right to the relief not granted on motion.

An appeal does not lie from the court's refusal to render any judgment on the pleading or summary judgment.

Source: Former R.S. 13:3601(4).

Cross References: Arts. 1034, 1111, 1915.

Comments

(a) The rules enunciated in this article were taken directly from former R.S. 13:3601, and extended so as to make them applicable to summary judgments as well as judgments on the pleadings.

(b) Under the Louisiana motion for summary judgment, differently from that governed by Fed. Rule 56(c), no interlocutory summary judgment can be rendered. See Comment (b) under Art. 966, *supra*.

(c) See Art. 2085, Comment (c), *infra*, with reference to the appealability of judgments rendered on the face of the pleadings notwithstanding the admissions contained in the answer.

(d) Since a trial court's action in overruling a motion for judgment on the pleadings, or for summary judgment, is merely an interlocutory judgment causing no irreparable injury, it cannot be appealed, except under the appeal from the final judgment rendered in the case. *Cf.* Art. 2083, *infra*.

(e) See, also, Comments under Arts. 965, 966, 967, *supra*, and Arts. 969, 2083, *infra*.

Art. 969. Judgment on pleadings and summary judgment not permitted in certain cases

Judgments on the pleadings and summary judgments shall not be granted in any action for divorce, separation from bed and board, or annulment of marriage, nor in any case where the community, paraphernal, or dotal rights may be involved in an action between husband and wife.

Source: Former R.S. 13:3601(4).

Cross References: Arts. 1034, 1111, 1915.

Comments

(a) The rules set forth in this article were taken directly from the Pleading and Practice Act, former R.S. 13:3601(4), under which they apply only to the motion for judgment on the pleadings. These rules were extended to the motion for summary judgment to prevent collusive judgments under the motion for summary judgment in divorce actions and other suits involving the rights of married women.

(b) When the motion for summary judgment was first developed, it was made available only to specified cases. However, by the adoption of the new Federal Rules of Civil Procedure, a precedent was established in making the device available in any case. The English rules permit the motion for summary judgment in all suits except those in libel, slander, malicious prosecution, false imprisonment, seduction, breach of promise, and actions in which the plaintiff alleges fraud. Eng. Rules of Supreme Court, Orders 3, r. 6(4), 14, 14a, and 15, Ann.Pract. (1950). Restrictions on the use of the motion for summary judgment in Louisiana were imposed for precisely the same reasons as required the restriction of the motion for judgment on the pleadings in this state.

(c) See Comments under Arts. 966, 967, and 968, *supra*.

CHAPTER 5. ANSWER

Art.
1001. Delay for answering.
1002. Answer filed prior to confirmation of default.
1003. Form of answer.
1004. Denials.
1005. Affirmative defenses.
1006. Alternative defenses.

Art. 1001. Delay for answering

A defendant shall file his answer within fifteen days after service of citation upon him, except as otherwise provided by law.

When an exception is filed prior to answer and is overruled or referred to the merits, or is sustained and an amendment of the petition ordered, the answer shall be filed within ten days after the exception is overruled or referred to the merits, or ten days after service of the amended petition.

The court may grant additional time for answering.

Source: C.P. Arts. 180, 316; former R.S. 13:3344; Fed. Rule 12(a).

Cross References: Arts. 1002, 1035, 1111, 1151, 1202.

Comments

(a) The article above adopts the simple flat delay allowed for answering regardless of the distance from the defendant's residence to the place where the court is held. In this day of rapid communication and transportation, there is no real need for any distance differential, and the difficulties of computing the time as provided in Art. 180, Code of Practice of 1870, make its retention inadvisable.

(b) The delay for answering, after the overruling of an exception, provided in this article is the same as that provided by former R.S. 13:3344.

(c) The last paragraph of this article is essentially the same as Art. 316, Code of Practice of 1870, which permits the trial judge to grant additional time for answering when necessary.

There is one change in Louisiana's procedural law effected by this Code, although not by the above article, which should be noted here. Under federal practice, when an enlargement of the delay for answering is granted, the order automatically extends the time for filing motions to dismiss. Fed. Rules 6(b) and 12(a); Orange Theatre Corp. v. Rayherstz Amusement Corp., 139 F.2d 871 (3 Cir. 1944); Blanton v. Pacific Mutual Life Ins. Co., 4 F.R.D. 200 (D.C. N.C.1944). This is contrary to the holding of the Louisiana cases that a defendant who moves for an extension of time to plead makes a general appearance which submits him to the jurisdiction of the court for all purposes. Modisette & Adams v. Lorenze, 163 La. 505, 112 So. 397 (1927); Stanley v. Jones, 197 La. 627, 2 So.2d 45 (1941). The result reached in these Louisiana cases is changed by the provisions of Art. 7, *supra*, which expressly provides that no general appearance results from the filing of a pleading praying for extension of time within which to plead.

(d) See, also, Comments under Art. 1701, *infra*.

Art. 1002. Answer filed prior to confirmation of default

Notwithstanding the provisions of Article 1001, the defendant may file his answer at any time prior to confirmation of a default judgment against him.

Source: C.P. Arts. 314, 317.

Cross References: Arts. 1111, 1701.

Art. 1002

Comments

(a) This article retains without change the rule of Art. 317, Code of Practice of 1870, which has worked satisfactorily in actual practice.

(b) See Art. 1035, *infra*, with reference to the delay for filing answers to incidental demands.

(c) See, also, Comments under Arts. 1035, 1701, *infra*.

Art. 1003. Form of answer

The answer shall comply with Articles 853, 854, and 863 and, whenever applicable, with Articles 855 through 861. It shall admit or deny the allegations of the petition as required by Article 1004, state in short and concise terms the material facts upon which the defenses to the action asserted are based, and shall set forth all affirmative defenses as required by Article 1005. It shall also contain a prayer for the relief sought. Relief may be prayed for in the alternative.

Source: C.P. Arts. 319, 328; former R.S. 13:3601; Fed. Rule 8(b).

Cross References: Arts. 1035, 1111.

Comments

(a) This is one of the basic articles retaining the system of fact pleading in Louisiana. See Comments under Art. 854, *supra*, and Arts. 1004 and 1032, *infra*.

(b) With the exception of the elimination of any necessity for a verifying affidavit (see Art. 854, *supra*), this article makes no change in the Louisiana rules on the requirements of the answer.

(c) The prohibition against the insertion of abusive, defamatory and impertinent expressions in the answer, contained in Art. 319, Code of Practice of 1870, is embodied in Art. 964, *supra*.

(d) Verbal answers in cases before courts of limited jurisdiction and in district courts in "clerk's book" cases are included in Book VIII.

(e) See, also, Comments under Arts. 856, 892, *supra*, and Art. 1154, *infra*.

Art. 1004. Denials

The answer shall admit or deny the allegations of fact contained in each paragraph of the petition, and all such allegations, other than those as to the amount of damages, are admitted if not denied in the answer. If the defendant is without knowledge or information sufficient to justify a belief as to the truth of an allegation of fact made in the petition, he shall so state and this shall have the effect of a denial. Denials shall fairly meet the substance of the allegations denied. When the defendant intends in good faith to deny only a part of or to qualify an allegation of fact, he shall admit so much of it as is true and material and shall deny or qualify the remainder.

Source: Fed. Rule 8(b), (d); *cf.* former R.S. 13:3601(2).

Cross References: Arts. 1003, 1035, 1111.

Comments

(a) This article is based primarily upon Fed. Rule 8(b), but does not include the federal provisions permitting the general denial. Further, this is one of the basic articles retaining the Louisiana system of fact pleading. See Comments under Art. 854, *supra*.

(b) While this article is generally in accord with the provisions of former R.S. 13:3601(2), it does make two changes in the Louisiana procedural rules:

(1) The second sentence of this article overrules the rule announced in Maddox v. Robbert, 165 La. 694, 115 So. 905 (1928), which held that the defendant's refusal either to admit or deny because of a lack of sufficient information to justify a belief constitutes an admission.

(2) The last sentence of this article, permitting the defendant to deny all allegations of fact except those contained in certain designated allegations or paragraphs likewise overrules the opposite rule announced in Emery v. Orleans Levee Board, 200 La. 285, 7 So.2d 912 (1942); and Middleton v. Humble, 154 So. 400 (La.App.1934).

(c) Another change in the law is effected by the language of this article which does not require a defendant to deny the plaintiff's allegations as to the amount of damages suffered. Such an allegation is not that of an ultimate fact. In the vast majority of cases, defendant will deny this allegation, but if, through inadvertence, he fails to do so, he is not subjected to the penalty of having judgment rendered against him for the full amount of damages claimed by plaintiff, when defendant has put at issue one or more of the ultimate facts alleged by plaintiff.

(d) This Code does not include the rules enunciated in Arts. 325 and 326 of the 1870 Code of Practice which relate to the defendant's denial of his signature. The penalty provided by those articles is harsh, and the provisions of Art. 1514, *infra*, imposing upon a defendant who denies his signature to a document the reasonable expenses of the plaintiff in proving the genuineness of the signature, suffice.

(e) See, also, Comments under Arts. 856, 892, *supra*, and Art. 1154, *infra*.

Art. 1005. Affirmative defenses

The answer shall set forth affirmatively arbitration and award, assumption of risk, contributory negligence, discharge in bankruptcy, division, duress, error or mistake, estoppel, extinguishment of the obligation in any manner, failure of consideration, fraud, illegality, injury by fellow servant, transaction or compromise, and any other matter constituting an affirmative defense. If a party has mistakenly designated an affirmative defense as an incidental demand, or an incidental demand as an affirmative defense, and if justice so requires, the court, on such terms as it may prescribe, shall treat the pleading as if there had been a proper designation.

Source: Fed. Rule 8(c).

Cross References: Arts. 1003, 1035, 1111.

Comments

(a) Except as noted in these Comments, this article is based upon Fed. Rule 8(c).

(b) The language of the source provision was changed to employ civilian, rather than common law, terminology. Thus, "extinguishment of the obligation in any manner" covers payment and release specified by the federal rule as well as all of the modes of extinguishing obligations provided in Art. 2130, Civil Code, except prescription. Compensation may also be urged through the reconventional demand (see Art. 1062, *infra*); while prescription is pleaded through the peremptory exception (see Art. 927, *supra*). Similarly res judicata is pleaded through the peremptory exception (see Art. 927, *supra*).

(c) The closest approach which our law has to the common law statute of frauds is in Arts. 2275 and 2276 of the Civil Code, and R.S. 13:3721 and 13:3722 and these are asserted as objections to the admission of evidence, rather than as affirmative defenses.

(d) Assumption of the risk as an affirmative defense in Louisiana was first applied in Satterly v. Morgan, 35 La.Ann. 1166 (1883), and has been employed many times since. See Radford v. Gibert, 12 So.2d 612 (La.App.1943). Injury by fellow servant occurs infrequently in actual practice because of the numerous exceptions to which it is subject, and because it is not available as a defense to cases falling within the Workmen's Compensation Act. The fellow servant rule, however, might still be applicable at times. See Weaver v. W. L. Goulden Logging Co., 116 La. 468, 40 So. 798 (1906). For these reasons, both assumption of risk and the fellow servant rules are retained in the enumeration of affirmative defenses.

(e) Certain common law concepts enumerated as affirmative defenses in Fed. Rule 8(c), such as accord and satisfaction, laches, license, and waiver, have been recognized and adopted in varying degrees by the jurisprudence of Louisiana. They have not been expressly included in the enumeration although to the extent that these concepts are recognized in our jurisprudence they are included within the omnibus phrase "any other matter constituting an affirmative defense."

For instance, accord and satisfaction has only recently been recognized and applied. The earlier cases treated this defense as an estoppel to deny compromise, Berger v. Quintero, 170 La. 37, 127 So. 356 (1930); Davis-Wood Lumber Co. v. Farnsworth & Co., 171 So. 622 (La.App.1937); Mall Tool Co. v. Poulan, 40 So.2d 512 (La.App.1949), although in one court of appeal case, accord and satisfaction was thrown in for good measure. Davis-Wood Lumber Co. v. Farnsworth & Co., *supra*. Henriques v. Vaccaro, 220 La. 216, 56 So.2d 236 (1951), was the first Louisiana case which could be found in which the decision rested solely and squarely on accord and satisfaction. Whether all of the rules of the common law on the subject of accord and satisfaction are to be applied in the future remains for future decisions.

(f) The peremptory exception of division has been changed to an affirmative defense to be governed by the above article. See Comments under Art. 927, *supra*.

(g) See, also, Comments under Arts. 856, 892, 927, *supra*, and Arts. 1062, 1154, *infra*.

Art. 1006. Alternative defenses

An answer may set forth two or more defenses in the alternative, even though the factual or legal bases thereof may be inconsistent or mutually exclusive. All allegations in such cases are made subject to the obligations set forth in Article 863.

Source: Fed. Rule 8(e) (2).

Cross References: Arts. 1035, 1111.

Comments

Heretofore, in Louisiana the pleading of inconsistent facts in the alternative has been prohibited, and only the alternative pleading of inconsistent legal conclusions or inferences based upon the same basic facts was permitted. Durham v. Williams, 32 La.Ann. 962 (1880); Patorno v. Baker, 14 La.App. 574, 130 So. 573 (1930). This article presents a much simpler rule. False and fraudulent averments are to be punished through the disciplinary power of the court. See Comments under Art. 922, *supra*.

See, also, Comments under Art. 1003, *supra*.

CHAPTER 6. INCIDENTAL ACTIONS

SECTION 1. GENERAL DISPOSITIONS

Art.
1031. Incidental demands allowed.
1032. Form of petition.
1033. Delay for filing incidental demand.
1034. Exceptions and motions.
1035. Answer.
1036. Jurisdiction; mode of procedure.
1037. Action instituted separately.
1038. Separate trial; separate judgment.
1039. Effect of dismissal of principal action.
1040. Words "plaintiff" and "defendant" include plaintiff and defendant in an incidental action.

SECTION 2. RECONVENTION

1061. Actions pleaded in reconventional demand.
1062. Pleading compensation.
1063. Service of reconventional demand; citation unnecessary.
1064. Additional parties.
1065. Reconventional demand exceeding principal demand.
1066. Action matured or acquired after pleading.

SECTION 3. INTERVENTION

1091. Third person may intervene.
1092. Third person asserting ownership of, or mortgage or privilege on, seized property.
1093. Service of petition; citation unnecessary.
1094. Intervener accepts proceedings.

SECTION 4. DEMAND AGAINST THIRD PARTY

1111. Defendant may bring in third person.
1112. Defendant in reconvention may bring in third person.
1113. Effect of failure to bring in third party.
1114. Service of citation and pleadings.
1115. Defenses of original defendant available to third party defendant.
1116. Third party defendant may bring in third person.

SECTION 1. GENERAL DISPOSITIONS

Art. 1031. Incidental demands allowed

A demand incidental to the principal demand may be instituted against an adverse party or against a third person.

Incidental demands are reconvention, intervention, and the demand against third parties.

Source: C.P. Arts. 362, 363.

Comments

This and succeeding articles reduce the incidental demands in Louisiana from five to three. The reconventional demand is used for the purpose of pleading compensation, and the intervention is broadened to encompass the third opposition.

It is to be noted that third party practice, enacted by the legislature in 1954 as former R.S. 13:3381–13:3386, has been incorporated into this Code. See Arts. 1111 through 1116, *infra*.

See, also, Comments under Arts. 1111, 1156, *infra*.

Art. 1032. Form of petition

An incidental demand shall be commenced by a petition which shall comply with the requirements of Article 891. An incidental demand instituted by the defendant in the principal action may be incorporated in his answer to the principal demand. In this event, the caption shall indicate appropriately the dual character of the combined pleading.

Source: C.P. Arts. 365, 377, 382, 393, 398.

Comments

This article does not change appreciably the Louisiana system of pleading incidental demands. It does, however, by the use of the word "petition" even where the incidental demand is to be incorporated in the answer of the defendant in the principal action, make it easier to apply uniform rules of pleading to the initial pleading in the incidental demand.

See, also, Comments under Arts. 1111, 1156, *infra*.

Art. 1033. Delay for filing incidental demand

An incidental demand may be filed without leave of court at any time up to and including the time the answer to the principal demand is filed.

An incidental demand may be filed thereafter, with leave of court, if it will not retard the progress of the principal action, or if permitted by Articles 1066 or 1092.

Source: New.

Comments

This article affords a definite time for the filing of all incidental demands as of right and without leave of court; and, with the exception noted below, permits the filing of the incidental demand thereafter and with leave of court, as long as the court thinks that the incidental demand would not retard the progress of the principal action. In the case of a third party's employing intervention to claim ownership of, or a superior privilege to the seizing creditor on seized property, the intervention may be filed at any time prior to the judicial sale of the property, without retarding or affecting the principal action. Compare Art. 1092, *infra*.

Under the 1870 Code of Practice the time in which an incidental demand may be filed varies with the particular demand. In theory, compensation may be pleaded at any stage of the proceedings, Art. 367, Code of Practice of 1870; though in practice it would have to be pleaded sufficiently in advance of trial to permit the defendant to introduce his evidence in support of the demand. The Code of Practice of 1870 is silent on the subject of when the reconventional demand may be filed, though being an incidental demand it would not be permitted to retard the progress of the principal action, and its filing after the original answer probably would be regarded as changing the issues. The call in warranty must be filed within the same delay as is given the defendant in warranty to answer under Art. 381, Code of Practice of 1870. The rule as to the intervention is that it shall not be permitted to retard the progress of the principal action, Art. 391, Code of Practice of 1870. No specific time is set forth in the 1870 Code for the filing of the third opposition, though as a practical matter it would have to be filed prior to the judicial sale of the seized property. The above article provides more uniform rules for the filing of the incidental demands.

See, also, Comments under Art. 283, *supra* and Art. 1111, *infra*.

Art. 1034. Exceptions and motions

A defendant in an incidental action may plead any of the exceptions available to a defendant in a principal action, and may raise any of the objections enumerated in Articles 925 through 927, except that an objection of improper venue may not be urged if the principal action has been instituted in the proper venue. Exceptions pleaded by the defendant in an incidental action shall be subject to all of the provisions of Articles 924 through 934.

A party to an incidental action may plead any of the written motions available to a party to a principal action, subject to the provisions of Articles 961 through 969.

Source: New; *cf.* C.P. Art. 384.

Comments

(a) This article changes the procedural law of Louisiana only to the extent that it permits the defendant in an incidental action to plead the same exceptions, and to use the same written motions, as is permitted the defendant in a principal action. This change is effected primarily by Art. 852, *supra*, and the reasons therefor are stated in the comments thereunder.

(b) The rule enunciated in the first sentence of this article that the defendant in an incidental action may urge all procedural objections available to a defendant in the principal action, except that improper venue may not be urged if the principal action is instituted in the proper venue, is simply declaratory of civilian theories of incidental actions. If the principal action is filed in the proper venue, then that court has ancillary jurisdiction to entertain jurisdiction over the defendant in the incidental action, even though the venue might have been improper had the incidental action been instituted as a separate suit. This is axiomatic, otherwise the venue of all incidental actions would be improper if instituted against a nonresident defendant. On this point, see Art. 384 Code of Practice of 1870.

(c) See, also, Comments under Art. 852, *supra* and Arts. 1036, 1111, 1156, *infra*.

Art. 1035. Answer

The answer in an incidental action shall be filed within the delay allowed by Article 1001, or at any time prior to a judgment by default against the defendant in the incidental action, and shall be subject to all of the rules set forth in Articles 1001 and 1003 through 1006.

Source: New.

Cross Reference: Art. 1111.

Comments

(a) This article is needed to implement the change made in Louisiana's procedural law by Art. 852, *supra*, in requiring answers to be filed in all incidental actions. For the extent of this change see Comments under Art. 852, *supra*.

(b) Under Art. 1002, *supra*, the defendant may file his answer to the original petition "at any time prior to *confirmation* of a default judgment against him." Under this article, the defendant in the incidental action may file his answer to the incidental demand "at any time prior to a judgment by default against the defendant in the incidental action." The phrase "judgment by default" in the above article was taken from Arts. 310, 311, and 333

Art. 1035   PLEADING   Bk. 2

of the 1870 Code of Practice and refers to what is known in the professional vernacular as the "preliminary default."

The reason why answers to incidental demands are required to be filed prior to judgment by default, under the above article, is that any rule permitting such answers to be filed prior to confirmation of the default judgment would place the plaintiff in these incidental actions under a tremendous disadvantage. If the plaintiff in the incidental action attempted to confirm his default judgment prior to trial, he would be compelled quite often to offer all of the evidence which would be submitted on the trial by both the original plaintiff and the plaintiff in the incidental action. If the plaintiff in the incidental action waited to confirm the default judgment against the defendant in the incidental action until the trial of the case on its merits, he might be faced with an answer to the incidental action filed a few minutes before such trial commenced, which might raise affirmative defenses which plaintiff in the incidental action would not be prepared to meet on the trial. For this reason, answers in incidental actions are to be filed prior to the judgment by default. The plaintiff in the incidental action would still have to confirm this default judgment, but it could be done on the trial without having to worry about last minute affirmative defenses pleaded in the answer to the incidental demand.

(c) See, also, Comments under Arts. 965, 1002, *supra*, and Arts. 1112, 1156, *infra*.

Art. 1036.   Jurisdiction; mode of procedure

A court shall have jurisdiction over an incidental demand only if it would have had jurisdiction over the demand had it been instituted in a separate suit. The only exceptions to this rule are those provided in the state constitution.

The mode of procedure employed in the incidental action shall be the same as that used in the principal action, except as otherwise provided by law.

Source: New; *cf.* Comments following.

Comments

The rule embodied in the first sentence of this article is supported by the decisions of the appellate courts. Heirs of Kempe v. Hunt, 4 La. 477 (1832); Cross v. Parent, 26 La.Ann. 591 (1874); Labarthe v. Mazzei, 2 Orl.App. 367 (La.App.1905); Feahney v. New Orleans Railways & Light Co., 4 Orl.App. 277 (La.App.1907). *Cf.* Hagan v. Hart, 6 Rob. 427 (La.1844); San-I-Baker Corporation v. Magendie, 157 La. 643, 102 So. 821 (1925). The exceptions referred to in the second sentence are those set forth in Const. Art. VII, §§ 91, 92, granting jurisdiction to the city courts of New Orleans over certain incidental demands. The "jurisdiction" referred to in this article is absolute competency, not venue. See Art. 1034, *supra*, concerning venue.

The general rule enunciated in the second paragraph of this article is declaratory of the traditional procedural rule of civilian jurisdictions, which was recognized and applied in Cepro v. Matulich, 152 La. 1072, 95 So. 226 (1923). The phrase "except as otherwise provided by law" serves to reserve the original exception to this rule, which permitted third oppositions to be filed in executory proceedings to enforce a mortgage, thus permitting this function to be performed by the broadened intervention. See Art. 1092, *infra*.

See, also, Comments under Art. 4, *supra*, and Arts. 1092, 1111, 1156, *infra*.

Art. 1037. Action instituted separately

When a person does not assert in an incidental demand the action which he has against a party to the principal action or a third person, he does not thereby lose this right of action, except as provided in Article 1113.

Source: C.P. Arts. 373, 377, 388, 391, 400.

Comments

(a) The rules embodied in the above article are in accord with the Louisiana rules respecting incidental demands.

(b) Under Louisiana law there is one instance in which a privilege on movables other than that of a valid chattel mortgage may be lost through the failure of the creditor to assert his privilege timely through the third opposition. When the creditor claims on only a part of the movables seized a privilege superior to that of the seizing creditor, and he fails to assert this superior privilege timely through the third opposition, the privilege will be lost. The privilege cannot follow the property into the hands of the purchaser at judicial sale, and if no third opposition is filed and separate sale and appraisement is had with respect to the movables on which this creditor claims his privilege, he cannot recover any portion of the proceeds of the sale of all seized movables sold in globo. Caldwell v. Laurel Grove Co., 179 La. 53, 153 So. 17 (1934). Thus, the privilege is lost when the property is acquired by a third person; and the creditor cannot recover any portion of the proceeds under any theory of unjust enrichment or privilege because he is unable to prove definitely the proportionate part of the proceeds attributable to the movables on which he held his privilege. Both of these results flow from the application of rules of substantive law, rather than procedure. Accordingly, this type of case is not included in the rules applicable to intervention, but the matter is left entirely to the courts' development and application of rules of substantive law.

(c) See, also, Comments under Arts. 1111, 1113, 1156, *infra*.

Art. 1038. Separate trial; separate judgment

The court may order the separate trial of the principal and incidental actions, either on exceptions or on the merits; and after adjudicating the action first tried, shall retain jurisdiction for the adjudication of the other.

When the principal and incidental actions are tried separately, the court may render and sign separate judgments thereon. When in the interests of justice, the court may withhold the signing of the judgment on the action first tried until the signing of the judgment on the other.

Source: Fed. Rule 13(i).

Cross Reference: Art. 1915.

Comments

(a) This article adopts the approach of federal procedure in permitting the court to order separate trials on the principal and incidental actions, in those cases where there is no connexity between the two, and it would be more convenient and orderly to have separate trials.

(b) While it would be more convenient in many instances to permit the court to render separate judgments where there have been separate trials of the principal and incidental actions, this may lead to two difficulties. First, it may permit piecemeal appeals, which are always undesirable. Second, it might permit the party who first obtained judgment to execute it, before his adversary obtains judgment on his demand. To avoid both of these difficulties, and to leave control of the matter in the hands of the trial court, this article authorizes the trial court to render judgment after the first separate trial, but to withhold signing thereof until judgment can be signed on the action subsequently tried.

(c) See, also, Comments under Art. 965, *supra*, and Arts. 1111, 1156, *infra*.

Art. 1039. Effect of dismissal of principal action

If an incidental demand has been pleaded prior to motion by plaintiff in the principal action to dismiss the principal action, a subsequent dismissal thereof shall not in any way affect the incidental action, which must be tried and decided independently of the principal action.

Source: Fed. Rule 41(a) (2).

Comments

There has been much uncertainty in Louisiana practice as to what happens when a plaintiff moves to dismiss or discontinue suit after the defendant has entered an incidental demand. Art. 491, Code of Practice of 1870, provides that the plaintiff has the right, in every stage of the suit previous to rendition of judgment, to discontinue the suit on paying the costs. However, one of the established exceptions to this rule has been that where a reconventional demand, or any defense urged "in the nature of a reconventional demand" has been filed prior to the motion to discontinue, the dismissal cannot be accomplished so as to affect the defendant's reconventional demand. Lanusse's Syndics v. Pimpienella, 4 Mart. (N.S.) 439 (La.1826); State ex rel. John T. Moore Planting Co. v. Howell, 139 La. 336, 71 So. 529 (1916); Stringfellow v. Nowlin Bros., 157 La. 683, 102 So. 869 (1925); Person v. Person, 172 La. 740, 135 So. 225 (1931); Rives v. Starcke, 195 La. 378, 196 So. 657 (1940), noted 3 La.L.Rev. 457 (1941); Senseley v. First Nat. Life Ins. Co., 205 La. 61, 16 So.2d 906 (1944); Alfonso v. Ruiz, 2 So.2d 480 (La.App.1941).

As to intervention, the Louisiana courts have held that the intervention falls with the dismissal of the suit by the plaintiff. Jones v. Lawrence, 4 La.Ann. 279 (1849); Barron v. Jacobs, 38 La.Ann. 370 (1886); Meyers v. Birotte, 41 La.Ann. 745, 6 So. 607 (1889); Gorman v. Gorman, 158 La. 274, 103 So. 766 (1925); Erskine v. Gardiner, 162 La. 83, 110 So. 97 (1926); St. Bernard Trappers' Assn. v. Michel, 162 La. 366, 110 So. 617 (1926); Seib v. Cooper, 170 La. 105, 127 So. 380 (1930); Miller v. Board of Com'rs of Port of New Orleans, 199 La. 1071, 7 So.2d 355 (1942). This rule has been severely criticized as being unnecessarily harsh. McMahon (1956 Supp.) 114. The remarks made by the supreme court in Lanusse's Syndics v. Pimpienella, 4 Mart. (N.S.) 439, 443 (La.1826), when the court refused plaintiff's dismissal after a reconventional demand made by the defendant, it seems, should apply equally well to the demand in intervention: "There would be few judgments, we imagine, rendered in this country, or any other, if the party against whom condemnation was prayed, and against whom it was about to be pronounced, could arrest the sentence, by the expression of a wish that it should be postponed to another time, or by desiring that the suit against him should be discontinued."

Although third opposition is a type of intervention the jurisprudential rule has been that it is a demand distinct from the original suit and such demand does not depend upon the outcome of the original suit between plaintiff and the defendant. Atkins v. Smith, 204 La. 468, 15 So.2d 855 (1943); Id., 21 So.2d 89 (La.App.1944). Cf. Art. 398, Code of Practice of 1870. The jurisprudence of Louisiana with respect to third opposition, therefore, is in accord with the

Art. 1039

above article. Even though a separate incidental demand for third opposition is not provided for in this Code, a discussion of the jurisprudence on this subject has been included to emphasize the point that to a considerable extent Louisiana already employs the rule set forth in the above article.

See, also, Comments under Arts. 1111, 1156, 1671, *infra*.

Art. 1040. Words "plaintiff" and "defendant" include plaintiff and defendant in an incidental action

Unless the context clearly indicates otherwise, wherever the words "plaintiff" and "defendant" are used in this Code, they respectively include a plaintiff and a defendant in an incidental demand.

Source: New.

SECTION 2. RECONVENTION

Art. 1061. Actions pleaded in reconventional demand

The defendant in the principal action may assert in a reconventional demand any action which he may have against the plaintiff in the principal action, even if these two parties are domiciled in the same parish and regardless of connexity between the principal and reconventional demands.

Source: New.
Cross Reference: Art. 1111.

Comments

This article permits a defendant to urge against the plaintiff any action which he might have. This practice has proved satisfactory in federal practice. See Fed. Rule 13(b). It prevents multiplicity of suits and encourages the settlement of all disputes between the parties at one time. Of course, this article changes the rule of Art. 375, Code of Practice of 1870, requiring either diversity of residence or connexity between the main and reconventional demands.

See, also, Comments under Art. 1156, *infra*.

Art. 1062. Pleading compensation

Compensation may be asserted in the reconventional demand.

Source: New.
Cross Reference: Art. 1111.

Comments

(a) While compensation is subject to certain substantive requirements (Arts. 2207–2216, Civil Code), there is no reason why it may not be urged through the reconventional demand. In fact, in at least one instance, compensation actually operates in precisely the same manner as reconvention. See Art. 371, Code of Practice of 1870; Moore v. Hamilton, 16 La.App. 630, 133 So. 790 (1931).

(b) Note, however, that under Art. 1005, *supra*, compensation may also be pleaded in the answer as an affirmative defense.

(c) See, also, Comments under Art. 1005, *supra*, and Arts. 1065, 1156, *infra*.

Art. 1063. Service of reconventional demand; citation unnecessary

The petition in reconvention, whether incorporated in the answer to the principal action or filed separately, shall be served on the plaintiff in the principal action in the manner prescribed by Article 1313. Citation of the plaintiff in the principal action shall not be necessary.

Source: Former R.S. 13:3345.

Cross Reference: Art. 1111.

Comments

(a) This article does not make any change in Louisiana's procedural law. Service of the petition in reconvention, or combined answer and reconventional demand, are made as required by former R.S. 13:3345. Since the plaintiff is already in court, there is no need for any citation.

(b) See Art. 1313, *infra*.

(c) See, also, Comments under Arts. 1156, 1314, *infra*.

Art. 1064. Additional parties

When the presence of parties other than those to the principal action is required for the granting of complete relief in the determination of a reconventional demand, the court shall order the plaintiff in reconvention to make such parties defendants in reconvention, if jurisdiction of them can be obtained.

Source: Fed. Rule 13(h).

Cross Reference: Art. 1111.

Comments

(a) This article makes a definite change in Louisiana law. Under Art. 374 of the 1870 Code of Practice, reconvention is defined as "[t]he demand which the defendant institutes in consequence of that which the plaintiff has brought against him, ..." Consequently, the defendant is not permitted to bring in a third person under the reconventional demand. Lyons v. Fry, 112 La. 759, 36 So. 674 (1904). Hence, in all cases where such third persons are indispensable parties to the action which the defendant would assert against the plaintiff, the court cannot proceed in the absence of these third persons. See cases cited at Comment (c) Art. 927, *supra*. The effect of this procedure leaves the plaintiff free to recover judgment against the defendant, although the latter may have a valid cause of action which may eventually result in a judgment against the plaintiff reducing or even exceeding that which the plaintiff may recover against the defendant. *Cf.* Lyons v. Fry, *supra*. This results in an undesirable multiplicity of action. The reconventional demand was broadened so as to permit the defendant to assert whatever action he may have against the plaintiff, even though this reconventional demand may require the presence of third persons indispensable to the action, if jurisdiction over the latter can be obtained.

(b) Jurisdiction in the last clause of this article "if jurisdiction of them can be obtained," is jurisdiction and not venue. Even though a third person may be brought into a pending suit under this article under circumstances where, if the action were asserted by a separate suit, he could object to the venue, yet he is brought in through an incidental demand over which the court has ancillary jurisdiction.

(c) See, also, Comments under Art. 1156, *infra*.

Art. 1065. Reconventional demand exceeding principal demand

The reconventional demand may or may not diminish or defeat the recovery sought in the principal demand. It may claim relief exceeding in amount that sought in the principal demand.

Source: Fed. Rule 13(c).

Cross Reference: Art. 1111.

Comments

(a) This article does not change the Louisiana procedural rules except to the extent that these rules are broadened under Art. 1061, *supra*, permitting the defendant to assert against the plaintiff any cause of action which he may have, regardless of connexity between the two actions or diversity of residence between plaintiff and defendant. See Comments under Art. 1061, *supra*.

(b) Fed.Rule 13(c) provides that the counterclaim "may claim relief exceeding in amount or different in kind from that sought in the pleading of the opposing party." Since Louisiana has never recognized any distinction between law and equity, there was no necessity to permit the reconventional demand to pray for "relief different in kind" from that prayed for in the original petition.

(c) See, also, Comments under Art. 1156, *infra*.

Art. 1066. Action matured or acquired after pleading

An action which either matured or was acquired by the defendant in the principal action after answer may be presented, with the permission of the court, as a reconventional demand by supplemental pleading.

Source: Fed. Rule 13(e).

Cross References: Arts. 1033, 1111.

Comments

While no case in point was found, it is believed that under the prior procedural law of Louisiana, a defendant could not reconvene to assert against the plaintiff any after-acquired action or any action which became exigible after defendant had filed his answer. But, *cf.* Arts. 15, 158 Code of Practice of 1870.

This article expressly permits the trial judge, within his discretion, to authorize assertion of these actions through reconvention, thus eliminating the multiplicity of actions which Louisiana procedure apparently has forced, and permitting plaintiff and defendant to adjudicate all of their respective controversies in a single suit.

See, also, Comments under Art. 1156, *infra*.

SECTION 3. INTERVENTION

Art. 1091. Third person may intervene

A third person having an interest therein may intervene in a pending action to enforce a right related to or connected with the object of the pending action against one or more of the parties thereto by:

(1) Joining with plaintiff in demanding the same or similar relief against the defendant;

(2) Uniting with defendant in resisting the plaintiff's demand; or

(3) Opposing both plaintiff and defendant.

Source: C.P. Art. 389; *cf.* Art. 105, Italian Code of Civil Procedure.

Comments

(a) The articles of the 1870 Code of Practice are so general and indefinite that they afford no adequate rule as to when a third person may intervene in a pending action. Art. 389 of the Code of Practice of 1870 defines intervention as "a demand by which a third person requires to be permitted to become a party in a suit between other persons; by joining the plaintiff in claiming the same thing, or something connected with it, or by uniting with the defendant in resisting the claims of the plaintiff, or, where his interest requires it, by opposing both." Art. 390 of the 1870 Code of Practice attempts to supply the needed rule but fails to do so through the generality of the language: "In order to be entitled to intervene, it is enough to have an interest in the success of either of the parties to the suit, or an interest opposed to both." Quite obviously, "interest" as used in this article includes but goes beyond the "real and actual interest" required under Art. 15, Code of Practice of 1870 to enable a party to institute the action.

The answer to this question has not been provided by the jurisprudence. *Cf.* Lincoln v. New Orleans Exp. Co., 45 La.Ann. 729, 12 So. 937 (1893) with H. B. Claflin Co. v. Feibleman, 44 La.Ann. 518, 10 So. 862 (1892).

(b) The concepts of "intervention of right" and "permissive intervention" of Fed.Rule 24 are not suitable for implementing the substantive law of a civil law jurisdiction; and the test of "a question of law or fact in common" of the federal permissive intervention is much too narrow and inflexible to define the traditional functions of intervention in the procedure of civilian jurisdictions.

(c) The Italian Code of Civil Procedure (1942) affords procedural rules which were designed to implement substantive rules of the civil law closely akin to the law of this state. For this reason, some of the concepts on which these rules are based are much more suitable for adoption in Louisiana than the corresponding concepts upon which the federal rules of intervention are predicated.

There was no necessity to adopt the rule of Art. 106 of the Italian Code of Civil Procedure, which permits any party to call a third person into the suit when he has a common right to be adjudicated, or pretends to have such a right. This function is performed by the demand against third parties. *Cf.* Arts. 1111 through 1116, *infra*.

The basic provision of the Italian Code, Art. 105, however, provides that

"Anyone may intervene in a suit between other persons in order to enforce, as against any or all of the parties, a right which relates to the object of, or which depends on the title asserted in, this suit.

"Anyone may also intervene in order to sustain the right of any one of the parties when he has an interest therein."

The first paragraph is declaratory of the requirement of connexity which for years has been the traditional basis of the incidental demands in civil jurisdictions. The second paragraph, while too general to afford much concrete assistance, nonetheless conveys the idea that a third person may enforce through intervention the rights of one of the original litigants when his own rights would be prejudiced by the non-enforcement thereof. Collectively, these two paragraphs provide a workable formula: a third person having a justiciable right related to or connected with the object of the principal suit may enforce that right through intervention. This concept and the provisions of Art. 389 of the 1870 Code of Practice have been combined in the above article.

(d) See, also, Comments under Art. 591, *supra,* and Arts. 1156, 2086, *infra.*

Art. 1092. Third person asserting ownership of, or mortgage or privilege on, seized property

A third person claiming ownership of, or a mortgage or privilege on, property seized may assert his claim by intervention. If the third person asserts ownership of the seized property, the intervention may be filed at any time prior to the judicial sale of the seized property, and the court may grant him injunctive relief to prevent such sale before adjudication of his claim of ownership.

If the third person claims a mortgage or privilege on the property seized, the intervention may be filed at any time prior to the distribution by the sheriff of the proceeds of the sale of the seized property, and the court may order the sheriff to hold such proceeds subject to its further orders; and when filed prior to the judicial sale, the court may further order the separate appraisement and sale of the property on which the intervener claims a mortgage or privilege.

An intervener claiming the proceeds of a judicial sale does not thereby admit judicially the validity, nor is he estopped from asserting the invalidity, of the claim of the seizing creditor.

Source: New; cf. C.P. Arts. 395–403.
Cross References: Arts. 1033, 2643.

Comments

(a) Except as noted in Comments (b) and (c), the broadened intervention operates in the same manner as the third opposition under Arts. 395 through 403, Code of Practice of 1870.

(b) Under Arts. 398 and 401 of the 1870 Code, the third opponent asserting ownership must plead it through a petition, whereas a superior mortgage or privilege may be pleaded through motion.

The intervention asserting ownership must be filed prior to the sale of the property seized under Art. 400 of the 1870 Code, which also gives the owner of the property sold the right to hold the sheriff and seizing creditor liable in damages. This same result obtains under this Code. See Art. 1037, *supra*.

The intervention asserting a privilege is filed at any time prior to distribution of the proceeds. See Art. 401, Code of Practice of 1870; Payne Dameron and Co. v. Eaton and Barstow, 27 La. Ann. 160 (1875). *Cf.* Comment (b) under Art. 1037, *supra*.

(c) Injunctive relief is not necessary when the intervener asserts a superior privilege or mortgage, but the court orders the sheriff to hold the proceeds subject to its further orders. Where the claim of the seizing creditor does not exhaust the proceeds of the judicial sale, the intervener asserting an inferior privilege or mortgage enforces his claim against the proceeds of the judicial sale remaining after satisfaction of the seizing creditor's claim. A junior privilege on movable property is lost after the sale of the property, and the junior privileged creditor loses his right to assert his privilege against the proceeds of the sale if the movable is sold without a separate appraisal. This article covers these situations.

(d) For the rules relating to intervention in an executory proceeding, see Art. 2643, *infra*.

(e) Heretofore, the third opposition was normally filed in the court which ordered the seizure. However, if the value of the claim of the third opponent was in excess of the jurisdictional amount of the court ordering the seizure, the third opposition could be filed as a separate suit in a court of general jurisdiction. Likewise, when the property was seized in one parish under a writ issuing from another parish, the third opposition could be filed as a separate suit in the district court of the parish where the property was seized. Hagan v. Hart, 6 Rob. 427 (La.1844); San-I-Baker Corporation v. Magendie, 157 La. 643, 102 So. 821 (1925). Neither of these jurisprudential exceptions was changed.

(f) The third paragraph of this article overrules the harsh and technical rule of Albert Pick & Co. v. Stringer, 171 La. 131, 129 So. 731 (1930) and Eddy v. Weathers, 16 La.App. 634, 134 So. 259 (1931), in so far as these cases hold that a third opponent judicially admits the validity of the principal demand and is estopped to claim the proceeds of the judicial sale, when he engrafts his third opposition upon the principal demand. *Cf.* Bomarito v. Max Barnett Furniture Co., 177 La. 1010, 150 So. 2 (1933).

(g) See, also, Comments under Art. 1036, *supra*, and Arts. 1093, 1156, 2299, 3601, *infra*.

Art. 1093. Service of petition; citation unnecessary

When the intervention asserts ownership of, or a mortgage or privilege on, the seized property, the petition shall be served on the sheriff and all parties to the principal action as provided in Article 1313. Any other petition of intervention shall be served on all parties to the principal action as provided in Article 1314. Citation is not necessary in intervention.

Source: *Cf.* C.P. Arts. 393, 398, 401.

Cross Reference: Art. 2643.

Comments

(a) This article conforms to the rules of its source provisions, except in the four respects mentioned below.

(b) Under prior law, citation was required in all cases of intervention. Art. 393, Code of Practice of 1870; Chism & Boyd v. Ong, 33 La.Ann. 702 (1881); Johnson v. City of New Orleans, 105 La. 149, 29 So. 355 (1901). In Hobson v. Woolfolk, 23 La.Ann. 384 (1871), *contra*, the court overlooked the provisions of Art. 393 of the Code of Practice of 1870.

(c) A petition is required under this article in all cases, while under prior law, if the third opposition asserted a privilege on the seized property, it could be asserted by motion. See Comment (b) of Art. 1092, *supra*.

(d) This article requires a joinder of all parties to the principal action where the intervention asserts ownership of, or a mortgage or privilege on, the seized property. Heretofore, there was no necessity for joining the defendant in the principal action when the third opponent asserted a superior privilege. See Wagner v. Newman, 18 La.Ann. 508 (1865). Since the intervener in such a case is actually asserting a right against the defendant in the principal action, this defendant is, under this article, made a party to the intervention.

(e) In permitting service by mail or delivery, the above article makes a change in Louisiana procedural law.

(f) See, also, Comments under Art. 1156, *infra*.

Art. 1094. Intervener accepts proceedings

An intervener cannot object to the form of the action, to the venue, or to any defects and informalities personal to the original parties.

Source: New; *cf.* Comment following.

Comments

The above article codifies the jurisprudential rule that an intervener takes the proceedings as he finds them. See Cahn v. Ford, 42 La.Ann. 965, 8 So. 477 (1890); Parish v. Holland, 166 La. 24, 116 So. 580 (1928). *Cf.* Art. 1292, *infra*.

See, also, Comments under Art. 1156, *infra*.

SECTION 4. DEMAND AGAINST THIRD PARTY

Art. 1111. Defendant may bring in third person

The defendant in a principal action by petition may bring in any person, including a codefendant, who is his warrantor, or who is or may be liable to him for all or part of the principal demand.

In such cases the plaintiff in the principal action may assert any demand against the third party defendant arising out of or connected with the principal demand. The third party defendant thereupon shall plead his objections and defenses in the manner prescribed in Articles 921 through 969, 1003 through 1006, and 1035. He may reconvene against the plaintiff in the principal action or the third party plaintiff, on any demand arising out of or connected with the principal demand, in the manner prescribed in Articles 1061 through 1066.

Source: La. Act 433 of 1954, §§ 1-6; cf. former R.S. 13:3381; C.P. Art. 380; Fed. Rule 14(a); Admiralty Rule 56.

Cross References: Arts. 1112, 1116.

Comments

(a) Probably the most radical change made in Louisiana's procedural law in recent years was effected by La. Act 433 of 1954, discarding the call in warranty and adopting the third party action based largely upon the third party practice of federal procedure. The call in warranty was always much narrower and much less effective than third party practice, and its usefulness had been reduced appreciably by the decisions in Bank of Baton Rouge v. Hendrix, 194 La. 478, 193 So. 713 (1940) and cases cited therein, holding that a defendant cannot call a third party in warranty unless a contract of warranty exists between the defendant and the third party sought to be called in warranty.

The 1954 legislation was based upon the work of the Louisiana State Law Institute in drafting the articles in the Title on Pleading. Through inadvertence the legislature in 1954 failed to adopt the provisions of Arts. 1031 through 1040, *supra*, intended to apply generally to all incidental actions, including the third party action. See Automotive Finance Company v. Daigle, 80 So.2d 579 (La. App.1955); Survey of 1954 Legislation—Courts and Judicial Procedure, 15 La.L.Rev. 38, 46-49 (1954). As a consequence, the rules on the subject in this Code are more complete than those embodied in the 1954 legislation.

Since the statute adopting the third party action is so recent, and the rules there adopted parallel some of those in this Code, the comments under the articles discuss only the differences between the procedure contained herein and that under the call in warranty for which it has been substituted.

(b) The third party demand embodied in Arts. 1111 through 1116, *infra*, is considerably broader than the third party action contemplated by Fed. Rule 14. Under the latter, the third party defendant is only "a person not a party to the action." Under the above article, the third party defendant may be "any person, including a codefendant . . ."

(c) One difference between this article and the federal rule is that in the latter whether a third party defendant may be brought in rests within the discretion of the trial judge, whereas under Art. 1033, *supra*, the defendant may bring in a third party as of right at any time up to and including the time for filing the answer. The rule embodied in Art. 1033 is substantially the same as that of Rule 56 of the Admiralty Rules. The call in warranty, under Art. 382 of the 1870 Code of Practice, may be included in the answer and hence filed as of right at the time the answer is filed.

(d) See, also, Comments under Arts. 1031, 1091, *supra* and Art. 1156, *infra*.

Art. 1112. Defendant in reconvention may bring in third person

The defendant in reconvention likewise may bring in his warrantor, or any person who is or may be liable to him for all or part of the reconventional demand, and the rules provided in Articles 1111, and 1113 through 1115 shall apply equally to such third party actions.

Source: La. Act 433 of 1954, §§ 1–6; *cf.* former R.S. 13:3382; C.P. Art. 380; Fed. Rule 14(b).

Cross Reference: Art. 1116.

Comments

Prior to the adoption of third party practice in 1954 there was considerable doubt as to whether the defendant in reconvention under the 1870 Code of Practice could call a third person in warranty. Under the third party practice as codified herein, however, there is no reason why the defendant in reconvention could not call in a warrantor, particularly since pleading by such defendant in reconvention is not considered replicatory under this Code. See Art. 1035, *supra*.

See, also, Comments under Arts. 1031, 1091, 1111, *supra*, and Art. 1156, *infra*.

Art. 1113. Effect of failure to bring in third party

A defendant who does not bring in as a third party defendant a person who is liable to him for all or part of the principal demand does not on that account lose his right or cause of action against such person, unless the latter proves that he had means of defeating the action which were not used, because the defendant either failed to bring him in as a third party defendant, or neglected to apprise him that the suit had been brought. The same rule obtains with respect to a defendant in reconvention who fails to bring in as a third party defendant a person who is liable to him for all or part of the reconventional demand.

Source: La. Act 433 of 1954, §§ 1–6; *cf.* former R.S. 13:3383; C.P. Art. 388.

Cross References: Arts. 1037, 1112, 1116.

Comments

This article retains the rule of its source provisions, and states an exception to the general rule consecrated by Art. 1037, *supra*.

See, also, Comments under Arts. 1031, 1091, 1111, *supra*, and Art. 1156, *infra*.

Art. 1114. Service of citation and pleadings

A citation and certified copies of the following pleadings shall be served on the third party defendant in the manner prescribed by Articles 1231 through 1265: the petition in the third party demand; the petition in the principal demand; the petition in the reconventional demand, if any; and the answers to the principal and reconventional demand filed prior to the issuance of citation in the third party action.

Source: La. Act 433 of 1954, §§ 1–6; *cf.* former R.S. 13:3384; C.P. Art. 383.

Cross References: Arts. 1112, 1116.

Comments

Under Fed. Rule 14 nothing but the summons and the third party complaint is served upon the third party defendant. Under Art. 383 of the Code of Practice of 1870 only the citation and a copy of the answer embodying the call in warranty are served upon the warrantor. Under the above article, in the demand against third parties copies of all the basic pleadings filed at the time of service upon the third party defendant are also served upon him.

See, also, Comments under Arts. 1031, 1091, 1111, *supra*, and Art. 1156, *infra*.

Art. 1115. Defenses of original defendant available to third party defendant

The third party defendant may assert against the plaintiff in the principal action any defenses which the third party plaintiff has against the principal demand.

Source: La. Act 433 of 1954, §§ 1-6; cf. former R.S. 13:3385; C.P. Art. 384; Fed. Rule 14(a).

Cross References: Arts. 1112, 1116.

Comments

When the legislature adopted the third party practice the language of Fed. Rule 14(a) providing that the third party defendant "may also assert any claim against the plaintiff arising out of the transaction or occurrence that is the subject matter of plaintiff's claim against the third party plaintiff," was omitted.

See, also, Comments under Arts. 1031, 1091, 1111, *supra*, and Art. 1156, *infra*.

Art. 1116. Third party defendant may bring in third person

A third party defendant may proceed under Articles 1111 through 1115 against any person who is or may be liable to him for all or any part of the third party demand.

Source: La. Act 433 of 1954, §§ 1-6; cf. former R.S. 13:3386; Fed. Rule 14(a); C.P. Art. 387.

Comments

No substantial change results from the above article in view of the fact that it is identical with former R.S. 13:3386 and Art. 387 of the 1870 Code of Practice which permits a defendant in warranty to call another in warranty.

See, also, Comments under Arts. 1031, 1091, 1111, *supra*, and Art. 1156, *infra*.

CHAPTER 7. AMENDED AND SUPPLEMENTAL PLEADINGS

Art.
1151. Amendment of petition and answer; answer to amended petition.
1152. Amendment of exceptions.
1153. Amendment relates back.
1154. Amendment to conform to evidence.
1155. Supplemental pleadings.
1156. Amended and supplemental pleadings in incidental action.

Art. 1151. Amendment of petition and answer; answer to amended petition

A plaintiff may amend his petition without leave of court at any time before the answer thereto is served. He may be ordered to amend his petition under Articles 932 through 934. A defendant may amend his answer once without leave of court at any time within ten days after it has been served. Otherwise, the petition and answer may be amended only by leave of court or by written consent of the adverse party.

A defendant shall plead in response to an amended petition within the time remaining for pleading to the original pleading or within ten days after service of the amended petition, whichever period is longer, unless the time is extended under Article 1001.

Source: C.P. Art. 419; Fed. Rule 15(a); cf. Comments following.

Cross Reference: Art. 1156.

Comments

This article effects a change in the procedural law of Louisiana, but it provides a simple, workable rule as to amendments after the filing of answer within the discretion of the trial judge, as is provided under the federal practice and under all of the newer rules of civil procedure in other American jurisdictions.

Probably the most unworkable rules contained in the 1870 Code of Practice are Arts. 419 and 420 relating to the amendment of the petition and answer. The concepts of "joinder of issue" and "altering the substance of the demand" are so nebulous and impractical as to make any rules dependent upon them wholly unworkable. On this subject see McMahon 43, 44, 95, and 96 (1956 Supp.). For these reasons, the above article leaves the decision to the discretion of the trial judge who is in the best position to determine the matter.

See, also, Comments under Art. 891, *supra*.

Art. 1152. Amendment of exceptions

A defendant may amend his declinatory or dilatory exceptions by leave of court or with the written consent of the adverse party, at any time prior to the trial of the exceptions, so as to amplify or plead more particularly an objection set forth or attempted to be set forth in the original exception. A declinatory or a dilatory exception may not be amended so as to plead an objection not attempted to be set forth in the original exception.

A defendant may amend his peremptory exception at any time and without leave of court, so as to either amplify an objection set forth or attempted to be set forth in the original exception, or to plead an objection not set forth therein.

Source: New.

Cross Reference: Art. 1156.

Comments

(a) The 1870 Code of Practice contains no rules relative to amendment of the exceptions, and the jurisprudence throws little light upon the subject. It is possible that the reason why there are no statutory or jurisprudential rules on the subject is because the vast majority of the exceptions pleaded were of the blanket type, and there was rarely any need of amending such a pleading. Under a system of particularized exceptions, however, there is a need for such rules. Yet the difficulty with a liberality of amendment, in so far as the declinatory and dilatory exceptions are concerned, is that it might actually restore the dilatory and pernicious practice of "stringing-out the exceptions". For this reason, amendment of the dilatory and declinatory exceptions is restricted sharply. Amendment of the peremptory exception is in accord with Succession of Howell, 177 La. 276, 148 So. 48 (1933).

(b) Under Art. 928, *supra,* since the peremptory exception may be pleaded at any stage of the proceeding, even in the appellate court, prior to a submission of the case to the court for a decision, a defendant may either plead the peremptory exception anew at any stage of the proceeding, or amend one filed earlier in the proceeding.

(c) See, also, Comments under Art. 932, *supra.*

Art. 1153. Amendment relates back

When the action or defense asserted in the amended petition or answer arises out of the conduct, transaction, or occurrence set forth or attempted to be set forth in the original pleading, the amendment relates back to the date of filing the original pleading.

Source: Fed. Rule 15(c); *cf.* Comment following.

Cross Reference: Art. 1156.

Comment

This article is in accord with the jurisprudence of Louisiana. See Reeves v. Globe Indemnity Co. of New York, 185 La. 42, 168 So. 488 (1936).

Art. 1154. Amendment to conform to evidence

When issues not raised by the pleadings are tried by express or implied consent of the parties, they shall be treated in all respects as if

Art. 1154   PLEADING   Bk. 2

they had been raised by the pleading. Such amendment of the pleadings as may be necessary to cause them to conform to the evidence and to raise these issues may be made upon motion of any party at any time, even after judgment; but failure to so amend does not affect the result of the trial of these issues. If evidence is objected to at the trial on the ground that it is not within the issues made by the pleadings, the court may allow the pleadings to be amended and shall do so freely when the presentation of the merits of the action will be subserved thereby, and the objecting party fails to satisfy the court that the admission of such evidence would prejudice him in maintaining his action or defense on the merits. The court may grant a continuance to enable the objecting party to meet such evidence.

Source: Fed. Rule 15(b).

Cross Reference: Art. 1156.

Comments

(a) Except as noted in Comment (c) hereof, the effect of this article and the jurisprudential rules in Louisiana are substantially identical.

(b) It is well settled that the pleadings may be enlarged by evidence adduced without objection, which is not pertinent to any of the issues raised by the pleadings, and hence would have been excluded if objected to timely. Hope v. Madison, 192 La. 593, 188 So. 711 (1939); Stanley v. Jones, 201 La. 549, 9 So.2d 678 (1942); Baden v. Globe Indemnity Co., 145 So. 53 (La.App.1932); Althans v. Toye Bros. Yellow Cab Co., 191 So. 717 (La.App.1939), noted 14 Tul.L.Rev. 306 (1940); Nezat v. General Outdoor Advertising Co., 24 So.2d 482 (La.App.1946); Randazzo v. Meraux, 27 So.2d 740 (La.App.1946); Guarisco Motor Co. v. Carline, 28 So.2d 364 (La. App.1946). Under the Louisiana jurisprudence, there is no opportunity for formal amendment in such cases. The second sentence of the above article permits such amendment at any time, whenever considered helpful, so as to have the pleadings amended to formally and expressly reflect the enlargement of the original pleadings effected by the evidence introduced without objection.

(c) Heretofore, under Louisiana law, all of the material facts upon which an affirmative defense is based had to be pleaded in the answer; and upon timely objection all evidence offered to support an affirmative defense pleaded generally or in terms of legal conclusion was excluded. Godchaux v. Hyde, 126 La. 187, 52 So. 269 (1910); Ouachita Nat. Bank v. McIlhenny, 169 La. 258, 125 So. 69 (1929); Masters v. Cleveland, 182 La. 483, 162 So. 51 (1935); Sellwood v. Phillips, 185 La. 1045, 171 So. 440 (1936); Arcadia Lumber Co. v. Austin, 15 La.App. 212, 131 So. 601 (1930); Quatray v. Wicker, 16 La.App. 515, 134 So. 313 (1931); Bloomenstiel v. McKeithen, 19 La.App. 513, 139 So. 519 (1932); Martin v. Toye Bros. Yellow Cab Co., 162 So. 257 (La.App.1935). Any amendment sought to be made at the trial under the jurisprudential rules was denied on the dual grounds that the amendment came too late and that it would have the effect of changing the issues. Martin v. Toye Bros. Yellow Cab Co., *supra*. *Cf.* Lobell v. Neal, 48 So. 2d 797 (La.App.1950).

In view of the retention of the Louisiana system of fact pleading effected by Arts. 854, 891, 1003 through 1005, *supra*, it is still necessary to plead in the answer all of the material facts on which all affirmative defenses are based. See Arts. 1003, 1005, *supra*. To this extent no change is made in the rules applied in all of the above cases. But the law is changed under the third sentence of the above article which authorizes the trial judge to permit amendments, even on the trial of the case, so as to plead the material facts supporting an affirmative defense pleaded only generally or as legal conclusions in the original answer.

(d) See, also, Comments under Arts. 854, 862, 891, 926, *supra*.

Art. 1155. Supplemental pleadings

The court, on motion of a party, upon reasonable notice and upon such terms as are just, may permit mover to file a supplemental petition or answer setting forth items of damage, causes of action or defenses which have become exigible since the date of filing the original petition or answer, and which are related to or connected with the causes of action or defenses asserted therein.

Source: Fed. Rule 15(d).

Cross Reference: Art. 1156.

Comment

The above article introduces to Louisiana law the much needed rule to permit claims for items of damage materializing after the filing of the initial pleading, and to permit a plaintiff suing on a series of notes containing no acceleration clause to amend his petition so as to include notes becoming exigible since the filing of the original petition.

Art. 1156. Amended and supplemental pleadings in incidental action

The petition, the answer, and the exceptions filed in an incidental action may be amended or supplemented in the manner provided in Articles 1151 through 1155.

Source: New.

Comment

The sole purpose of this article is to place the amendment and supplementing of pleadings in the incidental actions on the same basis as the amendment and supplementing of pleadings in the principal action, so as to implement the rules adopted in Arts. 852, 1031 through 1116, *supra*.

TITLE II
CITATION AND SERVICE OF PROCESS

Chap.		Art.
1.	Citation	1201
2.	Service on Persons	1231
3.	Service on Legal and Quasi Legal Entities	1261
4.	Persons Authorized to Make Service	1291
5.	Service of Pleadings	1311

CHAPTER 1. CITATION

Art.
1201. Citation; waiver.
1202. Form of citation.
1203. Citation to legal representative of multiple defendants.

PRELIMINARY STATEMENT

Most of the concepts contained in the 1870 Code of Practice and the Service of Process Act, former R.S. 13:3471, have been retained in this Chapter although somewhat modified in form. In addition, some new rules have been incorporated. Only a few provisions of the 1870 Code have been deleted as unnecessary; and the provision of Arts. 181, 183, and 184 of that Code which fix the duties of the clerk in connection with citation and service have been included in Arts. 251 through 288, *supra*, dealing with court officers and their duties.

This Chapter provides the basic general law governing citation in ordinary proceedings. However, special provisions of law providing for a particular mode of citation and service are not affected.

Art. 1201. Citation; waiver

Citation and service thereof are essential in all civil actions except summary and executory proceedings. Without them all proceedings are absolutely null.

The defendant may expressly waive citation and service thereof by any written waiver made part of the record.

Source: C.P. Arts. 177, 206.

Comments

(a) This article is substantially a combination of the 1870 Code of Practice Arts. 177 and 206.

(b) The 1870 Code does not define "citation" and no such definition is included in this Code.

(c) Art. 177 of the 1870 Code requires a waiver of citation to be on the back of the petition. Because that requirement is too restrictive, the above article provides that any written waiver made a part of the record is sufficient to waive citation.

(d) That portion of Art. 177 of the 1870 Code relating to clerk's and sheriff's fees has been transferred to Title 13 of the Revised Statutes.

(e) This article does not repeat the prohibition against waiver of citation prior to the maturity of an obligation for the reason that the provision of La.Const. Art. VII, § 44, is sufficient.

(f) See Comments under Art. 928, *supra*, for a discussion of waiver and the effect of filing exceptions. See, also, Comments under Art. 7, *supra*, for a discussion of waiver by general appearance.

(g) Acceptance of service must be dated; and when not dated, service is effective only when the acceptance is filed. R.S. 13:3471.

(h) See, also, Comments, under Arts. 2591, 2594, *infra*.

Art. 1202. Form of citation

The citation must be signed by the clerk of the court issuing it with an expression of his official capacity and under the seal of his office; must be accompanied by a certified copy of the petition, exclusive of exhibits, even if made a part thereof; and must contain the following:

(1) The date of issuance;

(2) The title of the cause;

(3) The name of the person to whom it is addressed;

(4) The title and location of the court issuing it; and

(5) A statement that the person cited must either comply with the demand contained in the petition or make an appearance, either by filing a pleading or otherwise, in the court issuing the citation within the delay provided in Article 1001 under penalty of default.

Source: C.P. Art. 179.

Comments

(a) Research on the form of citation used in other states shows that while some states specify particular forms, many others merely detail the general content of the citation. The latter provide the best system, and this article sets forth the content of the citation.

(b) Art. 179(2), Code of Practice of 1870, requires that the citation contain the address of the defendant. This is unnecessary and has been deleted since a defendant can be served anywhere.

(c) Arts. 179(4) and 179(5) of the 1870 Code were combined into paragraph (5) of the above article. The phrase "under penalty of default" was added to warn the defendant of the effect of his failure to answer. This provision is required in most states and by Fed.Rule 4(b).

(d) Art. 179(6) of the 1870 Code requires an expression of the date citation was "delivered." If this means "delivered to defendant," then that information is a part of the return and not the citation itself. On the assumption that Art. 179(6) was intended to require an expression of the date of "issuance" of the citation, paragraph (1) was included in the above article.

(e) The requirement that the citation bear the seal of court has been retained. It may be noted that this requirement also obtains in Fed.Rule 4(b).

(f) The provisions of Arts. 178 and 181 of the 1870 Code of Practice requiring the clerk of court to prepare the citation were considered an administrative detail and are retained in this Code at Art. 252, *supra*.

(g) Arts. 178 and 183, Code of Practice of 1870, indirectly require the petition to accompany the citation. Since the concept of simultaneous service of citation and petition is retained, it is stated expressly in the above article.

(h) The words "exclusive of exhibits even if made a part thereof" were added in order to make it clear that exhibits would not have to be served.

Art. 1203. Citation to legal representative of multiple defendants

When one person is the legal representative of several persons made defendant in the same cause, only one citation need be addressed to such representative.

Source: Former R.S. 13:3471(2).

Comment

Art. 182 of the Code of Practice of 1870, which contains the idea of singular citation in the case of associated defendants, is unrealistic and is not consonant with the more modern practice. Under the above article multiple citations are dispensed with only in the case of legal representatives.

Art. 1231 CITATION, SERVICE OF PROCESS Bk. 2

CHAPTER 2. SERVICE ON PERSONS

Art.
1231. Types of service; time of making.
1232. Personal service.
1233. Same; where made.
1234. Domiciliary service.
1235. Service on representative.

PRELIMINARY STATEMENT

This Chapter deals with personal and domiciliary service, and these two types cover all possible situations.

Art. 1231. Types of service; time of making

Service of citation or other process may be either personal or domiciliary, and except as otherwise provided by law, each has the same effect.

Service, whether personal or domiciliary, may be made at any time of day or night, including Sundays and holidays.

Source: C.P. Art. 186; former R.S. 13:3471.

Cross Reference: Art. 1314.

Comments

(a) The last clause of the first sentence is a general recognition that either type of service is sufficient to support a judgment; but that in particular cases, specially provided for, their effect may not be the same, *e. g.*, the requirement of personal service on a garnishee (Art. 2412); or, the different effects of personal and domiciliary service on the commencement of the delay for applying for a new trial (Art. 1974) and for taking an appeal (Arts. 1913 and 1916) where the defendant does not answer, and a default judgment is rendered against him.

(b) With reference to the service of process other than citation, see Arts. 1312, 1313, and 1314, *infra*.

(c) See Art. 2002, *infra*, which provides that a judgment shall be annulled if it is rendered against a defendant who has not been served with process as required by law.

(d) Domiciliary service on a resident of the state is considered personal service within the intendment of due process of law and full faith and credit.

(e) See, also, Comments under Arts. 323, 1063, *supra*.

Art. 1232. Personal service

Personal service is made when a proper officer tenders the citation or other process to the person to be served.

Source: C.P. Art. 188; former R.S. 13:3471(1).

Cross References: Arts. 1314, 3824.

Comments

(a) This is the usual method of personal service. See Arts. 1291 and 1293, *infra*, with reference to persons who may make service, who, within the intent of this article are "proper officers."

(b) This article introduces an innovation by making the "tendering" by the person authorized to make service the completion of service. Art. 188, Code of Practice of 1870, requires that the citation be "delivered" to the defendant. This apparently required the act of actual handing over to the person being served, whereas under the above article it is considered that a tender is sufficient.

(c) See Art. 2412, *infra*, dealing with service on garnishees.

(d) See, also, Comments under Art. 3781, *infra*.

Art. 1233. Same; where made

Personal service may be made anywhere the officer making the service may lawfully go to reach the person to be served.

Source: Former R.S. 13:3471(12)–13:3471(14).

Cross References: Arts. 1314, 3824.

Comments

Under the above article only unlawful entry by the serving officer is prohibited. Of course, if a nonresident defendant were to be fraudulently induced into the state for the purpose of effecting service, that service would be invalid. Fidelity and Deposit Co. of Md. v. Bussa, 207 La. 1042, 22 So.2d 562 (1945). R.S. 15:152.3, which provides a special immunity from service in a civil suit for nonresident witnesses summoned to attend criminal proceedings in this state, has been retained in the Revised Statutes.

See, also, Comments under Art. 6, *supra*, and Art. 3781, *infra*.

Art. 1234. Domiciliary service

Domiciliary service is made when a proper officer leaves the citation or other process at the dwelling house or usual place of abode of the person to be served with a person of suitable age and discretion residing therein as a member of his domiciliary establishment.

Source: C.P. Art. 189; former R.S. 13:3471(8); Fed. Rule 4(d) (1).

Cross Reference: Art. 1314.

Comments

(a) The above article is a combination of the Louisiana source provisions and Fed.Rule 4(d) (1).

(b) See Arts. 1291 and 1293, *infra*, with reference to persons authorized to make service.

(c) The requirement that domiciliary service may be made upon a person "of suitable age and discretion," adopted from Fed.Rule 4(d) (1), represents a change in the law which heretofore required service to be made upon a person apparently over a specified age.

(d) The last clause of the above article is a codification of the doctrine of Rehage v. Hayford, 141 La. 103, 74 So. 711 (1917), which held that merely living under the same roof with the defendant, such as in a boarding house, did not qualify a person to receive service, but that domiciliary service could be effected only by service upon a member of the defendant's personal domiciliary establishment.

(e) See, also, Comments under Art. 6, *supra*, and Art. 1261, *infra*.

Art. 1235. Service on representative

Service is made on a person who is represented by another by appointment of court, operation of law, or mandate, through personal or domiciliary service on such representative.

Source: New.

Cross Reference: Art. 1314.

Comments

(a) The purpose of the above article is to provide for service in all situations where legal representatives are cited in lieu of the defendant himself. It is intended to cover ad hoc as well as permanently appointed curators and tutors; receivers, liquidators, trustees, administrators, executors, and other persons appointed by law as representatives; and agents for service of process designated by mandate.

(b) This article does not give jurisdiction over an absent defendant where jurisdiction is not established in some other independent way; but once jurisdiction obtains, this article simply provides the citation procedure.

(c) R.S. 13:3474 and 13:3475, the Use of the Highway Statute, involves three types of service, *i. e.*, upon a curator, upon the secretary of state, and by registered letter. This statute and its counterpart regarding boats and watercraft, R.S. 13:3479 through 13:3481, being special in nature, are retained in the Revised Statutes.

(d) See, also, Comments under Art. 2031, *infra*.

CHAPTER 3. SERVICE ON LEGAL AND QUASI LEGAL ENTITIES

Art.
1261. Domestic or foreign corporation.
1262. Same; secretary of state.
1263. Partnership.
1264. Unincorporated association.
1265. Political entity; public officer.

Art. 1261. Domestic or foreign corporation

Service of citation or other process on a domestic or foreign corporation is made by personal service on any one of its agents for service of process.

If the corporation has failed to designate an agent for service of process, or if there is no registered agent by reason of death, resignation, or removal, service of the citation or other process may be made at any place where the business of the corporation is regularly conducted either:

(1) By personal service on any officer, director, or resident agent named in the articles of incorporation or in the last report previously filed with the secretary of state, or

(2) By personal service on any employee of suitable age and discretion.

Source: R.S. 12:37(C), former 13:3471(5) (a), (b), (c).

Cross References: Arts. 1262, 1314.

Comments

(a) This article deals with both domestic and foreign corporations and represents a consolidation of the source provisions.

(b) As noted at Art. 1234, *supra,* the person upon whom service is made in the case of domiciliary service or of service under the above article, must be merely "of suitable age and discretion". This test, borrowed from the Federal Rules of Civil Procedure, has been substituted for a fixed age requirement.

(c) The second paragraph supersedes R.S. 12:37(C), which deals with service where a corporation has failed to designate a process agent.

(d) R.S. 13:3471(5) (d), permitting the state to sue a foreign corporation for taxes, and R.S. 13:3471(5) (e), authorizing the secretary of state to keep a list of foreign corporations in order to facilitate service of process, have been retained in the Revised Statutes.

(e) See, also, Comments under Art. 1354, *infra.*

Art. 1262. Same; secretary of state

If the officer making service certifies that he is unable, after diligent effort, to have service made as provided in Article 1261, then the service may be made personally on the secretary of state, or on a person in his office designated to receive service of process on corporations. The secretary of state shall forward this citation to the corporation at its last known address.

Source: R.S. 12:37(C); former R.S. 13:3471(5).

Cross Reference: Art. 1314.

Art. 1263. Partnership

Service of citation or other process on a partnership is made by personal service on a partner. When the officer certifies that he is unable, after diligent effort, to make service in this manner, he may make personal service on any employee of suitable age and discretion at any place where the business of the partnership is regularly conducted.

Source: Former R.S. 13:3471(4).

Cross Reference: Art. 1314.

Comments

(a) This is substantially a restatement of former R.S. 13:3471 (4). However, it does allow service on a partner wherever he may be found, whereas the source provision is susceptible of more restrictive interpretation.

(b) Service on an employee has been clarified and instead of a fixed age limit, the "suitable age and discretion" limitation was substituted.

Art. 1264. Unincorporated association

Service on an unincorporated association is made by personal service on the agent appointed, if any, or in his absence, upon a managing official, at any place where the business of the association is regularly conducted. In the absence of all officials from the place where the business of the association is regularly conducted, service of citation or other process may be made by personal service upon any member of the association.

Source: Former R.S. 13:3471(22).

Cross References: Arts. 738, 1314.

Comments

(a) This article is a restatement of former R.S. 13:3471(22) omitting, however, that portion which in effect recognizes an unincorporated association as a legal entity for purpose of suits.

(b) The original language in Act 170 of 1918, the source of former R.S. 13:3471(22), was to the effect that an unincorporated association could be served through the managing official of the association in all cases where the action was based upon "any obligation incurred for the benefit of such association."

In the case of State ex rel. Doane v. General Longshore Workers, 61 So.2d 747 (La.App.1952) the Court of Appeal for the Parish of Orleans held that the quoted language had the effect of limiting the scope of the statute to actions on obligations incurred for the benefit of the association and that it could not apply in a case where a suit for mandamus was brought.

However, since the language on which the court based its decision has been eliminated, the above text is sufficiently broad to permit service on an unincorporated association through the managing official of the association in all cases.

See Art. 738, *supra*, and Comments thereunder.

Art. 1265.   Political entity; public officer

Service of citation or other process on any political subdivision, public corporation, or state, parochial or municipal board or commission is made at its office by personal service upon the chief executive officer thereof, or in his absence upon any employee thereof of suitable age and discretion. A public officer, sued as such, may be served at his office either personally, or in his absence, by service upon any of his employees of suitable age and discretion.

If the political entity or public officer has no established office, then service may be made at any place where the chief executive officer of the political entity or the public officer to be served may be found.

Source: New; *cf.* former R.S. 13:3471(6).

Cross References: Art. 1314.

Comments

(a) This is a rephrasing of the source provision. It has been specified that if a public officer, whether federal or state, is sued as such, and not as an individual, he can be served only at his public office. This was added to prevent the harassment which might follow if domiciliary service was allowed.

(b) The last paragraph of this article was included in order to provide for personal service in case the political entity or public officer in question does not have any established office.

CHAPTER 4. PERSONS AUTHORIZED TO MAKE SERVICE

Art.
1291. Service by sheriff.
1292. Sheriff's return.
1293. Service by private person.

Art. 1291. Service by sheriff

Except as otherwise provided by law, service shall be made by the sheriff of the parish where service is to be made or of the parish where the action is pending.

Source: Former R.S. 13:3471(12), 13:3471(13).

Cross Reference: Art. 322.

Comments

(a) Only a portion of the source provisions has been codified in the above article. Former R.S. 13:3471(12) and 13:3471(13) also deal with the transmission of the citation by the clerk of court of one parish to the sheriff of another parish, and that portion of the source provisions is incorporated in Book I, Title I, dealing with officers of court. Other purely administrative provisions have also been included at Book I, Title I, dealing with court officers.

(b) When service is required by the sheriff, it may be made by one of his deputies, or, when authorized by the sheriff, by a constable or marshal. Arts. 331, 332, *supra*.

(c) See, also, Comments under Arts. 1232, 1234, *supra*, and Art. 3742, *infra*.

Art. 1292. Sheriff's return

The sheriff shall endorse on a copy of the citation or other process the date, place, and method of service and sufficient other data to show service in compliance with law. He shall sign and return the copy promptly after the service to the clerk of court who issued it. The return, when received by the clerk, shall form part of the record, and shall be considered prima facie correct. The court, at any time and upon such terms as are just, may allow any process or proof of service thereof to be amended, unless it clearly appears that material prejudice would result to the substantial rights of the party against whom the process issued.

Source: C.P. Arts. 201–204; former R.S. 13:3471(8); Fed. Rule 4(h).

Comments

(a) The above article is a consolidation of the source provisions, but instead of detailed provisions regarding the content of the sheriff's return, this article requires only sufficient data to show compliance.

(b) Art. 202 of the 1870 Code of Practice, requiring service on banks, public institutions, and certain other establishments to be the same as service of ordinary citation, was deleted as unnecessary.

(c) Some states provide that the return be made to the plaintiff: N.Y.Civil Practice Act, § 220; S.C.Code, §§ 428, 433; Wis.Stats., §§ 262.03, 262.07. However, the Louisiana requirement that the return be made a part of the record is a preferable system and is more consonant with the theory of citation as the foundation of the action.

(d) The last sentence dealing with amendments was taken from Fed. Rule 4(h).

(e) See, also, Comments under Arts. 324, 1094, *supra*, and Art. 3823, *infra*.

Art. 1293. Service by private person

When the sheriff has not made service within five days after receipt of the process or when a return has been made certifying that the sheriff has been unable to make service, on motion of a party the court may appoint any person not a party over the age of majority, and residing within the parish where service is to be made, to make service of process in the same manner as is required of sheriffs. Service of process made in this manner must be proved like any other fact in the case.

Source: Former R.S. 13:3484.

Comment

See Comments under Arts. 1232, 1234, *supra*, and Arts. 1355, 3823, *infra*.

CHAPTER 5. SERVICE OF PLEADINGS

Art.
1311. Service of copy of exhibit to pleading unnecessary.
1312. Service of pleadings subsequent to petition; exceptions.
1313. Same; service by mail or delivery.
1314. Same; service by sheriff.

Art. 1311. Service of copy of exhibit to pleading unnecessary

A copy of any written instrument which is an exhibit to a pleading need not be served upon the adverse party unless the party who files the pleading expressly prays for such service.

Source: C.P. Art. 175.

Comment

This article is declaratory of its source provision, but is broader in view of the requirement of service of all pleadings on the adverse party.

See, also, Comments under Art. 853, *supra*.

Art. 1312. Service of pleadings subsequent to petition; exceptions

Except as otherwise provided in the second paragraph hereof, every pleading subsequent to the original petition shall be served on the adverse party as provided by Article 1313 or 1314, whichever is applicable.

No service on the adverse party need be made of a motion or petition for an appeal, of a petition for the examination of a judgment debtor, of a petition for the issuance of garnishment interrogatories in the execution of a final judgment, or of any pleading not required by law to be in writing.

Source: Former R.S. 13:3345.

Comments

(a) This article is a simplification of its source provision, containing, in its second paragraph, exceptions to cover cases where the adverse party either had no interest in being informed, or will receive this information in other ways.

(b) Contrary to federal practice, motions required by law to be in writing and rules to show cause are considered pleadings in Louisiana, and hence governed by this article. *Cf.* Arts. 852 and 963, *supra*.

(c) It was said in Doll v. R. P. Farnsworth Co., 49 So.2d 354 (La. App.1950), that the source provision of this article is directory, and not mandatory, since there is no penalty for noncompliance. While the result reached in this case is sound the reasons assigned therefor are questionable. The sanctions available for the enforcement of this provision are the refusal of the trial court to proceed when service of the pleading has not been made, or the annulment of its order or judgment when the trial court has acted without knowledge of the noncompliance. *Cf*. Alonso v. Bowers, 222 La. 1903, 64 So.2d 443 (1953).

(d) The source provision expressly excepts "garnishment process." As written, there is no reason for this article to include such a specific exception for the reason that garnishment interrogatories are not pleadings. However, the second paragraph of this article excepts "a petition for the issuance of garnishment interrogatories."

(e) A dual purpose is served by the language of the second paragraph of this article: "No service on the adverse party need be made . . . of any pleadings not required by law to be in writing." First, this article does not apply to cases in trial courts of limited jurisdiction where the law does not require certain pleadings to be in writing. Second, it also excepts the case where even though a written motion was required under a local rule of court, the law does not require such motion to be in writing. *Cf*. Doll v. R. P. Farnsworth Co., *supra*.

(f) See, also, Comments under Art. 1231, *supra*, and Arts. 2643, 2902, *infra*.

Art. 1313. Same; service by mail or delivery

A pleading which requires no appearance or answer, or which under an express provision of law may be served as provided in this article, may be served either by the sheriff or by:

(1) Mailing a copy thereof to the adverse party at his last known address, or to his counsel of record, this service being complete upon mailing;

(2) Delivering a copy thereof to the adverse party, or to his counsel of record; or

(3) Delivering a copy thereof to the clerk of court, if there is no counsel of record and the address of the adverse party is not known.

When service is made by mail or delivery, the party or counsel making the service shall file in the record a certificate of the manner in which service was made.

Source: Former R.S. 13:3345–13:3347.

Cross References: Arts. 1063, 1093, 1312, 2643, 2971.

Art. 1313 — CITATION, SERVICE OF PROCESS

Comments

(a) See Comments under Art. 1314, *infra*.

(b) This article is a simplification of its source provision, with the necessary adjustment to take care of cases where an article of this Code expressly permits service in accordance with the provisions of this article. Such articles include Arts. 1063, 1093, and 2643, permitting service as provided in this article of the reconventional demand, the intervention asserting ownership of or a privilege on property under seizure, and the intervention in an executory proceeding, respectively.

(c) The certificate of service required under the last paragraph may be made by endorsement on the face or reverse of the pleading served, or on a separate page annexed thereto.

(d) See, also, Comments under Art. 1231, *supra*, and Art. 2902, *infra*.

Art. 1314. Same; service by sheriff

A pleading which is required to be served, but which may not be mailed or delivered under Article 1313, shall be served by the sheriff, either on the adverse party in any manner permitted under Articles 1231 through 1265, or personally on the counsel of record of the adverse party.

Source: Former R.S. 13:3471(15).

Cross References: Arts. 1093, 1312, 1313, 1433, 1976, 2414, 3305.

Comments

(a) Domiciliary service on a counsel of record has been eliminated, since the delays for answering might expire before the counsel of record actually receives the papers served, *e. g.*, if he were out of town at the time of service.

(b) When service is required by the sheriff, it may be made by one of his deputies, or, when authorized by the sheriff, by a constable or marshal. Arts. 331, 332, *supra*.

(c) This article effects a change in the law, or at least overrules legislatively the interpretation of its source provision by the supreme court. When the original statute on the subject was adopted in 1944, it was generally understood to provide a supplementary method of service in so far as those pleadings which theretofore required service by the sheriff were concerned. Yet, in Alonso v. Bowers, 222 La. 1093, 64 So.2d 443 (1953), the supreme court interpreted the source provision of this article as prescribing the exclusive mode of service of pleadings of this character. Such a construction is unnecessarily restrictive, hence the express language of this article expressly provides that service of these pleadings may be made either by the sheriff or as provided in this article.

(d) See, also, Comments under Art. 1231, *supra*, and Arts. 3602, 4609, 4610, *infra*.

TITLE III
PRODUCTION OF EVIDENCE

Chap.	Art.
1. Subpoenas	1351
2. Proof of Official Records	1391
3. Depositions and Discovery	1421

Sec.	
1. General Dispositions	1421
2. Depositions upon Oral Examination	1451
3. Depositions upon Written Interrogatories	1471
4. Other Discovery Devices	1491
5. Refusal to Make Discovery	1511

CHAPTER 1. SUBPOENAS

Art.
1351. Issuance; form.
1352. Restrictions on subpoena.
1353. Prepayment of fees.
1354. Subpoena duces tecum.
1355. Service of subpoena.
1356. Subpoenas and subpoenas duces tecum for depositions.
1357. Failure to comply with subpoena.

Art. 1351. Issuance; form

The clerk or judge of the court wherein the action is pending, at the request of a party, shall issue subpoenas for the attendance of witnesses at hearings or trials. A subpoena shall issue under the seal of the court. It shall state the name of the court, the title of the action, and shall command the attendance of the witness at a time and place specified, until discharged.

Source: C.P. Art. 469; Fed. Rules 45(a), 45(e) (1).

Comments

(a) This article is a combination of Art. 469 of the 1870 Code of Practice and Fed.Rules 45(a) and 45(e) (1).

(b) The form of the subpoena is here detailed to a greater extent than in the 1870 Code. Most states and Fed.Rule 45(a) so specify these details. *Cf.* Texas Rule 177.

(c) The requirement that the subpoena should inform the witness that he is to attend until discharged has been added. See Ark. Stats. (1947), § 28–509; Texas Rule 179.

(d) That a judge may issue a subpoena has been clarified by a direct statement to this effect notwithstanding the fact that such a power is one of the inherent attributes of a court. As a practical matter, of course, the clerk will issue subpoenas in most cases.

(e) Some states (see N.Y.Civil Practice Act § 403) allow subpoenas to be issued by the attorney for a party without court authority; but since this system would be a radical departure from Louisiana practice and also introduce new problems of enforcement, it has been omitted in this Code.

(f) See R.S. 13:4 which provides that the clerk's seal will suffice on documents which this Code requires to be sealed by the "seal of the court."

Art. 1352. Restrictions on subpoena

A witness, whether a party or not, who resides or does business in this state may be subpoenaed to attend a trial or hearing wherever held in this state. If the place of the hearing or trial is over one hundred miles from both the place of residence of the witness and the place in which he does business, the subpoena shall not issue without a special ex parte order of the court, in which the court may prescribe such requirements and conditions as may be considered just and reasonable.

Source: New; cf. C.P. Art. 134, former R.S. 13:3661, Fed. Rule 45(e) (1)

Comments

(a) The one hundred mile limitation of former R.S. 13:3661 has been eliminated. However, where a witness neither resides nor does business within one hundred miles from the place of the trial or hearing, conditions might exist which would require special consideration. Hence, a special ex parte court order is required, but the article allows the court considerable latitude in fixing particular terms and conditions when the witness resides and does business more than one hundred miles from the place of trial.

(b) Rule 13(3) of the Rules of the Civil District Court, Parish of Orleans, provides that attendance cannot be required sooner than forty-eight hours after service of the subpoena. However, no such provision is included here for the reason that such requirements should be left to court rules.

(c) See, also, Comments under Art. 1354, *infra*.

Art. 1353. Prepayment of fees

No subpoena shall issue until the party who wishes to subpoena the witness first deposits with the clerk of court a sum of money sufficient to pay all fees and expenses to which the witness is entitled by law.

Source: Former R.S. 13:3661; Fed. Rule 45(c).

Comment

This article introduces a change in the law. Prepayment of any fee which may be due a witness is required in all cases, even if the witness resides within the parish. See R.S. 13:3661 for the fees, and the administrative details of subpoenaing witnesses who live outside of the parish.

Art. 1354. Subpoena duces tecum

A subpoena may order a person to produce at the trial or hearing, books, papers, documents, or any other tangible things in his possession or under his control, if a reasonably accurate description thereof is given; but the court in which the action is pending in its discretion may vacate or modify the subpoena if it is unreasonable or oppressive. Except when otherwise required by order of the court, certified copies, extracts, or photostatic copies may be produced in obedience to the subpoena duces tecum instead of the originals thereof.

When the person subpoenaed is an adverse party, the party requesting the subpoena duces tecum may accompany his request with a written statement under oath as to what facts he believes the books, papers, documents, or tangible things will prove, and a copy of such statement must be attached to the subpoena. If the party subpoenaed fails to comply with the subpoena, the facts set forth in the written statement shall be taken as confessed, and in addition the party subpoenaed shall be subject to the penalties set forth in Article 1357.

Source: C.P. Arts. 139–141, 473–475; Fed. Rule 45(b).

Comments

(a) The above article is a combination of the source provisions. It should be noted, however, that it is broader than Arts. 139 and 141 of the 1870 Code of Practice in that it allows a subpoena duces tecum of third persons to produce tangibles.

(b) The theory has been adopted that the production of documents and papers should be only an adjunct to the subpoenaing of a witness. Therefore, the idea contained in Art. 143 of the Code of Practice of 1870 to the effect that a person may simply deposit the subpoenaed objects with the clerk has been abolished. Since the above article requires the custodian of the documents to produce them, his testimony concerning his custody will be important in most cases. Of course, in many instances the testimony of the witness producing the documents will be pro forma only, and in fact all that he will be asked to do is produce the documents. The above article nevertheless fixes responsibility for the documents until produced in court.

(c) The last sentence of Art. 474 of the 1870 Code, providing that the party required to produce documents shall be given a reasonable time to search for and produce them, is unnecessary in view of the text providing for modification of an oppressive or unreasonable subpoena.

(d) That part of Art. 475, Code of Practice of 1870, providing that a party or person cannot be subpoenaed to produce incriminating objects is unnecessary in view of the constitutional protection against self-incrimination.

(e) That part of Art. 140, Code of Practice of 1870, which allows the subpoenaing of only those documents which are "material to the cause" is unnecessary in view of the above provision for a variation or modification of an unreasonable or oppressive subpoena. The burden of showing that a document is not material is upon the person subpoenaed.

As a practical matter this effects no change in the law since under the 1870 Code if a person subpoenaed wishes relief from the subpoena on the ground that it calls for immaterial matter, he must move to quash the subpoena.

(f) The limitations on a subpoena duces tecum are the same as those upon a regular subpoena, since the subpoena duces tecum is regarded as an adjunct of the subpoena. Thus, it would be impossible to issue a subpoena duces tecum for the production of documents in the custody of a witness who resides or does business over one hundred miles away except by special court order. See Art. 1352, *supra*.

(g) The provision for producing copies of documents instead of the originals requires that such copies, extracts or photostatic copies shall be certified. The above article does not include the production of notarial acts. Art. 142 of the 1870 Code has not been deleted, however, but is incorporated into Title 13 of the Revised Statutes.

(h) That part of Art. 143 of the 1870 Code of Practice dealing with the control and custody of documents after production is administrative in nature and is provided for in Art. 253, *supra*.

(i) In many parishes, a subpoena duces tecum is obtained by filing a formal written application therefor and obtaining a court order. This is unnecessary and the above article allows a subpoena duces tecum to issue in the same manner as any personal subpoena, *i. e.*, upon simple request.

(j) The word "person" in the first line of the above article applies also to any other legal entity in view of the definition of the word "person" at Art. 5251, *infra*. The Louisiana law has been that a corporation cannot be required to respond to a subpoena duces tecum, unless the order designates some officer thereof as the person required to respond: Keiffe v. LaSalle Realty Co., 163 La. 824, 112 So. 799 (1927); Rawlings v. Schwartz, 167 La. 61, 118 So. 692 (1928); Ascension Red Cypress Co. v. Drainage District, 169 La. 606, 125 So. 730 (1929); Kinnebrew v. La. Ice Co., Inc., 216 La. 472, 43 So.2d 798 (1949). The above article effects a change in this rule since the subpoena issues to the corporation as such. Service of the subpoena is made as in service of citation (see Art. 1261, *supra*). Therefore, the usual agents for service of process are to be served, but the response to the subpoena may be made by any person authorized by the corporation to appear.

The above text also solves the problem of issuing subpoenas duces tecum to foreign corporations doing business in Louisiana when the desired records are out of the state. *Cf.* Loeb v. Equitable Life Assurance Soc., 179 La. 566, 154 So. 453 (1934). The corporation itself, and not any particular person, is named in the subpoena, and since there can be no doubt that it would have possession and control of all its records, even those out of the state, it is required to obtain the documents for production in obedience to the subpoena.

(k) The second sentence of the article, providing for production of copies instead of originals, recognizes and relieves the practical difficulties often involved in carrying heavy or voluminous records into court when only a small part of them is pertinent to the case.

(*l*) See, also, Comments under Art. 1355, *infra*.

Art. 1355. Service of subpoena

A subpoena shall be served and a return thereon made in the same manner and with the same effect as a service of and return on a citation. When a party is summoned as a witness, service of the subpoena may be made by personal service on the witness' attorney of record.

Source: C.P. Art. 134.

Comments

(a) This article is a restatement of a portion of the source article which recognizes personal and domiciliary service on witnesses. It incorporates by reference Arts. 1231 through 1265, *supra*.

(b) Under the provisions of Art. 1357, *infra*, which recognizes a "reasonable excuse" for noncompliance, protection against contempt proceedings is given a witness who had no knowledge of the domiciliary service.

(c) Service of a subpoena duces tecum on a corporation is to be made in accordance with the articles on citation. See Comment (j), Art. 1354, *supra*.

(d) Under the provisions of Art. 1293, *infra*, service may be made by private individuals instead of the sheriff or his deputies. This procedure is similar to that found in several other states: Calif. Code of Civil Procedure, § 1987; Iowa Code, § 662.63; Minn. Stats.Anno., § 596.02. *Cf.* Fed.Rule 45(c). Oklahoma even allows a party to make service himself: Okla.Stats.Anno., T. 12, § 386.

(e) The last sentence of this article is a recognition that the calling of parties as witnesses should be easier than the calling of third persons as witnesses.

(f) See, also, Comments under Art. 1231, *supra*.

Art. 1356. Subpoenas and subpoenas duces tecum for depositions

Proof of service of a notice to take a deposition constitutes sufficient authorization for the issuance by the clerk or judge of the district court of the parish in which the deposition is to be taken of subpoenas and subpoenas duces tecum. All provisions applicable to subpoenas and subpoenas duces tecum shall apply to subpoenas and subpoenas duces tecum issued under the provisions of this article, except as otherwise provided by law.

Source: Fed. Rule 45(d) (1); *cf.* former R.S. 13:3741 *et seq.*

Comments

(a) Since the provisions of Arts. 1421 through 1515, *infra*, concerning depositions require a notice as the basis of all depositions with or without court order, it is clear that the presentation of a notice to the appropriate clerk of court should be the basis for the issuance of the subpoena.

(b) Regular subpoenas may be issued without special order to secure attendance of witnesses as far as one hundred miles from the place of trial. However, since the deposition articles require that a deposition be taken in the parish where the witness resides, the one hundred mile provision is usually inapplicable. All other provisions, including that relating to the confession of a party who disobeys a subpoena duces tecum, are applicable.

(c) See Art. 1422, *infra*.

Art. 1357. Failure to comply with subpoena

A person who, without reasonable excuse, fails to obey a subpoena may be adjudged in contempt of the court which issued the subpoena.

Art. 1357   PRODUCTION OF EVIDENCE

The court may also order a recalcitrant witness to be attached and brought to court forthwith or on a designated day.

Source: C.P. Arts. 134, 135; Fed. Rule 45(f).

Cross Reference: Art. 1354.

Comments

(a) The provision of Art. 134 of the 1870 Code of Practice stating that domiciliary service of subpoenas is to be considered equivalent to personal service has been deleted. Under the above article, domiciliary service is equivalent to personal service, but if the witness can show that in fact he never had notice of the domiciliary service, this would present a "reasonable excuse".

(b) Art. 227, *supra*, deals with the limitations on the penalty for contempt which may be imposed under the above article.

(c) See Art. 1633, *infra*, with reference to the penalty imposed upon witnesses who appear but refuse to testify.

(d) This article is applicable to subpoenas issued to witnesses to take depositions. The contempt, however, is to the authority of the court which issued the subpoena rather than to the authority of the court which ordered the deposition to be taken. This is administratively sound since, by reason of the rules concerning the place of taking depositions, the witness will be within the jurisdiction of the court issuing the subpoena. See Art. 1512, *infra*.

In addition to the penalty fixed in the above article for failure to obey a subpoena to take a deposition, Arts. 1513 through 1515, *infra*, are also applicable.

(e) See, also, Comments under Arts. 1425, 1512, *infra*.

CHAPTER 2. PROOF OF OFFICIAL RECORDS

Art.
1391. Judicial notice of laws.
1392. Proof of statutes.
1393. Proof of official records by official publication.
1394. Proof of official records by certified copy: Louisiana records.
1395. Same; out of state records.
1396. Proof of lack of record.
1397. Other proof.

PRELIMINARY STATEMENT

This Chapter deals with legislative, judicial and administrative records of Louisiana, the United States and its territories, other states and foreign countries.

With respect to some of these records, the federal government either under the "full faith and credit" clause, or under treaty provisions, has already effectively entered the field, thus precluding Louisiana's requiring *more* proof of official records than is required by federal law.

For example, 28 U.S.C. §§ 1738, 1739, provide definite methods of proof of state and territorial statutory, judicial and nonjudicial records; and 28 U.S.C. § 1741 makes provision for proof of foreign documents and records. However, such provisions would not prevent Louisiana's permitting proof of such records by *less* stringent requirements. For example, Art. 1392, *infra*, the Uniform Proof of Statutes Law, gives prima facie validity to the officially published statutes of other states, territories and foreign countries; likewise, under Art. 1393, *infra*, Louisiana admits the Federal Register or any officially published book or pamphlet as prima facie proof of the originals.

Since the Louisiana law tends to require less stringent proof than corresponding federal law, those portions of the Louisiana law which require less proof have been included in this Code.

This Chapter deals solely with the admissibility of documents and does not pertain to the probative evidentiary effect of such matter.

Art. 1391. Judicial notice of laws

Every court of this state shall take judicial notice of the common law and statutes of every state, territory and other jurisdiction of the United States.

The court may inform itself of such laws in any manner as it may deem proper, and the court may call upon counsel to aid it in obtaining such information.

The determination of such laws shall be made by the court, and not by the jury, and shall be reviewable.

A party may also present to the trial court any admissible evidence of such laws, but, to enable a party to offer evidence of the law in another jurisdiction or to ask that judicial notice be taken thereof, reasonable notice shall be given to the adverse parties either in the pleadings or otherwise.

The law of a jurisdiction other than those referred to in the first paragraph of this article shall be an issue for the court, but shall not be subject to the foregoing provisions concerning judicial notice.

Source: Uniform Judicial Notice of Foreign Law Act.

Comment

This article, which is the Uniform Judicial Notice of Foreign Law Act, with some stylistic changes, introduces a new idea of judicial

Art. 1391   PRODUCTION OF EVIDENCE   Bk. 2

notice of the common law of other states. It has been adopted by twenty-four states and its adoption is recommended by the American Bar Association in Recommendation No. 11. See Vanderbilt, Minimum Standards of Judicial Administration 360.

Art. 1392. Proof of statutes

Printed books or pamphlets purporting on their face to be the session or other statutes of any of the United States, or the territories thereof, or of any foreign jurisdiction, and to have been printed and published by the authority of any such state, territory or foreign jurisdiction, or proved to be commonly recognized in its courts, shall be received in the courts of this state as prima facie evidence of such statutes.

Source: R.S. 13:3717.

Comments

This article reproduces the text of R.S. 13:3717, the Uniform Proof of Statutes Act. In view of the second section of the uniform act, R.S. 13:3718, which provides that it is to be so construed as to make uniform the laws of the states enacting it, the source provision has been retained in the Revised Statutes.

See, also, Comments under Art. 1393, *infra*.

Art. 1393. Proof of official records by official publication

An official record, or an entry therein, of the United States, of this state, of any other state or territory of the United States, of any foreign country, or of any political subdivision, corporation or agency of any of the above, when admissible for any purpose, may be evidenced by an official publication thereof.

A regulation, report, proceeding, ruling, decision, or other official act of any officer, department, board, commission, or agency of the United States, when admissible for any purpose, may be evidenced by the Federal Register, or by a printed book, pamphlet, or periodical published by the United States Government Printing Office by authority.

Source: Fed.Rule 44(a); R.S. 13:3713.

Cross Reference: Art. 1397.

Comments to Articles 1393 through 1397

(a) Articles 1393 through 1397 substantially cover the source provisions, modified to show clearly that the official records of all agencies, bureaus, and political subdivisions of Louisiana, the United States, other states and foreign countries are subject to the provisions of this Chapter. Where copies are offered as evidence, a stricter degree of certification has been required with regard to records of other states. Thus, as to Louisiana records the custodian himself may execute the certificate and this is in accord with R.S. 13:3711. However, as to records outside of Louisiana, the certificate must be made by a judge, a public official, and in the case of foreign records, by a member of the U. S. diplomatic service. The American Bar Association, in Recommendation No. 10, advocates universal adoption of Fed.Rule 44. See Vanderbilt, Minimum Standards of Judicial Administration 357 (1949).

(b) According to Moore's interpretation of Fed.Rule 44, the term "official record" includes any paper which is "work done by a person in the employment of the government in the course of the performance of the duties of his position." See 5 Moore's Federal Practice (2d ed.) 1515 (1950). Minnehaha County, S. D. v. Kelley, 150 F.2d 356 (8 Cir.1945) involving weather bureau reports. Furthermore, the record need not be a public record, *i. e.*, the original need not be open to examination by the public.

(c) Under Fed.Rule 44, certified photographic copies are admissible. Vaughn v. U. S., 78 F.Supp. 494 (E.D.Tenn.1947). In this regard, see the Uniform Photographic Copies of Business and Public Records as Evidence Act, adopted by five states, one of which is Louisiana (R.S. 13:3733). This act provides among other things for the admission in evidence of microfilm records.

However, the term "copies" as used in Fed.Rule 44 and the above articles is broad enough to cover any sort of copy. Therefore, an article defining copies is not included in this Code.

(d) The last clause of Fed.Rule 44(c) reading "or by the rules of evidence at common law" was omitted to make the article conform to Louisiana law.

(e) Art. 1394, *infra*, taken from R.S. 13:3711, allows proof of records of Louisiana agencies simply by the production of certified copies thereof.

(f) R.S. 13:3713, which provides that the courts shall receive in evidence of federal laws and agency records an officially printed pamphlet or the Federal Register, is now unnecessary in civil cases in view of Arts. 1392, 1393, and 1395. Art. 1392, *supra*, covers the situation as to federal laws, Art. 1393 admits proof by the Federal Register or any other official publication, and Art. 1395, provides for the appropriate certification procedure where copies are offered in evidence.

(g) R.S. 13:3723, providing that certified copies of the records of a district court are admissible in evidence in that same court, and R.S. 13:3724, dealing with the duties of the clerk when the court has admitted a certified copy of its own records, have been retained in the Revised Statutes.

(h) Art. 1395, *infra*, supersedes the 1870 Code of Practice, Arts. 752 and 753, which provide for certification of federal and foreign judgments.

Art. 1394. Proof of official records by certified copy; Louisiana records

An official record, or an entry therein, of the State of Louisiana or of any political subdivision, corporation, or agency thereof, when admissible for any purpose, may be evidenced by copies certified as being true copies by the officer or employee having custody thereof.

Source: R.S. 13:3711.

Cross Reference: Art. 1397.

Comments

See Comments under Art. 1393, *supra*.
See, also, Comments under Art. 251, *supra*.

Art. 1395. Same; out of state records

An official record, or an entry therein, of the United States, of any state other than Louisiana, of any territory of the United States, of any foreign country, or of any political subdivision, corporation or agency of any of the above, when admissible for any purpose, may be evidenced by a copy attested by the officer having legal custody of the record, or by his deputy, and accompanied with a certificate that such officer has the custody. If the office in which the record is kept is within the United States or within a territory or insular possession subject to the dominion of the United States, the certificate may be made by a judge of a court of record of the district or political subdivision in which the record is kept, authenticated by the seal of the court, or may be made by any public officer having a seal of office and having official duties in the district or political subdivision in which the record is kept, authenticated by the seal of his office. If the office in which the record is kept is in a foreign state or country, the certificate may be made by a secretary of embassy or legation, consul general, consul, vice consul, or consular agent or by any officer in the foreign service of the United States stationed in the foreign state or country in which the record is kept, and authenticated by the seal of his office.

Source: C.P. Arts. 752, 753; Fed. Rule 44(a).

Cross Reference: Art. 1397.

Comments

See Comments under Art. 1393, *supra*.
See, also, Comments under Art. 2541, *infra*.

Art. 1396. Proof of lack of record

A written statement signed by an officer having the custody of an official record or by his deputy that after diligent search no record or entry of a specified tenor is found to exist in the records of his office, accompanied by a certificate as provided in Article 1395, is admissible as evidence that the records of his office contain no such record or entry.

Source: Fed. Rule 44(b).

Cross Reference: Art. 1397.

Comments

See Comments under Art. 1393, *supra*.

Art. 1397. Other proof

Nothing in Articles 1393 through 1396 shall prevent the proof of official records or of entry or lack of entry therein by any method authorized by law.

Source: Fed. Rule 44(c).

Comments

See Comments under Art. 1393, *supra*.

CHAPTER 3. DEPOSITIONS AND DISCOVERY

SECTION 1. GENERAL DISPOSITIONS

Art.
1421. Stipulation regarding the taking of depositions.
1422. Place of taking deposition.
1423. Person before whom deposition taken.
1424. Objection to irregularities in notice; waiver.
1425. Objection as to disqualification of officer; waiver.
1426. Objections to competency of witnesses, relevancy of testimony, manner or form of taking deposition.
1427. Objections as to completion and return of deposition.
1428. Use of deposition.
1429. Objection to admissibility.
1430. Effect of taking or using deposition.

PRODUCTION OF EVIDENCE — Bk. 2

Art.
1431. Deposition taken outside Louisiana.
1432. Perpetuation of testimony; petition.
1433. Notice and service of petition for perpetuation of testimony.
1434. Order and examination for perpetuation of testimony.
1435. Use of deposition to perpetuate testimony.
1436. Deposition pending action; scope of examination and cross examination of deponent.
1437. Deposition after trial.

SECTION 2. DEPOSITIONS UPON ORAL EXAMINATION

1451. Notice of examination; time and place.
1452. Orders for the protection of parties and deponents.
1453. Record of examination; oath; objections.
1454. Motion to terminate or limit examination.
1455. Submission to witness; changes; signing.
1456. Certification and filing by officer; copies; notice of filing.
1457. Failure to attend or to serve subpoena; expenses.

SECTION 3. DEPOSITIONS UPON WRITTEN INTERROGATORIES

1471. Notice and service of interrogatories.
1472. Taking of testimony and preparation of record; notice of filing of deposition.
1473. Orders for the protection of parties and deponents.

SECTION 4. OTHER DISCOVERY DEVICES

1491. Interrogatories to parties.
1492. Discovery and production of documents and things for inspection, copying, or photographing.
1493. Physical and mental examination of parties.
1494. Same; report of findings; delivery of copies to parties; waiver of privilege of party examined.
1495. Right of party examined to other medical reports.
1496. Admission of facts and of genuineness of documents.

SECTION 5. REFUSAL TO MAKE DISCOVERY

1511. Refusal of deponent to answer oral or written interrogatories; order compelling answer; costs of obtaining order.
1512. Contempt.
1513. Failure to comply with orders, penalty.
1514. Refusal to admit, expenses.
1515. Failure to attend or serve answers.

PRELIMINARY STATEMENT

The following articles are an adaptation of the discovery provisions contained in former R.S. 13:3741 through 13:3794 enacted into law by Act 202 of 1952. Prior thereto, the articles in the Code of Practice of 1870 and the provisions in the Revised Statutes on depositions were the means used for securing the testimony of absent witnesses not otherwise available during the trial; and the Code of Practice articles on interrogatories on facts and articles, though providing a limited discovery system, were not sufficiently adequate. This fact, coupled with the favorable reception given to the federal rules on discovery, was perhaps instrumental in precipitating the adoption of La.Act 202 of 1952, modeled almost exclusively on Fed.Rules 26 through 37.

In the majority of instances the federal rules have been adopted verbatim, except for the necessary mechanical changes to make them adaptable for use in the state courts. However, in this Code some federal policies were rejected as unworkable and others have been modified. In other instances, well established Louisiana concepts were added.

One of the most significant changes made in Louisiana was the adoption of the so-called Hickman amendment, recommended in 1946 by the advisory committee on the Federal Rules of Civil Procedure but rejected by the Supreme Court of the United States. The amendment clarifies the case of Hickman v. Taylor, 329 U.S. 495, 67 S.Ct. 385 (1947), holding that discovery could not be made of the "work product" of an attorney without showing good cause. This amendment is contained in the second paragraph of Art. 1452, *infra*.

Fed.Rule 28 permits the court to appoint anyone to take depositions, and confers upon such persons pro tempore authority to administer oaths. This provision was not included in the Louisiana statute. Art. 1423, *infra*, merely provides that depositions shall be taken before an officer authorized to administer oaths who is not an employee or attorney of any of the parties or otherwise interested in the outcome of the case. This avoids the problem of whether the legislature could constitutionally authorize the judiciary to confer upon private individuals the authority to administer oaths even under such limited circumstances.

Throughout the 1952 statute, the more flexible policy of the federal rules regarding the time for objecting to errors and irregularities has been adopted in preference to a more rigid "time" policy. *Cf.* Art. 1427, *infra*, providing that errors and irregularities in the manner of taking depositions are waived unless a motion to suppress is made with "reasonable promptness" after such defect is "or with due diligence might have been" ascertained.

In order to clarify the problem created in State ex rel. Batt v. Rome, 172 La. 856, 135 So. 610 (1931), to the effect that the deposition of an adverse party could not be taken as under cross examination prior to the filing of the suit, a sentence was added to Art. 1434, *infra*, providing that the deposition of an expected adverse party may be taken under the Louisiana statute which allows cross examination of an adverse party.

The prayer for oyer recognized by Art. 175 of the 1870 Code of Practice has been rendered obsolete by the new discovery devices contained in the statute of 1952, and for that reason is not included in this Code. *Cf.* Art. 1492, *infra.* In any case oyer was restricted to the "document declared upon" and was never available as a means of discovering other equally important documentary evidence.

The use of the subpoena duces tecum provided for in Art. 473 of the 1870 Code, though replaced in part by the 1952 statute as regards the parties to the litigation, is still effective as against third persons. See Arts. 1354 and 1356, *supra.*

Since the 1952 statute was originally designed as an integral part of this Code, no other changes were made in the provisions thereof upon their transfer to this Chapter, other than those which are specifically noted in the Comments. The sources shown for each of the articles are to the corresponding sections of former Title 13 of the Revised Statutes, as amended by La.Act 202 of 1952, with references to the Federal Rules of Civil Procedure from which they were originally adapted.

Full comments and explanations for each of the original provisions of the 1952 statute have already been published in the official 1952 cumulative supplement of the Revised Statutes of 1950, and are reproduced in permanent form in Hubert, The New Louisiana Statute on Depositions and Discovery, 13 La.L.Rev. 173 (1953).

SECTION 1. GENERAL DISPOSITIONS

Art. 1421. Stipulation regarding the taking of depositions

If the parties so stipulate in writing, a deposition may be taken by any person, at any time or place, upon any notice and in any manner, and when so taken may be used as any other deposition.

Source: Former R.S. 13:3741.

Cross Reference: Art. 2451.

Comment

See Comments under Arts. 854, 1356, *supra.*

Art. 1422. Place of taking deposition

A witness who is a resident of this state may be required to attend an examination to take his deposition only in the parish in which he resides or is employed or transacts his business in person, or at such other convenient place as may be fixed by order of court. A witness who is a nonresident of this state, but is temporarily in this state, may be required to attend an examination to take his deposition only in the parish where he is served with a subpoena or at such other convenient place as may be fixed by order of court.

Source: Former R.S. 13:3742; cf. Fed. Rule 45(d) (2).

Cross References: Arts. 2451, 2889.

Comment

See Comments under Arts. 854, 1356, *supra*.

Art. 1423. Person before whom deposition taken

A deposition shall be taken before an officer authorized to administer oaths, who is not an employee or attorney of any of the parties or otherwise interested in the outcome of the case.

Source: Former R.S. 13:3743; cf. Fed. Rule 28.

Cross References: Arts. 2451, 2889.

Comment

See Comments under Arts. 854, 1356, *supra*.

Art. 1424. Objection to irregularities in notice; waiver

All errors and irregularities in the notice for taking a deposition are waived unless written objection is promptly served upon the party giving the notice.

Source: Former R.S. 13:3744A; cf. Fed. Rule 32.

Cross Reference: Art. 2451.

Comment

See Comments under Arts. 854, 1356, *supra*.

Art. 1425. Objection as to disqualification of officer; waiver

An objection to taking a deposition because of disqualification of the officer before whom it is to be taken is waived unless made before the taking of the deposition begins or as soon thereafter as the disqualification becomes known or could be discovered with reasonable diligence.

Source: Former R.S. 13:3744B; cf. Fed. Rule 32.

Cross Reference: Art. 2451.

Comment

See Comments under Arts. 854, 1356, *supra*.

Art. 1426. Objections to competency of witnesses, relevancy of testimony, manner or form of taking deposition

Objections to the competency of a witness or to the competency, relevancy, or materiality of testimony are not waived by failure to make them before or during the taking of the deposition, unless the ground of the objection is one which might have been obviated or removed if presented at that time.

Errors and irregularities occurring at the oral examination in the manner of taking the deposition, in the form of the questions or answers, in the oath or affirmation, or in the conduct of parties, and errors of any kind which might be obviated, removed, or cured if promptly presented, are waived unless seasonable objection thereto is made of the taking of the deposition.

Objections to the form of written interrogatories submitted under Articles 1471 through 1473 are waived unless served in writing upon the party propounding them within the time allowed for serving the succeeding cross interrogatories and within three days after service of the last interrogatories authorized.

Source: Former R.S. 13:3744C; *cf.* Fed. Rule 32.

Cross References: Arts. 1429, 2451.

Comment

See Comments under Arts. 854, 1356, *supra*.

Art. 1427. Objections as to completion and return of deposition

Errors and irregularities in the manner in which the testimony is transcribed or the deposition is prepared, signed, certified, sealed, indorsed, transmitted, filed, or otherwise dealt with by the officer under Articles 1451 through 1473 are waived unless a motion to suppress the deposition or some part thereof is made with reasonable promptness after such defect is, or with due diligence might have been, ascertained.

Source: Former R.S. 13:3744D; *cf.* Fed. Rule 32.

Cross References: Arts. 1455, 2451.

Comment

See Comments under Arts. 854, 1356, *supra*.

Art. 1428. Use of deposition

At the trial or upon the hearing of a motion or an interlocutory proceeding, any part or all of a deposition, so far as admissible under the rules of evidence, may be used against any party who was present or represented at the taking of the deposition or who had due notice thereof, in accordance with any one of the following provisions:

(1) Any deposition may be used by any party for the purpose of contradicting or impeaching the testimony of deponent as a witness.

(2) The deposition of a party, of or his representative as defined in Article 1634, may be used by an adverse party for any purpose.

(3) The deposition of a witness, whether or not a party, may be used by any party for any purpose if the court finds: (a) that the witness is dead; or (b) that the witness is at a greater distance than one hundred miles from the place of trial or hearing or is outside of this state, unless it appears that the absence of the witness was procured by the party offering the deposition; or (c) that the witness is unable to attend or testify because of age, sickness, infirmity, or imprisonment; or (d) that the party offering the deposition has been unable to procure the attendance of the witness by subpoena; or (e) upon application and notice, that such exceptional circumstances exist as to make it desirable, in the interest of justice and with due regard to the importance of presenting the testimony of witnesses orally in open court, to allow the deposition to be used.

(4) If only part of a deposition is offered in evidence by a party, an adverse party may require him to introduce all of it which is relevant to the part introduced, and any party may introduce any other parts.

Substitution of parties does not affect the right to use depositions previously taken; and, when an action in any court of this state, or the United States or of any state has been dismissed and another action involving the same subject matter is afterward brought between the same parties or their representatives or successors in interest, all depositions lawfully taken and duly filed in the former action may be used in the latter as if originally taken therefor.

Source: Former R.S. 13:3745; *cf.* Fed. Rule 26(d).

Cross References: Arts. 1430, 1435, 1491, 2451, 2889.

Comments

Because of a conflict with former R.S. 13:3662 through 13:3664, Art. 1428(2) was modified so as to conform to the broader rule in effect in Louisiana for many years.

See, also, Comments under Arts. 854, 1356, *supra,* and Art. 1634, *infra.*

Art. 1429. Objection to admissibility

Subject to the provisions of Article 1426, objection may be made at the trial or hearing to receiving in evidence any deposition or part thereof for any reason which would require the exclusion of the evidence if the witness were then present and testifying.

Source: Former R.S. 13:3746; *cf.* Fed. Rule 26(e).

Cross Reference: Art. 2451.

Comment

See Comments under Arts. 854, 1356, *supra*.

Art. 1430. Effect of taking or using deposition

A party does not make a person his own witness for any purpose by taking his deposition. The introduction in evidence of the deposition or any part thereof for any purpose other than that of contradicting or impeaching the deponent makes the deponent the witness of the party introducing the deposition, but this shall not apply to the use by an adverse party of a deposition as described in Article 1428(2). At the trial or hearing any party may rebut any relevant evidence contained in a deposition whether introduced by him or by any other party.

Source: Former R.S. 13:3747; *cf.* Fed. Rule 26(f).

Cross References: Arts. 2451, 2889.

Comment

See Comments under Arts. 854, 1356, *supra*.

Art. 1431. Deposition taken outside Louisiana

If the witness whose deposition is to be taken resides out of this state, the law of the place where the deposition is to be taken shall govern the compulsory process to require the appearance and testimony of witnesses, but otherwise the provisions of this Chapter shall be applicable to such a deposition.

Source: Former R.S. 13:3748.

Cross References: Arts. 2451, 2889.

Comment

See Comments under Arts. 854, 1356, *supra*.

Art. 1432. Perpetuation of testimony; petition

A person who desires to perpetuate his own testimony or that of another person regarding any matter that may be cognizable in any court of this state may file a verified petition in a court in which the anticipated action might be brought. The petition shall be entitled in the name of the petitioner and shall show:

(1) That the petitioner expects to be a party to an action cognizable in a court of this state but is presently unable to bring it or cause it to be brought;

(2) The subject matter of the expected action and his interest therein;

(3) The facts which he desires to establish by the proposed testimony and his reasons for desiring to perpetuate it;

(4) The names or a description of the persons he expects will be adverse parties and their addresses so far as known; and

(5) The names and addresses of the persons to be examined and the substance of the testimony which he expects to elicit from each, and shall ask for an order authorizing the petitioner to take the depositions of the persons to be examined named in the petition, for the purpose of perpetuating their testimony.

Source: Former R.S. 13:3751A; *cf.* Fed. Rule 27(a).

Cross References: Arts. 1435, 2451.

Comment

See Comments under Arts. 283, 854, 1356, *supra.*

Art. 1433. Notice and service of petition for perpetuation of testimony

The petitioner shall thereafter cause to be served a notice upon each person named in the petition as an expected adverse party, together with a copy of the petition, stating that the petitioner will apply to the court, at a time and place named therein, for the order described in the petition. At least fifteen days before the date of hearing the notice shall be served as provided in Article 1314; but if such service cannot with due diligence be made upon any expected adverse party named in the petition, the court shall appoint an attorney to represent him who, in case he is not otherwise represented, shall cross examine the deponent.

Source: Former R.S. 13:3751B; *cf.* Fed. Rule 27(a).

Cross References: Arts. 1435, 2451.

Art. 1433

Comment

See Comments under Arts. 283, 854, 1356, *supra*.

Art. 1434. Order and examination for perpetuation of testimony

If the court is satisfied that the perpetuation of the testimony may prevent a failure or delay of justice, it shall make an order designating or describing the persons whose depositions may be taken and specifying the subject matter of the examination and whether the depositions shall be taken upon oral examination or written interrogatories. The depositions may then be taken in accordance with this Chapter, and the court may make orders of the character provided in Articles 1492 through 1495. The deposition of an expected adverse party may be taken under the provisions of Article 1634. For the purpose of applying these rules to depositions for perpetuating testimony, each reference therein to the court in which the action is pending shall be deemed to refer to the court in which the petition for such deposition was filed.

Source: Former R.S. 13:3751C; *cf.* Fed. Rule 27(a).

Cross References: Arts. 1435, 2451.

Comment

See Comments under Arts. 283, 854, 1356, *supra*, and Art. 1634, *infra*.

Art. 1435. Use of deposition to perpetuate testimony

A deposition to perpetuate testimony taken under Articles 1432 through 1434 may be used in any action involving the same subject matter subsequently brought in any court of this state, in accordance with the provisions of Article 1428.

Source: Former R.S. 13:3751D; *cf.* Fed. Rule 27(a).

Cross Reference: Art. 2451.

Comment

See Comments under Arts. 854, 1356, *supra*.

Art. 1436. Deposition pending action; scope of examination and cross examination of deponent

A party may take the testimony of any person, including a party, by deposition upon oral examination or written interrogatories for the purpose of discovery or for use as evidence in the action or for both purposes. After commencement of the action the deposition may be taken without leave of court, except that leave, granted with or without notice, must be obtained if notice of the taking is served by the plaintiff within fifteen days after commencement of the action. The attendance of witnesses may be compelled by the use of subpoena as for witnesses in trials. The deposition of a person confined in prison may be taken only by leave of court on such terms as the court prescribes.

Unless otherwise ordered by the court as provided by Article 1452 or 1454, the deponent may be examined regarding any matter, not privileged, which is relevant to the subject matter involved in the pending action, whether it relates to the demand or defense of the examining party or to the demand or defense of any other party, including the existence, description, nature, custody, condition, and location of any books, documents, or other tangible things and the identity and locations of persons having knowledge of relevant facts. It is not ground for objection that the testimony will be inadmissible at the trial if the testimony sought appears reasonably calculated to lead to the discovery of admissible evidence.

Examination and cross examination of deponents may proceed as permitted at the trial.

Source: Former R.S. 13:3752; *cf.* Fed. Rule 26(a), (b), (c).

Cross References: Arts. 1491, 1492, 2451.

Comment

See Comments under Arts. 283, 854, 1356, *supra*.

Art. 1437. Deposition after trial

If an appeal has been taken from a judgment or before the taking of an appeal if the time therefor has not expired, the court in which the judgment was rendered may allow the taking of the depositions of witnesses to perpetuate their testimony for use in the event of further proceedings. In such case the party who desires to perpetuate the testimony may make a motion in the court for leave to take the depositions, upon the same notice and service thereof as if the action was pending in the court. The motion shall show:

(1) The names and addresses of persons to be examined and the substance of the testimony which he expects to elicit from each; and

(2) The reasons for perpetuating their testimony.

If the court finds that the perpetuation of the testimony is proper to avoid a failure or delay of justice, it may make an order allowing the depositions to be taken and may make orders of the character provided for in Articles 1492 through 1495 and thereupon the depositions may be taken and used in the same manner and under the same conditions as are prescribed in this Chapter for depositions taken in actions pending in the court.

Source: Former R.S. 13:3753; cf. Fed. Rule 27(b).

Cross Reference: Art. 2451.

Comment

See Comments under Arts. 283, 854, 1356, *supra*.

SECTION 2. DEPOSITIONS UPON ORAL EXAMINATION

Art. 1451. Notice of examination; time and place

A party desiring to take the deposition of any person upon oral examination shall give reasonable notice in writing to every other party to the action. The notice shall state the time and place for taking the deposition and the name and address of each person to be examined, if known, and, if the name is not known, a general description sufficient to identify him or the particular class or group to which he belongs. On motion of any party upon whom notice is served, the court may enlarge or shorten the time, for cause shown.

Source: Former R.S. 13:3761; cf. Fed.Rule 30(a).

Cross References: Arts. 1427, 1473, 2451.

Comment

See Comments under Arts. 283, 854, 1356, *supra*.

Art. 1452. Orders for the protection of parties and deponents

After notice is served for taking a deposition by oral examination, upon motion seasonably made by any party or by the person to be examined and upon notice and for good cause shown, the court in which the action is pending may order that the deposition shall not be taken, or that it may be taken only at a designated time or place other than that stated in the notice, or that it may be taken on written interrogatories, or that certain matters shall not be inquired into, or that the scope of the examination shall be limited to certain matters, or that the examination shall be held with no one present except the parties to the action and their officers or counsel, or that after being sealed the deposition shall be opened only by order of the court, or that secret processes, developments, or research need not be disclosed, or

Tit. 3 DEPOSITIONS AND DISCOVERY Art. 1453

that the parties shall simultaneously file specified documents of information enclosed in sealed envelopes to be opened as directed by the court; or the court may render any other order which justice requires to protect the party or witness from annoyance, embarrassment, oppression, or undue expense.

The court shall not order the production or inspection of any writing obtained or prepared by the adverse party, his attorney, surety, indemnitor, expert, or agent in anticipation of litigation or in preparation for trial unless satisfied that denial of production or inspection will unfairly prejudice the party seeking the production or inspection in preparing his claim or defense or will cause him undue hardship or injustice. The court shall not order the production or inspection of any part of the writing that reflects the mental impressions, conclusions, opinions, or theories of an attorney or an expert.

Source: Former R.S. 13:3762; cf. Fed.Rule 30(b).

Cross References: Arts. 1427, 1436, 1451, 1473, 1491, 1492, 2451, 2889.

Comment

See Comments under Arts. 283, 854, 1356, *supra*.

Art. 1453. Record of examination; oath; objections

The officer before whom the deposition is to be taken shall put the witness on oath and shall personally, or by one acting under his direction and in his presence, record the testimony of the witness. The testimony shall be taken stenographically and transcribed unless the parties agree otherwise. All objections made at the time of the examination to the qualifications of the officer taking the deposition, or to the manner of taking it, or to the evidence presented, or to the conduct of any person, and any other objection to the proceedings, shall be noted by the officer upon the deposition. Evidence objected to shall be taken subject to the objections. In lieu of participating in the oral examination, parties served with notice of taking a deposition may transmit written interrogatories to the officer, who shall propound them to the witness and record the answers verbatim.

Source: Former R.S. 13:3763; cf. Fed.Rule 30(c).

Cross References: Arts. 1427, 1472, 1473, 2451, 2889.

Comment

See Comments under Arts. 854, 1356, *supra*.

Art. 1454. Motion to terminate or limit examination

At any time during the taking of the deposition, on motion of any party or of the deponent and upon a showing that the examination is being conducted in bad faith or in such manner as unreasonably to annoy, embarrass, or oppress the deponent or party, the court in which the action is pending or in which the judgment was originally rendered may order the officer conducting the examination to cease forthwith from taking the deposition, or may limit the scope and manner of the taking of the deposition as provided in Article 1452. If the order made terminates the examination, it shall be resumed thereafter only upon the order of the court. Upon demand of the objecting party or deponent, the taking of the deposition shall be suspended for the time necessary to make a motion for an order. In granting or refusing such order the court may impose upon either party or upon the witness the requirement to pay such costs or expenses as the court may consider reasonable.

Source: Former R.S. 13:3764; cf. Fed.Rule 30(d).

Cross References: Arts. 1427, 1436, 1473, 2451, 2889.

Comment

See Comments under Arts. 283, 854, 1356, *supra*.

Art. 1455. Submission to witness; changes; signing

When the testimony is fully transcribed the deposition shall be submitted to the witness for examination and shall be read to or by him, unless such examination and reading are waived by the parties. Any changes in form or substance which the witness desires to make shall be entered upon the deposition by the officer with a statement of the reasons given by the witness for making them. The deposition shall then be signed by the witness, unless the parties by stipulation waive the signing or the witness is ill or is absent from the parish where the deposition was taken or cannot be found or refuses to sign. If the deposition is not signed by the witness the officer shall sign it and state thereon the fact of the waiver or of the illness or absence of the witness or the fact of the refusal to sign together with the reason, if any, given therefor; and the deposition may then be used as fully as though signed, unless on a motion to suppress under Article 1427 the court holds that the reasons given for the refusal to sign require rejection of the deposition in whole or in part.

Source: Former R.S. 13:3765; cf. Fed.Rule 30(e).

Cross References: Arts. 1427, 1472, 1473, 2451, 2889.

Comment

See Comments under Arts. 854, 1356, *supra*.

Art. 1456. Certification and filing by officer; copies; notice of filing

The officer shall certify on the deposition that the witness was duly sworn by him and that the deposition is a true record of the testimony given by the witness. He shall then securely seal the deposition in an envelope, endorsing thereon the title of the action and the name of the deponent, and shall promptly file it with the court in which the action is pending or send it by registered mail to the clerk thereof for filing, where it shall remain available for inspection.

Upon payment of reasonable charges therefor, the officer shall furnish a copy of the deposition to any person.

The party taking the deposition shall give prompt notice of its filing to all other parties.

Source: Former R.S. 13:3766; cf. Fed.Rule 30(f).

Cross References: Arts. 1427, 1472, 1473, 2451, 2889.

Comment

See Comments under Arts. 854, 1356, *supra*.

Art. 1457. Failure to attend or to serve subpoena; expenses

If the party giving the notice of the taking of a deposition fails to attend and proceed therewith and another party attends in person or by attorney pursuant to the notice, the court may order the party giving the notice to pay to such other party the amount of the reasonable expenses incurred by him and his attorney in so attending, including reasonable attorney's fees.

If the party giving the notice of the taking of a deposition of a witness fails to serve a subpoena upon him and the witness because of such failure does not attend, and if another party attends in person or by attorney because he expects the deposition of that witness to be taken, the court may order the party giving the notice to pay to such other party the amount of the reasonable expenses incurred by him and his attorney in so attending, including reasonable attorney's fees.

Source: Former R.S. 13:3767; cf. Fed.Rule 30(g).

Cross References: Arts. 1427, 1473, 2451.

Comment

See Comments under Arts. 854, 1356, *supra*.

SECTION 3. DEPOSITIONS UPON WRITTEN INTERROGATORIES

Art. 1471. Notice and service of interrogatories

A party desiring to take the deposition of any person upon written interrogatories shall serve them upon every other party with a notice stating the name and address of the person who is to answer them and the name or descriptive title and address of the officer before whom the deposition is to be taken. Within five days thereafter a party so served may serve cross interrogatories upon the party proposing to take the deposition.

Source: Former R.S. 13:3771; cf. Fed.Rule 31(a).

Cross References: Arts. 1427, 1511, 2451.

Comment

See Comments under Arts. 854, 1356, *supra*.

Art. 1472. Taking of testimony and preparation of record; notice of filing of deposition

A copy of the notice and copies of all interrogatories served shall be delivered by the party taking the deposition to the officer designated in the notice, who shall proceed promptly, in the manner provided by Articles 1453, 1455, and 1456 to take the testimony of the witness in response to the interrogatories and to prepare, certify, and file or mail the deposition, attaching thereto the copy of the notice and the interrogatories received by him.

When the deposition is filed the party taking it shall promptly give notice thereof to all other parties.

Source: Former R.S. 13:3772; cf. Fed.Rule 31(b), (c).

Cross References: Arts. 1427, 1511, 2451, 2889.

Comment

See Comments under Arts. 854, 1356, *supra*.

Art. 1473. Orders for the protection of parties and deponents

After the service of interrogatories and prior to the taking of the testimony of the deponent, the court in which the action is pending or in which the judgment was originally rendered, on motion promptly made by a party or a deponent, upon notice and for good cause shown, may issue any order specified in Articles 1451 through 1457 which is appropriate and just or an order that the deposition shall not be taken before the officer designated in the notice or that it shall not be taken except upon oral examination.

Source: Former R.S. 13:3773; cf. Fed.Rule 31(d).

Cross References: Arts. 1427, 1511, 2451, 2889.

Comment

See Comments under Arts. 854, 1356, *supra*.

SECTION 4. OTHER DISCOVERY DEVICES

Art. 1491. Interrogatories to parties

Any party may serve upon any adverse party written interrogatories to be answered by the party served or, if the party served is a public or private corporation or a partnership or association, by any officer or agent, who shall furnish such information as is available to the party. Interrogatories may accompany the petition or be served after commencement of the action and without leave of court. The interrogatories shall be answered separately and fully in writing under oath. The answers shall be signed by the person making them; and the party upon whom the interrogatories have been served shall serve a copy of the answers on the party submitting the interrogatories within fifteen days from service thereof unless the court, on motion and notice and for good cause shown, enlarges or shortens the time. Within ten days after service of interrogatories a party may serve written objections thereto. Answers to interrogatories to which objection is made shall be deferred until the objections are determined.

Interrogatories may relate to any matters which can be inquired into under Article 1436, and the answers may be used to the same extent as provided in Article 1428 for the use of the deposition of a party. Interrogatories may be served after a deposition has been taken, and a deposition may be sought after interrogatories have been answered, but the court, on motion of the deponent or the party interrogated, may render such protective order as justice may require. The number of interrogatories or of sets of interrogatories to be served is not limited except as justice requires to protect the party from annoyance, embarrassment, oppression, or undue expense. The provisions of Article 1452 are applicable for the protection of the party from whom answers to interrogatories are sought under this article.

Source: Former R.S. 13:3781; cf. Fed.Rule 33.

Cross References: Arts. 1511, 1515, 2451.

Art. 1491.

Comment

See Comments under Arts. 854, 1356, *supra*.

Art. 1492. Discovery and production of documents and things for inspection, copying, or photographing

Upon motion of any party showing good cause therefor, and subject to the provisions of Article 1452, the court in which an action is pending or in which the judgment was originally rendered may:

(1) Order any party to produce and permit the inspection and copying or photographing, by or on behalf of the moving party, of any designated documents, papers, books, accounts, letters, photographs, objects, or tangible things, not privileged, which constitute or contain evidence relating to any of the matters within the scope of the examination permitted by Article 1436 and which are in his possession, custody, or control; or

(2) Order any party to permit entry upon designated land or other property in his possession or control for the purpose of inspecting, measuring, surveying, or photographing the property or any designated object or operation thereon within the scope of the examination permitted by Article 1436. The order shall specify the time, place, and manner of making the inspection and taking the copies and photographs and may prescribe such terms and conditions as are just.

Source: Former R.S. 13:3782; cf. Fed.Rule 34.

Cross References: Arts. 1434, 1437, 1513, 2451.

Comment

See Comments under Arts. 854, 1356, *supra*.

Art. 1493. Physical and mental examination of parties

In an action in which the mental or physical condition of a party is in controversy, the court in which the action is pending or in which the judgment was originally rendered may order him to submit to a physical or mental examination by a physician, except as otherwise provided by law. The order may be made only on motion for good cause shown and upon notice to the party to be examined and to all other parties and shall specify the time, place, manner, conditions, and scope of the examination and the person or persons by whom it is to be made.

Source: Former R.S. 13:3783A; cf. Fed.Rule 35(a).

Cross References: Arts. 1434, 1437, 1495, 1513, 2451.

Comment

See Comments under Arts. 854, 1356, *supra.*

Art. 1494. Same; report of findings; delivery of copies to parties; waiver of privilege of party examined

If requested by the person examined, the party causing the examination to be made shall deliver to him a copy of a detailed written report of the examining physician setting out his findings and conclusions. After such request and delivery the party causing the examination to be made shall be entitled upon request to receive from the party examined a like report of any examination, previously or thereafter made, of the same mental or physical condition. If the party examined refuses to deliver such report the court on motion and notice may make an order requiring delivery on such terms as are just, and if a physician fails or refuses to make such a report the court may exclude his testimony if offered at the trial.

By requesting and obtaining a report of the examination so ordered or by taking the deposition of the examiner, the party examined waives any privilege he may have in that action or any other involving the same controversy, regarding the testimony of every other person who has examined or may thereafter examine him in respect of the same mental or physical condition.

Source: Former R.S. 13:3783B; cf. Fed.Rule 35(b).

Cross References: Arts. 1434, 1437, 2451.

Comment

See Comments under Arts. 854, 1356, 1357, *supra.*

Art. 1495. Right of party examined to other medical reports

At the time of making an order to submit to a medical examination under Article 1493, the court shall upon motion of the party to be examined, order the party seeking such examination to furnish to the party to be examined a report of any examination previously made or medical treatment previously given by any physician employed directly or indirectly by the party seeking the order for a physical or mental examination, and at whose instance or request such medical examination, or treatment has previously been conducted. If the party seeking the examination refuses to deliver such report, the court on motion and notice may order the delivery on such terms as are just; and if a physician fails or refuses to make such a report the court may exclude his testimony if offered at the trial, or render such other order as authorized under Articles 1511 through 1515.

Source: Former R.S. 13:3783C; cf. Utah Rules of Civil Procedure, Rule 35.

Cross References: Arts. 1434, 1437, 2451.

Comment

See Comments under Arts. 854, 1356, 1357, *supra*.

Art. 1496. Admission of facts and of genuineness of documents

After commencement of an action a party may serve without leave of court upon any other party a written request for the admission by the latter of the genuineness of any relevant documents described in and exhibited with the request or of the truth of any relevant matters of fact set forth in the request. Copies of the documents shall be served with the request unless copies have already been furnished. Each of the matters of which an admission is requested shall be deemed admitted unless, within a period designated in the request, not less than fifteen days after service thereof or within such shorter or longer time as the court may allow on motion and notice, the party to whom the request is directed serves upon the party requesting the admission either:

(1) An affidavit denying specifically the matters of which an admission is requested or setting forth in detail the reasons why he cannot truthfully admit or deny those matters, or

(2) Written objections on the ground that some or all of the requested admissions are privileged or irrelevant or that the request is otherwise improper in whole or in part.

If written objections to a part of the request are made, the remainder of the request shall be answered within the period designated in the request. A denial shall fairly meet the substance of the requested admission, and when good faith requires that a party deny only a part or a qualification of a matter of which an admission is requested, he shall specify so much of it as is true and deny only the remainder.

Any admission made by a party pursuant to such request is for the purpose of the pending action only and neither constitutes an admission by him for any other purpose nor may be used against him in any other proceeding.

Source: Former R.S. 13:3784; cf. Fed.Rule 36.

Cross References: Arts. 1514, 2451.

Comment

See Comments under Arts. 854, 1356, 1357, *supra*.

SECTION 5. REFUSAL TO MAKE DISCOVERY

Art. 1511. Refusal of deponent to answer oral or written interrogatories; order compelling answer; costs of obtaining order

If a party or other deponent refuses to answer any questions propounded upon oral examination, the examination shall be completed on other matters or adjourned, as the proponent of the question may prefer. Thereafter, on reasonable notice to all persons affected thereby, he may apply to the court in which the action is pending or in which the judgment was originally rendered for an order compelling an answer. Upon the refusal of a deponent to answer any interrogatory submitted under Articles 1471 through 1473 or upon the refusal of a party to answer any interrogatory submitted under Article 1491, the proponent of the question may on like notice apply for such an order. If the written motion is granted and if the court finds that the refusal was without substantial justification the court shall require the refusing party or deponent and the party or attorney advising the refusal or either of them to pay to the examining party the amount of the reasonable expenses incurred in obtaining the order, including reasonable attorney's fees. If the motion is denied and if the court finds that the motion was made without substantial justification, the court shall require the examining party or the attorney advising the motion or both of them to pay to the refusing party or witness the amount of the reasonable expenses incurred in opposing the motion, including reasonable attorney's fees.

Source: Former R.S. 13:3791; cf. Fed.Rule 37(a).

Cross References: Arts. 1495, 1513, 2451, 2889.

Comment

See Comments under Arts. 854, 1356, 1357, *supra*.

Art. 1512. Contempt

If a party or other witness refuses to be sworn or refuses to answer any question after being directed to do so by the court in which the action is pending or in which the judgment was originally rendered, the refusal shall be considered a contempt of the court of the parish where the deposition is being taken.

Source: Former R.S. 13:3792A; cf. Fed.Rule 37(b).

Cross References: Arts. 1495, 2451, 2889.

Comment

See Comments under Arts. 854, 1356, 1357, *supra*.

Art. 1513. Failure to comply with orders, penalty

If any party or an officer or managing agent of a party refuses to obey an order made under Article 1511, or Article 1492, or Article 1493, the court may make such orders in regard to the refusal as are just, and among others the following:

(1) An order that the matters regarding which the questions were asked, or the character or description of the thing or land, or the contents of the paper, or the physical or mental condition of the party, or any other designated facts shall be taken to be established for the purposes of the action in accordance with the claim of the party obtaining the order;

(2) An order refusing to allow the disobedient party to support or oppose designated demands or defenses, or prohibiting him from introducing in evidence designated documents or things or items of testimony or from introducing evidence of physical or mental condition;

(3) An order striking out pleadings or parts thereof, or staying further proceedings until the order is obeyed, or dismissing the action or proceeding or any part thereof, or rendering a judgment by default against the disobedient party;

(4) In lieu of any of the foregoing orders or in addition thereto, the party may be adjudged guilty of contempt except for disobeying an order to submit to a physical or mental examination.

Source: Former R.S. 13:3792B; cf. Fed.Rule 37(b)(2).

Cross References: Arts. 1495, 2451, 2889.

Comment

See Comments under Arts. 854, 1356, *supra*.

Art. 1514. Refusal to admit, expenses

If a party, after being served with a request under Article 1496 to admit the genuineness of any documents or the truth of any matters of fact, serves a sworn denial thereof and if the party requesting the admissions thereafter proves the genuineness of any such document or the truth of any such matter of fact, he may apply to the court for an order requiring the other party to pay him the reasonable expenses incurred in making such proof, including reasonable attorney's fees. Unless the court finds that there were good reasons for the denial or that the admissions sought were of no substantial importance, the order shall be made.

Source: Former R.S. 13:3793; cf. Fed.Rule 37(c).

Cross References: Arts. 1495, 2451.

Comment

See Comments under Arts. 854, 1356, *supra*.

Art. 1515. Failure to attend or serve answers

If a party or an officer or managing agent of a party wilfully fails to appear before the officer who is to take his deposition, after being served with a proper notice, or fails to serve answers to interrogatories submitted under Article 1491, after proper services of such interrogatories, the court on motion and notice may strike out all or any part of any pleading of that party, or dismiss the action or proceeding or any part thereof, or enter a judgment by default against that party.

Source: Former R.S. 13:3794; cf. Fed.Rule 37(d).

Cross References: Arts. 1495, 2451.

Comment

See Comments under Arts. 854, 1356, 1357, *supra*.

TITLE IV

PRE-TRIAL PROCEDURE

Art.
1551. Pre-trial conference; order.

Art. 1551. Pre-trial conference; order

In any civil action in a district court the court may in its discretion direct the attorneys for the parties to appear before it for a conference to consider:

(1) The simplification of the issues;

(2) The necessity or desirability of amendments to the pleadings;

(3) What material facts and issues exist without substantial controversy, and what material facts and issues are actually and in good faith controverted;

(4) The possibility of obtaining admissions of fact and of documents which will avoid unnecessary proof;

(5) The limitation of the number of expert witnesses; or

(6) Such other matters as may aid in the disposition of the action.

The court shall render an order which recites the action taken at the conference, the amendments allowed to the pleadings, and the agreements made by the parties as to any of the matters considered, and which limits the issues for trial to those not disposed of by admissions or agreements of counsel. Such order controls the subsequent course of the action, unless modified at the trial to prevent manifest injustice.

Source: Former R.S. 13:5151; cf. Fed.Rule 16.

Comment

See Comments under Art. 854, *supra*.

TITLE V

TRIAL

Chap.		Art.
1.	Consolidation of Cases	1561
2.	Assignment of Cases for Trial	1571
3.	Continuance	1601
4.	Trial Procedure	1631
5.	Dismissal	1671
6.	Default	1701
7.	Jury Trial	1731

Sec.		
1.	Right to Trial by Jury	1731
2.	Selection of Jury	1751
3.	Procedure for Calling and Examining Jurors	1761
4.	Procedure in Jury Trials	1791
5.	Verdicts	1811

CHAPTER 1. CONSOLIDATION OF CASES

Art.
1561. Consolidation for trial; joint trial of common issues.

Art. 1561. Consolidation for trial; joint trial of common issues

When two or more separate suits involving a common issue of law or fact are pending in the same court, the court, at any time prior to trial, may order the consolidation of the suits for trial or may order a joint trial of any of the common issues.

Source: C.P. Arts. 422, 423; Fed.Rule 42(a).

Comments

(a) Despite the narrow wording of Arts. 422 and 423 of the Code of Practice, the jurisprudence permitted the consolidation of suits involving the same issues, even though the parties were different, and hence did not fall within the letter of these articles. Union Garment Co. v Newburger, 124 La. 820, 50 So. 740 (1909); Fried v. New York Life Ins. Co., 177 La. 132, 148 So. 5 (1933); Riggin v. Watson-Aven Ice Cream Co., 192 La. 469, 188 So. 144 (1939); Clifton v. Tri-State Transit Co. of Louisiana, 197 La. 222, 1 So.2d 84

(1941); Olivedell Planting Co. v. Town of Lake Providence, 209 La. 898, 25 So.2d 735 (1946); Maddox v. Pattison, 186 So. 894 (La. App.1939). The courts were held to have inherent judicial power to consolidate. Union Garment Co. v. Newburger, *supra*.

(b) Although this article is to a great extent declaratory of the Louisiana jurisprudence on the subject, it enlarges the jurisprudential rules in two respects: (1) by empowering the judge to order the consolidation on his own motion; and (2) by authorizing the judge to order the joint trial of common issues in separate suits, even though they are not otherwise consolidated.

CHAPTER 2. ASSIGNMENT OF CASES FOR TRIAL

Art.
1571. Assignment by court rule.
1572. Written request for notice of trial.

Art. 1571. Assignment by court rule

The district courts shall prescribe the procedure for assigning cases for trial, by rules which shall:

(1) Require adequate notice of trial to all parties; and

(2) Prescribe the order of preference in accordance with law.

These rules shall not allow the assignment of ordinary proceedings for trial except after answer filed.

Source: C.P. Art. 463; cf. Fed.Rule 40.

Comments to Articles 1571 and 1572

(a) Adequate notice is a minimum requirement for reasons of due process. Except as provided in Art. 1572, *infra*, no particular type or kind of notice is required, since the matter is to be regulated by the local rules of court.

(b) Art. 1572, *infra*, retains the rule of Art. 463 of the 1870 Code of Practice providing that the notice, when requested, must be in writing and mailed at least ten days prior to the date of the trial. In this connection *Cf.* Alford v. Glenn, 185 So. 720 (La.App.1939) holding that where counsel is entitled to ten days written notice, the case cannot be set for trial in less than ten days over his objection.

(c) The requirement in Art. 1571, that the rules prescribe the order of preference (heretofore applicable only to the Civil District Court for the Parish of Orleans under Const. Art. VII, § 81, and R.S. 13:1303) is extended to all district courts in conformity with the practice in these courts.

(d) These articles apply equally to nonjury as well as to jury cases. They do not, however, preclude variations in the local rules as between such cases.

(e) The minimum standards required by these articles are not applicable to summary cases. Neither are they applicable to default cases, although a confirmation of a default is, in a sense, a "trial." In this connection it is to be noted that the case cannot be set for trial prior to answer filed. Art. 463, Code of Practice of 1870. See Coltrano v. Lotuso, 147 La. 150, 84 So. 528 (1920); Bently v. Barrett, 146 So. 349 (La.App.1933).

Art. 1572. Written request for notice of trial

The clerk shall give written notice of the date of the trial whenever a written request therefor is filed in the record or is made by registered mail by a party or counsel of record. This notice shall be mailed by the clerk, properly stamped and addressed, at least ten days before the date fixed for the trial.

Source: C.P. Art. 463.

Comments

See Comments under Art. 1571, *supra*.

See, also, Comments under Art. 1914, *infra*.

CHAPTER 3. CONTINUANCE

Art.
1601. Discretionary grounds.
1602. Peremptory grounds.
1603. Motion for continuance.
1604. Prevention of continuance by admission of adverse party.
1605. Trial of motion; order.

Art. 1601. Discretionary grounds

A continuance may be granted in any case if there is good ground therefor.

Source: C.P. Art. 468.

Comments

(a) The general discretionary power of the court to grant continuances under the provisions of Art. 468 of the 1870 Code of Practice is retained by this article. See also the peremptory grounds set forth in Art. 1602, *infra*.

(b) The Federal Rules of Civil Procedure leave the grounds for a continuance to the rules of the various courts. See 5 Moore's

Federal Practice (2d ed.) 903 (1950), to the effect that while Equity Rule 57 regulated the subject of continuances and reinstatement of cases with some detail, the federal rules do not regulate these matters, but leave their regulation to each of the district courts under its rule making power pursuant to Fed. Rule 83.

(c) See, also, Comments under Art. 1603, *infra*.

Art. 1602. Peremptory grounds

A continuance shall be granted in the following cases:

(1) If the attorney of record in the case is a member of the legislature and his absence is caused by his attendance at a legislative session; or

(2) If at the time a case is to be tried, the party applying for the continuance shows that he has been unable, with the exercise of due diligence, to obtain evidence material to his case; or that a material witness has absented himself without the contrivance of the party applying for the continuance.

Source: C.P. Arts. 464, 465, 466; R.S. 13:4163; cf. C.P. Arts. 470, 471; Quebec Code of Civil Procedure, Art. 305.

Comments

(a) Although the grounds for continuance enumerated in this article are well recognized, they may be waived by laches. Davis v. Davis, 17 La. 259 (1841); Lejeune v. N. O. Land Co., 13 Orl. App. 108 (La.App.1916).

(b) A party applying for a continuance, although entitled to a reasonable delay and opportunity to procure his witnesses, must show due diligence. Morgan v. Leon, 14 La.App. 45, 129 So. 398 (1930); Borel v. Living, 28 So.2d 392 (La.App.1946).

(c) See, also, Comments under Art. 1601, *supra*.

Art. 1603. Motion for continuance

A motion for a continuance shall set forth the grounds upon which it is based, and if in writing shall comply with the provisions of Article 863.

Source: Cf. C.P. Arts. 464, 465; R.S. 15:321.

Comments

(a) Art. 863, *supra*, has dispensed with the necessity for verification, except as provided by law. Art. 1975, *infra*, retains the requirement of an affidavit in the case of applications for a new trial based on the grounds of newly discovered evidence. Under the above article one who applies for a continuance must comply with Art. 863, *supra*.

(b) R.S. 15:321 provides that applications for continuances in criminal cases shall be by written motion. However, Rule XIII, § 5, of the Rules of Orleans Civil District Court, sets up a procedure by which the court calls the cases on the trial docket for the day, and counsel who desire continuances may apply therefor by oral motion. Under Art. 961, *supra*, motions must be in writing unless made during trial or hearing or in open court. If a party desires a record for appellate review, he should under Art. 1601, *supra*, file a written motion.

Art. 1604. Prevention of continuance by admission of adverse party

When a party applies for a continuance on account of the absence of a material witness, the adverse party may require him to disclose on oath what facts he intends to prove by such witness, and if the adverse party admits that if the witness were present he would testify as stated in the affidavit, the court shall proceed to the trial of the case.

Source: C.P. Art. 466; cf. R.S. 15:325.

Comment

See Calif.Code of Civil Procedure, Art. 596, and Wis.Stats., § 270.145(3).

Art. 1605. Trial of motion; order

Every contested motion for a continuance shall be tried summarily and contradictorily with the opposite party.

Source: R.S. 15:323.

Comment

Although as a practical matter many continuances are granted ex parte by the court, the above article provides an opportunity for controverting the application.

CHAPTER 4. TRIAL PROCEDURE

Art.
1631. Power of court over proceedings.
1632. Order of trial.
1633. Oath or affirmation of witnesses; refusal to testify.
1634. Cross examination of party or representative by adverse party.
1635. Exceptions unnecessary.

Art.
1636. Evidence held inadmissible; record or statement as to nature thereof.
1637. Completion of trial; pronouncement of judgment.

Art. 1631. Power of court over proceedings

The court has the power to require that the proceedings shall be conducted with dignity and in an orderly and expeditious manner, and to control the proceedings at the trial, so that justice is done.

Source: Cf. C.P. Art. 486; R.S. 15:11, 15:369.

Cross Reference: Art. 371.

Comments

(a) This article is a restatement of the court's inherent power of supervision. See Succession of Robinson, 186 La. 389, 172 So. 429 (1937); Wyatt v. Texas Pipe Line Co., 9 La.App. 248, 120 So. 123 (1928). The matter is adequately covered by the rules of the various Louisiana courts which deal in varying detail with the subject.

(b) Only the first part of Art. 486 of the 1870 Code of Practice has been retained. The last part, which deals with the liability of attorneys for slanderous and libelous matter uttered, is substantive and has been incorporated in the Revised Statutes.

(c) See, also, Art. 371, *supra*, and Comments under Art. 1632, *infra*.

Art. 1632. Order of trial

The normal order of trial shall be as follows:

(1) The opening statements by the plaintiff and the defendant, in that order;

(2) The presentation of the evidence of the plaintiff and of the defendant, in that order;

(3) The presentation of the evidence of the plaintiff in rebuttal; and

(4) The argument of the plaintiff, of the defendant, and of the plaintiff in rebuttal, in that order.

This order may be varied by the court when circumstances so justify.

When an action involves parties in addition to the plaintiff and the defendant, the court shall determine the order of trial as to them and the plaintiff and the defendant.

Source: C.P. Arts. 476, 477, 485; cf. R.S. 15:333.

Tit. 5   TRIAL PROCEDURE   Art. 1633

Comments

(a) This article establishes the classical order of precedence. It does contain, however, a permissive clause which allows the court to vary this order when circumstances so justify.

In actual practice the privileges conferred by the 1870 Code of Practice Art. 485 are not insisted upon and the customary argument consists of an opening statement by the plaintiff, a reply by the defendant, and a rebuttal argument by the plaintiff. See McMahon 821.

(b) Art. 484 of the 1870 Code of Practice provides that: "After all incidental questions have been decided, and both parties have produced their respective evidence, the argument commences; no witness then can be heard, nor proof introduced except with the consent of all the parties."

It has been held that it is within the sound discretion of the court to allow testimony after both parties have closed their cases. See Succession of Robinson, 186 La. 389, 172 So. 429 (1937), where the supreme court held that the trial judge had arbitrarily exercised his discretion in refusing to reopen the case after the beginning of argument for the taking of evidence or to grant a new trial. See also Rawls v. Brotherhood of Railroad Trainmen Ins. Dept., 213 La. 899, 35 So.2d 809 (1948); *cf.* Ruiz v. Trocchiano, 38 So.2d 184 (La.App.1949); Walker v. Joyner, 45 So.2d 113 (La.App.1950).

Art. 1631, *supra*, permits a liberal interpretation of the Robinson case.

Art. 1633. Oath or affirmation of witnesses; refusal to testify

Witnesses shall be sworn to speak the truth and nothing but the truth. If the religious opinions of a witness are opposed to taking an oath, an affirmation to the same effect shall suffice.

A witness who appears but refuses to testify without proper cause shall be considered in contempt of court.

Source: C.P. Arts. 136, 478, 479.

Comments

(a) The first paragraph of this article is a combination of 1870 Code of Practice Arts. 478 and 479, with stylistic changes. However, the language "in open court" has been omitted.

(b) R.S. 13:3665 defines a competent witness as "a person of proper understanding," which controls as to the competency of witnesses.

(c) The second paragraph is taken from Art. 136 of the 1870 Code of Practice. The substantive provisions of Art. 137 of the

Art. 1633   TRIAL   Bk. 2

1870 Code were omitted for the reason that under Art. 2315 of the Civil Code a party aggrieved by the refusal of a witness to testify has an action for damages for the loss which the party may have sustained.

See, also, Comments under Art. 1357, *supra*.

Art. 1634. Cross examination of party or representative by adverse party

Any party or his representative may be called as a witness and cross examined by an adverse party without the latter vouching for his credibility, or being precluded from impeaching his testimony. The court may permit the recall and further cross examination of the party or of his representative as often as it deems in the interest of justice.

"Representative" as used in the paragraph above and in Article 1428(2) means an officer, agent, or employee having supervision or knowledge of the matter in controversy, in whole or in part, whether or not he is in the employ of or connected with the party at the time his testimony is taken.

Source: New; cf. former R.S. 13:3662, 13:3663.

Cross References: Arts. 1428, 1434.

Comments

(a) This article makes no change in the law.

(b) The testimony of a party or of his representative may be taken, as under cross examination, by deposition. See Arts. 1428 (2) and 1434, *supra*.

Art. 1635. Exceptions unnecessary

Formal exceptions to rulings or orders of the court are unnecessary. For all purposes it is sufficient that a party, at the time the ruling or order of the court is made or sought, makes known to the court the action which he desires the court to take or his objection to the action of the court and his grounds therefor; and, if a party has no opportunity to object to a ruling or order at the time it is made, the absence of an objection does not thereafter prejudice him.

Source: Fed.Rule 46; cf. C.P. Art. 488.

Art. 1636. Evidence held inadmissible; record or statement as to nature thereof

When a court rules against the admissibility of any evidence, it shall either permit the party offering such evidence to make a complete record thereof, or permit the party to make a statement setting forth the nature of the evidence. In all cases the court shall state the reason for its ruling as to the inadmissibility of the evidence. This ruling shall be reviewable on appeal without the necessity of further formality.

If the court permits a party to make a complete record of the evidence held inadmissible, it shall allow any other party to make a record in the same manner of any evidence bearing upon the evidence held inadmissible.

Source: Cf. former R.S. 13:4448; C.P. Art. 488.

Comments

In Brown v. Tauzin, 163 So. 764 (La.App.1935), it was held that testimony recorded in detail after the lower court had sustained an objection to the admissibility thereof would be considered by the appellate court when it found the lower court was in error in excluding such testimony. The court did not hold, however, that the party had an absolute right to the full recordation of testimony ruled inadmissible.

This article vests in the court discretion to determine whether evidence held inadmissible should be recorded verbatim or whether the record should contain only a statement as to the nature thereof.

Art. 1637. Completion of trial; pronouncement of judgment

After the trial is completed, the court may immediately pronounce judgment or take the case under advisement.

Source: C.P. Art. 490.

Comment

This article is subject to the provisions of R.S. 13:4207 which required that judges decide all cases taken under advisement within thirty days from the time the cases are submitted for their decision.

CHAPTER 5. DISMISSAL

Art.
1671. Voluntary dismissal.
1672. Involuntary dismissal.
1673. Effect of dismissal with or without prejudice.

Art. 1671. Voluntary dismissal

A judgment dismissing an action without prejudice shall be rendered upon application of the plaintiff and upon his payment of all

Art. 1671

costs, if the application is made prior to a general appearance by the defendant. If the application is made after a general appearance, the court may refuse to grant the judgment of dismissal except with prejudice.

Source: New; cf. C.P. Arts. 491, 492; R.S. 13:4201.

Cross Reference: Art. 1844.

Comments

(a) Under Art. 491, Code of Practice of 1870, the plaintiff was permitted to discontinue his suit upon payment of costs at any time prior to judgment, except after a reconventional demand had been filed. Smith v. New Orleans Public Service, 179 So. 606 (La.App. 1938). See also, Rives v. Starke, 195 La. 378, 196 So. 657 (1940); Barbara Inc. v. Billelo, 212 La. 937, 33 So.2d 689 (1948). *Cf.* State ex rel. Gondran v. Rost, 48 La.Ann. 455, 19 So. 256 (1896). Under the Federal Rules, voluntary discontinuance as of right is prohibited after the answer has been served. See Federal Rule 41.

This article is, of course, subject to the provisions of Art. 1039, *supra*, which when read with the above article, makes it clear that dismissals are allowed even when incidental demands are pending.

(b) After an appearance, the plaintiff's right to dismiss rests within the sound discretion of the court. In this connection it should be noted that if a plaintiff fails to make out his case for lack of sufficient evidence which it appears he will be able to supply later, his rights should be preserved for another occasion by granting a judgment of nonsuit. Logan v. Schuler, 220 La. 580, 57 So.2d 193 (1952). However, if it appears plaintiff will not be able to substantiate his claim, a judgment of absolute dismissal must be rendered. Strother v. Villere Coal Co., 15 So.2d 383 (La.App.1943).

(c) Under Art. 532 of the 1870 Code of Practice, the point of dismissal as of right in jury cases is at the time the jury retires. The above article changes this rule.

(d) This article requires an actual judgment of dismissal and thus prohibits independent and unilateral action by the plaintiff. See, however, In re Cox, 207 La. 228, 21 So.2d 43 (1945); Person v. Person, 172 La. 740, 135 So. 225 (1931), to the effect that dismissals are effective from the date plaintiff takes action.

(e) For the requirements of dismissal in which an indigent party has been relieved from the payment of costs, see Art. 5187, *infra*.

(f) See, also, Comments under Art. 1672, *infra*.

Art. 1672. Involuntary dismissal

A judgment dismissing an action shall be rendered upon application of any party, when the plaintiff fails to appear on the day set for

Tit. 5   **DISMISSAL**   **Art. 1672**

trial. In such case the court shall determine whether the judgment of dismissal shall be with or without prejudice.

Source: C.P. Art. 536.

Cross Reference: Art. 1844.

Comments

(a) This article is based partly upon the 1870 Code of Practice, Art. 536, but follows the basic principle of Art. 1671, *supra*, by allowing the court to determine prejudice, and to that extent deviates from Art. 536 of the 1870 Code.

(b) R.S. 13:1215 and 13:4522 with reference to dismissals for failure of the plaintiff to furnish security for costs are retained in the Revised Statutes.

(c) Under Civil Code Art. 3519 a failure to appear when the case is called for trial would be a tacit discontinuance, and therefore would cancel the interruption of prescription. However, it has been held that the failure of plaintiff to appear at the trial was not a sufficient discontinuance or abandonment as to destroy the interruption of prescription. See Norwood v. Devall, 7 La.Ann. 523 (1852); Wilson v. Marshall, 10 La.Ann. 327 (1855). But see Bell v. Elliott, 8 La.Ann. 453 (1853), which held that where plaintiff failed to appear and his absence was unexplained, prescription was not interrupted.

A dismissal on motion of defendant for plaintiff's failure to comply with a court order to furnish a cost bond will not prevent the suit from interrupting prescription. See Belden v. Butchers' Union Slaughter-House Co., 38 La.Ann. 391 (1886). It could be argued that a dismissal for nonpayment of costs would cancel the interruption of prescription.

(d) Another form of involuntary dismissal is abandonment by lack of prosecution for five years. However, in view of Art. 561, *supra*, no recognition of involuntary dismissal by abandonment is required here.

(e) R.S. 37:217, which deals with the liability of an attorney when a nonsuit is entered owing to his neglect, is retained in the Revised Statutes.

(f) This Title does not deal with dismissal on exceptions. These are specially provided for. See, *e. g.*, Code of Practice of 1870, Art. 158; Arts. 932–934, *supra*.

(g) The language in the indirect source of this article referring to the failure of the plaintiff to appear "either in person or by attorney" has not been retained in this article, as it is unnecessary. Appearance by a party is always either personally or through his counsel of record. *Cf.* Art. 7, *supra*.

Art. 1673. Effect of dismissal with or without prejudice

A judgment of dismissal with prejudice shall have the effect of a final judgment of absolute dismissal after trial. A judgment of dismissal without prejudice shall not constitute a bar to another suit on the same cause of action.

Source: Cf. C.P. Arts. 492, 536.

Cross Reference: Art. 1844.

Comment

A judgment of dismissal with prejudice is not a definitive judgment, but merely a final judgment and subject to the rules governing such judgments. See Arts. 1841 and 1842, *infra*. A case dismissed without prejudice can be reinstituted; the judgment rendered therein is neither final nor definitive.

CHAPTER 6. DEFAULT

Art.
1701. Judgment by default.
1702. Confirmation of default judgment.
1703. Scope of judgment.

Art. 1701. Judgment by default

If a defendant in the principal or incidental action fails to answer within the time prescribed by law, judgment by default may be rendered against him. This judgment must be obtained upon motion in open court, but shall consist merely of an entry in the minutes of the court.

Source: C.P. Arts. 310, 311.

Comments

(a) This article is based upon Arts. 310 and 311 of the 1870 Code of Practice. See Art. 1843, *infra*, which defines judgment by default.

(b) Arts. 314 and 333 of the 1870 Code of Practice have not been included in this Code, since Art. 928, *supra*, prevents the filing of a dilatory or declinatory exception after default; and Art. 1002, *supra*, permits an answer until confirmation of default.

(c) This article applies also to answers in incidental demands, which are now required under Art. 852, *supra*. *Cf.* Art. 1035, *supra*.

The above article, as well as Art. 1843, *infra*, which defines default, refers to a default against a "defendant" and the term "defendant" includes a defendant in reconvention.

Tit. 5 DEFAULT Art. 1702

(d) See Art. 4732, *infra*, which provides for a special default procedure in eviction cases.

(e) See, also, Comments under Art. 1671, *supra*, and Art. 1843, *infra*.

Art. 1702. Confirmation of default judgment

A judgment of default must be confirmed by proof of the demand sufficient to establish a prima facie case. If no answer is filed timely, this confirmation may be made after two days, exclusive of holidays, from the entry of the judgment of default.

When the demand is for a sum due on an open account, an affidavit of the correctness thereof shall be prima facie proof. When the demand is based upon a negotiable instrument, no proof of any signature thereon shall be required.

Source: C.P. Art. 312; cf. Comments following.

Comments

(a) This article is based upon Art. 312 of the 1870 Code of Practice with certain changes.

(b) In most jurisdictions a default taken in an action upon contract for a sum of money is clothed with less formality and is entered on filing an affidavit with the clerk. See Fed.Rule 55(b) (1); Calif.Code of Civil Procedure, §§ 407, 585; Florida Stats.Anno., § 50.11; Idaho Code, § 10–801; Nev.Rules of Civil Procedure, Rule 55; Wis.Stats., § 270.62.

(c) In federal procedure the grant or denial of a motion for the entry by the court of a default judgment lies within the sound discretion of the trial judge. See 6 Moore's Federal Practice (2d ed.) 1814 (1950).

A party may seek relief from a judgment of default for mistake, inadvertence, excusable neglect under Fed.Rule 60(b). See also Fed.Rule 55(c).

(d) The last sentence of this article is an attempt to clarify the situation with regard to proof of signatures on negotiable instruments. In Strange v. Albrecht, 190 La. 897, 183 So. 209 (1938) it was held that plaintiff did not need to prove endorsement by the payee in order to obtain a judgment by default. The case is cited with approval in 13 Tul.L.Rev. 303 (1939), where it is pointed out that the earlier cases held that in order for the holder of a promissory note endorsed in blank by the payee to recover on a default judgment it was necessary for him to prove both the maker's signature and the payee's endorsement. Bryan's Administrator v. Spruell, 16 La. 313 (1840) (maker's signature); D. Blum, Stern and Co. v. Sallis, 24 La.Ann. 118 (1872) (payee's signature). On the other

Art. 1702

hand, the later jurisprudence, applying Art. 324 of the 1870 Code of Practice, which requires that the defendant either avow or deny his signature, held that the plaintiff need not prove the signature of the maker in order to obtain a default judgment against him. Davis v. Davis, 8 La.Ann. 91 (1853). The author of the note states that this article should also apply where the holder sues the payee on his endorsement. See Miller v. Cohea, 1 La. 486 (1830); Union National Bank of New Orleans v. Lee, 33 La.Ann. 301 (1881).

The above article is restricted to negotiable instruments, since the reasoning of the cases was based upon the fact that the concept of negotiability required the result in those cases.

Art. 1703. Scope of judgment

A judgment by default shall not be different in kind from or exceed in amount that demanded in the petition.

Source: Fed.Rule 54(c); cf. C.P. Art. 315.

Cross Reference: Art. 862.

Comment

This article is essential to prevent the judgment by default from going beyond the scope of the prayer. A defendant may decide not to defend as to a particular prayer for relief, whereas he would defend if relief beyond the prayer were available. This necessary limitation is taken from the first part of Fed.Rule 54(c). Of course, if a judgment by default should exceed the amount demanded in the petition, it would be null to the extent of the excess.

CHAPTER 7. JURY TRIAL

SECTION 1. RIGHT TO TRIAL BY JURY

Art.
1731. Issues triable by jury.
1732. Demand for jury trial.
1733. Limitation upon jury trials.
1734. Specification of issues.
1735. Trial of less than all issues; stipulation.

SECTION 2. SELECTION OF JURY

1751. Qualification and exemptions of jurors.

SECTION 3. PROCEDURE FOR CALLING AND EXAMINING JURORS

1761. Procedure in general.
1762. Swearing of juror before examination.

Art.
1763. Examination of juror.
1764. Peremptory challenges.
1765. Challenges for cause.
1766. Time for peremptory challenge.
1767. Challenging or excusing jurors after acceptance.
1768. Swearing of jurors; selection of foreman.
1769. Alternate jurors.

SECTION 4. PROCEDURE IN JURY TRIALS

1791. Time for charging the jury; recordation of charge.
1792. Contents of charge to jury.
1793. Instruction to jury; objections.
1794. Taking evidence to jury room.
1795. Number required for verdict; stipulation.

SECTION 5. VERDICTS

1811. Special verdicts.
1812. General verdict accompanied by answer to interrogatories.
1813. Remittitur or additur as alternative to new trial; reformation of verdict.
1814. New trial on showing of misconduct by jury.

PRELIMINARY STATEMENT

Civil jury trials occupy a unique position in Louisiana. While the jury trial functions in substantially the same manner in criminal cases in this state as in other American jurisdictions, it plays a lesser and quite different role in the civil procedure of Louisiana. Appeals in civil cases are on both the law and the facts. Const., Art. VII, §§ 10, 29. Appellate courts review the findings of fact of the trial courts, whether made by the judge alone or by a jury; and if, after a study of the record of appeal, they conclude that the findings of fact appealed from are erroneous, the appellate courts substitute their own findings, even though there may be evidence in the record to support the findings of fact of the trial courts.

The result is that the civil jury trial in Louisiana is the relatively rare exception, and trial by the judge alone the general rule. Even in the relatively few civil cases tried by juries, there is no need for any elaborate system of controls over the irresponsibilities of the jury, since the latter's finding of fact or award of damages may be set aside if the appellate court concludes that these are not supported by a preponderance of the evidence.

For these reasons, this Code does not embody the excellent jury controls to be found in the Federal Rules of Civil Procedure, and in the procedural systems of other states based thereon. These controls are badly needed in the jurisdictions which have adopted them.

They would serve no particularly useful purpose in the civil procedure of Louisiana.

SECTION 1. RIGHT TO TRIAL BY JURY

Art. 1731. Issues triable by jury

Except as limited by Article 1733, the right of trial by jury is recognized.

The nature and amount of the principal demand shall determine whether any issue in the principal or incidental demand is triable by jury.

Source: New.

Comments

This article serves the same purpose as Fed.Rule 38(a), which provides that the right of trial by jury as declared by the Seventh Amendment to the Constitution or as given by a statute of the United States shall be preserved to the parties inviolate.

A troublesome question as to the right to jury trial might be presented in cases in which there are incidental demands. The second sentence of this article provides the test to be applied in such cases: whether any demand may be tried by a jury depends upon whether the principal demand is triable by jury under Art. 1733, *infra*. Thus, if the principal demand is for $800 damages, and the defendant reconvenes for $5,000 damages, neither demand may be tried by a jury. Conversely, if the principal demand is for $5,000 damages, and the defendant reconvenes for $800 damages, either or both demands may be tried by a jury, dependent on whether the plaintiff or defendant or both demand a jury trial under Art. 1732, *infra*.

Art. 1732. Demand for jury trial

A party may demand a trial by jury of any issue triable of right by a jury in a pleading filed not later than ten days after the service of the last pleading directed to such issue.

Source: Fed.Rule 38(b); cf. C.P. Arts. 494, 495.

Comments

(a) The former rule, permitting the request for jury trial to be made at any time before the case was assigned for trial, has proved difficult to administer, and was discarded in favor of the federal rule.

(b) Normally, the demand for a jury trial would be made by the plaintiff in his petition, or made by the defendant in his answer.

If not made then, under the above article it may be made in a supplemental pleading filed timely. This supplemental pleading would have to be filed not later than ten days after service of the answer, if there was no incidental demand; or not later than ten days after service of the answer to the incidental demand. However made, the pleading in which it was made would have to be served on the adverse party. See Art. 1312, *supra*.

(c) See, also Comments under Art. 1731, *supra*.

Art. 1733. Limitation upon jury trials

A trial by jury shall not be available in:

(1) A suit demanding less than one thousand dollars exclusive of interest and costs;

(2) A suit on an unconditional obligation to pay a specific sum of money, unless the defense thereto is forgery, fraud, error, want or failure of consideration;

(3) A summary, executory, probate, partition, mandamus, habeas corpus, quo warranto, injunction, concursus, workmen's compensation, emancipation, tutorship, interdiction, curatorship, legitimacy, filiation, separation from bed and board, annulment of marriage, or divorce proceeding;

(4) A proceeding to review an action by an administrative or municipal body; and

(5) All cases where a jury trial is specifically denied by law.

Source: C.P. Art. 494; cf. Comments following.

Cross Reference: Art. 1731.

Comments

(a) Art. 1733(1) is new as to district courts. However, in New Orleans, cases in city courts, which have jurisdiction up to $1,000, are tried without juries. See former R.S. 13:1971.

(b) Art. 1733(2) is a redraft of a portion of the 1870 Code of Practice Art. 494. The types of notes or bills of exchange referred to are not enumerated, since the source article is obviously intended to cover all unconditional obligations to pay, including bills and notes. See 11 Tul.L.Rev. 653 (1937); Boagni v. Anderson, 32 La. Ann. 920 (1880).

(c) The probate provision of Art. 1733(3) is the customary Louisiana practice. See Cafiero v. Cafiero, 154 La. 1076, 98 So. 672 (1923); Fellows v. Fellows, 220 La. 407, 56 So.2d 733 (1951). Of course, if a direct action were brought against the succession, it would not be regarded as a part of the succession proceeding itself and would not be governed by this limitation. On the other hand, a

Art. 1733 (continued)

succession creditor could assert his right by an opposition rather than a direct action, and in such cases he would waive his right to a jury trial.

(d) Adoption proceedings are not included in the above article for the reason that such proceedings are within the jurisdiction of juvenile courts to which this Code does not apply.

(e) In connection with summary proceedings referred to in this article, see Book V, Summary and Executory Proceedings. The word "summary" does not include actions which are not truly summary in nature, but are merely preference cases. Such cases are triable by jury provided they are not subject to any other of the limitations set by this article.

(f) R.S. 13:4792, which deals with civil rights cases and provides for a decision by the court when the jury fails to render a verdict, is retained in the Revised Statutes.

(g) Art. 1733(4) provides for cases involving review of the action of a city council or other municipal or administrative body. The majority of such issues come up in injunction or mandamus proceedings, but the above provision prohibits jury trials of such issues when they arise in other proceedings such as declaratory judgment actions, where jury trials are allowed. See Art.1879, *infra*.

(h) See, also, Comments under Art. 1731, *supra*, and Arts. 4662, 4842, *infra*.

Art. 1734. Specification of issues

In his demand a party may specify the issues which he wishes to be tried by jury; otherwise he shall be considered to have demanded trial by jury for all the issues so triable. If he has demanded trial by jury for only some of the issues, any other party, within ten days after service of the demand or such lesser time as the court may order, may demand trial by jury of any or all of the other issues in the action.

Source: Fed.Rule 38(c).

Comments

(a) This article is based on Fed.Rule 38(c) and provides that a party may, if he desires, ask for a jury trial as to certain issues only, provided the opposing party is allowed to demand a jury trial as to any other issues.

(b) With reference to reconventional demands, there will be no trial by jury unless the plaintiff in reconvention demands it or the defendant in reconvention does so within the time limit set in the article.

Tit. 5   JURY TRIAL   Art. 1761

Art. 1735. Trial of less than all issues; stipulation

The trial of all issues for which jury trial has been requested shall be by jury unless the parties stipulate that the jury trial shall be as to certain issues only, or unless the right to trial by jury as to certain issues does not exist, but in all cases there shall be but one trial.

Source: Fed.Rule 39(a).

Comments

Even though the parties have initially demanded a trial by jury on all issues, under this article they are granted the right to stipulate for trial by jury of less than all issues. See Fed.Rule 39.

The last clause was added to provide specific protection against piecemeal trial of cases. Otherwise the regulation of the procedure for trial of jury and nonjury issues is left to the discretion of the court.

See, also, Comment under Art. 1972, *infra*.

SECTION 2. SELECTION OF JURY

Art. 1751. Qualification and exemptions of jurors

The qualification and exemptions of jurors and the method of choosing and summoning the general venire in jury cases are provided by special laws.

Source: C.P. Art. 493.

Comment

The source provision refers to the various sections of the Revised Statutes of 1950 which prescribe the qualifications of jurors (R.S. 13:3041), provide for exemptions from jury service (R.S. 13:3042), set forth the requirements for eligibility of women for jury service (R.S. 13:3055, 13:3056), the methods of choosing and summoning jurors (R.S. 13:3043, 13:3050, 13:3101 and R.S. 15:191), and the grounds for attacking the general venire (R.S. 13:3051, 13:-3052).

SECTION 3. PROCEDURE FOR CALLING AND EXAMINING JURORS

Art. 1761. Procedure in general

In cases to be tried by jury, twelve jurors summoned in accordance with law shall be chosen by lot to try the case. The method of calling

Art. 1761

and drawing by lot shall be at the discretion of the court. The parties may stipulate for a lesser number of jurors to try the case; or that if one or more of the jurors dies or becomes disqualified the remaining jurors shall try the case.

Source: New; cf. C.P. Arts. 496–499; Fed.Rule 48; former R.S. 13:3050; R.S. 15:343–15:349.

Cross Reference: Art. 1795.

Comments

(a) This article establishes a single system for the actual empanelling of jurors from the general venire, called in accordance with law. This and the following articles provide the mechanics for narrowing the general venire down to the actual jury empanelled to try the case, and also the requirements for examination and challenge.

(b) This article does not retain the provisions of Arts. 496, 497, and 499 of the 1870 Code of Practice with reference to writing the names of jurors on separate tickets or calling the jurors by groups of three. Under this article, the details are left to the discretion of the court so long as selection is by chance and the jurors are sworn to answer on their voir dire.

(c) Following Fed.Rule 48, a stipulation for a jury of less than twelve is allowed under this article.

Art. 1762. Swearing of juror before examination

Every prospective juror, before being examined, shall be sworn to answer truthfully such questions as may be propounded to him.

Source: C.P. Art. 509; R.S. 15:356, 15:357.

Comment

See Art. 1633, *supra*, which provides that an affirmation may be substituted for an oath.

Art. 1763. Examination of juror

The court shall permit the parties or their attorneys to conduct the examination of a prospective juror and may itself conduct an examination, which shall be limited to ascertaining the qualifications of the juror.

Source: Cf. Fed.Rule 47(a).

Comment

This article is based in part on Fed.Rule 47(a). Many states follow this practice which is recommended by the American Bar Association. Others allow examination by the court alone. Heretofore, eleven states, including Louisiana, permitted only the attorneys to examine the jurors. See Art. 509 of the 1870 Code of Practice. See Vanderbilt, Standards of Judicial Administration 197 (1949) for a full discussion of this matter. Cf. 1 La.L.Rev. 67, 70 (1938).

Art. 1764. Peremptory challenges

Each side is allowed six peremptory challenges. If there is more than one party on any side, the court may allow each side additional peremptory challenges, not to exceed four. Each side shall be allowed an equal number of peremptory challenges. If the parties on a side are unable to agree upon the allocation of peremptory challenges among themselves, the allocation shall be determined by the court before the examination on the voir dire.

Source: Ill. Civil Practice Act, c. 110, § 66; cf. C.P. Arts. 511, 512; former R.S. 13:3050.

Comments

(a) This article is based upon § 66 of the Ill.Civil Practice Act and Arts. 511 and 512 of the 1870 Code of Practice are not adopted. It covers all possible variations, including multiple parties. The interests of the parties technically on the same side may be common or adverse to each other. It has been held that joint tortfeasors must share a single set of peremptory challenges. Driefus v. Levy, 140 So. 259 (La.App.1932). However, where the interests of the joint tortfeasors are opposed, the above article permits a more just resolution of the question.

(b) The initial number of challenges allowed to each side is six. The Ill.Civil Practice Act allows five; the 1870 Code of Practice provides for four; while former R.S. 13:3050, which applies to country parishes only, allows six.

(c) Under this article, if the intervener takes the side of either party he is regarded as being an extra party on that side. If the intervener is opposed to both parties, then the suit has three sides, and the above article takes care of that situation also. This is also true as to third parties under the third party practice articles, Arts. 1111–1116, *supra*.

Art. 1765. Challenges for cause

A juror may be challenged for cause based upon any of the following:

(1) When the juror lacks a qualification required by law;

(2) When the juror has formed an opinion in the case or is not otherwise impartial, the cause of his bias being immaterial;

(3) When the relations whether by blood, marriage, employment, friendship, or enmity between the juror and any party or his attorney are such that it must be reasonably believed that they would influence the juror in coming to a verdict;

(4) When the juror served on a previous jury, which tried the same case or one arising out of the same facts;

(5) When the juror refuses to answer a question on the voir dire examination on the ground that his answer might tend to incriminate him.

Source: C.P. Arts. 503, 506, 507; R.S. 15:350, 15:351.

Comments

(a) This article consolidates the 1870 Code of Practice Arts. 503, 506, and 507, and the rule of R.S. 15:350 and 15:351.

(b) The language "or his attorney" in Art. 1765(3) extends the restriction to counsel.

(c) Art. 510 of the 1870 Code provides that the judge shall decide upon the validity of the challenge for cause. This requirement is not included in the above article for the reason that no one but the trial judge could pass upon the point.

Art. 1766. Time for peremptory challenge

After the entire jury has been accepted and sworn, no party has the right to challenge peremptorily.

Source: R.S. 15:358.

Comment

Articles 1766, 1767, are taken from the Code of Criminal Procedure. They complete the system of challenges by placing limitations upon the time within which challenges may be exercised.

Art. 1767. Challenging or excusing jurors after acceptance

Although the entire jury may have been accepted and sworn, up to the beginning of the taking of evidence, a juror may be challenged for cause by either side or be excused either for cause or by consent of both sides, and the panel completed in the ordinary course.

Source: R.S. 15:359, 15:360.

Comment

See Comment under Art. 1766, *supra*.

Tit. 5　　　　　　　　JURY TRIAL　　　　　　　Art. 1769

Art. 1768. Swearing of jurors; selection of foreman

When the jury has been accepted by all parties, the jurors shall be sworn to try the case in a just and impartial manner, to the best of their judgment, and to render a verdict according to the law and the evidence. When the jury has retired, the jurors shall select a foreman to preside over them and sign the verdict which they may render.

Source: R.S. 15:398; cf. C.P. Art. 514, R.S. 15:361.

Comments

(a) R.S. 15:398 provides that in criminal cases the foreman is selected by the jurors themselves. This provision was adopted in preference to the 1870 Code of Practice Art. 514 which provides that the court shall select the foreman in civil cases.

(b) Art. 514 of the 1870 Code provides that the foreman is to be chosen as soon as the jury is sworn, whereas under the criminal procedure the foreman, being chosen by the jury after retiring, is unknown until a verdict is announced. The above article adopts the latter procedure.

Art. 1769. Alternate jurors

The court may direct that one or two jurors in addition to the regular panel be called and empanelled to sit as alternate jurors. Alternate jurors, in the order in which they are called, shall replace jurors who, prior to the time the jury retires to consider its verdict, become unable or disqualified to perform their duties. Alternate jurors shall be drawn in the same manner, shall have the same qualifications, shall be subject to the same examination and challenges, shall take the same oath, and shall have the same functions, powers, facilities, and privileges as the principal jurors. An alternate juror who does not replace a principal juror shall be discharged when the jury retires to consider its verdict. If one or two alternate jurors are called, each side shall have an equal number of peremptory challenges. The court shall determine how many challenges shall be allowed and shall allocate them among the parties on each side. The additional peremptory challenges may be used only against an alternate juror, and the other peremptory challenges allowed by law shall not be used against the alternate jurors.

Source: Fed.Rule 47(b).

Comments

This article is based upon Fed.Rule 47(b), and follows the recommendation of the American Bar Association that there should be provision made for the power of the court to swear alternate jurors

Art. 1769   TRIAL   Bk. 2

for prospective long trials. See Vanderbilt, Standards of Judicial Administration 200 (1949).

The statutes provide for alternate jurors only in criminal cases. See R.S. 15:362. However, in civil cases the court has allowed a substitution for a sick juror, where neither party objected. Lindsey v. Tioga Lumber Co., 108 La. 468, 32 So. 464 (1902).

SECTION 4. PROCEDURE IN JURY TRIALS

Art. 1791. Time for charging the jury; recordation of charge

After the trial of the case and the presentation of all the evidence and arguments, the court shall charge the jury in accordance with law. This charge shall be in writing or recorded in the same manner as testimony taken in the case.

Source: C.P. Art. 515.

Comments

This article specifically provides that the charge of the court to the jury should be either in writing or recorded in the same manner as the testimony.

See, also, Comments under Art. 1793, *infra*.

Art. 1792. Contents of charge to jury

In his charge to the jury the judge shall instruct the jurors on the law applicable to the cause submitted to them, but he shall not recapitulate or comment upon the evidence so as to exercise any influence upon their decision as to the facts.

Source: C.P. Art. 516.

Comment

This article retains the rule of the source provision which prohibits the court's commenting upon the facts in his charge.

Art. 1793. Instruction to jury; objections

At the close of the evidence or at an earlier time during the trial as the court reasonably directs, a party may file written requests that the court instruct the jury on the law as set forth in the requests. The court shall inform counsel of its proposed action upon the requests prior to their arguments to the jury.

A party may not assign as error the giving or the failure to give an instruction unless he objects thereto before the jury retires to consider its verdict, stating specifically the matter to which he objects and the grounds of his objection. Opportunity shall be given to make the objection out of the hearing of the jury.

Source: Fed.Rule 51; cf. C.P. Art. 517.

Comment

This article is based upon Fed.Rule 51. The language to the effect that the court shall instruct the jury after completion of the argument is omitted; that provision is covered in Art. 1791, *supra*.

Art. 1794. Taking evidence to jury room

In reaching a verdict the jurors must rely upon their memories, and, when they retire from the jury room to deliberate, they shall not be allowed access to any written evidence or to any notes of the testimony of any witness, but they may take with them any object or document received in evidence which requires a physical examination to enable them to arrive at a just conclusion.

Source: Cf. R.S. 15:395.

Comments

(a) The 1870 Code of Practice is silent with respect to the rules stated in this article which is based upon the criminal procedure source provision. It is also in accord with the English rule that depositions cannot be taken into the jury room on the theory that undue weight might be given them as against oral testimony. Cf. Wakeman v. Marquand, 5 Mart. (N.S.) 265 (La.1826) in which the court refused to set aside a verdict where the jury had taken depositions into the jury room holding that since all of the testimony was in writing as was then required by law, there was no reasonable basis for the application of the English rule.

(b) This article makes it clear that depositions may not be taken into the jury room under any circumstances, particularly since not all of the testimony is now required to be in writing.

Art. 1795. Number required for verdict; stipulation

In order to render any verdict, nine of the jurors must concur therein. The parties may stipulate, however, that the concurrence of a stated majority of the jurors shall be sufficient for a verdict, and must do so when they have stipulated for a trial by a lesser number in accordance with Article 1761.

Source: Former R.S. 13:3050; Fed.Rule 48.

Comments

The reference in the text to Art. 1761, *supra,* is necessary in view of the fact that under the latter article the parties may stipulate for a lesser number of jurors to try the case.

Under the 1870 Code of Practice Art. 527 and former R.S. 13:-3050, the concurrence of nine jurors is required to render a verdict. Under the Federal Rules of Civil Procedure, unanimity is required unless the parties stipulate to the contrary. See 5 Moore's Federal Practice (2d ed.) 2151 (1950). Under the above article, the concurrence of nine jurors is required, subject to the qualification that the parties may stipulate for a stated majority.

SECTION 5. VERDICTS

Art. 1811. Special verdicts

The court may require a jury to return only a special verdict in the form of a special written finding upon each issue of fact. In that event the court may submit to the jury written questions susceptible of categorical or other brief answer, or may submit written forms of the several special findings which might properly be made under the pleadings and evidence, or may use any other appropriate method of submitting the issues and requiring the written findings thereon. The court shall give to the jury such explanation and instruction concerning the matter submitted as may be necessary to enable the jury to make its findings upon each issue. If the court omits any issue of fact raised by the pleadings or by the evidence, each party waives his right to a trial by jury of the issue omitted unless, before the jury retires, he demands its submission to the jury. As to an issue omitted without such demand the court may make a finding; or, if it fails to do so, it shall be presumed to have made a finding in accord with the judgment on the special verdict.

Source: Fed.Rule 49(a); cf. C.P. Art. 521.

Cross Reference: Art. 1916.

Comments

(a) Articles 1811 and 1812 are taken from Fed.Rule 49 and follow the recommendation of the American Bar Association to the effect that the court should be permitted at its discretion to submit specific issues to the jury to be considered in connection with a general verdict. See Vanderbilt, Minimum Standards of Judicial Administration 237 (1949). The submission of specific issues to the jury is entirely within the discretion of the court. See 3 La.L.

Rev. 422 (1941) for a comparison between the federal and Louisiana practice, where the authors note that among other things the difference between federal and Louisiana law with regard to the right to determine the type of verdict a jury may render. See also, Fed.Rules 38(c) and 39(a).

(b) See Art. 1916, *infra*.

Art. 1812. General verdict accompanied by answer to interrogatories

The court may submit to the jury, together with appropriate forms for a general verdict, written interrogatories upon one or more issues of fact the decision of which is necessary to a verdict. The court shall give such explanation or instruction as may be necessary to enable the jury both to make answers to the interrogatories and to render a general verdict, and the court shall direct the jury both to make written answers and to render a general verdict.

When the general verdict and the answers are harmonious, the court shall direct the entry of the appropriate judgment upon the verdict and answers.

When the answers are consistent with each other but one or more is inconsistent with the general verdict, the court may direct the entry of judgment in accordance with the answers, notwithstanding the general verdict, or may return the jury for further consideration of its answers and verdict, or may order a new trial.

When the answers are inconsistent with each other and one or more is likewise inconsistent with the general verdict, the court shall not direct the entry of judgment but may return the jury for further consideration of its answers or may order a new trial.

Source: Fed.Rule 49(b); cf. C.P. Art. 521.

Cross Reference: Art. 1916.

Comment

See Comments under Art. 1811, *supra*.

Art. 1813. Remittitur or additur as alternative to new trial; reformation of verdict

If the trial court is of the opinion that the verdict is so excessive or inadequate that a new trial should be granted for that reason only, it may indicate to the party or his attorney within what time he may enter a remittitur or additur. This remittitur or additur is to be entered only with the consent of the plaintiff or the defendant as the case may be, as an alternative to a new trial, and is to be entered only if the

Art. 1813

amount of the excess or inadequacy of the verdict or judgment can be separately and fairly ascertained. If a remittitur or additur is entered, then the court shall reform the jury verdict or judgment in accordance therewith.

Source: New.

Comments

Neither the 1870 Code of Practice nor the Federal Rules of Civil Procedure contains specific provisions on remittitur, although the concept is recognized by both federal and Louisiana courts. See Dimick v. Schiedt, 293 U.S. 474, 55 S.Ct. 296 (1935); Landry v. New Orleans Shipwright Co., 112 La. 515, 36 So. 548 (1904); *Cf.* Vanderbilt, Minimum Standards of Judicial Administration 244 (1949).

The Vanderbilt treatise, *supra*, also deals with the problem of remittitur, in connection with the grossly inadequate verdict.

See, also, Comments under Art. 1971, *infra*.

Art. 1814. New trial on showing of misconduct by jury

A new trial shall be granted if it be proved that the jury was bribed or has behaved improperly so that impartial justice has not been done.

Source: C.P. Art. 560(3).
Cross Reference: Art. 1972.

Comments

(a) Art. 1972, *infra*, provides that a jury trial shall be granted, inter alia, "In jury cases as provided in Article 1814."

Art. 1972, *infra*, is based upon the 1870 Code of Practice Art. 560, which lists the peremptory grounds for new trial. Art. 1972 (3), *infra*, reads substantially as the above article. See Comments to Arts. 1971 through 1973, *infra*.

(b) For the requirements of the application for a new trial based on these grounds, see Art. 1975, *infra*.

Tit. 6 JUDGMENTS

TITLE VI

JUDGMENTS

Chap.		Art.
1.	General Dispositions	1841
2.	Declaratory Judgments	1871
3.	Rendition	1911
4.	Modification in Trial Court	1951
	Sec.	
	1. Amendment	1951
	2. New Trial	1971
	3. Action of Nullity	2001
5.	Revival	2031

INTRODUCTION

This Title introduces no radical changes in the law of Louisiana, although some have been made to simplify the procedure and attain greater uniformity.

Among the changes introduced is Art. 1971, *infra,* providing for partial new trials, following the recommendation of the American Bar Association. See Vanderbilt, Minimum Standards of Judicial Administration 243 (1949); Fed.Rule 59.

Apart from an article defining the judgment by default, this Title contains nothing regarding the procedure for obtaining such judgments and their confirmation. That procedure is set forth in Book II, Title V, of this Code.

The following subjects, although relating to judgments, are not treated in this Title, but have been relegated to other portions of this Code:

(1) The subject of judgments on the pleadings is covered by Arts. 965 and 968, *supra*.

(2) The provisions dealing with confession of judgment, in so far as it relates to executory process, are dealt with in Book V, Title II. The effect of confession of judgment on appeal is treated in Book III. *Cf.* Art. 2085, Comment (b).

(3) Judgment procedure in district courts in cases involving jurisdiction concurrent with justice of the peace courts is dealt with in Book VIII, Trial Courts of Limited Jurisdiction.

(4) The procedure regulating judgments by default is treated in Book II, Title V.

(5) The procedure for the rendition of judgments in cases tried before a jury is set forth in Book II, Title V.

The procedure for rescission of judgments has not been carried forward into this Code. In addition, former R.S. 13:4262 through 13:4264, providing for rehearings in the district courts, have been repealed. *Cf.* Comment (f), Arts. 1971 through 1973, *infra*.

CHAPTER 1. GENERAL DISPOSITIONS

Art.
1841. Judgments, interlocutory and final.
1842. Definitive judgment.
1843. Judgment by default.
1844. Judgment of dismissal; effect.

Art. 1841. Judgments, interlocutory and final

A judgment is the determination of the rights of the parties in an action and may award any relief to which the parties are entitled. It may be interlocutory or final.

A judgment that does not determine the merits but only preliminary matters in the course of the action is an interlocutory judgment.

A judgment that determines the merits in whole or in part is a final judgment.

Source: C.P. Arts. 537, 538; N.Y.Civil Practice Act § 472; cf. C.P. Art. 539.

Comments

(a) The first paragraph of the article is based upon Sec. 472 of the New York Civil Practice Act, with the addition, however, of the language "and may award any relief to which the parties are entitled" for the purpose of emphasizing the idea that a judgment includes the award of relief. The permissive "may" rather than the mandatory "shall" was used, since the article is applicable to declaratory judgments.

(b) The second paragraph of the article is a rephrasing of Art. 538 of the 1870 Code; while the third paragraph reflects the jurisprudential modification of Art. 539, which provides that final judgments are those which decide *all* points in controversy. See Cary v. Richardson, 35 La.Ann. 505 (1883).

(c) No attempt has been made to amplify the 1870 Code definitions of "final" and "interlocutory" judgments. The jurisprudence has fairly well delineated the areas covered by these terms. See Bossier's Heirs v. Hollingsworth and Jackson, 117 La. 221, 41 So. 553 (1906); Verrett v. Savoie, 174 La. 844, 141 So. 854 (1932); Metairie Bank in Liquidation v. Lecler, 4 So.2d 573 (La.App.1941). *Cf.* Comment (a) to Art. 2083, *infra*.

(d) Decrees of alimony, custody, costs, and like decrees are, of course, embraced within the general concept of the interlocutory judgment.

(e) See, also, Comments under Art. 1673, *supra*.

Art. 1842. Definitive judgment

A final judgment is definitive when it has acquired the authority of the thing adjudged.

Source: C.P. Art. 539.

Comments

The last paragraph of the source provision states that definitive judgments have the force of res judicata. However, no attempt has been made to define the term "res judicata," since the Civil Code definition is sufficient. See Civil Code Arts. 2286 and 3556(31). The term "thing adjudged" is employed in the above article to conform with the Civil Code terminology.

See, also, Comments under Art. 1673, *supra*.

Art. 1843. Judgment by default

A judgment by default is that which is rendered against a defendant who fails to plead within the time prescribed by law.

Source: Cf. C.P. Art. 534.
Cross Reference: Art. 1701.

Comments

(a) This article is a recognition of the general concept of default. The details and mechanics of taking defaults are set forth in Arts. 1701 through 1703, *supra*.

(b) Art. 534 of the 1870 Code of Practice defines a default judgment as one which also includes a default judgment against the plaintiff. However, this latter is more properly referred to as a dismissal. See Art. 1672, *supra*.

(c) See, also, Comments under Art. 1701, *supra*.

Art. 1844. Judgment of dismissal; effect

A judgment of dismissal with or without prejudice shall be rendered and the effects thereof shall be regulated in accordance with the provisions of Articles 1671 through 1673.

Source: New; cf. C.P. Art. 536.

Comments

This article recognizes the power of the court to enter judgments of dismissal, leaving the mechanics and details of procedure, and the effect of such judgments, to Arts. 1671 through 1673, *supra*.

See, also, Comments under Art. 1843, *supra*.

CHAPTER 2. DECLARATORY JUDGMENTS

Art.
1871. Declaratory judgments; scope.
1872. Interested parties may obtain declaration of rights, status, or other legal relations.
1873. Construction of contract.
1874. Interested person may obtain declaration of rights; purpose.
1875. Powers enumerated not exclusive.
1876. Court may refuse declaratory judgment.
1877. Review of judgments and decrees.
1878. Supplemental relief.
1879. Trial and determination of issue of fact.
1880. Parties.
1881. Construction.
1882. Provisions independent and severable.
1883. Uniformity of interpretation.

Art. 1871. Declaratory judgments; scope

Courts of record within their respective jurisdictions may declare rights, status, and other legal relations whether or not further relief is or could be claimed. No action or proceeding shall be open to objection on the ground that a declaratory judgment or decree is prayed for; and the existence of another adequate remedy does not preclude a judgment for declaratory relief in cases where it is appropriate. The declaration shall have the force and effect of a final judgment or decree.

Source: Former R.S. 13:4231; Fed.Rule 57.
Cross References: Arts. 1875, 1877, 1879, 1881, 1883, 3654.

Comments

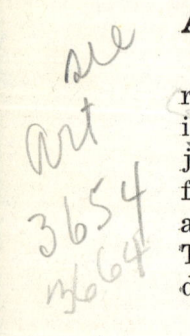

An important change in the procedural law is effected by the addition, to the language of former R.S. 13:4231, of the second clause of the second sentence above, borrowed from Fed.Rule 57. In Burton v. Lester, 227 La. 347, 79 So.2d 333 (1955), the supreme court held that the Declaratory Judgments Act could not be invoked where any other remedy is available to the plaintiff. While the result reached in this case is completely sound, and is the one which would be reached by every American jurisdiction which has adopted the Declaratory Judgments Act, the general rule announced by the court in the Burton case is most unfortunate, as it defeats one of the primary purposes of the adoption of the statute.

The conventional type of judgment embodies two elements: (1) an ascertainment or declaration of the rights of the parties (usually implied); and (2) a specific award of relief. The declaratory judgment embodies only the first element which, of course, is always express. There is actually no such thing as a declaratory action, even if the sole relief prayed for is a declaratory judgment. The action is identical, regardless of whether greater or lesser relief is prayed for; the difference is only as to the type of judgment to be rendered.

Further, even in the short time which has elapsed since the rule was announced, its unworkability in actual practice has been demonstrated. See 17 La.L.Rev. 382 (1957).

The specific purpose of the additional language in this article is to work a legislative overruling of Burton v. Lester, *supra*.

See, also, Comments under Art. 1872, *infra*.

Art. 1872. Interested parties may obtain declaration of rights, status, or other legal relations

A person interested under a deed, will, written contract or other writing constituting a contract, or whose rights, status, or other legal relations are affected by a statute, municipal ordinance, contract or franchise, may have determined any question of construction or validity arising under the instrument, statute, ordinance, contract, or franchise and obtain a declaration of rights, status, or other legal relations thereunder.

Source: Former R.S. 13:4232.

Cross References: Arts. 1875, 1877, 1879, 1881, 1883.

Comments to Articles 1872 through 1883

Except as pointed out in the Comments under Art. 1871, *supra*, Arts. 1871 through 1883 are virtually verbatim reproductions of the Uniform Declaratory Judgments Act, former R.S. 13:4231 through 13:4245, with the following omissions:

(1) Former R.S. 13:4240, empowering the court to make such an award of costs as may seem equitable and just was omitted as it would have been an unnecessary duplication of the provisions of Arts. 1920 and 2164, *infra*;

(2) Former R.S. 13:4243, defining "person" was omitted because it would have been an unnecessary duplication of the definition set forth in Art. 5251, *infra;* and

(3) Former R.S. 13:4245, providing that former R.S. 13:4231 through 13:4245 might be cited as the Uniform Declaratory Judgments Act, was omitted.

Art. 1873. Construction of contract

A contract may be construed either before or after there has been a breach thereof.

Source: Former R.S. 13:4233.

Cross References: Arts. 1875, 1877, 1879, 1881, 1882, 1883.

Comment

See Comments under Art. 1872, *supra.*

Art. 1874. Interested person may obtain declaration of rights; purpose

A person interested as or through an executor, administrator, trustee, guardian, or other fiduciary, creditor, devisee, legatee, heir, next of kin, or cestui que trust, in the administration of a trust, or of the estate of a decedent, an infant, lunatic, or insolvent, may have a declaration of rights or legal relations in respect thereto:

(1) To ascertain any class of creditors, devisees, legatees, heirs, next of kin or others;

(2) To direct the executors, administrators, or trustees to do or abstain from doing any particular act in their fiduciary capacity; or

(3) To determine any question arising in the administration of the estate or trust, including questions of construction of wills and other writings.

Source: Former R.S. 13:4234.

Cross References: Arts. 1875, 1877, 1879, 1881, 1882, 1883.

Comment

See Comments under Art. 1872, *supra.*

Art. 1875. Powers enumerated not exclusive

The enumeration in Articles 1872 through 1874 does not limit or restrict the exercise of the general powers conferred in Article 1871 in any proceeding where declaratory relief is sought, in which a judgment or decree will terminate the controversy or remove an uncertainty.

Source: Former R.S. 13:4235.

Cross References: Arts. 1877, 1879, 1881, 1882, 1883.

Comment

See Comments under Art. 1872, *supra*.

Art. 1876. Court may refuse declaratory judgment

The court may refuse to render a declaratory judgment or decree where such judgment or decree, if rendered, would not terminate the uncertainty or controversy giving rise to the proceeding.

Source: Former R.S. 13:4236.

Cross References: Arts. 1877, 1879, 1881, 1882, 1883.

Comment

See Comments under Art. 1872, *supra*.

Art. 1877. Review of judgments and decrees

All orders, judgments, and decrees under Articles 1871 through 1883 may be reviewed as other orders, judgments, and decrees.

Source: Former R.S. 13:4237.

Cross References: Arts. 1879, 1881, 1882, 1883.

Comment

See Comments under Art. 1872, *supra*.

Art. 1878. Supplemental relief

Further relief based on a declaratory judgment or decree may be granted whenever necessary or proper. The application therefor shall be by petition to a court having jurisdiction to grant the relief. If the application is considered sufficient, the court, on reasonable notice, shall require any adverse party whose rights have been adjudicated by the declaratory judgment or decree, to show cause why further relief should not be granted forthwith.

Source: Former R.S. 13:4238.

Cross References: Arts. 1877, 1879, 1881, 1882, 1883.

Comment

See Comments under Art. 1872, *supra*.

Art. 1879. Trial and determination of issue of fact

When a proceeding under Articles 1871 through 1883 involves the determination of an issue of fact, such issue may be tried and determined in the same manner as issues of fact are tried and determined in other civil actions in the court in which the proceeding is pending.

Source: Former R.S. 13:4239.

Cross References: Arts. 1877, 1881, 1882, 1883.

Comment

See Comments under Art. 1872, *supra*.

Art. 1880. Parties

When declaratory relief is sought, all persons shall be made parties who have or claim any interest which would be affected by the declaration, and no declaration shall prejudice the rights of persons not parties to the proceeding. In a proceeding which involves the validity of a municipal ordinance or franchise, such municipality shall be made a party, and shall be entitled to be heard. If the statute, ordinance, or franchise is alleged to be unconstitutional, the attorney general of the state shall also be served with a copy of the proceeding and be entitled to be heard.

Source: Former R.S. 13:4241.

Cross References: Arts. 1877, 1879, 1881, 1882, 1883.

Comment

See Comments under Art. 1872, *supra*.

Art. 1881. Construction

Articles 1871 through 1883 are declared to be remedial. Their purpose is to settle and afford relief from uncertainty and insecurity with respect to rights, status, and other legal relations, and they are to be liberally construed and administered.

Source: Former R.S. 13:4242.

Cross References: Arts. 1877, 1879, 1882, 1883.

Comment

See Comments under Art. 1872, *supra*.

Tit. 6 RENDITION

Art. 1882. Provisions independent and severable

Articles 1873 through 1883 are declared independent and severable, and the invalidity, if any, of any part or feature thereof shall not affect or render the remainder of the articles invalid or inoperative.

Source: Former R.S. 13:4244.

Cross References: Arts. 1877, 1879, 1881, 1883.

Comment

See Comments under Art. 1872, *supra*.

Art. 1883. Uniformity of interpretation

Articles 1871 through 1882 shall be interpreted and construed so as to effectuate their general purpose to make uniform the law of those states which enact them, and to harmonize, as far as possible, with federal laws and regulations on the subject of declaratory judgments and decrees.

Source: Former R.S. 13:4245.

Cross References: Arts. 1877, 1879, 1881, 1882.

Comment

See Comments under Art. 1872, *supra*.

CHAPTER 3. RENDITION

Art.
1911. Final judgments read and signed in open court.
1912. Final judgment read and signed in any parish in district.
1913. Notice of judgment.
1914. Interlocutory order or judgment when case under advisement; notice; delay for further action when notice required.
1915. Partial judgment.
1916. Jury cases; signature of judgment by the court.
1917. Written findings of fact and reasons for judgment.
1918. Form of final judgment.
1919. Judgment affecting immovable property; particular description.
1920. Costs; parties liable; procedure for taxing.
1921. Interest allowed by the judgment.

PRELIMINARY STATEMENT

One of the problems dealt with in this Chapter is the elimination of the confusion in Louisiana law regarding the rendition and signing of judgments and the time they become legally effective. This problem has been created by the uncertainty as to what actually constitutes the rendition of the judgment. It is obvious from the language of Arts. 491, 543, and 547 of the Code of Practice of 1870 that a distinction between rendition and signature was intended by giving the party cast an interval after the rendition of the judgment within which to apply for relief. On the other hand, although Art. 3547 of the Civil Code provides that money judgments shall prescribe in ten years from "rendition," the jurisprudence is to the effect that a judgment must be "signed" in order to be "rendered" for the purposes of prescription. Historically, the argument that a judgment is not rendered until it is signed antedates the introduction of Art. 3547 into the Civil Code of Louisiana. Brand v. Livaudais, 3 Mart. (O.S.) 389 (La.1814); cf. Sprigg v. Wells, 5 Mart. (N.S.) 104 (La.1826). Notwithstanding cases to the contrary, however, the majority of the Louisiana decisions are to the effect that a judgment of a trial court is not rendered until it is signed. See Viator v. Heinz, 201 La. 884, 10 So.2d 690 (1942) where the authorities are collected. For a full discussion of the problem see Comment, 24 Tul.L.Rev. 470 (1950).

Therefore, the question of fixing the date for the "effectiveness" of the judgment is of primary importance in order to determine, for example:

(1) The time for taking an appeal. See Art. 2087, *infra*, providing that an appeal can be taken only within ninety days, and Art. 3612, *infra*, regulating appeals in injunction cases;

(2) The time when a judgment operates as a property right and is entitled to recordation as a judicial mortgage;

(3) The time when a judgment may be legally executed. See Art. 2252, *infra*, providing that a judgment becomes executory after the delays for obtaining a suspensive appeal have elapsed; and

(4) The prescription of ten years under Art. 3547 of the Civil Code.

Art. 1911. Final judgments read and signed in open court

Except as otherwise provided by law, all final judgments shall be read and signed by the judge in open court.

Source: New; cf. C.P. Art. 543.

Comments

(a) While the rule of this article is substantially the same as the former rule on the subject, the articles in this Chapter make a radical change in the rules respecting the time when judgments may and shall be signed.

Under the articles in this Chapter, judgments are to be signed at the time of rendition or at any time thereafter. No time limit for the signing is imposed in any of these articles, but it is contemplated that all judgments will be signed within a reasonable time after rendition, which in turn depends upon the circumstances.

Heretofore, dichotomous rules on the subject obtained. In Orleans Parish the judgment could not be signed until three judicial days after rendition. Art. 546, Code of Practice of 1870. In the remainder of the state, the judgment was required to be signed within three calendar days of rendition. Former R.S. 13:4212. The delays for applying for a new trial or an appeal, as well as the time when the judgment might be executed, were all tied in with these dual rules as to the time the judgment was to be signed, and the problems presented forced the courts to formulate the "effective date of the judgment" concept. See 9 La.L.Rev. 509 (1949); 24 Tul.L.Rev. 470 (1950). Under this Code, the numerous and technical rules on this subject have been suppressed. See Arts. 1974 and 2087, *infra*.

(b) The exception at the beginning of this article avoids conflict with Arts. 194 and 196, *supra*, and with R.S. 13:4208, which authorize the signing of certain judgments in chambers and during vacation.

(c) Default judgments in cases involving $100 or less may be rendered and signed by the clerk of the district court. Art. 4972, *infra*.

(d) By stipulation, or other consent of all parties, the judgment may be signed in a manner different from that prescribed in this article.

(e) See, also, Comments under Arts. 1918, 1974, *infra*.

Art. 1912. Final judgment read and signed in any parish in district

Any final judgment may be read and signed in open court in any parish within the judicial district and shall be sent to the clerk of the parish in which the case was tried so that he may make minute entries of the signing of the judgment and mail notices thereof.

Source: New; cf. C.P. Art. 543.

Comments

(a) This article makes no change in the law.

(b) See Art. 1913, *infra*, requiring notices of judgment.

(c) See, also, Comments under Art. 1918, *infra*.

Art. 1913. Notice of judgment

Notice of the signing of a default judgment against a defendant on whom citation was not served personally, and who filed no exceptions or answer, shall be served on the defendant by the sheriff.

Art. 1913

Notice of the signing of all other final judgments shall be mailed by the clerk of court of the parish where the case was tried to the counsel of record for each party, and to each party not represented by counsel.

Source: C.P. Arts. 575, 624; cf. former R.S. 13:3344.

Cross Reference: Art. 1974.

Comments

(a) The first paragraph makes no change in the law.

(b) The second paragraph changes the law. Under the indirect source provision, notices of the rendition of the judgment were required to be issued by the clerk, and mailed to all counsel, only in cases which had been taken under advisement. This article requires the mailing of notices of the rendition of judgment by the clerk in all cases except those mentioned in the first paragraph, where service of notice of judgment on the defendant must be made by the sheriff.

(c) By stipulation, or other consent of all parties, the mailing of notice of the rendition of judgment may be waived. In such cases the delay for applying for a new trial commences to run the day after the judgment is signed.

(d) See, also, Comments under Arts. 1231, 1912, *supra*.

Art. 1914. Interlocutory order or judgment when case under advisement; notice; delay for further action when notice required

When a case has been taken under advisement by the court for the purpose of deciding whether an interlocutory order or judgment should be rendered, the clerk shall make an entry in the minutes of the court of any such interlocutory order or judgment rendered thereafter.

If a written request for notice of the rendition of the interlocutory order or judgment in such a case has been filed, the clerk shall mail notice thereof to the party requesting it; and the latter shall have ten days from the date of the mailing of the notice to take any action or file any pleadings he deems necessary, except as provided in the next paragraph.

If the interlocutory order or judgment is one refusing to grant a new trial, the delay for appealing commences to run only from the date of the mailing of such notice, as provided in Articles 2087 and 2123.

The provisions of this article do not apply to an interlocutory injunctive order or judgment.

Source: New; cf. former R.S. 13:3344.

Cross References: Arts. 2087, 2123.

Comments

(a) This article is restricted to cases taken under advisement so that the judge may decide whether to render an interlocutory order or judgment. The preceding article covers notice of the rendition of a final judgment.

(b) The indirect source of this article requires mailing of notice of the rendition of an interlocutory order or judgment in all cases taken under advisement. This article is narrower, and requires mailing of notice in such cases only when a party has requested it. However, it requires a minute entry of the rendition of such an order or judgment, which affords counsel a ready opportunity of checking on the matter.

(c) This article does not require any particular form for the written notice mentioned in the second paragraph. The most effective forms would be those prescribed by Art. 1572, *supra*.

(d) The unfortunate proviso in the indirect source, to the effect that the delays for applying for a new trial or appeal were not affected, left a real problem in its wake with respect to a case where an application for a new trial was taken under advisement, refused, and the clerk failed to notify the applicant of such refusal. The third paragraph of this article solves the former problem.

Art. 1915. Partial judgment

A final judgment may be rendered and signed by the court, even though it may not grant the successful party all of the relief prayed for, or may not adjudicate all of the issues in the case, when the court:

(1) Dismisses the suit as to less than all of the plaintiffs, defendants, third party plaintiffs, third party defendants, or interveners;

(2) Grants a motion for judgment on the pleadings, as provided by Articles 965, 968, and 969;

(3) Grants a motion for summary judgment, as provided by Articles 966 through 969; or

(4) Renders judgment on either the principal or incidental demand, when the two have been tried separately, as provided by Article 1038.

If an appeal is taken from such a judgment, the trial court nevertheless shall retain jurisdiction to adjudicate the remaining issues in the case.

Source: New.

Art. 1915

Comments

(a) Art. 1038, *supra,* referred to in the text above, provides that the court may order separate trials on the principal and incidental demands, in which case separate judgments may be rendered. The pleading article also authorizes the judge to withhold signing of the judgment first rendered, until the signing of the judgment on the demand tried last.

(b) Louisiana does not have a specific code provision for partial judgments, and a study of the Louisiana jurisprudence would indicate there is no precise rule concerning them. *Cf.* Regillo v. Lorente, 7 La. 140 (1834); State ex rel. Ikerd v. Judge of 8th District, 35 La.Ann. 212 (1883); State ex rel. Hearsey v. Talbot, 36 La.Ann. 981 (1884); Vicksburg S. & P. Ry. Co. v. Scott, 47 La.Ann. 706, 17 So. 249 (1895); Bossier's Heirs v. Hollingsworth, 117 La. 221, 41 So. 553 (1906); Swift & Co. v. Leon Cahn & Co., 151 La. 837, 92 So. 355 (1922); Williams v. DeSoto Bank and Trust Co., 185 La. 888, 171 So. 66 (1936); State ex rel. Knighton v. Derryberry, 188 La. 412, 177 So. 256 (1937); Motor Finance Co. v. Lynn, 142 So. 310 (La.App.1932); Robinson Mercantile Co. v. Freeman, 172 So. 797 (La.App.1937); Coreil v. Vidrine, 171 So. 199 (La.App.1937). But see State ex rel. Pflug v. Judge, 35 La.Ann. 765 (1883); Feitel v. Feitel, 169 La. 384, 125 So. 280 (1929).

The rule that there should be one final judgment is designed to prevent multiplicity of appeals and piecemeal litigation. In cases where the rules of joinder are liberal, however, injustice could result to parties who had clearly distinct claims and who were put to the trouble of awaiting the sometimes lengthy determination of the entire suit. Statutory exceptions have, therefore, been enacted. *Cf.* Fed.Rule 54(b).

Art. 1916. Jury cases; signature of judgment by the court

When a case has been tried by a jury, the following rules shall apply as to a judgment rendered on the verdict:

(1) When the jury returns a general verdict, the judge shall sign a judgment in accordance therewith within three days exclusive of holidays from the date of the verdict;

(2) When the jury returns a special verdict, the judge must sign a judgment in accordance therewith, but he shall have the same time for deliberating before signing the judgment as in cases tried without a jury.

In all other respects the provisions of this Chapter shall apply to a judgment rendered on a jury verdict.

Source: C.P. Arts. 520, 521, 541, 542.

Comments

(a) The source articles deal with two problems: (1) the type of judgment which may be rendered depending upon whether the jury returns a general or a special verdict; and (2) the time limitation upon the rendition of such judgments. The above article consolidates these ideas.

(b) Arts. 1811 and 1812, *supra*, retain the 1870 Code of Practice concepts concerning general and special verdicts.

(c) See, also, Comments under Arts. 1231, 1811, 1812, *supra*.

Art. 1917. Written findings of fact and reasons for judgment

In all appealable contested cases, other than those tried by a jury, the court when requested to do so by a party shall give in writing its findings of fact and reasons for judgment.

Source: Const. Art. VII, § 43.

Art. 1918. Form of final judgment

A final judgment shall be identified as such by appropriate language. When written reasons for the judgment are assigned, they shall be set out in an opinion separate from the judgment.

Source: New.

Comments

(a) In Louisiana the form and wording of judgments is not sacramental. See Louisiana Formulary Annotated 340, n. 2 (1951). Nonetheless, Louisiana courts require that a judgment be precise, definite and certain. See Russo v. Fidelity and Deposit Co., 129 La. 554, 56 So. 506 (1911); Falterman v. Prestenbach, 6 La.App. 563 (1927); Simon v. Hulse, 12 La.App. 450, 124 So. 845 (1929). However, it has been held that a judgment is not invalid on account of the insertions of an incorrect middle initial or the omission thereof, Jaubert Bros. Inc. v. Landry, 15 So.2d 158 (La.App.1943); or on account of failure to name specifically all defendants against whom it is rendered, Glen Falls Indemnity Co. v. Manning, 168 So. 787 (La.App.1936).

(b) The requirement of separate judgments and reasons for judgments in the second sentence will avoid the problem presented in Anderson v. Nugent, 16 So.2d 282 (La.App.1944).

(c) Arts. 1911, 1912, and 1916, *supra*, require that the judgment be signed by the trial judge, with certain exceptions.

Art. 1919. Judgment affecting immovable property; particular description

All final judgments which affect title to immovable property shall describe the immovable property affected with particularity.

This article does not apply to judgments in succession proceedings recognizing heirs or legatees and sending them into possession.

Source: Former R.S. 13:4202.

Comments

See Comment (e), Art. 1951, *infra*, with reference to amendment of judgments describing immovables.

See, also, Comments under Arts. 1951, 2089, 3061, *infra*.

Art. 1920. Costs; parties liable; procedure for taxing

Unless the judgment provides otherwise, costs shall be paid by the party cast, and may be taxed by a rule to show cause.

Except as otherwise provided by law, the court may render judgment for costs, or any part thereof, against any party, as it may consider equitable.

Source: C.P. Art. 550; Fed.Rule 54(d); cf. C.P. Arts. 549, 551.

Cross Reference: Art. 5188.

Comments

(a) At common law, neither party was entitled to costs and the right to recover these rested on statutes. Martin, Civil Procedure 320 (1899). By statute, most jurisdictions place liability for costs on the loser save in exceptional cases. Fla.Stats.Anno. (1943), § 58.04; Idaho Stats., § 12–102 (now embodied in court rules); Wis.Stats. (1953), § 271.01. The same rule obtains in many civilian codes. See French Code of Civil Procedure Art. 130; Italian Code of Civil Procedure Art. 91; Quebec Code of Civil Procedure Art. 549.

The Federal Rules of Civil Procedure place the matter within the discretion of the court. This rule has obvious advantages over the arbitrary rule in the trial courts of Louisiana, where costs are always imposed by the trial courts upon the party cast in accordance with Arts. 549, 551, and 552 of the 1870 Code of Practice. Flory & McMahon, The New Federal Rules, 1 La.L.Rev. 45 (1938).

(b) In Louisiana, it has been held that when there is a reconventional demand and both parties are cast, each must pay the costs occasioned by the demand of the other; and if the testimony has borne on both demands, the costs thereof will be divided. Hunter Canal Co. v. Robertson's Heirs, 113 La. 833, 37 So. 771 (1904). Also, when there are two distinct claims and demands, there is only one suit, and the rule is that if a plaintiff wins any part of his suit he is entitled to costs. Hart v. Polizzotto, 168 La. 356, 122 So. 64 (1929). When plaintiff asks for a judgment against defendants in solido, and the court condemns one defendant and the other is condemned on the call in warranty, the defendant condemned is liable for all costs, even though plaintiff does not receive a judgment entirely in accordance with his prayer. Derouen v. LeBleu, 18 So.2d 207 (La.App.1944).

(c) Since the above article makes the imposition of costs discretionary with the court, the provision of Art. 549, Code of Practice of 1870, excepting from the general rule cases where compensation has been allowed or real tender made, is unnecessary. Similarly, Art. 551 of the 1870 Code, to the effect that the costs are nonetheless due even though not mentioned in the judgment, is also unnecessary in view of the mandatory language of the above article.

(d) This article is intended to apply to both principal and incidental demands and Art. 550, Code of Practice of 1870, which specifically extends the provisions of the preceding article of the 1870 Code to the incidental demand, is unnecessary.

(e) The second part of Fed.Rule 54(d) sets a limitation on costs imposed against the United States. Louisiana also exempts the state from costs under R.S. 13:4521, which remains operative in the Revised Statutes.

(f) See, also, Comments under Art. 2825, *infra*.

Art. 1921. Interest allowed by the judgment

The court shall award interest in the judgment as prayed for or as provided by law.

Source: Cf. C.P. Art. 553.

Comments

(a) This article retains the requirement of Art. 553, Code of Practice of 1870, to the effect that interest may be awarded by the judgment only if prayed for.

The phrase "as provided by law" will cover the exception in the case of tort claims, since in these cases interest attaches automatically, without being prayed for. Grennon v. N. O. Public Service, 17 La.App. 700, 136 So. 309 (1931); Poulan v. Gallagher, 148 So. 511 (La.App.1933).

(b) Art. 554, Code of Practice of 1870, establishing the legal rate of interest, is unnecessary. This is a question of substantive law which is adequately covered by Arts. 1936 through 1944 of the Civil Code.

(c) The problem of when the running of interest begins is integrally bound up with substantive law, and for this reason should not be included in this project. The phrase "as provided by law" refers to the articles of the Civil Code and to R.S. 13:4203 and the considerable jurisprudence under these provisions.

CHAPTER 4. MODIFICATION IN TRIAL COURT

SECTION 1. AMENDMENT

Art.
1951. Amendment of judgment.

SECTION 2. NEW TRIAL

1971. Granting of new trial.
1972. Peremptory grounds.
1973. Discretionary grounds.
1974. Delay for applying for new trial.
1975. Application for new trial; verifying affidavit.
1976. Service of notice.
1977. Assignment of new trial.
1978. Method of procedure.
1979. Summary decision on motion; maximum delays.

SECTION 3. ACTION OF NULLITY

2001. Grounds in general.
2002. Annulment for vices of form; time for action.
2003. Same; action lost through acquiescence.
2004. Annulment for vices of substance; peremption of action.
2005. Annulment of judgments; effect of appeal.
2006. Court where action brought.

SECTION 1. AMENDMENT

Art. 1951. Amendment of judgment

A final judgment may be amended by the trial court at any time, with or without notice, on its own motion or on motion of any party:

(1) To alter the phraseology of the judgment, but not the substance; or

(2) To correct errors of calculation.

Source: C.P. Art. 547; Fed.Rule 60(a).

Comments

(a) This article is a combination of the source provisions. In order to obviate any danger of disturbing the body of jurisprudence defining the "nonsubstantial" changes which may be made to a judgment under Art. 547 of the Code of Practice of 1870, the language of the source article was retained, excluding, however, the illustrative language.

(b) The inclusion of the federal language "at any time" does not work a radical change in the Louisiana law, in view of the holding of the court in the case of Glen Falls Indemnity Co. v. Manning, 168 So. 787 (La.App.1936), to the effect that a judgment may be amended by the court even after signature, where the amendment takes nothing from or adds nothing to the original judgment.

(c) In view of Art. 2088, *infra*, providing for the divestiture of the trial court's jurisdiction upon the filing of the appeal bond, it is unnecessary to include in this Title a provision placing a limit upon the power of the trial court to correct errors after an appeal has been taken. *Cf.* Fed.Rule 60(a), which specifically limits the time for amendment of judgments by providing that "During the pendency of an appeal, such mistakes may be so corrected before the appeal is docketed in the appellate court, and thereafter while the appeal is pending may be so corrected with leave of the appellate court."

(d) It is well settled that appellate courts have power to correct appellate court judgments. State v. F. B. Williams Cypress Co., 132 La. 949, 61 So. 988 (1913); Levy v. Cappel, 39 So.2d 128 (La.App.1949). Likewise, the appellate court has the power to correct errors in calculation in judgments of the district court, which could have been corrected if brought to the notice of the court below. Union Sulphur Co. v. Campbell, 207 La. 514, 21 So.2d 626 (1945); International Paper Co. v. Rivers, 35 So.2d 677 (La.App.1948).

(e) The above article follows Fed.Rule 60(a) in providing for notice at the discretion of the court. Art. 547 of the 1870 Code does not contain a similar provision. However, it has been held that there is no error in correcting the name of a defendant, erroneously described, without citing him to show cause why the correction should not be made, where the error was of little or no importance. Town of Mandeville v. Paquette, 153 La. 33, 95 So. 391 (1922). A contradictory motion is required, however, to amend judgments giving incorrect description of realty. Jackson v. Brewster, 169 So. 166 (La.App.1936); *cf.* Succession of Corrigan, 42 La.Ann. 65, 7 So. 74 (1890). Art. 1919, *supra*, requires that judgments affecting title to immovable property shall describe with particularity the property affected.

(f) See, also, Comments under Art. 1919, *supra*.

SECTION 2. NEW TRIAL

Art. 1971. Granting of new trial

A new trial may be granted, upon contradictory motion of any party or by the court on its own motion, to all or any of the parties and on all or part of the issues, or for reargument only. If a new trial is granted as to less than all parties or issues, the judgment may be held in abeyance as to all parties and issues.

Source: C.P. Art. 557; Fed.Rule 59(a).

Comments to Arts. 1971 through 1973

(a) The Louisiana source provisions regarding the discretionary and peremptory grounds for a new trial were followed almost verbatim.

(b) See Arts. 1813 and 1814, *supra*, with reference to the granting of new trials in jury cases.

(c) The provisions in Art. 1971, authorizing the court to direct a new trial on its own motion, is a codification of the jurisprudence. Mitchell, to Use of Tartt, v. La. Industrial Life Ins. Co., 204 La. 855, 16 So.2d 458 (1944); Marks v. Leichner, 9 La.App. 563, 121 So. 685 (1928). It also follows the common law which gives the judge discretion in determining the causes for which a new trial will be granted. See Shipman, Common Law Pleading (3rd ed.) 536 (1923).

(d) Art. 560 of the 1870 Code lists the peremptory grounds for new trial. Art. 558 sets forth a discretionary provision for granting new trial. This Code adopts a similar form of presentation by providing for peremptory grounds in Art. 1972, *infra*, and the discretionary provision in Art. 1973, *infra*.

Although the trial judge has much discretion regarding applications for new trial, in a case of manifest abuse the appellate court will not hesitate to set the trial court's ruling aside, or grant a new trial when timely applied for. Succession of Robinson, 186 La. 389, 172 So. 429 (1937) *Cf.* Elchinger v. Lacroix, 192 La. 908, 189 So. 572 (1939); Weinberger Sales Co. v. Truett, 2 So.2d 699 (La.App. 1941).

(e) Art. 1971 incorporates the federal provision permitting partial new trials. This was one of the recommendations adopted by the American Bar Association in its Report of July, 1938. See Vanderbilt, Minimum Standards of Judicial Administration 243 (1949), where it is pointed out that the recommendation was based on the practice as regulated by Fed.Rule 59. The American Bar Committee, however, has recommended that this power should "be exercised sparingly in actual practice and then only where the several issues are clearly and fairly separable."

(f) Whether the partial new trial is treated as a phase of rehearing or as a reargument only, it would eliminate the need for provisions on rehearing in trial courts. Therefore, the repeal of former R.S. 13:4262 through 13:4264 has been recommended.

(g) Art. 1972(2), *infra*, includes the "due diligence" requirement of Art. 560(2) of the 1870 Code of Practice. Although there may be some question regarding the advisability of a hard and fast rule with regard to due diligence in this case, the wording of the 1870 Code was retained, since in any case it is believed that the courts will interpret this matter in the light of Succession of Robinson, 186 La. 389, 172 So. 429 (1937). The problem is one which can only be solved by following a middle course, which should be left to the courts to define. *Cf.* McMahon 912, and 163, n. 0.7 (1956 Supp.).

(h) With regard to the form of the motion for a new trial, see Art. 961, *supra*.

Art. 1972. Peremptory grounds

A new trial shall be granted, upon contradictory motion of any party, in the following cases:

(1) Where the judgment appears clearly contrary to the law and the evidence;

(2) Where the party has discovered, since the trial, evidence important to the cause, which he could not, with due diligence, have obtained before or during the trial; or

(3) In jury cases, as provided in Article 1814.

Source: C.P. Art. 560.

Cross Reference: Art. 1975.

Comments

See Comments under Art. 1971, *supra*.
See, also, Comments under Art. 1814, *supra*.

Art. 1973. Discretionary grounds

A new trial may be granted in any case if there is good ground therefor, except as otherwise provided by law.

Source: Cf. C.P. Art. 558.

Comment

See Comments under Art. 1971, *supra*.

Art. 1974. Delay for applying for new trial

The delay for applying for a new trial shall be three days, exclusive of holidays. This delay commences to run on the day after the clerk has mailed, or the sheriff has served, the notice of judgment as required by Article 1913.

Source: New.

Cross References: Arts. 2087, 2123.

Comments

(a) This article effects a needed uniformity in the delay for applying for a new trial. See Comment (a) under Art. 1911, *supra*.

(b) This article overrules the jurisprudence to the effect that in default cases, while the delays for taking appeal and executing judgment commence to run from the notification of the judgment, the same is not true with regard to the delay for applying for a new trial. McClelland v. District Household of Ruth, 151 So. 246 (La. App.1935); Meyer v. Esteb, 75 So.2d 421 (La.App.1955).

(c) See, also, Comments under Arts. 1231, 1911, *supra*, and Arts. 2087, 3942, *infra*.

Art. 1975. Application for new trial; verifying affidavit

A motion for a new trial shall set forth the grounds upon which it is based. When the motion is based on Article 1972(2) and (3), the allegations of fact therein shall be verified by the affidavit of the applicant.

Source: C.P. Arts. 559, 561.

Comments

(a) Art. 863, *supra*, has dispensed with the necessity for verification, except as otherwise provided by law. This article contains one of the exceptions contemplated in that it requires an affidavit in the cases where a new trial is sought on the grounds of newly discovered evidence. No affidavit is necessary, however, when the application for new trial is on the grounds that the judgment is contrary to the law and the evidence.

(b) The last sentence of Art. 561 of the 1870 Code, to the effect that the affidavit must be filed in the records, has been omitted since this would follow in any case as a matter of course.

(c) The above article does not include a provision regarding the form of application for a new trial, since this is governed by Arts. 961, 962, and 963, *supra*.

(d) No provision similar to R.S. 15:511 and 15:512, governing the procedure in criminal cases for obtaining a new trial on the grounds of newly discovered evidence, has been included in this Code. These provisions require, among others, that the motion for a new trial show affirmatively that the evidence is not merely cumulative or corroborative, that it is so material to the issue that a different verdict must be produced. It is also required that the motion disclose the names of the new witnesses and the facts to which they will testify.

The requirements for obtaining a new trial on the grounds of newly discovered evidence in civil cases is so well established by the jurisprudence that no positive legislation was thought necessary. See Vicknair v. Trosclair, 45 La.Ann. 373, 12 So. 486 (1893); Doiron v. Baker-Wakefield Cypress Co., 131 La. 618, 59 So. 1010 (1912); Miller v. Miller, 160 La. 936, 107 So. 702 (1926); Jefferson v. Caddo Transfer and Warehouse Co., 4 La.App. 377 (1926); Deimel v. Etheridge, 198 So. 537 (La.App.1940).

Art. 1976. Service of notice

Notice of the motion for new trial and of the time and place assigned for hearing thereon must be served upon the opposing party as provided by Article 1314.

Source: C.P. Art. 559; cf. Comments following.

Comments

(a) This article is more restrictive in application than the practice under former R.S. 13:3345, whereby service could be made by mail, since Art. 1314, *supra*, deals with service of papers where a response is required and provides that service in this case shall be in the same manner as service of citation or by personal service on the attorney of record.

(b) This article does not include the provision of Art. 559 of the 1870 Code of Practice regarding entry on the records of the court, since it would follow as a matter of course in accordance with the usual mechanical procedure of the court.

(c) Although Art. 559 of the 1870 Code of Practice provides that notice of new trials shall be given "in order that the adverse party may answer within the general delay prescribed for answering", the practice has been to apply for new trials by rule, the return date for which is fixed by the court. For this reason the language has been omitted from the above article.

Art. 1977. Assignment of new trial

When a new trial is granted, it shall be assigned for hearing in accordance with the rules and practice of the court.

Source: C.P. Art. 563.

Art. 1977

Comment

The source provision requiring the reassignment of cases on the docket has been carried forward in this article without change

Art. 1978. Method of procedure

It shall not be necessary to resummon the witnesses or to hear them anew at a new trial if their testimony has once been reduced to writing, but all such testimony and evidence received on the former trial shall be considered as already in evidence. Any party may call new witnesses or offer additional evidence, and with the permission of the court recall any witness for further examination or cross examination as the case may be. However, the parties shall not be precluded from producing new proofs, on the ground they have not been offered on the first trial. When a new trial is granted for reargument only, no evidence shall be adduced.

Source: C.P. Art. 563; former R.S. 13:4261.

Comments

(a) This article is a combination of the last part of the 1870 Code of Practice Art. 563 and of the greater part of former R.S. 13:4261.

(b) The terms of the order granting the new trial for reargument only will govern the scope of the new trial.

Art. 1979. Summary decision on motion; maximum delays

The court shall decide on a motion for a new trial within ten days from the time it is submitted for decision. The time may be extended for a specified period upon the written consent or stipulation of record by the attorneys representing all parties.

Source: C.P. Art. 563; cf. R.S. 13:4207.

Comments

(a) Art. 563 of the 1870 Code provides for a summary decision on applications for new trials; while former R.S. 13:4207 fixes the maximum delays for such decisions. This article represents a consolidation of the two source provisions.

(b) See Comments under Art. 5002, *infra*.

Tit. 6   MODIFICATION IN TRIAL COURT   Art. 2002

SECTION 3. ACTION OF NULLITY

Art. 2001. Grounds in general

The nullity of a final judgment may be demanded for vices of either form or substance, as provided in Articles 2002 through 2006.

Source: C.P. Art. 605.

Art. 2002. Annulment for vices of form; time for action

A final judgment shall be annulled if it is rendered:

(1) Against an incompetent person not represented as required by law;

(2) Against a defendant who has not been served with process as required by law and who has not entered a general appearance, or against whom a valid judgment by default has not been taken; or

(3) By a court which does not have jurisdiction over the subject matter of the suit.

Except as otherwise provided in Article 2003, an action to annul a judgment on these grounds may be brought at any time.

Source: C.P. Art. 606.

Cross References: Arts. 2001, 2003.

Comments

(a) This article carries forward the same grounds of nullity set forth in the source article.

(b) The illustrations of "incompetent person" were omitted as unnecessary.

(c) The omission of the references to "default" judgments where defendant has not been served is not intended to effect a change in the law.

(d) The above article covers judgments rendered in cases where there was no citation at all, cases involving defective citation, and cases where the defendant did not effect a waiver of service and citation by making a general appearance. *Cf.* Art. 7, *supra*, which sets forth the definition of "general appearance."

(e) This article incorporates the jurisprudence under Art. 606, Code of Practice of 1870, to the effect that the grounds for nullity enumerated therein are exclusive. Accardo v. Dimiceli, 226 La. 435, 76 So.2d 521 (1954). It adopts the jurisprudence to the effect that an action of nullity based on any of the grounds enumerated may be raised collaterally and at any time. Edwards v. Whited, 29 La.Ann. 647 (1877); Conery v. Rotchford, Brown and Co., 30 La.Ann. 698

(1878); State ex rel. Moyse v. Guion, 50 La.Ann. 492, 23 So. 614 (1898); Decuir v. Decuir, 105 La. 481, 29 So. 932 (1901); Andrews v. Sheehy, 122 La. 464, 47 So. 771 (1908); Brana v. Brana, 139 La. 305, 71 So. 519 (1916); McClelland v. District Household of Ruth, 151 So. 246 (La.App.1933); Key v. Jones, 181 So. 631 (La. App.1938).

(f) As regards an absolute nullity, *e. g.*, where the court is without jurisdiction over the subject matter, the last sentence of this article merely states the obvious, since a judgment absolutely null has no legal existence. Walworth v. Stevenson, 24 La.Ann. 251 (1872).

(g) See, also, Comments under Arts. 3, 1231, *supra*, and Art. 2004, *infra*.

Art. 2003. Same; action lost through acquiescence

A defendant who voluntarily acquiesed in the judgment, or who was present in the parish at the time of its execution and did not attempt to enjoin its enforcement, may not annul the judgment on any of the grounds enumerated in Article 2002.

Source: C.P. Art. 612; cf. Comment following.

Cross Reference: Art. 2001.

Comments

This article is an exception to the rule set forth in Art. 2002, *supra*. Voluntary acquiescence in the judgment precludes an action to annul it on the ground of vices of form. Succession of Corrigan, 42 La.Ann. 65, 7 So. 74 (1890); Andrews v. Sheehy, 125 La. 217, 51 So. 122 (1910).

See, also, Comments under Art. 3, *supra*.

Art. 2004. Annulment for vices of substance; peremption of action

A final judgment obtained by fraud or ill practices may be annulled.

An action to annul a judgment on these grounds must be brought within one year of the discovery by the plaintiff in the nullity action of the fraud or ill practices.

Source: C.P. Arts. 607, 613.

Cross Reference: Art. 2001.

Comments

(a) The source provisions were combined to provide the grounds of action as well as the time within which the action must be brought.

(b) The illustrations set forth in the source articles with reference to bribery, forged documents, and lost receipts have been omitted, pursuant to the policy of avoiding illustrations in the texts of the articles, except where absolutely necessary. In omitting these illustrative examples, however, there was no intention to change the law. Leaving the question to the discretion of the court is in accord with the jurisprudence which the above article is intended to ratify.

See Lazarus v. McGuirk, 42 La.Ann. 194, 8 So. 253 (1890); Miller v. Miller, 156 La. 46, 100 So. 45 (1924); Hanson v. Haynes, 170 So. 257 (La.App.1936).

Although the courts do not sanction negligence or laches, they have not hesitated "to afford relief against judgments irrespective of any issue of inattention or neglect, when the circumstances under which the judgment is rendered show the deprivation of the legal rights of the litigant who seeks relief, and when the enforcement of the judgment would be unconscientious and inequitable." City of New Orleans v. LeBourgeois, 50 La.Ann. 591, 23 So. 542 (1898); cf. Bell v. Holdcraft, 196 So. 379 (La.App.1940); Sandfield Oil and Gas Co. v. Paul, 7 So.2d 725 (La.App.1942); Vinson v. Picolo, 15 So. 2d 778 (La.App.1943).

(c) The qualification of Art. 607, Code of Practice of 1870, to the effect that the fraud must be on the part of the party in whose favor the judgment is rendered, was omitted and Clark v. Delta Tank Mfg. Co., 28 So.2d 62 (La.App.1946), in which it was held that a judgment could not be annulled for false testimony unless the petition alleged that the testimony was procured by the defendant or the latter had knowledge thereof and participated in the fraud, is thus overruled.

(d) No specific provision has been made regarding the manner of asserting the grounds of nullity in the above article. This was thought unnecessary in view of the established jurisprudence to the effect that such grounds must be asserted in a direct action and cannot be raised collaterally. Bruno v. Oviatt, 48 La.Ann. 471, 19 So. 464 (1896); Caldwell v. Caldwell, 164 La. 458, 114 So. 96 (1927). *Cf.* Art. 2002, Comment (e), *supra*.

(e) In the case of Cilluffa v. Monreale Realty Co., 209 La. 333, 24 So.2d 606 (1945), it was held that Art. 613 of the Code of Practice of 1870, providing that the action to annul on the grounds of fraud must be brought within the year after the discovery of the fraud, does not apply to a confession of judgment fraudulently obtained in violation of Const. Art. VII, § 44, since a transaction of this unlawful character cannot be made valid by ratification, either express or tacit. Of course this would also be true under the above article.

(f) Under the jurisprudence, the burden of proving that fraud or other ill practice was discovered within a year rests upon the plaintiff. Emuy v. Farr, 125 La. 825, 51 So. 1003 (1910). This rule still obtains, although it has not been codified specifically.

Art. 2005. Annulment of judgments; effect of appeal

A judgment may be annulled prior to or pending an appeal therefrom, or after the delays for appealing have elapsed.

A judgment affirmed, reversed, amended, or otherwise rendered by an appellate court may be annulled only when the ground for nullity did not appear in the record of appeal or was not considered by the appellate court.

An action of nullity does not affect the right to appeal.

Source: C.P. Arts. 604, 609, 611.

Cross Reference: Art. 2001.

Comments

(a) This article is a combination of the source provisions.

(b) The last sentence of the article makes it clear that the filing of an action of nullity does not affect the right to appeal. Thus, for instance, it has been held that the action of nullity is independent of the remedy by appeal and both remedies may be maintained at the same time without conflict. Succession of Lissa, 194 La. 328, 193 So. 663 (1940); Collins v. McCook, 17 La.App. 415, 136 So. 204 (1931). However, where an appeal is the proper remedy for the correction of a judgment, an action of nullity may not be substituted for it; thus, an action of nullity does not lie upon a general allegation that the judgment is contrary to the law and the evidence. Landry v. Bertrand, 48 La.Ann. 48, 19 So. 126 (1896); Conery v. His Creditors, 118 La. 864, 43 So. 530 (1907); Emuy v. Farr, 125 La. 825, 51 So. 1003 (1910). In the case of State v. Sommerville, 112 La. 1091, 36 So. 864 (1904), the court pointed out that the action of nullity was not to be used as a means of affording another day in court for a litigant, who has neglected his opportunity and that its purpose under Art. 607 of the 1870 Code of Practice was to furnish relief against fraud in the obtention of the judgment, which makes no appearance on the record, and for which an appeal would afford no remedy.

Art. 2006. Court where action brought

An action to annul a judgment must be brought in the trial court, even though the judgment sought to be annulled may have been affirmed on appeal, or even rendered by the appellate court.

Source: Cf. C.P. Arts. 608, 610, 611.

Cross References: Art. 44, 2001.

Comments

Arts. 608, 610, and 611 of the Code of Practice of 1870 provided that the action to annul a judgment should be brought in the court which rendered it.

The jurisprudence was unsettled, however, with respect to the annulment of a judgment which had either been affirmed on appeal, or rendered by an appellate court. Since the appellate courts have no such original jurisdiction, definitely the action to annul may not be instituted therein. Walker v. Barelli, 32 La.Ann. 1159 (1880). The jurisprudence was in conflict as to whether the action to annul such a judgment could be brought in the trial court. Melancton's Heirs v. Broussard, 2 La. 8 (1830) and Succession of Martin v. Succession of Hoggatt, 37 La.Ann. 340 (1885) held that such a judgment was one of the appellate court, and the trial court had no jurisdiction to annul it. *Cf.* Gajan v. Patout & Burguieres, 135 La. 156, 65 So. 17 (1914). But in Adkins' Heirs v. Crawford, Jenkins & Booth, 200 La. 561, 8 So.2d 539 (1942), although the issue was not squarely presented, the supreme court affirmed the trial court's annulment of such a judgment. Further, if the judgment is sought to be annulled because of an absolute nullity, it may be attacked collaterally. Decuir v. Decuir, 105 La. 481, 29 So. 932 (1901). The question is discussed in 3 La.L.Rev. 623 (1941) and 7 La.L.Rev. 272 (1947).

The above article removes all doubt on the question by expressly providing that the action may be filed in the trial court, even though it had been affirmed on appeal, or even rendered by the appellate court.

CHAPTER 5. REVIVAL

Art.
2031. Revival of judgments.

Art. 2031. Revival of judgments

A money judgment may be revived at any time before it prescribes by an interested party in an ordinary proceeding brought in the court in which the judgment was rendered.

The judgment debtor shall be made a defendant in the proceeding to revive the judgment, unless he is dead, in which event his legal representative or legal successor shall be made a defendant.

A judgment shall be rendered in such a proceeding reviving the original judgment, unless the defendant shows good cause why it should not be revived.

Source: New; cf. C.C. Art. 3547.

Comments

(a) The procedural provisions of Art. 3547 of the Civil Code have been transferred to the above article, and the Civil Code provision has been amended to delete therefrom all procedural provisions, and to reflect the change made by this Code with respect to the date prescription on such a judgment commences to run.

(b) If the defendant is a nonresident, absentee, or incompetent, the court may appoint an attorney at law to represent him, and the proceeding to revive conducted contradictorily against this attorney, under Art. 5091, *infra*.

(c) In interpreting Civil Code Art. 3547, the early cases held that an action to revive a judgment was the only way by which the accrual of prescription could be prevented. See Succession of Hardy, 25 La.Ann. 489 (1873); Smith v. Palfrey, 28 La.Ann. 615 (1876). However, in Succession of Patrick, 30 La.Ann. 1071 (1878), after considering Art. 3547 in connection with Art. 2278 of the Civil Code, the court held that the prescription on judgment debts was subject to the same rules regarding interruption of prescription as were applicable to other debts not reduced to judgment. The Patrick decision was either applied or cited with approval in Calhoun v. Levy, 33 La.Ann. 1296 (1881); Levy v. Calhoun, 34 La.Ann. 413 (1882); Succession of Saunders, 37 La.Ann. 769 (1885); Lelanne v. Payne, 42 La.Ann. 152, 7 So. 481 (1890); and Norres v. Hayes, 42 La.Ann. 857, 8 So. 606 (1890). In 1925, in the case of Bailey v. Louisiana and N. W. R. Co., 159 La. 576, 105 So. 626 (1925), the court reverted to the original construction placed upon Art. 3547 by the earlier decisions, and this was recently reaffirmed in Cassiere v. Cuban Coffee Mills, 225 La. 1003, 74 So.2d 193 (1954).

(d) The above article is predicated on the assumption that the courts will give Art. 3547 of the Civil Code the same interpretation as was given it in Cassiere v. Cuban Coffee Mills, *supra*.

BOOK III
PROCEEDINGS IN APPELLATE COURTS

TITLE I

APPELLATE PROCEDURE

Chap.		Art.
1.	General Dispositions	2081
2.	Procedure for Appealing	2121
3.	Procedure in Appellate Court	2161

INTRODUCTION

The appellate procedure set forth in this Title does not differ greatly from that in force prior to the adoption of this Code, and only four important changes are made:

(1) The responsibility for the lodging of all records on appeal in the appellate court is placed on the clerk of the trial court; and when the appellant has timely paid the required fees, the failure of the clerk of the trial court to prepare and lodge the record on appeal timely is not imputed to the appellant;

(2) The delay generally allowed for taking a devolutive appeal has been reduced from one year to ninety days;

(3) The trial court is given the power of extending the return day in all cases, thus making it unnecessary for the appellant to request an extension thereof in the appellate court; and

(4) The appellate court is given the power to render any judgment or decree which is proper, just, and legal upon the record on appeal, regardless of whether a particular legal point or theory was argued or passed on in the trial court.

This Title does not deal with the subject of appellate jurisdiction, since that is regulated by the constitution of the state.

Appeals from judgments of trial courts of limited jurisdiction are regulated in Book VIII.

CHAPTER 1. GENERAL DISPOSITIONS

Art.
2081. Applicability of Title.
2082. Definition of appeal.
2083. Judgments appealable.
2084. Legal representative may appeal.
2085. Limitations on appeals.
2086. Right of third person to appeal.
2087. Delay for taking devolutive appeal.
2088. Divesting of jurisdiction of trial court.
2089. Description required of immovable property affected by judgments or decrees.

Art. 2081. Applicability of Title

The provisions of this Title are applicable to all appeals to the supreme court and the courts of appeal, except as otherwise provided by law.

Source: Const. Art. VII, § 27, par. 2.

Cross Reference: Art. 2642.

Comments

(a) This provision is taken practically verbatim from the Louisiana Constitution of 1921.

(b) Art. 597 of the 1870 Code of Practice, which provided that the general appellate rules shall apply to all appeals to the supreme court, whether they are taken from judgments rendered by district courts or parish courts, is unnecessary, and furthermore, parish courts are now obsolete.

Art. 2082. Definition of appeal

Appeal is the exercise of the right of a party to have a judgment of a trial court revised, modified, set aside, or reversed by an appellate court.

Source: C.P. Arts. 556, 564.

Cross Reference: Art. 2642.

Comments

(a) This article embodies the principle that, except as otherwise provided by law, appeal from all final judgments is a matter of right. Const. Art. VII, §§ 10 and 29; Succession of Damico, 161 La. 725, 109 So. 402 (1925).

(b) The word "modified", which does not appear in Arts. 556 or 564 of the 1870 Code, was added in order to make it clear that revi-

Tit. 1   GENERAL DISPOSITIONS   Art. 2083

sion could entail an extension as well as a limitation of the judgment. See "modify" in Black's Law Dictionary, citing State v. Lincoln, 133 Minn. 178, 158 N.W. 50, 52 (1916); U. S. v. Felder, 13 F.2d 527, 528 (D.C.Cir.1926).

(c) The broad language of the above article is sufficient to cover all parties, and the terms "revised, modified, set aside, or reversed" include parts of judgments as well as entire judgments, and are applicable to incidental demands as well as principal demands.

(d) It should be noted that this article includes the idea of the remand. It was thought unnecessary, therefore, to spell out the word itself in the article. Note, also, that the idea of remand is covered by Art. 2164, *infra*.

(e) See, also, Comments under Art. 2085, *infra*.

Art. 2083. Judgments appealable

An appeal may be taken from a final judgment rendered in causes in which appeals are given by law whether rendered after hearing or by default, and from an interlocutory judgment which may cause irreparable injury.

Source: C.P. Arts. 565, 566.

Cross Reference: Art. 2642.

Comments

(a) The general concept that there is no appeal except in the case of final judgments is universal in order to prevent piecemeal appeals. Three Way Finance Co. v. McDonald, 213 La. 504, 35 So.2d 31 (1948); In re Canal Bank and Trust Co., 216 La. 410, 43 So.2d 777 (1949). However, the right to appeal certain interlocutory judgments, where irreparable injury would otherwise result, is retained in this Code.

The 1870 Code of Practice Art. 566 states that one may appeal an interlocutory judgment when "such judgment may cause him an irreparable injury." No attempt has been made to codify the jurisprudence in which interlocutory judgments have a final effect or may cause irreparable injury, since the jurisprudence has been largely a case by case process, rather than the development of a basic general rule.

For example, the following judgments, although interlocutory, have been held appealable: refusing to homologate partition proceedings and ordering a new sale, Hollingsworth v. Caldwell, 193 La. 638, 192 So. 83 (1939); dissolving an attachment and releasing the property seized, Pittman v. Lilly, 197 La. 233, 1 So.2d 88 (1941); denying right to jury trial, where irreparable injury would result, Wilson Sporting Goods v. Alwes, 17 So.2d 382 (La.App.

1944); ordering garnishees to hold and retain the amounts due by them on negotiable promissory notes originally given to the defendant pending the final determination of the suit, since notes were in the hands of third persons who could demand payment when due and seize security thus causing garnishees irreparable injury, Three Way Finance Co., Inc. v. McDonald, 213 La. 504, 35 So.2d 31 (1948).

A judgment requiring a defendant to account is appealable. Cary v. Richardson, 35 La.Ann. 505, 507 (1883). Compare, also, Maguire v. Fluker, 112 La. 76, 36 So. 231 (1902) and cases cited. Benham, Ziegler & Co. v. Mouledoux, 175 La. 711, 144 So. 428 (1932), holding that a judgment which requires a defendant to account is unappealable, is unsound in principle and has proven unworkable in practice. See Winsberg v. Winsberg, 233 La. 67, 96 So.2d 44 (1957), where the litigants were put to the trouble and expense of an accounting which the appellate court later held was not due. Although dependent on the facts of each case, usually a judgment refusing an accounting is appealable. See In re Canal Bank & Trust Co., 216 La. 410, 43 So.2d 777 (1949); Oliphint v. Oliphint, 219 La. 781, 54 So.2d 18 (1951).

On the other hand, the following judgments have been held to be nonappealable: granting a new trial or rehearing when application filed timely, Foster v. Kaplan Rice Mill, 203 La. 245, 13 So.2d 850 (1943); refusing to grant a new trial or rehearing even on the ground that the application therefor was not filed timely, State ex rel. Land v. Martin, 207 La. 410, 21 So.2d 481 (1945). Judgments overruling the following exceptions have been held to be interlocutory and unappealable: exceptions of no right or cause of action, Rapides Cent. Ry. Co. v. Mo. Pac. R. Co., 207 La. 870, 22 So.2d 200 (1945); exceptions to the jurisdiction rationae materiae and personae, Woodcock v. Crehan, 28 So.2d 61 (La.App.1946). Judgments maintaining exceptions of nonjoinder, Neal v. Hall, 28 So.2d 131 (La.App.1946), and no cause of action, Feitel v. Feitel, 169 La. 384, 125 So. 280 (1929), have been held to be nonappealable.

In many cases it is not easy to distinguish between which judgments are interlocutory and which are final. The supreme court, in Succession of Lissa, 194 La. 328, 193 So. 663 (1940), refused to say whether an ex parte judgment recognizing alleged heirs and sending them into possession of an estate was either final or interlocutory, but held it appealable since it was prima facie evidence of their right to the possession of the estate. In Oliphint v. Oliphint, 219 La. 781, 54 So.2d 18 (1951), the court commented on the omission of provisions in the 1870 Code of Practice relative to the twilight zone of decrees, which although interlocutory in nature are in effect final judgments in that they dispose of issues applicable solely to the merits of the case. See also, Cary v. Richardson, 35 La.Ann. 505, 507 (1883), where the court said, "If an interlocutory order will finally affect the merits of the case, or deprive a party of any benefit which he may have at the final hearing, an appeal is allowable. It is not always absolutely required to dispose of the entire merits of a cause and all the parties before the court, as a necessity to a final decree. Any order or decree finally settling any right or interest in controversy between the parties to a cause is final and reviewable."

(b) Some states avoid the problem of the distinction between final and interlocutory judgments by specifying which judgments are appealable: Arizona Rev.Stats.Anno., (1956), § 12–2101; Minn. Stats.Anno., § 605.09; Va.Code (1950), § 8–462.

Other states enumerate which interlocutory judgments are appealable: Idaho Stats., T. 11, Chap. 1, §§ 101, 201; *Cf.* Calif.Code of Civil Procedure, § 963.

Illinois makes appeals from orders granting new trials discretionary with the court. Ill.Ann.Stats., c. 110, § 201. The federal system takes a similar approach. Thus, 28 U.S.C. § 1291 makes all final judgments appealable; and 28 U.S.C. § 1292 specifies those interlocutory judgments which are appealable.

(c) Two jurisdictions attempt to solve the problem by defining interlocutory judgments. See Art. 46, Quebec Code of Civil Procedure (1947); New Mexico Stats.Anno., § 19–201(5) (2).

(d) This Code retains the Louisiana test of irreparable injury with respect to the appealability of interlocutory judgments.

(e) Art. 968, *supra*, does not permit appeals from the court's refusal to render a judgment on the pleadings or summary judgment.

Art. 3612, *infra*, denies appeal from any order relating to a temporary injunction, but specifically sets forth the bases for appeal from preliminary and final injunctions.

(f) This article retains the Louisiana concept of an appeal by the party against whom a default judgment has been rendered. While Arts. 604 through 613 of the 1870 Code of Practice provide an action of nullity which is similar to an appeal where there were jurisdictional, venue, and citation defects, as well as fraud in the trial below, the right of appeal of a defaulted defendant on the record as made has great protective value. In effect, it forces a plaintiff to make out his case even though the defendant has not answered. In addition, of course, certain defenses may be raised on appeal for the first time, such as no cause of action and prescription, and such an opportunity, under the above article, is available even to a defaulted party. See Comments under Art. 2163, *infra*.

(g) See, also, Comments under Arts. 968, 969, 1841, *supra*, and Art. 3612, *infra*.

Art. 2084. Legal representative may appeal

A legal representative may appeal any appealable judgment rendered against him or affecting the property which he is administering, for the benefit of the person whose property he administers or whom he represents, whenever he considers an appeal necessary or advisable.

Source: Cf. C.P. Art. 572.

Cross Reference: Art. 2642.

Comments

(a) For the definition of legal representative, see Art. 5251, *infra*.

(b) While this article broadens the language of its source provision, it actually makes no change in the procedural law of Louisiana, since it is merely declaratory of the judicial interpretation of Art. 572, Code of Practice of 1870.

Art. 2085. Limitations on appeals

An appeal cannot be taken by a party who confessed judgment in the proceedings in the trial court or who voluntarily and unconditionally acquiesced in a judgment rendered against him. Confession of or acquiescence in part of a divisible judgment or in a favorable part of an indivisible judgment does not preclude an appeal as to other parts of such judgment.

Source: C.P. Art. 567.

Cross Reference: Art. 2642.

Comments

(a) The prescription contained in the second numbered paragraph of Art. 567 of the 1870 Code of Practice was omitted. Art. 2087, *infra*, prescribes the time limitations for an appeal.

(b) The concept of a confession of judgment precluding an appeal is retained, but some of the problems connected with it are clarified. Thus, an extrajudicial confession would not preclude an appeal under this Code. Such a pre-trial confession should, of course, have probative value, but even though permitted by Const. Art. VII, § 44 after the maturity of an obligation, it should not bar an appeal. Cutting off an appeal where a person has made his confession while in open court is something quite apart from barring such appeal when the confession is privately made. Where there is a judicial confession, under the eye of the court, the danger of forced or pressured confessions is minimized. Therefore, the words "in the proceedings in the trial court" were added to make certain that no extrajudicial confessions would have the effect of cutting off an appeal.

(c) The term "confession" is not here defined. The jurisprudence has defined it as an admission by a party, in pleadings or in evidence, of the validity of his opponent's claim in such a way as to leave no issue to be tried. However, admissions in an answer sufficient to warrant a judgment on the face of the pleadings under former R.S. 13:3601(4) have been held not to be a confession so as to foreclose an appeal by the defendant, where his answer as a whole denied liability: Sample v. Wheless, 159 La. 844, 106 So. 325 (1925); Rosenberg v. Derbes, 161 La. 1070, 109 So. 841 (1926).

(d) With respect to the concept of acquiescence, the jurisprudence has enlarged the literal meaning of the text of Art. 567 of the 1870 Code of Practice, which would seem to limit acquiescence to a situation where a party voluntarily executes a judgment. However, the courts have interpreted this article to include various other forms of acquiescence: appellant who took record of suit ordered to be removed to federal court cannot subsequently appeal the removal, New Orleans City R. Co. v. Crescent City R. Co., 33 La.Ann. 1273 (1881); remarriage as an acquiescence in divorce, Barraco v. Barraco, 173 La. 81, 136 So. 95 (1931); the filing of a petitory action within the 60 days allowed after defeat of jactitory action held to be acquiescence in the judgment, Andrews v. McGee, 58 So.2d 561 (La.App.1952). This article eliminates the requirement that the acquiescence be *by execution*, and thus conforms to existing decisions. Of course, the term "acquiescence" obviously includes voluntary execution.

(e) The term "unconditionally" was also added to conform to the jurisprudence, which has added that qualification. See Saunders v. Busch-Everett Co., 138 La. 1049, 71 So. 153 (1916); Sanderson v. Frost, 198 La. 295, 3 So.2d 626 (1941); and Scott v. Scott, 218 La. 211, 48 So.2d 899 (1950), all of which held that the acquiescence must be unconditional, voluntary and absolute.

(f) The word "voluntarily" is retained as in Art. 567 of the 1870 Code and it is presumed that the jurisprudence on the meaning of this term will also follow the word into the above text. See Saunders v. Busch Everett Co., *supra*; Sanderson v. Frost, *supra*; and Scott v. Scott, *supra*. Thus, payment of a judgment with written reservation of right to appeal does not amount to voluntary acquiescence. Blanchard v. Donaldsonville Motors Co., 176 So. 669 (La.App.1937). Furthermore, there are certain situations where the law does not contemplate that the defendant should by acquiescence subject himself to various penalties, since the acquiescence cannot be considered voluntary: *viz.*, where an alternative judgment decreed that defendant should convey certain land within a fixed period, otherwise plaintiff would have the right to select the portion of land to be conveyed, defendant does not show acquiescence by electing the former course, Colvin v. Woodward, 40 La.Ann. 627, 4 So. 564 (1888); husband ordered to pay alimony who sought by rule to be relieved from making such payments did not show acquiescence in the judgment by paying the same, since he is not required to render himself liable to punishment for contempt and possible imprisonment in order to retain his right to appeal, Scott v. Scott, *supra*.

The supreme court has also held that there was no acquiescence such as to bar an appeal, where after an injunction against seizure and sale was dissolved and defendant's suspensive appeal bond was held invalid, defendant appeared at the sale and offered to repurchase the property, since at that point it was beyond his power to prevent the sale. La. Land and Immigration Co. v. Murff, 139 La. 808, 72 So. 284 (1916). *Cf.* Succession of Land, 209 La. 135, 24 So.2d 289 (1945).

(g) It is well established that a party may acquiesce in a part of a divisible judgment without forfeiting his right of appeal as to the other part of the judgment. Succession of Kaiser, 48 La. Ann. 973, 20 So. 184 (1896); Sanderson v. Frost, *supra*. Where a judgment is indivisible, acquiescence in any part precludes appeal. Jolley v. Vivian Oil Co., 131 La. 937, 60 So. 622 (1912). However, even as to indivisible judgments, one may acquiesce in a part favorable to him and yet appeal as to the remainder. Foster & Glassell Co. v. Harrison, 173 La. 550, 138 So. 99 (1931); State v. Baynard, 204 La. 834, 16 So.2d 451 (1943); Trimble v. Employers Mutual Casualty Co., 32 So.2d 479 (La.App.1947). The last sentence of the article was added in order to codify the latter jurisprudence.

(h) The text of the above article makes the confession or acquiescence effective only as to "the party" making either. This is in line with Louisiana jurisprudence. It is well settled that a confession or an acquiescence is binding only on the party making it, and has no effect on third parties. State ex rel. Blackman v. Strong, 32 La.Ann. 173 (1880). In Herring v. Price, 4 So.2d 17 (La.App.1941), where defendant's son acted as appraiser without defendant's authority and property was bought in by third party at sale, defendant, who was not present at sale, was not bound by act of his son and could subsequently appeal.

(i) The jurisprudence has added another limitation upon an appeal: that a party in whose favor a judgment has been rendered in strict accordance with his prayer for relief, cannot appeal. State ex rel. Moore Planting Co. v. Howell, 139 La. 336, 71 So. 529 (1916); Barbara, Inc. v. Billelo, 212 La. 937, 33 So.2d 689 (1947); Salassi v. Salassi, 220 La. 785, 57 So.2d 684 (1952). For a discussion of this matter see Comment (e) to Art. 2082, *supra*.

(j) See, also, Comments under Art. 968, *supra*.

Art. 2086. Right of third person to appeal

A person who could have intervened in the trial court may appeal, whether or not any other appeal has been taken.

Source: C.P. Arts. 571, 904; cf. Comments following.

Cross Reference: Art. 2642.

Comments

(a) In Haas v. Haas, 181 La. 265, 159 So. 384 (1935), it was held that Art. 904, Code of Practice of 1870, did not prevent an appeal by a judgment creditor, as his own appeal under Art. 571 of the 1870 Code, rather than as his debtor's appeal under Art. 904. It would seem, therefore, that as these articles are interpreted, there are contemplated two types of appeal by a third party: (1) his own independent appeal; (2) the exercise of his debtor's right of appeal. This distinction is unnecessary. A third party either has a right to appeal or he has not, and whether he exercises it as his own or as his debtor's should not make any difference. Therefore, the concept of Art. 904, Code of Practice of 1870, as interpreted by Haas v. Haas, has been rejected.

(b) Art. 1091, *supra*, requires that there be connexity between the intervention and the main case, and furnishes the criterion for determining the right of appeal of third persons under the above article.

(c) When a third person appeals, he takes the record as he finds it, and must show either that the judgment appealed from is erroneous or that it was the result of fraud and collusion between the original parties. Haas v. Haas, *supra*; Balis v. Mitchell, 48 So. 2d 691 (La.App.1950).

Art. 2087. Delay for taking devolutive appeal

Except as otherwise provided by law, an appeal which does not suspend the effect or the execution of an appealable order or judgment may be taken, and the security therefor furnished, only within ninety days of:

(1) The expiration of the delay for applying for a new trial, as provided by Article 1974, if no application has been filed timely;

(2) The court's refusal to grant a timely application for a new trial, if the applicant is not entitled to notice of such refusal under Article 1914; or

(3) The date of the mailing of notice of the court's refusal to grant a timely application for a new trial, if the applicant is entitled to such notice under Article 1914.

Source: New; cf. C.P. Arts. 578, 593.

Cross References: Arts. 1914, 1974, 2123, 2642, 3662, 3942, 4068, 4548.

Comments

(a) The principal change made by this article is to reduce the delay generally allowed for taking an appeal from the one year allowed for a devolutive appeal under Art. 593, Code of Practice of 1870, to ninety days. Under the former procedural law, the delay of one year for taking an appeal unnecessarily delayed final disposition of cases where the time element was extremely important, as in suits involving the title of immovables, or of mineral rights. The delay for appealing in most of the other states ranges from one to six months.

A delay of fifteen days is allowed for taking a suspensive appeal. Art. 2123, *infra*.

(b) The exception at the beginning of this article avoids conflict with a number of code and statutory provisions providing shorter delays for appeal from certain judgments. These provisions include: Art. 3612, *infra*, fifteen days to appeal from an interlocutory injunctive order; Arts. 3942 and 3943, *infra*, thirty days to appeal from a judgment of divorce, separation from bed and board, annulment of marriage, and alimony; Art. 4068, *infra*, thirty days to appeal from judgment confirming, appointing, or removing a tutor or undertutor; Art. 4548, *infra*, thirty days to appeal from judgment appointing or removing a curator, or revoking an interdiction; Art. 4735, *infra*, twenty-four hours to appeal from a judgment of eviction; Arts. 4899, 4942, 5002, *infra*, ten days to appeal from a judgment of a justice of the peace or a city court; R. S. 12:755, ten days to appeal from a judgment appointing, or refusing to appoint, a receiver; and R.S. 13:4453, thirty days to appeal from a judgment in cases involving the validity of bonds issued by public corporations or political subdivisions, or of servicing tax levies therefor.

(c) The above article omits the exception in Art. 593 of the Code of Practice of 1870 in favor of minors, which permits a minor to appeal an adverse judgment within one year after he reaches majority—which, in many cases, may be many years after the judgment was rendered. This exception produced incongruous results. For example, the prescriptions of one, three, and five years run against minors under Art. 3541 of the Civil Code—reserving to the minors their recourse against their tutors. So, if a tutor fails to file suit timely the minor's right is lost; yet if the tutor does file suit but fails to appeal, the case is open until the minor is twenty-two years old.

If the minor is not represented by the proper legal representative, any judgment in the case is a nullity. If he is represented properly, his legal representative should have the same delay for appealing as any one else, and the minor should be concluded by the judgment if no appeal is taken timely. The recourse of the minor in such cases should be against his tutor for failing to appeal timely, if an appeal should have been taken.

(d) See, also, Comments under Arts. 1911, 2082, 2085, *supra*, and Arts. 2121, 2123, 2252, 3942, 4068, *infra*.

Art. 2088. Divesting of jurisdiction of trial court

The jurisdiction of the trial court over the case shall be divested, and that of the appellate court shall attach, upon the timely filing of the appeal bond in the trial court, or if no bond is required, upon the granting of the order of appeal. Thereafter, the trial court shall have no jurisdiction over the case except: to tax the costs incurred in the trial court; to test the solvency of the surety on the appeal bond as of the date of its filing or subsequently; to consider objections to the form, substance, and sufficiency of the appeal bond, and permit the curing thereof, in accordance with Article 5124; and as provided by Articles 2125, 2131, and 2132.

Source: New; cf. Comments following.

Cross Reference: Art. 2642.

Comments

(a) The above article codifies the jurisprudence to the effect that when the appeal is perfected, the lower court retains jurisdiction to test the sufficiency of the appeal bond. Vacuum Oil Co. v. Cockrell, 177 La. 623, 148 So. 898 (1933); Mistich v. Holman, 205 La. 171, 17 So.2d 23 (1944).

However, the jurisdiction of the trial court is not divested by the filing of the appeal bond unless it is filed timely. Arnold v. Arnold, 217 La. 362, 46 So.2d 298 (1950); City of Baton Rouge v. Kiper, 96 So.2d 241 (La.App.1957).

(b) The last clause of the above article was inserted to recognize exceptions to the general rule stated. Art. 2125, *infra*, allows the trial court to grant an extension of time for filing the record on appeal. Art. 2131, *infra*, allows the trial court to narrate the facts after the appeal is taken. Art. 2132, *infra*, allows the trial court to correct irregularities in the record on appeal.

(c) The language "or if no bond is required, upon the granting of the order of appeal" was inserted in order to take care of cases where the law dispenses with the necessity for filing bond as in the cases of appeals by public bodies provided in R.S. 13:4581, and appeals in forma pauperis suits provided in Art. 5181 *et seq., infra*.

(d) Under the Louisiana jurisprudence the trial court has jurisdiction to test the appeal bond only as of the date of its filing; the appellate court has sole jurisdiction to test the sufficiency of such a bond as of a date subsequent to its filing. Harnischfeger Sales Corporation v. Sternberg Co., 177 La. 373, 148 So. 440 (1933). *Cf.* Borgnemouth Realty Co. v. Gulf Soap Corporation, 211 La. 255, 29 So.2d 841 (1947). *Cf.* Mistich v. Holman, 205 La. 171, 17 So.2d 23 (1944); Kennedy v. Perry Timber Co., 217 La. 401, 46 So.2d 312 (1950). In cases where the appellee moves to test the sufficiency of the appeal bond in the appellate court, the latter will remand the case to the trial court for that purpose, and to permit the appellant to furnish a new or supplemental bond, if the original one is found insufficient. Harnischfeger Sales Corporation v. Sternberg Co., *supra*. The above article avoids such circuity of procedure and permits the trial court to test the sufficiency of the appeal bond in all cases.

(e) See, also, Comments under Art. 1951, *supra*, and Art. 2125, *infra*.

Art. 2089. Description required of immovable property affected by judgments or decrees

All judgments and decrees which affect title to immovable property shall describe with particularity the immovable property affected.

Source: Former R.S. 13:4202.

Cross Reference: Art. 2642.

Comments

See Comments under Art. 1919, *supra*.

See, also, Comments under Art. 3061, *infra*.

CHAPTER 2. PROCEDURE FOR APPEALING

Art.
2121. Method of appealing.
2122. Appointment or removal of legal representative not suspended by appeal; effect of vacating appointment on appeal.
2123. Delay for taking suspensive appeal.
2124. Security to be furnished for an appeal.
2125. Return day.
2126. Payment of costs.
2127. Record on appeal; preparation; prepayment of fees.
2128. Same; determination of content.
2129. Assignment of errors unnecessary; exception.
2130. Record on appeal; statement of facts.
2131. Same; narrative of facts.
2132. Same; correction.
2133. Answer of appellee; when necessary.

Art. 2121. Method of appealing

An appeal is taken by obtaining an order therefor, within the delay allowed, from the court which rendered the judgment.

An order of appeal may be granted on oral motion in open court, or on petition; it shall show the return day of the appeal in the appellate court and shall provide the amount of security to be furnished, when the law requires the determination thereof by the court.

When the order is granted, the clerk of court shall mail a notice of appeal to counsel of record of all other parties, or to other parties not represented by counsel. The failure of the clerk to mail the notice does not affect the validity of the appeal.

Source: C.P. Arts. 573, 574; cf. Fed.Rule 73(b).

Cross Reference: Art. 2642.

Comments

(a) This article makes two important changes in the law as indicated in Comments (b) and (c).

(b) Under the 1870 Code of Practice an appeal could be taken by motion only in the same session as that in which the judgment was rendered. It could be taken by petition at any time, and had to be taken by petition if the appeal was applied for in the vacation period, or in the session following that in which the judgment was rendered.

Under this article the appeal may be taken either on petition, or on oral motion at any time court is open, regardless of when the judgment was rendered and the appeal is moved for. The court would not be open during the summer vacation unless a special session were called under its rules of court (*cf.* Art. 193, *supra*), but if such a special session were called the appeal might be moved for in open court. Art. 196(8), *supra*. The judge may grant an order of appeal on petition either in chambers or during vacation. Arts. 194(6) and 196(7), *supra*.

(c) Under the 1870 Code citation of appeal was required in all cases except when the order of appeal could be, and was, granted on oral motion in open court. Under this article, no citation of appeal is necessary, but as a substitute therefor the clerk of court is required to issue or to mail notices of appeal to all appellees. Failure of the clerk to issue and to mail these notices does not affect the validity of the appeal. If the appellees receive no notices of appeal, they will be entitled to obtain a delay of the proceedings in the appellate court, if necessary.

(d) See Arts. 2087, *supra*, and 2123, *infra*, relating to the delays for taking appeals.

Art. 2122. Appointment or removal of legal representative not suspended by appeal; effect of vacating appointment on appeal

A judgment or order of a trial court appointing or removing a legal representative shall be executed provisionally notwithstanding an appeal therefrom.

A judgment rendered on appeal vacating a judgment or order of the trial court appointing a legal representative does not invalidate any of his official acts performed prior to the rendition of the judgment of the appellate court.

Source: Cf. C.P. Art. 580.

Cross Reference: Art. 2642.

Comments

(a) For the definition of legal representative, see Art. 5251, *infra*.

(b) While the language of this article is broader than its source provision, it actually makes no change in the procedural law of Louisiana, since it is merely declaratory of the jurisprudential rules on the subject.

(c) See, also, Comments under Art. 2123, *infra*.

Art. 2123. Delay for taking suspensive appeal

Except as otherwise provided by law, an appeal which suspends the effect or the execution of an appealable order or judgment may be taken, and the security therefor furnished, only within fifteen days of:

(1) The expiration of the delay for applying for a new trial, as provided by Article 1974, if no application has been filed timely;

(2) The court's refusal to grant a timely application for a new trial, if the applicant is not entitled to notice of such refusal under Article 1914; or

(3) The date of the mailing of notice of the court's refusal to grant a timely application for a new trial, if the applicant is entitled to such notice under Article 1914.

Source: C.P. Arts. 575, 624; former R.S. 13:4212.

Cross References: Arts. 1914, 1974, 2087, 2124, 2642, 3662.

Comments

(a) The principal change made by this article was to increase the delay for taking a suspensive appeal from "ten days, not including Sundays" under the source provisions, to fifteen days. The primary reason for this change was the fact that the majority of suspensive appeal bonds today are surety company bonds, and more time is needed to obtain this type of bond.

(b) One of the principal exceptions to the general rule of this article is set forth in Art. 2122, *supra*, prohibiting a suspensive appeal from any judgment or order appointing or removing a legal representative. Other important exceptions to the general rule of this article are appeals from judgments or orders: awarding alimony or custody of children in divorce or judicial separation cases; ordering the release of a person in custody, or awarding his custody to another; granting interim allowance to surviving spouse, heirs, or legatees of deceased persons; issuing temporary restraining orders and preliminary injunction; and expropriating property of a defendant. See Arts. 3321, 3612, 3831, and 3943, *infra*; Art. 2634, Civil Code; and R.S. 19:13.

(c) See, also, Comments under Arts. 2087, 2121, *supra*, and Art. 2252, *infra*.

Art. 2124. Security to be furnished for an appeal

The security to be furnished for a devolutive appeal shall be fixed by the trial court at an amount sufficient to secure the payment of costs.

The security to be furnished for a suspensive appeal is determined in accordance with the following rules:

(1) When the judgment is for a sum of money, the amount of the security shall exceed by one-half the amount of the judgment, including the interest allowed by the judgment to the date the security is furnished, exclusive of costs;

(2) When the judgment distributes a fund in custodia legis, only security sufficient to secure the payment of costs is required; and

(3) In all other cases, the security shall be fixed by the trial court at an amount sufficient to assure the satisfaction of the judgment, together with damages for the delay resulting from the suspension of the execution.

A suspensive appeal bond shall provide, in substance, that it is furnished as security that the appellant will prosecute his appeal, that any judgment against him will be paid or satisfied from the proceeds of the sale of his property, or that otherwise the surety is liable for the amount of the judgment.

Both devolutive and suspensive appeal bonds shall afford security for the payment of all appellate costs paid by the appellee, and all costs due by the appellant, including those due the clerk of the trial court for the preparation of the record on appeal.

Source: C.P. Arts. 575–578; Fed.Rule 73(d); cf. Comments following.

Cross References: Arts. 2642, 3308, 4899, 4900, 5002.

Comments

(a) This article establishes the formulae for determining the proper amount of bond required to suspend execution. Subparagraphs (1) and (2) of the second paragraph are taken directly from Art. 575 of the 1870 Code of Practice.

(b) Those portions of Art. 575 dealing with the technicalities of the bond filed, *e. g.*, how it shall be payable, how tested, are not included in this Book. See Book IX, Title I, Chapter 3.

(c) Subparagraph (3) of the second paragraph is taken in principle from Fed. Rule 73(d). It is flexible in that it gives the court a wide discretion in fixing the bond in cases not involving a money judgment.

(d) Both Arts. 575 and 579 of the 1870 Code require that appeal bonds have sureties and that the sureties be held under the terms of the bonds. See Book IX, Title I, Chapter 3.

(e) This article applies to bonds in injunction cases, where appeals from such are available. See Art. 3612, *infra*.

(f) Under the Louisiana jurisprudence, only a cost bond is required for a suspensive appeal from a judgment distributing a fund in custodia legis. Blanchin v. Steamer Fashion, 10 La.Ann. 345 (1855); State ex rel. Block v. Rightor, 44 La.Ann. 564, 10 So. 866 (1892); Metropolitan Bank v. Blaise, 109 La. 92, 33 So. 95 (1902); Succession of Jones, 189 La. 693, 180 So. 489 (1938); State ex rel. Messina v. Cage, 152 So. 399 (La.App.1934). And, in such cases when the appellant has sued in forma pauperis where no cost bond is required, the suspensive appeal may be taken without furnishing any bond. Succession of Jones, *supra*; State ex rel. Messina v. Cage, *supra*. These rules of the jurisprudence are not changed by this Code.

(g) See, also, Comments under Arts. 2126, 2252, *infra.*

Art. 2125. Return day

The return day of the appeal shall be fixed by the trial court at not more than sixty days from the date the appeal is granted, but may be extended by the trial court for sufficient cause, on the application of the clerk, or of the deputy clerk preparing the record of appeal.

Source: C.P. Art. 574; former R.S. 13:4437, 13:4438.

Cross References: Arts. 2088, 2642.

Comments

(a) Under the source provisions the judge must fix the return date within the limitations of fifteen to sixty days for the supreme court and the courts of appeal of the first and second circuits, and fifteen to thirty days for the Orleans court of appeal. The above article makes a change in the law by eliminating the minimum limit.

(b) The above article establishes uniformity among the courts of appeal. *Cf.* Art. 2081, *supra*.

(c) This article gives the lower court some control over a case in which an appeal has been perfected. Under Louisiana jurisprudence, it is well settled that a lower court loses all jurisdiction over a case on appeal except as to the appeal bond. Mistich v. Holman, 205 La. 171, 17 So.2d 23 (1944). The above text extends the lower court's jurisdiction to a further point, at least in so far as adjusting the return date on the appeal. See Art. 2088, *supra*. Since the doctrine of the Mistich case and those cases which preceded it is not based upon any constitutional provision, the legislature has the power to extend the jurisdiction of the lower court to the extent provided by this article.

(d) See, also, Comments under Art. 2088, *supra*, and Art. 2127, *infra*.

Art. 2126. Payment of costs

The appellant shall pay to the clerk of the trial court, not later than three days prior to the return day or extended return day, all costs of preparing the record on appeal, and the filing fee required by the appellate court to lodge the appeal.

Source: R.S. 13:4445.

Cross Reference: Art. 2642.

Comments

(a) Under the above article, appeals are expedited, and a number of procedural technicalities are eliminated, which in some instances in the past have defeated the ends of justice. The above article applies generally to all appellate courts the procedure which has worked so well in the courts of appeal, first and second circuits, of imposing the duty of lodging the record of appeal in the appellate court on the clerk of the trial court, and requiring the appellant to pay the clerk of the trial court the filing fee in the appellate court, as well as all costs due the trial court clerk for preparing the record.

(b) Under R.S. 13:4445, which, prior to amendment, was applicable only to the courts of appeal, first and second circuits, the appellant was authorized, but not required, to pay the filing fee of the appellate court to the clerk of the trial court. If he failed to pay this fee to the clerk of the trial court, the appellant had the duty of lodging the record of appeal in the appellate court. Danna v. Yazoo & M. V. R. Co., 154 So. 365 (La.App.1934). Unfortunately, there was no time limit set for the payment of the appellate filing fee to the clerk of the trial court. As a result, even though a timely request for payment of the fee was made upon counsel for the appellant, and he neglected to pay it until after the original return day, the delay in lodging the record of appeal in the appellate court by the clerk of the trial court was not imputable to the appellant. Osborne v. Mossler Acceptance Corporation, 210 La. 1048, 29 So.2d 58 (1946). The case is criticized in 8 La.L.Rev. 272 (1948).

The new statute adopted to implement the above article accords with the latter, and specifies what fees the clerk of the trial court shall charge the appellant. See revised R.S. 13:4445 and 13:4446. Both this statute and the above article are intended to overrule legislatively the unfortunate and unworkable rule of Osborne v. Mossler Acceptance Corporation, *supra*, by: (1) making it the mandatory duty of the appellant to pay these fees to the clerk of the trial court; and (2) requiring such payment to be made not later than three days before the return day, or extended return day. If the appellant fails to pay such fees timely, any delay in lodging the record of appeal in the appellate court is imputable to the appellant.

(c) The last paragraph of Art. 2124, *supra*, gives full protection to the clerk of the trial court on all costs incurred and due him by the appellant for the preparation of the record on appeal.

Art. 2127. Record on appeal; preparation; prepayment of fees

The clerk of the trial court shall have the duty of preparing the record on appeal. He shall cause it to be lodged with the appellate court on or before the return day or any extension thereof, upon the timely payment to him by the appellant of all fees due in connection with the appeal, including the filing fee required by the appellate court to lodge the appeal. Failure of the clerk to prepare and lodge the record on appeal either timely or correctly shall not prejudice the appeal.

Source: C.P. Arts. 585, 883, 884; former R.S. 13:4437.1.

Cross Reference: Art. 2642.

Comments

(a) Although Art. 585 of the 1870 Code of Practice places the duty of preparing the record on appeal upon the clerk of the court from which the appeal was taken, Arts. 587, 883, and 884 indicate that it is the duty of the appellant to have the record lodged on time. It has been held that, in appeals to the supreme court and to the Orleans court of appeal, the responsibility is on the appellant. Cann v. Ruston State Bank, 155 La. 283, 99 So. 221 (1924); Stockbridge v. Martin, 162 La. 601, 110 So. 828 (1926); Gazzo v. Bisso Ferry Co., 174 So. 132 (La.App.1937). However, in appeals to the courts of appeal for the first and second circuits, it has been held that the responsibility is on the clerk. Succession of Bickham, 197 So. 924 (La.App.1940); Wilson v. Lee, 196 So. 373 (La.App. 1940). See 15 Tul.L.Rev. 304 (1941). Art. 2127, above, places the burden on the clerk in all cases.

(b) The last sentence of this article is a necessary supplement to the first sentence. If the whole responsibility for preparing and lodging the record is on the clerk, his negligence should not affect the appeal. See Art. 257, *supra*.

(c) The three day period of grace allowed by Art. 883 of the 1870 Code is unnecessary in view of the last sentence of this article. The clerk himself can obtain an extension of the return day.

(d) The above article uses the phrase "record on appeal" to describe the matter which is sent to the appellate court. The record on appeal includes copies of the pleadings, extracts from the minutes of the court, transcript of the testimony, bills of exception, instructions to juries, judgments and other rulings. The parties may designate what the record shall contain. See Art. 2128, *infra*.

(e) Art. 899, Code of Practice of 1870, requiring the judge or clerk to complete the record, and Art. 900 of the 1870 Code, requiring the judge to give a statement of facts or to sign exceptions from his opinion, are unnecessary in view of the full responsibility placed upon the clerk to see that the entire record is lodged in the appellate court.

Art. 2128. Same; determination of content

The form and content of the record on appeal shall be in accordance with the rules of the appellate court, except as provided in the constitution. However, within three days, exclusive of holidays, after taking the appeal the appellant may designate in a writing filed with the trial court such portions of the record which he desires to constitute the record on appeal. Within five days, exclusive of holidays, after service of a copy of this designation on the other party, that party may also designate in a writing filed with the trial court such other portions of the record as he considers necessary. In such cases the clerk shall prepare the record on appeal as so directed, but a party or the trial court may cause to be filed thereafter any omitted portion of the record as a supplemental record. When no designation is made, the record shall be a transcript of all the proceedings as well as all documents filed in the trial court.

Source: C.P. Art. 585; former R.S. 13:4443.

Cross Reference: Art. 2642.

Comments

(a) Former R.S. 13:4443 establishes the praecipe idea of preparing the record on appeal, *i. e.*, a designation by both parties in the absence of which the clerk prepares the record "as the law directs." Art. 585 of the 1870 Code of Practice states that the record shall be "a transcript of all the proceedings, as well as of all documents filed in the suit." However, Rule I of the supreme court rules establishes very detailed instructions as to what the form and content of the record on appeal shall be. In order to obtain flexibility, it is administratively sound to have the Code refer to the supreme court rules as to form and content of the record.

(b) The proviso in the first sentence of the above article has particular reference to Const. Art. VII, § 27, which requires that all cases on appeal to the courts of appeal shall be tried on the original record, pleadings, and evidence.

(c) The second concept embodied in this article regarding the designation of the record is taken directly from former R.S. 13:4443. However, a change was made in that this article allows a supplemental record to be filed by a "party or the trial court," whereas former R.S. 13:4443 required that it be filed by the parties and the court.

(d) Former R.S. 13:4439 provided for preparation of the record on appeal in triplicate. This was unnecessary in view of the supreme court's Rule I, and has been repealed. The supreme court determines the number of copies desired. With regard to the courts of appeal, this is also fixed by Const. Art. VII, § 27.

(e) See, also, Comments under Arts. 2088, 2127, *supra*.

Art. 2129. Assignment of errors unnecessary; exception

An assignment of errors is not necessary in any appeal. Where the appellant designates only portions of the record as the record on appeal, he must serve with his designation a concise statement of the points on which he intends to rely, and the appeal shall be limited to those points.

Source: Fed.Rule 75(d); cf. C.P. Arts. 896, 897.

Cross Reference: Art. 2642.

Comment

The jurisprudence has construed Arts. 896 and 897, Code of Practice of 1870, to the effect that where the transcript is certified as containing all the testimony and the grounds for reversal are apparent from the face of the record, no assignment of errors is necessary. Bossier v. Caradine, 18 La.Ann. 261 (1866); In re Fazende, 35 La.Ann. 1145 (1883); Havana American Co. v. Board of Assessors, 105 La. 471, 29 So. 938 (1901).

Art. 2130. Record on appeal; statement of facts

A party may require the clerk to cause the testimony to be taken down in writing and this transcript shall serve as the statement of facts of the case. The parties may agree to a narrative of the facts in accordance with the provisions of Article 2131.

Source: C.P. Art. 601.

Cross Reference: Art. 2642.

Comment to Arts. 2130 and 2131

Arts. 2130 and 2131, herein, are a consolidation of the systems set up by Arts. 601–603 of the 1870 Code of Practice, with the distinction, under the articles of this Code, that the trial court judge may make a narrative of the facts at any time prior to the lodging of the record in the appellate court. Under the 1870 Code the judge lost jurisdiction to settle the narrative of facts as soon as the appeal was perfected. Davis v. Ungerman, 150 So. 401 (La. App.1933). *Cf.* Comment (c), Art. 2125, *supra*.

Art. 2131. Same; narrative of facts

If the testimony of the witnesses has not been taken down in writing the appellant must request the other parties to join with him in a written and signed narrative of the facts, and in cases of disagreement as to this narrative or of refusal to join in it, at any time prior to the lodging of the record in the appellate court, the judge shall make a written narrative of the facts, which shall be conclusive.

Source: C.P. Arts. 602, 603.

Cross References: Arts. 2088, 2130, 2642.

Comment

See Comment under Art. 2130, *supra*.

Art. 2132. Same; correction

A record on appeal which is incorrect or contains misstatements, irregularities or informalities, or which omits a material part of the trial record, may be corrected even after the record is transmitted to the appellate court, by the parties by stipulation, by the trial court or by the order of the appellate court. All other questions as to the content and form of the record shall be presented to the appellate court.

Source: Fed.Rule 75(h); cf. C.P. Art. 898; R.S. 13:4433.

Cross References: Arts. 2088, 2642.

Comments

(a) The purpose of this article is to assure that the record on appeal is correct, irrespective of why or by whose fault it is found to be inaccurate. In all cases, the record should represent the truth.

(b) Fed. Rule 75(h) has been followed in part, but the above article is broader in that it allows the correction of irregularities and informalities as well as omissions and misstatements.

Art. 2133. Answer of appellee; when necessary

An appellee shall not be obliged to answer the appeal unless he desires to have the judgment modified, revised, or reversed in part or unless he demands damages against the appellant. In such cases, he must file an answer to the appeal, stating the relief demanded, not later than fifteen days after the return day or the lodging of the record, whichever is later. The answer filed by the appellee shall be equivalent to an appeal on his part from any portion of the judgment rendered against him and of which he complains in his answer.

Source: C.P. Arts. 591, 592, 886–891.

Cross Reference: Art. 2642.

Comments

(a) Arts. 591 and 592 of the 1870 Code of Practice seem to require an answer by appellee in all cases. Likewise, Arts. 886 through 889 of the 1870 Code seem to contemplate a formal answer by appellee even if he merely seeks confirmation of the judgment as rendered. However, all of these articles are negated by Arts. 890 and 891 of the 1870 Code. The result is that no answer by appellee is required under Louisiana law unless the appellee desires some modification of the judgment or damages for a frivolous appeal. The above article preserves the system set up by the 1870 Code. It may be noted that the courts adhere strictly to the time limitation on filing the answer. Ford v. Leonard Truck Lines, 26 So.2d 309 (La.App.1946).

(b) Under Louisiana jurisprudence if an appellant takes a limited appeal, this does not preclude the appellee from raising any other points on appeal by answer, even though such points are not embraced in the appellant's appeal as taken. Allengi v. Hartford Acc. & Indemnity Co., 183 La. 847, 165 So. 8 (1935); Shreveport v. Kahn, 194 La. 55, 193 So. 461 (1939). The above article is declaratory of this jurisprudential rule.

However, there is a division of authority on the question of whether defendant's answer to plaintiff's appeal brings up for appellate review a reconventional demand rejected by the lower court. Earlier cases held that in such a case, a distinct appeal by the defendant was necessary. The later cases take the position that an answer to the appeal is sufficient. See cases cited in McMahon 1023, n. 180. The above article is declaratory of the rule of the later cases.

(c) Art. 890 of the Code of Practice of 1870 required that the answer to an appeal be filed at least three days before the argument, and in the circuit courts of appeal permitted this answer to be filed prior to argument within the first three days of the term. This rule caused difficulty, as it permitted the answer to the appeal to be filed after the briefs had been filed, and usually required the appellant to file another brief in reply to the issues raised in the answer to the appeal.

For this reason, the above article requires the answer to the appeal to be filed "not later than fifteen days after the return day or the lodging of the record, whichever is later."

(d) See, also, Comments under Art. 2164, *infra*.

CHAPTER 3. PROCEDURE IN APPELLATE COURT

Art.
2161. Dismissal for irregularities.
2162. Dismissal by consent of parties, or because of lack of jurisdiction or right to appeal, or abandonment; transfer.
2163. Peremptory exception filed in appellate court; remand if prescription pleaded.
2164. Scope of appeal and action to be taken; costs.
2165. Dismissal of appeal for want of prosecution.
2166. Rehearing.
2167. Finality of judgment.

Art. 2161. Dismissal for irregularities

An appeal shall not be dismissed because of any irregularity, error, or defect unless it is imputable to the appellant. Except as provided

Art. 2161

in Article 2162, a motion to dismiss an appeal because of any irregularity, error, or defect which is imputable to the appellant must be filed within three days, exclusive of holidays, of the return day or the date on which the record on appeal is lodged in the appellate court, whichever is later.

Source: C.P. Art. 898; R.S. 13:4433.

Cross Reference: Art. 2642.

Comment

The above article makes no change in the law. See Comment (a) under Art. 2162, *infra*.

Art. 2162. Dismissal by consent of parties, or because of lack of jurisdiction or right to appeal, or abandonment; transfer

An appeal can be dismissed at any time by consent of all parties, or for lack of jurisdiction of the appellate court, or because there is no right to appeal, or if, under the rules of the appellate court, the appeal has been abandoned.

If an appeal is taken to an appellate court which has no jurisdiction over it, the court may transfer the appeal to the proper court, upon such terms and conditions as it may prescribe. If an appeal is transferred to the supreme court in error, the supreme court may transfer or retransfer it to the proper court.

Source: New; cf. former R.S. 13:4441.

Cross References: Arts. 2161, 2642.

Comments

(a) The first paragraph of the above article makes no change in the law. Cases illustrating the application of Art. 2161, *supra*, and the first paragraph of the above article are collected in McMahon (1956 Supp.) 198, n. 26.3.

(b) The second paragraph of the above article is broader than its indirect source provision. The latter authorized transfers only between the supreme court and the courts of appeal. See State v. Ginalva, 165 La. 304, 115 So. 571 (1928). Under the broad language of the above article a transfer by the supreme court to a district court, or vice versa, is authorized. Under the broad language of the above article, the supreme court may retransfer any appeal transferred to it in error.

(c) See, also, Comments under Art. 2164, *infra*.

Art. 2163. Peremptory exception filed in appellate court; remand if prescription pleaded

The appellate court may consider the peremptory exception filed for the first time in that court, if pleaded prior to a submission of the case for a decision, and if proof of the ground of the exception appears of record.

If the ground for the peremptory exception pleaded in the appellate court is prescription, the plaintiff may demand that the case be remanded to the trial court for trial of the exception.

Source: C.P. Art. 902.

Cross Reference: Art. 2642.

Comment

This article makes no change in the law, and is merely declaratory of the jurisprudence interpreting its source provision. See Gregory v. Hardwick, 218 La. 346, 49 So.2d 423 (1950); Succession of Douglass, 225 La. 65, 72 So.2d 262 (1954); and 15 La.L.Rev. 376, 393 (1955).

See, also, Comments under Arts. 928, 931, 2083, *supra*, and Art. 2164, *infra*.

Art. 2164. Scope of appeal and action to be taken; costs

The appellate court shall render any judgment which is just, legal, and proper upon the record on appeal. The court may award damages for frivolous appeal; and may tax the costs of the lower or appellate court, or any part thereof, against any party to the suit, as in its judgment may be considered equitable.

Source: Former R.S. 13:4444; cf. C. P. Arts. 894–897, 902, 905–907.

Cross References: Arts. 2642, 5188.

Comments

(a) The purpose of this article is to give the appellate court complete freedom to do justice on the record irrespective of whether a particular legal point or theory was made, argued, or passed on by the court below. This article insures that the "theory of a case" doctrine, which has served to introduce the worst features of the common law writ system into Louisiana is not applicable to appeals under this Code. See Hubert, The Theory of a Case in Louisiana, 24 Tul.L.Rev. 66 (1949).

(b) See Comment (b) to Art. 2133, *supra*, regarding reconventional demands.

(c) The above text is broad enough to permit affirmance in full and all revisions and modifications, as well as reversals or remandings. Hence, Arts. 905 and 906 of the 1870 Code, which specifically recognize those matters, seem unnecessary.

(d) Art. 902, Code of Practice of 1870, provides that in reversing a judgment the supreme court is to pronounce judgment on the case if it is able to do so, otherwise the case is to be reversed and remanded in accordance with Art. 906. Since Art. 2082, *supra*, is broad enough to cover the idea of remand, this procedure is adequately covered by this Code.

(e) The clause of this article which deals with damages for frivolous appeals is necessary to include the idea of Art. 907, Code of Practice of 1870. Art. 907 also dealt with costs, but this was omitted here because revised R.S. 13:4531 provides that appellant shall be primarily liable for costs. Furthermore, the above article gives the court discretion to award costs as it shall consider equitable. Art. 907 of the 1870 Code also spelled out the basis for the amount of damages for frivolous appeal (*i. e.*, damages caused by delay) and fixed a maximum of ten percent. Under the above article the scope of damages is broadened to other than money judgments.

(f) Art. 908 of the 1870 Code provided that in the case of reversal the appellee is to pay the costs. This would appear to be adequately covered by former R.S. 13:4531, which provides that on appeal the appellant is primarily liable for costs, and the appellee shall never be called on to pay the costs "unless he is condemned therefor by judgment on the appeal." The provision of former R.S. 13:4444 to the effect that appellate courts may tax costs as they deem equitable has been incorporated into the above article.

(g) See, also, Comments under Art. 2082, *supra*.

Art. 2165. Dismissal of appeal for want of prosecution

If five years elapse without any steps being taken in the prosecution of an appeal in the appellate court, the appeal shall be considered abandoned and shall be dismissed summarily.

Source: C.C. Art. 3519.

Cross Reference: Art. 2642.

Art. 2166. Rehearing

Within fourteen days of rendition of the judgment, in term time or out, a party may apply to the court for a rehearing. The court may act upon the application at any time.

In the courts of appeal the delay for applying for a rehearing commences to run the day after notice of the judgment has been given by the court to counsel of record in the case.

Source: Former R.S. 13:4446; La.Supreme Court Rule XII, § 1; Const. Art. VII, § 24.

Cross Reference: Art. 2642.

Comments

(a) This article is a consolidation of the source provisions. For the reason for the adoption of the supreme court rule, see 15 La.L.Rev. 49 (1954).

(b) Prior to 1958, the former Court of Appeal for the Parish of Orleans was not required to give notice of the rendition of its decisions to counsel of record, and the delay for applying for a rehearing commenced to run the day after the decision. Former R. S. 13:4446. Under Art. VII, § 24, of the Constitution, as amended in 1958, all courts of appeal are required to give such notice, so that the procedure is now uniform.

(c) The judgments of appellate courts become final and executory as provided in Art. 2167, *infra*.

Art. 2167. Finality of judgment

A judgment of an appellate court becomes final and executory when the delay for applying for a rehearing has expired and no application therefor has been made.

When an application for a rehearing has been applied for timely:

(1) A judgment of the supreme court becomes final and executory when this application is denied; and

(2) A judgment of a court of appeal becomes final and executory when the supreme court denies a timely application for a writ of certiorari in the case; or on the expiration of thirty days after the denial of a rehearing by the court of appeal, if no timely application has been made to the supreme court for a writ of certiorari.

Source: Former R.S. 13:4446; Const. Art. VII, § 11.

Cross Reference: Art. 2642.

Comments

(a) See Art. 5059, *infra*, relative to the calculation of delays.

(b) The above article is substantially the same as the Revised Statutes source provision, except that the time for applying for a rehearing applicable to appeals from the city courts of New Orleans to the Orleans court of appeal has not been retained.

(c) See, also, Comments under Art. 2166, *supra*

TITLE II

SUPERVISORY PROCEDURE

Art.
2201. Supervisory writs.

Art. 2201. Supervisory writs

Supervisory writs may be applied for and granted in accordance with the constitution and rules of the supreme court and other courts exercising appellate jurisdiction.

Source: Const. Art. VII, § 2.

Comment

This article represents the decision to eliminate from the procedural code all regulation of the supreme court's constitutionally granted supervisory power. Arts. 845, 846, and 857 of the 1870 Code, therefore, have been deleted as obsolete. *Cf.* Keegan v. Board of Commissioners, 154 La. 639, 98 So. 50 (1923).

BOOK IV
EXECUTION OF JUDGMENTS

INTRODUCTION

The 1870 Code of Practice, numerous statutes, and a large body of jurisprudence embody the law on execution of judgments which covers the collection of money judgments; the enforcement of other types of judgments, such as judgments for possession and specific performance; and, finally, the execution of foreign judgments.

The four articles of Title I, General Dispositions, apply to the enforcement of all judgments, and deal with the procedure for enforcing judgments of appellate courts, the delay for suspending execution pending appeal, the issuance of writs by the clerk and the sheriff's return.

The enforcement of money judgments by the writ of fieri facias is covered by Arts. 2291 through 2456. Among these are seven articles on garnishment and six articles on examination of the judgment debtor.

Only four articles are concerned with judgments other than money judgments. The last article is the only one on foreign judgments, a topic which heretofore has been covered in Louisiana by jurisprudence only.

TITLE I

GENERAL DISPOSITIONS

Art.
2251. Execution only in trial court; appellate court judgment.
2252. Delay before proceeding with execution.
2253. Writ from clerk to sheriff.
2254. Execution by sheriff; return.

Art. 2251. Execution only in trial court; appellate court judgment

A judgment can be executed only by a trial court.

A party seeking to execute a judgment of an appellate court must first file a certified copy with the clerk of the trial court. This filing may be made without prior notice to the adverse party.

Source: C.P. Arts. 617–621, 623, 915.

Comments

(a) Unnecessary language has been eliminated from the source provisions. For example, that portion of Art. 620, Code of Practice of 1870, giving the clerk power to receive, file and record judgments of the supreme court and issue process thereon is superfluous since clerks have that power without specific authority.

(b) The district court's functions in connection with recordation of appellate court judgments prior to execution is not changed; such functions are merely ministerial. Trial courts have no discretion to refuse to record appellate court judgments. State ex rel. Villavaso v. Judge of Second Judicial Dist. Ct., 20 La.Ann. 521 (1868); Gajan v. Patout & Burguieres, 135 La. 156, 65 So. 17 (1914).

(c) When a judgment is rendered after a change of venue, under R.S. 13:3276, the clerk of the court returns the file of the proceedings to the parish where the suit originated so that it can be executed there. The above article effects no change in that procedure. Likewise, this article does not affect R.S. 13:4434 through 13:4436, which provide that registry of the decree of an appellate court in the mortgage office creates a judicial mortgage.

(d) Arts. 588 and 589, Code of Practice of 1870, provide that where the appellant fails to file his record timely in the appellate court, the appellee can obtain a certificate from the clerk to the effect that the record has not been brought up, and upon filing the certificate in the district court, have execution issue.

Art. 2127, *supra*, places on the clerk the duty of preparing the record and filing it timely. Thus, the appellant's only duty is to pay the necessary costs, and failure to file a record timely will no longer be a ground for dismissal of an appeal. Therefore, the procedure of procuring a certificate from the appellate court that the record is not filed is no longer necessary.

(e) No mention is made of the execution of judgments rendered by the supreme court in the exercise of its original jurisdiction under Const. Art. VII, § 10. Such judgments are not subject to execution in the ordinary sense of the term, since the court's original jurisdiction extends only to disbarment cases, suits for removal of judges, and questions of fact involving its appellate jurisdiction.

(f) The choice of the term "judgment" for use in this article was the subject of considerable debate and research. Despite the fact that "judgment" and "decree" have been used interchangeably in Louisiana as well as in other jurisdictions as applied to appellate and trial court judgments, "judgment" was considered the more comprehensive term. Therefore, it is used in the above article.

Art. 2252. Delay before proceeding with execution

A judgment creditor may proceed with the execution of a judgment only after the delay for a suspensive appeal therefrom has elapsed.

Source: C.P. Art. 624.

Comments

(a) Art. 624, Code of Practice of 1870, provides, in effect, that no execution can issue until the expiration of the time for taking a suspensive appeal. Arts. 2123 and 2124, *supra*, relate to the suspension of execution of judgments and the requirements for a suspensive appeal bond. Under Art. 2123, *supra*, the delay within which to file the suspensive appeal bond has been increased to fifteen days.

(b) There is jurisprudence to the effect that an execution issued before the expiration of the delay for a suspensive appeal is not ipso facto null; the defendant ratifies the premature execution when he fails to appeal suspensively. Sowle v. Pollard, 14 La. Ann. 287 (1859); Wheeling Pottery Co. v. Levi, 48 La.Ann. 777, 19 So. 752 (1896); O'Keefe & Simpson v. Main Street Pharmacy, 8 La.App. 443 (1927).

A premature seizure under a writ of fieri facias is valid as between the judgment creditor and judgment debtor, but it creates no right in the seizing creditor as against a third person who may levy a seizure which is not premature. Kimber-Murphy Mfg. Co. v. Vestal, Inc., 43 So.2d 508 (La.App.1950). The rules of these cases are not changed by the above article. *Cf.* Art. 2292, *infra*.

(c) Art. 622 of the 1870 Code of Practice provides that judgments not appealable or judgments rendered on confession of judgment may be executed immediately after the close of the term of court. No provision similar to this article has been included because it was considered unnecessary and obsolete.

(d) Where property is sold under a writ of fieri facias and the judgment is subsequently reversed after a devolutive appeal, the validity of the sale is not affected by subsequent reversal of the judgment, and the defendant-appellant's only remedy is to sue the original judgment creditor for the return of the price for which the property was sold. Bomarito v. Barnett Furniture Co., 177 La. 1010, 150 So. 2 (1933); State v. Mutual Inv. Co., 214 La. 356, 37 So.2d 817 (1948). These cases are based upon Art. 578 of the 1870 Code of Practice which provides that a devolutive appeal does not stay the execution of judgment. Arts. 2087 and 2124, *supra*, furnish adequate basis for the retention of the above jurisprudential rule, although no provision similar to Art. 578, Code of Practice of 1870, has been included in this Code.

(e) See, also, Comments under Art. 2292, *infra*.

Art. 2253. Writ from clerk to sheriff

At the request of a judgment creditor, the clerk shall issue a writ bearing his signature, the seal of the court, and the date, and directing the sheriff of the parish where the judgment is to be executed to enforce it in the manner set forth in the writ. Concurrent writs may be directed to sheriffs of several parishes.

Source: C.P. Arts. 625, 626, 628; cf. C.P. Arts. 641–643.

Comments

(a) This article is a consolidation of the source articles. Art. 627 of the 1870 Code of Practice, requiring the sheriff to endorse on the order of execution the date on which it was delivered to him, has been relegated to those articles dealing with the duties of court officers generally. See Art. 324, *supra*.

(b) Art. 629 of the 1870 Code of Practice, which provides that the court, whether appellate or inferior, which has rendered the judgment must take cognizance of the manner of its execution, has been deleted as unnecessary in view of its interpretation by the supreme court as contemplating the exercise of the court's supervisory jurisdiction. Brown v. Pontchartrain Land Co., 49 La.Ann. 1779, 23 So. 292 (1896); Globe Realty Co. v. Vix, 120 La. 95, 44 So. 997 (1907).

(c) Art. 642 of this 1870 Code provides that the writ of fieri facias is directed to the sheriff of the parish where the property is situated and also permits several writs to exist in various parishes at the same time. The last sentence in the above article represents a change in the law in so far as it is made applicable to all types of execution.

(d) Under this article, a judgment rendered in one parish may be executed in another parish by sending the appropriate writ to the sheriff of the parish where the judgment is to be executed.

(e) See, also, Comments under Arts. 2254, 2291, 2416, *infra*.

Art. 2254. Execution by sheriff; return

The sheriff shall proceed promptly to execute the writ and make a return to the clerk who issued it, stating the manner in which it was executed.

Source: C.P. Art. 626.

Comments

Although the source article might have been included in those articles dealing with the duties of court officers generally, it was considered sufficiently important for inclusion in this Title. *Cf.*

Comment (a) under Art. 2253, *supra*. See Art. 2294, *infra*, which requires that a seizure under a writ of fieri facias must be made within one year after the date on which the writ was issued.

See, also, Comments under Art. 324, *supra*, and Art. 2294, *infra*.

TITLE II
MONEY JUDGMENTS

Chap.		Art.
1.	Writ of Fieri Facias	2291
2.	Judicial Sale Under Fieri Facias	2331
3.	The Adjudiciation and Its Effect	2371
4.	Garnishment Under a Writ of Fieri Facias	2411
5.	Examination of Judgment Debtor	2451

CHAPTER 1. WRIT OF FIERI FACIAS

Art.
2291. Money judgment; fieri facias.
2292. Privilege of creditor on seized property; successive seizures.
2293. Notice to judgment debtor.
2294. Time for seizure; return.
2295. Order of sale; sale in globo.
2296. Reduction of excessive seizure.
2297. Alias fieri facias.
2298. Injunction prohibiting sale.
2299. Order prohibiting payment of proceeds of sale.

Art. 2291. Money judgment; fieri facias

A judgment for the payment of money may be executed by a writ of fieri facias directing the seizure and sale of property of the judgment debtor.

Source: C.P.(1825), Arts. 641, 642; cf. C.P. Arts. 641, 642.

Comments

(a) This article is similar to the source articles as they were before amendment. The various additions to the original articles by subsequent legislation are treated elsewhere. See Art. 2253, *supra*, and Arts. 2294 and 2296, *infra*.

(b) The phrase "property of the judgment debtor" is used instead of "property real and personal, rights and credits," as in Art. 642, Code of Practice of 1870. See Art. 5251, *infra*, which defines property.

(c) Arts. 644 and 645, Code of Practice of 1870, are not included in this Code. These articles contain a partial list of the property of debtors which is exempt from seizure. Technically, the question of exemptions from seizure is not one of procedure, and proposed legislation has been submitted recommending that these articles of the 1870 Code of Practice be transferred without change to the Revised Statutes.

Art. 2292. Privilege of creditor on seized property; successive seizures

The seizing creditor, by the mere act of seizure, acquires a privilege on the property seized, which entitles him to a preference over ordinary creditors.

When several seizures of the same property are made by ordinary creditors, the seizing creditors acquire a privilege and are entitled to a preference among themselves according to the order of their seizures.

Source: C.P. Arts. 722, 723.

Comments

(a) This article combines the two source provisions with no change intended. The provision in Art. 722 of the 1870 Code referring to the creditor becoming bankrupt has been omitted because federal law now regulates the effect of bankruptcy on the claims of privileged creditors.

(b) See Art. 5251, *infra*, which defines the term "property."

(c) The provisions of the above article are modified by the provisions of Art. 2252, *supra*. See Comment (b) under Art. 2252.

Art. 2293. Notice to judgment debtor

After the seizure of property, the sheriff shall serve promptly upon the judgment debtor a written notice of the seizure and a list of the property seized, in the manner provided for service of citation.

Source: C.P. Art. 654.

Cross Reference: Art. 2331.

Comments

(a) The source article provides that notice shall be delivered to the debtor in person or left at his place of ordinary residence. The above article effects a change in this respect inasmuch as it provides that service of the notice shall be made in the manner provided for service of citation.

(b) A sale without notice of seizure is null. Lamorandier v. Meyer, 8 Rob. 152 (La.1844); Birch v. Bates, 22 La.Ann. 198 (1867); Graff v. Moylan, 28 La.Ann. 75 (1873). Under certain conditions the nullity may be cured by the prescription of five years. R.S. 9:5642. There is no intention to change these rules.

Art. 2294. Time for seizure; return

A seizure may be made under a writ of fieri facias only within one year from the date of its issuance.

At the expiration of that time the sheriff shall make a return on the writ unless a seizure has been made within the time. If a seizure has been made the sheriff shall proceed with the sale and thereupon make a return.

Source: C.P. Arts. 642, 700; former R.S. 13:4284, 13:4288.

Comments

(a) This article covers only the exceptional case when property seized by the sheriff during the effective life of the writ remains unsold on the expiration of the writ. The normal case of the seizure immediately after the issuance of the writ, and the judicial sale of the property seized within a few weeks thereafter, is covered by Art. 2254, *supra*.

(b) The seizure of property after the expiration of the seventy days fixed by Art. 642 of the 1870 Code of Practice as the return day for the writ of fieri facias is null. Latham v. Glasscock, 160 La. 1089, 108 So. 100 (1926). Thus, the return day actually fixes the expiration date of the writ. Nevertheless, property which has been seized, under the writ within the time permitted, may be sold after the expiration of the return day. Union National Bank v. Hyams, 50 La.Ann. 1110, 24 So. 774 (1898). No change in the rules of the Latham and Union National Bank cases is intended by this article, but the return day is extended by the increase in the period for valid seizure from seventy days to one year. *Cf.* Art. 2254, *supra*, which orders the sheriff to proceed promptly to execute the writ.

(c) Under Art. 642, Code of Practice of 1870, when the writ of fieri facias is returned before property seized under the writ has been sold, the sheriff, except in Orleans Parish, makes and retains a copy of the writ duly certified by himself, under which he proceeds to sell the property. This article simplifies the procedure by permitting the sheriff to make his return on the original writ after the sale of the property—thus eliminating the necessity for a return of the original writ on its expiration, the retention of a certified copy thereof, and a return on the latter after the sale.

(d) *Cf.* Art. 2343, *infra*, and Comment thereunder.

(e) See, also, Comments under Arts. 2254, 2291, *supra*, and Art. 2343, *infra*.

Art. 2295. Order of sale; sale in globo

If several items of property have been seized, or if one item of property which is divisible into portions has been seized, the judgment debtor, at any time prior to the first advertisement, may designate the order in which the items or portions of property will be sold, except that the judgment creditor can direct the sale of property on which he has a mortgage, or a privilege other than that resulting from the seizure.

If the judgment debtor does not designate the order of sale, the order of sale shall be at the discretion of the sheriff.

When property is offered by items or portions and the total price bid is insufficient to satisfy the judgment, with interest and costs, or if the judgment debtor so requests, the property shall be offered in globo and thus sold if a higher bid is obtained.

Source: C.P. Arts. 646 650, 676.

Comments

(a) Many states have statutes similar to the source articles permitting judgment debtors to designate which of the property seized shall be sold first.

(b) The requirement that the sheriff seize corporeal movables before immovables, and incorporeals only in the absence of corporeals has not been carried forward in these articles.

(c) Most of the source provisions give the judgment debtor the right to regulate the order of seizure prior to advertisement. This article gives the judgment debtor the right to regulate the order of sale at any time prior to the first advertisement.

(d) The third paragraph is new. The debtor's right to direct whether the property is to be sold separately or in globo is made to depend on the amount of the bids.

(e) This article governs the rights of the debtor only with respect to the sale of property seized under a single writ, and is not designed to give him the right to designate which of several successive seizures under other writs should be concluded first.

(f) See, also, Comments under Art. 2296, *infra*.

Art. 2296. Reduction of excessive seizure

If several items of property have been seized, or if one item of property which is divisible into portions has been seized, and if the value of the property seized exceeds what is reasonably necessary to satisfy the judgment, including interest and costs, the judgment debtor may obtain the release of the excess items or portion by contradictory motion filed not less than ten days before the day fixed for the sale.

Art. 2296. EXECUTION OF JUDGMENTS

The judgment debtor may not obtain the release of property on which the judgment creditor has a mortgage, or a privilege other than that resulting from the seizure.

Source: C.P. Arts. 642, 651–653.

Comments

(a) The above article is similar to Art. 3505, *infra*, providing for the reduction of excessive seizure under writs of attachment or sequestration. The source articles provide that the judge must determine the question of excessiveness vel non from the appraisal of the seized property. Under the above article, the judge may utilize appraisers as well as any other competent proof on trial of the motion.

(b) This article requires the motion to reduce to be filed at least ten days before the day fixed for the sale. This is more workable than the rule of Art. 653 of the 1870 Code, which permits the motion to be filed *at any time* before the day of the sale. Ten days best accomplishes the dual result desired: (1) to give the defendant as much time as possible to file the motion to reduce the seizure; and (2) to provide sufficient time to permit the court to dispose of the motion before the date fixed for the sale of the property. The debtor has at least three days after the notice of seizure within which to file the motion inasmuch as the sale cannot be fixed until ten days after the first advertisement, which cannot be placed until three days after service of the notice of seizure.

(c) Art. 2295, *supra*, contains a provision similar to the last sentence of this article. There is nothing in the 1870 Code or the Revised Statutes which deprives the debtor of his right to release the excess seizure where the property seized is subject to a mortgage or privilege.

(d) Under the 1870 Code an excessive seizure did not authorize an injunction to suspend the sale; the remedy was a reduction under Arts. 652 and 653, Code of Practice of 1870. Dabbs v. Hemken, 3 Rob. 123 (1842); Grenier v. Guillebert, 146 La. 277, 83 So. 553 (1920). The above article provides for a reduction action by means of a contradictory motion to reduce.

(e) See, also, Comments under Art. 2291, *supra* and Art. 4607, *infra*.

Art. 2297. Alias fieri facias

After a writ of fieri facias has been returned unsatisfied, another writ of fieri facias may be issued.

Source: Cf. C.P. Art. 728.

Comment

The source article applies to the imprisonment of the debtor on a money judgment. Although there are no particular provisions in the 1870 Code permitting an alias fieri facias, the right to such a writ is recognized. Marine Bank & Trust Co. v. Shaffer, 166 La. 164, 116 So. 838 (1928). There is no limitation on the number of writs of fieri facias which can be issued, and none is intended.

Art. 2298. Injunction prohibiting sale

Injunctive relief prohibiting the sheriff from proceeding with the sale of property seized under a writ of fieri facias shall be granted to the judgment debtor or to a third person claiming ownership of the seized property:

(1) When the sheriff is proceeding with the execution contrary to law;

(2) When subsequent to the judgment payment has been made, or compensation has taken place against the judgment, or it has been otherwise extinguished. If the payment, compensation, or extinguishment is for a part of the judgment, the injunction shall be granted to that extent, and the execution shall continue for the amount of the excess;

(3) When the judgment is for the payment of the purchase price of property sold to the judgment debtor and a suit for recovery of the property has been filed by an adverse claimant; or

(4) When the judgment sought to be executed is absolutely null.

Source: C.P. Arts. 298(7), 298(9), 298(10), 303, 739.

Comments

(a) The requirements of a bond and affidavit and the general procedure for issuing an injunction are set forth in Arts. 3601 through 3613, *infra*. Those provisions apply to all types of injunction, including those issued under this article.

(b) Art. 1092, *supra*, permits injunctive relief to third persons claiming ownership of seized property. The above article makes such an injunction mandatory, as does Art. 298 of the 1870 Code.

(c) The last part of Art. 298(10), Code of Practice of 1870, provides that where the injunction is based upon payment or compensation, the judge shall demand a bond in an amount double the amount of the alleged payment or set-off. This has been omitted because the general injunction articles require a bond in an amount within the court's discretion.

(d) Art. 2298(4) is new. It is based upon the recognized rule that where a judgment is absolutely null, its execution may be suspended by injunction. McInnis v. Wingate, 138 La. 682, 70 So. 610 (1916).

(e) Art. 739, Code of Practice of 1870, lists the various grounds upon which a sale under executory process may be enjoined. Some of those grounds are not included in Art. 298 of the 1870 Code, but should be available to a judgment debtor. Therefore, the language "or the debt has been otherwise extinguished" was added to the above article. Other grounds listed in Art. 739 of the 1870 Code, such as prescription of the original debt, are obviously unavailable after judgment. *Cf.* Arts. 2376 through 2378, *infra*.

(f) See, also, Comments under Art. 2299, *infra*.

Art. 2299. Order prohibiting payment of proceeds of sale

A third person claiming a privilege superior to that of the seizing creditor, may intervene and obtain a court order prohibiting the sheriff from paying to the judgment creditor a sum more than necessary to satisfy intervener.

Source: C.P. Arts. 300, 301.

Comments

(a) This article is permissive, thus retaining the provisions of Art. 300, Code of Practice of 1870. In this respect it differs from Art. 2298, *supra*, which is mandatory.

(b) Under this article, if the intervener claims a portion of the proceeds only, the payment of the balance should not be prohibited

(c) Art. 301, Code of Practice of 1870, appears to confer upon an ordinary creditor the right to an injunction against payment of the proceeds, but it has been interpreted as applying only to a creditor claiming a higher privilege than that of the seizing creditor. Thompson v. Daniel, 47 La.Ann. 1401, 17 So. 830 (1895).

See, also, Comments under Art. 3601, *infra*.

CHAPTER 2. JUDICIAL SALE UNDER FIERI FACIAS

Art.
2331. Publication of notice of sale.
2332. Appraisal.
2333. Sale of perishable property.
2334. Reading of advertisement and certificates.
2335. Superior mortgage or privilege.

Tit. 2   JUDICIAL SALE—FIERI FACIAS   Art. 2332

Art.
2336. Minimum price; second offering, if bid is less than two-thirds of appraised value.
2337. Price insufficient to discharge superior privileges; property not sold.
2338. Judgment creditor having superior privilege; price insufficient to satisfy inferior mortgage.
2339. Judgment debtor and creditor may bid.
2340. Payment of debt prior to adjudication.
2341. Sale when installment not due.
2342. Act of sale by sheriff.
2343. Sheriff's return after sale.

Art. 2331.   Publication of notice of sale

Notice of the sale of property under a writ of fieri facias shall be published at least once for movable property, and at least twice for immovable property, in the manner provided by law. The court may order additional publications.

The sheriff shall not order the advertisement of the sale of the property seized until three days, exclusive of holidays, have elapsed after service on the judgment debtor of the notice of seizure, as provided in Article 2293.

Source: New; cf. C.P. Arts. 655, 667, 670.

Cross Reference: Art. 2722.

Comments

(a) Art. 2293, *supra*, requires the sheriff to serve notice of seizure on the judgment debtor immediately after the seizure.

(b) Art. 670 of the 1870 Code of Practice, as construed by the courts, required three advertisements in a period of ten days for movables, and one advertisement a week for thirty days for immovables. This article reduces the number of judicial advertisements required in both cases. In the majority of cases one advertisement for movables, and two for immovables suffices. If, in any case, this number would not be sufficient, the court is authorized to increase the number of publications on motion of any interested party. The manner in which these notices must be published is provided in R.S. 43:203.

(c) See, also, Comments under Arts. 3264, 4607, *infra*.

Art. 2332.   Appraisal

The property seized must be appraised according to law prior to the sale.

Source: C.P. Arts. 671–676.

1 LSA–C.C.P.—23

Comment

This is the only provision dealing with appraisement included in this Code. The detailed provisions of Arts. 671 through 676, Code of Practice of 1870, regarding the procedure for the appointment of appraisers, have been transferred to the Revised Statutes.

Art. 2333. Sale of perishable property

The court, at the request of a party, may order the immediate sale at public auction, without advertisement or appraisement, of property that is perishable and subject to loss or deterioration pending compliance with the usual formalities. Notice of the time and place of the sale shall be given to all parties. The property shall be sold for cash to the highest bidder.

Source: C.P. Art. 261; former R.S. 13:4342.

Cross References: Arts. 2503, 2724, 3513.

Comment

Under Art. 261, Code of Practice of 1870, perishable property seized under attachment is required to be advertised before sale. However, former R.S. 13:4342, which regulates the sale of perishable property seized under writs of sequestration or fieri facias, provides for sale of the property without appraisement or advertisement, and the above article follows the Revised Statutes section in that it also dispenses with the requirements of appraisement or advertisement.

Art. 2334. Reading of advertisement and certificates

At the time and place designated for the sale, the sheriff shall read aloud the advertisement describing the property, and shall read aloud a mortgage certificate and any other certificate required by law.

Source: C.P. Arts. 677, 678.

Cross Reference: Art. 2724.

Comments

(a) The special provisions of Art. 678, Code of Practice of 1870, requiring the sheriff of Orleans Parish to read a conveyance certificate prior to the sale, has been omitted. Legislation has been submitted proposing that this provision and the requirement that the sheriff obtain a certificate from the vehicle commissioner when the property to be sold consists of motor vehicles subject to registration be transferred to the Revised Statutes.

Tit. 2   JUDICIAL SALE—FIERI FACIAS   **Art. 2337**

(b) The phrase "any other certificate required by law" has reference to the certificates referred to in Comment (a), *supra*.

(c) See, also, Comments under Art. 2372, *infra*.

Art. 2335. Superior mortgage or privilege

The sheriff shall announce that the property is to be sold for cash subject to any mortgage, lien, or privilege thereon superior to that of the seizing creditor.

Source: C.P. Arts. 679, 683.

Cross Reference: Art. 2724.

Comments

The provisions of Art. 683, Code of Practice of 1870, authorizing the judgment creditor "to subscribe his obligation at twelve months' credit" for the balance over and above the amount necessary to discharge superior privileges and mortgages, has been deleted on the grounds that there is no reason why the sale should not be made for cash.

See, also, Comments under Art. 2336, *infra*.

Art. 2336. Minimum price; second offering, if bid is less than two-thirds of appraised value

The property shall not be sold if the price bid by the highest bidder is less than two-thirds of the appraised value. In that event, the sheriff shall re-advertise the sale of the property in the same manner as for an original sale, and the same delay must elapse. At the second offering, the property shall be sold for cash for whatever it will bring, except as provided in Article 2337.

Source: C.P. Arts. 680, 682.

Cross Reference: Art. 2375.

Comment

This article changes the law in two respects. It abolishes the twelve months' credit sale procedure, and it increases to thirty days the time that must elapse between the first and second offering of immovables. See Comment under Art. 2335, *supra*.

Art. 2337. Price insufficient to discharge superior privileges; property not sold

If the price offered by the highest bidder at the first or subsequent offering is not sufficient to discharge the costs of the sale and the

Art. 2337.

mortgages, liens, and privileges superior to that of the seizing creditor, the property shall not be sold.

Source: C.P. Art. 684.

Cross References: Arts. 2336, 2724.

Comment

Although the source article makes no reference to the "costs of the sale," it would appear that the bid has to be sufficient to pay whatever costs are incurred over and above those advanced by the seizing creditor. The reason for this is that the claim of a superior mortgage holder cannot be reduced.

Art. 2338. Judgment creditor having superior privilege; price insufficient to satisfy inferior mortgage

If the mortgage, lien, or privilege of the seizing creditor is superior to other mortgages, liens, and privileges on the property, he may require that the property be sold, even though the price is not sufficient to satisfy his or the inferior mortgages, liens, and privileges.

Source: C.P. Art. 685.

Cross Reference: Art. 2724.

Art. 2339. Judgment debtor and creditor may bid

The judgment debtor and the seizing creditor may bid for the property.

Source: C.P. Art. 688.

Cross Reference: Art. 2724.

Art. 2340. Payment of debt prior to adjudication

The sale of the property may be prevented at any time prior to the adjudication by payment to the sheriff of the judgment, with interest and costs.

Source: C.P. Art. 663.

Cross Reference: Art. 2724.

Art. 2341. Sale when installment not due

When the seizing creditor has a mortgage, lien, or privilege on the property seized, for a debt of which all the installments are not due, he may demand that the property be sold for the entire debt, on the same terms for the payment of unmatured installments as provided in the original contract.

Source: C.P. Art. 686.

Cross Reference: Art. 2724.

Comment

The above provisions, found in the 1870 Code, have been retained to provide for such payments in the absence of an acceleration clause. As a practical matter, the widespread use of acceleration clauses has resulted in infrequent reference to Art. 686 of the 1870 Code.

Art. 2342. Act of sale by sheriff

Within five days after the adjudication, the sheriff shall pass an act of sale to the purchaser, in the manner and form provided by law.

The act of sale adds nothing to the force and effect of the adjudication, but is only intended to afford proof of it.

Source: C.P. Arts. 691, 695.

Cross Reference: Art. 2724.

Comment

This article is a combination of the first paragraphs of each of the source articles. No change was made except to extend from three to five days the period within which the act of sale is to be passed.

Art. 2343. Sheriff's return after sale

The sheriff shall make a signed return to the clerk who issued the writ, showing that all formalities have been complied with and stating the manner in which the writ was executed, a description of the property sold, the name of the purchaser, the purchase price, and the disposition thereof.

Source: C.P. Arts. 700–702.

Cross Reference: Art. 2724.

Comments

In the event the sale is completed before the expiration of the period within which a seizure may be effected, the details specified in the above article must be shown on the initial return.

See, also, Comments under Arts. 324, 2294, *supra*.

CHAPTER 3. THE ADJUDICATION AND ITS EFFECT

Art.
2371. Effect of adjudication.
2372. Sale subject to superior real charge or lease.
2373. Distribution of proceeds of sale.
2374. Property subject to superior mortgage; payment of price.
2375. Purchaser's liability; property subject to inferior mortgages.
2376. Release of inferior mortgages.
2377. Inferior mortgages; payment; reference to proceeds.
2378. Enforcement of mortgage or privilege superior to that of seizing creditor.
2379. Rights of buyer in case of eviction.
2380. Loss of recourse when purchaser fails to give judgment debtor timely notice.
2381. Action by seizing creditor who has been compelled to reimburse purchaser.

Art. 2371. Effect of adjudication

The adjudication transfers to the purchaser all the rights and claims of the judgment debtor as completely as if the judgment debtor had sold the property.

Source: C.P. Art. 690; C.C. Art. 2620.

Cross Reference: Art. 2724.

Comment

This article restates the settled rule under the source articles that the purchaser acquires the rights which the judgment debtor had, and no more. Perkins v. Louisiana Land & Exploration Co., 171 La. 913, 132 So. 499 (1931).

Art. 2372. Sale subject to superior real charge or lease

The property is sold subject to any real charge or lease with which it is burdened, superior to any mortgage, lien, or privilege of the seizing creditor.

Source: C.P. Art. 687.

Cross Reference: Art. 2724.

Comment

See Arts. 2334 and 2335, *supra*.

Art. 2373. Distribution of proceeds of sale

After deducting the costs, the sheriff shall first pay the amount due the seizing creditor, then the inferior mortgages, liens, and privileges on the property sold, and shall pay to the debtor whatever surplus may remain.

Source: C.P. Art. 704; former R.S. 13:4284.

Cross Reference: Art. 2724.

Comment

The language in Art. 704, Code of Practice of 1870, prohibiting the sheriff from paying the judgment creditor where he has been judicially enjoined from doing so, has been deleted as unnecessary.

Art. 2374. Property subject to superior mortgage; payment of price

If there is a mortgage, lien, or privilege on the property superior to that of the seizing creditor, the purchaser shall pay to the sheriff only that portion of the sale price which exceeds the amount of the superior mortgage, lien, or privilege.

Source: C.P. Arts. 679, 706.

Cross Reference: Art. 2724.

Comments

(a) Art. 710, Code of Practice of 1870, provides that the fact there is a general mortgage superior to that of the seizing creditor, does not authorize the purchaser to withhold payment of the purchase price, unless he has been evicted or "has just reason to fear eviction." No similar provision has been included in this Code on the theory that the purchaser should be able to protect himself against a general mortgage, just as he does in the case of a conventional mortgage.

(b) Art. 713 of the 1870 Code provides that if the purchaser is compelled to vacate the property on the hypothecary action of a general mortgagee, the purchaser has recourse only against the original judgment debtor and not against the seizing creditor. Under the above article the purchaser withholds payment as long as a prior general mortgage is recorded against the property. Hence, no provision similar to Art. 713 is necessary.

(c) See, also, Comments under Art. 2372, *supra*, and Art. 2378, *infra*.

Art. 2375. Purchaser's liability; property subject to inferior mortgages

The purchaser is liable for nothing beyond the purchase price. He shall pay the full purchase price to the sheriff, despite the existence of a mortgage, lien, or privilege on the property inferior to that of the seizing creditor.

Source: New; cf. C.P. Art. 708.

Cross Reference: Art. 2724.

Comments to Articles 2375 through 2377

Articles 2375 through 2377, herein, introduce a new system of dealing with inferior mortgages. Under Arts. 707 and 708, Code of Practice of 1870, the purchaser pays only the costs and the claim of the seizing creditor, and retains the balance for the payment of the inferior claims. The purchaser may also provoke a rule to refer the inferior claimants to the proceeds and thus obtain a cancellation of the inferior mortgages. Fortier v. Slidell, 7 Rob. 398 (La.1844). The above articles shift the burden of distributing the proceeds to the sheriff, and give the purchaser a clear title in all cases, and are intended to apply to all mortgages, including general mortgages, without restriction.

Art. 2376. Release of inferior mortgages

The sheriff shall give the purchaser a release from the mortgage, lien, or privilege of the seizing creditor, and from all inferior mortgages, liens, and privileges, and he shall direct the recorder of mortgages to cancel their inscriptions in so far as they affect the property sold.

Source: C.P. Art. 708.

Cross Reference: Art. 2724.

Comment

See Comment under Art. 2375, *supra*.

Art. 2377. Inferior mortgages; payment; reference to proceeds

The sheriff shall pay the inferior mortgages, liens, and privileges, after payment of the costs and the amount due the seizing creditor. When the sum remaining after payment of the costs and the amount due the seizing creditor is insufficient to pay such inferior claims in full, the sheriff may deposit the remainder with the court and proceed by contradictory motion against the inferior creditors to have their claims referred to the proceeds of the sale.

Source: New.

Cross Reference: Art. 2724.

Comment

See Comment under Art. 2375, *supra*.

Art. 2378. Enforcement of mortgage or privilege superior to that of seizing creditor

When the purchaser fails to pay a mortgage superior to the mortgage, lien, or privilege of the seizing creditor, the superior mortgage may be enforced under any of the applicable provisions of Articles 3721 through 3743.

When the purchaser fails to pay a lien or privilege superior to the mortgage, lien, or privilege of the seizing creditor, the superior lien or privilege may be enforced in an ordinary proceeding against the purchaser or, if the latter has sold the property, against the then owner thereof.

Source: New; cf. C.P. Art. 709.

Cross Reference: Art. 2724.

Comments

(a) This article covers the situation where an inferior creditor provokes the judicial sale and the purchaser withholds the amount of a superior mortgage or privilege under Art. 2374, *supra*, but fails to pay the superior mortgage or privilege.

(b) The change in the procedural law made in this article was necessary because of the suppression of the hypothecary action properly speaking. See Art. 3741 *et seq.*, *infra*.

Art. 2379. Rights of buyer in case of eviction

The purchaser who has been evicted from property sold under a writ of fieri facias shall have his recourse for reimbursement against the judgment debtor and the seizing creditor. If judgment is obtained against both, the purchaser shall issue execution first against the judgment debtor, and if his judgment remains unsatisfied, he may issue execution against the seizing creditor.

Source: C.P. Art. 711; C.C. Art. 2621.

Cross References: Arts. 2380, 2724.

Comments

(a) The provisions of the source articles, which contain almost identical language, have been retained without substantive change.

(b) It would appear that an actual eviction would not be a condition precedent to the reimbursement of the purchaser. The language used in this article is similar to the warranty provisions of the Civil Code under which an actual eviction is not a prerequisite for the action of the buyer against his vendor. Tennent v. Caffery, 163 La. 976, 113 So. 167 (1927).

Art. 2380. Loss of recourse when purchaser fails to give judgment debtor timely notice

The purchaser shall lose the right granted him by Article 2379 if a suit is filed to evict him and he neglects to notify the judgment debtor in time for him to defend the suit, and if the debtor could have successfully defended the suit.

Source: C.P. Art. 714.

Cross Reference: Art. 2724.

Comment

No change in the law is intended. Civil Code Arts. 2517 and 2518 cover the same subject matter with reference to warranty in conventional sales.

Art. 2381. Action by seizing creditor who has been compelled to reimburse purchaser

The seizing creditor may recover from his judgment debtor whatever he has had to pay to the purchaser who has been evicted.

Source: C.P. Art. 712.

Cross Reference: Art. 2724.

CHAPTER 4. GARNISHMENT UNDER A WRIT OF FIERI FACIAS

Art.
2411. Garnishee; effect of service.
2412. Method of service; delay for answering.
2413. Effect of garnishee's failure to answer.
2414. Notice of answer; traversing.
2415. Delivery of property or payment of indebtedness to sheriff.
2416. Venue of garnishment proceedings.
2417. Garnishment elsewhere than in parish of main action; procedure.

Tit. 2 GARNISHMENT Art. 2412

Art. 2411. Garnishee; effect of service

The judgment creditor, by petition and after the issuance of a writ of fieri facias, may cause a third person to be cited as a garnishee to declare under oath what property he has in his possession or under his control belonging to the judgment debtor and in what amount he is indebted to him, even though the debt may not be due. He may require the third person to answer categorically and under oath the interrogatories annexed to the petition within the delay provided by Article 2412.

The seizure shall take effect upon service of the petition, citation, and interrogatories.

Source: C.P. Arts. 246, 247, 250, 262, 642.

Comments

(a) This article is a consolidation of the source provisions with unnecessary language eliminated.

(b) The requirement for a petition and citation is taken from Arts. 246 and 250, Code of Practice of 1870. Strict compliance with this provision is necessary since a judgment pro confesso against a garnishee who has not been served with the petition for the issuance of garnishment process is null, even though service of the interrogatories has been made. Koningh v. Knecht, 48 So.2d 409 (La.App.1950). The provision of Art. 250 of the 1870 Code authorizing garnishment process to issue by supplemental petition has been omitted as unnecessary. Cf. Book II, Title I, Chapter 7, *supra*.

(c) Although the requirement of verification of ordinary pleadings has been deleted, Art. 863, *supra*, the provisions of Arts. 246 and 247, Code of Practice of 1870, requiring the garnishee's answer to be made under oath, have been retained. Art. 2412, *infra*.

(d) The provisions of Arts. 248 and 249, Code of Practice of 1870, authorizing the arrest of the garnishee, have not been carried forward into this Code since the writ of arrest of the debtor has been abolished.

(e) See, also, Comments under Art. 3503, *infra*.

Art. 2412. Method of service; delay for answering

The sheriff shall serve upon the garnishee the citation and a copy of the petition and of the interrogatories, together with a notice that a seizure is thereby effected against any property of or indebtedness to the judgment debtor.

Service shall be made in the manner provided for service of citation, except that if the garnishee is an individual, service must be personal. If the garnishee has concealed or absented himself with the purpose of avoiding personal service, the court may order that service be made in any other manner provided by law.

The garnishee shall file his sworn answers to the interrogatories within fifteen days from the date of service.

Source: C.P. Arts. 246, 251, 252, 256, 262; former R.S. 13:3471(10).

Cross References: Arts. 2411, 2413.

Comments

The complicated requirements of former R.S. 13:3471(10) relative to service upon corporations, partnerships, and boards have been eliminated by providing that the service of the petition and interrogatories is to be made in the manner provided for service of citation, except where the garnishee is an individual, in which case service must be personal.

See, also, Comments under Arts. 1231, 1232, 1233, *supra*, and Art. 3504, *infra*.

Art. 2413. Effect of garnishee's failure to answer

If the garnishee fails to answer within the delay provided by Article 2412, the judgment creditor may proceed by contradictory motion against the garnishee for the amount of the unpaid judgment, with interest and costs. The failure of the garnishee to answer prior to the filing of such a contradictory motion is prima facie proof that he has property of or is indebted to the judgment debtor to the extent of the judgment, interest, and costs.

Judgment shall be rendered against the garnishee on trial of the motion unless he proves that he had no property of and was not indebted to the judgment debtor. If on the trial of such motion, the garnishee proves the amount of such property or indebtedness, the judgment against the garnishee shall be limited to the delivery of the property or payment of the indebtedness, as provided in Article 2415.

Regardless of the decision on the contradictory motion, the court shall render judgment against the garnishee for the costs and a reasonable attorney's fee for the motion.

Source: New; cf. C.P. Art. 263.

Cross Reference: Art. 2415.

Comments

(a) This article changes the rule announced in Winnfield Furniture Company v. Peyton, 171 La. 519, 131 So. 657 (1930), authorizing the seizing creditor to obtain a judgment pro confesso against the garnishee by ex parte motion, by requiring a contradictory motion before judgment may be rendered against him.

(b) This article also codifies the rule announced in Victoria Lumber Co. v. Woodson, 13 La.App. 30, 127 So. 95 (1930), to the effect that the answers of the garnishee will be effective, if filed at any time before the seizing creditor has taken positive action against him, though he has failed to answer within the time prescribed by law.

(c) The last paragraph of the article relative to costs and attorney's fees is new.

Art. 2414. Notice of answer; traversing

The clerk shall cause written notice of the filing of the garnishee's answer to be served promptly upon the seizing creditor in the manner provided by Article 1314.

Unless the creditor files a contradictory motion traversing the answer of the garnishee within fifteen days after service upon him of the notice of the filing of the garnishee's answer, any property of the judgment debtor in the possession of the garnishee and any indebtedness to the judgment debtor which the garnishee has not admitted holding or owing shall be released from seizure. A new seizure may be made of such property or indebtedness by filing a supplemental petition and serving additional interrogatories.

Source: Former R.S. 13:3911.

Cross Reference: Art. 2415.

Comments

(a) The language in the source provision requiring the service of the notice to the creditor to be made "in the same manner that citations are served in ordinary suits" has been modified to conform with Art. 1314, *supra*, which regulates the method of serving pleadings requiring an appearance or response.

(b) The delay of twenty days given to the creditor for traversing the answers of the garnishee has been reduced to fifteen days to make it uniform with the delays for answering in ordinary suits.

Art. 2415. Delivery of property or payment of indebtedness to sheriff

When the garnishee admits in his answer, or when on trial of a contradictory motion under Article 2413 or Article 2414 it is found that he has in his possession property belonging to the judgment debtor or is indebted to him, the court shall order the garnishee to deliver the property immediately to the sheriff or to pay him the indebtedness when due. Delivery or payment to the sheriff discharges the gar-

Art. 2415 EXECUTION OF JUDGMENTS Bk. 4

nishee's obligation to the judgment debtor to the extent of the delivery or payment.

This article does not apply to garnishment of wages, salaries, or commissions.

Source: C.P. Arts. 246, 264.

Cross Reference: Art. 2413.

Comments

(a) The provision in Art. 264, Code of Practice of 1870, that the garnishee's answers can be disproved "either by positive written proof or by the oath of two witnesses worthy of belief" has been omitted. Any competent proof is sufficient if the court considers it of sufficient weight to prevail over the garnishee's answers.

(b) The last paragraph is necessary because of the specialized procedure contained in the law regulating the garnishment of wages. Cf. R.S. 13:3921 et seq.

Art. 2416. Venue of garnishment proceedings

The venue of a garnishment proceeding under a writ of fieri facias is the parish in which the garnishee may be sued under Article 42.

The venue of a garnishment proceeding under a writ of attachment or sequestration is any parish in which the defendant may be sued.

Source: New; cf. Comments following.

Comments

(a) Heretofore, the venue in garnishment proceedings has not been provided by code or statute. This article codifies the jurisprudential rules announced and applied in E. Marqueze & Co. v. Le Blanc, 29 La.Ann. 194 (1877) and cases cited, with respect to garnishments under the writs of fieri facias and attachment. See also, Manuel Motor Co. v. Gral·m, 69 So.2d 64 (La.App.1953). In view of the broadening of garnishment procedure to permit it to be used also under the writ of sequestration, this article includes the latter in providing rules of venue.

(b) The cross reference in the first paragraph is to the article providing the general rules of venue as to individuals, partnerships, corporations, etc.

(c) The word "defendant" in the second paragraph of this article refers only to the principal debtor who is sued, and not to any of the garnishees. Dependent on the facts of the case, the defendant may be sued in one or more parishes under the applicable provisions of Arts. 41–78, *supra*.

(d) In a nonresident attachment, the suit may be filed in any parish in which property of the defendant may be attached; and supplemental attachments may seize other property of the defendant in other parishes. Kahn & Bigart v. Sippili, 35 La.Ann. 1039 (1883). Hence, the petition in the attachment suit praying for the issuance of garnishment interrogatories may be filed at the domicile of the garnishee, and supplemental writs of attachment and garnishment interrogatories may be issued therein, so as to attach property in the hands of other garnishees in different parishes. Kahn & Bigart v. Sippili, *supra*.

(e) The venue for a garnishment proceeding against a nonresident, under a writ of attachment, is provided by Art. 3545, *infra*.

Art. 2417. Garnishment elsewhere than in parish of main action; procedure

Before garnishment proceedings under a writ of fieri facias can be filed in a parish other than that in which the principal action was filed, a writ of fieri facias must first be directed to the sheriff of the parish where the garnishment proceedings are to be filed. The pleadings and procedure shall be the same as if the garnishment were in the same parish as the principal action.

Source: New.

Comment

Where judgment is rendered in one parish and a writ of fieri facias issues to another parish, the clerk simply sends the writ to the sheriff of the parish where it is to be executed. See Art. 2253, *supra*. No pleadings need be filed in the parish where the execution is to take place. However, if there is to be a garnishment in a parish other than where the main action was brought, then the petition for garnishment will have to be filed in that parish, although no prior pleadings have been filed there. See Art. 2782, *infra*, and comments thereunder.

CHAPTER 5. EXAMINATION OF JUDGMENT DEBTOR

Art.
2451. Examination of judgment debtor; depositions.
2452. Court where motion filed and examination conducted.
2453. Motion; order; service.
2454. Oath; testimony not used in criminal proceedings.
2455. Costs.
2456. Contempt.

Art. 2451. Examination of judgment debtor; depositions

In aid of execution the judgment creditor may examine the judgment debtor, his books, papers, or documents, upon any matter relating to his property, either as provided in Articles 1421 through 1515 or as provided in Articles 2452 through 2456.

Source: Former R.S. 13:4311; Fed. Rule 69(a).

Comments

(a) The statutory provisions regulating examination of the judgment debtor have been incorporated into this Code because of their frequent use and their connexity with the garnishment procedure.

(b) The examination of the debtor by deposition represents a change in the Louisiana law. The source provision, Fed. Rule 69 (a), was adopted because examination by deposition is less inconvenient, and is no more burdensome than an examination in court.

Art. 2452. Court where motion filed and examination conducted

Except as provided in the next paragraph, the written motion for the examination of a judgment debtor shall be filed, and the proceedings conducted, in the court which rendered the judgment.

If the judgment debtor is an individual who is domiciled in the state but not in the parish where the judgment was rendered, or who has changed his domicile to another parish after the institution of the suit, the written motion for his examination shall be filed, and the examination conducted, in a court of competent jurisdiction in the parish of his then domicile. If the judgment debtor is a nonresident, the petition for his examination shall be filed, and the examination conducted, in a court of competent jurisdiction in any parish where he may be found. In any case mentioned in this paragraph, a certified copy of the judgment shall be attached to the written motion for examination.

Source: Cf. Former R.S. 13:4312(1) and (4).
Cross Reference: Art. 2451.

Comment

The first clause of the second paragraph of this article is not in its source provisions, and was added to avoid the inconvenience and expense to which a judgment debtor would be subjected in such an examination if his domicile was in Orleans Parish and the judgment was rendered against him in Caddo Parish.

Tit. 2 JUDGMENT DEBTOR EXAMINATION Art. 2454

Art. 2453. Motion; order; service

On ex parte written motion of the judgment creditor, personally or through his attorney, the court shall order the judgment debtor to appear in court for examination at a time fixed by the court, not less than five days from the date of service on him of the motion and order, and to produce any books, papers, and other documents relating to his property described in the motion.

Source: Former R.S. 13:4312.

Cross Reference: Art. 2451.

Comments

(a) The requirement in the source statute that the judgment creditor state under oath the facts he intends to establish by the books and papers has been deleted. The oath is particularly useless here, since obviously in all cases the judgment creditor is seeking to establish that the judgment debtor owns property subject to execution.

(b) Former R.S. 13:4312(2) provides that a "notice or summons" shall be served upon the judgment debtor, commanding him to appear. This article requires that the motion and order be served. Since the order will clearly specify what action the judgment debtor must take, an additional summons is unnecessary.

(c) In Rockholt Lumber Co. v. Mississippi Val. Const. Co., 66 So. 2d 359 (La.App.1953), the court held that the judgment creditor himself must verify the petition for examination requiring production of the debtor's books, papers, and other documents. This article permits the examination on ex parte written motion, but the first two lines thereof make it clear that this motion may be made by either the judgment creditor or his attorney.

Art. 2454. Oath; testimony not used in criminal proceedings

The debtor shall be sworn to tell the truth in the same manner as a witness in a civil action.

No testimony given by a debtor shall be used in any criminal proceeding against him, except for perjury committed at such examination.

Source: Former R.S. 13:4313.

Cross Reference: Art. 2451.

Comment

Former R.S. 13:4313 provides that if the debtor testifies falsely or makes any material alteration in his books, papers, or other documents, he shall be guilty of perjury and subject to the penalties prescribed by law for that offense. This provision is not included in the above article, as the offense is adequately covered by R.S. 14:123.

Art. 2455. Costs

Court costs in connection with the examination shall be taxed against the judgment debtor, except that if the court determines that the creditor invoked the remedy needlessly, the court may tax the costs against the creditor.

Source: Former R.S. 13:4315.

Cross Reference: Art. 2451.

Comment

The provision in former R.S. 13:4314 authorizing the "officers of the court [to] charge for their services in this proceeding the same fees and charges as provided for similar services in civil cases" has been deleted as unnecessary.

Art. 2456. Contempt

If the motion and order have been served personally on the judgment debtor, and he refuses to appear for the examination or to produce his books, papers, or other documents when ordered to do so, or if he refuses to answer any question held pertinent by the court, he may be punished for contempt.

Source: Former R.S. 13:4312.

Cross Reference: Art. 2451.

Comments

See Comments under Art. 3785, *infra*.

TITLE III

JUDGMENTS OTHER THAN MONEY JUDGMENTS

Art.
2501. Judgment ordering delivery of possession; writ of possession.
2502. Writ of distringas; contempt; damages.
2503. Distringas, execution and revocation.
2504. Specific performance; court directing performance by third party.

Art. 2501. Judgment ordering delivery of possession; writ of possession

A party in whose favor a judgment of possession has been rendered may obtain from the clerk a writ of possession directing the sheriff to seize and deliver the property to him if it is movable property, or to compel the party in possession to vacate the property by use of force, if necessary, if it is immovable.

Source: C.P. Arts. 630–634.

Comments

(a) The provisions of the five source articles are combined in the text above, unnecessary language having been deleted. The requirements in Arts. 632 and 634, Code of Practice of 1870, that a copy of the writ of possession be served on the judgment debtor and that three days elapse before the sheriff can execute the writ, have been deleted. Such a warning is not warranted, and if given, it affords the debtor an opportunity to dispose of the property.

(b) There is no requirement or authority for the sheriff to remove from the premises property belonging to the debtor such as is given in the case of eviction. *Cf.* former R.S. 13:4922. For the purpose of this article, the sheriff's authority to compel the defendant to vacate the premises seems sufficient.

Art. 2502. Writ of distringas; contempt; damages

If a judgment orders the delivery of a thing and the sheriff cannot seize it because the defendant has concealed or removed it from the jurisdiction of the court, or when the judgment orders a defendant to do or refrain from doing an act other than the delivery of a thing, and he refuses or neglects to comply with the order, the party entitled to performance may obtain by contradictory motion the following remedies:

Art. 2502   EXECUTION OF JUDGMENTS   Bk. 4

(1) A writ to distrain the property of the defendant;

(2) An order adjudging the disobedient party in contempt; or

(3) A judgment for any damages he may have sustained. He may likewise sue for damages in a separate action.

Source: C.P. Arts. 635, 636, 638, 639; Fed.Rule 70; cf. C.P. Art. 1058.

Cross Reference: Art. 3334.

Comments

(a) This article lists the grounds for the issuance of a distringas, a writ seldom used. Among the changes made is the elimination of the provision in Art. 636, Code of Practice of 1870, requiring, as a condition precedent to the issuance of the writ, that it be shown by the certificate of the sheriff that the debtor has refused to comply with the judgment.

(b) Under this article, the judgment creditor is entitled to damages in addition to the writ of distringas. This represents a change from the textual provisions of Art. 635, Code of Practice of 1870, which provides that the creditor has the "choice either of instituting an action for damages, or of compelling a specific execution of the judgment." Cf. Arts. 638 and 639, Code of Practice of 1870.

(c) Art. 636, Code of Practice of 1870, provides that the writ issues "on motion" of the judgment creditor, but does not indicate whether the proceedings are ex parte or contradictory with the judgment debtor. In accordance with the accepted practice, this article requires a contradictory motion or rule to show cause. Cf. Flemming's Formulary 166 (1933); Louisiana Formulary Annotated 215 (1951).

(d) Art. 1058, Code of Practice of 1870, authorizes distringas against curators, executors, or administrators failing to comply with judgment ordering specific performance. It has been deleted on the grounds that the above article was broad enough to cover the provisions of Art. 1058.

(e) By permitting the judgment creditor to rule the debtor into court as for contempt as a means of enforcing specific performance of his judgment, the above article affords the creditor a remedy heretofore denied to him. Cf. State ex rel. Hero, 36 La.Ann. 352 (1884); State ex rel. Duffy & Behan v. Civil District Court, 112 La. 182, 36 So. 315 (1904); Ansley v. Stuart, 119 La. 1, 43 So. 892 (1907); Manning v. Cohen, 128 La. 148, 54 So. 700 (1911). This change in the law is in line with the procedure in the federal courts. Cf. Fed.Rule 70. The general contempt provision, Art. 227, supra, provides the penalties incurred.

(f) See, also, Comments under Art. 2504, infra.

Art. 2503. Distringas, execution and revocation

In the execution of the writ of distringas, the sheriff shall seize the property of the defendant and retain it in his possession subject to the orders of the court.

The court shall revoke the writ, and order the sheriff to release and return to the defendant all property seized thereunder, when the defendant proves that he has complied with the judgment sought to be enforced through the distringas, and has also satisfied any judgment for damages which the plaintiff may have obtained against him because of his noncompliance with the judgment first mentioned.

Perishable property seized under a writ of distringas may be sold as provided in Article 2333. The proceeds of such a sale shall be held by the sheriff subject to the orders of the court.

Source: C.P. Arts. 637, 639.

Comments

(a) Art. 637 of the 1870 Code of Practice authorized the sheriff to "receive the rents, income, and other profits" of the property seized under distringas, and to keep the whole subject to the order of the court. The quoted language is now included within the general language of Art. 327, *supra*.

(b) Art. 640 of the 1870 Code required the sheriff to make a return stating the manner in which he executed the writ of distringas. This is now included within the general language of Art. 324, *supra*.

(c) The second paragraph of this article expressly authorizes the immediate sale of perishable property seized under a writ of distringas.

Art. 2504. Specific performance; court directing performance by third party

If a judgment directs a party to perform a specific act, and he fails to comply within the time specified, the court may direct the act to be done by the sheriff or some other person appointed by the court, at the cost of the disobedient party, and with the same effect as if done by the party.

Source: Fed.Rule 70; cf. C.P. Art. 308.

Comments

(a) Besides authorizing punishment for contempt for failure to perform a specific performance judgment, Fed.Rule 70 also permits the court to direct the act to be done by some other person at the defendant's cost. Although the court may have the implied power to order the sheriff, its "executive" officer, to perform such acts when the defendant refuses or fails to do so, in order to free the matter of doubt, a specific provision similar to Fed.Rule 70 has been included in this Code.

Fed.Rule 70 also permits the court to render a judgment divesting a party of title. Louisiana courts exercise such power without specific statutory authority, and for this reason that part of the federal source provision has been omitted.

(b) This article is not intended to cover a judgment affecting title to immovables situated in Louisiana—such a judgment is self-operative. An example of what is covered is a judgment ordering the defendant to demolish a fence or building. If the defendant fails to comply with such a judgment, the court should be able to order the act performed by a third party. For a provision similar to this article, see Art. 308, Code of Practice of 1870, which permits a court to cause to be destroyed whatever is done in violation of an injunction, if practicable.

(c) The above article gives an additional remedy to that provided by Art. 2502, *supra*, which authorizes a writ of distringas.

TITLE IV

FOREIGN JUDGMENTS

Art.
2541. Execution of foreign judgments.

Art. 2541. Execution of foreign judgments

A party seeking recognition or execution by a Louisiana court of a judgment or decree of a court of the United States or a territory thereof, or of any other state, or of any foreign country must bring an ordinary proceeding against the judgment debtor in the proper Louisiana court, to have the judgment or decree recognized and made the judgment of the Louisiana court.

A duly authenticated copy of the judgment or decree must be annexed to the petition.

Source: New; cf. R.S. 9:901.

Comments

(a) The above article codifies the jurisprudence to the effect that a foreign judgment cannot be executed in Louisiana until it is sued upon in Louisiana and recognized by and made the judgment of a Louisiana court, and that the procedure in such a suit is in all respects the same as in any other suit originally filed here. The foreign judgment is merely evidence of the debt. Douglass v. Gyulai, 144 La. 213, 80 So. 258 (1918). Thus, personal service or attachment of property is necessary, and a default judgment must be entered. The only differences between an action on a foreign judgment and one brought originally in Louisiana are that the Louisiana court cannot inquire into the merits of the foreign judgment, and the defenses to the suit on the foreign judgment are limited. Hockaday v. Skeggs, 18 La.Ann. 681 (1866). The question of jurisdiction of the foreign court can be raised. But these are matters governed by the principles of constitutional law and conflicts of law.

(b) R.S. 9:901 provides that foreign judgments of emancipation, authenticated according to the Acts of Congress, shall be given full faith and credit in Louisiana, and that upon presentation of a petition to the proper Louisiana court, the court shall "render judgment thereon." It should be noted that this provision does not deal with execution of a foreign judgment, since judgments of emancipation do not require execution.

(c) Arts. 752 and 753, Code of Practice of 1870, set forth rules for proper authentication of judgments of other state courts and foreign courts. Generally, the procedure is the same as that in the Act of Congress, 28 U.S.C. § 1738. The above article merely requires that the judgments be "duly authenticated". See Art. 1395, *supra*, which sets forth the requirements of due authentication.

(d) The phrase "proper Louisiana court" means a court of competent jurisdiction and proper venue, under the general rules pertaining to jurisdiction and venue.

(e) The Uniform Enforcement of Foreign Judgments Act, 9A U.L.A. 287 *et seq.*, sets forth in nineteen sections a procedure for "registration" of a foreign judgment. This uniform act has been adopted with minor changes in eight states: Arkansas, Illinois, Missouri, Nebraska, Oregon, Washington, Wisconsin, and Wyoming. The procedure is similar to a suit on a foreign judgment, such as is required by the above article. The Uniform Act requires either personal service or attachment, and also permits seizure of property before judgment even when personal service has been made. This was considered unnecessary in Louisiana, since if good cause exists for such a seizure, and the requirements for issuing an attachment or sequestration are present, seizure before judgment may be made under the general rules of attachment or sequestration.

(f) Consideration was given to the inclusion in this article of a requirement that the foreign judgment has to be final and executory in the jurisdiction where rendered, before it can be ordered executed in Louisiana. But it was felt that such a conclusion was implied from the general rules on conflicts of laws, and that a Louisiana court could not order a foreign judgment executed when it was not executory under the law of the jurisdiction in which it was rendered. This article sets forth only the procedure for obtaining recognition. The question of whether the judgment is executory is a substantive one.

BOOK V
SUMMARY AND EXECUTORY PROCEEDINGS

INTRODUCTION

Louisiana civil procedure employs three different modes of procedure in the trial courts: (1) ordinary procedure (regulated in this Code by the articles of Book II, Ordinary Proceedings); (2) summary procedure (governed herein by the provisions of Title I of this Book); and (3) executory procedure (regulated herein by the articles of Title II of this Book).

Summary procedure probably stems from the summatim cognoscere of Roman law, but its development in canonical procedure was accelerated by the Clementina saepe, the decretal of Pope Clement V in 1306 to expedite litigation in canonical courts. Subsequently, in some form or another, it became an important part of the procedural systems of all of the continental countries. The primary source of the applicable articles of the Louisiana Code of Practice of 1825 was Spanish procedure; but the influence of the adjective law of France thereon is quite evident. For a historical survey of the subject, see McMahon, Summary Procedure: A Comparative Study, 31 Tul.L.Rev. 573 (1957).

Executory procedure has its fountainhead in the Lombard custom permitting the extrajudicial enforcement of a pledge. Mediaeval Italian jurists, in an effort to provide a legitimate juridical ancestry, changed this custom into a judicial remedy, by analogizing it to the Roman law confession of judgment, and applying its rules thereto. As so developed in Italy, it afforded an expeditious and inexpensive mode of enforcing indisputable obligations, and was adopted by all of the procedural systems of the continent. It flourished for a while in France, but the adoption of the Ordinance of Moulins in 1566, requiring all contracts over one hundred livres to be evidenced by an authentic act, merged executory procedure into the ordinary procedure, leading to the eventual disappearance of the former. Executory procedure was brought into Louisiana by the O'Reilly Proclamation, which had annexed thereto a digest of the Spanish law to be applied in the future, containing numerous rules on executory procedure. In the Code of Practice of 1825, the redactors narrowed this procedure appreciably, restricting its use to the enforcement of mortgages and privileges, and providing the majority of the rules retained in this

Art. 2591   SUMMARY PROCEEDINGS   Bk. 5

Code. For a more complete discussion of the subject, see McMahon, The Historical Development of Executory Procedure, 32 Tul.L. Rev. 555 (1958).

TITLE I

SUMMARY PROCEEDINGS

Art.
2591. Proceedings conducted with rapidity.
2592. Use of summary proceedings.
2593. Pleadings.
2594. Service of process.
2595. Trial; decision.
2596. Rules of ordinary proceedings applicable; exceptions.

Art. 2591. Proceedings conducted with rapidity

Summary proceedings are those which are conducted with rapidity, within the delays allowed by the court, and without citation and the observance of all the formalities required in ordinary proceedings.

Source: C.P. Art. 98.

Comments

(a) The clause "within the delays allowed by the court" is declaratory of Louisiana procedural law. In the case of the extraordinary writs, this statement is in accord with the rule of Arts. 813, 841, 851, and 869 of the 1870 Code. Under the jurisprudence, the court always fixes the return day of rules to show cause and other contradictory motions.

(b) Art. 1201, *supra,* provides that "Citation and service thereof are essential in all civil actions except summary and executory proceedings." This goes beyond Art. 206 of the 1870 Code in so far as the exact language is concerned, but is in accord with prior law. *Cf.* Art. 98, Code of Practice of 1870.

(c) It has been consistently held that summary procedure is not unconstitutional, and clearly falls within the due process of law requirements of the Constitutions of Louisiana and of the United States. Kennard v. State of Louisiana, 92 U.S. 480, 23 L.Ed. 478 (1875); City of New Orleans v. Cannon, 10 La.Ann. 764 (1855); State ex rel. Morgan v. Kennard, 25 La.Ann. 238 (1873). Notice of the trial is required under Art. 2594, *infra,* to meet the requirements of due process.

Art. 2592. Use of summary proceedings

Summary proceedings may be used for the trial or disposition of the following matters only:

(1) An incidental question arising in the course of litigation;

(2) An application for a new trial;

(3) An issue which may be raised properly by an exception, contradictory motion, or rule to show cause;

(4) The homologation of a judicial partition, of a tableau of distribution or account filed by a legal representative, or of a report submitted by an auditor, accountant, or other expert appointed by the court; and an opposition to any of the foregoing, to the appointment of a legal representative, or to a petition for authority filed by a legal representative;

(5) A habeas corpus, mandamus, or quo warranto proceeding;

(6) The determination of the rank of mortgages and privileges on property sold judicially, and of the order of distribution of the proceeds thereof; and

(7) All other matters in which the law permits summary proceedings to be used.

Source: C.P. Arts. 98, 401, 754, 755, 786-790; cf. C.P. Arts. 819, 830, 871.

Comments

(a) More than one hundred and twenty-five code or statutory provisions permit the use of summary procedure in special cases. Only the most general and commonly used grounds for the use of summary proceedings have been enumerated in the above article. The limitation of summary procedure to these cases, however, does not in any way affect the special code and statutory provisions, as the above article excludes them from its operation through the exception in paragraph (7) thereof.

(b) Art. 754 of the 1870 Code of Practice, which provides that summary process is to be used in every case where it is expressly prescribed by law constitutes an exception to the enumerated summary proceedings of Art. 755.

In the above article, the same effect is achieved by limiting summary proceedings to those enumerated therein, including "all other matters in which the law permits summary proceedings to be used." There is one difference, however, in that the above article does not mention the word "expressly" as does Art. 754 of the 1870 Code. This omission was deliberate. In some cases the enforcement of statutory provisions has been sought through summary procedure, when the statute did not expressly permit the use thereof, although the circumstances were such that obviously the delays required in ordinary proceedings would make the remedy a very hollow one. In most instances summary procedure has been permitted, even though not expressly so provided by the statute, if it was apparent that the legislature intended to permit summary enforcement. Savage v. Jeter, 13 La.Ann. 239 (1858); Boos v. McClendon, 130 La. 813, 58 So. 582 (1912); Barrett v. Pierson, 163 La. 541, 112 So. 410 (1927). See, also, Succession of Carter, 32 So.2d 44 (La.App.1947). This position, however, cannot be reconciled with the holding of Fischel v. Mercier, 32 La.Ann. 706, 707 (1880), where the court said: "It was no doubt the intention of the statute that the proceedings authorized should be summary in their character; and had the proceeding by rule been expressly directed by the statute, it would not have been objectionable."

The omission of the word "expressly" in paragraph (7) of this article permits the court in each instance to give effect to the legislative intent where necessary.

(c) To some extent there may be some overlapping between the first and third enumerations of the above article. However, this does enable judges and lawyers to determine quickly and easily the availability of summary procedure.

(d) The "rule to show cause" in Louisiana is only one type of contradictory motion, in which the court orders the defendant in rule to appear and show cause on a date and hour fixed by the court why the relief prayed for should not be granted. Due to the very large number of code and statutory provisions permitting the use of summary proceedings and prescribing the rule to show cause as the initial pleading, it has been included specifically in the enumeration above.

(e) Different from Art. 755(2) of the 1870 Code, which provides for summary procedure only for the declinatory exceptions, the above article makes summary procedure available for the trial or determination of any issue raised by any exception. The reason for limiting summary procedure to the declinatory exceptions originally was because these were the only exceptions filed prior to answer, as dilatory and peremptory exceptions were included in the answer. Art. 333, Code of Practice of 1825. Hence, the dilatory and peremptory exceptions were disposed of on the trial of the case on its merits, and only the declinatory exceptions were tried preliminarily. After the 1836 amendment to Art. 333 of the 1825 Code, dilatory exceptions also had to be filed *in limine*, thus giving rise to the present practice of trying all exceptions preliminarily. The proposed article recognizes and gives effect to the present practice. See New Orleans Terminal Co. v. Teller, 113 La. 733, 37 So. 624, 2 Ann.Cas. 127 (1904); Briggs v. Aiken, 152 La. 607, 93 So. 917 (1922).

(f) See, also, Comments under Arts. 2593, 2643, 4603, *infra*.

Art. 2593. Pleadings

A summary proceeding may be commenced by the filing of a contradictory motion or by a rule to show cause, except as otherwise provided by law.

Exceptions to a contradictory motion, rule to show cause, opposition, or petition in a summary proceeding shall be filed prior to the time assigned for, and shall be disposed of on, the trial. An answer is not required, except as otherwise provided by law.

No responsive pleadings to an exception are permitted.

Source: New; cf. Comments following.

Cross Reference: Art. 2973.

Comments

(a) One of the difficulties concerning the use of summary procedure in Louisiana has been the absence of specific rules in the 1870 Code of Practice. The necessary rules are to be found in the jurisprudence, it is true, but it is important that they be made readily accessible from the provisions of the procedural code itself.

(b) Specific reference was made to the rule to show cause for the reason indicated in Comment (d) of Art. 2592, *supra*.

(c) The second paragraph of the above article is in accord with the practice and jurisprudence of Louisiana, except as stated in Comment (e), *infra*.

Under Arts. 810, 842, and 869, respectively, Code of Practice of 1870, an answer is required in habeas corpus, mandamus and quo warranto proceedings. Except for these and similar special provisions in the statutes, no answer is required under summary procedure, and if the defendant fails to appear at the trial, plaintiff may introduce his evidence immediately and secure whatever relief is justified thereby, without the necessity of taking a default. Succession of Porter, 5 Rob. 96 (La.1843); State v. McDonnell, 13 La.Ann. 231 (1858).

(d) The defendant waives any objection to the improper use of summary procedure if he enters upon the trial without excepting to the summary procedure. Butchert v. Ricker, 11 La.Ann. 489 (1856); Younger Bros. v. Spell, 194 La. 16, 193 So. 354 (1939); Alfonso v. Ruiz, 2 So.2d 480 (La.App.1941); Roper v. Brooks, 9 So.2d 497 (La.App.1941); Cryer v. Cryer, 44 So.2d 517 (La. App.1950). See, also, Dussin v. Delaroderie, 5 Rob. 202 (La. 1843); LeBouef v. Merle, 1 La.Ann. 144 (1846); Conery v. Heno, 9 La.Ann. 587 (1854); Succession of Moore, 18 La.Ann. 512 (1866); Succession of Esteves, 182 La. 604, 162 So. 194 (1935); Bloomenstiel v. Tridico, 156 So. 793 (La.App.1934);

Foret v. Stark, 16 So.2d 79 (La.App.1943). All other exceptions which, under ordinary procedure, are required to be filed prior to answer or default should be filed prior to the commencement of the summary trial, since there is no default in summary proceedings.

(e) Despite the well settled rule stated in Comment (d), *supra*, it has been held that, if the defendant does not make an appearance at the trial, he may appeal and urge his objections to the summary procedure in the appellate court. Sharp v. Bright, 14 La.Ann. 390 (1859); Succession of Esteves, *supra*. This rule appears undesirable for at least four reasons: (1) an appeal should be a review of the proceedings below, and if this issue was not presented to the trial judge, it should not be considered on appeal; (2) the rule throws an unnecessarily heavy burden upon the appellate courts, as it forces them to determine issues which were never presented to the trial courts; (3) there is no basis for different rules on the same subject; and (4) the rule militates against the expeditious settlement of the controversy, which is the very object of summary procedure. For these reasons, this article requires a defendant in a summary proceeding to urge his objections to the use of summary process by the dilatory exception filed prior to the commencement of the trial, under penalty of waiver, whether he appears at the trial or not. See Comment (d), *supra*, and Art. 926, *supra*.

Art. 2594. Service of process

Citation and service thereof are not necessary in a summary proceeding. A copy of the contradictory motion, rule to show cause, or other pleading filed by the plaintiff in the proceeding, and of any order of court assigning the date and hour of the trial thereof, shall be served upon the defendant.

Source: Cf. C.P. Art. 98; Comment following.

Comments

Under Art. 98, Code of Practice of 1870, citation is not required in summary proceedings. See also Art. 1201, *supra*. However, due process of law requires the service upon defendant of notice of plaintiff's demand, and of the date and hour appointed by the court for the trial of the summary proceeding. The rules embodied in the above article reflect the customary practice in Louisiana.

See, also, Comments under Art. 2591, *supra*.

Art. 2595. Trial; decision

Upon reasonable notice a summary proceeding may be tried in open court or in chambers, in term or in vacation; and shall be tried by preference over ordinary proceedings, and without a jury, except as otherwise provided by law.

The court shall render its decision as soon as practicable after the conclusion of the trial of a summary proceeding and, whenever practicable, without taking the matter under advisement.

Source: C.P. Arts. 756, 757; cf. Comments following.

Comments

(a) Express authority for the trial of summary proceedings in vacation, and in chambers, is necessary so as to conform with Arts. 195 and 196, *supra*, authorizing trial courts to try many additional matters in vacation as well as in chambers.

(b) The exception in the first paragraph accords with the provisions of certain special statutes, such as the Intrusion Into Office Act, R.S. 42:86, permitting a trial by jury.

(c) The last paragraph of the article is new, but is conducive to the expeditious determination of summary proceedings.

Art. 2596. Rules of ordinary proceedings applicable; exceptions

The rules governing ordinary proceedings are applicable to summary proceedings, except as otherwise provided by law.

Source: Art. 1151, Quebec Code of Civil Procedure; cf. Comment following.

Comment

The rule of this article is also declaratory of the Louisiana jurisprudence. See Love v. Banks, 3 La. 480 (1832).

TITLE II
EXECUTORY PROCEEDINGS

Chap.		Art.
1.	General Dispositions	2631
2.	Proceeding Against Surviving Spouse, Succession, or Heir	2671
3.	Proceedings when Property in Possession of Third Person	2701
4.	Execution of Writ of Seizure and Sale	2721
5.	Injunction to Arrest Seizure and Sale	2751
6.	Deficiency Judgment	2771
7.	Making Judgments of Other Louisiana Courts Executory	2781

CHAPTER 1. GENERAL DISPOSITIONS

Art.
2631. Use of executory proceedings.
2632. Act importing a confession of judgment.
2633. Venue.
2634. Petition.
2635. Authentic evidence submitted with petition.
2636. Authentic evidence.
2637. Evidence which need not be authentic.
2638. Order for issuance of writ of seizure and sale.
2639. Demand for payment.
2640. Citation unnecessary; service of demand for payment.
2641. Service upon, and seizure and sale prosecuted against, attorney for unrepresented defendant.
2642. Assertion of defenses; appeal.
2643. Third person claiming mortgage or privilege on property seized.
2644. Conversion to ordinary proceeding.

Art. 2631. Use of executory proceedings

Executory proceedings are those which are used to effect the seizure and sale of property, without previous citation and judgment, to enforce a mortgage or privilege thereon evidenced by an authentic act importing a confession of judgment, and in other cases allowed by law.

Source: C.P. Arts. 98, 732.
Cross Reference: Art. 3723.

Comments

(a) The two methods for the enforcement of conventional mortgages, *viz.:* by ordinary, and by executory procedure, are retained in this Code. See Arts. 3721, 3723, *infra.*

(b) The common law rule prohibiting confessions of judgment prior to the maturity of the obligation does not affect executory procedure in Louisiana. In an oblique fashion, the organic law of the state recognizes the validity of confessions of judgment made for the purposes of executory procedure. See Const. Art. VII, § 44, providing that judgment cannot be confessed prior to the maturity of the obligation sued on, "except for the purpose of executory process."

(c) The last clause of this article is based upon the language of Art. 98 of the 1870 Code. There are at least three possible exceptions to the general rule that executory procedure may be employed only when the mortgage or privilege is evidenced by an authentic act:

(1) Executory enforcement of judgments rendered by other Louisiana courts is permitted under Arts. 732, 747–751 of the Code of Practice of 1870 and is retained in Arts. 2781 and 2782, *infra.*

(2) Chattel mortgages on movables other than motor vehicles may be evidenced by an act under private signature duly acknowledged before a notary. R.S. 9:5353. Initially, such a mortgage could not be enforced by executory process. Osborne v. Mossler Acceptance Co., 214 La. 503, 38 So.2d 151 (1948); Martin-Wilkie Chevrolet Co. v. Wingart, 189 So. 309 (La.App.1939). *Cf.* West Louisiana Bank v. Dawson, 154 La. 830, 98 So. 262 (1923). See, also, Miller, The Louisiana Chattel Mortgage and Small Loan Acts, 23 Tul.L.Rev. 61, 70–73 (1948). But in 1952, R.S. 9:5363 was amended to include specific language conferring the right of executory process to all creditors on movable property, whether their rights arose by virtue of an authentic act or an act "under private signature duly acknowledged." La.Act 441 of 1952, § 1. See, also, General Motors Acceptance Corp. v. Anzelmo, 222 La. 1019, 64 So.2d 417 (1953), noted 14 La.L.Rev. 289 (1953).

(3) Although there may be some doubt in the matter, there is at least a possibility that a chattel mortgage on a motor vehicle executed under private signature duly acknowledged may be enforced by executory process. *Cf.* General Motors Acceptance Corp. v. Anzelmo, *supra.* Originally, all chattel mortgages were governed by the provisions of R.S. 9:5351 through 9:5365. But in 1950, when the Vehicle Certificate of Title Act was adopted, separate provisions, tracking the language of the Chattel Mortgage Act, were adopted. R.S. 32:710, as originally enacted, provided expressly that chattel mortgages on motor vehicles were governed

by the provisions of both the Chattel Mortgage Act and the Vehicle Certificate of Title Act. This, however, was in direct conflict with the provisions of R.S. 9:5366, adopted the same year, providing that "the sole and exclusive method of executing and recording certain mortgages as therein prescribed on certain vehicles as therein defined" would be governed by the provisions of the Vehicle Certificate of Title Act. This conflict was resolved in 1952, with the amendment of R.S. 32:710 so as to virtually track the language of R.S. 9:5366. However, the only provision in the Vehicle Certificate of Title Act is R.S. 32:710(K), which provides that "all laws and rules and all remedies and processes, including executory process under confessions of judgment as well as proceedings via ordinaria, now or hereafter made available to creditors for the protection or enforcement of their rights under mortgages affecting immovables shall be available to creditors of obligations secured by mortgages affecting vehicles."

This language is no more specific than that of R.S. 9:5363 prior to the 1952 amendment, or to that of the latter's source statute, La. Act 172 of 1944, § 9, which was in effect when Osborne v. Mossler Acceptance Co., *supra*, was decided. Under the strict construction of executory procedure, and the requirement that it be based upon authentic evidence unless otherwise expressly provided by statute, there was more than a possibility that the language "including executory process under confessions of judgment" now contained in R.S. 32:710(K) would be construed to mean that when the chattel mortgage is evidenced by an authentic act it can be enforced by executory process; otherwise, not. An amendment of R.S. 32:-710(K) to remove this objection is being recommended.

The authentic act, as defined by Art. 2234 of the Civil Code, must be passed in the presence of the parties, and signed by them in the presence of the witnesses and the notary. Colonial Trust Co. v. St. John Lumber Co., 138 La. 1033, 71 So. 147 (1916). See, also, Leibe v. Hebersmith, 39 La.Ann. 1051, 3 So. 283 (1887). But *cf.* Finance Security Co. v. Williams, 42 So.2d 902 (La.App.1949). It must appear from the face of the instrument that all requirements prescribed by law for authenticity have been complied with. Baker v. Baker, 125 La. 969, 52 So. 115 (1910); West Louisiana Bank v. Dawson, 154 La. 830, 98 So. 262 (1923); Demasi v. Whitney Trust & Savings Bank, 176 So. 703 (La.App.1937); Mossler Acceptance Co. v. Osborne, 14 So.2d 492 (La.App.1943).

By reason of the special statutes or code provisions cited, the following instruments, executed before persons other than Louisiana notaries public, have the force and effect of authentic acts in Louisiana: acts executed before clerks of court and their deputies, who are notaries public ex officio in Louisiana (R.S. 13:751 and 13:910, R.S. 44:101(B)); acts passed before a notary public and two witnesses in the District of Columbia, or in any other state

(R.S. 35:6); instruments executed in foreign countries before an American ambassador, minister, chargé d'affaires, secretary of legation, consul general, consul, vice consul, or commercial agent, even though not executed before two witnesses (R.S. 35:9); instruments executed by any person on active military duty before any commissioned officer of any of the armed forces of the United States, or the Coast Guard (R.S. 35:7); instruments of pledge passed before the cashiers of Louisiana banks (C.C. Art. 3159).

(d) See, also, Comments under Arts. 2632, 2635, *infra*.

Art. 2632.   Act importing a confession of judgment

An act evidencing a mortgage or privilege imports a confession of judgment when the obligor therein acknowledges the obligation secured thereby, whether then existing or to arise thereafter, and confesses judgment thereon if the obligation is not paid at maturity.

Source: C.P. Art. 733.

Cross Reference: Art. 3723.

Comment

Since chattel mortgages may now be enforced by executory process if evidenced by an authentic act or an act under private signature duly acknowledged, the language in the source provision requiring the act to be in authentic form has been omitted. See Comment (c) under Art. 2631, *supra*.

Art. 2633.   Venue

An executory proceeding to enforce a mortgage or privilege may be brought either in the parish where the property is situated, or as provided in the applicable provision of Article 42.

Source: C.P. Arts. 163, 736; R.S. 9:5363.

Cross References: Arts. 80, 3723.

Comments

In the only cases where the question was squarely presented, the Louisiana Supreme Court held that an executory proceeding to enforce the mortgage or privilege may be brought, at the option of the plaintiff, either in the parish where the property is situated, under Art. 736 of the 1870 Code of Practice, or in the parish of the domicile of the debtor, under Art. 163 of the 1870 Code. Roman v. Denney, 17 La.Ann. 126 (1865); Reugger v. De-Brueys, 146 La. 283, 83 So. 556 (1919). *Cf.* Miles Planting & Mfg. Co. v. Ware, 142 La. 1026, 78 So. 104, 108–109 (1918).

Art. 2633   EXECUTORY PROCEEDINGS   Bk. 5

In view of the clear and unambiguous language of Art. 163, Code of Practice of 1870, the law may be regarded as being settled. The above article is only declaratory of these rules. For the venue when a continuous tract of land in different parishes is involved, see R.S. 13:4111.

See, also, Comments under Art. 72, *supra*.

Art. 2634. Petition

A person seeking to enforce a mortgage or privilege on property in an executory proceeding shall file a petition therefor, praying for the seizure and sale of the property affected by the mortgage or privilege. This petition shall comply with Article 891, and the plaintiff shall submit therewith the exhibits mentioned in Article 2635.

Source: C.P. Art. 734; cf. Comments following.

Cross Reference: Art. 3723.

Comments

(a) While this article does not change prior practice in Louisiana, it does change procedural theory. Heretofore, the petition in an executory proceeding was not considered technically a "petition," and hence the provisions of the Pleading and Practice Act had no application. Advance Rumley Thresher Co. v. Shove, 7 La. App. 472 (1928). Under this article, however, the petition in an executory proceeding is governed by the rules applicable to petitions in ordinary proceedings.

(b) Under the jurisprudence of Louisiana, except when provided otherwise by statute, the plaintiff in an executory proceeding must submit with his petition, in authentic form, every link in the required chain of evidence. See the cases cited in Comment (b) under Art. 2635, *infra*. These are the exhibits referred to in the text of this article.

Art. 2635. Authentic evidence submitted with petition

The plaintiff shall submit with his petition the authentic evidence necessary to prove his right to use executory process to enforce the mortgage or privilege. These exhibits shall include authentic evidence of:

(1) The note, bond, or other instrument evidencing the obligation secured by the mortgage or privilege;

(2) The authentic act of mortgage or privilege importing a confession of judgment; and

(3) Any judgment, judicial letters, order of court, or authentic act necessary to complete the proof of plaintiff's right to use executory process.

This requirement of authentic evidence is relaxed only in those cases, and to the extent, provided by law.

Source: New; cf. Comments following.

Cross References: Arts. 2634, 3723.

Comments

(a) Although this article has no counterpart in the 1870 Code of Practice, its adoption effects no change in the law, since it is simply declaratory of well settled jurisprudential rules.

(b) The requirement of authentic evidence to support every link in the necessary chain of evidence in an executory proceeding is the very foundation of executory procedure. Its rigid application, in the absence of statute, is well illustrated in the leading case of Miller, Lyon & Co. v. Cappel, 36 La.Ann. 264 (1884) where it was held that: "To justify the order of seizure and sale every muniment of title, and every link of evidence must be in the authentic form. In such a proceeding the judge can entertain no matter in pais." To the same effect, see Ricks v. Bernstein, 19 La. Ann. 141 (1867).

(c) The mortgage note executed in connection with an act of mortgage must be described in and identified with the act of mortgage, and must be filed with the petition for executory process. Ricks v. Bernstein, 19 La.Ann. 141 (1867); Taylor v. Boedicker, 21 La.Ann. 170 (1869); Hackemuller v. Figueroa, 125 La. 307, 51 So. 207 (1910); Kreher v. Theisman's Estate, 125 La. 600, 51 So. 656 (1910). Under these authorities, any variance between the mortgage and the note precluded the use of an executory proceeding; but under R.S. 13:4104 and 13:4105 such a variance may be corrected if due to a typographical or clerical error.

(d) When the plaintiff sues in a representative capacity, or the defendant is sued in a representative capacity, as when they are executors, administrators, or curators, it is impossible to produce certified copies of any authentic act evidencing this capacity. In such cases, the plaintiff's right to sue, or his right to sue the particular defendant, can and should be evidenced by a certified copy of the judgment of possession, letters of administration, or letters testamentary, as the case may be. Such certified copies constitute evidence in authentic form, and since they are necessary to establish the right of the plaintiff to bring the executory proceeding, or to bring it against the defendant, they must be submitted with the petition; and the failure to so produce them is fatal to the executory proceeding. Landry v. Landry, 12 La.Ann. 167 (1857); DeBrueys v. Freret, 18 La.Ann. 80 (1866); Chaffe v. Carroll, 35 La.Ann. 115 (1883). *Cf.* Dosson v. Sanders, 12 Rob. 238 (La.1845).

Another situation where additional evidence in authentic form is needed to prove the plaintiff's right to bring the executory proceeding is where the mortgage note is made payable to a named mortgagee, who subsequently transfers the note to a third person, who in turn institutes the executory proceeding to enforce the mortgage. In such a case, the transfer and endorsement of the mortgage note to the plaintiff must be evidenced by an authentic act, and a certified copy annexed to the petition. Miller, Lyon & Co. v. Cappel, 36 La.Ann. 264 (1884). Of course, if the mortgage note is made payable to the order of the mortgagor and by him endorsed in blank, and the act of mortgage so recites, no authentic evidence of the transfer by the mortgagee is required. Miller, Lyon & Co. v. Cappel, *supra*. A similar requirement is made where the mortgagor acts through an agent, in the execution of the mortgage and note. In such instances, a certified copy of the authentic act of procuration must be attached to the petition for executory process. Crescent City Bank v. Blanque, 32 La.Ann. 264 (1880).

(e) The last paragraph of this article takes care of the statutory exceptions to the general rule requiring authentic evidence of the execution of the mortgage. See Art. 2631, *supra*, and Comments thereunder.

(f) See, also, Comments under Arts. 2636, 2637, *infra*.

Art. 2636. Authentic evidence

The following documentary evidence shall be deemed to be authentic for purposes of executory process:

(1) The note, bond, or other instrument evidencing the obligation secured by the mortgage or privilege, paraphed for identification with the act of mortgage or privilege by the notary or other officer before whom it is executed;

(2) A certified copy of an authentic act;

(3) A certified copy of any judgment, judicial letters, or order of court;

(4) A copy of a resolution of the board of directors, or other governing board of a corporation, authorizing the execution of a mortgage on its property, certified in accordance with the provisions of R. S. 13:4103; and

(5) All other documentary evidence recognized by law as authentic.

Source: Former R.S. 13:4103; cf. Comments following.
Cross Reference: Art. 3723.

Comments

(a) Paragraph (1) of this article reflects the prevailing custom and practice in Louisiana under which the mortgage note issued in connection with a mortgage, and identified therewith, is considered self-proving. This mortgage note must be annexed to the petition. See cases cited in Comment (c) under Art. 2635, *supra*.

(b) See Comment (d) under Art. 2635, *supra*. See also Dosson v. Sanders, 12 Rob. 238 (La.1845); Dobel v. Delavallade, 30 La. Ann. 604 (1878); and *cf*. Bank of Leesville v. Wingate, 123 La. 386, 48 So. 1005 (1909).

"Authentic evidence" is not limited to certified copies of authentic acts, as defined by Art. 2234 of the Civil Code. The term "authentic evidence" includes copies of any public act, certified as required by law. Woods v. Jastremski, 201 La. 1092, 11 So.2d 4 (1942).

(c) Paragraph (5) of this article is designed to include the following statutes: (1) R.S. 6:762, providing that the certificate of the secretary or assistant secretary of a building and loan association that the borrower, or the person who has assumed the borrower's loan, is in arrears, shall be considered authentic evidence of the default and arrears; (2) R.S. 6:763, providing that the certificate of the secretary or assistant secretary of a building and loan association, certifying the amount of advances made to the borrower, shall constitute authentic evidence of this indebtedness; (3) Art. 3159 of the Civil Code, providing that an act of pledge in favor of any bank passed before its cashier, is "authentic proof"; and, (4) R.S. 13:4104 and 13:4105 permitting the correction of any variance between the provisions of the act of mortgage and the mortgage note.

Art. 2637. Evidence which need not be authentic

Evidence as to the proper party defendant, or as to the necessity for appointing an attorney at law to represent an unrepresented defendant, or of the breach or occurrence of a condition of the act of mortgage or privilege maturing the obligation, need not be submitted in authentic form. These facts may be proved by the verified petition, or supplemental petition, or by affidavits submitted therewith.

A presumption of the judicial acceptance of the succession of the debtor by his heirs or legatees shall be established by a certified copy of the judgment of possession, recognizing these heirs or legatees and sending them into possession of the property of the deceased.

A presumption of the administration of the property by the legal representative of the debtor at the time of the institution of the executory proceeding shall be established by a certified copy of the letters issued by the court which has appointed or confirmed the legal representative.

Source: New; cf. C.P. Arts. 116, 734, 737, 964; C.C. Arts. 56, 313; former R.S. 13:3411, 13:3414.

Cross Reference: Art. 3723.

Comments

(a) This article is declaratory of the legal theory of executory process and customary Louisiana practice.

The requirements of authentic evidence, under the cases cited in the Comments under Art. 2635, *supra*, are limited to evidence of: (1) the mortgage or privilege on the property sought to be seized and sold; (2) the amount of the indebtedness sought to be enforced; and (3) the plaintiff's right to enforce the mortgage or privilege under the executory process.

As to facts relating to the proper defendant in the executory proceeding, and those necessary to authorize the appointment of an attorney at law to represent the absent, incompetent, or unrepresented defendant, there has never been any requirement as to their establishment by authentic evidence. From the very nature of things, there could be no such requirement. For example, under former R.S. 13:3414, in order to bring the action against the surviving spouse in community, plaintiff must show: (1) the mortgage or privilege affects property owned by the community; (2) the obligation secured by the mortgage or privilege is a community obligation; (3) the marriage of the spouses; and (4) the death of the deceased spouse. These facts could never be established by authentic evidence.

(b) Many acts of mortgage contain a condition that the entire obligation will be matured by the death or adjudication in bankruptcy of the mortgagor. This article provides the manner of proving the occurrence of such a condition. Other mortgages provide that the agreement of the mortgagor to maintain adequate insurance on the mortgaged property at all times is a condition of making the loan secured by the mortgage; and that the mortgage indebtedness will become due and exigible upon the breach of this condition by the mortgagor. This article likewise provides the manner of proving the breach of such a condition.

(c) The last two paragraphs of the article cover the cases where it is necessary to prove the right of plaintiff to proceed against the defendants named where actually no evidence could be obtained easily to prove that these parties are the proper defendants. In these instances it is necessary to require only the submission of a certified copy of the judgment of possession, or the letters, to establish a presumption that the parties sued are the proper defendants.

(d) See the definition of the term "legal representative" in Art. 5251, *infra*.

(e) See, also, Comments under Arts. 2672, 2673, *infra*.

Art. 2638. Order for issuance of writ of seizure and sale

If the plaintiff is entitled thereto, the court shall order the issuance of a writ of seizure and sale commanding the sheriff to seize and sell the property affected by the mortgage or privilege, as prayed for and according to law.

Source: New; cf. Comment following.

Cross Reference: Art. 3723.

Comments

Under recent Louisiana practice, the order rendered by the court on the petition and exhibits submitted therewith is either for the issuance of a writ of seizure and sale, or for the issuance of executory process; and the actual seizure and sale is made by the sheriff under authority of the "writ of seizure and sale" issued to him by the clerk of court. See Flemming's Formulary 520 (1933).

In the absence of any injunction to arrest the seizure and sale, the order rendered by the court directing the seizure and sale of the property is the only action taken by the court in an executory proceeding. It is the closest analogy to a judgment which can be found in executory procedure; and this is the order from which an appeal must be taken. *Cf.* State ex rel. Feibleman v. Judge, 45 La. Ann. 1426, 14 So. 428 (1893).

Art. 2639. Demand for payment

Before issuing the writ of seizure and sale, the clerk shall issue a demand upon the defendant for payment of the amount due and all costs of court. This demand shall notify the defendant that, in default of payment within three days of service, exclusive of holidays, a writ of seizure and sale will be issued and the property described in the petition will be seized and sold according to law.

The demand for payment need not be issued if it has been waived by the debtor in the act of mortgage or privilege; and in such event, the clerk shall issue the writ of seizure and sale immediately.

Source: New; cf. C.P. Art. 735.

Cross References: Arts. 2640, 2721, 3723.

Comments

(a) The language of this article is based largely upon the form of this demand and notice shown in Flemming's Formulary 519–520 (1933).

Substantially this same form of demand and notice is employed throughout Louisiana, and represents the settled practice in this state.

(b) The provision allowing five days for the payment of the amount due, if the defendant lives outside of the parish where the proceeding is brought, has been eliminated. In this era of efficient means of communication and transportation, it is no longer necessary.

(c) The demand and notice to the debtor must be signed and issued by the clerk of court or his authorized deputy; but if the sheriff has possession of the writ of seizure and sale, his issuance of this demand and notice, while improper, is not sufficient to invalidate any subsequent judicial sale. Hart v. Pike, 29 La.Ann. 262 (1877). See, to the same effect, Nash v. Johnson, 9 Rob. 8 (La. 1844); Billgery v. Ferguson, 30 La.Ann. 84 (1878); Sadler v. Henderson, 35 La.Ann. 826 (1883); Oriol v. Moss, 38 La.Ann. 770 (1886); Chase v. New Orleans Gaslight Co., 45 La.Ann. 300, 12 So. 308 (1893). This article does not change these jurisprudential rules.

(d) The demand and notice may be waived by the debtor in the act of mortgage or pledge. See cases cited in McMahon 1439, n. 10, and 273, n. 10 (1956 Supp.). In the case of immovable property, this waiver is not particularly advantageous, as the property cannot be removed from the jurisdiction or concealed pending the delay of three or five days. In the case of motor vehicles and other items of movable property, however, this waiver makes possible an immediate seizure by the sheriff; it also eliminates any need for an enforcement of the note via ordinaria, and the sequestration of the property subject to the mortgage or pledge.

Art. 2640. Citation unnecessary; service of demand for payment

Citation is not necessary in an executory proceeding.

The sheriff shall serve upon the defendant the demand for payment provided by Article 2639, unless waived by the debtor as provided therein.

Source: New; cf. Comment following.

Cross Reference: Art. 3723.

Comment

It is not necessary that a certified copy of the plaintiff's petition and of the court order rendered thereon be served upon the defendant in an executory proceeding. Exchange and Banking Co. v. Walden, 15 La. 431 (1840); Nash v. Johnson, 9 Rob. 8 (La. 1844); Aillet v. Henry, 2 La.Ann. 145 (1847); Snow v. Trotter, 3

La.Ann. 268 (1848); Hart v. Pike, 29 La.Ann. 262 (1877); Rogers v. St. Martin, 110 La. 80, 34 So. 137 (1903). For this reason service of a certified copy of the petition and court order is not required to be served on the defendant under this article.

Art. 2641. Service upon, and seizure and sale prosecuted against, attorney for unrepresented defendant

In all cases governed by Article 2674, all demands, notices, and other documents required to be served upon the defendant in an executory proceeding shall be served upon the attorney at law appointed by the court to represent him, against whom the seizure and sale shall be prosecuted contradictorily.

Source: C.P. Art. 737; former R.S. 13:3411; cf. C.P. Arts. 116, 964.

Cross Reference: Art. 3723.

Comment

This article makes no change in the procedural law of Louisiana. Art. 737 of the Code of Practice of 1870 expressly provides that "the judge, at the request of the plaintiff, shall appoint an attorney, to represent [the] debtor to whom notice of the demand shall be given in the manner above directed, and contradictorily with whom the seizure and sale shall be prosecuted."

Art. 2642. Assertion of defenses; appeal

Defenses and procedural objections to an executory proceeding may be asserted either through an injunction proceeding to arrest the seizure and sale as provided in Articles 2751 through 2754, or a suspensive appeal from the order directing the issuance of the writ of seizure and sale, or both.

A suspensive appeal from an order directing the issuance of a writ of seizure and sale shall be governed by the provisions of Articles 2081 through 2086 and 2088 through 2167, except that the security therefor shall be for an amount exceeding by one-half the balance due on the debt secured by the mortgage or privilege sought to be enforced, including principal, interest to date of the order of appeal, and attorney's fee, but exclusive of court costs.

Source: New; cf. Comments following.

Cross Reference: Art. 3723.

Comments

(a) The whole theory on which the civilian executory proceeding rests is that a seizure of the property subject to the mortgage or privilege may be made immediately on the order of the court issued on the ex parte application of the creditor. It is not a contradictory proceeding at all; but an ex parte one. The defendant can assert any valid defenses to the seizure, but he must do so either through an opposition to arrest the seizure and sale, or through an appeal from the order directing the seizure and sale. See Engelmann-Millar, A History of Continental Civil Procedure 498–501 (1927); General Motors Acceptance Corp. v. Anzelmo, 222 La. 1019, 64 So.2d 417 (1953), noted 14 La.L.Rev. 289 (1953); and Boatmen's Savings Bank v. Wagenspack, 12 F. 66, 4 Woods 130 (5 Cir. 1882).

(b) The second paragraph announces the Louisiana rule. State ex rel. Feibleman v. Judge, 45 La.Ann. 1426, 14 So. 428 (1893).

(c) Although theoretically a devolutive appeal from an order directing the issuance of a writ of seizure and sale is available to the defendant in an executory proceeding, if the property is sold prior to the time of the hearing on appeal, the appeal will be dismissed as presenting only a moot question. Bank of LaFourche v. Barrios, 167 La. 215, 118 So. 893 (1928). For this reason in this Code no devolutive appeal is permitted from an order directing the issuance of the writ of seizure and sale.

Art. 2643. Third person claiming mortgage or privilege on property seized

A third person claiming a mortgage or privilege on the property seized in an executory proceeding, superior to that of the plaintiff, may assert a preference in the distribution of the proceeds of the sale of the property by intervening, as provided in Article 1092.

A third person claiming a mortgage or privilege on the property seized in an executory proceeding, inferior to that of the plaintiff, similarly may assert by intervention a preference in the distribution of the surplus of the proceeds of the sale of the property remaining after the claim of the plaintiff has been paid in full.

The intervention shall be served as provided in Article 1093 and shall be tried summarily.

Source: C.P. Arts. 395–397, 401, 402, 755(4).

Cross Reference: Art. 3723.

Comments

(a) Since the intervention has been broadened to absorb third opposition, the remedies of a creditor having a mortgage or privilege on the property seized in an executory proceeding are retained through the intervention.

(b) Art. 755(4) of the 1870 Code of Practice permits summary proceedings to be used to determine "disputes relative to the creditors of a bankrupt." This language is not restrictive, however, as Art. 401 of the 1870 Code indicates that summary proceedings—proceedings by contradictory motion—are to be used in all third oppositions in which the third opponent seeks to assert a mortgage or privilege on the property seized superior to that of the seizing creditor. See also Art. 2592, *supra*, authorizing summary proceedings to determine the rank of mortgages and privileges on property judicially sold.

(c) In so far as mortgages and privileges on immovables and chattel mortgages were concerned, it was not necessary under the 1870 Code for the other creditors to file a third opposition, as their mortgages and privileges were preserved by recordation and would follow the property through into the hands of the adjudicatee at the judicial sale. Liquid Carbonic Co. v. Leger, 169 So. 170 (La.App. 1936). In the case of a creditor having only a privilege on movables, he had to enforce his claim by third opposition, because his privilege affected the movables only as long as they were owned by the original debtor; and if he permitted the movables to be sold, his privilege did not affect them in the hands of the adjudicatee. *Cf.* Art. 3228 of the Civil Code; Liquid Carbonic Co. v. Leger, *supra*.

(d) The second paragraph of the above article is necessary to protect a third party creditor who has a privilege on movables, inferior to that of the seizing creditor, who would otherwise lose his privilege when the sale is made to the adjudicatee. See Comment (c), *supra*.

(e) The first paragraph of this article would be invoked by a superior mortgagee only when his mortgage had matured and was in default. If his mortgage was not then due, the case would be governed by Art. 2374, *supra*. See Art. 2724, *infra*.

(f) See, also, Comments under Arts. 1092, 1313, *supra*.

Art. 2644. Conversion to ordinary proceeding

The plaintiff in an executory proceeding may convert it into an ordinary proceeding by amending his petition so as to pray that the defendant be cited and for judgment against him on the obligation secured by the mortgage or privilege.

The plaintiff in an ordinary proceeding may not convert it into an executory proceeding.

Source: New; cf. Comment following.

Cross References: Arts. 2772, 3723.

Comment

This article is declaratory of the jurisprudential rules. Board of Missions of Methodist Episcopal Church South v. C. D. Craighead

Art. 2671

Co., 130 La. 1076, 58 So. 888 (1912); Cathey, Inc. v. Henriques, 160 La. 692, 107 So. 493 (1926).

CHAPTER 2. PROCEEDING AGAINST SURVIVING SPOUSE, SUCCESSION, OR HEIR

Art.
2671. Proceeding against surviving spouse in community.
2672. Proceeding against heirs or legatees.
2673. Proceeding against legal representative.
2674. Attorney appointed to represent unrepresented defendant.
2675. Case falling within application of two or more articles; plaintiff may bring proceeding under any applicable article.

Art. 2671. Proceeding against surviving spouse in community

When a mortgage or privilege has been granted on community property to secure an obligation of the community, and one of the spouses in community has died subsequently, an executory proceeding to enforce the mortgage or privilege may be brought against the surviving spouse in community. It shall not be necessary to make the succession representative, heirs, or legatees of the deceased spouse parties to the proceeding.

Source: Cf. Former R.S. 13:3414.

Cross References: Arts. 2675, 3723.

Comments

(a) Even prior to 1926, it was the settled jurisprudence of this state that a mortgage affecting community property could be foreclosed under executory process against the surviving husband alone; and that it was not necessary to make the heirs of the deceased wife parties. Citizens' Bank of Louisiana v. Maureau, 37 La. Ann. 857 (1885); Oriol v. Herndon, 38 La.Ann. 759 (1886); Landreaux v. Louque, 43 La.Ann. 234, 9 So. 32 (1891); Gay v. Hebert, 44 La.Ann. 301, 10 So. 775 (1892); Luria v. Cote Blanche Co., 114 La. 385, 38 So. 279 (1905); Schlieder v. Boulet, 124 La. 658, 50 So. 617 (1909). See, also, Comment: Control of Property on Dissolution of the Community of Acquets and Gains, 22 Tul.L.Rev. 486, 492 (1948). The source provision broadened this rule to apply to the surviving wife also.

(b) This article is somewhat broader than former R.S. 13:3414, which merely provides that "it shall not be necessary to make the heirs of the deceased spouse parties to the proceedings." The above article goes further and provides that it "shall not be necessary to make the succession representative, heirs, or legatees of the deceased spouse parties to the proceeding." This language overrules the decision in Coreil v. Vidrine, 171 So. 199 (La.App.1936), which held that, when an administrator had qualified to administer the deceased's estate, he, and not the surviving spouse, must be proceeded against to enforce the mortgage; and that La.Act 57 of 1926 (former R.S. 13:3414) had no application in such cases. This was an unfortunate rule, as it invalidated a judicial sale when the appointment of an administrator was sought by the surviving wife and heirs solely for such purpose; and forced the attorney for the mortgage creditor to check the records of the court to determine whether an administrator had been appointed before filing his executory proceeding to enforce the mortgage. This was particularly onerous when the executory proceeding was brought in one parish, and the deceased spouse was domiciled in another prior to his death.

(c) This article does not disturb the ruling in Dixon v. Federal Land Bank of New Orleans, 196 La. 937, 200 So. 306 (1941), holding that the mortgage creditor could proceed, under La.Act 57 of 1926, against the surviving wife, and if she were absent to have an attorney at law appointed to represent her in the executory proceedings.

Art. 2672. Proceeding against heirs or legatees

When the original debtor is dead, and his heirs or legatees have accepted his succession, the executory proceeding may be brought against his heirs or legatees.

If an heir or legatee is dead, incompetent, or absent, his heirs, legatees, succession, or legal representative may be made a party defendant to the executory proceeding as provided above and in Articles 2673 and 2674, as the case may be.

Source: C.P. Art. 734; former R.S. 13:3411.

Cross References: Arts. 2675, 3723.

Comments

(a) The rules embodied in this article are those heretofore recognized in Louisiana.

(b) See Comment (b) under Art. 2637, *supra*.

Art. 2673. Proceeding against legal representative

When the property of the original debtor is under the administration of a legal representative, the executory proceeding may be brought against his legal representative, and no other person need be made a party to the proceeding.

Source: C.P. Art. 734; former R.S. 13:3411.

Cross References: Arts. 2672, 2675, 3723.

Art. 2673

Comments

(a) No change.

(b) Even prior to the adoption of the sources of this article, it had been held consistently that a mortgagee might enforce his mortgage in an executory proceeding, even if the mortgagor had died and his succession was then under administration. Boguille v. Faille, 1 La.Ann. 204 (1846); McCalop v. Fluker's Heirs, 12 La. Ann. 551 (1857). See, also, Succession of Wilson, 12 La.Ann. 591 (1857); and Berens v. Executors of Boutte, 31 La.Ann. 112 (1879). But if the mortgagee does not so enforce his mortgage, and the property is sold in the succession proceedings, the purchaser acquires the property free of the mortgage, and the mortgagee is paid in due course of the administration of the succession. Lafon's Executors v. Phillips, 2 Mart. (N.S.) 225 (La.1824); Hoey v. Cunningham, 14 La. 86 (1839); Childs v. Lockett, 107 La. 270, 31 So. 751 (1902); and Succession of Jessen v. Calcasieu Building & L. Ass'n, 172 La. 67, 133 So. 365 (1931). If the property is sold in the succession proceeding, the mortgagee must contribute to the costs of administration, if the succession is insolvent. Succession of Sussman, 168 La. 349, 122 So. 62 (1929). See also, Succession of Jessen v. Calcasieu Building & L. Ass'n, *supra*. Under R.S. 6:771 and 6:835, the vendor's privilege and first mortgage of a building and loan association cannot be affected in any way by a succession sale, unless prior written notice of intention to sell is given to the association. One of the purposes of R.S. 6:771 and R.S. 6:835 was to overrule the Sussman and Jessen cases, *supra,* so far as they applied to the privilege and mortgage of a building and loan association. This Code does not change the law with respect to any of the points discussed in this Comment.

(c) See, also, Comments under Art. 3196, *infra*.

Art. 2674. Attorney appointed to represent unrepresented defendant

The court shall appoint an attorney at law to represent the unrepresented defendant in an executory proceeding under the following circumstances:

(1) When the defendant is an absentee;

(2) When the debtor is dead, no succession representative has been appointed, and his heirs and legatees have not been sent into possession;

(3) When the debtor's property is under the administration of a legal representative, but the latter has died, resigned, or been removed from office, and no successor thereof has qualified;

(4) When the defendant is a corporation or a partnership upon which process cannot be served for any reason; and

(5) When the defendant is a minor, or a mental incompetent, who has no legal representative at the time of the institution of the proceeding.

Source: C.P. Arts. 116, 964; C.C. Arts. 56, 313; R.S. 9:841; former R.S. 13:3411.

Cross References: Arts. 2641, 2672, 2675, 3723.

Comments

(a) With the single exception noted in Comment (b), *infra*, no change is effected by the above article.

(b) Paragraph (3) goes beyond the source provisions, the latter being limited to a succession representative. This broadened provision will cover cases where a tutor, curator, receiver, liquidator, or trustee is no longer in office and no successor has been appointed for him.

(c) See Comment (b) under Art. 2637, *supra*.

(d) For the definition of an absentee, see Art. 5251, *infra*.

Art. 2675. Case falling within application of two or more articles; plaintiff may bring proceeding under any applicable article

If a case falls within the provisions of two or more of Articles 2671 through 2674, the plaintiff may bring the executory proceeding under any applicable article.

Source: New; cf. Comments following.

Cross Reference: Art. 3723.

Comment

If the mortgage secures a community obligation and one of the spouses is dead, the case would fall within Art. 2671, *supra*, or under Arts. 2672 through 2674, *supra*, depending upon whether the heirs of the decedent had been sent into possession, upon whether an administrator had been appointed, or upon whether the succession had been opened. This article insures the plaintiff's right to select the most convenient provisions applicable to his case.

CHAPTER 3. PROCEEDINGS WHEN PROPERTY IN POSSESSION OF THIRD PERSON

Art.
2701. Alienation of property to third person disregarded.
2702. Rights of third person who has acquired property and assumed indebtedness.
2703. Rights of third possessor.

Art. 2701. Alienation of property to third person disregarded

A mortgage or privilege evidenced by authentic act importing a confession of judgment, affecting property sold by the original debtor or his legal successor to a third person, may be enforced against the property without reference to any sale or alienation to the third person. The executory proceeding may be brought against the original debtor, his surviving spouse in community, heirs, legatees, or legal representative, as the case may be. The third person who then owns and is in possession of the property need not be made a party to the proceeding.

Source: New; cf. Comment following.

Cross Reference: Art. 3723.

Comments

(a) The purpose of this article is to provide a statutory pact de non alienando to eliminate in the future any necessity for a conventional one. See Art. 3741, *infra*.

Under the Louisiana jurisprudence, if the authentic act evidencing the mortgage or privilege contains a stipulation binding the mortgagor or debtor not to alienate the property affected to the prejudice of the mortgage or privilege, the creditor may disregard all subsequent alienations of the property, and proceed to enforce the mortgage or privilege against the original mortgagor or debtor, just as if he still owned it. Nathan v. Lee, 2 Mart. (N.S.) 32 (La. 1823); Citizens' Bank v. Miller, 44 La.Ann. 199, 10 So. 779 (1892). See, also, 21 Tul.L.Rev. 238 (1946). Under prior law if no such stipulation was contained in the act, the creditor was required to employ the hypothecary action against the third possessor to compel him either to pay the indebtedness or surrender the property.

(b) For a definition of legal representative, see Art. 5251, *infra*.

Art. 2702. Rights of third person who has acquired property and assumed indebtedness

When property sold or otherwise alienated by the original debtor or his legal successor has been seized and is about to be sold under executory process, a person who has acquired the property and assumed the indebtedness secured by the mortgage or privilege thereon may:

(1) Pay the balance due on the indebtedness, in principal, interest, attorney's fees, and costs; or

(2) Arrest the seizure and sale on any of the grounds mentioned in Article 2751.

Source: New; cf. Comment following.

Cross Reference: Art. 3723.

Comment

A person who has acquired the property from the original mortgagor, and assumed the payment of the mortgage, has only the rights which the mortgagor had to arrest the seizure and sale of the mortgaged property. See Art. 2703, *infra*, and Comments thereunder.

Art. 2703. Rights of third possessor

When property sold or otherwise alienated by the original debtor or his legal successor has been seized and is about to be sold under executory process, a person who has acquired the property subject to the mortgage or privilege thereon and who has not assumed the payment of the indebtedness secured thereby may:

(1) Pay the balance due on the indebtedness, in principal, interest, attorney's fees, and costs;

(2) Arrest the seizure and sale on any of the grounds mentioned in Article 2751, or on the ground that the mortgage or privilege was not recorded, or that the inscription of the recordation thereof had perempted; or,

(3) Intervene in the executory proceeding to assert any claim which he has to the enhanced value of the property due to improvements placed on the property by him, or by any prior third possessor through whom he claims ownership of the property. This intervention shall be a summary proceeding initiated by a petition complying with Article 891.

Source: New; cf. Comments following.

Cross Reference: Art. 3723.

Comments

(a) A "third possessor" is a third person who has acquired the property subject to the mortgage; and not one who has expressly assumed its payment. This is the sense in which the term is used by the jurisprudence. Duncan v. Elam, 1 Rob. 135 (La.1841); Twichel v. Andry, 6 Rob. 407 (La.1844); Boissac v. Downs, 16 La. Ann. 187 (1861); Thompson v. Levy, 50 La.Ann. 751, 23 So. 913 (1898); Federal Land Bank v. Cook, 179 La. 857, 155 So. 249 (1934).

(b) The third possessor always has the privilege of paying the plaintiff's claim in full, to avoid the seizure and sale of his property. *Cf.* Art. 3400 of the Civil Code.

(c) The grounds for an injunction to arrest the seizure and sale are set forth in Art. 2751, *infra*. Under this article the third possessor has these same rights. However, under prior law, when the third possessor sought an injunction to arrest the seizure and sale, he was required to furnish security. Only the mortgagor was allowed to obtain an injunction on certain grounds without furnishing security. Pepper v. Dunlap, 19 La. 491 (1841). Art. 2753, *infra*, retains this rule.

The alternative grounds mentioned in paragraph (2) of this article cover the cases where the mortgage or privilege, valid as against the mortgagor or debtor, is not binding upon the third possessor. No change in the law is made in this respect.

(d) Paragraph (3) of this article is declaratory of the settled jurisprudential rule in Louisiana. Citizens' Bank v. Miller, 44 La.Ann. 199, 10 So. 779 (1892); New Orleans Land Co. v. Southern States Fair-Pan-American Exposition Co., 143 La. 884, 79 So. 525 (1918); Glass v. Ives, 169 La. 809, 126 So. 69 (1930), noted 4 Tul. L.Rev. 633 (1930). *Cf.* Art. 3407 of the Civil Code.

(e) See, also, Comments under Art. 2702, *supra*, and Arts. 2753, 3743, *infra*.

CHAPTER 4. EXECUTION OF WRIT OF SEIZURE AND SALE

Art.
2721. Seizure of property; notice.
2722. Advertisement of sale.
2723. Appraisal of property, unless waived.
2724. Articles relating to sales under fieri facias applicable.

Art. 2721. Seizure of property; notice

The sheriff shall seize the property affected by the mortgage or privilege immediately upon receiving the writ of seizure and sale, but not before the expiration of the delay allowed for payment in the demand required by Article 2639, unless this demand has been waived.

The sheriff shall serve upon the defendant a written notice of the seizure of the property.

Source: New; cf. Comments following.

Cross Reference: Art. 3723.

Comments

(a) No change in the procedural law of Louisiana is made by the first paragraph of this article. Under Art. 735 of the 1870 Code, the defendant is served with a demand for payment of the indebtedness within three or five days, as the case may be; and the sheriff cannot seize the property until the expiration of this demand. Hawley v. Heyman, 28 La.Ann. 347 (1876); Billgery v. Ferguson, 30 La. Ann. 84 (1878). The first paragraph of this article is declaratory of this rule.

(b) A significant change in Louisiana procedure is made by the second paragraph of this article. Under Arts. 654 and 745 of the 1870 Code, the sheriff must serve upon the debtor notice of the seizure which he has made under the writ of seizure and sale. In this connection, see the form of notice of seizure in Flemming's Formulary 521 (1933); and Louisiana Formulary Annotated 226 (1951). In many mortgage forms, however, the debtor not only waives notice of the three day demand for payment, but also any notice of seizure by the sheriff. Since citation is not required in an executory proceeding, in such cases the debtor receives no notice whatever of either the institution of the executory proceeding, or the seizure of the property, unless he happens to read the fine print on the back pages of the local newspaper which carries the judicial advertisement of the sale of the property. Such a result is undesirable, not only from the viewpoint of the original mortgagor who is proceeded against, but even more so from the standpoint of a third possessor who purchased the property subject to the mortgage. The third possessor may have a substantial claim for the enhanced value of the mortgaged property due to improvements which he placed thereon, which may be completely lost through a judicial sale of the property before the third possessor ever learns of the institution of the executory proceeding. For this reason, the second paragraph prevents a waiver of the sheriff's notice of seizure in any case.

In the great majority of cases the third possessor will be informed of the seizure by the mortgagor on whom the sheriff has served notice thereof, yet occasionally the information may not be received in this manner. However, any requirement of service of seizure by the sheriff upon the person in possession of the property would destroy the efficacy of executory process.

Art. 2722. Advertisement of sale

After the seizure of the property, the sheriff shall proceed to advertise the sale of the property, in accordance with the provisions of the first paragraph of Article 2331.

Source: C.P. Art. 745.

Cross Reference: Art. 3723.

Comment

No change in the procedural law of Louisiana is effected by this article.

Art. 2723. Appraisal of property, unless waived

Prior to the sale, the property seized must be appraised in accordance with law, unless appraisal has been waived in the act evidencing the mortgage or privilege and plaintiff has prayed that the property be sold without appraisal, and the order directing the issuance of the writ of seizure and sale has directed that the property be sold as prayed for.

Source: C.P. Art. 745; cf. Comment following.

Cross References: Arts. 2724, 2771, 3723.

Comment

No change in the procedural law of Louisiana is effected by this article. The rule with respect to the waiver of appraisal is supported by Stockmeyer v. Tobin, 139 U.S. 176, 11 S.Ct. 504, 35 L.Ed. 123 (1891) and the Louisiana cases cited therein.

Art. 2724. Articles relating to sales under fieri facias applicable

The provisions of Articles 2333 through 2335, and 2337 through 2381, relating to a sale of property under the writ of fieri facias, shall apply to a sale of property under the writ of seizure and sale.

The provisions of Article 2336 shall also apply to a sale of property under the writ of seizure and sale, unless appraisement has been waived, as provided in Article 2723.

Source: C.P. Art. 745.

Cross Reference: Art. 3723.

Comment

This article makes specific, rather than general, cross-references to the articles on execution of judgments dealing with the formalities and requirements of the sheriff's sale, the price which must

Tit. 2 INJUNCTION Art. 2751

be offered to effect adjudication, the sheriff's act of sale, and the adjudication and its effect. No change in Louisiana law is intended.

See, also, Comments under Arts. 324, 2643, *supra*.

CHAPTER 5. INJUNCTION TO ARREST SEIZURE AND SALE

Art.
2751. Grounds for arresting seizure and sale.
2752. Injunction procedure.
2753. Security not required in certain cases.
2754. Security otherwise required.

Art. 2751. Grounds for arresting seizure and sale

The defendant in the executory proceeding may arrest the seizure and sale of the property by injunction when the debt secured by the mortgage or privilege is extinguished, or is legally unenforceable, or if the procedure required by law for an executory proceeding has not been followed.

Source: New; cf. C.P. Arts. 738, 739.

Cross References: Arts. 2642, 2702, 2703, 3723.

Comments

(a) See cases cited in Comment (a) of Art. 2752, *infra*.

(b) Despite the language of Arts. 738 and 739 of the Code of Practice of 1870, it is now definitely settled that the defendant in an executory proceeding is not limited to the specific grounds mentioned in Art. 739 to obtain an injunction to arrest the seizure and sale. Injunction can be obtained on any valid ground, but security must be furnished by the applicant for injunctive relief, unless he relies exclusively on the grounds mentioned in Art. 739. Kreher v. Theisman's Estate, 125 La. 600, 51 So. 656 (1910); Franek v. Brewster, 141 La. 1031, 76 So. 187 (1916); Jones v. Bouanchaud, 158 La. 27, 103 So. 393 (1925).

(c) The above article gives in general terms the grounds on which the seizure and sale may be arrested by injunction. Art. 2753, *infra*, gives the specific grounds on which injunction may be issued without bond. See the Comments thereunder.

(d) The provisions in the above article permitting injunctive relief to arrest the seizure and sale of the property in an executory proceeding when "the procedure required by law for an executory proceeding has not been followed" was inserted primarily to make injunctive relief available to the defendant when the order of seizure and sale was issued without sufficient authentic evidence. No change in the law is made in this respect. See Comment (b) under Art. 2753, *infra*.

(e) See, also, Comments under Art. 2298, *supra*.

Art. 2752. Injunction procedure

The petition for injunction shall be filed in the court where the executory proceeding is pending, either in the executory proceeding or in a separate suit. The injunction proceeding to arrest a seizure and sale shall be governed by the provisions of Articles 3601 through 3609, and 3612, except as provided in Article 2753.

Source: C.P. Arts. 738, 739; former R.S. 13:4062–4071; cf. Comments following.

Cross References: Arts. 2642, 3723.

Comments

(a) It is well established in the jurisprudence that the seizure and sale can be arrested only by a petition for an injunction, and not by a rule to set aside the order of seizure and sale. Clement v. Oakey, 2 Rob. 90 (La.1842); Minot v. Bank of the United States, 4 Rob. 490 (La.1843); Merchants Bank of Baltimore v. Bank of the United States, 4 Rob. 493 (La.1843); Koch v. Godchaux, 46 La.Ann. 1382, 16 So. 181 (1894). *Cf.* State v. Judge of the Fourth District Court, 18 La.Ann. 110 (1866); Levi v. Converse, 20 La.Ann. 558 (1868).

(b) Apparently no issue has been raised in the reported cases as to whether the petition for injunctive relief to arrest a seizure and sale should be filed in the executory proceedings or in a separate suit. Both practices appear to have been followed at one time or another in various sections of the state. The point is technical, and of no real importance, as long as it is settled definitely. The above article permits either practice.

(c) It is now settled that former R.S. 13:4062 through R.S. 13:-4071, regulating interlocutory injunctive orders, are applicable to injunctive relief granted to arrest the seizure and sale in an executory proceeding. American Nat. Bank v. Bauman, 173 La. 336, 137 So. 54 (1931). See, also, 17 Tul.L.Rev. 630 (1943).

(d) The exception as to Art. 2753, *infra*, is intended to preserve the exceptions embodied in Art. 739 of the 1870 Code permitting injunction without bond in certain cases.

(e) See, also, Comments under Arts. 2298, 2751, *supra*.

Art. 2753. Security not required in certain cases

The original debtor, his surviving spouse in community, heirs, legatees, and legal representative are not required to furnish security

Tit. 2 INJUNCTION Art. 2753

for the issuance of a temporary restraining order or preliminary injunction to arrest a seizure and sale, when the injunctive relief is applied for solely on one or more of the following grounds:

(1) The debt secured by the mortgage or privilege is extinguished or prescribed;

(2) The enforcement of the debt secured by the mortgage or privilege is premature, either because the original term allowed for payment, or any extension thereof granted by the creditor, had not expired at the time of the institution of the executory proceeding;

(3) The act evidencing the mortgage or privilege is forged, or the debtor's signature thereto was procured by fraud, violence, or other unlawful means;

(4) The defendant in the executory proceeding has a liquidated claim to plead in compensation against the debt secured by the mortgage or privilege; or

(5) The order directing the issuance of the writ of seizure and sale was rendered without sufficient authentic evidence having been submitted to the court, or the evidence submitted was not actually authentic.

Source: C.P. Arts. 739, 740; cf. Comments following.

Cross References: Arts. 2642, 2752, 2754, 3723.

Comments

(a) See Comment (c) under Art. 2703, *supra*, and Comment (a) under Art. 2754, *infra*.

(b) This article merely regroups and broadens the grounds for the issuance of an injunction to arrest the seizure and sale provided in Art. 739 of the 1870 Code. The latter mentions some, but not all, of the ways in which the obligation secured by the mortgage or privilege is extinguished. The above article groups all of these in the word "extinguished," which refers to Art. 2130 of the Civil Code, mentioning all of the ways in which obligations are extinguished. Prescription is expressly added, to eliminate the theoretical argument as to whether prescription extinguishes the obligation, or merely renders it legally unenforceable. On the other hand, there is some repetition. For example, although compensation is included in the term "extinguished," it has been included in paragraph (3) to make it clear that this ground for the issuance of injunctive relief is not abrogated.

(c) Prior to 1925, there were two lines of authority in Louisiana on the question of whether lack of sufficient authentic evidence was a matter which could be urged under a petition for injunctive relief to arrest the seizure and sale, or whether it could be raised only on

Art. 2753 EXECUTORY PROCEEDINGS Bk. 5

appeal. The various cases are set forth in the majority and dissenting opinions in Jones v. Bouanchaud, 158 La. 27, 103 So. 393 (1925); and in McMahon 1462–1464, nn. 15–17. In 1925, the supreme court held that lack of sufficient authentic evidence could be raised in the petition for injunction, and expressly overruled the earlier cases to the contrary. Jones v. Bouanchaud, *supra*. Despite this, however, the supreme court subsequently took the position that this defect in the executory proceeding could be raised only on an appeal. Weber v. Dawson, 172 La. 213, 133 So. 751 (1931); Bank of Coushatta v. Burch, 177 La. 465, 148 So. 680 (1933); Coreil v. Vidrine, 188 La. 343, 177 So. 233 (1937). Finally in 1953 the supreme court again considered the question, and held that lack of authentic evidence could be raised either under an application for injunctive relief to arrest the seizure and sale, or under an appeal from the order therefor. All cases to the contrary were again expressly overruled. General Motors Acceptance Corp. v. Anzelmo, 222 La. 1019, 64 So. 2d 417 (1953), noted 14 La.L.Rev. 289 (1953).

The position taken by the Supreme Court in the Anzelmo case is codified in this article. For the reasons supporting this position, see McMahon 1464, n. 17, and 14 La.L.Rev. 289 (1953).

(d) Under the above article, the applicant does not have to furnish security for an interlocutory injunctive order to arrest the seizure and sale on the grounds of lack of sufficient authentic evidence. This is contrary to the jurisprudence under Art. 740 of the Code of Practice of 1870. *Cf.* Jones v. Bouanchaud, *supra;* Kreher v. Theisman's Estate, *supra;* Franek v. Brewster, *supra*. This change is justified, however, since there is no more reason for compelling the applicant to furnish security when his application is based on this ground than when it is based on prescription.

(e) See, also, Comments under Arts. 2298, 2703, 2751.

Art. 2754. Security otherwise required

Except as provided in Article 2753, no temporary restraining order or preliminary injunction shall issue to arrest a seizure and sale unless the applicant therefor furnishes security as provided in Article 3610.

Source: New; cf. Comments following.

Cross References: Arts. 2642, 3723.

Comments

(a) This article codifies the jurisprudence to the effect that a bond is never required for the issuance of a final injunction, it being necessary only for the temporary restraining order or the preliminary injunction. Hankins v. Police Jury, 152 La. 1000, 95 So.

102 (1922); DeMaupassant v. Clayton, 214 La. 812, 38 So.2d 791 (1949); Hickman v. Branan, 151 So. 113 (La.App.1933).

(b) Except as noted in Comment (c), *infra*, no change is made in the law. Under the 1870 Code, though an injunction to arrest a seizure and sale could be issued on some ground other than those specified in Art. 738 thereof, the plaintiff was required to furnish the security required by the trial court for the issuance of an interlocutory injunctive order. Kreher v. Theisman's Estate, *supra*; Franek v. Brewster, *supra*; Jones v. Bouanchaud, *supra*.

(c) The same change effected in Art. 2753, *supra*, is made in this article. See Comment (d) under Art. 2753, *supra*.

(d) See, also, Comments under Art. 2753, *supra*, and Art. 2783, *infra*.

CHAPTER 6. DEFICIENCY JUDGMENT

Art.
2771. When deficiency judgment obtainable.
2772. Procedure to obtain deficiency judgment.

Art. 2771. When deficiency judgment obtainable

The creditor may obtain a judgment against the debtor for any deficiency due on the debt after the distribution of the proceeds of the judicial sale only if the property has been sold under the executory proceeding after appraisal in accordance with the provisions of Article 2723.

Source: R.S. 13:4106, 13:4107.

Cross Reference: Art. 3723.

Comments

(a) No change in the law is effected by this article.

(b) Since R.S. 13:4106 and 13:4107 are considerably broader than the proposed article, they have been retained in the Revised Statutes.

Art. 2772. Procedure to obtain deficiency judgment

A creditor may obtain a deficiency judgment against the debtor either by converting the executory proceeding into an ordinary proceeding as provided in Article 2644, or by a separate suit. In either case, the defendant must be cited, and all of the delays and formalities required in ordinary proceedings must be observed.

Source: New; cf. Comment following.

Cross Reference: Art. 3723.

Art. 2772   EXECUTORY PROCEEDINGS   Bk. 5

Comment

The above article is merely declaratory of established practices, and of the jurisprudence of Louisiana. Gordon v. Gilfoil, 99 U.S. 168, 25 L.Ed. 383 (1879); Liquidators of Prudential Savings & Homestead Society v. Nassans, 8 La.App. 712 (1928). *Cf.* Rogers v. Binyon, 124 La. 95, 49 So. 991 (1909); Beck v. Natalie Oil Co., 143 La. 153, 78 So. 430 (1918).

CHAPTER 7. MAKING JUDGMENTS OF OTHER LOUISIANA COURTS EXECUTORY

Art.
2781. When judgments may be made executory by other courts.
2782. Procedure; execution of executory judgment.
2783. Injunction to arrest execution of judgment made executory.

Art. 2781. When judgments may be made executory by other courts

A judgment rendered in a Louisiana court may be made executory in any other Louisiana court of competent jurisdiction, if its execution has not been and may not be suspended by appeal.

Source: C.P. Arts. 746, 747.

Cross Reference: Art. 2782.

Comments

(a) Arts. 746 and 747 of the Code of Practice of 1825 permitted the use of executory process for the enforcement of judgments rendered by all other courts, whether in this state, or another, or in a foreign country. La.Act 197 of 1846, however, repealed so much of these articles as authorized a judgment creditor from another state or country to enforce his judgment in Louisiana by executory process. Scott v. Duke, 3 La.Ann. 253 (1848); Ward v. Agricultural Bank of Mississippi, 3 La.Ann. 450 (1848); Kilgore v. Planters' Bank, 3 La.Ann. 693 (1848); Commercial Bank of Natchez v. Markham, 3 La.Ann. 698 (1848); Davis v. Dugas, 11 La.Ann. 118 (1856); Jones v. Jamison, 15 La.Ann. 35 (1860); Turley v. Dreyfus, 35 La.Ann. 510 (1883). Arts. 746 and 747 of the Code of Practice of 1870 were rewritten to delete therefrom the provisions which had been repealed by the 1846 legislation. See Turley v. Dreyfus, *supra*.

(b) Ordinarily the judgment rendered by another Louisiana court will be enforced through the writ of fieri facias authorizing the sheriff where the debtor's property is located to seize and sell it under this writ to satisfy a judgment. Art. 642, Code of Practice of 1870; Lafon v. Smith, 3 La. 473 (1832). Hence, usually there is no necessity to make the judgment of another Louisiana court executory. There are two instances where it is absolutely necessary to make the judgment of the other court executory: (1) in garnishment proceedings under the writ of fieri facias, where the garnishee is domiciled in another parish, Art. 2416, *supra;* and (2) in the examination of a judgment debtor domiciled in a parish other than the one in which the judgment was rendered. Art. 2452, *supra.*

(c) Under Arts. 746 and 747 of the Code of Practice of 1870, it is only the judgment of another Louisiana court having the force of res judicata which can be made executory. The above article provides that any judgment of another Louisiana court can be made executory if it has not been suspended by an appeal and the delay therefor has elapsed. Thus, if a judgment is executory in the court where it was rendered, there is no reason why it should not be made executory in any other Louisiana court necessary to its enforcement.

(d) See, also, Comments under Art. 2631, *supra.*

Art. 2782. Procedure; execution of executory judgment

A creditor wishing to have a judgment of a Louisiana court made executory, as provided in Article 2781, may file an ex parte petition complying with Article 891, with a certified copy of the judgment annexed, praying that the judgment be made executory. The court shall immediately render and sign its judgment making the judgment of the other Louisiana court executory.

The judgment thus made executory may be executed or enforced immediately as if it had been a judgment of that court rendered in an ordinary proceeding.

Source: New; cf. Comments following.

Cross Reference: Art. 2783.

Comments

(a) The 1870 Code provisions do not state exactly how the judgment of the other Louisiana court is to be made executory, other than to state that executory process can be employed. This article is based upon the customary practice followed in this state.

(b) The judgment thus made executory is enforced, not by the writ of seizure and sale, but by the writ of fieri facias. Canal Bank v. Copeland, 12 La. 34 (1838). Cf. Featherston'h v. Compton, 3 La. Ann. 380 (1848).

(c) See, also, Comments under Art. 2631, *supra.*

Art. 2783. Injunction to arrest execution of judgment made executory

The execution of a judgment made executory under the provisions of Article 2782 may be arrested by injunction if the judgment is extinguished, prescribed, or is otherwise legally unenforceable. No temporary restraining order or a preliminary writ of injunction may be issued, however, unless the applicant therefor furnishes security as provided in Article 3610.

Source: C.P. Arts. 748–751.

Comments

(a) The large bond required of the applicant for an injunction under Art. 750 of the 1870 Code, to restrain the judicial sale of movables, was required because the injunction pendente lite issued ex parte, and usually could not be dissolved until after the case had been tried on its merits. The judgment creditor was given ample protection, however, and there is no reason for requiring in this Code greater security than is required of the applicant in other injunction cases.

(b) Security is not required for the issuance of a permanent injunction, which issues only after a full and complete trial of the case on its merits. See Comment (a) under Art. 2754, *supra*.

BOOK VI.
PROBATE PROCEDURE

TITLE I
GENERAL DISPOSITIONS

Chap.		Art.
1.	Jurisdiction	2811
2.	Evidence of Jurisdiction and Heirship	2821
3.	Probate and Registry of Testaments	2851
	Sec.	
	1. Procedure Preliminary to Probate	2851
	2. Ex Parte Probate of Testaments	2881
	3. Contradictory Probate of Testaments	2901
4.	Annulment of Probated Testaments	2931
5.	Payment of State Inheritance Taxes	2951
6.	General Rules of Procedure	2971

INTRODUCTION

The adoption of the terminology "jurisdiction" and "venue" instead of the traditional civilian terminology "jurisdiction ratione materiae" and "jurisdiction ratione personae" is fully discussed at Book I, Title I, Chapter 1, Jurisdiction.

In the strictest sense, of course, the provisions relating to the jurisdiction of succession proceedings are to be found in Art. VII, §§ 35 and 81, of the Louisiana Constitution of 1921, conferring exclusive original jurisdiction upon the district courts "in all probate and succession matters." Yet venue has always been held to be jurisdictional in the succession procedure of Louisiana, and if the proceeding is brought in an improper parish, all of the orders and judgments rendered by the court are absolutely null. Succession of Williamson, 3 La.Ann. 261 (1848); Armstrong v. Bakewell, 18 La.Ann. 30 (1866); Miltenberger v. Knox, 21 La.Ann. 399 (1869); Clemens v. Comfort, 26 La.Ann. 269 (1874); Taylor v. Williams, 162 La. 92, 110 So. 100 (1926); Succession of Lewis, 174 La. 901,

142 So. 121 (1932); Succession of Dancie, 191 La. 518, 186 So. 14 (1939); Carter v. Cambrice, 1 La.App. 156 (1924); Taylor v. Williams, 3 La.App. 772 (1926); Succession of Bibbins, 152 So. 592 (La.App.1934).

Accordingly, in this Code the rules governing the place where a succession is to be opened judicially are treated as supplementary rules of jurisdiction, rather than as rules of venue.

There are included in Title I only those provisions of the Inheritance Tax Statute, R.S. 47:2401 *et seq.*, which relate to: (1) the procedural implementation for the payment of taxes due; (2) the submission of proof to the inheritance tax collector of the property of the succession and the value thereof; and (3) the procedure for determining the taxes due, and for evidencing the amount and payment thereof.

No effort has been made to integrate any of the procedure for the payment or collection of the state estate transfer tax, R.S. 47:2431 *et seq.*, for the reason that this tax, like the federal estate tax, normally is paid after the termination of the succession proceeding, or if paid during the administration of the succession, it requires nothing more than a court order permitting the succession representative to pay it.

CHAPTER 1. JURISDICTION

Art.
2811. Court in which succession opened.
2812. Proceedings in different courts; stay; adoption of proceedings by court retaining jurisdiction.

Art. 2811. Court in which succession opened

A proceeding to open a succession shall be brought in the district court of the parish where the deceased was domiciled at the time of his death.

If the deceased was not domiciled in this state at the time of his death, his succession may be opened in the district court of any parish where:

(1) Immovable property of the deceased is situated; or,

(2) Movable property of the deceased is situated, if he owned no immovable property in the state at the time of his death.

Source: C.P. Art. 929; C.C. Art. 935; Const. Art. VII, §§ 35, 81; cf. Restatement of Conflict of Laws, §§ 467, 469.

Cross References: Arts. 44, 3401.

Tit. 1 JURISDICTION Art. 2812

Comments

(a) Prior to 1952, probate jurisdiction could be alternatively established: (1) in the parish of the domicile of the deceased; (2) in the parish where deceased left immovable property, or in the parish of the situs of the principal immovable if he left immovables in more than one parish; or (3) in the parish where the deceased had died, if he had no domicile in the state. The last alternative was applicable in cases where the deceased had no Louisiana domicile, but died in Louisiana leaving movable property in the state. 1870 Code of Practice Art. 929; Civil Code Art. 935.

There was no provision, however, covering cases in which a decedent, domiciled in another state, had died in another jurisdiction, leaving only movable property in Louisiana. To remove this hiatus, Art. 929 of the Code of Practice of 1870 was amended by La.Act 87 of 1952 to provide that the succession could be opened in any parish where decedent had left movable property, if at the time of his death he was domiciled elsewhere and had left no immovable property in Louisiana.

The 1952 amendment also provided that if decedent had no domicile or property in Louisiana, his succession could be opened in the parish where he died, if death occurred in this state. It is clear, however, that this last provision could serve no useful purpose since the courts of Louisiana would have no jurisdiction to open a succession unless the decedent was either domiciled in this state at the time of his death, or had property in this state. Goodrich, Conflict of Laws (3rd ed.) 535 *et seq.* (1949). If the deceased was domiciled in Louisiana, or had property in this state at the time of his death, then paragraph 4 of Art. 929 of the 1870 Code of Practice could not be applied. Conversely, if there was neither domicile nor property in this state, then the Louisiana courts would not be vested with jurisdiction to open the succession. For these reasons, paragraph 4 of Art. 929 of the 1870 Code, as amended, was not retained in the above article.

(b) Nothing in the above article conflicts with or modifies the provisions of Art. 2315 of the Civil Code, as amended.

(c) See, also, Comments under Arts. 2812, 4031, 4032, 4033, *infra.*

Art. 2812. Proceedings in different courts; stay; adoption of proceedings by court retaining jurisdiction

If proceedings to open the succession of a deceased person who was not domiciled in this state at the time of his death are brought in two or more district courts of competent jurisdiction, the court in which the proceeding was first brought shall retain jurisdiction over the succession, and the other courts shall stay their proceedings.

The court retaining jurisdiction may adopt by ex parte order any of the proceedings taken in any other Louisiana court of competent jurisdiction, with the same force and effect as if these proceedings had been taken in the adopting court.

Source: Model Probate Code, § 61(b).

Cross Reference: Art. 44.

Comments

(a) This article solves the problem first presented under the 1952 amendment of Art. 929 of the 1870 Code. See Comment (a) under Art. 2811, *supra*. In the absence of a specific rule on the subject, the question would be governed by the application of the rules of judicial comity: that the court first seized of jurisdiction would retain it, and that the second and subsequent courts would stay their proceedings when the matter was called to their attention. But this is unsatisfactory; see McMahon, The Revision of Probate Procedure in Louisiana, 1 La.Bar J. 59, 60 (October, 1953).

(b) Sec. 61(b) of the Model Probate Code provides that "if proceedings are commenced in more than one county, they shall be stayed except in the county where first commenced until final determination of venue in the county where first commenced . . .", and although the section relates expressly to venue, the place where the proceedings should be filed is considered jurisdictional.

(c) Proceedings conducted in a Louisiana court of competent jurisdiction, other than the court which first opened the succession, are not null, but the court retaining jurisdiction has the power and authority to adopt any of these proceedings as its own, if deemed advisable. The court retaining jurisdiction is not compelled to adopt, but rather authorized to adopt, the proceedings of another court, and then with the same force and effect as if these proceedings had been taken in the adopting court.

CHAPTER 2. EVIDENCE OF JURISDICTION AND HEIRSHIP

Art.
2821. Evidence of jurisdiction, death, and relationship.
2822. Requirements of affidavit evidence.
2823. Additional evidence.
2824. No affidavit evidence of factual issues.
2825. Costs.
2826. Definition of certain terms used in Book VI.

Art. 2821. Evidence of jurisdiction, death, and relationship

The deceased's domicile at the time of his death, his ownership of property in this state, and all other facts necessary to establish the jurisdiction of the court may be evidenced by affidavits.

The deceased's death, his marriage, and all other facts necessary to establish the relationship of his heirs may be evidenced either by official certificates issued by the proper public officer, or by affidavits.

Source: New; cf. Comments following.

Cross References: Arts. 2822, 2823, 2824, 3003, 3361, 3371.

Comments

(a) The rule of the above article is declaratory of the established succession procedure in Louisiana since the days of Spanish dominion. "Yet the curious thing is that no provision of positive law either requires or sanctions this mode of proof. This probate custom has a legitimate ancestry in the 'proof and half-proof' of eighteenth century Spanish procedure—the affidavit of each 'good and credible' witness being half-proof, and the affidavits of both being full proof." McMahon 1484, n. 13.

(b) Certificates of birth, death, and marriage issued by the proper public official afford the most reliable proof of the facts recited. Due to the difficulty and, in the case of some older persons, the impossibility of obtaining these official certificates, the established custom of proof of these facts by affidavit has been retained.

(c) See, also, Comments under Arts. 2852, 3061, *infra*.

Art. 2822. Requirements of affidavit evidence

The affidavits referred to in Article 2821 shall be executed by two persons having knowledge of the facts sworn to. These affidavits shall be filed in the record of the succession proceeding.

Source: New; cf. Comments following.

Cross References: Arts. 2824, 3003, 3361, 3371.

Comments

(a) See Comments under Art. 2821, *supra*.

(b) The rationale of the custom of proving the facts in an ex parte succession by affidavits is that the latter constitute the depositions of "two good and credible witnesses." Since at the time this custom was adopted the parties to any judicial proceeding were deemed incompetent to testify, there was implicit in the customary practice the requirement that the affidavits annexed to the petition be those of disinterested witnesses. However, there is no requirement in the above article that the affiants be disinterested. In the case of old people, dying with few or no relatives here, the heirs and the attorney are often the only persons who can swear to the facts showing the relationship of the heirs. Furthermore, in certain parts of the state the practice heretofore has not been to require disinterested affiants, and if any requirement is made that the affidavits be those of disinterested witnesses doubt might be cast in many cases upon the legality of judgments of possession based upon completely accurate recitals of fact.

(c) See, also, Comments under Art. 3061, *infra*.

Art. 2823. Additional evidence

In any case in which evidence by affidavit is permitted under Article 2821, the court may require further evidence of any fact sworn to therein by the introduction of evidence as in ordinary cases.

Source: New; cf. Comments following.

Cross References: Arts. 3003, 3361, 3371.

Comments

(a) See Comments under Art. 2821, *supra*.

(b) Considering the facility by which alleged heirs may be placed in possession of the estate of the deceased, the court should not be compelled to accept at face value all recitals in the affidavits supporting the petition for possession, or a petition for the appointment of an administrator. Therefore, in cases in which the court may have some reason to desire further supporting evidence, it is permitted to require it. See also Comment (c) under Art. 2824, *infra*.

(c) See, also, Comments under Arts. 2824, 3095, 3783, *infra*.

Art. 2824. No affidavit evidence of factual issues

No fact which is an issue in a contradictory proceeding in a succession may be proved by affidavit under Articles 2821 and 2822. In all such contradictory proceedings, issues of fact shall be determined on the trial thereof only by evidence introduced as in ordinary cases.

Source: New; cf. Comments following.

Comments

(a) See Comments under Art. 2821, *supra*.

(b) The above article does not make any change in the succession procedure of Louisiana. In view of the express permission in this Code for the use of affidavit evidence, however, it is believed that its use should be expressly limited as provided above.

(c) The term "proof as in ordinary cases" is taken from the language of the Injunction Act of 1924, particularly former R.S. 13:4067. Under that statute, it means documentary evidence or testimony (either viva voce in open court or by deposition) introduced in open court on the trial of an ordinary proceeding. It is intended to have the same meaning in the above article and in Art. 2823, *supra*.

(d) See, also, Comments under Art. 2823, *supra*, and Arts. 3061, 3095, *infra*.

Art. 2825. Costs

In all succession proceedings conducted ex parte, the court costs are to be paid from the mass of the succession. In all contradictory succession proceedings, the court costs are to be paid by the party cast, unless the court directs otherwise.

Source: New.

Comments

The first sentence of this article is merely declaratory of prior Louisiana practice. Under Art. 157 of the Code of 1870, in the trial court, court costs are automatically imposed upon the party cast. This inflexible rule is unfortunate, and occasionally militates against the interests of justice. For this reason, in the second sentence of this article, the trial court is granted authority to assess court costs against any party, in the interests of justice. This accords with the general policy adopted with respect to the imposition of costs. See Art. 1920, *supra*, and Comments thereunder.

See, also, Comments under Art. 4322, *infra*.

Art. 2826. Definition of certain terms used in Book VI

Except where the context clearly indicates otherwise, as used in the articles of this Book:

(1) "Residuary legatee" includes a universal legatee, a legatee under a universal title, and an heir who inherits the residue of a testamentary succession in default of a valid disposition thereof by the testator; and

(2) "Succession representative" includes an administrator, provisional administrator, administrator of a vacant succession, executor, and dative testamentary executor.

Source: New.

Comments

(a) The term "residuary legatee" is used in a number of articles in this Book, and particularly Arts. 2931, 3031, through 3035, and

3372, for purposes of simplification of language, and to avoid repeated use of lengthy phrases.

(b) The term "succession representative" is used throughout the articles in this Book dealing with the rights, duties, power, and authority common to administrators, provisional administrators, administrators of vacant successions, executors, and dative testamentary executors, for purposes of brevity, and to avoid repeated enumeration of all of these succession representatives.

CHAPTER 3. PROBATE AND REGISTRY OF TESTAMENTS

SECTION 1. PROCEDURE PRELIMINARY TO PROBATE

Art.
2851. Petition for probate.
2852. Documents submitted with petition for probate.
2853. Purported testament must be filed, though possessor doubts validity.
2854. Search for testament.
2855. Return to order to search for testament.
2856. Probate hearing; probate forthwith if witnesses present.
2857. Proponent must produce witnesses; subpoenas.

SECTION 2. EX PARTE PROBATE OF TESTAMENTS

2881. Ex parte probate if no objection.
2882. Proceedings at probate hearing.
2883. Olographic testament.
2884. Nuncupative testament by private act.
2885. Mystic testament.
2886. Probate of nuncupative testament by private act or mystic testament, when witnesses dead or absent.
2887. Statutory testament.
2888. Foreign testament.
2889. Depositions of witnesses.
2890. Procès verbal of probate.
2891. Nuncupative testament by public act executed without probate.
2892. Use of probate testimony in subsequent action.
2893. Period within which will must be probated.

SECTION 3. CONTRADICTORY PROBATE OF TESTAMENTS

2901. Contradictory trial required; time to file opposition.
2902. Opposition to petition for probate.
2903. Proponent bears burden of proof.

SECTION 1. PROCEDURE PRELIMINARY TO PROBATE

Art. 2851. Petition for probate

If the deceased is believed to have died testate, any person who considers that he has an interest in opening the succession may petition a court of competent jurisdiction for the probate and execution of the testament.

Source: C.P. Art. 928.

Comments

This article does not change the probate procedure of Louisiana and does not require an actual justiciable interest, but permits the probate of the testament to be requested by any person who considers that he has an interest in its probate.

See, also, Comments under Art. 3095, *infra*.

Art. 2852. Documents submitted with petition for probate

The petitioner shall submit with his petition evidence of the death of the deceased, and of all other facts necessary to establish the jurisdiction of the court.

If the testament of the deceased is one other than a nuncupative testament by public act, and is in the possession of the petitioner, he shall present it to the court, and pray that it be probated and executed.

Source: Cf. C.P. Arts. 928, 932, 934; C.C. Art. 1645.

Comments

(a) To avoid the raising of any questions as to the validity of a testament contained in a sealed envelope, or the probate thereof, when this envelope was broken, no provision has been made in this Code, similar to Art. 934 of the 1870 Code of Practice, referring to the court's opening of the sealed envelope containing the testament.

(b) See Art. 2821, *supra*, for the requirement of the evidence necessary to establish the jurisdiction of the court.

(c) The above article refers to a case where the person having the possession of a testament of a decedent believes it to be authentic and valid. Under such circumstances it would be his duty to produce and file the testament, and to pray for its probate in due course. Art. 2853, *infra*, covers the case where a person finds himself in possession of what purports to be the testament of a decedent of which he doubts the authenticity or validity.

Art. 2853. Purported testament must be filed, though possessor doubts validity

If a person has possession of a document purporting to be the testament of a deceased person, even though he believes that the document is not the valid testament of the deceased, or has doubts concerning the validity thereof, he shall present it to the court with his petition praying that the document be filed in the record of the succession proceeding.

A person so presenting a purported testament to the court shall not be deemed to vouch for its authenticity or validity, nor precluded from asserting its invalidity.

Source: New: cf. Comment following.

Comment

This article covers the case of a person in possession of what purports to be the testament of the deceased of which the possessor doubts the validity or authenticity. In such a case the person in possession should file the instrument in court, but his act in filing the purported testament does not impose upon him the penalty of being considered as having vouched for its authenticity or validity.

Art. 2854. Search for testament

If the testament is not in the possession of the petitioner, he shall pray that the court direct that a search be made for the testament by a notary of the parish. In its order directing the search, the court may order any person having in his possession or under his control any books, papers, or documents of the deceased, or any bank box, safety deposit vault, or other receptacle likely to contain the testament of the deceased, to permit the examination of the books, papers, and documents, and of the contents of the bank box, safety deposit vault, or other receptacle, by the notary.

Source: C.P. Arts. 936, 937; R.S. 47:2409A.

Comments

(a) Testaments are usually kept in safety deposit vaults, or in safes at the office or home of the testator. For this reason, the search for the testament contemplated by R.S. 47:2409(A) is more effective than that provided in Arts. 936 and 937 of the 1870 Code. Even though the Revised Statutes provision was adopted to permit the inheritance tax collector to make a judicial search for the testament, since its enactment a similar practice has been customarily followed in practically all cases where the testament has not been found in the private papers of the testator in his home or office.

(b) It is not necessary to retain the provisions of Art. 937 of the 1870 Code of Practice. If the custodian of the testament proves contumacious, and refuses to deliver it to the notary appointed to make the service, the court has ample implied power to enforce its order through punishment for contempt.

(c) Under the provisions of the Inheritance Tax Act, R.S. 47:-2401–47:2435, and particularly under R.S. 47:2413, no bank or other depositary may deliver possession to any of the heirs or legatees of the deceased, nor permit entry by anyone into the bank box or other deposit vault until after three days' written notice to the inheritance tax collector. Because of the severe penalties provided for any violation of these provisions, banks and other depositaries rarely, if ever, permit entry into a bank box of the deceased by the notary searching for the will without a court order permitting the search and notification in advance thereof to the inheritance tax collector, so that he may have a representative present during the search, if he so desires.

Art. 2855. Return to order to search for testament

If the notary finds any document which purports to be a testament of the deceased, he shall take possession of it, and produce it in court with his written return to the order directing the search. The original petitioner, or any other interested person, may petition for the probate of the testament so produced.

If the search is unsuccessful, despite diligent effort, the notary shall make his written return to this effect to the court.

Source: R.S. 47:2409(B), (C).

Comment

The above article is merely declaratory of the usual practice in such cases.

Art. 2856. Probate hearing; probate forthwith if witnesses present

After the testament has been produced, the court shall order it presented for probate on a date and hour assigned. If all necessary witnesses are present in court at the time the testament is produced, the court may order it presented for probate forthwith.

Source: C.P. Art. 933; C.C. Art. 1644.

Comment

This article makes no change in the probate procedure of Louisiana. The notice of intention to probate the testament required by

Art. 935 of the 1870 Code of Practice has not been included. See Art. 2932, *infra*, and Comments thereunder.

Art. 2857. Proponent must produce witnesses; subpoenas

The petitioner for the probate of the testament shall produce all necessary witnesses at the time assigned for the probate hearing, and may cause them to be subpoenaed to appear and testify.

Source: C.P. Art. 935.

Comments

(a) No change in the probate procedure of Louisiana is intended.

(b) In addition to the specific provisions of this article, the proponent of the testament, of course, would also be responsible for having the testimony of unavailable witnesses taken timely, under the provisions of Art. 2889, *infra*.

SECTION 2. EX PARTE PROBATE OF TESTAMENTS

Art. 2881. Ex parte probate if no objection

The court shall proceed to probate the testament ex parte as provided in Article 2882, unless an objection thereto is made at the hearing.

An objection to the ex parte probate of a testament may be presented in an opposition, or made orally at the hearing. The opposition must comply with the provisions of Article 2902, and must be filed prior to the hearing. The oral objection must specify the grounds of invalidity of the testament asserted, and must be urged immediately after the objector has had an opportunity to examine the purported testament.

Source: New; cf. Comments following.

Cross Reference: Art. 2901.

Comments

(a) The 1870 Code does not expressly state that when an objection is made to the ex parte probate of a testament, the court shall refuse to proceed further, and assign a date and hour for the probate hearing at which the parties may introduce evidence. Yet, it has been recognized that the very purpose of requiring notice to the presumptive heirs living in the parish under Art. 935 of the 1870 Code of Practice, is to afford them an opportunity to oppose the probate. Succession of McDonogh, 18 La.Ann. 419 (1866); Succession of Theriot, 114 La. 611, 38 So. 471 (1905); Succession of Hagan, 150 La. 934, 91 So. 303 (1922); Succession of Wadsworth, 152 La. 131, 92 So. 760 (1922).

(b) Neither the 1870 Code provisions nor the jurisprudence provide the manner of opposing the ex parte probate of a testament. In most of the decided cases, the objections of the opponents have been set forth in an opposition filed prior to the commencement of the probate hearing. Yet there may be cases in which the opponent of the testament has no opportunity for determining in advance of the hearing whether the purported testament is either genuine or valid, particularly when it is sealed in an envelope and opened for the first time at the probate hearing. For this reason, under the above article an oral objection to the ex parte probate of a purported testament suffices to require the court to assign a date and hour for the contradictory probate thereof.

(c) The term "depositions" of the witnesses employed in Art. 939 of the Code of Practice of 1870 has not been retained either in this or in subsequent articles on the same subject matter. Actually, the reference in Art. 939 is to a recital in the procès verbal of the probate proceedings as to the declarations of the witnesses, not to the testimony of witnesses taken by deposition. Succession of Lewis, 177 La. 212, 148 So. 29 (1933).

(d) See, also, Comments under Art. 2883, *infra*.

Art. 2882. Proceedings at probate hearing

At the probate hearing the court shall open the testament, if it is enclosed in a sealed envelope, receive proof of the making of the testament as provided in Articles 2883 through 2889, read the testament to those present in a distinct and audible voice, and paraph the top and bottom of each page of the testament by inscribing it "Ne Varietur" over the judicial signature. All of these proceedings shall be conducted in the presence of two witnesses, in addition to those called in to prove the testament.

Source: C.P. Arts. 934, 939–941; C.C. Arts. 1656, 1657.

Cross References: Arts. 2881, 2890.

Comments

(a) The above article does not change the probate procedure of Louisiana, except possibly as noted in Comment (b).

(b) The practice differs in various localities of the state as to whether two witnesses to the probate proceeding, in addition to the two witnesses called to identify the testament, are needed. The last sentence of this article was added to clarify the rule on the subject.

(c) See Art. 2890, *infra*, with reference to the recitations required in the procès verbal.

Art. 2883. Olographic testament

The olographic testament must be proved by the testimony of two credible witnesses that the testament was entirely written, dated, and signed in the testator's handwriting. The court must satisfy itself, through interrogation or from the depositions of the witnesses, that the handwriting and signature are those of the testator, and must mention these facts in its procès verbal.

Source: C.C. Art. 1655.

Cross Reference: Art. 2882.

Comments

(a) This article is primarily an editorial revision of the source provision. One important change of language was made, however. The thing which the court should satisfy itself on is that the handwriting and signature in the purported testament are those of the testator, rather than merely that the witnesses are familar with the handwriting and signature of the testator.

(b) This article shows clearly that a testament may be probated through the depositions of witnesses, as well as through their testimony at the hearing. See Art. 2889, *infra*, and comments thereunder. These depositions should not be confused with those mentioned in Art. 939, Code of Practice of 1870, which are not retained in this Code. See Comment (c) of Art. 2881, *supra*.

Art. 2884. Nuncupative testament by private act

Except as provided in Article 2886, the nuncupative testament by private act must be proved by the testimony of at least three of the competent witnesses present when it was made. These witnesses must testify, in substance: that they recognize the testament presented to them as being the same that was written in their presence by the testator, or by another person at his direction, or which the testator had written or caused to be written out of their presence and which he declared to them contained his testament; and that they recognize their signatures and that of the testator, if they signed it, or the signature of him who signed for them, respectively, if they did not know how to sign their names.

Source: C.C. Arts. 1648, 1649.

Cross Reference: Art. 2882.

Comment

The above article is a consolidation and editorial revision of the source provisions.

Art. 2885. Mystic testament

Except as provided in Article 2886, the mystic testament must be proved by the testimony of at least three of the witnesses who were present at the act of superscription. These witnesses shall testify, in substance: that they recognize the sealed envelope presented to them to be the same that the testator delivered to the notary in their presence, declaring to the latter that it contained the testator's testament; and that they recognize their signatures and that of the notary in the act of superscription, if they signed it, or the signature of the notary and of the person who signed for them, if the witnesses did not know to sign their names.

The notary before whom the act of superscription has been passed may testify as one of the three witnesses required above.

Source: C.C. Arts. 1650–1652.

Cross Reference: Art. 2882.

Comment

The above article is a consolidation and editorial revision of the source provisions.

Art. 2886. Probate of nuncupative testament by private act or mystic testament, when witnesses dead or absent

If some of the witnesses to the nuncupative testament by private act, or to the act of superscription of the mystic testament, are dead, absent from the state, or cannot be located, so that it is not possible to procure the prescribed number of witnesses to prove the testament, it may be proved by the testimony of those witnesses then residing in the state and available.

If the notary and all of the subscribing witnesses are dead, absent from the state, or cannot be located, the testament may be proved by the testimony of two credible witnesses who recognize the signature of the testator, or of the notary before whom the act of superscription of the mystic testament was passed, or the signatures of two of the witnesses to the nuncupative testament by private act, or to the act of superscription of the mystic testament.

Source: Cf. C.C. Arts. 1650, 1653, 1654.

Cross References: Arts. 2882, 2884, 2885.

Comment

The second paragraph of the above article reflects a change from that enunciated in the source provisions, by deleting the requirement that the same two witnesses recognize all of the signatures on the act. Sometimes it is extremely difficult, if not impossible, to obtain two witnesses who are familiar with the signatures of the various persons who witnessed the act; but it is usually not difficult to produce two witnesses who could identify the signature of the testator, or of the notary, or identify the signatures of two of the witnesses. This was deemed sufficient proof of the authenticity of the testament, in those cases where it was not possible to produce any of the signatories to the act to testify.

Art. 2887. Statutory testament

A testament confected in accordance with R.S. 9:2442 must be proved by the testimony of the notary and one of the subscribing witnesses, or of two of these witnesses, that it was signed by the testator. If only the notary, or only one of these witnesses is living in the state and can be located, his testimony that the testament was signed by the testator will be sufficient.

If the notary and all of the subscribing witnesses are dead, absent from the state, or cannot be located, the testament may be proved by the testimony of two credible witnesses who recognize the signature of the testator, or of the notary, or the signatures of two of the subscribing witnesses.

Source: Cf. R.S. 9:2444.

Cross Reference: Art. 2882.

Comment

This article is primarily an editorial revision of the source provision. A change has been made, however, to relax the rigor of R.S. 9:2444(C) so as to make it possible to probate this type of testament, when the notary and all witnesses are dead, absent, or unavailable, by proving the signature of either the testator, the notary, or two of the witnesses.

Art. 2888. Foreign testament

A written testament subscribed by the testator and made in a foreign country, or in another state, or a territory of the United States, in a form not valid in this state, but valid under the law of the place where made, or under the law of the testator's domicile, may be probated in this state by producing the evidence required under the law of the place where made, or under the law of the testator's domicile, respectively.

Source: New; cf. CC. Art. 1596; R.S. 9:2401.

Cross Reference: Art. 2882.

Comments

(a) These rules are new, but are declaratory of the principles flowing from the substantive provisions of Art. 1596 of the Civil Code, and of the Uniform Foreign Wills Act, R.S. 9:2401.

(b) Normally, these testaments are probated by the courts of the foreign country, state, or territory in which the testator was domiciled, and are enforced in Louisiana under ancillary probate proceedings, through comity, if probated by a competent court of a foreign country, or under full faith and credit if probated by a competent American court. *Cf.* Arts. 1688 and 1689 of the Civil Code.

However, where the testator was domiciled in Louisiana at the time of his death, the testament must be probated by a competent Louisiana court. Succession of Drysdale, 121 La. 816, 46 So. 873 (1908).

(c) See, also, Comments under Art. 3405, *infra*.

Art. 2889. Depositions of witnesses

A petitioner for the probate of a testament under the provisions of Articles 2882 through 2888 may obtain leave of court ex parte for the taking of the deposition of any witness whose testimony otherwise would not be available. The provisions of Articles 1422, 1423, 1430, 1431, 1452 through 1456, 1472, 1473, and 1511 through 1513, so far as applicable, shall govern the taking of such deposition.

Source: New.

Cross Reference: Art. 2882.

Comments

(a) Despite the obvious necessity for such rules in a few cases, there appears to be some doubt as to whether the testimony of witnesses could have been taken heretofore by deposition for the purpose of probating a testament. *Cf.* Succession of Lewis, 177 La. 212, 148 So. 29 (1933); Succession of Wolf, 17 So.2d 495 (La.App.1944). But see Pfarr v. Belmont, 39 La.Ann. 294, 1 So. 681 (1887).

(b) The provisions of the Chapter on depositions and discovery referred to in the above article, of course, deal with the taking of depositions in a contradictory proceeding, and contemplate notice to the adverse party. For this reason, only specific provisions are referred to, and the above article qualifies even these specific references by the language "so far as applicable." This was done to eliminate the impossible requirement of notice when the depositions are taken in an ex parte succession proceeding to probate a testament.

(c) See, also, Comments under Arts. 2857, 2883, *supra*.

Art. 2890. Procès verbal of probate

A procès verbal of the hearing shall be prepared, signed by the judge or by the clerk, and by all of the witnesses, which shall be a record of the succession proceeding, and which shall recite or include:

(1) The opening of the testament, and the manner in which proof of its authenticity and validity was submitted;

(2) The names and surnames of the witnesses testifying, either personally or by deposition; the substance of the testimony of the witnesses who testify personally at the hearing; and that any depositions used are made a part thereof by attachment or by reference;

(3) The paraphing of the testament by the court, as set forth in Article 2882;

(4) The reading of the testament by the court in a distinct and audible voice; and

(5) An order that the testament be recorded, filed, and executed, if the court finds that it has been proved in accordance with law; or an order refusing to probate the testament, giving the substance of the court's reasons therefor.

Source: C.P. Arts. 939–942.

Comments

Except to the extent that it recognizes the right to use depositions to probate a testament, the above article effects no change in the probate procedure of Louisiana, but merely consolidates the source provisions, making them more specific.

See, also, Comments under Art. 2882, *supra*.

Art. 2891. Nuncupative testament by public act executed without probate

A nuncupative testament by public act need not be probated, and upon the production of either the original testament or a certified copy thereof, the court shall order the testament to be recorded and executed.

Source: C.P. Art. 930; C.C. Art. 1647.
Cross Reference: Art. 3081.

Comments

Art. 930 of the 1870 Code of Practice was adopted at a time when all notaries throughout Louisiana were the custodians of their own acts. Since the changing of this rule as to all parishes except Orleans, notaries are no longer the custodians of the acts passed before them. Hence, outside New Orleans, the original nuncupative testament by public act may either have been filed with the clerk of court, or it may have been retained by the testator. For this reason, a change of the rule has been made, so as to permit the production of either the original, or a certified copy, of the testament.

See, also, Comments under Art. 2933, *infra*.

Art. 2892. Use of probate testimony in subsequent action

When a testament has been probated in accordance with law, the record of the substance of the testimony of any witness at the hearing, and the deposition of any witness taken under Article 2889, shall be admissible in evidence in any subsequent action in which it is sought to annul the testament, if at the time of trial thereof the witness has died, or for any other reason his testimony cannot be taken again either by subpoenaing him to appear at the trial, or by deposition.

Source: C.P. Art. 943.

Comment

Two changes have been made in the rules enunciated in the source provisions and they constitute a statutory relaxation of the rule of evidence which precludes the admission of hearsay. The mere fact that one of the witnesses to the probate of a testament has left Louisiana permanently is no reason to wholly relax the rule of evidence, and deprive the opponent of the opportunity of cross examining him, if his testimony may be taken again by deposition. Conversely, the death of the witness should not be made the sole ground for using the substance of his testimony given at the probate hearing. Under the above article if, for any reason, his testimony cannot be taken again, either in open court or by deposition, the court trying an action to annul the testament will not be deprived of the witness's original testimony.

Art. 2893. Period within which will must be probated

No testament shall be admitted to probate unless a petition therefor has been filed in a court of competent jurisdiction within five years of the judicial opening of the succession of the deceased.

Source: New; cf. Model Probate Code, § 83.

Comments

The above article protects the titles to property deraigned from heirs of the decedent who may have opened his succession and caused themselves to be placed in possession, without knowing of the existence of a testament. Five years is considered ample to permit the location, production, and probate of any testament; and after the lapse of this period, third persons should be protected against failure of title caused by the tardy probate of a testament.

The reasons supporting and opposing the adoption of the rule provided in this article are summarized in McMahon, The Revision of Probate Procedure in Louisiana, 1 La.Bar J. 66, 67 (October, 1953).

SECTION 3. CONTRADICTORY PROBATE OF TESTAMENTS

Art. 2901. Contradictory trial required; time to file opposition

If an objection is made to the ex parte probate of a testament, as provided in Article 2881, the testament may be probated only at a contradictory trial of the matter. If only an oral objection is made to the ex parte probate, the court shall allow the opponent a reasonable delay, not exceeding ten days, to file his opposition.

Source: New; cf. Comment following.

Comments

Neither the Code of Practice nor the Civil Code prescribes the procedure for the contradictory probate of a testament after its ex parte probate has been opposed by an interested person. The rules set forth in the above article were observed in Succession of McDonogh, 18 La.Ann. 419 (1866); Succession of Farrell, 131 La. 719, 60 So. 203 (1912); Succession of White, 132 La. 890, 61 So. 860 (1913); Succession of Wadsworth, 152 La. 131, 92 So. 760 (1922); Succession of Richardson, 171 La. 828, 132 So. 360 (1931); and Succession of Lirette, 5 So.2d 197 (La.App. 1942).

See, also, Comments under Arts. 2902, 2972, *infra*.

Art. 2902. Opposition to petition for probate

The opposition to the petition for the probate of a testament shall comply with Article 2972, shall allege the grounds of invalidity of the testament relied on by the opponent, and shall be served upon the petitioner for the probate of the testament.

Source: New; cf. Comments following.

Cross Reference: Art. 2881.

Comments

(a) See Comment under Art. 2901, *supra*.

(b) Heretofore, the opposition has been served only on the petitioner for the probate, and this requirement is retained in the above article. This is an exception to the general rule of Art. 2971, *infra*, requiring service of oppositions on all adverse parties.

(c) Service of the opposition may be made as provided in Art. 1313, *supra*. See Art. 2971, *infra*.

Art. 2903. Proponent bears burden of proof

At the contradictory trial to probate a testament, its proponent bears the burden of proving the authenticity of the testament, and its compliance with all of the formal requirements of law.

Source: New; cf. Comment following.

Comment

See Comment under Art. 2901, *supra*.

CHAPTER 4. ANNULMENT OF PROBATED TESTAMENTS

Art.
2931. Annulment of probated testament by direct action; defendants.
2932. Burden of proof in nullity action.
2933. Action to annul nuncupative testament by public act.

Art. 2931. Annulment of probated testament by direct action; defendants

A probated testament may be annulled only by a direct action brought in the succession proceeding against the legatees, the residuary heir, if any, and the executor, if he has not been discharged. The

Art. 2931 — GENERAL DISPOSITIONS — Bk. 6

defendants shall be cited, and the action shall be tried as an ordinary proceeding.

Source: New.

Cross References: Arts. 2826, 2933.

Comments

(a) Neither the Code of Practice nor the Civil Code prescribes the procedure for the annulment of a probated testament. The rules set forth in the above article are those established by Succession of Hagan, 150 La. 934, 91 So. 303 (1922) and cases cited therein. Cf. Succession of Wadsworth, 152 La. 131, 92 So. 760 (1922); Succession of Lirette, 5 So.2d 197 (La.App.1942).

(b) The action to annul the probated testament is a new suit, requiring citation and service on all defendants, who have the same delay for answering as in any other ordinary proceeding. The requirement that the action be brought in the succession proceeding permits the judge who probated the testament to try the nullity action. All of these aspects of this article were observed in the cases cited in Comment (a) above.

(c) See, also, Comments under Art. 2826, *supra*.

Art. 2932. Burden of proof in nullity action

The plaintiff in an action to annul a probated testament has the burden of proving the invalidity thereof, unless the action was instituted within three months of the date the testament was probated. In the latter event, the defendants have the burden of proving the authenticity of the testament, and its compliance with all of the formal requirements of the law.

Source: New; cf. Comments following.

Comments

(a) Under Art. 935 of the Code of Practice, the proponents of the testament were required to notify all of the presumptive heirs who "reside in the place," of the hearing for the probate of the testament, so that they could attend if they wished. The quoted language has been interpreted to mean those presumptive heirs residing in the parish where the testament was to be probated. Succession of Dancie, 191 La. 518, 186 So. 14 (1939). The failure to give the required notice had the effect of requiring the proponents to prove the genuineness of the testament. See cases cited in Comment (a) under Art. 2931, *supra*; and Fox v. Succession of McDonogh, 18 La.Ann. 419 (1866); Succession of Theriot, 114 La. 611, 38 So. 471 (1905); Succession of Price, 197 La. 579, 2 So.2d 29 (1941).

Tit. 1 STATE INHERITANCE TAXES

(b) Art. 935 of the Code of Practice had two deficiencies: (1) it provided notice only to the presumptive heirs residing in the parish; and (2) it delayed the succession procedure in the innumerable cases where the presumptive heirs had no interest or desire to contest the probate of the testament.

This requirement for notice has been abolished, and the burden of proving the authenticity and formal validity of the probated testament has been made to depend upon the time when the action to annul is brought. Under the above article, the proponents have the burden of proving the genuineness of the testament except in cases of a delayed or belated attack upon the testament, in which case the burden of proving the invalidity of the testament is upon the opponents. Also, the ex parte probate of the testament is expedited, there being no necessity to serve notice upon the presumptive heirs.

(c) See, also, Comments under Art. 2856, *supra*.

Art. 2933. Action to annul nuncupative testament by public act

An action to annul a nuncupative testament by public act which has been ordered recorded and executed shall be governed by the provisions of Article 2931. The plaintiff always has the burden of proving the invalidity of the testament.

Source: New; cf. C.P. Art. 930.

Comment

There are no provisions in either the Code of Practice or in the Civil Code prescribing the procedure for annulling a nuncupative testament by public act. Under Art. 930 of the Code of Practice, and since this form of testament is a public act, it was presumed to be genuine and valid, and hence need not be probated.

CHAPTER 5. PAYMENT OF STATE INHERITANCE TAXES

Art.
2951. No judgment of possession or delivery of legacy or inheritance until inheritance taxes paid or deposited.
2952. Descriptive list of property, if no inventory.
2953. Evidence as to taxes due, receipt of payment.
2954. Rule to determine inheritance taxes due.

Art. 2951. No judgment of possession or delivery of legacy or inheritance until inheritance taxes paid or deposited

No judgment of possession shall be rendered, no inheritance or legacy shall be delivered, and no succession representative shall be discharged unless satisfactory proof has been submitted to the court that no inheritance taxes are due by the heirs or legatees, or that all such taxes have been paid, or that the maximum amount claimed by the inheritance tax collector has been deposited in the registry of the court pending judicial determination of the amount due.

Source: R.S. 47:2407(C), 47:2408(C).

Comments

(a) The Inheritance Tax Act, R.S. 47:2401 *et seq.*, does not expressly prohibit a court from rendering a judgment of possession in the absence of satisfactory proof of the payment of all inheritance taxes due, or that no such taxes are due. In actual practice, however, the rule of this article is followed by all district courts throughout Louisiana.

(b) When a dispute arises as to the amount due to the inheritance tax collector, the recognized practice in Orleans Parish is for the heirs to deposit into the registry of the court the maximum amount of taxes claimed by the collector and then to have the judgment of possession signed. Thereafter, the amount of the inheritance taxes due is determined judicially. If the court determines that a lesser amount of taxes is due, the judgment orders the payment to the inheritance tax collector of the amount due from the fund on deposit in the registry of the court, and further orders that the residue be paid over to the heirs and legatees. This practice has been incorporated in the last clause of the above article.

(c) See, also, Comments under Art. 3061, *infra*.

Art. 2952. Descriptive list of property, if no inventory

If no inventory of the property left by the deceased has been taken, any heir, legatee, or other interested party shall file in the succession proceeding a detailed, descriptive list, sworn to and subscribed by him, of all items of property composing the succession of the deceased, stating the actual cash value of each item at the time of the death of the deceased.

Source: R.S. 47:2408(A).

Comments

(a) No change in the law of Louisiana is intended or contemplated in the above article.

(b) This article dispenses with the necessity for a public inventory when the surviving spouse and heirs are sent into possession without an administration of the succession. Art. 3136, *infra*, similarly dispenses with the necessity of a public inventory even when it is necessary to administer the succession.

Art. 2953. Evidence as to taxes due, receipt of payment

The fact that no inheritance taxes are due by the heirs or legatees, or the amount of the taxes due when agreed upon by the inheritance tax collector and the heirs or legatees, may be proved by the acknowledgment of the inheritance tax collector or his attorney. The payment of the inheritance taxes due by the heirs or legatees may be proved by the receipt of the inheritance tax collector.

The acknowledgment and the receipt mentioned above shall be filed in the succession proceeding, or endorsed on any pleading therein or on the judgment of possession presented to the court for signature.

Source: New; cf. Comment following.

Comment

Heretofore, the only method for determining the inheritance taxes due was the rules contained in R.S. 47:2407(A) and 47:2409(A). That procedure is quite unnecessary and is merely perfunctory when the inheritance tax collector and all of the parties agree as to the amount of taxes due. The above article is based upon the simpler, more expeditious, and more practical custom followed in Orleans Parish. Cf. Art. 2954, *infra*.

Art. 2954. Rule to determine inheritance taxes due

If the succession representative, heirs, and legatees do not agree with the inheritance tax collector as to the taxes due, any party may rule the other interested parties into court to show cause why the inheritance taxes due by each heir or legatee should not be determined judicially. On the trial of this rule, the court shall render judgment against each heir and legatee for the tax due by him, or against the inheritance tax collector decreeing that no taxes are due.

Source: R.S. 47:2407(A), 47:2408(A).

Comments

This article effects no change in the probate procedure of Louisiana in those cases where the tax liability is in dispute.

See, also, Comments under Art. 2953, *supra*.

CHAPTER 6. GENERAL RULES OF PROCEDURE

Art.
2971. Pleading and service of process.
2972. Oppositions.
2973. Responsive pleadings to opposition.
2974. Appeals.

Art. 2971. Pleading and service of process

Except as otherwise provided by law, the rules of pleading and service of process applicable in ordinary proceedings shall apply to succession proceedings.

A certified copy of the petition, opposition, contradictory motion, or rule initiating a contradictory succession proceeding shall be served on the adverse party; but citation is necessary only in those cases in which it is specifically required by law.

An opposition may be served upon the adverse party as provided in Article 1313.

Source: New; cf. Comments following.

Comments

(a) Under the applicable articles in both the Code of Practice and the Civil Code, succession proceedings utilize both ordinary and summary process. No departure from this rule is made in this Code. Thus, the above article provides that the rules of pleading applicable to ordinary proceedings are likewise applicable to succession proceedings, except when summary process is expressly authorized.

(b) Service of process is necessary in all contradictory succession proceedings, but it is only in the rare case, such as the action to annul a probated testament under Art. 2931, *supra*, in which the issuance and service of citation are necessary.

(c) The last sentence of this article eliminates all doubts as to the validity of the service of an opposition made in accordance with Art. 1313, *supra*.

(d) See, also, Comments under Art. 2902, *supra*.

Art. 2972. Oppositions

An opposition to the petition, motion, or other application of a party to a succession proceeding for an order or judgment of the court shall be in writing and be filed within the delay allowed. It shall comply with the provisions of Articles 853 through 863; shall state the name, surname, and domicile of the opponent; shall allege the interest of opponent in filing the opposition, and the grounds for opposing the petition, motion, or other application; and shall conclude with a prayer for appropriate relief.

Source: New; cf. Comments following.

Cross References: Arts. 2902, 3095, 4066.

Comments

(a) Although the Civil Code and the Code of Practice frequently refer to the opposition to be filed in a succession proceeding, there are no provisions relating to its form except those of Arts. 971 and 972 of the Code of Practice dealing with oppositions to applications for the appointment of administrators. The above article supplies this deficiency. Its requirements are, in general, those of all other pleadings, and, in particular, those matters which relate peculiarly to the opposition.

(b) No person should be permitted to file an opposition in a succession proceeding unless he has a justiciable interest in doing so. The definition of this interest has been left for the determination of the courts, and the requirement has been stated only implicitly in the term "interested person."

(c) The delay allowed for the filing of an opposition may be: (1) provided by Code provision, (2) determined by the court, or (3) as under Art. 2901, *supra*, a maximum delay which the court has discretion to shorten. The term "within the delay allowed" is intended to cover all three types of delay.

Art. 2973. Responsive pleadings to opposition

Responsive pleadings to an opposition may be filed as provided in Article 2593.

Source: New; cf. Comments following.

Comment

Heretofore, no law expressly permitted and no cases could be found which specially authorized the filing of exceptions to an opposition. However, there is no reason why exceptions should not be permitted in the trial of an opposition filed by a person who had no right or interest in filing it. The trial might be

Art. 2974   GENERAL DISPOSITIONS   Bk. 6

shortened appreciably in some instances by the sustaining of an exception.

Art. 2974. Appeals

Appeals from orders or judgments rendered in succession proceedings shall be governed by the rules applicable to appeals in ordinary proceedings, except that an order or judgment confirming, appointing, or removing a succession representative, or granting an interim allowance under Article 3321 shall be executed provisionally, notwithstanding appeal.

The acts of a succession representative shall not be invalidated by the annulment of his appointment on appeal.

Source: C.P. Arts. 580, 1059; C.C. Art. 1120.

Comments

This article makes no change in the procedural law of Louisiana.

See, also, Comments under Arts. 3096, 3196, 3225, 4068, *infra*.

TITLE II

ACCEPTANCE OF SUCCESSIONS WITHOUT ADMINISTRATION

Chap.		Art.
1.	Intestate Successions	3001
2.	Testate Successions	3031
3.	Judgments of Possession	3061

CHAPTER 1. INTESTATE SUCCESSIONS

Art.
3001. Unconditional acceptance.
3002. Same; petition for possession.
3003. Same; evidence of allegations of petition for possession.
3004. Discretionary power to send heirs and surviving spouse into possession.
3005. Same; petition for possession; evidence.
3006. Same; when one of competent heirs cannot join in petition for possession.
3007. Creditor may demand security when heirs sent into possession.
3008. Administration in default of security.

Art. 3001. Unconditional acceptance

The heirs of an intestate shall be recognized by the court, and sent into possession of his property without an administration of the succession, on their ex parte petition, when all of the heirs are competent and accept the succession unconditionally, and the succession is relatively free of debt. A succession shall be deemed relatively free of debt when its only debts are succession charges, mortgages not in arrears, and debts which are small in comparison with the assets of the succession.

The surviving spouse in community of an intestate shall be recognized by the court on ex parte petition as entitled to the possession of an undivided half of the community, and of the other undivided half to the extent that he has the usufruct thereof, without an administration of the succession, when the community is accepted, and the succession is relatively free of debt, as provided above.

Source: New; cf. Comments following.

Cross References: Arts. 3002, 3004, 3007, 3031, 3362, 3462.

Art. 3001 UNCONDITIONAL ACCEPTANCE Bk. 6

Comments

(a) No provision of either the Civil Code or the Code of Practice expressly enunciates any of the rules embodied in the above article, but the jurisprudence definitely supports these rules. Succession of Ducloslange, 1 La.Ann. 181 (1846); Succession of Story, 3 La.Ann. 502 (1848); Alleman v. Bergeron, 16 La.Ann. 191 (1861); Succession of Hebert, 33 La.Ann. 1099 (1881); Succession of Baumgarden, 35 La.Ann. 675 (1883); *Id.*, 36 La.Ann. 46 (1884); Succession of Thibodeaux, 38 La.Ann. 716 (1886); Succession of Graves, 50 La.Ann. 435, 23 So. 738 (1898); Succession of Wintz, 111 La. 40, 35 So. 377 (1902); Succession of Weincke, 118 La. 206, 42 So. 776 (1907).

(b) In the majority of cases, the act of mortgage contains no provision accelerating the mortgage installment payments upon the death of the mortgagor; and in such cases, if all installments have been paid as they matured, the balance due should not be considered in the same category as debts of the succession which are past due and exigible, for purposes of determining whether an administration of the succession is necessary. In these cases, the mortgagee has no right to insist upon the mortgaged property being sold to pay the mortgage indebtedness; and if he had, he would prefer to have the mortgage enforced by a separate proceeding, so that he would not have to contribute to administration expenses if it developed that the succession was insolvent. For these reasons, "mortgages not in arrears" were excluded from the formula used to determine whether the succession is relatively free from debt.

Where the act of mortgage provides that the death of the mortgagor renders the entire mortgage indebtedness due and exigible, this indebtedness would have to be considered in determining whether an administration of the succession is necessary; and, in many of these cases, the surviving spouse and heirs desiring to dispense with an administration would have to invoke the provisions of Art. 3004, *infra*.

(c) If a debt of the succession is discovered after the heirs have been sent into possession, the recourse of the creditor is not against the succession, which has ceased to exist, but against the heirs, who have thus become debtors for their virile shares of the decedent's debts. Sevier v. Sargent, 25 La.Ann. 220 (1873); Succession of Hacker, 28 La.Ann. 446 (1876); Succession of Walker, 32 La.Ann. 321 (1880); Beauregard v. Lampton, 33 La.Ann. 827 (1881); Succession of Hebert, 33 La. Ann. 1099 (1881); Succession of Thibodeaux, 38 La.Ann. 716 (1886); Succession of Aronstein, 51 La.Ann. 1052, 25 So. 932 (1899). *Cf.* De la Ferriere v. Succession of England, 27 La.Ann. 686 (1875); Augustin v. Avila, 29 La.Ann. 837 (1877). Because this rule may work a hardship upon creditors in certain cases, Art. 3007, *infra*, permits the creditor to compel the heirs to furnish security for the payment of the debt.

(d) The heirs of an intestate have been sent into possession when the conditions of the above article could not have been met. For this reason, two sets of rules are set forth in this Code. The above article and Arts. 3002 and 3003, *infra*, embody the applicable rules in cases where all of the heirs are competent and unconditionally accept the succession which is relatively free of debt. In these cases no reason exists for an administration of the succession, and the heirs are entitled to a judgment of possession as of right. Arts. 3004 and 3005, *infra*, embody the applicable rules if some of the heirs are incompetent and hence cannot accept the succession unconditionally, or if the succession is not relatively free from debt, yet none of the succession creditors objects to the heirs being sent into possession. In these latter cases, ample reason exists for an administration of the succession, and if the heirs are sent into possession without an administration, it is only because the creditors do not care to exercise their privilege to demand an administration. To protect a creditor who may otherwise be prevented from demanding an administration, by the heirs presenting a petition for possession immediately after the death of decedent, Arts. 3007 and 3008, *infra*, permit the creditor to demand that the heirs furnish security for the payment of his claim, and to have the judgment of possession annulled and an administration had, in default of the furnishing of such security.

(e) See, also, Comments under Art. 3008, *infra*.

Art. 3002. Same; petition for possession

The petition of the heirs for possession under Article 3001 shall include allegations as to: the competency of the petitioners; the date of death of the deceased, and all other facts on which the jurisdiction of the court is based; the facts showing that petitioners are the sole heirs of deceased; and that the succession is relatively free of debt, as provided in Article 3001.

The petition of the surviving spouse in community for possession under Article 3001 shall include all of the above allegations except those relating to heirship; shall allege the facts showing that he is the surviving spouse in community; shall state what property belonged to the community; and if he claims the usufruct of any interest in the community property, shall allege the facts showing that he is entitled thereto.

The allegations of the petition for possession shall be verified by the affidavit of at least one of the petitioners. There shall be filed

Art. 3002 UNCONDITIONAL ACCEPTANCE

in the record of the succession proceeding written evidence of the acceptance of the community by the surviving widow if she did not execute this affidavit.

Source: New; cf. Comments following.

Cross References: Arts. 3003, 3005, 3032, 3362.

Comments

(a) See Comments under Art. 3001, *supra*.

(b) Since the petition for possession in an intestate succession in which all of the competent heirs accept unconditionally is usually the only pleading filed in the succession proceeding, it is necessary that it include all the allegations required in the above article. In a few cases, additional allegations may be necessary.

(c) Nothing in the probate procedure of Louisiana heretofore required the verifying affidavit of at least one of the petitioners, since the provisions of former R.S. 13:3601(5) were not applicable to petitions for possession. Under local practices, however, the verifying affidavit of at least one of the petitioners has usually been attached to the petition for possession.

This article requires some evidence of the acceptance of the community by the surviving widow in those instances where she did not execute any verifying affidavit to the petition for possession. This requirement is based upon the obvious advantage of having the record reflect expressly her acceptance of the community.

Art. 3003. Same; evidence of allegations of petition for possession

Evidence of the allegations of the petition for possession, under Articles 3002 or 3005, as to the death of the deceased, jurisdiction of the court, marriage of the spouses, and relationship of the petitioners to the deceased, shall be submitted to the court as provided by Articles 2821 through 2823.

Source: New; cf. Comment following.

Cross References: Arts. 3005, 3032, 3362.

Comments

See Arts. 2821 through 2823, *supra*, and the Comments thereunder.

See, also, Comments under Art. 3001, *supra*, and Art. 3361, *infra*.

Art. 3004. Discretionary power to send heirs and surviving spouse into possession

The heirs of an intestate may be recognized by the court, and sent into possession of his property without an administration of his succession, on the ex parte petition of those of the heirs who are competent, in all cases when the competent heirs accept the succession unconditionally, and none of the creditors of the succession has demanded its administration.

In such cases, the surviving spouse in community of the deceased may be recognized by the court as entitled to the possession of the community property, as provided in Article 3001.

Source: New; cf. Comments following.

Cross References: Arts. 3005, 3006, 3007, 3362, 3462.

Comments

(a) See Comment (c) under Art. 3001, *supra*.

(b) The purpose of the above article and of Art. 3005, *infra*, is to afford some degree of recognition to the fairly general practice of sending the heirs into possession without an administration even though some of them are incompetent, or the succession is not relatively free of debt, when none of the creditors of the succession opposes sending the heirs into possession.

In strict theory, putting the heirs into possession without an administration constitutes an unconditional acceptance and it should not be available except where all of the heirs are competent and can accept unconditionally. Also, there should be no sending into possession without an administration if the succession is heavily involved financially, for in such cases there would be a necessity for an administration. But if none of the creditors objects to the heirs being sent into possession, under either set of facts, no compelling reason appears to prevent such a practice. These articles protect the creditors by permitting them to demand an administration of the succession initially; or, under Arts. 3007 and 3008, *infra*, by permitting them to demand security for their claims, under penalty of the nullity of the judgment of possession and of having an administration of the succession. This article also gives the court discretion to refuse to send the heirs into possession, and to require an administration of the succession, whenever such a course is advisable.

(c) See, also, Comments under Art. 3008, *infra*.

Art. 3005. Same; petition for possession; evidence

The petition of the heirs for possession under Article 3004 shall include allegations as to: the competency of the petitioners; the date of death of the intestate, and all other facts on which the jurisdiction of the court is based; and the facts showing that petitioners and the incompetent heirs named in the petition, if any, are the sole heirs of the intestate.

The petition of the surviving spouse in community for possession under Article 3004 shall include all of the pertinent allegations of Article 3002.

The allegations of the petition for possession shall be verified by the affidavit of at least one of the petitioners. There shall be filed in the record of the succession proceeding written evidence of the acceptance of the community by the surviving widow if she did not execute this affidavit.

The allegations of the petition for possession shall be proved as provided in Article 3003.

Source: New; cf. Comments following.

Cross References: Arts. 3003, 3006, 3362.

Comments

(a) See Comments under Arts. 3001 and 3004, and Comment (c) under Art. 3002, *supra*.

(b) The allegations required by this article include all those which are necessary in the usual case, although in rare cases peculiar facts may require additional allegations.

Art. 3006. Same; when one of competent heirs cannot join in petition for possession

If a competent heir of an intestate resides out of the state and cannot be located, or his whereabouts are unknown, the other competent heirs may be sent into possession of the property without an administration of the succession, as provided herein and in Articles 3004 and 3005.

Upon the filing of the petition for possession, the court shall appoint an attorney at law to represent the absent heir, and shall order him to show cause why the heirs of the intestate should not be recognized, and sent into possession of the property of the intestate without an administration of the succession.

After a hearing on the rule against the attorney for the absentee, if the court concludes that the succession is thoroughly solvent and that there is no necessity for an administration, it may send all the heirs of the intestate, including the absentee, into possession.

Source: New; cf. Comment following.

Cross References: Arts. 3362, 3462.

Comment

This article covers those cases in which the absent heir cannot be contacted, or his whereabouts are unknown. An increasing number of successions have devolved, in part, upon persons who cannot be located. In some instances, there was no necessity for an administration, yet under the law one had to be had. The above article provides for the simpler and less expensive procedure of sending the heirs into possession and then having the property partitioned.

Art. 3007. Creditor may demand security when heirs sent into possession

When the heirs of an intestate, or the heirs and the surviving spouse thereof, have been sent into possession of the property of the intestate under Articles 3001 or 3004, any creditor having a claim against the succession may file in the succession proceeding, within three months of the date of the judgment of possession, a contradictory motion against all parties sent into possession to compel them to furnish security for the payment of his claim.

On the trial of this motion, the court may order the parties sent into possession to furnish such security as it deems necessary to protect the claimant.

Source: Cf. C.C. Arts. 1011, 1012, 1444, 1456.

Cross References: Arts. 3008, 3034, 3035, 3362.

Comments

(a) See Comments under Arts. 3001 and 3004, *supra*.

(b) This article combines the right of the succession creditor to demand security of the heirs who have accepted the succession, and the action of separation of patrimony. This combination is desirable as each of these remedies under prior law had deficiencies which made it unavailable to at least some of the creditors. Under Art. 1011 of the Civil Code, only a majority in amount of the creditors could demand security for the payment of their claims. This made it impossible for even a number of creditors, to assert the remedy, when a creditor having a large claim secured by a mortgage refused to join.

The action of separation of patrimony is largely theoretical. It can be invoked only in the rare case where one of the heirs is so heavily indebted that his acceptance of the succession would permit his individual creditors to jeopardize the enforcement of the claims of the succession creditors.

Art. 3007   UNCONDITIONAL ACCEPTANCE   Bk. 6

The above article: (1) removes the requirement that the majority in amount of the succession creditors must join in the demand for security; (2) makes the remedy available to creditors in all cases; (3) makes the provision more definite with respect to the time within which this demand must be asserted; and (4) gives the court discretion to prescribe the amount and conditions of the bond to be furnished by the heirs.

(c) No case could be found squarely holding that the succession creditors must demand security from the heirs for the payment of their claims within three months of the rendition of the judgment of possession. Under Civil Code Art. 1456, the action of "separation of patrimony must be instituted within three months from the express or tacit acceptance of the heirs." This provision appears to have been treated as being in pari materia with Art. 1011, and therefore applicable thereto. Succession of Bray, 50 La.Ann. 1209, 24 So. 601 (1898); Succession of Hart, 52 La.Ann. 364, 27 So. 69 (1899). At all events, some limitation is necessary, and three months is adequate and reasonable.

(d) The right of the succession creditors to employ summary procedure in compelling the heirs to furnish security was recognized in Succession of Bray, *supra*, and Succession of Hart, *supra*.

(e) To the extent that a mortgage or privilege does not fully protect the creditor, his claim is unsecured within the intendment of this article. Thus, if the creditor has a mortgage on a piece of property worth $1,000, to secure a $2,000 claim, his claim is unsecured to the extent of $1,000.

(f) Under the above article, there is no need to adopt any provision based upon Art. 1012 of the Civil Code. If there had been no actual seizure of the property or funds, or if no lis pendens had been recorded against the immovable property involved under Arts. 3751–3753, *infra*, the creditors could protect themselves by invoking this article. Moreover, under the above article, any single creditor may demand security of the heirs.

(g) If the surviving spouse or an heir is an unrepresented absentee, minor, or mental incompetent, the court can appoint an attorney at law to represent the unrepresented defendant in rule. See Art. 5091, *infra*.

Art. 3008.   Administration in default of security

If the security required by the court under Article 3007 is not furnished within the delay allowed, on ex parte motion of the creditor, the court shall render a judgment annulling the judgment of possession, directing the cancellation of all inscriptions of the registry thereof, ordering an administration of the succession, and ordering the parties sent into possession to surrender to the administrator to be appointed thereafter all of the property of the deceased which they have received, and which they have not alienated.

Conventional mortgages and other encumbrances placed by the heirs, legatees, or surviving spouse in community on property so surrendered, and recorded prior to the cancellation of the inscription of the registry of the judgment of possession, shall retain their initial force and effect despite the administration of the succession.

Source: New; cf. Comments following.

Cross References: Arts. 3034, 3035, 3362.

Comments

(a) See Comments under Arts. 3001, 3004, and 3007, *supra*.

(b) In so far as the above article permits the administration of the succession in default of security by the heirs, it goes no further than the rules announced in Succession of Hart, 52 La. Ann. 364, 27 So. 69 (1899); Succession of Barber, 52 La.Ann. 957, 27 So. 361 (1900); and *Id.*, 52 La.Ann. 960, 27 So. 363 (1900). See, also, Civil Code Art. 1011.

(c) This article reconciles the competing claims of succession creditors and third persons to the protection of the law. Under the judicial policy initiated by McDuffie v. Walker, 125 La. 152, 51 So. 100 (1909), protection should be afforded to transferees and mortgagees of the succession heirs, who had acted in reliance upon the judgment of possession registered in the conveyance records. The article provides the succession creditors with a supplemental remedy; but it also protects third persons who acquired interests in the succession property before the succession creditors exercise this supplemental remedy. The statutory substitute for the separation of patrimony, R.S. 9:5106 through 9:5111, gives complete protection to the succession creditors for a period of three months after the death of the deceased, in so far as succession immovables are concerned.

CHAPTER 2. TESTATE SUCCESSIONS

Art.
3031. Sending legatees into possession without administration.
3032. Same; petition for possession; evidence.
3033. Same; compensation of executor.
3034. Creditor may demand security when legatees sent into possession; administration in default of security.
3035. Particular legatee may demand security for delivery of legacy; administration in default of security.

Art. 3031. Sending legatees into possession without administration

When a testament has been probated, and subject to the provisions of Article 3033, the court may send the legatees into possession of their respective legacies without an administration of the succession, on their ex parte petition, when all of the legatees are either competent or are acting through their qualified legal representatives, all competent residuary legatees accept the succession unconditionally, and none of the creditors of the succession has demanded its administration.

In such cases, the surviving spouse in community of the testator may be recognized by the court as entitled to the possession of the community property, as provided in Article 3001.

Source: New; cf. Comments following.

Cross References: Arts. 2826, 3032, 3034, 3372.

Comments

(a) Succession of Dupuy, 4 La.Ann. 570 (1849) and Succession of Walker, 32 La.Ann. 321 (1880) support the proposition that the legatees may be sent into possession without any administration of the succession, if none of the creditors demands an administration. These cases, however, were expressly overruled by Succession of Serres, 135 La. 1005, 66 So. 342 (1914), holding that even though the testate succession is completely free of debt, and the residuary legatees are willing to accept it unconditionally, there must be an administration if only to permit the executor to execute the testament by delivering the legacies. In the Serres case, the petition of the legatees for possession was opposed by the person named in the testament as executor; and it is probable that the decision would have been otherwise, had the person named as executor waived his commission and joined with the legatees in the petition for possession. However, if none of the creditors demands an administration, and the residuary legatee is willing to deliver the particular legacies, there is no reason why the residuary legatee should be burdened with the unnecessary costs of administration, if the person named as executor has either waived his compensation or the residuary legatee is willing to pay it.

For this reason, the above article makes it discretionary with the court to send the legatees into possession without an administration, if the latter would be unnecessary and would only impose useless costs upon the residuary legatee.

(b) The requirement that all incompetent legatees be represented by their qualified legal representatives is necessary to permit the residuary legatee to receive a valid receipt for the delivery of particular legacies.

(c) When the testator makes only a few particular legacies, intending that the remainder of his estate should go to his heirs under the laws of descent and distribution, the procedure for permitting the residuary heir to be sent into possession is the same, under the above article, as in the case of the residuary legatee.

(d) See, also, Comments under Art. 2826, *supra*.

Art. 3032. Same; petition for possession; evidence

The petition of the legatees for possession under Article 3031 shall include allegations that all of the petitioners are either competent or are acting through their qualified legal representatives. The person named as executor in the testament shall join in the petition, except as otherwise provided by Article 3033.

The petition of the surviving spouse in community for possession under Article 3031 shall comply with all of the pertinent provisions of Article 3002.

The allegations of the petition for possession shall be verified by the affidavit of at least one of the petitioners. There shall be filed in the record of the succession proceeding written evidence of the acceptance of the community by the surviving widow if she did not execute this affidavit.

The allegations of the petition for possession shall be proved as provided in Article 3003.

Source: New; cf. Comment following.

Cross References: Arts. 3031, 3372.

Comment

See Comments under Arts. 2826 and 3031, *supra*, and Comment (c) under Art. 3002, *supra*.

Art. 3033. Same; compensation of executor

If the testament is dated prior to January 1, 1961, the person named therein as executor shall be entitled to the full compensation allowed by law for an executor's services in administering a testate succession, even though he may not have been confirmed as executor.

If the testament is dated subsequent to December 31, 1960, the person named therein as executor shall be entitled to reasonable compensation for the services which he has rendered, whether he has been confirmed as executor or not.

Art. 3033 UNCONDITIONAL ACCEPTANCE

Except as provided hereinafter, the legatees may be sent into possession only if the person named in the testament as executor joins in the petition thereof.

If the residuary legatee and the person named in the testament as executor cannot agree upon the compensation due him, or for any other reason he refuses to join in the petition for possession, the residuary legatee may rule him into court to show cause why the compensation due should not be determined judicially, and why the legatees should not be sent into possession of their legacies. The court shall not send the legatees into possession until satisfactory proof has been submitted that the compensation determined to be due the person named in the testament as executor has been paid.

Source: New; cf. Comments following.

Cross References: Arts. 2826, 3031, 3032, 3372.

Comments

(a) Heretofore, the testamentary executor could not be deprived of his commission by the legatees accepting the succession and being sent into possession, even though the succession was completely free of debt and there was no necessity for an administration. Succession of Serres, 135 La. 1005, 66 So. 342 (1914); 27 Tul.L.Rev. 87, 92 (1952). This is undesirable. The executor should recover a fair and reasonable compensation for all services performed, but the residuary legatee should not be forced to pay the full commission when the services of an executor are not actually necessary, unless it appears from the testament that it was intended as a legacy. However, the rule of this article will apply only in cases of testaments dated after December 31, 1960. This will give members of the legal profession reasonable time to familiarize themselves with the new rule.

(b) The person named as executor may have rendered valuable services to the succession in the probate of the testament and in conserving and protecting the property for the succession, even though not confirmed as executor. Under this article he will be entitled to receive reasonable compensation for these services.

(c) The purpose of this article is to afford compensation to a person named as executor in a testament, who either qualified as such or was eligible for confirmation but was prevented from being confirmed by the legatees being sent into possession. It is not intended to afford compensation to a person named as executor who would have been disqualified under Art. 3097, *infra*.

(d) See, also, Comments under Art. 2826, *supra*, and Art. 3352, *infra*.

Art. 3034. Creditor may demand security when legatees sent into possession; administration in default of security

When the legatees of a testator, or the legatees and the surviving spouse in community thereof, have been sent into possession of his property under Article 3031, any creditor having a claim against the succession may compel the parties sent into possession to furnish security for the payment of his claim, and may require an administration of the succession in default of such security, as provided by Articles 3007 and 3008.

Source: C.C. Arts. 1011, 1012, 1444, 1456.

Cross References: Arts. 2826, 2890, 3031, 3372.

Comment

See Comments under Arts. 2826, 3007, and 3008, *supra*.

Art. 3035. Particular legatee may demand security for delivery of legacy; administration in default of security

A particular legatee who has not received his legacy after being sent into possession by judgment may demand that the residuary legatee furnish security for the delivery of his legacy and may require an administration of the succession in default of such security, as provided by Articles 3007 and 3008.

Source: C.C. Arts. 1449, 3275.

Cross Reference: Art. 3031.

Comment

See Comments under Art. 2826, *supra*.

CHAPTER 3. JUDGMENTS OF POSSESSION

Art.
3061. Judgment rendered and signed immediately.
3062. Effect of judgment of possession.

Art. 3061. Judgment rendered and signed immediately

The court shall render and sign immediately a judgment of possession, if it finds from an examination of the petition for possession, and from the record of the proceeding, that the petitioners are entitled to the relief prayed for, and that all inheritance taxes due have been paid or deposited into the registry of the court, or that no such

Art. 3061. UNCONDITIONAL ACCEPTANCE

taxes are due. The judgment shall recognize the petitioners as the heirs, legatees, surviving spouse in community, or usufructuary, as the case may be, of the deceased, send the heirs or legatees into possession of the property owned by the deceased at the time of his death, and recognize the surviving spouse in community as entitled to the possession of an undivided one-half of the community property, and of the other undivided one-half to the extent that he has the usufruct thereof.

Source: New; cf. Comments following.

Cross References: Arts. 3381, 3462.

Comments

(a) See Comments under Art. 2951, *supra*. See also Arts. 2821 through 2824, and Comments thereunder, *supra*.

(b) In many instances, particularly in cases where the heirs are sent into possession of stock in corporations domiciled in other states, it is advisable to describe all items of property of which the heirs are sent into possession. See McMahon 1488, n. 20. As a practical matter, the description of all items of property of which the heirs are sent into possession is included in practically all judgments of possession rendered by the Civil District Court for the Parish of Orleans, under its Rule XXVI, § 4.

(c) The rule of Art. 1919, *supra*, that any final judgment affecting the title to immovables must describe the property affected with particularity has not been extended to judgments of possession because its strictness might invalidate a judgment of possession which does not contain a complete description of the immovables affected. Under this Code a particular description of the immovables affected is not essential to the validity of a judgment of possession.

(d) See, also, Comments under Arts. 1919, 2089, *supra*.

Art. 3062. Effect of judgment of possession

The judgment of possession rendered in a succession proceeding shall be prima facie evidence of the relationship to the deceased of the parties recognized therein, as heir, legatee, surviving spouse in community, or usufructuary, as the case may be, and of their right to the possession of the estate of the deceased.

Source: New; cf. Comments following.

Comments

(a) This article is merely declaratory of the prior jurisprudential rule. Succession of Lampton, 35 La.Ann. 418 (1883);

Taylor v. Williams, 162 La. 92, 110 So. 100 (1926); Dixon v. Commercial Nat. Bank, 13 La.App. 204, 127 So. 428 (1930); Succession of Fachan, 179 La. 333, 154 So. 15 (1934); Succession of Lissa, 194 La. 328, 193 So. 663 (1940); In re Liquidation of Reliance Homestead Ass'n, 181 So. 22 (La.App.1938); Curry v. Caillier, 37 So.2d 863 (La.App.1948). See also Dalton v. Wickliffe, 35 La.Ann. 355 (1883); Succession of Lorenz, 41 La.Ann. 1091, 6 So. 886, 7 L.R.A. 265 (1889); West v. Goodwin, 176 La. 873, 147 So. 20 (1933). *Cf.* Dugas v. Powell, 207 La. 316, 21 So.2d 366 (1945).

(b) By effect of special statutes, however, in certain cases corporations may rely completely upon the judgment of possession, if rendered by a court of competent jurisdiction. See R.S. 6:66 and R.S. 12:503. There is no intention to change any of these statutory rules.

TITLE III

ADMINISTRATION OF SUCCESSIONS

Chap.		Art.
1.	Qualification of Succession Representatives	3081
	Sec.	
	1. Executors	3081
	2. Administrators	3091
	3. Provisional Administrators	3111
	4. Administrators of Vacant Successions	3121
	5. Inventory of Succession Property	3131
	6. Security, Oath, and Letters of Succession Representative	3151
2.	Attorney for Absent Heirs and Legatees	3171
3.	Revocation of Appointment, and Removal of Succession Representative	3181
4.	General Functions, Powers, and Duties of Succession Representative	3191
	Sec.	
	1. General Dispositions	3191
	2. Collection of Succession Property	3211
	3. Preservation and Management of Succession Property	3221
5.	Enforcement of Claims Against Successions	3241
6.	Sale of Succession Property	3261
	Sec.	
	1. General Dispositions	3261
	2. Public Sale	3271
	3. Private Sale	3281
7.	Payment of Debts and Charges of Successions	3301
8.	Interim Allowance to Heirs and Legatees	3321
9.	Accounting by Succession Representative	3331
10.	Compensation of Succession Representative	3351
11.	Sending Heirs and Legatees into Possession	3361
	Sec.	
	1. Intestate Succession	3361
	2. Testate Succession	3371
	3. Judgment of Possession	3381
12.	Discharge of Succession Representative	3391

CHAPTER 1. QUALIFICATION OF SUCCESSION REPRESENTATIVES

SECTION 1. EXECUTORS

Art.
3081. Petition for confirmation.
3082. Order of confirmation; letters.
3083. Appointment of dative testamentary executor.

SECTION 2. ADMINISTRATORS

3091. Petition for notice of application for appointment.
3092. Form of petition for notice of application for appointment.
3093. Notice in compliance with petition.
3094. Order on application for appointment.
3095. Opposition to application for appointment.
3096. Appointment when no opposition; appointment after trial of opposition.
3097. Disqualifications.
3098. Priority of appointment.

SECTION 3. PROVISIONAL ADMINISTRATORS

3111. Appointment.
3112. Security; oath; tenure; rights and duties.
3113. Inventory taken when appointment made.

SECTION 4. ADMINISTRATORS OF VACANT SUCCESSIONS

3121. Clerk of court as administrator of vacant successions, Orleans Parish excepted.
3122. Public administrator as administrator of vacant successions in Orleans Parish.

SECTION 5. INVENTORY OF SUCCESSION PROPERTY

3131. Notary appointed for inventory in each parish.
3132. Public inventory.
3133. Procès verbal of inventory.
3134. Return of procès verbal of inventory.
3135. Procès verbal of inventory prima facie proof; traverse.
3136. Descriptive list of property in lieu of inventory.
3137. Descriptive list prima facie correct; amendment or traverse; reduction or increase of security.

SECTION 6. SECURITY, OATH AND LETTERS OF SUCCESSION REPRESENTATIVE

3151. Security of administrator.
3152. Security of provisional administrator.

Art.
3153. Security of testamentary executor.
3154. Forced heirs and surviving spouse in community may compel executor to furnish security.
3155. Creditor may compel executor to furnish security.
3156. Maximum security of executor.
3157. Special mortgage in lieu of bond.
3158. Oath of succession representative.
3159. Issuance of letters to succession representative.

PRELIMINARY STATEMENT

The office of provisional administrator of a succession heretofore has been a creature of jurisprudence, rather than of positive law. Succession of Clark, 30 La.Ann. 801 (1878); State ex rel. Gelpi v. King, 113 La. 905, 30 So. 871 (1905); Succession of Pavey, 124 La. 520, 50 So. 518 (1909); Succession of Coco, 184 La. 144, 165 So. 646 (1935). Normally, there is no need for the appointment of a provisional administrator since the succession representative is usually appointed expeditiously. In some instances, however, there is a need for the appointment of a provisional administrator. When an opposition has been filed to an application for the appointment of an administrator, or to a petition for the ex parte probate of a testament, the appointment of an administrator or the confirmation of an executor may be held up for months. For these reasons, express provision is made herein for the appointment of a provisional administrator, whenever necessary.

The majority of the Civil Code articles on succession procedure are in terms made applicable to the administration of vacant successions, and are made applicable to the administration of other successions by reference only. This has been a constant source of confusion to attorneys who are required to do extended research to determine the applicability of a particular article to the administration of other types of successions. The vacant succession is an extreme rarity in Louisiana today. Further, since a creditor may claim the right of administration if the heirs do not, there is little need for a body of rules applying to vacant successions only. In Orleans Parish, vacant successions are administered by the public administrator, but in other parishes apparently there has been no need for such an official.

For these reasons, the office of curator of vacant successions has been eliminated. In this Code, vacant successions in Orleans Parish will continue to be administered by the public administrator, and in other parishes by the clerk of court. All vacant successions are to be administered in the same manner as other successions, except as otherwise provided either in this Code or by special statute. See Arts. 3121, 3122, *infra*.

In recent years, considerable opposition has developed among practicing lawyers to the Louisiana rules relating to the taking of inventories in succession proceedings, due primarily to the expense thereof in certain parishes. For this reason, this Title contains twin sets of rules on the subject: the first retaining substantially the prior rules relating to the public inventory, and its use in connection with succession proceedings; and the second permitting the use, in lieu of a public inventory, and at the option of the party at whose instance the inventory is to be taken, of the detailed, descriptive list of property of the succession, based largely upon the pertinent provisions of the Inheritance Tax Statute.

SECTION 1. EXECUTORS

Art. 3081. Petition for confirmation

After the probate of the testament, or after its production into court as provided by Article 2891 if it is a nuncupative testament by public act, the person named as executor therein may petition the court for confirmation, and for the issuance of letters testamentary. If he files the original petition for the execution of the testament, he may pray therein for the issuance of letters.

Source: C.P. Art. 931; cf. Comments following.

Comments

(a) This article is based partly upon customary probate practices in Louisiana, and makes no change in the law except as noted in Comment (b), *infra*.

The word "execution" is employed in the same sense in which it was used in Art. 931 of the Code of Practice. *Cf.* Art. 928 of the Code of Practice. The word "probate" is not used, as this would have the effect of excluding the nuncupative testament by public act, which is self-proving and need not be probated.

(b) The last clause of Art. 931 of the Code of Practice is not retained. It provides that "if [the person named as executor] fail to pray for such letters testamentary, he shall be presumed to have declined the trust." In many instances the testament is sealed and is presented by an interested person other than the one named as executor, and the latter does not know of his appointment. In these instances, even if the named executor is the petitioner for probate, his petition will necessarily fail to contain the necessary prayer for the issuance of letters, and he should not be deprived of his office for this reason alone.

Art. 3082. Order of confirmation; letters

Unless the person named in the testament as executor is disqualified on any of the grounds assigned in Article 3097, the court shall render an order upon his petition for confirmation, confirming him as testamentary executor and directing the issuance of letters testamentary to him after he has taken his oath of office and furnished security, if required.

Source: New; cf. Comments following.

Comments

(a) No change in the law is made by this article except as indicated in Comment (b), *infra*.

(b) Heretofore there were no positive provisions granting the court the authority to refuse to confirm a testamentary executor. The first clause of this article expressly confers this authority on the court, which may, on its own motion, refuse to confirm an executor on any of the grounds which would disqualify him from office. See Art. 3097, *infra*.

Art. 3083. Appointment of dative testamentary executor

If no executor has been named in the testament, or if the one named is dead, disqualified, or declines the trust, on its own motion or on motion of any interested party, the court shall appoint a dative testamentary executor, in the manner provided for the appointment of an administrator of an intestate succession.

Source: C.P. Art. 924(7); C.C. Arts. 1678, 1679.

Comments

(a) Despite the language of Art. 1678 of the Civil Code to the effect that the judge may appoint a dative testamentary executor on his own motion, it has been repeatedly held that the judge is not given any untrammeled discretion in such appointment, but is governed by the rules relating to the publication of notice of an application for appointment as administrator, the Code preferences in such appointment, and other rules which govern the selection and appointment of an administrator. Girod's Heirs & Legatees v. Girod's Executors, 18 La. 394 (1841); King v. Lastrapes, 13 La.Ann. 582 (1858); Succession of Monaghan, 2 McGloin 35 (La.App.1884).

Further, while Art. 1679 of the Civil Code requires the dative testamentary executor to give the same security as the curator of a vacant succession, this is actually the same security required of the administrator of a succession. See Art. 1127 of the Civil Code.

(b) The language "or if the one named is dead, disqualified, or declines the trust" was intended to enumerate all of the reasons why an executor could not or would not accept the office. For the interpretation of the word "disqualified," see Art. 3097, *infra*.

(c) The general practice is to name one or more alternate executors in wills, with language indicating that if the person first named should die or decline the trust, the alternate shall serve as executor. Obviously, the testator has the privilege of naming his own executor, and the court is authorized to name a dative testamentary executor only if none is named in the testament, or the one named is disqualified, declines the trust, or dies. Under a testament naming alternate executors, the court would not be able to appoint a dative testamentary executor unless the person named and all alternates are dead or disqualified, or have declined the trust.

SECTION 2. ADMINISTRATORS

Art. 3091. Petition for notice of application for appointment

An interested person desiring to be notified of the filing of an application for appointment as administrator, at any time after the death of the deceased, may petition the court in which the succession has been opened, or may be opened, for such notice.

A petition for such notice shall comply with Article 3092, shall bear the number and caption of the succession proceeding, and shall be docketed and filed by the clerk in the record thereof.

When a petition for such notice has been filed within ten days of the death of the deceased, or prior to the application for appointment as administrator, the applicant for appointment shall serve the notice prayed for, as provided in Article 3093.

Source: New; cf. Model Probate Code, § 66.

Cross References: Arts. 3002, 3093, 3094.

Comments

(a) Under Arts. 967–973 of the Code of Practice and Art. 1117 of the Civil Code, an application for appointment as administrator must be advertised for ten days. This incurs unnecessary expense and produces unnecessary delay, especially in cases where no opposition to the application is made. In the rare case in which an interested party desires to oppose the application, his attorney either has to check the records of the court periodically, or gamble upon his ability to locate the judicial advertisement in the local newspaper.

For these reasons, rules similar to those contained in Sec. 66 of the Model Probate Code have been adopted. See Simes, Problems in Probate Law 94 (1946). These provisions will: (1) enable an interested person to receive notice of the application for appointment as administrator of the succession simply by filing the petition for notice; and (2) permit the expedition of the administration by granting discretion to the court to appoint the administrator forthwith, if no petition for notice has been filed. On this point, see McMahon, The Revision of Probate Procedure in Louisiana, 1 La.Bar J. 60–62 (October, 1953).

(b) The purpose of requiring a waiting period following the death of the deceased before any applicant can be appointed administrator is to afford a reasonable time for the filing of petitions for notice of the filing of an application for appointment.

(c) The reason for the express requirement that the petition for notice be docketed and filed by the clerk is to have this petition incorporated into the succession proceeding so effectively that counsel for any applicant for appointment can determine quickly and simply whether any such petitions have been filed, and thus enable him to comply with Art. 3093, *infra*, if he finds that such a petition has been filed.

(d) Neither Art. 3093 nor 3094, *infra*, requires or contemplates any court order upon the petition for notice. This is done to avoid throwing the burden of signing perfunctory and unnecessary orders upon district judges. Under these articles, the filing of the petition for notice automatically imposes the duty of serving notice upon any subsequent applicant for appointment, without the necessity for a court order.

(e) The sanction for the enforcement of the rule of the last paragraph of this article is the possibility of the removal of an administrator who fails to give notice of the filing of his application for appointment when required to do so, under the provisions of Art. 3182, *infra*.

(f) See, also, Comments under Art. 3442, *infra*.

Art. 3092. Form of petition for notice of application for appointment

A petition for notice under Article 3091 shall not be effective unless it is signed by the petitioner or his attorney, and sets forth: (1) the name, surname, and domicile of petitioner; (2) a statement of the interest of the petitioner; (3) the name, surname, and mailing address of the person to whom the requested notice shall be given; and (4) a prayer that the requested notice be given.

Source: New; cf. Model Probate Code, § 66.

Cross References: Arts. 3091, 3094.

Comment

See Comments under Arts. 3091, *supra*, and 3442, *infra*.

Art. 3093. Notice in compliance with petition

When notice has been petitioned for as provided in Article 3091, the applicant for appointment as administrator shall mail or deliver to the person designated to receive such notice a copy of his application for appointment, and shall notify him of the date and hour assigned by the court for a hearing thereon.

Source: New; cf. Model Probate Code, § 66.

Cross References: Arts. 3091, 3094, 3182.

Comments

(a) The purpose of the requirement that any subsequent applicant serve a copy of his application for appointment upon the person designated to receive it is to make the notice effective by giving full and complete information. Since service of a certified copy of the application is not required, an office copy will suffice.

(b) The penalty for failure to give the required notice is the removal of the administrator. See Art. 3182, *infra*.

(c) See, also, Comments under Art. 3442, *infra*.

Art. 3094. Order on application for appointment

The court shall order the taking of an inventory, or the filing of a descriptive list as provided in Article 3136, of the property of the deceased upon the filing of an application for appointment as administrator.

If notice of the application for appointment is required under Articles 3091 through 3093, the court shall assign a date and hour for a hearing on the application, which shall be held not earlier than the eleventh day after the mailing or delivery of such notice. If no such notice is required, and ten days have elapsed since the death of the deceased, the court may appoint the applicant as administrator forthwith, unless he is disqualified under Article 3097.

Source: New; cf. Comments following.

Art. 3094 ADMINISTRATION OF SUCCESSIONS Bk. 6

Comments

(a) Heretofore, orders appointing a notary to take the inventory and for the publication of notice of the application for appointment as administrator were usually rendered simultaneously upon the filing of the petition for appointment, and the inventory was usually completed and returned before the court appointed the administrator. Under the above article, in the normal case when no request for notice of an application for appointment has been filed within ten days of the death of the deceased, the administrator will be appointed forthwith at the same time as the court orders the taking of the inventory, or the filing of the descriptive list of assets. Although the administrator cannot qualify until the inventory or descriptive list has been taken and filed, and security furnished, the taking of the inventory or descriptive list will be expedited, and the administration accelerated accordingly.

(b) Under Art. 3093, *supra*, the applicant for appointment as administrator must notify the person requesting the notice of the date and hour assigned for a hearing on the application.

(c) See, also, Comments under Arts. 3096, 3442, *infra*.

Art. 3095. Opposition to application for appointment

The opposition to an application for appointment as administrator shall be filed prior to the hearing on the application and shall be served on the applicant for appointment. This opposition shall comply with Article 2972, and shall allege the prior right of opponent to the appointment, or the grounds on which it is claimed the applicant is disqualified. If the opposition is based on a prior right to the appointment, the opponent shall pray that he be appointed administrator.

Source: New; cf. C.P. Arts. 970–973; C.C. Arts. 1118, 1119.

Comments

(a) Under Art. 2972, *supra*, the opposition filed in a succession proceeding must comply with the pertinent provisions of the rules in Arts. 853 through 863, *supra*.

(b) Art. 3097, *infra*, sets forth the grounds for the disqualification of the person who is named in a testament as testamentary executor, or who applies for appointment as administrator. The opposition to the application for appointment may be made either on the ground of a prior right of opponent to the appointment, or on the ground that the applicant is disqualified.

Tit. 3   REPRESENTATIVES   Art. 3097

(c) Heretofore, a person opposing the application for appointment was required to allege and prove a prior right to the appointment and also claim the appointment himself. This last requirement has not been retained. A person having good reasons for opposing the application may not wish to claim the administration himself.

(d) See, also, Comments under Art. 3442, *infra*.

Art. 3096. Appointment when no opposition; appointment after trial of opposition

At the hearing on the application for appointment as administrator, if no opposition thereto has been filed, the court shall appoint the applicant, unless he is disqualified under Article 3097.

If an opposition to the application for appointment has been filed prior to the hearing thereon, the court shall assign the opposition for trial. After this trial, the court shall appoint as administrator the qualified claimant having the highest priority of appointment.

If all of the claimants are disqualified under Article 3097, the court shall appoint a qualified person who is willing to accept the administration of the succession.

Source: New; cf. C.P. Art. 973.

Comments

(a) Art. 3094, *supra*, provides for a hearing on the application for appointment if an interested party has petitioned for notice of the application. Under this article, if the notice has been petitioned for and given, the court may still make an ex parte appointment, if no opposition has been filed prior to the hearing. If an opposition has been filed, then it must be tried.

(b) For the effect of an appeal from a judgment dismissing the opposition, and appointing the applicant, see Art. 2974, *supra*.

(c) Under this article, the court may appoint dual or plural administrators. See Art. 5055(1), *infra*.

(d) See, also, Comments under Art. 3442, *infra*.

Art. 3097. Disqualifications

No person may be confirmed as testamentary executor, or appointed dative testamentary executor, provisional administrator, or administrator who is:

(1) Under twenty-one years of age;

(2) Interdicted, or who, on contradictory hearing, is proven to be mentally incompetent;

Art. 3097 ADMINISTRATION OF SUCCESSIONS Bk. 6

(3) A convicted felon, under the laws of the United States or of any state or territory thereof;

(4) A nonresident of the state who has not appointed a resident agent for the service of process in all actions and proceedings with respect to the succession, and caused such appointment to be filed in the succession proceeding;

(5) A corporation not authorized to perform the duties of the office in this state; or

(6) A person who, on contradictory hearing, is proved to be unfit for appointment because of bad moral character.

Source: New; cf. Model Probate Code, § 96(b).

Cross References: Arts. 3082, 3094, 3096, 3182, 3404, 4067.

Comments

(a) There are no positive provisions in the Civil Code which set forth the grounds for the disqualification of a testamentary executor. Art. 1123 of the Civil Code provides that "If several persons claim the curatorship, the judge shall appoint one of them as curator, provided he has the requisite qualifications, and offers sufficient security." An analysis of this article and others on the subject, however, indicates quite conclusively that the "qualifications" referred to relate to the qualifications for the necessary priority of appointment, such as "heir present or represented," "surviving partner," "surviving husband or wife," or "creditor." Despite the language used in Rust v. Randolph, 5 Mart. (O.S.) 89 (La.1817), to the effect that the rules of exclusion extend "only to those whom the law declares infamous," it would appear that other disqualifications, such as minority, mental incompetency, and the lack of authority in law for an ordinary business corporation to be appointed as a succession representative, would also be recognized, if actual cases arose. These disqualifications, however, are usually invoked obliquely in cases of competition for the appointment, and in such cases, it is held the unsuccessful applicant does not fall within the classes to whom any priority of appointment is provided by law.

It is simpler and more effective to list expressly the disqualifications which would preclude the appointment and even disqualify a person nominated as executor in the testament.

(b) While Arts. 1045 and 1158 of the Civil Code indicate the possibility of there being a nonresident administrator of a succession, by providing that the attorneys in fact who represent absent heirs may claim the administration in their behalf, they neither make provision for the filing of a copy of the power of attorney in the succession proceeding nor make it clear whether the procuration should authorize the agent to perform any acts of administration, although Art. 1158(3) of the Civil Code would appear to imply this.

It would seem, however, that the only necessary requirement is that the nonresident appoint a resident agent for service of process in all actions and proceedings with respect to the succession. The great majority of the matters relating to the administration of a succession are routine and perfunctory, and these can readily be handled by communication between the nonresident and his counsel. Matters requiring the actual presence of the nonresident administrator in Louisiana could be handled personally by him in short visits to this state.

(c) The disqualification of "a person whom the court finds unsuitable" in Sec. 96(b) (6) of the Model Probate Code has not been included in this article. If the testator nominates a person to serve as executor, the latter should not be disqualified generally unless he is proved to be of bad moral character.

(d) As used in this article, the word "person" does not include a partnership or association of persons. See Art. 5251, *infra*.

(e) See, also, Comments under Arts. 3033, 3083, 3095, *supra*, and Arts. 3111, 3404, 3442, 4231, *infra*.

Art. 3098. Priority of appointment

When the appointment as administrator or dative testamentary executor is claimed by more than one qualified person, except as otherwise provided by law, preference in the appointment shall be given by the court in the following order to:

(1) The best qualified among the surviving spouse and the major heirs of the deceased;

(2) The best qualified of the nominees of the surviving spouse and of the major heirs of the deceased;

(3) The best qualified of the creditors of the deceased; and

(4) Any other qualified person.

"Best qualified," as used in this article, means the claimant best qualified personally, and by training and experience, to administer the succession.

Source: New; cf. Model Probate Code, § 96(a).

Cross Reference: Art. 3404.

Comments

(a) Heretofore, the priority in appointment rested upon either: (1) close relationship, or (2) interest in the succession. If one of the competing applicants had the highest priority, he had to be appointed by the court whether he was qualified for the office or not. The court's authority for selecting the best qualified applicant for appointment was applicable only when two or more beneficiary heirs applied for appointment. Otherwise, appointment depended entirely upon the particular class into which the applicant fell; and if two or more applicants belonged to the same class, then upon the one who filed his application first.

The above article places more emphasis upon the qualifications for the office. While it retains a priority based upon close relationship and interest, it permits the court, to some extent, to select the best qualified of the applicants, and broadens the base of selection by permitting the surviving spouse and competent major heirs to nominate qualified third persons for the office. Appointment is to be made on the basis of qualifications, without regard to who may have filed the first application.

(b) The "except as otherwise provided by law" clause gives effect to the provisions of treaties between the United States and several foreign countries, recognizing the right of foreign consuls to be appointed administrators of the successions of their deceased nationals. These treaty provisions, of course, constitute the paramount law of the state.

(c) Though the above article uses the words "qualified nominees" in paragraph (2), the intention is that a person who is given the privilege of nominating a suitable person for the office may make only a single nomination.

(d) See, also, Comments under Arts. 3194, 3442, *infra*.

SECTION 3. PROVISIONAL ADMINISTRATORS

Art. 3111. Appointment

The court may appoint a provisional administrator of a succession, pending the appointment of an administrator or the confirmation of an executor, when it deems such appointment necessary to preserve, safeguard, and operate the property of the succession. On the application of an interested party, or on its own motion, when such an appointment is deemed necessary, the court may appoint a qualified person as provisional administrator forthwith.

Source: New; cf. Model Probate Code, § 105.

Comments

(a) The general language, "preserve, safeguard, and operate the property of the succession," is intended to give the court discretion in determining the necessity for the appointment of the provisional administrator.

(b) When the appointment of a provisional administrator is necessary, there will be no time available for the giving of notice to the heirs, creditors, and other interested parties, or to permit them to oppose the appointment of the particular person whom the court selects. The court must be empowered to act immediately, on the application of any interested person, and even on its own motion.

(c) The term "qualified person" in the second sentence means any competent person not disqualified on any of the grounds enumerated in Art. 3097, *supra*.

Art. 3112. Security; oath; tenure; rights and duties

A provisional administrator shall furnish security and take the oath of office required by Articles 3152 and 3158, respectively. He shall continue in office until an administrator or executor has been qualified, or until the heirs or legatees have been sent into possession.

Except as otherwise provided by law, a provisional administrator has all of the authority and rights of an administrator, and is subject to the same duties and obligations, in the discharge of his functions of preserving, safeguarding, and operating the property and business of the succession.

Source: New.

Comments

(a) *Cf.* Succession of Coco, 184 La. 144, 165 So. 646 (1935).

(b) The tenure of office of the provisional administrator may be further limited by his removal by the court, on any of the grounds assigned in Art. 3182, *infra*.

(c) The "except" clause in the second paragraph is necessary to avoid a conflict with the provisions relating exclusively to the provisional administrator, such as compensation, tenure, and security to be furnished.

(d) The functions of the provisional administrator are limited to those necessary for the performance of the duties of his office.

Art. 3113. Inventory taken when appointment made

When the court appoints a provisional administrator, it shall order the taking of an inventory of the property of the succession as provided in Article 3131, unless one has been ordered taken before.

Source: New.

Comments

(a) Although the qualification of a provisional administrator, unlike that of an administrator, need not be delayed until an inventory has been taken, it should be taken as soon as possible. Under this article, the inventory is taken at the same time as the appointment of a provisional administrator, if one has not been ordered previously.

(b) Art. 3152, *infra*, requires the provisional administrator to furnish security in the amount determined by the court. For his compensation, see Art. 3351, *infra*.

SECTION 4. ADMINISTRATORS OF VACANT SUCCESSIONS

Art. 3121. Clerk of court as administrator of vacant successions, Orleans Parish excepted

When no qualified person has petitioned for appointment as administrator of a vacant succession within three months of the death of the deceased, the court may appoint the clerk of court as administrator thereof.

When appointed administrator in such cases, the clerk's official bond shall provide security for his faithful performance of such duties. Otherwise, all of the provisions of law relating to the administrator of a succession shall apply to the clerk of court, when appointed administrator of a vacant succession.

This article does not apply to Orleans Parish.

Source: New.

Cross Reference: Art. 3122.

Comments

The term "vacant succession" has the identical meaning assigned to it by Art. 1095 of the Civil Code.

See, also, Comments under Art. 283, *supra*, and Art. 3442, *infra*.

Art. 3122. Public administrator as administrator of vacant successions in Orleans Parish

In Orleans Parish, the public administrator shall be appointed administrator of all successions of which, under Article 3121, the clerk of court in other parishes may be appointed administrator.

All provisions of law relating to the administrator of a succession shall apply to the public administrator, except as otherwise provided by R.S. 9:1581 through 9:1589.

Source: New.

Comments

(a) The duties of the public administrator, and the security which he is required to furnish, are governed by the provisions of R.S. 9:1581 through 9:1589.

(b) R.S. 9:1586 provides that the public administrator "shall be appointed curator of all vacant successions in the parish of Orleans." This provision is modified by the above article, which changes the title to "administrator of vacant successions." This, however, is not sufficiently important to require an express change of language in R.S. 9:1586.

(c) See, also, Comments under Art. 283, *supra*, and Art. 3442, *infra*.

SECTION 5. INVENTORY OF SUCCESSION PROPERTY

Art. 3131. Notary appointed for inventory in each parish

When the court orders the taking of an inventory of the property of the succession, it shall appoint a notary of each parish in which the deceased left property to take the inventory of such property in that parish.

Source: C.C. Art. 1112.

Cross References: Arts. 3113, 3136, 4102, 4604.

Comments

See Comments under Art. 4101, *infra*.

Art. 3132. Public inventory

The public inventory of the property of a deceased person, or of other estates under the administration of the court, shall be taken by a notary appointed by the court, in the presence of at least two competent witnesses, assisted by two competent appraisers appointed and sworn by the notary. The witnesses and appraisers need not be residents of the parish where the inventory is taken.

The taking of the inventory may be attended by any person interested in the estate to be administered, or by his attorney; and when timely requested to do so, the notary shall give such person, or his attorney, notice by ordinary mail of the time and place thereof.

Source: C.C. Arts. 1102, 1104, 1105, 1106(1), 1110.

Cross References: Arts. 3136, 4102, 4604.

Comments

(a) This article will be applicable to all public inventories of estates under the administration of the courts.

(b) The requirement of Civil Code Art. 1110 that the witnesses be residents of the parish where the inventory is being taken has not been included. In many cases a witness who works in the parish where the inventory is being taken may reside in an adjoining parish.

(c) Art. 1102 of the Civil Code provides for notice of the taking of the inventory by the notary to interested parties only if they reside within thirty miles of the place where the inventory is to be taken. This is unsatisfactory because: (1) the notary is compelled to notify the heirs within a radius of thirty miles whether or not they are interested in attending, and (2) no provision is made for notifying others living at a greater distance. The above article eliminates these objections by requiring notification only to interested persons who request it, no matter where they live.

(d) See, also, Comments under Art. 3133, *infra*.

Art. 3133. Procès verbal of inventory

The public inventory shall be evidenced by the notary's procès verbal of the proceedings, subscribed by him, and signed by the appraisers, witnesses, and other persons who have attended. This procès verbal shall contain:

(1) The names, surnames, domiciles, and qualities of the notary taking the inventory, of the witnesses thereto, of the appraisers who have valued the property, and of any other interested persons who have attended;

(2) The dates when and places where the inventory was taken;

(3) A description of the manner in which the inventory was taken;

(4) An adequate description of each item of property belonging to the estate and found in the parish where the inventory was taken, and the fair market value thereof estimated by the appraisers;

(5) An adequate description of all of the titles, account books, and written evidences of indebtedness due the estate, found during the taking of the inventory, and the amounts of the indebtedness, and the name, surname, and address of each debtor, as shown therein;

(6) An adequate description of any property owned in whole or in part by third persons, or claimed by third persons as having been left on loan, deposit, consignment, or otherwise; and

(7) A recapitulation of the aggregate value of all movable property, the aggregate value of all immovable property, and the total value of all property owned by the estate.

Source: C.C. Arts. 1105–1109.

Cross References: Arts. 3136, 4102, 4604.

Comments

(a) See Comment (a) under Art. 3132, *supra*.

(b) Art. 1107 of the Civil Code has been broadened so as to require the inventory of property owned in whole or in part, or claimed by third persons. See Art. 3133(6), *supra*.

(c) The value of the items of property should be the value without deduction for any mortgages or privileges. No change of prior practice is intended.

Art. 3134. Return of procès verbal of inventory

The notary who took the inventory, or the party at whose instance it was taken, shall return the procès verbal into the court which ordered it taken, immediately upon its completion and signing. A certified copy of the procès verbal of any inventory taken in Orleans Parish may be returned in the same manner, and with the same effect as the original.

Source: C.C. Arts. 1111, 1112; R.S. 9:1422.

Cross References: Arts. 3136, 4102, 4604.

Comment

As notaries in Orleans Parish are required to be the custodians of their notarial instruments, an exception has to be made with respect to inventories taken by them. *Cf.* R.S. 9:1422.

Art. 3135. Procès verbal of inventory prima facie proof; traverse

The procès verbal of a public inventory returned into court as provided in Article 3134 shall be accepted as prima facie proof of all matters shown therein, without homologation by the court.

An interested person at any time may traverse the procès verbal of a public inventory by contradictory motion served upon the notary and the person at whose instance the inventory was made.

Source: New.

Cross References: Arts. 3136, 4604.

Comments

(a) The description and values shown in a public inventory are not conclusive, but merely prima facie correct, and must always yield to proof showing the incorrectness thereof. Babin v. Nolan, 4 Rob. 278 (La.1843); Derouin v. Segura, 5 La.Ann. 550 (1850); Succession of Pipkin, 7 La.Ann. 617 (1852); Succession of Dean, 33 La.Ann. 867 (1887); Succession of Williams, 171 La. 151, 129 So. 807 (1930); Succession of Vance, 183 La. 760, 164 So. 792 (1935).

(b) Although in many cases the inventory is "approved and homologated" by the court ex parte, there is no statute or jurisprudential rule which either requires or gives any effect to such homologation. La.Act 337 of 1936 originally required the approval of the inventory by the court in Orleans Parish, but this statute was expressly repealed by La.Act 293 of 1940.

(c) The "homologation of the inventory" is a useless and unnecessary act, as it adds nothing to the prima facie correctness of the inventory resulting from the fact that the latter has complied with all of the requirements of law for the public inventory. To relieve the judges of the district court from any necessity of signing an unnecessary order, the above article expressly provides that the inventory is prima facie correct without the necessity of a judicial homologation.

(d) This article supplies the necessary machinery for traversing or correcting an inventory which is erroneous. Heretofore, this could be done only by the introduction of evidence to rebut its prima facie correctness whenever an attempt was made to use the inventory.

Art. 3136. Descriptive list of property in lieu of inventory

Whenever an inventory of succession property otherwise would be required by law, the person at whose instance the inventory would be taken may file in the succession proceeding, in lieu of an inventory complying with Articles 3131 through 3135, a detailed, descriptive list of all succession property. This list shall be sworn to and subscribed by the person filing it, shall show the location of all items of succession property, and shall set forth the fair market value of each item thereof at the date of the death of the deceased.

The privilege of filing a descriptive list of succession property, in lieu of an inventory thereof, may be exercised without judicial authority.

Source: New; cf. R.S. 47:2408(A).

Cross References: Arts. 3094, 3137, 4604.

Comments

See the explanation for the adoption of this rule set forth in the Preliminary Statement to Chapter 1 of Title III of Book VI.

See, also, Comments under Art. 2952, *supra*, and Art. 3442, *infra*.

Art. 3137. Descriptive list prima facie correct; amendment or traverse; reduction or increase of security

The descriptive list of succession property authorized by Article 3136 shall be accepted as prima facie proof of all matters shown therein, unless amended or traversed successfully.

The court may amend the descriptive list at any time to correct errors therein, on ex parte motion of the person filing it. Any interested person may traverse the descriptive list at any time, on contradictory motion served on the person filing it. If a descriptive list is amended, or successfully traversed, the court may order the reduction or increase of the security required of a succession representative to conform to the corrected total value of the property of the succession.

Source: New.

Cross Reference: Art. 4604.

Comment

Because the list of property and the values thereof are to be submitted by the person claiming office as succession representative, ample provision has been made for its correction in a contradictory proceeding at the instance of any person whose rights might be prejudiced by an incomplete list or by incorrect values.

SECTION 6. SECURITY, OATH, AND LETTERS OF SUCCESSION REPRESENTATIVE

Art. 3151. Security of administrator

Except as otherwise provided by law, the person appointed administrator shall furnish security for the faithful performance of his duties in an amount exceeding by one-fourth the total value of all property of the succession as shown by the inventory or descriptive list.

The court may reduce the amount of this security, on proper showing, whenever it is proved that the security required is substantially in excess of that needed for the protection of the heirs and creditors.

Source: C.C. Arts. 1048, 1127–1130.

Cross References: Arts. 3153, 3156, 3157.

Art. 3151

Comments

(a) No change in the law is made by this article.

(b) The requirements for the bond to be furnished are set forth in Arts. 3042 and 3064 of the Civil Code.

Art. 3152. Security of provisional administrator

The person appointed provisional administrator shall furnish security for the faithful performance of his duties in an amount determined by the court as being adequate for the protection of the heirs, legatees, surviving spouse in community, and creditors of the succession.

Source: New.

Cross References: Arts. 3112, 3157.

Comments

Since the duties of the provisional administrator are restricted in scope and limited in duration, the only security which he is called upon to furnish is in an amount determined by the court as adequate for the protection of all parties.

See, also, Comments under Art. 3113, *supra*.

Art. 3153. Security of testamentary executor

The person appointed dative testamentary executor shall furnish the same security as is required of the administrator under Article 3151.

The person named by the testator as executor is not required to furnish security, except when required by the testament or as provided in Articles 3154 through 3155.

Source: New; cf. C.C. Arts. 1127, 1677, 1679.

Cross References: Arts. 3156, 3157.

Comment

Under the Civil Code the person named in the testament as executor is not required to furnish any security "except on the demand of creditors or claimants of specific property in the succession, and then only in a sum exceeding by one-fourth the amount of said claims. Civil Code Art. 1677," Chretien v. Bienvenu, 41 La.Ann. 728, 729, 6 So. 552, 553 (1889). See also, Succession of Rassat, 157 So. 412 (La.App.1934).

Under the above article, the testator may require the testamentary executor to furnish security.

Art. 3154. Forced heirs and surviving spouse in community may compel executor to furnish security

Forced heirs and the surviving spouse in community of the testator may compel the executor to furnish security by an ex parte verified petition therefor. If the court finds that the petitioner is a forced heir, or the surviving spouse in community, it shall order the executor to furnish security, within ten days of the service of the order, in an amount determined by the court as adequate to protect the interest of the petitioner.

Source: New.

Cross References: Arts. 3153, 3156, 3157.

Comment

Usually the interests of the forced heirs and surviving spouse are much greater than those of any creditor; yet, heretofore, only the latter has been permitted to exact security of the executor, while the former were given no protection whatsoever. This article gives both the surviving spouse and the heirs this needed protection.

Art. 3155. Creditor may compel executor to furnish security

A person having a pecuniary claim against a testate succession, whether liquidated or not, or claiming the ownership of specific items of property in the possession of the succession, may compel the executor to furnish security in an amount exceeding by one-fourth the amount of the claim, or the value of the property as shown on the inventory or the descriptive list. His verified petition for security may be presented ex parte to the court, which shall order the executor to furnish such security within ten days of the service of the order upon him.

Source: C.C. Art. 1677.

Cross References: Arts. 3153, 3156, 3157.

Comments

(a) Art. 1677 of the Civil Code provides for the automatic removal of the executor who fails to furnish bond within thirty days when required to do so by the court. This harsh provision is suppressed and the court is authorized to remove the executor only under Arts. 3181 and 3182, *infra*. It is better to grant the court sufficient authority to remove the executor in cases where removal is justified, than to have an automatic removal for an inadvertence in furnishing bond.

(b) Art. 1677 of the Civil Code also gives the executor thirty days within which to furnish the security ordered by the court.

Since this long delay could cause irreparable damage to the creditors, forced heirs, and surviving spouse in community, under Arts. 3154 and 3155, *supra*, the executor is required to furnish security within ten days of the date the court order was served upon him.

Art. 3156. Maximum security of executor

The executor cannot be compelled to furnish security, under the provisions of Articles 3153 through 3155, in an amount in excess of the maximum security required of the administrator under Article 3151.

Source: New; cf. C.C. Art. 1677(5).

Comment

The above article makes no change in the probate procedure of Louisiana.

Art. 3157. Special mortgage in lieu of bond

The person appointed or confirmed as succession representative may give a special mortgage on unencumbered immovable property within the parish where the succession has been opened, in lieu of the security required by Articles 3151 through 3155. The mortgage shall be for the same amount as the security required, and shall be approved by the court before letters may be issued to him.

Source: C.C. Art. 1130.

Comment

No change in the law is made, except to make the rule of Art. 1130 of the Civil Code apply to executors as well as administrators.

Art. 3158. Oath of succession representative

Before the person appointed or confirmed as succession representative enters upon the performance of his official duties, he must take an oath to discharge faithfully the duties of his office.

Source: C.C. Arts. 1049, 1126.

Cross Reference: Art. 3112.

Comment

No change in the law is made except to extend the requirement of an oath of office to executors.

Tit. 3   ATTORNEY FOR ABSENT HEIRS

Art. 3159.   Issuance of letters to succession representative

After the person appointed or confirmed as succession representative has qualified by furnishing the security required of him by law, and by taking his oath of office, the clerk shall issue to him letters of administration or letters testamentary, as the case may be.

These letters, issued in the name and under the seal of the court, evidence the confirmation or appointment of the succession representative, his qualification, and his compliance with all requirements of law relating thereto.

Source: New.

Comments

(a) This article gives express recognition to the universal practice of issuing letters testamentary and letters of administration for which heretofore there was no express provision of law. *Cf.* Art. 931 of the Code of Practice.

(b) The last paragraph follows the language customarily used in these letters as set forth in Form 705, Louisiana Formulary Annotated (1954).

CHAPTER 2. ATTORNEY FOR ABSENT HEIRS AND LEGATEES

Art.
3171. Appointment.
3172. Duties.
3173. Removal; appointment of successor.
3174. Compensation.

PRELIMINARY STATEMENT

Heretofore, appointments of attorneys for absent heirs have often been made when there was no actual necessity therefor. However, the jurisprudence indicates that: (1) the court is not required to appoint an attorney for absent heirs unless the fact that some of the heirs are absent appears from the record, or is otherwise proved; (2) the court should not appoint an attorney for absent heirs unless it appears that the appointment is necessary; (3) the failure to appoint an attorney for absent heirs when one should have been appointed is a relative nullity which is prescribed in two years. See Lacey v. Newport, 3 La.Ann. 226 (1848); Succession of Harris, 29 La.Ann. 743 (1877); Heirs of Herriman v. Janney, 31 La.Ann. 276 (1879); Succession of Kellogg, 51 La.Ann. 1304, 26 So. 262 (1899); Succession of Price, 197 La. 579, 2 So.2d 29 (1941).

The articles in this Chapter reflect these jurisprudential rules rather than the language of the pertinent Civil Code provisions.

Art. 3171. Appointment

If it appears from the record, or is otherwise proved by an interested party, that an heir of an intestate, or a legatee or presumptive legal heir of a deceased testator, is an absentee, and there is a necessity for such appointment, the court shall appoint an attorney at law to represent the absent heir or legatee.

Source: Cf. C.C. Arts. 1210, 1661.

Cross Reference: Art. 3173.

Comments

(a) This article is declaratory of the jurisprudence to the effect that there must be proof of the existence of absent heirs to authorize the appointment of an attorney for them and that, in the absence of such proof, the appointment of an attorney for absent heirs will be revoked. Lacey v. Newport, 3 La.Ann. 226 (1848); Succession of Harris, 29 La.Ann. 743 (1877).

(b) The language, "there is a necessity for such appointment" is taken from the rule announced in Succession of Kellogg, 51 La.Ann. 1304, 26 So. 262 (1899), wherein it was held that the designation of an attorney for absent heirs is essential only in case the necessity therefor is shown during the course of a pending administration of a succession. See, to the same effect: Robouam's Heirs v. Robouam's Executor, 12 La. 73 (1838); Succession of Harris, *supra*; Heirs of Herriman v. Janney, 31 La.Ann. 276 (1879).

(c) For the definition of "absentee", see Art. 5251, *infra*.

(d) See, also, Arts. 5091, 5098, *infra*.

Art. 3172. Duties

The attorney at law appointed to represent an absent heir or legatee shall:

(1) Make all necessary efforts to determine the identity and address of the absent heir or legatee, and to inform him of the death of the deceased and of his interest in the succession;

(2) Represent the absent heir or legatee in the succession, and defend his interests in all contradictory proceedings brought against him therein; and

(3) Take any conservatory action necessary to protect the interests of the absent heir or legatee, including the filing of all necessary suits.

Source: C.C. Arts. 1210–1214.

Comment

The above article goes no further than its source provisions in enumerating the duties of the attorney for absent heirs.

Tit. 3   ATTORNEY FOR ABSENT HEIRS   Art. 3174

Art. 3173. Removal; appointment of successor

The attorney at law appointed to represent an absent heir or legatee may be relieved by the court of his trust for any lawful reason, shall be removed by the court for nonperformance of duty, and his office shall terminate when the absent heir or legatee by proper pleading advises the court of his appointment of an attorney in fact, or of the selection of his own counsel.

If the attorney appointed to represent an absent heir or legatee, as provided in Article 3171, is removed, resigns, or dies, the court may appoint another attorney at law to succeed him.

Source: C.C. Arts. 1216–1218.

Comments

(a) This article confers much greater authority upon the court to relieve the attorney at law appointed from his trust "for any lawful reason." It would make removal compulsory in the event the attorney for absent heirs fails to perform his duty.

(b) Another change is the provision for the termination of the office when the absent heir appoints either an attorney in fact or his own attorney at law.

(c) The strict requirement of Art. 1218 of the Civil Code which makes it mandatory for the judge to appoint another attorney for absent heirs if the one originally appointed dies, is absent, or is discharged, has been changed to give the court discretion in this respect. It may happen that, by that time, the necessity for the appointment of a successor may have ceased.

Art. 3174. Compensation

The court may allow the attorney at law appointed to represent an absent heir or legatee, upon the completion of his duties, reasonable compensation for the services rendered, payable out of the share of the absent heir or legatee in the succession.

If the person whom the attorney has been appointed to represent is not entitled to any share in the succession, or such share is insufficient to compensate him adequately for his services, his reasonable compensation shall be taxed as costs of court against the mass of the succession.

Such compensation may be determined judicially by contradictory motion against the absent heir or legatee, if he has appeared through counsel or an attorney in fact, or otherwise against the succession representative.

Source: C.C. Art. 1219; cf. Comments following.

Comments

(a) The second paragraph of this article reflects a change in the law. Valuable services might have been rendered by the attorney for absent heirs in defending the interests of the persons whom he was appointed to represent, and this article guarantees that he will not be left without compensation in those instances where the "absent heirs" were held not to have any interest in the succession.

(b) Another change is that the attorney for absent heirs will be permitted to proceed against them or against the succession representative by summary, instead of ordinary, proceedings.

CHAPTER 3. REVOCATION OF APPOINTMENT, AND REMOVAL OF SUCCESSION REPRESENTATIVE

Art.
3181. Revocation of appointment or confirmation; extension of time to qualify.
3182. Removal.

Art. 3181. Revocation of appointment or confirmation; extension of time to qualify

If a person appointed or confirmed as succession representative fails to qualify for the office within ten days after his appointment or confirmation, on its own motion or on motion of any interested person, the court may revoke the appointment or confirmation, and appoint another qualified person to the office forthwith.

The delay allowed herein for qualification may be extended by the court for good cause shown.

Source: C.C. Arts. 1041, 1159; cf. Comment following.

Comments

This article changes the law in three respects: (1) it gives the judge discretion to remove the succession representative, rather than have him removed solely by reason of his failure to furnish the required security and take his oath; (2) it grants the court authority to extend the ten days' delay for qualification, upon application and for good cause shown; and (3) it makes this rule applicable to executors as well as administrators.

See, also, Comments under Art. 3155, *infra*.

Art. 3182. Removal

The court may remove any succession representative who is or has become disqualified, has become incapable of discharging the duties

Tit. 3   SUCCESSION REPRESENTATIVE

of his office, has mismanaged the estate, has failed to perform any duty imposed by law or by order of court, has ceased to be a domiciliary of the state without appointing an agent as provided in Article 3097(4), or has failed to give notice of his application for appointment when required under Article 3093.

The court on its own motion may, and on motion of any interested party shall, order the succession representative sought to be removed to show cause why he should not be removed from office. The removal of a succession representative from office does not invalidate any of his official acts performed prior to his removal.

Source: Model Probate Code, § 98; C.P. Arts. 1013–1018; C.C. Arts. 1158, 1677.

Comments

(a) This article drops the requirement that a succession representative be removed only in an ordinary action commenced by a petition and citation, and permits his removal in a summary proceeding commenced by a contradictory motion of an heir, creditor, or other interested person. Cf. Art. 1017 of the Code of Practice. If the succession representative has committed some act serious enough to justify a court in removing him, then he should be removed expeditiously.

(b) This article also changes the law by granting the court the discretionary power to remove the succession representative for the causes specified, whereas, heretofore, some of the grounds for removal required an ipso facto removal whether such removal was justified or necessary.

(c) The last sentence effects no change in the law.

(d) See, also, Comments under Arts. 3091, 3093, 3112, 3155, *supra*, and Art. 3334, *infra*.

CHAPTER 4. GENERAL FUNCTIONS, POWERS, AND DUTIES OF SUCCESSION REPRESENTATIVE

SECTION 1. GENERAL DISPOSITIONS

Art.
3191. General duties.
3192. Duties and powers of multiple representatives.
3193. Powers of surviving representatives.
3194. Contracts between succession representative and succession prohibited; penalties for failure to comply.
3195. Contracts between succession representative and succession; exceptions.

Art. 3191   ADMINISTRATION OF SUCCESSIONS   Bk. 6

Art.
3196. Procedural rights of succession representative.
3197. Duty to close succession.
3198. Compromise and modification of obligations.

SECTION 2. COLLECTION OF SUCCESSION PROPERTY

3211. Duty to take possession; enforcement of claims and obligations.

SECTION 3. PRESERVATION AND MANAGEMENT OF SUCCESSION PROPERTY

3221. Preservation of succession property.
3222. Deposit of succession funds; unauthorized withdrawals prohibited; penalty.
3223. Investment of succession funds.
3224. Continuation of business.
3225. Continuation of business; interim order unappealable.
3226. Lease of succession property.
3227. Execution of contracts.
3228. Loans to succession representative for specific purposes; authority to mortgage and pledge succession property as security therefor.
3229. Notice by publication of application for court order; opposition.

SECTION 1. GENERAL DISPOSITIONS

Art. 3191.   General duties

A succession representative is a fiduciary with respect to the succession, and shall have the duty of collecting, preserving, and managing the property of the succession in accordance with law. He shall act at all times as a prudent administrator, and shall be personally responsible for all damages resulting from his failure so to act.

Source: C.C. Art. 1147; cf. R.S. 9:3801 et seq.

Comments

(a) This article is broad in scope and states the fiduciary relationship existing between the representative and the succession, which should pervade all his operations and should not be restricted to his functions in relation to the collection, preservation, and management of assets only. *Cf.* The Uniform Fiduciaries Law, R.S. 9:3801 *et seq.* The "prudent administrator" concept contained in Art. 1147 of the Civil Code has been retained.

(b) The responsibilities of the representative are stated in general terms. This follows the pattern of Civil Code Art. 1147, which provides that the succession representative is responsible for all damages resulting from his "misconduct". The liability of the representative for his failure to perform particular duties imposed upon him is covered in detail in other articles in this and other chapters of this Title. See for example Art. 3222, *infra*, imposing penalties for failure to deposit succession funds or withdrawing same without court authority.

(c) See, also, Comments under Arts. 3192, 4262, *infra*.

Art. 3192. Duties and powers of multiple representatives

If there are several succession representatives, all action by them shall be taken jointly, unless:

(1) The testator has provided otherwise; or

(2) The representatives have filed in the record a written authorization to a single representative to act for all.

Source: Model Probate Code, § 102; cf. C.C. Art. 1681.

Comments

(a) With respect to the duties and powers of multiple executors, Art. 1681 of the Civil Code provides that one of several executors has the power to bind the others, unless the testator has divided their functions. See Doriocourt v. Jacobs, 1 La.Ann. 214 (1846); *cf*. Allen v. Louisiana National Bank, 50 La.Ann. 366, 23 So. 360 (1898). The concept of Art. 1681 of the Civil Code has been rejected in favor of the system generally approved in the Model Probate Code, which is made applicable to succession representatives in general.

(b) Since the above article requires unanimity, it follows that unauthorized unilateral action would subject the offending representative to the penalty provisions of Art. 3191, *supra*.

Art. 3193. Powers of surviving representatives

Every power exercised by joint succession representatives may be exercised by the survivor of them in case of the death or termination of appointment of one or more of them, unless the testator has provided otherwise.

Source: Model Probate Code, § 101.

Cross Reference: Art. 3338.

Art. 3194. Contracts between succession representative and succession prohibited; penalties for failure to comply

A succession representative cannot in his personal capacity or as representative of any other person make any contracts with the succession of which he is a representative. He cannot acquire any property of the succession, or interest therein, personally or by means of third persons, except as provided in Article 3195.

All contracts prohibited by this article are voidable and the succession representative shall be liable to the succession for all damages resulting therefrom.

Source: C.C. Arts. 1146, 1790.

Cross Reference: Art. 3195.

Comments to Articles 3194 and 3195

(a) Arts. 3194 and 3195 are based on Arts. 1146 and 1790 of the Louisiana Civil Code. The purpose of Art. 3194 is strictly to preserve the fiduciary relationship. Art. 3195 contains the exceptions embodied in the amendments to Civil Code Art. 1146, which have been broadened and clarified. In this connection, it is believed that the succession representative should be permitted to do more than merely purchase property. A surviving spouse, for example, may wish to make other kinds of contracts with the succession, such as leases, loans, or service contracts. The same is true, although to a more limited extent, of the partner, the co-owner, legatee, or the mortgage or privileged creditor.

(b) Since the contracts prohibited by Art. 3194 do not preclude ratification, Prothro v. Prothro, 33 La.Ann. 598 (1881); Wood v. Nicholls, 33 La.Ann. 744 (1881), Art. 3194 simply states that these contracts are voidable.

(c) See, also, Comments under Art. 4263, *infra*.

Art. 3195. Contracts between succession representative and succession; exceptions

The provisions of Article 3194 shall not apply when a testament provides otherwise or to a succession representative who is:

(1) The surviving spouse of the deceased;

(2) A partner of the deceased, with respect to the assets and business of the partnership;

(3) A co-owner with the deceased, with respect to the property owned in common;

(4) A legatee of the deceased, with respect to property bequeathed in part to him; or

(5) A mortgage creditor or holder of a vendor's privilege, with respect to property subject to the mortgage or privilege.

Source: C.C. Art. 1146.

Cross Reference: Art. 3194.

Comments

See Comments under Art. 3194, *supra*, and Art. 4263, *infra*.

Art. 3196. Procedural rights of succession representative

In the performance of his duties, a succession representative may exercise all procedural rights available to a litigant.

Source: New; cf. C.P. Arts. 111, 122, 123; C.C. Arts. 1053, 1113, 1155, 1676.

Comment

See Comments under Arts. 428, 685, 734, *supra*, and Arts. 3211, 3249, *infra*.

Art. 3197. Duty to close succession

It shall be the duty of a succession representative to close the succession as soon as advisable.

Source: New; cf. Model Probate Code, § 173.

Comments

(a) This article does not go quite as far as Sec. 173 of the Model Probate Code, which provides that a representative shall close the estate as promptly as possible and also prescribes a nine months' limitation on the closing, subject to the court's discretion to extend the period for cause shown. Since there are cases where it is both necessary and advantageous to have a longer administration, there should be some flexibility in this matter. The standard prescribed by the above article accomplishes this flexibility.

(b) See Art. 3393, *infra*, which provides for the reopening of an administration in cases where property is discovered after the discharge or for any other proper cause.

Art. 3198. Compromise and modification of obligations

A succession representative may:

(1) Effect a compromise of an action or right of action by or against the succession; or

Art. 3198   ADMINISTRATION OF SUCCESSIONS   Bk. 6

(2) Extend, renew, or in any manner modify the terms of any obligation owed by or to the succession.

Any action taken under this article must be approved by the court after notice as provided by Article 3229.

Source: New; cf. Model Probate Code, §§ 126, 147.

Comments

(a) This article is based in part on Secs. 126 and 147 of the Model Probate Code. Heretofore, Louisiana courts frequently have been unwilling to issue orders authorizing succession representatives to effect compromises and hence, although such agreements may be subsequently ratified, the representative has been forced to proceed at his own risk. See St. Martin Land Co. v. Pinckney, 212 La. 605, 33 So.2d 169 (1947).

(b) Under this article, court authority to enter into compromise or modification agreements is not necessary, but the court must approve the completed agreement after due notice to the parties given in the manner provided by Art. 3229, *infra*.

(c) The Model Probate Code provides also for the authorization of a representative to submit to arbitration but the above article does not extend this far. In this connection, it should be noted that an arbitration agreement entered into by the representative may be subsequently ratified. See Lattier v. Rachal, 12 La.Ann. 695 (1857).

(d) See, also, Comments under Arts. 685, 734, 3193, *supra*, and Arts. 3229, 4264, *infra*.

SECTION 2. COLLECTION OF SUCCESSION PROPERTY

Art. 3211.   Duty to take possession; enforcement of claims and obligations

A succession representative shall be deemed to have possession of all property of the succession and shall enforce all obligations in its favor.

Source: New; cf. Model Probate Code, § 124.

Comments

(a) This article is a departure from the law relating to seizin. The utility of the concept of seizin in Louisiana law is doubtful, since as a practical matter the succession representative has full seizin of all the property of the deceased. McMahon 1688, n. 211.

(b) Since the language "all property of the succession" includes intangible property, it was deemed unnecessary to make specific provisions regarding the transfer to the representative of bank accounts and other incorporeals. In this connection, see the following statutory provisions authorizing the transfer of intangibles in specific cases: R.S. 6:66, bank deposits; R.S. 6:746, building and loan association memberships; R.S. 12:503, corporate stock; 38 U.S.C. § 451, war risk insurance.

(c) Art. 3196, *supra*, states the principle that a succession representative may exercise the rights of a litigant and has, therefore, the right to sue when necessary to protect the interests of the succession. The above article is broad enough to direct and empower the succession representative to bring all types of necessary actions which, under the jurisprudence, he is authorized to bring. No change in the jurisprudential rules in this respect is contemplated.

(d) The above article makes no provision as to the time when the representative should take possession. This point is covered by the "prudent administrator" concept, and thus he should be required to take possession as soon as practicable.

(e) No provision regarding the method of collecting succession property is necessary. This is likewise covered by the "prudent administrator" concept, and any expense incurred in connection therewith should be allowed if it is reasonable and necessary. See Succession of Schmidt, 16 La.Ann. 256 (1861).

(f) See, also, Comments under Arts. 428, 685, 3196, *supra*, and Arts. 3249, 4262, *infra*.

SECTION 3. PRESERVATION AND MANAGEMENT OF SUCCESSION PROPERTY

Art. 3221. Preservation of succession property

A succession representative shall preserve, repair, maintain, and protect the property of the succession.

Source: New; cf. Comments following.

Comments

(a) No change in the law is contemplated. It is the duty of the succession representative to make necessary expenditures for the preservation of succession property, as for instance, repairs, insurance, and taxes. Civil Code Art. 1147; Succession of Rhodes, 164 La. 488, 114 So. 107 (1927). Although a representative cannot by his contracts bind the succession, he is nevertheless entitled to reimbursement for proper expenditures. Succession of Whitehead, 3 La.Ann. 396 (1848); Succession of Nitch, 22 La.Ann. 316 (1870); Succession of Futch, 207 La. 807, 22 So.2d 125 (1945).

Art. 3221 ADMINISTRATION OF SUCCESSIONS Bk. 6

(b) No provision has been made requiring the succession representative to insure succession property. To require insurance in every case would be unwise and impractical since it would mean the insuring of every single succession effect, even one of very little or of no value.

On the other hand, the permissive provision in Sec. 124 of the Model Probate Code authorizing the representative to insure succession property is implicit in the text of this article requiring the representative to "protect" the property of the succession, and the duty to insure falls squarely within the implied duties of a prudent administrator. See Succession of Williams, 7 La.App. 465 (1928).

(c) See, also, Comments under Art. 4262, *infra*.

Art. 3222. Deposit of succession funds; unauthorized withdrawals prohibited; penalty

A succession representative shall deposit all moneys collected by him as soon as received, in a bank account in his official capacity, in a state or national bank in this state, and shall not withdraw the deposits or any part thereof, except in accordance with law.

On failure to comply with the provisions of this article, the court may render a judgment against the succession representative and his surety in solido to the extent of twenty percent interest per annum on the amount not deposited or withdrawn without authority, such sum to be paid to the succession. He may also be adjudged liable for all special damage suffered, and may be dismissed from office.

Source: C.C. Art. 1150.

Comment

This article is based on Civil Code Art. 1150, except that the source provision makes the penalty mandatory and the above article does not. This is in accordance with the prevailing jurisprudence. See Succession of Gandolfo, 173 La. 190, 136 So. 561 (1931); Succession of Lombardo, 204 La. 429, 15 So.2d 813 (1943); Succession of Baronet, 222 La. 1051, 64 So.2d 428 (1953).

See, also, Comments under Art. 3191, *supra*.

Art. 3223. Investment of succession funds

When it appears to the best interest of the succession, and subject to the representative's primary duty to preserve the estate for prompt distribution and to the terms of the testament, if any, the court may authorize a succession representative to invest the funds of the succession and make them productive.

Unless the testator has provided otherwise, such investments shall be restricted to the kinds of investments permitted to trustees by the laws of this state.

Source: New; cf. Model Probate Code, § 133.

Comments

(a) This article is a departure from the prevailing Louisiana practice. There are many instances where it is to the best interest of the succession to allow the representative to invest. In this way it is possible to build up a succession, especially where it is apparent that the funds will not be distributed for some time. An undue prolongation of the administration is guarded against by the requirement that authority to invest is subject to the primary duty of the representative to preserve the estate for "prompt distribution." In this connection, see Art. 3197, *supra*, providing that the representative has the duty of closing the succession as soon as advisable.

(b) The reference in the last paragraph is to the legal list of securities contained in the Trust Estates Law. See R.S. 9:2061.

(c) Under this article the succession representative may obtain court authority to invest succession funds on his own ex parte application.

(d) See, also, Comments under Art. 3261, *infra*.

Art. 3224. Continuation of business

When it appears to the best interest of the succession, and after compliance with Article 3229, the court may authorize a succession representative to continue any business of the deceased for the benefit of the succession; but if the deceased died testate and his succession is solvent, the order of court shall be subject to the provisions of the testament. This order may contain such conditions, restrictions, regulations, and requirements as the court may direct.

Source: New; cf. Model Probate Code, § 131.

Cross References: Arts. 3228, 3229, 3301.

Comments

(a) This article remedies what has been termed one of the greatest deficiencies of Louisiana probate procedure. McMahon, The Revision of Probate Procedure in Louisiana, 1 La.Bar J. 53, 63 (October, 1953).

(b) In the absence of express authority to continue the business of the decedent, an administrator may nevertheless be willing to do so, but under the prevailing jurisprudence he does so at his own

Art. 3224   ADMINISTRATION OF SUCCESSIONS   Bk. 6

risk. *Cf.* Carroll, Hoy and Co. v. Davidson, 23 La.Ann. 428 (1871); Succession of Worley, 40 La.Ann. 622, 4 So. 570 (1888). While the representative is authorized to perform conservatory acts for the business, express authority to continue the business as a going concern might prove essential, especially where it is apparent that the estate cannot be settled and the funds distributed for some time to come. *Cf.* Arts. 1138 and 1140 of the Civil Code, authorizing the administration of partnership effects for one year after dissolution.

(c) Under this article, the authority to continue the business includes the authority to pay debts incurred in connection with the operation of the business and to sell property in furtherance thereof. *Cf.* Arts. 3261 and 3301, *infra*.

(d) See, also, Comments under Art. 3225, *infra*.

Art. 3225. Continuation of business; interim order unappealable

When an application to continue business has been filed, the court may issue an interim ex parte order to the succession representative to continue the business immediately until such time as the procedure provided for by Article 3229 may be complied with.

No appeal shall lie from the granting or denial of the interim order.

Source: New.

Cross Reference: Art. 3229.

Comments

(a) This article allows the court to issue an interim authorization to conduct a business pending a final determination under Art. 3224, *supra*.

(b) The last sentence of this article is modeled on Art. 3513, *infra*, which provides that no appeal shall lie from any order relating to a temporary restraining order. Appeals from the final order after hearing are governed by Art. 2974, *supra*, which deals with appeals generally in succession matters.

(c) See, also, Comments under Art. 3301, *infra*.

Art. 3226. Lease of succession property

When it appears to the best interest of the succession, the court may authorize a succession representative to grant a lease upon succession property after compliance with Article 3229. No lease may be granted for more than one year, except with the consent of the heirs and interested legatees.

This article does not apply to the granting of mineral leases.

Source: New; cf. Comment following.

Cross Reference: Art. 3229.

Comment

Although there is no express authorization in the Civil Code for the representative to grant leases upon succession property, the courts have allowed it and, in certain instances, have even required the representative to make a diligent effort to do so. See 27 Tul. L.Rev. 95, 103, n. 86 (1952). A representative has even been held liable for the rental value of succession property which he might have rented. Succession of Hawthorne, 158 La. 637, 104 So. 481 (1925). However, to require the representative to lease succession property in every case might prove detrimental to the succession. For this reason the above article is couched in broad and permissive terms. The last sentence of the article was added in order to insure that R.S. 9:1491–9:1493, which allow a succession representative to grant mineral leases and prescribe the procedure therefor, will remain unaffected.

Art. 3227. Execution of contracts

If a person dies before performing an executory contract evidenced by writing, the court may authorize the succession representative to perform the contract, after compliance with Article 3229.

Source: New; cf. Model Probate Code, § 132.

Cross References: Arts. 685, 3229.

Comments

(a) A deficiency in the Louisiana probate procedure has been the lack of provisions in the law to authorize or direct a succession representative to execute a sale or lease entered into by the decedent prior to his death. The above article is based upon Sec. 132 of the Model Probate Code, but goes further in that it provides for the power of the representative to execute all written contracts, excepting those of a personal nature.

(b) The procedure set out in Arts. 3281 *et seq., infra,* governing the private sale of succession property is inapplicable to the enforcement of executory contracts contemplated by this article.

Art. 3228. Loans to succession representative for specific purposes; authority to mortgage and pledge succession property as security therefor

When it appears to the best interest of the succession, and after compliance with Article 3229, the court may authorize a succession representative to borrow money for the purposes of preserving the property or the orderly administration of the estate, of paying succession debts and charges, inheritance and estate taxes, and for expenditures in the regular course of business conducted in accordance with Article 3224. As security for such loans the court may authorize the succession representative to mortgage or pledge succession property upon such terms and conditions as it may direct.

Source: New.

Cross Reference: Art. 3229.

Comments

(a) Any possibility of abuse of the authority conferred by this article is counteracted by the fact that it is granted within the discretion of the court. Furthermore, the loans may be made only for the payment of debts, charges, and taxes and for expenditures in the regular course of business under Art. 3224, *supra*, and for the purpose of preserving the property or for the orderly administration of the estate.

(b) The language "upon such terms and conditions as the court may direct" is designed to give the court the authority to include the usual security clauses, such as confession of judgment and waiver of appraisal.

Art. 3229. Notice by publication of application for court order; opposition

When an application is made for an order under Articles 3198, and 3224 through 3228, notice of such application shall be published once in the parish where the succession proceeding is pending in the manner provided by law. The notice shall state that the order may be issued after the expiration of ten days from the date of publication and that an opposition may be filed at any time prior to the issuance of the order. If no opposition is filed, the court may grant the authority requested at any time after the expiration of ten days from the date of publication.

An opposition shall be tried as a summary proceeding.

Source: New.

Cross References: Arts. 3198, 3224, 3225, 3226, 3227, 3228.

CHAPTER 5. ENFORCEMENT OF CLAIMS AGAINST SUCCESSIONS

Art.
3241. Presenting claim against succession.
3242. Acknowledgment or rejection of claim by representative.
3243. Effect of acknowledgment of claim by representative.
3244. Effect of inclusion of claim in petition or in tableau of distribution.
3245. Submission of formal proof of claim to suspend prescription.
3246. Rejection of claim; prerequisite to judicial enforcement.
3247. Execution against succession property prohibited.
3248. Enforcement of conventional mortgage or pledge.
3249. Succession representative as party defendant.

Art. 3241. Presenting claim against succession

A creditor of a succession under administration may submit his claim to the succession representative for acknowledgment and payment in due course of administration.

Except for the purposes of Article 3245, no particular form is required for the submission of a claim by a creditor of the succession other than that it be in writing.

Source: New; cf. C.P. Art. 985.

Comment

See Comments under Arts. 3242, 3246, *infra*.

Art. 3242. Acknowledgment or rejection of claim by representative

The succession representative to whom a claim against the succession has been submitted, within thirty days thereof, shall either acknowledge or reject the claim, in whole or in part. This acknowledgment or express rejection shall be in writing, dated, and signed by the succession representative, who shall notify the claimant of his action. Failure of the succession representative either to acknowledge or reject a claim within thirty days of the date it was submitted to him shall be considered a rejection thereof.

Source: New; cf. C.P. Art. 985.
Cross Reference: Art. 3243.

Comments to Articles 3241 and 3242

(a) Art. 3241, *supra*, states the principle that claims may be presented in an informal manner and allows flexibility in the manner of presenting them. A formal method of presentation is permitted by Art. 3245, *infra*, and a creditor who follows it may suspend the running of prescription even though the claim is not subsequently acknowledged by the representative.

(b) Art. 3242, *supra*, merely develops further the system of processing claims. The succession representative is given a reasonable time within which to act, and if he does not, then the creditor may treat his failure to do so as a rejection, which under subsequent provisions frees the creditor to take other action. See Art. 3246, *infra*.

(c) The requirements of Art. 985 of the Code of Practice of 1870 regarding the approval of claims are not sacramental, and it has been held that the acknowledgment thereof may be made in several ways. See Comment (b) to Art. 3243, *infra*. The requirement that the claims be submitted in writing, however, has been retained.

(d) The notice provision of Art. 1133 of the Civil Code is unnecessary for the reason that the failure of the representative to give the required notice would not prevent a creditor from presenting his claim to the succession representative.

(e) See, also, Comments under Arts. 3244, 3246, *infra*.

Art. 3243. Effect of acknowledgment of claim by representative

The acknowledgment of a claim by the succession representative, as provided in Article 3242, shall:

(1) Entitle the creditor to have his claim included in the succession representative's petition for authority to pay debts, or in his tableau of distribution, for payment in due course of administration;

(2) Create a prima facie presumption of the validity of the claim, even if it is not included in the succession representative's petition for authority to pay debts, or in his tableau of distribution; and

(3) Suspend the running of prescription against the claim as long as the succession is under administration.

Source: New; cf. Comments following.

Comments

(a) Art. 3243(2) is an innovation in so far as it bears on the doctrine of In re Romero, 38 La.Ann. 947 (1886), which held that claims against a succession, although recognized by a representative and placed upon the tableau as succession debts, would nevertheless have to be proved when opposed by the heirs, and that claims unsupported by evidence would be rejected.

(b) Prescription is interrupted by the presentation of the claim and subsequent acknowledgment thereof by the representative. Succession of Dubreuil, 12 Rob. 507 (La.1846). The requirements of Arts. 984 through 987 of the Code of Practice of 1870 are not sacramental. Maraist v. Guilbeau, 31 La.Ann. 713 (1879). The acknowledgment can be made by a letter of the succession representative recognizing the claim. Succession of Yarborough, 16 La. Ann. 258 (1861). The claim is also acknowledged when it is placed on the tableau of distribution and the representative prays for homologation. Succession of Richmond, 35 La.Ann. 858 (1883). However, the mere placing of a claim in the hands of the attorney for the succession will not interrupt prescription. Succession of Egan, Mann.Unrep.Cas. 399 (La.1880). A confession of judgment is a sufficient acknowledgment. Succession of Mansion, 34 La.Ann. 1246 (1882).

(c) The procedure for the payment of debts and charges of the succession is provided for in Chapter 7 of this Title.

(d) The acknowledgment of the debt by the succession representative forms the basis for the introduction of parol evidence to prove the debt or liability of the deceased under the provisions of R.S. 13:3721, as amended.

(e) See, also, Comments under Art. 3242, *supra*, and Arts. 3244, 3245, *infra*.

Art. 3244. Effect of inclusion of claim in petition or in tableau of distribution

The inclusion of the claim of a creditor of the succession in the succession representative's petition for authority to pay debts or in his tableau of distribution creates a prima facie presumption of the validity of the claim; and the burden of proving the invalidity thereof shall be upon the person opposing it.

Source: New; cf. Comments following.

Comments

(a) Arts. 3242 and 3243, *supra*, apply to situations where a claim is presented informally. This article covers the situation where the representative places the claim on the petition for authority to pay debts or on the tableau of distribution on his own motion. In either case, such action amounts to an acknowledgment of the claim, and consequently, the same rule regarding prescription under Art. 3243, *supra*, is applicable under this article. See Maraist v. Guilbeau, *supra*; Morris v. Cain, 39 La.Ann. 712, 1 So. 797 (1887).

(b) See Comment (a) under Art. 3243, *supra*.

Art. 3245. Submission of formal proof of claim to suspend prescription

A creditor may suspend the running of prescription against his claim by delivering personally or by certified or registered mail to the succession representative a formal written proof of the claim, sworn to by the claimant, setting forth:

(1) The name and address of the creditor;

(2) The amount of the claim, and a short statement of facts on which it is based; and

(3) If the claim is secured, a description of the security and of any property affected thereby.

If the claim is based on a written instrument, a copy thereof with all endorsements must be attached to the proof of the claim. The original instrument must be exhibited to the succession representative on demand, unless it is lost or destroyed, in which case its loss or destruction must be stated in the claim.

The submission of this formal proof of claim, even though it be rejected subsequently by the succession representative, shall suspend the running of prescription against the claim as long as the succession is under administration.

Source: New; cf. Model Probate Code, § 137.

Cross Reference: Art. 3241.

Comments

(a) The short statement of facts on which the cause of action is based is sufficient to put the representative on notice of the claim. If the creditor complies with this article, it is unnecessary for him to do anything more in order to interrupt prescription.

(b) The submission of a formal proof of the claim under this article will establish the basis for the introduction of parol evidence to prove the debt or liability of the deceased under the provisions of R.S. 13:3721, as amended.

(c) This article does not affect R.S. 9:5621, which provides that all actions against administrators, curators, and executors are barred two years after the homologation of their final account, except in case of misappropriation of property or failure to pay the amounts shown in the final account.

Art. 3246. Rejection of claim; prerequisite to judicial enforcement

A creditor of a succession may not sue a succession representative to enforce a claim against the succession until the succession representative has rejected the claim.

If the claim is rejected in whole or in part by the succession representative, the creditor to the extent of the rejection may enforce his claim judicially.

Source: Cf. C.P. Arts. 984, 986.

Cross Reference: Art. 3248.

Comments

(a) The presentation required by this article as a prerequisite to the filing of suit is an informal presentation only, provided that it be in writing. See Art. 3241, *supra*.

(b) Although the article provides that the creditor cannot sue the representative until the latter has rejected his claim, if the representative fails to take any action for thirty days after the claim has been submitted to him, his failure to act will be considered as a rejection under Art. 3242, *supra*.

(c) The second paragraph of this article is based upon Art. 986 of the 1870 Code of Practice, which provides that if the claim is not liquidated or if the representative refuses to approve it, the creditor may bring an ordinary action or may proceed by way of opposition to the final account. The language "may enforce his claim judicially" is intended to cover both of these procedures.

(d) This article is applicable to all claims, whether liquidated or not, including damage suits.

(e) See Arts. 685 and 734, *supra*, as to proper party plaintiff or defendant in claims by or against successions.

(f) See, also, Comments under Art. 3242, *supra*.

Art. 3247. Execution against succession property prohibited

Execution shall not issue against any property of a succession under administration to enforce a judgment against the succession representative, or one rendered against the deceased prior to his death.

Source: Model Probate Code, § 145.

Cross Reference: Art. 3248.

Comments to Articles 3247 and 3248

(a) These articles are designed to withdraw the succession from ordinary execution by creditors and to subject it only to the orderly process of administration.

(b) It will be noted, however, that these articles do not prevent mortgage holders from enforcing their mortgage, either via executiva or via ordinaria, without reference to the succession proceedings. See Succession of Guillory, 167 So. 901 (La.App. 1936).

Art. 3248. **Enforcement of conventional mortgage or pledge**

The provisions of Articles 3246 and 3247 shall not prevent the enforcement of a conventional mortgage on or a pledge of movable or immovable property of the succession in a separate proceeding.

Source: Model Probate Code, § 145.

Comments

See Comments under Art. 3247, *supra*.

Art. 3249. **Succession representative as party defendant**

The succession representative shall defend all actions brought against him to enforce claims against the succession, and in doing so may exercise all procedural rights available to a litigant.

Source: New; cf. C.P. Arts. 120, 122, 123; C.C. Arts. 1113, 1155, 1676.

Cross Reference: Art. 731.

Comments

This article is a companion provision to Arts. 3196 and 3211, *supra*, which provide, respectively, that in the performance of his duties, the representative may exercise all procedural rights granted to a litigant, and that he shall enforce all obligations owed to the succession.

See, also, Comments under Art. 428, *supra*.

CHAPTER 6. SALE OF SUCCESSION PROPERTY

SECTION 1. GENERAL DISPOSITIONS

Art.
3261. Purpose of sale.
3262. No priority as between movables and immovables.
3263. Terms of sale.
3264. Perishable property; crops.

SECTION 2. PUBLIC SALE

3271. Petition; order.
3272. Publication of notice of sale; place of sale.
3273. Minimum price; second offering.

SECTION 3. PRIVATE SALE

3281. Petition.
3282. Publication.

Tit. 3 SALE OF SUCCESSION PROPERTY

Art.
3283. Who may file opposition.
3284. Order; hearing.
3285. Bonds and stocks.

PRELIMINARY STATEMENT

In the administration of successions by executors and administrators, sales are necessary in certain circumstances in order to reduce assets to cash so that the succession representative can pay taxes, debts, and legacies.

Under the 1870 Code of Practice, public sales by executors and administrators were permitted only in order to pay debts. There was no provision in the law authorizing private sales until 1890, when the legislature authorized the sale of stocks and bonds on the open market without advertisement and at prevailing rates. La. Act 21 of 1890.

This situation remained unchanged until 1934, when, as a depression measure, the legislature authorized a dation en paiement by the mortgagor to the mortgagee in full cancellation of the indebtedness if the value of the indebtedness was higher than the value of the property. La.Act 121 of 1934.

The next change in the law came when the legislature adopted La.Act 290 of 1938, opening the door wide to private sales by executors and administrators of any type of property and without priority. For the background of that statute, see Sarpy, Private Sale of Succession Property, 12 Tul.L.Rev. 412 (1938).

The 1938 Act (R.S. 9:1451 *et seq.*) was broadly interpreted by the supreme court in Succession of Pipitone, 204 La. 391, 15 So. 2d 801 (1943), holding that private sales were not restricted to situations where it was necessary to raise money to pay debts or legacies, and that sales could be made "for any other purpose."

Although opponents of the private sale, particularly auctioneers, have sought to have the law repealed or emasculated in almost every legislative session since its enactment, R.S. 9:1451 *et seq.* have not been changed.

In the following articles, the basic concepts of the statute have been retained. Thus, the right of the succession representative to sell at public sale, if he so elects, has been preserved. The one significant change that has been made is the reduction in the number of advertisements required prior to the sale of the property. Other minor modifications are noted under the articles where made.

Art. 3261   ADMINISTRATION OF SUCCESSIONS   Bk. 6

SECTION 1. GENERAL DISPOSITIONS

Art. 3261.   *Purpose of sale*

A succession representative may sell succession property in order to pay debts and legacies, or for any other purpose, when authorized by the court as provided in this Chapter.

Source: Former R.S. 9:1451; cf. Model Probate Code, § 152.

Comments

(a) Prior to the adoption of La.Act 290 of 1938 (R.S. 9:1451 *et seq.*) succession property could be sold only to pay debts or legacies. Civil Code Art. 1668; Succession of Barrios, 135 La. 241, 65 So. 229 (1914). In Succession of Pipitone, 204 La. 391, 15 So. 2d 801 (1943), the supreme court held that the language "or for any other purpose" in the source provision permitted a private sale to effect a partition.

Whether a succession representative should have authority to sell succession property for purposes other than to pay debts and legacies is a much debated question. There is dictum in the Pipitone case, *supra*, indicating that the 1938 Act applies also to public sales, in so far as it authorizes a sale "for any other purpose." However, under this article, the rule is made uniform as to both public and private sales.

(b) The articles in this Chapter do not apply to such sales of succession property as occur in the course of conducting a business owned by a succession. See Art. 3224, *supra*.

(c) See, also, Comments under Art. 3224, *supra*, and Art. 3281, *infra*.

Art. 3262.   *No priority as between movables and immovables*

There shall be no priority in the order of sale as between movable and immovable property.

Source: Former R.S. 9:1452; cf. Model Probate Code, § 150.

Comments

Originally, succession immovables could be sold only after the movables had been exhausted. Burney's Heirs v. Ludeling, 47 La. Ann. 73, 16 So. 507 (1894). La.Act 290 of 1938 abolished the priority with respect to private sales. This article, following R.S. 9:1521, abolishes the priority as to public sales also. An almost identical provision is contained in Sec. 150, Model Probate Code.

See, also, Comments under Art. 3281, *infra*.

Tit. 3   SALE OF SUCCESSION PROPERTY   Art. 3264

Art. 3263. Terms of sale

Sales of succession property shall be for cash, unless upon the petition of the succession representative the court authorizes a credit sale. When a credit sale is authorized, the order shall specify the terms of the sale and the security.

Source: New; cf. former R.S. 9:1451.

Cross Reference: Art. 3264.

Comments

(a) Civil Code Art. 1170 as interpreted by the supreme court in Succession of Hood, 33 La.Ann. 466 (1881), authorizes a credit sale of succession property at public auction if the property fails to bring the minimum price at the first offering. R.S. 9:1451 provides that private sales shall be for cash.

(b) The above article permits the greatest flexibility both for public and private sales, all subject to the supervision of the court. This flexibility is desirable, particularly in times of economic distress. When the time comes for the termination of the administration, the succession representative can always sell notes which have been received as part of the purchase price.

(c) See, also, Comments under Art. 3273, *infra*.

Art. 3264. Perishable property; crops

Upon the petition of the succession representative as provided in Articles 3263 and 3271, the court may order the immediate sale of perishable property and growing crops either at public auction or private sale, without appraisal, and without advertisement, or with such advertisement as the court may direct.

Source: Cf. C.C. Arts. 1051, 1162.

Comments

(a) Civil Code Arts. 1051 and 1162 authorize the public sale of perishable property, but apparently require advertisement. This article dispenses with advertisement. See also Art. 2333, *supra*.

(b) The provision allowing the *immediate* private sale of succession property is new.

(c) See, also, Comments under Art. 3282, *infra*.

SECTION 2. PUBLIC SALE

Art. 3271. Petition; order

A succession representative desiring to sell succession property at public auction shall file a petition setting forth a description of the property and the reasons for the sale.

The court shall render an order authorizing the sale at public auction after publication, when it considers the sale to be to the best interests of the succession.

Source: C.C. Arts. 1165, 1166; cf. R.S. 9:3001.

Cross Reference: Art. 3264.

Comments

(a) Civil Code Art. 1165 requires the succession representative to file a petition for authority to sell, and Art. 1166 of the Civil Code provides for an order by the court authorizing the sale.

(b) The qualifying language in the second paragraph of this article was included to grant the court discretionary power to refuse the necessary authority in cases where the sale is unnecessary or detrimental to the succession. The court does not have the power on its own motion to order a private sale rather than a public sale.

(c) Public sales may be made by the sheriff, an auctioneer, or by the legal representative of the succession. R.S. 9:3001.

Art. 3272. Publication of notice of sale; place of sale

Notice of the sale shall be published at least once for movable property, and at least twice for immovable property, in the manner provided by law. The court may order additional publications.

The notice of sale shall be published in the parish where the succession proceeding is pending. When immovable property situated in another parish is to be sold, the notice shall also be published in the parish where the property is situated. When movable property situated in another parish is to be sold, the court may require the notice to be published also in the parish where the property is situated.

The sale shall be conducted in the parish where the succession proceeding is pending, unless the court orders that the sale be conducted in the parish where the property is situated.

Source: New; cf. Comments following.

Comments

(a) Art. 1167 of the Civil Code requires three advertisements in a period of ten days for movables and one advertisement a week for

Tit. 3   SALE OF SUCCESSION PROPERTY   Art. 3273

thirty days for immovables. This article reduces the number of judicial advertisements required by law in both cases. In the majority of cases one advertisement for movables, and two for immovables, suffices. This article does not deny the right of the succession representative to request authority to spend money for extra advertisements when considered necessary to focus public attention on the sale.

The manner in which these notices must be published is provided in R.S. 43:203.

(b) This article fills in a hiatus in the law by designating the place where the advertisement is to be published. Because the advertisement also serves to notify the heirs and creditors, as well as prospective purchasers, the advertisement is required to be published in the parish where the succession proceeding is pending.

(c) R.S. 13:4351 is a special provision, providing that judicial sales which are required to be made in Jefferson, Plaquemines, or St. Bernard Parishes may, at the request of the parties concerned, be made in Orleans Parish, and is not affected by this article.

(d) This article does not affect R.S. 13:4341, which provides that succession sales shall be held at or near the court house, and that if the property to be sold consists of both movables and immovables, the succession representative may pray that the sale be made "on the premises."

(e) See, also, Comments under Arts. 3282, 3443, *infra*.

Art. 3273.   Minimum price; second offering

The property shall not be sold if the price bid by the last and highest bidder is less than two-thirds of the appraised value in the inventory. In that event, on the petition of the succession representative, the court shall order a readvertisement in the same manner as for an original sale, and the same delay must elapse. At the second offering the property shall be sold to the last and highest bidder regardless of the price.

Source: Cf. C.C. Art. 1170.

Comments

(a) The source article provides that the succession property must be sold for at least two-thirds of the appraised value at the first offering and provides for a credit sale at any price on the second offering. However, Civil Code Art. 1169 seems to be restricted to a sale by a curator of a vacant succession. Arts. 990 et seq. of the 1870 Code of Practice authorize a sale at the request of a creditor and provide that the sale must be for the appraised value. There is no general provision fixing a minimum price at an administrator's sale.

507

Art. 3273   ADMINISTRATION OF SUCCESSIONS   Bk. 6

In Succession of Hood, 33 La.Ann. 466 (1881), the supreme court relied upon Civil Code Art. 1170 and other provisions applicable to different types of judicial sales in reaching the conclusion that an administrator's sale must be for two-thirds of the appraised value. The case was cited with approval in Lacroix v. Crane, 133 La. 227, 62 So. 657 (1913).

(b) The above article codifies the rule as to minimum price as announced in the aforementioned cases. The entire question of credit sales is covered in Art. 3263, *supra*.

SECTION 3. PRIVATE SALE

Art. 3281. Petition

A succession representative who desires to sell succession property at private sale shall file a petition setting forth a description of the property, the price and conditions of and the reasons for the proposed sale.

Source: Former R.S. 9:1451, 9:1452.

Comments

(a) The requirement in the source provisions that the succession representative set forth a full description of the property and the provisions abolishing priority as between movables and immovables are contained in Arts. 3261 and 3262, *supra*. The provision requiring the succession representative to state the reasons for his recommendation to sell immovables before all movables are exhausted has not been adopted. *Cf.* Comment under Art. 3262, *supra*.

(b) The language in the former R.S. 9:1451 requiring the sale to be to the "manifest advantage of the succession" has not been included in order to avoid the possible interpretation that a public sale should be favored and that a private sale should be authorized only in unusual circumstances.

(c) See, also, Comments under Art. 283, *supra*.

Art. 3282. Publication

Notice of the application for authority to sell succession property at private sale shall be published at least once for movable property, and at least twice for immovable property, in the manner provided by law. The court may order additional publications.

The notice shall be published in the parish where the succession proceeding is pending. When immovable property situated in another parish is to be sold, the notice shall also be published in the parish where the property is situated. When movable property situated in another parish is to be sold, the court may require the notice to be published also in the parish where the property is situated.

The notice shall state that any opposition to the proposed sale must be filed within ten days from the date of the last publication.

Source: Former R.S. 9:1453.

Comments

(a) With respect to the number and place of the publications, see Art. 3272, *supra*, which contains similar provisions for public sales. For the requirements of the publication of the notice, see R.S. 43:203.

(b) Art. 3264, *supra*, dispenses with advertisement with respect to perishable property.

(c) See, also, Comments under Art. 283, *supra*, and Art. 3443, *infra*.

Art. 3283. Who may file opposition

An opposition to a proposed private sale of succession property may be filed only by an heir, legatee, or creditor.

Source: New; cf. Comments following.

Comments

(a) The question of who has the right to oppose an application for a private sale was squarely presented to the courts in Succession of Saxton, 72 So.2d 344 (La.App.1954). In that case, the district court had dismissed an opposition by a third person not an heir, creditor, or legatee, on the ground that the opponent had no interest in opposing the sale, although he had offered, in his opposition, to pay a higher price for the property. The court of appeal affirmed the judgment and the supreme court refused to grant writs. In Succession of Senkpiel, 227 La. 516, 79 So.2d 866 (1955), the supreme court considered the identical problem and approved the Saxton decision.

(b) This article codifies the holding of the Saxton case, which is based upon the principle that a third person should not be permitted to interfere with a decision reached in good faith by a succession representative as to how and for what price succession property should be sold.

(c) See, also, Comments under Art. 283, *supra*.

Art. 3284. Order; hearing

If no opposition has been filed timely, the court shall render an order authorizing the sale, when it considers the sale to be to the best interests of the succession.

An opposition shall be tried as a summary proceeding.

Source: Former R.S. 9:1454.

Comments

The source provision requires that the judge "shall fix the minimum price to be accepted." This language was deleted as unnecessary, for the petition must state the price for the proposed sale and the judge's order necessarily approves the sale at the price stated.

See, also, Comments under Art. 283, *supra*.

Art. 3285. Bonds and stocks

A succession representative may sell bonds and shares of stock at private sale at rates prevailing in the open market, by obtaining a court order authorizing the sale. No advertisement is necessary, and the order authorizing the sale may be rendered upon the filing of the petition.

The endorsement of the succession representative and a certified copy of the court order authorizing the sale shall be sufficient warrant for the transfer.

Source: Former R.S. 9:1455.

Comments

(a) This article is almost identical to the source provision, which also applies to tutors, curators, and syndics.

(b) If such stocks or bonds do not have a value in the open market, the provisions of this Code for private sales of movables apply.

(c) See, also, Comments under Art. 283, *supra*.

CHAPTER 7. PAYMENT OF DEBTS AND CHARGES OF SUCCESSIONS

Art.
3301. Payment of debts or charges; court order.
3302. Time for payment of debts; urgent debts.
3303. Petition for authority; tableau of distribution.
3304. Notice of filing of petition; publication.
3305. Petition for notice of filing of tableau of distribution.

DEBTS OF SUCCESSION   **Art. 3301**

Art.
3306. Notice of filing of tableau of distribution; effect of failure to serve.
3307. Homologation; payment.
3308. Appeal.

PRELIMINARY STATEMENT

The Civil Code articles dealing with payment of succession debts are not altogether clear. The system, however, appears to be as follows:

The administrator should pay no debts without court authority (Civil Code Arts. 1063 and 1150), nor should he pay any debts within three months after the succession is opened, with certain exceptions (Civil Code Arts. 1179 and 1189). If the funds are sufficient to pay all the debts, he merely files a petition for authority, annexing a list of the debts. If the estate is insolvent, he presents a tableau of distribution, showing the rank of the various privileges (Civil Code Arts. 1063, 1180, and 1181). Advertisement is required, whether or not the estate is insolvent (Civil Code Arts. 1064 and 1184), except with respect to certain privileged debts (Civil Code Art. 1189). If no opposition is filed, the petition for authority is homologated and the debts are paid (Civil Code Arts. 1065 and 1185). If an opposition is filed, it is tried summarily (Civil Code Arts. 1066 and 1186), and the judgment is appealable (Civil Code Arts. 1066 and 1187).

For the most part, the system prescribed by the Civil Code is retained in these articles. However, it should be noted that the customary practice, at least in Orleans Parish, is to combine the petition for authority to pay debts with the final account. Technically, a final account should show actual rather than proposed payments by the succession representative and should be filed only after authority has been granted to pay debts, after the debts are paid and the administration is complete. See Succession of Bofenschen, 29 La.Ann. 711 (1877). This Chapter does not deal with the account, but only with the payment of debts and the procedure therefor.

Art. 3301. Payment of debts or charges; court order

A succession representative may pay the debts or charges of the succession only with the authorization of the court, except as provided by Articles 3224 and 3302.

Source: C.C. Arts. 1063, 1150.

Art. 3301 ADMINISTRATION OF SUCCESSIONS Bk. 6

Comments

(a) Art. 1063 of the Civil Code also prohibits the payment of legacies without court authority.

(b) These articles do not apply to the payment of debts incurred in the operation of a business owned by a succession. Arts. 3224 and 3225, *supra*, authorize the representative to conduct such a business as a going concern under order of court. Debts incurred in the course of such an operation are paid in the regular course of business.

(c) R.S. 6:66, permitting banks to make transfers of funds of a succession predicated upon a judgment of court or letters of a succession representative, is not affected by this article.

(d) See, also, Comments under Art. 3224, *supra*.

Art. 3302. Time for payment of debts; urgent debts

Upon the expiration of three months from the death of the decedent, the succession representative shall proceed to pay the debts and charges of the succession as provided in this Chapter.

The court may authorize the payment at any time and without publication of debts the payment of which should not be delayed.

Source: C.C. Arts. 1179, 1189.

Cross Reference: Art. 3301.

Comments

(a) The purpose of the delay of three months is to give creditors an opportunity to present their claims. Art. 136 of the Civil Code of 1808, corresponding to Art. 1179 of the 1870 Civil Code, included a purpose clause: "for the purpose of allowing sufficient time to the creditors . . . to put in their claims . . .." Sec. 148 of the Model Probate Code provides a delay of four months before debts can be paid.

(b) Art. 1189 of the Civil Code makes a specific reference to funeral expenses, court costs, and expenses of the last illness as examples of debts "the payment of which cannot be retarded." No illustrations have been included in the above article in order to give the court broad discretion regarding debts the payment of which should not be delayed.

Art. 3303. Petition for authority; tableau of distribution

When a succession representative desires to pay charges or debts of the succession, he shall file a petition for authority and shall include in or annex to the petition a tableau of distribution listing those charges and debts to be paid.

If the funds in his hands are insufficient to pay all the charges and debts in full, the tableau of distribution shall show the total funds available and shall list the proposed payments according to the rank of the privileges and mortgages of the creditors.

Source: C.C. Arts. 1063, 1180, 1181.

Cross Reference: Art. 3306.

Comment

Civil Code Art. 1180 requires mention of the "places of residence of the creditors." This requirement has rarely been observed in actual practice and is omitted as unnecessary.

Art. 3304. Notice of filing of petition; publication

Notice of the filing of a petition for authority to pay debts and charges shall be published once in the parish where the succession proceeding is pending in the manner provided by law. The notice shall state that the petition can be homologated after the expiration of ten days from the date of publication and that any opposition to the petition must be filed prior to homologation.

Source: C.C. Arts. 1064, 1184.

Comments

(a) The source articles do not specify the number of advertisements required, but it has been held that in Orleans Parish there must be three advertisements in ten days. Succession of Greene, 158 La. 123, 103 So. 532 (1925). Under this article one advertisement of the petition for authority is sufficient.

(b) With respect to the effect of the failure to comply with the delay of ten days, it has been held that a judgment homologating an administrator's account before the expiration of ten days is a nullity. Succession of Taylor, 172 La. 1099, 136 So. 65 (1931).

(c) For the requirements of the publication of the notice, see R.S. 43:203.

(d) See, also, Comments under Art. 3442, *infra*.

Art. 3305. Petition for notice of filing of tableau of distribution

An interested person may petition the court for notice of the filing of a tableau of distribution.

The petition for such notice shall be signed by the petitioner or by his attorney, and shall set forth: (1) the name, surname, and address of the petitioner; (2) a statement of the interest of petitioner; (3) the name, surname, and office address of the attorney at law licensed to practice law in this state to whom the notice prayed for shall be mailed; and (4) a prayer that petitioner be notified, through his attorney, of the filing of the tableau of distribution.

A copy of this petition shall be served upon the succession representative, as provided in Article 1314.

Source: New.

Comments

(a) This article and Art. 3306, *infra*, afford additional protection by way of notice to those who request it.

(b) Art. 1314, *supra*, permits service upon an attorney. It applies to all pleadings which require appearance or answer on the part of the party served.

Art. 3306. Notice of filing of tableau of distribution; effect of failure to serve

When notice has been requested in accordance with Article 3303, the succession representative, without the necessity for a court order thereon, shall send a notice of the filing of a tableau of distribution by mail to the attorney designated by the person praying for notice at the address designated. Proof of mailing is sufficient; no proof of receipt is required.

If no notice of the filing of a tableau of distribution has been mailed when required under this article, a judgment homologating the tableau of distribution shall have no effect against the person praying for such notice.

Source: New.

Cross Reference: Art. 3307.

Comments

This article does not eliminate the necessity for the usual publication, but affords a creditor extra protection not heretofore available. Therefore, notice by ordinary mail suffices and no proof of receipt is required.

See, also, Comments under Art. 3305, *supra*.

Art. 3307. Homologation; payment

An opposition may be filed at any time before homologation. If no opposition has been filed, the succession representative may have the tableau of distribution homologated and the court may grant the authority requested at any time after the expiration of ten days from the date of publication or from the date the notice required by Article 3306 is mailed, whichever is later.

After the delay for a suspensive appeal from the judgment of homologation has elapsed, the succession representative shall pay the debts approved by the court.

An opposition shall be tried as a summary proceeding.

Source: C.C. Arts. 1065, 1066, 1185, 1186.

Comments

(a) An opposition may be filed ten days after notice, provided it is filed before homologation. Succession of Price, 35 La.Ann. 905 (1883). This article codifies that principle.

(b) The provisions for appeal are new; they were added in view of the fact that an appeal may be taken from a judgment homologating an unopposed account. See Art. 3308, *infra*.

(c) The provision prohibiting homologation until ten days after the mailing of the notice required by Art. 3306, *supra*, has been added to implement the system of notice by mail.

Art. 3308. Appeal

Only a suspensive appeal as provided in Article 2123 shall be allowed from a judgment homologating a tableau of distribution. The appeal bond shall comply with Article 2124.

The succession representative shall retain a sum sufficient to pay the amount in dispute on appeal until a definitive judgment is rendered. He shall distribute the remainder among the creditors whose claims have been approved and are not in dispute on appeal.

Source: Cf. C.C. Arts. 1066, 1187.

Comments

(a) In order not to delay the termination of the succession proceedings unnecessarily, only a suspensive appeal is permitted, which must be taken within the delays and under the conditions provided in Art. 2123, *supra*.

(b) Since the funds are in custodia legis, only a costs bond would be necessary. See Art. 2124, *supra*.

(c) See, also, Comments under Art. 3307, *supra*.

CHAPTER 8. INTERIM ALLOWANCE TO HEIRS AND LEGATEES

Art.
3321. Interim allowance for maintenance during administration.

Art. 3321. Interim allowance for maintenance during administration

When a succession is sufficiently solvent, the surviving spouse, heirs, or legatees shall be entitled to a reasonable periodic allowance in money for their maintenance during the period of administration, if the court concludes that such an allowance is necessary, provided the sums so advanced to the spouse, heirs, or legatees are within the amount eventually due them. Such payments shall be charged to the share of the person receiving them.

A surviving spouse, heir, or legatee may compel the payment of an allowance during the administration by contradictory motion against the succession representative.

Notice of the filing of a petition for authority to pay an allowance, or of a contradictory motion to compel the payment of an allowance, shall be published once in the manner provided by law. The notice shall state that any opposition must be filed within ten days from the date of publication.

Source: New; cf. Comments following.

Cross References: Arts. 2123, 2974.

Comments

(a) This article codifies the principles announced in Succession of Broadaway, 3 La.Ann. 591 (1848); Succession of Ledet, 175 La. 225, 143 So. 56 (1932); and Succession of Wengert, 180 La. 483, 156 So. 473 (1934). The Broadaway case holds that the administrator has the right to make reasonable advances to the widow and minor heirs and that such advances are chargeable to the persons who receive them. In Succession of Ledet, an order for the payment of $75.00 per month out of an estate of $50,000.00 for the support of two minor children was approved. In Succession of Wengert, the court affirmed a judgment ordering the executor to pay to the widow $120.00 in monthly installments of $40.00. The estate amounted to about $9,000.00, and the widow was a legatee of real estate valued at $3,000.00, and cash in the amount of $770.00.

The cited cases involved either the widow or minor heirs. The above article, however, extends the rule to any heir or legatee.

(b) This article does not affect Arts. 2382 and 3252 of the Civil Code regarding the rights of a widow in necessitous circumstances, nor R.S. 9:1513 regarding the authority of banks to pay over to the surviving spouse a portion of the deposits of the deceased.

(c) For the requirements of the publication of the notice, see R.S. 43:203.

CHAPTER 9. ACCOUNTING BY SUCCESSION REPRESENTATIVE

Art.
3331. Time for filing account.
3332. Final account.
3333. Contents of account.
3334. Failure to file account; penalty.
3335. Notice to heirs and residuary legatees.
3336. Opposition; homologation.
3337. Effect of homologation.
3338. Deceased or interdicted succession representative.

PRELIMINARY STATEMENT

Chapter 7 of this Title sets forth the procedure regulating the payment of succession debts and charges conformably to the petition for authority to pay the same. This Chapter deals with the account which should be filed after these debts and charges have been paid. The account is a report of the conduct of the succession representative with respect to the property entrusted to him.

Art. 3331. Time for filing account

A succession representative shall file an account annually and at any other time when ordered by the court on its own motion or on the application of any interested person.

Source: C.C. Arts. 1151, 1191, 1674.

Comments

(a) Despite the language in Art. 1191 of the Civil Code to the effect that an administrator who fails to file an annual account shall be dismissed from office and shall be compelled to pay a penalty, the supreme court has held that no such penalties can be imposed for the mere failure to do so, unless the administrator had been ordered to file an account and had failed to comply. Succession of Head, 28 La.Ann. 800 (1876). This principle, which has been consistently followed in later cases, is being retained. *Cf.* Art. 3334, *infra*.

(b) The heirs are "interested persons" within the meaning of this article. Succession of Weimann, 106 La. 387, 30 So. 893 (1901).

(c) The court has complete discretion, either on its own motion or upon request, to order the filing of an account at any time.

(d) See, also, Comments under Art. 283, *supra*.

Art. 3332. Final account

A succession representative may file a final account of his administration at any time after homologation of the final tableau of distribution and the payment of all debts and legacies as set forth in the tableau.

The court shall order the filing of a final account upon the application of an heir or residuary legatee who has been sent into possession or upon the rendition of a judgment ordering the removal of a succession representative.

Source: Cf. C.P. Art. 1000; C.C. Art. 1194.

Comments

(a) Civil Code Art. 1194 provides that as soon as the heirs have been sent into possession, the succession representative must file an account and pay the balance due to the heirs. The above article allows the filing of a final account at any time after homologation of the final tableau of distribution and payment of the debts and legacies.

(b) Art. 3334, *infra*, gives the heirs a right to be sent into possession under benefit of inventory at any time after the homologation of the final tableau of distribution. The right to a judgment of possession is not dependent upon the filing of a final account. Succession of Duffy, 50 La.Ann. 795, 24 So. 277 (1898). A final account is not required prior to the judgment of possession. Succession of Burbank, 126 La. 9, 52 So. 175 (1910). The heirs who have been sent into possession, however, have an absolute right to compel an account. Civil Code Art. 1194.

(c) Under this article, the order to file a final account is rendered ex parte and without a hearing or prior notice to the succession representative. *Cf.* Art. 1000 of the Code of Practice of 1870, which apparently requires the heirs to proceed by petition and citation.

(d) This article also codifies the jurisprudential rule that an administrator who has been removed can be required to file an account. Collins v. Hollier, 13 La.Ann. 585 (1858); Chaffe v. Farmer, 36 La.Ann. 813 (1884).

(e) See, also, Comments under Art. 283, *supra*, and Art. 4392, *infra*.

Art. 3333. Contents of account

An account shall show the money and other property received by and in the possession of the succession representative at the beginning of the period covered by the account, the revenue, other receipts, disbursements, and disposition of property during the period, and the remainder in his possession at the end of the period.

Source: Cf. C.C. Arts. 1147, 1191, 1194.

Cross Reference: Art. 4393.

Comments

(a) It is clear that under Civil Code Arts. 1147, 1191, and 1194, a full, true, and complete account of all assets and liabilities, and of the administration thereof is contemplated. Succession of D'Hebecourt, 189 La. 319, 179 So. 440 (1938).

(b) Under this article, the succession representative is not required to include a detailed list of the property on hand at the beginning and at the end of the period covered by the account. A reference to the inventory or descriptive list is sufficient to comply with the provisions of this article.

Art. 3334. Failure to file account; penalty

An interested person may proceed by contradictory motion to remove a succession representative who has failed to file an account after being ordered to do so by the court and may obtain the remedies provided by Article 2502.

Source: Cf. C.P. Arts. 1011, 1012; C.C. Arts. 1151, 1158, 1191.

Comments

(a) By treating the order to render an account like any other judgment ordering the performance of an act, the same results as under the source provisions are obtained, since under Art. 2502, *supra*, the debtor who fails to perform is subject to distringas or contempt proceedings or to damages.

(b) Although Art. 1191 of the Civil Code indicates that the administrator "shall be dismissed" if he fails to file an account timely, it has been consistently held that the imposition of penalties is discretionary with the court. Mount Carmel Church v. Farrelly, 34 La.Ann. 533 (1882); Succession of David, 213 La. 707, 35 So.2d 465 (1948). This article contemplates the imposition of penalties only after a court order to render an account has not been complied with.

(c) Although there is jurisprudential support for proceeding by rule to remove an administrator who has failed to file an ac-

Art. 3334 ADMINISTRATION OF SUCCESSIONS Bk. 6

count, Arts. 1017 and 1018 of the Code of Practice of 1870 seem to require that such a proceeding be commenced by petition and citation. On this point see Art. 3182, *supra*, providing for the removal, on contradictory motion, of a succession representative who has failed to perform any duty imposed on him by order of court.

(d) See, also, Comments under Arts. 3331, 3332, *supra*.

Art. 3335. Notice to heirs and residuary legatees

A copy of any account filed by a succession representative shall be served upon each heir or residuary legatee, together with a notice that the account may be homologated after the expiration of ten days from the date of service and that any opposition thereto must be filed before homologation. A copy of a final account shall be served in the manner provided for service of citation. Service of a copy of any other account may be made by mail.

Source: New; cf. C.P. Art. 1004.
Cross Reference: Art. 3336.

Comments

(a) This article clarifies the jurisprudence as to whether notice to the heirs is necessary prior to the homologation of the account of the succession representative which arises, no doubt, not only from the absence of statutory provisions on the point, but also from the apparent failure to distinguish between the account and the tableau of distribution. *Cf.* Succession of Taylor, 172 La. 1099, 136 So. 65 (1931), in which it was held that publication was necessary before an account could be homologated when, actually, advertisement is required only in the case of a tableau.

(b) Although Art. 1004 of the 1870 Code of Practice provides that the heirs should have three days from the filing of the account to file an opposition thereto, it makes no provision whatever for notice to them that the account has been filed. The supreme court has held, however, that a judgment homologating an account is ineffective as against the heirs in the absence of service upon them. Carter v. McManus, 15 La.Ann. 676 (1860); Succession of Conrad, 45 La.Ann. 89, 11 So. 935 (1893); Landry v. Landry, 105 La. 362, 29 So. 900 (1901).

(c) Formal service is required only in the case of a final account. In all other cases, service by mail is authorized since under Art. 3337, *infra*, the homologation of an interim account is only prima facie evidence of its correctness.

(d) Since heirs would have no interest when the succession is fully testate, service on the heirs is made only in the absence of a residuary legatee.

(e) See, also, Comments under Art. 4394, *infra*.

Art. 3336. Opposition; homologation

An opposition to an account may be filed at any time before homologation. An opposition shall be tried as a summary proceeding.

When no opposition has been filed, or to the extent to which the account is unopposed, the succession representative may have the account homologated at any time after the expiration of ten days from the date of service as provided in Article 3335.

Source: New; cf. Comments following.

Comments

(a) This article codifies the rule that an opposition may be filed at any time prior to homologation. Longbottom's Executors v. Babcock, 9 La. 48 (1836).

(b) Art. 1005 of the Code of Practice provides that where an opposition is filed to an account, the judge may decide it himself or refer it to auditors for a report. This provision is unnecessary, for the court has inherent authority to make use of experts.

(c) See, also, Comments under Art. 4395, *infra*.

Art. 3337. Effect of homologation

A judgment homologating any account other than a final account shall be prima facie evidence of the correctness of the account.

A judgment homologating a final account has the same effect as a final judgment in an ordinary action.

Source: C.C. Arts. 1191, 1674; cf. Comments following.

Comments

(a) The first paragraph of this article is similar to Arts. 1191 and 1674 of the Civil Code applying, respectively, to the annual account of administrators and executors.

(b) There are no statutory provisions dealing with the effect of homologation of a final account and, due to the confusion in the use of the terms "account" and "tableau," the jurisprudence is not clear. See, however, Bry v. Dowell, 1 Rob. 111, 113 (La.1841) where it is said:

"[An executor's] accounts cannot remain open, and his responsibility suspended for a number of years. When his accounts are settled and passed upon . . . contradictorily with the heirs . . . the decree is as final and binding on such heirs as any judgment in an ordinary suit, to which they may have been parties."

The rule of the Bry case has been codified in order for the succession representative to obtain a valid and final discharge by citing the heirs and giving them an opportunity to oppose his account.

(c) See, also, Comments under Art. 3335, *supra*, and Arts. 3392, 4396, *infra*.

Art. 3338. Deceased or interdicted succession representative

If a succession representative dies or is interdicted, an account of his administration may be filed by his heirs or by his legal representative; and upon the petition of an interested person the court shall order the filing of such an account.

Source: New; cf. Comment following.

Comment

Although there are no statutory provisions regarding the filing of an account on behalf of a deceased or interdicted representative, the above article represents the prevailing practice in Louisiana. *Cf.* Sec. 181 of the Model Probate Code and Sec. 932 of the Probate Code of California.

CHAPTER 10. COMPENSATION OF SUCCESSION REPRESENTATIVE

Art.
3351. Amount of compensation; when due.
3352. More than one succession representative.
3353. Legacy to executor.

Art. 3351. Amount of compensation; when due

An administrator or executor shall be allowed a sum equal to two and one-half percent of the amount of the inventory as compensation for his services in administering the succession. The court may increase the compensation upon proper showing that the usual commission is inadequate.

A provisional administrator or an administrator of a vacant succession shall be allowed fair and reasonable compensation by the court for his services.

The compensation of a succession representative shall be due upon the homologation of his final account. The court may allow an administrator or executor an advance upon his compensation at any time during the administration.

Source: Cf. C.C. Arts. 1069, 1194, 1200, 1683, 1684; Comments following.

Comments

(a) Arts. 1069, 1194, and 1200 of the Civil Code fix the compensation of an administrator and of an executor of a vacant succession at two and one-half percent on the amount of the inventory, deduction being made of the bad debts. Civil Code Art. 1683 likewise fixes the compensation of an executor with seizin at two and one-half percent on the inventory of the succession, "making deduction for what is not productive and for what is due by insolvent debtors." The executor without seizin is entitled, under Art. 1684 of the Civil Code, to two and one-half percent but only on the estimated value of the objects which he had in his possession "and on the sums put into his hands for paying the legacies and other charges of the will."

(b) The above article makes the commission uniform for the administrators and executors, regardless of whether the executor has seizin. No provision is made in this Code for the deduction of bad debts since, under the jurisprudence, the term "bad debts" is taken to mean debts due by persons who have been adjudged bankrupts, Succession of Blakey, 12 Rob. 155 (1845), and such debts would not be given any value in the inventory.

(c) It has also been held that, under the Civil Code articles cited, the succession representative cannot be allowed any more than the two and one-half percent commission therein provided. Succession of Sprowl, 21 La.Ann. 544 (1869). On the other hand, there is also authority for allowing a succession representative additional compensation out of income. In Succession of Robertson, 49 La.Ann. 80, 21 So. 197 (1896), the court allowed the usual two and one-half percent of the inventory value plus five percent of the revenues. However, in Succession of Rabasse, 51 La.Ann. 590 (1899), the court refused an extra commission out of income, pointing out that the Robertson case was an exceptional one and that it did not establish any new precedent.

To cover special circumstances in which the usual commission would not be adequate, a provision has been added authorizing the court, to increase the compensation of the representative upon proper showing.

(d) It has also been held, by analogy, that an administrator has no absolute right to his commission until he has completed the administration of the succession and has filed his final account. Succession of Marcour, 173 So. 587 (La.App.1937). Cf. Civil Code

Arts. 1194, 1200. See also, Art. 1069 of the Civil Code, which provides that the administrator's commission shall be allowed "on the settlement of his account."

(e) The provision in the above article relative to an advance prior to the final account conforms with a fairly common practice, which is sanctioned in Succession of Meyer, 44 La.Ann. 871, 11 So. 532 (1892).

(f) Art. 3033, *supra*, provides that, with respect to testaments dated prior to January 1, 1961, the person named as executor is entitled to full compensation even though he may not have been confirmed, but with respect to testaments dated subsequent to December 31, 1960, the person named as executor is entitled to "reasonable compensation for the services which he has rendered," even though he may not have been confirmed. It is intended that, when the executor does not qualify, the special article will govern, rather than the general one.

(g) Art. 3422, *infra*, fixes the fee of the administrator when the succession assets are less than $2000. R.S. 9:1589 fixes the fee of the public administrator in New Orleans. This article does not affect these provisions.

(h) There is no statutory provision dealing with forfeiture of compensation where the administrator has been guilty of maladministration. The supreme court has ruled that, where an administrator has been guilty of gross negligence in handling the succession, he is not entitled to his commission. Succession of Liles, 24 La.Ann. 490 (1872); Succession of Touzanne, 36 La.Ann. 420 (1884). The penalty is largely discretionary with the court. Succession of Gandolfo, 173 La. 190, 136 So. 561, 83 A.L.R. 720 (1931). Since the jurisprudence covers the question adequately, no specific article providing for forfeiture under such circumstances is necessary.

(i) The compensation to be paid a provisional administrator and an administrator of a vacant succession is left to the discretion of the court. The provisional administrator normally administers for a brief period, and the value of his services will vary. The administrator of a vacant succession may be confronted with difficulties of administration of a small estate where the two and one-half percent commission would not be adequate.

(j) See, also, Comments under Art. 3113, *supra*.

Art. 3352. More than one succession representative

If there is more than one succession representative, the compensation provided by Article 3351 shall be apportioned among them as the court shall direct.

Source: C.C. Arts. 1069, 1685.

Tit. 3   COMPENSATION   Art. 3353

Comments

(a) Art. 1069 of the Civil Code provides that where there are two administrators, they shall divide the commission. Art. 1685 provides that the commission shall be shared among the executors, but, if their functions are divided by the testator, each is entitled to a commission on what he has administered. The above article makes no provision for the situation in which the testator has divided the functions of the executors named in the will. By leaving the question of the proper division of compensation to the court, this article permits an equitable division under all circumstances.

(b) Where an administrator qualifies and thereafter dies, resigns, or is removed, and a successor is appointed, each administrator is entitled to a commission on such portions of the succession as have been administered by him. Succession of Milne, 1 Rob. 400 (1842); Succession of Girod, 4 La.Ann. 386 (1849). This article applies to both of these situations, that is, where there are either co-administrators or successive administrators.

Art. 3353. Legacy to executor

A testamentary executor who is a legatee shall be entitled to compensation, unless the testament provides to the contrary. If the legacy and the compensation of the executor together exceed the disposable portion, the executor shall receive only the disposable portion.

Source: New; cf. C.C. Arts. 1686, 1687.

Comments

(a) Art. 1686 of the Civil Code provides that the executor who is a legatee is entitled to compensation only if the testament so indicates. Under the above article this situation is reversed on the theory that the testator seldom intends that a legacy should deprive the executor of his commission. This article also eliminates the problems involved in Succession of Gilmore, 8 Orl.App. 295 (1911), in which it was held that if the legacy is of sentimental value only, the executor is entitled to a fee, although the will does not so provide, and in Succession of Fisk, 3 La.Ann. 705 (1848) to the effect that a bequest to an executor amounting to $5,000 must be considered as the equivalent to the testator's declaration of intention that the legacy was in lieu of commission (which would have amounted to $10,000), and that if the executor accepted the trust, he could expect no other compensation than the legacy itself.

(b) Art. 1687 of the Civil Code provides that in no case shall the executor's compensation affect the légitime reserved to forced heirs. The only situation in which this article is applicable is when the executor has been bequeathed the entire disposable portion. Cf. Succession of Manion, 143 La. 799, 79 So. 409 (1918). If any other person is the legatee of the disposable portion, the executor receives the normal compensation.

CHAPTER 11. SENDING HEIRS AND LEGATEES INTO POSSESSION

SECTION 1. INTESTATE SUCCESSION

Art.
3361. After homologation of final tableau of distribution.
3362. Prior to homologation of final tableau of distribution.

SECTION 2. TESTATE SUCCESSION

3371. After homologation of final tableau of distribution.
3372. Prior to homologation of final tableau of distribution.

SECTION 3. JUDGMENT OF POSSESSION

3381. Judgment of possession.

SECTION 1. INTESTATE SUCCESSION

Art. 3361. After homologation of final tableau of distribution

At any time after the homologation of the final tableau of distribution, an heir of an intestate succession may file a petition to be sent into possession under benefit of inventory, alleging the facts showing that he is an heir. Upon the filing of such a petition, the court shall order the administrator to show cause why the petitioner should not be sent into possession.

Evidence of the allegations as to heirship in the petition for possession shall be submitted to the court as provided by Articles 2821 through 2823.

Source: New; cf. Comments following.

Cross Reference: Art. 3462.

Comments

(a) After a succession has been fully administered, any heir has an absolute right to require the administration to be terminated and to be put into possession of the succession. Succession of Powell, 38 La.Ann. 181 (1886). After the final tableau of distribution has been homologated, the succession is complete except for the payment of debts, which the administrator must pay before he can deliver the property, and except for the final account.

Under the jurisprudence, the right to possession is not dependent upon or deferred until the filing of the account; an account may never be filed if the heirs are satisfied with an extrajudicial settlement. Succession of Duffy, 50 La.Ann. 795, 24 So. 277 (1898); Succession of Burbank, 126 La. 9, 52 So. 175 (1910). Therefore, the point at which heirs should be given an absolute right to go into possession under benefit of inventory is after the homologation of the final tableau of distribution, which is tantamount to a judgment in favor of the creditors and against the administrator.

(b) Since the jurisdictional facts of death and domicile will have already been established, the only proof which the heir must make is of the facts of heirship.

(c) If the administrator joins in the petition for possession, no contradictory proceeding is necessary and judgment is rendered forthwith. Cf. Art. 3381, *infra*.

(d) Under the provisions of Arts. 3002 and 3005, *supra*, a petition for unconditional possession must be verified by at least one of the petitioners. No verification is required when the administration has been completed and the acceptance is under the benefit of inventory.

(e) See, also, Comments under Arts. 3362, 3371, *infra*.

Art. 3362. Prior to homologation of final tableau of distribution

At any time prior to the homologation of the final tableau of distribution, the heirs of an intestate whose succession is under administration may be sent into possession of all or part of the property of the succession upon filing a petition for possession as provided in Articles 3001 through 3008, except that the proceeding shall be contradictory with the administrator. Upon the filing of such a petition, the court shall order the administrator to show cause why the heirs should not be sent into possession. If the heirs are sent into possession of a part of the property, the administrator shall continue to administer the remainder.

Source: C.C. Art. 1193; cf. Comments following.

Cross Reference: Art. 3462.

Comments

(a) This article applies only when the petition for possession is filed prior to the homologation of the final tableau of distribution. It complements Art. 3361, *supra*.

(b) Since acceptance under this article takes place before the completion of the administration, it is an unconditional acceptance, and the rules of Arts. 3001–3008, *supra*, governing acceptance without administration are, therefore, applicable. However, since an administrator has been appointed to represent creditors, the heirs are not sent into possession ex parte but only in a proceeding contradictory with the administrator, who may show to the satisfaction of the court that the heirs should not be sent into possession or that they should be compelled to furnish security. Art. 1193 of the Civil Code and the jurisprudence indicate that a contradictory proceeding is required. Calhoun v. McKnight, 39 La.Ann. 325, 1 So. 612 (1887).

(c) The provision permitting the heirs to go into possession of a part of the property, with the succession representative continuing to administer the balance, is new in Louisiana.

Under the substantive articles of the Civil Code an heir who takes possession of a part of the property of a succession before the administration is complete becomes personally liable for the debts. Therefore, the succession creditors could still hold the heirs liable and would not be affected. The above article does not change this fundamental rule.

(d) All competent heirs must join in the acceptance. See Art. 3004, *supra*.

(e) See, also, Comments under Art. 3372, *infra*.

SECTION 2. TESTATE SUCCESSION

Art. 3371. **After homologation of final tableau of distribution**

At any time after the homologation of the final tableau of distribution, a legatee or an heir may file a petition to be sent into possession under benefit of inventory, alleging the facts showing that he is a legatee or an heir. Upon the filing of such a petition, the court shall order the executor to show cause why the petitioner should not be sent into possession.

Evidence of the allegations in the petition for possession showing that the petitioner is a legatee or an heir shall be submitted to the court as provided by Articles 2821 through 2823.

Source: New; cf. Comment following.

Cross Reference: Art. 3462.

Comment

This article is analogous to Art. 3361, *supra*. After the final tableau of distribution is homologated, the residuary heirs and the legatees have an absolute right to be sent into possession. See Comments following Art. 3361, *supra*.

Art. 3372. Prior to homologation of final tableau of distribution

At any time prior to the homologation of the final tableau of distribution, the legatees in a testate succession may be sent into possession of all or part of their respective legacies upon filing a petition for possession as provided in Articles 3031 through 3035, except that the proceeding shall be contradictory with the executor. Upon the filing of such a petition, the court shall order the executor to show cause why the legatees should not be sent into possession. If the legatees are sent into possession of a part of their respective legacies, the executor shall continue to administer the remainder.

Source: New; cf. Comments following.

Cross Reference: Art. 3462.

Comments

(a) This article applies to a situation analogous to that covered by Art. 3362, *supra*. Prior to the homologation of the final tableau of distribution, the creditors are not protected and the acceptance is unconditional. Hence, the rules applicable to acceptance without administration apply. These rules are contained in the cross references given in the text of this article. See Art. 3362, *supra*, and Comments thereunder.

(b) Art. 1671 of the Civil Code provides that "the heirs can, at any time, take the seizin from the testamentary executor, on offering him a sum sufficient to pay the movable legacies and on complying with the requirements of Article 1012." Civil Code Art. 1012 requires the heirs, before they can terminate an administration, to furnish bond to cover suits actually pending against the succession. Apparently Art. 1671 does not contemplate the termination of the administration, for it requires the heirs to give the executor funds to pay legacies.

(e) See, also, Comments under Art. 2826, *supra*.

SECTION 3. JUDGMENT OF POSSESSION

Art. 3381. Judgment of possession

A judgment of possession shall be rendered and signed as provided in Article 3061. The judgment shall be rendered and signed only after a hearing contradictory with the succession representative, unless he joins in the petition, in which event the judgment shall be rendered and signed immediately.

Source: New; cf. Comments following.

Cross Reference: Art. 3462.

Comments

(a) See Art. 195, *supra*, with reference to signing judgments of possession in chambers in uncontested matters.

(b) See Comments under Art. 3061, *supra*.

(c) See, also, Comments under Art. 3361, *supra*.

CHAPTER 12. DISCHARGE OF SUCCESSION REPRESENTATIVE

Art.
3391. Discharge of succession representative.
3392. Effect of judgment of discharge.
3393. Reopening of succession.
3394. Refusal or inability to accept funds; deposit in bank.
3395. Disposition of movables not accepted by heir.

PRELIMINARY STATEMENT

Heretofore, there were virtually no code provisions, statutes, or jurisprudence on the subject of the discharge of a succession representative, although it was held that an administrator could not be discharged until his final account had been homologated or the homologation had been waived by the heirs. Succession of Taylor, 174 La. 822, 141 So. 847 (1932); Succession of Braun, 187 La. 185, 174 So. 257 (1937). The statutes dealing with the question treated it only obliquely, their principal purpose being to afford a method for the succession representative to dispose of unclaimed assets in his possession at the termination of the administration.

A new concept, namely, a provision to allow the succession representative to dispose of movable property if the heirs do not come forward to claim it, has been introduced in order to provide for the disposition of such property, since under prevailing conditions the cost of storing tangible movable property is prohibitive.

Art. 3391. Discharge of succession representative

After homologation of the final account, or upon proof that the heirs have waived a final account, the succession representative may petition for discharge.

Upon the filing of receipts or other evidence satisfactory to the court, showing that the creditors have been paid and that the balance of the property in the possession of the succession representative has been distributed to the heirs and legatees, the court shall render a judgment discharging the succession representative and cancelling his bond.

Source: New; cf. Comment following.

Tit. 3   DISCHARGE OF REPRESENTATIVE   **Art. 3393**

Comment

The above article does not adopt the custom, prevalent in some parts of the state, of having the court appoint an expert to examine the succession representative's receipts before approving the discharge. The court has that inherent right, but in many cases such procedure is unnecessary and involves needless expense.

Art. 3392. Effect of judgment of discharge

The judgment discharging the succession representative relieves him of further duty, responsibility, and authority as succession representative.

Source: New.

Comment

Since the judgment of discharge is rendered ex parte, it has no effect other than to relieve the representative of further responsibility and authority. Succession of Quaglino, 223 La. 171, 65 So.2d 127 (1953). Whatever liability of the representative or his surety may have existed prior to discharge remains in effect. In this connection, see Art. 3337, *supra*.

Art. 3393. Reopening of succession

After a succession representative has been discharged, if other property of the succession is discovered or for any other proper cause, upon the petition of any interested person, the court, without notice or upon such notice as it may direct, may order that the succession be reopened. The court may reappoint the succession representative or appoint another succession representative. The procedure provided by this Code for an original administration shall apply to the administration of a reopened succession in so far as applicable.

Source: New.

Comments

(a) Apparently there has been no statutory authority for reopening a succession after discharge of the succession representative, although there is dictum in the jurisprudence indicating that such a procedure is permitted. See Succession of Quaglino, 223 La. 171, 65 So.2d 127 (1953).

(b) Sec. 194 of the Model Probate Code has a similar though more detailed provision.

(c) See, also, Comments under Art. 3197, *supra*.

Art. 3394. Refusal or inability to accept funds; deposit in bank

When an heir or creditor is unwilling or unable to accept and receipt for the amount due him, on contradictory motion against the heir or creditor the court may order that the succession representative deposit in a state or national bank or in the registry of the court to the credit of the person entitled thereto the amount due him.

A receipt showing the deposit shall be sufficient in the discharge of the succession representative to the same extent as though distribution to the person entitled thereto had been made.

Source: C.C. Art. 1065; R.S. 9:1512.

Comment

This article applies to all persons who may refuse or be unable to accept funds due them, including minors not represented by tutors and incompetents not represented by curators.

Art. 3395. Disposition of movables not accepted by heir

If the succession representative has in his possession corporeal movable property the delivery of which an heir, legatee, or creditor is unwilling or unable to accept and receipt for, the succession representative may make such disposition thereof as the court may direct.

Source: New.

Comments

(a) This article introduces a new concept in the Louisiana law, based on the proposition that a succession representative should have the authority of disposing of movable property when the heirs refuse or are unable to accept it. *Cf.* Sec. 192(b) of the Model Probate Code.

It should be noted, however, that the article does not cover the situation where the heirs renounce the succession, but that it is limited to cases where they have refused to accept delivery of a particular piece of tangible property.

(b) If the property is not sufficiently valuable to warrant offering it for sale, it is clear that the "prudent administrator" concept would permit the succession representative to obtain court authority to destroy it or give it away.

TITLE IV

ANCILLARY PROBATE PROCEDURE

Art.
3401. Jurisdiction; procedure.
3402. Foreign representative; qualification.
3403. Capacity to sue.
3404. Priority in appointment.
3405. Testament probated outside Louisiana.

INTRODUCTION

It is fundamental that the domicile of a decedent at the time of his death determines the jurisdiction in which his succession will be principally administered, and that any other state where property of the decedent may be situated has ancillary jurisdiction only.

Recognizing the interest which it has in protecting the rights of local creditors to succession assets, Louisiana has always required ancillary administration proceedings and has taken the position that a succession representative appointed by a court of another state has no status in Louisiana unless he has first qualified in a Louisiana court. This concept is retained in this Title, except as indicated in Comment (a) under Art. 3403, *infra*.

Art. 3401. Jurisdiction; procedure

When a nonresident dies leaving property situated in this state, a succession proceeding may be instituted in a court of competent jurisdiction in accordance with Article 2811.

Except as otherwise provided in this Title, the procedure in such a succession shall be the same as provided by law for the succession of a Louisiana domiciliary.

Source: New; cf. C.P. Art. 929.

Comments

(a) This is a codification of the prevailing conflict of laws rule that the situs of property within the jurisdiction is necessary to support an ancillary probate proceeding.

(b) The second paragraph is intended to cover both simple possession proceedings and administrations. Except as otherwise provided herein, the general procedure should apply to ancillary proceedings.

(c) Art. 2811, *supra*, is the general article regulating the venue of succession proceedings, including those of nonresident decedents leaving only movable property in Louisiana.

Art. 3402. Foreign representative; qualification

A succession representative appointed by a court outside Louisiana may act with respect to property situated in Louisiana only after qualifying in a court of competent jurisdiction in Louisiana. He shall furnish bond upon the application of any interested person for good cause shown in the same amount as an administrator, even though in the case of a testamentary succession the testament dispenses with bond.

After such qualification the succession representative may exercise all of the rights and privileges of and has the same obligation as a succession representative originally qualified in Louisiana.

Source: New; cf. C.C. Art. 1220.

Comments

(a) Art. 1220 of the Civil Code provides that the succession of persons domiciled outside Louisiana shall be opened and administered as are those of Louisiana domiciliaries and that the judge shall appoint an administrator in the manner provided by law. By its terms, however, it does not apply to ancillary administrations nor does it make any reference to a succession representative appointed elsewhere.

(b) This article codifies the jurisprudence holding that a foreign representative has no status in Louisiana without first qualifying in a Louisiana court. Heirs of Henderson v. Rost, 15 La.Ann. 405 (1860); Succession of Butler, 30 La.Ann. 887 (1878); Warren v. Globe Indemnity Co., 216 La. 107, 43 So.2d 234 (1949).

(c) See, also, Comments under Arts. 2811, 2812, *supra*, and Art. 3403, *infra*.

Art. 3403. Capacity to sue

Except as otherwise provided by law, a succession representative appointed by a court outside Louisiana has no capacity to appear in court on behalf of the succession without first qualifying in a court of competent jurisdiction in Louisiana.

Source: New; cf. Comments following.

Comments

(a) The first clause of this article avoids a conflict with R.S. 13:3331, permitting an administrator or executor appointed or confirmed by a court of another jurisdiction, and in whom a right to recover damages for wrongful death vests, to sue in a Louisiana court without the necessity of qualifying as ancillary administrator or executor.

(b) Otherwise, this article is a codification of the rule announced in Agee v. Brent, 132 La. 821, 61 So. 837 (1913).

(c) This article does not affect the rule that, although the domiciliary administrator may not enforce collection of debts in Louisiana without qualifying, the voluntary payment by a Louisiana debtor to a foreign representative discharges the debt and is a bar to a subsequent suit by a local representative. Thorman v. Broderick, 52 La.Ann. 1298, 27 So. 735 (1900).

Art. 3404. Priority in appointment

When a succession representative has been appointed by a court of the decedent's domicile outside Louisiana, priority shall be given to him in the appointment of a representative in Louisiana, unless he is disqualified under Article 3097. Otherwise, priority shall be given in the appointment of a representative as provided in Article 3098.

Source: New.

Comments

(a) Although apparently the question has never arisen in Louisiana, it is clear that a domiciliary representative should be preferred over other applicants, so as to unify the domiciliary and ancillary administrations as far as possible. On the other hand, if an executor has been appointed in another state not the domiciliary state, he has no priority here as such and the usual rules of priority apply. A similar provision is found in the draft of the Uniform Ancillary Administration of Estates Act. See Simes, Model Probate Code 235.

(b) Arts. 3097 and 3098, *supra*, set forth, respectively, the grounds for disqualification, and the rules for priority in the appointment of succession representatives.

Art. 3405. Testament probated outside Louisiana

A testament admitted to probate outside Louisiana shall be governed by the provisions of R.S. 9:2421 through 9:2425.

Source: New.

Comments

(a) The cross reference is to the Uniform Probate Law, which has been incorporated by reference; no change in the law is made.

Art. 3405 ANCILLARY PROBATE PROCEDURE Bk. 6

(b) This article thus covers the ancillary probate of wills originally probated in another jurisdiction. Wills made in other jurisdictions and originally probated in Louisiana are covered by the provisions of Art. 2888, *supra*.

TITLE V

SMALL SUCCESSIONS

Chap.		Art.
1.	General Dispositions	3421
2.	When Judicial Proceedings Unnecessary	3431
3.	Judicial Proceedings	3441

INTRODUCTION

This Title regulates the procedure to be followed in the probate of small successions, which, for the purposes of this Title, are those having a gross value of two thousand dollars or less.

Of particular importance is an innovation incorporated in Chapter 2, whereby an administrative procedure for sending heirs into possession is permitted in those instances in which there is actually no need for judicial proceedings.

CHAPTER 1. GENERAL DISPOSITIONS

Art.
3421. Small succession defined.
3422. Court costs.

Art. 3421. Small succession defined

A small succession, within the intendment of this Title, is the succession of a person who dies leaving property in Louisiana having a gross value of two thousand dollars or less.

Source: New; cf. R.S. 47:2410.

Comments

(a) The line of demarcation between small successions and larger ones is drawn at $500 by Art. 1190 of the Civil Code and by the former R.S. 9:1551. This figure has been increased to $2,000. *Cf.* Inheritance Tax Act, R.S. 47:2410.

(b) The provisions of this Title apply only to cases where the deceased was domiciled in Louisiana at the time of his death. *Cf.* Art. 3432, *infra*. They have no application to cases where the deceased was domiciled in another state or foreign country at the time of his death, and where an ancillary administration of his succession must be had in Louisiana under the provisions of Book VI, Title IV.

(c) The provisions of this Title apply if the deceased owned property in other states or foreign countries, as long as the property left by the deceased having a Louisiana situs does not exceed $2,000 in value. As a practical matter, however, in the majority of instances where a Louisiana domiciliary dies leaving property in other jurisdictions, it will be preferable to have his succession opened and a succession representative qualified here, so that ancillary probate proceedings may be conducted in the other jurisdictions where he left property.

(d) See, also, Comments under Art. 4461, *infra*.

Art. 3422. Court costs

In judicial proceedings under this Title, the following schedule of costs, commissions, and fees shall prevail:

(1) Court costs shall be one-half the court costs in similar proceedings in larger successions, but the minimum costs in any case shall be five dollars; and

(2) The commission of the succession representative shall be not more than five percent of the gross assets of the succession.

Source: Cf. former R.S. 9:1557.

Comments

Two changes in the statutory source provision are effected by this article: (1) the fee of the succession representative is not a mandatory five percent, but this percentage is the maximum fee, and the court is empowered to fix a lower fee whenever such action is appropriate; and (2) minimum court costs of five dollars must be paid in all cases where the small succession is opened judicially.

See, also, Comments under Arts. 3441, 4464, *infra*.

CHAPTER 2. WHEN JUDICIAL PROCEEDINGS UNNECESSARY

Art.
3431. Small successions; judicial opening unnecessary.
3432. Submission of affidavit to inheritance tax collector.
3433. Endorsement that no inheritance taxes due.
3434. Endorsed copy of affidavit authority for delivery of property.

Art. 3431. Small successions; judicial opening unnecessary

It shall not be necessary to open judicially the small succession of a person who died intestate leaving no immovable property, and whose sole heirs are his descendants, ascendants, or surviving spouse.

Source: New; cf. Comments following.

Cross Reference: Art. 3432.

Comments

(a) An effective and beneficial change in the area of small successions is not to require judicial proceedings in those instances in which there is actually no need for such proceedings. Somewhat analogous provisions exist in R.S. 9:1513, which permits banks to pay to a surviving spouse funds on deposit belonging to the deceased.

(b) The public fisc is protected by requiring the heirs to submit an affidavit of the assets of the succession, and requiring the certificate of the inheritance tax collector that no inheritance taxes are due, before the procedure provided by this Chapter can be used. See Art. 3432, *infra*.

(c) Banks and other depositories paying money to these heirs, and persons delivering the property of the deceased to them are protected against double liability by the provisions of Art. 3434, *infra*. Creditors are exposed to no greater risks than they are exposed to in cases when the heirs are sent into possession, purely, simply, and unconditionally, and can always petition for an administration when there is an actual need for it.

(d) The above article recognizes the fact that in certain cases there will be a need for judicial proceedings, as in the case of a testate succession, where the testament must be probated to be given effect. Judicial proceedings are also required where immovable property is included in the assets of the succession, or where the heirs are relatives other than those of the immediate family of the deceased. This article expressly excludes all such cases from the scope of this Chapter.

Art. 3432. Submission of affidavit to inheritance tax collector

When it is not necessary under the provisions of Article 3431 to open judicially a small succession, the competent major heirs of the deceased, and the surviving spouse thereof, if any, may submit to the inheritance tax collector of the parish in which the deceased was domiciled at the time of his death one or more multiple originals of their affidavit setting forth:

(1) The date of death of the deceased, and his domicile at the time thereof;

(2) The fact that the deceased died intestate and left no immovable property;

(3) The marital status of the deceased, and the names and addresses of the surviving spouse, if any, and of the heirs and their relationship to the deceased; and

Art. 3432   SMALL SUCCESSIONS   Bk. 6

(4) A brief description of the movable property left by the deceased, and a showing of the value of each item thereof, and the aggregate value of all such property, at the time of the death of the deceased.

Source: New; cf. R.S. 47:2410.

Cross Reference: Art. 3434.

Comments

(a) Under the extrajudicial procedure contemplated by this Chapter, the affidavit should set forth all the facts necessary to enable the tax collector to determine his administrative jurisdiction. Thus, the affidavit is necessarily more extensive than the one required by R.S. 47:2410. The reason for the distinction is that, in a succession that has been opened judicially, the jurisdictional facts must be set forth in the petition for possession.

(b) The affidavit need not contain a separate allegation regarding adopted children since the terms "descendants" and "heirs" include children by adoption.

(c) See, also, Comments under Arts. 3421, 3431, *supra*.

Art. 3433.   Endorsement that no inheritance taxes due

If the inheritance tax collector is satisfied from the affidavit submitted to him that no inheritance taxes are due, he shall so certify by endorsement on the multiple originals of the affidavit provided by and to be returned to the heirs and surviving spouse, if any.

Source: New; cf. R.S. 47:2410.

Comments

(a) In view of the fact that this extrajudicial procedure may be used only in those cases where the descendants, ascendants, or surviving spouse of the deceased inherit, and that in such cases R.S. 47:2402 provides for an exemption of $5,000, there will never be any inheritance tax due, and all the collector need do is to certify this fact.

(b) Since the primary purpose of these articles is to minimize the costs and expenses of turning the small succession over to the heirs, the inheritance tax collector is not entitled to any compensation for checking the affidavits. See R.S. 47:2419.

Art. 3434.   Endorsed copy of affidavit authority for delivery of property

A multiple original of the affidavit required by Article 3432, bearing the endorsement of the inheritance tax collector that no inher-

Tit. 5　　　　　JUDICIAL PROCEEDINGS

itance taxes are due, shall be full and sufficient authority for the payment or delivery of any money or property of the deceased described in the affidavit by any bank, trust company, warehouseman, or other depositary, or by any person having such property in his possession or under his control. Similarly, a multiple original of this affidavit endorsed as required above shall be full and sufficient authority for the transfer to the heirs of the deceased, and surviving spouse, if any, or to their assigns, of any stock or registered bonds in the name of the deceased and described in the affidavit, by any domestic or foreign corporation.

The receipt of the persons named in the affidavit as heirs of the deceased, or surviving spouse thereof, constitutes a full release and discharge for the payment of money or delivery of property made under the provisions of this article. No inheritance tax collector, creditor, heir, succession representative, or other person whatsoever shall have any right or cause of action against the person paying the money, or delivering the property, or transferring the stock or bonds, under the provisions of this article, on account of such payment, delivery, or transfer.

Source: New; cf. R.S. 6:66, 9:1513, 12:503.

Comments

(a) The affidavit of the heirs and of the surviving spouse, if any, and the certificate of the inheritance tax collector are required in order to obtain the payment of money, or the delivery of property, or the transfer of stocks or bonds. This gives the public fisc ample protection, without imposing upon the heirs the expense of judicial proceedings and the drafting of appropriate pleadings.

(b) Banks and other depositories having possession of the property of the deceased are simply stakeholders, and are hereby given protection against double recovery. This article broadens the scope of R.S. 12:503 by extending the protection it affords to foreign corporations as well, whether they maintain transfer books in Louisiana or not.

(c) See, also, Comments under Art. 3431, *supra*.

CHAPTER 3.　JUDICIAL PROCEEDINGS

Art.
3441.　Acceptance without administration; procedure.
3442.　Administration of successions; procedure.
3443.　Sale of succession property; publication of notice of sale.

Art. 3441. Acceptance without administration; procedure

Except as otherwise provided by law, all of the rules applicable to the judicial opening of a succession, and its acceptance by the heirs or legatees without an administration, apply to the small succession.

Source: New; cf. Comments following.

Comments

(a) This article codifies customary Louisiana practice.

(b) There is no need for further simplification of the procedure, when the judicial opening of a small succession is necessary, and the acceptance of the heirs can be obtained and an administration dispensed with. Art. 3422, *supra*, reducing the court costs to one-half those charged for similar proceedings in larger successions, makes the proceedings hereunder even more economical.

Art. 3442. Administration of successions; procedure

Except as otherwise provided by law, all of the rules applicable to the judicial opening of a succession, its administration, and sending the heirs or legatees into possession on its termination apply to the small succession.

Source: New; cf. Comments following.

Comments

(a) Generally, the procedure applicable to the administration of larger successions is simple and economical enough to be made applicable to the administration of a small succession. The exception is with respect to the sale of property by the succession representative to pay debts and legacies, and this is covered by Art. 3443, *infra*.

(b) Under Arts. 3091 through 3098, *supra*, there is no need to publish the application for letters of administration; and under Art. 3136, *supra*, the applicant for appointment as administrator may submit a descriptive list instead of a formal inventory. Under Arts. 3121 and 3122, *supra*, the clerks of the district courts (and in Orleans Parish the public administrator) may be appointed administrators of vacant successions, with their official bond serving instead of a special bond. *Cf.* former R.S. 9:1552 through 9:1554.

(c) Art. 3304, *supra*, requires only a single publication of the succession representative's petition for authority to pay debts. *Cf.* former R.S. 9:1556.

Art. 3443. Sale of succession property; publication of notice of sale

Notice of the public sale of property, movable or immovable, by the succession representative of a small succession shall be published once and only in the parish where the succession is pending, and the property shall be sold not less than ten days nor more than fifteen days after publication.

Notice of the application of the succession representative of a small succession to sell succession property, movable or immovable, at private sale shall be published once and only in the parish where the succession proceeding is pending, and shall state that any opposition to the proposed sale must be filed within ten days of the date of publication.

Source: New; cf. former R.S. 9:1555.

Comments

(a) Because the articles regulating the sale of property of larger successions would impose unnecessary delay and expense upon the small succession, the above article reduces the time required for the sale as well as the number of publications. *Cf.* Arts. 3272 and 3282, *supra*.

(b) For the requirements of the publication of the notice, see R.S. 43:203.

(c) See, also, Comments under Art. 3442, *supra*.

TITLE VI

PARTITION OF SUCCESSIONS

Art.
3461. Venue; procedure.
3462. Partition of succession property.

Art. 3461. Venue; procedure

The petition for the partition of a succession shall be filed in the succession proceeding, as provided in Article 81(2).

In all other respects and except when manifestly inapplicable, the procedure for partitioning a succession is governed by the provisions of Articles 4601 through 4614.

Source: New; cf. Comments following.

Comments

(a) Prior to the advent of the inheritance tax, the partition of successions was employed quite frequently. Today, when heirs cannot be sent into possession of the property of the deceased except after the payment of the inheritance taxes due the state, it is seldom used. Now, it is usually easier to have the heirs recognized and sent into possession by a judgment of possession, and then have these heirs partition the property as co-owners, than it is to partition the succession. See Art. 3462, *infra*.

(b) Under the approach of the Civil Code, its articles generally apply expressly to partitions of successions, with a cross reference making these provisions applicable to the partition between co-owners. However, partitions between co-owners were not regulated by articles relating to the partition of successions when "manifestly inapplicable". Paul v. Lamothe, 36 La.Ann. 318 (1884).

The approach in this Code is diametrically opposite, for the reason which appears in Comment (a) hereof. The basic rules provided in this Code treat of partition between co-owners, and the above article makes these rules applicable to the partition of successions, except with respect to venue and when manifestly inapplicable.

(c) See, also, Comments under Art. 3462, *infra*.

Art. 3462. Partition of succession property

When a succession has been opened judicially, the coheirs and legatees of the deceased cannot petition for a partition of the succession property unless they could at that time be sent into possession of the

Tit. 6 PARTITION OF SUCCESSIONS Art. 3462

succession under Articles 3001, 3004, 3006, 3061, 3361, 3362, 3371, 3372, or 3381.

Source: New; cf. Comments following.

Comments

(a) Where succession property is under administration, an heir has no right of action against his coheir to provoke a partition of the property until the succession has been settled by the administrator. Robin v. Lob, 204 La. 983, 16 So.2d 541 (1944). Under this article, however, where the heirs desire to accept the succession unconditionally and can be sent into possession without an administration, as is provided in the articles referred to in the text above, the rule of Robin v. Lob, *supra*, does not apply, and they are allowed to partition at that point.

(b) Of course, once the heirs have been sent into possession, they can demand a partition as ordinary co-owners. Sometimes it may be necessary, however, to effect a partition before the heirs have actually been sent into possession. This article permits this to be done, but in order to meet the objection of the Lob case, *supra*, provides that the heirs may demand a partition as soon as, but not before, they can be sent into possession.

(c) Art. 1023 of the Code of Practice has not been included for the reason that it is substantive and its provisions are amply covered by the articles of the Civil Code.

(d) See Comments under Art. 3461, *supra*.

BOOK VII
SPECIAL PROCEEDINGS

TITLE I
PROVISIONAL REMEDIES

Chap.	Art.
1. Attachment and Sequestration	3501
Sec.	
1. General Dispositions	3501
2. Attachment	3541
3. Sequestration	3571
2. Injunction	3601

CHAPTER 1. ATTACHMENT AND SEQUESTRATION

SECTION 1. GENERAL DISPOSITIONS

Art.
3501. Petition; affidavit; security.
3502. Issuance of writ before petition filed.
3503. Garnishment under writs of attachment or of sequestration.
3504. Return of sheriff; inventory.
3505. Reduction of excessive seizure.
3506. Dissolution of writ; damages.
3507. Release of property by defendant; security.
3508. Amount of security for release of attached or sequestered property.
3509. Release of property by third person.
3510. Necessity for judgment and execution.
3511. Attachment and sequestration; privilege.
3512. Release of plaintiff's security.
3513. Sale of perishable property.
3514. Release not to affect right to damages

SECTION 2. ATTACHMENT

3541. Grounds for attachment.
3542. Actions in which attachment can issue.

Tit. 1   ATTACHMENT AND SEQUESTRATION

Art.
3543. Issuance of a writ of attachment before debt due.
3544. Plaintiff's security.
3545. Nonresident attachment; venue.

SECTION 3. SEQUESTRATION

3571. Grounds for sequestration.
3572. Sequestration before rent due.
3573. Sequestration by court on its own motion.
3574. Plaintiff's security.
3575. Lessor's privilege.
3576. Release of property under sequestration.

PRELIMINARY STATEMENT

The principal change effected by this Chapter is the elimination of the writs of provisional seizure and of arrest of the debtor. There is a need for two types of seizure before judgment: attachment and sequestration. Attachment is based upon some act, or anticipated act, of the debtor which would place the creditor at a disadvantage in the suit and which prompts the law to protect the creditor by permitting him to seize the debtor's property pending the suit, even though the creditor has no claim against the thing seized. Sequestration involves no intent on the part of the debtor to defraud the creditor or place him at a disadvantage, but it requires an element not found in attachment, namely, a claim to the ownership or possession of property seized, or to a privilege thereon. In sequestration, the creditor's right to seizure before judgment is predicated upon the claim to the property.

The only real distinction between the provisional seizure and sequestration was that the former issued without a bond. This distinction was not considered to be of sufficient importance to justify a separate writ. However, the concept of a seizure before judgment without the furnishing of security has been retained by providing for a sequestration *without* bond in those instances in which provisional seizure has been allowed by Louisiana law.

The articles in this Chapter set forth the grounds upon which and the type of action in which the writs may issue, as well as the procedure governing the seizure by the sheriff. This arrangement makes definitions unnecessary.

Little need be said in support of the proposition that the writ of arrest should be abolished and that it should form no part of Louisiana's civil procedure. It has been stated that:

"Although still available to the plaintiff in requisite cases, its harshness, its anachronism and its incompatability with modern ideas relative to procedural enforcement of obligations, has resulted in a tacit and universal agreement on the part of the Louisiana

Bar to ignore it. A much more desirable treatment would be the express legislative repeal of all code and statutory provisions concerning it." McMahon 1183, n. 1.

SECTION 1. GENERAL DISPOSITIONS

Art. 3501. Petition; affidavit; security

A writ of attachment or of sequestration shall issue only when the nature of the claim and the amount thereof, if any, and the grounds relied upon for the issuance of the writ clearly appear from specific facts shown by the petition verified by, or by the separate affidavit of, the petitioner, his counsel or agent.

The applicant shall furnish security as required by law for the payment of the damages the defendant may sustain when the writ is obtained wrongfully.

Source: C.P. Arts. 243, 245 and 276.

Cross References: Arts. 3502, 3544, 3574, 3575.

Comments

(a) The petition for a writ of attachment or of sequestration must contain allegations to support the principal cause of action as well as the provisional remedy. This article retains portions of Arts. 243, 245, and 276 of the Code of Practice, and it makes it clear that either a verified petition or an affidavit setting forth the facts will suffice. Except for the requirements of verification in the absence of an affidavit, the provisions of Book II, Title I are applicable to the petition required by this article.

(b) See Arts. 3544 and 3574, *infra,* for the security which the plaintiff must furnish to secure an attachment, and generally to secure a sequestration, respectively. A sequestration to enforce the lessor's privilege issues without security. Art. 3575, *infra.* The qualifications of the surety and other rules relative to the bond are provided in Arts. 5121 through 5127, *infra.* The provision in Art. 276 of the Code of Practice requiring the bond to be made "in favor of the defendant" has not been included because under Art. 5121, *infra,* all bonds are made in favor of the clerk of court.

(c) The words "as required by law" were added after "security" in order to provide for the two types of sequestration under this Code, namely, sequestration with bond, and sequestration without bond, which takes the place of the former provisional seizure.

Tit. 1   ATTACHMENT AND SEQUESTRATION   Art. 3503

Art. 3502.   Issuance of writ before petition filed

A writ of attachment or of sequestration may issue before the petition is filed, if the plaintiff obtains leave of court and furnishes the affidavit and security provided in Article 3501. In such a case the petition shall be filed on the first judicial day after the issuance of the writ of attachment or of sequestration, unless for good cause shown the court grants a longer delay.

Source: C.P. Art. 237.

Comment

Art. 237 of the 1870 Code of Practice required the filing of the petition on the day after the writ issued and this requirement has been retained in the above article. The computation of time is dealt with in Art. 5059, *infra*.

Art. 3503.   Garnishment under writs of attachment or of sequestration

Except as otherwise provided by law and in the second paragraph of this article, garnishment under a writ of attachment or of sequestration is governed by the rules applicable to garnishment under a writ of fieri facias.

In garnishment under a writ of sequestration the only property that can be seized is property the ownership or possession of which is claimed by the plaintiff or on which he claims a privilege.

Source: C.P. Arts. 246, 250.

Comments

(a) Arts. 246 and 250 of the Code of Practice authorize a garnishment in connection with a writ of attachment. There is no provision in the Code of Practice authorizing garnishment in connection with sequestration. See Ozan Lbr. Co. v. Goldonna Lbr. Co., 124 La. 1025, 50 So. 839 (1909). There seems to be no good reason to deny a plaintiff who is seeking a writ of sequestration the privilege of using garnishment interrogatories as an auxiliary remedy to determine whether a third party has property of the defendant in his possession.

(b) Property in the hands of a third person can be seized under a writ of sequestration without the necessity of a garnishment, for sequestration is not limited to property in the physical custody of the defendant, but extends to all property which the defendant can control and dispose of. A. F. Flournoy and Co. v. Milling, 15 La.Ann. 473 (1860); Lannes v. Courege, 31 La.Ann. 74 (1879); Blitz v. Guenin, 187 So. 690 (La.App.1939). This article effects no change in the rule set forth in the cited cases; it merely offers the plaintiff the additional procedural remedy of garnishment. Art. 3571, *infra*, recognizes the possibility of a seizure by sequestration when property is in the physical possession of a third person.

(c) In connection with the limitation contained in the second paragraph of this article, see Art. 3571, *infra*, which permits sequestration only when the plaintiff claims the ownership or the right to the possession of, or a privilege on the property.

Art. 3504. Return of sheriff; inventory

The sheriff, after executing a writ of attachment or of sequestration, shall deliver to the clerk of the court from which the writ issued a written return stating the manner in which he executed the writ. He shall annex to the return an inventory of the property seized.

Source: C.P. Arts. 256, 257, 282.

Comments

(a) The provisions in the source articles requiring the sheriff to serve copies of the petition and to seize the property have been omitted here as they are embodied in prior articles herein. *Cf.* Arts. 321 and 324, *supra*.

(b) For the requirements of the inventory, formerly covered in Arts. 257 and 282 of the Code, see R.S. 13:4408 *et seq.*

(c) The provision in Art. 257, Code of Practice, requiring the sheriff to "take charge and keep possession of all goods and effects which he may have attached" has been omitted as unnecessary. See Art. 326, *supra*.

(d) Heretofore, while the sheriff had the power of administration of property sequestered, he had no similar power with respect to property attached. He now has that power over all property seized, regardless of the type of writ. Art. 328, *supra*.

Art. 3505. Reduction of excessive seizure

If the value of the property seized under a writ of attachment or of sequestration exceeds what is reasonably necessary to satisfy the plaintiff's claim, the defendant by contradictory motion may obtain the release of the excess.

Source: New.

Comments

(a) This article is similar to the reduction of an excess seizure under a writ of fieri facias, except that this article contemplates

Tit. 1   ATTACHMENT AND SEQUESTRATION   Art. 3506

a finding by the court, after evidence is taken, that the seizure is excessive. Arts. 652 and 653 of the 1870 Code of Practice provided for the reduction of seizure under fieri facias and required the court to appoint appraisers to determine whether the seizure was excessive. This procedure is not required by the above article. However, the court may always appoint an expert to aid it in the determination of a case. This article does not affect the right of the defendant to release a seizure by furnishing bond.

(b) A proceeding contradictory with the plaintiff is contemplated; the sheriff is not a necessary party. See Art. 963, *supra*, defining "contradictory motion."

(c) See, also, Comments under Art. 2296, *supra*, and Art. 3542, *infra*.

Art. 3506.   Dissolution of writ; damages

The defendant by contradictory motion may obtain the dissolution of a writ of attachment or of sequestration, unless the plaintiff proves the grounds upon which the writ was issued. If the writ of attachment or of sequestration is dissolved, the action shall then proceed as if no writ had been issued.

The court may allow damages for the wrongful issuance of a writ of attachment or of sequestration on a motion to dissolve, or on a reconventional demand. Attorney's fees for the services rendered in connection with the dissolution of the writ may be included as an element of damages whether the writ is dissolved on motion or after trial on the merits.

Source: C.P. Art. 258.

Comments

(a) The source article seems to place the burden of proof upon the defendant and seems to require him to prove the falsity of the allegations upon which the writ was issued. The jurisprudence on this point is unsettled. *Cf.* Offut v. Edwards, 9 Rob. 90 (1844); Simons v. Jacobs, 15 La.Ann. 425 (1860); Swift & Co. v. Bonvillain, 139 La. 558, 71 So. 849 (1916); and Williams v. Ralph R. Miller Shows, 15 So.2d 249 (La.App.1943). Under these cases, it seems that when the defendant rebuts the prima facie case made out by the plaintiff's affidavit, the plaintiff then bears the burden of proving the truth of the facts upon which the writ was issued. The above article changes this rule by placing the burden of proceeding and the burden of proof on the plaintiff.

(b) The second sentence clearly establishes that the suit is not dismissed on the dissolution of the writ.

(c) This article retains the jurisprudential rule that only the grounds for the auxiliary remedy can be inquired into on the motion to dissolve, and not the merits of the main demand. Macarty v. Lepaullard, 4 Rob. 425 (La.1843); Hoss v. Williams, 24 La.Ann. 568 (1872); Young v. Guess and Swanson, 115 La. 230, 38 So. 975 (1905).

(d) This article overrules the jurisprudence to the effect that where the plaintiff objects, the defendant cannot obtain damages by the summary procedure of a motion to dissolve. See Younger Bros. v. Spell, 194 La. 16, 193 So. 354 (1939). The court is in a better position to decide the question of damages at the time the motion to dissolve is tried.

This article also overrules the jurisprudence which holds that attorney's fees are recoverable as an element of damage only where the writ is dissolved on motion and not where the writ is dissolved after trial on the merits. Mitchell v. Murphy, 131 La. 1040, 60 So. 677 (1913); Smith v. Wm. D. Keith Motors Co., 163 La. 395, 111 So. 798 (1927). The jurisprudence is based upon the assumption that it is impossible to distinguish between the services on the merits and those in connection with the question of whether there was ground for the issuance of the writ. The change which this article effects eliminates the necessity for two hearings if the claim to attorney's fees is to be asserted, *i. e.*, the hearing on the motion to dissolve the writ and the trial on the merits.

(e) Specific recognition of the right to recover damages by means of the reconventional demand was included in the above article to eliminate any possible doubt that such right existed under this Code.

(f) See, also, Comments under Art. 3608, *infra*.

Art. 3507. Release of property by defendant; security

A defendant may obtain the release of the property seized under a writ of attachment or of sequestration by furnishing security for the satisfaction of any judgment which may be rendered against him.

Source: C.P. Arts. 259, 279, 280, 281, 289.

Cross References: Arts. 3514, 3576.

Comments

The basic difference heretofore existing between the conditions of the bond furnished to release property under attachment and under sequestration has been eliminated. Under this article, the security is the same in both cases; the "forthcoming" feature of the bond to release property under sequestration has been eliminated; and in both instances, the security is similarly conditioned on the satisfaction of the judgment. This affords much greater protection to the plaintiff than a forthcoming bond. *Cf.* John M.

Parker Co. v. E. Martin and Co., 148 La. 791, 88 So. 68 (1921); Overland-Texarkana Co. v. Bickley, 1 La.App. 699 (1925); Mitchell v. Maxey, 11 La.App. 317, 123 So. 436 (1929).

Under the above article, the surety on the release bond is liable to the extent of the bond no matter what type of judgment the court rendered, whether the property is returned or not.

Art. 3508. Amount of security for release of attached or sequestered property

The security for the release of property seized under a writ of attachment or of sequestration shall exceed by one-fourth the value af the property as determined by the court, or shall exceed by one-fourth the amount of the claim, whichever is the lesser.

Source: C.P. Arts. 259, 279.

Cross Reference: Art. 3576.

Comments

(a) This article makes no change with respect to the writ of attachment. With respect to the writ of sequestration, however, the bond is based solely on the amount claimed rather than on the value of the property seized where the claim is substantially less than the value of the property. The reason for this is that in actions for money judgments, the most that the plaintiff can expect is protection up to the amount claimed.

(b) In cases of sequestration, where the relief sought is not a money judgment, the provisions of this article basing the bond on the amount claimed is inapplicable.

(c) See Art. 282, *supra*, retaining the right of the clerk under former R.S. 13:901 to fix the amount of release bonds.

Art. 3509. Release of property by third person

When property seized under a writ of attachment or of sequestration is in the possession of one not a party to the action, he may intervene in the action and, upon prima facie showing that he is the owner, pledgee, or consignee of the property, have the property released by furnishing security in the manner and amount, within the same delay, and with the same effect as a defendant.

Source: Former R.S. 13:3941.

Cross Reference: Art. 3514.

Comments

(a) As used in this article, "possession" includes constructive and actual possession, so that although the words "actual or con-

Art. 3509 ATTACHMENT AND SEQUESTRATION Bk. 7

structive" which appear in the source statute have been omitted, no change is thereby intended. See Art. 3571, *infra*. The defendant need not have manual custody of the property in order for sequestration to issue; it is only necessary that he have the right to control and dispose of it. Blitz v. Guenin, 187 So. 690 (La.App. 1939). *Cf.* Lannes v. Courege, 31 La.Ann. 74 (1879).

(b) A change in the law has been made with respect to the release bond. See Arts. 3507, *supra*, and 5127, *infra*.

Art. 3510. Necessity for judgment and execution

Except as provided in Article 3513, a final judgment must be obtained in an action where a writ of attachment or of sequestration has issued before the property seized can be sold to satisfy the claim.

Source: C.P. Art. 265.

Comments

(a) The source article is applicable only to attachment, whereas the above article has been made applicable to both types of writs.

(b) Under the above article, the plaintiff is required to obtain judgment and the issuance of a writ of fieri facias or other process in a case in which a writ of attachment or of sequestration has issued; he cannot merely have the seized property sold to satisfy his claim without the formality of judgment and execution.

Art. 3511. Attachment and sequestration; privilege

A creditor who seizes property under a writ of attachment or of sequestration acquires a privilege from the time of seizure if judgment is rendered maintaining the attachment or sequestration.

Source: C.P. Art. 724.

Comments

(a) Although Art. 724, Code of Practice of 1870, uses the words "provisional seizures", its application has been limited to attachment and sequestration. *Cf.* Beck v. Brady, 6 La.Ann. 444 (1851).

(b) This article codifies the jurisprudence to the effect that the judgment maintaining the writ is retroactive to the date of seizure. Board of Supervisors v. Hart, 210 La. 78, 26 So.2d 361 (1946).

Art. 3512. Release of plaintiff's security

The security required of the plaintiff for the issuance of a writ of attachment or of sequestration shall be released when judgment is rendered in his favor and is affirmed on appeal or when no appeal has been taken and the delay for appeal has elapsed.

Source: C.P. Art. 266.

Comments

(a) The source provision was applicable to attachment bonds only. The above article is applicable to both attachment and sequestration bonds. It also makes provision regarding the disposition of the bond during the pendency of an appeal or while the delays for an appeal are pending, as to which the Code of Practice was silent.

(b) The provisions in Arts. 266 and 267 of the Code of Practice providing longer delays in suits against absentees have been omitted in view of modern methods of communication and transportation.

Art. 3513. Sale of perishable property

Perishable property seized under a writ of attachment or of sequestration may be sold as provided in Article 2333. The proceeds of such a sale shall be held by the sheriff subject to the orders of the court.

Nothing contained herein shall be construed to prohibit the release of such property upon furnishing of security.

Source: C.P. Art. 261; former R.S. 13:4342.

Cross Reference: Art. 3510.

Comments

(a) The reference in the first paragraph of this article makes the procedure for the sale of perishable property seized under a writ of fieri facias available for the sale of such property seized under writs of attachment or of sequestration.

(b) See Comments under Art. 2333, *supra*.

(c) The second sentence of the first paragraph of this article, taken from former R.S. 13:4342, is needed to retain the proceeds of perishable property seized under writs of attachment or of sequestration to abide the rendition of final judgment. It is not needed in the case of the sale of such property seized under a writ of fieri facias.

(d) For a provision somewhat similar to this article, see 7 U.S.C. § 499.

(e) The term "perishable" is so difficult of definition in the abstract that its definition and application to the particular facts of each case is left to the courts.

Art. 3514. Release not to affect right to damages

The release of property upon furnishing security under Articles 3507, 3509, or 3576 shall not preclude a party from asserting the invalidity of the seizure, or impair his right to damages because of a wrongful seizure.

Source: Former R.S. 13:3944.

Comments

(a) The source provision applies only to releases obtained by third persons. The above article applies to all cases where property is released upon the furnishing of security, whether by the plaintiff, the defendant, or a third person. The scope of this article was broadened to preclude an interpretation that a party waives the right to damages by obtaining the release of seized property or by permitting another person to do so.

(b) This article does not affect the rule that a nonresident who obtains the release of property upon furnishing security submits himself to the jurisdiction of the court and permits a personal judgment to be rendered against him. Adams v. Ross Amusement Co., 182 La. 252, 161 So. 601 (1935). See Art. 7, *supra*, with reference to general appearances.

SECTION 2. ATTACHMENT

Art. 3541. Grounds for attachment

A writ of attachment may be obtained when the defendant:

(1) Has concealed himself to avoid service of citation;

(2) Has mortgaged, assigned, or disposed of his property or some part thereof, or is about to do any of these acts, with intent to defraud his creditors or give an unfair preference to one or more of them;

(3) Has converted or is about to convert his property into money or evidences of debt, with intent to place it beyond the reach of his creditors;

(4) Has left the state permanently, or is about to do so before a judgment can be obtained and executed against him; or

(5) Is a nonresident who has no duly appointed agent for service of process within the state.

Source: C.P. Art. 240; former R.S. 13:3952.

Comments

(a) The above article is essentially similar to Art. 240 of the Code of Practice.

Tit. 1   ATTACHMENT AND SEQUESTRATION   Art. 3543

(b) A person who has left the state permanently without having acquired a new domicile, thus retaining his Louisiana domicile, is not a "nonresident."

(c) The source article refers to the defendant's "property, rights, or credits." The simple term "property" is sufficient to include all species of property, and is used throughout this Title. *Cf.* Art. 5251, *infra*, which defines "property."

(d) See, also, Comments under Art. 3542, *infra*.

Art. 3542. Actions in which attachment can issue

A writ of attachment may be obtained in any action for a money judgment, whether against a resident or a nonresident, regardless of the nature, character, or origin of the claim, whether it is for a certain or uncertain amount, and whether it is liquidated or unliquidated.

Source: C.P. Arts. 239, 241, 242, 256; former R.S. 13:3952.

Comments

(a) The provision in Art. 256 of the Code requiring the sheriff to seize as much of the defendant's property as may be equal in value to the amount claimed has been deleted. Art. 3505, *supra*, which gives the defendant the right to obtain the release of any property in excess of what is necessary to protect the plaintiff's claim, is the only effective limitation upon the amount of property subject to seizure.

(b) This article changes the rule that an attachment would not lie in a tort action, Barrow v. McDonald, 12 La.Ann. 110 (1857); Childs v. Wilson, 15 La.Ann. 512 (1860); Hodges & Co. v. Pennsylvania R. R. Co., 171 La. 699, 132 So. 115 (1930), except where the defendant was a nonresident, former R.S. 13:3952 (Act 220 of 1932); Jackson State Bank v. Merchants' Bank, 177 La. 975, 149 So. 539 (1933). See also, Sondheimer Co. v. Richland Lumber Company, 121 La. 786, 46 So. 806 (1908); Christie & Lowe v. Pennsylvania Iron Works Co., 128 La. 208, 54 So. 742 (1911).

(c) This article is thus made applicable to all attachments, no matter what may be the basis for the writ. The defendant is protected by the strict requirements of Art. 3541, *supra*.

Art. 3543. Issuance of a writ of attachment before debt due

A writ of attachment may be obtained before the debt sued upon is due. If the debt is paid when it becomes due, the costs of the seizure shall be paid by the plaintiff.

Source: C.P. Arts. 244, 287.

Art. 3543   ATTACHMENT AND SEQUESTRATION   Bk. 7

Comments

Similar provisions in the source articles were applicable, respectively, to attachment and to provisional seizure in connection with the lessor's privilege. There were no provisions in the Code of Practice with respect to sequestration.

See Art. 3575, *infra*, authorizing sequestration without security based upon a lessor's privilege.

See, also, Comments under Art. 3572, *infra*.

Art. 3544. Plaintiff's security

The security required for the issuance of a writ of attachment shall be for the amount of the plaintiff's demand, exclusive of interest and costs. If the writ is obtained on the sole ground that the defendant is a nonresident, the security shall not exceed two hundred fifty dollars, but on proper showing the court may increase the security to any amount not exceeding the amount of the demand.

Source: C.P. Art. 245.

Comments

(a) The above article eliminates unnecessary language found in the source provision, but effects no substantive change.

(b) The phrase "on proper showing" is taken from Art. 245 of the Code of Practice and contemplates a contradictory proceeding. The last clause of this article, which permits the court to increase the bond in a nonresident attachment, is similar to the provisions in the Code. Under Art. 7, *supra*, a nonresident who moves to increase an attachment bond would thereby submit to the jurisdiction of the court, such a motion constituting an appearance. *Cf.* Comment (b), Art. 3514, *supra*.

(c) When the plaintiff voluntarily abandons an attachment or sequestration, he is liable for damages for the wrongful issuance of the writ. Cox v. Robinson, 2 Rob. 313 (1842); Steinhardt v. Leman, 41 La.Ann. 835 (1889); Coile v. Crawford, 162 So. 254 (La. App.1935). Under this article, failure to furnish an increased bond when ordered to do so will amount to an abandonment of the attachment so as to make plaintiff liable for damages.

Art. 3545. Nonresident attachment; venue

An action in which a writ of attachment is sought on the sole ground that the defendant is a nonresident may be brought in any parish where the property to be attached is situated.

Source: New.

Comments

(a) A resident attachment is an incident of the action against the defendant, and is brought in a parish of proper venue as to the latter.

(b) An action in which a writ of sequestration is sought against a resident defendant may be brought either in a parish of proper venue as to the defendant, or in the parish where the property is situated, as provided in Art. 72, *supra*.

(c) The venue for a garnishment proceeding against a resident defendant, under a writ of attachment or of sequestration, is provided in Art. 2416, *supra*.

(d) See, also Comments under Art. 42, *supra*.

SECTION 3. SEQUESTRATION

Art. 3571. Grounds for sequestration

When one claims the ownership or right to possession of property, or a mortgage, lien, or privilege thereon, he may have the property seized under a writ of sequestration, if it is within the power of the defendant to conceal, dispose of, or waste the property or the revenues therefrom, or remove the property from the parish, during the pendency of the action.

Source: C.P. Arts. 269, 275, 285; former R.S. 13:4001.

Cross Reference: Art. 3663.

Comments

(a) Under Art. 275(3) of the Code of Practice, in order for a sequestration to issue against immovable property, the plaintiff had to have good reason to fear that the defendant would perform some act which would deprive the plaintiff of the property. The same rule once applied to sequestration of movables. However, under the former R.S. 13:4001, the fact that the defendant had the power to conceal, part with, or dispose of a movable was sufficient ground for an affidavit by the plaintiff that he feared that defendant would do so. The former R.S. 13:4001 had the effect of eliminating, in the case of movables, the requirement that the plaintiff have reasonable ground to fear that the defendant would take certain action, and of substituting therefor the much more liberal requirement that the defendant have power to perform the act.

(b) Since the term "property" includes movable as well as immovable property, the same rule is applicable to both. See Art. 5251, *infra*.

(c) No change is intended by the reference in the above article to removal from the "parish", which is a condensation of the longer

Art. 3571 ATTACHMENT AND SEQUESTRATION Bk. 7

phrase "out of the jurisdiction of the court" used in the source provision, Art. 275(2).

(d) See, also, Comments under Arts. 3503, 3509, *supra*.

Art. 3572. Sequestration before rent due

A sequestration based upon a lessor's privilege may be obtained before the rent is due, if the lessor has good reason to believe that the lessee will remove the property subject to the lessor's privilege. If the rent is paid when it becomes due, the costs shall be paid by the plaintiff.

Source: C.P. Art. 287.

Comments

(a) Art. 287, Code of Practice of 1870, exempts the lessor from paying the costs of the seizure even if the rent is timely paid, if the lessor can prove that the lessee actually removed or attempted or intended to remove the property from the leased premises. This has been changed because it was considered too great a burden on the lessee. Under the above article, the lessor pays the cost of the seizure in all cases where the rent is paid when due.

(b) See Comment under Art. 3543, *supra*.

Art. 3573. Sequestration by court on its own motion

The court on its own motion may order the sequestration of property the ownership of which is in dispute without requiring security when one of the parties does not appear to have a better right to possession than the other.

Source: C.P. Art. 274.

Comment

The supreme court has recognized the judicial sequestration of movables. Ludwig v. Calloway, 191 La. 1000, 187 So. 4 (1939). Since the basis for the rule is the same for movables as for immovables, the above article is applicable to both. *Cf.* Art. 274, Code of Practice.

Art. 3574. Plaintiff's security

An applicant for a writ of sequestration shall furnish security for an amount determined by the court to be sufficient to protect the defendant against any damage resulting from a wrongful issuance, unless security is dispensed with by law.

Source: C.P. Art. 276.

Comments

(a) The loss of revenue is part of the damages sustained by the defendant, and is implicit in the words "any damage." *Cf.* Art. 277 of the Code of Practice.

(b) Art. 278 of the Code of Practice, dispensing with bond in cases of sequestration of property of insolvents, is considered obsolete in view of the federal bankruptcy laws.

(c) Art. 275(5) of the Code of Practice, authorizing sequestration of property of "one [who] has petitioned for a stay of proceedings," is considered obsolete.

Art. 3575. Lessor's privilege

A writ of sequestration to enforce a lessor's privilege shall issue without the furnishing of security.

Source: C.P. Arts. 285(2), 287, 295.

Comments

(a) Provisional seizure having been eliminated, the lessor's privilege is enforced by the writ of sequestration without bond under this Code. See Preliminary Statement, Book VII, Title I, Chapter 1.

(b) The above article is applicable only in the enforcement of the lessor's privilege. The other grounds listed in Art. 285 of the Code for the issuance of the writ have been omitted for the following reasons:

Art. 285(1) of the Code of Practice does not authorize a seizure prior to or independent of the seizure which issues under executory process; it simply recognizes the executory process seizure as another form of seizure prior to judgment. Milliken v. Sweet Home Co., 123 La. 998, 49 So. 669 (1909).

Art. 285(3) of the Code is obsolete in view of the exclusively federal admiralty jurisdiction. See McMahon 1242, n. 49. The first two paragraphs of Art. 289 of the Code deal with a similar situation and are also obsolete.

Art. 285(5) is very similar to R.S. 13:4032, which gives farm workers the right to seize provisionally. This is a special provision, which has been retained in the Revised Statutes.

(c) The provision in Art. 295 of the Code of Practice concerning personal liability in case the seizure has been wrongfully obtained has been omitted as unnecessary.

(d) See, also, Comments under Art. 3572, *supra*.

Art. 3576. Release of property under sequestration

If the defendant does not effect the release of property seized under a writ of sequestration, as permitted by Article 3507, within ten days of the seizure, the plaintiff may effect the release thereof by furnishing the security required by Article 3508.

Source: C.P. Arts. 279, 289; former R.S. 13:4031.

Cross Reference: Art. 3514.

Comments

(a) The above article applies only to sequestration, not to attachment. See Am. Nat. Bank v. Childs, 49 La.Ann. 1359, 22 So. 384, 385 (1897).

(b) Arts. 3507 and 3508, *supra*, fix the condition and the amount of the release bond required of the defendant.

CHAPTER 2. INJUNCTION

Art.
3601. Injunction, grounds for issuance; preliminary injunction; temporary restraining order.
3602. Preliminary injunction; notice; hearing
3603. Temporary restraining order; affidavit of irreparable injury.
3604. Form, contents, and duration of restraining order.
3605. Content and scope of injunction or restraining order.
3606. Temporary restraining order; hearing on preliminary injunction.
3607. Dissolution or modification of temporary restraining order or preliminary injunction.
3608. Damages for wrongful issuance of temporary restraining order or preliminary injunction.
3609. Proof at hearings; affidavits.
3610. Security for temporary restraining order or preliminary injunction.
3611. Penalty for disobedience; damages.
3612. Appeals.
3613. Jurisdiction not limited.

PRELIMINARY STATEMENT

Before 1924, almost the entire Louisiana law relating to injunctions was contained in Arts. 296 *et seq.* of the Code of Practice. Under these articles, preliminary injunctions issued without notice or hearing. Act 29 of 1924 (R.S. 13:4062–13:4071) established a new procedure for obtaining restraining orders and preliminary injunctions, modeled on the federal injunction provisions. Its purpose was "to rid the state of the abuse to which the ex parte issuance of the writ of injunction had been subjected for many years, by arranging the procedure for its issuance so that the judge would have to act no longer blindly on the face of the application for the writ, but would be placed in position to act with the crucial facts before him, . . . and with the right, in the exercise of sound discretion, to grant a temporary restraining order pending the hearing." American National Bank v. Bauman, 173 La. 336, 342, 137 So. 54, 55 (1931). For a discussion of the 1924 Act, see 26 La.Bar.Assn.Rep. 15, reprinted in part at McMahon 1280 ff.

Former R.S. 13:4062 et seq. are based upon the federal law in effect in 1924: former 28 U.S.C. § 381 et seq. and former Federal Equity Rules 73 and 74. The present federal provisions are based upon the same prior federal law. Since neither Fed.Rule 65 nor former R.S. 13:4062 et seq. deviate very much from the rules upon which both are modeled, the result is that the Louisiana statute and the federal rule are strikingly similar.

Experience has indicated that former R.S. 13:4062 et seq. have worked satisfactorily with respect to preliminary injunctions and restraining orders. For this reason most of the injunction statute has been retained in Chapter 2. In some instances, where Fed.Rule 65 differs from Louisiana law, the federal provision has been adopted; in others, the Louisiana law has been retained. One important change in the law is the inclusion of a provision similar to Fed. Rule 65 making suspensive appeals from judgments granting permanent injunctions discretionary with the trial judge. Heretofore, under former R.S. 13:4070 there was an absolute right to such an appeal.

Art. 3601. Injunction, grounds for issuance; preliminary injunction; temporary restraining order

An injunction shall issue in cases where irreparable injury, loss, or damage may otherwise result to the applicant, or in other cases specifically provided by law.

During the pendency of an action for an injunction the court may issue a temporary restraining order, a preliminary injunction, or both, in accordance with the provisions of this Chapter.

Except as otherwise provided by law, an application for injunctive relief shall be by petition.

Source: C.P. Art. 303; former R.S. 13:4064.

Cross Reference: Art. 2752.

Comments

(a) The jurisprudential rules governing the circumstances under which an injunction issues are not changed. Although Art. 298 of the Code of Practice lists ten specific grounds for injunction, these are not exclusive, State ex rel. Belden v. Fagan, 22 La.Ann. 545 (1870); State v. King, 49 La.Ann. 881, 21 So. 585 (1897); Pennington v. Drews, 209 La. 1, 24 So.2d 156 (1945); Minden

Syrup Co. v. Applegate, 150 So. 421 (La.App.1933); Rapides Dairy Dealers' Co-op Assn. v. Mathews, 158 So. 247 (La.App.1935), and there are other code articles and statutory provisions authorizing injunctive relief. See Art. 302, Code of Practice; La.Civil Code Arts. 149, 866–869, 1929. For this reason, no provisions similar to Art. 298 of the Code of Practice have been included in this Code, adopting instead the equitable rule established under Art. 303 of the Code of Practice. Wherever it has been considered desirable to authorize specifically the issuance of an injunction in connection with a particular procedural device, such provisions have been included elsewhere in this Code.

(b) The purposes served by Arts. 297, 299, and 302 of the Code of Practice are now accomplished under a different approach by the rules of Art. 1092, *supra*. See also, Art. 2299, *supra*, which codifies the rules of Arts. 300 and 301 of the Code of Practice.

Art. 3602. Preliminary injunction; notice; hearing

A preliminary injunction shall not issue unless notice is given to the adverse party and an opportunity had for a hearing.

An application for a preliminary injunction shall be assigned for hearing not less than two nor more than ten days after service of the notice.

Source: Former R.S. 13:4062, 13:4063; Fed. Rule 65(a).

Cross References: Arts. 2752, 3601, 3606.

Comments

(a) The first paragraph of this article is a fusion of the Revised Statutes source provisions and of Fed.Rule 65(a).

(b) Service of the notice of hearing is governed by the service of process article 1314, *supra*, but the injunction cannot be effective without actual notice to the party enjoined. See Art. 3605, *infra*.

Art. 3603. Temporary restraining order; affidavit of irreparable injury

A temporary restraining order shall be granted without notice when it clearly appears from specific facts shown by a verified petition or by supporting affidavit that immediate and irreparable injury, loss, or damage will result to the applicant before notice can be served and a hearing had.

The verification or the affidavit may be made by the plaintiff, or by his counsel, or by his agent.

Source: Former R.S. 13:4064; Fed. Rule 65(b).

Cross References: Arts. 2752, 3601.

Tit. 1 INJUNCTION Art. 3605

Comment

This article does not require the petition to be verified. It simply provides that the facts must be set forth either in the verified petition or an affidavit. Thus, if the petition is not verified, there must be an accompanying affidavit.

Art. 3604. Form, contents, and duration of restraining order

A temporary restraining order shall be endorsed with the date and hour of issuance; shall be filed in the clerk's office and entered of record; shall state why the order was granted without notice and hearing; and shall expire by its terms within such time after entry, not to exceed ten days, as the court prescribes. A restraining order, for good cause shown, and at any time before its expiration, may be extended by the court for one or more periods not exceeding ten days each. The party against whom the order is directed may consent that it be extended for a longer period. The reasons for each extension shall be entered of record.

Source: Former R.S. 13:4064; Fed. Rule 65(b).

Cross References: Arts. 2752, 3601.

Comments

(a) The provision that the party against whom the order is directed may consent to an extension in excess of ten days is taken from Fed.Rule 65(b) and represents a change in the Louisiana law.

(b) The above article applies only to restraining orders and sets forth only those requirements which are peculiar to restraining orders. Art. 3605, *infra*, gives all the requirements of a preliminary injunction, and applies to restraining orders also.

(c) Failure to comply with this rule concerning the contents of a restraining order does not render the order void. Druggan v. Anderson, 289 U.S. 36, 46 S.Ct. 14 (1925); Lawrence v. St. Louis-San Francisco Ry. Co., 274 U.S. 588, 47 S.Ct. 720 (1927).

(d) Under this article the number of extensions of a temporary restraining order is unlimited and the duration of each extension can be fixed by the court at any period not exceeding ten days.

Art. 3605. Content and scope of injunction or restraining order

An order granting either a preliminary or a final injunction or a temporary restraining order shall describe in reasonable detail, and not by mere reference to the petition or other documents, the act or acts sought to be restrained. The order shall be effective against the parties restrained, their officers, agents, employees, and counsel, and

Art. 3605   INJUNCTION   Bk. 7

those persons in active concert or participation with them, from the time they receive actual knowledge of the order by personal service or otherwise.

Source: Former R.S. 13:4064; Fed. Rule 65(d).

Cross References: Arts. 2752, 3601.

Comments

(a) The source provisions upon which the above article is based are substantially identical, with the exception that the clause referring to "persons in active concert" with the parties against whom the order is issued is found only in Fed.Rule 65(d).

(b) Former R.S. 13:4064 is applicable only to restraining orders, whereas the above article, following the Federal Rules of Civil Procedure, applies to all injunctive orders. The Louisiana jurisprudence indicates that most of the above provisions apply to injunctive orders: Avery v. Onillion, 10 La.Ann. 127 (1855), an injunction must be specific and detailed; Crucia v. Behrman, 147 La. 144, 84 So. 525 (1920), actual knowledge of an injunction is the test for effectiveness.

(c) The provision in the above article, that the order is effective from the time of "actual knowledge . . . by personal service or otherwise" is taken from Fed.Rule 65(d). It is clearer than the language of the Louisiana source provision, which makes a restraining order effective "from the time of service or of actual knowledge of the issuance thereon."

(d) See, also, Comments under Art. 3604, *supra*, and Art. 3610, *infra*.

Art. 3606.   Temporary restraining order; hearing on preliminary injunction

When a temporary restraining order is granted, the application for a preliminary injunction shall be assigned for hearing at the earliest possible time, subject to Article 3602, and shall take precedence over all matters except older matters of the same character. The party who obtains a temporary restraining order shall proceed with the application for a preliminary injunction when it comes on for hearing. Upon his failure to do so, the court shall dissolve the temporary restraining order.

Source: Former R.S. 13:4065; Fed. Rule 65(b).

Cross References: Arts. 2752, 3601.

Comments

(a) Former R.S. 13:4065 provides that the application for an injunction shall be set for hearing "on the date fixed"; the above arti-

Tit. 1   INJUNCTION   **Art. 3608**

cle follows the federal provision "at the earliest possible time." The words "without notice", which appear in Fed.Rule 65(b), have not been included in the above article since all temporary restraining orders are issued without notice.

(b) See Art. 196, *supra,* which authorizes the issuance of an injunction in vacation.

Art. 3607. Dissolution or modification of temporary restraining order or preliminary injunction

An interested person may move for the dissolution or modification of a temporary restraining order or preliminary injunction, upon two days' notice to the adverse party, or such shorter notice as the court may prescribe. The court shall proceed to hear and determine the motion as expeditiously as the ends of justice may require.

The court, on its own motion and upon notice to all parties and after hearing, may dissolve or modify a temporary restraining order or preliminary injunction.

Source: Former R.S. 13:4065, 13:4066; Fed. Rule 65(b).

Cross References: Arts. 2752, 3601.

Comments

(a) Fed.Rule 65(b) applies only to the dissolution or modification of a restraining order. The Revised Statutes source provisions overlap to some extent and apply to both the temporary restraining order and preliminary injunction. The above article is a consolidation of the source provisions. The provision permitting a notice of less than two days is new in Louisiana law and is taken from Fed.Rule 65(b).

(b) For the method of calculating the two days referred to in the text above, see Art. 5059, *infra.*

(c) The "adverse party" referred to in the above article means the person in whose favor the injunctive order was issued.

Art. 3608. Damages for wrongful issuance of temporary restraining order or preliminary injunction

The court may allow damages for the wrongful issuance of a temporary restraining order or preliminary injunction on a motion to dissolve or on a reconventional demand. Attorney's fees for the services rendered in connection with the dissolution of a restraining order or preliminary injunction may be included as an element of damages

Art. 3608

whether the restraining order or preliminary injunction is dissolved on motion or after trial on the merits.

Source: New; cf. C.P. Art. 375.

Cross References: Arts. 2752, 3601.

Comments

(a) The above article retains the provisions of Art. 375, Code of Practice of 1870, which gives the defendant in an injunction suit the right to claim damages by reconventional demand.

(b) Heretofore, attorney's fees could be recovered only where there was a dissolution of a restraining order or preliminary injunction on a motion prior to trial. Three Rivers Oil Co. v. Laurence, 153 La. 224, 95 So. 652 (1923); Edwards v. Wiseman, 198 La. 382, 3 So.2d 661 (1941). The above article, however, permits attorney's fees to be recovered even though the restraining order or preliminary injunction is dissolved after trial on the merits. *Cf.* Comments at Art. 3506, *supra*.

Art. 3609. Proof at hearings; affidavits

The court may hear an application for a preliminary injunction or for the dissolution or modification of a temporary restraining order or a preliminary injunction upon the verified pleadings or supporting affidavits, or may take proof as in ordinary cases. If the application is to be heard upon affidavits, the court shall so order in writing, and a copy of the order shall be served upon the defendant at the time the notice of hearing is served.

At least twenty-four hours before the hearing, or such shorter time as the court may order, the applicant shall deliver copies of his supporting affidavits to the adverse party, who shall deliver to the applicant prior to the hearing copies of affidavits intended to be used by such adverse party. The court, in its discretion, and upon such conditions as it may prescribe, may permit additional affidavits to be filed at or after the hearing, and may further regulate the proceeding as justice may require.

Source: Former R.S. 13:4067.

Cross References: Arts. 2752, 3601.

Art. 3610. Security for temporary restraining order or preliminary injunction

A temporary restraining order or preliminary injunction shall not issue unless the applicant furnishes security in the amount fixed by the court, except where security is dispensed with by law. The security shall indemnify the person wrongfully restrained or enjoined for the payment of costs incurred and damages sustained.

Source: C.P. Art. 304; former R.S. 13:4064, 13:4068; Fed. Rule 65(c).

Cross References: Arts. 2754, 2783, 3601.

Comments

(a) The above article covers the claim of any person restrained, including those under the terms of Art. 3605, *supra*, "in active concert" with the defendant in an injunction suit. *Cf.* Art. 5121, *infra*, which permits any person in interest to sue on a judicial bond even though he is not a named obligee.

(b) Fed.Rule 65(c) exempts the United States, its officers, and its agencies from furnishing bonds for injunctions. R.S. 13:4581 exempts state, parish, and municipal boards or commissions from furnishing bond in connection with judicial proceedings. It is broad enough to cover all instances in which the state is a litigant.

(c) Since a permanent injunction issues after a trial on the merits, it is unnecessary for the successful plaintiff to give security for a permanent injunction. See Hankins v. Police Jury, 152 La. 1000, 95 So. 102 (1922); Hickman v. Branan, 151 So. 113 (La.App. 1933).

(d) See, also, Comments under Art. 2298, *supra*.

Art. 3611. Penalty for disobedience; damages

Disobedience of or resistance to a temporary restraining order or preliminary or final injunction is punishable as a contempt of court. The court may cause to be undone or destroyed whatever may be done in violation of an injunction, and the person aggrieved thereby may recover the damages sustained as a result of the violation.

Source: C.P. Art. 308; former R.S. 13:4069; 18 U.S.C. § 401.

Cross Reference: Art. 3601.

Comments

(a) *Cf.* Arts. 221 through 227, *supra*, which contain the general contempt provisions. The above article emphasizes the availability of punishment for contempt as a method of enforcing an injunctive order.

(b) The provisions of Art. 307 of the Code of Practice, permitting the defendant to dissolve the injunctive order on bond where no irreparable injury is involved, are obsolete and unnecessary, and have not been included in this Code. In the majority of cases the injunctive order issues to avert irreparable injury. In a few cases where plaintiff is not threatened with irreparable injury, but the law expressly directs or authorizes the issuance of injunctive relief, the court may, in its discretion, grant a suspensive appeal from the injunctive order. See Art. 3612, *infra*.

Art. 3612. Appeals

There shall be no appeal from an order relating to a temporary restraining order.

An appeal may be taken as a matter of right from an order or judgment relating to a preliminary or final injunction, but such an order or judgment shall not be suspended during the pendency of an appeal unless the court in its discretion so orders.

An appeal from an order or judgment relating to a preliminary injunction must be taken and a bond furnished within fifteen days from the date of the order or judgment. The court in its discretion may stay further proceedings until the appeal has been decided.

Except as provided in this article, the procedure for an appeal from an order or judgment relating to a preliminary or final injunction shall be as provided in Book III.

Source: Former R.S. 13:4070; Fed. Rule 62(a), 62(c).

Cross References: Arts. 2752, 3601; R.S. 13:4061, 13:4431, 13:4432.

Comments

(a) The principal change effected by this article is that a suspensive appeal from a judgment granting a final injunction is made discretionary with the court. Heretofore, the trial court which granted a permanent injunction was compelled to allow a suspensive appeal even though the appeal had the effect of nullifying the judgment. Bujol v. Missouri Pac. R. Co., 207 La. 123, 20 So.2d 608 (1944); Borgnemouth Realty Co. v. Gulf Soap Corp., 211 La. 255, 29 So.2d 841 (1947).

(b) The third paragraph of the above article is limited to preliminary injunctions, and follows former R.S. 13:4070, except that the delay has been extended to fifteen days to coincide with the delay for suspensive appeals. *Cf.* Art. 2123, *supra*. The time for appeals from final injunctions is not affected.

(c) Under the last paragraph of this article, except where specific portions differ from the general procedure for appeals, the general rules are applicable.

(d) *Cf.* Arts. 194, 195, and 196, *supra*, which authorize hearings on the subjects covered by the above article in term time or in vacation, and in open court and in chambers.

(e) See Comments under Arts. 2083, 2087, 2123, 2124, 3611.

Art. 3613. Jurisdiction not limited

The provisions of this Chapter do not limit the issuance by a court of any writ, process, or order in aid of its jurisdiction.

Source: Cf. former R.S. 13:4070, 13:4071; Fed. Rule 62(g).

Cross References: Arts. 2752, 3601.

Comment

This article is a restatement of the constitutional provision authorizing the issuance of "needful writs" in aid of the courts' jurisdiction. Const. Art. VII, § 2.

TITLE II
REAL ACTIONS

Chap.		Art.
1.	Actions to Determine Ownership or Possession	3651
2.	Boundary Action	3691
3.	Hypothecary Action	3721
	Sec.	
	1. General Dispositions	3721
	2. Hypothecary Action against Third Person	3741
4.	Notice of Pendency of Action	3751

INTRODUCTION

Within the intendment of this Title, the term "real actions" is somewhat broader than the definition in Art. 4 of the Code of Practice.

Chapter 1 of this Title contains the rules regulating the actions to determine ownership or possession of immovable property or of a real right. The articles therein effect changes in the procedural law, yet accord with civilian concepts of property and possession, and with the basic principles on which the former procedural law was based.

Under the prior law, four actions were available to determine ownership or possession: (1) the petitory action to assert a right of ownership by a person out of possession against a person in possession; (2) the action to establish title to assert a right of ownership by a person out of possession against another out of possession; (3) the possessory action by a person entitled to possession against a person who physically disturbed that possession, to have the plaintiff maintained or restored to possession; and (4) the jactitory action by a person in possession against a person whose pretensions of ownership legally disturbed plaintiff's possession, to force the defendant to assert his pretensions in a petitory action. Because of the rigidity of the former actions, and the technical manner in which the rules applicable thereto were applied by the courts, they have been criticized as being unworkable and hypertechnical. Hubert, A Louisiana Anomaly—The "Writ" System in Real Actions, 22 Tul.L. Rev. 459 (1948). Simplification and liberalization were necessary in any revision of the procedural law worthy of the name.

The articles in Chapter 1 of this Title make two extremely important changes in the procedural law: (1) the petitory action is broadened to include both the former action of the same name and the former action to establish title, with the possession of the defendant merely determining the burden of proof to be imposed on the plaintiff; and (2) the possessory action is broadened so as to include both the former action of the same name and the former jactitory action, with some of the latter's procedural rules made applicable to the new possessory action. New rules are incorporated in the initial chapter which permit possession to perform its historic role of determining burden of proof in actions which actually or indirectly adjudicate rights of ownership, although not classified technically as real actions, such as concursus proceedings and actions for a declaratory judgment of ownership of immovable property. Minor changes in the procedural law are made in this Chapter so that the new petitory and possessory actions are better adapted to modern conditions.

No attempt has been made to include in this Title certain of the fringe actions which bear some resemblance to the real actions, such as the action of trespass, the action to remove a cloud from title, and the action of specific performance.

Chapter 2 contains the general procedural principles governing the action of boundary, which effect slight changes in the law to make the remedy less technical than under the former law.

Chapter 3 of this Title makes an important change in the procedural law by abolishing the cumbersome and circuitous hypothecary action, properly speaking, of the prior law and substituting therefor a simple and direct procedure for seizing the immovable property subject to a general mortgage in execution of a judgment liquidating the amount secured thereby, with notice of the seizure to the then owner of the property.

CHAPTER 1. ACTIONS TO DETERMINE OWNERSHIP OR POSSESSION

Art.
3651. Petitory action.
3652. Same; parties; venue.
3653. Same; proof of title.
3654. Proof of title in action for declaratory judgment, concursus, expropriation, or similar proceeding.
3655. Possessory action.
3656. Same; parties; venue.
3657. Same; cumulation with petitory action prohibited; conversion into or separate petitory action by defendant.
3658. Same; requisites.
3659. Same; disturbance in fact and in law defined.

Art. 3651 OWNERSHIP OR POSSESSION Bk. 7

Art.
3660. Same; possession.
3661. Same; title not at issue; limited admissibility of evidence of title.
3662. Same; relief which may be granted successful plaintiff in judgment; appeal.
3663. Sequestration; injunctive relief.
3664. Real rights under contracts to reduce minerals to possession.

Art. 3651. Petitory action

The petitory action is one brought by a person who claims the ownership, but who is not in possession, of immovable property or of a real right, against another who is in possession or who claims the ownership thereof adversely, to obtain judgment recognizing the plaintiff's ownership.

Source: New; cf. C.P. Arts. 5, 43; former R.S. 13:5062.

Comments

(a) This article combines the former petitory action and the former action to establish title, and hence would be brought by a person who claims ownership, but who is not in possession, against: (1) an adverse claimant of ownership who is in possession; (2) a person in possession who may not be asserting any adverse claim of ownership; or (3) an adverse claimant of ownership who is out of possession. The defendant's possession, or lack of it, determines the burden of proof imposed on the plaintiff. See Art. 3653, *infra*.

(b) Under this article, the action must be brought directly against the adverse claimant of ownership, or if there is no adverse claim, against the person in possession. There is no requirement that the action be brought against the tenant, since the latter does not possess for himself but only for his lessor. C.C. Art. 3441; *cf.* C.C. Arts. 3433, 3438. See, also, Art. 3656, *infra*. Art. 43 of the Code of Practice not only ran counter to civilian theory, but it was anachronistic as well. *Cf.* Lawrence v. Sun Oil Co., 166 F.2d 466 (5 C.C.A.1948). Today, with the conveyance records in each parish in good shape, it is a relatively simple matter to determine who is the adverse claimant of ownership, and even when there is no adverse claim of ownership it is not difficult to determine who is in possession.

The tenant may be joined as a co-defendant, if the plaintiff desires, under Art. 3652, *infra*.

Art. 3652. Same; parties; venue

A petitory action may be brought by a person who claims the ownership of only an undivided interest in the immovable property or real right, or whose asserted ownership is limited to a certain period which has not yet expired, or which may be terminated by an event which has not yet occurred.

A lessee or other person who occupies the immovable property or enjoys the real right under an agreement with the person who claims the ownership thereof adversely to the plaintiff may be joined in the action as a defendant.

A petitory action shall be brought in the venue provided by Article 80(1), even when the plaintiff prays for judgment for the fruits and revenues of the property, or for damages.

Source: New; cf. C.P. Arts. 43, 45, 163, and Comments following.

Comments

(a) The first paragraph of this article makes no change in the law.

(b) See Comment (b) under Art. 3651, *supra*. Even though not compelled to, there may be reasons why the plaintiff may wish to join the tenant as a co-defendant. If the tenant has a long-term lease, the plaintiff would wish to have his right of ownership established against the adverse claimant and his right to the possession established against the tenant in the same suit.

(c) Under the third paragraph of this article, venue is limited to the parish of the situs of the immovable; but if the action is brought in an improper venue, the defendant must except timely thereto, otherwise the objection is waived. See Arts. 44, 925, *supra*. Express provision is made in this paragraph for the venue of the mixed action.

Art. 3653. Same; proof of title

To obtain a judgment recognizing his ownership of the immovable property or real right, the plaintiff in a petitory action shall:

(1) Make out his title thereto, if the court finds that the defendant is in possession thereof; or

(2) Prove a better title thereto than the defendant, if the court finds that the latter is not in possession thereof.

Source: New; cf. C.P. Art. 44; Comments following.

Comments

(a) When the defendant is in possession, this article makes no change in the law. The words "make out his title" are taken from Art. 44 of the Code of Practice, and are intended to have the same meaning as given to them under the jurisprudence interpreting the source provision.

Art. 3653   OWNERSHIP OR POSSESSION   Bk. 7

(b) When the defendant is not in possession, this article may make a change in the procedural law. Under the prior law, there was a conflict in the jurisprudence as to the burden imposed on the plaintiff in the action to establish title. The earlier cases, applying the sounder rule, imposed on the plaintiff only the burden of proving a better title than defendant. Metcalfe v. Green, 140 La. 950, 74 So. 261 (1916). See, also, Ellis v. Louisiana Planting Co., 146 La. 652, 83 So. 885 (1920); and Doiron v. Vacuum Oil Co., 164 La. 15, 113 So. 748 (1927). The later cases held the plaintiff to the same burden as was imposed on a plaintiff in the former petitory action. Dugas v. Powell, 197 La. 409, 1 So.2d 677 (1941); Stockstill v. Choctaw Towing Corp., 224 La. 473, 70 So.2d 93 (1953); Albritton v. Childers, 225 La. 900, 74 So.2d 156 (1954). The later cases were erroneous. The reason why such a heavy burden of proving a valid title was visited on the plaintiff in the former petitory action was because the defendant admittedly had possession. In the former action to establish title, admittedly neither party was in possession, and there was not the same necessity for imposing the heavy burden of proof upon plaintiff as in the former petitory action. See 18 La.L.Rev. 360 (1958). This article works a legislative overruling of the later cases.

(c) In the occasional case where the pleadings will raise an issue as to the defendant's possession, this issue will have to be determined on the trial of the case on its merits.

Art. 3654. Proof of title in action for declaratory judgment, concursus, expropriation, or similar proceeding

When the issue of ownership of immovable property or of a real right is presented in an action for a declaratory judgment, or in a concursus, expropriation, or similar proceeding, or the issue of the ownership of funds deposited in the registry of the court and which belong to the owner of the immovable property or of the real right is so presented, the court shall render judgment in favor of the party:

(1) Who would be entitled to the possession of the immovable property or real right in a possessory action, unless the adverse party makes out his title thereto; or

(2) Who proves better title to the immovable property or real right, when neither party would be entitled to the possession of the immovable property or real right in a possessory action.

Source: New; cf. Comments following.

Comments

(a) This article adopts, implements, and broadens the suggestion made in Zengel, The Real Actions—A Study in Code Revision, 29 Tul.L.Rev. 617, 631 (1955).

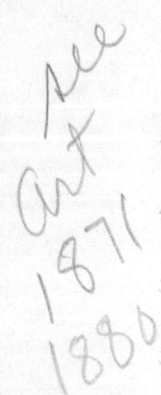

(b) As a practical matter, many issues of ownership are involved and adjudicated in concursus proceedings, where oil companies which have mineral leases from adverse claimants of ownership deposit royalties into the registry of the court and implead the adverse claimants. Rules which give effect to the historic role of possession in determining the burden of proof of ownership are needed in these cases.

This article does not constitute legislative approval of California Company v. Price, 234 La. 338, 99 So.2d 743 (1957) on the issue of res judicata, which many members of the legal profession in this state regard as erroneous. As a practical matter, this article would be needed even should the Price case be overruled. It is urgently needed as long as this decision is followed.

(c) In numerous cases, the action for a declaratory judgment has been used to adjudicate the ownership of land and mineral rights. See Horn v. Skelly Oil Co., 221 La. 626, 60 So.2d 65 (1952); Arkansas Louisiana Gas Co. v. Thompson, 222 La. 868, 64 So.2d 202 (1953); Horn v. Skelly Oil Co., 224 La. 709, 70 So.2d 657 (1954); Bierhorst v. Kelly, 225 La. 934, 74 So.2d 168 (1954); Calhoun v. Gulf Refining Company, 104 So.2d 547 (La.1958); Levenson v. Chancellor, 68 So.2d 116 (La.App.1953); Hastings v. McDowell, 75 So.2d 383 (La.App.1954). Since the broad dictum in Burton v. Lester, 227 La. 347, 79 So.2d 333 (1955) has been overruled legislatively in Art. 1871, *supra*, these actions will be used much more frequently for such purposes, and rules to give effect to the role of possession therein are needed.

(d) Much the same problems may be presented in expropriation suits and similar proceedings where adverse claimants of ownership are asserting conflicting claims to the compensation to be paid for the taking of immovable property. These rules are likewise made applicable to such cases.

(e) The possession required of a plaintiff in a possessory action was adopted here as the arbiter of burden of proof to prevent one of the parties from taking possession of the immovable property briefly prior to rendition of judgment, or from dispossessing the rightful possessor, so as to obtain the benefit of the rules as to burden of proof.

Art. 3655.   Possessory action

The possessory action is one brought by the possessor of immovable property or of a real right to be maintained in his possession of the property or enjoyment of the right when he has been disturbed, or to be restored to the possession or enjoyment thereof when he has been evicted.

Source: New; cf. C.P. Arts. 6, 46, and Comments following.

Art. 3655. OWNERSHIP OR POSSESSION

Comments

The articles on the possessory action in this Chapter make two important changes in the procedural law: (1) the present possessory action is a merger of the former possessory action and the former jactitory action; and (2) procedural rules heretofore applicable only to the former jactitory action have been made applicable to the new possessory action.

These changes have been effected primarily through: Art. 3659, *infra*, which broadens the definition of the disturbance in law; Art. 3657, *infra*, which permits the defendant to convert the suit into a petitory action; and Art. 3662, *infra*, which broadens the judgment to be rendered for the successful plaintiff in the new possessory action.

Art. 3656. Same; parties; venue

A plaintiff in a possessory action shall be one who possesses for himself. A person entitled to the use or usufruct of immovable property, and one who owns a real right therein, possesses for himself. A predial lessee possesses for and in the name of his lessor, and not for himself.

The possessory action shall be brought against the person who caused the disturbance, and in the venue provided by Article 80(1), even when the plaintiff prays for a judgment for the fruits and revenues of the property, or for damages.

Source: New; cf. C.P. Arts. 47, 48, 163; C.C. Art. 3441; and Comments following.

Cross Reference: Art. 3660.

Comments

(a) The first paragraph of this article is a consolidation and editorial revision of its indirect source provisions. No change in the law is made except through the broadening of the possessory action. See Comment under Art. 3655, *supra*.

(b) There is no conflict between this article and Art. 3660, *infra*. A person who is entitled to the use or usufruct possesses the property or right both for himself and for the naked owner, and hence either may bring the possessory action.

(c) Under the second paragraph of this article, venue is limited to the parish of the situs of the immovables. However, if the action is brought in an improper venue, the defendant must except timely thereto, otherwise the objection is waived. See Arts. 44, 925, *supra*. Further, express provision for the venue of the mixed action is provided in this paragraph of the above article.

Art. 3657. Same; cumulation with petitory action prohibited; conversion into or separate petitory action by defendant

The plaintiff may not cumulate the petitory and the possessory actions in the same suit or plead them in the alternative, and when he does so he waives the possessory action. If the plaintiff brings the possessory action, and without dismissing it and prior to judgment therein institutes the petitory action, the possessory action is abated.

When, except as provided in Article 3661(1)–(3), the defendant in a possessory action asserts title in himself, in the alternative or otherwise, he thereby converts the suit into a petitory action, and judicially confesses the possession of the plaintiff in the possessory action.

If, before executory judgment in a possessory action, the defendant therein institutes a petitory action in a separate suit against the plaintiff in the possessory action, the plaintiff in the petitory action judicially confesses the possession of the defendant therein.

Source: New; cf. C.P. Arts. 54–57, and Comments following.

Cross Reference: Art. 3661.

Comments

(a) The rules of this article are intended to keep the trial of the issues of possession and ownership as separate as possible, and to encourage the determination of the issue of possession before the institution of the petitory action.

(b) The first sentence of this article makes no change in the law, but is only a consolidation of its indirect sources.

(c) The second sentence of this article makes a change in the law.

Under the prior law, the penalty for the improper cumulation of the two actions was the judicial confession of the possession of the defendant. This not only worked a waiver of the possessory action when the two were cumulated, but it made it impossible for the plaintiff to dismiss the suit, and then to renew the possessory action alone in the second suit. This is too harsh a penalty when the improper cumulation, or alternative pleading, of the two actions results from a mere inadvertence of counsel.

Under the second sentence of this article, and subject to the provisions of Art. 1671, *supra*, where there is an improper cumulation or alternative pleading of the two actions in the same suit, plaintiff may have this suit dismissed without prejudice, and then renew his possessory action alone in a second suit, without being barred by a judicial confession of the possession of the defendant.

(d) The second paragraph of this article makes the procedural rule heretofore applicable to the former jactitory action applicable

Art. 3657   OWNERSHIP OR POSSESSION   Bk. 7

to the broadened possessory action. It not only permits the defendant to convert the suit into a petitory action, but provides that he does so whenever he injects the issue of ownership through his answer.

(e) Under the former jactitory action, the defendant could convert the suit into a petitory action: (1) through his answer, Board of Trustees of Ruston Circuit v. Rudy, 192 La. 200, 187 So. 549 (1939); Barrow v. LeBlanc, 35 So.2d 469 (La.App.1948); or (2) through a reconventional demand, Carmody v. Land, 207 La. 625, 21 So.2d 764 (1945); or (3) through a supplemental answer filed after judgment ordering the defendant to institute the petitory action, Sherburne v. Iberville Land Co., 192 La. 1091, 190 So. 227 (1939). It is intended that the word "answer" in the second paragraph of this article includes all three of these methods of converting the suit into a petitory action.

(f) The last paragraph of this article prevents a defendant in a possessory action from defeating the efforts of the plaintiff in the possessory action to have the issue of his possession adjudicated therein, or from relitigating the issue in a petitory action filed in a separate suit, and in which he would allege that the defendant was not in possession.

(g) The provisions of the former R.S. 13:5063 and 13:5064 would have been unnecessary and unworkable under the new procedure, and have been repealed.

Art. 3658.   Same; requisites

To maintain the possessory action the possessor must allege and prove that:

(1) He had possession of the immovable property or real right at the time the disturbance occurred;

(2) He and his ancestors in title had such possession quietly and without interruption for more than a year immediately prior to the disturbance, unless evicted by force or fraud;

(3) The disturbance was one in fact or in law, as defined in Article 3659; and

(4) The possessory action was instituted within a year of the disturbance.

    Source: New; cf. C.P. Art. 49; C.C. Arts. 3449, 3456; and Comment following.

    Cross Reference: Art. 3659.

Comment

This article makes no change in the law. The broadened statement of the applicable rule in Art. 3658(2) merely recognizes the established doctrine of the tacking of possession.

Art. 3659. Same; disturbance in fact and in law defined

Disturbances of possession which give rise to the possessory action are of two kinds: disturbance in fact, and disturbance in law.

A disturbance in fact is an eviction, or any other physical act which prevents the possessor of immovable property or of a real right from enjoying his possession quietly, or which throws any obstacle in the way of that enjoyment.

A disturbance in law is the execution, recordation, registry, or continuing existence of record of any instrument which asserts or implies a right of ownership or to the possession of immovable property or of a real right, or any claim or pretension of ownership or right to the possession thereof except in an action or proceeding, adversely to the possessor of such property or right.

Source: New; cf. C.P. Arts. 50–52, and Comments following.

Cross Reference: Art. 3658.

Comments

(a) The first two paragraphs of this article make no change in the law.

(b) The last paragraph makes an important change in the law which in turn makes it possible to merge the former jactitory action into the broadened possessory action.

The former jactitory action was borrowed from Spanish procedure by the jurisprudence to fill in a hiatus in our prior procedural law. No completely convincing evidence is available to account for this procedural hiatus, but it is not unreasonable to believe that it resulted from the extremely narrow and unrealistic definition of disturbance in law of Art. 53 of the Code of Practice. Under a much broader definition of disturbance in law of French procedure, its possessory action is broad enough to perform the functions of both of our former possessory and jactitory actions. The broadening of this definition in this article makes it possible to broaden the new possessory action so as to perform also the functions of the former jactitory action.

(c) The third paragraph makes another change in the law. Under Art. 53 of the Code of Practice, the institution of the possessory action was a disturbance in law of the defendant's possession, if the latter actually had possession. Under this article, it is not. However, this leaves no hiatus in the new procedure, since the defendant may reconvene and bring the possessory action against the plaintiff, and obtain the same relief as if he had filed a separate possessory action. See Comment (c) under Art. 3662, *infra*. The acts of possession on which the original plaintiff relied to prove his possession would constitute disturbances in fact, and any recorded title to

Art. 3660. Same; possession

the plaintiff would constitute a disturbance in law, of the original defendant's possession, if the latter actually had possession.

Art. 3660. Same; possession

A person is in possession of immovable property or of a real right, within the intendment of the articles of this Chapter, when he has the corporeal possession thereof, or civil possession thereof preceded by corporeal possession by him or his ancestors in title, and possesses for himself, whether in good or bad faith, or even as a usurper.

Subject to the provisions of Articles 3656 and 3664, a person who claims the ownership of immovable property or of a real right possesses through his lessee, through another who occupies the property or enjoys the right under an agreement with him or his lessee, or through a person who has the use or usufruct thereof to which his right of ownership is subject.

Source: New; cf. C.P. Art. 49; C.C. Arts. 3429–3431; and Comments following.

Cross References: Arts. 3656, 3664.

Comments

(a) This article makes no change in the law, but is a restatement of its indirect sources and is declaratory of the established jurisprudence on the subject.

(b) While it makes no change in the law, the first paragraph of this article does not retain the language "actual possession" and "real and actual possession" of Arts. 43 and 49 of the Code of Practice. These terms never accorded with the terminology and concepts of the Civil Code, and had to be defined by the jurisprudence. The first paragraph above accords with the terminology and concepts of the Civil Code and is declaratory of the jurisprudence. See Art. 3436 of the Civil Code; Ellis v. Prevost, 19 La. 251 (1841); Barnes v. Gaines, 5 Rob. 313 (La.1843).

(c) The second paragraph of this article applies not only to predial lessees, but to mineral lessees as well.

(d) See Comment (b) under Art. 3656, *supra,* and Comment (b) under Art. 3664, *infra.*

Art. 3661. Same; title not at issue; limited admissibility of evidence of title

In the possessory action, the ownership or title of the parties to the immovable property or real right is not at issue.

No evidence of ownership or title to the immovable property or real right shall be admitted except to prove:

(1) The possession thereof by a party as owner;

(2) The extent of the possession thereof by a party; or

(3) The length of time in which a party and his ancestors in title have had possession thereof.

Source: New; cf. C.P. Art. 53, and Comments following.

Cross Reference: Art. 3657.

Comments

(a) Although phrased differently from its indirect sources, this article makes no change in the law.

(b) One of the most convincing proofs that a party possesses the property for himself, and not for others, is a certified copy of the act of sale to him.

(c) Under Art. 3437 of the Civil Code, corporeal possession of a part of the property, with the intention of possessing all that is included within the boundaries called for by the act of sale, is possession of the whole. A certified copy of the act of sale to a party, showing the boundaries of the property acquired, is competent to prove the extent of his possession.

(d) Art. 3661(3) implements the doctrine of tacking of possession, under which a person who acquires property under a just title translative of ownership is permitted to add to his possession that of his ancestors in title.

Art. 3662. Same; relief which may be granted successful plaintiff in judgment; appeal

A judgment rendered for the plaintiff in a possessory action shall:

(1) Recognize his right to the possession of the immovable property or real right, and restore him to possession thereof if he has been evicted, or maintain him in possession thereof if the disturbance has not been an eviction;

(2) Order the defendant to assert his adverse claim of ownership of the immovable property or real right in a petitory action to be filed within a delay to be fixed by the court not to exceed sixty days after the date the judgment becomes executory, or be precluded thereafter from asserting the ownership thereof, if the plaintiff has prayed for such relief; and

(3) Award him the damages to which he is entitled and which he has prayed for.

A suspensive appeal from the judgment rendered in a possessory action may be taken within the delay provided in Article 2123, and

Art. 3662

a devolutive appeal may be taken from such judgment only within thirty days of the applicable date provided in Article 2087(1)-(3).

Source: New; cf. Comments following.

Cross References: Arts. 2087, 2123.

Comments

(a) A change in the law is made by this article by making available to the successful plaintiff in the broadened possessory action relief which heretofore has been available only in the former jactitory action.

(b) The plaintiff in a possessory action may not wish to have the defendant ordered to institute a petitory action, and may not wish to assert any claim for damages. For these reasons, the relief provided in Art. 3662(2) and (3) is optional, and to obtain it the plaintiff must specially pray for it.

(c) A defendant in a possessory action may reconvene and pray for any or all of the relief which is made available to the plaintiff under this article. This privilege of the defendant is necessary to prevent an adversary who fears a possessory action from instituting one himself first, then suspensively appealing from an adverse judgment, and thus preventing the party in possession from instituting and prosecuting a possessory action. See Comment (c) under Art. 3659, *supra*.

(d) By limiting the period for a devolutive appeal to thirty days, the last paragraph expedites a definitive judgment in the possessory action.

Art. 3663. Sequestration; injunctive relief

Sequestration of immovable property or of a real right involved in a possessory or petitory action during the pendency thereof is available under the applicable provisions of Chapter 1 of Title I of Book VII.

Injunctive relief, under the applicable provisions of Chapter 2 of Title I of Book VII, to protect or restore possession of immovable property or of a real right, is available to:

(1) A plaintiff in a possessory action, during the pendency thereof; and

(2) A person who is disturbed in the possession which he and his ancestors in title have had for more than a year of immovable property or of a real right of which he claims the ownership, the possession, or the enjoyment.

Source: New; cf. C.P. Arts. 58, 275(3), 298(5), and Comments following.

Cross References: Arts. 3501-3576; 3601-3613.

Comments

(a) This article makes no change in the law.

(b) Injunctive relief is made available in two separate and distinct types of cases: (1) as an ancillary remedy in a possessory action; and (2) as the relief to be granted in an injunction suit brought to enjoin trespassers and other disturbers, and which is neither a possessory nor a petitory action. See Churchill Farms v. Gaudet, 184 La. 984, 168 So. 123 (1936).

Art. 3664. Real rights under contracts to reduce minerals to possession

A mineral lessee or sublessee, owner of a mineral interest in immovable property, owner of a mineral royalty, or of any right under or obligation resulting from a contract to reduce oil, gas, and other minerals to possession, is the owner of a real right. These rights may be asserted, protected, and defended in the same manner as the ownership or possession of immovable property, and without the concurrence, joinder, or consent of the owner of the land.

Source: R.S. 9:1105.

Cross Reference: Art. 3660.

Comments

(a) The above article was included in this Chapter to show a clear and unmistakable legislative intent, despite any of the language of the majority opinion in Reagan v. Murphy, 105 So.2d 210 (La.1958), to permit the enforcement of any of the rights enumerated in the above article by the actions recognized in this Chapter.

(b) There is no conflict between this article and Art. 3660, supra. A mineral lessee, sublessee, or owner of a mineral or royalty interest possesses both for himself and for the owner of the land.

(c) R.S. 9:1105, which is both substantive and procedural, is not repealed.

CHAPTER 2. BOUNDARY ACTION

Art.
3691. Right to compel fixing of boundaries.
3692. Appointment of surveyor by court.
3693. Determination of boundary rights.

Art. 3691. Right to compel fixing of boundaries

If two contiguous lands have never been separated, or have never had their boundaries determined, or if the bounds which have been

Art. 3691. BOUNDARY ACTION

formerly fixed are no longer to be seen, or were wrongly placed, the owner of one of the contiguous lands may bring an action against the other to compel the fixing of the boundary.

Source: C.C. Arts. 823, 853.

Comment

This article formally recognizes the action of boundary and states when it may be used. It follows the language of Civil Code Art. 823, thus incorporating Louisiana jurisprudence and thereby avoiding difficulties of judicial interpretation.

Art. 3692. Appointment of surveyor by court

The court shall appoint a surveyor to inspect the lands in question and to make plans showing the respective contentions of the parties.

Source: C.C. Art. 841.

Comment

This article is substantially the same as Art. 841 of the Civil Code in that it makes the appointment of a surveyor mandatory upon the court.

Art. 3693. Determination of boundary rights

The fixing of bounds, the verifying of ancient boundaries, or the rectification of dividing lines shall be determined in an ordinary proceeding in accordance with the rights and titles of the parties.

Source: New; cf. Art. 1063, Quebec Code of Civil Procedure.

Comment

This article makes a significant change in the law. The language "in accordance with the rights and titles of the parties" was inserted in the above article to overrule legislatively the cases holding that questions of title and ownership cannot be determined in an action of boundary.

CHAPTER 3. HYPOTHECARY ACTION

SECTION 1. GENERAL DISPOSITIONS

Art.
3721. Methods of enforcing mortgage.
3722. Enforcement by ordinary proceeding.
3723. Enforcement by executory proceeding.

SECTION 2. HYPOTHECARY ACTION
AGAINST THIRD PERSON

Art.
3741. Right of enforcement.
3742. Notice of seizure.
3743. Rights of third possessor.

SECTION 1. GENERAL DISPOSITIONS

Art. 3721. Methods of enforcing mortgage

A conventional mortgage is enforced by ordinary or executory proceedings.

Source: New; cf. C.P. Arts. 61–63.

Cross References: Arts. 2378, 4705.

Comment

See Comments under Arts. 2631, *supra*, and 5155, *infra*.

Art. 3722. Enforcement by ordinary proceeding

When the mortgagee enforces a conventional mortgage by an ordinary proceeding, he must first obtain a judgment against the mortgagor and then execute the judgment.

Source: New.

Comment

See Comments under Art. 5155, *infra*.

Art. 3723. Enforcement by executory proceeding

When the mortgagee enforces a conventional mortgage by an executory proceeding, he must comply with Articles 2631 through 2724.

Source: New.

Comment

See Comments under Arts. 2631, *supra*, and 3741, 5155, *infra*.

SECTION 2. HYPOTHECARY ACTION AGAINST THIRD PERSON

Art. 3741. Right of enforcement

A legal mortgage, after judgment on the original obligation has been obtained, a judicial mortgage, or a conventional mortgage may be enforced without reference to any alienation or transfer of the mortgaged property from the original debtor, and the creditor may cause the property to be seized and sold as though it were still owned by the original debtor and in his possession.

Source: New.

Cross Reference: Art. 2378.

Comments

(a) This article supplies a statutory pact de non alienando which will henceforth be implicit in every mortgage, permitting the mortgage creditor to seize and sell the property in the hands of a third person as though it were still owned by his original debtor. It is to be noted, however, that in order to proceed *via ordinaria* under this article, the creditor must first reduce his claim to judgment against the original debtor.

(b) This article also eliminates the hypothecary action properly so called and the delays incident thereto. It permits the creditor to enforce his judicial mortgage against the present owner of the property by complying with Art. 3742, *infra*, and in a like manner it also permits the creditor to enforce his legal mortgage as soon as he has obtained judgment against the original debtor.

(c) Where the act of mortgage contains a confession of judgment, the enforcement of the mortgage may be governed by rules applicable to executory proceedings. See Art. 3723, *supra*.

(d) A privileged creditor may enforce his privilege on immovable property by an ordinary action against the debtor and the present owner of the property subject to the privilege.

Art. 3742. Notice of seizure

When property subject to a legal or a judicial mortgage is no longer owned by the original debtor, the seizing creditor shall cause notices of the seizure to be served by the sheriff upon both the original debtor and the present owner.

Source: New.

Cross References: Arts. 2378, 3743.

Comment

This article protects the present owner of the property since the seizure itself may not give him sufficient notice and time to assert the rights given him under Art. 3743, *infra*.

Art. 3743. Rights of third possessor

When property subject to a legal or a judicial mortgage is seized to enforce the mortgage, or is about to be seized for this purpose, and the property is no longer owned by the original debtor, the third possessor has the following rights:

(1) To arrest the seizure, or threatened seizure, and consequent judicial sale of the property by injunction on the grounds that the mortgage was not recorded, that the inscription of its recordation had peremped, or that the debt secured by the mortgage is prescribed or extinguished, or to plead discussion as provided in Articles 5154 and 5155; and

(2) All of the rights granted a third possessor under Article 2703 (1) and (3).

Source: C.P. Arts. 71–74; C.C. Arts. 3403, 3410.

Comments

(a) For a definition of "third possessor", see the cases cited in Comment (a) under Art. 2703, *supra*.

(b) This article is a consolidation of the pertinent provisions of its sources which relate to a third possessor who purchases property subject to a legal or a judicial mortgage.

(c) In view of Arts. 3741 and 3742, *supra*, granting to the judgment creditor the right to seize and sell the property in the hands of a third person without the necessity of bringing any action against the latter, it was necessary to allow the third possessor to plead discussion in an injunction proceeding brought to arrest the seizure and judicial sale of his property.

CHAPTER 4. NOTICE OF PENDENCY OF ACTION

Art.
3751. Notice to be recorded to affect third persons.
3752. Requirements of notice; recordation.
3753. Cancellation of notice of pendency.

Art. 3751. Notice to be recorded to affect third persons

The pendency of an action or proceeding in any court, state or federal, in this state affecting the title to, or asserting a mortgage or

Art. 3751 NOTICE OF PENDENCY OF ACTION

privilege on, immovable property does not constitute notice to a third person not a party thereto unless a notice of the pendency of the action or proceeding is made, and filed or recorded, as required by Article 3752.

Source: Former R.S. 13:3541.

Cross Reference: Art. 3752.

Comments

(a) No change in the law is made by this article, but see Comment (b) hereof.

(b) This article is declaratory of the rule of Soniat v. Whitmer, 141 La. 235, 74 So. 916 (1916), and is intended to overrule legislatively the contrary decision in Richardson Oil Co. v. Herndon, 157 La. 211, 102 So. 310 (1924).

Art. 3752. Requirements of notice; recordation

The notice referred to in Article 3751 shall be in writing, signed by the plaintiff, defendant, or other party to the action or proceeding who desires to have the notice recorded, or by a counsel of record for such party, showing the name of the court in which the action or proceeding has been filed, the title, docket number, date of filing, and object thereof, and the description of the property sought to be affected thereby.

This notice shall be recorded in the mortgage office of the parish where the property to be affected is situated, and has effect from the time of the filing for recordation.

Source: Former R.S. 13:3542.

Cross Reference: Art. 3751.

Comment

This article makes no change in the law and is merely an editorial revision of its source provision, as amended by La.Act 113 of 1958.

Art. 3753. Cancellation of notice of pendency

When judgment is rendered in the action or proceeding against the party who filed the notice of the pendency thereof, the judgment shall order the cancellation of the notice at the expense of the party who filed it, and as part of the costs of the action or proceeding.

Source: Former R.S. 13:3543.

Comment

This article makes no change in the law.

TITLE III
EXTRAORDINARY REMEDIES

Chap.		Art.
1.	General Dispositions	3781
2.	Habeas Corpus	3821
3.	Mandamus	3861
4.	Quo Warranto	3901

INTRODUCTION

The authority of the Louisiana courts to issue the extraordinary writs covered by this Title dates back to the Practice Act of 1805, the last section of which authorized the superior court of the territory of Orleans to issue writs of "quo warranto, procedendo, mandamus and prohibition." Although these writs were given their common law appellation, the rules governing their issuance, at least in the case of mandamus, were not necessarily those of the common law but rather those of the Spanish writs of incitativo, inhibición, and evocación, which were the counterpart thereof. Agnes v. Judice, 3 Mart. (O.S.) 182 (La.1813).

In England, mandamus was originally a mandate issuing directly from the sovereign to compel the performance of the royal will. The arbitrary issuance of the royal mandate later fell into disuse and gave place to the judicial writ. See City of Atlanta v. Wright, 119 Ga. 207, 45 S.E. 994 (1903). In Louisiana, the power of the courts to issue the writ was much more extensive than that of the common law courts. Hatch v. City Bank of New Orleans, 1 Rob. 470 (La. 1842). In this Title, the writ of mandamus is treated only as an extraordinary writ.

Originally, habeas corpus was the name given to a number of different writs the object of which was to bring a party before a court. As the term is now used, it applies to the writ directed against a person who has another in his custody, which, properly speaking, is a habeas corpus ad subjiciendum. The United States Constitution preserves the writ by providing that the privilege of the writ of habeas corpus shall not be suspended unless, when in cases of rebellion or invasion, the public safety may require it. U.S.Const. Art. I, § 9. The Louisiana Constitution, Art. I, § 13, contains a similar provision. R.S. 15:113 through 15:141, which govern the issuance of habeas corpus in criminal matters, are not affected by the provisions in this Title.

The writ of quo warranto is one of the most ancient writs known to the common law. Commonwealth v. Wherry, 302 Pa. 134, 152 A. 846 (1930). In State v. Kohnke, 109 La. 838, 846, 33 So. 793, 796 (1903), the supreme court made the observation that "our law [on quo warranto] is substantially an adoption of the common law on the same subject as modified by the statute of 9 Anne, c. 20." The original function of the writ was to determine who was the rightful holder of a public office. Since the adoption of the Intrusion Into Office Act, R.S. 42:76 et seq., the writ is seldom used in Louisiana to try title to public office, although it is probably still available for that purpose. Slater v. Blaize, 204 La. 21, 14 So.2d 872 (1943). Its principal use is to test office in a private corporation.

CHAPTER 1. GENERAL DISPOSITIONS

Art.
3781. Petition; summary trial; issuance of writs.
3782. Return date.
3783. Answer.
3784. Hearing.
3785. Disobedience of writ or judgment; contempt.

Art. 3781. Petition; summary trial; issuance of writs

A writ of habeas corpus, mandamus, or quo warranto may be ordered by the court only on petition. The proceedings may be tried summarily and the writ when ordered may be signed by the clerk under the seal of the court, or it may be issued and signed by the judge without further formality.

Source: C.P. Arts. 786, 801, 840, 841, 871, 872.

Comments

(a) Since summary procedure is available only where "expressly provided by law," the above provision authorizing summary trial in cases involving the extraordinary remedies is necessary.

(b) The phrase "may be tried summarily" was used to make it clear that a summary proceeding is not the exclusive form of procedure. Cf. State ex rel. Loraine, Inc. v. Adjustment Board of Baton Rouge, 220 La. 708, 57 So.2d 409 (1952). When summary proceedings are employed, the requirement of Arts. 794 and 840, Code of Practice, that the plaintiff initiate the proceedings by petition, has been retained.

(c) See Arts. 1232 and 1233, *supra*, which govern the method of serving process under the writ of habeas corpus, except as provided in Art. 3824, *infra*.

(d) Although under Arts. 791, 829, 867, and 872 of the Code of Practice the writs are to issue in the name of the state, there is no requirement that the suit be instituted in the name of the state. State ex rel. Dardenne v. Cole, 33 La.Ann. 1356 (1881); Davenport v. Sterling Lumber Co., 143 La. 671, 79 So. 215 (1918). See, also, State ex rel. Divens v. Johnson, 207 La. 23, 20 So.2d 412 (1944). *Cf.* R.S. 42:76, governing actions under the Intrusion into Office Act, and see State ex rel. Robinson v. Dranguet, 23 La.Ann. 784 (1871).

(e) Inasmuch as the defendant suffers no actual loss until after a hearing is had on an application for an extraordinary writ, no special provision requiring a verified petition has been included here. This represents a change in the law in view of Arts. 799, 810, and 840 of the 1870 Code, which require a verified petition and answer in a habeas corpus proceeding and a verified petition for the mandamus. *Cf.* Art. 863, *supra*, which dispenses with the verification of pleadings except where specifically provided by law.

(f) Art. 836 of the Code of Practice, providing that a mandamus can be issued only by courts whose jurisdiction exceeds one hundred dollars, is obsolete.

(g) See, also, Comments under Art. 3901, *infra*.

Art. 3782. Return date

A petition for a writ of habeas corpus, mandamus, or quo warranto shall be assigned for hearing not less than two nor more than ten days after the service of the writ, except that, upon proper showing, the court may assign the matter for hearing less than two days after the service of the writ.

Source: C.P. Art. 813.

Comment

The delay for the hearing fixed by this article is the same as the delay for a hearing on an application for a preliminary injunction, but the provision giving the court the right to fix a shorter delay is taken from Art. 813 of the Code of Practice.

Art. 3783. Answer

A written answer to a petition for a writ shall be filed not later than the time fixed for the hearing.

Source: C.P. Arts. 806, 842, 869.

Comment

This article is necessary in view of Art. 2593, *supra*.

Art. 3784. Hearing

The hearing may be held in open court or in chambers, in term or in vacation.

Source: C.P. Art. 830.

Comment

See Comments under Arts. 194–196, *supra*.

Art. 3785. Disobedience of writ or judgment; contempt

A person who fails to comply with a writ of habeas corpus, or with a judgment rendered after a hearing on a petition for a writ of habeas corpus, mandamus, or quo warranto may be punished for contempt. When a sentence of imprisonment is imposed for contempt, imprisonment may continue until the defendant obeys the writ or judgment.

Source: C.P. Arts. 814, 815, 843.

Comments

(a) Arts. 814 and 815 of the Code of Practice provide that failure to obey a writ of habeas corpus is punishable as a contempt, and Art. 843 is a similar provision applicable to a judgment on the return of a writ of mandamus. There is no similar provision in the Code of Practice applicable to quo warranto.

Disobedience of the writ of habeas corpus is punishable as a contempt, but with respect to the other two, the writ is, in effect, an order to show cause, and it is only the judgment which is enforceable by contempt process.

(b) The above article makes specific provision for continued imprisonment until the defendant has obeyed the order or judgment of the court. *Cf.* Art. 226, *supra*.

(c) In view of the fact that the general contempt penalty, Art. 227, *supra*, also applies, the defendant who is in contempt cannot escape punishment by complying with the judgment immediately after he is adjudged in contempt.

(d) The provision of Art. 815 of the Code of Practice that one who disobeys a habeas corpus is subject to an action in damages for false imprisonment has been omitted. See Art. 2315 of the Civil Code.

(e) Art. 844, Code of Practice, makes the writ of distringas available where a corporation disobeys a mandamus. Art. 1058 of the Code of Practice authorizes a distringas against an administrator, executor, or curator failing to comply with a mandamus. Neither of these provisions is necessary in view of Art. 2502, *supra*, which provides that a writ of distringas is available "when the judgment orders the defendant to do or refrain from doing an act other than the delivery of a thing."

CHAPTER 2. HABEAS CORPUS

Art.
3821. Definition.
3822. Venue.
3823. Persons authorized to make service; proof of service.
3824. Method of service.
3825. Answer; production of person in custody.
3826. Transfer of custody; answer.
3827. Inability to produce person in custody.
3828. Custody pendente lite.
3829. Notice of hearing.
3830. Judgment.
3831. Appeal not to suspend execution of judgment.

PRELIMINARY STATEMENT

After a careful study of the practice in other states, it was determined that this Code should include articles regulating the use of the writ of habeas corpus in civil proceedings, such as cases involving custody of children or civil commitment.

The articles in the Code of Criminal Procedure regulate the use of the writ where the applicant is confined as a result of a criminal proceeding against him.

Art. 3821. Definition

Habeas corpus is a writ commanding a person who has another in his custody to produce him before the court and to state the authority for the custody.

Custody, as used in this Chapter, includes detention and confinement.

A petition for a writ of habeas corpus may be filed by the person in custody or by any other person in his behalf.

Source: C.P. Arts. 787, 791, 794.

Comments

(a) In view of the fact that the writ of arrest is not provided for in this Code, all references to civil arrest found in the source articles were deleted. Art. 787, Code of Practice, speaks of habeas corpus as the right to be released "from illegal arrest or detention."

(b) Habeas corpus has been issued almost exclusively in civil matters involving custody of children. Numerous cases recognize this as a proper use of the writ. See, for example, State ex. rel. Jagneaux v. Jagneaux, 206 La. 107, 18 So.2d 913 (1944). Other possible civil uses of the writ are: to obtain the release of a person imprisoned for contempt, Craig v. Hecht, 263 U.S. 255, 44 S.Ct. 103, 68 L.Ed. 293 (1923); State v. Sauvinet, 24 La.Ann. 119 (1872); to obtain the release of persons confined on the ground of insanity, Oliver v. Terrall, 152 La. 662, 94 So. 152 (1922); and to question the legality of detention under quarantine or health regulations. See People v. Robertson, 302 Ill. 422, 134 N.E. 815, 22 A.L.R. 835 (1922).

(c) The general rules which require a petition to contain a statement of the cause of action and to state the name of the defendant make it unnecessary to include in this article the requirements of Arts. 794 and 795 of the Code of Practice that the petition must be "signed by the party" and must mention the "name of the party confined" and by whom. *Cf.* Art. 891, *supra.*

(d) See Comments under Art. 3781, *supra.*

Art. 3822. Venue

Habeas corpus proceedings may be brought in the parish in which the defendant is domiciled or the parish in which the person detained is in custody.

Source: C.P. Art. 792; cf. Comments following.

Comments

(a) This article codifies the rule of State ex rel. Jagneaux v. Jagneaux, 206 La. 107, 18 So.2d 913 (1944) that a habeas corpus proceeding can be brought at the defendant's domicile, even though the custody of the person is in another parish. *Cf.* Art. 792 of the Code of Practice.

(b) The first part of Art. 792 of the Code of Practice authorizing the district courts and the supreme court to issue writs of habeas corpus has been omitted. See Const. Art. VII, § 2.

(c) Where the habeas corpus proceeding is ancillary to another suit, this article is inapplicable. State ex rel. Steen v. Wade, 207 La. 177, 20 So.2d 747 (1944).

(d) Art. 793, Code of Practice, providing that when the judge of a district is absent or unable to act, a writ of habeas corpus may be issued by a judge in an adjoining district, has been deleted in view of R.S. 13:586, which gives judges of adjoining districts the power to grant any orders under such circumstances.

(e) See Comments under Art. 10, *supra.*

Art. 3823. Persons authorized to make service; proof of service

A writ of habeas corpus may be served by any person over the age of twenty-one who is capable of testifying.

If the writ is served by someone other than a sheriff, the affidavit of the person who served it shall be prima facie proof of such service.

Source: C.P. Arts. 802, 804.

Cross Reference: Art. 331.

Comments

(a) The requirement of Art. 802, Code of Practice, that the writ is to be served by a "male person" has been deleted. The requirement that the person making service must be over twenty-one years old is new.

(b) The source article provides for service of the writ by the sheriff or "by someone other than the sheriff." When service is made by the sheriff, Art. 1292, *supra*, governs both the method of service and the proof required. However, Art. 1293, *supra*, which permits service of process to be made by persons other than the sheriff in ordinary civil actions where the sheriff has not made service within the time provided, does not apply to the service of the writ because of its summary nature. Likewise, under Art. 1293, *supra*, where service is made by third persons in ordinary civil suits, proof of such service must be made "as any other fact in the case." The above article provides, however, that when the writ of habeas corpus is served by a person other than the sheriff, the affidavit of the server is "prima facie proof of such service."

Art. 3824. Method of service

A writ of habeas corpus shall be served upon the party to whom it is addressed or who has the person in custody in the manner provided by Articles 1232 and 1233. If personal service cannot be made, service may be made by attaching the writ to an entrance door of the residence of the party to be served or to a door of the place where the person is in custody.

Source: C.P. Art. 803.

Comments

(a) No change in the law is made.

(b) See Comments under Art. 3781, *supra*.

Art. 3825. Answer; production of person in custody

The person upon whom the writ has been served, whether it is directed to him or not, shall file an answer stating whether he has custody of the person named in the writ. If the person is in his custody, he shall produce him and state in his answer by what authority he holds the person detained.

Source: C.P. Arts. 805–807.

Cross Reference: Art. 3782.

Comments

(a) In many cases, particularly those involving custody of children, the requirement that the person in custody actually be produced in court is not always observed. Nevertheless, no change has been made in the provision requiring such production, since, historically, production of the person is the essential feature of the writ. *Cf.* State ex rel. Doran v. Doran, 215 La. 151, 39 So.2d 894 (1949).

(b) Art. 809, Code of Practice, provides that if the custody is by virtue of a judicial order, the original order must be annexed to the answer. A similar provision has not been included in this Title because it does not seem likely that an original civil custody order could be attached to the answer.

(c) Under Art. 818, Code of Practice, the person in custody may deny the allegations in the answer and may plead affirmatively himself. If the person in custody is the plaintiff in the habeas corpus proceeding, obviously no such provision is necessary. In other cases, the person in confinement may intervene in the proceeding if he desires to file pleadings. Therefore, no provision similar to Art. 818 has been included.

Art. 3826. Transfer of custody; answer

If the person upon whom the writ of habeas corpus is served has transferred the custody of the person detained prior to service of the writ, he shall state in his answer the name and address of the person to whom custody was transferred, the time of and the authority for the transfer, and the place where the person detained is then in custody.

Source: C.P. Art. 808.

Comments

(a) This article is of general application and is not limited to cases where the transfer of custody is made within three days of the service of the writ. *Cf.* Art. 808, Code of Practice.

(b) The requirement that the address of the person to whom custody is transferred and the place where the person is in custody be given is new and is for the purpose of giving the court the fullest information possible about the person detained.

Art. 3827. Inability to produce person in custody

If the person in custody cannot be brought before the court, the reasons therefor shall be stated in the answer. The hearing may proceed as if he had been produced.

Source: C.P. Arts. 816, 817.

Comment

In State ex rel. Doran v. Doran, 215 La. 151, 39 So.2d 894 (1949) it was pointed out that under Arts. 805 through 807 of the Code of Practice it is the duty of the respondent in a writ of habeas corpus to produce the subject of the writ, or to explain in the answer thereto the reason why he could not or should not be produced.

Art. 3828. Custody pendente lite

If judgment cannot be rendered immediately, the court may award the custody to a proper person until rendition of the judgment.

Source: C.P. Art. 820.

Comment

The term "proper person" includes welfare institutions as well as individuals. In all other respects this article is derived from the source provision.

Art. 3829. Notice of hearing

When a person is in custody by virtue of a prior court order, or at the request of any person, reasonable written notice of the hearing shall be given to the person who provoked the prior court order or requested the custody.

Source: C.P. Art. 821.

Art. 3830. Judgment

The judgment may order the person released or placed in the custody of a proper person.

Source: C.P. Art. 825.

Comment

See Comment under Art. 3828, *supra*.

Art. 3831. Appeal not to suspend execution of judgment

An appeal from a judgment ordering the release of a person from custody or placing him in the custody of another person shall not suspend the execution of the judgment.

Source: New; cf. Comments following.

Comments

(a) This article codifies the jurisprudential rule in State ex rel. Martinez v. Hattier, 192 La. 209, 187 So. 551 (1939).

(b) There is a similar article prohibiting suspensive appeals in custody matters incidental to divorce and separation suits. See Art. 3943, *infra*.

(c) See Comments under Art. 2123, *supra*.

CHAPTER 3. MANDAMUS

Art.
3861. Definition.
3862. Cases in which mandamus issues.
3863. Person against whom writ directed.
3864. Mandamus against corporation or corporate officer.
3865. Alternative writ.
3866. Judgment.

Art. 3861. Definition

Mandamus is a writ directing a public officer or a corporation or an officer thereof to perform any of the duties set forth in Articles 3863 and 3864.

Source: C.P. Arts. 789, 828(1), 829, 832, 841.

Comments

(a) This Chapter treats of mandamus only as an extraordinary writ, not as a supervisory remedy.

(b) Mandamus is defined in the source articles as an "order directing the performance of some specific act"; an order "to individuals or corporations to compel them to perform certain duties prescribed for them by law"; and an order "issued in the name of the state by a tribunal of competent jurisdiction, and addressed to an individual or corporation, or court of inferior jurisdiction, directing it to perform some certain act belonging to the place, duty or quality with which it is clothed." The above article states the essential features of the writ, all unnecessary language in the source articles having been deleted.

(c) This article does not modify the rule that mandamus may not be used to compel performance of contractual obligations. State ex rel. Brown v. United Gas Public Service Co., 197 La. 616, 2 So.2d 41 (1941).

(d) Mandamus may be directed to an officer or board member whose duty it is to perform the act involved. See Knoll v. Levert, 136 La. 241, 66 So. 959 (1914); Michel v. Michel, 151 La. 541, 92 So. 50 (1922).

(e) The term "duty" in this article is limited to those duties specified in Arts. 3863 and 3864, *infra*.

(f) See Comments under Art. 3901, *infra*.

Art. 3862. Cases in which mandamus issues

A writ of mandamus may be issued in all cases where the law provides no relief by ordinary means or where the delay involved in obtaining ordinary relief may cause injustice.

Source: C.P. Arts. 830, 831.

Comments

(a) The above article combines the source articles with changes of wording to achieve brevity.

(b) Mandamus will be denied where there has been an unreasonable delay in applying for it. State ex rel. McCabe v. Police Board of City of New Orleans, 107 La. 162, 31 So. 662 (1901); State ex rel. Boudreaux v. Alford, 205 La. 46, 16 So.2d 901 (1944). The same result obtains under this article.

(c) In some cases the distinction between a mandatory injunction and a writ of mandamus may not be clear. It should be noted that injunction is a much broader remedy and requires bond, whereas mandamus is restricted to the cases specified in this Code and no bond is required.

(d) Of necessity, constitutional provisions and special statutes governing the issuance of mandamus in particular cases remain in effect.

Art. 3863. Person against whom writ directed

A writ of mandamus may be directed to a public officer to compel the performance of a ministerial duty required by law, or to a former officer or his heirs to compel the delivery of the papers and effects of the office to his successor.

Source: C.P. Arts. 833, 834.

Cross Reference: Art. 3861.

Comments

(a) A typical and probably the most frequent use of the writ against a public officer is in a proceeding to compel the recorder of mortgages to cancel an illegal or unauthorized inscription. See State ex rel. Code v. Code, 215 La. 485, 41 So.2d 62 (1949).

(b) The following rules established by the jurisprudence are retained:

Mandamus will issue only when there is a clear and specific right to be enforced or a duty which ought to be performed. It never issues in doubtful cases. It may be used only to compel the performance of purely ministerial duties. State ex rel. Hutton v. City of Baton Rouge, 217 La. 857, 47 So.2d 665 (1950); State ex rel. Loraine, Inc. v. Adjustment Board, 220 La. 708, 57 So.2d 409 (1952).

(c) It has been held that a citizen taxpayer has no legal standing to enforce performance of a public officer's duty to the public at large, unless clearly shown to have special and peculiar interest, apart from the interest of the general public. Cleveland v. Martin, 29 So.2d 516 (La.App.1947).

Art. 3864. Mandamus against corporation or corporate officer

A writ of mandamus may be directed to a corporation or an officer thereof to compel:

(1) The holding of an election or the performance of other duties required by the corporate charter or bylaws or prescribed by law; or

(2) The recognition of the rights of its members or shareholders.

Source: C.P. Art. 835.

Cross Reference: Art. 3861.

Comments

(a) Mandamus has been used to compel a corporation to transfer stock, State ex rel. Pope v. Bunkie Coca Cola Bottling Co., 222 La. 603, 63 So.2d 13 (1953); to compel it to hold regular meetings as required by its charter, Alexis v. Coker, 35 So.2d 907 (La.App. 1948); to compel it to permit a shareholder to examine the corporate books, State ex rel. Carey v. Dalgarn Const. Co., 168 La. 620, 133 So. 884 (1929). The writ may not be used to compel the performance of obligations arising ex contractu. State ex rel. Arbour v. Board of Mgrs. of Presbyterian Hospital, 131 La. 163, 59 So. 108 (1912); State ex rel. Brown v. United Gas Public Service Co., 197 La. 616, 2 So.2d 41 (1941).

(b) The source article applies only to duties required by the corporate charter and makes no mention of bylaws or legal duties.

Many corporate duties required by statute but not by charter are enforceable by mandamus. See Tichenor v. Dr. G. H. Tichenor Co., Ltd., 161 So. 198 (La.App.1935).

(c) The service of the writ is governed by the provisions of this Code relative to service of process.

Art. 3865. Alternative writ

Upon the filing of a petition for a writ of mandamus, the court shall order the issuance of an alternative writ directing the defendant to perform the act demanded or to show cause to the contrary.

Source: C.P. Art. 841.

Comment

This article and Art. 3866, *infra*, perpetuate the system under which an alternative order issues at the outset and the peremptory writ issues only after a hearing.

Art. 3866. Judgment

After the hearing, the court may render judgment making the writ peremptory.

Source: C.P. Arts. 842, 843.

Comment

See Comment under Art. 3865, *supra*.

CHAPTER 4. QUO WARRANTO

Art.
3901. Definition.
3902. Judgment.

Art. 3901. Definition

Quo warranto is a writ directing an individual to show by what authority he claims or holds public office, or office in a corporation, or directing a corporation to show by what authority it exercises certain powers. Its purpose is to prevent usurpation of office or of powers.

Source: C.P. Arts. 789, 828(4), 867; cf. R.S. 42:76 et seq.

Comments

(a) This article is a combination of the definitions found in the source provisions.

Art. 3901   QUO WARRANTO

(b) The provision referring to public office was incorporated on the theory that the Intrusion into Office Act, R.S. 42:76 *et seq.*, does not give an individual the right to file suit except when he is claiming the office.

(c) At one stage in the development of the jurisprudence, it was held that quo warranto was not the proper procedure for trying title to an office in a private corporation. State ex rel. Jones v. Carradine, 147 So. 554 (La.App.1928). However, it is now well settled that a writ of quo warranto is the proper remedy. Leidenheimer v. Schutten, 194 La. 598, 194 So. 32 (1940); State ex rel. Palfrey v. Simms, 152 So. 395 (La.App.1934).

(d) Special statutes authorizing quo warranto proceedings are not affected by this article. *Cf.* R.S. 51:665.

(e) Art. 3866, *supra*, provides that after the hearing in a mandamus proceeding, the court may render judgment making the writ peremptory. A similar article would be unnecessary in quo warranto proceedings. Mandamus, by definition, is an order directing performance. A writ of quo warranto, on the other hand, does not direct the defendant to perform or to cease from performing some act, but it orders the defendant to show by what authority he is acting.

Art. 3902.   Judgment

When the court finds that a person is holding or claiming office without authority, the judgment shall forbid him to do so. It may declare who is entitled to the office and may direct an election when necessary.

When the court finds that a corporation is exceeding its powers, the judgment shall prohibit it from doing so.

Source: C.P. Arts. 870, 871.

Comment

This article combines the source articles. All unnecessary matter, such as the provision assessing costs against the defendant, has been deleted. The provision in Art. 871 of the Code of Practice requiring the judge to render judgment "in a summary manner" is unnecessary in view of Art. 3781, *supra*. The second paragraph of the above article is new.

TITLE IV

ANNULMENT OF MARRIAGE, SEPARATION FROM BED AND BOARD, AND DIVORCE

Art.
3941. Court where action brought; nullity of judgment of court of improper venue.
3942. Appeal from judgment granting or refusing annulment, separation, or divorce.
3943. Appeal from judgment awarding custody or alimony.
3944. Injunctive relief.
3945. Execution of alimony judgments in arrears.

INTRODUCTION

In this Code, and as a matter of public policy, the same principles applicable to actions for separation and divorce are made applicable to actions for the annulment of marriages. Consequently, the three actions have been consolidated in this Title.

Art. 3941. Court where action brought; nullity of judgment of court of improper venue

An action for an annulment of marriage, for a separation from bed and board, or for a divorce shall be brought in a parish where either party is domiciled, or in the parish of the last matrimonial domicile.

The venue provided in this article may not be waived, and a judgment rendered in any of these actions by a court of improper venue is an absolute nullity.

Source: New.

Cross Reference: Art. 44.

Comments

(a) This article provides a uniform rule of venue for these actions, and in so doing broadens the venue rules on the subject. The specific changes made in the law are pointed out in the following comments.

(b) Heretofore, there were only three provisions regulating the venue in actions for separation or divorce: Art. 142 of the Civil Code, dealing with a special situation which is discussed below; R.S. 9:301, providing that a suit for divorce on the ground of two years' separation may be brought by either spouse "in the courts of his or her residence within the state"; and R.S. 9:302, providing that after a judgment of separation a divorce may be obtained "from the same court" which rendered the separation judgment.

Art. 3941 ANNULMENT, DIVORCE, SEPARATION Bk. 7

Art. 142 of the Civil Code was adopted originally and primarily to permit a Louisiana woman who had married, and then moved out of the state to live with her husband, to return here to obtain a judgment of separation or divorce on grounds which occurred while the marital domicile was in another state or foreign country. As a practical matter, the above article will not conflict with this Civil Code provision, since the former recognizes the rule that the suit may be filed in the parish of plaintiff's domicile. Nevertheless, it has been recommended that Art. 142 of the Civil Code be amended, for two reasons: (1) to remove the second paragraph which was inserted by amendment to cover a single case; and (2) to remove the venue provision to make it clear that the wife does not have to return to the former Louisiana domicile of her husband or herself, but may establish a domicile anywhere in this state, and institute the suit therein.

The above article does not conflict with R.S. 9:301, which provides a venue at the plaintiff's domicile, for in Wreyford v. Wreyford, 216 La. 784, 44 So.2d 867 (1950), and Davidson v. Helm, 222 La. 759, 63 So.2d 866 (1953), the court held that an action under R.S. 9:301 might be brought at the domicile of a defendant, on the theory that a defendant may always be sued at his domicile.

In the great majority of cases, the action for a divorce after judgment of separation will be filed in the parish of the last matrimonial domicile, or in the parish where either plaintiff or defendant was domiciled at the time of the institution of the action for separation, *i. e.*, in "the same court" which rendered the judgment of separation, as provided in R.S. 9:302. The above article broadens this statute, except in the rare case where the court which rendered the separation judgment is not the parish of the last matrimonial domicile or the parish where either the plaintiff or defendant was domiciled at the time of the institution of the divorce action.

The exception in Art. 10(7), *supra*, avoids conflict with Art. 142 of the Civil Code, and R.S. 9:301, as interpreted in Davidson v. Helm, *supra*. See Comment (i) under Art. 10, *supra*.

(c) This article makes a change in the law with respect to actions for a separation or divorce, on grounds other than those provided in Art. 142 of the Civil Code, R.S. 9:301, and 9:302.

Heretofore, in the absence of a specific venue provision governing such actions, the courts have applied the general rule of venue, and have held that such suits must be instituted at the domicile of the defendant. Condran v. Boudreaux, 155 La. 662, 99 So. 521 (1924); Wallace v. Wallace, 164 La. 672, 114 So. 589 (1927); Switzer v. Elmer, 172 La. 850, 135 So. 608 (1931); McGee v. Gasery, 185 La. 839, 171 So. 49 (1936); Cotton v. Wright, 189 La. 686, 180 So. 487 (1938); Hymel v. Hymel, 214 La. 346, 37 So.2d 813 (1948). See also, McLean v. Janin, 45 La.Ann. 664, 12 So. 747 (1893); Wilcox v. Nixon, 115 La. 47, 38 So. 890 (1905). This rule has been applied even though the last matrimonial domicile was elsewhere, Wallace v. Wallace, *supra*, and even though the plaintiff was a nonresident. Cotton v. Wright, *supra*. The rule has also been applied where the husband abandoned the wife and set up a new domicile. He can be sued there either by a resident wife, Switzer v. Elmer, *supra*, or a nonresident one. George v. George, 143 La. 1032, 79 So. 832 (1918). Similarly, it has been held that when a husband establishes a new domicile he may sue his wife there since under the law that is likewise her domicile. Barrow v. Barrow, 160 La. 91, 106 So. 705 (1925). The effect of the wife being forced to leave the husband and establish a new domicile is discussed in Comment (d), *infra*.

In no case decided heretofore has the court held that an action for a separation or a divorce, on grounds other than those provided in Art. 142 of the Civil Code, R.S. 9:301, or R.S. 9:302, may be brought at the domicile of the plaintiff. Stevens v. Allen, 139 La. 658, 71 So. 936, L.R.A.1916E, 1115 (1916), may be distinguished on the ground that since the wife had been guilty of misconduct, she could not establish a separate domicile and the suit was actually filed at the domicile of the defendant.

By providing that all actions for separation or divorce may be brought at the domicile of either spouse, the above article makes a change in the law, by making the rule uniform in all cases.

(d) One exception to the general rule that the domicile of the husband is that of the wife is universally recognized in other American states. If the wife is forced to leave the matrimonial domicile because of the husband's misconduct, she may establish a separate domicile. Laiche v. His Wife, 156 La. 165, 100 So. 292 (1924), and Hymel v. Hymel, *supra*, left some doubt as to whether the Louisiana courts would recognize this exception and apply it to the determination of venue. This doubt, however, has been resolved by Bush v. Bush, 232 La. 747, 95 So.2d 298 (1957).

(e) There are cases which indicate that matrimonial domicile has played a role in determining proper venue. Zinko v. Zinko, 204 La. 478, 15 So.2d 859 (1943); Burgan v. Burgan, 207 La. 1057, 22 So.2d 049 (1945); Hymel v. Hymel, *supra;* Wreyford v. Wreyford, *supra*. A close study of these cases, however, discloses that at best these expressions are dicta. Hence, in providing that an action for separation or divorce may be brought in the parish of the last matrimonial domicile, the above article makes a change in the law.

Since this article also permits suits at the domicile of either party, the recent case of Bush v. Bush, *supra*, leaves some doubt as to whether the provision permitting suit at the last matrimonial domicile is necessary. However, the above article makes certain that a wife who has been abandoned may sue for a separation, and ultimately a divorce in the parish where the abandonment occurred.

Art. 3941 ANNULMENT, DIVORCE, SEPARATION Bk. 7

(f) The question of whether a court of improper venue has jurisdiction to render a valid judgment of separation or divorce is one which has troubled the Louisiana courts in the past. In the only case where the point was squarely presented, it was held that such a court had no jurisdiction to render a valid judgment. McGee v. Gasery, *supra*. *Cf.* Zinko v. Zinko, *supra;* and see Burgan v. Burgan, *supra*. In both of the latter cases, Chief Justice O'Niell wrote separate opinions in which he took the position that the question presented was not jurisdiction, but venue.

While venue generally may be waived, Art. 44, *supra*, there are instances where, because of public policy, it becomes jurisdictional and cannot be waived. The above article codifies the rule of McGee v. Gasery, *supra*.

(g) For the rules as to the jurisdiction of the Louisiana courts in these cases, see Art. 10(6), 10(7), and Comment (i) thereunder, *supra*.

Art. 3942. Appeal from judgment granting or refusing annulment, separation, or divorce

An appeal from a judgment granting or refusing an annulment of marriage, a separation from bed and board, or a divorce can be taken only within thirty days from the applicable date provided in Article 2087(1)–(3).

Such an appeal shall suspend the execution of the judgment in so far as the judgment relates to the annulment, separation, or divorce.

Source: C.P. Art. 573; former R.S. 13:4452.

Cross Reference: Art. 3943.

Comments

(a) This article is an exception to the general rule set forth in Art. 2087, *supra*, which provides that an appeal can be taken within ninety days after the dates set forth in Arts. 1914 and 1974, *supra*.

(b) This article makes no substantive change in the law, and, by providing that the delay shall commence (1) from the expiration of the time for applying for a new trial, or (2) from the date of the court's refusal to grant a new trial, or (3) from the date of the notice of refusal to grant a new trial where the applicant is entitled to such notice, it conforms with the general rule applicable in ordinary cases.

(c) See Comments under Art. 2087, *supra*.

Art. 3943. Appeal from judgment awarding custody or alimony

An appeal from a judgment awarding custody of a person or alimony can be taken only within the delay provided in Article 3942. Such an appeal shall not suspend the execution of the judgment in so far as the judgment relates to custody or alimony.

Source; New; cf. Comments following.

Comments

(a) This article codifies the jurisprudence denying a suspensive appeal in custody cases. Guidry v. Guidry, 206 La. 1049, 20 So.2d 309 (1944). However, it overturns the line of cases holding that a suspensive appeal may be taken from an alimony judgment. Ramos v. Ramos, 173 La. 407, 137 So. 196 (1927); Weyand v. Weyand, 169 La. 390, 125 So. 282 (1929); Demerell v. Gerlinger, 183 La. 704, 164 So. 633 (1935); Cotton v. Wright, 187 La. 265, 174 So. 351 (1937); Gravier v. Gravier, 200 La. 775, 8 So.2d 697 (1942); Forct v. Gautreaux, 213 La. 1083, 36 So.2d 393 (1948). Thus the wife will no longer be deprived of necessary support pending appeal.

(b) The above article also overturns the jurisprudential rule under which the judgment becomes unappealable within thirty days in so far as it relates to the divorce or separation, whereas an appeal may be taken within a year in so far as alimony or custody is concerned. Cressione v. Millet, 212 La. 691, 33 So.2d 198 (1947); Scott v. Scott, 218 La. 211, 48 So.2d 899 (1950).

Art. 3944. Injunctive relief

Either party to an action for separation from bed and board or divorce may obtain injunctive relief without bond prohibiting the other party from disposing of or encumbering community property.

Source: C.P. Art. 298; C.C. Art. 149; cf. Comments following.

Comments

(a) The right of a wife to an injunction without bond prohibiting her husband from alienating community property is recognized in Shipp v. Shipp, 180 La. 881, 158 So. 5 (1934). Although there is no Code article or statute dispensing with bond, the court reasoned that, since the husband could not sue the wife for damages if the injunction was issued wrongfully, a bond would be useless.

(b) The source articles both refer to the wife only. As a practical matter, the right of injunction should be recognized for both spouses. The reasoning of the Shipp case is equally applicable to an injunction in favor of the husband and against the wife.

(c) See Comments under Art. 3601, *supra*.

Art. 3945. Execution of alimony judgments in arrears

When the payment of alimony under a judgment is in arrears, the party entitled thereto may proceed by contradictory motion to have the amount of past due alimony determined and made executory. On the trial of the contradictory motion, the court shall render judgment for the amount of past due alimony.

Source: New; cf. Comments following.

Comments

(a) This article provides a method for making alimony judgments executory, and it codifies the jurisprudence recognizing the use of the rule to show cause as a method for determining the amount of alimony in arrears. Williams v. Williams, 211 La. 939, 31 So.2d 170 (1947). By this means, the clerk is able to determine the amount due for the purpose of the issuance of the writ of fieri facias.

(b) It should be noted, however, that the above article does not provide an exclusive method. *Cf.* Edwards v. Perrault, 170 La. 1011, 129 So. 619 (1930), holding that where the amount due on an alimony judgment has been admitted by the defendant in his answer to a proceeding for contempt for failure to pay, it is not necessary to require a separate proceeding to fix the amount due for purposes of execution, since the amount admitted is a sufficient basis for the issuance of the writ.

In Thornton v. Floyd, 229 La. 237, 85 So.2d 499 (1956), it was held that a subsequent judgment of divorce based upon a prior judgment of separation terminated a judgment of alimony pendente lite under the separation judgment, but did not affect the plaintiff's right to proceed by rule in order to obtain an executory judgment for the amount of alimony due prior to the divorce. There is no intention to change this rule, nor the principle that subsequent to a divorce judgment, the former wife may claim alimony only by a separate action. Player v. Player, 162 La. 229, 110 So. 332 (1926).

TITLE V

JUDICIAL EMANCIPATION

Art.
3991. Petition; court where proceeding brought.
3992. Consent of parent or tutor.
3993. Hearing; judgment.
3994. Expenses of proceeding.

INTRODUCTION

Of the three methods or types of emancipation, judicial emancipation is the only one requiring judicial proceedings. This Title, therefore, does not include any of the purely substantive provisions governing the other two types of emancipation.

Since there have been no particular problems in connection with emancipation proceedings, no substantial changes have been made in this Code.

Art. 3991. Petition; court where proceeding brought

The petition of a minor for judicial emancipation shall be filed in the district court in the parish of his domicile, and shall set forth the reasons why he desires to be emancipated and the value of his property, if any.

Source: C.C. Art. 385.

Cross Reference: Art. 44.

Comment

See Comments under Art. 3992, *infra*.

Art. 3992. Consent of parent or tutor

The petition of the minor shall be accompanied by a written consent to the emancipation and a specific declaration that the minor is fully capable of managing his own affairs, by the following:

(1) The father and mother if both are alive, or the survivor if one is dead. If either parent is absent or unable to act, the consent of the other parent alone is necessary. If the parents are judicially separated or divorced, and the custody of the minor has been awarded by judgment to one of the parents, the consent of that parent alone is necessary. A surviving parent is not required to qualify as natural tutor in order to give such consent, nor is the appointment of a special tutor necessary.

Art. 3992   JUDICIAL EMANCIPATION   Bk. 7

If the petition is filed on the ground of ill treatment, refusal to support, or corrupt examples, parental consent is unnecessary, but the parents or the surviving parent shall be cited to show cause why the minor should not be emancipated.

(2) The tutor of the minor if one has been appointed. If a tutor of his property and a tutor of his person have been appointed for the minor, the consent of both is necessary. If no tutor has been appointed, or if the tutor has died, resigned, or been removed, and there is no surviving parent who is able to act, a special tutor shall be appointed. If the tutor or special tutor refuses to give his consent, he may be cited to show cause why the minor should not be emancipated.

Source: C.C. Arts. 385, 387.

Comments to Articles 3991 and 3992

(a) Art. 3991 is a combination of the source articles. The provision requiring a proceeding contradictorily with the parents when the ground for the petition is cruel treatment is new.

(b) If both parents are alive and not judicially separated or divorced, both must consent. State ex rel. Billington v. Sacred Heart Orphan Asylum, 154 La. 883, 98 So. 406 (1923).

(c) A judgment of emancipation rendered without the consent of a tutor or special tutor when both parents are dead is a nullity. Gaston v. Rainach, 141 La. 162, 74 So. 890 (1917). The consent of the tutor is required even when a bank is tutor of the property and the mother is tutrix of the person. In re Webster's Tutorship, 188 La. 623, 177 So. 688 (1937). For the protection of the minor, this article requires the consent of the tutor of the property and of the tutor of the person.

Art. 3993.   Hearing; judgment

If the judge is satisfied that there is good reason for emancipation and that the minor is capable of managing his own affairs, he shall render a judgment of emancipation, which shall declare that the minor is fully emancipated and relieved of all the disabilities which attach to minority, with full power to perform all acts as fully as if he had reached the age of twenty-one.

Source: C.C. Art. 386.

Comments

(a) Art. 386 of the Civil Code provides no test for the court, but simply states that the judge, "after hearing the parties, shall render judgment in the premises." The above article provides a standard, and deletes the provision regarding "hearing," leaving it to the judge to determine in whatever manner he wishes whether the minor should be emancipated. This includes the power to emancipate a minor who may be temporarily absent, such as in the armed forces.

(b) The provision in Art. 386 of the Civil Code authorizing the judge to render the judgment in open court or in chambers, in term time or in vacation, has been deleted. But see Arts. 194 through 196, *supra*.

Art. 3994. Expenses of proceeding

Whether the minor succeeds or fails in obtaining a judgment of emancipation, all expenses which he may have incurred shall be paid out of his estate.

Source: C.C. Art. 388.

TITLE VI

TUTORSHIP

Chap.		Art.
1.	Court Where Proceedings are Brought	4031
2.	Appointment of Particular Tutors	4061
3.	Inventory of Minor's Property	4101
4.	Security of Tutor	4131
5.	Oath and Letters of Tutorship	4171
6.	Undertutor	4201
7.	Disqualification, Revocation of Appointment, Resignation, and Removal	4231
8.	General Functions, Powers and Duties of Tutor	4261
9.	Sale of Minor's Property	4301
	Sec.	
	1. General Dispositions	4301
	2. Public Sale	4321
	3. Private Sale	4341
	4. Adjudication to Parent	4361
10.	Accounting by Tutor	4391
11.	Ancillary Tutorship Procedure	4431
12.	Small Tutorships	4461

INTRODUCTION

A paramount consideration in the drafting of this Title was to preserve the traditional protection which the law affords minors. To this end, very little change has been made in the nature of the security to be furnished by the tutor. To further protect the minor's property, new articles have been included giving the court discretion in exceptional cases to require a bond even from a natural tutor or to appoint a separate tutor of the property.

There is a new chapter dealing with provisional tutors to take care of emergency situations which could arise pending the appointment of a tutor. There is also a new provision by which the procedure for legal and dative tutorship is combined, with no change of the substantive differences between the two types of tutorship.

The most significant change is the discarding of the "legal list" for investment of minor's funds in favor of the prudent man rule, which gives the tutor wide latitude in the choice of investments, subject to the approval of the court.

A number of Civil Code articles were encountered which have been made obsolete by the Married Women's Emancipation Act, R.S. 9:51, and by the statute abolishing family meetings, the former R.S. 9:651–9:653. These articles are not included. There are also several articles which apply both to tutorship and interdiction. These are included in this Title but will also remain applicable to interdiction by appropriate cross reference.

Where possible, an attempt has been made to make tutorship procedure similar to succession procedure.

CHAPTER 1. COURT WHERE PROCEEDINGS ARE BROUGHT

Art.
4031. Minor domiciled in the state.
4032. Minor not domiciled in the state.
4033. Petitions filed in two or more courts; stay of proceedings in second and subsequent courts; adoption of proceedings by first court.
4034. Proceedings subsequent to appointment of tutor.

Art. 4031. Minor domiciled in the state

A petition for the appointment of a tutor of a minor domiciled in the state shall be filed in the district court of the parish where the surviving parent is domiciled, if one parent is dead, or in the parish where the parent or other person awarded custody of the minor is domiciled, if the parents are divorced or judicially separated.

In all other cases, the petition shall be filed in the parish where the minor resides.

Source: Cf. C.P. Arts. 944–946; C.C. Art. 307.

Cross References: Arts. 44, 4433, 4502.

Comment

See Comments under Art. 4032, *infra*.

Art. 4032. Minor not domiciled in the state

If the minor is not domiciled in the state, a petition for the appointment of a tutor may be filed in any parish where:

(1) Immovable property of the minor is situated; or

(2) Movable property of the minor is situated, if he owns no immovable property in the state.

Source: Cf. C.P. Arts. 944–946; C.C. Art. 307.

Art. 4032

Comments to Arts. 4031 and 4032

(a) Because of the overlapping and somewhat confused articles of the 1870 Codes, it is difficult to state what the law actually is as to venue of tutorship proceedings. Arts. 944–946 of the Code of Practice fix the venue as the parents' domicile or that of the survivor; if both are dead, at their last domicile or that of the nearest relative; if the minor is a nonresident, in the parish where he has interests to assert or defend. Civil Code Art. 307 establishes the venue at the minor's domicile; or, if he is a nonresident, in the parish of his principal estate. It is preferable, in view of the provisions of Art. 39 of the Civil Code, under which the domicile of the minor is that of his father, mother, or tutor, to specifically provide the venue in each particular situation. The "principal property" concept of Art. 307 of the Civil Code was discarded as too indefinite and as likely to promote attacks on the jurisdiction of the court subsequent to the termination of the proceeding.

(b) See Comments under Arts. 10, 4433.

Art. 4033. Petitions filed in two or more courts; stay of proceedings in second and subsequent courts; adoption of proceedings by first court

If petitions for the appointment of a tutor are filed in two or more competent courts, the court in which a petition was first filed shall proceed to a determination of the issues and the proceedings in the other courts shall be stayed. However, the first court may adopt as its own any of the proceedings taken in the other courts.

Source: New.

Comment

This article is similar to Art. 2812, *supra*. It is necessary in view of the possibility that proceedings may be brought in more than one court, each of which would be a proper court under Art. 4032, *supra*

Art. 4034. Proceedings subsequent to appointment of tutor

Proceedings relative to a tutorship subsequent to the appointment of a tutor shall be brought in the parish of his domicile if he is living at the time or, if he is dead, in the parish where he was last domiciled.

If the proceedings are brought in a court other than the one which appointed the tutor, the court may require the filing of certified copies of all or any part of the proceedings in the other court.

Source: New; cf. Comment following.

Comment

This article codifies the jurisprudential rule announced in State v. Judge, 2 Rob. 418 (La.1842); Boissac v. Petit, 14 La.Ann. 565 (1859); and Fraser v. Zylicz, 29 La.Ann. 534 (1877).

CHAPTER 2. APPOINTMENT OF PARTICULAR TUTORS

Art.
4061. Natural tutor; general obligations.
4062. Tutorship by will.
4063. Legal tutor.
4064. Dative tutor.
4065. Legal or dative tutor; petition for appointment; publication of notice.
4066. Opposition to application of legal or dative tutor.
4067. Appointment of legal or dative tutor.
4068. Appeal from judgment confirming, appointing, or removing tutor or undertutor; effect.
4069. Separate tutor of property.
4070. Provisional tutor.
4071. Security, oath, and tenure of provisional tutor.
4072. Inventory on appointment of provisional tutor.
4073. Functions, duties, and authority of provisional tutor.

Art. 4061. Natural tutor; general obligations

Before a natural tutor enters upon the performance of his official duties, he must take an oath to discharge faithfully the duties of his office, cause an inventory to be taken, and cause a legal mortgage in favor of the minor to be inscribed, or furnish security, in the manner provided by law.

Source: C.P. Arts. 949, 950; C.C. Art. 251.

Comments

(a) Although the surviving parent has an absolute right to be appointed natural tutor, he must qualify as such before he can exercise the authority conferred on tutors. This principle was first decided over a hundred years ago and has been followed consistently. See Mitchell v. Cooley, 12 Rob. 636 (La.1846).

(b) Although all of the obligations enumerated above are set forth in detail in other articles, it was considered advisable to specify them as is done in Art. 251 of the Civil Code.

Art. 4062. Tutorship by will

The court shall appoint as tutor the person nominated as such in a testament or an authentic act, upon his furnishing security and taking an oath, as provided in Articles 4131 and 4171, unless he is disqualified or unless for some other reason the court determines that the appointment would not be for the best interest of the minor.

Source: C.C. Art. 260.

Comments

(a) Art. 956 of the Code of Practice requires the parent's nominee to attach to his petition for appointment a copy of the will. This is an unnecessary requirement, for any proof of the nomination should suffice.

(b) For the grounds for disqualification, see Art. 4231, *infra*.

Art. 4063. Legal tutor

The court shall appoint a legal tutor under the circumstances and according to the rules for priority provided by law, and in the manner provided in Articles 4065 through 4068.

Source: New; cf. C.C. Art. 263.

Comment

The rules of priority are found in Arts. 263 *et seq.* of the Civil Code, which provide for the order of preference in the appointment of the tutor. This article regulates only the procedure governing the application and the appointment of the tutor.

Art. 4064. Dative tutor

The court shall appoint a dative tutor under the circumstances provided by law and in the manner provided in Articles 4065 through 4068.

Source: C.P. Art. 957.

Comments

(a) The circumstances under which dative tutors may be appointed are governed by the substantive provisions of Civil Code Art. 270.

(b) There is no time limit which must elapse before an application may be filed for appointment as dative tutor. As long as no application for legal tutorship is pending, the application for dative tutorship may be filed. Anyone who desires appointment as legal tutor may file an opposition to the appointment of a dative tutor.

(c) Although the Civil Code treats legal and dative tutorship in separate sections, for procedural purposes the two are combined in this Code and the provisions relative to notice, opposition, and appointment are applicable to both legal and dative proceedings.

(d) There is apparently no reported decision involving the question as to whether or when the dative tutor must furnish security. *Cf.* Civil Code Art. 271 and Art. 957, Code of Practice of 1870. This Code requires a bond from all dative tutors except where the assets under administration amount to less than $2,000. See Art. 4463, *infra*.

Art. 4065. Legal or dative tutor; petition for appointment; publication of notice

When a petition for appointment as legal or dative tutor is filed, an affidavit by the applicant listing the ascendants of the minor who are alive and who reside in the state shall be annexed to the petition. A copy of the petition for appointment shall be served on each such ascendant in the manner provided for service of citation.

Notice of the application shall be published once in the parish where the petition was filed, in the manner provided by law.

Source: New; cf. C.P. Arts. 952, 953.

Cross References: Arts. 4063, 4065, 4067.

Comments

(a) The source articles require the applicant to state under oath the names of all other relatives who are in an equal or nearer degree than the applicant and require them to be cited. This procedure is too expensive and also provides too much opportunity for fatal error, for a failure to serve one of a number of relatives would probably be a ground for annulling the appointment. The difficulty in approving title to property sold by a dative or legal tutor is obvious.

The above article adopts a middle approach between the requirement of service and that of publication. Ascendants, of course, are the most likely relatives to oppose an application for appointment and, therefore, service on them is required.

(b) The manner in which this notice must be published is provided in R.S. 43:203.

Art. 4066. Opposition to application of legal or dative tutor

An opposition to an application for appointment as legal or dative tutor may be filed at any time prior to the appointment, as provided

Art. 4066

in Article 4067. The opposition shall comply with Article 2972, and shall allege the prior right of the opponent to the appointment, or the grounds upon which it is claimed the applicant is disqualified. If the opposition is based on a prior right to the appointment, the opponent shall pray that he be appointed tutor.

Source: New; cf. C.P. Art. 954.

Cross References: Arts. 4063, 4064.

Comments

(a) This article and Art. 4067, *infra*, combine the procedure adopted with respect to an opposition to an application for appointment as administrator in Arts. 3091 through 3095, *supra*, and that provided in the Code of Practice for tutorship.

The above article is similar to Art. 3095, *supra*, dealing with an opposition to an application for appointment as administrator.

(b) Art. 4231, *infra*, sets forth the grounds for disqualification.

Art. 4067. Appointment of legal or dative tutor

At any time after the expiration of ten days from service or publication as provided in Article 4065, whichever period is longer, if no opposition has been filed, the court shall appoint the applicant, unless he is disqualified under Article 4231.

If an opposition has been filed, it shall be tried in a summary manner. After the trial, the court shall appoint as tutor the qualified applicant having the highest priority of appointment. If two or more applicants have the same priority, the court shall appoint the one best qualified, personally, and by training and experience, to serve as tutor.

Source: New; cf. C.P. Art. 955.

Cross References: Arts. 4063, 4064, 4066.

Comments

The only test given by the Louisiana law for the appointment of a tutor other than the priority arising from relationship is included in Art. 955 of the Code of Practice, which provides that the judge shall appoint the person "he thinks to have the best right."

The test provided in the above article for selecting among applicants with equal priority is taken largely from Art. 3098, *supra*.

Art. 4068. Appeal from judgment confirming, appointing, or removing tutor or undertutor; effect

An appeal from a judgment confirming, appointing, or removing a tutor or an undertutor can only be taken within thirty days from the applicable date provided in Article 2087(1)–(3).

Such judgment shall not be suspended during the pendency of an appeal. The acts of a tutor or of an undertutor shall not be invalidated by the annulment of his appointment on appeal.

Source: C.C. Art. 307; C.P. Arts. 580, 1059.

Cross References: Arts. 4063, 4064.

Comments

(a) Art. 2087, *supra*, provides that an appeal can be taken within ninety days after the dates set forth in paragraphs (1), (2), and (3). This article provides an exception to the general rule, employing the substance of Art. 307, Civil Code, and limiting appeals to thirty days in divorce and separation cases. See Art. 3942, *supra*.

(b) The source articles do not apply specifically to undertutors, but the principle involved is applicable. State v. Judge, 17 La. 432 (1841); Succession of Menendez, 29 La.Ann. 408 (1877). The above article also makes the limitation of thirty days applicable to appeals from judgments of removal and to all judgments relating to undertutors.

(c) For a similar provision relating to the acts of a succession representative whose appointment is annulled on appeal, see Art. 2974, *supra*.

Art. 4069. Separate tutor of property

In exceptional cases and for good cause shown, the court may appoint a bank as tutor of the property of the minor pursuant to the provisions of R.S. 6:322(6). This appointment may be made upon the court's own motion or upon motion of the tutor or other person entitled to the tutorship if no tutor has been previously appointed, or upon motion of any interested person after a contradictory hearing with the tutor or person entitled to the tutorship.

In such cases, a tutor previously appointed shall continue as tutor of the person to whom the custody and care of the minor shall be entrusted. If no tutor has been appointed at the time of the appointment of the bank, the court shall appoint a tutor of the person of the minor.

Source: New; cf. R.S. 6:322(6).

Cross Reference: Art. 4550.

Art. 4069

Comments

(a) There has been statutory authority for a bank to act with consent of all concerned since 1902. See R.S. 6:322(6).

This article changes the law by giving the court the right in exceptional cases to appoint a bank as tutor of the property even though the person otherwise entitled to the tutorship objects. The appointment of a bank does not, however, take the care and custody of the minor from the person entitled to it by law.

(b) This article is not restricted to the initial appointment of a tutor. The court may appoint a bank as tutor of the property at any time provided there is sufficient showing of exceptional circumstances.

(c) All articles in this Title dealing with the care of the minor's person apply to the custodian of the person; whereas those dealing with the administration of property apply to the tutor of the property.

Art. 4070. Provisional tutor

On the application of an interested person or on its own motion, pending the appointment of a tutor, the court may appoint a qualified person as provisional tutor of a minor, if such appointment is necessary for the welfare of the minor or for the preservation of his property.

Source: New.

Comments

(a) Heretofore, there has been no statutory basis in Louisiana for the appointment of a temporary tutor, nor any reported decision on the subject. However, Art. 335 of the Civil Code permits an applicant for the tutorship to preserve the minor's property pending the issuance of letters "in cases which admit of no delay."

(b) This article is similar to Art. 3111, *supra*, dealing with provisional administrators.

(c) The article applies not only pending the appointment of a tutor, but also pending the appointment of a successor in the event of a vacancy. There is no corresponding provision for the appointment of a provisional undertutor.

Art. 4071. Security, oath, and tenure of provisional tutor

A provisional tutor shall take an oath to discharge faithfully the duties of his office and shall furnish security as provided in Article

4132 for the faithful performance of his duties, in an amount determined by the court as adequate for the protection of the minor.

A provisional tutor shall continue in office until his appointment is terminated by the court or until a tutor has been qualified.

Source: New.

Comment

The basis for the fixing of the bond of a provisional tutor is the same as that approved for a provisional administrator's bond, Art. 3152, *supra*. Since no inventory will have been taken at this stage of the proceeding, the amount of the bond is left to the court's discretion.

Art. 4072. Inventory on appointment of provisional tutor

When the court appoints a provisional tutor, it shall order the taking of an inventory of the minor's property as provided in Articles 4101 and 4102.

Source: New.

Art. 4073. Functions, duties, and authority of provisional tutor

The functions of a provisional tutor are limited to the care of the person of the minor and the preservation of his rights and property. In the performance of his functions, a provisional tutor has the same authority, and is subject to the same duties and obligations, as a tutor.

Under specific authority of the court which appointed him, a provisional tutor may:

(1) Institute and prosecute an action to enforce judicially a right of the minor; and

(2) Operate a business belonging to the minor.

A provisional tutor shall file an account upon the termination of his authority.

Source: New.

Comments

(a) This article is based partly upon Art. 3112, *supra*, dealing with provisional administrators. The provisional tutor's job is to keep matters in the status quo pending the appointment and qualification of a permanent tutor.

(b) A provisional tutor is a tutor within the intendment of Art. 683, *supra*.

CHAPTER 3. INVENTORY OF MINOR'S PROPERTY

Art.
4101. Inventory and appraisement.
4102. Procedure for inventory; procès verbal; return.

Art. 4101. Inventory and appraisement

When any person applies to be appointed as tutor, the court shall order the taking of an inventory and an appraisal of the minor's property, which shall be begun not later than ten days after the order is signed. The court shall appoint a notary of each parish in which property of the minor has a situs to take the inventory of such property in that parish.

Source: C.C. Art. 316.

Cross Reference: Art. 4072.

Comment

Civil Code Art. 316 is silent on the question of whether a separate notary must be appointed for each parish, and the procedure in this respect varies in different parts of the state. This article follows the rule approved in connection with succession inventories. See Art. 3131, *supra*.

Art. 4102. Procedure for inventory; procès verbal; return

In so far as applicable, Articles 3131 through 3134 shall govern the procedure for the taking of the inventory, procès verbal, and the return and effect of the procès verbal.

Source: New.

Cross Reference: Art. 4072.

Comment

This article incorporates by reference all provisions adopted concerning succession inventories except the authority to substitute a sworn, descriptive list for the inventory. In view of the minor's inability to protect himself, and because the inventory serves as a basis for the liability of the tutor at the end of the tutorship, a formal inventory and appraisal is required in all cases, except where the small amount of the minor's property brings the proceeding within the provisions of Arts. 4461 through 4464, *infra*.

CHAPTER 4. SECURITY OF TUTOR

Art.
4131. Amount.
4132. Nature of security.
4133. Special mortgage instead of bond.
4134. Natural tutor; bond; recordation of certificate of inventory.
4135. Security instead of legal mortgage.
4136. Substitution of one kind of security for another.

Art. 4131. Amount

The person appointed tutor, except the natural tutor, shall furnish security for the faithful performance of his duties in an amount equal to the total value of the minor's movable property as shown by the inventory, plus such additional sum as the court may consider sufficient to cover any loss or damage which may be caused by the bad administration of the tutor.

Upon proper showing that the security required is substantially in excess of that needed for the protection of the minor, the court may fix the security at any amount which it considers sufficient for the protection of the minor.

The court may order the security to be increased or diminished at any time as the movable property may increase or diminish in value or for other circumstances which the court may consider proper.

Source: Cf. C.C. Arts. 317, 318.

Cross References: Arts. 4062, 4132, 4133, 4135.

Comment

This article retains the basic test for the amount of bond, but gives the court discretion in exceptional cases to set a lower bond. Where there are extensive holdings in stocks and bonds, and the cost of a bond would be considerable, this will be particularly useful.

Art. 4132. Nature of security

The security required by Article 4131 shall be in the form of a bond, to be approved by the court, and secured by:

(1) A surety company authorized to do business in this state; or

(2) Bonds of this state or of any political subdivision or any municipality thereof, or of the United States, or shares of any building or loan or homestead association domiciled in this state and insured

by an agency of the United States, in an amount at par value equal at least to the amount of the security required; or

(3) No less than two personal sureties signing in solido, each having unencumbered property in an amount amply sufficient to secure the amount of the bond.

Bonds or homestead shares posted as security shall be deposited for safekeeping with the clerk of court or in a bank or other recognized depositary as directed by the court, and may not be withdrawn without an order of court. The form of the act under which such bonds or shares are given in security shall be substantially that of a bond, in which the principal binds himself and declares that instead of furnishing sureties, he deposits, as directed by the court, such bonds or shares to be subject to any claim the minor may have.

Insured homestead shares may not be furnished as security in excess of the amount insured.

The bond shall not be recorded in the mortgage records nor operate as a mortgage.

Source: Former R.S. 9:801, 9:802.

Cross References: Arts. 4072, 4133, 4135, 4363.

Comments

(a) The authority for furnishing homestead shares as security is new. Such shares have been included in the "legal list" for minor's investments since 1940. See Art. 348 of the Civil Code.

(b) Art. 319 of the Civil Code requires a recordation of a personal surety bond, which creates a general mortgage. R.S. 9:801 provides that the bond need not be recorded, but R.S. 9:802 permits personal sureties only for natural tutors. The above article permits any tutor to furnish the dual personal surety, and does away with recordation entirely.

Art. 4133. Special mortgage instead of bond

Instead of the security required by Articles 4131 and 4132, the tutor may furnish a special mortgage in favor of the minor on immovable property otherwise unencumbered. The mortgage shall be for the same amount as the security required by Article 4131 and shall be approved by the court as provided in Article 4271.

The costs occasioned by the furnishing of a special mortgage shall be borne by the tutor.

Source: C.C. Arts. 320, 325, 329, 331.

Cross References: Arts. 4135, 4363.

Comments

(a) The above article supersedes Arts. 320, 325, 326, 330, 331, and 332 of the Civil Code.

(b) Art. 331 of the Civil Code required the judge to appoint appraisers to value the property to be mortgaged. The court has the right under this Code to appoint experts to determine any question before it, but should not be compelled to do so.

Art. 4134. Natural tutor; bond; recordation of certificate of inventory

Except as provided in Article 4135, a natural tutor shall not be required to furnish bond, but shall record in the mortgage records of the parish of his domicile a certificate of the clerk setting forth the total value of the minor's property according to the inventory filed in the tutorship proceeding. A certificate of the recorder of mortgages setting forth the recordation of the clerk's certificate shall be filed in the tutorship proceedings before the tutor is appointed or letters of tutorship are issued.

Within thirty days after his appointment, the natural tutor shall cause the clerk's certificate to be recorded in the mortgage records of every other parish in the state in which he owns immovable property.

The recordation operates as a legal mortgage in favor of the minor on all the immovable property of the tutor situated within any parish where recorded.

Source: C.C. Arts. 321–323.

Cross References: Arts. 4135, 4204.

Comment

This article codifies the Louisiana law, with some stylistic changes. However, the exception provided in Art. 4135, *infra*, is new.

Art. 4135. Security instead of legal mortgage

Instead of the legal mortgage provided in Article 4134, a natural tutor may furnish bond in the amount provided by Article 4131 and of the nature provided by Article 4132, or a special mortgage as provided in Article 4133.

If the court determines that the legal mortgage will not be sufficient protection for the minor, and that substantial loss to the minor may result unless a bond is furnished, the court may order that the natural tutor furnish a bond or a special mortgage instead of the legal mortgage.

Source: C.C. Art. 320; former R.S. 9:802; cf. Comments following.

Comments

(a) The first paragraph retains the Louisiana law.

(b) The second paragraph is entirely new and represents a basic change in the Louisiana law in that it gives the court discretion to require the natural tutor to furnish bond in the unusual cases where bond is indicated.

Art. 4136. Substitution of one kind of security for another

Any tutor who desires to give bond or security and thus release from an existing general or special mortgage the whole or a portion of the property covered thereby may do so with the approval of the court as provided in Article 4271, provided the bond or security tendered fully protects the minor.

Any of the securities enumerated in Articles 4132 and 4133 may be substituted at any time either in whole or in part for any other kind, at the option of the tutor, and with the approval of the court as provided in Article 4271, which shall enter the necessary orders to render the substitutions effective. If other security has been furnished instead of a general mortgage, the tutor may not revert to a general mortgage.

When a bond or security is substituted only in part for the general or special mortgage, the amount thereof may be proportionately smaller based on the value of the property to be released from mortgage.

Source: Former R.S. 9:803, 9:804.

Comments

(a) This article makes no substantial change in the law. The procedure for substituting securities requires either the concurrence of the undertutor or a rule against him.

(b) Under the last sentence of the second paragraph of this article, a tutor cannot substitute other security for a general mortgage, dispose of all or a portion of his property, and then release the other security by reverting to a general mortgage. If the tutor in such a situation owns property, he can furnish a special mortgage and obtain the release of the other security.

CHAPTER 5. OATH AND LETTERS OF TUTORSHIP

Art.
4171. Oath.
4172. Issuance of letters.

Art. 4171. Oath

Before the person appointed as tutor enters upon the performance of his official duties, he must take an oath to discharge faithfully the duties of his office. A natural tutor shall include in his oath a list of the parishes in which he owns immovable property.

Source: C.C. Art. 334.

Cross Reference: Art. 4062.

Comments

(a) The first sentence of this article parallels Art. 3157, *supra*, dealing with the oath of a succession representative.

(b) The list of parishes which must be included in the oath of the natural tutor is to serve as the basis for the recordation of the minor's legal mortgage which is required only of the natural tutor under Arts. 4134 and 4135, *supra*.

Art. 4172. Issuance of letters

After the person appointed as tutor has qualified by furnishing the security required of him by law, and by taking his oath of office, the clerk shall issue to him letters of tutorship.

These letters, issued in the name and under the seal of the court, evidence the appointment of the tutor, his qualification, and his compliance with all requirements of law relating thereto.

Source: C.C. Art. 335.

Comment

Without making any substantial change in the law, this article closely parallels Art. 3159, *supra*, dealing with the issuance of letters to a succession representative.

CHAPTER 6. UNDERTUTOR

Art.
4201. Appointment; oath.
4202. General duties of undertutor.
4203. Compelling tutor to account.
4204. Security of tutor, undertutor's duty regarding sufficiency.
4205. Vacancy in tutorship, duty of undertutor.
4206. Termination of duties.

Art. 4201. Appointment; oath

At the time judgment is rendered appointing a tutor, the court shall also appoint a responsible person as undertutor.

Before entering upon the performance of his official duties, the undertutor must take an oath to discharge faithfully the duties of his office.

Source: C.C. Arts. 273, 274.

Cross Reference: Art. 4553.

Comments

(a) The Civil Code does not prescribe any qualifications for the undertutor. The above article provides for the appointment of a "responsible person" as undertutor whose office differs from that of the tutor in that it is always dative, compulsory to no one, and there are no preferences by reason of relationship. See State v. Judge, 2 Rob. 418 (La.1842); Undertutor of Walker, 14 La.Ann. 631 (1859).

(b) Civil Code Art. 273 indicates that the appointment of an undertutor should be made "at the time the letters of tutorship are certified for the tutor." In practice, the appointment is made at the same time as the appointment of the tutor, and this is the procedure contemplated by the above article.

(c) Under Louisiana law, an undertutor has never been required to furnish bond. No change is made in this respect.

Art. 4202. General duties of undertutor

The undertutor shall express his concurrence or nonconcurrence in action suggested by the tutor to the court, as set forth in Article 4271, and shall act for the minor whenever the minor's interest is opposed to that of the tutor.

Source: C.C. Art. 275; cf. Comments following.

Cross Reference: Art. 4553.

Comments

(a) This article sets forth the general rule that the undertutor is the "watch dog" for the minor. The last sentence is nearly identical to Civil Code Art. 275, which has been in use since 1808.

(b) See Art. 4234, *infra*, and Comments thereunder.

Art. 4203. Compelling tutor to account

The undertutor shall apply to the court for an order compelling the tutor to file an account whenever the tutor has failed to file his annual account or at any other time when the circumstances indicate that an account should be filed.

Source: C.C. Art. 275; C.P. Art. 999.

Cross Reference: Art. 4553.

Comment

Because one of the tutor's most important duties is to file accounts, the duty of the undertutor to compel the tutor to do so is set forth specifically. In Art. 4391, *infra*, the court is empowered to order an account at any time, and to implement it this article makes it the duty of the undertutor to cause an order to issue whenever circumstances indicate that an account is necessary.

Art. 4204. Security of tutor, undertutor's duty regarding sufficiency

The undertutor shall:

(1) Cause the natural tutor to record the legal mortgage in favor of the minor as provided in Article 4134;

(2) Require the tutor to furnish evidence that he has a valid and merchantable title to property offered as security under a special mortgage instead of bond and that the value of the property is at least equal to the amount of security required; otherwise the undertutor shall oppose the tutor's application to furnish a special mortgage; and

(3) Apply to the court for an order compelling the tutor to furnish additional security whenever the security has become insufficient for any reason.

Source: C.C. Arts. 278, 324, 328.

Cross Reference: Art. 4553.

Comments

(a) This article combines the three different Civil Code source provisions dealing with duties of the undertutor relative to the security furnished by the tutor.

(b) Civil Code Art. 328 makes it the undertutor's duty to apply for a court order compelling the tutor to furnish additional security whenever the value of the property specially mortgaged diminishes in value. This provision has been expanded to impose the same duty upon the undertutor whenever the security has become insufficient for any reason.

Art. 4205. Vacancy in tutorship, duty of undertutor

The tutorship does not devolve upon the undertutor when it is vacant. If a vacancy occurs, the undertutor shall apply to the court for the appointment of a new tutor.

Source: C.C. Art. 279.

Cross Reference: Art. 4553.

Comment

The above article makes no change in the law.

Art. 4206. Termination of duties

The undertutor is relieved of further duty and authority as undertutor when the minor reaches majority or is fully emancipated. However, his liability for acts prior thereto shall not be affected.

Source: C.C. Art. 280.

Cross Reference: Art. 4553.

Comments

(a) Because Art. 280 is substantive, it is retained in the Civil Code, even though the above article covers the same subject matter. This article is similar to Art. 3392, *supra*, dealing with the effect of a judgment discharging the succession representative. Of course, any liability of the undertutor for actions prior to the termination of his authority will not be affected.

(b) The termination of the undertutor's duty is not related exactly to the discharge of the tutor, whose responsibility continues until the approval of his final account.

(c) Art. 999 of the Code of Practice provides that, even though emancipated, the minor shall be assisted by the undertutor in making demand for an accounting, unless he is married. No similar provision is included in this Code. Once a minor is fully emancipated, the undertutor's task ceases and the minor deals directly with the tutor.

CHAPTER 7. DISQUALIFICATION, REVOCATION OF APPOINTMENT, RESIGNATION, AND REMOVAL

Art.
4231. Disqualification of tutor.
4232. Revocation of appointment; extension of time to qualify.
4233. Resignation of tutor.
4234. Removal of tutor.
4235. Authority and liability of tutor after resignation or removal.

Art.
4236. Undertutor, grounds for disqualification, revocation, or removal.
4237. Appointment of successor tutor or undertutor.
4238. Heirs of tutor; responsibility.

Art. 4231. Disqualification of tutor

No person may be appointed tutor who is:

(1) Under twenty-one years of age;

(2) Interdicted, or who, on contradictory hearing, is proved to be mentally incompetent;

(3) A convicted felon, under the laws of the United States or of any state or territory thereof;

(4) Indebted to the minor, unless he discharges the debt prior to the appointment;

(5) An adverse party to a suit to which the minor is a party; or

(6) A person who, on contradictory hearing, is proved to be incapable of performing the duties of the office, or to be otherwise unfit for appointment because of his physical or mental condition or bad moral character.

The provisions of paragraphs (1), (4), and (5) do not apply to the parent of the minor.

Source: C.C. Arts. 302, 303.

Cross References: Arts. 4236, 4502.

Comments

(a) This article preserves much of the Louisiana law, with stylistic changes to conform to Art. 3097, *supra*. Paragraph (6), which is based largely on the successions article, is new.

(b) For obvious reasons, the provision of Art. 302 of the Civil Code disqualifying women from serving as tutors, except for the mother and grandmother of the minor, has not been included. See R.S. 9:51.

(c) The last paragraph of this article makes inapplicable to the parent the grounds enumerated in paragraphs (1), (4), and (5). Civil Code Art. 302(1) provides that minors, except the father and mother, cannot be tutors. Although Art. 302(6) of the Civil Code provides that a person who is an adverse party to a suit in which the minor is interested cannot be his tutor, this prohibition does not apply to the father. In re Rupp, 171 La. 866, 132 So. 405 (1931). On the basis of this case, a parent should not be disqualified simply because he is an adverse party to a suit to which the minor is a party or because he is indebted to the minor.

(d) For the provisions imposing the duty to accept and for the causes which excuse a person from the obligation of accepting the tutorship, see Civil Code Arts. 292 *et seq.*

(e) See Comments under Arts. 4062, 4066, *supra,* and Arts. 4234, 4392, *infra.*

Art. 4232. Revocation of appointment; extension of time to qualify

If a person who is not a parent of the minor is appointed tutor and fails to qualify for the office within ten days from his appointment, on its own motion or on motion of any interested person, the court may revoke the appointment and appoint another qualified person to the office forthwith.

The delay allowed in this article for qualification may be extended by the court for good cause shown.

Source: New.

Cross Reference: Art. 4236.

Comments

(a) Heretofore, there was apparently no procedure for revocation of the appointment of a tutor for failure to qualify, although Art. 303 of the Civil Code provides that a person who has neglected to have an inventory taken timely is "excluded from the tutorship." The above article is based upon the parallel provisions of Art. 3181, *supra.*

(b) In most instances, particularly with respect to legal tutors, the court would allow a reasonable additional delay. The parents of the minor have been excepted from the application of the above article. Otherwise, a father by not complying with the required formalities could excuse himself from the obligation of serving as tutor to his own children.

(c) See Comments under Art. 4234, *infra.*

Art. 4233. Resignation of tutor

A tutor other than the father of the minor may resign when authorized by the court under Article 4271:

(1) If subsequent to his appointment as tutor he has been invested with an office or engaged in a service or occupation which excuses him from the obligation of serving as tutor;

(2) If he has reached the age of seventy years;

(3) If because of infirmity he has become incapable of discharging the duties of his office; or

(4) For any other reason which the court in its discretion may deem sufficient.

The resignation by a tutor shall become effective when a successor is appointed, as provided in Article 4237, and when his final account has been filed and homologated.

Source: C.C. Arts. 294, 296, 297; cf. Comments following.

Comments

(a) Civil Code Arts. 294, 296, and 297 specify the only grounds for resignation of a tutor. These grounds are covered by paragraphs (1), (2), and (3) of the above article. Under Civil Code Art. 301 these reasons do not apply to the father, who may not resign at all. See Succession of Watt, 111 La. 937, 36 So. 31 (1903). See, also, In re Minors Long, 118 La. 689, 43 So. 279 (1907), holding that the mother cannot resign once she is appointed, although apparently she did not allege one of the grounds specified in the Code.

(b) The fourth paragraph gives the court discretion to accept any excuse deemed sufficient. A tutor who is unwilling to continue in office is not likely to afford the best care to the minor or his property. Cf. Model Probate Code, § 217.

(c) Art. 4271, *infra*, requires concurrence of the undertutor or a contradictory proceeding against him.

(d) See Comments under Art. 4231, *supra*.

Art. 4234.   Removal of tutor

The court may remove any tutor who is or has become disqualified, has left the state permanently, has become incapable of discharging the duties of his office, has mismanaged the minor's property, or has failed to perform any duty imposed by law or by order of court.

The court on its own motion may order, and on motion of any interested party shall order, the tutor to show cause why he should not be removed from office. The removal of a tutor from office does not invalidate any of his official acts performed prior to his removal.

Source: C.C. Arts. 303, 304; cf. Comments following.

Cross Reference: Art. 4236.

Comments

(a) This article effects two important procedural changes which are beneficial to a minor. Under Art. 1017 of the Code of Practice a tutor could be removed only in an ordinary action commenced by a petition and citation. Castille v. Gallagher, 206 La. 904, 20 So.2d 175 (1944). This article permits more expeditious action

Art. 4234

by contradictory motion. It also permits the proceeding to be instituted by the court on its own motion or by any interested person. Code of Practice Art. 1016 provided that the judge, if he considered that probable cause existed, should direct the undertutor to commence an action for removal or appoint a curator ad hoc to do so. Pursuant to these provisions, the supreme court has held that an undertutor cannot commence a suit for removal without permission from the court, Lillard v. Kemp, 9 Rob. 113 (La. 1844); and that a grandparent cannot sue for removal under any circumstances, Succession of Desina, 135 La. 402, 65 So. 556 (1914).

(b) Arts. 3069 and 3070 of the Civil Code, under which the surety on the bond of an administrator, executor, curator, or tutor, upon proof of mismanagement by the principal, may obtain a court order requiring the principal to furnish new security, in default of which the principal is removed, are not necessary in view of this article, giving the surety the right to file a rule to remove the principal.

(c) Unlike Art. 304 of the Civil Code, this article does not include insolvency per se as a ground for removal, although the tutor may be removed if, because of his insolvency, the court considers him unfit to serve. See Ozanne v. Delile, 5 Mart.(N.S.) 21 (La.1826).

(d) Art. 305 of the Civil Code provides that no cause of exclusion or removal is applicable to the father except: (1) unfaithfulness of his administration; (2) notoriously bad conduct; (3) abandonment of his children and failure to support and maintain them for more than one year. There are three situations to be considered: (1) disqualification under Art. 4231, *supra*; (2) revocation under Art. 4232, *supra*; and (3) removal under the above article. In so far as disqualification is concerned, all of the grounds in Art. 4231 necessarily apply to the father, except those where specific exception is made. As to revocation, the court would be compelled to revoke the appointment of a father as tutor if he refused to take the proper steps to qualify. Finally, the various grounds for removal in the above article are also applicable to the father, particularly since the existence of such a ground does not make it mandatory for the court to remove the tutor.

(e) This article does not affect the principle that action by a tutor cannot be collaterally attacked.

(f) See Comments under Art. 4202, *supra*, and Art. 4273, *infra*.

Art. 4235. Authority and liability of tutor after resignation or removal

A tutor who has resigned or has been removed shall have no further authority as such, and no further duty except as provided by

Article 4392. However, his liability for acts prior to his resignation or removal shall not be affected thereby.

Source: New.

Comment

This article strips the tutor of further authority after resignation or removal and of further duty except to file an account. See Art. 4392, *infra*.

Art. 4236. Undertutor, grounds for disqualification, revocation, or removal

The grounds for disqualification, revocation, and removal provided in Articles 4231, 4232, and 4234, other than indebtedness to the minor, apply also to an undertutor.

An undertutor may resign at any time with the approval of the court, but the resignation shall not be effective until a successor has been appointed and qualified.

Source: C.C. Art. 306.

Comment

An undertutor may resign without having to allege and prove any excuse. In re Walker, 14 La.Ann. 631 (1859).

Art. 4237. Appointment of successor tutor or undertutor

When a tutor or undertutor dies, is removed, or resigns, another tutor or undertutor shall be appointed in his place in the manner provided for an original appointment.

Source: C.C. Art. 314; cf. Comment following.

Comment

Art. 314 of the Civil Code covers the death of a tutor and indefinite absence from the state. It has been expanded to cover removal and resignation also.

Art. 4238. Heirs of tutor; responsibility

Tutorship is a personal trust, which does not descend to the heirs of the tutor upon his death. However, the representative of the tutor's succession or the major heirs who have accepted his succession are responsible for the administration of the minor's property until another tutor has been appointed.

Source: C.C. Art. 315.

Art. 4238 TUTORSHIP Bk. 7

Comment

The source article provides that the major heirs of the tutor are responsible during the interim until a successor tutor is appointed. The above article has a more realistic approach, *i. e.*, to hold responsible the tutor's succession representative or his major heirs who have accepted his succession. There may be some major heirs, for example, who may reside a great distance away and who do not even know the tutor who has died.

CHAPTER 8. GENERAL FUNCTIONS, POWERS, AND DUTIES OF TUTOR

Art.
4261. Care of person of minor; expenses.
4262. Administration of minor's property.
4263. Contracts between tutor and minor.
4264. Tutor's administration in his own name; procedural rights.
4265. Compromise and modification of obligations.
4266. Continuation of business.
4267. Loans to tutor for specific purposes; authority to mortgage and pledge minor's property.
4268. Lease of minor's property; mineral contracts.
4269. Investment and management of minor's property.
4270. Procedure for investing funds.
4271. Court approval of action affecting minor's interest.
4272. Court approval of payments to minor.
4273. Temporary absence; appointment of agent.
4274. Compensation of tutor.
4275. Donations to or by minor.

Art. 4261. Care of person of minor; expenses

The tutor shall have custody of and shall care for the person of the minor. He shall see that the minor is properly reared and educated in accordance with his station in life.

The expenses for the support and education of the minor should not exceed the revenue from the minor's property. However, if the revenue is insufficient to support the minor properly or to procure him an education, with the approval of the court as provided in Article 4271, the tutor may expend the minor's capital for these purposes.

Source: C.C. Arts. 337, 350.

Art. 4262. Administration of minor's property

The tutor shall take possession of, preserve, and administer the minor's property. He shall enforce all obligations in favor of the minor and shall represent him in all civil matters. He shall act at all times as a prudent administrator, and shall be personally responsible for all damages resulting from his failure so to act.

Source: C.C. Art. 337; cf. Comments following.

Comments

(a) There is no specific recognition in the Code of Practice or Civil Code of the tutor's duty to take possession of the minor's property, but it can be inferred from several articles. The language in the above article concerning responsibility for damages is taken partly from the parallel provisions in Art. 3191, *supra*. Arts. 3211 and 3221, *supra*, cover the administrator's obligation to collect, preserve, and manage the property of a succession.

(b) The term "obligations" means those which are enforceable. The tutor, for example, has no duty to enforce a debt against a bankrupt debtor. See Art. 3211, *supra*.

(c) Civil Code Art. 355 provides that the tutor must insure all "houses or other buildings" owned by the minor. No similar provision has been included since the duty to insure is covered by the prudent administrator concept.

Art. 4263. Contracts between tutor and minor

A tutor cannot in his personal capacity or as representative for any other person make any contracts with the minor. He cannot acquire any property of the minor, or interest therein, personally or by means of a third person, except as otherwise provided by law.

Contracts prohibited by this article shall be null, and the tutor shall be liable to the minor for damages resulting therefrom.

Source: C.C. Arts. 337, 1790; cf. Comments following.

Comments

(a) Civil Code Art. 337 provides that the tutor cannot purchase or lease the minor's property, or accept the assignment of any claim against the ward. The above article has been expanded to apply generally to all types of contracts. See Art. 3194, *supra*.

(b) Because of the fiduciary relationship between the tutor and the ward, a parent co-owner can acquire the minor's interest in property only through an adjudication. Wenk v. Ansimann, 211 La. 641, 30 So.2d 567 (1947).

(c) One exception to the prohibition against a tutor purchasing property of the minor is where the minor's property is adjudicated to the tutor under Art. 4361, *infra*. The general exception clause, "except as otherwise provided by law," was used to cover any other possible exceptions as well as any statutory exceptions which may later be enacted.

Art. 4264. Tutor's administration in his own name; procedural rights

The tutor acts in his own name as tutor, and without the concurrence of the minor. The tutor may act through a mandatary or attorney in fact outside the parish of his residence.

In the performance of his duties, the tutor may exercise all procedural rights available to a litigant.

Source: C.P. Arts. 108, 109, 115; C.C. Art. 351.
Cross References: Arts. 683, 732.

Comments

(a) This article clarifies the question as to when the tutor may act through an attorney in fact. *Cf.* Becnel v. Louisiana Cypress Lumber Co., 134 La. 467, 64 So. 380 (1914).

(b) The second paragraph parallels Art. 3196, *supra*.

Art. 4265. Compromise and modification of obligations

With the approval of the court as provided in Article 4271, a tutor may compromise an action or right of action by or against the minor, or extend, renew, or in any manner modify the terms of an obligation owed by or to the minor.

Source: C.C. Arts. 353, 3072.

Comments

(a) The above article retains the rule of Civil Code Art. 353, substituting the contradictory proceedings between the tutor and the undertutor for the family meeting.

(b) Generally, this article is parallel to Art. 3198, *supra*.

(c) A compromise by a tutor without court authority is a nullity. Chambers v. Chambers, 41 La.Ann. 443, 6 So. 659 (1889).

(d) See Comments under Art. 4271, *infra*.

Art. 4266. Continuation of business

The court may authorize a tutor to continue any business in which the minor has an interest, when it appears to the best interest of the minor, and after compliance with Article 4271. The order of court may contain such conditions, restrictions, regulations and requirements as the court may direct.

Source: New; cf. Model Probate Code, § 222.
Cross Reference: Art. 4267.

Comments

This article is similar to a parallel provision in Art. 3224, *supra*. Art. 4271, *infra*, referred to in the text, regulates the procedure for obtaining court approval on matters affecting the minor's interest.

In the articles dealing with successions it is provided that the court may render an ex parte order permitting the continuation of a business pending issuance of the final order, because the final order could issue only after advertisement and the attendant delays. No similar provision is needed here, for two reasons: the procedure for obtaining the final order will not involve more than a few days' delay and the minor will not ordinarily acquire such a business except through inheritance. If an emergency exists, it will be in connection with the succession proceeding, not the tutorship.

See Comments under Art. 4271, *infra*.

Art. 4267. Loans to tutor for specific purposes; authority to mortgage and pledge minor's property

When it appears to the best interest of the minor, and after compliance with Article 4271, the court may authorize a tutor to borrow money for the purpose of preserving or administering the property, of paying debts, for expenditures in the regular course of a business conducted in accordance with Article 4266, or for the care, maintenance, training, or education of the minor. As security for such a loan, the court may authorize the tutor to mortgage or pledge property of the minor upon such terms and conditions as it may direct. Before authorizing a loan, the court may require the tutor to furnish additional security in an amount fixed by the court.

Source: C.C. Arts. 339, 353.

Comments

(a) Some of the purposes for which the court has authorized the sale or mortgage of a minor's property are as follows: (1) To pay debts or claims against the minor's property—Succession of Hickman, 13 La.Ann. 364 (1858); Lalanne's Heirs v. Moreau, 13 La. 431 (1839); (2) To operate a plantation owned by a minor— Leisey v. Tanner & Helm, 28 La.Ann. 299 (1876); (3) To pay taxes, to repair and to improve the minor's property—Spence & Goldstein v. Clay, 169 La. 1030, 126 So. 516 (1930).

(b) The last sentence, giving the court the right to increase the tutor's bond, is new. A similar provision is included in Art. 4304, *infra*, relative to sale of a minor's property. Since the proceeds of

Art. 4267

a loan will sometimes be expended almost immediately, in this instance the increased bond should be discretionary with the court.

(c) See Comments under Art. 4304, *infra*.

Art. 4268. Lease of minor's property; mineral contracts

When it appears to the best interest of the minor, and after compliance with Article 4271, the court may authorize a tutor to grant a lease upon property of the minor. The term of the lease may extend beyond the anticipated duration of the tutorship.

In addition to the requirements of Article 4271, the petition of the tutor shall set forth the terms and conditions of the proposed lease.

This article does not apply to mineral leases.

Source: C.C. Art. 346.

Comments

(a) The source article provides for the granting of a lease either at public auction or by private act, with the approval of the judge. The provision for public auction has been omitted as impractical. To eliminate any doubt, the language specifically authorizing a lease to extend beyond the minority was added. In many instances beneficial leases can be negotiated only on a long term basis.

(b) R.S. 9:711–9:713 set forth the procedure for a tutor to execute mineral leases and other forms of contracts affecting minerals.

(c) Art. 4271, *infra*, referred to in the above text, governs the procedure for submitting all proposals affecting the minor to the court.

Art. 4269. Investment and management of minor's property

In acquiring, investing, reinvesting, exchanging, retaining, selling, and managing property for the benefit of a minor, a tutor shall exercise the judgment and care, under the circumstances then prevailing, which men of prudence, discretion, and intelligence exercise in the management of their own affairs, not in regard to speculation but in regard to the permanent disposition of their funds, considering the probable income as well as the probable safety of their capital. Within the limitations of the foregoing standard, a tutor is authorized to acquire and retain every kind of property and every kind of investment, specifically including but not by way of limitation, bonds, debentures, and other corporate obligations, and stocks, preferred or common, and securities of any open-end or closed-end management type investment company or investment trust registered under 15

U.S.C. §§ 80a–1 through 80a–52, as from time to time amended, which men of prudence, discretion, and intelligence acquire or retain for their own account.

Source: New; cf. Model Statute for Fiduciary Investments.

Comments

(a) The above article represents a change in the Louisiana law which has always restricted fiduciaries to prescribed lists of approved investments. However, this is a change which is long overdue and which will be of great benefit to minors. A similar change is recommended for other fiduciaries, particularly curators of interdicts. See, The Development of the Prudent Man Rule for Fiduciary Investment in the United States in the Twentieth Century, 12 Ohio State L.J. 491 (1951); Why the Prudent Man?, 7 Vand.L.Rev. 74 (1953).

(b) This article renders obsolete the provisions of Civil Code Arts. 347, 348, and 353.

Art. 4270. Procedure for investing funds

An investment of funds of a minor may be made or changed only with the approval of the court after compliance with Article 4271.

Source: C.C. Art. 348.

Comments

(a) This article retains the Louisiana law, with a specific reference to Art. 4271, *infra*, requiring approval of the undertutor or a rule against him.

(b) The provision in Civil Code Art. 348 requiring notice to the insurance company before a change can be made in a policy or before the policy can be changed to another company has been deleted.

Art. 4271. Court approval of action affecting minor's interest

The tutor shall file a petition setting forth the subject matter to be determined affecting the minor's interest, with his recommendations and the reasons therefor, and with a written concurrence by the undertutor. If the court approves the recommendations, it shall render a judgment of homologation. The court may require evidence prior to approving the recommendations.

If the undertutor fails to concur in the tutor's recommendations, the tutor shall proceed by contradictory motion against him. After

Art. 4271

such hearing and evidence as the court may require, the court shall decide the issues summarily and render judgment.

Source: Former R.S. 9:651–9:653.

Cross References: Arts. 4133, 4136, 4233, 4261, 4265, 4266, 4267, 4268, 4270, 4301, 4321, 4341, 4361, 4556, 4642.

Comments

(a) This article is taken practically verbatim from the source statute, with the following exceptions:

1. The provision in the former R.S. 9:651 specifically dispensing with the family meeting has been deleted on the theory that it is no longer necessary. Although this article does not specify what matters require submission to the court for approval, many of the foregoing articles contain a cross reference to this one. For example, see Arts. 4265 and 4266, *supra*, dealing with compromise of a minor's claim and continuation of a business in which the minor has an interest.

2. See Art. 4554, *infra*.

3. The provision in the former R.S. 9:653 permitting the hearing to be held "in chambers or in open court, in term time or in vacation" has been omitted. See Arts. 195 and 196, *supra*.

4. The language in the former R.S. 9:652 requiring an "appearance" by the undertutor, has been changed to a "written concurrence." Any written document indicating concurrence in the proposal and filed in the record will suffice. Furthermore, instead or requiring the undertutor to set forth the reasons for his concurrence, the above article requires the tutor to set forth the reasons for his reconsideration, and the undertutor need merely concur therein.

(b) See, also, Comments under Arts. 4266, 4268, 4270, *supra*.

Art. 4272. Court approval of payments to minor

In approving any proposal by which money will be paid to the minor, the court may order that the money be paid directly into the registry of the court for the minor's account, to be withdrawn only upon approval of the court and to be invested directly in an investment approved by the court.

Source: New.

Comment

This article provides a method of preventing the tutor from receiving the minor's funds and never investing same or accounting therefor.

Art. 4273. Temporary absence; appointment of agent

A tutor who will be absent from the state temporarily may execute a power of attorney appointing a resident of the parish where the tutor resides to represent him in any matter relating to the tutorship during the absence of the tutor.

Source: C.C. Art. 314.

Comments

(a) This article gives the tutor specific authority to appoint an agent to act for him during a temporary absence. Permanent absence is a ground for removal under Art. 4234, *supra*.

(b) See Comments under Art. 4237, *supra*.

Art. 4274. Compensation of tutor

The tutor may retain as compensation for his services a sum to be fixed by the court, not to exceed ten percent of the annual revenue from the property committed to his charge.

Source: C.C. Art. 349.

Cross References: R.S. 6:322, 29:362.

Comments

In order to retain the benefit of the jurisprudence interpreting Civil Code Art. 349, almost identical language is used in the above article. It has been held that the tutor's commission applies to the net and not the gross proceeds from the sale of crops. Succession of Hargrove, 9 La.Ann. 505 (1854). The tutor is not entitled to a commission on the proceeds of the sale of personal property of the minor, nor on the principal collected on notes inherited by the minor. In re Hollingsworth, 45 La.Ann. 134, 12 So. 12 (1893). Neither is the tutor entitled to a commission on rents due before the property was "committed to his charge," even though collected during the tutorship. Sims v. Billington, 50 La.Ann. 968, 24 So. 637 (1898).

Provision is made giving the court the right to fix the compensation at less than ten percent because in some cases the flat ten percent is excessive.

Art. 4275. Donations to or by minor

The tutor may accept donations made to the minor, but he cannot make donations of any property of the minor.

Source: C.C. Art. 354.

Comment

This article effects no change in the law.

CHAPTER 9. SALE OF MINOR'S PROPERTY

SECTION 1. GENERAL DISPOSITIONS

Art.
4301. Purpose of sale.
4302. Terms of sale.
4303. Perishable property; crops.
4304. Additional bond prior to sale of immovables.

SECTION 2. PUBLIC SALE

4321. Petition; order.
4322. Publication; place of sale.
4323. Minimum price; subsequent offering.

SECTION 3. PRIVATE SALE

4341. Petition.
4342. Bonds and stocks.

SECTION 4. ADJUDICATION TO PARENT

4361. Adjudication of minor's interest to parent co-owner.
4362. Recordation of judgment; mortgage in favor of minor.
4363. Security instead of mortgage.

SECTION 1. GENERAL DISPOSITIONS

Art. 4301. Purpose of sale

A tutor may sell or exchange any interest of a minor in property, owned either in its entirety or in indivision, for any purpose, when authorized by the court as provided in Article 4271.

Source: Former R.S. 9:671.

Cross References: Art. 4641; C.C. Art. 2231.

Comments

(a) The source statute applies only to private sales; however, the above article authorizes both public and private sales. The power to exchange the minor's property has been made specific.

(b) The phrase "any purpose" includes a partition. See Succession of Pepitone, 204 La. 391, 15 So.2d 801 (1943); Art. 4641, *infra*.

Art. 4302. Terms of sale

A sale of minor's property shall be for cash, unless upon the petition of the tutor the court authorizes a credit sale. When a credit sale is authorized, the order shall specify the terms of the sale and the security.

Source: New; cf. C.C. Art. 340.

Cross Reference: Art. 4461.

Comment

In view of the fact that there is no more reason to prohibit sales of minor's property on credit than there is to prevent comparable sales of succession property, the above article was adopted. See Comments under Art. 4341, *infra*.

Art. 4303. Perishable property; crops

Upon the petition of the tutor as provided in Article 4321 or 4341, the court may order the immediate sale of perishable property and growing crops either at public auction or private sale, without appraisal, and without advertisement, or with such advertisement as the court may direct.

Source: New.

Cross Reference: Art. 4641.

Comment

This article is almost identical with Art. 3264, *supra*.

Art. 4304. Additional bond prior to sale of immovables

Before authorizing a sale of a minor's immovable property, the court may require the tutor to furnish additional security in an amount fixed by the court.

Source: New.

Cross Reference: Art. 4641.

Comments

(a) Many other states have similar provisions to protect the additional cash which the tutor will obtain as the result of a sale, *e. g.*, Code of Alabama (1940), T. 21, § 28; California Probate Code, § 1534a; Illinois Anno.Stats., § 3:307; Indiana Stats.Anno. (1953); § 8–122; Code of Iowa (1954), § 668.19; Minn.Stats.Anno., § 525.-652; N. Dakota Rev.Code, (1943), § 30:1109; Oregon Compiled Laws Anno. (1940), § 22–213; Utah Code Anno., (1953), § 75–5–3.

Since a loan on behalf of the minor will also produce additional funds in the hands of the tutor, a similar provision was included in Art. 4267, *supra*, relative to loans.

(b) See Comments under Art. 4267, *supra*.

SECTION 2. PUBLIC SALE

Art. 4321. Petition; order

In addition to the requirements of Article 4271, a petition for authority to sell property of a minor at public sale shall set forth a description of the property and the reasons which make it advantageous to the minor to sell at public sale.

The court shall render an order authorizing the sale at public auction after publication, when it considers the sale to be to the best interest of the minor. The order shall specify the minimum price to be accepted.

Source: Former R.S. 9:672.

Cross References: Arts. 4303, 4641.

Comments

(a) This article is very similar to the former R.S. 9:672, governing private sales.

(b) The rule on minimum price is that at the first sale the property must bring "the amount of its appraised value mentioned in the inventory." Civil Code Art. 342. Under the above article, the court order shall specify the minimum price, permitting the court to use any assistance available, including the inventory appraisal.

Art. 4322. Publication; place of sale

Notice of the sale shall be published in the parish in which the tutorship proceeding is pending, at least twice for immovable property and at least once for movable property, in the manner provided by law. The court may order additional advertisements.

When immovable property situated in another parish is to be sold, the notice shall also be published in the parish where the property is situated. When movable property situated in another parish is to be sold, the court may require the notice to be published also in the parish where the property is situated.

The sale shall be conducted in the parish in which the tutorship proceeding is pending, unless the court orders that the sale be conducted in the parish where the property is situated.

Source: New; cf. C.C. Art. 341.

Cross Reference: Art. 4641.

Tit. 6 SALE OF MINOR'S PROPERTY **Art. 4341**

Comments

(a) The source provision is deficient in that it does not specify the place where the advertisement is to be published, nor the number of advertisements.

(b) This article supplies another deficiency in the law by specifically stating the place where the sale is to be conducted. *Cf.* In re Pierce, 9 Mart. (O.S.) 461 (La.1821); Cole v. Richmond, 156 La. 262, 100 So. 419 (1924).

(c) For the requirements of the publication of the notice, see R.S. 43:203.

Art. 4323. Minimum price; subsequent offering

The property shall not be sold if the price bid by the last and highest bidder is less than the minimum price fixed by the court. In that event, on the petition of the tutor, the court may order another offering, with the same formalities as for an original offering, at a lower minimum price.

Source: New; cf. C.C. Art. 342.

Cross Reference: Art. 4641.

Comments

(a) The source article provides that if the court is satisfied that a sale cannot be made at the original appraisal, it can order another appraisement. The above article adopts a more realistic approach and permits the court to authorize a sale at a lower price, without the intervening step of ordering a lower appraisal.

(b) The minimum price limitation has no application to sale of property owned partly by the minor, in a partition proceeding. Life Assn. of America v. Hall, 33 La.Ann. 49 (1881).

SECTION 3. PRIVATE SALE

Art. 4341. Petition

In addition to the requirements of Article 4271, a petition for authority to sell property of a minor at private sale shall set forth a description of the property, the price and conditions of the proposed sale, and the reasons which make it advantageous to the minor to sell at private sale.

Source: Former R.S. 9:672–9:674.

Cross References: Arts. 4303, 4641.

Art. 4341 — TUTORSHIP — Bk. 7

Comment

The following matters are covered by the source provisions, but have been omitted from this article: (1) The authority of the court to appoint experts to examine into the condition and value of the property. Under this Code, the court has the inherent right to appoint experts. (2) The provision which permits the hearing to be had "in open court or in chambers, in term or in vacation." Under this Code, the necessity for this special authority has been eliminated, see Arts. 195, 196, *supra*. (3) The requirement in the former R.S. 9:674 that the order approving the sale "shall fix the minimum price to be accepted, the terms of the sale, and the security to be given for the credit portion of the purchase price." This language is unnecessary, in view of the fact that the petition must state the price and terms of the proposed sale and the judge's order necessarily approves the sale at the price and under the terms stated. The credit portion of the sale is covered by Art. 4302, *supra*.

Art. 4342. Bonds and stocks

A tutor may sell bonds and stocks of the minor at rates prevailing in the open market, by obtaining a court order authorizing the sale.

The endorsement of the tutor and a certified copy of the court order authorizing the sale shall be sufficient warrant for the transfer.

Source: Former R.S. 9:1455.

Cross Reference: Art. 4641.

Comments

This article is almost identical to the source provision, which also applies to tutors, curators, and syndics.

The provision in the source statute dispensing with advertisement has been deleted as unnecessary, since no advertisement is required for any private sale by a tutor.

SECTION 4. ADJUDICATION TO PARENT

Art. 4361. Adjudication of minor's interest to parent co-owner

The parent of a minor who owns property in common with him may obtain a judgment adjudicating the share of the minor either in all of the property or any part thereof to the parent at a price fixed under oath by experts appointed by the court. The adjudication may be made even though there are other co-owners. The proposed adjudication must be approved by the court after compliance with Article 4271.

Source: C.C. Art. 343.

Comments

(a) The concept of adjudication of minor's property which dates back to La.Acts of 1809, c. 21, § 2, is retained.

(b) Both movables and immovables can be adjudicated to the parent. Succession of Schwabacher, 130 La. 631, 58 So. 414 (1912). The judgment of the court operates as a sale for the price fixed and transfers the property without the necessity of an act of sale. Krone v. Krone, 138 La. 666, 70 So. 605 (1916).

(c) The source article does not make it clear whether the parent who owns property in common with minor children and others, such as major children, can cause the minor's share to be adjudicated to him. In Brewer v. Brewer, 145 La. 835, 83 So. 30 (1919), it was held that Art. 343 did not authorize such an adjudication. As a matter of policy, the law should permit such an adjudication; hence, specific provision therefor is made.

(d) See, also, Comments under Art. 4263, *supra*.

Art. 4362. Recordation of judgment; mortgage in favor of minor

A judgment adjudicating immovable property shall be effective only after it is recorded in the mortgage records of the parish where the property is situated. The recordation shall operate as a mortgage and vendor's privilege against the property adjudicated in favor of the minor, for the price of the adjudication.

Source: C.C. Arts. 343, 3317, 3353; former R.S. 9:5501.

Cross Reference: Art. 4263.

Comment

This article effects no substantial change in the law.

Art. 4363. Security instead of mortgage

Instead of the mortgage provided in Article 4362, the parent may furnish security as provided in Article 4132 or a special mortgage as provided in Article 4133. The amount of the security or special mortgage shall be equal to the price of the adjudication.

Source: C.C. Art. 343; former R.S. 9:804.

Comments

(a) No change in the law is effected by this article.

(b) The two articles referred to in the text specify the types of security which a tutor can furnish, and the procedure for substituting a special mortgage.

CHAPTER 10. ACCOUNTING BY TUTOR

Art.
4391. Duty to account; annual accounts.
4392. Final account.
4393. Contents of account.
4394. Service of account.
4395. Opposition; homologation.
4396. Effect of homologation.
4397. Deceased or interdicted tutor.
4398. Cost of accounting.

Art. 4391. Duty to account; annual accounts

A tutor shall file an account annually, reckoning from the day of his appointment, and at any other time when ordered by the court on its own motion or on the application of any interested person.

Source: C.C. Arts. 356, 357.

Cross Reference: R.S. 14:354.

Comments

(a) The only substantial change effected by this article is the omission of the unnecessary requirement in Art. 356 of the Code of Practice that the tutor annex to each annual account an affidavit specifying the parishes in which he owns immovable property.

(b) There is no express provision in Art. 356 for the court to order an account on its own motion or on application of any interested person, but Art. 357 requires the tutor to file an account "whenever he is ordered to do so by the judge."

(c) See Art. 4392, *infra*, and Comments under Art. 4203, *supra*.

Art. 4392. Final account

A tutor may file a final account at any time after expiration of the tutorship.

The court shall order the filing of a final account upon the application of the former minor after the expiration of the tutorship, or upon the rendition of a judgment ordering the removal of a tutor or authorizing his resignation.

Source: C.C. Art. 357.

Cross Reference: Art. 4235.

Comments

(a) Art. 357 of the Civil Code requires the tutor to file a final account on the expiration of his tutorship. The above article makes a change in the law. It is similar to Art. 3332, *supra*, which gives the succession representative the right to file a final account, but imposes no absolute duty upon him to do so except after an order of court on the application of any party in interest. In many instances, the minor who has just attained majority may be completely satisfied with an extrajudicial settlement.

(b) It is contemplated that included in every judgment of removal or resignation will be an order by the court compelling a final account.

(c) Art. 358 of the Civil Code provides for a final account by a tutor who is about to leave the state permanently and authorizes his arrest for failure to comply. The arrest portion is obsolete. A tutor who is to leave the state permanently will have to resign, and a part of his resignation procedure will be the filing of a final account. See Art. 4233, *supra*.

(d) See Comments under Arts. 4235, 4391, *supra*.

Art. 4393. Contents of account

The account of a tutor shall contain the same matters required by Article 3333 for an account of a succession representative.

Source: New.

Comment

Heretofore, nothing in the Louisiana law specified the nature of the tutor's account.

Art. 4394. Service of account

A copy of an account filed by a tutor, together with a notice that the account can be homologated after the expiration of ten days from the date of service and that any opposition must be filed before homologation, shall be served in the manner provided for service of citation:

(1) Upon the undertutor, if an annual account or other interim account is ordered by the court;

Art. 4394

(2) Upon the former minor, if a final account is rendered after expiration of the tutorship; or

(3) Upon the successor tutor, if a final account is rendered after removal, resignation, death, or interdiction of a tutor.

Source: New.

Cross Reference: Art. 4395.

Comments

(a) Art. 356 of the Civil Code requires that an annual account be rendered "contradictorily with the undertutor." The above article is similar to Art. 3335, *supra*.

(b) Civil Code Art. 369 requires the rendition of the account "to the emancipated minor assisted by a curator ad hoc, who shall be assigned to him by the judge." This provision implemented Civil Code Art. 375, providing that the minor emancipated otherwise than by marriage cannot appear in court without the assistance of a curator ad litem. The latter article was repealed by Art. 958 of the Code of Practice. Richardson v. Richardson, 38 La.Ann. 639 (1886). *Cf.* Beauchamp v. Whittington, 10 La.Ann. 646 (1855).

An emancipated minor, regardless of how he has been emancipated, may sue and be sued individually. Arts. 682 and 731, *supra*. Hence it would be anomalous to require the court to appoint an attorney to represent him in the matter of an accounting to him by his former tutor. For this reason, this article does not follow the language of Civil Code Art. 369.

Art. 4395. Opposition; homologation

An opposition to an account may be filed any time prior to homologation. An opposition shall be tried as a summary proceeding.

If no opposition has been filed, the court may homologate the account at any time after the expiration of ten days from the date of service as provided in Article 4394.

Source: New.

Comment

Heretofore, there has been no positive law on this subject. However, the above article establishes the same system for tutors as for succession representatives. See Art. 3336, *supra*.

Art. 4396. Effect of homologation

A judgment homologating any account other than a final account shall be prima facie evidence of the correctness of the account.

A judgment homologating a final account has the same effect as a final judgment in an ordinary action.

Source: C.C. Art. 356; cf. Comments following.

Cross References: C.C. Arts. 360, 361.

Comment

Civil Code Art. 356 provides that a judgment homologating an annual account is prima facie evidence of correctness. However, there is no provision dealing with the effect of homologation of the final account of a tutor nor apparently any reported decision directly in point. The final account would serve little purpose unless it is given the effect proposed in the above article, and therefore the same effect is provided herein as for an account filed by a succession representative. See Art. 3337, *supra*.

Art. 4397. Deceased or interdicted tutor

If a tutor dies, an account of his administration may be filed by his succession representative or heirs. If a tutor is interdicted, such an account may be filed by his curator.

The court shall order the filing of such an account in either case, on the petition of an interested person.

Source: New; cf. Comments following.

Comments

(a) This article is similar to Art. 3338, *supra*.

(b) The duty of a deceased tutor's administrator to render an account to his successor, and the duty of the undertutor and the successor tutor to require such an account to be rendered has been judicially recognized. Angelloz v. Angelloz, 204 La. 988, 16 So.2d 654 (1944).

Art. 4398. Cost of accounting

Accounts filed by a tutor are at the expense of the minor, except that an account filed by a tutor who has been removed or an account not filed timely is at the expense of the tutor.

Source: C.C. Art. 359.

Comment

The source article includes a provision requiring the tutor to advance the costs of an account. There is no more reason to require the tutor to advance this expense than any other. However, under this article the tutor pays the expense when he has been removed or when an account is filed late.

CHAPTER 11. ANCILLARY TUTORSHIP PROCEDURE

Art.
4431. Foreign tutor; authority and powers.
4432. Possession or removal of property from state.
4433. Foreign tutor qualifying in Louisiana; authority.

Art. 4431. Foreign tutor; authority and powers

Upon producing proof of his appointment, a tutor or guardian of a minor residing outside Louisiana, appointed by a court outside Louisiana, may appear in court on behalf of the minor without qualifying as tutor according to the law of Louisiana, when no tutor has been appointed in this state. He may perform acts affecting the minor's property in Louisiana, when authorized by the court of the parish in which the property is situated, in the same manner as a tutor appointed by a court in Louisiana.

Whenever the action of an undertutor would be necessary, an undertutor ad hoc shall be appointed by the court.

Source: C.C. Art. 363.

Cross References: Arts. 683, 684, 732, 733; R.S. 9:603.

Comments

(a) A foreign succession representative has always been required to qualify as such according to Louisiana law before performing any act in Louisiana. On the other hand, over 100 years ago the legislature abolished this requirement for foreign tutors. La.Act 145 of 1843 first dispensed with the requirement of previous qualification in this state. Civil Code Art. 363, which is similar to the above article, retains the rule of the 1843 statute.

(b) Art. 363 of the Civil Code provides that the foreign tutor may perform acts affecting the minor's property in Louisiana "when properly authorized according to the laws of this state." The meaning of the quoted language is not clear. However, orderly procedure would require the usual petition for court authority, which in this circumstance would have to be brought at the situs of the property, plus the usual concurrence of the undertutor or rule against him.

Art. 4432. Possession or removal of property from state

In order to take possession of or remove the minor's property from this state, a tutor or guardian appointed by a court outside Louisiana shall file a petition for authority to do so in the court of the parish where the property is situated. Notice of the petition directed to the creditors of the minor shall be published twice in the manner provided for judicial advertisements, with an interval of not less than twenty days between publications. After the expiration of ten days from the second publication, the court shall render judgment authorizing the tutor or guardian to take possession of the property and remove it from the state, upon proof that all creditors who have filed claims have been paid or that no claims have been filed.

Source: New; cf. C.C. Art. 364.

Comments

(a) Although the above procedure is somewhat cumbersome, it does give some protection to local creditors.

(b) The procedure contemplated by Civil Code Art. 364 is similar to that provided in this article, but is too vague.

Art. 4433. Foreign tutor qualifying in Louisana; authority

A tutor or guardian of a minor residing outside Louisiana, appointed by a court outside Louisiana, may be appointed as tutor by a court of competent jurisdiction in Louisiana, as provided in Article 4031.

The procedure shall be the same as provided by law for the tutorship of a minor residing in Louisiana.

After such qualification the tutor has the same rights and responsibility as a tutor originally qualified in Louisiana.

Source: New; cf. C.C. Art. 363.

Comment

Although Civil Code Art. 363 dispenses with the requirement that a foreign tutor qualify in Louisiana, there is nothing in the law which would prevent such a procedure. Under the above article there is recognized expressly the right to institute such an ancillary proceeding, which would prove particularly helpful in cases where the minor owns property in several parishes. Art. 4031, *supra*, referred to above, establishes the jurisdiction for all tutorship proceedings, including those involving nonresidents.

CHAPTER 12. SMALL TUTORSHIPS

Art.
4461. Small tutorship defined.
4462. Inventory dispensed with.
4463. Dative tutor without bond.
4464. Court costs.

Art. 4461. Small tutorship defined

For the purposes of this Chapter, a small tutorship is the tutorship of a minor whose property in Louisiana has a value of two thousand dollars or less.

Source: New; cf. former R.S. 9:821–9:823.

Comments

(a) The former R.S. 9:821–9:823 provided for the use of a descriptive list instead of an inventory in tutorships involving less than five hundred dollars. The two thousand dollars limit in the above article is the same placed on small successions. See Art. 3421, *supra*.

(b) Questions as to the situs of the minor's property are determinable by the rules of conflict of laws.

(c) See Comments under Art. 4102, *supra*.

Art. 4462. Inventory dispensed with

In a proceeding under this Chapter, the applicant for the tutorship may file a detailed descriptive list of the property instead of an inventory. The list shall be sworn to and subscribed by the applicant, and shall set forth the location and fair market value of each item of property.

The list has the same effect as an inventory, and an abstract thereof recorded in the mortgage records preserves the legal mortgage of the minor.

Source: Former R.S. 9:821–9:823.

Cross Reference: Art. 3136.

Comment

This article effects no change in the law. See Comments under Art. 4102, *supra*.

Art. 4463. Dative tutor without bond

If the court is satisfied that no one will accept the dative tutorship of a minor in a proceeding under this Chapter and furnish the usual security, it shall appoint a dative tutor, who shall comply with all requirements except that of furnishing security.

Source: New; cf. C.C. Art. 271.

Comments

(a) Art. 271 of the Civil Code provides for a dative tutor without bond whenever no one will accept with bond, with no limitation as to the amount of the minor's property. Under this article, such appointments are limited to small tutorships, on the theory that where more than $2,000 is involved, it should be possible to obtain a surety company bond or some other form of security. Where less than $2,000 is involved, no bond will be required and no legal mortgage will be recorded.

(b) See Comments under Arts. 4064, 4102, *supra*.

Art. 4464. Court costs

In proceedings under this Chapter, court costs shall be one-half the court costs in similar proceedings in larger tutorships, provided that the minimum costs in any case shall be five dollars.

Source: New; cf. former R.S. 9:1557.

Comments

(a) Heretofore, there has been no provision for reduced costs in small tutorships. However, a similar provision dealing with small successions has been included in Art. 3422, *supra*, and there is no reason why small tutorships should not be given the same cost advantage.

(b) See Comments under Art. 4102, *supra*.

TITLE VII

ADMINISTRATION OF MINOR'S PROPERTY DURING MARRIAGE OF PARENTS

Art.
4501. Father as administrator of minor's property.
4502. Rights of mother when father is a mental incompetent or absentee.

Art. 4501. Father as administrator of minor's property

When both parents are alive and not divorced or judicially separated, property belonging to a minor may be sold or mortgaged, a claim of a minor may be compromised, and any other step may be taken affecting his interest, in the same manner and by pursuing the same forms as in case of a minor represented by a tutor, the father occupying the place of and having the powers of a tutor.

Whenever the action of an undertutor would be necessary, an undertutor ad hoc shall be appointed by the court, who shall occupy the place of and have the powers of an undertutor.

Source: C.C. Arts. 221, 222.

Cross References: Arts. 683, 732, 4501.

Comments

(a) No change, except to overrule legislatively Blades v. Southern Farm Bureau Casualty Ins. Co., 237 La. 1, 110 So.2d 116 (1959). The retention of most of the language of Art. 222 of the Civil Code was intended to retain the remainder of the jurisprudence construing this Civil Code article. See Darlington v. Turner, 202 U.S. 195, 26 S.Ct. 630, 50 L.Ed. 992 (1906); Succession of Allen, 48 La.Ann. 1240, 20 So. 683 (1896); In re Monrose, 187 La. 739, 175 So. 475 (1937).

(b) See Comments under Arts. 683, 732, *supra*.

Art. 4502. Rights of mother when father is a mental incompetent or absentee

If the father of a minor is a mental incompetent or an absentee, the mother shall occupy the place of and have the powers of the tutor, instead of the father, as provided in Article 4501.

Source: C.C. Arts. 81–85, 221.

Cross References: Arts. 683, 732.

Tit. 7 ADMINISTRATION BY PARENT Art. 4502

Comments

(a) The above article is slightly broader than its source provisions, which limit the mother's right to act as administratrix of the estate of her minor child only when the father has been interdicted or is absent.

(b) See Comments under Arts. 683, 732, *supra*.

TITLE VIII

INTERDICTION AND CURATORSHIP OF INTERDICTS

Art.
4541. Court in which interdiction proceedings brought.
4542. Proceedings subsequent to appointment of curator.
4543. Who may file petition.
4544. Service of process; appointment of attorney.
4545. Defendant confined outside Louisiana.
4546. Summary trial.
4547. Interrogation and examination of defendant.
4548. Effect of appeal.
4549. Appointment and qualification of provisional curator; functions, duties, authority.
4550. Appointment of curator.
4551. Costs.
4552. Recordation of notice of suit and of judgment.
4553. Undercurator.
4554. Tutorship rules applicable.
4555. Custody of interdict.
4556. Expenses for care of interdict and legal dependents.
4557. Termination of interdiction.

INTRODUCTION

Much of the procedure for curatorship is contained in the Civil Code and, in many instances, the procedures are nearly identical for tutorship and curatorship. Civil Code Art. 415, for example, provides expressly that the tutorship rules relating to the oath, security, recording of legal mortgage, sale of property, compensation of curator, accounting, "and the other obligations" apply also to curatorship. Under Art. 4554, *infra*, the provisions of this Title on tutorship apply to interdiction and curatorship also, except as otherwise specifically provided.

The principal difference between interdiction and tutorship is that, in the former, a contradictory proceeding is necessary to establish the fact of the disability of the interdict; whereas, in a tutorship proceeding, the question of minority is never an issue. Most of the articles in this Title deal with the procedure in the suit to obtain a judgment of interdiction. The cross reference in Art. 4554, *infra*, to the tutorship articles solves practically all of the problems of administration subsequent to the judgment of interdiction. Although the procedural rules contained in the Civil Code have been incorporated in this Code, the substantive rules pertaining to interdiction and curatorship are not disturbed.

Judicial commitment is governed by the Mental Health Law, R.S. 28:1 et seq.

Art. 4541. Court in which interdiction proceedings brought

A petition to have a person interdicted shall be filed in the district court of the parish of his domicile.

Source: New; cf. C.C. Art. 392.

Cross Reference: Art. 44.

Comment

See Comments under Art. 4542, *infra*.

Art. 4542. Proceedings subsequent to appointment of curator

All subsequent proceedings relative to the interdiction and curatorship shall be brought in the court in which the original petition was filed.

Source: New; cf. C.C. Art. 392.

Comments to Articles 4541 and 4542

(a) These articles overrule the jurisprudential rules announced in Interdiction of Dumas, 33 La.Ann. 679 (1880); Interdiction of Lepine, 160 La. 953, 107 So. 708 (1926), to the effect that the proceedings must be instituted in the parish of the residence of the defendant. See Comments under Art. 10, *supra*.

(b) See R.S. 9:1001 *et seq.*, authorizing the interdiction of inebriates or habitual drunkards. This is a special statute not affected by the articles in this Title.

(c) R.S. 33:4767, 38:1627, and 38:1644 are special provisions not affected by this Code.

Art. 4543. Who may file petition

A proceeding for interdiction may be brought by the spouse or any relative of the person sought to be interdicted, or by any other person.

Source: C.C. Arts. 390, 391.

Comments

(a) This article emphasizes the right of the spouse or a relative to initiate the proceeding, but no order of preference is intended.

(b) The provision in Art. 391 of the Civil Code to the effect that an interdiction may be "pronounced ex officio by the judge," has been omitted from this Code. See Interdiction of Escat, 207 La. 228, 21 So.2d 43 (1945).

Art. 4544. Service of process; appointment of attorney

Citation and service of process upon the defendant shall be made as in ordinary proceedings. If the defendant makes no appearance through an attorney, the court, after the expiration of the delay for answering, shall appoint an attorney to represent the defendant, upon whom citation and a copy of the petition shall be served.

Source: C.C. Art. 391; cf. Comments following.

Comments

(a) While no statute expressly so provides, the jurisprudence makes it clear that the defendant must be served as in ordinary cases. Unless he makes an appearance through an attorney, the court must appoint one to represent him, upon whom service must then be made. Segur v. Pellerin, 16 La. 63 (1840); Gernon v. Dubois, 23 La.Ann. 26 (1871); Gore v. Barrow, 137 La. 320, 68 So. 625 (1915).

(b) Under this article the appointment of counsel to represent a defendant does not prevent the latter from appearing in proper person.

Art. 4545. Defendant confined outside Louisiana

If the defendant is domiciled in Louisiana but is receiving treatment outside of Louisiana for an alleged condition which would justify interdiction, regardless of the duration of his absence, the court, upon the filing of the original petition, shall appoint an attorney to represent him and all service shall be made upon such attorney.

Source: New; cf. C.C. Art. 391.

Comments

(a) This article overrules Interdiction of Toca, 217 La. 465, 46 So.2d 737 (1950). See Comments under Art. 10, *supra*.

(b) See R.S. 9:1021, a special statute applicable only to veterans confined in government institutions outside the state, permits service to be made upon the defendant through the officer in charge of the government institution.

Art. 4546. Summary trial

Interdiction suits shall be tried summarily and by preference.

Source: Former R.S. 13:4158.

Tit. 8   INTERDICTION AND CURATORSHIP   **Art. 4548**

Art. 4547.   Interrogation and examination of defendant

The judge may interrogate the defendant and may appoint an expert to examine the defendant and make a report under oath as to his condition. When the defendant is outside the state the judge shall appoint such an expert.

Either party may cross examine an expert appointed by the court.

Source: C.C. Art. 393.

Comments

(a) Under this article the right of either party to cross examine an expert appointed by the court is specifically preserved. Without objection, of course, a written report may be introduced. See Stafford v. Stafford, 1 Mart. (N.S.) 551 (1823); Segur v. Pellerin, 16 La. 63 (1840).

(b) If the defendant is out of the state, and a nonresident expert is appointed, cross examination may be conducted under the deposition and discovery articles of this Code.

Art. 4548.   Effect of appeal

An appeal from a judgment appointing or removing a curator or undercurator, or a judgment revoking a judgment of interdiction, can be taken only within thirty days from the applicable date provided in Article 2087(1)–(3).

Such judgment shall not be suspended during the pendency of an appeal, and the acts of a curator or of an undercurator shall not be invalidated by the annulment of his appointment on appeal.

Source: C.C. Art. 395; C.P. Arts. 580, 1059.

Comments

(a) Heretofore there was no specific provision limiting the time for taking an appeal from a judgment of interdiction, as there was in tutorship proceedings. See Art. 307, Civil Code. Art. 4068, *supra*, limits the time for appeal from judgments confirming, appointing, or removing a tutor or undertutor to thirty days, and prohibits suspensive appeals from such judgments. The above article is parallel to Art. 4068, *supra*.

(b) The source articles do not apply specifically to undercurators, but the principle involved is applicable. See Succession of Menendez, 29 La.Ann. 408 (1877).

(c) Civil Code Art. 396 provides that on appeal in an interdiction suit, the appellate court may hear new evidence and may question the defendant. In Bland v. Edwards, 52 La.Ann. 822, 27 So. 289 (1900), the supreme court termed the article "a dead letter," pointing out that while it may have had effect when courts of appeal had wide original jurisdiction, it is at variance with subsequent laws regulating appellate procedure.

Art. 4549. Appointment and qualification of provisional curator; functions, duties, authority

On the application of an interested person or on its own motion, pending the trial of a suit for interdiction or pending the appointment of a curator, the court may appoint a qualified person as provisional curator, if such appointment is necessary.

A provisional curator is subject to the same requirements as to qualification, oath, security, and inventory, and has the same functions, duties, and authority, as a provisional tutor. He shall continue in office until his appointment is terminated by the court or until a curator has been qualified.

Source: C.C. Arts. 394, 405.

Cross References: Arts. 4070–4073.

Comment

This article is intended to apply not only pending the trial of the interdiction suit but also pending the appointment of an original curator or a successor in the event of a vacancy. A provisional curator may be appointed upon removal of a curator, pending qualification of a successor. State ex rel. Gelpi v. King, 113 La. 905, 37 So. 71 (1905).

Art. 4550. Appointment of curator

Within thirty days after the judgment of interdiction the court shall appoint a curator for the person interdicted.

The spouse of an interdicted person has the prior right to be appointed curator.

If the interdict has no spouse or if the spouse does not apply for appointment as curator within ten days after the judgment of interdiction, the court shall appoint the applicant best qualified, personally, and by training and experience, to serve as curator. Article 4069 governs the appointment of a separate curator of the property and person.

Source: C.C. Arts. 404, 412, 413.

Comments

(a) Civil Code Art. 404 provides for the appointment of a curator within a month after the judgment if no appeal is taken or within a month after the rendition of the final judgment on appeal. On the other hand, Art. 395 of the Civil Code and Art. 580 of the 1870 Code of Practice require a judgment of interdiction to be executed despite an appeal. It has been held that these articles are not in conflict; that Civil Code Art. 404, being specific, controls the appointment of a curator, whereas the other articles apply to all other results which flow from the judgment. In re Jones, 116 La. 776, 41 So. 89 (1906). The above article requires the appointment of a curator even though an appeal is pending.

(b) Under Civil Code Arts. 412 and 413, only the husband has a preference in the appointment of a curator. In all other cases, the appointment is dative, the rules of priority for the appointment of tutors being inapplicable. Bradley v. Commercial National Bank, 170 La. 59, 129 So. 371 (1930). The wife may be appointed, but has no priority, and she is not required to furnish bond. It has been held that the Married Women's Emancipation Act had no effect upon Art. 413. Castille v. Gallagher, 206 La. 904, 20 So.2d 175 (1945). The above article gives priority to either spouse to serve as curator for the other. It also repeals the exemption of the wife from furnishing bond. Since the court will have complete control over the amount of the bond (see Art. 4131, *supra*), a requirement that the wife furnish bond should not result in great hardship.

(c) There is a question whether under the existing law a husband may refuse to serve as curator for his interdicted wife. There is apparently no reported decision in point. Civil Code Art. 412 provides merely that a married woman who is interdicted is "of course" under the curatorship of her husband. Art. 415 of the Civil Code provides inter alia that the tutorship rules concerning "excuses" apply to interdiction. However, the supreme court has held that the rules governing tutorship have no application in the selection and appointment of a curator. Bradley v. Commercial National Bank, 170 La. 859, 129 So. 371 (1930). Moreover, a husband appointed curator for his interdicted wife must give security. Woodward v. Woodward, 15 La.Ann. 162 (1860). Under this article a husband is not compelled to serve as curator of his interdicted wife.

(d) Art. 4069, *supra*, to which reference is made in this article, provides for the appointment of a bank as separate tutor of the property. The principles involved apply also to curatorship of interdicts.

(e) See Civil Code Art. 414, providing that no one except a spouse, ascendant, or descendant of the interdicted person can be compelled to serve as curator for over ten years, at the expiration of which any other person may petition for his discharge as curator. See, also, Civil Code Arts. 292–301, which set forth the causes which excuse him from the obligation of accepting a tutorship.

(f) See, also Comments under Art. 4554, *infra*.

Art. 4551. Costs

The costs of an interdiction proceeding shall be paid from the estate of the defendant, if a judgment of interdiction is rendered. If judgment is rendered in favor of the defendant, the court in its discretion may tax the costs, or any part thereof, against any party.

Source: C.C. Art. 397.

Comments

(a) Under Civil Code Art. 397, the court is given no discretion in assessing costs; the estate of the interdict pays if a judgment of interdiction is rendered, and the plaintiff pays if the suit is dismissed. The above article gives the court discretion to assess costs if the suit is dismissed.

(b) Where the suit is abated by the death of the defendant prior to final judgment, the usual result which follows generally from abatement applies, and each party pays his own costs. Ruiz v. Pons, 141 La. 110, 74 So. 713 (1917).

Art. 4552. Recordation of notice of suit and of judgment

The clerk of court shall cause to be recorded in the conveyance records of the parish in which an interdiction suit is filed a notice of the filing of the suit.

Within ten days of his appointment, the curator shall cause the judgment of interdiction to be recorded in the conveyance records of the parish in which the judgment was rendered and in each parish in which the interdict owns immovable property.

If either the clerk or the curator fail to perform this duty, he shall be liable for the damages sustained by any person who contracts with the interdict through ignorance of the interdiction proceedings.

Source: New; cf. C.C. Arts. 398, 401.

Comments

(a) Heretofore, there was no statutory requirement that the curator record a notice of the judgment. However, that duty is imposed upon the clerk by former R.S. 13:911 and 13:912. Since the date of the filing of the suit is the critical date for determining the invalidity of acts performed by the interdict, Civil Code Art. 401, it is more advisable from the standpoint of third parties to require the clerk's notice to be recorded upon the filing of suit.

(b) Civil Code Art. 398, which requires the curator to cause a notice of the judgment to be published three times, has not been included in this article.

(c) See Civil Code Arts. 401 through 403, as to the validity of acts done by a person interdicted.

Art. 4553. Undercurator

At the time the court appoints a curator, the court shall also appoint a responsible person as undercurator, who shall have the same duties and responsibilities as an undertutor. In so far as applicable, Articles 4201 through 4206 apply also to undercurators.

The undercurator is relieved of further duty and responsibility as undercurator upon the death of the interdict or upon rendition of judgment revoking the interdiction. However, his liability for acts prior thereto shall not be affected.

Source: C.C. Arts. 406–411.

Art. 4554. Tutorship rules applicable

Except as otherwise provided in this Title, the relationship between an interdict and his curator is the same as that between a minor and his tutor, with respect to the person and property of the interdict.

The rules provided in Articles 4032, 4033, 4067, 4101 through 4172, 4231 through 4342, and 4391 through 4464 apply likewise to the curatorship of an interdict.

Source: C.C. Art. 415.

Cross References: Arts. 684, 733.

Comments

(a) The source article not only contains a general cross reference to the rules governing tutors, but also specifically refers to the oath, the inventory, the security, the mode of administering, "and the other obligations." To avoid uncertainty, specific reference has been made to the applicable articles on tutorship.

(b) The changes thus effected by this article in the rules governing the administration of an interdict's property are the same as those in tutorship proceedings.

(c) Under this article, guardians of mental incompetents domiciled outside of Louisiana may act in this state on producing proof of their appointments, without qualifying in Louisiana. In re Parker, 39 La.Ann. 333, 1 So. 891 (1887); Vick v. Voltz, 47 La. Ann. 42, 16 So. 568 (1895). See, also, Art. 4431, *supra*.

Art. 4555. Custody of interdict

The court may order that an interdict be attended in his own home, in a hospital, or in any other place, within or without the state, taking into consideration the nature of his incapacity and the value of his property. If necessary, the court may order that an interdict be confined in safe custody.

Source: C.C. Art. 417.

Comments

(a) A confinement by order of court under the provisions of this article would not be governed by the Mental Health Act, R.S. 28:1 *et seq.* The institution which accepts care of the interdict under order of court would be obligated to hold the interdict subject to the further orders of the court.

(b) The provisions of Civil Code Arts. 424 and 425, making it mandatory for the court to appoint a superintendent and for the judge to visit the interdict whenever he deems it expedient, have not been included in this Code. The judge's right to visit the interdict is, of course, inherent, but the appointment of a superintendent is unnecessary in view of the fact that an undercurator must be appointed.

(c) Under this article, the court is given complete discretion in controlling the person of the interdict. *Cf.* Civil Code Art. 423, which is superseded by this article.

Art. 4556. Expenses for care of interdict and legal dependents

The curator shall expend that portion of the revenue from the interdict's property as is necessary to care properly for his person and, with the approval of the court, to support his legal dependents. If the revenue is insufficient for these purposes, with the approval of the court in the manner provided in Article 4271, the curator may expend the interdict's capital.

Source: C.C. Art. 418; cf. Comments following.

Comments

This article is in accord with the jurisprudential rule on the subject. See In re Leech, 45 La.Ann. 194, 12 So. 126 (1893).

Under the rules of tutorship, which apply also to interdiction, approval of the court is necessary before expenditures may be made in excess of revenues. Succession of Sangfried, 114 La. 878, 38 So. 593 (1905).

Article 4271, *supra*, sets forth the general procedure for obtaining court approval of any action affecting a minor.

Art. 4557. Termination of interdiction

A judgment of interdiction may be revoked only by a judgment rendered in the interdiction proceeding, contradictorily with the curator. The interdict has procedural capacity to sue in his own name to revoke the interdiction.

Source: New; cf. C.C. Art. 421.

Cross Reference: Art. 684.

Comments

(a) In Oliver v. Terrall, 152 La. 662, 94 So. 152 (1923), it was held that in an action to revoke the interdiction the proper plaintiff was the interdict and the proper defendant, the curator.

(b) As to the time the interdiction terminates, see Civil Code Art. 420.

TITLE IX

PARTITION BETWEEN CO-OWNERS

Chap.		Art.
1.	General Dispositions	4601
2.	Partition When Co-owner an Absentee	4621
3.	Partition When Co-owner a Minor or Interdict	4641

INTRODUCTION

Prior to the adoption of this Code, the law of partitions was scattered through the Code of Practice, the Civil Code, and in different chapters of Titles 9 and 13 of the Revised Statutes. This Title incorporates all of the procedural law relating to partitions between co-owners, and the procedural provisions of the codifications mentioned above were repealed on the adoption of this Code.

The substantive law of partitions has been left intact in the Civil Code, as have all of the rules regulating the manner in which a notary effects the partition when appointed to do so by the court. Under the Civil Code, the procedural rules were couched in terms of their applicability to the partition of successions, with a cross reference making them apply, so far as practicable, to partitions between co-owners. This Title adopts the opposite, but a much more realistic, approach. Chapter 1 thereof sets forth the specific rules regulating the judicial partition between co-owners, while Title VI of Book VI contains the rules governing the infrequently-used partition of successions, with a cross reference therein adopting the rules of Chapter 1 of this Title, except when manifestly inapplicable.

The principal change made in the procedural law of the subject by this Title has been with respect to the partition by sale of property in which an absentee has an interest. The former R.S. 9:171–178, and the former R.S. 13:4976–4983, permitting the private sale of property in which an absentee had an interest to effect a partition, did not provide adequate protection of the rights of the absentee, and have proven unworkable in practice. The former R.S. 13:4971–4975, permitting a partition by licitation of property in which an absentee had an interest, offered much greater protection of the latter's rights, but was so extremely narrow in its application that it was not available in any large number of cases. Chapter 2 of this Title provides solutions of the problems presented by permitting the partition by licitation in all cases where an absentee owns an interest in property, and makes no provision for the private sale

Tit. 9   PARTITION BETWEEN CO-OWNERS   Art. 4601

thereof. Its articles contain additional safeguards to protect the rights of an absentee.

The former R.S. 13:4984, which authorized the partition in kind without the necessity of drawing lots of property in which a minor or an interdict had an interest, really sanctioned a conventional partition. Similarly, the former R.S. 9:671–674, which authorized the sale of the interest of a minor or an interdict in property owned in indivision with others to effect a partition, actually did not constitute a judicial partition. Both of these partitions technically were nonjudicial. But since these modes of partition require judicial authority, and must be considered by attorneys in determining the type of partition best suited to their clients' needs, the substance of both are included in this Title.

CHAPTER 1. GENERAL DISPOSITIONS

Art.
4601. Methods of partition.
4602. Judicial partition.
4603. Same; procedure; venue.
4604. Inventory.
4605. Preference; appointment of notary; discretion of court.
4606. Partition in kind.
4607. Partition by licitation.
4608. Controversy before notary effecting partition.
4609. Homologation of partition.
4610. Opposition to homologation.
4611. Supplementary partition when rule to reject or opposition to homologation sustained.
4612. Finality of partition when rule to reject or opposition unfounded.
4613. Attorney's fee in uncontested proceedings.
4614. Purchase by co-owner of property or interest sold.

Art. 4601. Methods of partition

Partition of property may be made either nonjudicially or judicially.

Source: New; cf. C.C. Art. 1294.

Cross Reference: Art. 3461.

Comments

(a) The source provision classifies partitions as being either voluntary or judicial. The nonjudicial partition of this article is somewhat broader than the voluntary partition of the source provision. See Introduction to this Title, *supra*, and Comments under Art. 4602, *infra*.

(b) See Arts. 3401 and 3462, *supra*, for the basic rules regulating the partition of successions.

Art. 4602   PARTITION BETWEEN CO-OWNERS   Bk. 7

Art. 4602.   Judicial partition

Partition must be judicial when:

(1) A party is an unrepresented absentee, minor, or mental incompetent; or

(2) All the interested parties cannot agree upon a nonjudicial partition.

Source: C.P. Art. 1021; C.C. Art. 1323.

Cross Reference: Art. 3461.

Comments

(a) An absentee represented by an attorney in fact may join his co-owners in a nonjudicial partition. Partition of property in which an unrepresented absentee has an interest must be made judicially, either under the provisions of this Chapter and of Art. 5091(1), *infra*, or under the provisions of Chapter 2 of this Title.

For the definition of absentee, see Art. 5251, *infra*.

(b) Property in which a minor or interdict who has a legal representative has an interest may be partitioned judicially under the provisions of this Chapter and of Arts. 732 or 733, *supra*.

If the legal representative is authorized to act by the court, the property may be: (1) sold to effect a partition under Art. 4641, *infra;* or (2) partitioned in kind without the necessity of drawing lots, under Art. 4642, *infra*. While judicial authority for both is required, neither of these is technically a judicial partition.

If the minor or mental incompetent has no legal representative, the partition must be judicial, and under the provisions of this Chapter and of Article 5091(2), *infra*.

Art. 4603.   Same; procedure; venue

A person desiring a judicial partition of property shall petition for it in a court of competent jurisdiction. The partition proceeding shall be brought in the venue provided by Article 80(2) if the property sought to be partitioned is immovables, or both movables and immovables; or in the parish where some of the property is situated, if it consists only of movables.

Except as otherwise provided by law, a partition proceeding is subject to the rules regulating ordinary proceedings.

Source: C.P. Arts. 1024–1027; C.C. Art. 1328.

Cross References: Arts. 3461, 4629.

Comments

(a) Arts. 1024–1027 of the Code of Practice contemplate that the action to provoke a partition is an ordinary proceeding. Although

674

Art. 1328 of the Civil Code provides that in an action for partition "the judge is bound to pronounce thereon in a summary manner," all that this means is that he will proceed with the least possible delay and "in preference to the ordinary suits pending before him." In this connection, see Art. 4605, *infra*, providing that partition suits are to be tried by preference.

(b) The exception at the beginning of the second paragraph refers to: (1) the use of summary proceedings in the homologation of a judicial partition or in the trial of an opposition thereto, under Arts. 4609 and 4610, *infra;* and (2) the trial of partition proceedings in vacation, under Art. 196(4), *supra*.

Art. 4604. Inventory

The court may order that an inventory be made of all property sought to be partitioned, in accordance with the provisions of Articles 3131 through 3137.

Source: C.C. Art. 1324.

Cross Reference: Art. 3461.

Comment

Art. 1324 of the Civil Code provides that every partition shall be preceded by an inventory, in which the effects to be divided shall be appraised according to the form prescribed for public inventories. The taking of inventories in succession matters is governed by Arts. 3131 through 3137, *supra*, which are made applicable for the taking of inventories for partition purposes. Under Art. 3136, *supra*, the public inventory required by those articles may be dispensed with and a descriptive list of property substituted therefor.

Art. 4605. Preference; appointment of notary; discretion of court

A partition proceeding shall be tried with preference over other ordinary proceedings.

After the trial of the proceeding, if the court finds that the plaintiff is entitled to a partition of the property, the court shall appoint a notary to make the partition in accordance with law.

Except as otherwise provided in Article 4606, the court has discretion to direct the manner and conditions of effecting the partition, so that it will be most advantageous and convenient to the parties.

Source: C.P. Art. 1027; C.C. Arts. 1328, 1345; cf. C.C. Art. 1336.

Cross References: Arts. 3461, 4629.

Art. 4605 PARTITION BETWEEN CO-OWNERS

Comments

(a) The first sentence of this article is based upon Civil Code Art. 1328, which provides that the judge is bound to proceed with the least possible delay and in preference to the ordinary suits pending before him.

(b) The remainder of this article is based on Art. 1027 of the Code of Practice and Art. 1345 of the Civil Code. Unlike Art. 1336 of the Civil Code, which subjects the discretion of the court in the mode of effecting a partition to other provisions of that Code, the above article gives the court full and unrestricted discretion in directing the manner in which the partition is to be made, except as provided in Art. 4606, *infra*, which requires the partition to be made in kind unless the property is indivisible by nature or cannot be conveniently divided. In this connection, see Fertel v. Fertel, 226 La. 307, 76 So.2d 377 (1954) in which the court held that, under Art. 1336 of the Civil Code, the court was without authority to order the sale of property in a manner other than as listed in the inventory and suggested in the petition.

(c) This article does not affect the practice, observed in some parishes, whereby, although a notary is appointed, the co-owners and coheirs simply sign the act of sale and divide the proceeds in cases of no contest.

(d) See Comments under Art. 4603, *supra*.

Art. 4606. Partition in kind

Except as otherwise provided by law, or unless the property is indivisible by nature or cannot conveniently be divided, the court shall order the partition to be made in kind.

Source: C.C. Arts. 1339, 1340.

Cross References: Arts. 3461, 4605.

Comments

(a) The exception at the beginning of this article refers to Art. 4621, *infra*. See, also, Art. 4641, *infra*.

(b) This article makes no change in the law. The question as to whether the property is susceptible of division or cannot be conveniently divided is governed by the jurisprudential rules developed under the source provisions.

Art. 4607. Partition by licitation

When a partition is to be made by licitation, the sale shall be conducted at public auction and after the advertisements required for judicial sales under execution. At any time prior to the sale, the parties may agree upon a nonjudicial partition.

Source: C.C. Arts. 1339, 1346.

Cross References: Arts. 3461, 4629.

Comments

(a) No change in the law is made by this article. Art. 1339 of the Civil Code provides that, when the property is indivisible by nature or cannot be conveniently divided, the judge shall order that it be sold at public auction, and Art. 1346 provides that, if the heirs who have instituted the partition suit are of age and present, they may continue the partition amicably and in the manner they think proper.

(b) The procedure in cases involving property of absentees, minors, and interdicts is governed by the articles in Chapters 2 and 3 of this Title.

(c) See, also, Comments under Arts. 4609 and 4610, *infra*.

(d) The requirements for judicial sales under execution are set forth in Art. 2331, *supra*.

Art. 4608. Controversy before notary effecting partition

If there should be any controversy between the parties in the course of the proceedings before the notary effecting the partition, he shall record the objections and declarations of the parties in his proces verbal. Unless otherwise ordered by the court, such objections shall not suspend the proceedings before the notary, but any party may present his objections to the court in his opposition to the homologation of the partition.

Source: Cf. C.P. Art. 1028; C.C. Art. 1368.

Cross Reference: Art. 3461.

Comments

(a) Under Art. 1368 of the Civil Code, if, in the course of the partition, contestations arose, the officer to whom the partition had been referred was required to suspend the proceedings and refer the matter to the judge for his decision thereon. The above article changes this rule by providing that the proceedings shall continue. Once the objections have been noted in the procès verbal, emergency relief, if necessary, may always be obtained from the court.

(b) See, also, Comments under Art. 4607, *supra*.

Art. 4609. Homologation of partition

When the partition has been completed by the notary, he shall file his procès verbal of the partition, or a copy thereof, in the court which ordered the partition. Any party may rule all other parties into court to show cause why the partition should not be homologated or rejected.

Source: C.P. Art. 1029; C.C. Art. 1374.

Cross References: Arts. 3461, 4611.

Comment

See Comments under Art. 4610, *infra*.

Art. 4610. Opposition to homologation

An opposition may be filed at any time prior to the homologation of the partition. If no opposition has been filed, the partition may be homologated at any time after ten days from the service of the rule to show cause.

Source: C.P. Arts. 1029, 1030; C.C. Arts. 1374, 1375.

Cross References: Arts. 3461, 4611.

Comments to Arts. 4609 and 4610

(a) Except for the minor changes noted below, these articles follow their source provisions. See 3 La.L.Rev. 98, 133, 134 (1940).

(b) Art. 1029 of the Code of Practice and Art. 1374 of the Civil Code required that the procès verbal be filed by an interested party. Art. 4609, *supra*, requires that it, or a copy thereof, be filed by the notary. In Orleans Parish, where the notary is the custodian of his own records, a copy of the procès verbal would be filed. In all other parishes, the notary would file the procès verbal.

There may be occasions, of course, when the partition as made by the notary is accepted by all parties without filing the procès verbal in court, or having it homologated. *Cf.* Art. 4607, *supra*, and Art. 1346 of the Civil Code.

(c) Art. 4609, *supra*, differently from its source provisions, permits a dissatisfied party to file a rule for the rejection of the partition.

(d) Service of the rule to show cause is made in accordance with Art. 1314, *supra*.

Tit. 9 PARTITION BETWEEN CO-OWNERS Art. 4613

Art. 4611. Supplementary partition when rule to reject or opposition to homologation sustained

When a rule to reject the partition, or an opposition to its homologation, is sustained in whole or in part, the court shall rectify the partition, or refer the parties to the same or another notary who shall prepare a supplementary act of partition in conformity with the order of the court.

Articles 4609 and 4610 apply to this supplementary partition.

Source: C.P. Art. 1031; C.C. Art. 1376.

Cross Reference: Art. 3461.

Comments

(a) This article follows substantially the text of its source provisions. However, under the above article, it is within the discretion of the court to rectify the partition or to refer it to a notary for a supplementary partition.

(b) The opposition referred to in this article does not pertain to the sale made to effect the partition. See Hollingsworth v. Caldwell, 195 La. 30, 196 So. 10 (1940).

Art. 4612. Finality of partition when rule to reject or opposition unfounded

When the court finds that a rule to reject the partition, or an opposition to its homologation, is unfounded and that all legal formalities have been observed, it shall homologate the act of partition.

Source: C.P. Art. 1032; C.C. Art. 1377.

Cross Reference: Art. 3461.

Comment

This article is a restatement of the source provisions and effects no change in the law.

Art. 4613. Attorney's fee in uncontested proceedings

When there is no contest of the partition proceeding by any defendant, the court shall allow the attorney for the plaintiff a reasonable fee for his services. Except as provided in the second paragraph of this article, the fee shall be taxed as costs of court and paid out of the mass of the funds or the property partitioned, or the proceeds of the latter if sold.

Art. 4613 PARTITION BETWEEN CO-OWNERS

No portion of the fee may be paid out of the share of any party represented in the proceeding by an attorney, whether appointed by the court or selected by the party.

Source: Former R.S. 13:4524.

Cross Reference: Art. 3461.

Comment

No change in the law is made by this article.

Art. 4614. Purchase by co-owner of property or interest sold

Any property or interest therein sold to effect a partition, whether by licitation or by private sale, may be purchased by a co-owner.

Source: New; cf. former R.S. 9:177, former R.S. 13:4982.

Cross References: Arts. 3461, 4629.

Comments

(a) This article makes no change in the law, except as noted below.

(b) Under this article, property in which a minor or an interdict has an interest, and which is sold to effect a partition, may be purchased by his tutor or curator if authorized by the court as a prudent investment, under Arts. 4269, 4270, and 4554, *supra*.

CHAPTER 2. PARTITION WHEN CO-OWNER AN ABSENTEE

Art.
4621. Partition by licitation.
4622. Petition.
4623. Order; service of citation; contradictory proceedings.
4624. Publication of notice.
4625. Trial; judgment ordering sale.
4626. Judgment ordering reimbursement or payment of amounts due co-owner out of proceeds of sale.
4627. Effect of judgment and sale.
4628. Deposit of absentee's share into registry of court.
4629. Articles applicable to partition by licitation.
4630. Partition in kind when defendant appears and prays therefor.

Art. 4621. Partition by licitation

When one of the co-owners of property sought to be partitioned is an absentee, the partition may be effected by licitation, as provided in this Chapter, whether the property is divisible in kind or not.

Source: New; cf. former R.S. 13:4971.

Comments

(a) For the definition of "absentee", see Art. 5251, *infra*.

(b) The articles in this Chapter are much broader than their indirect source provisions. Under the former R.S. 13:4973, the indirect source provisions of these articles were limited to cases where the absentee had not, to the knowledge of the plaintiff, paid taxes on the property or exercised any acts of ownership thereof for the past ten years. No such limitation is contained in the articles in this Chapter, which are intended to be available in all cases where an absentee owns property in indivision with others.

(c) The former R.S. 9:171–178 and the former R.S. 13:4976–4983, which permitted the private sale of property owned by an absentee in indivision with others, provided inadequate protection of the rights of the absentee. For this reason, no corresponding provisions have been incorporated into this Chapter, which is limited to authority for a partition by licitation.

Property owned by an absentee in indivision with others may also be partitioned under the provisions of Chapter 1 of this Title. See Comment (a) under Art. 4602, *supra*.

(d) See, also, Comments under Art. 4606, *supra*.

Art. 4622. Petition

The petition for the partition of property in which an absentee owns an interest, under the articles of this Chapter, shall allege the facts showing that the absent and unrepresented defendant is an absentee, as defined in Article 5251, shall describe the property sought to be partitioned and allege the ownership interests thereof, and shall be supported by an affidavit of the petitioner or of his counsel that the facts alleged in the petition are true.

Source: New; cf. former R.S. 13:4971 and 13:4972.

Comment

This article simplifies the statement of the required allegations of the petition, and makes no change in the law.

Art. 4623. Order; service of citation; contradictory proceedings

When the petition for a partition discloses that the plaintiff is entitled thereto, and that the absent and unrepresented defendant is an absentee who owns an interest in the property, the court shall appoint an attorney at law to represent the absent defendant, and

Art. 4623 PARTITION BETWEEN CO-OWNERS

shall order the publication of notice of the institution of the proceeding.

The citation to the absent defendant and all other process shall be served on or service thereof accepted by the attorney at law appointed to represent him, and all proceedings shall be conducted contradictorily against this attorney.

Source: New; cf. former R.S. 13:4971 and 13:4972.

Comments

(a) The principal change in the law made by this article is the requirement of publication of notice of the institution of the proceeding, as was required by the former R.S. 9:172 and 13:4977, instead of service by posting on the bulletin board of the court, as was required by the former R.S. 13:4971. The latter service is ineffective, and notice by publication affords better protection of the rights of the absentee.

(b) For the rules regulating the appointment of the attorney at law to represent the absentee, and the duties of this attorney, see Arts. 5091 *et seq., infra.*

Art. 4624. Publication of notice

Notice of the institution of the proceeding shall be published at least once in the parish where the partition proceeding is instituted, in the manner provided by law. This notice shall set forth the title and docket number of the proceeding, the name and address of the court, and a description of the property sought to be partitioned, and shall notify the absent defendant that the plaintiff is seeking to have the property partitioned by licitation, and that the absent defendant has fifteen days from the date of the publication of notice, or of the initial publication of notice if there is more than one publication, to answer the plaintiff's petition.

Source: New; cf. former R.S. 9:172, 13:4971, and 13:4977.

Comments

(a) See Comment (a) under Art. 4623, *supra.*

(b) For the requirements of publication generally, see R.S. 43:-203.

Art. 4625. Trial; judgment ordering sale

Except as otherwise provided in Article 4630, if the petitioner proves on the trial of the proceeding that he is a co-owner of the property and entitled to the partition thereof and that the defendant is an absentee who owns an interest therein, the court shall render judgment ordering the public sale of the property for cash by the sheriff to effect a partition, after the advertisement required by law for a sale under execution.

The judgment shall determine the absentee's share in the proceeds of the sale, and award a reasonable fee to the attorney appointed to represent him to be paid from the absentee's share of the proceeds of the sale.

Source: New; cf. former R.S. 13:4974.

Comments

(a) This article makes no change in the law, but see Art. 4628, *infra*, and Comments thereunder.

(b) The requirements of publication of notice of a judicial sale under execution are set forth in Art. 2331, *supra*.

Art. 4626. Judgment ordering reimbursement or payment of amounts due co-owner out of proceeds of sale

A judgment ordering the public sale of property to effect a partition under the provisions of this Chapter shall order, out of the proceeds of such sale:

(1) The reimbursement to a co-owner of the amount proven to be due him for the payment of taxes on the property, and the expenses of preservation thereof; and

(2) The payment to a co-owner of the amount proven to be due him by another co-owner who has received and retained the fruits and revenues of the property.

Source: New; cf. former R.S. 13:4975.

Comments

This article is considerably broader than its indirect source provision, and makes it possible for a co-owner to obtain judgment not only for taxes paid, but for the expenses of preservation, and for his share of the fruits and revenues collected by another co-owner.

This article does not retain the language of its indirect source provision "if . . . the claim for the same shall not have been prescribed." This language makes it doubtful as to who has the burden of proving prescription. Under this article, if the claim is prescribed, the adverse party has the burden of pleading and proving the prescription.

Art. 4627. Effect of judgment and sale

The judgment ordering the public sale of the property to effect a partition, and the sale made in compliance therewith, has the same force and effect as to the absentee, his succession representative and heirs, as if he had been served personally with process and the judgment had been rendered against him personally. Thereafter, the absentee, his succession representative and heirs are precluded from asserting any right, title, or interest in the property partitioned.

Source: New; cf. former R.S. 9:175, 13:4980.

Comment

This article is declaratory of what would be the jurisprudential rules on the subject, if the validity of the judgment or sale were questioned.

Art. 4628. Deposit of absentee's share into registry of court

After deducting the portion of the court costs and expenses of the sale to be paid by the absentee, the fee awarded by the court to the attorney appointed to represent him, and any amount required by the judgment to be paid a co-owner, the absentee's share of the proceeds of the sale shall be deposited into the registry of the court for the account of the absentee, his succession representative or heirs. This deposit may be withdrawn only on order of the court, in accordance with the law regulating such deposits.

Source: New; cf. former R.S. 9:176 and 13:4981.

Comment

This article accords with the provisions of the former R.S. 9:176 and 13:4981, rather than with those of the former R.S. 13:4974. If the net share of the absentee is paid to the state treasurer, it may require a legislative appropriation to pay it to the absentee, his personal representative or heirs. Cf. Art. IV, § 1, of the Constitution.

Art. 4629. Articles applicable to partition by licitation

Article 4603, the first paragraph of Article 4605, and Articles 4607 and 4614 are applicable to a partition by licitation under the provisions of this Chapter.

Source: New.

Comment

The provisions referred to in this article are the rules of venue, ordinary procedure, trial by preference, partition by licitation, and permitting a co-owner to purchase the property sold to effect a partition.

Art. 4630. Partition in kind when defendant appears and prays therefor

If the property sought to be partitioned is divisible in kind, and the defendant timely answers through counsel of his own selection and prays therefor, the court shall render judgment ordering the partition to be made in kind, under the applicable provisions of Chapter 1 of this Title.

Source: New; cf. Comments following.

Cross Reference: Art. 4625.

Comments

This article makes a change in the law: (1) to meet the objection which otherwise would be raised by Roy O. Martin Lumber Co. v. Strange, 106 So.2d 723 (La.1958); and (2) to afford greater protection of the rights of an absentee.

In the case cited, it was held that the former R.S. 9:171–178 could not be employed if the defendant appeared through counsel of his own selection. Such an appearance would have forced the plaintiff to institute a new proceeding against the absentee to effect a partition under the general laws; and in this new proceeding, the property, of course, would have had to be partitioned in kind, if susceptible of division. Under this article, a new proceeding is not required if the defendant appears personally, and the property can still be partitioned by licitation unless the defendant prays for a partition in kind and the property is divisible.

Since a Louisiana domiciliary is entitled to a partition in kind if the property is divisible, an absentee should be entitled to the same privilege if he appears personally and claims it.

CHAPTER 3. PARTITION WHEN CO-OWNER A MINOR OR INTERDICT

Art.
4641. Sale of interest of minor or interdict to effect partition.
4642. Partition in kind, dispensing with drawing of lots when authorized by court.

Art. 4641. Sale of interest of minor or interdict to effect partition

The undivided interest of a minor or interdict in property owned in common with others may be sold to effect a partition, as provided

Art. 4641   PARTITION BETWEEN CO–OWNERS   Bk. 7

in Articles 4301 through 4304, 4321 through 4323, 4341, 4342, and 4554.

The interest of the minor or interdict in the property may be purchased by a co-owner.

Source: Former R.S. 9:671–9:674.

Comments

(a) This article makes no change in the law. Its inclusion in this Title is for the sake of completeness. The articles referred to therein are in the Titles on Tutorship and on Interdiction and Curatorship of Interdicts, and regulate the public and private sale of property in which a minor or an interdict has an undivided interest.

(b) The source of this article is also the source of the articles referred to in the above article.

(c) See, also, Comments under Arts. 4602, 4606, *supra*.

Art. 4642.   Partition in kind, dispensing with drawing of lots when authorized by court

Property may be divided in kind without the necessity of drawing lots therefor when all of the co-owners who are competent agree to the proposed partition, and the court has authorized it on behalf of the incompetent co-owner, as provided in Articles 4271 and 4554.

In such event there is no necessity for a judicial partition, and the division of the property may be made by agreement of the co-owners, with the legal representative of an incompetent co-owner executing the act of partition in behalf of the incompetent whom he represents.

Source: New; cf. former R.S. 13:4984.

Comments

(a) No change in the law is made by the first paragraph of this article.

(b) The second paragraph makes it clear that the partition may be made nonjudicially, once authority is obtained from the court to permit the legal representative to act for the incompetent he represents.

(c) See, also, Comments under Art. 4602, *supra*.

TITLE X

CONCURSUS PROCEEDINGS

Art.
4651. Definition.
4652. Claimants who may be impleaded.
4653. Parish where proceeding brought.
4654. Petition.
4655. Service of process; delay for answer.
4656. Each defendant both plaintiff and defendant; no responsive pleadings to answer; no default required.
4657. Failure of defendant to answer timely.
4658. Deposit of money into registry of court.
4659. Costs.
4660. Injunctive relief.
4661. Applicability of articles to proceedings under certain special statutes.
4662. Rules of ordinary proceeding applicable.

INTRODUCTION

The concursus procedure of civilian jurisdictions can be readily traced back to Romano-canonical law. McMahon 1747, n. 3. The parentage of the concursus procedure of Louisiana is left in some doubt. A few cases suggest the possibility that it was an inheritance from Spanish law. See Clarke v. Saloy, 2 La.Ann. 987 (1847); and Lauterbach v. Seikman, 125 La. 839, 51 So. 1008 (1910). However, it is more probable that it was derived from the French *procédure en concours* used in the administration of insolvent estates by syndics. In the first place, the insolvency laws of this state were lifted almost bodily from Arts. 1265–1270 of the French Civil Code. *Cf.* Arts. 166–172, Digest of the Civil Laws 294 (1808); Arts. 2166–2180, Civil Code of 1825. Secondly, the earliest use of concursus procedure in Louisiana was in the administration of insolvent estates, as attested by cases too numerous to permit citation. Its use in this area was curtailed when the state insolvency laws were suspended by the adoption of the first National Bankruptcy Act, but the repeal of the latter in 1860 revived its primary utility. On the adoption of the National Bankruptcy Act of 1898, the state insolvency laws were again suspended and the usefulness of the procedural remedy was again restricted. But by this time, the potentialities of concursus procedure had been recognized, and the jurisprudence extended it to other areas of the law. See Lauterbach v. Seikman, *supra*; State v. Alexander, 106 La. 460, 31 So. 60 (1901); Dunlap v. Whitmer, 137 La. 792, 69 So. 737 (1914); New York Life Ins. Co. v. Dorsett, 152 La. 67, 92 So. 737 (1922); and Seal v. Gano, 160 La. 636, 107 So. 473 (1926). During this period, the legislature likewise extended its use by making it available in cases involving construction contracts, both private and public, for the adjudication of the numerous claims of the owner, contractor, laborers, and materialmen against each other. See La.Act 167 of 1912 and La.Act 224 of 1918. Long prior to the adoption of the Interpleader Act, concursus procedure provided a most effective counterpart of interpleader in Louisiana. See Lauterbach v. Seikman, *supra*; Dunlap v. Whitmer, *supra*; and New York Life Ins. Co. v. Dorsett, *supra*. But even though there was no actual need for an interpleader statute, one was adopted in La.Act 123 of 1922. This statute led to the reception of limitations imposed on interpleader in other jurisdictions, see American Surety Co. of New York v. Brim, 175 La. 959, 144 So. 727 (1932); and it discouraged the jurisprudential development of concursus procedure.

The fountain-head of Anglo-American interpleader is the old common law writ of the same name. Chafee, Cases on Equitable Remedies 1 (1938). But it was in the chancery courts that the principles of interpleader were developed, and the use of the remedy became common. Limitations on the use of the equitable remedy were imposed by four technical requirements: (1) the same thing, debt, or duty had to be claimed by all the parties interpleaded; (2) all of the claims had to be derived from a common source; (3) the plaintiff could not claim any interest in the subject matter; and (4) the plaintiff must have had no independent liability to any defendant, but must be a mere stakeholder. 4 Pomeroy, Equity Jurisprudence (5th ed.) 906 *et seq.* (1941). These restrictions curtailed the usefulness of interpleader to such an extent that the equitable bill in the nature of interpleader was developed to provide a remedy where the plaintiff claimed something himself, or denied liability in whole or in part, or where the defendants claimed different amounts.

"The most modern and liberal method of obtaining interpleader to be found" is Fed.Rule 22, supplementing and broadening 28 U. S.C. § 1335. 1 Moore's Federal Practice (2d ed.) 3007 (1948). It removes the technical restrictions on interpleader by combining it with the bill in the nature of interpleader.

The articles in this Title: (1) codify those jurisprudential rules on concursus procedure which have been found to be useful and workable; (2) broaden the base of the procedural remedy by borrowing some of the broad and flexible principles of federal interpleader; (3) provide workable substitutes for two of the prior rules which experience has proven to be unworkable; and (4) provide, so far as practicable, a single set of rules to govern concursus procedure regardless of the use to which it may be put.

Art. 4651. Definition

A concursus proceeding is one in which two or more persons having competing or conflicting claims to money, property, or mortgages or privileges on property are impleaded and required to assert their respective claims contradictorily against all other parties to the proceeding.

Source: New.

Cross References: Arts. 3654, 4661.

Comments

No code or statutory provision heretofore has defined concursus, and no adequate definition has been provided by the jurisprudence of the state. The definition of the term in the above article is broad enough to embrace all recognized uses of the proceeding.

See, also, Comments under Art. 591, *supra*.

Art. 4652. Claimants who may be impleaded

Persons having competing or conflicting claims may be impleaded in a concursus proceeding even though the person against whom the claims are asserted denies liability in whole or in part to any or all of the claimants, and whether or not their claims, or the titles on which the claims depend, have a common origin, or are identical or independent of each other.

No claimant may be impleaded in a concursus proceeding whose claim has been prosecuted to judgment. No person claiming damages for wrongful death or for physical injuries may be impleaded in a concursus proceeding, except by a casualty insurer which admits liability for the full amount of the insurance coverage, and has deposited this sum into the registry of the court.

Source: New; cf. Fed.Rule 22(1).

Cross Reference: Art. 4661.

Comments

(a) The first paragraph of this article removes the jurisprudential limitations on the remedy made possible when La.Act 123 of 1922 introduced the concept of interpleader, and thus paved the way for the recognition of all of the limitations on interpleader in the common law. See American Surety of New York v. Brim, 175 La. 959, 144 So. 727 (1932). The language of this paragraph is based on Fed.Rule 22(1), which combines interpleader with the bill in the nature of interpleader and removes the former limitations and restrictions on the use of the remedy.

Under the first paragraph of the above article, the remedy is no longer limited to a stakeholder, or to an obligor who admits his indebtedness but does not know to whom a fund in his hands should be distributed. The remedy may now be used not only to prevent multiple liability, but to prevent multiple litigation, and thus may be used by a person against whom multiple claims are asserted, although liability on some or all of these claims is denied.

(b) The prohibition against impleading a claimant who has prosecuted his claim to judgment is universal. American Surety Co. of New York v. Brim, *supra*. This prohibition is retained for the protection of a claimant who has prosecuted his claim to judgment, and otherwise would be forced to relitigate the matter, not only with the obligor, but with all other adverse claimants.

(c) The prohibition contained in the last sentence of this article prevents an abuse of the remedy by a tortfeasor or his insurer, so as to deprive claimants for damages for wrongful death or physical injuries of their right of separate suits against the tortfeasor or his insurer, to select the jurisdiction and the venue, and to a trial by jury.

(d) See, also, Comments under Art. 4658, *infra*.

Art. 4653. Parish where proceeding brought

Except as provided in the second paragraph of this article, a concurcus proceeding may be brought in any parish of proper venue, under Article 42, as to any claimant impleaded therein.

If the competing or conflicting claims are for money due or claimed to be due on account of, or otherwise involve, any sale, lease, or other transaction affecting or pertaining to immovable property or any character of interest therein, the proceeding shall be brought in the parish where the immovable property or any part thereof is situated.

Source: New; cf. former R.S. 13:4811.

Cross Reference: Art. 4661.

Comments

(a) Prior to its amendment in 1954, former R.S. 13:4811 provided merely that the proceeding should be filed in a court "having jurisdiction." Under this language it was held that since a concursus proceeding is essentially a proceeding in rem, the proper venue was at the domicile of the person who owed the money deposited, *i. e.*, the plaintiff; but where mineral rights were involved, it was held that the proceeding could be brought in the parish where the land was situated. See 15 La.L.Rev. 44 (1954), and cases cited therein.

(b) The first paragraph of this article changes the rule of venue. The situation covered by this paragraph is closely analogous to the case where joint or solidary obligors are sued, and the plaintiff is given the option to sue at the domicile of any obligor made a defendant. *Cf.* Art. 73, *supra*. This analogy has been followed.

The cross references in the first paragraph of this article are to articles stating the general rules of venue with respect to the various types of defendants, *e. g.*, individuals, corporations, partnerships, et al.

(c) The second paragraph is based on La.Act 523 of 1954, which amended former R.S. 13:4811.

Art. 4654. Petition

The petition in a concursus proceeding shall comply with Article 891, shall allege the nature of the competing or conflicting claims, and shall include a prayer that all of the persons having such claims be required to assert their respective claims contradictorily against all other parties to the proceeding.

Source: New; cf. former R.S. 13:4812, 13:4813.

Cross Reference: Art. 4661.

Comments

(a) The cross reference is to the article providing the requisites of the petition in an ordinary proceeding.

(b) In Bland v. Good Citizens Mut. Ben. Ass'n, 64 So.2d 29 (La. App.1953), the court permitted the defendant to convert the suit into a concursus proceeding through what was, in effect, a reconventional demand. There is no intention to overrule this decision or to prohibit the procedure employed. R.S. 45:920 and R.S. 54:17 specifically authorize a defendant to employ this procedure in the cases there provided for. Since none of the provisions of this Title prohibit such procedure, under Art. 4662, *infra*, a defendant may always convert a suit against him into a concursus proceeding by reconvention. In such a case, his petition in reconvention must comply with the above article.

Art. 4655. Service of process; delay for answer

Service of citation and a copy of the petition in a concursus proceeding shall be made in the same form and manner, and the delays for answering are the same, as in an ordinary proceeding.

Source: Former R.S. 13:4814.

Cross Reference: Art. 4661.

Art. 4656. Each defendant both plaintiff and defendant; no responsive pleadings to answer; no default required

Each defendant in a concursus proceeding is considered as being both a plaintiff and a defendant with respect to all other parties. No exceptions or responsive pleadings may be filed to the answer of a defendant, and every fact alleged therein is considered as denied or avoided by effect of law as to all other parties. If a defendant fails to answer, issue need not be joined by default.

Source: New; cf. Comments following.

Cross Reference: Art. 4661.

Comments

(a) This article codifies the jurisprudential rules stated and applied in State v. Alexander, 106 La. 460, 31 So. 60 (1901), and Graphic Arts Bldg. Co. v. Union Indemnity Co., 163 La. 1, 111 So. 470 (1926). From the very nature of the proceeding, and the large number of claimants which may be impleaded, there can be no application of the rules of an ordinary proceeding to the matters covered in the above article. See Comment (a) under Art. 4657, *infra*.

(b) Since every defendant in a concursus proceeding is both a plaintiff and a defendant, his right to the fund deposited, or to the amount claimed to be due by the plaintiff, may be asserted in his answer, and the proper judgment prayed for therein. Hence, since he may not inject issues which are extraneous to the subject matter of the proceeding and with which the other claimants impleaded are not concerned, there is neither a need for nor a possibility of the defendant reconvening.

(c) Nothing in the above article prevents a defendant from excepting to the plaintiff's petition, to raise the objections of lack of jurisdiction, improper venue, no right to implead the defendants, and so forth.

(d) The order in which the plaintiff, and the various claimants, should present their evidence, both in chief and in rebuttal, will vary, and depends to a considerable extent upon the circumstances and issues in the particular case. For this reason, it has been left to the discretion of the trial judge. In more complicated cases where a large number of claimants have been impleaded, this should be done at a pretrial conference.

Art. 4657. Failure of defendant to answer timely

If a defendant fails to answer within the delay allowed by law, any party may move for an ex parte order of court limiting the time in which an answer may be filed in the proceeding. In such event, the court shall order all defendants who have not answered to file their answers within a further delay to be assigned by the court, not exceeding ten days from the service or publication of the order.

If not more than five defendants have failed to answer timely, a copy of this order of court shall be served on each. If more than five defendants have failed to answer timely, a notice of the order of court limiting the delay for answering shall be published once in the parish in which the proceeding was filed, in the manner provided by law.

The failure of a defendant to file an answer within the delay as extended by the court precludes him thereafter from filing an answer, or from asserting his claim against the plaintiff.

Source: New; cf. Comments following.

Cross Reference: Art. 4661.

Comments

(a) The former R.S. 13:4815 provided that the "failure of anyone cited under R.S. 13:4814 to appear and answer within the time required by law, shall thereafter estop the person from claiming the money." Probably because of the harshness of the penalty imposed, the courts refused to enforce this statutory estoppel. American Surety Co. of New York v. Ryan, 185 La. 678, 170 So. 34 (1936); American Nat. Ins. Co. v. Cook, 14 La.App. 665, 130 So. 667 (1930).

Despite the prior rulings in State v. Alexander, 106 La. 460, 31 So. 60 (1901) and Graphic Arts Bldg. Co. v. Union Indemnity Co., 163 La. 1, 111 So. 470 (1926) that in a concursus proceeding issue was joined as to all parties tacitly and that the taking of defaults was unnecessary, the court in both the Ryan and Cook cases refused to apply the statutory estoppel on the ground that defaults were not taken and confirmed against the defendants who did not answer timely. The facts of the Ryan case illustrate vividly the unworkability of the decision. There were over fifty claimants impleaded and twenty-seven failed to answer timely. Had one of the claimants taken and confirmed defaults against those who failed to answer timely, it would not have affected the rights of the other claimants who answered timely against those who did not. The tardy claimants would have been estopped to claim any portion of the fund as to one, but not estopped as to the others who answered timely. This obvious difficulty was precisely the reason for the adoption of the statutory estoppel.

The harsh penalty imposed by former R.S. 13:4815 has been tempered. This article gives every claimant ample opportunity before the trial to study the pleadings of all other claimants, so that there will be ample opportunity afforded to rebut the evidence presented on the trial by each claimant. Under this article a defendant who

Art. 4657 CONCURSUS PROCEEDINGS Bk. 7

does not file his answer timely is given a second opportunity to do so, but he is estopped if he neglects to take advantage of this second opportunity.

(b) The requirements for the publication of the notice referred to in the second paragraph of the above article are set forth in R.S. 43:203.

Art. 4658. Deposit of money into registry of court

With leave of court, the plaintiff may deposit into the registry of the court money which is claimed by the defendants, and which plaintiff admits is due one or more of the defendants.

When sums of money due one or more of the defendants accrue from time to time in the hands of the plaintiff after the institution of the proceeding, with leave of court he may deposit the money as it accrues into the registry of the court.

After the deposit of money into the registry of the court, the plaintiff is relieved of all liability to all of the defendants for the money so deposited.

Source: Former R.S. 13:4811, 13:4817.

Cross Reference: Art. 4661.

Comment

The sources of this article required the deposit into court of the fund in dispute, as the former statute could be used only when the plaintiff admitted liability. As the procedure is broadened under Art. 4652, *supra*, to permit the use of the remedy even though the person against whom the claims have been asserted denies liability thereon, this article makes the deposit into the registry of the court permissive.

Art. 4659. Costs

When money has been deposited into the registry of the court by the plaintiff, neither he nor any other party shall be required to pay any of the costs of the proceeding as they accrue, but these shall be deducted from the money on deposit. The court may award the successful claimant judgment for the costs of the proceeding which have been deducted from the money on deposit, or any portion thereof, against any other claimant who contested his right thereto, as in its judgment may be considered equitable.

In all other instances, the court may render judgment for costs as it considers equitable.

Source: New; cf. former R.S. 13:4816.

Cross Reference: Art. 4661.

Art. 4703. Delivery or service when premises abandoned or closed, or whereabouts of tenant or occupant unknown

If the premises are abandoned or closed, or if the whereabouts of the lessee or occupant is unknown, all notices, process, pleadings, and orders required to be delivered or served on the lessee or occupant under this Title may be attached to a door of the premises, and this shall have the same effect as delivery to, or personal service on, the lessee or occupant.

Source: Former R.S. 13:4916, 13:4923.

Comment

This article effects no change in the law.

Art. 4704. Definitions

Unless the context clearly indicates otherwise, as used in this Title the following terms have the following meanings:

"Lease" means any oral or written lease, and includes a sublease;

"Lessee" includes a sublessee, whether the person seeking to evict is a lessor or sublessor; and an assignee of a lessee;

"Lessor" includes a sublessor, assignee, or transferee;

"Occupant" includes a sharecropper; half hand; day laborer; former owner; and any person occupying immovable property by permission or accommodation of the owner, former owner, or another occupant, except a mineral lessee, owner of a mineral servitude, or a lessee of the owner;

"Owner" includes a lessee; and

"Premises" includes the land and all buildings and improvements thereon leased by a tenant, or possessed by an occupant.

Source: New.

Art. 4705. Lessors' rights or real actions not affected

Nothing in this Title shall be construed to deprive any lessor of any remedy heretofore allowed him either for the payment of rent due to him or for the seizure of any furniture found on the leased premises; and nothing in this Title shall be construed to conflict with the provisions of Articles 3651 through 3664.

Source: Former R.S. 13:4917, 13:4926.

CHAPTER 2. PROCEDURE

Art.
4731. Rule to show cause why possession should not be delivered.
4732. Trial of rule; judgment of eviction.
4733. Warrant for possession if judgment of eviction not complied with.
4734. Execution of warrant.
4735. Appeal; bond.

Art. 4731. Rule to show cause why possession should not be delivered

If the lessee or occupant fails to comply with the notice required to vacate required under this Title, the lessor or owner, or agent thereof, may cause the lessee or occupant to be cited summarily by a court of competent jurisdiction to show cause why he should not be ordered to deliver possession of the premises to the lessor or owner.

Source: Former R.S. 13:4912, 13:4919.

Comments

(a) This article follows the source provisions and provides the procedure to be followed after the notice to vacate has been given.

(b) Under the provisions of R.S. 37:213, it is necessary for the agent to engage an attorney to institute the eviction proceeding.

Art. 4732. Trial of rule; judgment of eviction

The court shall make the rule returnable not earlier than the third day after service thereof, at which time the court shall try the rule and hear any defense which is made.

If the court finds the lessor or owner entitled to the relief sought, or if the lessee or occupant fails to answer or to appear at the trial, the court shall render immediately a judgment of eviction ordering the lessee or occupant to deliver possession of the premises to the lessor or owner.

Source: Former R.S. 13:4913, 13:4920; cf. former R.S. 13:4912, 13:4919.

Comment

The only change effected by this article is the clarification of the return day.

Art. 4733. Warrant for possession if judgment of eviction not complied with

If the lessee or occupant does not comply with the judgment of eviction within twenty-four hours after its rendition, the court shall

TITLE XI

EVICTION OF TENANTS AND OCCUPANTS

Chap.		Art.
1.	General Dispositions	4701
2.	Procedure	4731

INTRODUCTION

These articles were drawn from former R.S. 13:4911, dealing with "occupants holding by accommodation of the owner or any other occupant" and 13:4918, dealing with persons as to whom the lessor-lessee relationship exists. As to the procedure after the initial notices, there is provided one system applicable to both of these basic situations, drawn from former R.S. 13:4911–13:4916 and 13:4918–13:4925.

CHAPTER 1. GENERAL DISPOSITIONS

Art.
4701. Termination of lease; notice to vacate.
4702. Notice to occupant other than tenant to vacate.
4703. Delivery or service when premises abandoned or closed, or whereabouts of tenant or occupant unknown.
4704. Definitions.
4705. Lessors' rights or real actions not affected.

Art. 4701. Termination of lease; notice to vacate

When a lessee's right of occupancy has ceased because of the termination of the lease by expiration of its term, action by the lessor, non-payment of rent, or for any other reason, and the lessor wishes to obtain possession of the premises, the lessor or his agent shall cause written notice to vacate the premises to be delivered to the lessee. The notice shall allow the lessee not less than five days from the date of its delivery to vacate the leased premises.

If the lease has no definite term, the notice required by law for its termination shall be considered as a notice to vacate under this article. If the lease has a definite term, notice to vacate may be given not more than thirty days before the expiration of the term.

Source: New; cf. former R.S. 13:4918.

Comments

(a) This article covers all cases of termination of lease, regardless of the cause, and fixes a notice period of five days. It represents a change in the prior law under which the notice was five, ten, or thirty days, depending upon the circumstances. The article also permits the lessor in the case of a lease having a fixed term to anticipate that the tenant will not vacate the premises at the end of the term and to give him the necessary notice prior to its expiration, so that he may take court action as soon as the term is over.

(b) The word "limitation", which appears in former R.S. 13:4918, has been omitted. See 2 La.L.Rev. 161 (1940). See, also, 21 Tul.L. Rev. 256 (1946).

(c) If the lease has already terminated and the tenant remains on the premises, the substantive problem of reconduction then enters the picture. See 21 Tul.L.Rev. 256 (1946). The above text applies to the "reconducted" lease, which is a new lease and not a continuation of the old lease. See 1 La.L.Rev. 439 (1939). The term of this reconducted lease is fixed by Civil Code Arts. 2686–2691, and it is not necessary to include these substantive provisions in an article on eviction. The notice of ten days provided for by Art. 2686 of the Civil Code is a device to prevent reconduction, and is not to be confused with the ten day notice of eviction, although presumably one notice could serve both purposes.

Art. 4702. Notice to occupant other than tenant to vacate

When an owner of immovable property wishes to evict the occupant therefrom, after the purpose of the occupancy has ceased, the owner, or his agent, shall first cause a written notice to vacate the property to be delivered to the occupant.

This notice shall allow the occupant five days from its delivery to vacate the premises.

Source: Former R.S. 13:4911.

Comments

(a) No change in the law is made by this article.

(b) See Art. 3663, *supra*, which makes injunctive relief available against squatters.

(c) In a judicial sale, the vendor can obtain possession by eviction by use of the applicable provisions of R.S. 13:4346.

(d) See Comments under Art. 4704, *infra*.

issue immediately a warrant directed to and commanding its sheriff, constable, or marshal to deliver possession of the premises to the lessor or owner.

Source: Former R.S. 13:4914, 13:4921.

Cross Reference: Art. 4734.

Comment

This article follows the source provisions except that the language relating to the payment of costs "out of any goods and chattels of the defendant subject to seizure" has been deleted as unworkable and unrealistic.

Art. 4734. Execution of warrant

The sheriff, constable, or marshal shall execute a warrant rendered under Article 4733 in the presence of two witnesses, by clearing the premises of any property therein, in order to put the lessor or owner in possession of the premises.

If the sheriff, constable, or marshal finds the windows, doors, or gates of the premises locked or barred, he shall break open any of these when necessary to effect convenient entry into the premises.

Source: Former R.S. 13:4915, 13:4922.

Comment

This article effects no change in the law.

Art. 4735. Appeal; bond

An appeal does not suspend execution of a judgment of eviction unless the defendant has answered the rule under oath, pleading an affirmative defense entitling him to retain possession of the premises, and the appeal has been applied for and the appeal bond filed within twenty-four hours after the rendition of the judgment of eviction. The amount of the suspensive appeal bond shall be determined by the court in an amount sufficient to protect the appellee against all such damage as he may sustain as a result of the appeal.

Source: Former R.S. 13:4924; cf. Comments following.

Comments

(a) Heretofore, the source provision was applicable only where the lessor-lessee relationship existed. This article applies to all cases regardless of the relationship between the parties.

(b) This article codifies the jurisprudential rule that a suspensive appeal from the judgment must be taken within twenty-four hours. Audubon v. Brounig, 119 La. 1070, 44 So. 891 (1907); State ex rel. Mallu v. Judge, 128 La. 914, 55 So. 574 (1911).

BOOK VIII.
TRIAL COURTS OF LIMITED JURISDICTION

TITLE I

GENERAL DISPOSITIONS

Art.
4831. Applicability of Book VIII.
4832. Jurisdiction of city courts in municipalities of less than 10,000 population, and justice of the peace courts.
4833. Jurisdiction of city courts in municipalities of 10,000 to 20,000 population.
4834. Jurisdiction of city courts in municipalities of 20,000 or more population, New Orleans city courts excepted.
4835. Jurisdiction of New Orleans city courts.
4836. Limitations on jurisdiction.
4837. Limitations on power and authority.
4838. Power to punish for contempt.
4839. Venue.
4840. Jury trial prohibited.
4841. Illness or absence of justice of the peace, or judge of city court; New Orleans city courts excepted.
4842. Illness or absence of judge of New Orleans city court.
4843. Recusation; grounds.
4844. Recusation of justice of the peace or city court judge; trial of motion to recuse; exceptions.
4845. Trial of motion to recuse; judges of city courts having more than one judge; Second City Court of New Orleans.
4846. Power and authority of judge ad hoc.
4847. Rules of court.

Art. 4831. Applicability of Book VIII

The provisions of this Book apply only to suits in justice of the peace and city courts, and to suits in the district courts within their jurisdiction concurrent with that of justices of the peace.

Except as otherwise provided in this Book, civil proceedings in a city court, and the enforcement of judgments rendered therein, shall be governed as far as practicable by the other provisions of this Code.

Source: New; cf. former R.S. 13:3339.

Comment

See Comments under Art. 4836, *infra*.

Art. 4832. Jurisdiction of city courts in municipalities of less than 10,000 population, and justice of the peace courts

The civil jurisdiction of city courts where the population within their respective territorial jurisdiction is less than ten thousand, and of justice of the peace courts, is concurrent with that of district courts in cases where the amount in dispute, or the value of the movable property involved, does not exceed one hundred dollars, exclusive of interest, including suits by landlords for the possession of leased premises where the monthly or yearly rent, or the rent for the unexpired term of the lease, does not exceed this amount.

Source: Const. Art. VII, §§ 48, 51.

Comment

See Comments under Art. 4836, *infra*.

Art. 4833. Jurisdiction of city courts in municipalities of 10,000 to 20,000 population

The civil jurisdiction of city courts where the population within their respective territorial jurisdictions is ten thousand or more but less than twenty thousand is concurrent with that of the district courts in cases where the amount in dispute, or the value of the movable property involved, does not exceed five hundred dollars, exclusive of interest and attorney's fees, including suits by landlords for the possession of leased premises where the monthly or yearly rent, or the rent for the unexpired term of the lease, does not exceed this amount.

Source: Const. Art. VII, § 51.

Comment

See Comments under Art. 4836, *infra*.

Art. 4834. Jurisdiction of city courts in municipalities of 20,000 or more population, New Orleans city courts excepted

The civil jurisdiction of city courts where the population within their respective territorial jurisdiction is twenty thousand or more is concurrent with that of district courts in cases where the amount in dispute, or the value of the movable property involved, does not exceed one thousand dollars, exclusive of interest and attorney's fees, including suits by landlords for the possession of leased premises where the monthly or yearly rent, or the rent for the unexpired term of the lease, does not exceed this amount.

This article does not apply to the city courts of New Orleans.

Source: Const. Art. VII, § 51.

Comment

See Comments under Art. 4836, *infra.*

Art. 4835. Jurisdiction of New Orleans city courts

The city courts of New Orleans have exclusive original jurisdiction of all cases, including suits for the ownership or possession of movable property where the amount in dispute, fund to be distributed, or value of the movable property, does not exceed one hundred dollars, exclusive of interest, and of suits by landlords for the possession of leased premises where the monthly rent does not exceed this amount.

These courts have concurrent jurisdiction with the Civil District Court for the Parish of Orleans in all cases, including suits for the ownership or possession of movable property where the amount in dispute, fund to be distributed, or value of the movable property, exceeds one hundred dollars but does not exceed one thousand dollars, exclusive of interest, penalties, and attorney's fees.

These courts have jurisdiction of reconventional demands and interventions filed therein and necessarily connected with or growing out of the main demand, irrespective of the amount in dispute or the value of the property.

Source: Const. Art. VII, §§ 91, 92.

Comment

See Comments under Art. 4836, *infra.*

Art. 4836. Limitations on jurisdiction

A justice of the peace, or city court other than one in New Orleans, has no jurisdiction of any of the following cases or proceedings:

(1) A case involving title to immovable property, the right to public office or position, or civil or political rights;

(2) A case in which it is sought to obtain judgment of annulment of marriage, separation from bed and board, divorce, separation of property, or for alimony;

(3) A succession, tutorship, curatorship, emancipation, partition, receivership, liquidation, habeas corpus, or quo warranto proceeding;

(4) A case in which the state, a parish, municipal, or other political corporation, or a succession, is a defendant;

(5) Any other case or proceeding excepted from the jurisdiction of these courts by law.

New Orleans city courts have no jurisdiction of any of the cases or proceedings enumerated in paragraphs (1), (2), (3), and (5) of this article.

Source: Const. Art. VII, §§ 35, 48, 91, 92.

Comments to Articles 4831 through 4836

(a) The term "city court" includes a municipal court having civil jurisdiction. Art. 5251, *infra*.

(b) Art. 4831, *supra*, makes all provisions of this Code governing the procedure in trial courts applicable to city courts, except those which are inconsistent with specific provisions of Book VIII and those which are manifestly inapplicable to city courts.

(c) Arts. 4832 through 4836, *supra*, merely restate the constitutional provisions on the same subject.

(d) The jurisdiction articles use varying elements in computing the jurisdictional amount, *viz.*, "exclusive of interest", in Art. 4832, *supra*; "exclusive of interest and attorney's fees", in Arts. 4833 and 4834, *supra*; and "exclusive of interest, penalties, and attorney's fees", in Art. 4835, *supra*. These exceptions are inconsistent but accord with the constitutional provisions on which they are based.

Art. 4837. Limitations on power and authority

A justice of the peace may not issue a writ of seizure and sale in executory process. A city court may issue a writ of seizure and sale in an executory proceeding to enforce a privilege or mortgage on movable or immovable property. The procedure shall conform with that required by this Code for an executory proceeding, except that

Art. 4837

written pleadings shall not be required if the seizure is of movable property and the claim is for not more than one hundred dollars exclusive of interest.

A justice of the peace or city court may not issue any injunctive order except to arrest the execution of its own writ.

Source: New; cf. former R.S. 13:1879, 13:1923, 13:2621; La. Act 196 of 1916.

Comments

(a) This article prohibits the use of executory process by justice of the peace courts. These courts did not have such power until 1916, when Act 196 conferred it upon justice of the peace courts in cities having a population of over 50,000. However, Act 196 of 1916 was repealed by Act 2 of the Extra Session of 1950. Thus, this article does not effect any change with respect to the use of executory process.

(b) The third sentence of the above article provides appropriate limitations on the exercise of the power of city courts to issue executory process on immovable property.

(c) The constitution does not confer on justice of the peace or city courts specific injunctive powers, and under the second paragraph of this article such power is restricted to arresting the execution of their own writs.

Art. 4838. Power to punish for contempt

A justice of the peace may punish a direct contempt of court as defined in Art. 222 by a fine of not more than ten dollars, or imprisonment in the parish jail for not more than twenty-four hours, or both.

A city court has the same power to punish a contempt of court as a district court.

Source: New; cf. C.P. Art. 1154.

Comment

This article limits specifically the contempt powers of justices of the peace.

Art. 4839. Venue

The rules of venue provided in Articles 41 through 45, and 71 through 79, apply to suits brought in a justice of the peace or city court, except that where these articles use the word "parish" it shall be construed to mean the territorial jurisdiction of the respective court.

Source: C.P. Arts. 1069, 1070, 1071.

Comment

This article adopts the general venue concepts. Technical considerations required that the geographical limits of venue in justice of the peace and city courts which are smaller units than in the case of district courts be specifically stated. Otherwise, the basic concepts of the general venue articles are retained.

Art. 4840. Jury trial prohibited

There shall be no trial by jury in any case in a justice of the peace or city court.

Source: New.

Comment

Art. 1733, *supra*, excludes jury trials in cases involving less than $1,000.00.

Art. 4841. Illness or absence of justice of the peace, or judge of city court; New Orleans city courts excepted

If a justice of the peace cannot try a case within a reasonable time because of illness or absence, the district court of the parish shall appoint a qualified person to act as justice of the peace ad hoc to try the case.

A judge of a city court, judges of the First and Second City Courts of the City of New Orleans excepted, who cannot try a case within a reasonable time because of illness or absence shall appoint a person having the qualifications required for election to the office and domiciled in the parish to try the case.

Source: New; cf. former R.S. 13:2018, 13:2080.

Comment

See Comment under Art. 4842, *infra*.

Art. 4842. Illness or absence of judge of New Orleans city court

If a judge of the First City Court of the City of New Orleans cannot try a case within a reasonable time because of illness or absence, the case shall be reallotted to another judge of the court for trial.

If a judge of the Second City Court of the City of New Orleans cannot try a case within a reasonable time because of illness or absence, the case shall be tried by a judge of the First City Court of the City of New Orleans upon his order or the order of the Civil District Court for the Parish of Orleans.

Source; New; cf. former R.S. 13:1922.

Comment to Articles 4841 and 4842

These articles provide a procedure, apart from recusation, for the appointment of ad hoc judges where a justice of the peace or a city court judge is unable to try a case because of illness or absence.

Art. 4843. Recusation; grounds

A justice of the peace or a city court judge may recuse himself or be recused for the same reasons and on the same grounds as provided in Article 151.

Comment

See Comment under Art. 4845, *infra*.

Art. 4844. Recusation of justice of the peace or city court judge; trial of motion to recuse; exceptions

Except as provided in Article 4845, when a motion is made to recuse a justice of the peace or a city court judge, he shall either recuse himself or the motion to recuse shall be tried by the district court. In case of recusation, the district court shall appoint a person domiciled in the parish to try the case, who is otherwise qualified to hold the office.

This article does not apply to New Orleans city courts.

Comment

See Comment under Art. 4845, *infra*.

Art. 4845. Trial of motion to recuse; judges of city courts having more than one judge; Second City Court of New Orleans

A motion to recuse a judge of any city court which has more than one judge shall be tried by another judge of the court, in accordance with its rules. A motion to recuse the judge of the Second City Court of the City of New Orleans shall be tried by a judge appointed as provided in Article 4842.

Source of Arts. 4843–4845: New; cf. C.P. Art. 1072; former R.S. 13:2018, 13:2043, 13:2080.

Comment to Articles 4843 through 4845

These articles set up a recusation system specifically applicable to justice of the peace and city courts. The grounds of recusation are the same as in Art. 151, *supra*.

Art. 4846. Power and authority of judge ad hoc

A judge ad hoc appointed in place of a recused judge or justice of the peace, or one appointed under Article 4841 or 4842, has the same power and authority to dispose of the case as the justice of the peace or judge for whom he was appointed.

Source: New.

Comment

This article affirmatively sets forth the power of a judge ad hoc in case of transfer or recusation.

Art. 4847. Rules of court

A city court may adopt, and from time to time amend, rules for the conduct of judicial business before it, as provided in Article 193.

Article 193 has no application to justices of the peace.

Source: New: cf. former R.S. 13:1921, 13:2017, 13:2148, 13:2220, 13:2260, 13:2343.

Comment

This article permits city courts to adopt rules in the same way as district courts do. However, it expressly prohibits justice of the peace courts from making such rules.

TITLE II

CASES INVOLVING ONE HUNDRED DOLLARS OR LESS

Chap.	Art.
1. City Courts	4891
Sec.	
1. City Courts, New Orleans Excepted	4891
2. New Orleans City Courts	4921
2. Justice of the Peace Courts	4941
3. District Courts Where Jurisdiction Concurrent with Justice of the Peace Courts	4971

CHAPTER 1. CITY COURTS

SECTION 1. CITY COURTS, NEW ORLEANS EXCEPTED

Art.
- 4891. Procedure.
- 4892. Pleadings.
- 4893. Record of case; subsequent entries.
- 4894. Citation.
- 4895. Delay for answering.
- 4896. Defendant's failure to answer or parties' failure to appear; effect; proof of open account; judgment.
- 4897. Form of judgment; new trial not permitted; execution of judgment.
- 4898. Notice of judgment.
- 4899. Appeal.
- 4900. Appeal bond.
- 4901. Record on appeal.

SECTION 2. NEW ORLEANS CITY COURTS

- 4921. Procedure in cases involving less than twenty-five dollars.
- 4922. Procedure in cases involving twenty-five to one hundred dollars.

SECTION 1. CITY COURTS, NEW ORLEANS EXCEPTED

Art. 4891. Procedure

The filing and trial of a suit in a city court, and the rendition of judgment, execution, and appeal therefrom, are governed by the provisions of Articles 4892 through 4901 in cases where the amount involved is one hundred dollars or less, exclusive of interest and attorney's fees.

If a city court has no clerk of court, the duties and powers given by these articles to clerks of court shall be performed by the judge.

Source: New.

Comment

See Comments under Art. 4894, *infra*.

Art. 4892. Pleadings

A party or his attorney may state the claim, exceptions, defenses, or other pleas orally to the clerk of court, and no written pleadings are required, except:

(1) When an attachment or sequestration is demanded, an affidavit setting forth the grounds thereof must be filed;

(2) When executory process as to an immovable is demanded, the pleadings shall be in writing.

A party may file other written pleadings if he so desires, but additional fees resulting from written pleadings not required shall not be imposed upon the party cast as costs of court.

A defendant must include in his answer, whether oral or in writing, all of the exceptions upon which he intends to rely.

Source: New; cf. C.P. Arts. 1073, 1117, 1124; former R.S. 13:3331, 13:4001.

Cross References: Arts. 4891, 4921, 4941, 4971.

Comment

See Comments under Art. 4894, *infra*.

Art. 4893. Record of case; subsequent entries

The clerk of court shall record in a permanent book the title of the case, the docket number, the name and address of all parties, a brief statement of the nature and amount of the claim, the issuance and service of citation, the defenses pleaded, motions and other pleas made, the names of witnesses who testified, a list of the documents offered at the trial, the rendition of judgment, and any appeal therefrom.

The failure to record any entry in this book shall not affect the validity of the proceedings or the judgment rendered therein.

Source: New; cf. C.P. Art. 1074; former R.S. 13:3332, 13:3340.

Cross References: Arts. 4891, 4921, 4941, 4971.

Art. 4893

Comment

See Comments under Art. 4894, *infra*.

Art. 4894. Citation

The citation shall summon the defendant to comply with the demand of the plaintiff against him, or to state his answer to this demand to the clerk within five days, exclusive of legal holidays, of service of citation upon him; and shall state the location where the court is to be held.

When a written petition has been filed, a copy thereof shall be attached to the citation.

When the plaintiff has not filed a written petition, the citation shall:

(1) State the amount and nature of the claim, the year or years in which the indebtedness was contracted or arose, and shall describe sufficiently to place the defendant on notice any promissory note or other written evidence of indebtedness on which the demand is based; and

(2) Describe the movable property and state the value thereof, if the suit is for the ownership or possession of movable property.

Except as provided hereinabove, the citation shall conform to the requirements for citation issuing out of a district court.

Source: New; cf. C.P. Art. 1078; former R.S. 13:3333.

Cross References: Arts. 4891, 4921, 4941, 4971.

Comments to Articles 4891 through 4894

(a) These articles are an adaptation of the Code articles relating to procedure in justice of the peace courts and provisions dealing with "Clerks' Book Cases" contained in former R.S. 13:3331 *et seq.*

(b) Particular attention is invited to two provisions of Art. 4892, *supra:*

1. That requiring all exceptions to be included in the answer. This has been a successful practice in the New Orleans city courts.

2. That requiring all pleadings to be in writing where executory process as to an immovable is demanded. Since executory process as to an immovable affects title, all aspects of the case, including pleadings, should be of record.

Art. 4895. Delay for answering

The defendant shall answer within five days, exclusive of legal holidays, of the service of citation. A garnishee shall answer garnishment interrogatories within five days, exclusive of legal holidays, of the service of the interrogatories.

The judge or clerk may grant additional time for answering for good reason.

Source: New; cf. C.P. Art. 1082; former R.S. 13:1951, 13:1971.

Cross References: Arts. 4891, 4921, 4941, 4971.

Comment

This article reduces the delay for answering from ten to five days. Cf. C.P. Art. 1082.

Art. 4896. Defendant's failure to answer or parties' failure to appear; effect; proof of open account; judgment

If the defendant fails to answer timely, or if he fails to appear at the trial, and the plaintiff proves his case, a final judgment in favor of plaintiff may be rendered. No prior default is necessary. In such instances, when the suit is for a sum due on an open account, or other conventional obligation, prima facie proof may be submitted by affidavit.

If, after answer, the plaintiff fails to appear at the trial, judgment may be rendered dismissing the suit with prejudice, at plaintiff's cost.

Source: New; cf. C.P. Art. 1085; former R.S. 13:1877.

Cross References: Arts. 4891, 4921, 4922, 4941, 4971, 4972, 5002.

Comments

(a) This article is merely a restatement of present procedure in so far as default judgments are concerned. It spells out the nature of proof, which is sufficient in open account cases. However, the article broadens the provision for proof by affidavit so as to apply to all conventional obligations, instead of merely open accounts.

(b) The last paragraph of the article is not intended to preclude a dismissal without prejudice.

Art. 4897. Form of judgment; new trial not permitted; execution of judgment

The judgment shall be in writing and signed by the judge. No new trial may be granted.

Art. 4897 CITY COURTS Bk. 8

The judgment may be executed when the delay for appealing therefrom has elapsed unless a suspensive appeal has been taken as provided in Articles 4899 and 4900.

Source: New.

Cross References: Arts. 4891, 4921, 4941, 4971.

Comments

New trial in a case in a justice of the peace court, or in a city court where the amount involved is $100 or less, is abolished. Any error in the judgment may be corrected on appeal; and a new trial is unnecessary and productive of delay in cases which should be concluded speedily.

A new trial in a case involving $100 or less in a district court is retained, as there is no appeal from the judgment in such a case. See Art. 4972, *infra*.

Art. 4898. Notice of judgment

Notice of judgment shall be served on a defendant against whom judgment is rendered if the citation was not served on him personally, and he failed to answer.

Notice of judgment need not be given in any other case.

Source: C.P. Art. 1131.

Cross References: Arts. 4891, 4899, 4921, 4941, 4942, 4971, 4972, 5002.

Comment

This is an adaptation for city courts of the source provision relating to judgments in justice of the peace courts.

Art. 4899. Appeal

An appeal from a judgment rendered by a city court can be taken only within ten days from the date of judgment or of the service of notice of judgment when necessary under Article 4898.

An oral request for an appeal may be made of the judge. When a request for an appeal is made, the judge shall fix the return day no later than ten days from the request for an appeal. The date of the request for an appeal, the return day, and the amount of the appeal bond when determined by the judge as provided in Articles 2124 and 4900 shall be entered in the permanent record book.

The appeal is to the district court of the parish, where the case is tried de novo.

Source: New; cf. C.P. arts. 1128, 1129.

Cross References: Arts. 4891, 4897, 4921, 4941.

Comments

(a) The ten day return day is the same as that provided by the Code of Practice Art. 1128.

(b) In cases under $100.00, the Code of Practice Art. 1129 provides for a trial de novo. See, however, Art. VII, § 36, of the Louisiana Constitution, as amended in 1958.

(c) See, also, Comments under Art. 2087, *supra*.

Art. 4900. Appeal bond

When the appellant takes a suspensive appeal, he shall file with the clerk, within the delay allowed for taking the appeal, a written appeal bond with solvent surety in the amount provided by the applicable provisions of Article 2124.

No appeal bond is required where the appeal is devolutive only.

Source: New; cf. C.P. 1131.

Cross References: Arts. 4891, 4897, 4899, 4921, 4941.

Comment

This article follows the general procedure for suspensive appeals. However, it dispenses with a bond in devolutive appeal cases as provided by Art. 1132 of the Code of Practice.

Art. 4901. Record on appeal

When an appeal has been taken, the clerk of the city court shall transmit to the clerk of the district court, on or before the return day, the citation and return thereon, all written pleadings which may have been filed and all documents offered in evidence, the judgment, and a certificate showing all proceedings in the case.

Source: New; cf. C.P. Art. 1135.

Cross References: Arts. 4891, 4921, 4941.

Comments

(a) This article broadens the provisions of Art. 1135 of the Code of Practice. Its purpose is to bring before the appellate court a record of all procedural steps, together with the original of all documents which may have been filed.

(b) Art. 1130 of the Code provides that the parties may stipulate the facts for the appeal. This is not here codified, because it is manifest that the parties may do so without specific authorization.

Art. 4921

SECTION 2. NEW ORLEANS CITY COURTS

Art. 4921. Procedure in cases involving less than twenty-five dollars

Except as otherwise provided in this article, the rules provided in Articles 4892 through 4901 apply to a case in a New Orleans city court where the amount involved is less than twenty-five dollars.

An appeal in such a case granted prior to July 1, 1960, shall be to the Court of Appeal for the Parish of Orleans; and an appeal in such a case granted on or after July 1, 1960, shall be to the Civil District Court for the Parish of Orleans. On appeal the case shall be tried de novo by a judge of the appellate court.

Source: Const. Art. VII, § 91; former R.S. 13:1951.

Comment

See Comments under Art. 4922, *infra*.

Art. 4922. Procedure in cases involving twenty-five to one hundred dollars

The procedure in a case in a New Orleans city court within its exclusive original jurisdiction, but involving twenty-five dollars or more, is the same as that provided by law for a case in the Civil District Court for the Parish of Orleans, except that:

(1) The delay for answering shall be five days, exclusive of legal holidays, and the citation shall so state;

(2) A defendant shall incorporate in his answer all of the exceptions which he intends to plead;

(3) No prior default is necessary, and judgment may be rendered as provided in Article 4896;

(4) No notice of the rendition of judgment need be given, except as required by Article 4898;

(5) The delays for answering garnishment interrogatories shall be five days, exclusive of legal holidays;

(6) An appeal may be granted only if a written motion or petition therefor is filed, or an oral motion therefor is made in open court, within ten days of the date of judgment, or of the service of notice of judgment when necessary; and

(7) The appeal, if granted prior to July 1, 1960, shall be to the Court of Appeal for the Parish of Orleans, and if granted on or

after July 1, 1960, shall be to the Civil District Court for the Parish of Orleans, where the case shall be tried de novo by a judge thereof.

Source: New; cf. former R.S. 13:1951; Const. Art. VII, § 91.

Comments to Articles 4921 and 4922

(a) Sec. 91 of Art. VII of the Constitution of 1921, creating city courts in New Orleans, requires written pleadings in cases involving more than $25.00. Therefore it is impossible to use the procedure provided in Arts. 4892 through 4901, *supra*, for such cases in the New Orleans city courts. Instead, the above articles adopt the procedure of city courts in cases involving less than $25.00 and, with certain exceptions, the general district court procedure in cases involving more than $25.00, for New Orleans city courts.

(b) The above article requires all exceptions to be filed as part of the answer, which is essential for the expeditious handling of small cases.

(c) The above article changes the delay for answering in New Orleans city courts from three to five days.

CHAPTER 2. JUSTICE OF THE PEACE COURTS

Art.
4941. Procedure.
4942. Appeal.

Art. 4941. Procedure

The filing and trial of a suit in a justice of the peace court, and the rendition of judgment, execution and appeal therefrom, are governed by the provisions of Articles 4892 through 4901, except as provided in Article 4942.

Source: New.

Comment

See Comments under Art. 4942, *infra*.

Art. 4942. Appeal

An appeal from a judgment of a justice of the peace court can be taken only within ten days from the date of the judgment or of service of notice of judgment when necessary under Article 4898.

Source: New; cf. C.P. Arts. 1128, 1129.

Cross Reference: Art. 4941.

Art. 4942 JUSTICE OF THE PEACE COURTS Bk. 8

Comments to Articles 4941 and 4942

These articles adopt for justice of the peace courts the procedure set up in Arts. 4892 through 4901, *supra*, for city courts. The delay for answering has been reduced from ten to five days. See Art. 4895, *supra*. The new trial concept has been rejected in so far as justice of the peace court cases are concerned.

CHAPTER 3. DISTRICT COURTS WHERE JURISDICTION CONCURRENT WITH JUSTICE OF THE PEACE COURTS

Art.
4971. Procedure.
4972. Rendition of judgment; cases where judgment rendered by clerk; time for applying for new trial.

Art. 4971. Procedure

Except as otherwise provided in Article 4972, the rules provided in Articles 4892 through 4898 apply to a suit in a district court, when a justice of the peace would have concurrent jurisdiction thereof.

No appeal lies from the judgment rendered in such a case.

Source: New.

Comment

See Comments under Art. 4972, *infra*.

Art. 4972. Rendition of judgment; cases where judgment rendered by clerk; time for applying for new trial

When a defendant does not answer timely, or when he has confessed judgment, a final judgment may be rendered and signed by either the judge or the clerk of the district court, in the manner provided by Article 4896. When the judgment is rendered by the clerk, a note of all documents offered in evidence shall be made, and the oral evidence offered shall be reduced to writing in narrative form by the clerk.

When a defendant does not answer timely a rule to show cause in an eviction case, the judge and not the clerk shall render judgment therein.

A new trial may be applied for, whether the case is tried originally or on appeal de novo in the district court, within three days of judgment, or within three days of the service of notice of judgment when required by Article 4898.

Source: New; cf. former R.S. 13:3331 et seq.

Cross References: Arts. 284, 4971.

Comments to Articles 4971 and 4972

(a) These articles do not apply to New Orleans at all, since there are no justice of the peace courts in New Orleans, and since the New Orleans district court does not have jurisdiction in cases involving less than $100.00. See Const. Art. VII, §§ 81 and 91.

(b) The procedure for cases in a district court involving less than $100.00 follows the procedure set up in Arts. 4892 through 4898, *supra*, for city courts. See Art. 4971, *supra*. However, certain exceptions are necessary and these are covered in Art. 4972.

(c) The procedure in district courts in cases involving less than $100.00 is substantially that provided for such cases by the "clerks book" statute, former R.S. 13:3331 *et seq.*

(d) There is no appeal at all from judgments in cases in district courts involving less than $100.00. The only remedy is a new trial. In this connection see Comment under Art. 4897, *supra*.

(e) Authority for adoption of the provision giving the clerk power to render and sign judgments, in case of a default or when confessed by the defendant, is provided in Const. Art. VII, § 37.

TITLE III

CASES INVOLVING MORE THAN ONE HUNDRED DOLLARS

Art.
5001. Procedure.
5002. Delays for answering; incorporation of exceptions in answer; prior default unnecessary; notice of judgment; new trial; appeals.

Art. 5001. Procedure

Except as otherwise provided in Article 5002, the procedure in a civil case in a city court of which a justice of the peace does not have concurrent jurisdiction is the same as that provided by law for a civil case in the district court of the parish in which the municipality is situated.

Source: Cf. former R.S. 13:1877, 13:3601.

Comments

See Comments under Art. 5002, *infra*.

Art. 5002. Delays for answering; incorporation of exceptions in answer; prior default unnecessary; notice of judgment; new trial; appeals

The delay for answering shall be stated in the citation and shall be five days, exclusive of legal holidays. A defendant shall incorporate in his answer all of the exceptions on which he intends to rely. No prior default is necessary, and judgment may be rendered as provided in Article 4896. Notice of the rendition of judgment is not necessary, except as provided in Article 4898. The delay for answering garnishment interrogatories shall be five days, exclusive of legal holidays.

A new trial may be applied for within three days, exclusive of legal holidays, of the date of judgment, or within three days of the service of notice of judgment when necessary.

A devolutive or suspensive appeal to the proper appellate court may be granted if applied for within ten days after the expiration of the delay for applying for a new trial, or within ten days of the denial of a new trial.

The suspensive appeal bond, as required by the applicable provisions of Article 2124, must be filed within the delays allowed above for a suspensive appeal.

Source: New; cf. former R.S. 13:1877.

Comments to Articles 5001 and 5002

(a) These articles cover the procedure for cases in city courts where the amount involved is over $100.00. Art. 5001 ties in the general procedure used in district courts to such cases; but certain exceptions are essential, and these are covered by Art. 5002. The principal changes are the reduction of the delay for answering and the requirement of filing exceptions with the answer.

(b) It will be noted that the delay for answering in New Orleans city courts in cases over $100.00 will also be five days instead of three days as at present.

BOOK IX.
MISCELLANEOUS PROVISIONS AND DEFINITIONS

TITLE I
MISCELLANEOUS PROVISIONS

Chap.		Art.
1.	Rules of Construction	5051
2.	Attorney Appointed to Represent Unrepresented Defendants	5091
3.	Bonds in Judicial Proceedings	5121
4.	Discussion	5151
5.	Waiver of Costs for Indigent Party	5181

CHAPTER 1. RULES OF CONSTRUCTION

Art.
5051. Liberal construction of articles.
5052. Unambiguous language not to be disregarded.
5053. Words and phrases.
5054. Clerical and typographical errors disregarded.
5055. Number; gender.
5056. Conjunctive, disjunctive, or both.
5057. Headings, source notes, cross references.
5058. References to code articles or statutory sections.
5059. Computation of time.

Art. 5051. Liberal construction of articles

The articles of this Code are to be construed liberally, and with due regard for the fact that rules of procedure implement the substantive law and are not an end in themselves.

Source: New.

Comment

This article expresses the procedural philosophy of this Code and serves as a constant reminder to the bench and bar that procedural rules are only a means to an end, and not an end in themselves.

Art. 5052. Unambiguous language not to be disregarded

When the language of an article is clear and free from ambiguity, its letter is not to be disregarded under the pretext of pursuing its spirit.

Source: New; cf. C.C. Art. 13; R.S. 1:4.

Art. 5053. Words and phrases

Words and phrases are to be read in their context, and are to be construed according to the common and approved usage of the language employed.

The word "shall" is mandatory, and the word "may" is permissive.

Source: New; cf. C.C. Art. 15; R.S. 1:3.

Art. 5054. Clerical and typographical errors disregarded

Clerical and typographical errors in this Code shall be disregarded when the legislative intent is clear.

Source: New: cf. R.S. 1:5.

Art. 5055. Number; gender

Unless the context clearly indicates otherwise:

(1) Words used in the singular number apply also to the plural; words used in the plural number include the singular; and

(2) Words used in one gender apply also to the others.

Source: New; cf. R.S. 1:7, 1:8.

Comment

See Comment (c) under Art. 3096, *supra*.

Art. 5056. Conjunctive, disjunctive, or both

Unless the context clearly indicates otherwise:

(1) The word "and" indicates the conjunctive;

(2) The word "or" indicates the disjunctive; and

(3) When the article is phrased in the disjunctive, followed by the words "or both", both the conjunctive and disjunctive are intended.

Source: New; cf. R.S. 1:9.

Art. 5057. Headings, source notes, cross references

The headings of the articles of this Code, and the source notes and cross references thereunder, are used for purposes of convenient arrangement and reference, and do not constitute parts of the procedural law.

Source: New; cf. R.S. 1:13.

Art. 5058. References to code articles or statutory sections

Unless the context clearly indicates otherwise:

(1) A reference in this Code to a book, title, chapter, section, or article, without further designation, means a book, title, chapter, section, or article of this Code; and

(2) A reference in this Code to an article of a code, or to a statutory section, applies to all prior and subsequent amendments thereof.

Source: New; cf. R.S. 1:14.

Art. 5059. Computation of time

In computing a period of time allowed or prescribed by law or by order of court, the date of the act, event, or default after which the period begins to run is not to be included. The last day of the period is to be included, unless it is a legal holiday, in which event the period runs until the end of the next day which is not a legal holiday.

A half-holiday is considered as a legal holiday. A legal holiday is to be included in the computation of a period of time allowed or prescribed, except when:

(1) It is expressly excluded;

(2) It would otherwise be the last day of the period; or

(3) The period is less than seven days.

Source: New; cf. Fed. Rule 6(a).

Comments

(a) The inclusion of a half-holiday as a holiday is contrary to the rule of the indirect source provision of this article, but in accord with what would probably be the jurisprudential rule. See Evans v. Hamner, 209 La. 442, 24 So.2d 814 (1946); Vicknair v. Vicknair, 211 La. 159, 29 So.2d 706 (1947); and Frank v. Currie, 172 So. 843 (La.App.1937).

(b) The rule excluding holidays if the delay is less than a week accords with the jurisprudence. State ex rel. State Pharmaceutical

Ass'n v. Michel, 52 La.Ann. 936, 27 So. 565, 49 L.R.A. 218, 78 Am.St.Rep. 364 (1900); Fellman v. Mercantile Fire & Marine Ins. Co., 116 La. 723, 41 So. 49 (1906); Johnson v. Murphy, 124 La. 143, 49 So. 1007 (1909); State ex rel. Marcade v. City of New Orleans, 216 La. 587, 44 So.2d 305 (1949); and Frank v. Currie, *supra*.

(c) See Comments under Arts. 1001, 2087, 2123, 2125, 2133, 2167, 3502, 3607, *supra*.

CHAPTER 2. ATTORNEY APPOINTED TO REPRESENT UNREPRESENTED DEFENDANTS

Art.
5091. Appointment; contradictory proceedings against attorney; improper designation immaterial.
5092. Qualifications; suggestions for appointment not permitted.
5093. Oath not required; waiver of citation and acceptance of service.
5094. Duties; notice to nonresident or absentee.
5095. Same; defense of action.
5096. Compensation.
5097. Attorney appointed to represent claimant in workmen's compensation case.
5098. Validity of proceeding not affected by failure of attorney to perform duties; punishment of attorney.

PRELIMINARY STATEMENT

The Louisiana procedural practice of appointing an attorney at law to represent an unrepresented defendant stems back to Partida 3. 2. 12, requiring the appointment of a curator to represent an absent defendant. See Millar, Jurisdiction Over Absent Defendants: Two Chapters in American Civil Procedure, 14 La. L.Rev. 321, 329 (1954).

The procedures of the various American states make provision for the appointment of a guardian ad litem for a defendant minor or other incompetent for whom no guardian has been appointed. But the practice is not generally extended to afford representation to an absent defendant. Here, the pattern is service by publication, with some states affording the absentee a definite period of time to set aside the default judgment by proving that he has a defense to the action, and others requiring the plaintiff to furnish security for the protection of the absent defendant who subsequently proves that he has a defense to the action.

The appointment of an attorney at law to represent an absent defendant is provided for in the modern procedural codes of three other American states. The applicable procedure of Texas can be traced, through Mexican law, to the same source as our own practice. Millar, *op. cit.* at 335–338. The appointment of an attorney at law to represent an absent defendant in the "warning order" procedure of Kentucky and Arkansas are believed to have been borrowed by the former from Louisiana, and in turn taken by Arkansas from Kentucky practice.

For well over a century, this representation of an unrepresented defendant by an attorney appointed by the court was a very real and effective representation. The reported decisions indicate the industry, zeal, and ability brought into the defense of these cases by appointed attorneys and the seriousness with which the latter took their professional responsibilities. See, for instance, Stevens v. Allen, 139 La. 658, 71 So. 936 (1916); Lepenser v. Griffin, 146 La. 584, 83 So. 839 (1919); Mathews v. Mathews, 157 La. 930, 103 So. 267 (1925); and Succession of Baragona, 231 La. 1016, 93 So.2d 542 (1957). In some instances, the appointed attorneys took their professional responsibilities so seriously that appeals were taken and appellate briefs printed at their personal expense. See, for instance, Mathews v. Mathews, *supra*, where the appointed attorney appealed and reversed an adverse judgment.

While the system has always worked well in New Orleans and most of the state, the purpose of the appointment has been so far overlooked in recent years in one or two sections of the state that the defendant receives virtually no representation in the action. No answers are filed, and judgments against the defendants are taken and confirmed by default. The only service rendered in some cases is notifying the defendant of the institution of the suit against him, but even then only if his address can be obtained readily. Three factors appear to contribute to this unfortunate result: (1) there is nothing in our positive law which informs the young lawyer what his duties will be in such a case; (2) appointments are being made of attorneys whose names are suggested to the court by counsel for the plaintiff; and (3) the attorneys so appointed are reluctant to make any actual defense for fear that opposing counsel will not suggest their appointment in future cases.

For these reasons, the articles in this Chapter set forth the duties and responsibilities of attorneys appointed by the court to represent unrepresented parties. However, no judgment or title to property will be invalidated by the failure to discharge the duties of his office. Other sanctions are provided to ensure compliance with these provisions.

Art. 5091. **Appointment; contradictory proceedings against attorney; improper designation immaterial**

When the court has jurisdiction over the person or property of the defendant, or over the status involved, on the petition or ex parte written motion of plaintiff, it shall appoint an attorney at law to represent the defendant if he is:

(1) A nonresident or absentee who has not been served with process, either personally or through an agent for the service of process, and who has made no general appearance; or

(2) An unemancipated minor or mental incompetent who has no legal representative, and who may be sued through an attorney at law appointed by the court to represent him.

All proceedings against such a defendant shall be conducted contradictorily against the attorney at law appointed by the court to represent him.

The improper designation of the attorney appointed by the court to represent such a defendant as curator ad hoc, tutor ad hoc, special tutor, or by any other title, does not affect the validity of the proceeding.

Source: C.P. Arts. 116, 964; C.C. Arts. 56, 313; former R.S. 9:841.

Comments

(a) This article makes no change in the law.

(b) The requirement that the court have jurisdiction over the person or property of the defendant, or over the status involved, before it may make a valid appointment of an attorney to represent such a defendant is one of constitutional due process, which is merely declaratory of the Louisiana jurisprudence. See Laughlin v. Louisiana & New Orleans Ice Co., 35 La.Ann. 1184 (1883); Bracey v. Calderwood, 36 La.Ann. 796 (1894); West v. Lehmer, 115 La. 213, 38 So. 969 (1905).

(c) Not all emancipated minors or mental incompetents may be sued through an attorney appointed by the court to represent them. Cf. Arts. 732 and 733, supra.

(d) For the definitions of "nonresident" and "absentee", see Art. 5251, infra.

(e) See, also, Comments under Arts. 6, 8–10, 4602, 4623, supra.

Art. 5092 UNREPRESENTED DEFENDANTS Bk. 9

Art. 5092. Qualifications; suggestions for appointment not permitted

When the court appoints an attorney at law to represent an unrepresented party, it shall appoint an attorney qualified to practice law in this state.

The court shall not accept any suggestion as to the name of the attorney to be appointed, unless manifestly in the interest of the unrepresented party.

Source: New; cf. Kentucky Code of Practice of 1876, § 59(1) (Carroll's ed. 1948).

Cross References: Arts. 5097, 5098.

Comments

(a) See Preliminary Statement to this Chapter.

(b) Under exceptional circumstances, a suggestion to the court as to the attorney to be appointed may be manifestly in the interest of the party to be represented, *e. g.*, when counsel for the plaintiff suggests that the court appoint the lawyer who has in the past represented the absent defendant, and who is generally familiar with his business affairs in the locality. For this reason the above article does not constitute an absolute prohibition against suggestions by counsel for plaintiffs, and acceptance of these suggestions by the court, as to the attorney to be appointed, as under the Kentucky Code of Practice. However, in the majority of cases suggestions as to the attorneys to be appointed are not in the interest of the parties to be represented, and the court should not entertain the suggestions.

Art. 5093. Oath not required; waiver of citation and acceptance of service

An attorney at law appointed by the court to represent an unrepresented party need not take an oath before entering on the performance of his duties, as his oath of office as an attorney applies to all of his professional duties.

An attorney appointed to represent a defendant may waive citation and accept service of process, but may not waive any defense. No further action may be taken by the court after service or acceptance thereof until after the expiration of the delay allowed the defendant to answer, even though the appointed attorney may have filed an exception or answer prior thereto.

Source: C.P. Art. 116; cf. Comment following.

Cross References: Arts. 5097, 5098.

Comment

The last sentence of this article accords with the local rules of some district courts. The purpose of this prohibition is to allow an unrepresented defendant the full delay to appear and defend the suit through counsel of his own choice.

Art. 5094. Duties; notice to nonresident or absentee

When an attorney at law is appointed by the court to represent a defendant who is a nonresident or an absentee, the attorney shall use reasonable diligence to communicate with the defendant and inform him of the pendency and nature of the action or proceeding, and of the time available for the filing of an answer or the assertion of a defense otherwise.

Source: New.

Cross Reference: Art. 5098.

Comments

(a) Notice of the pendency of the suit, and of the time available to the defendant for asserting his defense, are two of the most important duties of the appointed attorney in such cases.

(b) The phrase "the assertion of a defense otherwise" applies to executory proceedings, where no exceptions or answer may be filed, and all defenses must be asserted either in a suit for an injunction to arrest the seizure and sale, or through a suspensive appeal.

(c) For the definitions of "nonresident" and "absentee", see Art. 5251, *infra*.

Art. 5095. Same; defense of action

The attorney at law appointed by the court to represent a defendant shall use reasonable diligence to inquire of the defendant, and to determine from other available sources, what defense, if any, the defendant may have, and what evidence is available in support thereof.

Except in an executory proceeding, the attorney may except to the petition, shall file an answer in time to prevent a default judgment from being rendered, may plead therein any affirmative defense available, may prosecute an appeal from an adverse judgment, and generally has the same duty, responsibility, and authority in defend-

Art. 5095. UNREPRESENTED DEFENDANTS

ing the action or proceeding as if he had been retained as counsel for the defendant.

Source: New.

Cross Reference: Art. 5098.

Comments

(a) This article is based upon customary practices which are regarded as proper. The appointed attorney has no authority to force the defendant to become the actor by filing a separate suit in his name, or by calling in a third party defendant, or by reconvening. His function, and his sole authority under the law, is to defend the pending action or proceeding, and he may not commit the person he is appointed to represent in any other manner.

(b) Defenses to an executory proceeding may be raised only through the action to enjoin the seizure and sale, or through a suspensive appeal. The appointed attorney has no legal authority to act for the person he is representing by exercising either remedy. His sole function in an executory proceeding is to receive service of all process and to notify the defendant of the pendency of the proceeding. See Art. 5094, *supra*.

Art. 5096. Compensation

The court shall allow the attorney at law appointed to represent a defendant a reasonable fee for his services, which shall be paid by the plaintiff, but shall be taxed as costs of court.

The attorney so appointed may require the plaintiff to furnish security for the costs which may be paid by, and the reasonable fee to be allowed, the attorney.

If the attorney so appointed is retained as counsel for the defendant, the attorney shall immediately advise the court and opposing counsel of such employment.

Source: New; cf. Comment following.

Cross Reference: Art. 5098.

Art. 5097. Attorney appointed to represent claimant in workmen's compensation case

Articles 5092, 5093, and 5098 apply to an attorney at law appointed by the court to represent a claimant in a workmen's compensation case who seeks authority to compromise or to accept a lump sum settlement.

Source: New.

Comment

See R.S. 23:1272. A reasonable fee, not to exceed $15, may be granted by the court to the attorney appointed to represent an unrepresented claimant.

Art. 5098. Validity of proceeding not affected by failure of attorney to perform duties; punishment of attorney

The failure of an attorney appointed by the court to represent an unrepresented party to perform any duty imposed upon him by, or the violation by any person of, the provisions of Articles 5092 through 5096 shall not affect the validity of any proceeding, trial, order, judgment, seizure, or judicial sale of any property in the action or proceeding, or in connection therewith.

For a wilful violation of any provision of Articles 5092 through 5096 an attorney at law subjects himself to punishment for contempt of court, and such further disciplinary action as is provided by law.

Source: New.

Comments

Imposing the penalty of the nullity of the proceedings because of the failure of the appointed attorney to perform any of his duties would be visiting the punishment upon an innocent person, rather than on the offender. Further, to impose upon a title examiner the burden of satisfying himself that the appointed attorney has performed all of the duties imposed upon him by these articles would make title examination unduly burdensome and perilous, and would lessen the security of any title coming through such a proceeding.

For these reasons, the article provides that the wilful failure of the appointed attorney to perform any of his duties, or the violation of any of the provisions of these articles by any person, counsel for the plaintiff or the judge, does not affect the validity of the proceedings. If an attorney at law has been appointed by the court in a case where required by law, and the attorney so appointed has been served with process or has accepted service, no one need look behind such appointment and the judgment rendered in the action or proceeding.

CHAPTER 3. BONDS IN JUDICIAL PROCEEDINGS

Art.
5121. Bond payable to clerk; person in interest may sue.
5122. Oath of surety and principal on bond.
5123. Testing sufficiency and validity of bond.
5124. Furnishing new or supplemental bond to correct defects of original.
5125. Insufficiency or invalidity of bond; effect on orders or judgments; appeal from order for supplemental bond.
5126. Insufficiency or invalidity of new or supplemental bond.
5127. Release bond.

Art. 5121. Bond payable to clerk; person in interest may sue

When a party to a judicial proceeding is required by law or order of court to furnish security, any bond so furnished shall be made payable to the clerk of the trial court in which the proceeding was brought.

Any person in interest may sue thereon. No error, inaccuracy, or omission in naming the obligee on the bond is a defense to an action thereon.

Source: Former R.S. 13:4571.

Cross Reference: Art. 5127.

Comment

See Comments under Arts. 3501, 3610, *supra*.

Art. 5122. Oath of surety and principal on bond

Except as otherwise provided in this article, no bond shall be accepted in a judicial proceeding unless accompanied by affidavits of:

(1) Each surety that he is worth the amount for which he bound himself therein, in assets subject to execution, over and above all of his other obligations; and

(2) The party furnishing the bond that he is informed and believes that each surety on the bond is worth the amount for which the surety has bound himself therein, in assets subject to execution, over and above all of the other obligations of the surety.

This article does not apply to a bond executed by a surety company licensed to do business in this state.

Source: Former R.S. 13:4574.

Cross Reference: Art. 5127.

Art. 5123. Testing sufficiency and validity of bond

Any person in interest wishing to test the sufficiency, solvency of the surety, or validity of a bond furnished as security in a judicial proceeding shall rule the party furnishing the bond into the trial court in which the proceeding was brought to show cause why the bond should not be decreed insufficient or invalid, and why the order, judgment, writ, mandate, or process conditioned on the furnishing of security should not be set aside or dissolved. If the bond is sought to be held invalid on the ground of the insolvency of a surety other than a surety company licensed to do business in this state, the party furnishing the bond shall prove the solvency of the surety on the trial of the rule.

Source: New; cf. former R.S. 13:4573.

Cross Reference: Art. 5127.

Art. 5124. Furnishing new or supplemental bond to correct defects of original

Within four days, exclusive of legal holidays, of the rendition of judgment holding the original bond insufficient or invalid, or at any time if no rule to test the original bond has been filed, the party furnishing it may correct any defects therein by furnishing a new or supplemental bond, with either the same surety if solvent, or a new or additional surety.

The new or supplemental bond is retroactive to the date the original bond was furnished, and maintains in effect the order, judgment, writ, mandate, or process conditioned on the furnishing of security.

The furnishing of a supplemental bond, or the furnishing of a new bond by a different surety, does not discharge or release the surety on the original bond; and the sureties on both are liable in solido to the extent of their respective obligations thereon and may be joined in an action on the bond.

Source: Former R.S. 13:4572, 13:4576, 13:4577.

Cross References: Arts. 5125, 5126, 5127.

Comment to Articles 5121 through 5124

These articles effect no change in the Louisiana law.

Art. 5125. Insufficiency or invalidity of bond; effect on orders or judgments; appeal from order for supplemental bond

No appeal, order, judgment, writ, mandate, or process conditioned on the furnishing of security may be dismissed, set aside, or dissolved on the ground that the bond furnished is insufficient or invalid unless the party who furnished it is afforded an opportunity to furnish a new or supplemental bond, as provided in Articles 5124 and 5126.

No suspensive appeal is allowed from an order or ruling of a trial court requiring or permitting a new or supplemental bond to be furnished as provided in Articles 5124 and 5126.

Source: Former R.S. 13:4579, 13:4580.

Cross Reference: Art. 5127.

Comment

This article makes no change in the law, except as effected in Art. 5126, *infra*.

Art. 5126. Insufficiency or invalidity of new or supplemental bond

The party furnishing a new or supplemental bond under the provisions of Article 5124 may correct an insufficiency or invalidity therein by furnishing a second new or supplemental bond within four days, exclusive of legal holidays, of rendition of judgment holding the new or supplemental bond insufficient or invalid, or at any time if no rule to test the new or supplemental bond has been filed.

If the second new or supplemental bond is insufficient or invalid, the party furnishing it may not correct the defects therein by furnishing a further new or supplemental bond.

Source: New; cf. former R.S. 13:4573, 13:4575.

Cross References: Arts. 5125, 5127.

Comments

Originally, La.Act 112 of 1916, § 5, permitted a further bond to be furnished, if for any reason the new or supplemental bond furnished to correct errors or deficiencies of the original bond was itself deficient, and apparently this process of substituting bonds could be carried on ad infinitum. Because of the abuse of this privilege, the statute was amended by La.Act 284 of 1928 to provide that if the new or supplemental bond furnished to correct an error or deficiency of the original bond was itself insufficient or invalid, no further bond might be furnished. However, instead of amending Sec. 5 and removing all conflicting language therein, the 1928 act amended Sec. 3, with the result that the language of these two sections conflicted. Since Sec. 3 was the later expression of legislative will, it had the effect of repealing the conflicting language of Sec. 5 by implication. However, in the revision of the statutes in 1950, this conflicting language of the two sections was overlooked through inadvertence, with the result that the language of the former R.S. 13:4573 conflicted with that of the former R.S. 13:4575.

Neither the original statute nor the 1928 amendment provided workable solutions of the problem. Since the surety on the new or supplemental bond might not be worth the amount for which he bound himself, or the surety company which executed it might subsequently become insolvent, it was felt that a party furnishing a judicial bond should have two opportunities of correcting insufficiencies or invalidities therein. This article represents a compromise between the original statute and the 1928 amendment.

Art. 5127. Release bond

No property seized under any order, judgment, writ, mandate, or process of a court may be released from seizure under a release or forthcoming bond unless it is executed by:

(1) A surety company licensed to do business in this state; or

(2) An individual surety, and has been approved by the sheriff after the latter has satisfied himself of the solvency of the surety.

Articles 5121 through 5126 apply to a release or forthcoming bond.

Source: New.

Comment

Under the Code of Practice, release bonds were required to be made payable and delivered to the sheriff, and the latter was liable if he accepted an insufficient bond or one with an insolvent surety. Arts. 219, 225, 226, 259, 279, and 287. This rule was changed by the adoption of La.Act 112 of 1916, § 1, requiring all judicial bonds to be made payable to the clerk, and requiring the adverse party to object to any error, invalidity, or insufficiency of the bond, which had the effect of relieving the sheriff of any liability under a release bond.

The difficulty about the latter rule was that a bond with an insolvent surety might be furnished to obtain the release of property under seizure, and the property might have been run out of the jurisdiction or otherwise disposed of long before the adverse party had any opportunity to test the solvency of the surety on the release bond. The principal reason why the 1916 statute worked was because most sheriffs did not realize that they had been relieved of absolute liability by its adoption, and they continued to take all precautions to accept only a bond with a solvent surety.

The above article provides additional safeguards to protect the adverse party in these cases. Although the sheriff is under no absolute liability in accepting an insolvent surety, as he was prior to 1916, he would still be liable to the injured party for negligence in satisfying himself of the solvency of the surety.

CHAPTER 4. DISCUSSION

Art.
5151. Discussion defined.
5152. Surety's right to plead.
5153. Transferee in revocatory action; right to plead discussion.
5154. Third possessor's right to plead.
5155. Pleading discussion.
5156. Effect of discussion.

Art. 5151. Discussion defined

Discussion is the right of a secondary obligor to compel the creditor to enforce the obligation against the property of the primary obligor or, if the obligation is a legal or judicial mortgage, against other property affected thereby, before enforcing it against the property of the secondary obligor.

Source: New.

Comment

The fact that a surety is a secondary obligor is apparent. It is not quite so obvious that a third possessor and the transferee in a revocatory action similarly are secondary obligors. While a third possessor is not liable personally on the principal obligation secured by the legal or judicial mortgage, he is under the obligation of either relinquishing the property so that the creditor might enforce his mortgage against it, or paying the debt due the creditor. He is only a secondary obligor since, of course, the primary obligor is the debtor who owes the principal obligation. The transferee in a revocatory action has a similar obligation, and is also a secondary obligor.

Art. 5152. Surety's right to plead

When a surety is sued by the creditor on the suretyship obligation, the surety may plead discussion to compel the creditor to obtain and execute a judgment against the principal before executing a judgment against the surety.

Discussion may not be pleaded by a surety who is obligated solidarily with the principal, or who has renounced the benefit of discussion.

Source: C.C. Art. 3045.

Comment

This article effects no change in the law.

Art. 5153. Transferee in revocatory action; right to plead discussion

When a revocatory action is brought by a creditor to set aside a transfer of property made by his debtor, the transferee may plead discussion to compel the creditor to obtain and execute a judgment against the debtor before setting the transfer aside.

Source: C.C. Art. 1973.

Comment

No change in the law is made by this article.

Art. 5154. Third possessor's right to plead

When a legal or judicial mortgage securing an indebtedness due by a former owner of property is sought to be enforced against the property after its acquisition by a third possessor, the latter may plead discussion to compel the mortgagee to enforce the mortgage against other property affected thereby, which is owned by the mortgagor, or which has been acquired from the mortgagor by a third person after the third possessor acquired his property.

Source: C.P. Arts. 71–73, 715; C.C. Art. 3403.
Cross Reference: Art. 3743.

Comments

(a) This article makes no change in the law.

(b) There is no necessity for a counterpart of Art. 73 of the Code of Practice, providing that discussion may not be opposed to the privileged creditor, or to one having a special mortgage, since this article by its terms is limited to general mortgages, and does not include privileges.

Art. 5155. Pleading discussion

A third possessor may plead discussion in an injunction suit to restrain the enforcement of a legal or judicial mortgage against his

Art. 5155

property. Discussion may be pleaded by a surety or transferee in a revocatory action only in the dilatory exception.

In pleading discussion, the secondary obligor shall:

(1) Point out by a description sufficient to identify it, property in the state belonging to the primary obligor, or otherwise subject to discussion, which is not in litigation, is not exempt from seizure, is free of mortgages and privileges, and is worth more than the total amount of the judgment or mortgage; and

(2) Deposit into the registry of the court, for the use of the creditor, an amount sufficient to defray the costs of executing the judgment or enforcing the mortgage against the property discussed.

Source: New; cf. C.P. Art. 72; C.C. Arts. 1973, 3047.

Cross Reference: Art. 3743.

Comments

(a) The hypothecary action, properly speaking, is abolished by this Code. See Arts. 3721 through 3743, *supra*. The third possessor must urge his defenses to the seizure of his property through an injunction proceeding to arrest the seizure and judicial sale and he can plead discussion as a ground for the injunction. See Art. 3743, *supra*. The first sentence of this article recognizes the latter right.

(b) There was a conflict between Arts. 1973 and 3047 of the Civil Code, on the one hand, and Art. 72 of the Code of Practice, on the other. The former two exclude from discussion property of the debtor situated out of the state; the latter excludes therefrom property out of the jurisdiction of the court. While the Code of Practice is the later expression of legislative will, the rule of the Civil Code is the sounder. Execution runs throughout the state, and there is no reason to limit discussion to the property of the debtor situated within the territorial jurisdiction of the court. This article restores the rule of the Civil Code.

Art. 5156. Effect of discussion

When discussion is pleaded successfully by a third possessor, or by the transferee in a revocatory action, the court shall stay proceedings against the third possessor or transferee until the creditor has executed his judgment against the property discussed.

When discussion is pleaded successfully by a surety and the principal is joined, the court may render judgment against both the principal and the surety, but shall order the creditor to execute his judgment against the property discussed. If the principal is not joined in the action initially, the court shall order his joinder if he is subject to its jurisdiction, and may then proceed as provided in this paragraph.

If the creditor is not able to satisfy his judgment out of the proceeds of the judicial sale of the property discussed, he may thereafter proceed as if discussion had not been pleaded.

Source: New; cf. C.P. Art. 71; C.C. Arts. 1973, 3051.

CHAPTER 5. WAIVER OF COSTS FOR INDIGENT PARTY

Art.
5181. Privilege of litigating without prior payment of costs.
5182. Restrictions on privilege.
5183. Affidavits of poverty; order.
5184. Traverse of affidavits of poverty.
5185. Rights of party permitted to litigate without payment of costs.
5186. Account and payment of costs.
5187. Compromise; dismissal of proceeding prior to judgment.
5188. Unsuccessful party condemned to pay costs.

Art. 5181. Privilege of litigating without prior payment of costs

A person who is unable to pay the costs of court, because of his poverty and lack of means, may prosecute or defend a judicial proceeding, other than an action for a divorce or for a separation from bed and board, in any trial or appellate court without paying the costs in advance, or as they accrue, or furnishing security therefor.

As used in this chapter, "person" means an individual who is a citizen of this state, or an alien domiciled therein for more than three years.

Source: New; cf. former R.S. 13:4525.
Cross Reference: Art. 283.

Comment

This article makes no change in the law.

Art. 5182. Restrictions on privilege

The privilege granted by this Chapter shall be restricted to litigants who are clearly entitled to it, with due regard to the nature of the proceeding, the court costs which otherwise would have to be paid, and the ability of the litigant to pay them or to furnish security therefor, so that the fomentation of litigation by an indiscriminate resort thereto may be discouraged, without depriving a litigant of its benefits if he is entitled thereto.

Source: New; cf. former R.S. 13:4525.

Comment

The former prohibition against attorneys charging fees in these cases except those contingent on the amount recovered, contained in the indirect source of this article, has not been retained in the Code. This prohibition was both unnecessary and unrealistic. The provisions of this Chapter will be used primarily in damage suits and workmen's compensation cases in which, under the universal custom throughout the state, contingent fees are the only ones charged. To this extent, the prohibition was unnecessary. Further, there are some types of cases in which there are no pecuniary demands, and hence no amount which can ever be recovered. There is no reason why small fees should not be charged in such cases. To this extent, the former prohibition was unrealistic.

Art. 5183. Affidavits of poverty; order

A person who wishes to exercise the privilege granted in this Chapter shall apply to the court for permission to do so in his first pleading, or in an ex parte written motion if requested later, to which he shall annex:

(1) His affidavit that he is unable to pay the costs of court in advance, or as they accrue, or to furnish security therefor, because of his poverty and lack of means; and

(2) The affidavit of a third person other than his attorney that he knows the applicant, knows his financial condition, and believes that he is unable to pay the costs of court in advance, or as they accrue, or to furnish security therefor.

When the application and supporting affidavits are presented to the court, it shall inquire into the facts, and if satisfied that the applicant is entitled to the privilege granted in this Chapter, it shall render an order permitting the applicant to litigate, or to continue the litigation of, the action or proceeding without paying the costs in advance, or as they accrue, or furnishing security therefor.

Source: New: cf. former R.S. 13:4526.

Cross Reference: Art. 283.

Comment

Under the indirect source provision of this article, it has been held that the attorney for an indigent plaintiff may execute the supporting affidavit as to the plaintiff's poverty. Harrison v. Jones,

187 La. 489, 175 So. 37 (1937). This rule is undesirable and the above article is intended to overrule legislatively the Harrison case.

Art. 5184. Traverse of affidavits of poverty

An adverse party may traverse the facts alleged in the affidavits of poverty, and the right of the applicant to exercise the privilege granted in this Chapter, by a rule against him to show cause why the order of court permitting him to litigate, or to continue the litigation, without paying the costs in advance, or as they accrue, or furnishing security therefor, should not be rescinded.

The court shall rescind its order if, on the trial of the rule to traverse, it finds that the litigant is not entitled to exercise the privilege granted in this Chapter.

Source: New; cf. former R.S. 13:4526.

Comment

No change in the law is made by this article.

Art. 5185. Rights of party permitted to litigate without payment of costs

When an order of court permits a party to litigate without the payment of costs, until this order is rescinded, he is entitled to:

(1) All services required by law of a sheriff, clerk of court, court reporter, notary, or other public officer in, or in connection with, the judicial proceeding, including but not limited to the filing of pleadings and exhibits, the issuance of certificates, the certification of copies of notarial acts and public records, the issuance and service of subpoenas and process, the taking and transcribing of testimony, and the preparation of a record of appeal;

(2) The right to a trial by jury, and to the services of jurors, when allowed by law and applied for timely; and

(3) The right to a devolutive appeal, and to apply for supervisory writs.

He is not entitled to a suspensive appeal, or to an order or judgment, required by law to be conditioned on his furnishing security other than for costs, unless he furnishes the necessary security therefor.

No public officer is required to make any cash outlay to perform any duty imposed on him under any article in this Chapter.

Source: New; cf. former R.S. 13:4525.

Art. 5185

Comments

(a) This article has not retained the provision of its indirect source which purported to give the indigent party the right to the services of a court reporter in depositions taken out of court. Actually, there is no statutory provision which imposes on a court reporter the duty of taking such depositions. The matter is left to agreement between counsel for the indigent party and the court reporter. If the latter is willing to take and transcribe testimony under deposition, and to take his chances on being paid if the indigent party obtains judgment, the reporter is entitled to recover his fees in such cases. However, no duty is imposed upon the official court reporter to take such depositions.

(b) The second to last paragraph is declaratory of the jurisprudence. See Muller v. Johnson, 140 La. 902, 74 So. 189 (1917); Orgeron v. Lytle, 180 La. 646, 157 So. 377 (1934); Succession of Wolfe, 180 La. 688, 157 So. 391 (1934); Succession of Jones, 189 La. 693, 180 So. 489 (1938); State ex rel. Messina v. Cage, 152 So. 399 (La.App.1934); Wicks v. Metropolitan Life Ins. Co., 169 So. 101 (La.App.1936); Cook v. Pickering, 14 So.2d 110 (La.App. 1943); and Bonnelucq v. Bernard, 29 So.2d 486 (La.App.1947).

Art. 5186. Account and payment of costs

An account shall be kept of all costs incurred by a party who has been permitted to litigate without the payment of costs, by the public officers to whom these costs would be payable. If judgment is rendered in favor of the indigent party, the party against whom this judgment is rendered shall be condemned to pay all costs due these officers, who have a privilege on the judgment superior to the rights of the indigent party or his attorney.

Source: New; cf. former R.S. 13:4527.

Comment

No change in the law is made by this article.

Art. 5187. Compromise; dismissal of proceeding prior to judgment

No compromise shall be effected unless all costs due these officers have been paid. Should any compromise agreement be entered into in violation of this article, each party thereto is liable to these officers for all costs due them at the time.

No judicial proceeding in which a party has been permitted to litigate without the payment of costs shall be dismissed prior to judgment, unless all costs due these public officers have been paid, or there is annexed to the written motion to dismiss the certificates of all counsel of record that no compromise has been effected or is contemplated.

Source: New; cf. former R.S. 13:4527.

Comment

This article implements the preceding one, and offers further protection to the sheriff, clerk, and court reporter to whom court costs may be due, by preventing, as far as possible, the dismissal of such an action to effect a compromise which may have been agreed to, but which would be consummated by the dismissal.

Art. 5188. Unsuccessful party condemned to pay costs

Except as otherwise provided by Articles 1920 and 2164, if judgment is rendered against a party who has been permitted to litigate without the payment of costs, he shall be condemned to pay the costs incurred by him, and those recoverable by the adverse party.

Source: New; cf. former R.S. 13:4528.

Comments

(a) The exceptions in this article avoid conflict with those which empower the trial and appellate courts to award costs as they deem equitable. This power of the trial court effects a change in the law, and to this extent requires this article likewise to effect a change in the law.

(b) In a number of cases decided by the appellate courts, the indirect source provision of this article has been overlooked, and the courts have held that costs may not be imposed on an unsuccessful plaintiff. See cases cited in Coulon v. Anthony Hamlin, Inc., 233 La. 798, 98 So.2d 193 (1957). Obviously, the result reached in these cases is erroneous. Coulon v. Anthony Hamlin, Inc., *supra*.

TITLE II

DEFINITIONS

Art.
5251. Words and terms defined.

Art. 5251. Words and terms defined

Except where the context clearly indicates otherwise, as used in this Code:

(1) "Absentee" means a person who is either a nonresident of this state, or a person who is domiciled in but has departed from this state, and who has not appointed an agent for the service of process in this state in the manner directed by law; or a person whose whereabouts are unknown, or who cannot be found and served after a diligent effort, though he may be domiciled or actually present in the state; or a person who may be dead, though the fact of his death is not known, and if dead his heirs are unknown.

(2) "Agent for the service of process" means the agent designated by a person or by law to receive service of process in actions and proceedings brought against him in the courts in this state.

(3) "City court" includes a municipal court which has civil jurisdiction.

(4) "Competent court", or "court of competent jurisdiction", means a court which has jurisdiction over the subject matter of, and is the proper venue for, the action or proceeding.

(5) "Corporation" includes a private corporation, domestic or foreign, a public corporation, and, unless another article in the same Chapter where the word is used indicates otherwise, a domestic, foreign, or alien insurance corporation.

(6) "Foreign corporation" means a corporation organized and existing under the laws of another state or a possession of the United States, or of a foreign country.

(7) "Insurance policy" includes all policies included within the definition in R.S. 22:5, and a life, or a health and accident policy, issued by a fraternal benefit society.

(8) "Insurer" includes every person engaged in the business of making contracts of insurance as provided in R.S. 22:5, and a fraternal benefit society.

DEFINITIONS — Art. 5251

(9) "Law" as used in the phrases "unless otherwise provided by law" or "except as otherwise provided by law" means an applicable provision of the constitution, a code, or a statute of Louisiana.

(10) "Legal representative" includes an administrator, provisional administrator, administrator of a vacant succession, executor, dative testamentary executor, tutor, administrator of the estate of a minor child, curator, receiver, liquidator, trustee, and any officer appointed by a court to administer an estate under its jurisdiction.

(11) "Nonresident" means an individual who does not reside in this state, a foreign corporation which is not licensed to do business in this state, or a partnership or unincorporated association organized and existing under the laws of another state or a possession of the United States, or of a foreign country.

(12) "Person" includes an individual, partnership, unincorporated association of individuals, joint stock company, or corporation.

(13) "Property" includes all classes of property recognized under the laws of this state: movable or immovable, corporeal or incorporeal.

Comments

(a) Absentee: When a person defined as an absentee under this article appears in the action or proceeding personally or through counsel of his own selection, he ceases to be an absentee, and submits himself to the jurisdiction of the court. Roy O. Martin Lumber Co. v. Strange, 106 So.2d 723 (La.1958); Art. 7, *supra*.

See, also, Comments under Arts. 6, 2674, 4602, 4621, 5091, and 5094, *supra*.

(b) Agent for the service of process: See Comments under Art. 6, *supra*.

(c) Competent court: See Comments under Art. 8, *supra*.

(d) Insurance policy: See Comments under Art. 76, *supra*.

(e) Insurer: See Comments under Arts. 690, 693, 739 and 741, *supra*.

(f) Legal representative: See Comments under Arts. 194, 195, 374, 805, 2084, 2122, 2637, and 2701, *supra*.

(g) Nonresident: See Comments under Arts. 5091, and 5094, *supra*.

(h) Person: See Comments under Arts. 42, 330, 1354, and 3097, *supra*.

(i) Property: See Comments under Arts. 8, 326, 2291, 2292, and 3541, *supra*.

SECTION 2. (A) The Louisiana State Law Institute, as the official advisory law revision commission of the State of Louisiana, shall direct and supervise the continuous revision, clarification, and coordination of the Louisiana Code of Civil Procedure in a manner not inconsistent with the provisions of this section.

(B) At the close of each legislative session, the Louisiana State Law Institute shall prepare printer's copy, either for a supplement to the Louisiana Code of Civil Procedure, or for a volume to be called "Louisiana Code of Civil Procedure" containing the text of the Louisiana Code of Civil Procedure as it may have been amended, and omitting therefrom or noting therein those articles which have been repealed. There shall also be incorporated therein, in an appropriate place and classification, the text of all the new procedural legislation applicable generally to civil actions or proceedings, or to those actions or proceedings regulated by the Louisiana Code of Civil Procedure, assigning to these new laws an appropriate book, title, chapter, section, subsection, and article number, and indicating the source of the legislative acts from which they are taken.

(C) In preparing the printer's copy provided in this section, the Louisiana State Law Institute shall not alter the sense, meaning, or effect of any act of the legislature, but it may:

(1) Re-number and re-arrange articles;

(2) Transfer or divide articles or statutory sections so as to give to distinct subject matters a separate article number, but without changing the meaning;

(3) Insert or change the wording of headnotes;

(4) Change reference numbers to agree with the re-numbered articles;

(5) Substitute the proper book, title, chapter, section, subsection, or article number for the terms "this act", "the preceding section", and the like;

(6) Strike out figures where they are merely a repetition of written words and vice-versa;

(7) Change capitalization for the purpose of uniformity;

(8) Correct manifest typographical and grammatical errors; and

(9) Make any other purely formal or clerical changes in keeping with the purposes of the continuous revision.

The Institute shall omit all titles of acts, all enacting, resolving, and repealing clauses, all temporary statutes, all declarations of emergency, and all validity, declaration of policy, and construction clauses, except when the retention thereof is necessary to preserve the full meaning and intent of the law. Whenever any validity, declaration of policy, or construction clause is omitted, proper notation of the omission shall be made.

(D) The printer's copy for any edition of the Louisiana Code of Civil Procedure, or for any supplement thereof, prepared in the manner provided in this section shall be delivered to the secretary of state together with the certification of the Louisiana State Law Institute that each article therein has been compared with the original act enacted after the adoption of the Louisiana Code of Civil Procedure, with the original provisions of the enrolled acts from which the articles were derived, and that with the exception of the changes of form permitted in this section, the articles in the printer's copy are correct. Upon receipt of the printer's copy, the secretary of state shall order the printing of an edition sufficient in number to supply the demand. When the edition has been printed, the secretary of state, after making the necessary comparison with the original printer's copy, shall affix to a copy of the printed edition the Institute's original certificate and file the same for record in his office. All other copies of the same edition may contain a printed facsimile of the Institute's certificate.

(E) Any article in any subsequent edition or supplement of the Louisiana Code of Civil Procedure prepared by the Louisiana State Law Institute may be amended or repealed by reference to the article number, without reference to the legislative act from which the article was taken.

(F) The secretary of state is authorized to enter into contracts with private publishers for the printing, publication, sale, and distribution of any edition or supplement of the Louisiana Code of Civil Procedure prepared by the Louisiana State Law Institute and certified by it pursuant to the provisions of this section. Those editions or supplements so authorized by the secretary of state and containing the printed facsimile of the Institute's certificate of correctness shall be admissible as prima facie evidence of the laws contained therein.

LOUISIANA CODE OF CIVIL PROCEDURE

SECTION 3. If, for any reason, any provision of this act, including any provision of the Louisiana Code of Civil Procedure enacted by Section 1 hereof, is declared unconstitutional or invalid, the other separable provisions thereof shall not be affected thereby.

SECTION 4. (A) This act is hereby declared to be remedial legislation.

(B) The provisions of the Louisiana Code of Civil Procedure enacted by Section 1 hereof, so far as applicable, shall govern and regulate the procedure in all civil actions and proceedings:

(1) Instituted on or after the effective date of this act; and

(2) Pending on the effective date of this act, except that none of the provisions thereof shall:

(a) Decrease or shorten any procedural delay granted or allowed by any law in existence immediately prior to, and which had commenced to run but had not yet completely elapsed on, the effective date of this act; or

(b) Affect the validity or change the legal effect of any judicial, official, or procedural act done or attempted, or of any failure to act, prior to the effective date of this act in any civil action or proceeding, including but not limited to any: citation, writ, mandate, summons, subpoena, notice, or other process issued or served; pleading filed; security furnished; oral motion made; testimony taken, by deposition or otherwise; evidence introduced or offered; ruling made by the court; order or judgment rendered; appeal taken or requested; execution of any judgment, writ, or mandate; seizure made by the sheriff or other executive officer of a court; publication of a judicial notice or advertisement; or judicial sale, whether actually completed or not.

SECTION 5. The Code of Practice of the State of Louisiana, and all other laws or parts of laws in conflict or inconsistent with the Louisiana Code of Civil Procedure enacted by Section 1 hereof, are hereby repealed; but nothing contained herein, or in the code enacted hereby, shall be construed to repeal, supersede, or otherwise affect, the provisions of Sections 4438, 4441, 4442, 4445, and 4446 of Title 13 of the Revised Statutes of 1950, as amended or adopted by the Legislature at its Regular Session of 1960.

SECTION 6. In the event of any conflict between the provisions of this act, and those of any other act adopted by the Legislature at its Regular Session of 1960, regardless of which act is adopted later or signed later by the Governor, the provisions of this act, and of the Louisiana Code of Civil Procedure hereby enacted, shall control and prevail on the effective date hereof.

SECTION 7. All of the provisions of this act shall become effective on January 1, 1961.

Approved June 16, 1960.

TABLES

Table	Page
1. Concordance — Articles of the Code of Practice	751
2. Concordance — Articles of the Civil Code	761
3. Concordance — Sections of the Revised Statutes	765
4. Implementation Table	769

INDEX
Page 773

CONCORDANCE TABLE 1

REPLACEMENT IN THE CODE OF CIVIL PROCEDURE, THE CIVIL CODE, AND IN THE REVISED STATUTES OF ARTICLES IN THE CODE OF PRACTICE

(Unless otherwise indicated, references in replacement columns below are to articles in the Code of Civil Procedure)

C.P. Art.	Replacement	C.P. Art.	Replacement	C.P. Art.	Replacement
1	421	50	3659	93	925
2	422	51	3659	94	531
3	422	52	3659		925
4	422	53	3661	95	None
5	3651	54	3657	96	None
6	3655	55	3657	97	851
7	422	56	3657	98	851
8 to 11	None	57	3657		2591
		58	3663		2592
		59	See 3658(4)		2594
12	422	60	None		2631
13	None	61	3721	99	None
14	423	62	3721	100	None
15	681	63	3721	101	See 1031
16	See 5059	64 to 70	See 3741	102	682
17 to 19	None			103	None
		71	3743	104	R.S. 9:571
			5154	105	R.S. 9:271
20	424		5156	106	None
21	421	72	3743	107	See 682
22	426		5154		686
23	426		5155	108	683
24	426	73	3743		684
25	427		5154		4264
26	422	74	3743	109	683
27	427	75	See 1		684
28	422	76	1		4264
29 to 39	None	77 to 85	None	110	682
				111	685
					3196
40	427	86	5251(4)	112	690
41	422	87	2		691
42	None	88	2	113	See 685
43	3651	89	42	114	731
	3652	90	See 41	115	732
44	3653	91	2		733
45	3652		4		4264
46	3655		5	116	2637
47	3656		425		2641
48	3656	92	3		2674
49	3658		925		5091
	3660				5093

CODE OF CIVIL PROCEDURE

C.P. Art.	Replacement	C.P. Art.	Replacement	C.P. Art.	Replacement
117	None	159	None	195	1235
118	731	160	854	196	1235
	735	161	See 854	197	None
119	739	162	42	198	Obsolete
120	428		44	199	1235
	734	163	72	200	1292
121	2672		2633	201	1292
	3741		3652	202	1292
122	3196		3656	203	1292
123	3196	164	81	204	1292
124	851	165	42	205	None
125	None		72	206	1201
126	None		73	207	288
127	Obsolete		74		323
128	Obsolete		76	208	3501
129	None		78		3602
130	191		79	209	3501
131	227		80		3602
132	225		R.S. 13:3239	210	
133	222	166	None	to	None
	224	167	71	236	
134	1352	168	71	237	3502
	1355	169	421	238	None
	1357	170	421	239	3542
135	1357		852	240	3541
136	1633	171	891	241	3542
137	None	172	853	242	3542
138	None		891	243	3501
139	1354	173	891	244	3543
140	1354	174	None	245	3501
141	1354	175	1311		3544
142	R.S. 13:3671	176	253	246	2411
143	1354	177	1201		2412
144	None	178	252		2415
145	193	179	1202		3503
146	None	180	1001	247	2411
147	421	181	See 252	248	None
148	461	182	1203	249	None
149	462	183	252	250	2411
	463	184	252		3503
150	3657	185	324	251	2412
151	462	186	1231	252	2412
152	464	187	1232–	253	See 3504
153	See 1031		1234	254	None
154	1034	188	1232	255	None
	1036	189	1234	256	2412
155	None	190	1232–		3504
156	425		1234		3542
157	1920	191	1232		R.S. 13:3913
	1921	192	1234	257	3504
158	423	193	Obsolete	258	3506
	933	194	1235		

CONCORDANCE TABLE 1

C.P. Art.	Replacement	C.P. Art.	Replacement	C.P. Art.	Replacement
259	3507	298	2298	337	151
	3508		3663		161
260	5091		3944	338	152
261	2333	299	1092		153
	3513	300	1092		154
262	2411		2299		161
	2412	301	2299	339	155
263	2413	302	1092		157
264	2415	303	2298		161
265	3510		3601	340	156
266	3512	304	3610		157
267	None	305	252		161
268	None	306	3605	341	158
269	3571	307	None		161
270	None	308	2504	342	157
271	3571		3611		161
272	3571	309	5121	343	922
273	3573	310	1701		923
274	3573	311	1701		927
275	3571	312	1702		934
	3663	313	Obsolete	344	Obsolete
276	3501	314	1002	345	927
	3574	315	1703	346	928
277	3574	316	1001		929
278	None	317	1002		931
279	3507	318	5059	347	
	3508	319	852	to	See 1491
	3576		1003	356	
280	3507	320	926	357	
281	3507	321	933	to	None
282	3504	322	925	360	
283	326	323	1003	361	1031
284	See 3571	324	See 1003	362	1031
285	3571	325	None	363	1031
	3575	326	None	364	1091
286	None	327	852	365	852
287	3543	328	854		1032
	3572		1003	366	See 1062
	3575	329	852	367	
288	3575	330	921	to	See 1062
	C.C. Art. 2709	331	921	372	
289	3507	332	923	373	1037
	3576		926	374	See 1061
290	See 3571		933	375	3608
291		333	926	376	None
to	None		928	377	1032
294		334	923		1037
295	3575		925	378	Obsolete
296	None		932	379	Obsolete
297	See 3605	335	531	380	1111
			925	381	Obsolete
		336	925	382	1032

1 LSA–C.C.P.—48

CODE OF CIVIL PROCEDURE

C.P. Art.	Replacement	C.P. Art.	Replacement	C.P. Art.	Replacement
383	1114	442	192	497	1761
384	1034, 1115	443	192	498	1761
385	See 1111	444	192	499	1761
386	None	445	None	500 to 502	None
387	1116	446	192		
388	1037, 1113	447 to 461	None	503	1765
				504	None
389	1091	462	192	505	None
390	1091	463	1571, 1572	506	1765
391	1037			507	1765
392	See 1034	464	1602, 1603	508	None
393	1032, 1093	465	1602, 1603	509	1762
				510	None
394	None	466	1602, 1604	511	1764
395	1092, 2643			512	1764
				513	Obsolete
396	1092, 2643	467	See 1603	514	1768
		468	1601	515	1791
397	1092, 2643	469	1351	516	1792
		470	1602	517	1792
398	1032, 1092, 1093, R.S. 13:3882	471	1602	518	None
		472	R.S. 13:365	519	1811, 1812, 1916
		473	1354		
399	1092	474	1354	520	1916
400	1037, 1092	475	1354	521	1811, 1812, 1916
		476	1632		
401	1092, 1093, 2592, 2643	477	1632		
		478	1633	522 to 529	None
		479	1633		
402	1092, 2643	480 to 482	Obsolete	530	See 1769
				531	See 1769
403	1092	483	None	532	See 1671
404 to 418	None	484	1632	533	None
		485	1632	534	1843
		486	371, 1631, R.S. 13:3416	535	None
419	1151			536	1672, 1673, 1844
420	1151	487	None		
421	None	488	1636	537	1841
422	1561	489	1635, 1636	538	1841
423	1561			539	1841, 1842
424	See 1421–1473	490	1637		
		491	1671	540	None
425	See 1421–1473	492	1671, 1673	541	1916
				542	1916
426 to 439	See 1471–1473	493	1751	543	1911, 1912
		494	1732, 1733		
				544	254
440	1432	495	1732	545	None
441	192	496	1761	546	1911

754

CONCORDANCE TABLE 1

C.P. Art.	Replacement	C.P. Art.	Replacement	C.P. Art.	Replacement
547	1951	588 ⎫		638	2502
548	None	to ⎬	None	639	2502
549	1920	590 ⎭			2503
550	1920	591	2133	640	324
551	1920	592	2133	641	2253
552	None	593	2087		2291
553	1921		R.S. 13:4452	642	2253
554	None	594	See 2088		2291
555	None	595	See 2088		2294
556	2082	596	See 2124		2296
557	1971	597	None		2411
558	1973	598	Obsolete		R.S. 13:3881
559	1975	599	Obsolete	643	2253
560	1814	600	None	644	13:3881
	1972	601	2130	645	None
561	1975	602	2131	646 ⎫	
562	1971	603	2131	to ⎬	2295
563	1977	604	2005	650 ⎭	
	1978	605	2001	651 ⎫	
	1979	606	2002	to ⎬	2296
564	2082	607	2004	653 ⎭	
565	2083	608	2006	654	2293
566	2083	609	2005	655	2231
567	2085	610	2006	656	327
568 ⎫		611	2005	657	326
to ⎬	Obsolete		2006		328
570 ⎭		612	2003	658	328
571	2086	613	2004	659	326
572	2084	614 ⎫		660	326
573	2121	to ⎬	None	661	329
	3942	616 ⎭		662	328
574	2121	617 ⎫		663	2340
	2125	to ⎬	2251	664 ⎫	
575	1913	621 ⎭		to ⎬	Obsolete
	2123	622	None	666 ⎭	
	2124	623	2251	667	2331
576	2124	624	1913	668	Obsolete
577	2124		2123	669	None
578	2087		2252	670	2331
	2124	625	2253	671 ⎫	
579	See 2124	626	2253	to ⎬	2332
580	2122	627	324	675 ⎭	R.S. 13:4363–4366
	2074	628	2253	676	2295
	4068		2254		2332
	4545	629	None	677	2334
581 ⎫		630 ⎫		678	2334
to ⎬	See 2121	to ⎬	2501	679	2335
584 ⎭		634 ⎭			2374
585	2127	635	2502	680	2336
	2128	636	2502	681	See 2336
586	Obsolete	637	2503	682	2336
587	See 2127			683	2335

755

CODE OF CIVIL PROCEDURE

C.P. Art.	Replacement	C.P. Art.	Replacement	C.P. Art.	Replacement
684	2337	734	2634	773	None
685	2338		2635	774	252
686	2341		2672	775	251
687	2372		2673	to	254
688	2339	735	2639	779	
689	None	736	2633	780	257
690	2371	737	2635	781	R.S. 13:4534
691	2342		2641	782	255
692	2342	738	2751		256
693	R.S. 13:4353		2752	783	None
694	R.S. 13:4353	739	2298	784	333
695	2342		2751	785	None
	R.S. 13:4354		2752	786	256
696	See 2336		2753		2592
697	R.S. 13:4356	740	2753		3781
698	R.S. 13:4355	741	2752	787	2592
699	R.S. 13:4357	742	See 2751		3821
700	2294	743	See 2751	788	2592
	2343	744	2701	789	2592
701	2343	745	2722		3861
702	2343		2723		3901
703	None		2724	790	2592
704	2373	746	2781	791	3821
705	See 2336	747	2781	792	3822
706	2374	748	2783	793	None
707	None	749	2783	794	3821
708	2375	750	2783	795	See 3821
	2376	751	2783	796	
709	2378	752	1395	to	None
710	See 2374	753	1395	800	
711	2379	754	2592	801	3781
712	2381	755	2592	802	3823
713	None		2643	803	3824
714	2380	756	2595	804	3823
715	5154	757	2595	805	3825
716		758	333	806	3783
to	See 2336	759	None		3825
720		760	321	807	3825
721	See 2136	761	322	808	3826
722	2292	762	325	809	None
723	2292	763	323	810	See 3825
724	3511	764	Obsolete	811	See 3825
725		765	332	812	None
to	None	766	334	813	3782
727		767	334	814	3785
728	2297	768	330	815	3785
729	None		334	816	3827
730	Obsolete	769	330	817	3827
731	None		334	818	See 852
732	2631	770	None	819	2592
733	2632	771	331	820	3828
		772	None	821	3829

CONCORDANCE TABLE 1

C.P. Art.	Replacement	C.P. Art.	Replacement	C.P. Art.	Replacement
822 to 824	None	881	151	928	2851
			152		2852
			159	929	2811
825	3830		160		3401
826	None	882	None	930	2891
827	None	883	2127		2933
828	3861	884	2127	931	3081
	3901	885	2125	932	2852
829	3861	886 to 891	2133	933	2856
830	2592			934	2852
	3784				2882
	3862	892	None	935	2857
831	3862	893	None	936	2854
832	3861	894	2164	937	2854
833	3863	895	2164	938	2821
834	3863	896	2129		2901
835	3864		2164	939	2882
836	None	897	2129		2890
837 to 839	See 2201		2164	940	2882
		898	2132		2890
			2161	941	2882
840	3781	899	2132		2890
841	3781	900	See 2201	942	2890
	3861	901	See 2162	943	2892
	3865	902	928	944	4031
842	3782		929	945	4031
	3783		931	946	4031
	3865		2163	947	None
843	3785	903	821	948	None
	3865	904	2086	949	4061
844	None	905 to 908	2164	950	4061
845 to 866	See 2201			951	Obsolete
		909	None	952	4065
867	3901	910	None	953	4065
868	See 3901	911	2167	954	4066
869	3783	912	See 2166	955	4067
870	3902	913	See 2166	956	4062
871	2592	914	None	957	4064
	3902	915	2251	958 to 963	None
872	252	916	None		
	321	917 to 919	Obsolete	964	732
873	None				733
874 to 876	Obsolete	920	None		2637
		921 to 923	Obsolete		2041
877	191				2674
878	See 2201	924	3083		5092
879	Obsolete	925 to 927	Obsolete	965	Obsolete
880	Obsolete			966 to 969	None
				970	3095

757

CODE OF CIVIL PROCEDURE

C.P. Art.	Replacement	C.P. Art.	Replacement	C.P. Art.	Replacement
971	3095	1024 to 1026	4603	1069 to 1071	4839
972	3095	1027	4603, 4605	1072	151, 4843–4845
973	3095, 3096	1028	4608	1073	4892
974	See 3081 et seq.	1029	4609, 4610	1074	4893
975	3131, 3137	1030	4610	1075	4893
976 to 983	See 3081 et seq.	1031	4611	1076	4901, 4941
984	3246 et seq.	1032	4612	1077	4894, 4941
985	3241, 3242	1033	See 2971	1078	4894
986	3246	1034	See 2971	1079 to 1081	None
987	See 3247	1035	Obsolete	1082	4895
988	Obsolete	1036	1733	1083	4892
989	None	1037	See 191	1084	None
990 to 992	3261 et seq.	1038	Obsolete	1085	4896
993	3303	1039	Obsolete	1086	None
994	Obsolete	1040	193	1087	None
995	None	1041	Obsolete	1088	Obsolete
996	None	1042 to 1044	None	1089	None
997	3331	1045	See 254	1090	4899
998	3334	1046	Obsolete	1091 to 1094	None
999	4203	1047	See 321	1095	1920
1000	3332	1048	See 333	1096 to 1115	None
1001	3361	1049	Obsolete	1116	See 4892
1002	None	1050	2974	1117	3501, 4831
1003	See 3381	1051	Obsolete	1118	3544, 4831
1004	3335	1052	Obsolete	1119 to 1123	None
1005 to 1007	See 3336	1053	See 3307	1124	4892
1008	None	1054	See 3307	1125	3571, 3575, 4831
1009	See 3171	1055 to 1057	Obsolete	1126	3501, 4831
1010	3332	1058	2502, 2504	1127	3507, 4831
1011	3334	1059	2974, 4068, 4548	1128	4899, 4942
1012	3334	1060 to 1062	Obsolete		
1013 to 1018	3182	1063	4832		
1019	See 3172	1064	4832		
1020	See 3461	1065	None		
1021	4602	1066	Obsolete		
1022	81	1067	4, 4831		
1023	See 3461	1068	4836		

CONCORDANCE TABLE 1

C.P. Art.	Replacement	C.P. Art.	Replacement	C.P. Art.	Replacement
1129	4899, 4942	1137 to 1142	None	1153	227, 4838
1130	Obsolete	1143	Obsolete	1154	227, 4838
1131	4898, 4900	1144 to 1149	None	1155	None
1132	4900	1150	Obsolete	1156	Obsolete
1133	4899	1151	Obsolete	1157 to 1160	None
1134	None	1152	191, 4831		
1135	4901				
1136	Obsolete			1161	Obsolete

CONCORDANCE TABLE 2

REPLACEMENT IN THE CODE OF CIVIL PROCEDURE AND IN THE REVISED STATUTES OF CIVIL CODE ARTICLES REPEALED

(Unless otherwise indicated, references in replacement columns below are to articles in the Code of Civil Procedure)

C.C. Art.	Replacement	C.C. Art.	Replacement	C.C. Art.	Replacement
56	2637	316 to 318	4101, 4131	347	4269
	2674			348	4269
	5091				4270
141	5091	319	4132	349	4274
222	4501	320	4133	350	4261
251	4061		4135		4262
	4101	321	4134	351	4264
	4131	323	4134	353	4265
	4133	324	4204		4267
	4134	325	4133		4270
254	Obsolete		4135	354	4275
255	Obsolete	326	4133	355	4262
258	4062		4135	356	4391
260	4062	327	Obsolete		4394
271	4064	328	4204		4396
	4463	329	4133	357	4391 to 4393
274	4201	330	4133		
275 to 277	4202		4204	358	4392
		331	4133	359	4398
		332	4133	363	4431
279	4205	334	4171		4433
281 to 291	Obsolete	335	4070	364	4432
			4172	369	4394
		336	None	375	682
302	4231	337	4261 to 4263	386	195
303	4231				196
	4232				3003
	4234	338	None		
304	4234	339	4267	387	3992
305	4234		4301	388	3994
306	4236	340	4271	408	4553
307	4031	341	4322	415	4550
	4032	342	4321		4554
	4068		4323	935	2811
312	None	343	4361 to 4363	1011	3007
					3034
313	732			1012	3007
314	4234	344	4361 to 4363		3034
	4237			1019	R.S. 9:101
	4273	346	4266	1041	3094
315	4238		4268		3098
					3181

CODE OF CIVIL PROCEDURE

C.C. Art.	Replacement	C.C. Art.	Replacement	C.C. Art.	Replacement
1042 to 1046	3098	1131	None	1190	3121
		1132	3181		3122
		1133	3242		3421 et seq.
1048	3151	1134	3121	1191	3331
1049	None	1135	None		3333
1051	3261	1136	None		3337
	3262	1137	80	1193	3361
	3264		81		3362
1053	None	1146	3194	1194	3332
1063	3301		3195		3333
	3303	1147	3191		3351
1064	3304		3333	1195	3391
1065	3307	1149	None	1196 to 1199	3391 / 3394 / 3395
	3394	1150	3222		
1066	3307	1151	3331	1200 to 1202	3351
	3308		3334		
1069	3351	1152	None		
	3352	1153	3097	1203	3395
1070	2825		3182	1204 to 1208	3394 / 3395
1075 to 1094	R.S. 9:1424	1154	3097		
		1155	3196		
		1156	3211	1209	3182
1098	None	1157	3121	1210 to 1219	3171 to 3174
1099	None		3211		
1101	None	1158	3182		
1102	3132	1159	3181		
1104	3132	1160	3181		3401 to 3405
1105 to 1110	3132 / 3133	1161	Obsolete	1220	
		1162	3264		
		1163	None		
1111	3134	1164	None	1221 to 1226	Obsolete
1112	3131	1165	3271		
	3134	1166	3271		
1113	81	1167	3272	1316	Obsolete
1114 to 1116	None		3282	1317	Obsolete
			R.S. 43:203	1324	4604
		1168	None	1327	81
1117	3091 et seq.	1169	3273		3461
	R.S. 43:203	1170	3273	1368	4608
1118	3095	1172 to 1178	None	1374	4609
1119	3095				4610
1120	3096			1375	4610
1121 to 1124	3098	1179	3302	1376	4611
		1180 to 1183	3303	1377	4612
1125	2825			1444 to 1464	R.S. 9:5011 to 9:5016
1126	3158	1184	3304		
1127 to 1129	3151	1185	3307		
		1186	3307	1596	2888
		1187	3308	1648	2884
1130	3157	1189	3302	1649	2884

CODE OF CIVIL PROCEDURE

C.C. Art.	Replacement	C.C. Art.	Replacement	C.C. Art.	Replacement
1650 to 1654	2885 / 2886	1675	3394	1689	3405
		1676	3196	3275	3035
		1677	3153		R.S. 9:5011 to 9:5016
1655	2883		3155		
1656	2882		3156		
1657	2882	1678	3083	3316	R.S. 9:101
1659	3211	1679	3153	3351	4061
1660	3211	1681	3192		4101
1666	R.S. 9:1424	1682	2825		4134
1667	3132	1683	3351	3352	R.S. 9:101
1668 to 1670	3261	1684	3351	3400 to 3402	2378 / 3721 to 3743
		1685	3352		
1671	3272	1686	3353		
1673	Obsolete	1687	3353	3403	3743
1674	3331 / 3337	1688	3405	3404	3743

CONCORDANCE TABLE 3

REPLACEMENT IN THE CODE OF CIVIL PROCEDURE OF REPEALED SECTIONS OF THE REVISED STATUTES

Section	C.C.P. Art.	Section	C.C.P. Art.	Section	C.C.P. Art.
9:171 to 9:178	4621 to 4630	9:1551 to 9:1557	3121, 3122, 3421 to 3443	13:2584	See 4841
9:303	5098			13:2621	4837
9:651 to 9:653	4271, 4554	9:2662	None	13:3050	1761 to 1764, 1795
		9:4867	72	13:3234	42, 74, 77
9:671	4301, 4321, 4341, 4554, 4641	9:5501	4362		
		13:101	None	13:3235	42, 74, 77
		13:901 to 13:909	281 to 286, 4972	13:3236	77
9:672	4301, 4321, 4341, 4554, 4641	13:911	See 4552	13:3238	75
		13:912	See 4552	13:3271 to 13:3279	121, 122, See amended 13:3271 to 13:3277
		13:1877	4896, 5001, 5002		
9:801 to 9:804	4132, 4135, 4136, 4363, 4554	13:1879	4837		
		13:1921	4847		
		13:1922	4842	13:3331 to 13:3343	284, 286, 4971, 4972
		13:1923	4837		
		13:1951	4895, 4922		
9:821 to 9:825	4461 to 4464, 4554	13:1971	4895	13:3344	1001, 1913, 1914
		13:2017	4847		
		13:2018	4841, 4843 to 4845	13:3345	1063, 1312, 1313
9:841	5091				
9:1421	None	13:2043	4843 to 4845	13:3346	1313
9:1431	3421 to 3443			13:3347	1313
				13:3349	428
9:1451 to 9:1454	3261, 3263, 3281, 3284	13:2080	4841, 4843 to 4845	13:3381 to 13:3386	1111 to 1116
9:1455	3285, 4342, 4554	13:2148	4847	13:3411 to 13:3413	2637, 2041, 2672 to 2074
		13:2220	4847		
		13:2260	4847		
9:1512	3395	13:2343	4847		

765

CODE OF CIVIL PROCEDURE

Section	C.C.P. Art.	Section	C.C.P. Art.	Section	C.C.P. Art.
13:3414	2637	13:3748	1431	13:4063	3602
	2671	13:3751	194	13:4064	3603
13:3471	42		1432		to
	1203		to		3605
	1231		1435		3610
	to	13:3752	194	13:4065	3606
	1234		1436		3607
	1261	13:3753	1437	13:4066	3607
	to	13:3761	1451	13:4067	3609
	1265	13:3762	1452	13:4068	3610
	1291	13:3763	1453	13:4069	3611
	1292	13:3764	1454	13:4070	196
	1314	13:3765	1455		3612
	2412	13:3766	1456		3613
	See amended	13:3767	1457	13:4071	3613
	13:3471	13:3771	1471	13:4108	None
	to	13:3772	1472	13:4158	4546
	13:3473	13:3773	1473	13:4202	1919
13:3484	1293	13:3781	1491		2089
13:3541	3751	13:3782	194	13:4212	1911
to	to		1492		1912
13:3543	3753	13:3783	194		2123
13:3601	852		1493	13:4213	1974
	to		to	13:4214	2087
	865		1495		2123
	891	13:3784	1496		2252
	965	13:3791	1511	13:4231	1871
	968	13:3792	1512	to	to
	969		1513	13:4246	1883
	1003	13:3793	1514	13:4261	1971
	1004	13:3794	1515		1978
	5001	13:3851	See amended	13:4262	
13:3661	1352	to	13:3851	to	1971
	1353	13:3861	to	13:4264	
	See amended		13:3861	13:4311	2451
	13:3661	13:3911	2414	to	to
13:3662	1436	13:3912	2414	13:4315	2456
to	1634	13:3941		13:4342	2333
13:3664		to	3509		3513
13:3670	None	13:3943		13:4352	None
13:3741	1421	13:3944	3514	13:4401	See amended
to	to	13:3952	3541	to	13:4359
13:3794	1515		3542	13:4406	to
13:3741	1356	13:3954	3501		13:4362
	1421	13:4001	3571	13:4437	2125
13:3742	1422		4892	13:4437.1	2127
13:3743	1423	13:4031	3574	13:4438	2125
13:3744	1424	13:4033	None		See amended
	to	13:4062	3601		13:4438
	1427	to	to	13:4441	2162
13:3745	1428	13:4071	3613	13:4442	2162
13:3746	1429			13:4443	2128
13:3747	1430	13:4062	3602		2164

CONCORDANCE TABLE 3

Section	C.C.P. Art.	Section	C.C.P. Art.	Section	C.C.P. Art.
13:4444	2164	13:4612	221 to 227	13:4971 to 13:4983	4621 to 4630
13:4446	2166, 2167		371	13:4984	4642
13:4448	1635	13:4811 to 13:4816	4651 to 4662	13:5061	None, See 3657
13:4452	3942	13:4817	4658 See amended 13:4817	13:5062	3651 to 3654
13:4524	4613			13:5063	None
13:4525 to 13:4528	5181 to 5188			13:5064	None
13:4571 to 13:4580	5121 to 5127	13:4911 to 13:4926	4701 to 4735	13:5151	1551

IMPLEMENTATION TABLE 4

Acts 1960, Nos. 30–35, both inclusive, effective January 1, 1961, implemented the adoption of the Louisiana Code of Civil Procedure by amending, repealing and adding designated sections and articles of the Revised Civil Code and the Louisiana Revised Statutes.

The articles and sections affected by the implementing Acts and the effect on such articles and sections are shown in this Table for convenient reference in evaluating the impact of the new Code of Civil Procedure on the procedural law formerly found in the Revised Civil Code and the Louisiana Revised Statutes.

A. REVISED CIVIL CODE

LSA–C.C. Articles	Effect Acts 1960, No. 30	LSA–C.C. Articles	Effect Acts 1960, No. 30
56	Repealed	1041–1046	Repealed
141	Repealed	1048, 1049	Repealed
142	Amended	1051	Repealed
222	Repealed	1053	Repealed
248	Amended	1063–1066	Repealed
251	Repealed	1060, 1070	Repealed
254, 255	Repealed	1075–1094	Repealed
258	Amended	1097	Amended
260	Repealed	1098, 1099	Repealed
265	Amended	1101, 1102	Repealed
267	Amended	1104–1137	Repealed
270	Amended	1146, 1147	Repealed
271	Repealed	1149–1170	Repealed
273	Amended	1172–1187	Repealed
274–277	Repealed	1189–1191	Repealed
279	Repealed	1193–1226	Repealed
281–291	Repealed	1316, 1317	Repealed
302–307	Repealed	1324	Repealed
312–321	Repealed	1327	Repealed
322	Amended	1348	Amended
323–332	Repealed	1368	Repealed
333	Amended	1374–1377	Repealed
334–344	Repealed	1444–1464	Repealed
346–351	Repealed	1596	Repealed
353–359	Repealed	1648–1657	Repealed
363, 364	Repealed	1659, 1660	Repealed
369	Repealed	1666–1671	Repealed
375	Repealed	1672	Amended
385	Amended	1673–1679	Repealed
386–388	Repealed	1681–1689	Repealed
408	Repealed	2103	Amended
415	Repealed	2315	Amended
935	Repealed	2621	Amended
1011, 1012	Repealed	2709	Amended
1019	Repealed		

CODE OF CIVIL PROCEDURE

LSA–C.C. Articles	Effect Acts 1960, No. 30	LSA–C.C. Articles	Effect Acts 1960, No. 30
3275	Repealed	3400–3404	Repealed
3316	Repealed	3519	Amended
3351, 3352	Repealed	3532	Amended
3399	Amended	3547	Amended

B. LOUISIANA REVISED STATUTES

LSA–R.S. Sections	Effect Acts 1960, No. 31	LSA–R.S. Sections	Effect Acts 1960, No. 32
9:171–9:178	Repealed	13:1213	Amended
9:271	Added	13:1870	Repealed
9:301, 9:302	Amended	13:1871–13:1885	Repealed Added
9:303	Repealed		
9:304	Added	13:1886–13:1902	Added
9:571	Added	13:1921–13:1930	Repealed
9:603	Amended	13:1951, 13:1952	Repealed Added
9:651–9:653	Repealed		
9:671–9:674	Repealed	13:1953–1958	Repealed
9:731, 9:732	Amended	13:1971	Repealed
9:801–9:804	Repealed	13:1981–13:1993	Repealed
9:821–9:823	Repealed	13:2001	Added
9:841	Repealed	13:2001.1–13:2001.11	Repealed
9:1421	Repealed	13:2002–13:2010	Added
9:1424	Added	13:2011–13:2021	Repealed
9:1431	Repealed	13:2031–13:2044	Repealed
9:1441–9:1443	Added	13:2071–13:2080	Repealed Added
9:1451–9:1455	Repealed		
9:1512	Repealed	13:2081–13:2089	Added
9:1551–9:1557	Repealed	13:2091–13:2095	Repealed
9:2441	Repealed	13:2111–13:2127	Repealed
9:2662	Repealed	13:2131–13:2138	Repealed
9:2701	Added	13:2141–13:2148	Repealed
9:4501, 9:4502	Amended	13:2151–13:2158	Repealed Added
9:4601	Amended		
9:4622	Amended	13:2159–13:2160	Added
9:4721	Amended	13:2161, 13:2162	Repealed Added
9:4866	Amended		
9:4867	Repealed	13:2163–13:2175	Repealed
9:5011–9:5016	Added	13:2191–13:2196	Repealed
9:5501	Repealed	13:2211–13:2228	Repealed
9:5651	Added	13:2251–13:2261	Repealed
9:5801	Amended	13:2281–13:2289	Repealed
LSA–R.S. Sections	Effect Acts 1960, No. 32	13:2301–13:2313	Repealed
13:4	Repealed Added	13:2331–13:2343	Repealed
		13:2361–13:2372	Repealed
13:101	Repealed	13:2381–13:2388	Repealed
13:752	Amended	13:2401–13:2411	Repealed
13:841	Amended	13:2421–13:2431	Repealed
13:901–13:909	Repealed	13:2441–13:2452	Repealed
13:910	Amended	13:2471–13:2481	Repealed
13:911, 13:912	Repealed	13:2482.1–13:2482.18	Repealed
		13:2483.1–13:2483.17	Repealed

770

IMPLEMENTATION TABLE 4

LSA–R.S. Sections	Effect Acts 1960, No. 32	LSA–R.S. Sections	Effect Acts 1960, No. 32
13:2581–13:2584	Repealed	13:4101	Amended
	Added	13:4102	Repealed
13:2585–13:2587	Added	13:4103	Amended
13:2601	Repealed	13:4106	Amended
13:2621	Repealed	13:4108	Repealed
13:2641, 13:2642	Repealed	13:4111	Added
13:3234–13:3236	Repealed	13:4158	Repealed
13:3238	Repealed	13:4202	Repealed
13:3239	Added	13:4212–13:4214	Repealed
13:3271–13:3276	Amended	13:4231–13:4246	Repealed
13:3277–13:3279	Repealed	13:4261–13:4264	Repealed
13:3331	Repealed	13:4283–13:4285	Amended
	Added	13:4290	Added
13:3332–13:3347	Repealed	13:4311–13:4315	Repealed
13:3349	Repealed	13:4342	Repealed
13:3381–13:3386	Repealed	13:4344–13:4346	Amended
13:3411–13:3414	Repealed	13:4352	Repealed
13:3415	Added	13:4353–13:4357	Added
13:3471–13:3473	Amended	13:4359–13:4366	Added
13:3484	Repealed	13:4401–13:4404	Repealed
	Added	13:4406	Amended
13:3485	Added	13:4437	Repealed
13:3541–13:3543	Repealed	13:4437.1	Repealed
13:3601	Repealed	13:4443, 13:4444	Repealed
13:3661	Amended	13:4448	Repealed
13:3662–13:3664	Repealed	13:4452	Repealed
13:3670	Repealed		Added
13:3671, 13:3672	Added	13:4522	Amended
13:3721–13:3723	Amended	13:4524–13:4528	Repealed
13:1953–13:1958	Repealed	13:4529	Amended
13:3741–13:3748	Repealed	13:4534	Added
13:3751–13:3753	Repealed	13:4571–13:4580	Repealed
13:3761–13:3767	Repealed	13:4611	Repealed
13:3771–13:3773	Repealed		Added
13:3781–13:3784	Repealed	13:4612	Repealed
13:3791–13:3794	Repealed	13:4811–13:4816	Repealed
13:3851–13:3862	Repealed	13:4817	Amended
	Added	13:4911–13:4926	Repealed
13:3874	Amended	13:4971–13:4984	Repealed
13:3875	Repealed	13:4991	Repealed
13:3879	Amended	13:5061–13:5064	Repealed
13:3881, 13:3882	Added	13:5151	Repealed
13:3911, 13:3912	Repealed	LSA–R.S. Sections	Effect Acts 1960, No. 33
13:3913	Added	32.710	Amended
13:3941–13:3944	Repealed	LSA–R.S. Sections	Effect Acts 1960, No. 34
13:3952	Repealed	43:203	Repealed
13:3954	Repealed		Added
13:3957	Added	LSA–R.S. Sections	Effect Acts 1960, No. 35
13:4001	Repealed	47:2413	Amended
13:4002	Added		
13:4031–13:4033	Repealed		
13:4062–13:4071	Repealed		

INDEX TO CODE OF CIVIL PROCEDURE

References are to Articles

ABANDONMENT
Actions, 561.
Appeals, 561, 2162.

ABATEMENT OF ACTIONS
Death of party, 428.

ABSENCE AND ABSENTEES
Attachment, leaving state permanently, grounds, 3541.
Attorney appointed to represent absentee, 5091–5098.
City court judges, 4841.
    New Orleans city court, 4842.
Defined, 5251(1).
Executory proceeding against absentee, 2672, 2674.
Heirs and legatees, attorney for, 3171–3174.
Justice of the peace, ad hoc appointment, 4841.
Partition, co-owner an absentee, 4621–4630.
Tutors, temporary absence, agent, 4273.

ACCEPTANCE
Intestate successions, 3001–3008, 3061, 3062.
Testate successions, 3031–3035, 3061, 3062.

ACCIDENT INSURANCE
Venue, action on policy, 76.

ACCOUNTS AND ACCOUNTING
City courts, proof of open account, 4896.
Costs for indigent party, 5186.
Curators, 4391–4398, 4554.
Discovery and production for inspection, 1492.
Executors and administrators, 3331–3338.

ACCOUNTS AND ACCOUNTING—C't'd
Opposition,
    Curator, 4395, 4554.
    Succession representative, 3336.
    Tutor, 4395.
Provisional tutor, duties, 4073.
Succession representative, 3331–3338.
Tutors, 4391–4398.
Undertutor, 4203.

ACKNOWLEDGMENTS
Claims against succession, representative, 3242–3244.

ACT
Act importing confession of judgment, executory proceeding, 2632.

AD HOC
Curator, attorney appointed to represent unrepresented absentee or mental incompetent, 5091–5098.
Judge,
    Appointment, 158.
    Power, 157.
    Recusation, 161.
Tutor, attorney appointed to represent unrepresented minor, 5091–5098.

ADDITUR
Alternative to new trial, 1813.

ADJUDICATION
Minor's property to parent, 4361–4363.

ADMINISTRATION
Curatorship, 4262–4272, 4554.
Minor's property during marriage of parents, 4501, 4502.
Successions, 3081–3395.
Tutorship, 4262–4272.

INDEX—CODE OF CIVIL PROCEDURE
References are to Articles

ADMINISTRATIVE REVIEW
Jury trial, limitation, 1733.

ADMINISTRATORS
See Executors and Administrators.

ADMISSIBILITY OF EVIDENCE
Common law and statutes of other states, 1391.
Depositions, 1428, 1429.
Order prohibiting on failure to comply with discovery orders, 1513.
    Possessory actions, limited, title, 3661.

ADMISSIONS
Answer, 1003, 1004.
Continuance, prevention by, 1604.

ADOPTION
Jurisdiction of proceedings, 10(1).

ADOPTION BY REFERENCE
Pleading, 853.

ADVERSE PARTY
Amendment of exceptions, consent unnecessary, 1152.
Continuance, prevention by admission, 1604.
Cross-examination, party or representative, 1634.
Deposition, use, 1428.
Interrogatories on discovery, 1491.
Pleadings, service, 1311–1314.
Successions, service of papers on, 2971.
Summary judgment, affidavits opposing motion, service, 966.

AFFIDAVITS
Attachment, 3501.
Poverty, waiver of costs for indigent party, 5183.
    Traverse, 5184.
Preliminary injunction, hearing, 3609.
Sequestration, 3501.
Small successions,
    Endorsed copy, authority for delivery of property, 3434.
    Inheritance tax, 3432, 3433.
Successions, evidence, 2821–2823.
Summary judgment, motion for, 966.
    Supporting and opposing affidavits, 967.
Temporary restraining order, issuance, 3603.

AFFIRMATIVE DEFENSES
Answer, 1003, 1005.
Pleading, 1005.

AGENTS
Capacity to sue, 694, 695.
Process, agent for service of process, defined, 5251(2).
Service of process or citation, 6(1), 1235, 5251(2).

AGRICULTURAL PRODUCTS
Sale, succession property, 3264.
Tutors, minor's property, sale, 4303.

ALIEN INSURER
Proper defendant, 739, 741.
Proper plaintiff, 691.
Receivership,
    Ancillary receiver generally proper plaintiff, 693.
    Receiver proper defendant, 741.
Venue in suit against, general rule, 42(7).

ALIMONY
Appeal, 3943.
Judgment, 3943, 3945.

ALLOWANCES
Succession, interim, heirs and legatees, 3321.

ALTERNATIVE DEFENSES
Answer, 1006.

ALTERNATIVE PLEADING
Petition, 892.
Petitory and possessory actions prohibited, 3657.

AMBIGUITY OR VAGUENESS
Pleading, 926.

AMENDMENT
Answer, 1151.
Exceptions, 1152.
Judgment, 1951.
Petition, 1151.
    Joinder of necessary or indispensable party, 646.
Pleadings,
    Generally, 646, 932–934, 1151–1156.
    Conformity to evidence, 1154.
    Joinder of necessary or indispensable party, 646.
    Pre-trial conference, 1551.
    Relation back to date of filing, 1153.

AMICABLE DEMAND
Generally not required, 421.
Pleading want, 926.

ANCILLARY CURATORSHIP PROCEEDING
Procedure, 4431–4433, 4554.

INDEX—CODE OF CIVIL PROCEDURE
References are to Articles

ANCILLARY PROBATE PROCEEDING
Procedure, 3401–3405.

ANCILLARY TUTORSHIP
Procedure, 4431–4433.

ANNULMENT
Judgments, 2001–2006.
Probated testaments, 2931–2933.

ANNULMENT OF MARRIAGE
    Generally, 3941–3945.
Appeal from judgment, 3942.
Judgment on pleadings not permitted, 969.
Jurisdiction of proceeding, 10(6).
Jury trial, limitation, 1733.
Procedure, 3941–3945.
Summary judgment not permitted, 969.
Venue, may not be waived, 44, 3941.

ANSWER
    Generally, 1001–1006.
Admissions, 1003, 1004.
Affirmative defenses, 1003, 1005.
Allowed pleading, 852, 1001–1006.
Alternative defenses, 1006.
Amendment, 1151.
Appeals, 2133.
Concursus proceeding, 4655, 4657.
Delay, filing,
    Appeal, 2133.
    City court, 4895, 5002.
    Concursus proceeding, 4655, 4657.
    District court, 1001, 1002.
        Less than $100, 4895, 4971.
    Incidental demand, 1033.
    Justice of the peace court, 4895, 4941.
Demand against third party, 1035.
Denials, 1003.
    Plaintiff's allegations, 1004.
Form, 1003.
Garnishment interrogatories, 2412, 2414.
Habeas corpus, 3783, 3825, 3826.
Incidental actions, 1035.
Intervention, 1035.
Mandamus, 3783.
Petition, answer to amended petition, 1151.
Quo warranto, 3783.
Reconvention, 1035.
Supplemental answer, 1155.
Time, filing, 1001.

APPEALS
    Generally, 2081–2167.
Abandonment, 561, 2162.
Alimony judgment, 3943.
Annulment of judgments, 2005.

APPEALS—Cont'd
Annulment of marriage, judgment, 3942.
Answer to appeal,
    Delay for filing, 2133.
    Necessity, 2133.
Appealable judgments, 2083.
Assignment of errors unnecessary, 2129.
City courts,
    Cases involving more than $100, 5002.
    Cases involving $100 or less, 4899–4901, 4921, 4922.
Consent of parties, dismissal, 2162.
Contents of record, determination, 2128.
Correction of record, 2132.
Costs,
    Appellate court may tax, 2164.
    Payment to clerk of district court, 2126.
Custody of child judgment, 3943.
Declaratory orders, judgments and decrees, 1877.
Defects, dismissal, 2161.
Definition of appeal, 2082.
Delay,
    Annulment of marriage, 3942.
    Answer, filing, 2133.
    City courts, 4899, 4921, 4922, 4942.
    Devolutive appeal, 2087.
    Divorce judgment, 3942.
    Separation from bed and board judgment, 3942.
    Suspensive appeal, 2123.
Description of immovables affected, 2089.
Devolutive appeal,
    Delay for appealing, 2087.
    Delay for taking, 2087.
    None in executory proceeding, 2642.
    Possessory action, 3662.
    Security, 2124.
Dismissal,
    Consent of parties, 2162.
    Irregularities, 2161.
    Lack of jurisdiction, 2162.
    No right to appeal, 2162.
    Want of prosecution, 2165.
Divesting of jurisdiction of trial court, 2088.
Divorce case, judgment, 3942.
    Alimony judgment, 3943.
    Awarding custody, 3943.
Eviction of tenants and occupants, 4735.
Exceptions filed in appellate court, 2163.
Failure to prosecute, dismissal, 2165.
Fees, preparation of record, prepayment, 2127.
Finality, 2167.
Form of record, 2128.
Habeas corpus, not suspensive, 3831.

INDEX—CODE OF CIVIL PROCEDURE
References are to Articles

APPEALS—Cont'd
Injunctive order or judgment, 3612.
Interdiction, effect, 4548.
Judicial notice of common law and statutes, 1391.
Jurisdiction,
    Trial court, divesting, 2088.
    Transfer for lack, 2162.
Justice of the peace courts, 4942.
Legal representative, 2084.
    Appointment or removal not suspended by, 2122.
Limitations, 2085.
Method of appealing, 2121.
Narrative of facts, record, 2131.
Order homologating tableau of distribution, 3308.
Pleading, judgment on pleading not to lie on refusal, 968.
Possessory action, 3662.
Procedure in appellate courts, 2161–2167.
Proceedings in appellate courts, 2081–2167.
Preparation of record, 2127.
Record, 2127, 2128, 2130–2132.
Remand, prescription pleaded, 2163.
Return day,
    Extension, 2125.
    Original, 2125.
Scope of appeal, 2164.
Security, 2124.
Separation from bed and board, judgment, 3942.
    Alimony, 3943.
    Awarding custody, 3943.
Service of motion or petition unnecessary, 1312.
Statement of facts, transcript of record, 2130.
Substitution of parties, 821.
Succession proceedings, 2974.
Summary judgment, appeal not to lie on refusal, 968.
Suspensive,
    Delay for taking, 2123.
    Effect, 2123.
    Executory proceeding, 2642.
    Possessory action, 3662.
    Security, 2124.
Temporary restraining order, 3612.
Third person, right to appeal, 2086.
Transfer, when court lacks jurisdiction, 2162.
Tutors or undertutors, appointment or removal, 4068.
Vacation of appointment of legal representative, effect, 2122.

APPEARANCE
City courts, parties' failure to appear, 4896.
Implied waiver of objections by general appearance, 7.
Pleading, no general appearance, 7.
Waiver, objections,
    Jurisdiction over person, 7.
    Raised by declinatory exception, 925.

APPELLATE COURT
Proceedings, 2081–2167.

APPRAISAL
Executory proceedings, seizure and sale, 2723.
Judicial sales, fieri facias, bid less than appraised value, 2336.
Property seized, 2332.
Succession property, 3132, 3133, 3136.

ARBITRATION AND AWARD
Pleaded as affirmative defense, 1005.

ARREST
Abolished, 3501–3613.

ASSIGNMENTS
Cases for trial, 1571, 1572.
Errors on appeal, necessity, 2129.
New trial, 1977.
Proper plaintiff to enforce assigned right, 698.

ASSOCIATIONS
    See, also, Unincorporated Association.
Discovery, 1491.
Party defendant, 738.
Party plaintiff, 689.

ASSUMPTION OF RISK
Pleaded as affirmative defense, 1005.

ATTACHMENT
Actions in which it may issue, 3542.
Affidavit, 3501.
Damages for dissolution, 3506.
Dissolution on motion, 3506.
Garnishment, 3503.
Grounds for issuance, 3501, 3541, 3542.
Inventory of property seized, 3504.
Issuance before debt due, 3543.
Issuance before filing of petition, 3502.
Motion to dissolve nonresident, no general appearance, 7(4).
Necessity for judgment and execution, 3510.
Nonresident, venue, 3545.
Orders, signing in chambers, 194.
Perishable property, sale, 3513.

INDEX—CODE OF CIVIL PROCEDURE
References are to Articles

ATTACHMENT—Cont'd
Petition, 3501.
    Issuance of writ before filing, 3502.
Plaintiff's security, 3544.
Privilege resulting from seizure, 3511.
Property of nonresident, jurisdiction, 9.
Reduction of excessive seizure, 3505.
Release,
    Bond, 5127.
    Property seized,
        Defendant, 3507.
        Not to effect right to damages, 3514.
        Security, 3507, 3508.
        Third person, 3509.
    Security for issuance, 3512.
Security,
    Issuance,
        Amount, 3501, 3544.
        Cancellation, 3512.
    Release of property, 3507, 3508.
Sheriff's return, 3504
Third person, release of property seized, 3509.
Venue,
    Garnishment proceeding under writ, 2416.
    Nonresident, 3545.

ATTORNEYS
Absent heirs and legatees, successions, 3171–3174.
Appointment by court,
    Absentee co-owner, partition, order appointing, 4623.
    Absentees, represent absentees, 5091–5098.
    Citation, waiver, 5093.
    Compensation, 5096.
    Designation immaterial, 5091.
    Duties,
        Defense of action, 5095.
        Notice to nonresident or absentee, 5094.
    Executory proceeding, 2641, 2674.
    Failure to perform duties,
        Does not affect validity of proceeding, 5098.
        Punishment, 5098.
    Jurisdiction based upon service of process on, 6.
    Oath not required, 5093.
    Order appointing, signing in chambers, 194.
    Partition between co-owners, 4605.
    Pleadings filed by, no general appearance, 7.
    Qualifications, 5092.

ATTORNEYS—Cont'd
Appointment by court—Cont'd
    Represent unrepresented defendant, 5091–5098.
    Suggestions for appointment not permitted, 5092.
    Waiver of citation, acceptance of service, 5093.
    Workmen's compensation case, 5097.
Compensation,
    Appointment by court, 5096.
    Attorney for absent heirs and legatees, 3174.
Court officers, 371.
Disciplinary action, deceit, 863, 864.
District court officers, 371.
Entry or removal of name as counsel of record no general appearance, 7(1).
Executory proceedings, 2641, 2674.
Fees,
    Class actions, 595.
    Depositions, failure to attend, 1457.
    Genuineness of documents, refusal to admit in discovery, 1514.
    Jurisdiction, amount in dispute, 4.
    Partition between co-owners uncontested, 4613.

AUTHENTIC EVIDENCE
Executory proceedings, 2635–2637.

BANKRUPTCY
Discharge pleaded as affirmative defense, 1005.

BANKS AND BANKING
Safety deposit vaults, examination on search for testament, 2854.

BED AND BOARD
See Separation From Bed and Board.

BILL IN NATURE OF INTERPLEADER
Concursus, 4652.

BILL OF EXCEPTIONS
Not necessary, 1635.

BILLS OF LADING
Concursus, 4661.

BOARDS AND COMMISSIONS
Official acts, etc., proof, 1303.
Service, citation or process, 1265.

BONDS
    See, also, Security.
Judicial bonds, 5121–5127.
Succession property sale, 3285.
Tutors, sale of minor's bonds, 4342.
Venue, judicial bond, 75.

INDEX—CODE OF CIVIL PROCEDURE
References are to Articles

BOUNDARIES
Actions, boundary actions, 3691–3693.

BRIBERY
Jury, ground for new trial, 1814.

BUILDINGS
Eviction. See Eviction of Tenants and Occupants.

BURDEN OF PROOF
Annulment of probated testaments, 2932, 2933.
Concursus, immovables, 3654.
Declaratory judgments, immovables, 3654.
Expropriations, immovables, 3654.
Petitory action, plaintiff, 3653.
Possessory action, 3658.
Probate of testaments, proponent, 2903.

BUSINESS
Succession representative, continuation, 3224, 3225.
Tutors, continuation, 4266.
Provisional tutor, 4073.

CALL IN WARRANTY
See Demand Against Third Party.

CAPACITY
Agents, capacity to sue, 694, 695.
Pleadings, allegations, 855.

CAPTION
Pleadings, 853.

CASUALTY INSURER
Claimants may be impleaded, 4652.

CAUSE OF ACTION
Raising objection through peremptory exception, 927.
Splitting, effect, 425.
Use as defense, 424.

CERTIFIED COPIES
Judgment, execution, filing, 2251.
Official records, proof by, 1394, 1395.
Subpoena duces tecum to produce, 1354.

CESTUI QUE TRUST
Declaratory judgments, 1874.

CHALLENGES
Jurors, 1764–1767, 1769.

CHAMBERS
Extraordinary remedies, hearing in chambers, 3784.
Judicial proceedings, 195.
Signing orders and judgments, 194.
Vacation, during vacation, 196.

CHAMBERS—Cont'd
Summary proceedings, trial in chambers, 2595.

CHANGE OF VENUE
Generally, 121, 122.
Vacation, trial of motion for change during, 196.

CHARGE TO JURY
Generally, 1791–1793.

CHARGES
Judicial sales subject to real charge, 2372.
Succession, payment, 3301–3308.

CHILDREN
See Minors.

CITATION
See, also, Service.
Generally, 1201–1203.
City courts,
Cases involving $100 or less, 4894, 4921, 4922.
Cases involving more than $100, 5002.
Clerk of court,
Issuance, 252.
Signature, 1202.
Concealment to avoid service, grounds for attachment, 3541.
Corporations, service, 1261.
Demand against third party, 1114.
Eviction, notice to vacate, 4703.
Executory proceedings, no necessity, 1201, 2640.
Foreign corporations, service, 1261.
Form, 1202.
Garnishment, 2411, 2412.
Intervention, 1093.
Legal representative of multiple defendants, 1203.
Necessity in ordinary proceedings, 1201–1314.
Pleading insufficiency, 925.
Reconvention, unnecessary, 1063.
Service,
Legal and quasi legal entities, 1261–1265.
Persons, 1231–1235.
Persons authorized to make, 1291–1293.
Substitution of parties, 802, 803.
Summary proceedings, no necessity, 1201.
Waiver,
Acceptance of service, 1201.
Attorney appointed by court, 5093.

778

INDEX—CODE OF CIVIL PROCEDURE
References are to Articles

CITY COURTS
Appeal, 4899–4901, 4921, 4922.
    Cases involving more than $100, 5002.
Appearance, parties' failure to appear, 4896.
Application of law, 4831.
Cases involving more than $100, procedure, 5001, 5002.
Cases involving $100 or less, procedure,
    New Orleans city courts, 4921, 4922.
    Other than New Orleans, 4891–4901.
Citation,
    Cases involving more than $100, 5002.
    Cases involving $100 or less, 4894, 4921, 4922.
Contempt, power to punish, 4838.
Defined, 5251(3).
Evidence, proof of open account, 4896.
Execution of judgment, 4897.
Form, judgment, 4897.
Illness or absence of judge,
    All courts other than New Orleans, 4841.
    New Orleans city courts, 4842.
Judgment, 4896, 4897.
Jurisdiction,
    Limitations, 4836.
    Municipalities of less than 10,000, 4832.
    Municipalities of 10,000 to 20,000, 4833.
    Municipalities of 20,000 or more, 4834.
    New Orleans city courts, 4835.
Jury trial prohibited, 4840.
Limitations,
    Jurisdiction, 4836.
    Power and authority, 4837.
New Orleans city courts,
    Absence or illness of judge, 4842.
    Cases involving less than $25, 4921.
    Cases involving more than $100, 5001, 5002.
        New trial, 5002.
    Cases involving $25 to $100, 4922.
    Jurisdiction, 4835.
New trial not permitted, 4897.
Notice of judgment, 4898.
Open account, proof, 4896.
Pleadings, cases involving $100 or less, 4892, 4921, 4922.
Record of case, 4893.
Record on appeal, 4901.
Recusation of judge, 4844–4846.
Rules of court, 4847.
Security on appeal, 4900.
Venue, 4839.

CLAIMS
Concursus proceedings, 4651–4662.
Succession representative, enforcement, 3211.
Successions, enforcement of claims against, 3241–3249.

CLASS ACTIONS
    Generally, 591–597.
Compromise, 594.
Dismissal, 594.
Expenses, 595.
Judgments, 597.
Security, costs, 595.
Shareholders, 593.
Venue, 593.

CLERKS OF COURT
    See, also, District Court Clerks.
    Generally, 251–288.
Administrator of vacant successions, 3121.
Citation, signature, 1202.
District courts, 281–288.
Judicial bonds payable to clerk of trial court, 5121.

CODE
Rules of construction, 5051–5059.

COMMENCEMENT
Civil action, 421.

COMMON LAW
Judicial notice, 1391.

COMMUNITY PROPERTY
Enforcement,
    Community right, 686, 695.
    Obligation of community, 735.
Executory proceeding against surviving spouse in community, 2671.
Judgment on pleadings not permitted, 969.
Partition, venue, 82.
Summary judgment not permitted, 969.
Venue, partition, 82.

COMPENSATION
Attorney,
    Absent heirs and legatees, 3174.
    Appointed by court, 5096.
Curator, 4274, 4554.
Executors and administrators, 3351.
    Succession not administered, 3033.
Now pleaded through reconvention, 1062.
Succession representative, 3033, 3351–3353.
Tutor, 4274.

COMPETENCY
Competent court, defined, 5251(4).

INDEX—CODE OF CIVIL PROCEDURE
References are to Articles

COMPROMISE
Action against joint or solidary obligors, venue, 73.
Affirmative defense in pleading, 1005.
Class action, 594.
Forma pauperis case, payment of costs, 5187.
Indigent party action, 5187.
Succession representative, power, 3198.
Tutorship, compromise of obligations, 4265.

CONCURSUS PROCEEDING
Answer, delay, 4655, 4657.
Bills of lading, applicability, 4661.
Burden of proof, immovables, 3654.
Claimants who may be impleaded, 4652.
Claims, 4651–4662.
Costs, 4659.
Definition of concursus, 4651.
Delay for answering, 4655, 4657.
Deposit of money into registry of court, 4652, 4658.
Each defendant both plaintiff and defendant, 4656.
Failure of defendant to answer timely, 4657.
Injunctive relief, 4660.
Jury trial, limitation, 1733.
No default required, 4656.
No responsive pleadings to answer, 4656.
Petition, 4654.
Private work lien act, applicability, 4661.
Process, service, 4655.
Public work lien act, applicability, 4661.
Rules of ordinary procedure applicable, 4662.
Service of process, 4655.
Venue, 4653.
Warehouse receipts, applicability, 4661.

CONDITION OF MIND
Pleading, 856.

CONDITIONS
Pleading, suspensive conditions, 857.

CONFERENCES
Pre-trial conference, 1551.

CONFESSION OF JUDGMENT
Act importing, 2632.
Limitations on appeals, 2085.

CONSENT
Appeals, parties, dismissal, 2162.
Judicial emancipation, parent or tutor, 3992.

CONSERVATORY WRITS
Arrest abolished, 3501–3613.
Attachment, 3501–3545.
Injunction, 3601–3613.
Provisional seizure now merged with sequestration, 3572, 3575.
Sequestration, 3501–3514, 3571–3576.

CONSIDERATION
Affirmative defense, failure of consideration, pleading, 1005.

CONSOLIDATION
Cases for trial, 1561.

CONSTRUCTION
Declaratory relief, 1881, 1883.
Pleadings, 865.
Rules for construing code provisions, 5051–5059.

CONSTRUCTIVE CONTEMPT
Defined, 224.
Imprisonment until performance, 226.
Procedure for punishing, 225.

CONSUL OR CONSULAR AGENT
Official records, certification, 1395.

CONTEMPT
City courts, 4838.
Clerks of court, 257.
Collection of fines by sheriff, 330.
Constructive contempt,
    Acts constituting, 224.
    Imprisonment until performance, 226.
    Procedure for punishing, 225.
Courts, power to punish, 221–227.
Defined, 221.
Direct contempt,
    Acts constituting, 222.
    Procedure for punishing, 223.
Discovery,
    Failure to comply with orders, 1513.
    Refusal to make, 1512.
Disobedience, habeas corpus, mandamus, quo warranto, 3785.
District court, 221–227.
    Experts, punishment, 375.
    Legal representative, punishment, 375.
Examination of judgment debtor, 2456.
Expert, punishment for nonperformance, 375.
Habeas corpus, disobedience of writ, 3785.
Imprisonment by sheriff of contumacious persons, 330.
Judgment ordering delivery of possession, concealment or removal, 2502.

INDEX—CODE OF CIVIL PROCEDURE
References are to Articles

CONTEMPT—Cont'd
Justices of the peace, power to punish for, 4838.
Legal representatives, nonperformance of duties, 375.
Mandamus, disobedience of writ, 3785.
Preliminary injunction, disobedience, 3611.
Punishment, 227.
Quo warranto, disobedience of writ, 3785.
Sheriffs, 334.
Subpoena, failure to comply, 1357.
Summary judgment proceeding, delay, 967.
Temporary restraining order, disobedience, 3611.

CONTINUANCE
Generally, 1601–1605.
Discretionary grounds, 1601.
Motion, 1603, 1605.
Order, 1605.
Peremptory grounds, 1602.
Prevention by admission of adverse party, 1604.
Summary trial of motion, 1605.
Trial of motion, 1605.

CONTRACTS
Declaratory judgments, 1872.
    Construction, 1873.
Succession representative,
    Contracts with succession prohibited, 3194, 3195.
    Executory contracts, performance, 3227.
Tutorship, contracts between minor and tutor prohibited, 4263.

CONTRADICTORY MOTION
Defined, 963.
Rule to show cause, 963.
Summary proceedings, 2592–2594.

CONTRADICTORY PROBATE
Testaments, 2901–2903.

CONTRIBUTORY NEGLIGENCE
Affirmative defense in pleading, 1005.

CONTROVERSY
Partition between co-owners, notary effecting, 4608.

CONVERSION
Executory proceeding to ordinary proceeding, 2644.

CONVEYANCE
Declaratory judgments, 1872.

CO-OWNERS
Partition, 4601–4642.

COPIES
Depositions on oral examination, 1456.
Discovery, production of documents for, 1492.

CORPORATIONS
Agents or officers, personal service, citation or process, 1261.
Defined, 5251(5).
Discovery, 1491.
Foreign,
    Defined, 5251(6).
    Proper defendant, 739.
    Proper plaintiff, 691.
    Receivership, ancillary receiver,
        Proper defendant, 740.
        Proper plaintiff, 692.
    Service, citation or process, 1261.
Liquidation,
    Proper defendant, 740.
    Proper plaintiff, 692.
Mandamus against corporation or officer, 3864.
Official records, certified copy, proof by, 1393–1395.
Proper defendant, 739.
Proper plaintiff, 690.
Receivership,
    Receiver proper defendant, 740.
    Receiver proper plaintiff, 692.
Secretary of state, service of citation or process upon, 1262.
Service, citation or process, 1261.
Shares and shareholders,
    Class actions, 593.
    Mandamus to compel recognition, 3864.
    Sale of succession property, 3285.
    Secondary actions,
        Petition, 596, 611.
        Venue, 593.
    Tutors, sale of minor's stock, 4342.
    Venue of class action, 593.
Shareholder's derivative action, 593, 596, 611.
Venue in suit against, general rule, 42(2).

COSTS
Appeals, 2126, 2164.
Appellate court may tax in discretion, 2164.
Concursus proceeding, 4659.
Depositions upon oral examination, 1454.
Discovery, refusal to make, 1511.
Examination of judgment debtor, 2455.

INDEX—CODE OF CIVIL PROCEDURE
References are to Articles

COSTS—Cont'd
Forma pauperis case,
    Account and payment, 5186.
    Payment, when case compromised or dismissed, 5187.
    Unsuccessful party condemned, 5188.
    Waiver, 5181–5188.
Interdiction, 4551.
Motion for security for, no general appearance, 7(3).
Parties liable, 1454, 1457, 1511, 1514, 1920, 2164.
Procedure for taxing, 1920.
Small successions, court costs, 3422.
Small tutorship, court costs, 4464.
Succession proceedings, court costs, 2825.
Tutorship, accounting, 4398.
Voluntary dismissal, 1671.
Waiver for indigent party, 5181–5188.

COUNSEL OF RECORD
Entry or removal of name of attorney no general appearance, 7(1).

COURT CRIER
Generally, 333.

COURT OFFICERS
    Generally, 251–375.
Attorneys, 371.
Clerks, 251–288.
Court reporters, 372.
Experts, 373
Legal representatives, 374.
Minute clerk, 256.
Sheriffs, 321–334.

COURT REPORTER
Generally, 372.

COURT RULES
Assignment of cases, 1571.
District Court, adoption and publication of local rules, 193.

COURTS
    See, also,
        City Courts.
        Courts of Appeal.
        District Courts.
        Justice of the Peace Courts.
        Supreme Court.
Clerk's failure to perform duties, 257.
Competent court, defined, 5251(4).
Contempt, power to punish, 221–227.
Declaratory judgment, refusal, 1876.
Deputy clerks, 255.
Docket books, 254.
Inherent judicial power, 191.
Minute books, 254.
Minute clerks, 256.

COURTS—Cont'd
Officers, 251–375.
    Attorneys, 371.
    Clerks, 251–288.
    Court reporters, 372.
    Experts, 373.
    Legal representatives, 374.
    Minute clerk, 256.
    Sheriffs, 321–334.
Power to punish for contempt, 221–227.
Recusation of judge, 151–161.
Reporter, court reporter, 372.

COURTS OF APPEAL
Appellate procedure, 2081–2167.
Clerks, power, generally, 251–257.
Inherent judicial power, 191.
Recusation of judge, 151, 160.
Substitution of parties in pending action, 821.
Supervisory jurisdiction, 2201.

CREDITORS
See Debtors and Creditors.

CROPS
Sale, succession property, 3264.
Tutors, minor's property, sale, 4303.

CROSS EXAMINATION
Adverse party or representative, 1634.
Depositions, pending action, 1436.

CUMULATION OF ACTIONS
    Generally, 461–465.
Defined, 461.
Improper,
    Effect, 464.
    Pleading, 926.
Joinder of parties, permissive, 463–465, 647.
Objective, 462.
Permissive joinder governed by rules of, 647.
Petitory and possessory actions prohibited, 3657.
Plural plaintiffs or defendants, 463.
Separate trial of cumulated actions, 464, 465.
Single plaintiff against single defendant, 462.
Subjective, 463.

CURATOR AD HOC
Attorney appointed to represent unrepresented absentee or mental incompetent, 5091–5098.

CURATORSHIP OF INTERDICTS
Accounting by curator, 4391–4398, 4554.
Ancillary curatorship proceeding, 4431–4433, 4554.

782

INDEX—CODE OF CIVIL PROCEDURE
References are to Articles

CURATORSHIP OF INTERDICTS—Cont'd
Appointment of curator, 4549, 4550.
    Legal or dative curator, 4067, 4554.
Custody of interdict, 4555.
Disqualification of curator or undercurator, 4231–4238, 4554.
Duties of curator, 4261–4275, 4554.
Expenses, care of interdict and dependents, 4556.
Functions of curator, 4261–4275, 4554.
Inventory, 4101, 4102, 4454.
Judgment, curator must file in conveyance office, 4552.
Jurisdiction, 10(4).
Jury trial, limitation, 1733.
Letters of curatorship, 4172, 4554.
Oath of curator, 4171, 4554.
Powers of curator, 4261–4275, 4554.
Proper defendant, 733.
Proper plaintiff, 684.
Provisional curator, 4549.
Removal of curator or undercurator, 4231–4238, 4554.
Resignation of curator or undercurator, 4231–4238, 4554.
Revocation of appointment of curator or undercurator, 4231–4238, 4554.
Sale of interdict's property, 4301–4342, 4554.
Security of curator, 4131–4136, 4554.
Small curatorships, 4461–4464, 4554.
Termination of interdiction, 4557.
Undercurator, 4553.
Venue, may not be waived, 44, 4032, 4033, 4541, 4554.

CUSTODY
Appeals, child custody judgment, 3943.
Defined, habeas corpus, 3821.
Interdict, 4555.

DAMAGES
Attachment, dissolution, 3506.
Injunction, disobedience, 3611.
Judgment ordering delivery of possession, concealment or removal, 2502.
Petitory action, 3662.
Pleading special damage, 861.
Possessory action, 3662.
Preliminary injunction, wrongful issuance, 3608.
Sequestration, dissolution, 3506.
Temporary restraining order, wrongful issuance, 3608.

DEATH
Abatement of actions, 428.
Evidence in probate procedure, 2821–2824.

DEATH—Cont'd
Parties, 428.
    Compulsory substitution, 802.
    Voluntary substitution, 801.
Tutor, accounting, 4397.
Witnesses, deposition, use, 1428.

DEATH ACTIONS
Claimants may not be impleaded in concursus proceeding, 4652.

DEBTORS AND CREDITORS
Acts with intent to defraud creditors, grounds for attachment, 3541.
Compelling executor to furnish security, 3155.
Declaratory judgments, 1874.
Discussion, 5151–5156.
Joint debtors,
    Necessary parties, 643.
    Venue in action against, **73**.
Judgment creditor,
    Bid at judicial sales, fieri facias, 2339.
    Superior privilege, judicial sales, fieri facias, 2338.
Judgment debtor,
    Bid at judicial sales, fieri facias, 2339.
    Examination, 2451–2456.
    Seizure under fieri facias, notice, 2293.
Money judgment, execution, 2291–2456.
Successions, acceptance without administration, demand of security, 3007, 3008, 3034.
Venue, action against solidary debtors, 73.

DEBTS
Succession, payment, 3301–3308.

DECEDENT'S ESTATE
Declaratory judgments, 1874.

DECLARATORY JUDGMENTS
    Generally, 1871–1883.
Appeals, 1877.
Burden of proof, immovables, 3654.

DECLINATORY EXCEPTIONS
See Exceptions.

DEEDS
Declaratory judgments, 1872.

DEFAULT JUDGMENT
    Generally, 1701–1703, 1843.
Concursus proceeding, none required, 4656.
Confirmation, 1702.

INDEX—CODE OF CIVIL PROCEDURE
References are to Articles

DEFAULT JUDGMENT—Cont'd
Defined, 1843.
Discovery,
   Failure to attend or serve answers, 1515.
   Failure to comply with orders, 1513.
Notice of signing, 1913.
Preliminary, 1701.
Scope, 1703.

DEFENDANTS
See Parties.

DEFENSES
Affirmative defenses, answer, 1005.
Alternative defenses, answer, 1006.
Attorney appointed by court, duty to defend action, 5095.
Cause of action, use, 424.
Demand against third party, available to third party defendant, 1115.
Executory proceedings, assertion, 2642.
Motion to strike, 964.
Real rights under contracts to reduce minerals to possession, 3664.
Supplemental pleadings, 1155.
Third party defendant, pleading, 1111.
Unconditional obligation to pay specific sum of money, jury trial, 1733.

DEFICIENCY JUDGMENT
Generally, 2771, 2772.

DEFINITIONS
See Words and Phrases.

DEFINITIVE JUDGMENT
Generally, 1842.

DELAY
Appealing,
   Annulment of marriage judgment, 3942.
   City courts, justice of the peace courts, 4899, 4921, 4922, 4942.
   Devolutive appeal, 2087.
   Divorce judgment, 3942.
   Separation from bed and board judgment, 3942.
   Suspensive appeal, 2123.
Applying for new trial,
   City courts, "clerk's book" cases, 4972, 5002.
   District courts, generally, 1974.
Extension of time to plead no general appearance, 7(2).
Filing answer,
   Appeal, 2133.
   City court, 4895, 5002.
   Concursus proceeding, 4655, 4657.

DELAY—Cont'd
Filing answer—Cont'd
   District court, 1001, 1002.
      Less than $100, 4895, 4971.
   Incidental demand, 1033.
   Justice of the peace court, 4895, 4941.
Filing incidental demands, 1033.
Filing exceptions,
   City courts, justice courts, "clerk's book" cases, 4892, 4895, 4921, 4941, 4971.
   District courts, generally, 928.
Further action after interlocutory judgment, 1914.
Garnishment interrogatories, answer.
   City courts, justice courts, "clerk's book" cases, 4892, 4895, 4921, 4922, 4941, 4971.
   District court, generally, 2412, 2413.

DELIVERY
Garnishment, money or property to sheriff, 2415.
Legacy or inheritance, payment of inheritance taxes, necessity, 2951.
Service by delivery, 1313, 1314.

DEMAND
Executory proceedings, demand for payment, 2639.
   Service, 2640.
Jury trial, 1732.

DEMAND AGAINST THIRD PARTIES
Generally, 1031–1040, 1111–1116.
Action instituted separately, 1037.
Amended and supplemental pleadings, 1156.
Answer, 1035.
Citation, 1114.
Defendant may bring in third party, 1111.
   Reconvention, 1112.
Defenses of defendant available to third party defendant, 1115.
Delay for filing, 1033.
Dismissal of principal action, effect, 1039.
Exceptions and motions, 1034.
Failure to bring in third party, effect, 1113.
Form of petition, 1032.
Jurisdiction, 1036.
Mode of procedure, 1036.
Motions, 1034.
Pleadings, service, 1114.
Separate judgments, 1038.
Separate trial, 1038.
Service of process, 1114.

INDEX—CODE OF CIVIL PROCEDURE
References are to Articles

DEMAND AGAINST THIRD PARTIES
—Cont'd
Supplemental pleadings, 1156.
Third party defendant may bring in third person, 1116.
Venue, 1034.

DENIALS
Answer, 1003, 1004.

DEPOSIT
Registry of court,
    Concursus proceeding, 4652, 4658.
    Maximum inheritance tax claimed, 2951.
    Partition, absentee co-owner's share, 4628.
Succession funds, 3222.

DEPOSITIONS
    See, also, Witnesses.
Adjournment of examination, refusal to answer questions, 1511.
Adverse party, use, 1428.
After suit filed, 1436.
After trial, 1437.
Before suit filed,
    Generally, 1432–1435.
    Notice and service of petition, 1433.
    Order and examination, 1434.
    Petition, 1432.
    Use of deposition, 1435.
Cross-examination of deponents, pending action, 1436.
Effect of taking or using, 1430.
Examination,
    Deponents, pending action, 1436.
    Judgment debtor, 2451.
    Perpetuation of testimony, 1434.
Nonresidents, place of taking, 1422.
Notice,
    Application to compel answer to interrogatories, 1511.
    Objections to irregularities, 1424.
    Oral examination, 1451 et seq.
    Perpetuation of testimony, petition, 1433.
    Stipulations regarding taking, 1421.
    Waiver, objection to irregularities, 1424.
    Written interrogatories, 1471 et seq.
Objections,
    Admissibility, 1429.
    Competency, relevancy, 1426.
    Completion and return, 1427.
    Disqualification of officer, 1425.
    Form of taking, 1426.
    Irregularities in notice, 1424.
    Manner of taking, 1426.
    Waiver, 1424–1427.

DEPOSITIONS—Cont'd
Oral examination,
    Generally, 1451–1457.
    Certification and filing of deposition, 1456.
    Changes in deposition, 1455.
    Copies of deposition, 1456.
    Costs, 1454.
    Expenses imposed on negligent party, 1457.
    Failure to attend taking, 1457.
    Failure to serve subpoena, 1457.
    Motion to terminate or limit examination, 1454.
    Notice,
        Examination, 1451.
        Filing deposition, 1456.
    Oath, 1453.
    Objections, 1453.
    Orders for protection of parties and deponent, 1452.
    Place of taking, 1451.
    Record of examination, 1453.
    Refusal to answer questions, 1511.
    Scope, limiting, 1454.
    Signing by deponent, 1455.
    Submission of deposition to deponent, 1455.
    Time of taking, 1451.
Orders,
    Compelling answer to interrogatories, 1511.
    Failure to comply with order, 1513.
    Perpetuation of testimony, 1434.
    Protection of parties and witnesses, 1452, 1473.
    Taking, signing in chambers, 194.
Out of state, 1431.
Party who may use, 1428, 1430.
Pending action, 1436.
Perpetuation of testimony,
    Generally, 1432–1435.
    Notice and service of petition, 1433.
    Order and examination, 1434.
    Petition, 1432, 1433.
    Use of deposition, 1435.
Person before whom taken, 1423.
Place of taking, 1422.
Probate of testament, 2889.
    Admissibility in subsequent action, 2892.
Production of evidence, 1421–1515.
Rebuttal of evidence, 1430.
Scope of examination, 1436.
Stipulations regarding taking, 1421.
Subpoena and subpoena duces tecum, 1356.

INDEX—CODE OF CIVIL PROCEDURE
References are to Articles

DEPOSITIONS—Cont'd
Summary judgment, supplementing affidavit supporting or opposing motion, 967.
Use, 1428, 1430.
Waiver of objections,
    Competency, relevancy, 1426.
    Completion and return, 1427.
    Disqualification of officer, 1425.
    Irregularities in notice, 1424.
Written interrogatories,
    Generally, 1471–1473.
    Notice, 1471.
        Filing of depositions, 1472.
    Orders for protection of parties and deponent, 1473.
    Preparation of record, 1472.
    Refusal to answer, 1511.
    Service of interrogatories, 1471.
    Taking of testimony, 1472.

DESCRIPTIVE LIST
Succession property, in lieu of inventory, 2952, 3136, 3137.

DEVISEES
Declaratory judgments, 1874.

DEVOLUTIVE APPEAL
Delay for taking, 2087.
None in executory proceeding, 2642.
Possessory action, 3662.
Security, 2124.

DILATORY EXCEPTIONS
See Exceptions

DIRECT CONTEMPT
Defined, 222.
Procedure for punishing, 223.

DISCHARGE
Succession representative, 3391–3395.

DISCOVERY
    See, also,
        Depositions.
        Witnesses.
Accounts, production for inspection, 1492.
Admission of facts, 1496.
Admission of genuineness of documents, 1496.
Associations, 1491.
Books and papers, production for inspection, 1492.
Contempt,
    Failure to comply with orders, 1513.
    Refusal to make, 1512.
Corporations, party served, 1491.
Costs, refusal to make, 1511.

DISCOVERY—Cont'd
Default judgment, failure to comply with orders, 1513.
Depositions,
    After trial, 1437.
    Before suit filed, 1432–1435.
    Effect of taking or using, 1430.
    Objections,
        Admissibility, 1429.
        Competency, relevancy, 1426.
        Completion and return, 1427.
        Disqualification of officer, 1425.
        Irregularities in notice, 1424.
        Waiver, 1424–1427.
    Oral examination, 1451–1457.
    Out of state, 1431.
    Party who may use, 1428, 1430.
    Perpetuation of testimony, 1432–1435.
    Person before whom taken, 1423.
    Place of taking, 1422.
    Stipulations regarding taking, 1421.
    Use, 1428, 1430.
    Waiver of objections,
        Competency, relevancy, 1426.
        Completion and return, 1427.
        Disqualification of officer, 1425.
        Irregularities in notice, 1424.
    Written interrogatories, 1471–1473.
Dismissal, refusal to make, 1513, 1515.
Documents,
    Admission of genuineness, 1496.
    Production for inspection, copying, 1492.
Facts, admission, 1496.
Interrogatories, 1491.
    Adverse party, 1491.
    Refusal to make, 1511.
Letters, production for inspection, 1492.
Mental examination of parties, 1493 et seq.
Notice,
    Application to compel answer to interrogatories, 1511.
    Mental examination of parties, 1493, 1494.
    Objections to irregularities, 1424.
    Oral examination, 1451 et seq.
    Perpetuation of testimony, petition, 1433.
    Physical examination of parties, 1493, 1494.
    Stipulations regarding taking, 1421.
    Waiver, objection to irregularities, 1424.
    Written interrogatories, 1471 et seq.
Oral examination, refusal to answer, 1511.

INDEX—CODE OF CIVIL PROCEDURE
References are to Articles

DISCOVERY—Cont'd
Orders,
    Compelling answer to interrogatories, 1511.
    Failure to comply with order, 1513.
    Perpetuation of testimony, 1434.
    Protection of parties and witnesses, 1452, 1473.
    Taking, 194.
Partnership, 1491.
Physical examination of party, 1493–1495.
Production of evidence, 1421–1515.
Refusal to make discovery,
    Admission of facts, 1514.
    Admission of genuineness of documents, 1514.
    Contempt, 1512.
    Dismissal, 1513, 1515.
    Failure to attend taking of deposition, 1515.
    Failure to comply with order, 1513.
    Interrogatories, 1511.
        Adverse party, 1515.
Summary judgment, motion for, continuance to permit, 967.
Surveys, orders to permit, 1492.
Things, production for inspection and photographing, 1492.
Written interrogatories, refusal to answer, 1511.

DISCUSSION
Defined, 5151.
Effect, 5156.
Pleading, 5155.
    In exception, 926.
Surety, 5152.
Third possessor, 5154.
Transferee in revocatory action, 5153.

DISMISSAL
    Generally, 1671–1673, 1844.
Absolute dismissal, 1673, 1844.
Action against joint or solidary obligors, venue, 73.
Appeals, 2161, 2162, 2165.
Class action, 594.
Court without jurisdiction, no general appearance, 7(5).
Cumulation of actions, failure to amend, 464.
Declinatory exception, effect of sustaining, 932.
Demand against third party, dismissal of principal action, 1039.
Dilatory exception, effect of sustaining, 933.
Discovery, refusal to make, 1513, 1515.

DISMISSAL—Cont'd
Forma pauperis case, payment of costs, 5187.
Incidental action, 1039.
Intervention, dismissal of principal action, 1039.
Involuntary, 1672, 1844.
Judgment, 1844.
Mental examination of party, 1493–1495.
Miscellaneous discovery devices, 1491–1496.
Nonsuit, 1673, 1844.
Peremptory exception, 923.
    Effect of sustaining, 934.
Prematurity, 423.
Reconvention, dismissal of principal action, 1039.
Voluntary, 1671, 1844.
With prejudice, 1673, 1844.
Without prejudice, 1673, 1844.

DISSOLUTION
Attachment on motion, 3506.
Preliminary injunction, 3607.
    Hearing, 3609.
Sequestration on motion, 3506.
Temporary restraining order, 3607.

DISTRICT COURT CLERKS
    See, also, District Courts.
Chief deputy, powers, Orleans Parish excepted, 255, 286.
Book cases, 4971, 4972.
Deputy clerks, 255, 256, 286.
Enumeration of acts which may be done by, 282.
Functions which may be exercised on holiday, 288.
General powers, 251–257, 281–288.
Judicial powers, Orleans Parish excepted, 281–287.
Minute clerks, 256.
Notaries public ex officio, 287.
Orders and judgments, Orleans Parish excepted, 281, 283, 285.
Orleans Parish, 251–257, 281, 287, 288.
Powers and authority, Orleans Parish excepted, 281–287.
Punishment for contempt, 257.
Subpoena duces tecum for taking of depositions, 1356.
Subpoenas for attendance of witnesses, 1351.

DISTRICT COURTS
Application of law, 4831.
Assignment of cases under local rules, 1571.
Attorneys officers of court, 371.

INDEX—CODE OF CIVIL PROCEDURE
References are to Articles

DISTRICT COURTS—Cont'd
Chambers,
    Extraordinary remedies, hearing, 3784.
    Judicial proceedings, 195.
    Orders and judgments which may be signed, 194.
        Vacation, during vacation, 196.
    Summary proceedings, trial, 2595.
Citation, 1201–1203.
Clerks,
        See, also, District Court Clerks.
    Chief deputy's powers, Orleans Parish excepted, 286.
    "Clerk's book" cases, 4971, 4972.
    Deputy clerks, 255, 256, 286.
    Enumeration, acts which may be done by, 282.
    Functions to be exercised on holiday, 288.
    General powers, 251–257, 281–288.
    Judicial acts, Orleans Parish excepted, 281–287.
    Minute clerks, 256.
    Notaries public ex officio, 287.
    Orders and judgments, Orleans Parish excepted, 281, 283, 285.
    Orleans Parish, 251–257, 281, 287, 288.
    Powers and authority, Orleans Parish excepted, 281–287.
    Punishment for contempt, 257.
    Subpoenas,
        Attendance of witnesses, 1351.
        Taking of depositions, 1356.
Concurrent jurisdiction with justice of the peace courts, 4971, 4972.
Contempt,
        Generally, 221–227.
    Experts, punishment, 375.
    Legal representatives, punishment, 375.
Court reporters, 372.
Crier, 333.
Docket books, 254.
Experts,
    Appointment, 373.
    Power to appoint, 192.
Judgments, rendition and signing, 1911–1921.
Judicial emancipation, petition, filing, 3991.
Legal representative, officers of appointing court, 374.
Minute books, 254.
Minute clerks, duties, 256.
Pending action, substitution of parties, 821.

DISTRICT COURTS—Cont'd
Powers and authority, generally, 191–196.
Pre-trial conference, 1551.
Reasons for judgment, 1917.
Recusation of judge, 151–158.
Rules,
    Power to adopt local, 193.
    Publication of local, 193.
Service of citation or other process, 1231–1314.
Sheriffs,
        Generally, 321–324.
    Administration of property seized, 328.
    Collection of contempt fines, 330.
    Constable's service or execution, 332.
    Deputies and other employees, 331.
    Functions generally only in own parish, 322.
    Imprisonment of contumacious persons, 330.
    Nonperformance of duties, contempt, 334.
    Protection and preservation of property seized, 326, 329.
    Returns on process served and writs executed, 324.
    Right of entry for execution, 325.
    Seizure of rents, fruits, and revenues, 327.
    Service of process, generally, 321, 322, 324.
    Writs executed on holiday, 323.
Substitution of parties, 801–807, 821.
Vacation, power to act during, 196.

DISTRICT JUDGES
Chambers,
    Extraordinary remedies, hearing, 3784.
    Judicial proceedings, 195.
    Signing orders and judgments, 194.
        Vacation, during vacation, 196.
    Summary proceedings, trial, 2595.
Powers and authority generally, 191–196.
Recusation, 151–158.
Subpoena,
    Attendance of witnesses, 1351.
    Subpoena duces tecum for taking of depositions, 1356.
Vacation, power to act during, 196.

DISTRINGAS
Execution and revocation, 2503.
Issuance of writ, 2502.

DISTURBANCE IN FACT
Defined, 3659.
Possessory action, requisite, 3658.

INDEX—CODE OF CIVIL PROCEDURE
References are to Articles

DISTURBANCE IN LAW
Defined, 3659.
Possessory action, requisite, 3658.

DIVISION
Pleaded as affirmative defense, 1005.

DIVORCE
Alimony,
    Appeal, 3943.
    Judgment, 3943, 3945.
Appeal, judgment, 3942.
    Alimony, 3943.
    Awarding custody, 3943.
Executing alimony judgment in arrears, 3945.
Injunctive relief, 3944.
Judgment on pleadings not permitted, 969.
Jurisdiction of proceeding, 10(7).
Jury trial, limitation, 1733.
Summary judgment not permitted, 969.
Venue, may not be waived, 44, 3941.

DOCUMENTS
Admissions, pre-trial conference, 1551.
Discovery,
    Admission of genuineness, 1496.
    Production for inspection, copying, 1492.
Judgment debtor, examination, 2451.
    Contempt, refusal to appear, 2456.
    Motion for order, service, 2453.
Pleading, official documents, 858.
Probate of testaments, submitted with petition, 2852.
Subpoena duces tecum to produce, 1354.

DOMESTIC CORPORATIONS
    See, also, Corporations.
Citation or process, service on agents or officers, 1261.
Defined, 5251(5).
Discovery, 1491.
Liquidation,
    Proper defendant, 740.
    Proper plaintiff, 692.
Mandamus against corporation or officer, 3864.
Official records, proof, 1393–1395.
Proper defendant, 739.
Proper plaintiff, 690.
Receivership,
    Receiver proper defendant, 740.
    Receiver proper plaintiff, 692.
Secretary of state, service of citation or process upon, 1262.
Service, citation or process, 1261.
Shareholders, derivative action, 593, 596, 611.

DOMESTIC CORPORATIONS—Cont'd
Venue in suits against, general rule, 42 (4, 5).

DOMESTIC INSURER
Casualty insurer, claimants may be impleaded, 4652.
Defined, 5251(8).
Proper defendant, 739.
Proper plaintiff, 690.
Receiver,
    Proper defendant, 741.
    Proper plaintiff, 693.
Policy, defined, 5251(7).
Venue in suit against, general rule, 42(2).

DOMICILE
Venue, 42, 73.

DOMICILIARY SERVICE
Citation or process, 1231, 1234.

DURESS
Pleaded as affirmative defense, 1005.

EMANCIPATION
Judicial emancipation, 3991–3994.
    Jury trial, limitation, 1733.
    Jurisdiction, 10(2).
    Petition, 3991.
    Venue, may not be waived, 44, 3991.
Minor,
    Party defendant, 731.
    Party plaintiff, 682.

ENTRY
Name of attorney as counsel of record, no general appearance, 7(1).

ERROR OR MISTAKE
Assignment of errors on appeal, necessity, 2129.
Pleading, 856.
    Affirmative defense, 1005.

ESTOPPEL
Pleaded as affirmative defense, 1005.

EVICTION OF TENANTS AND OCCUPANTS
Appeal and appeal bond, 4735.
Definition of terms, 4704.
Judgment of eviction, 4732.
Judicial sales, eviction of purchaser subsequently, 2379, 2380.
Lessor's rights or real actions not affected, 4705.
Notice to vacate,
    Delivery or service, 4703.
    Occupants, 4702.
    Tenants, 4701.
Rule for possession, 4731.

INDEX—CODE OF CIVIL PROCEDURE
References are to Articles

EVICTION OF TENANTS AND OCCUPANTS—Cont'd
Termination of lease, 4701.
Trial of rule for possession, 4732.
Warrant for possession, 4733, 4734.

EVIDENCE
Admissibility,
    Common law and statutes of other states, 1391.
    Depositions,
        Objection, 1429.
        Use, 1428.
    Order prohibiting on failure to comply with discovery orders, 1513.
    Possessory action, limited, title, 3661.
Amendments, conformity, 1154.
Authentic evidence, executory proceedings, 2635–2637.
Burden of proof,
    Annulment of probated testaments, 2932, 2933.
    Concursus, immovables, 3654.
    Declaratory judgments, immovables, 3654.
    Expropriations, immovables, 3654.
    Petitory action, plaintiff, 3653.
    Possessory action, 3658.
    Probate of testaments, proponent, 2903.
Certified copies of official records, 1394.
City courts, proof of open account, 4896.
Confirmation of default judgment, 1702.
Death, probate procedure, 2821–2824.
Declinatory exception, trial, 930.
Dilatory exception, trial, 930.
Inadmissible, introduction into record, 1636.
Inheritance taxes due, successions, 2953.
Injunction hearings, proof, 3609.
Jury trial,
    Charge to jury, no comment on evidence, 1792.
    Taking into jury room, 1794.
Official records, 1391–1397.
Order of trial, presentation, 1632.
Orders for production of documentary evidence, signing in chambers, 194.
Peremptory exception, trial, 931.
Perpetuation of testimony, 1432–1435.
Petitory action, proof of title, 3653.
Possessory action, limited admissibility of evidence of title, 3661.
Presumptions,
    Parties plaintiff, representative's authority presumed, 700.
    Pleading, capacity, 855.

EVIDENCE—Cont'd
Prima facie evidence, statutes of other states, 1392.
Probate, admissible in subsequent action, 2892.
Production of evidence,
    Depositions and discovery, 1421–1515.
        Miscellaneous discovery devices, 1491–1496.
        Oral examination, 1451–1457.
        Refusal to make discovery, 1511–1515.
        Written interrogatories, 1471–1473.
    Examination of judgment debtor, 2451–2456.
    Orders, signing in chambers, 194.
    Proof, official records, 1391–1397.
    Subpoenas, 1351–1357.
Proffer of evidence excluded, 1636.
Records, proof of official records, 1391–1397.
Statutes, other states, prima facie evidence, 1392.
Successions, affidavits, 2821–2823.
Summary judgment, affidavits supporting and opposing motion, 967.

EXAMINATION
See Depositions.

EXCEPTIONS
See, also, Objections.
Generally, 921–934.
Amendment, 1152.
Appellate court, 2163.
Bills of, unnecessary, 1635.
Declinatory exceptions,
    Amendment, 1152.
    Effect of sustaining, 932.
    Evidence on trial, 930.
    Form, 924.
    Objections raised, 925.
        Venue, waiver by failure to plead, 44.
    Pleading, no general appearance, 7.
    Time,
        Pleading, 928.
        Trial, 929.
Defined, 921.
Delay, filing,
    City courts, clerk's book cases, 4892, 4895, 4921, 4941, 4971.
    District courts, 928.
Delay for pleading, 928.
Demand against third party, 1034.
Dilatory exceptions,
    Amendment, 1152.

INDEX—CODE OF CIVIL PROCEDURE
References are to Articles

EXCEPTIONS—Cont'd
Dilatory exceptions—Cont'd
  Capacity, challenging, 855.
  Effect of sustaining, 933.
  Evidence, 930.
  Form, 924.
  Objections raised, 926.
  Time,
    Plead, 928.
    Trial, 929.
Incidental actions, 1034.
Intervention, 1034.
Overruling, time for answer, 1001.
Peremptory exception,
  Amendment, 1152.
  Effect of sustaining, 934.
  Evidence, 931.
  Filing in appellate court, 2163.
  Form, 924.
  Objections raised, 927.
  Time,
    Pleading, 928.
    Trial, 929.
Pleading, 852, 921–934.
Reconvention, 1034.
Service on plaintiff, 1312–1314.
Summary proceedings,
  Filing, 2593.
  Issue raised by, 2592.

EXECUTIONS
  Generally, 2251–2417.
Alias writ, 2297.
Attachment, necessity, 3510.
Certified copy, filing, 2251.
City court judgment, 4897.
Constable, when authorized by sheriff, 332.
Delay before proceeding, 2252.
Executory judgment, 2782.
Fieri facias,
  Generally, 2291–2299.
  Alias writs, 2297.
  Injunction to arrest, 2298.
  Judicial sales, 2331–2343.
  Life of writ, 2294.
  Money judgments, 2291–2299.
    Adjudication and effect, 2371–2381.
    Attachment, issuance in action for, 3542.
    Examination of judgment debtor, 2451–2456.
    Garnishment, 2411–2417.
      Judicial sale under, 2331–2343.
    Notice of seizure, 2293.
    Order in which property sold, 2295.
    Privilege of seizing creditor, 2292.

EXECUTIONS—Cont'd
Fieri facias—Cont'd
  Prohibiting payment of proceeds, 2299.
  Reduction of excessive seizure, 2296.
  Sale in globo, 2295.
  Sheriff's return after seizure, 2294.
  Successive seizures, 2292.
  Time for seizure, 2294.
Foreign judgments, 2541.
Life of writ, 2294.
Marshal, when authorized by sheriff, 332.
Money judgments, 2291–2417.
Other than money judgments, 2501–2504.
Sequestration, necessity, 3510.
Sheriff, 321, 332, 2254.
  Return, 2254.
Trial courts only, 2251.
Writ issued by clerk to sheriff, 2253.

EXECUTORS AND ADMINISTRATORS
  See, also,
    Probate Procedure.
    Successions.
Accounting, 3331–3338.
Advances, compensation, 3351.
Ancillary probate procedure, 3401–3405.
Claims against successions, enforcement, 3241–3249.
Compensation, 3351.
  Succession not administered, 3033.
Dative testamentary executor, appointment, 3083.
Declaratory judgments, 1874.
Discharge, succession representative, 3391–3395.
Disqualifications, 3097.
Form, petition for notice of application for appointment, 3092.
General functions, powers and duties, 3191–3198.
Inventory, succession property, 3131–3137.
Letters testamentary, order, 3082.
Mortgages, special mortgage in lieu of bond, 3157.
Oppositions, application for appointment of administrator, 3095.
Orders,
  Application for appointment as administrator, 3094.
  Confirmation, 3082.
Payment of debts and charges of successions, 3301–3308.
Petition,
  Confirmation, 3081.

INDEX—CODE OF CIVIL PROCEDURE
References are to Articles

EXECUTORS AND ADMINISTRATORS —Cont'd
Petition—Cont'd
  Notice of application for appointment, 3091–3193.
Preservation and management of succession property, 3221–3229.
Priority of appointment, 3098.
Provisional administrator, security, 3152.
Qualification,
  Administrator, 3091–3098, 3111–3122, 3151–3159.
  Administrator of vacant succession, 3121, 3122, 3151–3159.
  Executor, 3081–3083, 3151–3159.
  Letters, 3159.
  Oath, 3158.
  Provisional administrator, 3111–3113, 3151–3159.
  Security, 3151–3157.
Revocation of appointment or removal, 3181, 3182.
Sale of succession property,
  Private, 3261–3264, 3281–3285.
  Public, 3261–3264, 3271–3273.
Testamentary administrator, compensation, 3353.
Testamentary executor, security, 3153.

EXECUTORY PROCESS
See Executory Proceedings.

EXECUTORY PROCEEDINGS
  Generally, 2631–2754, 2781–2783.
Absence and absentees, proceedings against, 2672, 2674.
Act importing confession of judgment, 2632.
Appeal from order for seizure and sale, 2642.
Appraisal, seizure and sale, 2723.
Arrest of seizure and sale by third possessor, 2703.
Assumption of indebtedness by third person, rights, 2702.
Attorney,
  Appointed by court, service, 2641.
  Represent unrepresented defendant, 2641, 2674.
Authentic evidence, 2635–2637.
Citation unnecessary, 1201, 2640.
Community property, proceeding against surviving spouse in community, 2671.
Conflict between code provision, reconciliation, 2675.
Conventional mortgage, enforcement by, 3721, 3723.
Conversion to ordinary proceeding, 2644.
Defenses, assertion, 2642.

EXECUTORY PROCEEDINGS—Cont'd
Deficiency judgment, 2771, 2772.
Demand for payment, 2639.
Execution, writ of seizure and sale, 2721–2724.
Heirs, proceeding against, 2672, 2674.
Husband and wife, proceeding against surviving spouse, 2671.
Injunction to arrest,
  Generally, 2642, 2751–2754.
  Grounds, 2751.
  Procedure, 2752.
  Security, 2753, 2754.
  Seizure and sale, 2642.
Intervention,
  Third parties, 2643.
  Third possessor, summary proceeding, 2703.
Judgments of other Louisiana courts, making executory, 2781–2783.
Judicial sale, rules applicable, 2724.
Jury trial, limitation, 1733.
Legal representative, proceeding against, 2673.
Legatees, proceeding against, 2672, 2674.
Objections, assertion, 2642.
Order for issuance of writ, 2638.
Parties, 2671–2674.
Petition, 2634.
  Injunction to arrest, 2752.
Seizure and sale, writ,
  Advertisement of sale, 2722.
  Appraisal, when necessary, 2723.
  Notice of seizure mandatory, 2721.
  Order for issuance of writ, 2638.
  Rules of fieri facias sales applicable, 2724.
  Seizure by sheriff, 2721.
Service of demand for payment, 2640.
Service of process, 2640, 2641.
Succession, proceeding against, 2671–2675.
Surviving spouse, proceeding against, 2671.
Third person,
  Alienation to, disregarded, 2701.
  Intervention, 2643.
  Pact de non alienando unnecessary, 2701.
  Rights of one who has assumed mortgage, 2702.
  Rights of third possessor, 2703.
Three-day notice, 2639.
Use, 2631.
Venue, 2633.

EXHIBITS
Pleading, 853.
Service of copy unnecessary, 1311.

INDEX—CODE OF CIVIL PROCEDURE
References are to Articles

EXPENSES
Care of interdict and dependents, 4556.
Class actions, 595.
Judicial emancipation proceeding, 3994.
Subpoena, prepayment of witnesses, 1353.
Tutorship, care of person of minor, 4261.

EXPERTS
Appointment, 373.
Contempt, punishment, 375.
District Court,
    Appointment, 373.
    Power to appoint, 192.
Officers of appointing court, 373.
Pre-trial conference, limitation of number, 1551.
Trial court, power to appoint, 192.

EXPROPRIATION
Burden of proof, immovables, 3654.

EXTENSION OF TIME TO PLEAD
No general appearance, 7(2).

EXTRAORDINARY REMEDIES
Habeas corpus, 3781–3785, 3821–3831.
Mandamus, 3781–3785, 3861–3866.
Quo warranto, 3781–3785, 3901, 3902.

FACTS
Admission, through discovery, 1496.

FAILURE OF CONSIDERATION
Pleaded as affirmative defense, 1005.

FATHER
Administrator of estate of minor child, 4501, 4502.

FEES
See Attorneys.

FELLOW SERVANT
Injury by, pleaded as affirmative defense, 1005.

FIDUCIARIES
Declaratory judgments, 1874.
Succession representative, 3191.

FIERI FACIAS
See,
    Executions.
    Judicial Sales.

FINAL JUDGMENT
    Generally, 1841–1842.
Appeals, 2167.
Form, 1918.
Rendition, 1911, 1912.

FINES AND PUNISHMENT
See, also, Contempt.
Habeas corpus, disobedience, 3785.
Injunction, disobedience, 3611.
Mandamus, disobedience, 3785.
Successions, failure to file account, 3334.

FOREIGN CORPORATION
Defined, 5251(6).
Proper defendant, 739.
Proper party plaintiff, 691.
Receivership, ancillary receiver,
    Proper defendant, 740.
    Proper plaintiff, 692.
Service, citation or process, 1261.
Venue in suits against, general rule, 42(4, 5).

FOREIGN COUNTRIES
Judgments, execution, 2541.
Official records, proof, 1393.
    Certified copies, 1395.
Probate of testament, 2888.

FOREIGN GUARDIAN
Mental incompetent, may act here, 4431, 4554.
Minor, may act here, 4431.

FOREIGN INSURERS
Party defendant, 739, 741.
Party plaintiff, 691.
Receivership,
    Ancillary receiver, generally, proper plaintiff, 693.
    Receiver proper defendant, 741.
Venue in suit against, general rule, 42(7).

FOREIGN JUDGMENT
Enforcement in Louisiana, 2541.

FOREIGN LAW
Uniform judicial notice of foreign law, 1391.

FOREIGN REPRESENTATIVE
Ancillary probate procedure, 3402.

FOREIGN STATES
Execution of foreign judgments, 2541.
Official records, proof, 1393.
    Certified copies, 1395.
Probate of testament, 2888.

FOREIGN TESTAMENT
Probate, 2888.

FORM
Annulment of judgment for vices of form, 2002.
Answer, 1003.
Citation, 1202.

INDEX—CODE OF CIVIL PROCEDURE
References are to Articles

FORM—Cont'd
Contradictory motion, 962, 963.
Exceptions, 924.
Executors and administrators, petition for notice of application for appointment, 3092.
Final judgment, 1918.
Intervener cannot object to form of action, 1094.
Judgment, city courts, 4897.
Petition,
    Generally, 891.
  Demand against third party, 1032.
  Incidental actions, 1032.
  Intervention, 1032.
    Pleading noncompliance with requirements, 926.
  Reconventional demand, 1032.
Pleading, 854.
Record on appeal, 2128.
Rule to show cause, 962, 963.
Subpoenas, 1351.
Temporary restraining order, 3604.
Written motion, 962.

FORMA PAUPERIS
Waiver of costs for indigent party, 5181–5188.

FRANCHISES
Declaratory judgments, 1872.

FRAUD
Pleading, 856, 1005.

FUNDS
Deposited in registry of court, burden of proof, title, 3654.
Successions, deposit and withdrawal, 3222.

GARNISHMENT
Answers to interrogatories, 2412–2414.
Attachment, 3503.
Citation, 2411, 2412.
Delay for answering interrogatories, 2412, 2413.
  City courts, 4892, 4895, 4921, 4922, 4941, 4971.
Delivery of money or property to sheriff, 2415.
Fieri facias, under writ of, 2411–2417.
Interrogatories, 2411, 2412.
Notice of filing answers to interrogatories, 2414.
Parish other than where judgment rendered, 2417.
Petition, service, 2411, 2412.
  Interrogatories, service unnecessary, 1312.

GARNISHMENT—Cont'd
Sequestration, 3503.
Service on garnishee,
  Effect, 2411.
  Method, 2412.
Sheriff,
  Delivery of money or property, 2415.
  Interrogatories, service, 2412.
Third persons, 2411.
Traversing answers to interrogatories, 2414.
Venue, 2416.

GENERAL APPEARANCE
Implied waiver of objections by, 7.

GENUINENESS
Documents,
  Admission on discovery, 1496.
  Refusal to make discovery, 1514.

GUARDIANS
Declaratory judgments, 1874.
Foreign,
  Mental incompetent, may act here, 4431, 4554.
  Minor, may act here, 4431.

HABEAS CORPUS
Answer or return, 3783, 3825, 3826.
Appeal not suspensive, 3831.
Chambers, hearing in, 3784.
Contempt, disobedience of writ, 3785.
Definition, 3821.
Disobedience, punishment, 3785.
Extraordinary remedy, 3781–3785, 3821–3831.
Hearing on petition, 3782.
Issuance of writ, 3781.
Judgment, 3830.
  Disobedience, contempt, 3785.
Jury trial, limitation, 1733.
Notice of hearing, 3829.
Person in custody, 3825–3828.
Persons who may file petition, 3821.
Petition, 3781.
Process, service, 3823, 3824.
Return date, 3782.
Service of process, 3823, 3824.
Summary trial, 2592, 3781, 3784.
Time,
  Answer to petition, filing, 3783.
  Hearing petition, 3782.
Vacation, trial by district court during, 196.
Venue, 3822.

HEALTH AND ACCIDENT INSURANCE
Venue, action on policy, 76.

INDEX—CODE OF CIVIL PROCEDURE
References are to Articles

HEIRS
Attorney for absent heirs, successions, 3171–3174.
Deceased's obligation, enforcement, 427.
Declaratory judgments, 1874.
Enforcement of right by obligee's heirs, 426.
Executory proceeding against, 2672, 2674.
Forced heirs, compelling executor to furnish security, 3154.
Inheritance taxes, 2951–2954.
Intestate successions, 3001–3008.
Notice of account to, 3335.
Obligee, enforcement of right by heirs of, 426.
Succession,
    Administration, sending into possession, 3361–3381.
    Interim allowance, 3321.
Tutors, responsibility, 4238.

HEIRSHIP
Probate procedure, evidence, 2821–2826.

HOLIDAYS
Functions which district clerk may exercise, 288.
Service of citation or process, 1231.
Sheriff's execution of writs, 323.

HOLOGRAPHIC WILL
Probate, 2883.

HUSBAND AND WIFE
Community,
    Proper defendant to be sued, 735.
    Proper plaintiff to enforce rights, 686, 695.
Executory proceeding against surviving spouse, 2671.
Parties, enforcement of community right, 686, 695.
Wife may sue as agent of husband, 695.

HYPOTHECARY ACTION
    Generally, 2378, 3721–3743.
Enforcement of mortgage or privilege against third person, 2378, 3741–3743.

ILLEGALITY
Pleaded as affirmative defense, 1005.

IMMOVABLES
Actions to determine ownership or possession, 3651–3664.
Appeals, description of immovables affected, 2089.
Eviction, tenants and occupants, 4701–4735.

IMMOVABLES—Cont'd
Injunction to prevent interference with possession, 3663.
Judgment affecting, 1919.
Partition between co-owners, 4601–4642.
Possessory action, defined, 3655.
Sale of succession property, no priority, 3262.
Tutors, sale of minor's immovables, additional bond, 4304.
Venue of action to assert interest, 80.
Writ of possession, judgment, 2501.

IMPRISONMENT
Contempt of court, 227.

INCIDENTAL ACTIONS
    See, also,
        Demand Against Third Party,
        Intervention,
        Reconvention.
    Generally, 1031–1116.
Amended and supplemental pleadings, 1156.
Answer, 1035.
Demand against third party, 1031–1040, 1111–1116.
General dispositions, 1031–1040.
Intervention, 1031–1040, 1091–1094.
Reconvention, 1031–1040, 1061–1066.

INCIDENTAL DEMANDS
Parties, 771.

INCOMPETENT
See Mental Incompetent.

INDIGENT PARTY
Waiver of costs, 5181–5188.

INDISPENSABLE PARTIES
Joinder, 641, 644–646.
Pleading nonjoinder, 927.

INDIVIDUAL
Party defendant, 731.
Party plaintiff, 682.
Service by private person, 1293.
Venue in suit against,
    General rule, 42(1).
    When domicile changed, 71.

INFANTS
See Minors.

IN FORMA PAUPERIS
Waiver of cost for indigent party, 5181–5188.

INHERENT JUDICIAL POWER
Courts, 191.

INDEX—CODE OF CIVIL PROCEDURE
References are to Articles

INHERITANCE TAXES
Probate procedure, payment, 2951–2954.
Small successions, affidavit, 3432, 3433.

INJUNCTION
Appeals from order or judgment, 3612.
Arresting executory proceedings, 2751–2754.
Concursus proceeding, 4660.
Damages, disobedience, 3611.
Disobedience of order, penalty, 3611.
Divorce case, 3944.
Evidence, hearings, proof, 3609.
Executory proceedings, arrest, 2642, 2751–2754.
Judgments, arrest execution of judgment made executory, 2783.
Judicial sale, prohibiting, 2298.
Jurisdiction not limited by rules regulating, 3613.
Jury trial, limitation, 1733.
Petitory or possessory actions, 3663.
Preliminary injunction,
    Generally, 3601, 3602, 3605–3612.
  Affidavits, hearing, 3609.
  Contempt, disobedience, 3611.
  Damages for wrongful issuance, 3608.
  Dissolution or modification, 3607.
    Hearing, 3609.
  Grounds for issuance, 3601.
  Hearing on rule, 3602, 3606.
  Notice, 3602.
  Pleadings, 3609.
  Proof at hearings, 3609.
  Security for issuance, 3610.
  Trial of rule, 3602, 3606.
  Vacation, trial by district court during, 196.
Preventing interference with possession of immovables, 3663.
Security,
  Arrest of executory proceeding, 2753, 2754.
  Interlocutory injunctive order, 3610.
Separation from bed and board proceeding, 3944.
Temporary restraining order,
    Generally, 3601, 3603–3612.
  Affidavit for issuance, 3603.
  Appeals, 3612.
  Contempt, disobedience, 3611.
  Content, 3604, 3605.
  Damages for wrongful issuance, 3608.
  Dissolution or modification, 3607.
  Duration, 3604.
  Form, 3604.
  Grounds for issuance, 3601.

INJUNCTION—Cont'd
Temporary restraining order—Cont'd
  Scope, 3605.
  Security for issuance, 3610.
Vacation, trial by district court during, 196.

IN PERSONAM
Jurisdiction, 6, 7.

IN REM, JURISDICTION
Jurisdiction, 8.

INSOLVENTS
Declaratory judgments, 1874.

INSPECTION
Discovery, production of documents for, 1492.

INSTALLMENTS
Judicial sales, fieri facias, sale when installment not due, 2341.

INSTRUCTIONS TO JURY
Generally, 1791–1793.

INSURANCE COMPANIES
Casualty insurer, claimants may be impleaded, 4652.
Foreign or alien,
  Proper defendant, 739, 741.
  Proper plaintiff, 691.
  Receivership,
    Ancillary receiver, generally, proper plaintiff, 693.
    Receiver proper defendant, 741.
  Venue in suit against, general rule, 42(7).
Insurer, defined, 5251(8).
Policy, defined, 5251(7).
Proper defendant, 739.
Proper plaintiff, 690.
Receiver,
  Proper defendant, 741.
  Proper plaintiff, 693.
Venue in action to enforce policy, 76.

INTENT
Pleading, 856.

INTERDICTION
See, also, Curatorship of Interdicts.
Appeal, effect, 4548.
Appointment of attorney for defendant, 4544.
Costs, 4551.
Curatorship, 4541–4557.
Custody of interdict, 4555.
Defendant confined out of state, 4545.
Interrogation and examination of defendant, 4547.
Jurisdiction, 10(3).

INDEX—CODE OF CIVIL PROCEDURE
References are to Articles

INTERDICTION—Cont'd
Jury trial, limitation, 1733.
Notice of suit must be filed by clerk, 4552.
Partition when co-owner an interdict, 4641, 4642.
Petition, 4543.
Process, service, 4544.
Service of process, 4544.
Summary trial, 4546.
Termination, 4557.
Venue, may not be waived, 44, 4032, 4033, 4541, 4554.
Who may file petition, 4543.

INTEREST
Judgments, 1921.

INTERLOCUTORY JUDGMENT
Generally, 1841.
Rendition, 1914.

INTERPLEADER
Concursus proceedings, 4651–4662.

INTERPRETATION
Declaratory relief, 1881, 1883.
Pleadings, 865.
Rules for interpreting code provisions, 5051–5059.

INTERROGATORIES
Depositions upon written interrogatories, 1471–1473.
Discovery, 1491.
    Adverse party, 1491.
    Refusal to make discovery, 1511.
Garnishment, 2411, 2412.

INTERVENTIONS
Generally, 1031–1040, 1091–1094.
Acceptance of proceeds by intervener, 1094.
Action instituted separately, 1037.
Amended and supplemental pleadings, 1156.
Answer, 1035.
Citation unnecessary, 1093.
Delay for filing, 1033.
Effect of dismissal of principal action, 1039.
Exceptions and motions, 1034.
Executory proceedings, 2643.
    Third possessor, summary proceeding, 2703.
Form of petition, 1032.
Judicial sale, claim of proceeds, 1092.
Jurisdiction, 1036.
Mode of procedure, 1036.
Mortgages, third person claiming on seized property, 1092.

INTERVENTIONS—Cont'd
Motions, 1034.
New Orleans city courts, jurisdiction, 4835.
Privilege on seized property, third person claiming, 1092.
Proceeds of sale, prohibiting payment, 2299.
Seized property, third person asserting ownership, mortgage or privilege on, 1092.
Separate judgments, 1038.
Separate trial, 1038.
Service of petition, 1093.
Supplemental pleadings, 1156.
Third party intervention, 1091.
    Asserting ownership, mortgage or privilege on seized property, 1092.
    Executory proceeding, 2643.
Venue, 1034.

INTESTATE
Succession, administration, sending heirs and legatees into possession, 3361, 3362.

INVENTORY
Attachment, property seized, 3504.
Judicial partition, 4604.
Minor's property, tutorship, 4101, 4102.
Natural tutor, 4061.
Orders and judgments, signing in chambers, 194.
Procès verbal, 3133–3135.
    Minor's property, 4102.
Property of interdict, curatorship, 4101, 4102, 4554.
Provisional tutor, 4072, 4549.
    Taking on appointment, 3113.
Public inventory, 3132.
Sequestration, property seized, 3504.
Small tutorship, necessity, 4462.
Succession property, 2952, 3131–3137.

INVESTMENTS
Succession representative, funds, 3223.
Tutors, minor's funds, 4269, 4270.

IRREPARABLE INJURY
Injunction, grounds for issuance, 3601.
Temporary restraining order, affidavit, 3603.

JACTITORY ACTION
Now included within possessory action, 3655–3662.

JOINDER OF ACTIONS
See Cumulation of Actions.

INDEX—CODE OF CIVIL PROCEDURE
References are to Articles

JOINDER OF PARTIES
Compulsory, 641–647.
Indispensable or necessary party who refuses to sue, 644.
Permissive, 463, 647.
Pleading improper, 926.

JOINT DEBTORS
Necessary parties, 643.
Venue in action against, 73.

JOINT TRIAL
Common issues, 1561.

JUDGES
See, also, District Judges.
Acting until recusation or motion to recuse filed, 153.
Ad hoc,
   Appointment, 158.
   Power, 157.
   Recusation, 161.
City court judge, recusation, 4844–4846.
Courts of appeal, recusation, 151, 160.
Judge ad hoc, recusation, 161.
Justices of the peace, recusation, 4844, 4846.
Power of judge ad hoc, 157.
Selection of judge to replace recused judge, 155–157.
Supreme court, recusation, 151, 159.
   Judge ad hoc, appointment on, 158.

JUDGMENT DEBTOR OR CREDITOR
See Debtors and Creditors.

JUDGMENTS
   See, also, Executions.
Absolute dismissal, 1673, 1844.
Action of nullity, 2001–2006.
Alimony, 3943, 3945.
Amendment, 1951.
Annulment, 2001–2006.
Appealable, 2083.
Attachment, necessity, 3510.
City courts, 4896, 4897.
Class actions, 597.
Completion of trial, pronouncement, 1637.
Confession of judgment,
   Act importing, 2632.
   Limitations on appeals, 2085.
Costs, 1920.
Declaratory judgments, 1871–1883.
   Burden of proof, immovables, 3654.
Default judgment,
   Generally, 1701–1703, 1843.
   Concursus proceeding, none required, 4656.
   Confirmation, 1702.
   Defined, 1843.

JUDGMENTS—Cont'd
Default judgment—Cont'd
   Discovery, 1513, 1515.
   Notice of signing, 1913.
   Preliminary, 1701.
   Scope, 1703.
Deficiency judgment, 2771, 2772.
Defined, 1841, 1842.
Definitive, 1842.
Demand against third parties, separate judgments, 1038.
Discussion, effect, 5156.
Dismissal,
   With prejudice, 1673, 1844.
   Without prejudice, 1673, 1844.
Distringas, execution, 2503.
Effect dependent on venue in certain actions, 72.
Emancipation, 3993.
Eviction, tenants and occupants, 4732.
Examination of judgment debtor, 2451–2456.
Executory, making judgments of other Louisiana courts executory, 2781–2783.
Final, 1841, 1842.
   Appeals, 2167.
   Form, 1918.
   Rendition, 1911, 1912.
Foreign, enforcement in Louisiana, 2541.
Form of final judgment, 1918.
Forma pauperis case, 5187, 5188.
Garnishment, 2411–2417.
Habeas corpus, 3830.
   Disobedience, contempt, 3785.
Immovable property, particular description, 1919.
Injunction, arrest execution of judgment made executory, 2783.
Interest, 1921.
Interlocutory,
   Definition, 1841.
   Notice of rendition, 1914.
Intervention, separate judgments, 1038.
Involuntary dismissal, 1672, 1844.
Judgment on pleadings, motion, 965, 968, 969.
Judicial emancipation, 3993.
Jury cases, 1916.
Mandamus, 3866.
   Disobedience, contempt, 3785.
Modification in trial court, 1951–2006.
Money judgments,
   Adjudication and effect, 2371–2381.
   Attachment, issuance in action for, 3542.
   Examination of judgment debtor, 2451–2456.
   Execution, 2291–2456.

INDEX—CODE OF CIVIL PROCEDURE
References are to Articles

INTERDICTION—Cont'd
Jury trial, limitation, 1733.
Notice of suit must be filed by clerk, 4552.
Partition when co-owner an interdict, 4641, 4642.
Petition, 4543.
Process, service, 4544.
Service of process, 4544.
Summary trial, 4546.
Termination, 4557.
Venue, may not be waived, 44, 4032, 4033, 4541, 4554.
Who may file petition, 4543.

INTEREST
Judgments, 1921.

INTERLOCUTORY JUDGMENT
Generally, 1841.
Rendition, 1914.

INTERPLEADER
Concursus proceedings, 4651–4662.

INTERPRETATION
Declaratory relief, 1881, 1883.
Pleadings, 865.
Rules for interpreting code provisions, 5051–5059.

INTERROGATORIES
Depositions upon written interrogatories, 1471–1473.
Discovery, 1491.
    Adverse party, 1491.
        Refusal to make discovery, 1511.
Garnishment, 2411, 2412.

INTERVENTIONS
    Generally, 1031–1040, 1091–1094.
Acceptance of proceeds by intervener, 1094.
Action instituted separately, 1037.
Amended and supplemental pleadings, 1156.
Answer, 1035.
Citation unnecessary, 1093.
Delay for filing, 1033.
Effect of dismissal of principal action, 1039.
Exceptions and motions, 1034.
Executory proceedings, 2643.
    Third possessor, summary proceeding, 2703.
Form of petition, 1032.
Judicial sale, claim of proceeds, 1092.
Jurisdiction, 1036.
Mode of procedure, 1036.
Mortgages, third person claiming on seized property, 1092.

INTERVENTIONS—Cont'd
Motions, 1034.
New Orleans city courts, jurisdiction, 4835.
Privilege on seized property, third person claiming, 1092.
Proceeds of sale, prohibiting payment, 2299.
Seized property, third person asserting ownership, mortgage or privilege on, 1092.
Separate judgments, 1038.
Separate trial, 1038.
Service of petition, 1093.
Supplemental pleadings, 1156.
Third party intervention, 1091.
    Asserting ownership, mortgage or privilege on seized property, 1092.
    Executory proceeding, 2643.
Venue, 1034.

INTESTATE
Succession, administration, sending heirs and legatees into possession, 3361, 3362.

INVENTORY
Attachment, property seized, 3504.
Judicial partition, 4604.
Minor's property, tutorship, 4101, 4102.
Natural tutor, 4061.
Orders and judgments, signing in chambers, 194.
Procès verbal, 3133–3135.
    Minor's property, 4102.
Property of interdict, curatorship, 4101, 4102, 4554.
Provisional tutor, 4072, 4549.
    Taking on appointment, 3113.
Public inventory, 3132.
Sequestration, property seized, 3504.
Small tutorship, necessity, 4462.
Succession property, 2952, 3131–3137.

INVESTMENTS
Succession representative, funds, 3223.
Tutors, minor's funds, 4269, 4270.

IRREPARABLE INJURY
Injunction, grounds for issuance, 3601.
Temporary restraining order, affidavit, 3603.

JACTITORY ACTION
Now included within possessory action, 3655–3662.

JOINDER OF ACTIONS
See Cumulation of Actions.

INDEX—CODE OF CIVIL PROCEDURE
References are to Articles

JOINDER OF PARTIES
Compulsory, 641–647.
Indispensable or necessary party who refuses to sue, 644.
Permissive, 463, 647.
Pleading improper, 926.

JOINT DEBTORS
Necessary parties, 643.
Venue in action against, 73.

JOINT TRIAL
Common issues, 1561.

JUDGES
See, also, District Judges.
Acting until recusation or motion to recuse filed, 153.
Ad hoc,
  Appointment, 158.
  Power, 157.
  Recusation, 161.
City court judge, recusation, 4844–4846.
Courts of appeal, recusation, 151, 160.
Judge ad hoc, recusation, 161.
Justices of the peace, recusation, 4844, 4846.
Power of judge ad hoc, 157.
Selection of judge to replace recused judge, 155–157.
Supreme court, recusation, 151, 159.
  Judge ad hoc, appointment on, 158.

JUDGMENT DEBTOR OR CREDITOR
See Debtors and Creditors.

JUDGMENTS
See, also, Executions.
Absolute dismissal, 1673, 1844.
Action of nullity, 2001–2006.
Alimony, 3943, 3945.
Amendment, 1951.
Annulment, 2001–2006.
Appealable, 2083.
Attachment, necessity, 3510.
City courts, 4896, 4897.
Class actions, 597.
Completion of trial, pronouncement, 1637.
Confession of judgment,
  Act importing, 2632.
  Limitations on appeals, 2085.
Costs, 1920.
Declaratory judgments, 1871–1883.
  Burden of proof, immovables, 3654.
Default judgment,
  Generally, 1701–1703, 1843.
  Concursus proceeding, none required, 4656.
  Confirmation, 1702.
  Defined, 1843.

JUDGMENTS—Cont'd
Default judgment—Cont'd
  Discovery, 1513, 1515.
  Notice of signing, 1913.
  Preliminary, 1701.
  Scope, 1703.
Deficiency judgment, 2771, 2772.
Defined, 1841, 1842.
Definitive, 1842.
Demand against third parties, separate judgments, 1038.
Discussion, effect, 5156.
Dismissal,
  With prejudice, 1673, 1844.
  Without prejudice, 1673, 1844.
Distringas, execution, 2503.
Effect dependent on venue in certain actions, 72.
Emancipation, 3993.
Eviction, tenants and occupants, 4732.
Examination of judgment debtor, 2451–2456.
Executory, making judgments of other Louisiana courts executory, 2781–2783.
Final, 1841, 1842.
  Appeals, 2167.
  Form, 1918.
  Rendition, 1911, 1912.
Foreign, enforcement in Louisiana, 2541.
Form of final judgment, 1918.
Forma pauperis case, 5187, 5188.
Garnishment, 2411–2417.
Habeas corpus, 3830.
  Disobedience, contempt, 3785.
Immovable property, particular description, 1919.
Injunction, arrest execution of judgment made executory, 2783.
Interest, 1921.
Interlocutory,
  Definition, 1841.
  Notice of rendition, 1914.
Intervention, separate judgments, 1038.
Involuntary dismissal, 1672, 1844.
Judgment on pleadings, motion, 965, 968, 969.
Judicial emancipation, 3993.
Jury cases, 1916.
Mandamus, 3866.
  Disobedience, contempt, 3785.
Modification in trial court, 1951–2006.
Money judgments,
  Adjudication and effect, 2371–2381.
  Attachment, issuance in action for, 3542.
  Examination of judgment debtor, 2451–2456.
  Execution, 2291–2456.

INDEX—CODE OF CIVIL PROCEDURE
References are to Articles

JUDICIAL SALES—Cont'd
Fieri facias—Cont'd
    Payment of debt prior to adjudication, 2340.
    Perishable property, 2333.
    Publication, notice, 2331.
    Reading of advertisement and certificates, 2334.
    Sale in globo, 2295.
    Sale of perishable property, 2333.
    Sale when instalment not due, 2341.
    Sheriffs,
        Act of sale, 2342.
        Return after sale, 2343.
    Superior mortgage or privilege, 2335, 2338.
Inferior mortgage or privilege, 2375–2377.
Intervention, claim of proceeds, 1092.
Judgment creditor's recourse against debtor, 2381.
Money judgments, execution, sale under fieri facias, 2331–2343.
Payment,
    Inferior mortgages, liens and privileges, 2377.
    Price, 2374.
Proceeds, order of distribution, summary proceedings, 2592.
Property subject to inferior mortgages, 2375.
Property subject to superior mortgage, 2374, 2378.
Purchasers,
    Liability, 2375.
    Rights in case of eviction, 2379, 2380.
Release of inferior mortgages, 2376.
Sale subject to real charge or lease, 2372.
Summary proceeding to determine rank of mortgages and privileges, 2592.
Superior mortgage or privilege, 2374, 2378.
Writ of seizure and sale, 2721–2724.

JUDICIAL SEQUESTRATION
Issues on court's own motion, 3573.

JURISDICTION
    Generally, 1–10.
Adoption proceedings, 10(1).
Ancillary probate proceedings, 3401.
Annulment of marriage proceeding, 10(6).
Appeals,
    Divesting of trial court, 2088.
    Transfer for lack, 2162.
Attorney's fees, amount in dispute, 4.
City courts, 4832–4836.
Cumulation of actions, test, 462, 463.
Curatorship proceeding, 10(4).

JURISDICTION—Cont'd
Custody of minors proceedings, 10(5).
Definition, 1.
Demand against third party, 1036.
Divorce suit, 10(7).
Incidental action, 1036.
Injunction, not limited by rules of, 3613.
In personam, 6, 7.
In rem, 8.
Interdiction proceeding, 10(3).
Intervention, 1036.
Justice of the peace courts, 4832.
    Limitations, 4836.
Over person of defendant,
    Generally, 6, 7.
    Pleading lack of jurisdiction, 925.
    Waiver of objections by general appearance, 7.
Over property, 8, 9.
Over status, 10.
Over subject matter,
    Generally, 2–5.
    Amount in dispute, 2.
        Determination, 4.
        Jury trial, limitation, 1733.
    Cannot be conferred by consent, 3.
    Claim, reduction to confer, remittance, 5.
    Consent of parties cannot confer, 3.
    Demand, based upon object, 2.
    Determination, 4.
    Effect of reduction of claim to confer, 5.
    Pleading lack of jurisdiction, 925.
    Value of right asserted, 2.
        Determination, 4.
Probate, evidence, 2821–2826.
Process, based upon service, 6.
Quasi in rem, 9.
Reconvention, 1036.
Separation from bed and board suit, 10(7).
Successions, 2811, 2812.
Tutorship proceeding, 10(4).

JURISDICTION RATIONE MATERIAE
Over subject matter. See Jurisdiction.

JURISDICTION RATIONE PERSONAE
Over person of defendant. See Jurisdiction; Venue.

JURORS
See Jury Trial.

INDEX—CODE OF CIVIL PROCEDURE
References are to Articles

JUDGMENTS—Cont'd
Money judgments—Cont'd
    Garnishment under writ of fieri facias, 2411–2417.
    Judicial sales,
        Adjudication and effect, 2371–2381.
        Under fieri facias, 2331–2343.
        Writ of fieri facias, 2291–2299.
New trial, 1971–1979, 4897, 5002.
Nonsuit, 1673, 1844.
Notice of signing, 1913.
Nullity action, 2001–2006.
Other Louisiana courts, making executory, 2781–2783.
Other than money judgments, execution, 2501–2504.
Partial judgment, 1915.
Parties liable for costs, 1920.
Partition, when co-owner absent, 4625 to 4627.
Pleading, 859.
Possession,
    Legacy or inheritance, payment of taxes, necessity, 2951.
    Ordering delivery, execution, 2501.
    Succession, 3061, 3062, 3381.
Procedure, appellate courts, 2081–2167.
Quo warranto, 3902.
    Disobedience, contempt, 3785.
Reconvention, separate judgments, 1038.
Rehearing on appeal, 2166.
Rendition of final judgments, 1911, 1912.
Revival, 2031.
Separate judgments, incidental action, 1038.
Sequestration, necessity, 3510.
Signing, 1911, 1912.
    Chambers, 194.
Specific performance, execution, 2504.
Succession, possession, after administration, 3381.
Summary judgment, motion, 966–969.
Summary proceeding, 2595.
Taxing costs, 1920.
Voluntary dismissal, 1671, 1844.
Writ of fieri facias, execution, 2291–2299.
    Adjudication and effect, 2371–2381.
Written reasons for judgment, 1917.

JUDICIAL ADVERTISEMENT
Notice,
    Filing tableau of distribution, 3304.
    Partition suit, when co-owner absent, 4624.
Sale under,
    Executory process, 2722.
    Writ of fieri facias, 2331.

JUDICIAL ADVERTISEMENT—Cont'd
Succession property,
    Private sale, 3282.
    Public sale, 3272.

JUDICIAL BONDS
Furnishing new or supplemental bond, 5124, 5126.
Invalid or insufficient bond, 5125, 5126.
Oaths of principal and surety, 5122.
Payable to clerk of trial court, 5121.
Release bond, 5127.
Testing sufficiency and validity, 5123.
Venue in action, 75.

JUDICIAL EMANCIPATION
Consent of parent or tutor, 3992.
Expenses, 3994.
Hearing, 3993.
Judgment, 3993.
Jurisdiction, 10(2).
Jury trial, limitation, 1733.
Petition, 3991.
Venue, may not be waived, 44, 3991.

JUDICIAL MORTGAGE
Hypothecary action against third person, 3741–3743.

JUDICIAL NOTICE
Common law and statutes, 1391.
Law and statutes of other American states, 1391.
Uniform Judicial Notice of Foreign Law Act, 1391.

JUDICIAL POWER
See Courts.

JUDICIAL SALES
Adjudication and effect, 2371–2381.
Distribution of proceeds, 2373.
Effect of adjudication, 2371.
Eviction of purchaser subsequently, 2379, 2380.
Executory proceedings, 2721–2724.
Fieri facias,
    Appraisal, 2332.
        Value, bid less than, 2336.
    Executory proceedings, rules applicable, 2724.
    Inferior mortgages and privileges, 2338.
    Judgment debtor or creditor may bid, 2339.
    Minimum price to be paid, 2336, 2337.
    Notice of sale,
        Perishable property, 2333.
        Publication, 2331.
    Order in which property sold, 2295.

INDEX—CODE OF CIVIL PROCEDURE
References are to Articles

JURY TRIAL
Alternative jurors, 1769.
Calling and examining jurors, 1761–1769.
Challenges, 1764–1767, 1769.
    After acceptance, 1767.
    Cause, 1765.
Charge to jury,
    Contents, 1792.
    No comment on evidence, 1792.
    Objections, 1793.
    Recordation, 1791.
    Time, 1791.
City courts, prohibited, 4840.
Evidence which may be taken into jury room, 1794.
Examination, 1763.
    Alternate jurors, 1769.
Instructions to jury, 1791–1793.
Issues triable by jury, 1731, 1732.
Judgment, rendition, 1916.
Justices of the peace, prohibited, 4840.
Misconduct of jury, ground for new trial, 1814.
Peremptory challenges, 1764.
    Alternate jurors, 1769.
Procedure, 1791–1795.
Right to trial by jury,
    Generally, 1731–1735.
    Demand for jury trial, 1732.
    Issues triable, 1731, 1732.
    Limitations, 1733.
    Specification of issues, 1734.
    Trial of less than all issues, 1735.
Selection of foreman, 1768.
Selection of jury, 1751.
Stipulation,
    Less than all issues, 1735.
    Lesser number of jurors, 1761.
    Verdict, number of jurors, 1795.
Swearing,
    After acceptance, 1768.
    Before examination, 1762.
Time for peremptory challenges, 1766.
Verdicts,
    Generally, 1795, 1811–1814.
    Additur, 1813.
    General, with answers to interrogatories, 1812.
    Reformation, 1813.
    Remittitur, 1813.
    Special, 1811.

JUSTICE OF THE PEACE COURTS
Absence or illness, ad hoc appointment, 4841.
Appeal, 4942.
Application of law, 4891.

JUSTICE OF THE PEACE COURTS—Cont'd
Concurrent jurisdiction with district courts, 4971, 4972.
Contempt, power to punish for, 4838.
Delay, filing answer, 4895, 4941.
District courts, concurrent jurisdiction, 4971, 4972.
Jury trial prohibited, 4840.
Limitations on jurisdiction, 4836.
Pleading, 4892, 4941.
Power and authority, limitations, 4837.
Procedure, 4892–4901, 4941, 4942.
Recusation, 4844, 4846.
Time, delay,
    Appealing, 4899, 4921, 4922, 4942.
    Filing answer, 4895, 4941.
Venue, 4839.

KNOWLEDGE
Pleading, 856.

LACK OF PROCEDURAL CAPACITY
Pleading, 926.

LAW
Defined, 5251(9).

LEASES
Eviction, tenants and occupants, procedure, 4701–4735.
Judicial sales subject to real charge or lease, 2372.
Succession property, 3226, 3229.
Tutors, minor's property, 4268.

LEGAL MORTGAGE
Hypothecary action against third person, 3741–3743.
Natural tutor, 4061, 4134.

LEGAL REPRESENTATIVE
Appeals, 2084.
    Appointment not suspended by, 2122.
Appointment, opposition, summary proceedings, 2592.
Authority or qualification to sue, 700.
Citation, 1203.
Contempt, punishment, 375.
Defined, 5251(10).
Executor and administrator. See Executors and Administrators.
Executory proceeding against, 2673.
Hearing on application for authority in chambers, 195.
Officer of appointing court, 374.
Order confirming or appointing, signing in chambers, 194.
Petition for authority, summary proceedings, 2592.
Removal not suspended by appeal, 2122.

1 LSA–C.C.P.—51

INDEX—CODE OF CIVIL PROCEDURE
References are to Articles

LEGAL REPRESENTATIVE—Cont'd
Service, process or citation, 1235.
Substitution of parties, 805.
Summary proceedings of tableau of distribution or account, 2592.
Tutors. See Tutors and Tutorship.
Vacating appointment, effect on appeal, 2122.

LEGAL SUCCESSOR
Defined, substitution of parties, 801, 805.

LEGATEES
Attorney for absent legatees, successions, 3171–3174.
Declaratory judgments, 1874.
Executory proceeding against, 2672, 2674.
Inheritance taxes, 2951–2954.
Notice of account to residuary legatees, 3335.
Succession,
    Administration, sending into possession, 3361–3381.
        Interim allowance, 3321.
Testamentary executor, 3353.
Testate successions, 3031–3035.

LEGITIMATE FILIATION
Jury trial, limitation, 1733.

LETTERS
Administration, intestate succession, 3159.
Curatorship, interdicts, 4172, 4554.
Discovery and production for inspection, 1492.
Testamentary, testate succession, 3159.
Tutorship, 4172.

LIFE INSURANCE
Venue, action on policy, 76.

LIMITATIONS
Appeals, 2085.
City courts,
    Jurisdiction, 4836.
    Power and authority, 4837.
Jury trials, 1733.
Justices of the peace, power and authority, 4837.

LIQUIDATION
Corporation or partnership,
    Party defendant, 740.
    Party plaintiff, 692.

LIS PENDENS
Actions, 531, 532.
Notice of pendency of real action, 3751–3753.

LIS PENDENS—Cont'd
Pleading, 925.
Statute, 3751–3753.

LOANS
Succession representative, 3228, 3229.
Tutors, 4267.

MAIL
Service of pleadings, 1313, 1314.

MAJORS
Party defendant, 731.
Party plaintiff, 682.

MALICE
Pleading, 856.

MANAGEMENT
Interdict's property, curator, 4262–4275, 4554.
Minor's property,
    Father as administrator of estate, 4501.
    Tutor, 4262–4275.
Succession property, 3221–3229.

MANDAMUS
Alternative writ, 3865.
Answer or return, 3783.
Cases where issued, 3862.
Chambers, hearing in, 3784.
Contempt, disobedience of writ, 3785.
Corporation or corporate officer, 3864.
Definition, 3861.
Disobedience, punishment, 3785.
Extraordinary remedy, 3781–3785, 3861–3866.
Hearing on petition, 3782.
Issuance of writ, 3781.
Judgment, 3866.
    Disobedience, contempt, 3785.
Jury trial, limitation, 1733.
Person against whom directed, 3864.
Petition, 3781.
Public officers, directing writ against, 3863.
Return date, 3782.
Shareholders, compel recognition, 3864.
Summary trial, 2592, 3781, 3784.
Time,
    Answer to petition, filing, 3783.
    Hearing petition, 3782.
Vacation, trial by district court during, 196.

MARITAL COMMUNITY
Party defendant, 735.
Party plaintiff, 686, 695.

INDEX—CODE OF CIVIL PROCEDURE
References are to Articles

MARRIAGE
Administration of minor's property during marriage of parents, 4501, 4502.
Annulment, 3941–3945.
    Appeal from judgment, 3942.
        Judgment on pleadings not permitted, 969.
    Jurisdiction of proceeding, 10(6).
    Jury trial, limitation, 1733.
    Summary judgment not permitted, 969.
Divorce, 3941–3945.
Separation from bed and board, 3941–3945.
Venue, may not be waived, 44, 3941.

MARSHAL
Service or execution, when authorized by sheriff, 332.

MARSHALLING OF ASSETS
See Discussion.

MATURITY
Reconventional demand, action matured after pleading, 1066.

MENTAL EXAMINATION
Contempt, exception on disobedience of order to submit to, 1513.
Parties, 1493–1495.

MENTAL INCOMPETENT
    See, also,
        Curatorship of Interdicts.
        Interdiction.
Attorney appointed to represent unrepresented, 5091–5098.
Declaratory judgments, trust or estate, 1874.
Party defendant, 733.
Party plaintiff, 684.

MINERAL RIGHTS
Real rights, 3664.

MINORS
    See, also, Tutors and Tutorship.
Accounting by tutor, 4391–4398.
Adjudication of property to parent, 4361–4363.
Administration of property during marriage of parents, 4501, 4502.
Ancillary tutorship procedure, 4431–4433.
Appeal, judgment awarding custody, 3943.
Appointment of tutors, 4061–4073.
Attorney appointed to represent unrepresented, 5091–5098.
Care of person by tutor, 4261.

MINORS—Cont'd
Custody, jurisdiction of proceeding, 10(5).
Disqualification, revocation, removal, or resignation of tutor, 4231–4238.
Donations to or by, 4275.
Emancipated minor,
    Party defendant, 731.
    Party plaintiff, 682.
Foreign tutor or guardian may act, 4431.
Functions, powers, and duties of tutor, 4261–4275.
Inventory of property, tutorship, 4101, 4102.
Judicial emancipation,
    Generally, 3991–3994.
    Jurisdiction, 10(2).
    Jury trial, limitation, 1733.
Letters of tutorship, tutor, 4172.
Management of property,
    Father as administrator of estate, 4501.
    Tutor, 4262–4275.
Oath of tutor, 4171.
Partition when co-owner a minor, 4641, 4642.
Party defendant, 732.
Procedural capacity to sue, 683.
Sale of property, tutors,
    Private sale, 4301, 4304, 4341, 4342.
    Public sale, 4301–4304, 4321–4323.
Security of tutor, 4131–4136.
Separate tutor of property, 4069.
Small tutorships, 4461–4464.
Trust or estate, declaratory judgments, 1874.
Undertutor, 4201–4206, 4236, 4237.
Venue of tutorship proceedings, may not be waived, 44, 4031–4034.

MISCONDUCT
Jury, ground for new trial, 1814.

MISJOINDER OF ACTIONS
Cumulation, improper, 461–465.

MISJOINDER OF PARTIES
Cumulation, improper, 463–465.
Pleading, 926.

MISTAKE
Assignment of errors on appeal, necessity, 2129.
Pleading, 856.
    Affirmative defense, 1005.

MIXED ACTION
Definition, 422.
Venue, 3652, 3656.

MODIFICATION
Judgments in trial court, 1951–2006.

803

INDEX—CODE OF CIVIL PROCEDURE
References are to Articles

MONEY JUDGMENT
Adjudication and effect, 2371-2381.
Attachment, issuance in action for, 3542.
Examination of judgment debtor, 2451-2456.
Execution, generally, 2291-2456.
Garnishment under writ of fieri facias, 2411-2417.
Judicial sale,
    Adjudication and effect, 2371-2381.
    Under fieri facias, 2331-2343.
Writ of fieri facias, 2291-2299.

MORTGAGES
    See, also, Judicial Sales.
Enforcement,
    Executory proceeding, 2631-2754.
    Hypothecary action, 2378, 3741-3743.
Executors and administrators, special mortgage in lieu of bond, 3157.
Executory proceeding, conventional mortgage, enforcement by, 3721, 3723.
Hypothecary actions, 3721-3743.
Intent to defraud creditors, grounds for attachment, 3541.
Legal mortgage,
    Hypothecary action against third person, 3741-3743.
    Natural tutor, 4061, 4134.
Natural tutor's legal mortgage, 4061, 4134.
Notice of pendency of action to enforce, 3751-3753.
Ordinary proceeding, enforcement by, 3722.
Pendency of action to enforce, 3751-3753.
Sequestration on claim, 3571.
Succession representative, secure loan, 3228, 3229.
Third persons, intervention, claiming on seized property, 1092.
Tutors, minor's property, 4267.
Venue, action to enforce by ordinary proceeding, 72.

MOTIONS
Attachment, motion to dissolve, nonresident, no general appearance, 7(4).
Contempt rule,
    Constructive contempt, 225.
    Direct contempt, 223.
Continuance, 1603, 1605.
Contradictory, 963.
    Summary proceeding,
        Commencement by filing, 2593.
        Issue raised by, 2592.
        Service, 2594.
Demand against third party, 1034.

MOTIONS—Cont'd
Depositions on oral examination, terminate or limit examination, 1454.
Ex parte, 963.
Examination of judgment debtor, court where filed, 2452.
Incidental actions, 1034.
Interim allowance to heirs or legatees, 3321.
Intervention, 1034.
Judgment on pleadings, 965, 966, 968, 969.
Judgment pro confesso in garnishment, 2413.
New trial, 1971-1979.
Physical or mental examination of parties, 1493.
    Report, 1495.
Pleading, written motions, 961-969.
Reconvention, 1034.
Recusation,
    City court judge, 4844.
    Court of appeal judge, 160.
    District judge, 153, 154.
    Justice of the peace, 4844.
    Supreme court justice, 159.
Rule to show cause, 963.
Security for costs, no general appearance, 7(3).
Strike, 964.
Summary judgment, 966-969.
Time,
    Judgment on pleadings, 964.
    Motion to strike, 964.
    Summary judgment, 966.
Traverse,
    Affidavits of poverty, forma pauperis cases, 5183.
    Answers to garnishment interrogatories, 2414.
    Descriptive list of property, successions, 3137.
    Public inventory, 3135.
    Sufficiency or validity of judicial bond, 5123.
Written motions, 961-969.

MOVABLES
Sale of succession property, no priority, 3262.

MYSTIC TESTAMENT
Probate, 2885, 2886.

NAMES
Party defendant, 736.
Party plaintiff, 687.

INDEX—CODE OF CIVIL PROCEDURE
References are to Articles

NECESSARY PARTIES
Joinder, 642–646.
Joint obligees or obligors, 643.
Pleading nonjoinder, 926.

NEGLIGENCE
Contributory negligence, affirmative defense, pleading, 1005.

NEW ORLEANS, CITY COURTS
Absence or illness of judge, 4842.
Cases involving less than $25, 4921.
Cases involving more than $100, 5001, 5002.
Cases involving $25 to $100, 4922.
Jurisdiction, 4835.

NEW TRIAL
Additur as alternative, 1813.
Application, 1975, 1979.
Assignment for new trial, when granted, 1977.
City courts, new trial not permitted, 4897.
Delay for applying, 1974.
    City courts, clerk's book cases, 4972, 5002.
Discretionary grounds, 1973.
Granting, 1971.
Grounds, 1814, 1972, 1973.
Misconduct of jury, 1814.
Motion, 1975, 1979.
New Orleans city courts, cases involving more than $100, 5002.
Notice of filing application, 1976.
Peremptory grounds, 1972.
Procedure when new trial granted, 1978.
Remittitur as alternative, 1813.
Service of notice of application, 1976.
Summary decision on motion, 1979.
Summary proceedings on application, 2592.

NEXT OF KIN
Declaratory judgments, 1874.

NO CAUSE OF ACTION
Pleading in exception, 927.

NO RIGHT OF ACTION
Pleading in exception, 927.

NON-ALIENATION PACT
Unnecessary in executory proceeding, 2701.

NONJOINDER OF PARTIES
Pleading, 926.
    Indispensable or necessary parties, 645, 927.

NONRESIDENT
Attachment, grounds, 3541.
Defined, 5251(11).
Depositions, place of taking, 1422.
Succession, jurisdiction, 2811, 2812.
Venue in suits against, general rule, 42(6).

NON-SUIT
Judgment, 1673, 1844.

NOTARIES
Probate of testaments, search for testament,
    Appointment, 2854.
    Return, 2855.

NOTICE
City courts, judgment, 4898.
Depositions and discovery,
    Application to compel answer to interrogatories, 1511.
    Filing deposition, 1456.
    Mental examination of parties, 1493, 1494.
    Oral examination, 1451.
    Perpetuation of testimony, 1433.
    Physical examination of parties, 1493, 1494.
    Taking, 1421.
    Waiver of irregularities, 1424.
    Written interrogatories, 1471.
        Filing of depositions, 1472.
Eviction of tenants and occupants, notice to vacate, 4701–4703.
Executory proceedings,
    Seizure, 2721.
    Three-day notice, 2639.
Garnishment, filing answers to interrogatories, 2414.
Habeas corpus, hearing, 3829.
Interdiction, notice of suit, filing by clerk, 4552.
Judgment, 1913, 1914, 4998, 5002.
Judicial notice,
    Common law and statutes, 1391.
    Law and statutes of other states, 1391.
    Uniform act, 1391.
Judicial sales, fieri facias, publication, 2331.
Lis pendens, 531, 532.
    Pendency of real actions, 3751–3753.
    Pleading, 925.
Oral examination, depositions on, filing, 1456.
Partition suit, when co-owner absent, 4624.
Pendency of real actions, 3751–3753.

INDEX—CODE OF CIVIL PROCEDURE
References are to Articles

NOTICE—Cont'd
Physical or mental examination of parties, 1493.
    Report, 1495.
Preliminary injunction, 3602.
Sale under writ of fieri facias, 2331.
Succession property,
    Private sale, 3282.
    Public sale, 3272.
Tableau of distribution, filing, 3304.
Trial, 1571.
    Written request for, 1572.
Written request for notice of trial, 1572.

NULLITY
Action, 2001–2006.

NUNCUPATIVE TESTAMENT
Probate, 2884, 2886.
    Necessity, 2891.

OATHS
Affidavits of poverty, forma pauperis cases, 5183.
Attorney appointed by court, necessity, 5093.
Curator of interdict, 4171, 4554.
Depositions on oral examination, 1453.
Examination of judgment debtor, 2454.
Jurors, 1762, 1768.
Natural tutor, 4061.
Principal and surety on judicial bonds, 5122.
Provisional administrator, 3112.
Provisional curator, 4549.
Provisional tutor, 4071.
Succession representative, 3158.
Tutors, 4171.
Undertutor, 4201.
Witnesses at trial, 1633.

OBJECTIONS
    See, also, Exceptions.
Declinatory exception, objections raised by, 925.
Depositions, 1424–1427.
    Admissibility, 1429.
    Irregularities in notice, 1424.
    Waiver, 1424–1427.
Dilatory exception, objections raised by, 926.
Executory proceedings, assertion, 2642.
Oral examination, depositions on, 1453.
Peremptory exception, objections raised by, 927.
Probate of testaments, ex parte probate, 2881, 2901.
Third party defendant, pleading, 1111.
Venue, waiver, 44.

OBJECTIONS—Cont'd
Waiver,
    Objections which should have been raised in exceptions, 925, 926.
    Venue, 44.

OBLIGATION
Deceased enforced against heirs, 427.
Extinguishment, pleaded as affirmative defense, 1005.
Personal obligation, abatement on death of party, 428.
Right to enforce, 423.
Succession representative, enforcement, 3211.

OCCUPANTS
Eviction, procedure, 4701–4735.
Judicial sales, eviction of purchaser subsequently, 2379, 2380.

OFFENSE
Venue in action, 74.

OFFICERS
Courts,
    Generally, 251–375.
    Attorneys, 371.
    Clerks, 251–288.
    Court reporters, 372.
    Experts, 373.
    Legal representatives, 374.
    Minute clerk, 256.
    Sheriffs, 321–334.
Evidence of regulations, 1393.
Mandamus, directing writ against, 3863.
Service, citation or process, 1265.
Substitution of parties, 806.

OFFICIAL RECORDS
Proof,
    Generally, 1391–1397.
    Certified copies, 1395.
    Lack of record, 1396, 1397.
    Louisiana records, 1394.
    Other proof, 1397.
    Out of state records, 1395.

OIL AND GAS
Contracts to reduce to possession as real rights, 3664.

OLOGRAPHIC TESTAMENT
Probate, 2883.

OPPOSITIONS
    Generally, 2971–2973.
Account,
    Curator, 4395, 4554.
    Succession representative, **3336**.
    Tutor, 4395.

INDEX—CODE OF CIVIL PROCEDURE
References are to Articles

OPPOSITIONS—Cont'd
Appointment of administrator, 3095.
Probate of testament, 2881, 2901, 2902.
Sale of succession property, 3283.
Tableau of distribution, succession, 3307.
Third opposition, now included in intervention, 1092.

ORAL EXAMINATION
See Depositions.

ORDERS
Appeal, homologating tableau of distribution, 3308.
Application,
    Appointment as administrator, 3094.
    Authority, succession representative, 3229.
Authorizing payment of debts in successions, 3301, 3307.
Confirmation of executor, 3082.
Contempt,
    Guilty of constructive, 225.
    Guilty of direct, 223.
Continuance, 1605.
Court's approval of action affecting,
    Interdict's interest, 4271, 4554.
    Minor's interest, 4271.
Depositions and discovery,
    Compelling answer to interrogatories, 1511.
    Failure to comply with order, 1513.
    Perpetuation of testimony, 1434.
    Protection of parties and witnesses, 1452, 1473.
    Taking, 194.
Examination of judgment debtor, 2453.
Forma pauperis cases, 5183.
Granting new trial, 1977.
Interim allowance to heirs or legatees, 3321.
Issuance of writ, executory proceedings, 2638.
Joint trial of common issues, 1561.
Partition, appointment of attorney for absent co-owner, 4623.
Permitting party to litigate without payment of costs, 5183.
Physical or mental examination of parties, 1493.
    Report, 1495.
Pre-trial conference, 1551.
Prohibiting payment of proceeds of judicial sale, 2299.
Recusation of judge, 152, 157, 158.
Rendered by district court clerk, Orleans Parish excepted, 283.

ORDERS—Cont'd
Sale,
    Interdict's property, 4321, 4341, 4342, 4554.
    Minor's property, tutorship, 4321, 4341, 4342.
    Succession property, 3271, 3284, 3285.
Signing in chambers, 194.
Subpoena duces tecum, 1354.
Taking inventory in succession proceedings, 3131.
Temporary restraining orders, 3601–3612.

ORDINANCES
Declaratory judgments, 1872.

ORDINARY PROCESS
See Ordinary Proceedings.

ORDINARY PROCEEDINGS
Generally, 851–2031.
Annulment of probated testament, 2931.
Citation and service of process, 1201–1314.
Concursus proceeding, 4662.
Conventional mortgage, enforcement by, 3722.
Executory proceedings, conversion to, 2644.
Judgments, 1841–2031.
Pleading, 851–1156.
Pre-trial procedure, 1551.
Production of evidence, 1351–1515.
Trial, 1561–1814.

OTHER STATES
Execution of foreign judgments, 2541.
Official records, proof, 1393.
    Certified copies, 1395.
Probate of testament, 2888.

OWNERSHIP
See, also, Partition.
Actions to determine, 3651–3664.

PACT DE NON ALIENANDO
Unnecessary in executory proceeding, 2701.

PARTIES
See, also,
    Adverse Party.
    Third Parties.
Abatement on death of party, 428.
Concursus proceeding,
    Claimants who may be impleaded, 4652.
    Each defendant both plaintiff and defendant, 4656.

INDEX—CODE OF CIVIL PROCEDURE
References are to Articles

PARTIES—Cont'd
Consent, dismissal of appeal, 2162.
Costs, liability, 1454, 1457, 1511, 1514, 1920, 2164.
Cumulation of actions, 463, 647.
Death of party, 428.
    Compulsory substitution, 802.
    Voluntary substitution, 801.
Declaratory judgments, 1880.
Declaratory relief, 1880.
Defendants,
    Generally, 731–742.
    Associations, 738.
    Attorney, appointment to represent unrepresented defendants, 5091–5098.
    Community, marital, 735.
    Defined, incidental action, 1040.
    Domestic corporation, 739.
        Receivership, 740.
    Domestic insurance company, 739.
        Receivership, 741.
    Emancipated minor, 731.
    Foreign corporation, 739.
        Receivership, 740.
    Foreign or alien insurance company, 739.
        Receivership, 741.
    Interdict, 733.
    Major having procedural capacity, 731.
    Members of unincorporated association, 738.
    Mental incompetent, 733.
    Minor, 732.
    Partners, 737.
    Partnership, 737.
        Liquidation, 740.
    Person doing business under trade name, 736.
    Succession, 734, 3249.
    Trust estate, 742.
    Unincorporated association, 738.
Demand against third party, 1031–1040, 1111–1116.
Executory proceedings, 2671–2674.
Incidental demands, 771.
Indispensable,
    Joinder, 641, 644–646.
    Pleading nonjoinder, 927.
Joinder,
    Generally, 641–647.
    Indispensable or necessary party who refuses to sue, 644.
    Permissive, 463, 647.
    Pleading improper, 926.
Misjoinder,
    Cumulation, improper, 463–465.
    Pleading, 926.

PARTIES—Cont'd
Necessary,
    Joinder, 642–646.
    Pleading nonjoinder, 926.
    Solidary obligees or obligors, 643.
Nonjoinder of necessary or indispensable party, 926.
    Pleading, 645, 927.
Petitory action, 3652.
Physical and mental examination, 1493–1495.
Plaintiffs,
    Generally, 681–700.
    Agent, 694, 695.
    Assignor or assignee, 698.
    Associations, 689.
    Community, marital, 686, 695.
    Corporation in receivership or liquidation, 692.
    Defined, incidental action, 1040.
    Domestic corporation, 690.
    Domestic insurance company, 690.
    Emancipated minor, 682.
    Foreign corporation, 691.
    Foreign or alien insurance company, 691.
    Insurance company in receivership, 693.
    Interdict, 684.
    Major, 682.
    Mandatary, 694, 695.
    Mental incompetent, 684.
    Minor, 683.
    Partnership, 688.
        Liquidation, 692.
    Person doing business under trade name, 687.
    Pledgor or pledgee, 696.
    Real and actual interest required, 681.
    Representative's authority presumed, 700.
    Subrogor or subrogee, 697.
    Succession, 685.
    Trust estate, 699.
    Unincorporated association, 689.
    Wife as agent of husband, 695.
Possessory action, 3656.
Public officers, substitution, 806.
Reconvention, 1064.
Stipulation, taking of depositions, 1421.
Substitution,
    Appellate courts, 821.
    Courts of Appeal, 821.
    Depositions, use, 1428.
    District court, 821.
    Trial courts, 801–807.
Waiver of costs for indigent party, 5181–5188.

INDEX—CODE OF CIVIL PROCEDURE
References are to Articles

PARTITION
Between co-owners, 4601–4642.
    Absentee, when co-owner an absentee, 4621–4630.
        Contradictory proceeding, 4623.
        Deposit of absentee's share, 4628.
        Effect of judgment and sale, 4627.
        Judgment ordering sale, 4625.
        Order appointing attorney, 4623.
        Other articles applicable, 4629.
        Partition by licitation, 4621.
        Partition in kind when defendant prays for, 4630.
        Petition, 4622.
        Process service, 4623.
        Publication of notice, 4624.
        Reimbursement of co-owner, 4626.
        Service of citation, 4623.
        Trial, 4625.
    Appointment of attorney, 4605.
    Attorney's fee in uncontested partition, 4613.
    Controversy before notary effecting partition, 4608.
    Homologation of partition, 4609–4612.
    Interdict, when co-owner an interdict,
        Partition in kind, 4642.
        Sale of interest, 4641.
    Inventory, 4604.
    Judicial partition, 4602, 4603.
    Licitation, 4607.
    Methods, 4601.
    Minor when co-owner a minor,
        Partition in kind, 4642.
        Sale of interest, 4641.
    Partition in kind, 4606.
    Procedure in judicial partition, 4603.
    Purchase by co-owner, 4614.
    Trial by preference, 4605.
    Venue of judicial partition, 1603.
Community property, 82.
Judgments, signing in chambers, 194.
Jury trial, limitation, 1733.
Partnership property, 83.
Successions, 81, 3461, 3462.
Summary proceedings, homologation of judicial partition, 2592.
Vacation, trial by district court during, 196.
Venue,
    Generally, 80–83, 4603.
    Between co-owners, 4603.

PARTITION—Cont'd
Venue—Cont'd
    Community property, 82.
    Partnership property, 83.
    Successions, 81, 3461.

PARTNERSHIP
Discovery, 1491.
Liquidation,
    Party defendant, 740.
    Party plaintiff, 692.
Partition of property, venue, 83.
Partners proper defendants, 737.
Party defendant, 737.
Party plaintiff, 688.
Service, citation or process, 1263.
Venue,
    Action against partnership, 42(3).
    Action to dissolve partnership, 79.
    Existing partnership, suit against, 78.
    Partition of property, 83.

PAYMENT
Debts and charges, successions, 3301–3308.
Judicial sales, price, 2374.
State inheritance taxes, successions, 2951–2954.
Tutors, payments to minors, court approval, 4272.

PENDENCY OF ACTION
Another action, pleading, 925.
Mortgage, notice of action to enforce, 3751–3753.
Notice,
    Action to enforce mortgage, 3751–3753.
    Real action, 3751–3753.
Real actions, notice, 3751–3753.

PEREMPTORY EXCEPTION
See Exceptions.

PERISHABLE PROPERTY
Sale,
    Attachment or sequestration, 3513.
    Fieri facias, 2333.
    Succession property, 3264.
    Tutors, 4303.

PERPETUATION OF TESTIMONY
Generally, 1432–1435.

PERSONAL ACTION
Definition, 422.

PERSONAL INJURIES
Claimants cannot be impleaded in concursus proceedings, 4652.

INDEX—CODE OF CIVIL PROCEDURE
References are to Articles

PERSONAL SERVICE
Citation or process, 1231–1233.
   Corporations, 1261.
   Partnership, 1263.
   Unincorporated associations, 1264.

PERSONS
Person defined, 5251(12).
Process, service,
   Persons authorized to make, 1291–1293.
   Private person, 1293.

PETITION
   Generally, 891, 892.
Administrator, application for appointment, 3094.
Allowed pleadings, 852.
Alternative causes of action, 892.
Amendment,
   Generally, 1151.
   Joinder of necessary or indispensable party, 646.
Answer, amended petition, 1151.
Attachment, 3501.
   Issuance of writ before filing, 3502.
Concursus proceeding, 4654.
Executor,
   Confirmation, 3081.
   Notice of application for appointment, 3091–3093.
Executory proceeding, 2634.
   Injunction to arrest, 2752.
Form, 891.
   Demand against third party, 1032.
   Incidental actions, 1032.
   Intervention, 1032.
   Pleading noncompliance with requirements, 926.
   Reconventional demand, 1032.
Garnishment, service, 2411, 2412.
Habeas corpus, 3781.
Incidental actions, form, 1032.
Interdiction, 4543.
Interim allowance to heir or legatee, 3321.
Intervention, service, 1093.
Joinder of indispensable or necessary party, 646, 926.
Judicial emancipation, 3991.
Mandamus, 3781.
Noncompliance with requirements, 926.
Notice,
   Application for appointment as administrator, 3091, 3092.
   Filing tableau of distribution, petition for, 3305.
Partition between co-owners, when co-owner absent, 4622.

PETITION—Cont'd
Payment of succession debts and charges, submitting tableau of distribution, 3303.
Perpetuation of testimony, 1433.
Possession, succession proceedings, 3002, 3005, 3032, 3361, 3362, 3371, 3372.
Prayer for relief in the alternative, 891.
Probate of testament, 2851.
   Documents submitted with, 2852.
   Opposition, 2902.
   Time for filing, 2893.
Quo warranto, 3781.
Reconvention, service, 1063.
Sequestration, 3501.
   Issuance of writ before filing, 3502.
Service unnecessary, 1312.
Shareholder's secondary action, 596, 611.
Submitting tableau of distribution, 3303.
Succession representative. See Successions.
Supplemental petition, 1155.
Tutorship, appointment of tutor, 4031–4033.

PETITORY ACTION
   Generally, 3651–3653, 3663, 3664.
Burden of proof on plaintiff, 3653.
Cumulation with possessory action prohibited, 3657.
Damages, 3662.
Definition, 3651.
Evidence, proof of title, 3653.
Injunctive relief, 3663.
Mineral right real right, 3664.
Notice of pendency, 3751–3753.
Parties, 3652.
Possession, 3660.
Possessory action, conversion by defendant, 3657.
Proof of title, 3653.
Sequestration, 3663.
Venue, 3652.

PHOTOGRAPHS
Discovery, production of documents and things for, 1492.

PHOTOSTATIC COPIES
Subpoena duces tecum to produce, 1354.

PHYSICAL EXAMINATION
Contempt, exception on disobedience of order to submit to, 1513.
Parties, 1493–1495.

PLACE
Pleading, allegations, 860.

PLAINTIFFS
See Parties.

INDEX—CODE OF CIVIL PROCEDURE
References are to Articles

PLEADING
  See, also,
    Answer.
    Motions.
    Petition.
Adoption by reference, 853.
Adverse party, service, 1311–1314.
Affirmative defense erroneously pleaded as incidental demand, 1005.
Alternative causes of action, 892.
  Petitory and possessory actions prohibited, 3657.
Amended pleadings, 646, 932–934, 1151–1156.
  Conformity to evidence, 1154.
  Joinder of necessary or indispensable party, 646.
  Pre-trial conference, 1551.
  Relation back to date of filing, 1153.
Amicable demand, want, 926.
Arbitration and award as affirmative defense, 1005.
Assumption of risk as affirmative defense, 1005.
Attorneys, disciplinary action, deceit, 863, 864.
Capacity, allegations, 855.
Caption, 853.
Citation, insufficiency, 925.
City courts, cases involving $100 or less, 4892, 4921, 4922.
Clerk of court, filing with, 253.
Compensation, 1062.
Compromise or transaction as affirmative defense, 1005.
Concursus proceeding, no responsive pleadings to answer, 4656.
Condition of mind, 856.
Construction, 865.
Contradictory motion, 963.
Contributory negligence as affirmative defense, 1005.
Demand against third party, 1031–1040, 1111–1116.
Discharge in bankruptcy as affirmative defense, 1005.
Discussion,
  Generally, 5155.
  In exception, 926.
Division as affirmative defense, 1005.
Duress as affirmative defense, 1005.
Error or mistake as affirmative defense, 1005.
Estoppel as affirmative defense, 1005.
Exceptions, 852, 921–934.
Exhibits attached, 853.
Extinguishment of obligation as affirmative defense, 1005.

PLEADING—Cont'd
Failure of consideration as affirmative defense, 1005.
Fellow servant doctrine as affirmative defense, 1005.
Form, 854.
Forma pauperis cases, 5181–5188.
Fraud, 856, 1005.
Illegality as affirmative defense, 1005.
Incidental actions, 1031–1116.
Incidental demand pleaded erroneously as affirmative defense, 1005.
Intent, 856.
Intervention, 1031–1040, 1091–1094.
Judgment on pleadings, motion, 965, 968, 969.
Judgment or decision, 859.
Jurisdiction over person of defendant, lack, 925.
Jurisdiction over subject matter, lack, 925.
Justice of the peace court, 4892, 4941.
Knowledge, 856.
Lack of cause of action in exception, 927.
Lis pendens, 925.
Malice, 856.
Maturity of action after, reconventional demand, 1066.
Misjoinder of parties, 926.
Mistake, 856.
Motions, written motions, 961–969.
Necessary parties, nonjoinder, 926.
No cause of action in exception, 927.
No right of action in exception, 927.
Nonjoinder,
  Indispensable party, 645, 927.
  Necessary party, 645, 926.
Official documents or acts, 858.
Opposition,
    Generally, 2971–2973.
    Account,
      Curator, 4395, 4554.
      Succession representative, 3336.
      Tutor, 4395.
    Appointment of administrator, 3095.
    Probate of testament, 2881, 2901, 2902.
    Sale of succession property, 3283.
    Tableau of distribution, successions, 3307.
Pendency of another action, 925.
Prayer, 862.
Preliminary injunction, 3600.
Prematurity, 926.
Prescription in exception, 927.
Presumptions, capacity, 855.
Procedural capacity, lack, 926.
Process, insufficiency of service, 925.

INDEX—CODE OF CIVIL PROCEDURE
References are to Articles

PLEADING—Cont'd
Reconvention, 1031–1040, 1061–1066.
Redundant matter, motion to strike, 964.
Reference, adoption by reference, 853.
Relief granted under, 862.
Replicatory pleadings prohibited, 852.
Res judicata in exception, 927.
Rule to show cause, 963.
Scandalous or indecent matter, 864.
  Motion to strike, 964.
Service, 1311–1314.
Service of process, insufficiency, 925.
Signature, 863.
Special damages, 861.
Special matters, 855–861.
Strike, motion, 964.
Striking out,
  Depositions, failure to attend or serve answers, 1515.
  Discovery, failure to comply with orders, 1513.
Succession representative, secure loan, 3228, 3229.
Successions, 2971.
Summary judgment, motion, 966–969.
Summary proceedings, 2593.
  Unauthorized use, 926.
Supplemental pleadings, 1151–1156.
  Reconventional demand, action matured or acquired after, 1066.
Suspensive condition, 857.
Technical forms required, 854.
Third party, demand against, 1031–1040, 1111–1116.
Time and place, allegations, 860.
Tutors, minor's property, 4267.
Vagueness or ambiguity of petition, 926.
Venue improper, 925.
Want of interest in exception, 927.
Written motions, 852, 961–969.
  Form, 962.

PLEDGES
Proper plaintiff to enforce, 696.

PLURAL ACTIONS
Same cause of action, 531, 532.

POLITICAL SUBDIVISIONS
Official records, certified copy, proof by, 1393–1395.
Service, citation or process, 1265.

POSSESSION
Actions to determine, 3655–3664.
Defined, 3660.
Disturbance, 3658.
Eviction, tenants and occupants, 4701–4735.

POSSESSION—Cont'd
Injunction to prevent interference, immovables, 3663.
Judgment,
  Legacy or inheritance, payment of taxes, necessity, 2951.
  Ordering delivery, execution, 2501.
  Succession, 3061, 3062, 3381.
Real actions to determine, 3655–3664.
Succession,
  Administration, sending heirs and legatees into, 3361–3381.
  Petition, 3001–3006, 3031–3033, 3371, 3372.
Succession representative, duty to take possession of property, 3211.

POSSESSORY ACTION
  Generally, 3655–3662.
Appeal, devolutive or suspensive, 3662.
Burden of proof, 3658.
Cumulation with petitory action prohibited, 3657.
Damages, 3662.
Definition, 3655.
Disturbance in fact, 3658.
Disturbance in law, 3658.
Eviction, tenants and occupants, 4701–4735.
Evidence, limited admissibility of evidence of title, 3661.
Injunctive relief, 3663.
Mineral right real right, 3664.
Parties, 3656.
Petitory action, conversion by defendant, 3657.
Possession required of plaintiff, 3658, 3660.
Relief which may be granted, 3662.
Requisites, 3658.
Sequestration, 3663.
Title,
  Limited purposes of admissible evidence, 3661.
  Not at issue, 3661.
Venue, 3656.

PREFERENCE
Executors and administrators, appointment, 3098.
Partition between co-owners, trial, 4605.
Sale of succession property, 3262.

PRELIMINARY INJUNCTION
See Injunction.

PREMATURITY
Dismissal because action premature, 423.
Pleading, 926.

INDEX—CODE OF CIVIL PROCEDURE
References are to Articles

PRESCRIPTION
Claims against successions, suspension on submission of formal proof, 3245.
Pleading in exception, 927.

PRESERVATION
Minor's property, tutor, 4262–4275.
Succession property, 3221–3229.

PRESUMPTIONS
Parties plaintiff, representative's authority presumed, 700.
Pleading, capacity, 855.

PRE-TRIAL CONFERENCE
Generally, 1551.

PRICE
Judicial sales, fieri facias, minimum price, 2336, 2337.

PRINCIPAL AND SURETY
Discussion pleaded by surety, 5151, 5152, 5155, 5156.

PRINCIPAL DEMAND
Reconventional demand exceeding, 1065.

PRIORITIES
Executors and administrators, appointment, 3098.
Partition between co-owners, trial, 4605.
Sale of succession property, 3262.

PRISONERS
Deposition pending action, leave of court, 1436.

PRIVILEGES
See, also, Judicial Sales.
Attachment and sequestration, 3511.
Hypothecary action to enforce, 2378, 3741–3743.
Intervention, third person claiming on seized property, 1092.
Private work, concursus, 4661.
Public work, concursus, 4661.
Seizing creditor, 2292.
Sequestration on claim, 3571.
Venue, action to enforce by ordinary proceeding, 72.

PROBATE OF TESTAMENTS
See, also,
   Probate Procedure.
   Successions.
Annulment of probated testaments, 2931–2933.
Books and papers, examination on search for testament, 2854.

PROBATE OF TESTAMENTS—Cont'd
Burden of proof,
   Annulment of probated testaments, 2932, 2933.
   Proponent, 2903.
Contradictory probate, 2901–2903.
Depositions of witnesses, 2889.
   Admissibility in subsequent action, 2892.
Documents submitted with petition, 2852.
Evidence admissible in subsequent action, 2892.
Ex parte probate, 2881–2893.
Executors and administrators, see Executors and Administrators.
Foreign testament, 2888.
Hearing, 2856, 2882, 2901.
Judgments, signing in chambers, 194.
Jury trial, limitation, 1733.
Mystic testament, 2885, 2886.
Nuncupative testament,
   Private act, 2884, 2886.
   Public act, not necessary, 2891.
Olographic testament, 2883.
Opposition to petition for probate, 2901, 2902.
Orders and judgments, signing in chambers, 194.
Period within which must be probated, 2893.
Petition for probate, 2851.
   Documents submitted with, 2852.
   Opposition, 2902.
   Time for filing, 2893.
Preliminary procedure, generally, 2851–2857.
Procès verbal of probate, 2890.
Proponent bears burden of proof, 2903.
Purported testament must be filed, 2853.
Safe deposit vaults, examination on search for testament, 2854.
Search for testament,
   Appointment of notary, 2854.
   Notary's return, 2855.
Statutory testament, 2887.
Subpoena of witnesses, 2857.
Time, opposition to ex parte probate, filing, 2901.
Venue, action to annul, 81.
Witnesses, proponent must produce, 2857.

PROBATE PROCEDURE
See, also,
   Probate of Testaments.
   Successions.

INDEX—CODE OF CIVIL PROCEDURE
References are to Articles

PROBATE PROCEDURE—Cont'd
Acceptance of successions without administration,
    Creditor may demand security or administration, 3007, 3008, 3034.
    Intestate successions, 3001–3008, 3061, 3062.
    Judgments of possession, 3061–3062, 3381.
    Small successions, 3441.
    Testate successions, 3031–3035, 3061, 3062.
Accounting by succession representative, 3331–3338.
Administration of successions, 3081–3395.
    Small successions, 3442.
Administrator,
    Compensation, 3351.
    Discharge, 3391–3395.
    Qualification, 3091–3098, 3111–3122, 3151–3159.
Administrator of vacant succession,
    Compensation, 3351.
    Discharge, 3391–3395.
    Qualification, 3121, 3122, 3151–3159.
Ancillary probate procedure, 3401–3405.
Annulment of probated testaments, 2931–2933.
Attorney for absent heirs and legatees, 3171–3174.
Claims against succession, enforcement,
    Generally, 3241–3249.
    Acknowledgment by representative, 3242–3244.
    Effect of listing on tableau, 3244.
    Formal proof, effect of submission, 3245.
    Judicial enforcement after rejection, 3246–3248.
    Presentation, 3241.
Compensation, succession representative, 3351–3353.
Evidence of jurisdiction and heirship, 2821–2826.
Executors and administrators, see Executors and Administrators.
General rules of procedure, 2971–2974.
Heirs and legatees, interim allowances, 3321.
Heirs' refusal or inability to accept funds, 3394, 3395.
Inheritance taxes, payment, 2951–2954.
Intestate successions, acceptance without administration, 3001–3008, 3061, 3062.
Inventory, 2952, 3131–3137.
Jurisdiction, 2811, 2812.

PROBATE PROCEDURE—Cont'd
Letters of succession representative, 3159.
Nuncupative testament, 2884, 2886.
Oath of succession representative, 3158.
Olographic testament, 2883.
Partition of successions, 3461, 3462.
Payment of succession debts and charges,
    Generally, 3301–3308.
    Appeal from order of homologation, 3308.
    Court order necessary, 3301, 3307.
    Homologation of tableau of distribution, 3307.
    Notice of filing tableau of distribution, 3304.
    Payment after homologation of tableau, 3307.
    Petition, 3303.
        Notice of filing, publication, 3304.
        Submitting tableau of distribution, 3303.
    Publication, filing tableau of distribution, 3304.
    Time for payment, 3302.
    Urgent debts, 3302.
Petition for possession, 3001–3006, 3031–3033, 3371, 3372.
Preliminary procedure, 2851–2857.
Provisional administrator,
    Compensation, 3351.
    Discharge, 3391–3395.
    Qualification, 3111–3113, 3151–3159.
Reopening succession, 3393.
Sale of succession property,
    Generally, 3261–3285.
    Bonds and stocks, 3285.
    Private sale, 3261–3264, 3281–3285.
    Public sale, 3261–3264, 3271–3273.
Security of succession representative, 3151–3157.
Sending heirs and legatees into possession, administration, 3361–3381.
Small successions,
    Generally, 3421–3443.
    Judicial proceedings, 3441–3443.
    When judicial proceedings unnecessary, 3431–3434.
Succession representative,
    Claims and obligations, enforcement, 3211.
    Compromise, power, 3198.
    Continuation of business, 3224, 3225.
    Contracts with succession prohibited, 3194, 3195.
    Defendant, 3249.

INDEX—CODE OF CIVIL PROCEDURE
References are to Articles

PROBATE PROCEDURE—Cont'd
Succession representative—Cont'd
    Deposit and withdrawal of funds, 3222.
    Discharge, 3391–3395.
    Duty to close succession, 3197.
    Duty to take possession of property, 3211.
    General functions, powers and duties, 3191–3198.
    Investment of funds, 3223.
    Lease of property, 3226, 3229.
    Loans to representative, 3228, 3229.
    Mortgage or pledge to secure loan, 3228, 3229.
    Multiple representatives, 3192.
    Performance of executory contract, 3227.
    Preservation of property, 3221.
    Procedural rights, 3196.
    Qualification, 3081–3159.
    Revocation of appointment or removal, 3181, 3182.
    Survivor, 3193.
Testate successions, acceptance without administration, 3031–3035, 3061, 3062.

PROCEDURAL CAPACITY
Pleading lack, 926.

PROCÈS VERBAL
Inventory, 3133–3135.
    Minor's property, 4102.
Probate of testament, 2890.

PROCESS
Agent for service of process defined, 5251(2).
Citation, 1201–1203.
City courts,
    Cases involving $100 or less, 4894, 4921, 4922.
    Cases involving more than $100, 5002.
    Signature, 1202.
Clerk of court,
    Issuance, 252.
Concealment to avoid service, grounds for attachment, 3541.
Corporations, 1261.
Demand against third party, 1114.
Eviction, service of notice to vacate, 4703.
Executory proceedings, 1201, 2640.
Foreign corporations, 1261.
Form, 1202.
Garnishment, 2411, 2412.
Intervention, 1093.
Legal and quasi-legal entities, 1261–1265.

PROCESS—Cont'd
Legal representative of multiple defendants, 1203.
Ordinary proceedings, necessity, 1201–1314.
Persons, 1231–1235.
Persons authorized to make service, 1291–1293.
Pleading insufficiency of citation, 925.
Reconvention, 1063.
Service. See Service.
Summary proceedings, necessity of service, 1201.
Summons, substitution of parties, 802, 803.
Waiver,
    Acceptance of service, 1201.
    Attorney appointed by court, 5093.

PRODUCTION OF EVIDENCE
Depositions and discovery,
    Generally, 1421–1515.
    Depositions upon oral examination, 1451–1457.
    Depositions upon written interrogatories, 1471–1473.
    Miscellaneous discovery devices, 1491–1496.
    Refusal to make discovery, 1511–1515.
Examination of judgment debtor, 2451–2456.
Orders, signing in chambers, 194.
Proof, official records, 1391–1397.
Subpoenas, 1351–1357.

PROOF
Official records, 1391–1397.

PROPERTY
Defined, 5251(13).

PROTECTION
Real rights under contracts to reduce minerals to possession, 3664.

PROVISIONAL REMEDIES
Attachment, 3501–3514, 3541–3545.
Injunction, 3601–3613.
Sequestration, 3501–3514, 3571–3576.

PROVISIONAL SEIZURE
Now merged with sequestration, 3572, 3575.

PRUDENT MAN RULE
Investment of minor's funds, 4269.
Succession representative, 3191.

PUBLIC ADMINISTRATOR
Vacant successions in Orleans Parish, 3122.

INDEX—CODE OF CIVIL PROCEDURE
References are to Articles

PUBLIC INVENTORY
Generally, 3132–3135.

PUBLIC OFFICERS
Evidence of regulations, 1393.
Mandamus, directing writ against, 3863.
Service, citation or process, 1265.
Substitution of parties, 806.

PUBLICATION
See Judicial Advertisement.

PUNISHMENT
See Fines and Punishment.

QUALIFICATION
Curators of interdicts, 4067–4172, 4554.
Executors and administrators, 3091–3098, 3111–3122, 3151–3159.
Succession representatives, 3081–3159.
Tutors, 4061–4172.

QUASI IN REM
Jurisdiction, 9.

QUASI OFFENSE
Venue in action, 74.

QUESTIONS
Summary proceedings on incidental questions in course of litigation, 2592.

QUO WARRANTO
Answer, 3783.
Chambers, hearing in, 3784.
Contempt, disobedience of writ, 3785.
Definition, 3901.
Disobedience, punishment, 3785.
Extraordinary remedy, 3781–3785, 3901, 3902.
Hearing on petition, 3782.
Issuance of writ, 3781.
Judgment, 3902.
  Disobedience, contempt, 3785.
Jury trial, limitation, 1733.
Petition, 3781.
Return date, 3782.
Summary trial, 2592, 3781, 3784.
Time,
  Answer to petition, filing, 3783.
  Hearing petition, 3782.
Vacation, trial by district court during, 196.

REAL ACTIONS
Boundary action, 3691–3693.
Definition, 422.
Determination of ownership or possession, 3651–3664.
Establish title, now within petitory action, 3651.
Hypothecary action, 2378, 3721–3743.

REAL ACTIONS—Cont'd
Jactitory action included within possessory action, 3655–3662.
Notice of pendency, 3751–3753.
Petitory action, 3651–3653, 3663, 3664.
Possessory actions, 3655–3662.

REASONS FOR JUDGMENT
District court, 1917.

RECEIVERSHIP
Corporations,
  Receiver proper defendant, 740.
  Receiver proper plaintiff, 692.
Defined, parties plaintiff, 693.
Foreign or alien insurer in receivership, parties plaintiff, 693.
Parties defendant,
  Corporate or partnership receivership, 740.
  Insurer in receivership, 741.

RECONVENTION
Generally, 1031–1040, 1061–1066.
Additional parties, 1064.
Amended and supplemental pleadings, 1156.
Answer, 1035.
Citation unnecessary, 1063.
Compensation, pleading, 1062.
Delay for filing reconventional demand, 1033.
Effect of dismissal of principal action, 1039.
Exceptions and motions, 1034.
Form of petition, 1032.
Instituted separately, 1037.
Jurisdiction, 1036.
Matured or acquired after pleading, 1066.
Mode of procedure, 1036.
Motions, 1034.
New Orleans city courts, jurisdiction, reconventional demands, 4835.
Petition, service, 1063.
Pleading actions in reconventional demand, 1061.
Reconventional demand exceeding principal demand, 1065.
Separate judgments, 1038.
Separate trial, 1038.
Service of reconventional demand, 1063.
Supplemental pleadings, 1156.
Third party defendant, 1111.
Venue, 1034.

RECORD
Appeals, 2127, 2128, 2130–2132.
City court case, 4893.
City courts, appeal, 4901.

INDEX—CODE OF CIVIL PROCEDURE
References are to Articles

RECORD—Cont'd
Clerk of court, duties, 251.
Depositions,
    Oral examination, 1453.
    Written interrogatories, preparation, 1472.
Official records, proof, 1391–1397.
Proof of official records, 1391–1397.

RECUSATION
Acting by judge until recusation or motion to recuse filed, 153.
City court judge, 4844–4846.
Court of appeal, 151, 160.
District court, 151–158.
District judge,
    Own motion, 152.
    Supreme court, 152.
Judge ad hoc, 161.
Justice of the peace, 4844, 4846.
Power of judge ad hoc, 157.
Procedure for recusing district judge, 154.
Selection of judge to replace recused judge, 155–157.
Supreme court justice, 151, 159.
    Appointment of judge ad hoc, 158.

REFERENCE
Pleadings, adoption by reference, 853.

REGISTRATION
Curator of interdict, 4233, 4554.

REGISTRY OF COURT
Concursus proceeding, deposit, 4652, 4658.
Deposit of maximum inheritance tax claimed, successions, 2951.
Partition, absentee co-owner's share, 4628.

REHEARING
Abolished in trial court, 1951–2006.
Appeal, 2166.

RELEASE
Attachment,
    Bond, 5127.
    Property seized, 3507.
        Not to effect right to damages, 3514.
        Security, 3507, 3508.
        Third person, 3509.
    Security for issuance, 3512.
Bond, sequestration, 5127.
Judicial sales, inferior mortgages, 2376.
Sequestration, property seized, 3507.
    Damages, not to affect right to, 3514.
    Plaintiff, 3576.

RELEASE—Cont'd
Sequestration, property seized—Cont'd
    Security for issuance, 3507, 3508, 3512.
    Third person, 3509.

REMAND
Appeals, prescription pleaded, 2163.

REMITTITUR
Alternative to new trial, 1813.

REMOVAL
Name of attorney as counsel of record, no general appearance, 7(1).
Tutors, 4234–4236.

RENDITION
Judgments, 1911–1921.

REOPENING
Successions, 3393.

REPAIR
Succession property, 3221–3229.

REPLICATORY PLEADINGS
Prohibited, 852.

REPORTERS
Court reporter, 372.

REPORTS
Physical or mental examination of parties, 1494, 1495.
Summary proceedings on report of auditor, accountant or expert, 2592.

REPRESENTATION
Class actions, 592.

REPRESENTATIVE
Defined, cross examination at trial, 1634.
Succession representative. See, Probate Procedure.
    Successions.

RESIGNATION
Tutor, 1233, 1235.

RES JUDICATA
Pleading in exception, 927.

RETURN
See Sheriffs.

REVENUE AND TAXATION
Payment, state inheritance taxes, 2951–2954.

REVIVAL
Judgments, 2031.

1 LSA-C.C.P.—52   817

INDEX—CODE OF CIVIL PROCEDURE
References are to Articles

REVOCATION
Appointment,
    Curators of interdicts, 4232–4236, 4554.
    Succession representatives, 3181.
    Tutors, 4232–4236.

ROYALTIES
Real rights under contracts to reduce minerals to possession, 3664.

RULE TO SHOW CAUSE
Contradictory motion, 963.
Eviction of tenants and occupants, 4731.
Motions, 963.
Signing in chambers, 194.
Summary proceedings,
    Commencement by filing, 2593.
    Issue raised by, 2592.
    Service, 2594.

SAFETY DEPOSIT VAULTS
Probate of testaments, examination on search for testament, 2854.

SALES
Execution of writ, executory proceedings, 2721–2724.
Fieri facias, money judgments, execution, 2331–2343.
Judicial sales. See Judicial Sales.
Probate procedure, succession property, 3261–3285.
    Bonds and stocks, 3285.
    Private sale, 3261–3264, 3281–3285.
    Public sale, 3261–3264, 3271–3273.
Property of minors, tutors, 4301–4363.
Successions, property, 3261–3285.
    Bonds and stocks, 3285.
    Crops, 3264.
    Minimum price, 3273.
    Opposition, 3283.
    Orders, 3271, 3284, 3285.
    Perishable property, 3264.
    Petition, 3271, 3281, 3285.
    Priority between movables and immovables, 3262.
    Private, 3261–3264, 3281–3285.
    Public sale, 3261–3264, 3271–3273.
    Publication of notice, 3272, 3282.
        Small successions, 3443.
    Purpose, 3261.
    Small successions, 3443.
    Terms, 3263.
Tutorship, minor's property,
    Bonds and stocks, 4342.
    Immovables, additional bond, 4304.
    Perishable property, 4303.
    Private sale, 4301–4303, 4341, 4342.
    Public sale, 4301–4304, 4321–4323.

SALES—Cont'd
Tutorship, minor's property—Cont'd
    Purpose, 4301.
    Terms, 4302.

SECONDARY ACTIONS
Generally, 596, 611.
Shareholder in corporation, 596, 611.
Venue, 593.

SECRETARY OF STATE
Service, citation or process, 1262.

SECURITY
Appeals, 2124.
Attachment,
    Issuance, 3501, 3544.
        Cancellation, 3512.
    Release of property attached, 3507, 3508.
City courts, appeal, 4900.
Class actions, costs, 595.
Curator of interdict, 4131–4136, 4554.
Eviction of tenants and occupants, appeal bond, 4735.
Executory proceedings, injunction to arrest, 2753, 2754.
Injunction,
    Arrest of executory proceeding, 2753, 2754.
    Interlocutory injunctive order, 3610.
Natural tutor, 4061.
Preliminary injunction, 3610.
Provisional administrator, 3112, 3152.
Provisional curator, 4549.
Sequestration,
    Cancellation of bond, 3512.
    Issuance, 3501, 3574, 3575.
    Release of property sequestered, 3507, 3508.
Succession representative, 3151–3157.
Temporary restraining order, 3610.
Tutors, 4131–4136.
Undertutor, 4204.

SEIZURE
Constable, when authorized by sheriff, 332.
Execution of writ, executory proceeding, 2638, 2721–2724.
Intervention, third person asserting ownership, mortgage or privilege on seized property, 1092.
Inventory of property seized, attachment or sequestration, 3504.
Orders in chambers, signing, 194.
Reduction of excessive seizure, attachment or sequestration, 3505.
Sheriffs, 326–329.
Writ, 2638, 2721–2724.

818

INDEX—CODE OF CIVIL PROCEDURE
References are to Articles

SEPARATION FROM BED AND BOARD
Generally, 3941–3945.
Appeal,
    Alimony judgment, 3943.
    Judgment, 3942.
        Awarding custody, 3943.
Executing alimony judgment in arrears, 3945.
Injunctive relief, 3944.
Judgment on pleadings not permitted, 969.
Jurisdiction of proceeding, 10(7).
Jury trial, limitation, 1733.
Summary judgment not permitted, 969.
Venue, may not be waived, 44, 3941.

SEQUESTRATION
Affidavit, 3501.
Court's own motion, issuance, 3573.
Damages for dissolution, 3506.
Dissolution on motion, 3506.
Garnishment, 3503.
Grounds for issuance, 3501, 3571.
Inventory of property seized, 3504.
Issuance before filing of petition, 3502.
Judicial, 3573.
Lessor's privilege, 3572.
    Security, 3575.
Necessity for judgment and execution, 3510.
Orders, signing in chambers, 194.
Perishable property, sale, 3513.
Petition, 3501.
    Issuance of writ before filing, 3502.
Petitory or possessory actions, 3663.
Plaintiff's release of property seized, 3576.
Privilege resulting from seizure, 3511.
Provisional seizure, substitute, 3572, 3575.
Reduction of excessive seizure, 3505.
Release bond, 5127.
Release of property seized,
    Defendant, 3507.
    Not to affect right to damages, 3514.
    Plaintiff, 3570.
    Security, 3507, 3508, 3512.
    Third person, 3509.
Rent, enforcement of claim, 3572, 3575.
Security,
    Issuance,
        Amount, 3501, 3574, 3575.
        Cancellation of bond, 3512.
    Release of property, 3507, 3508.
Sheriff's return, 3504.
Third person, release of property seized, 3509.

SEQUESTRATION—Cont'd
Venue,
    Effect of judgment, 72.
    Garnishment proceeding under writ, 2416.

SERVICE
See, also, Citation.
Acceptance, 1201.
    Attorney appointed by court, 5093.
Agent for service of process defined, 5251(2).
Appeals, motion or petition, 1312.
Depositions, written interrogatories, 1471.
Eviction, notice to vacate, 4703.
Executory proceedings, demand for payment, 2640.
Motion for examination of judgment debtor, 2453.
Pleadings,
    Delivery, 1313–1314.
    Mail, 1313, 1314.
    Sheriff, 1313, 1314.
Process,
    Acceptance of service, 1201.
        Attorney appointed by court, 5093.
    Agents, 6(1), 1235, 5251(2).
    Boards or commissions, 1265.
    By sheriff, 321, 322, 324, 1291–1293, 1314.
    Concursus proceedings, 4655.
    Constable, when authorized by sheriff, 332.
    Corporation, 1261.
    Demand against third party, 1114.
    Domestic corporation, 1261.
    Domiciliary, 1231, 1234.
    Executory proceedings, 2640, 2641.
    Foreign corporations, 1261.
    Habeas corpus proceeding, 3823, 3824.
    Holidays, 1231.
    Interdiction proceeding, 4544.
    Jurisdiction based upon service, 6.
    Legal and quasi legal entities, 1261–1265.
    Marshal, when authorized by sheriff, 332.
    Partition proceeding, when co-owner absentee, 4623.
    Partnership, 1262.
    Personal, 1231–1233.
    Persons authorized to make, 1291–1293.
    Petition of intervention, 1093.
    Pleading insufficiency, 925.

INDEX—CODE OF CIVIL PROCEDURE
References are to Articles

SERVICE—Cont'd
Process—Cont'd
  Pleadings,
    Delivery, 1313, 1314.
    Mail, 1313, 1314.
    Sheriff, 1313, 1314.
  Political entity, 1265.
  Private person, 1293.
  Public officer, 1265.
  Reconventional demand, 1063.
  Return, sheriff, 1292.
  Sheriffs, 321, 322, 324, 1291–1293, 1314.
  Succession proceedings, 2971.
  Summary proceedings, 2594.
  Unincorporated association, 1264.
Sheriff,
  Pleading, 1313, 1314.
  Process or citation, 321, 322, 324, 1291–1293, 1314.
Subpoena, 1355.
Subpoena duces tecum, 1355.
Summary judgment, motion, time, 966.
Summons, substitution of parties, 802, 803.

SHARES AND SHAREHOLDERS
Class actions, 593.
Mandamus to compel recognition, 3864.
Sale of succession property, 3285.
Secondary actions,
  Petition, 596, 611.
  Venue, 593.
Tutors, sale of minor's stock, 4342.
Venue of class action, 593.

SHERIFFS
  See, also, District Courts.
Act of sale, 2342.
Administration, power of, over seized property, 328.
Advertisements and certificates, judicial sales, fieri facias, 2334.
Collection of fines for contempt, 330.
Constable's service or execution under authority, 332.
Crier, sheriff may act as, 334.
Deed of sale, 2342.
Deputies and other employees, 331.
Execution,
  Judgments, 2253, 2254.
  Writ of fieri facias, 2291–2299.
Functions exercised generally in own parish, 322.
Garnishment,
  Delivery of money or property, 2415.
  Interrogatories, service, 2412.
Imprisonment of contumacious persons, 330.

SHERIFFS—Cont'd
Injunction prohibiting sale under fieri facias, 2298.
Inventory of property seized, attachment or sequestration, 3504.
Nonperformance of duties, contempt, 334.
Notice of seizure,
  Seizure under fieri facias, 2293.
  Seizure under seizure and sale, 2721.
Pleadings, service, 1313, 1314.
Powers and duties generally, 321–334.
Protection and preservation of property seized, 326, 329.
Release bonds, 5127.
Return,
  After judicial sale, 2343.
  Attachment or sequestration, 3504.
  Fieri facias, 2294.
  Process served, generally, 324.
  Seizure and sale, executory proceeding, 2721.
  Writs executed, generally, 324, 2254.
Right of entry for execution, 325.
Seizure,
  Executory proceeding, 2721.
  Rents, fruits, or revenues, 327.
Service,
  Pleading, 1313, 1314.
  Process or citation, 321, 322, 324, 1291–1293, 1314.
Writs executed on holiday, 323.

SIGNATURE
Pleadings, 863.

SLANDER OF TITLE
Now included within possessory action, 3655–3662.

SMALL CURATORSHIP
Generally, 4461–4464, 4554.

SMALL SUCCESSIONS
Generally, 3421–3443.
Affidavit,
  Endorsed copy, authority for delivery of property, 3434.
  Inheritance tax, 3432, 3433.
Defined, 3421.
Judicial proceedings, 3441–3443.
When judicial proceedings unnecessary, 3431–3434.

SMALL TUTORSHIPS
Generally, 4461–4464.

SOLIDARY DEBTORS
Venue in action against, 73.

INDEX—CODE OF CIVIL PROCEDURE
References are to Articles

SPECIAL MATTERS
Pleading, 855–861.

SPECIAL TUTOR
Attorney appointed to represent unrepresented minor, 5091–5098.

SPECIAL VERDICTS
Jury trial, 1811.

SPECIFIC PERFORMANCE
Judgments, execution, 2504.

SPLITTING
Cause of action, effect, 425.

STATUTES
Declaratory judgments, 1872.
Judicial notice, 1391.
Proof, 1392.

STATUTORY TESTAMENT
Probate, 2887.

STAY
Order on failure to comply with discovery orders, 1513.

STIPULATIONS
Depositions, 1421.
Jury trial,
    Less than all issues, 1735.
    Lesser number of jurors, 1761.
    Verdict, number of jurors required, 1795.

STOCK AND STOCKHOLDERS
See Shares and Shareholders.

STRIKE
Motion, 964.
Pleading,
    Depositions, failure to attend or serve answers, 1515.
    Discovery, failure to comply with orders, 1513.

SUBPOENAS
    Generally, 1351–1357.
Attend taking of depositions, 1356.
Deposition pending action, 1436.
Expenses of witnesses, 1353.
Nonresident of parish, 1352, 1353.
Penalty for failing to comply, 1357.
Probate of testaments, witnesses, 2857.

SUBPOENAS DUCES TECUM
Penalty for failure to comply, 1354, 1357.
Production of documents at taking of deposition, 1356.
Service, 1355.
Use, 1354.

SUCCESSIONS
See, also,
    Probate of Testaments.
    Probate Procedure.
Acceptance without administration,
    Creditor may demand security or administration, 3007, 3008, 3034.
    Intestate, 3001–3008, 3061, 3062.
    Judgments of possession, 3061–3062, 3381.
    Small successions, 3441.
    Testate, 3031–3035, 3061, 3062.
Accounting by succession representative, 3331–3338.
Administration, 3081–3395.
    Small successions, procedure, 3442.
Administrator,
    Compensation, 3351, 3352.
    Discharge, 3391–3395.
    Qualification, 3091–3098, 3111–3122, 3151–3159.
Administrator of vacant succession,
    Compensation, 3351.
    Discharge, 3391–3395.
    Qualification, 3121, 3122, 3151–3159.
Adverse party, service of papers on, 2971.
Affidavits, evidence, 2821–2823.
Allowances, interim, heirs and legatees, 3321.
Ancillary probate procedure, 3401–3405.
Annulment of probated testaments, 2931–2933.
Appeals, 2974.
Appraisal of property, 3132, 3133, 3136.
Attorney for absent heirs and legatees, 3171–3174.
Business, continuation, 3224, 3225.
Claims against, enforcement,
    Generally, 3241–3249.
    Acknowledgment by representative, 3242–3244.
    Effect of listing on tableau, 3244.
    Formal proof, effect of submission, 3245.
    Judicial enforcement after rejection, 3246–3248.
    Presentation, 3241.
    Suspension of prescription, submission of formal proof, 3245.
Compensation of succession representative, 3033, 3351–3353.
Compromise, power of succession representative, 3198.
Contents of account, 3333.
Contracts, performance of executory, 3227.
Costs, 2825.

INDEX—CODE OF CIVIL PROCEDURE
References are to Articles

SUCCESSIONS—Cont'd
Defendant, succession representative, 734, 3249.
Descriptive list of property,
  Amendment, 3137.
  In lieu of inventory, 3136, 3137.
  Prima facie correct, 3137.
  Traverse, 3137.
Evidence of jurisdiction and heirship, 2821–2826.
Executor,
  Compensation, 3033, 3351–3353.
  Discharge, 3391–3395.
  Qualification, 3081–3083, 3151–3159.
Executory proceeding against, 2671–2675.
Failure to file account, penalty, 3334.
Fees, prepayment of witnesses, 1353.
Final account, succession representative, 3331–3338.
Funds,
  Deposit and withdrawal, 3222.
  Investment, 3223.
Heirs,
  Refusal or inability to accept funds, 3394, 3395.
  Sending into possession, administration, 3361–3381.
Homologation of accounts, 3336, 3337.
Inheritance taxes, payment, 2951–2954.
Interim allowance to heirs and legatees, 3321.
Intestate,
  Acceptance without administration, 3001–3008, 3061, 3062.
  Administration sending heirs and legatees into possession, 3361–3381.
Inventory,
    Generally, 3131–3137.
  Descriptive list in lieu, 2952, 3136, 3137.
  Prima facie proof, 3135.
  Procès verbal, 3133–3135.
  Public inventory, 3132.
  Traverse, 3135.
Judgments of possession, 3061, 3062, 3381.
Jurisdiction,
  Determination, 2811, 2812.
  Evidence to establish, 2821, 2822.
Lease of succession property, 3226, 3229.
Legal successor, substitution for deceased party, 801.
  Failure to appear, 804.
Legatees, sending into possession, administration, 3371–3381.
Letters, succession representative, 3159.

SUCCESSIONS—Cont'd
Loans to succession representative, 3228, 3229.
Management of property, 3221–3229.
Mortgage or pledge to secure loans, 3228, 3229.
Nonresidents, jurisdiction, 2811, 2812.
Oath of succession representative, 3158.
Orders for administration and settlement, signing in chambers, 194.
Partition, 81, 3461, 3462.
Payment of debts and charges,
  Generally, 3301–3308.
  Appeal from order of homologation, 3308.
  Court order necessary, 3301, 3307.
  Homologation of tableau of distribution, 3307.
  Notice of filing tableau of distribution, 3304.
    Failure to serve, effect, 3306.
    Petition for, 3305.
  Payment after homologation of tableau, 3307.
  Petition, 3303.
    Notice of filing, publication, 3304.
    Submitting tableau of distribution, 3303.
  Publication, filing tableau of distribution, 3304.
  Time for payment, 3302.
  Urgent debts, 3302.
Petition for possession, 3001–3006, 3031–3033, 3371, 3372.
Preservation and management of property, 3221–3229.
Procedure,
    Generally, 2971–2974.
  Appeals, 2974.
  Oppositions, 2971–2973.
  Pleadings, 2971.
  Service of process, 2971.
Process service, 2971.
Provisional administrator,
  Compensation, 3351.
  Discharge, 3391–3395.
  Qualification, 3111–3113, 3151–3159.
Reopening, 3393.
Repair of property, 3221–3229.
Residuary legatee defined, 2826.
Responsive pleadings to opposition, 2973.
Sale of property,
    Generally, 3261–3285.
  Bonds and stocks, 3285.
  Crops, 3264.
  Minimum price, 3273.
  Opposition, 3283.

INDEX—CODE OF CIVIL PROCEDURE
References are to Articles

SUCCESSIONS—Cont'd
Sale of property—Cont'd
  Orders, 3271, 3284, 3285.
  Perishable property, 3264.
  Petition, 3271, 3281, 3285.
  Priority between movables and immovables, no priority, 3262.
  Private, 3261–3264, 3281–3285.
  Public sale, 3261–3264, 3271–3273.
  Publication of notice, 3272, 3282.
    Small successions, 3443.
  Purpose, 3261.
  Small successions, 3443.
  Terms, 3263.
Security of succession representative, 3151–3157.
Small successions,
  Generally, 3421–3443.
  Affidavit,
    Endorsed copy, authority for delivery of property, 3434.
    Inheritance tax, 3432, 3433.
  Defined, 3421.
  Judicial proceedings, 3441–3443.
  When judicial proceedings unnecessary, 3431–3434.
Succession representative,
  Ancillary probate procedure, 3401–3405.
  Claims and obligations, enforcement, 3211.
  Compensation, 3033, 3351–3353.
  Compromise, power, 3198.
  Continuation of business, 3224, 3225.
  Contracts with succession prohibited, 3194, 3195.
  Death or interdiction, account, 3338.
  Defendant, 3249.
  Defined, 2826.
  Deposit and withdrawal of funds, 3222.
  Discharge, 3391–3395.
  Duty to close succession, 3197.
  Duty to take possession of property, 3211.
  General functions, powers, and duties, 3191–3198.
  Invalidation of acts by annulment of appointment, 2974.
  Investment of funds, 3223.
  Lease of property, 3226, 3229.
  Loans to representative, 3228, 3229.
  Mortgage or pledge to secure loan, 3228, 3229.
  Multiple representatives, 3192.
  Performance of executory contract, 3227.

SUCCESSIONS—Cont'd
Succession representative—Cont'd
  Petition,
    Borrow money, 3228, 3229.
    Continuation of business, 3225, 3229.
    Lease of succession property, 3226, 3229.
    Performance of executory contract, 3227, 3229.
    Sale of succession property, 3271, 3281, 3285.
  Plaintiff, 685.
  Preservation of property, 3221.
  Private sale, 3261–3264, 3281–3285.
  Procedural rights, 3196.
  Qualification, 3081–3159.
  Removal, 3182.
  Revocation of appointment, 3181.
  Survivor, 3193.
Tableau of distribution,
  Appeal from order of homologation, 3308.
  Claims against succession, listing on, effect, 3244.
  Distribution, summary proceedings, 2592.
  Failure to serve notice of filing, 3306.
  Homologation, 3307.
  Petition,
    Notice of filing, 3305.
    Submitting, 3303.
  Publication of notice of filing, 3304.
Testate successions,
  Acceptance without administration, 3031–3035, 3061, 3062.
  Administration sending heirs and legatees into possession, 3371, 3372.
Time for filing account, 3331.
Traverse, descriptive list in lieu of inventory, 3136, 3137.
Venue, may not be waived, 44, 2811, 2812.

SUBROGATION
Proper plaintiff to enforce subrogated right, 697.

SUBSTITUTION OF PARTIES
Appellate courts, 821.
Courts of appeal, 821.
Depositions, use, 1428.
District court, pending action, 821.
Trial courts, 801–807.

SUMMARY JUDGMENT
Motion, 966–969.

INDEX—CODE OF CIVIL PROCEDURE
References are to Articles

SUMMARY PROCEEDINGS
Generally, 2591–2596.
Chambers, trial in, 2595.
Continuance, trial of motion, 1605.
Contradictory motion,
    Commencement by filing, 2593.
    Issue raised by, 2592.
    Service, 2594.
Decision, 2595.
Definition, 2591.
Exceptions, filing, 2593.
Habeas corpus, 2592, 3781, 3784.
Interdiction, 4546.
Intervention by third possessor in executory proceeding, 2703.
Judgment, 2595.
Jury trial, limitation, 1733.
Mandamus, 2592, 3781, 3784.
Pleadings, 2593.
    Unauthorized use, 926.
Process, service, 2594.
Quo warranto, 2592, 3781, 3784.
Rule to show cause,
    Commencement by filing, 2593.
    Issue raised by, 2592.
    Service, 2594.
Rules of ordinary proceedings, applicability, 2596.
Service of process, 2594.
Trial, 2595.
Use, 2592.
Vacation, trial during, 2595.

SUMMARY PROCESS
See Summary Proceedings.

SUMMONS
See, also, Subpoenas.
Jury venire, 1751.
Substitution of parties, 802, 803.

SUPERVISORY JURISDICTION
Appellate courts, 2201.

SUPERVISORY WRITS
Generally, 2201.

SUPPLEMENTAL PLEADINGS
Generally, 1151–1156.
Reconventional demand, 1066.

SUPPLEMENTAL RELIEF
Declaratory judgments, 1878.

SUPREME COURT
Appellate procedure, 2081–2167.
Clerk, power generally, 251–257.
Inherent judicial power, 191, 2201.
Recusation of judge, 151, 159.
    Judge ad hoc, appointment on, 158.
Supervisory jurisdiction, 2201.

SURVEYS AND SURVEYORS
Boundary action, appointment by court, 3692.
Discovery, orders to permit, 1492.

SURVIVORS
Spouse, compelling executor to furnish security, 3154.
Succession representative, powers, 3193.

SUSPENSIVE APPEAL
Delay for taking, 2123.
Executory proceeding, 2642.
Possessory action, 3662.
Security, 2124.

TABLEAU
See Successions

TEMPORARY INJUNCTION
See Injunction.

TENANTS
Eviction, procedure, 4701–4735.

TERMINATION
Lease, eviction of tenants and occupants, 4701.

TESTAMENTS
See Probate of Testaments.

THIRD PARTIES
    See, also, Demand Against Third Party.
Appeals, 2086.
Attachment, release of property seized, 3509.
Discussion by third possessor, 5154.
Executory proceedings, property in possession of, 2701–2703.
    Intervention, 2643.
Garnishment, 2411.
Hypothecary action against, 2378, 3741–3743.
Intervener claiming privilege on property seized, 2299.
Intervention, 1091.
    Asserting ownership, mortgage or privilege on seized property, 1092.
    Executory proceeding, 2643.
    Third opposition now included in, 1092.
Legal mortgage, hypothecary action against third person, 3741–3743.
Sequestration, release of property seized, 3509.
Specific performance, court directing, 2504.
Third possessor, 2703, 3743, 5154.
    Discussion, 5154.

INDEX—CODE OF CIVIL PROCEDURE
References are to Articles

THIRD PARTIES—Cont'd
Third possessor—Cont'd
Hypothecary action, 3743.
Pleading discussion, 5155.
Rights, in executory proceedings, 2703.

THIRD PARTY DEMAND
See Demand Against Third Party.

THIRD POSSESSOR
See Third Parties.

TIME
Annulment of judgment for vices of form, 2002.
Answer, filing, 1001.
Declinatory exception,
Pleading, 928.
Trial, 929.
Delay for appealing,
Annulment of marriage judgment, 3942.
City courts, justice of the peace courts, 4899, 4921, 4922, 4942.
Devolutive appeal, 2087.
Divorce judgment, 3942.
Separation from bed and board judgment, 3942.
Suspensive appeal, 2123.
Delay for applying for new trial,
City courts, "clerk's book" cases, 4972, 5002.
District courts, generally, 1974.
Delay for filing answer,
Appeal, 2133.
City court, 4895, 5002.
Concursus proceeding, 4655, 4657.
District court,
Generally, 1001, 1002.
Less than $100, 4895, 4971.
Incidental demand, 1033.
Justice of the peace court, 4895, 4941.
Delay for filing exceptions,
City courts, justice courts, "clerk's book" cases, 4892, 4895, 4921, 4941, 4971.
District courts, generally, 928.
Delay for further action after interlocutory judgment, 1914.
Dilatory exception,
Pleading, 928.
Trial, 929.
Garnishment interrogatories, delay for answering,
City courts, justice courts, "clerk's book" cases, 4892, 4895, 4921, 4922, 4941, 4971.

TIME—Cont'd
Garnishment interrogatories, delay for answering—Cont'd
District courts, generally, 2412, 2414.
Habeas corpus,
Answer to petition, filing, 3783.
Hearing petition, 3782.
Incidental demands, filing, 1033.
Jury trial, charge to jury, 1791.
Mandamus,
Answer to petition, filing, 3783.
Hearing petition, 3782.
Motions,
Judgment on pleadings, 964.
Motion to strike, filing, 964.
Summary judgment, 966.
Payment of succession debts and charges, 3302.
Peremptory exception,
Pleading, 928.
Trial, 929.
Period within which testament must be probated, 2893.
Pleading,
Extension of, no general appearance, 7(2).
Time and place, 860.
Probate of testaments, opposition to ex parte probate, filing, 2901.
Quo warranto,
Answer to petition, filing, 3783.
Hearing petition, 3782.
Service of process, 1231.
Successions, filing account, 3331.
Trial of exceptions, 929.

TITLE
Action to establish included within petitory action, 3651.
Possessory action, not at issue, 3661.
Slander of title, now included within possessory action, 3655–3662.

TRADE NAMES
Party defendant, person doing business under, 736.
Party plaintiff, person doing business under, 687.

TRANSFER
Appeals, court lacks jurisdiction, 2162.
Interest in subject matter of action, substitution of party, 807.

TRIAL
See, also, Jury Trial.
Generally, 1631–1637.
Absentee co-owner, partition, 1623, 1625.
Assignment of cases, 1571, 1572.

INDEX—CODE OF CIVIL PROCEDURE
References are to Articles

TRIAL—Cont'd
Calling and examining jurors, 1761–1769.
Consolidation of cases, 1561.
Continuance, 1601–1605.
Cumulated actions, separate trial, 464, 465.
Declaratory judgment, 1879.
Default, 1701–1703, 1843.
Demand against third parties, separate trial, 1038.
Dismissal, 1671–1673, 1844.
Eviction, rule for possession, 4732.
Evidence excluded, proffer or introduction, 1636.
Exceptions, 929–934.
Interdiction, summary, 4546.
Intervention, separate trial, 1038.
Joint trial of common issues, 1561.
Judgments, 1637, 1841–1921.
Judicial emancipation proceeding, 3993.
Jury trial, 1731–1814.
Notice, 1571.
    Written request for, 1572.
Oath or affirmation of witness, 1633.
Order of trial, 1632.
Partition,
    Co-owner absent, 4623, 4625.
    Proceeding, preference, 4605.
Power of court to regulate procedure, 1631.
Preliminary injunction, rule, 3602, 3606.
Pre-trial procedure, 1551.
Probate of testament, contradictory, 2901.
Reconvention, separate trial, 1038.
Refusal of witness to testify, 1633.
Right to trial by jury, 1731–1735.
Selection of jury, 1751.
Separate trial, incidental action, 1038.
Summary proceedings, 2591–2595.
    Habeas corpus, mandamus, quo warranto, 2592, 3781, 3784.
Vacation, power of district court, 196.
Verdicts, 1795, 1811–1814.
Written request for notice, 1572.

TRUSTS
Declaratory judgments, 1874.
Party defendant, 742.
Party plaintiff, 699.

TUTOR AD HOC
Attorney appointed to represent unrepresented minor, 5091–5098.

TUTORS AND TUTORSHIP
Absence, temporary absence of tutor, agent, 4273.
Accounting by tutor, 4391–4398.

TUTORS AND TUTORSHIP—Cont'd
Action affecting minor's property, court approval, 4271.
Adjudication of minor's property to parent, 4361–4363.
Administration of minor's property by tutor, 4262, 4264.
Ancillary tutorship proceeding, 4431–4433.
Appointment of tutor,
    Appeal not suspensive, 4068.
    Dative tutor, 4064–4068.
    Legal tutor, 4063, 4065–4068.
    Natural tutor, 4061, 4068.
    Provisional tutor, 4068, 4070–4073.
    Successor tutor, 4237.
    Testamentary tutor, 4062, 4068.
    Tutor of property, 4069.
Attorney appointed to represent unrepresented defendant, 5091–5098.
Bond, substitution for legal mortgage, 4134, 4136.
Care of person of minor by tutor, 4261.
Compensation of tutor, 4274.
Compromise of obligation, 4265.
Continuation of business, 4266.
Contracts between minor and tutor prohibited, 4263.
Cost of accounting, 4398.
Court approval of action affecting minor's property, 4271.
Dative tutor without bond, small tutorship, 4463.
Death of tutor, accounting, 4397.
Disqualification of tutor, 4231.
Donations to or by minor, 4275.
Expenses, care of person of minor, 4261.
Foreign tutor, 4431–4433.
Foreign tutor or guardian may act, 4431.
Functions, duties, and power, 4261–4275.
Heirs of tutor, responsibility, 4238.
Inventory of minor's property, 4101, 4102.
Investment of minor's funds, 4269, 4270.
Jurisdiction, 10(4).
Jury trial, limitation, 1733.
Lease of minor's property, 4268.
Legal mortgage, substitution of bond, 4134, 4136.
Letters, 4172.
Loans to tutor, 4267.
Management of minor's property, 4269, 4270.
Mineral rights owned by minor, 4268.
Mortgage or pledge of property to secure loan, 4267.
Oath of tutor, 4171.
Payments to minor, court approval, **4272.**

INDEX—CODE OF CIVIL PROCEDURE
References are to Articles

TUTORS AND TUTORSHIP—Cont'd
Petition, appointment of tutor, 4031–4033.
Procedural rights of tutor, 4264.
Prudent man rule, liability of tutor, 4269.
Removal of tutor, 4068, 4234, 4235.
Resignation of tutor, 4233, 4235.
Revocation of appointment of tutor, 4232.
Sale of minor's property,
    Bonds and stocks, 4342.
    Immovables, additional bond, 4304.
    Perishable property, 4303.
    Private sale, 4301–4303, 4341, 4342.
    Public sale, 4301–4304, 4321–4323.
    Purpose, 4301.
    Terms, 4302.
Security of tutor, 4071, 4131–4136.
Separate tutor of property, 4069.
Small tutorship, 4461–4464.
Special mortgage substituted for bond, 4134, 4136.
Substitution of bond for mortgage, 4134, 4136.
Successor tutor, 4237.
Undertutor, 4068, 4201–4206, 4236, 4237.
Venue, may not be waived, 44, 4031–4034.
    Disqualification, revocation of appointment, resignation and removal, 4231–4238.

UNCONDITIONAL ACCEPTANCE
Intestate successions, 3001–3008, 3061, 3062.
Testate successions, 3031–3035, 3061, 3062.

UNDERCURATOR
Curatorship proceedings, interdicts, 4553.

UNDERTUTOR
    Generally, 4068, 4201–4206, 4236, 4237.
Disqualification, revocation of appointment, resignation, and removal, 4231–4238.

UNIFORM ACTS
Uniform Declaratory Act, 1871–1883.
Uniform Foreign Wills Act, 2888.
Uniform Judicial Notice of Foreign Law Act, 1391.

UNINCORPORATED ASSOCIATION
Party defendant, 738.
Party plaintiff, 680.
Service of citation or process, 1264.
Venue in suit against, general rule, 42(3).

UNITED STATES
Official record, proof, 1393.
    Certified copies, 1395.

VACANT SUCCESSION
Administrator, 3121, 3122.

VACATION
District courts, power to act during, 196.
Extraordinary remedies, hearing during, 3784.
Habeas corpus, hearing during, 3784.
Mandamus, hearing during, 3784.
Quo warranto, hearing during, 3784.
Summary proceedings, trial during, 2595.

VAGUENESS OR AMBIGUITY
Pleading, 926.

VENUE
    Generally, 41–122.
Action of nullity, may not be waived, 44, 2006.
Alien insurer, suit against, general rule, 42(7).
Annulment of marriage proceeding, may not be waived, 44, 3941.
Attachment,
    Garnishment proceeding under writ, 2416.
    Nonresident, 3545.
Bond, judicial bond, 75.
Change of venue, 121, 122.
    Vacation, trial of motion for change during, 196.
City courts, 4839.
Class action, 593.
Community property, partition, 82.
Compromise, action against joint or solidary obligors, 73.
Concursus proceedings, 4653.
Conflict between articles, determination, 45.
Curatorship, may not be waived, 44, 4032, 4033, 4541, 4554.
Definition, 41.
Demand against third party, 1034.
Dismissal of action against joint or solidary obligors, 73.
Divorce case, may not be waived, 44, 3941.
Domestic corporation, suit against, general rule, 42(2).
Domestic insurer, suit against, general rule, 42(2).
Exceptions to general rule, 43, 71–83.
Executory proceeding, 2633.
Foreign corporations, suits against, general rule, 42(4, 5).

INDEX—CODE OF CIVIL PROCEDURE
References are to Articles

VENUE—Cont'd
Foreign insurer, suit against, general rule, 42(7).
Garnishment, 2416.
Habeas corpus, 3822.
Health and accident insurance, action on policy, 76.
Immovable property, action to assert interest, 80.
Individual,
    General rule, 42(1).
    When domicile changed, 71.
Insurance policy, venue in action to enforce, 76.
Interdiction proceeding, may not be waived, 44, 4032, 4033, 4541, 4554.
Intervener cannot object to, 1094.
Intervention, 1034.
Joint debtors, suits against, 73.
Judgment, effect in certain actions, 72.
Judicial bond, 75.
Judicial emancipation, may not be waived, 44, 3991.
Judicial partition between co-owners, 4603.
Justice of the peace courts, 4839.
Life insurance policy, action on, 76.
Mixed actions, 3652, 3656.
Mortgage, venue in action to enforce by ordinary proceeding, 72.
Nonresident,
    Appointed agent, general rule, 42(6).
    Attachment, 3545.
Offense, 74.
Partition,
    Generally, 80–83, 4603.
    Between co-owners, 4603.
    Community property, 82.
    Partnership property, 83.
    Succession, 81, 3461.
Partnership,
    Action against partnership, 42(3).
    Action to dissolve, 79.
    Existing partnership, suit against, 78.
    Partition of property, 83.
    Suits against domestic, 42(3).
Person doing business in another parish, suit against, 77.
Petitory action, 3652.
Pleading improper, 925.
Possessory action, 3656.
Privilege, venue in action to enforce by ordinary proceeding, 72.
Quasi offense, 74.
Reconventional demand, 1034.
Separation from bed and board, may not be waived, 44, 3941.

VENUE—Cont'd
Sequestration,
    Effect of judgment, 72.
    Garnishment proceeding under writ, 2416.
Shareholder's class action, 593.
Solidary debtors, suit against, 73.
Succession proceeding, may not be waived, 44, 2811, 2812.
Testament, action to annul, 81.
Tutorship proceeding, may not be waived, 44, 4031–4034.
Unincorporated association, suits against domestic, general rule, 42(3).
Vacation, trial by district court on motion for change during, 196.
Waiver of objections, 44.

VERDICTS
Jury trial, 1795, 1811–1814.

VIA EXECUTIVA
See Executory Proceedings.

VIA ORDINARIA
See Ordinary Proceedings.

VIA SUMMARIA
See Summary Proceedings.

WAIVER
Annul judgment, action may not be waived, 44, 2006.
Appearance, objections which can be raised by declinatory exception, 924.
Citation, 1201.
    Attorney appointed by court, 5093.
Costs for indigent party,
    Account and payment of costs, 5186.
    Affidavits of poverty, 5183.
    Compromise of case, 5187.
    Court order, 5183.
    Dismissal, payment of costs, 5187.
    Privilege, 5181, 5182.
    Rights to litigate when costs waived, 5185.
    Traverse of affidavits of poverty, 5184.
    Unsuccessful party condemned to pay costs, 5188.
Depositions, objections, 1424–1427.
Jurisdiction, objections by general appearance, 7.
Objections to venue, 44.
Objections which should have been raised in exceptions, 925, 926.
Physical or mental examination of parties, report, 1494.

WANT OF INTEREST
Pleading plaintiff's, in exception, 927.

INDEX—CODE OF CIVIL PROCEDURE
References are to Articles

WAREHOUSE RECEIPTS
Concursus, 4661.

WARRANTS
Eviction of tenants and occupants, warrant for possession, 4733, 4734.

WARRANTY, CALL
See Demand Against Third Party.

WILLS
    See, also,
        Probate of Testaments.
        Probate Procedure.
Declaratory judgments, 1872.
Probate and registry of testaments, 2851–2903.

WITHDRAWALS
Succession funds, 3222.

WITNESSES
Depositions and discovery, 1421–1515.
    After trial, 1437.
    Contradiction, use, 1428, 1430.
    Impeachment, use, 1428.
    Miscellaneous discovery devices, 1491–1496.
    Oral examination, 1451–1457.
    Pending action, 1436.
    Perpetuation of testimony, 1432–1435.
    Refusal to make discovery, 1511–1515.
    Written interrogatories, 1471–1473.
Oath or affirmation, 1633.
Probate evidence admissible in subsequent action, 2892.
Probate of testament,
    Depositions, 2889.
        Admissibility in subsequent action, 2892.
    Proponent must produce, 2857.
Public inventory, 3132.
Refusal to testify, 1633.
Subpoenas,
    Generally, 1351–1357.
    Nonresident of parish, 1352, 1353.
    Probate of testaments, 2857.
Subpoenas duces tecum, 1354–1357.
    Taking of deposition, 1356.

WORDS AND PHRASES
Absentee, 5091(1).
Act importing confession of judgment, 2632.
Agent for service of process, 5251(2).
Appeal, 2082.
Authentic evidence, 2635, 2637.
Best qualified, executors or administrators, 3098.

WORDS AND PHRASES—Cont'd
City court, 5251(3).
Competent court, 5251(4).
Concursus, 4651.
Constructive contempt, 224.
Contempt, 221.
Corporation, 5251(5).
Cumulation of actions, 461.
Declinatory exception, 922, 923.
Default judgment, 1843.
Defendant, incidental action, 1040.
Definitive judgment, 1842.
Dilatory exception, 922, 923.
Direct contempt, 222.
Discussion, 5151.
Disturbance in fact, 3659.
Disturbance in law, 3659.
Domiciliary service, 1234.
Exceptions, 921.
Executory proceeding, 2631.
Final judgment, 1841.
Foreign corporation, 5251(6).
Habeas corpus, 3821.
Indispensable parties, 641.
Insurance policy, 5251(7).
Insurer, 5251(8).
Interlocutory judgment, 1841.
Judgment, 1841.
Jurisdiction, 1.
Law, 5251(9).
Lease, 4704.
Legal representative, 5251(10).
Legal successor, substitution of parties, 801, 805.
Lessee, 4704.
Lessor, 4704.
Mandamus, 3861.
Mineral rights as real rights, 3664.
Mixed action, 422.
Necessary parties, 642.
Nonresident, 5251(11).
Occupant, 4704.
Ordinary proceeding, 851.
Owner, 4704.
Partition by licitation, 4607.
Partition in kind, 4606.
Peremptory exception, 922, 923.
Person, 5251(12).
Personal action, 422.
Personal service, 1232.
Petitory action, 3651.
Plaintiff, incidental action, 1040.
Possession, 3660.
Possessory action, 3655.
Premises, 4704.
Property, 5251(13).
Quo warranto, 3901.
Real action, 422.
Receiver, parties plaintiff, 693.

INDEX—CODE OF CIVIL PROCEDURE
References are to Articles

WORDS AND PHRASES—Cont'd
Representatives, cross-examination at trial, 1634.
Residuary legatee, 2826.
Rule to show cause, 963.
Small succession, 3421.
Small tutorship, 4461.
Succession representative, 2826.
Summary proceeding, 2591.
Third possessor, 2703.
Venue, 41.

WORKMEN'S COMPENSATION
Attorney appointed by court, 5097.
Jury trial, limitation, 1733.

WRITTEN INTERROGATORIES
Depositions, 1471–1473.

WRITTEN MOTIONS
Generally, 852, 961–969.
Form, 962.

WRITS
Conservatory writs,
    Arrest abolished, 3501–3613.
    Attachment, 3501–3545.
    Injunction, 3601–3613.
    Provisional seizure now merged with sequestration, 3572, 3575.
    Sequestration, 3501–3514, 3571–3576.
Supervisory writs, 2201.

WRONGFUL DEATH
Claimants may not be impleaded in concursus proceeding, 4652.

END OF VOLUME